FAMILIAR ALLUSIONS:

A Hand-Book of

MISCELLANEOUS INFORMATION,

INCLUDING

THE NAMES OF CELEBRATED STATUES, PAINTINGS, PALACES, COUNTRY-SEATS, RUINS, CHURCHES, SHIPS, STREETS, CLUBS, NATURAL CURIOSITIES, AND THE LIKE.

BEGUN (BUT LEFT UNFINISHED)

BY WILLIAM A. WHEELER.

COMPLETED AND EDITED

BY CHARLES G. WHEELER.

He that undertakes to compile a Dictionary undertakes that which, if it comprehends the full extent of his design, he knows himself unable to perform. Yet his labors, though deficient, may be useful. — JOHNSON.

Les monuments sont les crampons qui unissent une génération à une autre. — JOUBERT.

BOSTON:
JAMES R. OSGOOD AND COMPANY.
1882.

REPUBLISHED BY GALE RESEARCH COMPANY, BOOK TOWER, DETROIT, 1966

BIBLIOGRAPHICAL NOTE

Familiar Allusions, originally published by James R. Osgood & Co. (predecessor of Houghton, Mifflin and Co.), went through some eight editions—or more accurately "printings"—between 1882 and 1896. The present reprint is made from the first edition which is identical with all later "editions."

Library of Congress Catalog Card Number 66-24371

PAPER USED IN THIS EDITION IS
A FINE ACID FREE PERMANENT/DURABLE PAPER
COMMONLY REFERRED TO AS "300-YEAR" PAPER

Electrotyped and Printed by Rand, Avery, & Co.,
117 Franklin Street, Boston.

PREFACE.

THIS Handbook of Miscellaneous Information was first announced by Mr. William A. Wheeler in the preface to his "Dictionary of the Noted Names of Fiction," to which it was designed to be a companion volume. Its design and scope are sufficiently indicated by the title it bears and by the words of the original announcement referred to above: viz., "the author has been urged to extend his plan so as to include . . . the names of celebrated statues, paintings, palaces, country-seats, churches, ships, streets, clubs, and the like; inasmuch as such names are of very common occurrence in books and newspapers, and, for the most part, are not alphabetically entered and explained in encyclopædias, dictionaries, or gazetteers."

A large amount of notes and memoranda in a considerably advanced state (as well as completed MS.) was left by Mr. Wheeler at his death; and the present editor has endeavored to carry out the work in strict accordance with the original plan.

One only needs to glance at the pages of any prominent writer, or at the citations here given, to see how full they are of allusions to buildings, pictures, statues, streets, and the like, for which the ordinary reader has no explanation at hand, and which this book aims so far as possible to explain. The same holds true of the columns of the magazines and daily newspapers, where there are repeated allusions to objects of interest—and unaccompanied by any explanation—of which a very well-informed person might excusably be ignorant, and concerning which he has no ready means of obtaining information, unless through the medium of a book like this. The rapid increase of travel, bringing with it acquaintance with foreign treasures of art, together with the growing taste for photographic and heliotype reproductions of works of art, have made many persons familiar with the names of pictures, statues, and buildings, while, at the same time, they may be ignorant of the artists, or the situations of the objects.

As the number of objects, in the classes above mentioned, to which reference is made in books, newspapers, and conversation, is almost innumerable, the task of selection has been very difficult. As a rule, institutions, buildings, and other objects which bear names closely identified with those of the places where they are situated, have been excluded, for the reason that information in regard to such can be found with comparative ease by any ordinary reader. Geographical names have also been, for the most part, excluded; it not being the intention to encroach to any considerable extent upon the province of the gazetteer or geography. Some purely geographical objects, however, which are the subject of frequent allusion in literature, have been included. Names in foreign languages have been frequently omitted, and the objects entered under the English equivalents, as the latter are more generally known to the ordinary reader. This is the case particularly with the names of works of art.

As regards the insertion of names which may possibly be considered by some of minor importance, the words of the preface to the companion volume (the "Noted Names of Fiction") are precisely applicable here, and will explain the principle which has governed the compilers' action: "To what extent names of secondary importance should be included, was a question difficult to determine. . . . Some favored a selected list of the more important names only; others, and the greater number, recommended a much wider scope. A middle course is the one that has been actually followed. It is evident that many articles which may seem to one person of very questionable importance, if not wholly unworthy of insertion, will be held by another to be of special value, as throwing light upon passages which to him would otherwise be perplexing or obscure."

The sources of the information used in the preparation of this Dictionary are far too numerous to be here specified. Whenever a statement has been taken in great part from any one author, it has been carefully collated and verified with information obtained from independent sources, and has been changed and abridged according to circumstances. No hesitation has been felt, however, in the occasional use of an author's exact language when the desired information has been found already stated in what seemed the form best suited to the requirements of the case.

It is evident that a work of this kind, which, like its predecessor, is believed to be unique, and which, like that volume, must be compiled without having the advantage of any similar work upon which it might be based, and from which materials might be drawn, must of necessity be more or less imperfect. No pretence is made to completeness, for the field of survey is indefinitely large, while the size of the book is definitely limited; but it is hoped and confidently believed that there will be found comparatively few omissions of the most noteworthy objects of interest in the several classes which are treated.

CHARLES G. WHEELER.

BOSTON, June, 1881.

FAMILIAR ALLUSIONS.

A.

Aaron's Tomb. The time-honored tomb of the Hebrew high-priest is situated upon Mount Hor, in Arabia Petræa. The present tomb is of comparatively modern date, but is composed of the ruins of an older structure. The place has been held sacred for many centuries, and unbroken tradition tends to substantiate the belief that this is really the place where Aaron died and was buried.

Abbaye. [Fr. *Prison de l'Abbaye.*] A military prison, near St. Germain des Prés, in Paris, built in 1522, and demolished in 1854. Here the French Guards who had refused to fire on the people were imprisoned in 1789, but soon released by the mob. One of the well-known revolutionary cries was "À l'Abbaye!" Here 164 prisoners were murdered in September, 1792, by infuriated republicans under Maillard.

Abbey. For names beginning with the word Abbey, see the next prominent word of the title.

Abbotsford. The residence of Sir Walter Scott (1771–1832), near Melrose in Scotland. It is on the banks of the Tweed, but does not command a fine view. It is interesting chiefly from its connection with the great novelist, and because it contains some valuable relics. The expense of the purchase and building of Abbotsford, and the extended hospitality which Scott practised there, was the chief source of his subsequent pecuniary difficulties. It was Scott's ambition to attempt to revive old times in this mansion on the Tweed, and to play the part of one of those feudal lords whom he has so well portrayed in his works.

☞ "Viewed as a mere speculation, or, for aught I know, as an architectural effort, this building may perhaps be counted as a mistake and a failure. I observe that it is quite customary to speak of it, among some, as a pity that he ever undertook it. But viewed as a development of his inner life, as a working out in wood and stone of favorite fancies and cherished ideas, the building has to me a deep interest. The gentle-hearted poet delighted himself in it; this house was his stone and wood poem, as irregular perhaps, and as contrary to any established rule, as his 'Lay of the Last Minstrel,' but still wild and poetic. The building has this interest, that it was throughout his own conception, thought, and choice; that he expressed himself in every stone that was laid, and made it a kind of shrine, into which he wove all his treasures of antiquity, and where he imitated, from the beautiful old mouldering ruins of Scotland, the parts that had touched him most deeply. The walls of one room were of carved oak from the Dunfermline Abbey; the ceiling of another imitated from Roslin Castle; here a fireplace was wrought in the image of a favorite niche in Melrose; and there the ancient pulpit of Erskine was wrought into a wall. To him, doubtless, every object in the house was suggestive of poetic fancies."
Mrs. H. B. Stowe.

Abelard and Eloise. See Tomb of Abelard and Eloise.

Aberbrothock. See Arbroath Abbey.

Aboosee? See Rock of Aboo-seer.

Aboo-Simbel. See TEMPLE OF ABOO-SIMBEL.

Aboshek, Lady of. See LADY OF ABOSHEK.

Abraham, Heights (*or* Plains) of. An eminence in the vicinity of Quebec, Canada, where on the 13th of September, 1759, was fought a battle between the English (who were victorious), under Gen. Wolfe, and the French, under the Marquis de Montcalm. Both commanders were killed, and a monument 40 feet in height, to the memory of Wolfe, marks the spot where he fell.

To many the rock over which Wolfe climbed to the *Plains of Abraham*, and on the summit of which he fell in the hour of victory, gives to Quebec its chiefest charm. *Anthony Trollope.*

Abraham's House. The name given by the Jews to a ruined structure at Ramet-el-Khulil, Syria, which they identify as the spot where the patriarch pitched his tent beneath the oak of Mamre.

Abraham's Oak. An ancient oak or terebinth which long stood on the plain of Mamre, near Hebron in Syria, and was believed to be that under which the patriarch pitched his tent. It was for centuries an object of worship, to put an end to which the Emperor Constantine is said to have ordered a basilica to be erected. A writer of the seventh century speaks of the church, and of the oak which stood by it.

Absalom's Tomb. A sepulchral monument near Jerusalem, popularly called by this name. It has a structural spire in place of the usual pyramidal roof.

☞ "The capitals and frieze are so distinctly late Roman, that we can feel no hesitation as to the date being either of the age of Herod, or subsequent to that time." *Fergusson.*

Abydos, Tablet of. See TABLET OF ABYDOS.

Academia. [Academy.] A suburban and rural gymnasium in ancient Athens, said to have been named from one Hecademus. It was here that Plato established his famous school, B.C. 388. The place retained something of its old repute as late as to the second or third century of the Christian era, and has bequeathed its name to the modern institutes of learning and art.

See there the olive grove of *Academe*,
Plato's retirement, where the Attick bird
Trills her thick-warbled notes the summer long. *Milton.*

No round-robin signed by the whole main-deck of the *Academy* or the Porch. *De Quincey.*

Nearer and dearer to the poet's heart,
Than the blue ripple belting Salamis,
Or long grass waving over Marathon,
Fair *Academe*, most holy *Academe*,
Thou art, and hast been, and shalt ever be. *Edwin Arnold.*

Academy, Académie, *or* Accademia. For names beginning with either of these words, see the next prominent word of the title. See also *infra*.

Academy of Design. See NATIONAL ACADEMY OF DESIGN.

Académie Française. [French Academy.] One of the five academies embraced in the *Institut*, the most important learned society of France. It is devoted to matters relative to the French language, and particularly to the composition of its Dictionary. This celebrated society owes its origin to the Cardinal Richelieu. The first edition of the Dictionary appeared in 1694, the last in 1835. The Academy is composed of forty members, called the forty *Immortels*. In consequence of often having recruited its numbers from the ranks of those literary men whose careers were ended, the Academy has been sometimes called the *Hôtel des Invalides* of literature.

Acadia. The original name of Nova Scotia, and that by which it is often poetically designated. The forced removal of the French inhabitants of Acadia, in 1755, has been made by Longfellow the subject of his poem of "Evangeline."

Aceldama. [Field of Blood.] The reputed site of the "field of blood," bought with the "thirty pieces of silver," the price of the betrayal of the Saviour (Matt. xxvii.), is on the side of the hill opposite the Pool of Siloam, near Jerusalem. There is here a long vaulted structure, of heavy masonry, in front of a precipice of rock. The interior is dug out to a depth of perhaps 20 feet, forming a huge charnel-house into which the bodies of the dead were thrown. It is traditionally of the time of Jerome. The soil was thought to consume the bodies within twenty-four hours. The place is no longer used for burial.

And it was known unto all the dwellers at Jerusalem; insomuch as that field is called, in their proper tongue, *Aceldama*, that is to say, The field of blood.
Acts i. 19.

Achilles. A noted colossal statue in the corner of Hyde Park, London, nearly opposite Apsley House. It was cast from cannon taken at Salamanca and Vittoria.

Achilles, The. An armor-plated ship of the British navy, launched Dec. 24, 1863.

Achilles and Briseis. A celebrated picture painted in distemper, found at Pompeii, Italy, of which there is a well-known engraving. Now in the Museum at Naples.

Acrocorinthus. A hill nearly 1,900 feet in height, near Corinth, Greece, which for 3,000 years has served as the citadel of that place. Hieron writes of the Corinth of ancient times, "There was hardly a stronger fortress in all Greece, and perhaps no spot afforded a more splendid view than the Acrocorinthus. Beneath it might be seen the busy city and its territory, with its temples, its theatres, and its aqueducts; its two harbors, Lechæum on the western bay, Cenchreæ on the eastern, filled with ships, and the two bays themselves, with the isthmus between them, all in sight."

Stranger, wilt thou follow now,
And sit with me on *Acro-Corinth's* brow?
Byron.

I stood upon that great *Acropolis*,
The turret-gate of Nature's citadel,
Where once again, from slavery's thick abyss
Strangely delivered, Grecian warriors dwell.
Lord Houghton

Acropolis. [The upper or higher city.] **1.** The ancient citadel of Athens, Greece, said to have been built by the mythical Cecrops. It was at the same time the fortress, sanctuary, and museum of the city. Here are the remains, in a ruined state, of three temples, — the Temple of Victory, the Parthenon, and the Erectheum. Fragments of the Propylæa are still standing.

☞ "Imagine a rocky height, rising precipitously from the plain, so as to be inaccessible on all sides but the west, where it is approached by a gentle slope; give it an elevation of 350 feet above the vale of Athens, and 569 above the sea, a length of about 950 feet from east to west, and a breadth of 430 from north to south. This is the Acropolis."
T. Chase.

☞ "From the gates of its Acropolis, as from a mother-city, issued intellectual colonies into every region of the world. These buildings now before us, ruined as they are at present, have served for 2,000 years as models for the most admired fabrics in every civilized country of the world."
C. Wordsworth.

Or could the bones of all the slain,
Who perished there, be piled again,
That rival pyramid would rise
More mountain-like, through those clear skies,
Than yon tower-capped *Acropolis*,
Which seems the very clouds to kiss.
Byron.

He said to the young lady, however, that the State House was the Parthenon of our *Acropolis*, which seemed to please her, for she smiled, and he reddened a little, — so I thought.
Holmes.

2. [Of Argos.] A conical hill in Greece, nearly 1,000 feet in height. It was called Larissa in ancient times. A ruined castle on the summit preserves some fragments of the noted Acropolis of Argos.

3. [Of Corinth.] See ACROCORINTHUS.

Actæon. See DIANA AND ACTÆON.

Adam and Eve. An engraving by Albert Dürer (1471–1528). In the gallery of Vienna, Austria. There is also a painting on the same subject by the same artist in the Madrid gallery. Still another example, of great beauty, is in the Pitti Palace in Florence. An early copy or replica, which has sometimes passed for an original, is in the gallery of Mayence.

Adam and Eve. Celebrated frescoes by Michael Angelo Buonarotti (1475–1564), representing the creation of Adam and Eve. In the Sistine Chapel, Rome.

Adam and Eve. A picture by Jacopo Palma, called Palma Vecchio (1480–1528), which has been attributed to Giorgione. It is in the Brunswick gallery.

Adam and Eve. A fresco in the Loggie of the Vatican, Rome, executed by Giulio Romano (1492–1546), after a design by Raphael.

Adam and Eve. A picture by Jacopo Robusti, called Tintoretto (1512–1594). In the Academy at Venice, Italy.

Adam and Eve. See FALL OF ADAM AND EVE.

Adams, Fort. See FORT ADAMS.

Adelphi, The. The name given to a series of streets on the south side of the Strand, London. See ADELPHI TERRACE.

> He [Martin Chuzzlewit] found himself, about an hour before dawn, in the humbler regions of the *Adelphi;* and, addressing himself to a man in a fur cap, who was taking down the shutters of an obscure public-house, inquired if he could have a bed there. *Dickens.*

Adelphi Terrace. This terrace in London occupies part of what was formerly the site of Durham House and its gardens, and is so called from the Greek ἀδελφοί (brothers) in commemoration of its founders, John, Robert, James, and William Adam (1768). It is approached by four streets, known as John, Robert, James, and William streets, after the Christian names of the brothers. David Garrick and Topham Beauclerk died in the terrace.

☞ "There is always, to this day, a sudden pause in that place to the roar of the great thoroughfare. The many sounds become so deadened that the change is like putting cotton in the ears, or having the head thickly muffled." *Dickens.*

Adelphi Theatre. A well-known place of dramatic entertainment in the Strand, London, first opened in 1806, rebuilt and enlarged in 1858.

> Bless me! when I was a lad, the stage was covered with angels who sang, acted, and danced. When I remember the *Adelphi*, and the actresses there! *Thackeray.*

Adelsberg Grotto. See GROTTO OF ADELSBERG.

Adersbach Rocks. A remarkable natural curiosity, perhaps unequalled in its kind in Europe, near the village of the same name in Bohemia. It consists of masses of sandstone extending over a tract five or six miles in length by three in breadth, and divided by all manner of openings and clefts. "You walk, as it were, in a narrow street, with immense smooth walls on each side of you, opening here and there into squares, whence is obtained a view of the countless number of giant rocks which surround you on all sides." Such is the intricacy of the passages, that the region is a perfect labyrinth, from which extrication is very difficult, unless one is attended by a guide.

Admiralty, The. The building in which is conducted the business of the Admiralty, in Whitehall, London. It occupies the site of Wallingford House. The street front was built about 1726 by Thomas Ripley, and the stone screen towards the street was designed in 1776 by the brothers Adam.

> See under Ripley rise a new Whitehall,
> While Jones' and Boyle's united labors fall. *Pope.*

Admiralty Pier. A magnificent breakwater of granite at Dover, England, one of the greatest works of the kind in the world. It extends nearly half a mile into the sea. The work was begun in 1844, and is not yet finished.

Admiralty Square. A famous square in St. Petersburg, Russia, around which are grouped the most important buildings and monuments of the city. It is about one mile in length by a quarter of a mile in breadth.

Adonis. An admired statue by Thorwaldsen (1770–1844). In the Glyptothek at Munich, Bavaria.

Adoration of the Kings. See ADORATION OF THE MAGI.

Adoration of the Lamb. A remarkable altar-piece begun by Hubert van Eyck (1366–1426), the Flemish painter, but left unfinished by him. It was painted for Jodocus Vydts, burgomaster of Ghent, and his wife Elizabeth, for their mortuary chapel in the Cathedral of St. Bavon at Ghent, Belgium. It consisted of two rows of separate panels, the subject of the upper picture being the Triune God with the Holy Virgin and the Baptist at his side, and the lower central picture showing the Lamb of the Revelation, "whose blood flows into a cup; over it is the dove of the Holy Spirit; angels who hold the instruments of the Passion worship the Lamb, and four groups, each consisting of many persons, advance from the sides. . . . In the foreground is the fountain of life; in the distance the towers of the heavenly Jerusalem." This work no longer exists as a whole, the separate parts having been dispersed, and some of them lost. The céntre pictures and two of the panels are still at Ghent, while others of the pictures are among the chief attractions of the Museum of Berlin. After the death of Hubert van Eyck, the pictures which were unfinished were completed by his younger brother Jan van Eyck. An excellent copy of this altar-piece was made, about a century after its completion, for Philip II. of Spain; but the panels of this work, like those of the original, have been dispersed, some being in the Berlin Museum, others being in the possession of the King of Bavaria, and others still at the Hague. There is also a copy in the Antwerp Museum.

☞ "This [Van Eyck's Adoration of the Lamb] . . . may be considered as in some respects the highest exposition of all representations of this class, however marked by the then growing corruptions and inconsistencies of religious art. The merit of this picture, which is exquisite in execution and expression, is the earnest reality of certain portions: its fault is the incongruous symbolism and convention of others." *Lady Eastlake.*

Adoration of the Magi (Kings). [Ital. *L'Adorazione de' Magi, L'Epifania;* Ger. *Die Anbetung der Weisen aus dem Morgenland, Die heilige drei Königen;* Fr. *L'Adoration des Rois Mages.*] A very common subject of representation by the great mediæval painters, who portrayed the visit of the three wise men from the East to Bethlehem, with their gifts of gold and frankincense and myrrh, according to the account in Matt. ii. 1–12.

☞ "In the first place, who were these Magi, or these kings as they are sometimes styled? 'To suppose,' says the antique legend, 'that they were called Magi because they were addicted to magic, or exercised unholy or forbidden acts, would be, heaven save us! a rank heresy.' No! Magi, in the Persian tongue, signifies 'wise men.' They were in their own country kings or princes, as it is averred by all the ancient fathers. . . . In the legends of the fourteenth century, the kings had become distinct personages, under the names of Caspar (or Jasper), Melchior, and Balthasar." *Mrs. Jameson.*

Of numerous compositions on this subject, the following may be named as among the more noted.

Adoration of the Magi (Kings). A picture by Gentile da Fabriano (1370–1450 ?). In the Academy at Florence, Italy.

☞ "The first real picture in the series is the Adoration of the Magi by Gentile da Fabriano, a really splendid work in all senses, with noble and beautiful figures in it." *Hawthorne.*

Adoration of the Magi (Kings). A remarkable altar-picture by Jan van Eyck (1390–1440). In the gallery of Munich, Bavaria.

Adoration of the Magi (Kings).

An altar-piece, with wings, by Stephan Lochner, called Meister Stephan (d. 1451), a German painter, and regarded as his principal work. It was originally painted for a chapel of the Hôtel de Ville, but has been for many years in a chapel of the choir of Cologne Cathedral.

Adoration of the Magi (Kings). A picture by Giovanni da Fiesole, called Fra Angelico (1387–1455). In the Museum of St Mark, Florence, Italy.

Adoration of the Magi (Kings) 1. A celebrated picture by Roger van der Weyden (d. 1464), the Flemish painter, and one of the largest and finest works of that master. The Annunciation and the Presentation in the Temple are represented in the wings of the picture. It is said to have been painted for the church of St. Columba in Cologne, and was afterwards in the Boisserée collection, but is now in the gallery of Munich, Bavaria.

2. A picture by the Flemish painter, Roger van der Weyden (d. 1464). For centuries it adorned the altar of a church at Middelburg, but has been transferred to the Museum of Berlin, Prussia.

Adoration of the Magi (Kings). The travelling altar-piece of Charles V., with wings representing the Nativity and the Presentation in the Temple. It was executed by Hans Memling (d. 1495), the Flemish painter, and is now in Madrid, Spain. There is a smaller altar-piece by this painter, bearing the title of the "Adoration," now in St. John's Hospital at Bruges, Belgium.

Adoration of the Magi (Kings). A picture by Domenico Ghirlandajo (1449–1498?). In Florence, Italy.

Adoration of the Magi (Kings). A noted picture by Pietro Perugino (1446–1524), and one of his best works. In the church of S. Francesco del Monte, at Perugia, Italy.

Adoration of the Magi (Kings). An admired picture by Francesco Francia (1450–1518), in which the landscape is very beautiful. In the gallery at Dresden. There is an excellent engraving of this fine picture.

Adoration of the Magi (Kings). A large altar-piece by Raphael Sanzio (1483–1520). It has been much injured by dampness. It was formerly in the possession of the Ancajini family at Spoleto, Italy, but is now in the Museum of Berlin, Prussia.

☞ "In a composition upon the same subject by Raphael, in the Vatican, the worshippers wear the classical, not the oriental costume; but an elephant with a monkey on his back is seen in the distance, which at once reminds us of the far East."

Mrs. Jameson.

Adoration of the Magi (Kings). A picture by Raphael Sanzio (1483–1520). Now at Copenhagen, Denmark.

Adoration of the Magi (Kings). A picture by Albert Dürer (1471–1528), the German painter, originally executed for the Elector of Saxony, and now in the Tribune of the Uffizi, at Florence, Italy.

Adoration of the Magi (Kings). An admired picture by Paolo Cagliari, called Paul Veronese (1528–1588). In the gallery at Dresden, Saxony.

Adoration of the Magi (Kings). A picture by Jan (or Jannyn) Gossart (d. 1532), a Flemish painter, and considered to be his principal work. It is now at Castle Howard, the seat of the Earl of Carlisle, England.

Adoration of the Magi (Kings). A picture by Peter Paul Rubens (1577–1640), one of fifteen by him upon this subject, and the finest of all. Now in the gallery at Madrid, Spain.

Adoration of the Shepherds. A common subject of representation by the religious painters of the Middle Ages. Of compositions upon this subject those mentioned below are among the better known.

Adoration of the Shepherds. A picture by Albert Altdorfer (d. 1538), a German painter. In the collection of the Historical Society at Regensburg, Bavaria.

Adoration of the Shepherds. A picture by Alessandro Bonvicino, called Il Moretto di Brescia (1500–1547). In the Museum of Berlin, Prussia.

Adoration of the Shepherds. A picture by Diego Rodriguez de Silva y Velasquez (1599–1660), the Spanish painter. Now in the Louvre, Paris.

Adoration of the Shepherds. A well-known picture by Anton Rafael Mengs (1728–1779). It was brought to the United States by Joseph Bonaparte, and is now in the Corcoran Gallery, Washington.

Adoration of the Shepherds. See NOTTE, LA.

Adoration of the Trinity. A celebrated picture by Albert Dürer (1471–1528), the German painter and engraver, regarded as one of his masterpieces. It was painted for the chapel of the Landauer Brüderhaus in Nuremberg, was afterwards removed to Prague, and is now in the Belvedere at Vienna, Austria.

Adorno Palace. [*Palazzo Adorno.*] A noted palace in Genoa, Italy.

Adrian VI. 1. A portrait of this pope by Sebastian del Piombo (1485–1547), the "realization," according to Sir C. L. Eastlake, "of what is usually attributed to Michael Angelo." It has been wrongly named Alexander VI. Now in the Museum of Naples, Italy.

2. There is another picture of this pope by Sebastian (often miscalled Amerigo Vespucci) in the collection of the late Lord Taunton.

Adrian's Mole. See ST. ANGELO.

Adrian's Wall. See HADRIAN'S WALL.

Adullam, Cave of. See CAVE OF ADULLAM.

Advance, The. A noted vessel in which Elisha Kent Kane (1820–1857) set sail from New York, in May, 1853, on a voyage of Arctic discovery, and in search of Sir John Franklin. The *Advance* was beset with ice, and abandoned in higher latitude than any vessel had ever before reached.

Adventure, The. The ship in which the notorious pirate Capt. William Kidd (——1701) cruised.

Ægina Marbles. A collection of casts from groups of figures on the Temple of Jupiter in the island of Ægina, now preserved in the British Museum, London. The originals are now in Munich, Bavaria. They have been skilfully restored by Thorwaldsen, and arranged as far as possible in the order in which they originally stood.

☞ "These sculptures may be classed among the most valuable remains of ancient art that have reached us." *R. Westmacott.*

Æneas, Shipwreck of. See SHIPWRECK OF ÆNEAS.

Æschines. A famous statue discovered at Herculaneum, and now in the Museum at Naples, Italy. By some it is considered to be a statue of Aristides.

Age of Innocence. A picture by Sir Joshua Reynolds (1723–1792). Now in the National Gallery, London.

Ages. See THREE AGES.

Agger of Servius Tullius. A celebrated rampart of ancient Rome, a few remains of which still exist in the rear of the Baths of Diocletian.

Agincourt, The. An armor-plated ship of the British navy, launched March 27, 1865.

Agnes, St. See ST. AGNES.

Agora, The. [The Market-place or Forum.] The public place of Athens, Greece, situated in a valley partially enclosed by the hills known as the Acropolis, Areopagus, Pnyx, and Museum. It is an elliptical area about one-third of a mile in length. The Gate of the so-called New Agora, also known as Hadrian's Arch, is of comparatively recent date.

☞ "All the buildings connected with the civil processes employed in the enactment of laws at Athens are, from its neighborhood to the Pnyx, fitly grouped together in this place. Here is the *Bouleuterion*, or Council Chamber, in which the Senate of Five Hundred meet to discuss measures before they are submitted to the assembly of the people in the Pnyx. Here are the statues of the ten Heroes of Athens, — Cecrops, Erectheus, Pandion, Ægeus, Hippothoon, Acamas, Leon, Œneus, Ajax, Antiochus, — the Eponymi, as they are called, because they give their names to the ten tribes of Athens. Here is the refectory of the *Prytanes*, or Presidents of the Assembly, — a building which may be distinguished from the crowd of other fabrics in the same place by its hemispherical dome, and in which the most distinguished citizens of Athens are entertained at the public charge. In the centre of the area which we are describing stands the altar of the Twelve Gods, being the point to which all the roads of Attica converge, and from which distances are measured. . . . Such are the most remarkable objects contained in the Agora of Athens. We speak of the early times of its glory." *C. Wordsworth.*

Ahmed ebn Tooloon. See MOSQUE OF AHMED EBN TOOLOON.

Aignan. See HÔTEL ST. AIGNAN.

Ain Moosa. See FOUNTAINS OF MOSES.

Aird's Moss. A tract of moorland in the county of Ayr, Scotland, famous in the history of the Scottish Covenanters as being the scene of numerous gatherings, or "conventicles," "where men came armed to the teeth to hear the Bible read."

Airlie Castle. A residence of the Earl of Airlie, near Meigle, Scotland. It forms the subject of the ballad of "The Bonnie House of Airlie."

Akbar's Palace. A famous palace, built by the renowned emperor of that name, in the city of Akbar, or Agra, in Hindostan.

☞ "It would be difficult to describe in detail its many courts, its separate masses of buildings, and its detached pavilions. . . . Akbar's palace is far more complete than the Alhambra. No part has been utterly destroyed, and the marks of injury by time and battle are comparatively slight. The substructions of the palace are of red sandstone, but nearly the whole of its corridors, chambers, and pavilions are of white marble, wrought with the most exquisite elaboration of ornament. There are precious caskets of marble, glittering all over with jasper, agate, cornelian, blood-stone, and lapis-lazuli, and topped with golden domes. Balustrades of marble, wrought in open patterns of such rich design that they resemble fringes of lace when seen from below, extend along the edge of the battlements." *Bayard Taylor.*

Alabama, The. A Confederate privateer, built by Laird of Liverpool, and commanded by Raphael Semmes, who set out on a cruise with her in 1862. This ship, during her career, inflicted immense damage on the American mercantile marine. She is reported to have captured over 60 vessels, destroyed 45 others, and taken millions of property. She was sunk on the 19th of June, 1864, off the harbor of Cherbourg, France, in a battle with the Union vessel *Kearsarge*, commanded by Capt. Winslow. For the complicity of the British government in the ravages of this English-Confederate privateer, a tribunal of arbitration, chosen by the United States and Great Britain jointly, adjudged that the latter should pay to the former, for damages, the sum of $15,-500,000 in gold, and this sum was paid. [Also known as the "290."]

☞ "The most famous of the English-American cruisers during the civil war was the *Alabama*, Capt. Raphael Semmes. She was built by Laird near Liverpool, was armed, provisioned, and chiefly manned in a British port, and sailed under British colors. She was watched while in port by the national ship *Tuscarora;* but, favored by the British government in keeping the latter vessel back until the *Alabama* had got well to sea, she was allowed to go on her destructive errand without molestation. For a year and a half afterward, while carefully avoiding contact with armed vessels of the United States, the *Alabama* illuminated the sea with blazing American merchantmen which she had captured and set on fire. During the last 90 days of 1862 she captured and destroyed 28 helpless vessels. After a prosperous voyage in the South Atlantic and Indian oceans, during which she captured 67 vessels, and destroyed a greater portion of them, the *Alabama* took shelter in the French harbor of Cherbourg, in the early summer, 1864. There the United States steamship *Kearsarge* found her at or near the middle of June." *Lossing.*

Alabaster Cave. A natural curiosity in California, on Kidd's Ravine near its junction with American River. This remarkable cave was discovered Aug. 19, 1860.

☞ "On our first entrance we descended about 15 feet gradually to the centre of the room, which is 100 x 30 feet. At the north end there is a most magnificent pulpit. . . . It is completed with the most beautiful drapery of alabaster sterites of all colors, varying from white to pink-red, overhanging the beholder. Immediately under the pulpit is a beautiful lake of water extending to an unknown distance. . . . On arriving at the centre of the first room we saw an entrance to an inner chamber still more splendid, 200 x 100 feet, with most beautiful alabaster overhangings, in every possible shape of drapery." *Gwinn.*

Alameda. In Spanish towns the usual name for the public walk, or promenade. The word is derived from *alamo*, poplar.

A walk in Broadway or Fifth Avenue will show you damsels and dames who will remind you of those you have met in the Cascine or Corso, in the Prado or *Alameda.* *Galaxy.*

Alaric's Grave. According to tradition the grave of the Visigothic chief (d. 410) was dug in the bed of the river Busento, in Italy, the stream being diverted from its course for the purpose; and after the burial the waters were let back into their former channel.

Alba Madonna. See MADONNA DELLA CASA D'ALBA.

Albani. See VILLA ALBANI.

Albany Chambers. A well-known row of buildings in Piccadilly, London, named after the Duke of York.

In the quiet avenue of the *Albany*, memories of the illustrious dead crowd upon you. *Jerrold.*

Albany, Fort. See FORT ALBANY.

Albero d'Oro. [Golden Tree.] The name given to one of the most beautiful palaces in Venice, Italy, from a tradition that one of its owners staked and lost all his fortunes except a single tree in the garden of this palace. The tree finally being staked also, fortune turned, and the owner recovered all that he had lost, including the palace.

Albert Dürer. A well-known autograph portrait of the painter, in the collection of artists' portraits painted by themselves, in the Uffizi Gallery at Florence, Italy. He is represented as standing at a window, with his hands resting on the window-sill, dressed in a holiday suit. There is also another portrait of him in the gallery of Munich, Bavaria, which represents him as much more mature in features and character, although he was but two years older when it was taken. This picture gives a front view of him, with his hand laid upon the fur lining of his robe.

Albert Embankment. See THAMES EMBANKMENTS.

Albert Memorial. This monument to the memory of the Prince Consort, Albert of Saxe Gotha (d. 1861), was built from designs of Sir Gilbert Scott. It is situated opposite the Albert Hall in London, and on the site of the Crystal Palace of 1851. Monuments in memory of the Prince have also been erected in other places in Great Britain.

☞ "If the Prince had united the genius of Napoleon to the virtues of Washington, there might, with more show of reason, have been such a literary and such a sculptured monument raised to him so soon after the close of his blameless and useful life. But even then something more simple and sober would have been more effective than this gilded, enthroned, enshrined, and canopied effigy of the demi-god of commonplace. In fact, this is the most obtrusively offensive monument in London." *Richard Grant White.*

Albert Park. See FINSBURY PARK.

Albertina Bronze. See CALIGULA.

Albion, The. 1. A noted London tavern famous for its Corporation banquets, and other public dinners, and for the annual trade-sales of the principal London publishers.

2. A London club founded in the first part of the present century, and dissolved in 1841.

Alcala, Gate of. See PUERTA DE ALCALA.

Alcantara, Bridge of. See PUENTE DE ALCANTARA.

Alderney Bull, Cow, and Calf. An admired picture by James Ward (1769-1859), often compared with Paul Potter's Young Bull (*q. v.*). It is in the National Gallery, London.

Aldersgate. One of the gates in the old city walls of London. It was restored after the Great Fire of 1666, and somewhat resembled Temple Bar.

> He [Clennam] turned slowly down *Aldersgate Street*, and was pondering his way along towards St. Paul's, . . . when a crowd of people flocked towards him. *Dickens.*

Aldgate. One of the old Roman gates of London, so called from its antiquity (Aeld or Old gate). From the time of the Romans to 1760 (when it was demolished), it formed the main outlet to the eastern counties. The barons, using money from the monks' coffers, and building material from the Jews' houses, rebuilt the structure during the time of John. This gate was torn down in 1606, and again built up in 1609. The poet Chaucer (1328-1400) held a life lease of the dwelling-house above the gate.

> If the brutalizing effect of such scenes as the storming of St. Sebastian may be counteracted, we may hope, that, in a Christian Utopia, some minds might be proof against the kennels and dresses of *Aldgate.* *Macaulay.*

> Old Father Baldpate,
> Say the slow bells at *Aldgate.*
> *Mother Goose.*

Aldine Press. The name given to the press established about 1490, at Venice, by Aldo Manuzio (Aldus Manutius), an Italian printer of the fifteenth and sixteenth centuries, and the inventor of *Italic* type. The highly-esteemed Aldine editions of the classics issued by Manutius and his descendants led to the publication of counterfeit Aldine editions in Florence and Lyons as early as 1502. The name *Aldine* has also been used by the English publisher Pickering.

> As for the foundlings like my Hedericus, they go among their peers: it is a pleasure to take them from the dusty stall where they were elbowed by plebeian school-books and battered odd volumes, and give them *Alduses* and Elzevirs for companions. *Holmes.*

Aldobrandini Madonna. See MADONNA ALDOBRANDINI.

Aldobrandini Marriage. [*Nozze Aldobrandini.*] A celebrated fresco painting, and one of the most valuable relics of ancient art. It was found in 1606 among the ruins of the Baths of Titus in Rome, and is now in the Vatican. It derives its name from the Aldobrandini family, by whom it was purchased. It represents a marriage-scene, as the name implies. Winckelmann thinks that it represents the nuptials of Peleus and Thetis. In the Palazzo Doria, there is a copy by Nicholas Poussin.

Aldobrandini, Villa. See VILLA ALDOBRANDINI.

Aletsch Glacier. A celebrated glacier in Switzerland surrounded by the Aletschhorn, Jungfrau, and other peaks. It is about sixteen miles in length.

Alexander. See TRIUMPHAL MARCH OF ALEXANDER and VICTORY OF ALEXANDER THE GREAT OVER DARIUS.

Alexander and Diogenes. A noted picture by Sir Edwin Landseer (1803-1873), the celebrated painter of animals. In the National Gallery, London.

Alexander and Roxana. See MARRIAGE OF ALEXANDER AND ROXANA.

Alexander Column. A red granite monolith and memorial pillar, 160 feet in height, situated in the Admiralty Square, St. Petersburg, Russia. It was erected to the Emperor Alexander, and was the work of Montferrand.

It is one of the greatest memorial monoliths of modern times.

Taller than Luxor's shafts, and grander,
Looms the *pillar of Alexander*,
Guarding the palace that fronts the square.
E. D. Proctor.

Alexander in the Tent of Darius. A fresco-painting by Gianantonio Razzi, or Bazzi, called Il Sodoma (1474–1549). In the Farnesina, Rome.

Alexander's Tomb. A small structure at Alexandria, Egypt, traditionally identified with the tomb of Alexander. The existence of Alexander's tomb has long been recorded by Arab tradition. Leo Africanus speaks of it as being highly honored by the Moslems, and as being visited with religious veneration by great numbers of strangers from foreign lands.

Alexandrian Library. This celebrated library at Alexandria, Egypt, was founded, like the Museum, by Ptolemy Soter. Ptolemy Philadelphus, his successor, made great additions to it, and at his death there were 100,000 volumes in the library. A great deal of trouble was taken and expense incurred in forming and adding to this collection, in which it was said that a copy of every known work was included. Here was deposited the Septuagint translation of the Bible. The Alexandrian Library consisted of about 700,000 volumes, of which 400,000 were in the Museum and 300,000 in the Serapeum. The former collection was destroyed by fire during the war between Julius Cæsar and the Alexandrians, and the latter by order of Caliph Omar in 640. By this act the Caliph Omar is said to have provided the 4,000 baths of the city with fuel for six months.

Alfred Club. A club in London, established in Albemarle Street in 1808, and dissolved about the middle of the century.

☞ Lord Byron, who was a member, characterized it as "pleasant, a little too sober and literary," and "in the whole, a decent resource in a rainy day, in a dearth of parties, or Parliament, or in an empty season."

☞ "The Alfred received its *coup-de-grâce* from a well-known story to the effect that Mr. Canning, whilst in the zenith of his fame, dropped in accidentally at a house dinner of twelve or fourteen, staid out the evening, and made himself remarkably agreeable, without any one of the party suspecting who he was."
Quarterly Review.

Alfred dividing his Loaf with the Pilgrim. A picture by Benjamin West (1738–1820), well known by engravings. In the Hall of the Stationers' Company, London.

Alfred Jewel. A remarkable jewel found near Ethelney Abbey in Somersetshire, England, and a rare specimen of Anglo-Saxon art. It bears this inscription in Saxon characters: "Alfred had me wrought."

Alhambra. [The Red Castle.] The palace-fortress of the Moorish kings in Granada, Spain. It was begun in 1248, and finished in 1314. The exterior is plain, and affords little indication of the unrivalled splendor which once characterized the interior apartments. The building has suffered greatly from decay, neglect, and wanton injury, but is still an object of attraction to travellers, as one of the finest existing specimens of Moorish architecture, abounding in colonnades, pavilions, baths, fountains, gilded ceilings, and every kind of Oriental ornamentation. Around the palace and gardens were scattered the establishments of the court and nobility, so that the whole population of the Alhambra consisted of some 40,000 souls. The preservation from absolute ruin of this, the most interesting and beautiful of the historical monuments of Spain, is due to the French, who, when Granada was in their hands, did much to repair and restore the Alhambra.

☞ "To the traveller imbued with a feeling for the historical and poetical, so inseparably intertwined in the annals of romantic Spain, the Alhambra is as much an object of devotion as is the Caaba to all true Moslems. How many legends and traditions, true and fabulous, — how many songs and ballads, Arabian and Spanish, of love and war and chivalry, — are associated with this Oriental pile! It was the royal abode of the Moorish kings, where, surrounded with the splendors and refinements of Asiatic luxury, they held dominion over what they vaunted as a terrestrial paradise, and made their last stand for empire in Spain. The royal palace forms but a part of a fortress, the walls of which, studded with towers, stretch irregularly round the whole crest of a hill, a spur of the Sierra Nevada or Snowy Mountains, and overlook the city: externally it is a rude congregation of towers and battlements, with no regularity of plan nor grace of architecture, and giving little promise of the grace and beauty which prevail within. . . . After the kingdom had passed into the hands of the Christians, the Alhambra continued to be a royal demesne, and was occasionally inhabited by the Castilian monarchs. The Emperor Charles V. commenced a sumptuous palace within its walls, but was deterred from completing it by repeated shocks of earthquakes. The last royal residents were Philip V. and his beautiful queen, Elizabetta of Parma, early in the eighteenth century. . . . The desertion of the court, however, was a fatal blow to the Alhambra. Its beautiful halls became desolate, and some of them fell to ruin; the gardens were destroyed, and the fountains ceased to play." *Irving.*

☞ "The *Alhambra*, a name which will make my blood thrill if I live to the frosts of a century, not that the pleasure I received, on wandering over the immense extent of these most graceful and most picturesque of all ruins, was like the quiet, hallowed delight of a solitary visit to the Coliseum or the Forum, . . . but it was a riotous, tumultuous pleasure, which will remain in my memory like a kind of sensual enjoyment." *George Ticknor.*

Lonely and still are now thy marble halls,
Thou fair *Alhambra!* there the feast is o'er;
And with the murmur of thy fountain falls
Blend the wild tones of minstrelsy no more. *Felicia Hemans.*

And there the *Alhambra* still recalls
Aladdin's palace of delight:
Allah il Allah! through its halls
Whispers the fountain as it falls,
The Darro darts beneath its walls,
The hills with snow are white. *Longfellow.*

On to *Alhambra*, strong and ruddy heart
Of glorious Morisma, gasping now,
A maimèd giant in his agony. *George Eliot.*

All Hallows Church. A celebrated old London church, destroyed in 1877. In this church Milton was baptized.

All Saints. A modern church in London, the interior of which is said to be the most gorgeous of any in the kingdom. Finished in 1859.

☞ "Though I have a rather large acquaintance with English and foreign works executed since the revival of Pointed art, I cannot hesitate for an instant in allowing that this church is not only the most beautiful, but the most vigorous, thoughtful, and original, of them all." *G. A. Street.*

Allée Verte. [The Green Walk.] A fine promenade in Brussels, Belgium, extending along the canal from Brussels to the Scheldt.

Alloway Kirk. A ruined church near Ayr, Scotland, immortalized in Burns's poem of "Tam O'Shanter." The old bell of the kirk is still hanging in it, though hardly more than the four walls of the structure are now standing.

She prophesy'd that late or soon,
Thou would be found deep drown'd in Doon;
Or catch'd wi' warlocks in the mirk,
By *Alloway's auld haunted kirk.* *Burns.*

Almack's. Noted assembly-rooms in King Street, St. James's, London, so called after the proprietor, Almack, a Scotchman. They were opened Feb. 12, 1765, with an assembly at which the Duke of Cumberland, the hero of Culloden, was present. The house continued to be the fashionable place of entertainment during the early part of the present century, but has now lost its former importance, — "a clear proof that the palmy days of exclusiveness are gone by in England" (*Quarterly Review*). The rooms are let for public meetings, dramatic readings, lectures, concerts, balls, and dinners. Almack's is now called "Willis's," from the name of the present proprietor. A novel entitled

"Almack's" was issued in 1831, and followed by "A Key to Almack's," by Benjamin Disraeli.

☞ "We could, however, stay there but a short time; for we were to go to Almack's, where, with some exertion, we arrived just before the doors were closed at midnight. It was very brilliant, as it always is; and the arrangements for ease and comfort were perfect, — no ceremony, no supper, no regulation or managing, brilliantly lighted large halls, very fine music, plenty of dancing. . . . It struck me, however, that there were fewer of the leading nobility and fashion there than formerly, and that the general cast of the company was younger."
George Ticknor (*in* 1835).

The Fraction asked himself: How will this look in *Almack's*, and before Lord Mahogany? The Winklemann asked himself: How will this look in the Universe, and before the Creator of Man?
Carlyle.

Almack's Club. This club in Pall Mall, London, was founded in 1764, and was celebrated for the gambling which took place there. Walpole writes, in 1770, that the gaming at Almack's is "worthy the decline of our empire, or commonwealth, which you please." He adds: "The young men of the age lose ten, fifteen, twenty thousand pounds, in an evening there." Charles Fox was a member, and also Gibbon. The latter wrote, that, notwithstanding the rage of play, he found there more entertainment and rational society than in any other club to which he belonged. Almack's afterwards became Goosetree's Club, of which, in 1780, Pitt and Wilberforce were members. See BROOKES'S CLUB.

Almeidan. The largest and handsomest square in Constantinople, Turkey.

Almond Glen. See GLEN ALMOND.

Alnwick Castle. The ancient seat of the Duke of Northumberland, in the town of the same name, and historically one of the most interesting baronial mansions in England. It dates from before the Conquest, but has undergone several restorations.

☞ "As no pains or expense was spared to make the new part harmonize with the old, so far as it was possible to combine ancient architecture with modern requirements, the structure, as a whole, presents the most magnificent specimen in Great Britain — perhaps in the world — of the feudal castle of mediæval days."
The Times, 1869.

Home of the Percy's high-born race,
Home of their beautiful and brave,
Alike their birth and burial place,
Their cradle and their grave!
Still sternly o'er the castle's gate
Their house's Lion stands in state,
As in his proud departed hours;
And warriors frown in stone on high,
And feudal banners "flout the sky,"
Above his princely towers.
Fitz-Greene Halleck.

Alphonsine Tables. A series of astronomical tables intended to correct those contained in Ptolemy's "Almagest," composed by order of Alphonso of Castile in 1252.

Alsatia. See WHITEFRIARS.

Alster, The. A basin or lake in the city of Hamburg, Germany, surrounded with fine buildings. It is a favorite pleasure-resort of the inhabitants.

Alte Markt. [Old Market.] A public square in Dresden, Germany.

Altenahr Castle. An ancient feudal fortress, now in ruins, in the valley of the Ahr, in Germany.

Altenberg Abbey. A very interesting monastic establishment of the Cistercian order in a sequestered valley near Cologne, Germany. The church is of the thirteenth century.

Altenburg. An ancient and noted castle near Bamberg, in Franconia, Germany. It is now in ruins.

Althorp. A noble manor near Weedon in England, the seat of Earl Spencer.

Alton Towers. A noble mansion, the seat of the Earl of Shrewsbury, in the parish of Alton, England.

Altötting. See SHRINE OF THE BLACK VIRGIN.

Altoviti, Bindo. A portrait of this youth, which has been wrongly taken to be that of the painter himself, by Raphael Sanzio (1483–1520). It was formerly in the Casa Altoviti, Rome, but is now in the gallery at Munich, Bavaria.

Amalienborg. A royal palace in Copenhagen, Denmark. It is the ordinary residence of the royal family.

Amazon, The. 1. A celebrated work of ancient sculpture in the Vatican, Rome. Also another in the Museum of the Capitol.

2. A celebrated relic of ancient sculpture in the Museum of Berlin, Prussia. It has been by some ascribed to Polycleites the Elder (452?–412? B. C.), the Greek statuary.

Amazons, Battle of the. See BATTLE OF THE AMAZONS.

Ambassadors, The. See TWO AMBASSADORS.

Ambassadors' Club. See COVENTRY CLUB.

Ambras Armoury. [Ger. *Ambraser Sammlung.*] A famous collection of ancient armor, jewels, and curiosities, in the Belvedere, Vienna, Austria. It derives its name from the Castle of Ambras in the Tyrol, from which place it was brought to Vienna in the early part of this century.

Ambrosian Library. [Ital. *Bibliotéca Ambrosiana.*] A noted library in Milan, Italy, containing some celebrated manuscripts. It was founded in 1602, and was named after St. Ambrose, the patron saint of the city.

Ambush, The. A picture by George H. Boughton, a contemporary painter of landscapes and *genre*.

Amer, Mosque of. See MOSQUE OF AMER.

America, The. 1. A war-vessel of the old American navy, built between 1775 and 1783. She carried 74 guns, and was pronounced by Commodore Jones "the largest of seventy-fours in the world." She was presented to the French government before she went to sea, and was finally captured from the French by the British.

2. A noted schooner-rigged yacht, celebrated for her speed and the excellence of her model. The victory of this yacht over R. Stephenson's iron yacht *Titania* in a race, August, 1851, demonstrated the superiority of the model upon which the *America* was built. She is now in the possession of Gen. Benjamin F. Butler.

Amiens Cathedral. See NOTRE DAME [d'Amiens].

Amphion, The. A British frigate destroyed by an explosion in the harbor of Plymouth, England, Sept. 22, 1796. Nearly all on board perished.

Amphitrite, The. A ship which was wrecked off Boulogne, France, in 1833, with a loss of over 100 passengers.

Amrita Saras. [Fount of Immortality.] A famous temple in Amritsar, India, one of the sacred places of the Hindus. The temple is situated on an island in the centre of a reservoir or tank about 150 paces square. It was constructed in 1581.

Amsterdam Vegetable Market. A picture by Gabriel Metzu (b. 1630), a Dutch *genre*-painter. In the Louvre, Paris.

Ananias, Death of. See DEATH OF ANANIAS.

Anatomical Lecture. A celebrated picture by Rembrandt van Ryn (1607–1669), the Dutch painter. It bears date 1632, and is now in the Museum of the Hague, Holland.

Ancajani Madonna. See MADONNA ANCAJANI.

Ancaster House. See LINDSEY HOUSE.

Ancient and Honorable Artillery Company. The oldest regular military company in the United States, organized in 1638. Its armory and interesting collection of military and other relics are in Faneuil Hall, Boston. An Artillery Company was incorporated in England under Henry VIII.

And the old books in uniforms as varied as those of the *Ancient and Honorable Artillery Company* used to be, if my memory serves me right. *Holmes.*

Ancient Italy. A picture by Joseph Mallord William Turner (1775–1857), the eminent English painter.

Andersonville Prison. A noted military prison in Sumter Co., Georgia, in which, during the civil war in the United States, many Union soldiers were confined, and subjected to great cruelty.

Andes, Heart of the. See HEART OF THE ANDES.

Andrea del Sarto. A portrait of himself by the painter (1488–1530). In the collection of autograph portraits in the Uffizi, Florence, Italy.

Andromeda. A picture by Guido Reni (1575–1642), in the casino, or summer-house, of the Rospigliosi palace, in Rome.

Angel, The. An old and famous inn in the parish of Islington, London, rebuilt in 1819.

☞ This name has been a common designation of inns and public-houses in England, which were formerly known by the various devices upon their signs.

Angel appearing to the Shepherds. A picture by Thomas Cole (1801–1848). In the Boston Athenæum.

Angelo. See BRIDGE OF ST. ANGELO, MICHAEL ANGELO, MICHAEL ANGELO'S HOUSE, and ST. ANGELO.

Angels, Fall of the. See FALL OF THE ANGELS.

Angels' Heads. 1. A well-known picture, called by this name, by Sir Joshua Reynolds (1723–1792). "The head of Miss Gordon, the niece of 'No-Popery' Lord Gordon, appears in five different positions, with cherubs' wings." This picture is in the National Gallery, London, and has been often reproduced.

2. Picture-groups bearing this name, by Correggio, and by others, are very familiar through photographic reproductions.

Angerstein Gallery. The collection of pictures which formed the nucleus of the present National Gallery, London. See NATIONAL GALLERY.

Animali, Sala degli. See SALA DEGLI ANIMALI.

Anna, St. See ST. ANNA.

Anne Hathaway's Cottage. A house in the village of Shottery, near Stratford-on-Avon, England, which is pointed out as the cottage in which Anne Hathaway lived prior to her becoming the wife of Shakespeare.

☞ "It is a timber and plaster house, like John Shakespeare's, standing on a bank, with a roughly paved terrace in front. The parlor is wainscoted high in oak, and in the principal chamber is an enormous and heavily carved bedstead. Though a rustic and even rude habitation when measured by our standard, it was evidently a comfortable home for a substantial yeoman in the time of Queen Elizabeth, and is picturesque enough for the cradle of a poet's love."
Richard Grant White.

Anne's, St. See ST. ANNE'S.

Annitshkoff Palace. A noted palace in St. Petersburg, Russia, a favorite residence of the imperial family. It is situated on the Nevskoi Prospekt, the main avenue of the city.

Annunciation, The. [Ital. *L'Annunciazione*, Fr. *L'Annonciation*, Ger. *Die Verkündigung*.] A very common subject of representation by the mediæval painters, exhibiting the interview between the angel and the Virgin Mary, according to the account in Luke i. 26-29. Of numerous compositions treating of this subject, the following may be mentioned as among the more celebrated.

Annunciation, The. A picture regarded as miraculous, and formerly held in the highest veneration by all Christendom. It is in a chapel of the church styled *della Santissima Nunziata* in Florence, Italy. It is concealed from the public, and only exhibited to the devout on great occasions. There is a copy of this picture in the Pitti Palace, by Carlo Dolce.

☞ "The name of the painter is disputed; but, according to tradition, it is the work of a certain Bartolomeo, who, while he sat meditating upon the various excellencies and perfections of Our Lady, and most especially on her divine beauty, and thinking with humility how inadequate were his own powers to represent her worthily, fell asleep; and, on awaking, found the head of the Virgin had been wondrously completed, either by the hand of an angel, or by that of St. Luke, who had descended from heaven on purpose. Though this curious relic has been frequently restored, no one has presumed to touch the features of the Virgin, which are, I am told, — for I have never been blessed with a sight of the original picture, — marvellously sweet and beautiful. It is concealed by a veil, on which is painted a fine head of the Redeemer, by Andrea del Sarto; and forty-two lamps of silver burn continually round it." *Mrs. Jameson.*

Annunciation, The. A picture by Giovanni da Fiesole, called Fra Angelico (1387–1455). In the Museum of St. Mark, Florence, Italy.

Annunciation, The. A picture by Hans Memling (d. 1495), the Flemish painter, bearing date 1482, and described as a work of very original conception and marvellous delicacy. It is in possession of Prince Radzivil at Berlin, Germany.

Annunciation, The. A remarkable picture by Baccio della Porta, called Fra Bartolommeo (1469–1517), representing the Virgin on a throne, the angel descending with a lily, and around the throne various saints. In the gallery at Bologna, Italy.

Annunciation, The. A picture by Francesco Francia (1450–1517). In the Brera, Milan, Italy.

Annunciation, The. A small picture by Fra Bartolommeo (1469–1517), the Italian painter. Now in the Louvre, Paris.

Annunciation, The. A picture by Francesco Albani (1578–1660). In the church of S. Bartolomeo, Bologna, Italy.

Anthony's Nose. A well-known promontory on the Hudson River, at the entrance to the Highlands, said to have been so called from Anthony Van Corlear, a trumpeter of Gov. Stuyvesant.

☞ "It must be known, then, that the nose of Anthony, the trumpeter, was of a very lusty size. . . . Now thus it happened, that, bright and early in the morning, the good Anthony, having washed his burly visage, was leaning over the quarter-railing of the galley, contemplating it in the glassy wave below. Just at this moment the illustrious sun, breaking in all his splendor from behind a high bluff of the Highlands, did dart one of his most potent beams full upon the refulgent nose of the sounder of brass, the reflection of which shot straightway down hissing hot into the water, and killed a mighty sturgeon that was disporting near the vessel. The huge monster, being with infinite labor hoisted on board, furnished a luxurious repast to the crew. . . . When this astonishing miracle became known to Peter Stuyvesant, and that he tasted of the unknown fish, he, as may be supposed, marvelled exceedingly, and as a monument thereof he gave the name of Anthony's Nose to a stout promontory in the neighborhood, and it has continued to be called Anthony's Nose ever since that time." *Irving.*

☞ There is also an Anthony's Nose on the shore of Lake George, and another on the Mohawk in Montgomery Co., N.Y.

Antinous, The. A name given to several statues supposed to represent a young Bithynian of distinguished beauty, and a friend of the Emperor Hadrian. According to some historians he drowned himself in the Nile. Hadrian wept for him, and caused the most famous artists to reproduce his image. Among the statues which represent him, there are two *chefs d'œuvre*. One (Belvedere Antinous) is now in the Belvidere of the Vatican, Rome, the other in the Capitol. (See *infra*, 2.) The former, which is now called Mercury, was found near S. Martino ai Monti, a church on the Esquiline, and is a statue of great beauty. Its just proportions and graceful posture have received unqualified praise.

☞ "The Belvedere Antinous is an exquisite image of blooming youth. For soft and delicate beauty, — beauty which, like that of the vernal rose, the sunset cloud, and the breaking wave, is suggestive of brief continuance and early decay, — this statue has no superior, hardly an equal." *Hillard.*

☞ "Poussin declared the Mercury, which at that time was called without reason the *Antinous*, the most perfect model of the proportions of the human body." *Ampère, Trans.*

☞ "The Belvedere 'Mercury,' a young man standing like the Meleager, but still more beautiful. The torso is more vigorous, and the head more refined. A smiling expression flickers lightly over the countenance, the grace and modesty of a well-born youth capable of expressing himself properly, because he is of an intelligent and select race, but who hesitates to speak because his soul is still fresh. Setting aside the Venus of Milo and the statues of the Parthenon, I know of nothing comparable to it." *Taine, Trans.*

Look long enough
On any peasant's face here, coarse and lined,
You'll catch *Antinous* somewhere in that clay,
As perfect-featured as he yearns at Rome
From marble pale with beauty.
Mrs. Browning.

2. An admired statue of Antinous, found in Hadrian's villa, and now in the Capitol, Rome.

☞ "In the Antinous the anatomist would look in vain to detect even the slightest mistake or misconception; yet such is the simplicity of the whole composition, so fine and undulating the forms, that a trifling error would appear a gross fault." *John Bell.*

☞ "The identity of the Capitoline Antinous has only once, I think, been seriously questioned; and yet it may be reckoned more than doubtful. The head is almost certainly not his. How it came to be placed upon a body presenting so much resemblance to the type of Antinous, I do not know. Careful comparison of the torso and the arms with an indubitable portrait will raise the question whether this fine statue is not a Hermes or a hero of an earlier age." *J. A. Symonds.*

3. A famous bas-relief of Antinous, from the Villa Adriana, now in the Villa Albani at Rome, representing the youth crowned with lotus. Winckelmann pronounces it, after the Apollo and the Laocoon, the most beautiful monument of antiquity which time has transmitted to us, "as fresh and as highly finished as if it had just left the studio of the sculptor."

☞ "The bas-relief of the Villa Albani, restored to suit the conception of a Vertumnus, has even more of florid beauty, but whether the restoration was wisely made may be doubted." *J. A. Symonds.*

4. A bust in the Louvre, Paris.

☞ "Among the simple busts, by far the finest, to my thinking, are the colossal head of the Louvre and the ivy-crowned bronze at Naples. The latter is not only flawless in its execution, but is animated with a pensive beauty of expression. The former, though praised by Winckelmann as among the two or three most precious masterpieces of antique art, must be criticised for a certain vacancy and lifelessness." *J. A. Symonds.*

5. A bronze bust in the Museum at Naples, Italy. (See *supra*, 4.)

6. Among other statues of Antinous, is that called the Braschi Antinous, from having belonged to Duke Braschi. This colossal statue, found on the site of the ancient Gabii, is now in the Rotunda of the Vatican, Rome.

Antiope. See JUPITER AND ANTIOPE.

Antiparos, Grotto of. See GROTTO OF ANTIPAROS.

Antoine, Faubourg St. See FAUBOURG ST. ANTOINE.

Antonia, Fortress of. The site of this structure at Jerusalem has been a subject for controversy, but it is thought to have occupied the whole northern section of the Haram. Josephus describes it as being the fortress of the Temple, as the Temple was that of the city, and as having the apartments and conveniences of a palace. He says that the "general appearance was that of a tower, with other towers at each of the four corners, three of which were 50 cubits high, while that at the south-east angle rose to an elevation of 70 cubits, so that from thence there was a complete view of the Temple."

Antonine Column. A celebrated relic of ancient Rome, now standing in the Piazza Colonna, to which it gives its name. It was erected to the Emperor Marcus Aurelius Antoninus by the Senate and Roman people, A.D. 174. The column is surmounted by a statue of St. Paul, placed there by Sixtus V., and the shaft is surrounded by bas-reliefs arranged in a spiral form. One of these bas-reliefs, a figure of Jupiter Pluvius, representing him sending down rain which falls from his outstretched arms, is celebrated from its supposed connection with an old legend that a Christian legion from Mitylene caused rain to fall as the result of their prayers. This story is told by Eusebius, and corroborated by Justin Martyr.

Antoninus and Faustina. See TEMPLE OF ANTONINUS AND FAUSTINA.

Antoninus, Wall of. See WALL OF ANTONINUS.

Antony, St. See ST. ANTONY.

Antwerp Citadel. A famous fortress in Antwerp, Belgium, erected for the Duke of Alva. It has undergone several sieges, and at different times has fallen into the hands of the English and the French.

Apis Mausoleum. A large subterranean tomb at Sakkárah, Egypt, also known as the Serapeum, although the latter title is more properly applied to the temple (no longer in existence) which was built over the excavated tomb. M. Mairette discovered the site of the Serapeum and the Apis Mausoleum in 1860-61. He found them buried in the sand; and the remains of the Serapeum, which he excavated with great difficulty, are now re-buried. The discovery of the Apis Mausoleum was, historically, of much importance. In it were found many inscribed tablets, the most important of which are now in the Louvre at Paris. See SERAPEUM.

☞ "An avenue of sphinxes led up to it [the Serapeum], and two pylons stood before it; round it was the usual enclosure. But it was distinguished from all other temples by having in one of its chambers an opening, from which descended an inclined passage into the rock below, giving access to the vaults in which reposed the mummied representatives of the god Apis. Living, the sacred bull was worshipped in a magnificent temple at Memphis, and lodged in a palace adjoining, — the Apieum: dead, he was buried in excavated vaults at Sakkárah, and worshipped in a temple built over them — the Serapeum." *Murray's Handbook.*

Apollinare in Classe. See SANT' APOLLINARE IN CLASSE.

Apollinarisberg. A hill on the banks of the Rhine, well known to travellers, and crowned with a beautiful modern Gothic church.

Apollino, The. [The little Apollo.] An ancient and admired statue, now in the Tribune of the Uffizi Palace, Florence, Italy.

☞ "After the vivid truth of these two remarkable works [the Wrestlers, and the Knife-Grinder], we are hardly prepared to do full justice to the soft, ideal beauty of the *Apollino*. It is like taking up the Phèdre of Racine, after laying down the first part of King Henry IV." *Hillard.*

Apollo. An ancient statue in the Louvre, Paris, supposed to be a copy of a work by Praxiteles, the Greek sculptor (b. B.C. 392 ?). There is another in the Tribune of the Uffizi, Florence, Italy.

Apollo and Daphne. A work of sculpture by Giovanni Lorenzo Bernini (1598-1680). In the Villa Borghese, Rome.

Apollo and Python. A picture by Joseph Mallord William Turner (1775-1851), the English landscape-painter, regarded one of his best works.

Apollo and the Muses. See PARNASSUS.

Apollo Belvidere. A celebrated statue of Apollo found about the beginning of the sixteenth century at Porto d'Anzio, the ancient Antium. It was purchased by Julius II., when Cardinal, and was placed in the Belvidere of the Vatican, Rome, whence it derives its present name. Connoisseurs now think that this statue is not the original work of a Greek sculptor, but a copy.

☞ "Ardently excited, and filled with divine anger, with which is mingled a touch of triumphant scorn, the intellectual head is turned sideways, while the figure with elastic step is hastening forward. The eye seems to shoot forth lightning; there is an expression of contempt in the corners of the mouth; and the distended nostrils seem to breathe forth divine anger."
Lübke, Trans.

☞ "The Apollo Belvidere belongs to a more recent and a less simple age. Whatever its merit may be, it has the defect of being a little too elegant: it might well please Winckelmann and the critics of the eighteenth century. His plaited locks fall behind the ear in the most charming manner, and are gathered above the brow in a kind of diadem, as if arranged by a woman. This Apollo certainly displays *savoir-vivre*, also consciousness of his rank — I am sure he has a crowd of domestics."
Taine, Trans.

Or view the Lord of the unerring bow,
The God of life, and poesy, and light, —
The sun in human limbs arrayed, and brow
All radiant from his triumph in the fight;
The shaft has just been shot — the arrow bright
With an immortal's vengeance; in his eye
And nostril beautiful disdain, and might
And majesty, flash their full lightnings by,
Developing in that one glance the Deity.
Byron.

Apollo Club. Ben Jonson appears to have been the founder of this club, which met at the noted Devil Tavern, between Temple Bar and the Middle Temple gate, in London. The principal room at the tavern was known as the "Oracle of Apollo." The *Welcome* in gilded letters upon a black-board, and the rules of the Club inscribed in the same manner, were placed over the door and fireplace of the Apollo. The Welcome and the *Leges Conviviales* are to be found in Jonson's works. See DEVIL TAVERN.

☞ "The Club at the Devil does not appear to have resembled the higher one at the Mermaid, where Shakespeare and Beaumont used to meet him [Jonson]. He most probably had it all to himself."
Leigh Hunt.

Apollo Gallery. See GALERIE D'APOLLON.

Apollo Room. An apartment in the Raleigh Tavern, an ancient building in Williamsburg, Va., in which the House of Burgesses met to take into consideration the insurrectionary proceedings then occurring in Massachusetts.

Apollo Sauroctonos. [Lizard-killer.] A bronze statue of Apollo in the Villa Albani at Rome, which in the judgment of Winckelmann is the original statue by Praxiteles, described by Pliny, and the most beautiful bronze statue left in the world. It was found upon the Aventine Mount. There is another statue of the same name in the Vatican.

Apollo, Temple of. See TEMPLE OF APOLLO.

Apollonicon. An immense organ first exhibited in 1817 at the manufactory of the builders, Messrs. Flight and Robson, St. Martin's Lane, London. The instrument was self-acting, and could also be played in the ordinary manner by one or by several performers. The Apollonicon was five years in course of construction, and cost about £10,000.

Apostles, The. See CALLING OF THE APOSTLES, COMMUNION OF THE APOSTLES, and TWELVE APOSTLES.

Apotheosis of Hercules. A well-known picture by François Lemoine (1688–1737), the French historical painter. It is 64 feet by 54 feet in size, and is said to be the largest in Europe. "There are 142 figures in it, and it is probably the most magnificent *pittura di machina* of the decorative period in which it was executed." It is painted on the ceiling of a room in the palace at Versailles.

Apotheosis of Trajan. See TRIUMPH OF TRAJAN.

Apotheosis of Washington. An immense fresco on the interior of the dome of the Capitol in Washington, painted by Brumidi. It covers some 5,000 feet, and cost $40,000.

Apoxyomenes. A celebrated statue of an athlete by Lysippus (flourished time of Alexander the Great), the Greek sculptor; a marble copy of which, found at Trastevere in 1846, is now in the Vatican, Rome.

The legs and arms [of the Antinous] are modelled with exquisite grace of outline; yet they do not show that readiness for active service which is noticeable in the statues of the Meleager, the *Apoxyomenos*, or the Belvedere Hermes. *J. A. Symonds.*

Appian Way. See VIA APPIA.

Apprentices. See IDLE AND INDUSTRIOUS APPRENTICES.

Approach to Venice. A picture by Joseph Mallord William Turner (1775-1851), the eminent English painter.

Apsley House. The former well-known residence of the Duke of Wellington, Piccadilly, London. It immediately adjoins Hyde Park. It was built about 1785 for Charles Bathurst, Lord Apsley, and was purchased by Marquis Wellesley, elder brother of the great Duke, in 1828. It contains a collection of pictures.

Ara Cœli. [Altar of Heaven.] A very interesting church in Rome, of high antiquity, occupying the site of the temple of Jupiter Capitolinus. It was in this church that Gibbon, as he himself informs us, on the 15th of October, 1764, as he sat musing amidst the ruins of the Capitol, while the barefooted friars were singing vespers, first meditated writing the history of the Decline and Fall of the city. The name Ara Cœli is traditionally derived from the altar consecrated by Augustus in consequence of the sibyl's prophecy about the coming of the Redeemer, a monkish invention wholly unsupported by historical evidence. Some say, however, that in the middle ages the church was called "S. Maria in *Aurocœlio*." The church of Ara Cœli is held in great reverence by the people, on account of the famous wooden image called the *Santissimo Bambino*, supposed to be of great efficacy in curing the sick. The steps of this church are the identical ones which formed the ascent to the temple of Jupiter Capitolinus. See BAMBINO.

☞ "On the steps of Ara-Cœli, nineteen centuries ago, the first great Cæsar climbed on his knees after his first triumph. At their base Rienzi, the last of the Roman tribunes, fell. . . . Standing on a spot so thronged with memories, the dullest imagination takes fire." *W. W. Story.*

☞ "A flight of 124 steps of marble leads to the church of Ara-Cœli, one of the oldest and ugliest in Rome. But no one is held in greater reverence by the people, and none is more frequented by throngs of worshippers." *G. S. Hillard.*

☞ "A staircase of extraordinary width and length stretches upward to the red façade of the church of Ara-Cœli. On these steps hundreds of beggars, as ragged as those of Callot, clad in tattered hats and rusty brown blankets, are warming themselves majestically in the sunshine. You embrace all this in a glance, the convent and the palace, the colossi and the *canaille;* the hill, loaded with architecture, suddenly rises at the end of a street, its stone masses spotted with crawling human insects. This is peculiar to Rome." *Taine, Trans.*

Returning home by *Ara Cœli*, we mounted to it by more than 100 marble steps, not in devotion,—as I observed some to do on their bare knees,—but to see those two famous statues of Constantine in white marble, placed there out of his Baths. *John Evelyn*, 1644.

Arbroath Abbey. This ruin of the most spacious abbey in Scotland is in Aberbrothwick. It was built in 1178, and dedicated to St. Thomas à Becket. There is a tradition that the Abbots of Aberbrothwick placed a bell on a dangerous reef in the German Ocean, and this story gave rise to a ballad of Southey's.

The Abbot of Aberbrothock
Had placed that bell on the Inchcape rock.
Southey.

See INCHCAPE ROCK.

Arc de l'Étoile, *or* **Arc de Triomphe.** A very large and fine triumphal arch at the west end of the Champs-Elysées, Paris. It is one of the chief ornaments of the city, and, from its high situation, commands an extensive view over Paris. In 1806 Napoleon resolved to build this arch, and its construction was begun; but the work as now seen was not finished until 1836, after the accession of Louis Philippe. It is of a classical design; and the whole structure is 161 feet high, 145 feet wide, and 110 feet deep.

☞ "It was not, however, till we stood almost beneath it that we really felt the grandeur of this great arch, including so large a space of the blue sky in its airy sweep. At a distance it impresses the spectator with its solidity; nearer, with the lofty vacancy beneath it." *Hawthorne.*

She [Mme. de B——] is not a cabinet minister, she is not a marshal of France, she has no appointments in her gift, she lives beyond the *Arc de l'Étoile*; but, for all that, people go to visit her from the four corners of Paris. *Taine, Trans.*

With every respect for Kensington turnpike, I own that the *Arc de l'Etoile* at Paris is a much finer entrance to an imperial capital. *Thackeray.*

You find here [in Rome] less space and stone-work, less material grandeur than in the Place de la Concorde, and in the *Arc de Triomphe*, but more invention and more to interest you. *Taine, Trans.*

Arc de Triomphe. See ARC DE L'ÉTOILE.

Arc du Carrousel. A triumphal arch in the centre of the Place du Carrousel, Paris, 48 feet high, 65 feet wide, begun in 1806. It is a copy, with alterations, of the Arch of Severus at Rome. Formerly the Arc du Carrousel was surmounted by four horses of bronze from St. Mark's, Venice; but these were returned to Venice in 1814.

Arcade, The. A well-known building in Providence, R.I., being an immense granite bazaar 225 feet in length by 80 feet in depth (in parts 130 feet deep), containing under one glass roof 78 stores. The building was erected in 1828.

Arcadian Academy. [Ital. *Accademia degli Arcadi.*] A literary institute at Rome, founded in 1690, which still holds its meetings in the Capitol. Its aim, which it failed to reach, was to improve the literary taste of the time, and at one period it numbered some 2,000 members. Its laws were drawn out in ten tables, its constitution was republican, its first magistrate was called *custos*, and its members shepherds. Goethe was enrolled as an Arcadian in 1788.

☞ "Each person on his admission took a pastoral name, and had an Arcadian name assigned to him: the business of the meetings was to be conducted wholly in the allegorical language, and the speeches and verses as much so as possible. . . . The Arcadia has survived all the changes of Italy; it still holds its meetings in Rome, listens to pastoral sonnets, and christens Italian clergymen, English squires, and German counsellors of state, by the names of the heathens. It publishes moreover a regular journal, the *Giornale Arcadico*, which, although it was a favorite object of ridicule with the men of letters in other provinces, condescends to follow slowly the progress of knowledge, and often furnishes foreigners with interesting information, not only literary but scientific." *Spalding.*

Arch of Augustus. An old Roman memorial arch in Rimini, Italy.

Arch of Constantine. One of the most imposing monuments of ancient Rome, standing over the Via Triumphalis. It is ornamented with bas-reliefs and medallions illustrating the history of Trajan. These were taken from an arch of Trajan to decorate that of Constantine, though some writers have regarded the whole structure of Constantine as a transformed arch of Trajan. The frieze and sculptures upon the arch, which are of the time of Constantine, show plainly the decay which the art of sculpture had suffered since the age of Trajan.

☞ "The Arch of Constantine . . . is, I think, by far the most noble of the triumphal arches of Rome. Its superiority arises partly, no doubt, from its fine preservation. Its ancient magnificence still stands unimpaired." *C. A. Eaton.*

Arch of Drusus. A triumphal arch near the gate of San Sebastiano in Rome, the oldest monument of this kind now in existence in the city.

Arch of Hadrian. This gate, on the outskirts of the modern city of Athens, Greece, is inscribed on the side toward the Acropolis, "This is Athens, the ancient city of Theseus;" on the other side, "This is the city of Hadrian, and not of Theseus."

Arch of Janus. (Quadrifrons.) This structure, which is rather inaccurately called an arch, since it consists of four arches, is now standing in what was once the Forum Boarium, Rome. It is a large square mass, each of its four fronts being pierced with an arch, which gives rise to the belief that it was a *Compitum*, a kind of structure which was generally erected at the meeting of four roads. It is supposed to have been used as a shelter from the sun and rain, and as an exchange or place of business for those trading in the Forum. The date of its construction is unknown, though it has been usually assigned to the time of Septimius Severus (146–211), and by some to as late an age as that of Constantine.

☞ "I know few ruins more picturesque and venerable than this. That this arch is a work of imperial Rome, there can be no doubt, but the date of its erection is purely conjectural." *Eaton.*

Arch of Septimius Severus. 1. A noted monument of ancient Rome, standing at the north-west angle of the Forum. It was built of marble, A.D. 205, in honor of the emperor Septimius Severus and his sons Caracalla and Geta, and consists of one large and two smaller arches. It is ornamented with bas-reliefs relating to the Eastern wars of the emperor, and was formerly surmounted by a car drawn by six horses abreast, and containing statues of Septimius Severus and his two sons. The part of the inscription of the arch relating to Geta was obliterated after his murder by his brother.

☞ "The heavy and clumsy style of its architecture is sufficiently striking when viewed beside the noble buildings of the Forum, in which it stands. Indeed, I know few ancient edifices in which the arts have been so completely tortured out of their native graces. The whole building is covered with a profusion of bas-reliefs, and their deformity of design and execution is sufficiently evident through all the injuries of time and accident. . . . Though this arch is entire, the sculpture has evidently suffered from fire." *Eaton.*

☞ "In the later days of the Empire two side arches were added for foot-passengers, in addition to the carriage-way in the centre. This added much to the splendor of the edifice, and gave a greater opportunity for sculptural decoration than the single arch afforded. The Arch of Septimius Severus is perhaps the best specimen of the class." *Fergusson.*

2. There is also a smaller Arch of Septimius Severus in the Velabrum, Rome, near the church of S. Giorgio in Velabro. It was erected to the emperor Severus, his wife Julia, and his sons Caracalla and Geta, by the silversmiths (*Argentarii;* hence it is also called *Arcus Argentarius*) and tradespeople of the Forum Boarium. The dedication of this arch was changed after the death of Geta, as in the case of the larger arch described above.

Arch of Titus. The most elegant triumphal arch in Rome. It stands upon the summit of the Via Sacra, and was erected by the Roman Senate and people in honor of Titus to commemorate the destruction of Jerusalem. As a record of Bible history it is the most interesting ruin in Rome, containing as it does a representation in bas-relief of the spoils brought from the Temple; among which may be recognized the table of shew-bread, the silver trumpets, and the golden seven-branched candlestick which is said to have fallen into the Tiber during the flight of Maxentius from the onslaught of

Constantine. There is a close resemblance between the bas-reliefs on this arch representing the trophies brought from Jerusalem, and the account of them given by the Jewish historian Josephus.

☞ "The Arch of Titus — the most ancient and perhaps the most faultless of the Triumphal Arches — was the work of an age when the arts, which in the age of Domitian had degenerated from their ancient simplicity into a style of false and meretricious ornament, had revived in their fullest purity and vigor, beneath the patronage of Trajan. But we now see it to great disadvantage. The hand of Time has robbed it of much of its ancient beauty, his 'effacing fingers' have obliterated much of the expression and grace and even outline of the bas-reliefs, the design and composition of which we can yet admire." *Eaton.*

☞ "Over the half-worn pavement, and beneath this arch, the Roman armies had trodden in their outward march to fight battles, a world's width away. Returning victorious, with royal captives and inestimable spoil, a Roman triumph, that most gorgeous pageant of earthly pride, has streamed and flaunted in hundred-fold succession over these same flagstones and through this yet stalwart archway." *Hawthorne.*

☞ "The Arch of Titus is the most graceful in its form of all the Roman arches. . . . The Jews to this day, it is said, never pass under this arch; avoiding the sight of this mournful record of the downfall of their country and the desecration of their religion." *Hillard.*

I stood beneath the *Arch of Titus* long;
On Hebrew forms there sculptured long I pored;

Titus! a loftier arch than thine hath spanned
Rome and the world with empery and law;
Thereof each stone was hewn from Israel!
Aubrey de Vere.

Arch of Trajan. 1. A fine relic of Roman times at Benevento, Italy. The arch, which is nearly perfect, is now called the *Porta Aurea*.

2. An old Roman triumphal arch in Ancona, Italy.

Archery Guild. [Dutch, *het Doclenstück.*] A celebrated picture by Bartholomew van der Helst (1613–1670), the Dutch painter. It is now in the Amsterdam Gallery. There is a replica of the same now in the Louvre in Paris.

Archimedes, The. The first vessel propelled by a screw. She was built by the English Admiralty in 1838, and made her first trip in 1839.

Arctic, The. A vessel of the Collins line of transatlantic steamers which sank in 1854, with a loss of many lives, in consequence of a collision with the *Vesta.*

☞ "In that mysterious shroud, that vast atmosphere of mist, both steamers were holding their way with rushing prow and roaring wheels, but invisible. At a league's distance, unconscious, and at nearer approach, unwarned; within hail, and bearing right towards each other, unseen, unfelt, till in a moment more, emerging from the gray mists, the ill-omened *Vesta* dealt her deadly stroke to the *Arctic*. . . . In a wild scramble that ignoble mob of firemen, engineers, waiters, and crew, rushed for the boats, and abandoned the helpless women, children, and men, to the mercy of the deep! Four hours there were from the catastrophe of collision to the catastrophe of SINKING!" *H. W. Beecher.*

Ardennes. [Written also poetically *Arden.*] An ancient forest of vast extent in Belgium and the North of France, of which but little remains at the present time. The Forest of Arden is familiar to readers of "As You Like It." There was an ancient forest named Arden in the central part of England, which has now entirely disappeared. Shakespeare's "Arden" is by some identified with the English forest.

☞ "The wood of Soignies is supposed to be a remnant of the forest of Ardennes, famous in Boiardo's Orlando, and immortal in Shakespeare's 'As You Like It.' It is also celebrated in Tacitus as being the spot of successful defence by the Germans against the Roman encroachments." *Byron.*

Oli. Where will the old Duke live?
Cha. They say he is already in the *Forest of Arden*, and a many merry men with him; and there they live like the old Robin Hood of England. *Shakespeare.*

And *Ardennes* waves above them her green leaves,
Dewy with nature's tear-drops as they pass. *Byron.*

That motley clown in *Arden* wood,
Whom humorous Jaques with envy viewed,
Not even that clown could amplify
On this trite text so long as I. *Scott.*

The forest-walks of *Arden's* fair domain,
Where Jaques fed his solitary vein,
No pencil's aid as yet had dared supply,
Seen only by the intellectual eye.
Charles Lamb.

Ardfert Abbey. An interesting and picturesque monastic ruin in the county of Kerry, Ireland, near Tralee, of high antiquity.

Ardtornish Castle. An ancient ruined castle of the fourteenth century, in the island of Mull, formerly a place of great consequence as a stronghold, and as the headquarters of the "Lords of the Isles." Its situation, on a low basaltic promontory overlooking the sea, is very picturesque. [Written also *Artornish* and *Ardtonish.*]

Ardtornish on her frowning steep,
'Twixt cloud and ocean hung. *Scott.*

Wake, Maid of Lorn! the minstrels sung.
Thy rugged halls, *Artornish*, rung;
And the dark seas thy towers that lave,
Heaved on the beach a softer wave. *Ibid.*

Arena, The [of Arles]. A Roman ruin in the city of Arles, France. This amphitheatre is thought to have surpassed in the days of its splendor that at Nîmes.

There, the huge Coliseum's tawny brick,
The twin arcs hand in hand. But there is one
In mine own country I saw clearer yet.
Thou art the *Arles arena* in my eyes,
Great ruin! *Aubanel, Trans.*

Arena, The [of Nîmes]. A remarkable Roman ruin at Nîmes, in Southern France. The amphitheatre is 437 feet long, 332 feet broad, and 72 feet high, and is one of the finest remains of the kind in existence.

☞ "Rousseau, in the last century, complained of the neglected state in which the arenas of Nîmes were allowed to lie. . . . Not till the year 1810 was an act passed for the clearing of this great amphitheatre, and now there is no obstruction to the view. Situated in the middle of the town, and not far from the ancient wall, the arenas [Fr. *Les Arènes*] of Nîmes have long been famous for their size and preservation. They are supposed to be contemporaneous with the Coliseum. . . . The interior presents only a picturesque mass of ruins, but the principal parts may even yet be easily distinguished."
Le Fèvre, Trans. Donald.

☞ "If the arena of Arles is better preserved in the interior, the wall of that of Nîmes is more intact, and its crown has not suffered so much. . . . Taken together these two amphitheatres furnish almost complete details of the construction of these buildings, the purpose of which, and their gigantic proportions, argue a state of things so different from our own." *Mérimée.*

Arena, The [of Verona]. A celebrated Roman ruin in Verona, Italy, being an amphitheatre of the age probably of Diocletian, and in a remarkable state of preservation. It is still used for theatrical purposes.

☞ "In the midst of Verona is the great Roman amphitheatre. So well preserved, and carefully maintained, that every row of seats is there, unbroken. Over certain of the arches the old Roman numerals may yet be seen; and there are corridors, and staircases, and subterranean passages for beasts, and winding ways above ground and below, as when the fierce thousands hurried in and out, intent upon the bloody shows of the arena." *Dickens.*

☞ "The amphitheatre is interesting from the excellent preservation in which the interior still continues. . . . We see here that root of utility out of which the flower architecture springs. The idea of an amphitheatre is simply that of a building in which he who is the most distant, in a horizontal line, shall have the highest place. This is the way in which a crowd, on any occasion of interest, dispose themselves. The amphitheatre is still used for public exhibitions. I could not help thinking what a capital place it would be for a political caucus or a mass-meeting. It will hold twenty-two thousand spectators."
Hillard.

☞ "The arena of this amphitheatre [at Verona] is very nearly perfect, owing to the care taken of it during the Middle Ages, when it was often used for tournaments and other spectacles. Its dimensions are 502 feet by 401, and 98 feet high, in three stories, beautifully proportioned." *Fergusson.*

☞ "This edifice seen from above looks like an extinct crater. If one desires to build for eternity it must be in this fashion." *Taine, Trans.*

Arena Chapel. A celebrated chapel in Padua, Italy, noted for the fine fresco decorations of Giotto (1276-1336), with which its walls are covered.

Areopagus. [Hill of Mars.] A hill in Athens, Greece, on the north-east side of the Agora, and between the Pnyx and the Acropolis.

☞ "Above the steps [by which the hill is ascended], on the rocky pavement of the hill, are the stone seats on which the court of the Areopagus sits. In this spot, distinguished by rude simplicity, is assembled the council by whose predecessors heroes and deities are said to have been judged, and whose authority commands respect and enforces obedience when other means fail, and whose wisdom has saved their country in times of difficulty and danger, when there appeared to be no longer any opportunity for deliberation."
C. Wordsworth.

Then Paul stood in the midst of *Mars' Hill*, and said, Ye men of Athens, I perceive that in all things ye are too superstitious. *Acts xvii. 22.*

Pallas in figures wrought the heavenly powers,
And *Mars's Hill* among the Athenian towers. *Ovid, Trans.*

Arethusa, Fountain of. See FOUNTAIN OF ARETHUSA.

Argus, The. A noted vessel of the United States Navy, built at Washington, and in service in the war of 1812. She was captured by the English *Pelican*, Aug. 14, 1813.

Argyll House. A mansion in Argyll Street, London, formerly the residence of the Duke of Argyll, taken down in 1862.

Or hail at once the patron and the pile
Of vice and folly, Greville and *Argyle!*
Where yon proud palace, Fashion's hallow'd fane,
Spreads wide her portals for the motley train,
Behold the new Petronius of the day,
Our arbiter of pleasure and of play!
Byron.

Argyll Rooms. Formerly a fashionable place of entertainment in London, where balls, concerts, etc., were held. The buildings were burnt down in 1830.

While walking through the nightly procession of the Haymarket, I thought about the *Argyll Rooms*, a sort of pleasure casino which I had visited the night before. *Taine, Trans.*

Ariadne. A famous Greek statue, representing Ariadne sleeping. It was at one time thought to be a figure of Cleopatra. In the Gallery of Statues in the Vatican, Rome.

☞ "The effect of sleep, so remarkable in this statue, and which could not have been rendered by merely closing the lids over the eyes, is produced by giving positive form to the eyelashes, a distinct ridge being raised at right angles to the surface of the lids."
Shakspere Wood.

☞ "One of the finest works of antiquity . . . especially admirable for the drapery, which hangs in the most natural folds, revealing the fine outline of the limbs which it veils, but managed with great refinement."
G. S. Hillard.

Ariadne. A well-known and much admired group of statuary, representing Ariadne on a panther, by Johann Heinrich Dannecker (1758–1841). In the Ariadneum, or Museum of Bethmann, in Frankfort-on-the-Main.

Ariadne. See BACCHUS AND ARIADNE.

Ariosto's House. The house of the poet (1474–1533) is still standing in the Via dei Ariostei, Ferrara, Italy.

Arkansas, The. A monster armor-plated "ram" of the Confederate Navy, in the war of the Rebellion. Her mission was to "drive the Yankees from New Orleans." For that purpose she went down the river; but encountering the three Union gunboats, the *Essex*, *Cayuga*, and *Sumter*, she was driven ashore and set on fire.

Arkhangelski Sabor. See ST MICHAEL'S.

Arles Amphitheatre [or Arena]. See ARENA.

Arlington House. A noted mansion on the heights opposite Washington, D.C., overlooking the Potomac. It was once the property of Gen. Washington, who left it to his adopted son, George Washington Parke Custis, from whom it descended to Robert E. Lee, the General of the

Confederate Army. During the war of the Rebellion the estate was a camp-ground for the Federal troops, and the house was occupied as a headquarters. In 1863 the place was sold, and came into the possession of the United States.

Armada, The Spanish. This famous naval armament, or expedition, known as the *Invincible Armada*, was collected by Philip II. of Spain, and by him sent against England in 1588. The Armada, consisting of 130 ships, about 2,500 great guns, nearly 5,000 quintals of powder, about 20,000 soldiers, besides volunteers, and more than 8,000 sailors, arrived in the Channel on the 19th of July, and in the first engagement was defeated by the English fleet, which was commanded by Howard, Drake, Frobisher, and others. Several of the Spanish vessels were captured, and others destroyed. Afterwards fire-ships were sent into the Spanish fleet, which caused so much alarm that the Armada put to sea in disorder, closely pursued by the English fleet, which attacked it so vigorously and kept up so persistent an engagement that the immense armament was fairly routed. A number of the Spanish ships were destroyed, many were injured, a large number of men were killed; and the Spanish commanders received such a fright that they did not dare return home the way they had come, but resolved to sail through the North Sea and round Scotland to avoid risking another engagement. In this passage they suffered from storms and disasters, many of the vessels were wrecked, and of the whole fleet but 53 shattered vessels and a little more than one-third of the army reached Spain. The attack of the Armada cost the English only one ship.

☞ "There was never any thing that pleased me better than seeing the enemy flying with a southerly wind to the northward." *Drake.*

Armadale Castle. The seat of Lord Macdonald in the island of Skye, one of the Hebrides.

Armenian Convent [in Jerusalem]. This conventual establishment, which is the most aristocratic in Syria, was formerly the property of the Georgians, by whom it was founded in the eleventh century. The convent has accommodations for three thousand pilgrims. Here are reputed to be the tomb of St. James, the stone which closed the Holy Sepulchre, the spot where Peter denied the Saviour, and the court where the cock crew. It contains a very gorgeous chapel. The Armenian Patriarchs of Jerusalem are buried here.

Armourers' Hall. The building of the Armourers' Company, one of the old city companies of London. In Coleman Street.

Armoury. See HORSE ARMOURY.

Army and Navy Club. A house opposite the War Office, in Pall Mall, London, opened in 1851, is occupied by this well-known club. It is a superb edifice, and, including the land, cost not far from £100,000. In 1837, Sir Edward Barnes and others originated the idea of founding a military club; and the Duke of Wellington became a patron, under the stipulation that the navy and marines should be included in the scheme of the club.

Arnolfini, Jean. See JEAN ARNOLFINI.

Arnstein Abbey. An ancient ruined monastery with a church still preserved of the fourteenth century, near Dietz, in Germany.

Arques Castle. A ruined fortress a few miles from Dieppe, France. It was an important stronghold in the Middle Ages. Under its walls Henri IV. gained a great victory over the army of the League.

Arrotino, L'. [The Slave sharpening his Knife.] An ancient statue, now in the Uffizi Palace, Florence. The figure is represented as suspending his employment, and looking up as if to listen to something that is said to him. [Often called the *Knife-Grinder*.]

☞ "I found in the figure of the *Knife-Grinder* quite a new revelation of the power of art. As is well known, this statue is an enigma, to which no satisfactory solution has ever been offered. Indeed, whether he is whetting his knife seems somewhat doubtful. But as to its power there can be no doubt. The figure is unideal, and the face and head coarse; but every line glows with the fire of truth. . . . It seemed to me that a single look at this figure had given me a new insight into Roman life and manners, as if one of Terence's characters had been turned into marble for my benefit." *Hillard.*

To be made a living statue of,—nothing to do but strike an attitude. Arm up—so—like the one in the Garden. John of Bologna's Mercury—thus—on one foot. Needy *knife-grinder* in the Tribune at Florence. No, not "needy," come to think of it. *Holmes.*

Arsenal of Venice. This interesting structure is a work of the fourteenth century, of great extent, and containing many memorials of the early power and naval supremacy of Venice.

☞ "No reader of Dante will fail to pay a visit to the Arsenal, from which, in order to illustrate the terrors of his 'Inferno,' the great poet drew one of those striking and picturesque images, characteristic alike of the boldness and the power of his genius. Besides, it is the most characteristic and impressive spot in Venice. The Ducal Palace and St. Mark's are symbols of pride and pomp, but the strength of Venice resided here. . . . Here was the index-hand which marked the culmination and decline of her greatness." *Hillard.*

As in the *Arsenal* of the Venetians
Boils in the winter the tenacious pitch
To smear their unsound vessels o'er again.
Dante, Longfellow's Trans.

Arsenal. See BIBLIOTHÈQUE DE L'ARSENAL.

Arthur's Club. This club in London, referred to by Lady Hervey as "the resort of old and young" in 1756, is so called from Mr. Arthur, the proprietor of White's Chocolate House, who died in 1761. The club-house in St. James's Street was built in 1811, and reconstructed in 1825.

Arthur's Palace. See KING ARTHUR'S PALACE.

Arthur's Round Table. See ROUND TABLE and KING ARTHUR'S ROUND TABLE.

Arthur's Seat. An eminence in Edinburgh, Scotland, 820 feet in height, the most conspicuous feature in the view of the city. It derives its name from Prince Arthur.

☞ "Arthur's Seat, a huge double-headed hill, presenting, from some directions, peculiar resemblance to a recumbent lion." *J. F. Hunnewell.*

Whose muse, whose cornemuse sounds with such plaintive music from *Arthur's Seat*, while . . . the mermaids come flapping up to Leith shore to hear the exquisite music? *Thackeray.*

Why do the injured unresisting yield
The calm possession of their native field?
Why tamely thus before their fangs retreat,
Nor hunt the bloodhounds back to *Arthur's Seat?* *Byron.*

Traced like a map the landscape lies,
In cultured beauty stretching wide;
There ocean with its azure tide;
There *Arthur's Seat.* *D. M. Moir.*

Artist and the Easel. A picture by Adrian van Ostade (1610–1683), the Dutch *genre*-painter, and considered one of his chief works. In the Dresden Gallery.

Artornish Castle. See ARDTORNISH CASTLE.

Arundel Castle. An ancient baronial mansion, the property of the Duke of Norfolk, situated on the River Arun, in Sussex, England. There are references to it as early as the time of King Alfred. The castle stands upon a knoll overlooking the sea. Of the original structure, the gateway, part of the walls, and the keep are still standing. The latter, which is covered with ivy, is a stone tower of a circular form, 68 feet in diameter, and is one of the most interesting feudal remains in England. The castle was mainly in ruins till 1815, when it was restored by the owner at great expense. The buildings and grounds are magnificent.

Arundel House. A celebrated mansion which formerly stood in the Strand, London, and was

taken down in 1678. It was here that the celebrated collection known as the Arundelian Marbles was gathered. See ARUNDELIAN MARBLES.

Arundel Library. A well-known collection now merged in the library of the British Museum, to which it was added in 1831.

Arundelian Marbles. A celebrated collection of ancient Greek statues and monuments, brought to England in 1627 from the island of Paros, and purchased by the Earl of Arundel. After the Restoration in 1660, they were presented by the grandson of the Earl to the University of Oxford. [Called also *Oxford Marbles.*]

How a thing grows in the human Memory, in the human Imagination, when love, worship, and all that lies in the human Heart, is there to encourage it. And in the darkness, in the entire ignorance, without date or document, no book, no *Arundel-marble;* only here and there some dumb monumental cairn. *Carlyle.*

Ascension, Convent of the. A convent on the summit of Mount Olivet, near Jerusalem.

Ascension of Christ. [Ital. *L'Ascensione*, Fr. *L'Ascension*, Ger. *Die Himmelfahrt.*] A favorite subject of representation by the early painters. The following may be mentioned as among the more celebrated and familiar examples.

Ascension, The. A picture by Giotto di Bordone (1276–1336). In the Chapel of the Arena at Padua, Italy.

Ascension, The. A grand altar-picture by Pietro Perugino (1446–1524), originally painted for the church of S. Pietro Maggiore, at Perugia, Italy, and afterwards presented by Pope Pius VII. to the city of Lyons, France, and now preserved in the museum of that city.

Ascension, The. A picture by Antonio Allegri, surnamed Correggio (1494–1534). In the church of S. Giovanni, Parma, Italy.

Ashburnham House. A mansion in London, so named because formerly the residence of Lord Ashburnham. It was built by Inigo Jones.

Asher Place. See ESHER PLACE.

Ashmolean Museum. A building connected with the University of Oxford, England, built by Sir Christopher Wren in 1682, to contain the collections of Ashmole, the antiquary.

Asinelli, Torre degli. See TORRE DEGLI ASINELLI.

Assistance, The. An Arctic exploring vessel which sailed under Commander Austin, in 1850.

Assumption, The. [Ital. *L'Assunzione*, Fr. *L'Assomption*, Ger. *Mariä Himmelfahrt.*] A very common and favorite subject of representation by the early painters, in which is portrayed the exaltation of the Virgin Mary. Of the great number of pictures called by this name, the following may be mentioned as among the more celebrated and familiar.

Assumption, The. A picture by Pietro Perugino (1446–1524). In the Academy at Florence, Italy.

Assumption, The. A celebrated picture by Albert Dürer (1471–1528), the German painter and engraver. The sum of 10,000 florins was paid for this picture by Maximilian, the Elector of Bavaria; but it was destroyed by fire at Munich in 1674. A copy of it by Paul Juvenel of Nuremberg is still preserved in the Stahlhof at Frankfort-on-the-Main.

Assumption, The. A noted picture by Guido Reni (1575–1642), now in the Gallery of Munich, Bavaria.

☞ "The fine large Assumption in the Munich Gallery may be regarded as the best example of Guido's manner of treating this theme." *Mrs. Jameson.*

Assumption, The. A picture bearing this title by Guido Reni (1575–1642) in the National Gallery, London, is, according to the best authorities, an Immaculate Conception.

Assumption, The. A large altar-piece by Domenico di Bartolo (fl. 1440). Now in the Gallery of Berlin, Prussia.

☞ "This is one of the most remarkable and important pictures of the Siena school." *Mrs. Jameson.*

Assumption, The. A picture by Fra Bartolommeo (1477-1517), the Italian painter. It is now in the Museum at Naples, Italy. There is another upon the same subject by this master in the Museum at Naples, and another at Besançon, France.

Assumption, The. A picture by Antonio Allegri, called Correggio (1494-1534). In the cupola of the Duomo at Parma, Italy.

☞ "One glow of heavenly rapture is diffused over all; but the scene is vast, confused, almost tumultuous." *Mrs. Jameson.*

Assumption, The. A celebrated picture by Titian (1477-1576), and regarded as his masterpiece, now in the Accademia delle Belle Arti in Venice, Italy, to which it was removed from the church of S. Maria Gloriosa de' Frari. It is one of the best examples of the work of this renowned master of coloring.

☞ "The injury and neglect this marvellous picture had suffered in the keeping of the Roman Church protected it from the rapacity of the French. The lower part was literally burnt with candles, and the whole so blackened with smoke, that the French commissioners did not think it worth the transport to Paris. It continued in this state till 1816, when, all danger being over, Count Cicognara drew attention to Titian's masterpiece, which was then cleaned and restored." *Eastlake, Handbook of Painting, Note.*

☞ "And Titian's angels impress me in a similar manner. I mean those in the glorious *Assumption* at Venice, with their childish forms and features, but with an expression caught from beholding the face of 'our Father that is in heaven:' it is glorified infancy. I remember standing before this picture, contemplating those lovely spirits one after another, until a thrill came over me like that which I felt when Mendelssohn played the organ, and I became music while I listened." *Mrs. Jameson.*

Assumption, The. A celebrated picture by Peter Paul Rubens (1577-1640). Of a number of compositions upon this subject by Rubens, the most famous and splendid is that in the Museum at Brussels, Belgium.

Astankina. A summer palace and park in the immediate neighborhood of Moscow, Russia, belonging to the noble family of Cheremetieff. The grounds are laid out after the manner of Versailles.

☞ "Here was the scene of one of those gigantic pieces of flattery by which the courtiers of Catherine II. sought to keep or win her favor. During a visit of that empress to Astankina, she remarked to the proprietor, 'Were it not for the forest, you would be able to see Moscow.' The latter immediately set some thousands of serfs to work, and in a few days afterward prevailed upon the empress to pay him another visit. 'Your majesty,' he said, 'regretted that the forest should shut out my view of Moscow. It shall do so no longer.' He thereupon waved his hand, and there was a movement among the trees. They rocked backward and forward a moment, tottered, and fell crashing together, breaking a wide avenue through the forest, at the end of which glittered in the distance the golden domes of the city." *Bayard Taylor.*

Astley's. A well-known place of entertainment, Westminster Bridge Road, London, so called from Philip Astley, the builder of nineteen theatres. It was originally built for equestrian exhibitions. The present theatre, which is the fourth erected upon this site, has been remodelled for performances of the regular drama.

☞ "There is no place which recalls so strongly our recollections of childhood as Astley's. It was not a 'Royal Amphitheatre' in those days, nor had Ducrow arisen to shed the light of classic taste and portable gas over the sawdust of the circus; but the whole character of the place was the same, the pieces were the same, the clown's jokes were the same, the riding-masters were equally grand, the comic performers equally witty, the tragedians equally hoarse, and the 'highly-trained chargers' equally spirited. Astley's has altered for the better — we have changed for the worse." *Dickens.*

He [Canning] came, but said he hated the whole thing; that he had come only because he had given his word; and then, turning suddenly on the Secretary, "Now

if you will let me off from this business to-night, I will treat you to *Astley's*."
George Ticknor.

We have four horses and one postilion, who has a very long whip, and drives his team something like the Courier of St. Petersburg in the circle at *Astley's* or Franconi's. *Dickens.*

Base Buonapartè, filled with deadly ire,
Sets, one by one, our playhouses on fire.
Some years ago he pounced with deadly glee on
The Opera House, then burnt down the Pantheon;
Thy hatch, O Halfpenny! passed in a trice,
Boiled some black pitch, and burnt down *Astley's* twice. *Rejected Addresses.*

Astor Library. A library in New York City, containing more than 100,000 volumes, so named after John Jacob Astor (1763–1848), by whom it was endowed with $400,000.

Astrologer, The. A picture by Giorgio Barbarelli, commonly called Giorgione (1477–1511), in the Manfrin palace, Venice, Italy.

Astrologers, The. See GEOMETRICIANS, THE.

Athassel Priory. A beautiful ruined priory of the thirteenth century, in Tipperary County, Ireland.

Athenæum. In ancient Athens a temple or gymnasium sacred to Minerva, where philosophers, poets, and rhetoricians were accustomed to recite their works. Hence applied in later times to an association or a building devoted to purposes of literature or art.

Athenæum. A noted club-house and club situated in Pall Mall, London, belonging to an association instituted in 1823, and composed of individuals distinguished for their literary or scientific attainments, or as patrons of science, literature, and art. The club-house was built in 1829. The Athenæum has the best club library in London.

☞ "The only club I belong to is the Athenæum, which consists of 1,200 members, among whom are to be reckoned a large proportion of the most eminent persons in the land, in every line — civil, military, and ecclesiastical, peers spiritual and temporal (95 noblemen and 12 bishops), commoners, men of the learned professions, those connected with science, the arts, and commerce in all its principal branches, as well as the distinguished who do not belong to any particular class. Many of these are to be met with every day, living with the same freedom as in their own houses. For six guineas a year every member has the command of an excellent library, with maps, of the daily papers, English and foreign, the principal periodicals, and every material for writing, with attendance for whatever is wanted. The building is a sort of palace, and is kept with the same exactness and comfort as a private dwelling. Every member is a master, without any of the trouble of a master. He can come when he pleases, and stay away as long as he pleases, without anything going wrong. He has the command of regular servants, without having to pay or to manage them. He can have whatever meal or refreshment he wants, at all hours, and served up with the cleanliness and comfort of his own house. He orders just what he pleases, having no interest to think of but his own. In short, it is impossible to suppose a greater degree of liberty in living."
Walker's Original.

☞ "Ninety-nine hundredths of this club are people who rather seek to obtain a sort of standing by belonging to the Athenæum, than to give it lustre by the talent of its members. Nine-tenths of the intellectual writers of the age would be certainly black-balled by the dunces. Notwithstanding all this, and partly on account of this, the Athæneum is a capital club."
New Quarterly Review.

His [M. Guizot's] name was immediately proposed as an honorary member of the *Athenæum*. M. Guizot was black-balled. Certainly, they knew the distinction of his name. But the Englishman is not fickle. He had really made up his mind, now for years as he read his newspaper, to hate and despise M. Guizot; and the altered position of the man as an illustrious exile, and a guest in the country, make no difference to him, as they would instantly to an American.
Emerson.

Every day after leaving the *Athenæum*, I go and sit for an hour in St. James's Park. *Taine, Trans.*

The broad steps of the *Athenæum* are as yet unthronged by the shuffling feet of the literati whose morning is longer and more secluded than that of idler men, but who will be seen in swarms, at four, entering that superb edifice in company with the *employés* and politicians who affect their society. *N. P. Willis.*

Athenæum. A building on Beacon Street, Boston, belonging to the Athenæum corporation, and containing a library of more than 115,000 volumes, and until recently a good collection of paintings and statuary. A great part of the works of art formerly in the Athenæum are now in the Museum of Fine Arts, in Boston. It contains also the library of the American Academy of Arts and Sciences.

Athenæum. A building in Baltimore, Md., containing several libraries, a picture gallery, reading-room, and museum of curiosities

Athenæum. A very common name applied to numerous associations and buildings devoted to purposes connected with literature or art. See *supra*.

Athens, School of. See School of Athens.

Athlone Castle. This castle at Athlone, Ireland, has been prominent in the military history of the island. It underwent a long siege in the reign of James II., and was at last taken by the English.

Atlanta, The. A powerful Confederate ram in the Civil War of 1861–65. She was under the command of Capt. Webb, formerly of the United States Navy. She was captured by the United States vessel-of-war *Weehawken*.

☞ "The *Atlanta* was in the Wilmington River. It was the pleasant month of June. She went down to meet the two monitors [the *Weehawken* and the *Nahant*], accompanied by gunboats crowded with citizens of Savannah, who went to see the fight and enjoy the victory. When her intended victims appeared in sight, Webb assured his 'audience' that the monitors would be 'in tow of the *Atlanta* before breakfast.' As she pushed swiftly toward the *Weehawken*, Capt. Rodgers sent a solid shot that carried away the top of the *Atlanta's* pilot-house and sent her aground. Fifteen minutes afterwards she was a prisoner to the *Weehawken*. 'Providence, for some good reason,' said the astonished Webb pathetically to his crew, 'has interfered with our plans.'" *Lossing.*

Atlas. A noted statue representing Atlas sustaining a globe. This figure is of value as exhibiting the ancient ideas of astronomy. Now in the Museum at Naples, Italy.

Attila. A fresco by Raphael Sanzio (1483–1520) in the Stanza of the Heliodorus, in the Vatican, Rome.

☞ "Raphael's fresco styled 'the Attila' is rather historically than religiously treated: it is, in fact, an historical picture." *Mrs. Jameson.*

Auburn. A place celebrated in Goldsmith's poem of "The Deserted Village." The situation of this village has been much in doubt; but it is now generally supposed to be the same as Lissoy, or Lishoy, in the county of Westmeath, near Athlone, Ireland. There is a village named Auburn (sometimes spelt Albourne) in Wiltshire, near Marlborough, which has by some been identified, but without any apparent reason, with the scene of the poem.

☞ "The village of Lissoy, now and for nearly a century known as Auburn, and so 'marked on the maps,' stands on the summit of a hill. . . . The circumstances under which he [Goldsmith] pictured 'Sweet Auburn' as a *deserted* village, remain in almost total obscurity. If his picture was in any degree drawn from facts, they were in all likelihood as slender as the materials which furnished his description of the place, surrounded by all the charms which poetry can derive from invention. . . . The poem bears ample evidence, that, although some of the scenes depicted there had been stamped upon his memory, . . . the *story* must either be assigned to some other locality, or traced entirely to the creative faculty of the poet." *Mr. and Mrs. Hall.*

☞ "The village in its happy days is a true English village. The village in its decay is an Irish village. The felicity and the misery which Goldsmith has brought close together belong to two different countries and to two different stages in the progress of society. He had assuredly never seen in his native island such a rural paradise, such a seat of plenty, content, and tranquillity, as his *Auburn*. He had assuredly never seen in England all

the inhabitants of such a paradise turned out of their homes in one day, and forced to emigrate in a body to America. The hamlet he had probably seen in Kent; the ejectment he had probably seen in Munster; but by joining the two, he has produced something which never was and never will be seen in any part of the world."
Macaulay.

☞ "He [Goldsmith] paints the friends and scenes of his youth, and peoples Auburn and Wakefield with remembrances of Lissoy." *Thackeray.*

Sweet *Auburn!* loveliest village of the plain. *Goldsmith.*

Auburn, Mount. See MOUNT AUBURN.

Auchinleck House. The mansion of the Boswell family, near Cumnock, Scotland, often alluded to in the memoirs of Johnson, and associated with the name of his biographer.

Audley Castle. A picturesque ruined fortress in the county of Down, Ireland.

Audubon Avenue. A subterranean passage in the Mammoth Cave, Kentucky. It is one mile in length, 50 feet high, and 50 or 60 feet in width.

Auerbach's Cellar. A place of public entertainment, where beer and wine are sold, under an old house in Leipzig, Germany. It is noted as the scene of the traditional feats of the famous magician, Doctor Faustus. His magical exploits of drawing various wines from gimlet-holes bored for the purpose in the table, of making the members of the company seize each other's noses under the delusion that they were grasping bunches of grapes, and his finally riding out of the door upon a cask, are told by Goethe in his dramatic poem of "Faust," one scene of which is laid in Auerbach's Cellar. Two pictures painted upon the walls of the vault are supposed to commemorate the adventures of Faust.

☞ "I supped there during my last visit to Germany, and took some pains to ascertain the traditions connected with it, which the waiter seemed to have a particular pleasure in communicating. He assured me that there was not the shadow of a doubt as to my being seated in the very vault in which both Faust and Goethe had caroused."
Hayward.

☞ "Another interesting place in Leipsic is Auerbach's cellar, which it is said contains an old manuscript history of Faust, from which Goethe derived the first idea of his poem. He used to frequent this cellar." *Bayard Taylor.*

As grosser spirits gurgled out
From chair and table with a spout,
In *Auerbach's Cellar* once, to flout
The senses of the rabble rout,
Where'er the gimlet twirled about
Of cunning Mephistopheles:
So did these cunning spirits seem in store,
Behind the wainscot or the door.
Lowell, Biglow Papers.

Auerback. A ruined castle on the road between Darmstadt and Heidelberg, Germany.

Augustan Age. A picture by Jean Léon Gérôme (b. 1824), the French painter.

Augusteum. A palace in Dresden, Saxony. It contains a valuable collection of works of art and scientific treasures. [Called also the *Japanese Palace.*]

Augustus. See ARCH OF AUGUSTUS, MAUSOLEUM OF AUGUSTUS, PALACE OF THE CÆSARS.

Aurea Domus. See GOLDEN HOUSE.

Aurora. 1. A celebrated fresco by Guido Reni (1575-1642) in the casino, or summer-house, of the Rospigliosi Palace in Rome. It is painted upon the ceiling, and represents Aurora scattering flowers before the chariot of the Sun, while the Hours advance in rapid motion. The engraving of this picture by Raphael Morghen (1758-1833) has made it very familiar. According to Lanzi, the Venus de' Medici and the Niobe were the favorite models of Guido, and there are few of his large pictures in which the Niobe or one of her children is not introduced, yet with such skill that the imitation can hardly be detected.

☞ "Guido's *Aurora* is the very type of haste and impetus; for surely no man ever imagined such hurry and tumult, such sounding and clashing. Painters maintain that it is lighted from two sides: they have my full permission to light *theirs* from three, if it will improve them, but the difference lies elsewhere." *Mendelssohn's Letters.*

☞ "The God of Day is seated on his chariot, surrounded by a choir of dancing Hours, preceded by the early morning Hour, scattering flowers. The deep blue of the sea, still obscure, is charming. There is a joyousness, a complete pagan amplitude, about these blooming goddesses, with their hands interlinked, and all dancing as if at an antique festival." *Taine, Trans.*

What is Guido's Rospigliosi *Aurora* but a morning thought, as the horses in it are only a morning cloud. *Emerson.*

2. A well-known fresco-painting by Giovanni Francesco Barbieri, called Guercino (1590–1666). In the Villa Ludovisi, Rome.

☞ "The Aurora of Guercino fills the ceiling and its curves. She is a young, vigorous woman, her vigor almost inclining to coarseness. Before her are three female figures on a cloud, all large and ample, and much more original and natural than those of the Aurora of Guido . . . A ray of morning light half traverses their faces, and the contrast between the illuminated and shadowed portions is charming. . . . Guercino did not, like Guido, copy antiques · he studied living models, like Caravaggio, always observing the details of actual life, the changes of impression from grave to gay, and all that is capricious in the passion and expression of the face." *Taine, Trans.*

☞ "The work of Guido [see *supra*] is more poetic than that of Guercino, and luminous and soft and harmonious." *Forsyth.*

An *Aurora* by Jean-Louis-Hamon (1821–1874) is known through reproductions.

Aurora, The [of Michael Angelo]. See MORNING, THE.

Aurungzebe Mausoleum. A celebrated tomb erected by Aurungzebe to his daughter, in Aurungabad, Hindostan. It has clustering domes of white marble similar to those of the Taj Mahal, but inferior to the latter in size and splendor. See TAJ MAHAL.

Austerlitz, Battle of. See BATTLE OF AUSTERLITZ.

Austin Friars. The name given to a court or place in London, in which formerly stood a celebrated Augustinian convent, now converted into a Dutch church.

Austria, The. A screw steamer sailing from Hamburg, Germany, destroyed by fire on the open sea in 1858, with a loss of nearly 400 persons, for the most part Germans.

Auto da Fé. A noted picture by Francisco Rizi (1608–1685). In the gallery at Madrid, Spain.

Avalon. The poetical name of Glastonbury, Somersetshire, England, spoken of as an *island*, which, it is conjectured, the place may once have been at certain seasons. Avalon is intimately connected with the romances of King Arthur.

Clustered upon the western side
Of *Avalon's* green hill,
Her ancient homes and fretted towers
Were lying, bright and still.
Henry Alford.

Glory and boast of *Avalon's* fair vale,
How beautiful the ancient turrets rose!
W. L. Bowles.

Ave-Cæsar-Imperator. A picture by Jean Léon Gérôme (b. 1824), the French painter.

Aventine Mount. [Lat. *Mons Aventinus.*] One of the seven hills of Rome. Under the kings two orders had been established at Rome, the Patricians and Plebeians. The revolution which substituted the consular republic for royalty destroyed the equilibrium between these two orders. The plebeians, revolting against the severity of the poor-laws, broke the peace of the city, B.C. 493, by an armed secession to the Aventine Mount. Ancus Martius added the hill to Rome, and peopled it with captives from neighboring Latin villages, thus originating the order of *plebs.* Of the many temples and buildings which once covered the Mount, but very little remains, and its summit is now crowned by the three churches of Sant' Alessio, Il Priorato, and Santa Sabina. The name of the hill is said to be derived from Aventinus, a king of Alba; but some regard it as taken from Avens, a Sabine river; while others give it a more legendary derivation from the story of Romulus and Remus watching the auspices after the foundation of the city. A cliff of the Aventine is famed as the supposed place where the giant Cacus had his cave. The story of his robbery of the oxen of Hercules, and of his subsequent destruction by that hero, is told by Virgil in the eighth book of the Æneid. The poets Ennius, Gallus, and Livius Andronicus lived upon the Aventine.

☞ "Mount Aventinus indemnifies the mind for all the painful recollections the other hills awake; and its aspect is as beauteous as its memories are sweet. The banks at its foot were called the Lovely Strand (*pulchrum littus*). Poetry also has embellished this spot: it was there that Virgil placed the cave of Cacus; and Rome, so great in history, is still greater by the heroic fictions with which her fabulous origin has been decked." *Madame de Staël.*

Abelard had his school, his camp as he called it, upon the mountain, then almost deserted, where now rises the temple of St. Geneviève. This was the *Aventine Mount* of a nation of disciples leaving the ancient schools in order to listen to the fresh and strong words of Abelard. *Lamartine Trans.*

Amidst these scenes. O pilgrim! seek'st thou Rome?
Vain is thy search, — the pomp of Rome is fled;
Her silent *Aventine* is glory's tomb;
Her walls, her shrines, but relics of the dead. *Francisco de Quevedo, Trans.*

Avoca. A beautiful valley in the county of Wicklow, Ireland, celebrated in the verse of Moore. The name signifies the "meeting of the waters."

There is not in the wide world a valley so sweet,
As that vale in whose bosom the bright waters meet.

Axum. See OBELISK OF AXUM.

Ayoon Moosa. See FOUNTAINS OF MOSES.

Ayr, Twa Brigs of. See TWA BRIGS OF AYR.

Azhar, Mosque of. See MOSQUE OF AZHAR.

B.

Babel, Tower of. See BIRS NIMROOD and TOWER OF BABEL.

Babele, Tor di. See TOR DI BABELE.

Babi Humayon. See SUBLIME PORTE.

Babuino, Via. See VIA BABUINO.

Bacchanal, The. 1. A picture by Dosso Dossi (1474–1558), the Italian painter. In the Pitti Palace, Florence, Italy.

2. A picture by Peter Paul Rubens (1577–1640), now at Blenheim, England.

Bacchante. A famous picture by Annibale Caracci (1560–1609). In the Tribune at Florence, Italy.

Bacchus. 1. A famous relic of ancient sculpture, a masterpiece by some attributed to Phidias. In the Museum at Naples, Italy. [Also called the *Torso Farnese*.]

2. A celebrated colossal statue in the Vatican, Rome.

☞ "The same personality [Antinous], idealized it is true, but rather suffering than gaining by the process, is powerfully impressed upon the colossal Dionysus [Bacchus] of the Vatican. What distinguishes this great work is the inbreathed spirit of divinity." *J. A. Symonds.*

3. A statue by Jacopo Sansovino (1477–1570), pronounced "one of the finest statues conceived by any modern in the style of the antique." It is in the Uffizi Gallery, Florence, Italy.

Bacchus. See DRUNKEN BACCHUS and NARCISSUS.

Bacchus and Ariadne. An admired mythological picture by Titian (1477–1576), now in the National Gallery, London.

☞ "The creation of the Bacchus and Ariadne may be said to make a third with that of Shakespeare's Midsummer Night's Dream and Milton's Comus; each given in their own proper language." *Eastlake.*

☞ "Is there any thing in modern art in any way analogous to what Titian has effected in the wonderful bringing together of two times in the *Ariadne* of the National Gallery?" *Charles Lamb.*

Back Bay. An expansion of Charles River, the principal stream flowing into Boston Harbor. On the new made land in this region of the city (to which quarter the name Back Bay is commonly applied) are some of the finest streets and buildings.

The crowds filled the decorous streets, and the trim pathways of the Common and the Public Garden, and flowed in an orderly course towards the vast edifice on the *Back Bay*, presenting the interesting points which always distinguish a crowd come to town from a city crowd. *W. D. Howells.*

Bacon's Brazen Head. See FRIAR BACON'S BRAZEN HEAD.

Badia, La. A celebrated abbey church in Florence, Italy. It was founded in the middle of the thirteenth century. In the immediate neighborhood of Florence is another church built by the Medici, in the fifteenth century, known as La Badia di Fiesole.

Badminton. The seat of the Duke of Beaufort, 10 miles from Chippenham, England.

Bagnigge Wells. Formerly a noted mineral spring in Islington, London. It was much visited by Londoners in the latter part of the eighteenth and first part of the nineteenth century. Its gardens were extensive, and laid out in the fashion of the times; but its mineral springs were the principal attraction. Miss Edgeworth alludes to it as a place of popular resort, and it is often spoken of by authors of the last century. It has ceased to exist.

☞ "Bagnigge Wells were situated on a little stream called the River Bag-

nigge, though scarcely better than a ditch. The House of Bagnigge was at one time inhabited by Nell Gwynn. On an inscription on the front of it stood: 'T. S. This is Bagnigge House near the Pindar a Wakefeilde, 1680.'"
W. Howitt.

Baiæ, Bay of. See BAY OF BAIÆ.

Bailey, Old. See OLD BAILEY.

Baker Street. A well-known street in London, leading north from Portman Square. In Baker Street is Madame Tussaud's celebrated exhibition of wax-work figures. See MADAME TUSSAUD'S EXHIBITION.

What would they say in *Baker Street* to some sights with which our new friends favored us? *Thackeray*

Balbi Palace. [Ital. *Palazzo Balbi.*] A well-known palace in Genoa, Italy, containing some treasures of art.

Balbi. See STRADA BALBI.

Baldacchino. [*The Canopy.*] The bronze canopy which covers the high altar in St. Peter's Church, Rome. It was cast after designs by Bernini in 1633, and made chiefly from the bronze taken from the Pantheon, and partly from metal which Pope Urban VIII. procured from Venice.

☞ "It is difficult to imagine on what ground, or for what purpose, this costly fabric was placed here. It has neither beauty nor grandeur, and resembles nothing so much as a colossal four-post bedstead without the curtains. . . . It is a pursuing and intrusive presence. . . . We wish it anywhere but where it is, under the dome, rearing its tawdry commonplace into that majestic space, and scrawling upon the air its feeble and affected lines of spiral." *Hillard.*

☞ "It only looked like a considerably magnified bedstead — nothing more. Yet I knew it was a good deal more than half as high as Niagara Falls. It was overshadowed by a dome so mighty that its own height was snubbed." *Mark Twain.*

Balduinstein. A feudal fortress on the river Lahn, near Dietz, in Germany. It was built in 1325.

Balgownie, Bridge of. See BRIG O' BALGOWNIE.

Baliol College. A noted college in Oxford, England, being one of the nineteen colleges included in the University. It was founded about the year 1263.

1637. 10 May, I was admitted a fellow communer of *Baliol College*. . . . The fellow communers were no more exempt from exercise than the meanest commoners there. *John Evelyn, Diary.*

Ball's Cave. A natural curiosity in Schoharie County, N.Y. It is traversed in boats which follow the course of a subterranean river at a depth of one hundred feet below the surface of the ground.

Ballybunian. A series of noted caves which are among the most remarkable of the natural wonders of Ireland. They are situated not far from Tralee, in the county of Kerry, Ireland.

Balmoral Castle. A castle in Scotland, on the river Dee, about 40 miles south-west of Aberdeen, belonging to the Queen of England, and occupied by her as a Highland residence.

Baltimore Street. A main avenue in Baltimore, Md., and a favorite promenade.

Baltony. A Druidical temple in the county of Donegal, Ireland, somewhat resembling that at Stonehenge in size and structure.

Bambino Santissimo. [The Holy Infant.] A wooden figure of the infant Saviour, preserved in the church of Ara Cœli at Rome, whose miraculous powers in curing the sick have caused it to be held in wonderful repute. According to the legend it was carved by a Franciscan pilgrim out of a tree from the Mount of Olives, and was painted by St. Luke while the pilgrim was sleeping over his work. The image is extremely rich in gems and jewelry, and is held in such esteem in cases of severe sickness that it has been said by the Italians to receive more fees than any physician in Rome. The festival of the Bambino, which occurs at the Epiphany, attracts crowds of peasantry from all parts of the surrounding country.

☞ "On the 6th of January, the lofty steps of Ara Cœli looked like an ant-hill, so thronged were they with people. . . . Il Bambino, a painted image of wood, covered with jewels, was carried by a monk in white gloves, and exhibited to the people. Everybody dropped down upon their knees." *Frederika Bremer.*

☞ "The disposition of the group and the arrangement of the lights are managed with considerable skill. On this occasion the church is always thronged, especially by peasants from the country." *G. S. Hillard.*

☞ "The miraculous Bambino is a painted doll, swaddled in a white dress, which is crusted over with magnificent diamonds, emeralds, and rubies. The Virgin also wears in her ears superb diamond pendants. The general effect of the scenic show is admirable, and crowds flock to it and press about it all day long." *W. W. Story.*

Garnished from throat to foot with rings
And brooches and precious offerings,
And its little nose kissed quite away
By dying lips. . . .
. . . for you must know
It has its minions to come and go,
Its perfumed chamber, remote and still,
Its silken couch, and its jewelled throne,
And a special carriage of its own
To take the air in, when it will.
T. B. Aldrich.

Banbury Cross. In Oxfordshire, England. The place was famous for its cakes and ale, and also for its Puritanic zeal. In the latter part of Elizabeth's reign an attempt was made to revive the shows and pageants of the Catholic Church in Banbury; but when the performers reached the high cross in Banbury, a collision occurred between them and the Puritans, in which the latter were victorious. The high cross, and three smaller ones, were cut down and hacked in pieces. The magnificent church met with a similar fate.

Ride a cock-horse to *Banbury Cross*,
To see a fine lady ride on a white horse,
Rings on her fingers, and bells on her toes,
That she may make music wherever she goes. *Mother Goose.*

Bangor House. An old ecclesiastical mansion in London — the residence of the Bishops of Bangor — which stood until 1828.

Bâniâs. A noble deserted castle in Syria, of very high antiquity, one of the finest examples of Phœnician architecture. Portions of the building are of the period of the Middle Ages. It was occupied by the Christians at the time of the Crusades, after which it fell into the hands of the Moslems, and in the seventeenth century was allowed to go to ruin. [Called also *Castle of Subeibeh.*]

Bank of England. The great national moneyed institution of England, and the principal bank of deposit and circulation in the world, situated in Threadneedle Street, London. It is sometimes jocularly styled "The Old Lady of Threadneedle Street." It was founded in 1694. The process of weighing gold and printing bank-notes is one of the most wonderful results of mechanical invention. The chief halls of the Bank are open to the public.

The finished glaze of life in Paris is less invariable, and the full tide of trade round the *Bank of England* is not so inexorably powerful. *Anthony Trollope.*

Bank of Ireland. A noble building — formerly the Houses of Parliament — in Dublin.

☞ "The Bank of Ireland is universally classed among the most perfect examples of British architecture in the kingdom; and indeed is, perhaps, unsurpassed in Europe. Yet, strange to say, little or nothing is known of the architect — the history of the graceful and beautiful structure being wrapt in obscurity almost approaching to mystery. It is built entirely of Portland stone, and is remarkable for an absence of all meretricious ornament, attracting entirely by its pure, classic, and rigidly simple architecture. In 1802 it was purchased from government by the governors of the Bank of Ireland, who have since subjected it to some alterations, with a view to its better application to its present purpose. These changes, however, have been effected without impairing its beauty either externally or internally; and it unquestionably merits its reputation as 'the grandest, most convenient, and most extensive edifice of the kind in Europe.'" *Mr. and Mrs. Hall.*

Banks, The. A name familiarly given to the shoal, or submarine table-land, extending some 300 miles eastward of Newfoundland, and much frequented by fishing-craft. The depth of water varies from 25 to 60 fathoms.

The good ship darts through the water, all day, all night, like a fish, quivering with speed, gliding through liquid leagues, sliding from horizon to horizon. She has passed Cape Sable; she has reached the *Banks*, the land-birds are left; no fishermen — and still we fly for our lives.
R. W. Emerson.

Banque de France. [Bank of France.] The Bank of France, in the Rue de la Vrillière, Paris, was founded in 1803. Its capital is 182,500,000 francs, and the average amount of bullion in the large and carefully guarded vaults has been of late years about 300,000,000 francs (£12,000,000). The Bank has branches in the chief large towns.

Banqueting House. A building in Whitehall, London, forming part of a magnificent design by Inigo Jones, but of which only this portion was completed. The ceiling is adorned with paintings by Rubens. Upon a scaffold erected in front of the Banqueting House, Charles I. was led forth to execution.

Baphomet. A small human figure which served among the Templars as an idol, or, more accurately, as a symbol. This figure, of which specimens are to be found in some Continental museums, was carved of stone, and had two heads, one male and the other female, while the body was that of a female. The image was covered with mysterious emblems. The name Baphomet is thought to be an accidental corruption of Mahomet.

Baptism of Christ. A picture by Giotto di Bondone (1276–1336). In the Accademia at Florence, Italy.

Baptism of Christ. A picture by Rogier van der Weyden (1400–1464). In the Museum at Berlin, Prussia.

Baptism of Christ. A fresco by Pietro Perugino (1446–1524), in the Sistine Chapel, Rome.

Baptism of Christ. A well-known picture by Gheerardt David (1484–1523), a Flemish painter. Now in the Academy of Bruges, Belgium.

Baptism of Christ. A picture by Francesco Albani (1578–1660). In the church of S. Georgio, Bologna, Italy.

Baptism of Pocahontas. A picture in one of the panels of the Rotunda in the Capitol of Washington, representing the well-known scene in the early history of Virginia, which is now regarded as destitute of truth, or mainly legendary. This painting was executed by John G. Chapman (b. 1808) under commission from Congress, and is not considered a work of merit. It has become very familiar to the general public by its reproduction as an engraving upon the back of the twenty-dollar note of the national currency.

Baptist. See ST. JOHN THE BAPTIST.

Baptistery of Pisa. A well-known building in Pisa, Italy, forming one of the beautiful and noted group of marble structures which includes the Cathedral, the Baptistery, the Leaning Tower, and the Campo Santo. See PISA CATHEDRAL, LEANING TOWER, CAMPO SANTO.

☞ In this building hangs the celebrated lamp whose measured swinging suggested to Galileo the theory of the pendulum.

Baptistery of San Giovanni. A famous religious edifice in Florence, Italy, noted especially for its beautiful gates — the work of Andrea Pisano and of Lorenzo Ghiberti.

Barbara, St. See ST. BARBARA.

Barberi, Course des. See COURSE DES BARBERI.

Barberini Faun. A celebrated work of ancient sculpture, so called from having once belonged to the Barberini family in Rome, but now preserved in the Glyptothek at Munich, Bavaria. See FAUN, SLEEPING FAUN, DANCING FAUN, etc.

☞ "A colossal male figure of the Satyr class, sleeping, half sitting, half reclining, on a rock. The peculiar merits of this work claim particular notice. It is essentially a work of character. The expression of heavy sleep is admirably given in the head and falling arm. . . . The precise date of this fine statue has not been determined; but the style of form, and excellent technical treatment of the marble, leave little doubt of its having emanated from the best school of sculpture. If not from the hand even of Scopas or Praxiteles, it may without disparagement be considered the work of a scarcely inferior scholar."
R. Westmacott, jun.

Barberini Juno. A colossal statue of the goddess. In the Vatican, Rome. See JUNO.

Barberini Palace. [Ital. *Palazzo Barberini.*] One of the largest palaces in Rome, begun by Pope Urban VIII., and finished by Bernini in 1640. It contains a valuable library, museum, and gallery of paintings. Among the latter is the celebrated portrait of Beatrice Cenci, by Guido. See BEATRICE CENCI.

Barberini Vase. See PORTLAND VASE.

Barbican. A locality in London, so called, as the name indicates, from a former watch-tower of which nothing now remains. Milton lived here in 1616 17, and here wrote some of his shorter poems.

Barcaccia, Fontana della. See FONTANA DELLA BARCACCIA.

Barclay's Brewery. [Barclay, Perkins, and Co.] The largest and most famous brewery in London (Park Street, Southwark), extending over 11 acres, and in which 600 quarters of malt are brewed daily. It is one of the sights of London. It is said to occupy the site of the Globe Theatre of Shakespeare's time.

Therefore, I freely acknowledge that when I see a Jolly young Waterman representing a cherubim, or a *Barclay and Perkins's* Drayman depicted as an Evangelist, I see nothing to commend or admire in the performance, however great its reputed Painter. *Dickens.*

Bardi, Via de'. See VIA DE' BARDI.

Bargello. A palace in Florence, otherwise called the *Palazzo del Podestà*, the seat of the chief tribunal of justice, built in the year 1250. In the sixteenth and seventeenth centuries, the palace, no longer needed for the dwelling of the chief magistrate of a free city, was turned into a jail for common criminals, and what had been once a beautiful chapel was occupied as a larder or store-room. In this room, in 1840, some ancient and precious frescos by Giotto were discovered, among others the now famous portrait of Dante, the only one known to have been made of the poet during his life, and on that account of inestimable value. The palace also contains many treasures of sculpture.

☞ "We went yesterday forenoon to see the *Bargello*. I do not know any thing in Florence more picturesque than the great interior court of this ancient Palace of the Podesta with the lofty height of the edifice looking down into the enclosed space, dark and stern."
Hawthorne.

He [Dante] has been down to hell, and come back as the women in Verona saw him, scarred and singed; far otherwise, truly, than as Giotto painted him on the wall of the *Bargello*, with the clear-cut features, and fresh look of early manhood, and pomegranates of peace in his hand.
Chr. Examiner.

Barnard Castle. A ruined fortress, now the property of the Duke of Cleveland, on the river Tees in England. It gives its name to the town in which it stands.

While, as a livelier twilight falls,
Emerge from *Barnard's* bannered walls.
Scott.

Barnard's Inn. A law establishment, one of the Inns of Chancery, in London.

☞ "I [Pip] was still looking sideways at his block of a face . . . when he [Mr. Wemmick] said here we were at 'Barnard's Inn.' My depression was not alleviated by the announcement, for I had supposed that establishment to be an hotel kept by Mr. Barnard, . . . whereas I now found Barnard to be a disembodied spirit or fiction, and his inn the dingiest collection of shabby buildings ever squeezed together in a rank corner as a club for Tom-cats. . . . A frowsy mourning of soot and smoke attired this forlorn creation of Barnard, and it had strewed ashes on its head, and was undergoing penance and humiliation as a mere dust-hole. Thus far my sense of sight; while dry rot, and wet rot, and all the silent rots that rot in neglected roof and cellar — rot of rat, and mouse, and bug, and coaching stables near at hand besides — addressed themselves faintly to my sense of smell, and moaned, 'Try Barnard's Mixture.'" *Dickens.*

Barrack Bridge. An ancient and noted bridge over the Liffey in Dublin, Ireland. It was formerly called the Bloody Bridge, from a sanguinary conflict fought in its vicinity between the Irish and the English, A.D. 1408.

Barricades, Les. A picture by Ferdinand Victor Eugène Delacroix (1799–1863). In Paris.

He [the painter] is bound to be veracious and dramatic; if he shows us a battle, let it be the *Barricades* of Delacroix. *Taine, Trans.*

Barrière de Vincennes. See Barrière du Trône.

Barrière de Clichy. A noted picture by Horace Vernet (1789–1863). In the Luxembourg, Paris.

Barrière du Combat. An old barrier, corner of the Boulevard du Combat and the Boulevard de la Butte Chaumont, Paris. It is on the line of the fortifications of old Paris.

One of them said of the dancers on the platform [at the Mabille]: They turn like caged beasts, that is the *Barrière du Combat.* *Taine, Trans.*

Barrière du Trône. One of the old gates of Paris, so called from the throne used by Louis XIV. in 1660, at the upper end of the Faubourg St. Antoine, on the road to Vincennes. It was formerly the *Barrière de Vincennes.*

As I wished to see every thing, I went over to the bai Perron at the *Barrière du Trône.* *Taine, Trans.*

Barrogill Castle. A seat of the Earl of Caithness, in the North of Scotland, not far from Wick.

Bartholomew Close. A passage in London, where for a time Milton was secreted.

Bartholomew Fair. A famous fair formerly held at Smithfield, London. It was one of the leading fairs of England, and was established under a grant from Henry I. to the priory of St. Bartholomew. The original grant was for the eve of St. Bartholomew, and the two succeeding days (N. S. Sept. 3 to Sept. 6), but the duration of the fair was afterwards extended to 14 days. Bartholomew Fair was proclaimed for the last time in 1855, and for a long period previous to its abolition was a scene of much license. Many of its customs and abuses are pictured in Ben Jonson's comedy of "Bartholomew Fair." Morley's "Memoirs of Bartholomew Fair" contains many details upon the subject. See Smithfield.

Doll. I' faith, and thou followedst him like a church. Thou whoreson little tidy *Bartholomew* boar-pig, when wilt thou leave fighting o' days, and foining o' nights, and begin to patch up thine old body for heaven? *Shakespeare, Henry IV.*

Not that of pasteboard which men shew
For groats at *Fair of Barthol'mew.* *Butler.*

A countryman coming one day to Smithfield, in order to take a slice of *Bartholomew Fair,* found a perfect show before every booth. The drummer, the fire-eater, the wire-walker, and the salt-box were all employed to invite him in. *Goldsmith.*

To Johnson Life was as a Prison, to be endured with heroic faith: to Hume it was little more than a foolish *Bartholomew-Fair* Show-booth, with the foolish crowdings and elbowings of which it was not worth while to quarrel; the whole would break up, and be at liberty, so *soon.* *Carlyle.*

Bartholomew's Hospital. See St. Bartholomew's Hospital.

Bartolomeo Colleoni. A celebrated equestrian statue in Venice, Italy, designed by Andrea Verrocchio (1432–1488).

☞ "I do not believe that there is a more glorious work of sculpture existing in the world." *Ruskin.*

Basil, St. See St. Basil.

Bass Rock. A fortress on the Frith of Forth, near Edinburgh. It is celebrated as the prison in which the Covenanters were immured.

☞ "It was this fortress that Habakkuk Mucklewrath [a fanatic preacher in Scott's 'Old Mortality'] speaks of in his ravings when he says, 'Am I not Habakkuk Mucklewrath, whose name is changed to Major-Missabib, because I am made a terror unto myself, and unto all that are around me? I heard it: when did I hear it? Was it not in the tower of the Bass, that overhangeth the wide, wild sea? and it howled in the winds, and it roared in the billows, and it screamed, and it whistled, and it clanged, with the screams and the clang and the whistle of the sea-birds, as they floated and flew, and dropped and dived on the bosom of the waters.'"
Mrs. H. B. Stowe.

Bastei, The. A remarkable and noted precipice on the Elbe, in the region called the "Saxon Switzerland."

Bastille. This name — a general term for a strong fortress, protected by bastions or towers — is commonly applied to the structure which was originally a castle for the defence of Paris, but which in later times became the famous prison known as the Bastille. The castle was built in the fourteenth century for the defence of the gate of St. Antoine against the English. It was a stone building of an oblong shape, with eight circular semi-engaged towers, in which (and also in the cellars) the prisons were situated. The Bastille, though not a strong fortress, regarded in the light of modern military science, commanded with its guns the Faubourg St. Antoine, the workmen's quarter. Although by its lofty walls, its guns, and its moat, it seemed proof against any assaults of the people, it was attacked, July 14, 1789, by a mob of 50,000 persons, with twenty cannon, and the assistance of the Gardes Françaises, and was soon taken, after a feeble defence by the governor Delaunay and his small garrison of 82 invalids and 32 Swiss. On the following day the destruction of the building was begun by the exasperated multitude. Although only seven prisoners were found in the Bastille at the time of its destruction, it had been the place of confinement of many persons of the upper classes, — many victims of intrigue, family quarrels, political despotism, and various forms of tyranny, — many noblemen, *savans*, authors, priests, publishers. The position of this famous prison is now marked by the Place de la Bastille. The Bastille was always to the people of Paris a threatening emblem of arbitrariness and oppression. See PLACE DE LA BASTILLE.

☞ "The history of the Bastille would comprehend, strictly speaking, all the intellectual and political movements of France." *Mongin.*

When silent zephyrs sported with the dust
Of the *Bastille*, I sat in the open sun,
And from the rubbish gathered up a stone,
And pocketed the relic, in the guise
Of an enthusiast. *Wordsworth,*

The dark foundations of the *Bastille* walls
Were banked with lengthy, crisp, white, sloping drifts
Of hailstones multitudinous, that lay
Thick as the pebbles on a moonlit beach.
George Gordon McCrae.

There were censors then for those who attempted to write, and the *Bastille* for those who were refractory
Thiers, Trans.

In order to write well on liberty, I should wish to be in the *Bastille*.
Voltaire, Trans.

Bastille, Place de la. See PLACE DE LA BASTILLE.

Bates College. An institution of learning in Lewiston, Me., organized in 1864.

Bates Hall. The main library room in the Public Library building, Boylston Street, Boston, Mass. This room contains the most valuable part of the large collection of books belonging to the city, and was named after the principal benefactor of the institution, Joshua Bates (1788-1864), who contributed largely towards its endowment.

Bath House. The town residence of Lord Ashburton, Piccadilly, London. It contains a fine collection of Dutch and Flemish pictures.

Bathiaz, La. An ancient feudal stronghold in the neighborhood of Martigny, Switzerland.

Bathing Soldiers. See SOLDIERS BATHING IN THE ARNO.

Baths of Caracalla. The most perfect of all the Roman Thermæ, and one of the most impressive ruins of the ancient city, situated on the Via di S. Sebastiano, under the eastern slopes of the Aventine. They were begun by Caracalla about 212 A.D.; and the portions devoted to the baths, which were supplied by the Antonine Aqueduct, are said to have accommodated 1,600 persons at one time, while the whole edifice was nearly a mile in circuit. Many pieces of sculpture, among others the Farnese Hercules, were discovered in these baths. The ruins were a favorite resort of the poet Shelley.

☞ "In the Baths of Caracalla, there is no unity of impression: a mass of details is heaped up like rubbish shot from a cart. They are a town-meeting of ruins without a moderator." *Hillard.*

☞ "They now present an immense mass of frowning and roofless ruins abandoned to decay; and their fallen grandeur, their almost immeasurable extent, the tremendous fragments of broken wall that fill them, the wild weeds and brambles which wave over them, their solitude and their silence; the magnificence they once displayed and the desolation they now exhibit, — are powerfully calculated to affect the imagination." *Eaton.*

☞ "There is nothing with which to compare its form, while the line it describes on the sky is unique. You enter, and it seems as if you had never seen any thing in the world so grand. The Colosseum itself is no approach to it, so much do a multiplicity and irregularity of ruins add to the vastness of the vast enclosure." *Taine, Trans.*

☞ "From these stately palaces [the Thermæ, or Baths of Caracalla] issued fo th a swarm of dirty and ragged plebeians, without shoes and without mantle, who loitered away whole days in the streets or Forum to hear news and to hold disputes; who dissipated in extravagant gaming the miserable pittance of their wives and children, and spent the hours of the night in the indulgence of gross and vulgar sensuality." *Gibbon.*

☞ "This poem [the Prometheus Unbound] was chiefly written upon the mountainous ruins of the Baths of Caracalla, among the flowery glades and thickets of odoriferous blossoming trees which are extended in ever-widening labyrinths upon its immense platforms and dizzy arches." *Shelley.*

Baths of Diocletian. A vast collection of ruins in Rome, covering, it is said, a space of 440,000 square yards. The construction of these baths was begun under the Emperors Diocletian and Maximian about A.D. 302; and 40,000 Christians, it is related, were employed upon them. The Thermæ are said to have had twice the capacity of the Baths of Caracalla, and the ruins with the surrounding buildings cover a space which is nearly a mile in circumference. The great central hall was converted by Michael Angelo into a church (Sta. Maria degli Angeli), which was, however, altered by Vanvitelli in the last century.

☞ "We drove this morning to the Baths of Diocletian, which are scattered over the summit of the Quirinal and Viminal Hill, and which in extent as well as splendor are said to have surpassed all the Thermæ of ancient Rome. Though they do not stand in the same imposing loneliness of situation as those of Caracalla, the wide space of vacant and grass-grown ground over which their ruins may be traced tells a melancholy tale of departed magnificence." *Eaton.*

Baths of Titus. The ruins of celebrated baths built by the Emperor Titus (A.D. 79-81) upon the southern slope of the Esquiline Hill in Rome, overlooking the northern side of the Coliseum. They occupy an area of about 1,150 feet by 850 feet. The Baths of Titus and those of Trajan occupy part of the site of the palace of Nero, which in turn was erected on that part of the Esquiline covered by the house and gardens of Mæcenas. Merivale says that the Golden House of Nero "was still the old mansion of Augustus and the villa of Mæcenas connected by a long series of columns and arches;" and as Titus in constructing his baths made use of the works of his predecessors, parts of the ruins now to be seen are thought to be undoubtedly older than the time of that emperor. In these baths were discovered the famous Nozze Aldobrandini (*q.v.*); and there are still remaining interesting arabesques, though their color and outline are fast fading away. They were a favorite study of Raphael.

☞ "That part of these interesting ruins which has been excavated is near the Colosseum. We passed the mouths of nine long corridors . . . and entered the portal of what is called the House of Mæcenas, a name so justly dear to every admirer of taste and literature, that we did not feel disposed too scrupulously to question the grounds of the belief that we actually stood within the walls of that classic habitation where Horace and Virgil and Ovid and Augustus must have so often met."

Eaton.

Battersea Park. A pleasure-ground on the right bank of the Thames, facing Chelsea Hospital, London, laid out with ornamental plantations, a fine sheet of water, a sub-tropical garden of four acres, cricket-grounds, etc.

☞ The district of Battersea, thought to be a corruption of Peter's Eye (or Island), was once a portion of the inheritance of St. Peter's Abbey, Westminster. It had great celebrity for the asparagus which was there raised.

Battery, The. A park of 10½ acres in New York City, at the south end of Manhattan Island. A fine view of the Bay is obtained from the promenade which runs along the water-front. The immigrant station here was originally built for a fort in 1807, was granted to the city in 1823, and afterwards became an opera-house. In it were held civic receptions of Marquis Lafayette, Gen. Jackson, President Tyler, and others, and here (while an oppera-house) appeared Jenny Lind, Sontag, Parodi, Jullien, and others. See CASTLE GARDEN.

☞ "He [Peter Stuyvesant] fortified the city, too, with pickets and palisadoes, extending across the island from river to river, and, above all, cast up mud batteries, or redoubts, on the point of the island where it divided the beautiful bosom of the bay. These latter redoubts, in process of time, came to be pleasantly overrun by a carpet of grass and clover, and overshadowed by wide-spreading elms and sycamores, among the branches of which the birds would build their nests and rejoice the ear with their melodious notes. Under these trees, too, the old burghers would smoke their afternoon pipe, contemplating the golden sun as he sank in the west, an emblem of the tranquil end toward which they were declining. Here, too, would the young men and maidens of the town take their evening stroll, watching the silver moonbeams as they trembled along the calm bosom of the bay, or lit up the sail of some gliding bark, and peradventure interchanging the soft vows of honest affection, — for to evening strolls in this favored spot were traced most of the marriages in New Amsterdam. Such was the origin of that renowned promenade, THE BATTERY, which, though ostensibly devoted to the stern purposes of war, has ever been consecrated to the sweet delights of peace."

Irving (Knickerbocker).

What would a Boston or New York mother think of taking chairs for her whole family, grown-up daughters and all, in the Mall, or upon the *Battery*, and spending the day in the very midst of the gayest promenade of the city? People of all ranks do it here [in Paris].

N. P. Willis.

Where nowadays the *Battery* lies,
New York had just begun,
A new-born babe, to rub its eyes,
In Sixteen Sixty-One.

E. C Stedman.

The visitor, I may say without flattery,
Finds few, if any, ports to match the view
(When the wind's up, the walk is slightly spattery)
Of bustling, white-winged craft and laughing blue,
Which fixes him enchanted on the *Battery*, —
So full of life, forever fresh and new.

T G. Appleton.

Battle between Constantine and Maxentius. A well-known fresco representing the battle between the Emperor Constantine and Maxentius at the Ponte Molle, near Rome. The design of this composition was by Raphael (1483-1520), but it was executed by Giulio Romano (1492-1546). It is in a room, called after this picture the Sala di Costantino, in the Vatican, Rome.

Battle Hill. An eminence in Greenwood Cemetery, commanding a grand view of the cities of

New York and Brooklyn, and the Bay.

Battle Monument. A memorial structure in Baltimore, Md., built in 1815, to commemorate the soldiers who were engaged in the defence of the city against the British troops in September, 1814. The total height of the monument is 72 feet.

Battle of Austerlitz. A celebrated picture by François Gérard (1770-1836), the eminent French painter. It is of great size (30 feet wide by 16 feet high), and is much admired. It was painted by request of Napoleon I.

Battle of Bunker Hill. A well-known picture by John Trumbull (1756-1843).

☞ "Not surpassed [this and his 'Death of Montgomery'] by any similar works in the last century, and thus far stand alone in American historical paintings." *Harper's Magazine.*

Battle of Cadore. A picture by Titian (1477-1576), no longer existing, but of which there is a drawing in the Uffizi Gallery in Florence, Italy.

Battle of Darius and Alexander. A celebrated mosaic found at Pompeii, and now preserved in the Museum at Naples, Italy.

Battle of Gettysburg. An immense picture by Peter F. Rothermel (b. 1817), the American artist. It was painted under commission from the State of Pennsylvania, and is much admired. It is now in Fairmount Park, Philadelphia.

Battle of Hercules with the Centaurs. A marble bas-relief by Michael Angelo (1475-1564).

Battle of Isly. A noted picture by Horace Vernet (1789-1863), the celebrated French painter.

Battle of Lepanto. A picture by Titian (1477-1576), believed to have been painted by him at the age of ninety-four. At Madrid, Spain.

Battle of the Amazons. A celebrated picture by Peter Paul Rubens (1577-1640). In the Munich gallery.

Battle of the Huns. [Ger. *Hunnenschlacht.*] A celebrated picture by Wilhelm von Kaulbach (1805-1874), regarded as a masterpiece. In the museum at Berlin, Prussia. It is "founded upon the tradition of the battle before the gates of Rome, between the Romans and the spirits of the Huns who were slain, which, rising in the air, continued the fight."

Battle of the Issus. A famous mosaic, representing the battle between Alexander and Darius at the river Issus. This mosaic was discovered at Pompeii in 1831, and is the finest ancient relic of the kind in existence. It is now in the Museum at Naples, Italy.

Battle of the Standard. A celebrated cartoon by Leonardo da Vinci (1452-1520). The subject is the victory of the Florentines under the Patriarch of Aquileja, at Anghiari, over Niccolò Piccinino, general of Filippo Visconti. The cartoon is no longer in existence. There is a sketch by Rubens, and an engraving taken from it by Edelinck, called the "Battle of the Standard."

☞ "Leonardo's work, both cartoon and painting, partook of the evil destiny, which, not unaccountably, presided over all he did. He repeated the same process so fatal to the Last Supper, only apparently with still fewer precautions, painted in oil on so defective a ground that the surface gave way under his own hand, and the work, for which he had already received a considerable sum, was finally abandoned." *Eastlake.*

Battle of Waterloo. A picture by Sir William Allan (1782-1850). In the possession of the Duke of Wellington.

Baumann's Cave. A curious cavern in the Harz Mountains, Germany, very interesting in a geological regard, on account of the fossil remains that have been discovered in it.

Bavaria. A colossal bronze statue by Ludwig Schwanthaler (1802-

1848). It is 54 feet in height, larger than any other work of modern sculpture. In the Hall of Fame at Munich, Bavaria.

Bavon, St. See St. Bavon.

Bay of Baiæ. A picture by Joseph Mallord William Turner (1775–1851), the English landscape painter, and regarded one of his best works. In the National Gallery, London.

Bayenthurm. A picturesque Gothic tower of the fourteenth century in Cologne, Germany. From its position, projecting into the river Rhine, it serves as a sort of barrier against the drifting ice.

Bayeux Tapestry. [Fr. *Tapisserie de Bayeux.*] This tapestry, now preserved at Bayeux near Caen, France, is traditionally said to have been wrought by Matilda, queen of William the Conqueror. It is the oldest known work of the kind. It is 214 feet long by 19 inches wide, and represents the history of the conquest of England by William of Normandy, in a series of scenes, the subject of each of which is indicated by a Latin inscription. The series extends from the visit of Harold to the Norman court to his death at Hastings.

☞ "The most celebrated, if not the most ancient piece of needlework tapestry — *real* tapestry, being entirely wrought by the needle, as was usual in the earliest period of its history — which time has spared us, is the 'Bayeux tapestry,' and called at Bayeux the 'Toilet of Queen Matilda,' or of 'Duc Guillaume.'" *L. Jewitt.*

☞ "Of Norman armor and arms in England, the *Bayeux tapestry* affords every detail, and may be looked upon as a valuable storehouse of information." *L. Jewitt.*

Beacon Hill. An eminence north of the Common in Boston, Mass., now covered with streets and houses. It was so called from the circumstance, that, in the early days of the city, beacon-fires were lighted here to arouse the people in case of danger.

And, sunlike, from her *Beacon-height*
The dome-crowned city spreads her rays.
Holmes.

Beacon Street. A well-known street of residences in Boston, Mass. It was originally known as the lane leading to the almshouse, at which it terminated.

☞ "The name of Beacon Street was applied very early to that portion north and east of the State House, and to the westerly part before the Revolution. At this time there were not more than three houses between Charles Street and the upper end of the Common. The rest of the hill was covered with small cedars and native shrubbery with here and there a cow-path through which the herds ranged unmolested." *Drake.*

Beacon Street, very like Piccadilly, as it runs along the Green Park, and there is the Green Park opposite to this Piccadilly, called Boston Common. *Anthony Trollope.*

The lack-lustre eye, rayless as a *Beacon-street* door plate in August, all at once fills with light; the face flings itself wide open, like the church-portals when the bride and bridegroom enter. *Holmes.*

The bore is the same, eating dates under the cedars of Lebanon, as over a plate of baked beans in *Beacon Street.* *Holmes.*

Bean Feast. A well-known picture by Jacob Jordaens (1593–1678), of which there are numerous specimens, the best being that in the Vienna Gallery.

Bears of Berne. The armorial device of the city of Berne, Switzerland, is a bear (the name itself signifying bear), and the animal is a favorite effigy throughout the city. In addition many living bears are still kept and supported at public expense. At the time of the French Revolution the bears of Berne were carried as prisoners to Paris.

I have forgotten the famous *bears*, and all else. *Holmes.*

Beatrice. A picture by Ary Scheffer (1795–1858), well known through engravings.

Beatrice Cenci. 1. The subject of a well-known and exquisite portrait by Guido Reni, in the Barberini Palace at Rome. It is said, according to the family tradition, to have been taken on the night before her execution. Other accounts represent that it was painted from memory, after Guido had seen her on the scaffold.

The tragic story has been treated by Shelley in his poem entitled with her name.

☞ "I think no other such magical effect can ever have been wrought by pencil. . . . The picture can never be copied. Guido himself could never have done it over again. The copyists get all sorts of expression, gay as well as grievous; some copies have a coquettish air, a half-backward glance, thrown alluringly at the spectator; but nobody ever did catch, or ever will, the vanishing charm of that sorrow. I hated to leave the picture, and yet was glad when I had taken my last glimpse, because it so perplexed and troubled me not to be able to get hold of its secret." *Hawthorne.*

☞ "The picture of Beatrice Cenci represents simply a female head; a very youthful, girlish, perfectly beautiful face. . . . The whole face is very quiet, there is no distortion or disturbance of any single feature, nor is it easy to see why the expression is not cheerful, or why a single touch of the artist's pencil should not brighten it into joyousness. But, in fact, it is the very saddest picture ever painted or conceived; it involves an unfathomable depth of sorrow, the sense of which comes to the observer by a sort of intuition." *Hawthorne.*

☞ "The picture of Beatrice Cenci is a picture almost impossible to be forgotten. Through the transcendent sweetness and beauty of the face there is a something shining out that haunts me." *Dickens.*

2. A life-size statue by Harriet Hosmer (b. 1831). In the Mercantile Library, St. Louis, Mo.

Beaudesert Park. The seat of the Marquis of Anglesea, near Rugeley, England.

Beaumarchais, Boulevart. One of the boulevards of Paris, so called from the author of that name, who built here a fine mansion. See BOULEVARDS.

Beauvais Cathedral. A fine Gothic church in Beauvais, France. It was begun in 1225, and has the loftiest choir in the world.

Beaux Arts, Académie des. [Academy of Fine Arts.] One of the five academies embraced in the *Institut*, the most important learned society of France. It is devoted to painting, sculpture, architecture, engraving, and music, and is, accurately speaking, the most ancient of the academies in Paris, traces of an association among painters being found as early as the fourteenth century. It was regularly founded by the Cardinal Mazarin in 1655. See INSTITUT.

Bed of Justice. [Fr. *Lit de Justice.*] Formerly the seat or throne occupied by the French monarchs when they attended parliament. Afterwards the term was applied to parliament itself. The last Bed of Justice was held at Versailles by Louis XVI., Aug. 5, 1788.

Was not every soul, or rather every body, of these Guardians of our Liberties, naked, or nearly so, last night; "a forked Radish with a head fantastically carved"? And why might he not, did our stern fate so order it, walk out to St. Stephen's, as well as into bed, in that no-fashion; and there, with other similar Radishes, hold a *Bed of Justice?* *Carlyle.*

Bed of Ware. See GREAT BED OF WARE.

Bedford Coffee-house. A noted house in Covent Garden, London, formerly much frequented. Goldsmith, John and Henry Fielding, Hogarth, Churchill, Foote, Garrick, and others resorted to the Bedford. It is no longer standing.

☞ "Almost every one you meet is a polite scholar and a wit." *Connoisseur*, 1754.

Bedford Head. An old London tavern, Covent Garden.

When sharp with hunger, scorn you to be fed
Except on pea-chicks at the *Bedford Head?* *Pope.*

Bedford House. A noble mansion in Belgrave Square, London, the residence of the Duke of Bedford. It was taken down in 1704.

Most of the peers who were in town met in the morning at *Bedford House*, and went thence in procession to Cheapside. *Macaulay.*

Bedford Level. A tract of land in England, situated in the counties of Norfolk, Suffolk, Huntingdon, Northampton, Lincoln, Cambridge, and the Isle of Ely, consisting of about 400,000 acres, a large portion of it being marshy ground. It was drained and reclaimed in the seventeenth century by the Duke of Bedford and others. It produces fine crops of grain, flax, and colé-seed.

Bedford Square. A well-known square in London, near Oxford Street.

Bedlam. See BETHLEM HOSPITAL.

Bednall - green. See BETHNAL GREEN.

Bee Hive House. A building in Salt Lake City, Utah Territory, used as a seraglio of the Mormon leaders. It derives its name from an emblematic bee-hive carved over the entrance.

Beef-steak Society [Club]. **1.** The first club with this name is thought to have been established at London in the time of Queen Anne. The meetings "composed of the chief wits and great men of the nation" seem to have been noted for their jovial character. The first Providore of the Club was Dick Estcourt, the actor, who was valued for his gayety and humor, and who wore, as the badge of the Club, a small golden gridiron.

2. The Sublime Society of the Steaks was established in 1735 by Henry Rich. According to an early rule of the Society the diet was restricted to beef-steaks, port-wine, and punch. The meetings were first held in a room at the Covent Garden Theatre, but later at various places, and finally at a room in the Lyceum Theatre — "ornamented with gridirons as thick as Henry the Seventh's Chapel with the portcullis of the founder. Every thing assumes the shape, or is distinguished by the representation, of their emblematic implement, the gridiron. The cook is seen at his office through the bars of a spacious gridiron, and the original gridiron of the Society (the survivor of two terrific fires) holds a conspicuous position in the centre of the ceiling." Many persons distinguished for rank or social powers have been "Steaks," as the members were accustomed to call themselves, and many are included in the list of guests of the Society.

☞ "On Saturday, the 14th of May [1785], the Prince of Wales was admitted a member of the Beef-steak Club [Society]. His Royal Highness having signified his wish of belonging to that Society, and there not being a vacancy, it was proposed to make him an honorary member; but that being declined by his Royal Highness, it was agreed to increase the number from 24 to 25, in consequence of which his Royal Highness was unanimously elected. The Beef-steak Club [Society] has been instituted just 50 years, and consists of some of the most classical and sprightly wits in the kingdom."
Annual Register, 1785.

☞ "The Beef-steak and October Clubs are neither of them averse to eating or drinking, if we may form a judgment of them from their respective titles." *Spectator.*

3. A Beef-steak Club became an institution in almost every theatre. Dr. Johnson's club in Ivy Lane was at first a Beef-steak Club. About 1749 a Beef-steak Club was founded at the Theatre Royal, Dublin, and was presided over by the celebrated "Peg Woffington." There was also a Beef-steak Club at the Bell Tavern, Houndsditch. In 1733-34 there existed in London the *Rump-steak, or Liberty Club*, a political club in opposition to Sir Robert Walpole.

Beersheba. See DAN.

Beethoven. A statue by Thomas Crawford (1813-1857). In the Music Hall, Boston, Mass.

Befana, La. A wooden figure placed outside the doors of houses in Italy at the opening of Lent. This name is perhaps derived from La Befana (a corruption of Epiphany, Gr. Ἐπιφάνια), which in Italy is a common personification of the Epiphany, differently represented as a saint, as a fairy, and as the bugbear of naughty children, and who at Epiphany is supposed to go about at night like

Santa Claus, bearing presents to the children.

☞ "On the eve of Twelfth-Day, the *Crature* (the children), with trembling mingled with hope, anticipate a midnight visit from a frightful old woman, called the *Befana* (an obvious corruption of *Epifania*, the Epiphany), for whom they always take care to leave some portion of their supper, lest she should eat them up; and when they go to bed, they suspend upon the back of a chair a stocking, to receive her expected gifts. This receptacle is always found in the morning to contain some sweet things, or other welcome presents, — which, I need scarcely say, are provided by the mother or the nurse." *C. A. Eaton.*

Beffroi [Ghent]. An ancient and celebrated belfry or watch-tower in the city of Ghent, Belgium. It was erected in 1183, and is a lofty square structure, containing a fine chime, and surmounted by a gilt dragon brought from Constantinople. One of the bells in the belfry weighs nearly five tons.

Beggar Boy. A picture by Diego Rodriguez de Silva y Velasquez (1599–1660), the Spanish painter. In the Louvre, Paris. There is another upon the same subject in the Pinakothek at Munich, Bavaria.

Béguinage, The. A famous nunnery in Ghent, Belgium.

Béguinage, Grand. A fine church of the seventeenth century in Brussels, Belgium

Beheading of St. John. A picture by Michelangelo Amerighi, surnamed Caravaggio (1569-1609), and one of his principal works. In the Cathedral of Malta.

Beheading of St. John the Baptist. A picture by the Swiss painter, Nicolas Manuel, surnamed Deutsch (1484–1531). Now in the Museum at Basle, Switzerland.

Beheading of St. Paul. A picture by Niccolo dell' Abbate, called also Niccolo da Modena (1509–1571). In the Gallery of Dresden, Germany.

Bekaa. A valley in Syria, sometimes called Hollow Syria. It is between the Antilibanus range and the higher Lebanon. It was by this way that the ancient armies used to march, the Syrians to Samaria, and the Egyptians against Damascus.

Belfort. An ancient and venerable fortress of unknown origin, situated on the summit of a bare rock in northern Palestine. Portions of the castle are thought to have been built by the Crusaders, who, at different times, took refuge in it. In 1189 it was besieged by Saladin. In 1260 it was purchased by the Templars, who, however, were soon compelled to relinquish it. It is a stronghold of great size, with massive walls, and moats, and drawbridges, and the other means of defence common in the Middle Ages. The original building is believed to have been of Phœnician origin. The place is first mentioned under its European name by William of Tyre in the twelfth century The castle is now deserted.

Belfry of Bruges. See HALLES, LES. For the BELFRY OF GHENT, see BEFFROI. See also CAMPANILE.

Belgrave Square. See BELGRAVIA.

Belgravia. Formerly a *sobriquet* applied to Belgrave and Eaton Squares, Grosvenor Place, and the radiating streets, London, but now received as the legitimate name of this aristocratic quarter. Belgrave Square was so called from Belgrave, Lincolnshire

But the ordinary residences of fashionable life — the mansions of *Belgravia*, Tyburnia, and Mayfair — are mere shells of brick and stucco, which present such a dreary appearance outside that one is surprised sometimes to find them palaces of comfort within. *C L Eastlake.*

Crouched on the pavement close by *Belgrave Square*,
A tramp I saw, ill, moody, and tongue-tied;
A babe was in her arms, and at her side
A girl; their clothes were rags, their feet were bare. *Matthew Arnold.*

That is a source of prospective pleasure in which the inhabitants of *Belgravia* and Tyburnia cannot indulge. *Eastlake.*

Belisarius. A noted picture by François Gérard (1770–1836), the eminent French painter. It was executed about 1795.

Bell, The. 1. A noted inn at Edmonton, near London, famous in connection with John Gilpin's ride, and a favorite stopping-place of Charles Lamb.

'To-morrow is our wedding-day,
And we will then repair
Unto the *Bell* at Edmonton,
All in a chaise and pair.' *Cowper.*

2. A noted old inn in Warwick Lane, London. The present building is modern.

And he [Archbishop Leighton] obtained what he desired; for he died at the *Bell Inn*, in Warwick Lane. *Burnet.*

☞ The name has been a frequent designation of inns and public-houses in England, which were formerly distinguished by the various devices of their signs.

Bell Rock (*or* **Inchcape Rock) Lighthouse.** This important lighthouse — built upon the famous rock of the same name in the German Ocean, on the northern side of the entrance of the Firth of Forth, and about twelve miles from land — was begun in 1807, under the charge of the celebrated engineer Robert Stevenson. After much very difficult work and many discouraging hinderances the structure was finished in October, 1810. Its total height is 115 feet, and diameter at the base 42 feet. See INCHCAPE ROCK.

Far in the bosom of the deep,
O'er these wild shelves my watch I keep;
A ruddy gem of changeful light,
Bound on the dusky brow of night;
The seaman bids my lustre hail,
And scorns to strike his timorous sail.
Scott.

Bella di Tiziano. [Titian's Beauty.] A picture in the Sciarra Palace, Rome, now attributed to Jacopo Palma, called Palma Vecchio (1480–1528). There is another picture of the same name in the Pitti Palace, Florence, Italy.

Bella Donna, La. A noted picture by Titian (1477–1576). In the Palazzo Pitti, Florence, Italy.

Bellamy's Kitchen. An establishment which was situated near the Old House of Commons, London, and is described as a plain apartment, with an immense fire, meat-screen, gridirons, and a small tub under the window for washing the glasses, — a place where "the statesmen of England very often dine, and men, possessed of wealth untold, and with palaces of their own, in which luxury and splendor are visible in every part, are willing to leave their stately dining-halls and powdered attendants, to be waited upon, while eating a chop in Bellamy's kitchen, by two unpretending old women."

☞ "But let us not omit to notice Bellamy's kitchen, or, in other words, the refreshment-room, common to both Houses of Parliament, where Ministerialists and Oppositionists, Whigs and Tories, Radicals, Peers, and destructives, strangers from the gallery, and the more favored strangers from below the bar, are alike at liberty to resort." *Dickens.*

Belle Arti, Accademia delle. [Academy of Fine Arts.] A name applied in Italy to buildings in nearly all the principal cities, containing collections of art. Among the more celebrated are the Accademias of Florence, Venice, and Bologna.

Belle Ferronière. A celebrated portrait of Lucrezia Crivelli by Leonardo da Vinci (1452–1519), the Italian painter. It is now in the Louvre, Paris, and is known by the title above given, from a tradition that it is the picture of a blacksmith's wife, mistress of Francis I. There is a fine copy of this portrait believed to be by Beltraffio.

Belle Jardinière. [The Fair Gardener.] A beautiful and well-known picture of the Madonna by Raphael Sanzio (1483–1520), in which the Virgin is represented as sitting among flowering shrubs as in a garden (from which circumstance the picture may have derived its name). The infant Christ stands at her knee, while St. John kneels in childlike devotion. There is an early copy of this picture, probably by a

Flemish artist, sometimes taken for the original, which latter is now in the gallery of the Louvre, Paris.

Belle Joconde. The name given to the celebrated portrait of Mona Lisa, wife of Francesco del Giocondo, by Leonardo da Vinci (1452-1519). It is regarded as one of the most beautiful and highly-finished works of art existing. It is stated that the lady sat for her portrait during a period of four years. This picture is now in the Louvre, Paris. The Duke d'Aumale has a black chalk cartoon of the same by Leonardo.

☞ "As the countenance of the Sistine Madonna represents the purest maidenliness, so we see here the most beautiful woman — worldly, earthly, without sublimity, without enthusiasm, but with a calm, restful placidity, a smile, a mild pride about her, which makes us stand before her with endless delight." *Grimm, Trans.*

Belle Sauvage. A noted old London tavern which formerly stood on Ludgate Hill.

☞ "A few of these quaint old figures still remain in London town. You may still see there, and over its old hostel in Ludgate Hill, the 'Belle Sauvage,' to whom the *Spectator* so pleasantly alludes, and who was probably no other than the sweet American Pocahontas who rescued from death the daring Captain Smith." *Thackeray.*

Belle Tout. A celebrated lighthouse on the south coast of England near Beachy Head, built in 1831.

Bellerophon. An English line-of-battle ship in which, on the 15th of July, 1815, while lying at anchor in the roadstead of Rochefort, France, the emperor Napoleon I. took passage for England, having vainly endeavored to escape to America.

2. A formidable armor-plated ship of the British navy, launched April 26, 1865.

Bellevue Avenue. A broad road at Newport, R. I., lined with country-seats, many of which are very magnificent. It is a fashionable drive, where may be seen a display of elegant equipages, affording in the season one of the gayest spectacles to be seen in the country.

Bellini, Giovanni. A portrait of himself by the painter (1426–1516). In the collection of autograph portraits of the painters in the Uffizi, Florence, Italy.

Bellosguardo. A hill in the neighborhood of Florence, Italy. From this eminence Galileo is said to have observed the planetary movements.

From Tuscan *Bellosguardo*, wide awake,
When standing on the actual, blessed sward
Where Galileo stood at nights to take
The vision of the stars, we find it hard,
Gazing upon the earth and heaven, to make
A choice of beauty. *Mrs. Browning.*

Belmont. A noted mansion in what is now Fairmount Park, Philadelphia, Penn. It was erected in 1745, and was a favorite resort of Washington, Lafayette, Franklin, Jefferson, Talleyrand, Louis Philippe, and other distinguished men.

Belœil. A celebrated Gothic castle near Ath, in Belgium, built in 1146, and containing some valuable works of art.

Belœil tout à la fois magnifique et champêtre. *Delille.*

Belrespiro. See Villa Pamfili-Doria.

Belshazzar's Feast. A picture by Washington Allston (1779–1843), the American painter. It was left unfinished at his death. Now in the Athenæum, Boston, Mass.

☞ "A mighty sovereign surrounded by his whole court, intoxicated with his own state, in the midst of his revelry, palsied in a moment under the spell of a preternatural hand suddenly tracing his doom on the wall before him; his powerless limbs, like a wounded spider's, shrunk up to his body, while his heart, compressed to a point, is only kept from vanishing by the terrific suspense that animates it, during the interpretation of his mysterious sentence." *Allston.*

Belus, Temple of. See Birs Nimrood.

Belvedere Antinous. See ANTINOUS.

Belvedere Palace. A celebrated palace in Vienna, Austria, consisting of two buildings, an upper and a lower, with a public garden between them. The upper Belvedere contains a gallery of pictures, filling 35 halls; the lower, an armory and museum of sculptures.

Belvidere Apollo. See APOLLO BELVIDERE.

Belvidere, *or* **Cortile del Belvidere.** [Court of the Beautiful View.] A famous octagonal court in the palace of the Vatican, Rome, built by Bramante, out of which open several cabinets containing some of the most precious remains of ancient art, as the Antinous, the Laocoon, and the Apollo.

☞ The name Belvidere (Belvedere) is frequently applied to apartments in palaces and galleries of art.

☞ "The view from the balcony in front of the windows is that which gave the name of *Belvidere* to this Museum, and in consequence to the Apollo, and some of its finest pieces of sculpture. It commands a prospect over the vale of the Tiber to the pine-covered height of Monte Mario, but the hues which the brilliant sky of Italy sheds over it must be seen before its beauty can be imagined." *Eaton.*

Belvidere Torso. See TORSO BELVIDERE.

Belvoir Castle. An ancient and noble mansion, the seat of the Duke of Rutland, near Grantham, Leicestershire, England. It contains one of the best collections of pictures in England.

Till *Belvoir's* lordly terraces
The sign to Lincoln sent,
And Lincoln sped the message on
O'er the wide vale of Trent.
Macaulay.

The lord of *Belvoir* then his castle viewed,
Strong without form, and dignified but rude. *George Crabbe.*

Belzoni's Tomb. The common appellation, from its discoverer, of the tomb of Sethi I., in Thebes, Egypt. This tomb is regarded as the most noteworthy in Thebes for its sculpture and preservation.

Bema. [Gr. Βῆμα.] A tribune or raised platform in ancient Greek buildings, from which speeches were made before a court of law. Especially applied to a place of this kind in the Pnyx, at Athens.

Bemerside. A mansion in Scotland, near the town of Dryburgh, memorable for the fact that it has been for 700 years the seat of the family of Haig, in verification of a prophecy of Thomas of Ercildoune, called Thomas the Rhymer.

"Betide, betide, whate'er betide,
Haig shall be Haig of *Bemerside.*"

Ben, Big. See BIG BEN.

Bench. See KING'S BENCH AND QUEEN'S BENCH.

Bengal, Little. See LITTLE BENGAL.

Beni Hassan, Caves *or* **Tombs of.** These ancient tombs excavated in the rock on the shore of the Nile are the oldest known monuments in Egypt, excepting the Pyramids. They are numerous and spacious, and some of them are exceedingly interesting. The sculptures and paintings are of great variety, representing the occupations and amusements of the people, and throwing much light on their modes of life. The paintings are of various and very brilliant coloring. [Written also *Benee Hasan.*]

☞ "The character of the sculptures which adorn their walls approaches that found in the tombs surrounding the Pyramids, but the architecture differs widely. They are all cheerful-looking halls open to the light of day, many of them with pillared porches, and all possessing pretensions to architectural ornament, either internal or external." *Fergusson.*

Benjamin West. A portrait by Washington Allston (1779–1843), the American painter. It was placed in the Boston Athenæum, but is now in the Museum of Fine Arts in that city.

Bentivoglio, Cardinal. A well-known portrait by Anthony van Dyck (1599–1641). In the Pitti Palace, Florence, Italy.

Bergstrasse. [Mountain Road.] A famous post-road from Darmstadt to Heidelberg, Germany, now superseded in great part by the railway, but formerly very celebrated for its beautiful views of mountains and of the river Rhine, and for the rich cultivation of the district it overlooks.

Bergüner Stein. A deep and narrow ravine in Switzerland, in which is a carriage-road 600 feet above the Albula. This road is a triumph of engineering skill.

Berkeley Castle. A noted Norman fortress and baronial mansion, the former residence of the Berkeley family, near the river Severn, in England, between Bristol and Gloucester. It was founded soon after the Conquest, and has been the scene of many historical events, including the murder of Edward II. It is regarded as one of the finest feudal structures in Great Britain.

☞ "The room shown for the murder of Edward II., I verily believe to be genuine. It is a dismal chamber, almost at the top of the house, almost detached, and to be approached only by a kind of footbridge." *Horace Walpole.*

Mark the year, and mark the night,
When Severn shall re-echo with affright
The shrieks of death through *Berkeley's* roof that ring, —
Shrieks of an agonizing king. *Gray.*

Berkeley Square. A well-known public square in London.

Bermondsey. A district in the borough of Southwark, London, a great seat of the tanning trade.

Bermudas, The. A name given to some narrow and intricate alleys in London. These passages, which are thought to have been north of the Strand, near Covent Garden, are no longer in existence.

Pirates here at land
Have their *Bermudas* and their Streights in the Strand. *Ben Jonson.*

Bernard, St. See HOSPICE OF THE ST. BERNARD and VISION OF ST. BERNARD.

Berne, Bears of. See BEARS OF BERNE.

Bethesda, Pool of. See POOL OF BETHESDA.

Bethlem (Bethlehem) Hospital. A lunatic hospital, founded in 1547, in the reign of Henry VIII., and popularly called *Bedlam.* It has been situated at the junction of Kensington and Lambeth Roads, London, since 1810–'15, but was formerly in Moorfields, near Bishopsgate. Until 1770 it was one of the sights of the city. The patients, before 1815, were kept chained to the walls; but now their treatment is all that could be wished. The entrance-hall contains the famous statues of Melancholy and Madness by Caius Gabriel Cibber (father of Colley Cibber). See MELANCHOLY.

He [Fox] was then a youth of pure morals and grave deportment, with a perverse temper, with the education of a laboring man, and with an intellect in the most unhappy of all states, that is to say, too much disordered for liberty, and not sufficiently disordered for *Bedlam.* *Macaulay.*

Why, there are passions still great enough to replenish *Bedlam,* for it never wants tenants; to suspend men from bed-posts, from improved-drops at the west end of Newgate. *Carlyle.*

——The river proudly bridged; the dizzy top
And Whispering Gallery of St. Paul's; the tombs
Of Westminster; the giants of Guildhall;
Bedlam, and those carved maniacs at the gates
Perpetually recumbent. *Wordsworth.*

Bethnal Green. A district in London to the east of Spitalfields, celebrated in the old English ballad of Bednall-Green. Great numbers of silk-weavers reside in this quarter. It was made a parish in 1743.

☞ "Numerous blind courts and alleys form a densely crowded district in Bethnal Green. Among its inhabitants may be found street venders of every kind of produce, travellers to fairs, tramps, dog-fanciers, dog-stealers, men and women sharpers, shoplifters, and pickpockets. It abounds with the young Arabs of the streets, and its outward moral degradation is at once apparent to any one who passes that way." *Athenæum.*

☞ Dickens, in "Oliver Twist," places the home of Bill Sikes in one of a "maze of mean and dirty streets, which abound in the close and densely populated quarter of Bethnal Green."

26 June, 1663. By coach to *Bednall-green*, to Sir W. Rider's to dinner. A fine merry walk with the ladies alone after dinner in the garden; the greatest quantity of strawberries I ever saw, and good.
Pepys' Diary.

My father, shee said, is soone to be seene:
The seely blind beggar of *Bednall-greene*,
That daylye sits begging for charitie,
He is the good father of pretty Bessee.
The Beggar's Daughter of Bednall-Green. Percy's Reliques. [According to Percy, this popular old ballad was written in the reign of Elizabeth.]

'Twas August, and the fierce sun overhead
Smote on the squalid streets of *Bethnal Green*,
And the pale weaver, through his windows seen
In Spitalfields, looked thrice dispirited.
Matthew Arnold.

Bevis Marks. A thoroughfare in London, near Houndsditch. A part of the scene of Dickens's "Old Curiosity Shop" is laid here.

I intended calling on you this morning on my way back from *Bevis Marks*, whither I went to look at a house for Sampson Brass. *Charles Dickens to Mr. Forster.*

Bezetha. A hill in Jerusalem mentioned by Josephus, but not mentioned in the Bible. It is identified with a broad uneven ridge which extends north from the Haram, and descends into the Valley of Jehoshaphat. At the present time it is cultivated and covered with olive-trees.

Bibiena, Cardinal. A portrait by Raphael Sanzio (1483-1520). In the Pitti Palace, Florence, Italy.

Bibliotéca Ambrosiana. See AMBROSIAN LIBRARY.

Bibliotéca Casanatense. [Casanatense Library.] The largest library in Rome, next to that of the Vatican, named after its founder Cardinal Casanate, and kept in the Dominican convent of the Minerva, Sta. Maria sopra Minerva. It contains more than 120,000 bound volumes and 4,500 MSS.

Bibliothèque de l'Arsenal. One of the principal public libraries of Paris.

Bibliothèque Mazarine. [Mazarin Library.] One of the principal public libraries of Paris, situated in the Palais de l'Institut. Its foundation was the library of Cardinal Mazarin, bequeathed by him to the city of Paris.

Bibliothèque Nationale. [It has been known as the *Bibliothèque du roi, Bibliothèque royale, nationale, impériale,* according to the changes of government.] A public library in Paris, perhaps the richest and most extensive in the world. The collection is supposed to include 1,000,000 printed books, 1,300,000 engravings, 300,000 maps and charts, 150,000 MSS. The Palais Mazarin, originally the palace of the Cardinal Mazarin, was purchased for the library in 1724.

Bicêtre. An ancient hospital near Paris, founded in 1364, was destroyed in the fifteenth century, but afterwards restored and converted into a hospital for old men and those afflicted with mental diseases. The name is a corruption of Winchester, a Bishop of Winchester having lived here in 1290. The word Bicêtre has passed into common language to express a notion of folly or extravagance. Thus the French say of one who gives himself up to acts of folly: "He has escaped from *Bicêtre*." Compare BEDLAM.

Bielshöhle. A cave in the Harz Mountains, Germany, very interesting in a geological regard on account of the fossil remains found in it.

Big Ben. This is the largest bell in England. It hangs in the clock-tower of the new Houses of Parliament, in London. The first bell of this name was cast in 1856, but was cracked by being struck for amusement before it was raised to its place in the tower. The weight of this bell, which was broken up and re-cast, was more than 16 tons, its height 7 feet 10½ inches, and its diameter at the mouth 9 feet 5½ inches; the thickness of the metal at the sound bow was 9¾ inches. The present "Big Ben" was cast in 1857, and is slightly cracked. Its weight is more than 13 tons. See GREAT TOM (2).

Big Bonanza. See CONSOLIDATED VIRGINIA.

Big Trees of California. See CALAVERAS.

Biga, Sala della. See SALA DELLA BIGA.

Billingsgate. The noted fish-market of London, near London Bridge, long famous for the coarse language indulged in by the venders. According to Geoffrey of Monmouth, the name Billingsgate was derived from Belin, king of the Britons about 400 B.C., who, says Geoffrey, built here a water-gate, with an immense tower above it, and a haven for ships beneath. The market was destroyed by fire in 1715, and rebuilt. A new market was erected in 1852, and it has been since rebuilt in 1856.

That strength of body is often equal to the courage of mind implanted in the fair sex, will not be denied by those who have seen the water-women of Plymouth; the female drudges of Ireland, Wales, and Scotland; the fisherwomen of *Billingsgate*. *Goldsmith.*

One may term *Billingsgate* the Esculine gate of London. *Fuller.*

There stript, fair Rhetoric languish'd on the ground;
Her blunted arms by Sophistry are borne,
And shameless *Billingsgate* her robes adorn. *Pope.*

Some less fastidious Scotchman shall be found,
As bold in *Billingsgate*, though less renown'd. *Byron.*

No song is heard, save, haply, the strain of some siren from *Billingsgate*, chanting the eulogy of deceased mackerel. *Irving.*

While Lady Thrifty scolds in French,
And Cis in *Billingsgate*. *Praed.*

Bilton Hall. A noted mansion near Rugby, England, once the residence of Addison.

Birds of America. A series of drawings of American birds, of the size and color of life, by John James Audubon (1782–1851). Cuvier is said to have pronounced it (the book containing them) "the most gigantic and most magnificent monument that had ever been erected to Nature."

Birkenhead, The. An English steamer employed to carry troops to South Africa, and wrecked off the Cape of Good Hope, Feb. 26, 1852. Less than 200 were saved out of more than 600 who were on board.

☞ "'The women and children to the boats,' says the captain of the Birkenhead; and, with the troops formed on the deck, and the crew obedient to the word of glorious command, the immortal ship goes down." *Thackeray.*

But courage like this, or let us say the ever-memorable noble behavior of the soldiers on the sinking *Birkenhead*, was not greater than was exhibited by those 20 poor nuns who, in the French Revolution, stood together on the scaffold chanting the *Te Deum*, till one by one the sweet voices dropped in silence beneath the axe of the guillotine. *Frances Power Cobbe.*

Birmingham Tower. The ancient keep or ballium of the Castle of Dublin, Ireland, and the only part which now bears a character of antiquity. It is associated with many romantic histories. It is now used as the State Paper Office.

Birnam Hill *and* **Wood.** An eminence about 1,500 feet high, near the town of Dunkeld, and about 16 miles from Perth, Scotland. It is famous from its association with Shakespeare's tragedy of "Macbeth."

☞ "Birnam hill is at present almost bare of trees, though an attempt is being made to clothe it again with fir saplings taken from the original 'Birnam wood.' In the rear of the hotel are two trees, an oak and a plane, which are believed to be a remnant of this famous forest." *W. J. Rolfe.*

I pull in resolution, and begin
To doubt the equivocation of the fiend
That lies like truth: 'Fear not till *Birnam wood*
Do come to Dunsinane; and now a wood
Comes toward Dunsinane. *Shakespeare.*

Before I can sit down in my own chamber, and think it of the dampest, the door opens, and the Brave comes moving in, in the middle of such a quantity of fuel that he looks like *Birnam Wood* taking a winter walk. *Dickens.*

Biron. A large and well-preserved feudal fortress in southern France, not far from Cahors. It is of the eleventh century.

Birs Nimrood. A ruin in the neighborhood of ancient Babylon, thought to be the same as the Tower of Babel, or the Temple of Belus mentioned by Herodotus. This tower is over 2,000 feet in circumference at the base. The existing remains are of brick laid in beautiful masonry, and are some 28 feet in width. See TOWER OF BABEL.

☞ "The tower of the great temple of Belus was amongst the most remarkable monuments of Babylon. Eight gradually diminishing stories gave it the look of a pyramid with enormous gradients. Upon the summit stood the temple, surmounted by a platform, where the priests assiduously devoted themselves to the study of the celestial bodies. They believed that science was the supreme aim of man, and was the crown of religion. This temple was still in existence in the second century of our era."
Lefèvre, Trans.

☞ "It is true that as it now stands, every brick bears the stamp of Nebochadnassar, by whom it was repaired, perhaps nearly rebuilt; but there is no reason for supposing that he changed the original plan, or that the sacred form of these temples had altered in the interval. It owes its more perfect preservation to the fact of the upper story having been vitrified after erection by some process we do not quite understand. This now forms a mass of slag which has to a great extent protected the lower stories from atmospheric influences." *Fergusson.*

Nay, the whole Encyclopédie, that world's wonder of the eighteenth century, the *Belus' Tower* of an age of refined Illumination, what has it become! *Carlyle.*

Birth of Venus. 1. A mythological fresco in the Vatican, Rome, designed by Raphael (1483–1520), and executed by his scholars.

2. A picture by Alexandre Cabanel (b. 1823). In the collection of H. C. Gibson, Philadelphia, Penn.

Bishopsgate. An old and quaint street in London.

Black Brunswicker. A picture by John Everett Millais (b. 1829).

Black Butte. A natural curiosity in Wyoming Territory, being a mound of rock and earth standing on the level plain, one of the more celebrated of the huge monumental mountains which are found along the line of the Union Pacific Railroad in this part of its course.

Black Forest. An extensive wooded district in Germany, sloping down to the banks of the Rhine, and containing the most varied and beautiful scenery. The heights are covered with forests, and vegetation is most luxuriant in the valleys.

Black Forests, and the glories of Lubberland; sensuality and horror, the spectre nun, and the charmed moonshine, shall not be wanting. *Carlyle.*

And you, with braided queues so neat,
Black-Forest maidens, slim and brown,
How careful on the stoop's green seat
You set your pails and pitchers down.
Ferdinand Freiligrath, Trans.

Black Hole. A small dungeon, so called, in Fort William, Calcutta. When Calcutta was captured by Surajah Dowlah, in June, 1756, he shut up at night in this confined and ill-ventilated space the British garrison of 146 men. The Black Hole was only 18 feet square; and the sufferings from heat, want of air, and thirst, were so terrible that but 23 of the prisoners were found alive in the morning. The Black Hole now serves as a warehouse. Mr. Holwell, one of those imprisoned, gives a narrative of the excruciating sufferings of the unfortunate garrison, in the "Annual Register" for 1758.

Must the indomitable millions, full of old Saxon energy and fire, lie cooped up in this Western Nook, choking one another, as in a *Blackhole* of Calcutta, while a whole fertile untenanted Earth, desolate for want of the ploughshare, cries: Come and till me, come and reap me? *Carlyle.*

Black Maria. A name popularly applied to the covered van in which criminals are conveyed to and from the court-house and the jail in cities. It is often painted black.

Black Prince. An armor-plated ship of the British navy, launched Feb. 27, 1861.

Black Rod. The title of a gentleman-usher who bears a black rod surmounted with a gold lion, and who in the time of a parliamentary session attends in the House of Lords, and summons the House of Commons when a royal assent is to be given, and on other occasions.

The House, therefore, on the last day of the session, just before the *Black Rod* knocked at the door, unanimously resolved that William Fuller was a cheat and a false accuser. *Macaulay.*

Black Rood [of Scotland]. A famous gold cross, believed to contain a piece of the true cross, brought to Scotland by Queen Margaret in 1067, and held in reverence by the whole Scottish people. Since the Reformation it has disappeared.

Black Stone of Mecca. A dark colored stone contained in a small oratory of the temple of the Caaba at Mecca, Arabia, and held in the utmost veneration by the Mohammedans as having been given by an angel to Abraham. See CAABA.

☞ "To the idolatrous Arabs one of the most ancient universal objects of worship was that Black Stone, still kept in the building called Caabah at Mecca. Diodorus Siculus mentions this Caabah in a way not to be mistaken, as the oldest, most honored temple in his time; that is, some half century before our Era. Silvestre de Sacy says there is some likelihood that the Black Stone is an aërolite. In that case, some man might *see* it fall out of Heaven! It stands now beside the Well Zemzem: the Caabah is built over both." *Carlyle.*

Black Virgin. See SHRINE OF THE BLACK VIRGIN.

Blackfriars. The district in London between Ludgate Hill and the Thames, so called from the Dominican monks who built a monastery and church here. Here (June 21, 1529) was decided the divorce of Henry VIII. from Catherine of Arragon, and here assembled the parliament which condemned Cardinal Wolsey. Under Edward VI. part of the monastic buildings was converted into Blackfriars Theatre. See BLACKFRIARS THEATRE.

Dead long since, but *not* resting; daily doing motions in that Westminster region still,—daily from Vauxhall to *Blackfriars*, and back again; and cannot get away at all! *Carlyle.*

Blackfriars Bridge. An iron bridge across the river Thames, at London, erected in 1760–69 by Robert Mylne, and rebuilt in 1867 by Cubitt.

Blackfriars Theatre. A playhouse in London, built in 1575 upon the site of the monastery of Blackfriars. Shakespeare was one of the proprietors, and acted here in 1598. In 1655 the theatre was taken down, and dwelling-houses were built upon the ground.

In 1598 Ben Jonson's first and best comedy, *Every Man in his Humour*, was produced at the *Blackfriars;* and the author of *King Henry the Fourth* and *Romeo and Juliet* might have been seen for two pence by any London prentice who could command the coin, playing an inferior part, probably that of *Knowell*, in the new play. *Richard Grant White.*

In that year [1603] Ben Jonson's *Sejanus* was produced at the *Blackfriars*, and the author of *Hamlet* might have been seen playing a subordinate part in it. *Richard Grant White.*

Blackwell's Island. An island within the city limits of New York, noted for its penitentiary and for its public hospitals.

Blair Castle. The seat of the Duke of Athole, near Blair-Athole, in Scotland.

Blanche Nef. The ship in which William, the only son of Henry I. of England, with 140 noblemen was wrecked in 1120 upon the rocks of Barfleur, Normandy.

Blarney Stone. About four miles north-west of the city of Cork, in Ireland, are the celebrated remains of the ancient Blarney Castle, in which is a wondrous stone, thought to possess the power of imparting to any one who kisses it a fluent, persuasive, and not over-honest tongue. The exact position of the stone in the ruins is a matter of dispute. Some say that it is lying loose on the ground; others allege that it is at the summit of the large square tower which was originally the donjon or keep of the castle; while there are yet others who maintain that it is inserted in the wall at such a height that he who would kiss it must consent to be suspended by his heels from the top. When or how it first got its singular reputation is not known; but the superstition concerning it is firmly fixed in the minds of the Irish peasantry, hundreds of whom resort to the castle every year for the purpose of kissing a stone endued with a property so marvellous. It is said that, in the early part of the seventeenth century, the lord of Castle Blarney, having been taken prisoner by the English, made repeated promises that he would surrender the fortress; but, whenever the fulfilment of his pledges was demanded, he invented some smooth and plausible excuse for delay; and thus the term *blarney* became a byword, and was used to denote a soft, insinuating, and deceitful manner of speech.

☞ "When or how the stone obtained its singular reputation, it is difficult to determine: the exact position among the ruins of the castle is also in doubt; the peasant-guides humor the visitor according to his capacity for climbing, and direct either to the summit or the base the attention of him who desires to 'greet it with a holy kiss.'" *Mr. and Mrs. Hall.*

There is a stone there
That whoever kisses,
O, he never misses
To grow eloquent.
Don't hope to hinder him
Or to bewilder him,
Sure he's a pilgrim
From the *Blarney Stone.*
R. A. Milliken.

O say, would you find this same '*Blarney*'?
There's a castle, not far from Killarney,
On the top of its wall
(But take care you don't fall)
There's a stone that contains all this Blarney.
Like a magnet, its influence such is,
That attraction it gives all it touches;
If you kiss it, they say,
From that blessed day
You may kiss whom you please with your Blarney. *Samuel Lover*

Blenheim. A noble mansion and estate at Woodstock, near Oxford, England. It was erected in the reign of Queen Anne, and was presented by the British Parliament to the Duke of Marlborough in commemoration of the victory achieved by him at the battle of Blenheim, Aug. 13, 1704.

☞ "I saw Blenheim Palace, near Woodstock, belonging to the Duke of Marlborough. This is a sort of Louvre, formerly presented by this nation to the great captain, built in the style of the period, much ornamented." *Taine, Trans.*

See, here's the grand approach,
That way is for his Grace's coach;
There lies the bridge, and there the clock,
Observe the lion and the cock;
The spacious court, the colonnade,
And mind how wide the hall is made;
The chimneys are so well designed,
They never smoke in any wind;
The galleries contrived for walking,
The windows to retire and talk in;
The council-chamber to debate,
And all the rest are rooms of state.
"Thanks, sir," cried I, "'tis very fine,
But where d'ye sleep, or where d'ye dine?
I find by all you have been telling,
That 'tis a house, but not a dwelling."
Swift.

Blennerhasset's Island. A little island in the Ohio River, not far from Parkersburg, W. Va., celebrated as the residence of Harman Blennerhasset (1770-1831), a wealthy Irishman, who ruined his fortune by aiding Aaron Burr, of whose designs, suspected to be treasonable, he was an associate or accomplice.

Who is Blennerhasset? A native of Ireland, a man of letters, who fled from the storms of his own country, to find quiet in ours. On his arrival in America, he retired, even from the population of the Atlantic States, and sought quiet and solitude in the bosom of our western forests. But he brought with him taste, and science, and wealth; and "lo, the desert smiled!" Possessing himself of a beautiful island in the Ohio, he rears upon it a palace, and decorates it with every romantic embellishment of fancy. A shrubbery that Shenstone might have envied blooms around him. Music that might have charmed Calypso and her nymphs is his. An extensive library spreads its treasures before him. A philosophical apparatus offers to him all the secrets and mysteries of Nature. Peace, tranquillity, and innocence shed their mingled delights around him. *Wm. Wirt.*

Blois Castle. An ancient royal fortress and residence in Blois, France, possessing great historic interest. It has been within a few years restored by the government to something like its former condition.

Blood of St. Januarius. In the Church of San Gennaro (St. Januarius), at Naples, are preserved in a tabernacle behind the altar, two phials, containing a solid, reddish substance, said to be the dried blood of St. Januarius, Bishop of Benevento, in the latter part of the third century, who suffered martyrdom under Diocletian. The tradition runs, that when the saint was exposed to be devoured by lions in the amphitheatre at Pozzuoli, the animals became tame, and prostrated themselves before him. This miracle converted so many to Christianity that the Roman commander ordered him to be decapitated. After death the body was removed to Naples. At the time of the removal, a woman, who collected the blood of the saint, delivered it, in two bottles, to St. Severus, in whose hands it immediately melted. According to the belief of many Catholics, this miracle of liquefaction still takes place at least three times every year; and the occurrence of it is the occasion of the greatest religious festivals observed by the Neapolitans. The head of the martyr, and the phials containing his blood, are carried in solemn procession to the high altar; and, prayer having been offered, the head is brought into contact with the phials, the blood in which is thereupon believed to liquefy. The phenomenon, however, does not always take place immediately, and occasionally it fails altogether. The excitement of the congregation, when the pretended miracle takes place, is only surpassed by that caused by its non-occurrence, which is considered an omen of the worst possible import.

☞ "At the same moment [that of liquefaction], the stone (distant some miles) where the saint suffered martyrdom becomes faintly red. It is said that the officiating priests turn faintly red also, sometimes, when these miracles occur." *Dickens.*

☞ "The first day the blood liquefies in forty-seven minutes: the church is crammed, then, and time must be allowed the collectors to get around; after that it liquefies a little quicker and a little quicker every day, as the houses grow smaller, till on the eighth day, with only a few dozens present to see the miracle, it liquefies in four minutes." *Mark Twain.*

At Naples they [the English] put *St. Januarius' blood* in an alembic. *Emerson.*

But as it was then, so it is now; so will it always be. Does not the *blood of St. Januarius* become liquid once a year? *Bayard Taylor.*

——as I lay
Watching Vesuvius from the bay,
I besought *St. Januarius.*
But I was a fool to try him;
Nought I said could liquefy him.
T. W. Parsons.

Bloody Brook. A locality in Deerfield, Mass., noted as the scene of a terrible battle with the Indians in the early days of New England. On the 18th of September, 1675, Capt. Lathrop, with a company of 84 men, was here attacked by 700 Indian warriors; and all perished with the exception of seven who escaped. In 1835 a marble monument was erected on this battle-field, and an address delivered by Edward Everett.

Bloomsbury Square. A London square, built in 1665, and formerly called Southampton Square from Southampton House, which stood there until 1800. This square was once so fashionable that it was considered one of the wonders of England. On the northern side is a bronze statue of Charles James Fox by Westmacott.

In Palace-yard, at nine, you'll find me there,
At ten, for certain, sir, in *Bloomsbury Square.* *Pope.*

Blue Boy. A celebrated portrait-picture by Thomas Gainsborough (1727–1788). In the Grosvenor Gallery, London.

☞ "Reynolds had laid down the law that blue ought not to be employed in masses in a picture, when, more from a spirit of malice which led Gainsborough to show that such a law was not without an exception, than with the intention of expressing his grave dissent from the view, Gainsborough painted the son of Mr. Buttall in an entire suit of blue. The result was a triumph of Gainsborough's art in the treatment of a difficult subject, so as to produce an agreeable effect under dis-

advantages, rather than an upsetting of Sir Joshua's theory."
Sarah Tytler.

☞ "Gainsborough's *Blue Boy* already possesses the expressive and wholly modern physiognomy by which a work falling within the painter's province oversteps the limits of painting."
Taine, Trans.

Blue Coat School. See CHRIST'S HOSPITAL.

Blue Grotto. [Ital. *Grotta Azzura.*] A celebrated cavern on the island of Capri, in the Bay of Naples. The walls and roof of the grotto, as well as the water within it, are of a beautiful ultramarine color, produced by the light from without entering the water, and being refracted upwards into the grotto.

☞ "Here, under a rough round bastion of masonry, was the entrance to the Blue Grotto. We were now trans-shipped to the little shell of a boat which had followed us. The swell rolled rather heavily into the mouth of the cave, and the adventure seemed a little perilous, had the boatmen been less experienced. We lay flat in the bottom, the oars were taken in, and we had just reached the entrance, when a high wave rolling up threatened to dash us against the iron portals. The young sailor held the boat back with his hands, while the wave rolled under us into the darkness beyond; then, seizing the moment, we shot in after it, and were safe under the expanding roof. At first, all was tolerably dark; I only saw that the water near the entrance was intensely and luminously blue. Gradually, as the eye grew accustomed to the obscurity, the irregular vault of the roof became visible, tinted by a faint reflection from the water. The effect increased, the longer we remained. . . . The silvery, starry radiance of foam or bubbles on the shining blue ground was the loveliest phenomenon of the grotto. To dip one's hand in the sea, and scatter the water, was to create sprays of wonderful, phosphorescent blossoms, jewels of the sirens, flashing and vanishing garlands of the Undines."
Bayard Taylor.

☞ "The Blue Grotto loses nothing of its beauty, but rather gains by contrast, when passing from dense fog you find yourselves transported to a world of wavering subaqueous sheen. It is only through the opening of the very topmost arch that a boat can glide into this cavern; the arch itself spreads downward through the water, so that all the light is transmitted from beneath, and colored by the sea. . . . The flesh of a diver in this water showed like the faces of children playing at snapdragon; all around him the spray leapt up with a living fire; and, when the oars struck the surface, it was as though a phosphorescent sea had been smitten, and the drops ran from the blades in blue pearls."
J. A. Symonds.

Many an archèd roof is bent
  Over the wave,
But none like thine, from the firmament
  To the shells that at thy threshold lave.
What name shall shadow thy rich-blue sheen,
Violet, sapphire, or ultramarine?
W. Gibson.

Blue-Stocking Clubs. Boswell describes the origin of Blue-Stocking Clubs: "About this time [1781] it was much the fashion for several ladies to have evening assemblies, where the fair sex might participate in conversation with literary and ingenious men, animated by a desire to please. One of the most eminent members of these societies, when they first commenced, was Mr. Stillingfleet (grandson of the Bishop), whose dress was remarkably grave; and in particular it was observed that he wore blue stockings. Such was the excellence of his conversation, that his absence was felt so great a loss that it used to be said, 'We can do nothing without the *blue stockings;*' and thus by degrees the title was established. Miss Hannah More has admirably described a *Blue-Stocking Club* in her *Bas-Bleu*, a poem in which many of the persons who were most conspicuous there are mentioned." The club which met at Mrs. Montagu's, in London, is described as having consisted originally of Mrs. Montagu, Mrs. Vesey, Mrs. Carter, Miss Boscawen, Lord Lyttelton, Mr. Pulteney, Horace Walpole, and Mr. Stillingfleet, and, according to Forbes, derived its name from the fact that Mr. Stillingfleet, "being somewhat of an humorist in his habits and manners, and a little negligent in his dress, literally wore gray stockings; from which circumstance Admiral Boscawen used, by way of pleasantry, to call them 'The Blue-Stocking Society,' as if to intimate that when these brilliant friends met, it was not for the purpose of forming a dressed assembly. A foreigner of distinction, hearing the expression, translated it literally, 'Bas-Bleu,' by which these meetings came to be afterwards distinguished."

☞ Mills (History of Chivalry) refers the use of the term Blue-Stocking, applied to a literary body, to the Society de la Calza, established at Venice in 1400, the members of which, "when they met in literary discussion, were distinguished by the color of their stockings. The colours were sometimes fantastically blended; and at other times one color, particularly *blue*, prevailed." The name was afterward applied in France to ladies of literary tastes, as a derisive appellation to denote female pedantry. From France the title crossed over to England. Byron (1788–1824), in "The Blues: a Literary Eclogue," ridicules the blue-stockings of that period.

Boar, Calydonian. See CHACE OF THE CALYDONIAN BOAR.

Boar Hunt. See WILD-BOAR HUNT.

Boar's Head. A celebrated tavern which formerly stood in Eastcheap, London, said to have been the oldest in the city. It was here that Shakespeare represents Prince Henry and his companions indulging their revels before A.D. 1413. The celebrated Boar's Head Tavern of Shakespearean fame was destroyed (afterwards rebuilt) by the great fire of 1666, a fact forgotten by Goldsmith, Boswell, and Washington Irving, in their references to the tavern as the identical structure frequented by Falstaff.

☞ "The earliest notice of this place occurs in the testament of Sir William Warden, who, in the reign of Richard II., gave 'all that his tenement, called the Boar's Head, Eastcheap,' to a college of priests or chaplains, founded by Sir William Walworth, Lord Mayor, in the adjoining church of St. Michael, Crooked-lane. Whether at that time it was a tavern or a cook's residence, does not appear; but very early in the next reign, if any confidence can be reposed in the locality of Shakespeare's scenes, it became the resort of old Jack Falstaff and Prince Hal; but subsequently it was converted into a residence for the priests, to whose college it had been devised." *Brayley's Londiniana.*

☞ "Falstaff absolutely requires the frame of an inn to make his portrait intelligible, with the buxom figure of Mrs. Quickly in the background; and it may be safely affirmed that no public house of entertainment has afforded such world-wide mirth as the *Boar's Head*, Eastcheap."

H. T. Tuckerman.

Such were the reflections that naturally arose while I sat at the *Boar's Head* tavern, still kept at Eastcheap. Here, by a pleasant fire, in the very room where old Sir John Falstaff cracked his jokes, in the very chair which was sometimes honored by Prince Henry, and sometimes polluted by his immoral merry companions, I sat and ruminated on the follies of youth.

Goldsmith.

[See Goldsmith's essay entitled, *A Reverie at the Boar's Head Tavern.*]

Boboli Gardens. Beautiful and well-known pleasure-grounds contiguous to the Pitti Palace, in Florence, Italy; so named from the Boboli family, who formerly possessed a mansion here; and affording fine views of the city with its domes and towers.

☞ "All is formal and regular. Trees are planted in rectangular rows, and their branches so trained and interlaced as to form long cathedral aisles of foliage, as if a lateral shaft had been cut in a solid mass of fresh green. In these very gardens Milton may have had suggested to him his image of the Indian herdsman,

—'that tends his pasturing herds
At loop-holes cut through thickest shade.'" *Hillard.*

☞ "I went into the Boboli Gardens, which are contiguous to the Palace; but found them too sunny for enjoyment. They seem to consist partly of a wilderness; but the portion into which I strayed was laid out with straight walks, lined with high box-hedges, along which there was only a narrow margin of shade."

Hawthorne.

At Florence, too, what golden hours
In those long galleries were ours;
What drives about the fresh Cascinè,
Or walks in *Boboli's* ducal bowers.

Tennyson.

Bocca della Verità. [Truth's Mouth.] A huge mask of white marble in the portico of the church of S. Maria in Cosmedin, Rome, which has given its name to the adjoining piazza. This mask is a slab of stone with holes for the eyes, nose, and mouth, and resembles the common representations of the face of the sun or moon. It had great fame among the vulgar of Rome, who believed in it as a sort of touchstone of truth, from which notion it derived its name. The belief was, that a witness of doubted veracity, having been required to place his hand in the mouth of the mask, would be unable to remove it in case he swore falsely. This truth-loving stone is thought to have been the opening to a drain.

☞ "This Bocca della Verita is a curious relic of the Middle Ages. It served the purpose of a divine ordeal. Imagine a windmill which resembles not a human countenance, but the face of the moon: we can distinguish in it eyes, a nose, and an open mouth into which the accused person placed his hand to take an oath. This mouth bit all liars, at least so the tradition goes. I put my right hand into it, saying the Ghetto was a delightful place, and have not been bitten." *About, Trans.*

Bocca di Leone. See LION'S MOUTH.

Bodleian Library. A famous library belonging to the University of Oxford, England, founded, or rather restored, by Sir Thomas Bodley, near the close of the sixteenth century. It is one of the most valuable collections of books and manuscripts in Europe. The founder expended large sums upon the building, which is magnificent, furnished it with a large quantity of books, and bequeathed a large sum to be devoted to its annual replenishment. It has been enriched, also, by many valuable gifts of books and manuscripts.

☞ "No candle or fire is ever lighted in the Bodleian. Its catalogue is the standard catalogue on the desk of every library in Oxford. In each several college, they underscore in red ink on this catalogue the titles of books contained in the library of that college, —the theory being that the Bodleian has all books." *Emerson.*

The walls and roofs [of the Vatican library] are painted not with antiques and grotescs, like our *Bodleian* at Oxford, but emblems, figures, diagrams, and the like learned inventions. *John Evelyn*, 1644.

Each college has been developed by itself, each age has built in its fashion . . . close to the *Bodleian Library*, a mass of edifices, sculptured portals, lofty bell-towers. *Taine, Trans.*

Bohême, La. See BOHEMIA.

Bohemia. A cant name (from the Fr. *Bohémien*, gypsy) given to certain quarters of London largely occupied by roving wits and people who have no fixed occupation. The appellation *La Bohême* is similarly used in Paris.

Bois de Boulogne. A beautiful and extensive promenade in Paris, covering nearly 2,500 acres. Previous to 1852 it was a sort of forest, with walks and rides; but in that year Napoleon III. determined to improve it, and, together with the municipality, built new roads, dug out the lakes, made the waterfalls, and otherwise diversified the surface, converting it into a delightful promenade — the Hyde Park of Paris.

☞ "The Bois de Boulogne is a level wood of small trees covering a mile or two square, and cut from corner to corner with straight roads for driving. The soil is sandy, and the grass only in tufts. Barring the equipages and the pleasure of a word in passing an acquaintance, I find a drive to this famous wood rather dull business. I want either one thing or the other, — cultivated grounds like the Tuileries or the wild wood." *N. P. Willis.*

☞ "In 1319 some pilgrims, having erected at Mem-lez-Saint-Cloud (a little hamlet situated in the midst of a clearing of woods) a church modelled after that of Boulogne-sur-Mer, the name of the hamlet was changed to that of Boulogne. The wood, too, following the fortunes of the first habitations erected upon its territory, took the name of Boulogne, which it has retained to this day." *Alphaud, Trans.*

About four o'clock he takes a turn in the *Bois*. He has a fair horse. He rides well, and does not look badly.
Taine, Trans.

His [Béranger's] geography did not go far beyond the Tuileries, the Champs Elysées, and the *Bois de Boulogne;* and his true home was the circle in which the self-supporting citizen toiled for his daily bread and butter and his weekly holiday. *Daily Advertiser.*

Come, Albert, said he, if you will take my advice, let us go out: a turn in the *Bois* in a carriage or on horseback will divert you. *Dumas, Trans.*

Boisserée Gallery. A celebrated collection of paintings (often referred to in works upon art) begun at Cologne, Prussia, in 1804 by two brothers of that name, during the confiscation of property and the dispersion of works of art at the time of the Napoleonic wars. The best part of this collection is now in the Pinakothek at Munich, having been purchased in 1827 by King Lewis.

Boisson. See GLACIER DE BOISSON.

Bolingbroke House. A building at Battersea, about three miles from London. It was formerly the residence of Henry St. John, Viscount Bolingbroke, and was the frequent resort of Pope, Swift, Arbuthnot, Thomson, Mallet, and other men of genius. The greater part of the mansion was taken down in 1778. In the wing remaining is a parlor lined with cedar, in which Pope composed his "Essay on Man." It is said to have been called "Pope's Parlor."

Bolsena, Mass of. See MASS OF BOLSENA.

Bolt Court. A street in London. Dr. Johnson lived here (at No. 8) from 1776 until his death in December, 1784.

☞ "When we read of Johnson's house in Bolt Court, although we do not think of the doctor as living in any state, we do not imagine a place like a flagged yard, reached through a dark, narrow alley, and in which we should expect to see clothes drying on the lines. Bolt Court is a representative place — an example of those nooks and secluded recesses found in the towns all over England." *R. G. White.*

The plate-licker and wine-bibber [Boswell] dives into *Bolt Court*, to sip muddy coffee with a cynical old man, and a sour-tempered blind old woman (feeling the cups, whether they are full, with her finger;) and patiently endured contradictions without end; too happy so he may but be allowed to listen and live. *Carlyle.*

There, in the Rue Taranne, for instance, the once noisy Denis Diderot has fallen silent enough. Here also, in *Bolt Court*, old Samuel Johnson, like an over-wearied giant, must lie down and slumber without dream. *Carlyle.*

Can this be Sir Allan McLean?

. . . .

Ah, no! It is only the Rambler,
The Idler, who lives in *Bolt Court*,
And who says, were he Laird of Inchkenneth,
He would wall himself round with a fort.
Anonymous.

Bolton Priory. The ruins of this celebrated priory are situated in one of the most beautiful spots in England, near Skipton on the banks of the Aire.

From *Bolton's* old monastic tower
The bells ring loud with gladsome power;

. . . .

And thus in joyous mood they hie
To *Bolton's* mouldering Priory.
Wordsworth.

Entranced with varied loveliness, I gaze
On *Bolton's* hallowed fane. Its hoary walls,
More eloquent in ruin, than the halls
Of princely pomp. *Newman Hall.*

Bon Homme Richard. [Good Man Richard.] A noted ship in which Capt. John Paul Jones of the American navy sailed in 1779 to the coast of England, and engaging the much superior British frigate *Serapis* captured her after a desperate fight of two hours. The Bon Homme Richard was named after Benjamin Franklin's "Poor Richard."

☞ "In his earlier writings, he [Benjamin Franklin] often uttered wise sayings in this form: '"A bird in the hand is worth two in the bush," as Poor Richard says.' By these sayings in this form he came to be known at home and abroad as 'Poor Richard;' and when, in the summer of 1779, the French government and the American ambassador jointly fitted out an expedition to be commanded by Jones, the flag-ship was named *Bonhomme Richard*, or 'Good Man Richard.'" *Lossing.*

Who, in the darkest days of our Revolution, carried your flag into the very chops of the British Channel, bearded the lion in his den, and woke the echoes of old Albion's hills by the thunders of his cannon, and the shouts of his triumph? It was the American sailor. And the names of John Paul Jones, and the *Bon Homme Richard*, will go down the annals of time forever. *R. F. Stockton.*

Bonanza, Big. See CONSOLIDATED VIRGINIA.

Bonaparte at Cairo. A picture by Jean Léon Gérôme (b. 1824), the French painter.

Bonaventure. A noted cemetery near Savannah, Ga. It is planted with native live-oaks.

Bond Street. A street in London named after its builder, Sir Thomas Bond.

It is natural to me to go where I please, to do what I please. I find myself at eleven o'clock in the day in *Bond Street*, and it seems to me that I have been sauntering there at that very hour for years past. *Charles Lamb.*

Why should we call them from their dark abode
In broad St. Giles's or in Tottenham-road?
Or (since some men of fashion nobly dare
To scrawl in verse) from *Bond-street* or the Square? *Byron.*

Is this the sublime? Mr. Angelo of *Bond Street* might admire the attitude; his namesake, Michel, I don't think would. *Thackeray.*

The expressive word 'quiet' defines the dress, manner, bow, and even physiognomy, of every true denizen of St. James's and *Bond Street*. *N. P. Willis.*

Bone Compagnie. See COURT DE BONE COMPAGNIE.

Bonne Nouvelle, Boulevart. One of the boulevards of Paris. On this street is the Théâtre du Gymnase. See BOULEVARDS.

Bonsecours Market. A stone building three stories high, with a dome, in Montreal, Canada. It is unsurpassed for its purposes by any building in America.

Boodle's Club. This club in St. James's Street, London, first known as the *Savoir Vivre Club*, was established about 1764. Gibbon was a member of Boodle's.

☞ "Boodle's Club-house, designed by Holland, has long been eclipsed by the more pretentious architecture of the club edifices of our time; but the interior arrangements are well planned. Boodle's is chiefly frequented by country gentlemen, whose status has been thus satirically insinuated by a contemporary: 'Every Sir John belongs to Boodle's — as you may see; for when a waiter comes into the room, and says to some aged student of the *Morning Herald*, "Sir John, your servant has come," every head is mechanically thrown up in answer to the address.'" *Timbs.*

So, when some John his dull invention racks,
To rival *Boodle's* dinners or Almack's,
Three uncouth legs of mutton shock our eyes,
Three roasted geese, three buttered apple-pies. *William Mason.*

Rank weeds will sprout between yon stones,
And owls will roost at *Boodle's*,
And Echo will hurl back the tones
Of screaming Yankee Doodles. *Frederick Locker.*

Book of Revelation. A series of wood-cuts illustrating the Book of Revelation, by Albert Dürer (1471-1528), the German painter and engraver.

Booth's. An elegant theatre on Twenty-third Street, New York. It is chiefly used for standard tragedy.

Bora, The. A name locally given to the north or north-east wind which at times rages over the Carnic and Julian Alps, in Southern Austria, with extreme violence.

Border, The. The name often applied to the common boundary line (or more generally to the whole of the common frontier region) of England and of Scotland. The position of this dividing line was, until comparatively recent times, dependent upon the changes of war or diplomacy; and the border, from the eleventh century until about the beginning of the eighteenth century, was the scene of almost constant wars, forays, feuds, and various disturbances. After the legislative union of 1707, these wars and troubles of the border were finally terminated. Sir Walter Scott is often called the "Border Minstrel," and he and some of his poetical followers, who celebrated various plundering chiefs of the border, have been sometimes referred to as the "Border-thief School."

O, young Lochinvar is come out of the West!
Through all the wide *Border* his steed is the best;
And save his good broadsword he weapon had none;
He rode all unarmed, and he rode all alone.
Scott.

Sophia [Scott] shares and enjoys these local feelings and attachments, and can tell as many *Border* stories as her father, and repeat perhaps as many ballads, and certainly more Jacobite songs.
George Ticknor.

Borestone, The. 1. A spot on the field of Bannockburn, in Scotland, now enclosed by an iron railing, where, according to tradition, Bruce's standard was planted during the contest.

2. A monumental stone preserved at Edinburgh, Scotland, into which, according to tradition, the standard of James IV. was stuck before he marched to the battle-field of Flodden.

Borghese Chapel. See CAPELLA BORGHESE.

Borghese Gladiator. A celebrated statue, representing a warrior contending with a horseman, and supposed to have made part of a large battle-group. It is attributed to Agasias (400 B.C.?), an Ephesian sculptor, whose name appears on the statue. Now in the Louvre, Paris. See DYING GLADIATOR and WOUNDED GLADIATOR.

Borghese Palace. [Ital. *Palazzo Borghese.*] A Roman palace of immense size, containing one of the richest collections of art in the city. It was begun in 1590, and completed by Paul V., one of the Borghese family.

☞ "The Palazzo Borghese contains the finest private collection of pictures in Rome, upwards of six hundred in number. . . . The Borghese family is still rich, and the suite of apartments devoted to the collection is taken good care of." *G. S. Hillard.*

Borghese Villa. See VILLA BORGHESE.

Borgia, Cæsar. See CÆSAR BORGIA.

Borgo. [Suburb, or borough.] See LEONINE CITY.

See also INCENDIO DEL BORGO and STANZE OF RAPHAEL.

Borough, The. A general term, but applied specifically to Southwark, a parliamentary borough of England, on the southern side of the Thames, directly opposite the City of London.

And Gower, an older poet whom
The *Borough* church enshrines.
Horace Smith.

Indeed, it is evident that the curious little passage which leads in to the "Cock" must have been originally an entrance to one of these courts on which the tavern gradually encroached. Much the same are found in the *Borough*, only these lead into great courts and innyards.
Fitzgerald.

"Borrachos," The. [The topers.] A famous picture by Diego Rodriguez de Silva y Velasquez (1599–1660). In the gallery at Madrid, Spain.

Borromean Colossus. See CARLO BORROMEO.

Borromean Islands. See ISOLA BELLA.

Borromeo, Carlo. See CARLO BORROMEO.

Borthwick Castle. A Scotch fortress of the fifteenth century, in the parish of the same name, in the county of Edinburgh.

☞ "This building is believed to be the largest specimen of that class of architecture [a simple square block] in Scotland." *Billings.*

Bosch, The. See HUIS IN'T BOSCH.

Boston Common. See COMMON, THE.

Bothwell Bridge. A bridge over the Clyde, near Glasgow, the scene of the battle between the Royalists and the Covenanters, June 22, 1679, described in Sir Walter Scott's tale of "Old Mortality."

☞ "We went to the famous Bothwell Bridge, which Scott has immortalized in 'Old Mortality.' We walked up and down, trying to recall the scenes of the battle, as there described, and were rather mortified, after we had all our associations comfortably located upon it, to be told that it was not the same bridge — it had been newly built, widened, and otherwise made more comfortable and convenient."
Mrs. H. B. Stowe.

Bothwell Castle. An old baronial fortress on the Clyde, near Glasgow, Scotland, belonging to the Earl of Home. The modern mansion adjoining contains a valuable art-collection.

☞ "The name had for me the quality of enchantment. . . . I remembered the dim melodies of 'The Lady of the Lake.' Bothwell's lord was the lord of this castle, whose beautiful ruins here adorn the banks of the Clyde. Whatever else we have, or may have, in America, we shall never have the wild poetic beauty of these ruins. The present noble possessors are fully aware of their worth as objects of taste, and therefore with the greatest care are they preserved."
Mrs. H. B. Stowe.

Immured in *Bothwell*'s towers, at times the brave
(So beautiful is Clyde) forgot to mourn
The liberty they lost at Bannockburn.
Wordsworth.

Botolph's, St. See St. Botolph's.

Bouc, La. A strong fortification at Luxemburg, Holland. It is an excavation in the solid rock capable of holding four thousand men.

Boucherie. See St. Jacques la Boucherie.

Bouffes Parisiens. A little theatre in Paris, known for the first production of Offenbach's operettes. It is much frequented, and is devoted to comedies and vaudevilles.

Do you suppose that I do not know that your club appointment is at the *Bouffes Parisiens* or somewhere else?
Taine, Trans.

Bouillon Castle. An extensive feudal mansion in Belgium, once the seat of the famous Godfrey de Bouillon (1058?-1100). It is now used as a prison.

Boulevards. A name given in French cities to the public promenade, and chiefly applied to the wide and magnificent streets of Paris, which occupy the site of the former fortifications, or *Bulwarks* (whence the name), once devoted to the defence of the city. In the centre is a road which is lined with trees, and between each row of trees and the houses are wide sidewalks. They became a general promenade in the reign of Louis XIV. Each of these streets has a distinctive name, as the Boulevart des Italiens, de la Madeleine, des Capucines, de Montmartre, Poissonière, Bonne Nouvelle, St. Denis, St. Martin, du Temple, des Filles du Calvaire, Beaumarchais. Napoleon III. built several great streets which traverse the city in different directions, and to which the name Boulevart is applied. The principal of these new streets are: Boulevart de Prince Eugène, Boulevart de Malesherbes, Boulevart de la Reine Hortense, Boulevart de Haussman, Boulevart de Richard Lenoir, Boulevart de Sèbastopol. The *boulevards extérieurs* constitute a line of broad, continuous road on the site of the ancient *octroi* wall.

☞ For the more celebrated boulevards of Paris, see the next prominent word: *e.g.*, Boulevart des Italiens, see Italiens, Boulevart des.

☞ "The *Boulevarts Intérieurs*, the oldest in Paris, and those best known to the visitor, extend from the Madeleine to the Bastille, and occupy the site of the old walls of Paris, which were pulled down about 1670, when the ground was levelled and trees were planted, and the broad and handsome street thus formed soon became, and still continues, the gayest and most brilliant part of Paris. Some of the trees had attained large size, but they were cut down to form barricades in the revolutionary struggle of 1830; fresh ones were planted, but many of these were again cut down in 1848, and the Boulevarts thus deprived of their chief ornament. These Boulevarts are thronged with carriages and pedestrians, especially in the evening, when the hosts of people sitting outside cafés, the throng of loungers along the pavement, the lofty houses, the splendid shops, the brilliantly lighted cafés, and the numerous theatres, form a scene which will be quite new to an Englishman." *Murray's Handbook.*

Under pretence of doing his duty, he passed his time in walking to the Tuileries and on the *Boulevard.*
Alfred de Musset.

Que ma gloire s'etende
Du Louvre aux *boulevards*
Béranger.

Would ten rubles buy a tag
Of ribbon on the *boulevard*, worth a sou?
Mrs. Browning.

Boulogne Flotilla. A naval armament assembled at Boulogne, France, in 1804, by Napoleon I., with the design of invading England. It included over 1,200 vessels, with a large force of seamen, infantry, cavalry, and artillery In consequence of Nelson's success, the expedition was abandoned, and the flotilla was dispersed.

Bounty, The. A noted ship which sailed from England in 1787 for the Society Islands in the South Pacific Ocean. On the 28th of April, 1789, a mutiny occurred on board, as a result of which the commander, Capt. Bligh, was bound and placed with 18 of his crew in an open boat with 140 pounds of bread, a little meat, and a few gallons of water. They landed at Otaheite, but were driven off, and finally reached New Holland, after having been 46 days in a small boat upon the open sea on short allowances of food. After his return to England, Capt. Bligh published "A Narrative of the Mutiny which occurred on H. M. S. the Bounty," which excited great interest. Lord Byron wrote a poem entitled "The Island," suggested by the adventure.

> With slow, despairing oar, the abandon'd skiff
> Ploughs its drear progress to the scarce-seen cliff,
> Which lifts its peak a cloud above the main:
> *That* boat and ship shall never meet again! *Byron.*

Bourbon, Gros. [The Great Bourbon.] An orange-tree in the gardens of Versailles, France, said to have reached an age of over 400 years.

> When France with civil wars was torn,
> And heads, as well as crowns, were shorn
> From royal shoulders,
> One *Bourbon*, in unaltered plight.
> Hath still maintained its regal right,
> And held its court, — a goodly sight
> To all beholders. *Horace Smith.*

Bourbon Museum. See MUSEO BORBONICO.

Bourdon, Gros. See GROS BOURDON.

Bourse, La. [Exchange, or Stock Exchange.] A stately edifice in the Place de la Bourse, Paris. It is in the form of a parallelogram, with a surrounding colonnade of Corinthian pillars, and is one of the finest examples of classical architecture in Paris. In it is the Salle de la Bourse, a large and handsome hall with a gallery. The hours for business at the Bourse are from one to five.

☞ Bourse is a general term corresponding to the English 'Change. While the Bourse of Paris is the most prominent and best known, these exchanges exist in the other French cities.

> Each year the number of real artists grows less and less. Taste has declined since the division of patrimonies has broken fortunes into crumbs, and the great profits of the *Bourse* soil society with new and vulgar wealth. *Taine, Trans.*

> When I observe the Parisians on the boulevard, at the *Bourse*, at the café or theatre, I always seem to see a pêle-mêle of busy and maddened ants, on whom pepper has been sprinkled. *Taine, Trans.*

> Well-shaven, buxom merchants, looking as trim and fat as those on the *Bourse* or on 'Change. *Thackeray*

> J'ai fréquenté, jusqu'à présent,
> La *Bourse* plus que le Parnasse. *Scribe.*

> . . . La *Bourse* est un champ clos
> Où c'est, au lieu de sang, de l'or qui coule à flots. *Ponsard.*

> Paris, like Sparta, has its temple of Fear, — it is the *Bourse*. *Heine, Trans.*

> The *Bourse* is the temple of speculation. *Proudhon, Trans.*

> The *Bourse* is the sibyl's cave of Paris. *Viennet, Trans.*

Bow Bells. The famous set of bells in the belfry of the Church of St. Mary-le-Bow, Cheapside, London. It was from the extreme fondness of the citizens in the old times for these bells, that a genuine cockney has been supposed to be born within the sound of Bow Bells. The Bow Bells being rung somewhat late for the closing of shops, the young men, 'prentices, and others in Cheap made this rhyme: —

> "Clarke of the Bow Bells with the yellow locks,
> For thy late ringing thou shalt have knocks."

To which the clerk replied: —

> "Children of Cheape, hold you all still,
> For you shall have the Bow Bells rung at your will."

The Bow Bells were the ones that rung the famous rhyme in the nursery tale: —

Turn again, Whittington,
Lord Mayor of London.

See Bow CHURCH.

Far as loud *Bow's* stupendous bells resound. *Pope.*

I am sure I don't know,
Says the great bell at *Bow.*
Mother Goose.

Bow Church, *or* **St. Mary-le-Bow.** A celebrated church in Cheapside, London. According to Stow, an ancient church upon the same site was originally named St. Mary *de Arcubus,* from its being built on arches of stone. The Ecclesiastical Court, "The Court of Arches," was formerly held in this church, and hence derived its name. The bells of this church, which was built by Wren, have long been famed for their sweetness of tone. See Bow BELLS.

Tillotson was nominated to the Archbishopric, and was consecrated on Whitsunday, in the church of *St. Mary Le Bow.* *Macaulay.*

There has been a saying current among the ancient sibyls, who treasure up these things, that when the grasshopper on the top of the Exchange shook hands with the dragon on the top of *Bow Church* steeple, fearful events would take place. *Irving.*

Bow Street. A once fashionable street in Covent Garden, London, so called from its shape being that of a bent bow. Here in the eighteenth century was Will's well-known coffee-house. Bow Street is especially familiar in connection with the Bow-street Police Office. In this street Fielding wrote his novel "Tom Jones;" and here lived Edmund Waller, Wycherley, and Dr. Radcliffe.

I've had to-day a dozen billets-doux
From fops, and wits, and cits, and *Bow-street* beaux. *Dryden.*

Through this dingy, ragged, bustling, beggarly, cheerful scene, we began now to march towards the *Bow Street* of Jaffa. *Thackeray.*

Can none remember that eventful day,
That ever glorious, almost fatal fray,
When Little's leadless pistol met his eye,
And *Bow-street* myrmidons stood laughing by? *Byron.*

At home, our *Bow-street* gemmen keep the laws,
And here a sentry stands within your calling. *Byron.*

Bowariyeh. The oldest Chaldæan temple of which any remains exist. It is at Warka (Erek), and was erected at least 2,000 years before Christ.

Bowdoin College. An institution of learning in Brunswick, Me., named after Gov. James Bowdoin of Massachusetts, who endowed it with gifts in land and money, together with his library and picture-gallery. The latter contains some valuable works of the old masters. The college was incorporated in 1794.

Bowery, The. A well-known thoroughfare in New York, nearly parallel with Broadway. It is chiefly populated by the lower classes. At one time it gained notoriety by the ruffian bands known as the Bowery Boys.

Bowery Theatre. A theatre on the Bowery, New York, devoted to German plays and operas.

Bowling Green. An enclosure just north of the Battery, in the city of New York. It was "the cradle" of the infant city. Here formerly stood an equestrian statue of King George III. It was torn down by the people in 1776, and, after being removed to Connecticut, was melted into bullets for the national army.

Is this the *Bowling Green?* I should not know it,
So disarrayed, defaced, and gone to seed,
Like some un-Pegasused and prosy poet,
Whose Helicon is now the bowl and weed;
Its Green, if grass, does not precisely show it,
So changed to worse from that once lovely mead.

. . . .

The iron fence, its once proud decoration,
The street, the mansions round, share the disgrace. *T. G. Appleton.*

The road is continuous. It is as if Broadway had half a dozen names between the *Bowling Green* and Thirty-fourth Street. *R. G. White.*

Bowood. A seat of the Marquis of Lansdowne, near Calne, England.

Bowyer, Fort. See FORT BOWYER.

Boxers, The. See TWO BOXERS.

Boy and the Dolphin. A statue executed by Raphael (1483–1520), the Italian painter, and pronounced "a remarkable work of sculpture." It is in the possession of Sir Hervey Bruce, London.

Boy Blowing Bubbles. A well-known and beautiful picture by Franz van Mieris (1635–1681). At the Hague, Holland.

Boy Praying. A bronze statue, considered one of the finest relics of ancient sculpture, discovered in the bed of the Tiber. It was purchased by Frederic II. of Prussia for 10,000 thalers, and placed in his palace at Potsdam. Now in the Museum at Berlin. It is known of Boëdas, son of Lysippus, the celebrated Greek sculptor, that he executed the statue of a praying figure, and by many this is believed to be his work.

O genius of new days!
Hail from thine ancient tomb;
Now let thy spirit's blaze
Chase the old world of gloom.

Bright one! thine influence pour
On man, so prone and sad;
And teach him how to adore,
And to be free and glad.
N. L. Frothingham.

Boy with a Squirrel. A picture by John Singleton Copley, the American painter (1737–1815). In possession of Mrs. James S. Amory.

Braccio Nuovo. A hall in the Vatican, Rome, built in 1817 under Pius VII., filled with valuable works of sculpture.

☞ "This noble hall is upwards of 200 feet in length, and admirably lighted from a roof supported by Corinthian columns. It is impossible for works of sculpture to be better disposed; and, out of 72 busts and 43 statues which are here, there is hardly one which is not excellent." *Hillard.*

All this shows itself in the *Braccio Nuovo* and in countless statues besides, such as the Augustus and the Tiberius. *Taine, Trans.*

This statue [the Sleeping Ariadne], the Demosthenes and the Minerva Medica in the *Nuovo Braccio*, are worthy of peculiar attention to the modern artist, as showing what may be done by a skilful management of drapery. *Hillard.*

Brae-Mar. A picture by Sir Edwin Landseer (1803–1873), the celebrated English painter of animals. It is pronounced the noblest single figure which he has painted, — "a stately stag, standing clearly out on a misty hill-top, and bellowing defiance, while near him are several does." This picture was sold for $21,000 in 1868.

Brambletye House. An ancient mansion of the reign of Henry VII., near the royal forest of Ashdown, in Sussex, England. With its gables and chimneys, moat and drawbridge, it remained an object of interest and curiosity till about 60 years since. About the middle of the seventeenth century Sir Henry Compton erected an elegant baronial mansion, but after the Civil War it was deserted. It is now only a picturesque ruin. Horace Smith's romance of "Brambletye House" has its opening scenes laid here.

Bramfield Oak. A noted tree of great size, not far from Norwich, in England, the age of which exceeded 1,000 years. It fell in 1843, from simple decay.

Brancacci Chapel. See CAPELLA BRANCACCI.

Brandenburg Gate. [Ger. *Das Brandenburger Thor.*] A noted gate and entrance-way into the city of Berlin, Prussia. It is said to have been modelled after the Propylæum at Athens. On the summit is a triumphal car, which was carried by Napoleon to Paris, but afterwards recovered.

Brandywine, The. A noted frigate of the United States navy, in service in the war of 1812. She was fitted up to convey Lafayette home to France in 1824 on his return from his visit to this country.

Branksome Hall. A mansion near Hawick, Scotland, belonging to the Duke of Buccleuch, and associated with Scott's poem of the "Lay of the Last Minstrel."

Such is the custom of *Branksome Hall.*
Scott.

Why did I leave fair *Branksome's* towers,
Why did I leave sweet Teviot glen?
William Wilson.

Braschi Antinous. See ANTINOUS, THE (6).

Braschi Palace. [Ital. *Palazzo Braschi.*] A well-known palace in Rome, built near the end of the last century by Pius VI. for his nephew, the Duke of Braschi.

☞ "As you ascend the staircase, you will be struck with its noble architecture, which is in the most chaste and classical taste. The stairs are led up between a colonnade of columns of red Oriental granite, the high polish of which accords well with the lustre of the variegated marbles, and with the graceful symmetry and just design of the whole." *Eaton.*

Brazen Head. See FRIAR BACON'S BRAZEN HEAD.

Brazen Nose College. One of the colleges included in the University of Oxford, England. The tradition is, that its quaint name is derived from the circumstance that it was erected on the site of two ancient halls, one of which was called Brazen Nose Hall on account of an iron ring fixed in a nose of brass, and serving as a knocker to the gate.

Bread and Cheese Land. The name given to a piece of ground, twenty acres in extent, in the parish of Biddenden, Kent, England, where, it is said, pursuant to the will of two maiden sisters, born in 1110 (and traditionally said to have been joined together by the shoulders and hips), "on the afternoon of Easter Sunday, 600 rolls are distributed to strangers, and 270 loaves, weighing three pounds and a half each, are given to the poor of the parish, — the expense being defrayed by the rental of the land."

Bread Street. A street in London, so named from the market in which bread was formerly sold. Stow says that in the year 1302, which was the 30th of Edward I., the bakers of London were forced to sell no bread in their shops or houses, but in the market. In this street John Milton was born, Dec. 9, 1608; and in the Church of All Hallows (now destroyed), at the corner of Bread Street and Watling Street, he was baptized. Dec. 20, 1608. See MERMAID TAVERN.

Brèche de Roland. [Roland's Breach.] A famous mountain pass in the Pyrenees, deriving its name from the tradition that Roland opened the passage with a blow of his sword, *Durandal.* It is the colossal entrance way from France to Spain, 200 feet wide, 300 feet high, and 50 feet long, at an elevation of more than 9,000 feet above the level of the sea.

Breda, Surrender of. See SURRENDER OF BREDA.

Brède, La. An interesting and ancient château, in the vicinity of Bordeaux, France. It is the seat of the Montesquieu family. It was here that the great historian and philosopher of that name was born and wrote.

Brederode Castle. A picturesque ruined fortress of the Middle Ages, in the neighborhood of Haarlem, Holland.

Breed's Hill. An eminence (formerly so called) in Charlestown, now a part of Boston, Mass. See BUNKER HILL MONUMENT.

Brera, La. A palace in Milan, Italy, containing a famous gallery of paintings, together with a museum of antiquities. The building was erected in 1618, and is said to derive its name from the Latin *prædium,* meadow.

Leonardo da Vinci's angels do not quite please me, elegant, refined, and lovely as they are: "methinks they smile too much." By his scholar Luini there are some angels in the gallery of the *Brera,* swinging censers and playing on musical instruments, which, with the peculiar character of the Milanese school, combine all the grace of a purer, loftier nature.
Mrs. Jameson.

Breton Club. A political association formed at Versailles, France, in 1789. The name was subsequently changed to that of the Jacobin Club.

Bridal Veil. 1. A noted fall in the Yosemite Valley, Cal. The water falling from a height of 1,000 feet is converted into mist before reaching the bottom.

2. A slender fall on the American shore, at Niagara Falls.

Bride's, St. See St. Bride's.

Bridewell. Formerly a workhouse and prison, now a hospital in London. The prison was founded upon the ancient palace of Bridewell, in which is laid the whole third act of Shakespeare's "Henry VIII." The name is derived from the famous well (St. Bride's, or St. Bridget's Well) in the vicinity of St. Bride's Church; and, this prison being the first of its kind, other houses of correction upon the same plan were called Bridewells.

Bridge of Alcantara. See Puente de Alcantara.

Bridge of Balgownie. See Brig o' Balgownie.

Bridge of Lodi. A bridge over the river Adda, at Lodi, in Italy, famous in military history in connection with the wars of Napoleon.

> Battles and bloodshed, September massacres, *Bridges of Lodi*, retreats of Moscow, Waterloos, Peterloos, ten-pound franchises, tar-barrels and guillotines.
> *Carlyle.*

> Shall future ages tell this tale
> Of inconsistence faint and frail?
> And art thou He of *Lodi's bridge*,
> Marengo's field, and Wagram's ridge?
> *Scott.*

Bridge of St. Angelo. This bridge — the ancient *Pons Ælius* — which crosses the Tiber immediately opposite the Castle of St. Angelo in Rome, was erected by Hadrian as a passage to his mausoleum. At the end are the statues of St. Peter and St. Paul. See St. Angelo.

☞ "The piers and arches are ancient, but have been a good deal repaired; not, indeed, till it was necessary, for in the Pontificate of Clement VII., when crowds were pressing forward to St. Peter's to share in the benefits and indulgences offered to the pious there, the bridge gave way, and 172 persons are said to have perished in the Tiber." *Eaton.*

> Even as the Romans, for the mighty host,
> The year of jubilee, upon the bridge,
> Have chosen a mode to pass the people over;
> For all upon one side towards the Castle
> Their faces have, and go unto St. Peter's;
> On the other side they go towards the Mountain.
> *Dante (Inferno), Longfellow's Trans.*

> I may be wrong; but the Tiber has a voice for me, as it whispers to the piers of the *Pons Ælius*, even more full of meaning than my well-beloved Charles eddying round the piles of West Boston Bridge.
> *Holmes.*

Bridge of Segovia. See Puente del Diablo.

Bridge of Sighs. [Ital. *Ponte dei Sospiri.*] This bridge over the Rio Canal in Venice, Italy, connecting the Doge's palace and the state prisons, is so called because the condemned passed over it on the way to execution. "The Bridge of Sighs" is also the title of a well-known poem by Thomas Hood (1798–1845), which begins:—

> "One more unfortunate,
> Weary of breath."

☞ "The Venice of modern fiction and drama is a thing of yesterday, a mere efflorescence of decay, a stage-drama, which the first ray of daylight must dissipate into dust. No prisoner whose name is worth remembering, or whose sorrows deserved sympathy, ever crossed that Bridge of Sighs, which is the centre of the Byronic ideal of Venice." *Ruskin.*

☞ "The Bridge of Sighs was not built till the end of the sixteenth century, and no romantic episode of political imprisonment and punishment (except that of Antonio Foscarini) occurs in Venetian history later than that period. But the Bridge of Sighs could have nowise a savor of sentiment from any such episode; being, as it was, merely a means of communication between the criminal courts sitting in the Ducal Palace and the criminal prison across the little canal. Housebreakers, cut-purse knaves, and murderers do not commonly impart a poetic interest to places which have known them; and yet these are the only sufferers on whose Bridge of Sighs the whole sentimental world has looked with pathetic sensation ever since Byron drew attention to it. The name of the bridge was given by the people from that opulence of compassion which enables the Italians to pity even rascality in difficulties." *W. D. Howells.*

I stood in Venice, on the *Bridge of Sighs:*
A palace and a prison on each hand.
Byron.

Bridgewater Gallery. See BRIDGEWATER HOUSE.

Bridgewater House. The town residence of the Earl of Ellesmere, London, built in 1847-49 on the site of Cleveland House, where once resided Barbara Villiers, Duchess of Cleveland, and which had at different times belonged to the great Earl of Clarendon, and to the Earls of Bridgewater. It contains a very celebrated collection of pictures, called the Bridgewater Gallery, and sometimes the Stafford Gallery; it having been left by the Duke of Bridgewater to his nephew, the Marquis of Stafford. It is the finest private collection in England; comprising some of the best works of Raphael, Titian, Guido, Domenichino, Rubens, Rembrandt, Vandyke, and other masters, as well as those of the modern artists.

☞ "From the time of Raphael the series is more complete than in any private gallery I know, not excepting the Lichtenstein Gallery at Vienna. The Caracci school can nowhere be studied to more advantage."
Mrs. Jameson.

Bridgewater Madonna. See MADONNA OF THE BRIDGEWATER GALLERY.

Brig o' Balgownie. A famous bridge of a single arch near Aberdeen, Scotland, built in the time of Robert Bruce (1274-1329). It has been made familiar by Byron, who alludes to it in his poem of "Don Juan."

☞ "It is a single gray stone arch, apparently cut from solid rock, that spans the brown rippling waters, where wild overhanging banks, shadowy trees, and dipping wild flowers, all conspire to make a romantic picture. This bridge, with the river and scenery, were poetic items that went, with other things, to form the sensitive mind of Byron, who lived here in his earlier days. He has some lines about it: —

'As "Auld lang Syne" brings Scotland, one and all,
Scotch plaids, Scotch snoods, the blue hills, and clear streams,
The Dee, the Don, Balgownie's brig's black wall,
All my boy-feelings, all my gentler dreams,
. . . .
Like Banquo's offspring — floating past me seems
My childhood.'" *Mrs. H. B. Stowe.*

Brig o' Doon. A bridge across the river Doon, in Scotland, near the town of Ayr, made famous by the poetry of Burns.

Now do thy speedy utmost, Meg,
And win the key-stane of the brig:
There at them thou thy tail may toss,
A running stream they darena cross!
Tam O'Shanter.

Brignole Sale Palace. [Ital. *Palazzo Brignole Sale.*] A beautiful palace in Genoa, Italy, now the property of the city, and containing many fine treasures of art. It derives its name *rosso* from being painted of a red color. It formerly belonged to the Brignole family.

Britain, Little. See LITTLE BRITAIN.

Britannia Bridge. A famous iron tubular bridge across Menai Strait, which separates the island of Anglesea from Carnarvon, Wales. It consists of two lines of tubes, each 1,513 feet long, supported on three piers, in addition to the abutments, 100 feet above the sea. It is situated one mile from the Menai suspension bridge.

A fourth [stone in the substructure of a temple at Baalbec] of similar dimensions is lying in the quarry, which it is calculated must weigh alone more than 1,100 tons in its rough state, or nearly as much as one of the tubes of the *Britannia Bridge.* *Fergusson.*

Britannia Theatre. A well-built theatre in London, opened in 1858.

British Coffee-house. A London coffee-house, formerly frequented by Scotchmen.

British Museum. This celebrated institution, formed of three collections, — the Cottonian, the Harleian, and the Sloane, — occupies the site of Montague House in Great Russell Street, London. It has been the growth of a century, the first purchase for the collection having been made in 1753, and it having been opened to the public 1759. It was at first divided into three departments, viz.: Printed Books, Manuscripts, and Natural History. To these have since been added other departments, as Antiquities and Arts, Medals and Coins, Prints and Drawings, Zoölogical Collections, etc. The Elgin marbles, the Egyptian antiquities, and the Assyrian sculptures collected by Layard, are among the chief curiosities of the institution. The Library is one of the largest and most valuable in Europe.

Brittany Sheep. A picture by Rosa Bonheur (b. 1822), the celebrated French painter of animals.

Broad Street. One of the great thoroughfares of Philadelphia, Penn. It is over 100 feet in width, and runs in a straight line 15 miles.

Broadway. A noted street, and the great thoroughfare of New York, extending from the Battery, at the extreme lower end of the island, to Central Park. In respect of length, the imposing character of its buildings, and the importance of the business transacted in it, this avenue is unequalled in the world.

> Princes' Street, the *Broadway* of the new town, is built along the edge of the ravine facing the long, many-windowed walls of the Canongate. *N. P. Willis.*

> He's so innate a cockney, that had he been born
> Where plain bare-skin's the only full-dress that is worn,
> He'd have given his own such an air that you'd say
> 'T had been made by a tailor to lounge in *Broadway*. *Lowell.*

> Tell me not, in half-derision,
> Of your Boulevards Parisian,
> With their brilliant broad *pavés*,
> Still for us the best is nearest,
> And the last love is the dearest,
> And the Queen of Streets—*Broadway*.
> *W. A. Butler.*

> For the wide sidewalks of *Broadway* are then
> Gorgeous as are a rivulet's banks in June,
> That, overhung with blossoms, through its glen
> Slides soft away beneath the sunny noon,
> And they who search the untrodden wood for flowers
> Meet in its depths no lovelier ones than ours. *Bryant (Spring in Town).*

Brocken, Spectre of the. See Spectre of the Brocken.

Brohlthal. This lovely valley of the Rhine is surrounded by mountains, and a rapid brook runs through it. It is especially remarkable that the whole bottom of the valley consists of tuffstone 15 to 50 feet in thickness.

Brömserburg. A well-known ruined castle at Rüdesheim, on the Rhine.

Bronze Door [of the Capitol at Washington]. A work of art, forming the entrance to the Rotunda of the Capitol. It is entirely of bronze, weighing 20,000 pounds, and was designed by Randolph Rogers, an American artist. The casting was executed at Munich in 1861. The door is 17 feet in height by 9 feet in width. It contains 8 panels with reliefs exhibiting scenes in the life of Columbus.

Bronze Gates [of Ghiberti]. Famous gates of bronze in the Baptistery of St. John at Florence, Italy, executed from designs furnished by Lorenzo Ghiberti (1378–1455?), the greatest sculptor of his time. These gates represent scenes from the New Testament. Ghiberti is said to have spent more than 20 years on these bronze gates, which were pronounced by Michael Angelo worthy to be the Gates of Paradise.

Bronze Horses. Four celebrated figures of horses, in bronze, which were brought by the Venetians from Constantinople, and which now stand over the vestibule of the Cathedral of St. Mark, in Venice, Italy.

> He [the doge Dandolo] went to die;
> But of his trophies four arrived ere long,
> Snatched from destruction,—the four steeds divine,
> That strike the ground, resounding with their feet,
> And from their nostrils snort ethereal flame
> Over that very porch. *Rogers.*

☞ "A glorious team of horses,— what seemed strange to me was, that, closely viewed, they appear heavy, while from the piazza below they look light as deer." *Goethe, Trans.*

☞ "It should seem that the horses are irrevocably Chian, and were transferred to Constantinople by Theodosius." *Byron.*

☞ "We have seen no bravoes with poisoned stilettos, no masks, no wild carnival; but we have seen the ancient pride of Venice, the grim Bronze Horses that figure in a thousand legends. Venice may well cherish them, for they are the only horses she ever had." *Mark Twain.*

Before St. Mark still glow his *steeds of brass*,
Their gilded collars glittering in the sun;
But is not Doria's menace come to pass?
Are they not *bridled?* *Byron.*

Bronze Wolf. See WOLF OF THE CAPITOL.

Brook Farm. A celebrated community or association organized for agricultural and also for educational purposes, at West Roxbury, Mass., in 1841. Nathaniel Hawthorne and George Ripley were among its founders. In his preface to the "Blithedale Romance," which is thought to embody a description of the community, Hawthorne says that he has "ventured to make free with his old and affectionately-remembered Brook Farm, as being certainly the most romantic episode of his own life." The characters introduced into this romance are wholly fictitious, though they may naturally enough be thought to harmonize well with the scene of the story.

☞ "The self-conceited philanthropist; the high-spirited woman bruising herself against the narrow limitations of her sex; the weakly maiden whose tremulous nerves endow her with sibylline attributes; the minor poet beginning life with strenuous aspirations which die out with his youthful fervor: all these might have been looked for at Brook Farm, but, by some accident, never made their appearance there." *Hawthorne.*

☞ "While our enterprise lay all in theory, we had pleased ourselves with delectable visions of the spiritualization of labor. It was to be our form of prayer and ceremonial of worship. Each stroke of the hoe was to uncover some aromatic root of wisdom, heretofore hidden from the sun. . . . In this point of view, matters did not turn out quite so well as we anticipated. . . . The clods of earth which we so constantly belabored and turned over and over, were never etherealized into thought. Our thoughts, on the contrary, were fast becoming cloddish." *Hawthorne.*

Here is a new enterprise of *Brook Farm*, of Skeneateles, of Northampton; why so impatient to baptize them Essenes, or Port Royalists, or Shakers, or by any known and effete name? *Emerson.*

Between the generality of these theorists and Emerson there was a wide gap, although he, like Hawthorne, if less practically, sympathized with Ripley's *Brook Farm* experiment. *Lathrop, Harper's Mag.*

Brooks's. A Whig club in London, founded as Almack's Club in 1764. The club-house in St. James's Street was opened in 1778. Sir Joshua Reynolds, Burke, Hume, Garrick, Gibbon, Horace Walpole, Sheridan, and Wilberforce were among the noted men of Brooks's. See ALMACK'S CLUB.

The choicest wines are enhanced in their liberal but temperate use by the vista opened in Lord Holland's tales of bacchanalian evenings at *Brooks's* with Fox and Sheridan, when potations deeper and more serious rewarded the statesman's toils, and shortened his days. *Talfourd.*

Not to know Brown was, at the West End, simply to be unknown. *Brookes* was proud of him, and without him the Travellers would not have been such a Travellers as it is. *Anthony Trollope.*

Brothers, The. A political club in London, the rules for which were framed, in 1713, by Dean Swift, who declared that the end of the club was "to advance conversation and friendship, and to reward learning without interest or recommendation;" and that it was to take in "none but men of wit, or men of interest; and if we go on as we began, no other club in this town will be worth talking of." The meetings of the club were held every Tuesday, first at the Thatched House Tavern, and latterly at the Star and Garter. The Brothers Club having to a great extent served its purpose was succeeded, in 1714, by the Scriblerus Club. See SCRIBLERUS CLUB.

Brothers, The. [Ger. *Die Brüder*.] See STERNBERG.

Brougham Hall. The ancient and picturesque seat of Lord Brougham in the neighborhood of Penrith, Cumberland, England. It is called, from its situation and beautiful view, the "Windsor of the North."

Broughton Castle. A noted mansion of the Elizabethan age, the seat of Lord Saye and Sele, near Banbury, in the county of Oxford, England.

Brown University. An institution of learning in Providence, R. I. It was originally founded in 1764, at Warren, as Rhode Island College, removed to Providence in 1770, and in 1804 named Brown University. Here is a library of about 40,000 volumes, a museum of natural history, and a portrait-gallery.

Broxbourne House. The seat of the Duke of Roxburghe, near Dunbar, Scotland.

Bruce's Castle. This castle on Rathlin Island, between Ireland and Scotland, derives its name from the fact that Robert Bruce was long concealed here. Here occurred the well-known incident of the spider and the web.

Bruce's Tomb. See HARPERS' TOMB.

Bruges, Belfry of. See BELFRY OF BRUGES.

Brühl Palace. A well-known building in Dresden, Saxony. In front of the palace is the Brühl terrace overlooking the Elbe.

Brunswick Square. A well-known public square in London, England.

Brunswick Theatre. This theatre in London, built upon the site of the Royalty Theatre, and opened in 1828, fell to the ground, from defective construction, during a rehearsal, a few days after the opening.

Bteddin. A ruined palace of the Emir Beshir (b. 1764), "Prince of Lebanon," in Northern Palestine. It was once gorgeously furnished in the highest style of Damascene art, with marble pavements and gilded arabesqued ceilings, but is now entirely abandoned to decay.

Bubastis, Temple of. See TEMPLE OF BUBASTIS.

Bucentaur, The. The name of the famous galley in which the Doge of Venice went out once a year to wed the Adriatic. The name is said to be a corruption of Ducentorum, i.e., a vessel having two hundred oars. There have been only three Bucentaurs. One was built in 1520. Another, still more splendid, was built in the following century. The third and last was constructed in 1725, and destroyed in 1797. It is said that the gilding alone of this last cost $40,000. The ceremony of the Espousal of the Adriatic is of higher antiquity than the construction of the first Bucentaur. This wedding ceremony, symbolizing the naval supremacy of Venice, owes its origin to the victory of the Venetians over the fleet of Frederick Barbarossa. A consecrated ring was each year thrown into the sea in the presence of the papal Nuntio and the diplomatic corps, with the declaration by the Doge that, "We wed thee, O sea, in sign of true and perpetual dominion" (*Desponsamus te, mare, in signum veri perpetuique dominii*).

☞ "In the model-room [of the Arsenal at Venice] are miniature representations of all forms of navigable craft, from ancient galleys down to modern frigates. There is also a model of the Bucentaur, made from drawings and recollections after the original had been destroyed. This must have been a gorgeous toy, but very unseaworthy. A bit of the mast of the original structure is still preserved." *Hillard.*

The spouseless Adriatic mourns her lord;
And, annual marriage now no more renewed,
The *Bucentaur* lies rotting unrestored,
Neglected garment of her widowhood!
Byron.

As bright as in a blue lagune,
When gondolas from shore to shore
Swam round the golden *Bucentaur*
On a Venetian holiday,
What time the Doge threw in the tide
The ring which made the sea his bride.
T. B. Read.

Buckingham Palace. The town residence of the sovereign of England, situated in London, on the west side of St. James's Park. It was built between 1825 and 1837, upon the site of Buckingham House. Queen Victoria took up her residence here July 13, 1837.

Buen Retiro. [Pleasant Retreat.] Extensive pleasure-grounds in Madrid, Spain, laid out as a place of retirement for Philip IV., in order to divert his attention from politics. Here were formerly situated a palace and a theatre in which the plays of Lope de Vega were acted. These gardens have been thrown open to the public since the revolution of 1868.

Building of Carthage. A well-known and admired picture by Joseph Mallord William Turner (1775–1851), the English landscape-painter, and regarded one of his best works. Now in the National Gallery, London.

☞ "The principal object in the foreground of Turner's '*Building of Carthage*,' is a group of children sailing toy-boats." *Ruskin.*

Bull, The Young. A celebrated picture by Paul Potter (1625–1654), the Dutch painter. It represents a young bull with a cow, reposing, and a sheep and a shepherd, in a landscape. "All these figures are as large as life, and the cattle so extraordinarily true to nature as not only to appear real at a certain distance, but even to keep up the illusion when seen near; the single hairs on the cow's head being seemingly palpable to the touch. The plastic element and the energy of execution are particularly imposing upon so large a scale. There is but one fault, — the legs of the bull, and the bent foreleg of the cow, are a little stiff." It is in the Museum of the Hague, Holland.

☞ "There cannot be a greater contrast to a very generalized mode of treatment than that displayed in the celebrated picture of 'The Bull' by Paul Potter, which approaches the nearest to deception of any really fine work of art I have seen. . . . Throughout the picture, indeed, we see that the hand has been directed by the eye of a consummate artist, and not merely by a skilful copyist." *C. R. Leslie.*

Bull, The. See Farnese Bull and Alderney Bull.

Bull and Mouth Inn. A noted hostelry of London in former days, in the street of the same name.

Also the bumpkins from Norfolk just disgorged by the *Bull and Mouth*, — the soldiers, the milliners, the Frenchmen, the swindlers, the porters with four-post beds on their backs, who add the excitement of danger to that of amusement. *N. P. Willis.*

Bull of Phalaris. Phalaris, tyrant of Agrigentum, in Sicily, who lived in the sixth century before Christ, is said to have employed an Athenian artist to make for him a brazen bull so constructed as to contain a man, and a small fire by which he would be burned to death. History adds that the artist was the first victim of the punishment he had himself invented. Phalaris subjected his enemies and many citizens of Agrigentum to this punishment, but finally the people revolting caused him to be destroyed by the same means.

Lettres de cachet, that masterpiece of ingenious tyranny, are more dangerous to men than the *brazen bull*, that infernal invention of Phalaris, because they unite to the most odious uniformity an imposing appearance of justice. *Mirabeau.*

Bunhill Fields. A burial-ground in London, and the place of interment of several eminent men. It was opened as a suburban place for burial in 1665, and was closed in 1850. According to Southey, Bunhill-Fields' burial-ground is the *Campo Santo* of the Dissenters. It was one of the chief places for burial in the time of the Great Plague. John Bunyan, Daniel DeFoe, Isaac Watts, and Nathaniel Lardner were buried here. Its original name of "Bonehill Fields" is supposed to have arisen from its having been made a place of deposit for more than 1,000 cart-loads of human bones removed from the charnel-house of St. Paul's.

He [Milton] used also to sit in a gray, coarse cloth coat, at the door of his house in *Bunhill Fields*, in warm sunny weather, to enjoy the fresh air; and so, as well as in his room, received the visits of people of distinguished parts as well as quality. *J. Richardson.*

Bunker Hill. See BATTLE OF BUNKER HILL.

Bunker Hill Monument. A lofty obelisk of Quincy granite, on what is now called Bunker Hill, formerly Breed's Hill, in Charlestown (now a part of Boston), Mass. It is erected upon the site of the battle between the British and American forces which took place June 17, 1775. The monument is 221 feet in height, and is a conspicuous object from all points. The corner-stone was laid in 1825 by Gen. La Fayette. It was finished in 1842, when an oration was delivered by Daniel Webster.

☞ "We wish that whosoever, in all coming time, shall turn his eye hither, may behold that the place is not undistinguished where the first great battle of the Revolution was fought. . . . We wish that this column, rising towards heaven among the pointed spires of so many temples dedicated to God, may contribute also to produce, in all minds, a pious feeling of dependence and gratitude. We wish, finally, that the last object to the sight of him who leaves his native shore, and the first to gladden his who revisits it, may be something which shall remind him of the liberty and the glory of his country. Let it rise! let it rise, till it meet the sun in his coming; let the earliest light of the morning gild it, and the parting day linger and play on its summit." *Daniel Webster.*
[*Address on Laying the Corner-Stone of the Bunker Hill Monument, 1825.*]

There is a stone now standing in very good order that was as old as a monument of Louis XIV. and Queen Anne's day is now when Joseph went down into Egypt. Think of the shaft on *Bunker Hill* standing in the sunshine on the morning of January 1st. in the year 5872! It won't be standing, — the Master said. — We are poor bunglers compared to those old Egyptians. *Holmes.*

I have seen Taglioni, — he answered. — She used to take her steps rather prettily. I have seen the woman that danced the cap-stone on to *Bunker Hill Monument*, as Orpheus moved the rocks by music, — the Elssler woman, — Fanny Elssler. *Holmes.*

And when the prowling man-thief came
hunting for his prey
Beneath the very shadow of *Bunker's shaft* of gray,
How, through the free lips of the son, the
father's warning spoke;
How, from its bond of trade and sect, the
Pilgrim city broke! *Whittier.*

Burghley House. The fine Elizabethan manorial mansion erected by the Lord Treasurer Burleigh, now the seat of the Marquis of Exeter. It is situated on the borders of the two counties of Lincoln and Northampton, England. The interior is very magnificent, and the building has many historical and legendary associations connected with it.

Weeping, weeping, late and early,
Walking up and pacing down,
Deeply mourned the Lord of Burghley,
Burghley House by Stamford town.
Tennyson.

Burgomaster Meier Madonna. See MADONNA OF THE BURGOMASTER MEYER.

Burgoyne, Surrender of. See SURRENDER OF BURGOYNE.

Burlington Arcade. A double row of shops in London, built in 1819 for Lord George Cavendish, and, according to Leigh Hunt, famous for "small shops and tall beadles."

When I first descended into the cabin of the New York, it looked, in my unaccustomed eyes, about as long as the *Burlington Arcade.* *Dickens.*

Burlington House. A mansion in Piccadilly, London, originally built for the second Earl of Burlington. It is celebrated as having been the rendezvous of the leading artists, poets, and philosophers of the last century. Handel resided here for a time. In 1854 it was purchased by the British government, and is now occupied by the Royal Society and other literary and scientific institutions.

— *Burlington's* fair palace still remains
Beauty within — without, proportion
reigns;
Beneath his eye declining art revives,
The wall with animated pictures lives.
There Handel strikes the strings, the melting strain
Transports the soul, and thrills through
every vein,
There oft I enter (but with cleaner shoes),
For *Burlington's* beloved by every Muse.
Gay, Trivia.

Burnet House. A noble mansion in London, in which lived the celebrated Bishop of Salisbury (1643–1715). It was taken down a few years ago.

Burning Bush. See MOSES AND THE BURNING BUSH.

Burns's Cottage. A small house about two miles from the town of Ayr, in Scotland, where, on the 25th of January, 1759, Robert Burns, the poet, was born. The original building, which was nothing more than a "clay bigging," was rebuilt by the poet's father. The cottage is now converted into a public-house.

Burns's Monument. 1. A memorial structure in honor of the poet Burns (1759–1796), erected in 1820 near the town of Ayr, in Scotland. It is in the form of a circular temple, surrounded by nine Corinthian pillars, symbolical of the nine Muses. Within are preserved some relics of the poet.

2. A memorial in honor of the poet, erected in 1830, in Edinburgh. The cupola is designed after the monument of Lysicrates at Athens.

Burying Hill. A hill in Plymouth, Mass., where many of the Pilgrims were buried. On this hill, which commands a fine view of the harbors of Plymouth and Duxbury and the adjacent country, a fortified church was built in 1622 with six cannon on its flat roof.

Bushnell Park. A beautiful pleasure-ground in Hartford, Conn. The new State Capitol is situated in it, and it contains some fine statues.

Bushy Park. A well-known royal park near Twickenham, England.

Busrah. A noble fortress in Syria, once a great stronghold, but now abandoned, or occupied only by roving bands of Arabs. It contains within its enclosure a great theatre, portions of which are still perfect, and which dates without doubt from Roman times.

Button's. A sort of successor to Will's coffee-house, and the great place of resort for the wits in London after the death of Dryden. Button's was in Russell Street, on the side opposite to Will's. Addison (who was the chief patron), Steele, Pope, Swift, Arbuthnot, Garth, and others frequented Button's. Here was a letter-box, with its opening in the form of a lion's head, into which were put contributions for the "Guardian." Button's declined after Addison's death and Steele's retirement from London. See WILL'S.

> On Sunday morning, died, after three days' illness, Mr. Button, who formerly kept Button's Coffee-house, in Russell Street, Covent Garden; a very noted house for wits, being the place where the Lyon produced the famous *Tatlers* and *Spectators*. *Daily Advertiser* (1731).

> Addison usually studied all the morning, then met his party at *Button's*, dined there, and stayd five or six hours; and sometimes far into the night. *Pope, Spence's Anecdotes.*

> Our fate thou only canst adjourn
> Some few short years, no more!
> E'en *Button's* wits to worms shall turn,
> Who maggots were before. *Pope.*

C.

Ca' Doro. One of the most beautiful palaces in Venice, Italy. It was built in the fifteenth century, and is so named after its ancient owners, the Doro family.

Caaba. A Mohammedan temple at Mecca, Arabia. It contains a small oratory within which is a black stone held sacred by all Mussulmans. [Written also *Kaabah.*] See BLACK STONE.

☞ "Neither its ordonnance, nor, so far as we can understand, its details, render the temple an object of much architectural magnificence. Even in size it is surpassed by many, and is less than its great rival, the great temple of Jerusalem, which was 600 feet square. Still it is interesting, as it is in reality the one temple of the Moslem world; for though many mosques are now reputed sacred, and as such studiously guarded against profanation, this pretended sanctity is evidently a prejudice borrowed from other religions, and is no part of the doctrine of the Moslem faith, which, like the Jewish, points to one only temple as the place where the people should worship, and towards which they should turn in prayer."
Fergusson.

☞ "The celebrated Kaabah at Mecca, to which all the Moslem world now bow in prayer, is probably a third [fire-temple of the ancient Persians]."
Fergusson.

☞ "A curious object, that Caabah! There it stands at this hour, in the black cloth-covering the Sultan sends it yearly; '27 cubits high;' with circuit, with double circuit of pillars, with festoon-rows of lamps and quaint ornaments: the lamps will be lighted again *this* night, — to glitter again under the stars. An authentic fragment of the oldest Past. It is the *Keblah* of all Moslem: from Delhi all onwards to Morocco, the eyes of innumerable praying men are turned towards *it*, five times, this day and all days: one of the notablest centres in the Habitation of Men. *Carlyle.*

They . . measure with an English footrule every cell of the Inquisition, every Turkish *caaba*, every Holy of holies.
Emerson.

To the traveller imbued with a feeling for the historical and poetical, so inseparably intertwined in the annals of romantic Spain, the Alhambra is as much an object of devotion as is the *Caaba* to all true Moslems. *Irving.*

Cadzow Castle. A ruined baronial mansion in Scotland, near Hamilton, and the ancient seat of the family of that name. Sir Walter Scott has a ballad entitled "Cadzow Castle."

Caerlaverock Castle. An ancient and noted feudal fortress near Dumfries, Scotland, the former seat of the Maxwells, celebrated for its siege by King Edward I. of England, and for the brave resistance made by its garrison. This castle suggested to Scott his description of Ellengowan.

Cæsar. See CLEOPATRA AND CÆSAR, DEATH OF JULIUS CÆSAR, TRIUMPHS OF JULIUS CÆSAR.

Cæsar Borgia. A portrait often ascribed to Raphael, and said to be the likeness of the Prince, in the Borghese gallery at Rome. It is now ascertained to be neither the work of the one nor the portrait of the other.

Cæsars, Palace of the. See PALACE OF THE CÆSARS.

Cæsar's Tower. A remarkable keep of immense size and impressive effect, at Kenilworth Castle, of which it forms a part. See KENILWORTH CASTLE.

Café (Caffè) Grecco. [The Greek Café.] A well-known café at Rome, in the Via Condotti, famous as the rendezvous of artists of all nations.

☞ "In the morning we breakfast at the *café Greco;* this is a long, low, smoky apartment, not brilliant or attractive, but convenient: it appears to be like the rest throughout Italy."
Taine, Trans.

Caffegiolo. A royal villa, the ancient residence of the Medicis, about 15 miles from Florence, Italy.

Cagliari, The. A Sardinian steamer trading between Genoa and Tunis. She was seized by some Sicilian adventurers in June, 1857, who with her effected a landing on the territory of Naples. Afterwards the vessel was surrendered to the Neapolitans, who imprisoned with the crew two English engineers who were on board. The affair became a matter of diplomatic correspondence between England and Naples.

Caiaphas' Palace. This name is applied to a building, now a convent, on Zion, which seems to have been built by the Armenians. The credulous see here the stone which closed the Saviour's sepulchre, the spot where Peter was standing when he denied his Master, and even the very stone upon which the cock roosted when he crew.

Caius Cestius, Pyramid of. See PYRAMID OF CAIUS CESTIUS.

Caius College. A foundation of the University of Cambridge, England. The college was instituted in 1348.

Calais Pier. A noted picture by Joseph Mallord William Turner (1775–1851). In the National Gallery, London.

Calaveras Pines. A celebrated grove of mammoth pine-trees (*Sequoia gigantea*) in Calaveras County, California. Some of these are about 320 feet high and 30 feet in diameter. A similar grove, likewise much visited by tourists, is found in Mariposa County. These trees are believed to be over 2,300 years of age. By an act of Congress this grove was granted to the State of California on condition that it should be kept as a public domain. The grant was accepted, and the locality is now under the charge of commissioners.

Caledonia, The. An armor-plated ship of the British navy, launched Oct. 24, 1862.

Caledonian Forest. A remnant of the ancient wood which once, under the name of the Caledonian Forest, covered the whole of southern Scotland, from sea to sea, still exists on the bank of the Avon near Hamilton. A few large oaks are all that is now left.

California. A statue by Hiram Powers (1805–1873).

California Street. One of the principal streets in San Francisco, Cal., in which the chief banking offices are situated.

Caligula. A noted bronze bust of the Roman emperor Caligula, now in Turin, Italy. [Called also the *Albertina Bronze*.]

☞ "One of the most precious portraits of antiquity, not only because it confirms the testimony of the green basalt in the Vatican, but also because it supplies an even more emphatic and impressive illustration to the narrative of Suetonius." *J. A. Symonds.*

Caligula's Palace and Bridge. A picture by Joseph Mallord William Turner (1775–1851), the English landscape-painter, and regarded one of his best works. In the National Gallery, London.

Calisto. See DIANA AND CALISTO.

Calixtus, St. See CATACOMB OF ST. CALIXTUS.

Calling of St. Peter. See MIRACULOUS DRAUGHT OF FISHES.

Calling of the Apostles. A fresco-painting by Domenico Ghirlandajo (1449–1498 ?). In the Sistine Chapel, Rome.

Callirrhöe. The fountain — and according to Pausanias the only one — which supplied sweet running water to Athens, Greece. Also known as *Enneacrunus*, from the nine pipes in which the water was conveyed. A small spring still called καλλιῤῥόη now issues from a ridge of rock crossing the bed of the Ilissus.

Calton Hill. A well-known eminence in Edinburgh, Scotland, crowned with monuments.

Calvary. A rock so called, now within the Church of the Sepulchre, at Jerusalem. The Saviour was crucified at a place known as Golgotha (Hebrew for "a skull"), the Latin equivalent for which is *Calvaria*, whence our English Calvary.

☞ "It may be well to remind the reader that there are two errors implied in the popular expression 'Mount Calvary.' 1. There is in the Scriptural narrative no mention of a mount or hill. 2. There is no such name as 'Calvary.' The passage from which the word is taken in Luke xxiii. 33, is merely the Latin translation ('Calvaria') of what the Evangelist calls 'a skull,'—κρανιον." *A. P. Stanley.*

According to Mr. Bulwer, Glory is a *Calvary* on which the poet is crucified.
Gustave Planche, Trans.

Calves-Head Club. This club, "in ridicule of the memory of Charles I," consisting of Independents and Anabaptists, and formed in the times of the Revolution, was in existence as late as the eighth year of the reign of George II. They met annually, and dined upon calves' heads prepared in various ways, by which they represented the King and his friends. Their meetings were at length broken up by a mob.

Indeed, his [George Saville, Viscount Halifax] jests upon hereditary monarchy were sometimes such as would have better become a member of the *Calf's Head Club* than a privy councillor of the Stuarts.
Macaulay.

Calvin's House. The house in which the Reformer lived from 1543 to 1564. It is situated in the Rue des Chanoines, Geneva, Switzerland.

Calydonian Boar. See CHACE OF THE CALYDONIAN BOAR.

Camaldoli, Convent of. A celebrated monastic establishment at Camaldoli, Italy, founded near the beginning of the eleventh century.

☞ "This monastery is secluded from the approach of woman, in a deep, narrow, woody dell. Its circuit of dead walls, built on the conventual plan, gives it an aspect of confinement and defence; yet this is considered as a privileged retreat, where the rule of the order relaxes its rigor, and no monks can reside but the sick or the superannuated, the dignitary or the steward, the apothecary or the bead-turner. *Forsyth.*

Oh, joy for all, who hear her call
From gray *Camaldoli's convent-wall*,
And Elmo's towers to freedom's carnival!
Whittier.

Cambiaso Palace. [Ital. *Palazzo Cambiaso.*] A noted palace in Genoa, Italy.

Cambio, Sala del. See SALA DEL CAMBIO.

Cambridge House. A mansion in London, where Adolphus, Duke of Cambridge, youngest son of George III., died in 1850. It was afterwards the town residence of Viscount Palmerston, and is now a Naval and Military Club House.

Cambuskenneth Abbey. A ruined monastery in Scotland, near Alloa, founded in the twelfth century, and once the richest abbey in the kingdom.

Camden House. A mansion in London, built in 1612, and interesting from its historic associations connected with the young Duke of Gloucester, who lived here with his mother, Queen Anne. Camden House was burnt in 1862, and has since been rebuilt.

Back in the dark, by Brompton Park,
He turned up thro' the Gore,
And slunk to *Campden-house* so high,
All in his coach and four. *Swift.*

Camelot. A hill in what is now known as the parish of Queen's Camel, England, famous in the Arthurian legends.

Goose, if once I had thee upon Sarum plain,
I'd drive thee cackling home to *Camelot*.
Shakespeare.

Camera della Segnatura. One of the four chambers known as the Stanze of Raphael, in the Vatican, Rome, because adorned with paintings by that master.

Camere di Raffaello. See STANZE OF RAPHAEL.

Campagna. [The country.] A name given, in particular, to the undulating plain which extends on all sides around Rome, including portions of ancient Latium and Etruria. The name is said to have been first applied in the Middle Ages. The whole region is now very unhealthy in summer, owing to the miasmata which rise from it. Pliny speaks of the healthfulness and perennial salubrity of this now desolate region, which was once adorned with Roman villas and gardens. Pius VI. (1775-1799) drained a portion of this plain.

☞ "Of all kinds of country that could, by possibility, lie outside the gates of Rome, this is the aptest and fittest burial-ground for the Dead City." *Dickens.*

☞ "Over this region of the Campagna a light still hangs more beautiful than its golden mists or the purple shadows that lie upon its distant hills. The spirit of the past dwells here, and breathes over the landscape the consecrating gleams of valor, patriotism, and filial duty." *Hillard.*

☞ "Nothing can be more heart-rending than the contrast which the immediate and the present here form with the recollections of the past, gilded as they are by the feelings and the fancy. I cannot express the sinking of heart which I felt in passing so many hours over this dreary waste — these *lugentes campi*, so different from all the deserts nature has elsewhere left or created." *Ticknor.*

Nothing impresses the traveller more, on visiting the once imperial city, than the long lines of aqueducts that are everywhere seen stretching across the now deserted plain of the *Campagna.*
Fergusson.

Groves, temples, palaces,
Swept from the sight; and nothing visible,
Amid the sulphurous vapors that exhale
As from a land accurst, save here and there
An empty tomb, a fragment like the limb
Of some dismembered giant.
Samuel Rogers.

No wreaths of sad *Campagna's* flowers
Shall childhood in thy pathway fling;
No garlands from their ravaged bowers
Shall Terni's maidens bring. *Whittier.*

The priest, and the swart fisher by his side,
Beheld the Eternal City lift its domes
And solemn fanes and monumental pomp
Above the waste *Campagna.* *Whittier.*

Campana Museum. An old Roman collection, now forming part of the Musée Napoleon III., in the Louvre, Paris. It was bought by the French Government in 1861. This museum contains a fine collection of antique statues, and is rich in jewels of gold and precious stones.

Mlle. d'Estang had earrings like those in the *Campana Museum*, with emeralds. *Taine, Trans.*

Campanile. In Italy, the general name for the belfry or bell-tower of a church, usually in that country a separate building from the church itself. The more noted campaniles are those of Florence, Pisa, and Venice. See GIOTTO'S CAMPANILE, the LEANING TOWER, and ST. MARK'S CAMPANILE.

Campbell. See CASTLE CAMPBELL.

Campidoglio, Piazza del. See PIAZZA DEL CAMPIDOGLIO.

Campo di Sangue. See FIELD OF BLOOD.

Campo Marzo. The modern Italian name of the ancient Campus Martius, or Field of Mars, a low irregular plain in the city of Rome, between the Corso and the Tiber, surrounded by the Pincian, Quirinal, Viminal, and Capitoline hills, including the principal portion of the modern city. See CAMPUS MARTIUS.

Campo Santo. [The Holy Field.] A celebrated cemetery in Pisa, Italy, adjoining the Cathedral and Baptistery. It was founded by Archbishop Ubaldo de' Lanfranchi, about the year 1200, who, retreating from Palestine, whence he had been expelled by Saladin, returned with 53 vessels laden with earth from Mount Calvary, which he deposited in this place. The present building was begun in 1278. It has given its name to every similar burial-place in Italy. It contains a museum of sepulchral monuments, and frescos of much celebrity.

☞ "Giovanni Pisana, having been appointed to enclose the space with walls, designed and built the first, as well as the most beautiful, Campo Santo in Italy. Following the ground-plan marked out by Archbishop Lanfranchi, Giovanni raised his outer walls without windows, and with only two doors looking towards the Duomo, that the frescos, with which they were to be covered on the inside, might be protected as far as possible from the injurious effect of the salt and damp sea-winds. Between these outer walls, which he decorated with arches and pilasters, and the inner, directly contiguous to the quadrangle, he made a broad-roofed corridor paved with marble, lighted by Gothic windows and four open doorways." *Perkins.*

The Cemetere cal'd *Campo Santo* is made of divers gally ladings of earth formerly brought from Jerusalem, said to be of such a nature as to consume dead bodies in forty hours. 'Tis cloistered with marble arches. *John Evelyn*, 1644.

Love, long remembering those she could not save,
Here hung the cradle of Italian Art:
Faith rocked it: like a hermit child went forth
From hence that power which beautified the earth.
She perished when the world had lured her heart
From her true friends, Religion and the Grave.
. . . . . . Monumental marbles,
Time-clouded frescos, mouldering year by year,
Dim cells in which all day the night-bird warbles,—
These things are sorrowful elsewhere, not here:
A mightier Power than Art's hath here her shrine:
Stranger! thou tread'st the soil of Palestine. *Aubrey de Vere.*

Even the slumberers in the churchyard of the *Campo Santo* seemed
Scarce more quiet than the living world that underneath us dreamed.
T. W. Parsons.

A signal example is the fine enthroned Madonna in the *Campo Santo*, who receives St. Rani ri when presented by St. Peter and St. Paul. *Mrs. Jameson.*

Campo Vaccino. [The Cow-Pasture.] The modern Italian name of the Forum Romanum, or Roman Forum, derived, it is supposed, from the greater part of the area having become, as far back as the fifteenth century, the resort of cattle, "a kind of Roman Smithfield;" but according to others the name is derived from one Vitruvius Vacco, who is said to have lived there. See FORUM ROMANUM.

1844, Nov. 7. We went into the *Campo Vaccino* by the ruins of the Temple of Peace built by Titus Vespasianus.
John Evelyn.

Campus Esquilinus. [Esquiline Field.] A burial-ground for the poor in ancient Rome. It now makes a part of the grounds of the Villa Massimo.

Campus Martius. [Field of Mars.] 1. The ancient name of the irregular plain in the city of Rome surrounded by the Pincian, Quirinal, Viminal, and Capitoline hills, now including the principal portion of the modern city. This region did not come within the walls of ancient Rome, and it is thought that settlements were first made here during the Lombard invasion, when, the supply of water through the aqueducts having been cut off, the people were compelled to desert the hills and seek the plain below where they could use the water of the Tiber. The Pantheon and a few fragments of other structures are all that is now left of the buildings which were erected upon the Campus. Campo Marzo is the modern Italian name of the ancient Field of Mars.

—There of old
With arms and trophies gleamed the *field of Mars:*
There to their daily sports the noble youth rushed emulous. *John Dyer.*

2. A large open square in Detroit, Mich.

Campus Sceleratus. [The Accursed Field.] A field in ancient Rome where unchaste virgins were buried alive.

Cana, Marriage at. See MARRIAGE AT CANA.

Canadian Fall. See HORSE-SHOE FALL.

Canal of the Giudecca. A picture of a scene in Venice, by Joseph Mallord William Turner (1775-1851). In the National Gallery, London.

Canal Street. A noted street in New Orleans, La. It has a breadth of nearly 200 feet, with a grass-plot 25 feet in width in the centre, extending the entire distance.

Canale Grande. See GRAND CANAL.

Cancelleria, Palazzo della. A magnificent palace in Rome, completed in 1495, the official residence of the Vice-Chancellor.

Cane, Grotta del. See GROTTA DEL CANE.

Cannon Street. A well-known modern street in London, leading out of St. Paul's Churchyard.

Canon, The. A celebrated print by Albert Dürer (1471–1528) which is thought to be the first example of the art of etching.

Cañon. See GRAND CAÑON OF THE YELLOWSTONE.

Canonbury Tower. A building in London, formerly the resort and lodging-place of many literary men.

Canongate. A noted street and the principal thoroughfare in the Old Town of Edinburgh, Scotland (bearing different names at other points of its course), and terminating at the rocky eminence on which stands the palace of Holyrood. Sir Walter Scott published two series of tales entitled "Chronicles of the Canongate."

Strew'd were the streets around with milk-white reams,
Flow'd all the *Canongate* with inky streams. *Byron.*

Canons Park. A palatial residence built by the "Great Duke of Chandos," near Edgeware, England. It was a favorite resort of literary men, including Pope, who often alludes to it. The original building is no longer standing.

Canopus, Decree of. See STONE OF SÂN.

Canterbury Cathedral. A magnificent cathedral at Canterbury, England. It was designed by Sir James Burrough, was begun in 1174, and finished in the reign of Henry V. It contains the shrine of Thomas à Becket, in former times a great resort of pilgrims. See SHRINE OF THOMAS À BECKET.

And specially from every shire's ende
Of Engle lond to *Canterbury* they wende.
Chaucer.

Cape Horn. A name given to a locality on the line of the Central Pacific Railroad, in California.

☞ "The bluffs at this point are so precipitous that when the railroad was made the workmen had to be lowered down the face of the rock by ropes, and held on by men above, until they were enabled to blast for themselves a foothold on the side of the precipice." *Samuel Smiles.*

Capella Borghese. [Borghese Chapel.] A gorgeous chapel, so called from the Borghese family, in the church of Santa Maria Maggiore in Rome, built for Paul V. in 1608, rich in marbles, alabasters, and frescos.

☞ "The splendor of the opposite Borghese chapel so far surpasses my feeble powers of description that I shall leave it all to your imagination, to which you may give abundance of latitude, for it can scarcely surpass the reality. It contains one of St. Luke's precious performances, a miraculous image of the Virgin." *Eaton.*

Capella Brancacci. [Brancacci Chapel.] A chapel in the convent of the Carmine, Florence, Italy, celebrated for its fine frescos by Masaccio (1402?–1443).

☞ "The importance of these frescos arises from the fact that they hold the same place in the history of art during the fifteenth century, as the works of Giotto, in the Arena chapel at Padua, hold during the fourteenth. Each series forms an epoch in painting." *Layard.*

People at the present day still go to the *Brancacci Chapel* to contemplate this isolated creator [Masaccio] whose precocious example no one followed *Taine, Trans.*

He came to Florence long ago
And painted here these walls, that shone
For Raphael and for Angelo
With secrets deeper than his own,
Then shrank into the dark again,
And died, we know not how or when.
Lowell.

Capella Clementina. See CLEMENT'S CHAPEL.

Capella Corsini. See CORSINI CHAPEL.

Capella della Colonna Santa. [Chapel of the Holy Pillar.] A chapel in St. Peter's Church, Rome, so called from an inscribed pillar in it, concerning which the church tradition is that it is the one against which Christ leaned when teaching in the Temple at Jerusalem.

Capella Paolina. [Pauline Chapel.] An apartment in the Vatican Palace, Rome, built in 1540 for Paul III. It contains two frescos by Michael Angelo.

☞ "Two excellent frescos executed by Michael Angelo on the side walls of the Pauline Chapel are little cared for, and are so much blackened by the smoke of lamps that they are seldom mentioned. The Crucifixion of St. Peter, under the large window, is in a most unfavorable light, but is distinguished for its grand, severe composition. That on the opposite wall — the Conversion of St. Paul — is still tolerably distinct." *Kugler.*

Capella Sistina. See SISTINE CHAPEL.

Capitol, The [Rome]. See CAPITOLINE HILL and PIAZZA DEL CAMPIDOGLIO.

Capitol [of the United States]. The immense and magnificent building in Washington, D.C., devoted to the uses of the American Congress. The centre building is of freestone painted white. Its corner-stone was laid by Washington in 1792. The marble extensions were begun in 1851. The total length of the original Capitol, together with the wings and corridors, is 737 feet. The building covers an area of 3½ acres, and the cost of erection has been over $13,000,000. It is surmounted by an iron dome which is 287 feet above the base of the building, and 135½ feet in diameter, being surpassed in size only by four domes in Europe, — that of St. Peter's at Rome, of St. Paul's in London, St. Isaac's in St. Petersburg, and that of the Invalides in Paris. The dome is surmounted by a colossal statue of Liberty in bronze, 19 feet in height, standing upon a globe which bears the inscription *E Pluribus Unum.* Within the Capitol are included the Senate Chamber, the Hall of the House of Representatives, the Supreme Court room, and the Library of Congress.

☞ "We have built no national temples but the *Capitol;* we consult no common oracle but the Constitution." *R. Choate.*

When, lo! in a vision I seemed to stand
In the lonely *Capitol.* On each hand
Far stretched the portico; dim and grand
Its columns ranged, like a martial band
Of sheeted spectres whom some command
Had called to a last reviewing.
Bret Harte.

Capitol [of New York]. An immense and imposing building in the city of Albany, the capital of the State of New York, designed for legislative purposes and the uses of the executive department of the State. The structure is of the Renaissance architecture, and one of the best finished and most costly edifices of the kind in the world.

Capitoline Hill. [Lat. *Mons Capitolinus.*] One of the original seven hills of ancient Rome, immediately contiguous to the Forum, and still bearing the same name. The Church of Ara Cœli is supposed to mark the site of the Temple of Jupiter Capitolinus, which formerly stood upon the summit. There is a depression called the Intermontium, upon the top of the hill, forming two heights, upon the summit of one of which the Temple of Jupiter Capitolinus is thought to have stood, and upon the summit of the other the Arx Capitolii. Upon the latter mount is placed the temple which Romulus is said to have built and to have dedicated to Jupiter Feretrius. The hill was originally called Mons Saturnius, and afterwards (or certainly the whole of one side of it) Mons Tarpeia, from her who, during the war with the Sabines, longing for the golden bracelets of the enemy, and allured by the promise of receiving that which they wore upon their arms, treacherously opened the fortress to the Sabines, and was rewarded by being crushed by the shields which they threw upon her in passing. It lastly received the name of Mons Capitolinus (or Capitolium), because in digging the foundations for the Temple of Jupiter (Capitolinus) a bloody human head was found, which the augurs declared to be an omen that Rome was destined to become the head of Italy. The famous Tarpeian Rock was also upon this side of the Intermontium, though its exact situation is not definitely determined. See PIAZZA DEL CAMPIDOGLIO.

☞ "But when we think of its invulnerable citadel, its vanished temples, its triumphal arches, its splendid porticos, its golden statues, and all its unparalleled but forgotten splendors — it is indeed a contrast to look round on the scattered ruins of that seat of empire which awed the world; to behold a convent of barefooted friars usurping the proud temple of Jupiter Optimus Maximus, a few miserable hovels crowning the Tarpeian Rock, and the palace of a modern Roman patrician occupying the site of the house of Ovid and the School of Philosophers." *C. A. Eaton.*

☞ "No language contains a word of more expression and significance than the Capitol, nor is there a spot on earth more full of historical interest. It was at once a fortress and a temple; the head of the Roman state and the shrine of their religion. The Capitol was the symbol of ancient Rome, as St. Peter's and the Vatican are the symbols of the modern and mediæval city." *G. S. Hillard.*

Unsexed, but foul with barren lust,
  Marshalled her powers to overwhelm
  Our *Capitol* and ancient realm,
And lay Rome's glories in the dust?
Horace, Trans.

Cal. Cæsar, I never stood on ceremonies,
Yet now they fright me. There is one within,
Besides the things that we have heard and seen,
Recounts most horrid sights seen by the watch.
A lioness hath whelped in the streets;
And graves have yawn'd. and yielded up their dead;
Fierce fiery warriors fought upon the clouds,
In ranks, and squadrons, and right form of war,
Which drizzled blood upon the *Capitol*.
Shakespeare.

Capitoline Museum. See MUSEO CAPITOLINO.

Capitolium. See CAPITOLINE HILL and PIAZZA DEL CAMPIDOGLIO.

Cappuccini, Convent, Church, and Cemetery of the. One of the largest and most populous convents in Rome, belonging to the monks of the order of St. Francis. The conventual Church contains a number of fine pictures, including that of the "Archangel Michael and the Devil" by Guido. Adjoining the Church is the famous Cemetery of the Cappuccini. It is a sort of museum of bones, consisting of four chambers decorated with human bones, and bodies that have become mummified. The earth was brought hither from Jerusalem. Several skeletons are standing upright, dressed in their monastic robes. Whenever a brother dies, he is buried in the oldest grave, and the bones which have been displaced to make room for him are removed to the general collection.

Caprino, Monte. See MONTE CAPRINO.

Capucines, Boulevart des. One of the boulevards of Paris. See BOULEVARDS.

Caracalla, Baths of. See BATHS OF CARACALLA.

Card Party. A small but very interesting picture, representing a company of men and women at a card-table, by Luc Jacobsz, commonly called Lucas van Leyden (1494–1533), a Flemish painter. It is now in the collection of the Earl of Pembroke, at Wilton House, England.

Cardiff Giant. A noted piece of trickery in the shape of a colossal statue of gypsum disinterred at a little place called Cardiff, near Lafayette, N.Y., in October, 1869, and successfully palmed off upon some of the most distinguished antiquaries and palæontologists of America as being either a work of ancient sculpture, or more probably a fossilized man. It was carried about the country, and publicly exhibited to great crowds in all the principal cities. At last the fact came out, that it had been cut from a quarry in Iowa not long before, wrought into shape in Chicago, and buried in Cardiff, where it was soon after alleged to have been accidentally discovered.

Cardinal Bentivoglio. See BENTIVOGLIO.

Cardinal Bibiena. See BIBIENA.

Cardinal Pole. See POLE.

Cardross Castle. A ruined castle in Scotland, on the Clyde, near

Dumbarton. In this castle Robert Bruce died in 1329.

Carinæ. A fashionable quarter in ancient Rome, situated upon the Esquiline Hill, where many of the nobles and principal citizens had their residences.

Carisbrooke Castle. A magnificent feudal mansion, now in ruins, in the village of Carisbrooke on the Isle of Wight. Charles I. was confined here after his flight from Hampton Court. The castle contains a well said to be over 300 feet in depth.

Carità. [Charity.] A picture by Andrea Vannucchi, called Andrea del Sarto (1487-1531), the Italian painter, and considered one of his best works. In the Louvre, Paris.

Carità. [Charity.] A striking picture by Bartolommeo Schedone (1560-1615). In the Museum at Naples, Italy.

Carlisle Castle. An ancient feudal fortress in Carlisle, England, now in a state of decay. It was built by William Rufus (1056-1100). The castle is at present used as a barrack and armory.

Musing on this strange hap the while,
The King wends back to fair *Carlisle;*
And cares, that cumber royal sway,
Wore memory of the past away. *Scott.*

Carlo Borromeo. A statue in bronze and copper, of colossal size, near Arona, Italy, erected to the memory of the saint in 1697. It is 106 feet in height including the pedestal.

Far off the Borromean saint was seen,
Distinct, though distant, o'er his native town,
Where his Colossus with benignant mien,
Looks from its station on Arona down;
To it the inland sailor lifts his eyes,
From the wide lake, when perilous storms arise. *Southey.*

Carlo Felice. A noted theatre in Genoa, Italy, opened in 1828.

Carlo, San. See San Carlo.

Carlsbrücke, Die. [Charles' Bridge.] A famous bridge over the Moldau in Prague, Austria. It was begun in 1357, and was 150 years in building. The piers are surmounted with groups of saints and martyrs, 28 in number, including the celebrated statue of St. John Nepomuck. See St. John Nepomuck.

Carlton Club. A noble building of Italian architecture (from St. Mark's Library in Venice), in Pall Mall, London, is occupied by the famous political club of this name, founded in 1831 by the Duke of Wellington. The first meeting of the club was held in Charles Street, St. James's. It removed to Carlton Gardens in 1832, and in 1836 a club-house was built in Pall Mall. The present house was built in 1854.

☞ "The Carlton contains Conservatives of every hue, from the good old-fashioned Tory to the liberal progressist of the latest movements,—men of high position in fortune and politics." *Timbs.*

No *Carlton Clubs*, Reform Clubs, nor any sort of clubs or creatures, or of accredited opinions or practices, can make a Lie Truth, can make Bribery a Propriety. *Carlyle.*

Carlton House. A noted mansion which formerly stood in Waterloo Place, south of Pall Mall, London. It was built in 1709, and was taken down in 1827. Upon the Ionic columns of this house an Italian epigram was written by Bonomi:—

"Care colonne, che fatti quà?
Non sapiamo, in verità,"

which has been translated as follows:—

"Dear little columns, all in a row,
What do you do there?
Indeed we don't know."

☞ "We went to see the Prince's new palace in Pall Mall, and were charmed. It will be the most perfect in Europe. . . . In all the fairy tales you have been, you was never in so pretty a scene. I forgot to tell you how admirably all the carving, stucco, and ornaments are executed, but whence the money is to come I conceive not. All the tin-mines in Cornwall could not pay a quarter." *Horace Walpole, 1785.*

With the same childish attendant, I remember peeping through the colonnade at *Carlton House* and seeing the abode of the great Prince Regent. *Thackeray.*

I have a state-coach at *Carlton House,*
A chariot in Seymour Place;
But they're lent to two friends, who make me amends
By driving my favorite pace. *Byron.*

I remember Alvanley eating three suppers once at *Carlton House* — one night *de petite comité*. *Thackeray.*

Carmine, The. A noted church in Florence, Italy, of the fifteenth century, containing some fine frescos which are of great importance in the history of art.

Carnac. A collection of stones or monumental blocks of granite, several thousand in number, in the town of the same name, in the Department of Morbihan, France. They are of unknown origin and antiquity, and their use and meaning are involved in great obscurity. By some they are thought to be Druidic remains, and by others to be of earlier date. They are probably not sepulchral monuments, and it is quite as probable that they were intended for military as for religious purposes. In their general appearance they resemble the monuments found in the Orkney Islands.

Caroccio. A famous car of great size, drawn by two beautiful oxen, which, in the old days of Florence, accompanied the citizens to the field of battle. It bore the standard of the city, and is supposed to have been built in imitation of the ark carried before the Israelites.

☞ "This vehicle is described, and also represented in ancient paintings, as a four-wheeled, oblong car, drawn by two, four, or six bullocks. . . . A platform ran out in front of the car, spacious enough for a few chosen men to defend it, while behind, on a corresponding space, the musicians gave spirit to the combat: mass was said on the Caroccio, ere it quitted the city, the surgeons were stationed near it, and not unfrequently also a chaplain attended it to the field. The loss of the Caroccio was a great disgrace, and betokened utter discomfiture." *Napier.*

Caroline, The. A United States steamer burned Dec. 29, 1837, by the loyal Canadians, for having brought aid to the rebels. The affair became a subject of diplomatic correspondence.

Caroll, Fort. See FORT CAROLL.

Carondelet, The. An armor-plated ship of the United States Navy during the war of the Rebellion.

Carré. See SALON CARRÉ.

Carrickfergus Castle. One of the most perfect castellated structures in Ireland, standing on a rock which projects into the sea, and is nearly surrounded by water. It is in the county of Antrim.

Carrig-a-droid Castle. A ruined stronghold of the Middle Ages, in the county of Cork, Ireland. It successfully resisted for a time the arms of Oliver Cromwell.

Carrig-o-gunnell. [Rock of the Candle.] An interesting castle in the county of Limerick, Ireland, and one of the most romantic ruins in the island. It is said to have been built by the O'Brien family in 1530, and has undergone many sieges.

Carrousel. See ARC DU CARROUSEL and PLACE DU CARROUSEL.

Carthage, Building of. See BUILDING OF CARTHAGE.

Cartoons of Raphael. A collection of seven (a number of others are now lost) drawings in distemper colors by Raphael (1483-1520), being original designs executed by order of Leo X., for tapestries to adorn the lower walls of the Sistine Chapel in Rome. The tapestries still hanging in the Vatican, for which the Cartoons were designed, were called *Arazzi*, from Arras in Flanders, the place where they were executed. The seven Cartoons lay neglected until about 1630, when Charles I. bought them by the advice of Rubens. After the death of Charles, they were purchased by Cromwell, and were subsequently removed by William III. to Hampton Court, where they remained until 1865, when they were placed in a gallery specially prepared for them in the South Kensington Museum, London. These cartoons are ranked among the grandest productions of Christian art. The subjects are "Christ's Charge to St. Peter," "The Miraculous Draught of Fishes," "Elymas the Sorcerer struck Blind," "Peter and John healing the Cripple at the Beautiful Gate," "The Death of Ananias," "The Sacrifice at Lystra," and "Paul preaching at Athens." A number of copies of the Cartoons have been executed in tapestry, and the drawings have been twice cut into strips by tapestry-workers.

☞ "When I first went to see them, I must confess I was but barely pleased; the next time I liked them better; but at last, as I grew better acquainted with them, I fell deeply in love with them: like wise speeches, they sank deep into my heart."
Steele: Spectator, No. 244.

☞ "In the set of Cartoons for the tapestries of the Sistine Chapel, as originally prepared by Raphael, we have the foundation, the heaven-bestowed powers, the trials and sufferings of the early Church, exhibited in the calling of St. Peter, the conversion of St. Paul, the acts and miracles of the apostles, the martyrdom of St. Stephen; and the series closed with the Coronation of the Virgin, placed over the altar, as typical of the final triumph of the Church, the completion and fulfilment of all the promises made to man, set forth in the exaltation and union of the mortal with the immortal, when the human Mother and her divine Son are re-united and seated on the same throne." *Mrs. Jameson.*

Casa Blanca. [White House.] An old Spanish mansion in New Orleans, La. It was formerly the residence of Bienville, the first governor of Louisiana.

Casa del Labrador. [Laborer's Cottage.] A curious and noted building erected for Charles IV. of Spain, at Aranjuez.

☞ "A little plaything of Charles IV. It is the merest little jewel. There is but one suite of apartments in it, all the rest being divided into small rooms, cabinets, etc., the roofs painted in miniature frescos, and the floors paved in mosaic. In the richness of its ornaments, which are often of gold, and sometimes of platina, it is absolutely unrivalled." *Ticknor.*

Casa d'Oro. [The Golden House.] A noble palace in Venice, Italy.

☞ "It has no trace of the high roofs or aspiring tendencies of the Northern buildings of the same age, no boldly-marked buttresses in strong vertical lines; but, on the contrary, flat sky-lines, and every part is ornamented with a fanciful richness far more characteristic of the luxurious refinement of the East than of the manlier appreciation of the higher qualities of art which distinguished the contemporary erections on this side of the Alps." *Fergusson.*

Oh, yes, to be sure, Venice built her Ducal Palace, and her church of St. Mark, and her *Casa d'Oro*, and the rest of her golden houses. *O. W. Holmes.*

Slow, underneath the *Casa d'Oro's* wall,
Three searchers and three peering shadows came. *Walter Thornbury.*

Casa Guidi. A building in Florence, Italy, best known to English-speaking people from its connection with Elizabeth Barrett Browning, the poetess, who lived here for some years, and who wrote here her well-known poem of "Casa Guidi Windows," — a poem giving her impressions upon events in Tuscany of which she was a witness. There is a tablet here inscribed to the memory of Mrs. Browning (died in Florence in 1861), — "who in a woman's heart united the learning of a scholar and the spirit of a poet, and by her verse joined with a golden link Italy and England."

She came, whom *Casa Guidi's* chambers knew,
And know more proudly, an immortal, now.
. . . .
And life, new lighted, with a lark-like glee
Through *Casa Guidi* windows hails the sun,
Grown from the rest her spirit gave to me.
Bayard Taylor

And peradventure other eyes may see,
From *Casa Guidi* windows, what is done
Or undone. Whatsoever deeds they be,
Pope Pius will be glorified in none.
Mrs. Browning

Casa Santa. See SANTA CASA.

Casanata Library. See BIBLIOTÉCA CASANATENSE.

Cascine. A beautiful and well-known public park in Florence, Italy.

☞ "This is quite the loveliest public pleasure-ground, a wood of three miles in circumference, lying on the banks of the Arno just below the town, not like most European promenades, a bare field of clay or ground, but full of sward paths green and embowered. . . . The whole place is more like a half-redeemed wild wood in America, than a public promenade in Europe." *N. P. Willis.*

☞ "If . . . his tastes are for companionship and society, he will find the Cascine, during a portion of the day, a most agreeable place of resort. Here, in the afternoon, assemble all the gay world of Florence, native and foreign. . . . Here may be seen the equipages and the manners of all Europe." *Hillard.*

At Florence, too, what golden hours
In those long galleries were ours;
What drives about the fresh *Cascinè*,
Or walks in Boboli's ducal bowers.
Tennyson.

Caserta (Royal Palace). A noted palace at Caserta, in Southern Italy, begun in 1752 by Vanvitelli for Charles III., and regarded as one of the finest royal residences in Europe.

☞ "The chief productions of this period [the eighteenth century] are the colossal palaces of princes in which the spirit of modern despotism declares itself in a grandiose manner, but also with the utmost caprice. Perhaps there is no better example of these vast buildings than the Villa of Caserta, built by Luigi Vanvitelli at Naples, with its huge three stories, imposing staircase, and park with its aqueduct and superb fountains." *Lübke.*

When London shall have become the Rome or Athens of a fallen empire, the termini of the railways will be among its finest ruins. That of the Birmingham and Liverpool track is almost as magnificent as that flower of sumptuousness, the royal palace of *Caserta.* *N. P. Willis.*

Cashel, Rock of. See ROCK OF CASHEL.

Casino, Monte. See MONTE CASINO.

Cassiobury House. The seat of the Earl of Essex, near Watford, England.

Castalian Fountain. See FOUNTAIN OF CASTALIA.

Castel Nuovo. [The New Castle.] A massive stronghold in Naples, Italy, bearing some resemblance to the Tower of London. It was begun in the thirteenth century.

Castel Sant' Elmo. See ST. ELMO; and for other names beginning with the word CASTEL, see the next prominent word.

Castiglione, Count. A portrait of his friend by Raphael Sanzio (1483–1520). In the Louvre, Paris.

Castle. For names beginning with the word CASTLE, see the next prominent word; e.g., CASTLE OF CHILLON, see CHILLON. See also *infra.*

Castle Campbell. A ruined castle near the village of Dollar in Scotland, of romantic and historic interest.

☞ "The origin of this castle is unknown; but it was originally called the Castle of Gloom, situated in the parish of Dolour, surrounded by the glen of Care, and watered by the rivers of Sorrow."

O Castell Gloom! thy strength is gone,
The green grass o'er thee growin';
On hill of Care thou art alone,
The Sorrow round thee flowin'.
Carolina, Baroness Nairne.

Castle Clinton. See CASTLE GARDEN.

Castle Garden. A singular building of a circular form, situated on the Battery in New York City, and now used as a receiving station for immigrants. On landing here, they are received, cared for, furnished with instruction and guidance in regard to their routes of travel, and forwarded to their destination. The building was originally a fort, and known as Castle Clinton. It was built in 1807, and made over to the city in 1823. After having been put to various uses (at one time as an opera-house), it finally was appropriated to its present object as a place of reception for immigrants. See BATTERY, THE.

The arrivals of immigrants at *Castle Garden* for the month of August [1880] numbered 25,300. This aggregate exceeds by 4,000 the figures for the same month in any year for a quarter of a century. *Boston Journal.*

If, as a boy I did, I make my haunt in
Dear *Castle Garden*, soon I find a check
In two policemen, who, my courage daunting,
Stand sentinels beside that piteous wreck,

And point to signs; I read, *Für Emigranten*,
And just beyond I see an emptying deck.
T. G. Appleton.

Castle Hill. An eminence in Edinburgh, Scotland, on which stand the Castle of Edinburgh and other buildings of interest.

While danderin' cits delight to stray
To *Castlehill* or public way,
Where they nae other purpose mean,
Than that fool cause o' being seen,
Let me to Arthur's Seat pursue,
Where bonnie pastures meet the view.
R. Fergusson.

Castle Howard. The magnificent seat of the Earl of Carlisle, near New Malton, England.

Castle Kennedy. An interesting ivy-clad ruin near Stranrear, Scotland. The ancient castle was burned in the seventeenth century. The gardens are celebrated for the beautiful groves of pines, the finest in Scotland.

Castle Rising. An ancient English castle supposed to have been built by Alfred the Great (849-901). The keep and portions of the walls and embankments remain. Queen Isabella was confined in this castle for the rest of her life, after the death of her husband, King Edward II.

Castle Roche. A remarkable ruin in the county of Louth, Ireland, formerly one of the frontier castles of the English Pale. The name is a corruption of Rose Castle. This fortress was destroyed by Oliver Cromwell in 1649.

Castle Thunder. A military prison in Richmond, Va., during the war of the Rebellion. Here many Federal prisoners were confined, and subjected to great hardships. The building was simply a warehouse converted to the uses of a jail.

Castor and Pollux. 1. Two well-known marble statues, of colossal size, which stand at the head of the modern ascent to the Capitol in Rome.

2. Two statues which were found in the Baths of Constantine, and now stand in the Piazza di Monte Cavallo. There are copies of these statues in the Museum at Berlin. See QUIRINAL HILL.

Castor and Pollux carrying off the daughters of Leucippus. A picture by Peter Paul Rubens (1577-1640), now in the Munich Gallery.

Castor and Pollux. See TEMPLE OF CASTOR AND POLLUX.

Caswell, Fort. See FORT CASWELL.

Cat and Bagpipes. A well-known tavern which was situated in London.

A *bon-mot*, for instance, that might be relished at White's, may lose all its flavor when delivered at the *Cat and Bagpipes* in St. Giles's. *Goldsmith.*

Catacombs [of Alexandria]. Extensive subterranean cemeteries in Alexandria, Egypt.

☞ "Nothing which remains of Alexandria attests its greatness more than these catacombs. The entrance to them is close to a spot once covered with the habitations and gardens of the town, or suburb of the city, which, from the neighboring tombs, was called the Necropolis. The extent of these catacombs is remarkable; but the principal inducement to visit them is the elegance and symmetry of the architecture in one of the chambers, having a Doric entablature and mouldings, in good Greek taste, which is not to be met with in any other part of Egypt." *Murray.*

Catacombs [of Paris]. One tenth of the city is said to be undermined by quarries out of which building-stone was taken in former times. In 1784, after interment in the Cemetery of the Innocents was given up, vast quantities of bones were removed and deposited in these old quarries. In the first part of the present century the bones were arranged in the form of walls, altars and chapels were built of them, and the catacombs have become one of the sights of Paris. From the labyrinthine arrangement of the caverns, and the consequent danger of being lost in them, the catacombs were for many years closed to the public; but they may now be visited at certain times and with proper precautions.

Catacombs [of Rome]. The name given to the vast excavations which formed the burial-places of the early Christians. They were begun in the times of the Apostles, and continued to be used for the purpose of interment until the capture of Rome by Alaric in 410. The catacombs were usually named after those who owned the land. Among the more important catacombs in Rome are those of S. Calisto, S. Sebastian, and Sta. Priscilla.

Catacombs [of St. Calixtus]. One of the most interesting and most frequently visited of the Roman catacombs. The cemetery is of considerable extent, and comprises several tiers of galleries. In early times it was a favorite resort of pilgrims. It contains some curious paintings and sepulchral inscriptions.

Catacombs [of St. Sebastian]. A well-known subterranean cemetery in Rome. It was to a part of this cemetery that the term catacomb was first applied.

Catelan, Pré. See PRÉ CATELAN.

Cathedra Petri. See CHAIR OF ST. PETER.

Catherine Cornaro, The Nobles of Venice paying Homage to. A picture by Hans Makart (b. 1840). In the National Gallery, Berlin.

☞ "A grandiose composition, which, when displayed in London, was looked upon less as grave history than as phantasmagoria." *J. B. Atkinson.*

Catherine, St. See ST. CATHERINE.

Catherine Docks. See ST. KATHERINE DOCKS.

Catherine's House. See ST. CATHERINE'S HOUSE.

Catiline, Conspiracy of. See CONSPIRACY OF CATILINE.

Cato Street. A street in London, now called Homer Street, from which the Cato-Street Conspiracy derived its name.

There had been radical meetings in all parts of the kingdom; the bloody scenes at Manchester; the great plot in *Cato Street;* and, above all, the Queen had returned to England! *Irving.*

Cattle of Brittany. A picture by Rosa Bonheur (b. 1822), the celebrated French painter of animals.

Caudine Forks. [Lat. *Furculæ Caudinæ.*] A famous pass, in the form of two lofty fork-shaped defiles, in the valley of Caudium, in the Apennines, into which a Roman army was enticed by the Samnites, B. C. 321, and, being hemmed in and unable to retreat, was obliged to capitulate.

Cauter, The. A fine public square or parade in Ghent, Belgium.

Cautionary Towns. The towns of Briel, Flushing, Rammekins, and Walcheren, were held, in 1585, by Queen Elizabeth as security for the payment of troops with which she supplied the Netherlands. These four towns were called the Cautionary Towns; and although only one-third of the sum due on account of the troops was refunded by the Dutch, they were nevertheless delivered to them July 16, 1616, in accordance with a treaty for the purpose signed May 22.

Cavallo, Obelisk of the. See OBELISK OF THE MONTE CAVALLO.

Cave Canem, House of the. [Also called *House of Homer*, and *House of the Tragic Poet.*] A very interesting disinterred private residence at Pompeii, Italy, famous for the beautiful wall-paintings discovered in it. On the threshold of this house was a mosaic representing a chained dog, with the words "Cave Canem" (Beware of the Dog), from which the house derives its name. This mosaic is now at Naples.

Cave of Adullam. A large cavern at Khureitûn, Syria, traditionally identified with the "cave of Adullam" into which David retreated after his adventure at Gath (1 Sam. xxii. 1). There is no intrinsic improbability in the monastic tradition, and many circumstances favor the conclusion that this may have been the cave.

Cave of Jeremiah. This cave near Jerusalem is a very interesting natural curiosity. It is entered by a door cut in the side of a hill; and the whole interior of the hill seems to be occupied by a series of caverns, separated from one another by pillars and screens wholly natural. There are vaulted chapels, crypts, and chambers, in one of which the Latin monks sometimes perform mass. The whole place would be as sombre as the meditations of Jeremiah, were it not relieved by an abundance of graceful weeds.

Cave of Machpelah. The burial-place of Abraham, Isaac, and Jacob, in Hebron. Over it stands a Mohammedan mosque to which Christians cannot under any pretence obtain access. It is regarded as reasonably certain that the cave underlies the venerable Haram, and there is no intrinsic improbability in the supposition that the embalmed remains of the patriarchs may still be lying there, as the excessive sanctity of the place would naturally guard it from pillage and profanation.

Cave of the Nativity. A cave in Bethlehem, which was, according to tradition, the residence of Mary, and the birthplace of Jesus. Over it is a fine church arranged for Greek, Latin, and Armenian worship. One is shown here the silver star in the spot where Jesus was born, the corner where the manger was, and the place where the Magi presented their offerings.

Cave of the Winds. A wet cave or grotto at Niagara Falls. It is under the great Centre Fall. The entrance to it is attended with difficulty, but with proper precaution, and the company of the guide, is not necessarily dangerous.

☞ "A cavern deep below roaring seas, in which the waves are there, though they do not enter in upon him; or rather not the waves, but the very bowels of the ocean. He will feel as though the floods surrounded him, coming and going with their wild sounds, and he will hardly recognize that though among them he is not in them. And then as they fall with a continual roar, not hurting the ear, but musical withal, will seem to move as the vast ocean waters may perhaps move in their internal currents. . . . And as he looks on, strange colors will show themselves through the mist; the shades of gray will become green or blue, with ever and anon a flash of white; and then, when some gust of wind blows in with greater violence, the sea-girt cavern will become all dark and black. Oh, my friend, let there be no one there to speak to thee then; no, not even a brother. As you stand there, speak only to the waters."
Anthony Trollope.

Cave of Trophonius. A dark subterranean cave beneath frowning rocks in a dark ravine near the city of Lebadea, Greece, so called as the place chosen for the seat of the oracle of the Bœotian hero, Trophonius.

☞ "This [the cave of Trophonius], according to the most reasonable conjecture, is yet to be discovered within the walls of the modern castle on the top of the hill, where it may exist choked up with rubbish."
Murray's Handbook.

☞ "The mouth of this cave was three yards high and two wide. Those who consulted the oracle had to fast several days, and then to descend a steep ladder till they reached a narrow gullet. They were then seized by the feet and dragged violently to the bottom of the cave, where they were assailed by the most unearthy noises, howlings, shrieks, bellowings, with lurid lights and sudden glares, in the midst of which uproar and phantasmagoria the oracle was pronounced. The votaries were then seized unexpectedly by the feet, and thrust out of the cave without ceremony. If any resisted, or attempted to enter in any other way, he was instantly murdered." *Plutarch.*

Cave-temples of Elephanta. See ELEPHANTA, CAVE-TEMPLES OF.

Caveau. A literary and convivial society founded at Paris in 1729-35 by Piron, Collé, Gallet, and the younger Crébillon. It was so called from the sort of *cabaret* or *café*, called Le Caveau, in the Rue de Bussy, where, about 1735, many men of letters and song-writers were accustomed to meet. The society dissolved in 1817, started up again in 1834, and still exists. Recently Caveau has become a general name for societies similar to the original Caveau.

☞ "In 1813 there had existed for for many years a *réunion* of song-writers and literary men, which had taken the name of Caveau, after the Caveau rendered illustrious by Piron, Panard, Collé, Gallet, and the elder and younger Crébillon." *Béranger.*

Au *Caveau* je n'osais frapper;
Des méchants m'avaient su tromper.
Béranger.

Cavendish Square. This square in London, laid out in 1717, was so called from the wife of Harley, second Earl of Oxford.

Caves of Beni Hassan. See BENI HASSAN.

Cecilia Metella, Tomb of. See TOMB OF CECILIA METELLA.

Cecilia, St. See ST. CECILIA.

Cedarcroft. The former residence of Bayard Taylor at Kennett Square, Penn.

Cedars of Lebanon. An interesting and venerable group of patriarchal cedar-trees, standing in a completely solitary situation, with no other tree or hardly a bush in sight, upon the central ridge of Lebanon, or Libanus, in Northern Palestine. There are in all in this grove about 350 trees, of which a few only are very ancient. These last are inscribed with the names of many visitors. The place is much resorted to, and annually in August is celebrated the "Feast of the Cedars," when multitudes gather in the grove, and pass the time in prayer and in festivity. The cedars of Lebanon are a frequent subject of allusion in the Old Testament writings, were regarded with religious reverence, and furnished to King David some of the most beautiful images in the Psalms.

☞ "In ancient days, the grove must have been much more extensive, or rather, perhaps, the great trees then overspread the whole. Now they are huddled together upon two or three of the central knolls, and the peculiar grace of the cedar, as we see it in Europe, with its long sweeping branches feathering down to the ground, is there unknown. In one or two instances the boughs of these aged trees are upheld by a younger tree; others again of the smaller ones whose trunks are decayed, are actually supported in the gigantic arms of their elder brethren." *A. P. Stanley.*

Cemetery Hill. An eminence in Gettysburg, Penn., famous in connection with the great battle of July 3, 1863. The hill was held by the Federal troops, and was the centre of a most violent attack by the rebel army under Gen. Lee. Howard's artillery, massed at this point, aided in the final repulse and overthrow of the insurgent forces. This hill where so many Union soldiers fell has since been consecrated as a great national cemetery. See NATIONAL MONUMENT.

Cemetery of the Cappuccini. See CAPPUCCINI.

Cemetery of San Lorenzo. See SAN LORENZO.

Cenacolo. See LAST SUPPER.

Cenci, Beatrice. See BEATRICE CENCI.

Cenci Palace. [Ital. *Palazzo Cenci.*] An immense palace in an obscure quarter near the Ghetto, in Rome, famous as the ancient residence of the Cencis, and as the scene of many of the frightful crimes and atrocities connected with that ill-fated family.

☞ "The Cenci Palace is of great extent; and though in part modernized, there yet remains a vast and gloomy pile of feudal architecture in the same state as during the dreadful scenes which it once witnessed, . . . and from the upper windows you see the immense ruins of Mount Palatine, half hidden under the profuse undergrowth of trees." *Shelley.*

Central Park. A noble pleasure-ground in New York City, one of the largest and most beautiful parks in the world. It comprises 863 acres, and is in the form of a parallelogram, two and a half miles long, by half a mile in breadth. It is crossed from east to west by four sunken roads which provide for communication between the avenues which bound it on either side. It includes 12 miles of carriage-roads, 9 miles of bridle-paths, and some 25 miles of walks. By a lavish expenditure of money, this tract of land, which in 1856 was a most uninteresting region of ledges and swamps, without natural advantages, has been converted into one of the most delightful public pleasure-grounds of which any city can boast; affording also, by its natural-history collections, instruction as well as recreation to the thousands who visit it.

Cerreto Guidi. A famous villa near Empoli, Italy, once belonging to the Medici family.

Certosa [di Pavia]. A celebrated Carthusian convent near Pavia, Italy, founded near the close of the fourteenth century, and regarded as the most splendid monastic establishment in Europe.

☞ "The Certosa of Pavia leaves upon the mind an impression of bewildering sumptuousness; nowhere else are costly materials so combined with a lavish expenditure of the rarest art. Those who have only once been driven round together with the crew of sight-seers can carry little away but the memory of lapis-lazuli and bronze-work, inlaid agates, and labyrinthine sculpture, cloisters tenantless in silence, fair painted faces smiling from dark corners on the senseless crowd. . . . All the great sculptor-architects of Lombardy worked in succession on this miracle of beauty, and this may account for the sustained perfection of style. . . . It remains the triumph of North Italian genius. . . . The Certosa is a wilderness of lovely workmanship." *J. A. Symonds.*

Approach, for what we seek is here.
Alight, and sparely sup, and wait
For rest in this outbuilding near;
Then cross the sward, and reach that gate;
Knock; pass the wicket! Thou art come
To the Carthusians' world-famed home.
Matthew Arnold.

Certosa of the Val d'Emo. A noted Carthusian convent near Florence, Italy, founded about the middle of the fourteenth century.

Cesnola Collection. A fine collection of Egyptian, Phœnician, and Greek antiquities, gathered by Gen. di Cesnola, an Italian nobleman, while serving as United States consul in Cyprus. This collection is now preserved in the Metropolitan Museum of Art in New York.

Cestius. See PYRAMID OF CAIUS CESTIUS.

Chace of the Calydonian Boar. A picture by Peter Paul Rubens (1577-1640) regarded as one of his most admirable works in this kind. It is in the Imperial Gallery at Vienna, Austria.

Chair of Coronation. See CORONATION CHAIR.

Chair of St. Peter. [Lat. *Cathedra Petri.*] A famous chair of bronze in the Tribune of St. Peter's at Rome, the work of Bernini, enclosing, according to the Church tradition, the identical chair which St. Peter and many of his successors used as their official throne.

Peter's chair is shamed
Like any vulgar throne the nations lop
To pieces for their firewood unreclaimed;
And, when it burns too, we shall see as well
In Italy as elsewhere. Let it burn.
Mrs. Browning.

Chaldean Sages. A picture by Giorgio Barbarelli, commonly called Giorgione (1477-1511), in the Belvidere, Vienna, Austria.

Chalk Farm. A former well-known tea-garden near London, and a place where a number of duels have been fought.

☞ "Chalk Farm, by the by, is probably a corruption of Chalcote Farm, the Chalcote estate extending thence to Belsize Lane. There is no chalk in the neighborhood to originate the name." *W. Howitt.*

Nay, oftener it is Cowardice rather that produces the result: for consider. Is the *Chalk-Farm* Pistoleer inspired with any reasonable Belief and Determination; or is he hounded on by haggard, indefinable Fear, — how he will be *cut* at public places, and "plucked geese of the neighborhood" will wag their tongues at him a plucked goose? *Carlyle.*

The Courage that can go forth, once and away, to *Chalk-Farm*, and have itself shot, and snuffed out, with decency, is nowise wholly what we mean here. *Ibid.*

Challenge, The. A picture by Sir Edwin Landseer (1803-1873), the most celebrated modern painter of animals. In the possession of the Duchess of Northumberland, and well known through reproductions.

Chalmette, Plains of. See PLAINS OF CHALMETTE.

Chambord. A magnificent château, — "the Versailles of La Tourraine," — about 12 miles from Blois, France. It was built by Francis I. in 1526. Its architecture is intermediate between that of a mediæval fortress and an Italian palace. It was pillaged during the Revolution, and confiscated as public property. Subsequently it was purchased by national subscription, and presented to the Comte de Chambord, to whom it now belongs.

Chamouni-Needles. A term sometimes applied to the mountain-range of the Aiguilles Rouges (red needles) which bound the vale of Chamouni, in Savoy, on the north.

> Over all which *Chamouni-needles* and Staubbach Falls, the great Persifleur skims along in this his little poetical air-ship, more softly than if he travelled the smoothest of merely prosaic roads.
> *Carlyle.*

Champ de Mars. [Field of March.] A large open space in Paris, three-quarters of a mile long, and about one-third of a mile broad. Here occurred the Fête de la Fédération, on the 14th July, 1790, and here Louis XVI. swore to observe the new constitution. In this place also Napoleon held his famous Champ de Mai, in 1815, before setting out on his fatal campaign in Belgium. On this field military exercises take place, and horse-racing on Sunday. Much of its area was occupied by the buildings of the Great International Exhibition of 1867.

> Far over the waters there have been federations of the *Champ de Mars;* guillotines, portable-guillotines, and a French people risen against tyrants; there has been a *Sansculottism*, speaking at last in cannon-volleys and the crash of towns and nations over half the world. *Carlyle.*

> Imminent blood-thirsty Regiments camped on the *Champ de Mars;* dispersed National Assembly; red-hot cannon-balls; the mad War-god and Bellona's sounding thongs. *Carlyle.*

Champs-Elysées. [Elysian Fields.] A delightful and popular promenade in Paris. The Avenue, which begins at the Place de la Concorde, and rises by a gradual slope to the Arc de Triomphe, is more than a mile and a quarter in length. In 1616 it was laid out as a promenade by Marie de Medicis; and it has been gradually embellished and adorned with trees, graceful fountains, and gardens. On pleasant afternoons carriages throng the central road of the Champs-Elysées, and promenaders the foot-paths. In the evening the place is crowded with the middle and lower classes. The greatest crowd is on Sunday, though Thursday is the most fashionable day. See also ELYSIAN FIELDS.

☞ "The grand display of the year is in Passion Week, and is called *Promenade de Longchamps.* There was formerly an abbey of that name in the Bois de Boulogne, and it became the fashion to attend vespers there during Passion Week. The abbey is gone; but the fashion of driving on the road to Longchamps during the last week of Lent remains, though somewhat fallen off of late years." *Murray's Handbook.*

☞ "The strangest peculiarity of this place, however, to eyes fresh from moist and verdant England, is, that there is not one blade of grass in all the Elysian Fields, nothing but hard clay, now covered with white dust. It gives the whole scene the air of being a contrivance of man, in which Nature has either not been invited to take any part, or has declined to do so."
Hawthorne (Jan., 1858).

> Their cashmere shawls, their silks and jewels, and the gay Oriental liveries of the footmen gave the display [on the Esplanade in Calcutta] an air of pomp and magnificence which threw Hyde Park and the *Champs Elysées* into the shade.
> *Bayard Taylor.*

> The word goes round the ranks,
> Resounds along the line;
> That word they give, is — France,
> The answer — St. Hélene.
> 'Tis there at midnight hour
> The grand review, they say,
> Is by dead Cæsar held,
> In the *Champs-Elysées.*
> *J. C. von Zedlitz, Trans.*

Chancellor's Mace. A richly ornamented and elaborately carved staff which is laid before the Lord

Chancellor of England when sitting as Speaker of the House of Lords.

Chancery Lane. A well-known "legal thoroughfare" in London, extending from Fleet Street to Holborn. Part of the scene of Dickens's novel of "Bleak House" is laid in Chancery Lane and its neighborhood.

Change Alley. A famous alley between Cornhill and Lombard Street, London. Strype describes Exchange-alley (now 'Change Alley) as a place "of a very considerable concourse of merchants, seafaring men, and other traders, occasioned by the great coffee-houses that stand there. Chiefly now brokers, and such as deal in buying and selling of stocks, frequent it." During the eighteenth century it was the centre for all the monetary operations of England, and, to a great extent, for those of Europe.

There is in it [generosity] something of what we admire in heroes, and praise with a degree of rapture. Justice, on the contrary, is a mere mechanic virtue, fit only for tradesmen, and what is practised by every broker in *Change Alley*.
Goldsmith.

There is a gulf where thousands fall,
There all the bold adventurers came;
A narrow sound, though deep as hell,
Change Alley is the dreadful name.
Swift.

If you had seen him [a banker] first in his suburban retreat, you would wonder how the deuce such a cordial, joyous, spare-nothing sort of a good fellow could ever reduce himself to the cautious proportions of *Change Alley*. *N. P. Willis.*

Changer of Money weighing Gold. A picture by Quentin Massys (1466–1530), the Flemish painter. It is now in the Louvre, at Paris.

Changing Pasture. A picture by Rosa Bonheur (b. 1822), the celebrated French painter of animals.

Chanteloup. A magnificent château, once the residence and retreat of the Duc de Choiseul, the minister of Louis XV., near Amboise, France. It was destroyed in 1830.

Chanting Cherubs. A marble group by Horatio Greenough (1805–1852).

☞ "One day they [Greenough and James Fenimore Cooper, the novelist] paused, in one of the saloons of the Pitti Palace, before a *capo d'opera* of Raphael; and the artist pointed out to his companion the fine drawing exhibited in two little angelic figures in the foreground, in the act of holding an open book, and singing. Cooper inquired if a subject like this was not well adapted to sculpture; afterwards one of his daughters copied the figures, and the result of their mutual interest in the design was an order from Cooper for a group, which in a few months Greenough executed in marble. It was afterwards exhibited in America under the name of the 'Chanting Cherubs.' . . . The grace, truth to nature, and infantile beauty of the Cherubs were at once and warmly recognized."
H. T. Tuckerman.

Chapeau de Paille. [The Straw Hat.] A celebrated picture by Peter Paul Rubens (1577–1640) in the National Gallery, London, the chief charm of which "consists in the marvellous triumph over a great difficulty, that of painting a head entirely in the shadow cast by the hat, and yet in the clearest and most brilliant tones."

Chapel. For names beginning with the word CHAPEL, see the next prominent word.

Chapelle, Sainte. See SAINTE CHAPELLE.

Chapter Coffee-house. An establishment in Paternoster Row, London, converted into a tavern in 1854, and famous in the last century as a place of resort for literary characters. Goldsmith and Chatterton frequented it.

☞ "This then was the Chapter Coffee-house, which a century ago was the resort of all the booksellers and publishers, and where the literary hacks, the critics, and even the wits, used to go in seach of ideas or employment. . . . Years later it became the tavern frequented by university men, and country clergymen, who were up in London for a few days."
Mrs. Gaskell (in 1848).

Chapultepec. A strong fortress situated on a rocky hill, 150 feet high, near the city of Mexico, and forming the principal defence of the place. The castle was taken by Gen. Scott in 1847.

Charing Cross. The large area at the meeting of the Strand, Whitehall, and Cockspur Street, London, supposed to be so named from the village of Cherringe, Westminster. A fanciful tradition refers the name to the stone cross set up there after her death to Eleanor, the *Chère Reine* of Edward I., to whom her husband erected a cross at each of the nine resting-places of her body on its way from Lincolnshire to Westminster. The name is also said to be derived from the Saxon word Charan, to turn, "both the road and river making a bend here." There is now in front of the Charing Cross Railway Station a modern cross designed as a reproduction of the old one, which was destroyed by the Long Parliament. Here the Regicides were put to death in 1660, and here was erected in 1674 a statue of Charles I. Charing Cross is called by Sir R. Peel the finest site in Europe. See ELEANOR CROSSES.

☞ "Why, Sir, Fleet-street has a very animated appearance, but I think the full tide of human existence is at Charing Cross." *Dr. Johnson.*

'Methinks the common-council should
Of it have taken pity,
'Cause good old Cross, it always stood
So firmly to the City.
Since crosses you so much disdain,
Faith, if I were as you,
For fear the king should rule again,
I'd pull down Tyburn too.'
The Dounefall of Charing Cross.

Each man an Ascapart, of strength to toss
For quoits both Temple-bar and *Charing-cross.* *Pope.*

Where all that passes inter nos
May be proclaimed at *Charing Cross.*
Swift.

Charlatan, The. A picture by Franz van Mieris (1635–1681), the Dutch *genre*-painter, and considered one of his best productions. In the gallery of the Uffizi, at Florence, Italy.

Charlecote House. A country mansion, the seat of the Lucy family, in Warwickshire, England, near Stratford-on-Avon. It is greatly resorted to by pilgrims on account of its associations with Shakespeare — especially the legendary deer-stealing incident in the poet's life. In one of the halls of this mansion he is said to have been tried.

☞ "My mind had become so completely possessed by the imaginary scenes and characters connected with it [Charlecote House], that I seemed to be actually living among them. Every thing brought them, as it were, before my eyes; and, as the door of the dining-room opened, I almost expected to hear the feeble voice of Master Silence quavering forth his favorite ditty: —

'Tis merry in the hall, when beards
wag all,
And welcome merry Shrove-tide.'"
Irving.

Charlemagne. A bronze statue at Aix-la-Chapelle, Prussia, erected in 1620.

Charlemagne crowned by Leo III. A well-known fresco by Raphael Sanzio (1483–1520), in the Stanza del Incendio, in the Vatican, Rome.

Charlemagne's Tomb. A vault under the dome of the cathedral of Aix-la-Chapelle, Prussia, covered with a slab of marble, inscribed CAROLO MAGNO. The throne upon which the body of the emperor was seated alone remains.

Amid the torch-lit gloom of Aachen's aisle
Stood Otho, Germany's imperial lord,
Regarding with a melancholy smile,
A simple stone, where, fitly to record
A world of action by a single word,
Was graven "Carlo Magno."
Aubrey de Vere.

Charles I. A portrait by Anthony Van Dyck (1599–1641), representing the king as hunting. In the Louvre, Paris. There is another portrait of the king by Van Dyck, and considered one of his finest works, in the Vienna Gallery; and still another and very imposing figure of the king on horseback, in Windsor Castle.

2. A well-known statue in Charing Cross, London, erected in 1674. It was for a time secreted under a church, but was brought out and placed upon its present pedestal, at the time of the Restoration.

Charles V. An equestrian portrait by Titian (1477-1576). This famous picture is known as "della Gloria." It was painted for the great emperor, who gave orders that it should always be hung up where his body was buried. In the Gallery at Madrid, Spain.

☞ "This is perhaps the most remarkable picture existing of any individual, for here Titian has sounded a greater depth of individual expression than any other of his works exhibits."
Eastlake.

Charles the Bold of Burgundy. A well-known portrait, of which there are several replicas, by Giorgio Barbarelli, commonly called Giorgione (1477-1511). The best example is in the Städel Institut, Frankfort, Germany.

Charlottenborg. A palace in Copenhagen, Denmark. It is now used as an academy of arts, and contains a museum of Northern antiquities which is unrivalled of its kind.

Charlottenhof. A villa in the gardens of Sans Souci at Potsdam, near Berlin, built after the Pompeian style, and with ornaments brought from that place.

Charter Oak. A tree celebrated in American history, which formerly stood in Hartford, Conn. It derived its name from the circumstance that the Colonial Charter, securing the liberties of the people, and of which Gov. Andrews had in vain endeavored to obtain possession, was for some time secreted in it. While the Assembly was in session at Hartford, in 1688, and debating the Governor's proposition for a surrender of the charter, suddenly the lights were extinguished, and in the darkness that ensued, a patriot named Wadsworth escaped with the instrument through the crowd, and concealed it in the hollow of the oak, which ever after bore the name of the Charter Oak, and was carefully preserved until overthrown by a violent storm in the year 1856.

The charter was renewed when William III. came to the throne, and now hangs triumphantly in the State House at Hartford. The *Charter Oak* has, alas! succumbed to the weather.
Anthony Trollope.

The years are many since, in youth and hope,
Under the *Charter Oak*, our horoscope
We drew thick-studded with all favoring stars.
Whittier.

From Mississippi's fountain-head
A sound as of the bison's tread!
There rustled freedom's *Charter Oak!*
Whittier.

Charterhouse, The. [A corruption of Chartreuse.] A celebrated public school in London. Upon the register of its pupils are many illustrious names. Oliver Cromwell was elected governor of it in 1652. It is under the direction of the Queen, fifteen governors selected from the great officers of state, and the Master of the Hospital. Among the more eminent pupils have been Richard Crashaw, Isaac Barrow, Sir William Blackstone, Joseph Addison, Richard Steele, John Wesley, Thackeray, Grote, Thirwall, Sir Charles Eastlake, John Leech, and others. The school was removed in 1872 to Godalming.

Chartres Cathedral. A splendid Gothic church in Chartres, France, considered the most perfect in that country. It was built about 1200.

☞ "At Chartres there is a simplicity of design and a grandeur of conception seldom surpassed. . . . Its two spires of different ages are unsurpassed in France. The new or northern spire was erected by John Texier between the years 1507 and 1514, and, notwithstanding the lateness of its date, it must be considered as, on the whole, the most beautifully designed spire on the Continent of Europe; and, though not equal in height, certainly far surpassing in elegance of outline and appropriateness of design those at Strasburg, Vienna, or even Antwerp. If it has rivals, it has that at Freiburg, or those designed for Cologne; but, were its details of the same date, it can hardly be doubted that it would be considered the finest spire of the three."
Fergusson

☞ "There is not in France a church so rich in sculptures. Calculating only the exterior, there are to be counted 1,800 figures, without including arabesques, gargoiles, corbels, masks, and consols. These stone figures narrate, as in an allegorical poem, the history of this world and the next. Add to the statues the thousand figures that shine in the colored glass, and we can comprehend why the cathedral of Chartres appeals more to the mind than its rivals, and why it seems animated with a mysterious life."

Lefèvre, Tr. Donald.

Eluding these, I loitered through the town,
With hope to take my minster unawares
In its grave solitude of memory.

. . . .

With outward senses furloughed and head bowed,
I followed some fine instinct in my feet,
Till, to unbend me from the loom of thought,
Looking up suddenly, I found mine eyes
Confronted with the minster's vast repose.
Silent and gray as forest-leaguered cliff
Left inland by the ocean's slow retreat,
That hears afar the breeze-borne rote, and longs,
Remembering shocks of surfs that clomb and fell,
Spume-sliding down the baffled decuman,
It rose before me, patiently remote
From the great tides of life it breasted once.

Lowell.

Chartreuse, La Grande. See GRANDE CHARTREUSE.

Charybdis. A celebrated whirlpool, now known as Galofaro, in the strait between Italy and Sicily, near Messina. Its dangers are very much diminished.

See SCYLLA.

☞ "Scylla and Charybdis are farfamed names. Our ship glided away over the eddying Charybdis; we had no foreboding of it. Where is that wild maelstrom? They pointed to the sea close by where we sailed; but there was no particular motion of the waves to be seen."

Hans Christian Andersen.

☞ "Even at the present day, small vessels are sometimes endangered by its eddies; but it has long lost the terrors with which it is invested in ancient song, whether from the superiority of modern navigation, or from some of the geological changes frequent in this volcanic region; and we noticed, as we sailed calmly over it, only a slight agitation in the water, contrasting with the unruffled surface of the broader sea."

T. Chase.

Chase, The. A picture by Jacob Ruysdael (1625?-1682), the Dutch landscape-painter. In the Dresden Gallery.

Chase of Diana. A celebrated landscape by Domenico Zampieri, called Domenichino (1581-1641). In the Palazzo Borghese, Rome. This picture is well known by Raphael Morghen's engraving.

Chasm of the Colorado. A picture by Thomas Moran (b. 1837). Purchased by Congress, and now in the Capitol at Washington.

Chastisement of Heliodorus. See EXPULSION OF HELIODORUS.

Chat Moss. Formerly a dangerous and treacherous bog, some 6,000 acres in extent, about ten miles from Manchester, England, and crossed by the Manchester and Liverpool Railway. It has been reclaimed by filling and drainage, and is now cultivated with profit.

☞ "Chat Moss and the fens of Lincolnshire and Cambridgeshire are unhealthy and too barren to pay rent. By cylindrical tiles, and gutta-percha tubes, 5,000,000 of acres of bad land have been drained and put on equality with the best, for rape-culture and grass. The climate too, which was already believed to have become milder and dryer by the enormous consumption of coal, is so far reached by this new action, that fogs and storms are said to disappear."

Emerson.

Château. For names beginning with the word CHÂTEAU, see the next prominent word of the title: e.g., CHÂTEAU DE FERNAY, see FERNAY. See also *infra*.

Château d'Eau. The best known of the fountains which bear this name is that at Paris, on the Boulevart St. Martin, built in 1812, and rebuilt in 1869. In 1848 there was much fighting near this fountain, and in 1872 a bloody Communist struggle.

Château des Fleurs. A garden in the Champs Elysées, near the Arc de l'Etoile, Paris, charmingly laid out, and brilliantly illuminated by jets of light of various colors, and Chinese lanterns hanging from the trees. It is open to the people for dancing and other amusements, and is a favorite place of resort. The Jardin Mabille is now combined with this garden. See JARDIN MABILLE.

Mabille at the present day is so well known both in France and in other countries, it is so frequented by people of fashion, by princes even, who in their passage through the city visit it with as much interest as Notre Dame and the Sainte Chapelle, and give it renown, that to call the *Château des Fleurs* its brother, is to confer upon it the highest eulogy.
Larousse, Trans.

Chatelherault. A miniature castle on the bank of the Avon near Hamilton, Scotland, built in the early part of the last century by the Duke of Hamilton, in imitation of the French château from which one of his titles is derived.

Chatsworth. The splendid seat of the Duke of Devonshire, situated in the county of Derby, England. It is regarded as one of the most magnificent residences in Europe. It stands in a beautiful park some ten miles in circumference, and contains fine collections of books, paintings, and statuary.

☞ "Few country residences ever existed comparable with this in the variety of its treasures and decorations. . . . It is the perfection of a modern home in its most brilliant development of wealth, refinement, and education."
J. F. Hunnewell.

☞ "Even peers, who are men of worth and public spirit, are overtaken and embarrassed by their vast expense. The respectable Duke of Devonshire, willing to be the Mæcenas and Lucullus of his island, is reported to have said that he cannot live at Chatsworth but one month in the year."
Emerson.

Chatsworth! thy stately mansion, and the pride
Of thy domain, strange contrast do present
To house and home in many a craggy rent
Of the wild Peak. *Wordsworth.*

Cheapside. A celebrated street and crowded thoroughfare in London, famous many years ago for its "Ridings," its Cross, its Standard, and its Conduit. Three centuries ago it was called "The Beauty of London," and was noted for its shops of goldsmiths, linen-drapers, etc. It is named from the Saxon word *Chepe*, or market. It is still the greatest thoroughfare in London, and, excepting London Bridge, perhaps the busiest thoroughfare in the world.

When there any ridings were in *Chepe*
Out of the shoppe thider would he lepe
And till that he had all the sight ysein
And danced wel, he would not come again. *Chaucer.*

In short, the inhabitants of St. James's, notwithstanding they live under the same laws and speak the same language, are a distinct people from those of *Cheapside*.
Addison.

Smack went the whip, round went the wheels,
Were never folk so glad;
The stones did rattle underneath
As if *Cheapside* were mad.
Cowper (John Gilpin).

'Tis a note of enchantment; what ails her? she sees
A mountain ascending, a vision of trees;
Bright volumes of vapor through Lothbury glide,
And a river flows on through the vale of *Cheapside*. *Wordsworth.*

Cheating Gamesters. A picture by Michelangelo Amerighi, surnamed Caravaggio (1569–1609). In the Spada Palace, Rome.

Cheese Wring. A natural curiosity, and one of the principal sights of Cornwall, England, near the town of Liskeard. It consists of a pile of rocks thirty-two feet in height, resembling a child's top, the smaller end being at the bottom. The immense stones, though apparently so insecure, are perfectly immovable.

Chehil Minar. See XERXES.

Chelsea Hospital. A Royal Hospital for disabled and aged soldiers, Chelsea, London, built from designs by Sir Christopher Wren. The foundation stone was laid by Charles II. in 1681-82. The founding of the hospital originated with Sir Stephen Fox, though it is traditionally said to be due to the influence of Nell Gwynne with King Charles. On the frieze runs this inscription: "In subsidium et levamen emeritorum senio belloque fractorum, condidit Carolus Secundus, auxit Jacobus Secundus, perfecere Gulielmus et Maria Rex et Regina, MDCXCII."

Chenany. See JEAN ARNOLFINI.

Cheops, Pyramid of. See GREAT PYRAMID.

Cherbourg. See DIGUE DE CHERBOURG.

Cherubs. See CHANTING CHERUBS.

Chesapeake, The. An American vessel of war attacked and disabled by the British ship *Leopard* in 1813. She afterwards engaged in a desperate encounter off Marblehead, Mass., with the *Shannon*, and was captured and carried to Halifax. Her brave commander James Lawrence was mortally wounded in the action, and expired with the memorable saying, "Don't give up the ship."

Cheshire Cheese. A tavern in "Wine Office Court," Fleet Street, London. It was a frequent resort of Dr. Johnson, while living at Bolt Court.

☞ "It is an interesting locality, and a pleasing sign — the 'Old Cheshire Cheese Tavern,' which will afford the present generation, it is hoped, for some time to come, an opportunity of witnessing the kind of tavern in which our forefathers delighted to assemble for refreshment." *Fitzgerald.*

Chess-Players, The. An admired picture by Jean Louis Ernest Meissonier (b. 1811).

Chesterfield House. The town house of the Earl of Chesterfield, London. It was built for the celebrated Lord Chesterfield, who wrote his famous *Letters* in the library, a room of which he boasted that it was the "finest in London."

Chestnut Street. A noted and fashionable street in Philadelphia, Penn.

Cheyne Row. A well-known street in Chelsea, London.

Thomas Carlyle, who died full of years and of honors on Saturday morning, February 5 [1881], at the house in *Cheyne-Row*, Chelsea, where he had resided for nearly 47 years, . . . had overpassed by fully two months the ripe age of 85 years, on the day of his death.

☞ "We have broken up our old settlement, and after tumult enough, formed a new one here [in Cheyne-Row]. The house pleases us much. It is in the remnant of genuine old Dutch-looking Chelsea, looks out mainly into trees. We might see at half a mile's distance, Bolingbroke's Battersea, could shoot a gun into Smollett's old house, where he wrote 'Count Fathom,' and was wont every Saturday to dine a company of hungry authors." *Carlyle, 1834.*

Chiaja. A long and somewhat narrow strip of streets and squares in Naples, Italy, of which a broad street called the *Riviera di Chiaia* passes along the entire length, running parallel to the shore, bordered on the one side by handsome houses, and on the other by the public gardens called the Villa Reale. It is the modern and fashionable quarter of the city.

☞ "At six o'clock every evening, all Naples turns out to drive on the *Riviere di Chiaja* (whatever that may mean); and for two hours one may stand there and see the motliest and the worst mixed procession go by that ever eyes beheld. Princes (there are more princes than policemen in Naples — the city is infested with them), — princes who live up seven flights of stairs and don't own any principalities, will keep a carriage and go hungry; and clerks, mechanics, milliners, and strumpets will go without their dinners, and squander the money on a hack-ride in the Chiaja; the rag-tag and rubbish of the city stack themselves up, to the number of twenty or thirty, on a rickety little go-cart hauled by a donkey not much bigger than a cat, and *they* drive in the Chiaja; dukes and bankers, in sumptuous carriages, and with gorgeous drivers and footmen, turn out also, and so the furious procession goes." *Mark Twain.*

To me, the Prado is an inexhaustible source of amusement. In the first place, it is in itself the finest public walk I have ever seen within the walls of any city, not excepting either the Tuileries or the *Chiaja.* *George Ticknor.*

Chiaramonti. See MUSEO CHIARAMONTI.

Chiaravalle. A celebrated old monastic church near Milan, Italy.

Chief Mourner. See OLD SHEPHERD'S CHIEF MOURNER.

Chief's return from Deer-Stalking. A well-known picture by Sir Edwin Landseer (1803-1873), the most celebrated modern painter of animals.

Chigi Palace. [Ital. *Palazzo Chigi.*] A well-known palace in Rome, on the north side of the Piazza Colonna. It was erected in 1526, and contains some pictures and statues of note.

Child of the Regiment. A picture by John Everett Millais (b. 1829).

Childe Harold's Pilgrimage. A picture by Joseph Mallord William Turner (1775-1851), the English landscape-painter, and regarded one of his best works. In the National Gallery, London.

Children of the Mist. A famous picture by Sir Edwin Landseer (1803-1873), the celebrated painter of animals, regarded as one of his masterpieces.

Child's Bank. A financial house in Fleet Street, London, celebrated as the oldest banking institution in England. Charles II., among many others, kept his account here.

Child's Coffee-house. An establishment in St. Paul's Churchyard, London, which was much frequented by professional men.

Chillingham. See WILD DEER OF CHILLINGHAM.

Chillon. This massive castle, the scene of Byron's "Prisoner of Chillon," is built on a solitary rock, almost surrounded by water, near the shore of Lake Geneva. The name of Francis Bonnivard, prior of St. Victor, is intimately connected with it. By his warm defence of the republic of Geneva, he incurred the hostility of the Duke of Savoy, into whose hands he unfortunately fell in 1530, and by whom he was imprisoned in the Castle of Chillon for six years. The castle contains gloomy dungeons in which the early reformers and prisoners of state were confined.

☞ "Across one of the vaults is a beam black with age, on which we were informed that the condemned were formerly executed. In the cells are seven pillars, or, rather, eight, one being half merged in the wall; in some of these are rings for the fetters and the fettered: in the pavement the steps of Bonnivard have left their traces. He was confined here several years. It is by this castle that Rousseau has fixed the catastrophe of his Héloïse, in the rescue of one of her children by Julie from the water: the shock of which, and the illness produced by the immersion, is the cause of her death. The château is large, and seen along the lake for a great distance. The walls are white." *Byron.*

☞ "First into the dungeon with the seven pillars described by Byron. . . . One of the pillars in this vault is covered with names. I think it is Bonnivard's pillar. There are the names of Byron, Hunt, Schiller, and many other celebrities." *C. Beecher.*

☞ "It appears to sit right upon the water, and does not rise very loftily above it. I was disappointed in its aspect, having imagined this famous castle as situated upon a rock, a hundred, or, for aught I know, a thousand feet, above the surface of the lake; but it is quite as impressive a fact — supposing it to be true — that the water is eight hundred feet deep at its base. . . . The castle is wofully in need of a pedestal. If its site were elevated to a height equal to its own, it would make a far better appearance. As it now is, it looks, to speak profanely of what poetry has consecrated, when seen from the water, or along the shore of the lake, very like an old whitewashed factory or mill." *Hawthorne.*

Chillon! thy prison is a holy place,
And thy sad floor an altar — for 'twas trod
Until his very steps have left a trace,
Worn, as if the cold pavement were a sod,
By Bonnivard! may none those marks efface,
For they appeal from tyranny to God.
Byron.

Chillon, Prisoner of. See PRISONER OF CHILLON.

Chimborazo. A well-known picture by Frederic Edwin Church (b. 1826), the American landscape-painter.

Chinon Castle. An interesting ruined castle in Chinon, France, once a favorite residence of the French kings.

Choragic Monument of Lysicrates. A small circular building of graceful proportions at Athens, Greece. It is interesting as the only surviving relic of a series of temples forming a street, which was called the Street of the Tripods, from the Tripods (gained by victorious Choragi in the neighboring Theatre of Dionysus) by which the temples were surmounted. This monument, the first authentic instance of Corinthian architecture, is about eight feet in diameter and 34 feet high.

☞ "Notwithstanding the smallness of its dimensions, one of the most beautiful works of art of the merely ornamental class to be found in any part of the world." *Fergusson.*

Where every thing is square and rugged, as in a Druidical trilithon, the effect may be sublime, but it cannot be elegant; where every thing is rounded, as in the *Choragic Monument of Lysicrates*, the perfection of elegance may be attained, but never sublimity. *Fergusson.*

Christ. 1. A marble statue by Michael Angelo Buonarotti (1475–1564). In the church of Sopra Minerva in Rome.

☞ "In its outward finish and as a representation of a naked human form in the prime of beauty, it is a most admirable work; but as an image of Him whom it is to call to mind, it is the first statue of Michael Angelo's which we must designate as full of mannerism." *Grimm, Trans.*

2. A famous statue by Johann Heinrich von Dannecker (1758–1841), the sculptor of Ariadne. The statue is in a tower, built to imitate a ruined abbey, in the grounds attached to the palace of Tzarko Selo, near St. Petersburg, Russia.

☞ "The longer I looked upon it, the more I was penetrated with its wonderful representation of the attributes of Christ, — Wisdom and Love. The face calmly surveys and comprehends all forms of human passion, with pity for the erring, joy in the good, and tenderness for all. I have seen few statues like this, where the form is lost sight of in the presence of the idea. In this respect it is Dannecker's greatest, as it was his favorite work." *Bayard Taylor.*

Christ amid the Doctors. A picture by Albert Dürer (1471–1528), the German painter. According to the inscription upon it, it was executed in five days. In the Barberini Palace at Rome.

Christ and the Parable of the Vineyard. A picture by Rembrandt van Ryn (1607–1669), the Dutch painter. Now in the Hermitage at St. Petersburg, Russia.

Christ and the Scoffers. A picture by Anthony van Dyck (1599–1641), now in Madrid, Spain.

Christ appearing to the Magdalen. A picture by Rembrandt van Ryn (1607–1669), the Dutch painter. Now in Buckingham Palace, London.

Christ, Ascension of. See ASCENSION OF CHRIST.

Christ at the Table of Simon the Publican. An immense picture by Paul Veronese (1500–1588), now in the Louvre, Paris. There is another upon the same subject at the Brera in Milan, Italy; and another in the Marcello Durazzo Palace, at Genoa.

Christ, Baptism of. See BAPTISM OF CHRIST.

Christ before Pilate. An admired picture by Gherardo della Notte. In Lucca, Italy.

Christ borne to the Sepulchre. 1. A well-known picture by Raphael Sanzio (1483–1520). In the Palazzo Borghese, Rome.

☞ "Raphael's picture of this subject . . . though meriting all its fame in respect of drawing, expression, and knowledge, has lost all signs of reverential feeling in the persons of the bearers." *Lady Eastlake.*

2. A well-known picture by Titian (1477–1576). In the Louvre, Paris.

3. A picture by Jacopo Robusti, called Tintoretto (1512–1594). Now in the Stafford Gallery, London.

Christ Church. 1. An ancient and venerable church edifice in Philadelphia, Penn. It was built near the beginning of the last century. Gen. Washington was a regular attendant here. In the lofty tower is the oldest chime of bells in the United States, brought from England in 1754, and which proclaimed the Declaration of Independence in 1776.

2. A religious edifice in Boston, Mass., memorable as the oldest church structure now standing in the city (having been consecrated in 1723), and possessing an ancient chime of bells.

—and in the steeple of *Christ Church*, hard by, are the sweet chimes which are the Boston boy's *Ranz des Vaches*, whose echoes follow him all the world over.
Holmes

And here the patriot hung his light,
Which shone though all that anxious night,
To eager eyes of Paul Revere.
E. B. Russell.

3. A venerable church in Alexandria, Va., built in 1766, in which George Washington worshipped, and in which the pew he occupied is still shown.

Christ Church College. The largest and most splendid of the colleges included in the University of Oxford. It was founded in 1524 by Cardinal Wolsey. Its hall is one of the finest in Great Britain.

☞ "Each college has been developed by itself, each age has built in its fashion; here the imposing quadrangle of Christ Church, with its turf, its fountains and its staircases."
Taine, Trans.

Francis [Atterbury] was educated at Westminster School, and carried thence to *Christ Church* a stock of learning which, though really scanty, he through life exhibited with such judicious ostentation that superficial observers believed his attainments to be immense. *Macaulay.*

Christ Consolateur. See CHRISTUS CONSOLATOR.

Christ crowned with Thorns. A well-known picture by Titian (1477–1576) unsurpassed as an example of his art in coloring. In the Louvre, Paris.

Christ disputing with the Doctors. A picture attributed to Leonardo da Vinci (1452–1519). In the National Gallery, London.

Christ giving the Keys to Peter. A fresco by Pietro Perugino (1446–1524). In the Sistine Chapel, Rome.

Christ healing the Sick. A picture by Benjamin West (1738–1820). In the Pennsylvania Hospital.

Christ in Pilgrim's Dress. A noted picture by Fra Angelico Giovanni (*da Fiesole*) (1387–1455). In the Museum of St. Mark, Florence, Italy.

Christ in the Garden. A picture by Giovanni Bellini (1426–1516?), the Italian painter. Now in the National Gallery, London.

Christ in the Garden with the Magdalene. A picture by Antonio Allegri, surnamed Correggio (1494–1534). In the Gallery of Madrid, Spain.

Christ in the Temple. A picture by William Holman Hunt (b. 1827).

☞ "When 34 years of age, Holman Hunt painted *Christ discovered in the Temple*, which thousands flocked to see, not only in London, but in every town where it was exhibited."
Mrs. Tytler.

☞ "Yet neither that picture [Christ in the Temple], great as it is, nor any other of Hunt's, is the best he could have done." *Ruskin.*

☞ "There it hangs before us [an engraving of the picture], but without its glorious color as Holman Hunt gave it forth from the years' study of his earnest soul. I wish you could have seen the picture all aglow with those wonderful hues, somewhat, perhaps, too rainbow-like and shifty in gleams, but yet no tint without meaning, and all conspiring to one of the most glorious effects." *Dean Alford.*

Christ mocked by the Soldiers. A picture by Anthony van Dyck (1599–1641). In the Museum of Berlin, Prussia.

Christ on the Mount of Olives. 1. An admired picture by Antonio Allegri, surnamed Correggio (1494–1534). It was "taken in Joseph Buonaparte's carriage at the battle of Vittoria, returned to the King of Spain, and by him presented to the Duke of Wellington." Now in Apsley House, London.

2. A picture by Raphael Sanzio (1483–1520). Now in England.

3. A noted picture by Friedrich Overbeck (1789–1869). At Hamburg, Germany.

Christ presented by Pilate to the People. A noted picture by Antonio Allegri, called Correggio (1494–1534). In the National Gallery, London.

Christ rejected by the Jewish People. A picture by Benjamin West (1738–1820). In Fairmount Park, Philadelphia.

Christ with the Tribute Money. A celebrated picture by Titian (1477–1576). In the Dresden Gallery.

☞ "This is a finely executed and delicately colored head, but too cold and commonplace in expression to merit the stereotyped praise bestowed upon it."
Eastlake: Handbook of Painting.

2. Another expressive and admirable picture upon the same subject by Guercino (1590–1666). In the Palazzo Durazzo, Genoa, Italy.

Christian Martyrs (in the Coliseum). A picture by Peter F. Rothermel (b. 1817), an American artist. In Fairmount Park, Philadelphia, Penn.

Christianity in the Arts. See INFLUENCE OF CHRISTIANITY IN THE ARTS.

Christiansborg Palace. The royal palace of Denmark, in the city of Copenhagen. It is decorated with many fine works of Thorwaldsen, the Danish sculptor, and contains a gallery of paintings and a museum of Northern antiquities.

Christopher, St. See ST. CHRISTOPHER.

Christ's Charge to Peter. The subject of one of the famous cartoons by Raphael Sanzio (1483–1520), from which the tapestries in the Vatican at Rome were executed.

Christ's College. A foundation of the University of Cambridge, England. Established in 1505.

Christ's Entrance into Jerusalem. A noted picture by Friedrich Overbeck (1789–1869). In the Marienkirche at Lübeck, Germany.

Christ's Hospital. A celebrated public school — upon the site of the monastery of the Grey Friars — in London, at which many eminent men have been educated. It is often called the "Blue-coat School," from the antique uniform which has been worn by the pupils since the foundation of the school in the time of Edward VI. It was not originally founded as a school: its object was to rescue young children from the streets, to shelter, feed, clothe, and lastly educate them. The number of pupils is at present about 800. Coleridge, Charles Lamb, Richardson the novelist, and Leigh Hunt are among the more distinguished "Blues," as the scholars of Christ's Hospital are termed. Charles Lamb has essays entitled "Recollections of Christ's Hospital," and "Christ's Hospital Five and Thirty Years Ago."

☞ "Christ's Hospital is an institution to keep those who have yet held up their heads in the world from sinking; to keep alive the spirit of a decent household, when poverty was in danger of crushing it; to assist those who are the most willing, but not always the most able, to assist themselves; to separate a child from his family for a season, in order to render him back hereafter, with feelings and habits more congenial to it, than he could ever have attained by remaining at home in the bosom of it." *Charles Lamb.*

Christus Consolator. [Christ the Consoler.] A celebrated picture, well-known by reproductions. executed by Ary Scheffer (1795–1858).

The country itself is a *Consolator* colored too heartily for the thin-blooded palette of Scheffer. *John Weiss.*

Christus Remunerator. A picture by Ary Scheffer (1795–1858).

Chrysostom, St. See ST. CHRYSOSTOM.

Church Butte. A natural curiosity in Wyoming Territory, being a mound of rock and earth standing on the level plain, one of the more celebrated of the huge monumental and often fantastically shaped mountains which are found along the line of the Union Pacific Railroad in this part of its course.

☞ "Seen under favorable lights, it imposes upon the imagination like a grand old cathedral going into decay, quaint in its crumbling ornaments, majestic in its height and breadth. They [the Buttes] seem, like the more numerous and fantastic illustrations of nature's frolicsome art in Southern Colorado, to be the remains of granite hills that wind and water, and especially the sand whirlpools which march in lordly force through the air, — literally moving mountains, — have left to hint the past and tell the story of their own achievements. Not unfitly, there as here, they have won the title of "Monuments to the Gods."

Samuel Bowles.

Church Militant and Triumphant. A noted picture by Simone de Martini (Memmi) (1283–1344). In the church of Sta. Maria Novella, Florence, Italy.

Cincinnati, The. A patrician military order or society established in this country at the close of the Revolutionary war, about 1783, by the officers of the American army. The name was derived from the Roman dictator Cincinnatus (456 B.C.), and was adopted in allusion to the change made by them from military to agricultural pursuits. Provision was made that the privilege of membership should pass by descent to the eldest son of each deceased member. The society aimed "to preserve inviolate the rights and liberties of human nature," to promote friendly feeling between the different States, and to aid suffering officers and their families. George Washington was the first president of the order. It was at one time large and popular, but is now fast declining.

Circe. [Lat. *Promontorium Circæum.*] A famous promontory of antiquity, now called *Monte Circello*, situated at the extremity of the Pontine Marshes, in Southern Italy. It was much celebrated by the Latin poets.

Circe. A picture by Dosso Dossi (1474–1558). In the Borghese Gallery, Rome.

Circus Maximus. The famous circus of ancient Rome, founded in the time of the kings, and rebuilt with great splendor by Julius Cæsar. It was in the valley between the Palatine and Aventine mounts. This circus, which was burned in Nero's time, was restored by Vespasian, and enlarged by Constantine. It is said that 250,000 spectators could be accommodated with seats. A confused mass of brickwork is all that now remains of this ruin.

Circus Maximus. A picture by Jean Léon Gérôme (b. 1824), the French painter.

Cirque, La. [The Circle.] A natural curiosity in Southern France, near Gavarnie. It consists of an immense semicircle of rocks, the sides of which are lofty precipices, and the floor of which is strewn with the detritus of the neighboring mountains. It is one of the most remarkable scenes in the Pyrenees, and marks the limits of the French territory.

Cité, Ile de la. See Ile de la Cité.

Città Leonina. See Leonine City.

City Cross. See Dun-Edin's Cross.

Civil Club. This London society was established in the city in 1669, three years after the Great Fire. No record is to be found of the circumstances of its establishment or of the name of the founder. This is the only club which can boast of having the reputed office of a chaplain attached to its staff. All the members are citizens; and the records show, as former members, Parliament men, baronets, and aldermen. One of the rules is, that "but one person of the same trade or profession should be a member of the club." This association, which is now in existence, met for years at the Old

Ship Tavern, in Water Lane, and afterwards at the New Corn Exchange Tavern, in Mark Lane.

Claddagh, The. A populous district, forming one of the suburbs of Galway, Ireland, noted for the peculiarity of its inhabitants, chiefly fishermen, who enjoy certain hereditary "rights," of which they are very tenacious, and any infringement of which is resisted with violence.

☞ "This singular community is still governed by a 'king,' elected annually, and a number of by-laws of their own. At one time this king was absolute, — as powerful as a veritable despot; but his power has yielded, like all despotic powers, to the times. He has still, however, much influence, and sacrifices himself, literally without fee or reward, for 'the good of the people:' he is constantly occupied hearing and deciding causes and quarrels, for his people never by any chance appeal to a higher tribunal. . . . His majesty was at sea; but we were introduced to his royal family, — a group of children and grandchildren, who for ruddy health might have been coveted by any monarch in Christendom."
Mr. and Mrs. Hall.

Clarendon House. A noted mansion which formerly stood in Piccadilly, London, but which was taken down soon after 1675, the name surviving in the modern Clarendon Hotel.

Clarendon Press. A well-known establishment at Oxford, England.

Clava, Stones of. See STONES OF CLAVA.

Clement XIII. A celebrated statue by Antonio Canova (1757-1822). In St. Peter's Church, Rome.

Clement Danes. See ST. CLEMENT DANES.

Clement's Chapel. [Ital. *Capella Clementina.*] A chapel in St. Peter's, Rome, containing, among other things, the tomb of Pius VII., and a monument to him by Thorwaldsen.

Clement's Inn. One of the nine Inns of Chancery in London, so named from its proximity to the church of St. Clement Danes and St. Clement's Well.

Shallow. — I was once of *Clement's Inn*, where I think they will talk of mad Shallow yet. *Silence.* — You were called lusty Shallow then, cousin. *Shallow.* — By the mass, I was called any thing; and I would have done any thing indeed, and roundly too. There was I and Little John Doit of Staffordshire, and Black George Barnes of Staffordshire, and Francis Pickbone, and Will Squele, a Cotswold man: you had not four such swinge bucklers in all the Inns of Court again. . . . *Shallow* — Nay, she must be old; she cannot choose but be old; certain she's old, and had Robin Nightwork by old Nightwork, before I came to *Clement's Inn*. . . . *Shallow.* — I remember at Mile-end green (when I lay at *Clement's Inn*). I was then Sir Dagonet in Arthur's show. . . *Falstaff* — I do remember him at *Clement's Inn*, like a man made after supper of a cheese-paring
Shakespeare.

Clement's Well. See ST. CLEMENT'S WELL.

Cleopatra. A statue by William W. Story (b. 1819).

☞ "The two conceptions, 'Cleopatra' and the 'Libyan Sibyl,' have placed Mr. Story in European estimation at the head of American sculptors." *Jarves.*

☞ "In a word, all Cleopatra, — fierce, voluptuous, passionate, tender, wicked . . . was kneaded into what, only a week or two before, had been a lump of wet clay from the Tiber. Soon, apotheosized in an indestructible material, she would be one of the images that men keep forever, finding a heat in them that does not cool down through the centuries." *Hawthorne.*

Cleopatra and Cæsar. A picture by Jean Léon Gérôme (b. 1824), the French painter.

Cleopatra's Needle. This ancient Egyptian obelisk, one of two which were brought from Heliopolis to Alexandria by one of the Cæsars, stood on the sands near the new fortification wall. The companion obelisk, having fallen, was embedded and preserved in these sands. The obelisks are of red granite of Syene, and Cleopatra's Needle is 70 feet high. It has been recently taken to New York, and is now set up in Central Park.

What obelisk northward meets the curious eye?
Rich as an orient gem it courts the sky;
Its tapering sides a myriad sculptures grace,
Dark mystic writing of earth's early race.

Brought from far Thebes, it decked the splendid pile
Where Beauty, famed forever, shed her smile;
Hence to yon shaft cling memories sweet and rare,
And lore and love their souls are breathing there. *Nicholas Michell.*

Clepsydra. A famous fountain in ancient Athens, Greece. It was so named from its intermittent character, being dependent upon the Etesian winds. It was thought to have an underground communication with Phalerum. The name clepsydra is older than the water-clock of Andronicus.

Clerkenwell. A now thickly settled district in London, so called from a well where the parish clerks (*clerken*) were accustomed to meet for the acting of Scripture plays. A great number of clockmakers, watchmakers, and jewellers, are now to be found in Clerkenwell.

Not content with the easy victories which he [Dr William Sherlock] gained over such feeble antagonists as those who were quartered at *Clerkenwell* and the Savoy, he had the courage to measure his strength with no less a champion than Bossuet, and came out of the conflict without discredit. *Macaulay.*

Clermont, The. The steamer built by Robert Fulton (1765-1815), which ascended the Hudson in September, 1807, the first vessel propelled by steam. The Clermont made regular passages between New York and Albany at the rate of five miles an hour. After the introduction of improved machinery this rate was increased.

Clichy. An old debtor's prison, formerly standing in the Rue de Clichy, Paris. It is now demolished, and imprisonment for debt has now been done away with.

My nephew gives bouquets to Mademoiselle X——, but he will not go to *Clichy* for her. *Taine, Trans.*

Clichy. See BARRIÈRE DE CLICHY.

Cliefden. A seat of the Duke of Sutherland, near Maidenhead, England.

Clifford-street Club. A debating society in London, "which boasted for a short time a brighter assemblage of talent than is usually found to flourish in societies of this description." The club, of which George Canning was a member, met once a month, in the last century, at the Clifford-street Coffee-house.

Clifford's Inn. One of the Inns of Chancery in London, so named from Robert de Clifford, to whom the land was left in the time of Edward II. Clifford's Inn was granted to students-at-law in the reign of Edward III.

Clinton. See CASTLE GARDEN and FORT CLINTON.

Clisson Castle. A ruined castle in the town of Clisson on the Sèvre-Nantaise, near its confluence with the Maine, in France.

It was a dark autumnal day
When first to *Clisson* I would stray.
. . . .
Long grass-grown steps cut o'er the rock,
Which shelves down in a mighty block,
Conduct you to the portals grand,
Which green with ivy proudly stand.
Kenelm H. Digby.

Clisson! thy towers, thy depth of sunless caves,
Thy humid corridors that smother sound,
And thy gapped windows whence the violet waves
A sweet farewell to Legend lingering round,
And mingling whispers echoed from afar,
Invite and chain my steps here where thy mysteries are. *T. G. Appleton.*

Cloaca Maxima. A subterranean canal, well known as the great common sewer of ancient Rome. It is of Etruscan architecture, and, still serving its original purpose, is as firm as when its foundations were laid. It was built at least twenty-four hundred years ago, and is one of the few monuments of Rome whose antiquity has never been assailed.

☞ "Modern scepticism, which has overturned so much of the old faith, has not laid its withering touch upon this venerable monument. Romulus and Numa have been changed into thin shadows, but the stones of the Cloaca are still alive to speak of an antiquity of at least 2,400 years." *G. S. Hillard.*

As a general thing, you do not get elegance short of two or three removes from the soil, out of which our best blood doubtless comes,—quite as good, no doubt, as if it came from those old prize-fighters with iron pots on their heads, to whom some great people are so fond of tracing their descent through a line of small artisans and petty shopkeepers whose veins have held "base" fluid enough to fill the *Cloaca Maxima*.

Holmes.

Clock-tower (of Berne). A noted tower in Berne, Switzerland, formerly a watch-tower at the eastern extremity of the city, but now almost in the centre of the town. The tower is the scene of the following curious spectacle. Three minutes before the hour a cock crows, and claps its wings, whereupon a number of bears (the bear being the heraldic device of Berne) walk around a seated figure; then the cock repeats his signal; and at the striking of the hour the seated figure, which is an old man with a beard, turns an hourglass, raises his sceptre, and opens his mouth as many times as the clock strikes, while the bear on his right inclines his head. The hour is then struck on a bell by a hammer, and the performance is closed as it began by the crowing of a cock.

Closeburn Castle. An ancient feudal mansion in Scotland, near the town of the same name, the seat of the Kirkpatricks, from whom Eugénie, the late Empress of France, traces her Scottish descent.

Cloth Fair. A district in London, formerly much frequented by foreign merchants.

Clotilde, Sainte. See SAINTE CLOTILDE.

Cloud, St. See ST. CLOUD.

Club, The. 1. A celebrated association in London, founded in 1764 by Sir Joshua Reynolds and Dr. Johnson. It originally consisted of nine members, — Sir Joshua Reynolds, Dr. Johnson, Edmund Burke, Dr. Nugent, Mr. Beauclerk, Mr. Langton, Oliver Goldsmith, Mr. Chamier, and Sir John Hawkins. The number was afterwards increased, and the club has included men very distinguished in literature and in science. From 1799 until the removal of that tavern, they met at the Thatched House in St. James's Street. At Garrick's funeral in 1779 the club was entitled the "Literary Club," and subsequently the name was again changed to the "Johnson Club."

☞ "The verdicts pronounced by this conclave on new books were speedily known over all London, and were sufficient to sell off a whole edition in a day, or to condemn the sheets to the service of the trunk-maker and the pastry-cook. Nor shall we think this strange when we consider what great and various talents and acquirements met in the little fraternity. Goldsmith was the representative of poetry and light literature, Reynolds of the arts, Burke of political eloquence and political philosophy. There, too, were Gibbon, the greatest historian, and Jones, the greatest linguist, of the age. Garrick brought to the meetings his inexhaustible pleasantry, his incomparable mimicry, and his consummate knowledge of stage effect. . . . To predominate over such a society was not easy. Yet even over such a society Johnson predominated." *Macaulay.*

☞ "The room is before us. . . . There are the spectacles of Burke, and the tall, thin form of Langton, the courtly sneer of Beauclerk, the beaming smile of Garrick, Gibbon tapping his snuff-box, and Sir Joshua with his trumpet in his ear. In the foreground is that strange figure which is as familiar to us as the figures of those among whom we have been brought up, — the gigantic body, the huge massy face, seamed with the scars of disease; the brown coat, the black worsted stockings, the gray wig with the scorched foretop; the dirty hands, the nails bitten and pared to the quick. We see the eyes and the nose moving with convulsive twitches; we see the heavy form rolling; we hear it puffing; and then comes the 'Why, Sir?' and the 'What then, Sir?' and the 'No, Sir!' and the 'You don't see your way through the question, Sir!'"

Macaulay.

2. The appellation of "The Club" was also given in the time of William III. to a society in Edinburgh, including Sir James Montgomery, Lord Ross, the Earl of Annandale, and other disappointed Whigs, who were, as Macaulay says, dishonest malcontents, who merely desired to

annoy the government and to get places. They formed a union with the Jacobites; and, after giving much trouble to William and Mary, the chiefs betrayed one another, and the club finally broke up in disgrace.

Club of Kings. See KING CLUB.

Club of 1789. See FEUILLANT CLUB.

Clumber Park. The seat of the Dukes of Newcastle, near Worksop, England.

Cluny. See HÔTEL CLUNY.

Clytie. A beautiful relic of Greek sculpture, well known through frequent reproductions. It is one of the Townley marbles in the British Museum. It exhibits the water-nymph, who, according to the Greek legend, fell in love with Apollo, but, meeting with no reciprocation of her passion, became changed into a sunflower, and constantly keeps her face turned towards him. It is said that this image was carried away in his hands by Mr. Townley, its former owner, as being his most valued treasure, at the time when his house was threatened with destruction by a mob.

> I will not have the mad *Clytie*,
> Whose head is turned by the sun.
> *Hood.*

> But to hear her wonder and lament and suggest, with soft, liquid inflections, and low, sad murmurs, in tones as full of serious tenderness for the fate of the lost key as if it had been a child that had strayed from its mother, was so winning, that, had her features and figure been as delicious as her accents, — if she had looked like the marble *Clytie*, for instance, — why, all I can say is— *Holmes*

Cnidian Venus. 1. A famous statue in Cnidus, of the goddess of love, by Praxiteles, the Greek sculptor (fl. B. C. 364), known through report of its beauty. It was burnt in the palace of Lausiacus, in Constantinople, A.D. 475. There are existing copies of some of the works of Praxiteles, and there is a statue in the Vatican supposed to be a copy of this.

2. A celebrated ancient statue, surnamed the Cnidian Venus, considered by some to be the work of Praxiteles, and his masterpiece. Now in the Glyptothek at Munich, Bavaria.

Coach. See CORONATION COACH and LORD MAYOR'S COACH.

Coat, Holy. See HOLY COAT.

Cobbler, The. A popular name in Scotland of the mountain known as Ben Arthur, which rises at the head of Loch Long to the height of over 2,000 feet, and is said to resemble the figure of a cobbler.

> Far away, up in his rocky throne,
> The gaunt old *Cobbler* dwells alone;
> Around his head the lightnings play,
> Where he sits with his lapstone night and day. *Charles Mackay.*

Cobham Hall. A seat of the Earl of Darnley, at Gad's Hill, near London.

Cock, The. 1. A famous old tavern in Fleet Street, London, which still retains some internal decoration of the time of James I.

> ☞ "It is, perhaps, the most primitive place of its kind in the metropolis." *Timbs.*

> ☞ "You go through a little squeezed and panelled passage to enter; and at the end of the passage you pass the little window of the 'snuggery,' or bar, of a most inviting sort on a winter's night, with something simmering on the hob. There sits one whom we might call 'Miss Abbey,'—like Dickens's directress of the 'Fellowship Porters,' — to whom come the waiters, to receive the good hunches of bread 'new or stale'— which she, according to old unvarying rule, chalks down, or up, on the mahogany sill of the door. All is duly sawdusted. The ceiling of the long low tavern room is on our heads. The windows are small, like sky-lights, and give upon the hilly passage or lane outside. There are 'boxes' or pews all round, with green curtains, of mahogany black as ebony. Both the coveted places — say about a sharp Christmas time — are the two that face the good fire, on which sings a huge kettle. The curious old chimney-piece over it is of carved oak, with strange grinning faces, one of which used to delight Dickens, who invited people's attention to it particularly. There is a quaintness, too, in the china trays for the pewter mugs, each decorated with an effigy of a cock. On application, those in office produce to you a well-thumbed copy of Defoe's 'History of the Plague,' where the allusion is made to the establishment, and

also a little circular box, in which is carefully preserved one of the copper tokens of the house — a little lean, battered piece, with the device of a cock, and the inscriptions 'The Cock Alehouse' and 'C. H. M. ATT. TEMPLE BARR. 1655.'" *Fitzgerald.*

☞ "Through a narrow portal, a few doors north-east of Temple Bar, over which a gilt bird proudly struts, have entered many generations of hungry Englishmen. There is no *habitué* of the 'Cock' Tavern in Fleet Street who has not at some period or another of his prandial existence been informed of the extreme antiquity of that ancient dining-place." *Thornbury.*

Thence by water to the Temple, and there to the *Cock* Alehouse, and drank, and eat a lobster, and sang, and mightily merry. *Pepys,* 1668.

O plump head-waiter at *The Cock*,
To which I must resort,
How goes the time? 'Tis five o'clock.
Go fetch a pint of port;
But let it not be such as that
You set before chance-comers,
But such whose father-grape grew fat
On Lusitanian summers.
Tennyson.

2. A well-known public-house in Threadneedle Street, London, taken down in 1841. It was noted for its excellent soups.

3. An old London tavern of unenviable notoriety. It was situated in Bow Street.

☞ The Cock has been a frequent designation for English taverns, which were formerly distinguished by the devices of their signs.

Cock Lane. A lane in London, well known from its association with the "Cock-lane Ghost."

The public were too strenuously employed with their own follies, to be assiduous in estimating mine; so that many of my best attempts in this way have fallen victims to the transient topics of the times, the Ghost in *Cock Lane*, or the siege of Ticonderoga. *Goldsmith.*

Every one must have heard of the *Cock Lane* ghost, and the apparition that guards the regalia in the Tower, which has frightened so many bold sentinels almost out of their wits. *Irving.*

The shade of Denmark fled from the sun,
And the *Cock-lane* ghost from the barn-loft cheer. *Whittier.*

Cockloft Hall. An old mansion in the vicinity of Newark, N.J., celebrated by Washington Irving under this name in the "Salmagundi" papers.

Cockpit, *or* **Phœnix Theatre.** A theatre in London, altered from a cockpit. It occupied the site of Cockpit-alley, now Pitt Place, opposite the Castle Tavern, St. Giles's-in-the-Fields. Knight refers to this as being in 1583 one of the chief London theatres.

Cocoa-Tree. The Tory Chocolate-house in London, of the reign of Queen Anne, was converted into the Cocoa-Tree Club, it is thought before 1746, at which time the house served for the headquarters of the Jacobites in Parliament. Gibbon and Lord Byron were members of the club.

☞ "That respectable body, of which I have the honor of being a member, affords every evening a sight truly English. Twenty or thirty, perhaps, of the first men in the kingdom in point of fashion and fortune, supping at little tables covered with a napkin, in the middle of a coffee-room, upon a bit of cold meat, or a sandwich, and drinking a glass of punch." *Gibbon* (1762).

A Whig will no more go to the *Cocoa-Tree* or Ozinda's, than a Tory will be seen at the Coffee-house, St. James's. *Journey through England,* 1714.

Cocos Castle. A fine ruined fortress in Castile, Spain.

☞ "Its tall towers and clustering turrets still attest its former magnificence, and point to a local style of defensive architecture differing from that of any other part of Europe, but even more picturesque than the best examples of either France or England." *Fergusson.*

Cœlian Hill. [Lat. *Mons Cœlius.*] One of the seven hills of ancient Rome. It is not inhabited at the present day, except by some orders of monks.

Cœnaculum. An ancient building in Jerusalem, known for many centuries by this name, and believed to be the building within which, in an upper chamber (50 feet by 30 feet), Jesus partook of the last supper with his disciples. The building, which is unquestionably very ancient, is also associated by believers with other incidents in the life of Christ and his apostles.

Cold Bath Fields Prison. A jail in London, to which the nickname of the English Bastille was given, about the beginning of the present century, from the number of state prisoners confined in it.

"As he went through *Cold Bath Fields* he saw
A solitary cell;
And the Devil was pleased, for it gave him a hint
For improving his prisons in hell."
Coleridge.

Cold Harbor. A tavern at a country cross-road near the Chickahominy River, and a few miles from Richmond, Va., where, on the 3d of June, 1864, a short but very sanguinary battle took place between the Union and Confederate armies, in which the former are said to have lost over 12,000 men in half an hour. There is another Cold Harbor, nearer the Chickahominy, which consists of a solitary country store.

Coliseum. The most celebrated relic of ancient Rome, now a ruin. It was begun by Vespasian in A.D. 72, and continued by Titus, by whom it was dedicated with a great display of magnificence in A.D. 80. Additions were made by Domitian, and the Coliseum was for nearly 400 years the scene of gladiatorial combats. The building was originally called the *Flavian Amphitheatre*, in honor of its founders; and the first reference to the name Coliseum is found in the fragments of the Venerable Bede, who records the memorable prophecy of Anglo-Saxon pilgrims: —

"While stands the Coliseum, Rome shall stand;
When falls the Coliseum, Rome shall fall;
And when Rome falls, the world."

Large portions of the amphitheatre were removed after the Middle Ages, and were used as material for building palaces and other structures; and the building suffered much spoliation and desecration until it was consecrated in 1750 by Benedict XIV., to the memory of the Christian martyrs who had been sacrificed in it. The popes have of late endeavored to preserve the ruin from further destruction. The name Coliseum is probably derived from the vast size of the building, though some have thought that it was so called from a colossal statue which stood near it. • See COLOSSEUM.

☞ "As it now stands, the Colosseum is a striking image of Rome itself, decayed, vacant, serious, yet grand, half gray and half green, exact on one side and fallen on the other, with consecrated ground in its bosom, inhabited by a beadsman, visited by every cast, for moralists, antiquaries, painters, architects, devotees, all meet here to meditate, to examine, to draw, to measure, and to pray." *Forsyth.*

☞ "Under all aspects, in the blaze of noon, at sunset, by the light of the moon or stars, — the Colosseum stands alone and unapproached. It is the monarch of ruins. It is a great tragedy in stone, and it softens and subdues the mind like a drama of Æschylus or Shakespeare. It is a colossal type of those struggles of humanity against an irresistible destiny, in which the tragic poet finds the elements of his art." *G. S. Hillard.*

☞ "Fast tottering to its fall, but beautiful even in decay, we beheld the grandest remains of antiquity in the world, the majestic ruins of the mighty Colosseum. No relic of former greatness, no monument of human power, no memorial of ages that are fled, ever spoke so forcibly to the heart, or awakened feelings so powerful and unutterable. . . . What solitude and desertion! On that wide arena, so often deep in blood, were now only to be seen the symbols and the worship of a religion then unknown, but which, even in its most corrupted state, had banished from the earth the fiend-like sports and barbarous sacrifices that disgraced human nature." *Eaton.*

☞ "It is the most impressive, the most stately, the most solemn, grand, majestic, mournful sight conceivable. Never, in its bloodiest prime, can the sight of the gigantic Coliseum, full and running over with the lustiest life, have moved one heart, as it must move all who look upon it now, a ruin, — God be thanked: a ruin!" *Dickens.*

Arches on arches! as it were that Rome,
Collecting the chief trophies of her line,
Would build up all her triumphs in one dome,
Her *Coliseum* stands. *Byron.*

—Upon such a night
I stood within the *Coliseum's* wall,
Midst the chief relics of almighty Rome;
The trees which grew along the broken arches
Waved dark in the blue midnight, and the stars
Shone through the rents of ruin. *Byron.*

An amphitheatre's amazing height
Here fills my eye with terror and delight,
That on its public shows unpeopled Rome,
And held uncrowded nations in its womb.
Addison.

2. An immense wooden building erected in Boston, Mass., in 1872, for a Universal Peace Jubilee, and taken down the following year. It was capable of accommodating 50,000 persons. The musical entertainment consisted of American and foreign bands, with an orchestra of 2,000 musicians and a chorus of some 20,000 voices. The "Jubilee" lasted three weeks.

If there were a building on it [the moon] as big as York Minster, as big as the Boston *Coliseum*, the great telescopes like Lord Rosse's would make it out. *Holmes.*

Collége de France. [College of France.] A large building in Paris, where gratuitous lectures on subjects connected with the higher departments of science and literature are delivered by various professors selected from among the most eminent men of France.

Collége Louis-le-Grand. See LOUIS-LE-GRAND.

College of Arms. See HERALDS' COLLEGE.

College of Cardinals. See SACRED COLLEGE.

College of Heralds. See HERALDS' COLLEGE.

College of Physicians. The Royal College of Physicians, London, was founded by Linacre, physician to Henry VIII. The present building in Pall Mall East, corner of Trafalgar Square, was opened in 1825.

College of Surgeons. The Royal College of Surgeons, London, was incorporated by royal charter in 1800. The building (containing the Museum) of the College, in Lincoln's Inn Fields, was first erected in 1800, and rebuilt by Barry in 1835-37.

Collegio di Propaganda Fede. See PROPAGANDA.

Collegio Romano. [Roman College.] A college in Rome, under the superintendence of the Jesuits, built in 1582 for Gregory XIII., and containing, besides a valuable library, the Kircherian Museum, in which is an interesting collection of antiquities.

Cologne Cathedral. This superb edifice at Cologne, in Rhenish Prussia, holds the first rank among German cathedrals, and is one of the most magnificent buildings in the world. It was, according to the common belief, begun in 1248, and progressed slowly till the sixteenth century, when work upon it was for a time abandoned. It fell more and more into decay until Frederick William IV. began its restoration. It was consecrated six hundred years after its foundation. Work upon this edifice has been vigorously prosecuted within the last few years, and it is now substantially completed.

☞ "Externally, its double range of stupendous flying buttresses, and intervening piers, bristling with a forest of purpled pinnacles, strike the beholder with awe and astonishment. If completed, this would be at once the most regular and most stupendous Gothic monument existing." *Hope.*

☞ "The great typical cathedral of Germany, certainly one of the noblest temples ever erected by man in honor of his Creator . . . Generally speaking, it is assumed that the building we now see is that commenced by Conrad de Hochsteden in 1248; but more recent researches have proved that what he did was to rebuild or restore the old double-apse cathedral of earlier date. . . . It seems that the present building was begun about the year 1270-1275, and that the choir was completed in all essentials as we now find it by the year 1322. Had the nave been completed at the same rate of progress, it would have shown a wide deviation of style, and the western front, instead of being erected according to the beautiful design preserved to us, would have been covered with stump tracery, and other vagaries of the late German school, all of which are even now observable in the part of the north-west tower actually erected. . . . In dimensions it is the largest cathedral of Northern Europe; its extreme length being 468, its extreme breadth 275, and its superficies 91,464 feet, which is 20,000 feet more than are covered by Amiens . . . The noblest as well as the most original part of the design of this cathedral is the western façade. This front, considered as an independent feature, without reference to its position, is a very grand conception. . . . We see in Cologne the finest specimen of masonry attempted in the Middle Ages; and, notwithstanding its defects, we may hope to see in the completed design a really beautiful and noble building, worthy of its builders and of the religion to which it is dedicated." *Fergusson.*

Cathedral of Cologne!
Memorial of eld,
When German art excelled,
Long grown with age so gray,
Unfinished till this day,
Cathedral of Cologne!
Friedrich Rückert, Trans.

Cologne, Shrine of the Three Kings of. See SHRINE, etc.

Colombine, La. A picture in the Hermitage at St. Petersburg, thought by some to be a representation of Mona Lisa, whose portrait, known as *La Belle Joconde*, by Leonardo da Vinci, is in the Louvre at Paris. It is ascribed by some to Solario, by others to Bernardo Luini (1460–1530?). See BELLE JOCONDE.

Colonna della Vergine. [Column of the Virgin.] A fine column of the Corinthian order of architecture, formerly belonging to the Basilica of Constantine, now standing in the Piazza di Sta. Maria Maggiore, in Rome.

Colonna Palace. [Ital. *Palazzo Colonna.*] A palace in Rome belonging to the Colonna family, containing a fine picture-gallery, with many art treasures.

☞ "The immense length and beautiful proportions of this building, the noble Corinthian columns and pilasters of *giallo antico* marble that support it, the splendor of its painted roof, and the lustre of its marble pavement, delight the eye with the rare union of magnificence and taste, and well accord with the ancient greatness of the 'Gloriosa Colonna.'" *Eaton.*

We will
Convey her unto the *Colonna Palace*,
Where I have pitched my banner.
Byron.

Colonna. See CAPELLA DELLA COLONNA SANTA, PIAZZA COLONNA, and TRAJAN'S COLUMN.

Colonne de Joux. A marble pillar, thought to be of Celtic origin, on the Pass of the Little St. Bernard, Switzerland.

Colonne de Juillet. [Column of July.] A famous monument of bronze erected on the site of the Bastille, in the square of that name in Paris, France. It is 154 feet in height, and was reared by Louis Philippe, July 28, 1831, in honor of those who fell in the Revolution of 1830. Napoleon's purpose had been to rear a colossal elephant on this spot, and a model plaster-cast of the same might be seen even so late as 1846 at the entrance of the Faubung St. Antoine. After the July revolution a resolution was adopted to supersede the elephant; and the column, the first stone of which had been laid by Louis Philippe, was inaugurated on the 28th of July, 1840. The bassirilievi of the July column are by Barye; the Genius of Liberty by Duret. The names of 615 of the combatants of July, 1830, are recorded upon the column; and in the vault beneath their ashes rest, together with those of combatants who fell in the insurrection of February, 1848.

O July!
A tall and stately shaft, with classic scrolls
Wrought on its antique capital, where stands,
Poised airily a-tiptoe on one foot,
That scarcely presses on the golden globe,
A mighty-winged divinity!
George Gordon McCrae.

Colonne de la Grande Armée. [Column of the Grand Army.] A monument to Napoleon I., erected at Boulogne, France, by the soldiers of the Grand Army. The corner-stone was laid by Marshal Soult in 1804. It is a marble pillar 165 feet in height, crowned by a statue of the Emperor.

Colonne Vendôme. [Column of Vendôme.] A celebrated monumental pillar in the Place Vendôme, Paris. It was erected by Napoleon I. in 1805, to supersede a statue of Louis XIV. by Girardon, which was pulled down in 1792. The column is the work of the architects Denon, Gondouin, and Lépère; and the work was inaugurated on the 15th of August, 1810. It is of stone, and is 143 feet in height, including the pedestal. The shaft is cased with bronze from captured cannon, in the form of a spiral riband, 890 feet in length, on which is represented, in a series of bas-reliefs by Bergeret, the contests and victories of the French during Napoleon's campaigns of 1805. It was surmounted by a statue of Napoleon. In 1871, the column and statue were both pulled down by the Commune. A few days later the republic of M. Thiers resolved to put it in repair and replace it.

Colorado, Chasm of the. See CHASM OF THE COLORADO.

Colosseum, The. 1. A large domed building in London, so named from its colossal size, and not from any resemblance to the Coliseum at Rome. It was built for the exhibition of panoramic views, and other curiosities. See COLISEUM.

☞ "The most varied show in the world, the Colosseum in the Regent's Park, is such an aggregation of wonders, that the visitor must have very small compassion not to be sorry for everybody who has not been there. . . If one were conjured bodily for five minutes to the ruins of Athens, the next five minutes left lounging in a Moorish palace, then dropped into Switzerland, then held in an angel's lap high over London, — winding up with a wilderness of galleries, aviaries, conservatories, statuary, and grottos, — it would probably be not a bit more astonishing than a visit to the Colosseum. The Swiss valley (which has a *real* waterfall, 40 feet high, and a *real* lake) is a complete illusion. And there is another illusion quite as complete, — a view down upon London by night with all the streets illuminated, the shop-windows glittering, the markets crowded, and the moon shining over all. . . . It is next to impossible that any person can lean over the balustrade for five minutes, and mark the fleecy clouds sailing steadily along, lighted as they come within the influence of the halo-encircled moon which has just emerged from the smoke of the great city, and then fading from sight, or occasionally obscuring the stars that twinkle here and there in the apparently illimitable space, — it is next to impossible that they can, after such contemplation, recall themselves immediately to the conviction that the scene before them is but an illusion."

N. P. Willis.

2. An immense iron building in New York, designed for panoramic exhibitions.

Colossus, Borromean. See CARLO BORROMEO.

Colossus of Rhodes. One of the seven "wonders of the world," built, according to Pliny and Strabo, by Chares, a native of Lindos, in the early part of the third century B. C., and overthrown by an earthquake fifty-six years after its erection. This famous statue of Apollo is traditionally supposed to have been placed at the entrance to the harbor of Rhodes, where it served the purpose of a light-house, or pharos; and to have been of such immense size that ships under full sail passed between its legs, which were separated in a straddling attitude. But the traditions of its use as a light house, and of the ungraceful posture of the legs, are not verified by the ancient authors, and may be regarded as fables of comparatively modern growth. According to Strabo and Pliny, the brazen statue of Helios — known popularly as the Colossus — was seventy cubits in height: its thumb was so large that but few men could embrace it with their arms. Pliny says that it cost 300 talents; and the Saracens, who captured Rhodes in 672, are said to have sold the brass of which it was composed to a Jewish merchant for £36,000.

The antique Rhodian will likewise set forth
The great *Colosse*, erect to memorie;
And what else in the world is of like worth,
Some greater learned wit will magnify.

Spenser.

Colossus of the Apennines. A gigantic statue by John of Bologna (1524–1608), at Pratolino, a little place among the Apennines.

☞ "This remarkable figure impresses one like a relic of the Titans. He is represented as half-kneeling, supporting himself with one hand, while the other is pressed upon the head of a dolphin, from which a little stream falls into the lake. The height of the figure when erect would amount to more than sixty feet. The limbs are formed of pieces of stone joined together, and the body of stone and brick. His rough hair and eyebrows, and the beard which reached nearly to the ground, are formed of stalactites, taken from caves and fastened together in a dripping and crusted mass. These hung also from his limbs and body, and gave him the appearance of Winter in his mail of icicles. . . . We entered his body, which contains a small-sized room: it was even possible to ascend through his neck, and look out at his ear. The face is stern and grand, and the architect has given to it the majestic air and sublimity of the Apennines." *Bayard Taylor.*

Columba, Church and Abbey of. A famous religious and monastic establishment at Bobbio, Italy, founded by St. Columba in the early part of the seventh century. It became a celebrated seat of learning in the Middle Ages.

Columba's Isle. A name sometimes given to the island Iona, near Scotland, from the fact that here St. Columba founded a monastery and introduced Christianity into Scotland. It was formerly the favorite royal cemetery. Macbeth was probably the last Scotch monarch buried here. The island contains many ecclesiastical ruins and antiquities, of which St. Oran's Chapel is the finest.

Columbia, The. A noted frigate of the United States Navy, in service in the war of 1812. She was built at Washington.

Columbus at the Council of Salamanca. An historical picture by Emmanuel Leutze (1816–1868). In the Gallery at Düsseldorf in Rhenish Prussia.

Columbus. See FORT COLUMBUS and LANDING OF COLUMBUS.

Column of July. See COLONNE DE JUILLET.

Column of M. Aurelius Antoninus. See ANTONINE COLUMN.

Column of Phocas. See PHOCAS, COLUMN OF.

Column of Trajan. See TRAJAN'S COLUMN.

Column of the Flagellation. A broken shaft of porphyry in the Church of the Holy Sepulchre at Jerusalem. It is traditionally identified with the pillar to which Jesus was bound when he was delivered by Pilate to be scourged.

Column of Vendôme. See COLONNE VENDÔME.

Combat, Barrière du. See BARRIÈRE DU COMBAT.

Comédie Française. The former name of the Théâtre Français, and one which is still sometimes given to it. See THÉÂTRE FRANÇAIS.

La *Comédie-Française* a des retours inattendus de faveur et de vogue. *Ste.-Beuve.*

Coming through the Rye. A picture by George H. Boughton, the landscape and *genre* painter.

Common, The. A well-known and beautiful public park in Boston, Mass. It comprises about 48 acres.

☞ "The Common is now, as under the government of John Winthrop, the common land of the inhabitants of Boston. Its original purpose was for pasturage and military parade. From the earliest times, until after Boston became a city, the tinkling of bells and lowing of cattle might be heard across its hills and dales. . . . No other city of America has fifty acres of green turf and noble forest trees in its very midst. Its central position renders it accessible from every quarter of the town; and although it is not dignified with the name of a park, it is at once the glory and beauty of the ancient peninsula." *Drake.*

☞ "On the south there is a small but pleasant Common, where the Gallants a little before sunset walk with their *Marmalet-Madams*, as we do in Moorfields, etc., till the nine o'clock Bell rings them home to their respective habitations, when presently the

Constables walk their rounds to see good order kept, and to take up loose people." *John Josselyn*, 1675.

Commons, House of. See HOUSE OF COMMONS.

Commonwealth Avenue. A fine street in Boston, Mass., the widest in the city, and lined with elegant buildings.

Communion of St. Francis. A picture by Peter Paul Rubens (1577–1640), and regarded as one of his finest works. It is now in the Antwerp Museum.

Communion of St. Jerome. 1. A celebrated painting in the Vatican at Rome, the masterpiece of Domenico Zampieri, surnamed Domenichino (1581–1641), and regarded by many as one of the three greatest pictures in the world, which honor it shares with the Transfiguration and the Sistine Madonna of Raphael. It was originally designed for the church of Ara Cœli, Rome.

☞ "The last communion of St. Jerome is the subject of one of the most celebrated pictures in the world, — the *St. Jerome* of Domenichino, which has been thought worthy of being placed opposite to the Transfiguration of Raphael in the Vatican." *Mrs. Jameson.*

2. A picture by Agostino Caracci (1558–1602). In the gallery of Bologna, Italy.

Communion of the Apostles. An altar-piece, executed for the brotherhood of Corpus Christi, by Justus of Ghent, a Flemish painter, and now in the town gallery of Urbino, Italy.

Compagnie, La Court de bone. See COURT DE BONE COMPAGNIE.

Compass Hill. The name given to a hill in the island of Canna, one of the Hebrides, from the remarkable variation in the compass experienced by the vessels which pass it.

Compostella, Shrine at. See SHRINE OF ST. JAMES.

Comstock Lode. A famous mine of silver-and-gold-bearing quartz, situated under Virginia City and Gold Hill, Nev. It is said to be the most profitable mining deposit in the world. It has depths of 1,000 feet, and there are more miles of streets underground than in the city above. The ledge or lode was discovered in 1859. It is reported to have yielded at times over $10,000,000 of silver in a year.

Conception. See GREAT CONCEPTION OF SEVILLE and IMMACULATE CONCEPTION.

Concert Champêtre. A picture by Giorgio Barbarelli, commonly called Giorgione (1477–1511). In the tribune of the Louvre, Paris. There is a similar picture in the Pitti Palace, Florence, Italy.

Conciergerie, La. The ancient prison of the Palais de Justice, Paris. During the Reign of Terror the prisoners were confined here before being sent to the guillotine. 288 prisoners were killed here by the mob in September, 1792. It was from here that the fatal carts took their daily loads (*fournées*, batches) to the guillotine. Here Marie Antoinette was confined from Aug. 1, 1793, until her execution, Oct. 26. Here Malesherbes, Bailly, Madame Roland, Danton, and also Robespierre and 17 followers, were confined before being taken to execution. Napoleon III. was imprisoned here after the failure of the attempt on Boulogne. The prison is now used for the temporary confinement of criminals.

Concorde, Place de la. See PLACE DE LA CONCORDE.

Conduit House. See WHITE CONDUIT HOUSE.

Confiance, La. The flag-ship of Commodore Downie, the commander of the British fleet, in the naval battle on Lake Champlain in September, 1814. She surrendered to the American flagship *Saratoga*, commanded by Commodore Macdonough.

Confusion of Tongues. A picture by Wilhelm Kaulbach (b. 1805). In Berlin, Prussia.

Congress, The. 1. The flag-ship of the American fleet on Lake Champlain in 1776. After a desperate engagement, the *Congress*, which had fought four hours surrounded by the enemy's ships, was run ashore and blown up by her commander.

2. A vessel of the United States Navy destroyed by the Confederate ram *Merrimack*, in Hampton Roads, March 8, 1862.

Congress. See MÜNSTER CONGRESS.

Congress Park. A low ridge around the Congress and Columbian Springs at Saratoga Springs, N.Y. It is a pleasant ground, opposite the principal hotels, well laid out, and beautified with fine elms.

Congressional Cemetery. A beautifully situated burial-ground in Washington, containing monuments to those members of Congress who have died while in office.

Congressional Library. A collection of books intended primarily for the use of members of Congress, and kept in the Capitol at Washington. It is now the largest library in the United States. The library was founded by Congress in 1800. In 1814 it was destroyed by the British. It underwent a partial loss by fire in 1851, when 35,000 volumes were burned, since which time it has rapidly increased in size.

Conisborough Castle. An ancient Norman castle, supposed to have been built within the first century after the conquest of England. The most remarkable part of it is a grand tower strengthened by six massive buttresses, which is made the scene of one of the chapters in Sir Walter Scott's novel of "Ivanhoe."

Connoisseurs, The. A noted picture by Sir Edwin Landseer (1803–1873), the most celebrated modern painter of animals. It was painted in 1865, and presented by the artist to the Prince of Wales, its present owner.

☞ "The man behind his work was seen through it, — sensitive, variously-gifted, manly, genial, tender-hearted, simple and unaffected; and, if any one wishes to see at a glance nearly all we have written, let him look at his own portrait painted by himself with a canine *connoisseur* on each side."

Monkhouse.

Consecration of Thomas à Becket. A picture attributed to Jan Van Eyck (1370–1441). It is now in the collection of the Duke of Devonshire at Chatsworth, England.

Conseil Paternal. [Paternal Advice.] A celebrated picture by Gerard Terburg (1608–1681), the Dutch *genre*-painter. It is now in the Amsterdam Gallery. There are replicas of this picture in the Museum at Berlin, and in the Bridgewater Gallery.

Conservative Club. A Tory club in London, founded in 1840. The club-house, opened in 1845, is in St. James's Street, partly upon the site of the old Thatched House Tavern.

☞ "This is the second Club of the Conservative party; and many of its chiefs are honorary members, but rarely enter it: Sir Robert Peel is said never to have entered this Club-house except to view the interior. Other leaders have, however, availed themselves of the Club influences to recruit their ranks from its working strength. This has been political ground for a century and a half; for here, at the Thatched House Tavern, Swift met his political Clubs, and dined with Tory magnates; but with fewer appliances than in the present day: in Swift's time 'the wine being always brought by him that is president.'" *Timbs.*

Was it never thy hard fortune, good Reader, to attend any Meeting convened for Public purposes; any Bible Society, Reform, *Conservative*, Thatched-Tavern, Hogg-Dinner, or other such Meeting?

Carlyle.

Conservators, Palace of the. See PIAZZA DEL CAMPIDOGLIO.

Consolator. See CHRISTUS CONSOLATOR.

Consolidated Virginia. One of the richest silver-mines in America, situated at Virginia City, Nev. It is said to have at times yielded $10,000,000 of silver in a year. Also known as the Big Bonanza.

Conspiracy of Catiline. A picture by Salvator Rosa (1615-1673), one of the best of his works. In the Pitti Palace, Florence, Italy.

Constant-Warwick, The. The first frigate in the British navy. She was built in 1649.

Constantine. See ARCH OF CONSTANTINE and VICTORY OF CONSTANTINE.

Constantine and Maxentius. See BATTLE BETWEEN CONSTANTINE AND MAXENTIUS.

Constantino, Sala di. See SALA DI CONSTANTINO.

Constellation, The. A noted vessel of the United States navy, built in 1798. She was the flagship of Commodore Truxtun, and was sent in pursuit of French cruisers. In 1799 she captured the famous French frigate *Insurgente*, 40 guns, — a victory which caused great exultation throughout the United States. The London merchants sent Truxtun a service of silver plate, and the papers were filled with his praises.

We sailed to the West Indies, in order to annoy
The invaders of our commerce, to burn, sink, or destroy;
Our *Constellation* shone so bright,
The Frenchmen could not bear the sight,
And away they scampered in affright,
From the brave Yankee boys.

Old Song.

Constitution, The. A famous frigate of the United States navy, launched at Boston in 1797, and noted for the brilliant service she rendered in the attack upon Tripoli, in 1804, and for the part she took in the second war with Great Britain. On the 19th of August, 1812, the *Guerrière* frigate was captured by her; and on the 29th of December, in the same year, the frigate *Java* surrendered to her. The well-known poem entitled "Old Ironsides," by Oliver Wendell Holmes (b. 1809), which begins: —

"Ay, tear her tattered ensign down!"

was printed at the time of the proposal to break up the frigate Constitution as being no longer fit for service. This renowned frigate now lies at one of the piers of the United States Navy Yard in Philadelphia. She has been of late used as a school-ship.

☞ "In the course of two years and nine months [July, 1812, to March, 1815] this ship had been in three actions, had been twice critically chased, and had captured five vessels of war, two of which were frigates, and a third frigate-built. In all her service . . . her good fortune was remarkable. She never was dismasted, never got ashore, and scarcely ever suffered any of the usual accidents of the sea. Though so often in battle, no very serious slaughter ever took place on board her. One of her commanders was wounded, and four of her lieutenants had been killed, two on her own decks, and two in the *Intrepid*; but, on the whole, her entire career had been that of what is usually called 'a lucky ship.' Her fortune, however, may perhaps be explained in the simple fact, that she had always been well commanded. In her two last cruises, she had probably possessed as fine a crew as ever manned a frigate. They were principally from New England; and it has been said of them that they were almost qualified to fight the ship without her officers."

James Fenimore Cooper.

In the year 1812, when your arms were covered by disaster, — when Winchester had been defeated, when the army of the North-west had surrendered, and when the feeling of despondency hung like a cloud over the land, — who first relit the fires of national glory, and made the welkin ring with the shouts of victory? It was the American sailor. And the names of Hull and the *Constitution* will be remembered as long as we have left any thing worth remembering.

R. F. Stockton.

Old Ironsides at anchor lay
In the harbor of Mahon;
A dead calm rested on the bay, —
The waves to sleep had gone;
When little Hal, the captain's son,
A lad both brave and good,
In sport, up shroud and rigging ran,
And on the main truck stood!

G. P. Morris.

Constitution Hill. An eminence bearing this name in London, near Buckingham Palace.

Conti, Torre dei. See TORRE DEI CONTI.

Convent. For names beginning with the word CONVENT, see the next prominent word of the title; e.g., CONVENT OF MONSERRAT, see MONSERRAT.

Conversazione, La. A celebrated picture by Niccolo dell' Abbate, called also Niccolo da Modena (1512–1571). In the Institute of Bologna, Italy.

Conversazione. See SACRA CONVERSAZIONE.

Conversion of St. Maurice by Erasmus. A picture by Matthew Grunewald (d. 1530), a German painter. It was executed for a church at Halle, but is now at Munich, Bavaria.

Conversion of St. Paul. A large fresco painting by Michael Angelo (1475–1564). In the Vatican, Rome.

Conversion of St. Paul. One of the famous cartoons by Raphael Sanzio (1483-1520), from which the tapestries in the Vatican were executed.

Cooper Institute. This institution in New York City was so named after Peter Cooper (b. 1791), by whom it was founded and endowed. It has a large library and reading-room, and occupies a brown-stone building which covers an entire square. The Institute was designed especially for the benefit of the working classes, and furnishes free instruction to some 3,000 pupils annually.

Coppet. This château, near Geneva, formerly belonged to Necker, the banker of Paris, afterwards minister of finance to Louis XVI., who died here in 1804. His daughter, Madame de Staël, also lived here many years, and her desk, and portrait by David, are exhibited here. She and her father were buried in a chapel near the castle. The whole now belongs to Madame de Staël's son-in-law, the Duc de Broglie.

Copp's Hill. An elevation in the north-east part of Boston, Mass. In the early period of the Revolutionary war it was occupied by a British fort, from which hot shot were thrown into Charlestown, at the battle of Bunker's Hill, setting the town on fire. An ancient burial-ground on the summit of the hill, containing the graves of several of the early Puritan ministers, is reverentially preserved.

> Perhaps you sometimes wander in through the iron gates of the *Copp's Hill* burial-ground. You love to stroll round among the graves that crowd each other in the thickly peopled soil of that breezy summit. *Holmes.*

Corcoran Gallery. A fine art-building in Washington, erected and endowed by W. W. Corcoran, a banker of Washington. It contains a rich collection of bronzes, casts, and statues, and a gallery of paintings.

Cordonnata, La. [Ital. *Cordoni*, steps.] The name given to the imposing staircase which leads by an easy ascent from the Piazza di Ara Cœli to the Capitol, in Rome. It was opened on the occasion of the entrance of the Emperor Charles V. in 1536. See ARA CŒLI.

Cordouan, Tour de. See TOUR DE CORDOUAN.

Cordova, Mosque of. See MOSQUE OF CORDOVA.

Corfe Castle. An ancient and celebrated fortress, formerly one of the strongest in the country, on the isle of Purbeck in the county of Dorset, England. It is now in ruins.

Cor-Gawr. See DANCE OF THE GIANTS.

Cork Convent. A curious hermitage, so called, near Cintra in Portugal, situated on the brow of a precipice nearly 3,000 feet above the level of the sea, and lined with cork as a protection against the moisture that prevails there.

Cornaro Family. A picture by Titian (1477–1576), representing a family-group in the performance of religious functions. It was in Northumberland House, London, previous to the destruction of that mansion.

Cornell University. An institution of learning in Ithaca, N.Y. It was founded in 1865 by Ezra Cornell.

Corinna at the Cape of Miseno. A noted picture by François Gérard (1770–1836), the eminent French painter.

Cornfield, The. A picture by John Constable (1776–1837). In the National Gallery, London.

Cornhill. One of the principal streets of London, named from a corn-market which in ancient times was there held. Chaucer speaks of a high May-pole which was set up here, as the "great shaft of Cornhill." Here was also the Standard, a conduit set up in 1582. Thomas Gray (1716–1771) was born in Cornhill.

Cornice Road. A famous coast-road between Nice and Genoa, running along the shore of the Mediterranean Sea, at a considerable elevation. It derives its name from its situation on the cornice or edge of the shore, and is noted for its beautiful views.

> Upon the *Cornice Road* with Italy behind him and home before (such home as he knows), he thinks once more of those he has left. *D. G. Mitchell.*

Cornwallis's Cave. An excavation in a bluff at Yorktown, Va., said on good authority to have been made and used as a council-chamber by Gen. Cornwallis during the siege of Yorktown.

Cornwallis, Surrender of. See SURRENDER OF CORNWALLIS.

Coronation Chair. There are two Coronation Chairs, so called, in Westminster Abbey, London. One, the older of the two, contains the famous Coronation Stone (the Prophetic or Fatal Stone of Scone), and is the chair in which all the kings of England from the time of Edward I. have been crowned. The other chair was made for the coronation of Mary, queen of William III. See STONE OF SCONE.

> ☞ "The chair is of oak, carved and hacked over with names, and on the bottom some one has recorded his name with the fact that he once slept in it." *Bayard Taylor.*

> Methinks I sate in seat of majesty
> In the Cathedral Church of Westminster,
> And in that *Chair* where kings and queens are crowned. *Shakespeare.*

Coronation Coach. [*or* Queen's State Coach.] An elaborate and ornate carriage used by the sovereigns of England for state purposes on occasion of coronations and the like. The cost of it is said to have been £8,000. It is kept at the Royal Mews, Pimlico, and is exhibited on application. See LORD MAYOR'S COACH.

> ☞ "It is a beautiful object though crowded with improprieties. Its supports are Tritons, not very well adapted to land carriage; and formed of palm-trees, which are as little aquatic as Tritons are terrestrial. The crowd to see it, on the opening of the Parliament, was greater than at the coronation, and much more mischief done." *Walpole.*

Coronation of Charlemagne. See CHARLEMAGNE CROWNED BY LEO III.

Coronation of the Virgin. [Ital. *Maria Coronata dal divin suo Figlio*, Fr. *Le Couronnement de la Sainte Vierge.*] A favorite subject of representation by the great painters of the Middle Ages, in which Christ is exhibited in the act of crowning his Mother. Of the numerous compositions upon this subject, the following may be named as being among the more celebrated.

Coronation of the Virgin. A picture by Angelico da Fiesole (1387–1455), the Italian painter. It is now in the Louvre, Paris.

> ☞ "One of the most beautiful and celebrated of the pictures of Angelico da Fiesole is the 'Coronation,' now in the Louvre. Formerly it stood over the high altar of the Church of St. Dominic at Fiesole. The composition is conceived as a grand regal ceremony, but the beings who figure in it are touched with a truly celestial grace. The spiritual beauty of the heads, the delicate tints of the coloring, an ineffable charm of brightness and repose shed over the whole, give to this lovely picture an effect like that of a church hymn sung at some high festival." *Mrs. Jameson.*

Coronation of the Virgin. A noted picture by Fra Angelico,

Giovanni (*da Fiesole*) (1387-1455). In the Museum of St. Mark, Florence, Italy.

Coronation of the Virgin. A picture by Giovanni da Fiesole, called Fra Angelico (1387-1455). In the Uffizi Palace, Florence, Italy.

Coronation of the Virgin. A picture by Fra Filippo Lippi (1412-1469). In the Academy at Florence, Italy.

Coronation of the Virgin. A picture undertaken by Raphael Sanzio (1483-1520). In the Vatican, Rome.

☞ "In the Vatican is the *Coronation* attributed to Raphael. That he designed the cartoon, and began the altar-piece, for the nuns of Monte-Luce, near Perugia, seems beyond all doubt; but it is equally certain that the picture as we see it was painted almost entirely by his pupils Giulio Romano and Gian Francesco Penni. . . . Thus in highest heaven, yet not out of sight of earth, in beatitude past utterance, in blessed fruition of all that faith creates and love desires, amid angel hymns and starry glories, ends the pictured life of Mary, Mother of our Lord." *Mrs. Jameson.*

Coronation of the Virgin. A cartoon executed for one of the tapestries of the Sistine Chapel in the Vatican, by Raphael Sanzio (1483-1520). Both the cartoon and the tapestry have disappeared.

Coronation of the Virgin. A picture by Annibale Caracci (1560-1609). Formerly belonging to Rogers the poet. Now in the National Gallery, London.

☞ "This picture shows how deeply Annibale Caracci had studied Correggio in the magical chiaro-oscuro, and the lofty but somewhat mannered grace of the figures." *Mrs. Jameson.*

Coronation of the Virgin. A picture by Peter Paul Rubens (1577-1640). Now at Brussels, Belgium.

Coronation Stone. See STONE OF SCONE.

Corps Législatif. See PALAIS DU CORPS LÉGISLATIF.

Corpus Christi College. 1. A foundation of the University of Cambridge, England. Established in 1352.

2. One of the colleges of the University of Oxford. It was founded in 1516.

Corsham House. A noble mansion near Chippenham, England, the seat of Lord Methuen, and celebrated for its choice collection of pictures.

Corsini Chapel. [Ital. *Capella Corsini.*] A chapel in the church of St. John Lateran, in Rome, erected in 1729, in honor of St. Andrea Corsini. It is very richly decorated, ranking perhaps next to the Borghese Chapel in this respect.

Corsini Palace. [Ital. *Palazzo Corsini.*] 1. A splendid palace in Rome, built for the Riario family, and changed to its present form by Clement XII., in 1729, for his nephew, Cardinal Corsini. It was the resort of Michael Angelo and of Erasmus, among others, and was the residence of Christina, Queen of Sweden, who died here in 1689. It contains a library and picture-gallery.

2. A palace in Florence, Italy, containing an interesting gallery of pictures.

Corso. [The Course.] The principal street in modern Rome, about a mile in length, extending from the Porta del Popolo to near the foot of the Capitoline Hill. It is the great thoroughfare of the city, and the scene of the festivities of the Carnival.

☞ "The reader will have the goodness to walk with me into the Corso at about half-past two on a carnival day. . . . The usually commonplace and unexpressive fronts of the houses have suddenly put on life and bloom like that which a mass of multiflora in full flower gives to a dead wall." *G. S. Hillard.*

☞ "The Corso is a street a mile long; a street of shops, and palaces, and private houses, sometimes opening into a broad piazza. There are verandas and balconies, of all shapes and sizes, to almost every house, — not on one story alone, but often to one room or another on every story, — put there in general with so little order or regularity, that if, year after year, and season after season, it had rained balconies, hailed balconies, snowed balconies, blown balconies, they could scarcely have come into existence in a more disorderly manner." *Dickens.*

Cortes, Plaza de las. See PLAZA DE LAS CORTES.

Corykian Cave. A grotto or cavern in Greece about 300 feet long, nearly 200 feet wide, and about 40 feet in height. It contains fine stalactite and stalagmite formations. In this cave the inhabitants sought refuge when the Persians marched upon Delphi, and in the Greek revolution it again served as a retreat. The inhabitants say that this cavern which they call Σαράντ' Ἀυλαί, the Forty Courts, will hold 3,000 people.

Cosmo I. An equestrian statue by Giovanni da Bologna, called Il Fiammingo (1530–1608). In the Piazza della Signoria, Florence, Italy.

Costanza, Strada di. See STRADA DI COSTANZA.

Cothele House. An ancient and beautiful mansion, belonging to the Earl of Edgecumbe, one of the most interesting of the historic halls of England. It is near Plymouth.

Cotopaxi. A well-known picture by Frederic Edwin Church (b. 1826), the American landscape-painter.

☞ "In this picture the artist represents Cotopaxi in continuous but not violent eruption; the discharges of thick smoke occur in successive but gradual jets, and, seen at a distance, the column rises slow and majestic." *Tuckerman.*

Cottage City. A name by which the village of Oak Bluffs on Martha's Vineyard is often known. It was laid out in 1868, and contains a large number of summer cottages and seashore residences.

Cottonian Library. A very valuable collection of ancient charters, records, and other MSS., gathered by Sir Robert Bruce Cotton. The collection was purchased by Parliament in 1700, and in 1757 it was transferred to the British Museum, of which it now makes a part.

Count Castiglione. See CASTIGLIONE.

Count of Toulouse, Pilgrimage of the. A picture by Jan (or Jannyn) Gossart (d. 1532), the Flemish painter. It is now in the possession of Sir John Nelthorpe at his seat, Scawby, Lincolnshire, England.

Coup de Canon. [The Cannon-shot.] A picture by Jan Joseph Wynand Nuyen (1813–1839), and one of his best.

Couriers of the Pasha. A picture by Jean Léon Gérôme (b. 1824), the French painter.

Course de Barberi. A famous picture by Emile-Jean-Horace Vernet (1789–1863), representing the horses setting out for the carnival race, in the Corso, Rome.

Course of Empire. An allegorical painting by Thomas Cole (1801–1848), the American painter. Now in the Gallery of the New York Historical Society.

Court de bone Compagnie. A society in England, of the time of Henry IV., regarded as the earliest instance of an English "Club," although that name did not come into use until a later period. The poet Occleve belonged to this society, and Chaucer was probably a member.

☞ "This society of four centuries and a half since was evidently a jovial company." *Timbs.*

Court, Inns of. See INNS OF COURT.

Court of Lions. A celebrated apartment in the palace of the Alhambra, in Spain, originally a Moorish cloister, and luxuriously adorned with Arabian sculptures, mosaics, and paintings. See ALHAMBRA.

☞ "This is the gem of Arabian art in Spain — its most beautiful and most perfect example. It has, however, two defects which take it entirely out of the range of monumental art; the first is its size, which is barely that of a modern parish church, and smaller than many ball-rooms; the second, its materials, which are only wood covered with stucco. In this respect the Alhambra forms a perfect contrast to such a building as the Hall at Karnac, or any of the greater monumental edifices of the ancient world. But in fact no comparison is applicable between objects totally different. Each is a true representative of the feeling and character of the people by whom it was raised. The Saracenic plaster-hall would be totally out of place and contemptible beside the great temple-palace of Thebes; while the granite works of Egypt would be considered monuments of ill-directed labor if placed in the palaces of the gay and luxurious Arab fatalist, to whom the present was every thing, and the enjoyment of the passing hour all in all." *Fergusson.*

Court of the Great Mogul. A most elaborate and costly trinket in the Green Vault at Dresden, consisting of some 138 figures wrought in gold, and representing the Great Mogul upon his throne surrounded by his court.

Courtesan. See YOUNG COURTESAN.

Coussin Vert. See VIERGE A L'OREILLER VERD.

Coutts's Bank. An establishment in London which has been used by the royal family since the time of Queen Anne.

Covent Garden. A locality in London, lying between the Strand and Long Acre, and which has been of much interest and celebrity for centuries. According to Strype, it was so named from the garden belonging to the large convent where Exeter House formerly stood. It was formerly occupied by taverns and coffee-houses, which were much resorted to by the wits and literary characters of the time, among whom were Addison, Butler, Sir Richard Steele, Dryden, Otway, Pope, Cibber, Fielding, Warburton, Churchill, Bolingbroke, Dr. Johnson, Rich, Woodward, Booth, Garrick, Wilkes, Macklin, Peg Woffington, Kitty Clive, Mrs. Pritchard, the Duchess of Bolton, Lady Derby, Lady Thurlow, the Duchess of St. Albans, Sir Godfrey Kneller, Sir Peter Lely, Sir James Thornhill, Lambert, Hogarth, and Samuel Foote. See also COVENT GARDEN MARKET and COVENT GARDEN THEATRE.

☞ "The convent becomes a play-house; monks and nuns turn actors and actresses. The garden, formal and quiet, where a salad was cut for a lady abbess, and flowers were gathered to adorn images, becomes a market, noisy and full of life, distributing thousands of fruits and flowers to a vicious metropolis." *Walter Savage Landor.*

☞ "Courtly ideas of Covent Garden as a place with famous coffee-houses, where gentlemen wearing gold-laced coats and swords had quarrelled and fought duels; costly ideas of Covent Garden, as a place where there were flowers in winter at guineas apiece, pine-apples at guineas a pound, peas at guineas a pint; picturesque ideas of Covent Garden, as a place where there was a mighty theatre, showing wonderful and beautiful sights to richly-dressed ladies and gentlemen, and which was forever far beyond the reach of poor Fanny, or poor uncle; desolate ideas of Covent Garden, as having all those arches in it, where the miserable children in rags, among whom she had just now passed, like young rats, slunk and hid, fed on offal, huddled together for warmth, and were hunted about; . . . teeming ideas of Covent Garden, as a place of past and present mystery, romance, abundance, want, beauty, ugliness, fair country gardens, and foul street gutters, all confused together, — made the room dimmer than it was, in Little Dorrit's eyes, as they timidly saw it from the door." *Dickens.*

Where *Covent Garden's* famous temple stands,
That boasts the work of Jones' immortal hands,
Columns with plain magnificence appear,
And graceful porches lead along the square;
Here oft my course I bend, when lo! from far
I spy the furies of the football war.
Gay.

All the town was in an uproar of admiration of his poem, the 'Campaign,' which Dick Steele was spouting at every coffee-house in Whitehall and *Covent Garden.* *Thackeray.*

Covent Garden Market. The great fruit, vegetable, and herb-market of London, originated about 1656. The present market-place was erected in 1830 by the Duke of Bedford. See also Cov-

ENT GARDEN and COVENT GARDEN THEATRE.

☞ "The two great national theatres on one side, a churchyard full of mouldy but undying celebrities on the other; a fringe of houses studded in every part with anecdote and history; an arcade, often more gloomy and deserted than a cathedral aisle; a rich cluster of brown old taverns — one of them filled with the counterfeit presentment of many actors long since silent, who scowl or smile once more from the canvas upon the grandsons of their dead admirers; a something in the air which breathes of old books, old pictures, old painters, and old authors; a place beyond all other places one would choose in which to hear the chimes at midnight; a crystal palace — the representative of the present — which peeps in timidly from a corner upon many things of the past; a withered bank, that has been sucked dry by a felonious clerk; a squat building, with a hundred columns and chapel-looking fronts, which always stands knee-deep in baskets, flowers, and scattered vegetables; a common centre into which Nature showers her choicest gifts, and where the kindly fruits of the earth often nearly choke the narrow thoroughfares; a population that never seems to sleep, and does all in its power to prevent others sleeping; a place where the very latest suppers and the earliest breakfasts jostle each other on the footways, — such is Covent Garden Market, with some of its surrounding features." *Thackeray.*

☞ "Such stale, vapid, rejected cabbage-leaf and cabbage-stalk dress, such damaged orange countenance, such squashed pulp of humanity, are open to the day nowhere else." *Dickens.*

Covent Garden Theatre. The Italian Opera House, Bow Street, London. The first building of this name was opened by Rich, the celebrated harlequin, in 1732. The present house, the third theatre upon this spot, was constructed in 1858 for operatic performances, and is one of the largest theatres in the world. See also COVENT GARDEN and COVENT GARDEN MARKET.

Coventry *or* Ambassadors' Club. A London club, founded about 1853, and closed in March, 1854.

☞ "The Coventry Club was a club of most exclusive exquisites, and was rich in diplomacy; but it blew up in admired confusion." *New Quarterly Review.*

Cowgate, The. A well-known street in the Old Town of Edinburgh, Scotland. It was once a fashionable quarter, now occupied only by the poorest class of inhabitants.

Cradle of Liberty. See FANEUIL HALL.

Craig-crook Castle. This pleasantly situated castle overlooking Edinburgh, Scotland, was formerly the residence of Lord Jeffrey.

Craigenputtoch. A farm in a lonely region, among granite hills and black morasses, fifteen miles north-west of Dumfries, Scotland. It was the former home of Thomas Carlyle (1795–1881). It was here that his first great original work, "Sartor Resartus," was written. It was during his seclusion in Craigenputtoch also that the brilliant series of essays contributed to the Edinburgh, Westminster, and Foreign Reviews were mainly produced.

☞ ". . . I found the house amid desolate heathery hills, where the lonely scholar [Carlyle] nourished his mighty heart." *Emerson.*

☞ "In this wilderness of heath and rock, our estate stands forth a green oasis — a tract of ploughed, partly enclosed and planted ground, where corn ripens and trees afford a shade, although surrounded by sea-mews and rough-wooled sheep. Here, with no small effort, have we built and furnished a neat, substantial mansion; here, in the absence of a professional or other office, we live to cultivate literature with diligence, and in our own peculiar way. Two ponies which carry us everywhere, and the mountain air, are the best medicines for weak nerves. This daily exercise is my only dissipation; for this nook of ours is the loneliest in Britain — six miles removed from every one who in any case might visit me." *Carlyle to Goethe.*

☞ "Once, in the winter time, I remember counting that for three months there had not been any stranger, not even a beggar, called at Craigenputtoch door." *Carlyle.*

Craigmiller Castle. A mediæval mansion near Edinburgh, Scotland, associated with the name and memory of Mary, Queen of Scots, who once lived here.

Craignethan. A castle on the river Clyde in Scotland. It is the "Tillietudlem Castle" in Scott's novel of "Old Mortality."

☞ "It is stated in Lockhart's life of Scott, that the ruins of this castle excited in Scott such delight and enthusiasm, that its owner urged him to accept for his lifetime the use of a small habitable house, enclosed within the circuit of the walls."
Mrs. H. B. Stowe.

Cranes in the Vintry. See THREE CRANES IN THE VINTRY.

Crawford Notch. See NOTCH, THE.

Creation, The. A fresco in the Loggie of the Vatican, Rome, executed by Giulio Romano (1492?–1556), after a design by Raphael.

Creation of Adam and Eve. See ADAM AND EVE.

Creation of Light. One of the frescos of Michael Angelo (1475–1564) in the Sistine Chapel, Rome.

Creation of the World. One of the frescos of Michael Angelo (1475–1564) in the Sistine Chapel, Rome.

Cremorne Gardens. A place of entertainment (a kind of Vauxhall) on the Thames near London, greatly frequented on summer evenings.

About eleven o'clock in the evening we proceed to *Cremorne Gardens*, a sort of Bal Mabille, and where the folly of the day is continued throughout the night.
Taine, Trans.

Crepuscolo, Il. See EVENING, THE.

Creux du Vent. A remarkable eminence between Pontarlier in France, and Neuchâtel, Switzerland, the summit of which is hollowed into a vast cavity 1,000 feet deep, occasioning remarkable echoes. See also CAVE OF THE WINDS.

☞ "At times the crater of the mountain is seen to become suddenly filled with a cloud of white vapor, rising and falling, until the whole hollow presents the appearance of an immense caldron of boiling vapor, which seldom rises above the edge."
Latrobe.

Crichton Castle. A ruined castellated building in the county of Edinburgh, Scotland, associated with the poems of Sir Walter Scott.

Crichton, though now thy miry court
But pens the lazy steer and sheep,
Thy turrets rude, and tottered keep
Have been the minstrel's loved resort.
Marmion.

Crime pursued by Justice. See JUSTICE AND DIVINE VENGEANCE PURSUING CRIME.

Cripplegate. A gate in London of great antiquity, said to have been so called from the cripples who congregated there to beg. It is referred to under this name in the early part of the eleventh century, and was pulled down in the latter part of the eighteenth century. Part of the postern was for some time used as a prison for trespassers and debtors.

Three crooked cripples went through *Cripplegate*,
And through *Cripplegate* went three crooked cripples. *Mother Goose.*

Cristo della Monetà. See CHRIST WITH THE TRIBUTE MONEY.

Croce Greca, Sala a. See SALA A CROCE GRECA.

Croce, Santa. See SANTA CROCE.

Crockford's. A famous gaming club-house in St. James's Street, London, so called from the proprietor, who began life as a fishmonger, and finally amassed an immense fortune by gambling. He died in 1844. It was opened in 1849 for the Military, Naval, and County Service Club, but was closed in 1851, and has for some years served for a dining-house. Crockford's was celebrated for its *cuisine*.

☞ "It [the club-house] rose like a creation of Aladdin's lamp; and the genii themselves could hardly have surpassed the beauty of the internal decorations, or furnished a more accomplished *maître d'hôtel* than Ude. To make the company as select as possible, the establishment was regularly organized as a club, and the election

of members vested in a committee. 'Crockford's' became the rage; and the votaries of fashion, whether they liked play or not, hastened to enroll themselves. The Duke of Wellington was an original member, though (unlike Blücher, who repeatedly lost every thing he had at play) the great captain was never known to play deep at any game but war or politics. Card-tables were regularly placed, and whist was played occasionally; but the aim, end, and final cause of the whole was the hazard-bank, at which the proprietor took his nightly stand, prepared for all comers. . . . A vast sum, perhaps half a million, was sometimes due to him; but as he won, all his debtors were able to raise, and easy credit was the most fatal of his lures. He retired in 1840, much as an Indian chief retires from a hunting country where there is not game enough left for his tribe."
Edinburgh Review.

Truly this same world may be seen in Mossgiel and Tarbolton, if we look well, as clearly as it ever came to light in *Crockford's* or the Tuileries itself. *Carlyle.*

The *plats* at White's, the play at *Crock's*,
The bumpers to Miss Gunning;
The *bonhomie* of Charlie Fox,
And Selwyn's ghastly funning.
Frederick Locker.

Cromwell Gardens. A place in London much frequented in the last century.

Crosby Hall. An interesting house in Bishopsgate Street, London, built in the fifteenth century by Sir John Crosby. Here lived Richard, Duke of Gloucester, and here is laid the scene of a portion of Shakespeare's "Richard III." Sir Thomas More lived for some years in Crosby Place, and also the Countess of Pembroke, "Sidney's sister, Pembroke's mother." Crosby Hall is now a restaurant, having variously served of late years as a Methodist meeting, an auction-room, the meeting-place for a literary society, and a wine-store.

☞ "Crosby Hall is a witness of this unwillingness to improve a house off the face of the earth. The name of this house is known to all readers of 'Richard III.' . . . I knew something of its beauty and its history, and it was one of the buildings in London I was curious to see. . . . It is now a common eating-house chiefly frequented by commercial people. . . . As it is said to be the only remnant of the ancient domestic architecture of London, it is a building of peculiar interest." *Richard Grant White.*

When you have done, repair to *Crosby Place.* *Shakespeare.*

Crosby Place. See CROSBY HALL.

Cross, The True. The instrument of torture upon which Christ suffered death was believed to have lain "dishonored and unknown for three centuries" on a spot now covered by the Church of the Holy Sepulchre at Jerusalem, and to have been dug up together with the crown of thorns, the nails, and the inscription, in the presence of the Empress Helena, the mother of Constantine the Great, at the time of the building of the church. An altar and a crucifix now mark the place of the discovery, and the *Chapel of the Invention of the Cross* is regarded with peculiar veneration by the pious pilgrims to Jerusalem.

Cross. See DEPOSITION FROM THE CROSS, DESCENT FROM THE CROSS, ELEVATION OF THE CROSS, MIRACLE OF THE CROSS, VISION OF THE HOLY CROSS.

Cross and the World. An impressive allegorical picture by Thomas Cole (1801–1848), the American painter. It was left unfinished at his death.

Crowland Bells. A famous peal of bells once connected with the Abbey of Crowland. They were named Pega, Bega, Tatwin, Turketyl, Betelin, Bartholomew, and Guthlac.

Nunc erat turre tanta consonantia campanarum in tota Anglia. *Ingulphus.*

Crown and Anchor. A noted tavern in the Strand, London, formerly much frequented.

At half-past eight we adjourned in mass from the tavern, which was the well-known '*Crown and Anchor*,' in the Strand, to the Geological Rooms at Somerset House. *George Ticknor.*

Crown. See HOLY AND APOSTOLICAL CROWN and IRON CROWN.

Crown Point Fortress. A fortification on Lake Champlain, now in ruins, memorable as the scene of an engagement in 1775, when the fort was captured by the Vermont militia under the lead of Ethan Allen and Benedict Arnold.

Crown Tavern. A former house of London. Its site is now occupied by the Bank of England, Threadneedle Street.

☞ The Crown has been a frequent designation for public houses in England, which were formerly distinguished by the devices of their signs.

Crucifixion [of Christ], The. Of the great number of compositions which treat of this subject, the following may be named as among the more celebrated and better known.

Crucifixion, The. A noted picture by Fra Angelico, Giovanni (*da Fiesole*) (1387-1455). In the Museum of St. Mark, Florence, Italy.

Crucifixion, The. A triptych, representing, together with the crucifixion, the Raising of the Brazen Serpent, and Moses striking the Rock, executed by Gerard van Meire (1627-1691), the Flemish painter, and said to be the only picture in existence with which his name is intimately connected. It is in a chapel of the Cathedral of St. Bavon at Ghent.

Crucifixion, The. A picture of the Crucifixion, Expulsion, and Last Judgment, by Roger van der Weyden (d. 1464), the Flemish painter, and considered a fine example of that master. It has recently been transferred from the Monastery de los Angelos to the Museum of Madrid, Spain.

Crucifixion, The. A large altar-picture by Hans Memling (d. 1495), the Flemish painter. It is in the Palais de Justice at Paris.

Crucifixion, The. An altar-piece, with wings representing the Sacrifice of Abraham and the Brazen Serpent, by Cornelis Engelbrechtsen (1468-1533), the Flemish painter. It is now in the town-hall at Leyden, Holland.

Crucifixion, The. A picture by Guido Reni (1575-1642), and one of that painter's finest creations. In the gallery at Bologna, Italy. Another striking picture on the same subject by that artist is in the gallery of Modena. Another in Rome, in the Church of S. Lorenzo in Lucina. Of this last Robert Browning writes:

> "Beneath the piece
> Of Master Guido Reni, Christ on Cross,
> Second to nought observable in Rome."

Crucifixion, The. A picture by Anthony van Dyck (1599-1641). In the Cathedral of Mechlin, Belgium. There are also several other paintings upon the same subject by that artist.

Crucifixion, The. A picture by Jacopo Robusti, called Il Tintoretto (1512-1594). In the School of St. Roche, Venice, Italy.

Crucifixion, The. A large altar-piece, with wings representing scenes from the life of Christ, executed by Hans Memling (d. 1495), the Flemish painter, and pronounced the most important representation of this subject which the Flemish school offers, "full of original motives and admirable carrying out." It is now in the cathedral at Lubeck, Germany.

Crucifixion, The. A picture by Gheerardt David (1484-1523), the Flemish painter. In the Museum of Berlin, Prussia.

Crucifixion, Descent from the Cross, and Entombment. Portions of an altar-piece of eighteen or twenty panels, painted in 1502 by Hans Holbein the Elder (d. 1524). This picture was originally in the Abbey of Keisheim, but is now at Munich, Bavaria.

Crucifixion, The. An altar-piece at Weimar, Germany, by Lucas Cranach (1472-1553). It includes admirable portraits of Luther, Melanchthon, and the painter himself.

Crucifixion, The. A well-known picture by Peter Paul Rubens (1577-1640). In the museum at Antwerp, Belgium.

Crucifixion, The. A picture by Jacopo Robusti, called Il Tintoretto (1512-1594), and regarded as one of his finest and most perfect works. It is in a room of the Scuola di S. Rocco, at Venice, Italy.

Crucifixion, The. A picture by Albert Dürer (1471–1528), the German painter and engraver, and regarded as one of his best works. It is in the gallery of Dresden, Germany.

Crucifixion, The. A picture by Tintoretto (1512–1594). In the Schleissheim Palace, near Munich, Bavaria.

Crucifixion, Chapel of the. One of the chapels in the Church of the Holy Sepulchre at Jerusalem. It is believed to stand upon the spot where Christ was nailed to the cross.

Crucifixion of St. Peter. 1. A large fresco painting by Michael Angelo (1475–1564), and one of his last. In the Vatican, Rome.

2. A well-known picture by Peter Paul Rubens (1577–1640), in the Church of St. Peter, in Cologne, Germany.

Crusaders, The. A picture by Wilhelm Kaulbach (b. 1805), the eminent German painter.

Crutched Friars. A street in London, named after a convent of Crouched Friars.

Crystal Palace. A building which originally stood in Hyde Park, London, constructed for the Exhibition of the World's Industry, held in that city, and opened for that purpose May 1, 1851. It is said to have received its name from Douglas Jerrold, its roof and sides being made of glass. The entire area of the building was about 17 acres. It was subsequently taken down, re-erected and enlarged at Sydenham in Kent, where it is still an object of attraction.

☞ "The Alhambra and the Tuileries would not have filled up the eastern and western nave; the National Gallery would have stood beneath the transept; the palace of Versailles (the largest in the world) would have extended but a little way beyond the transept; and a dozen metropolitan churches would have stood erect under its roof of glass." *Athenæum.*

But a few years ago we believed the world had grown too civilized for war, and *Crystal Palace* in Hyde Park was to be the inauguration of a new era. Battles bloody as Napoleon's are now the familiar tale of every day, and the arts which have made greatest progress are the arts of destruction. *Froude.*

Solvency is in the ideas and mechanism of an Englishman. The *Crystal Palace* is not considered honest until it pays; no matter how much convenience, beauty, or *éclat*, it must be self-supporting.
Emerson.

Just now, the world is busy: it has grown
A Fair-going world. Imperial England draws
The flowing ends of the earth, from Fez, Canton,
Delhi and Stockholm, Athens and Madrid,
The Russias and the vast Americas,
As a queen gathers in her robes amid
Her golden cincture, — isles, peninsulas,
Capes, continents, far inland countries hid
By jasper sands and hills of chrysopras,
All trailing in their splendors through the door
Of the new *Crystal Palace.*
Mrs. Browning.

Culla, Santa. See SANTA CULLA.

Culzean Castle. The seat of the Marquis of Ailsa, in the neighborhood of Maybole, Scotland. It is a Gothic castle of the last century. It is alluded to in the poems of Burns.

Cumæan Sibyl. 1. A well-known picture by Domenico Zampieri, called Domenichino (1581–1641). In the Palazzo Borghese, Rome.

2. A picture by Guido Reni (1575–1642). In the Uffizi Palace, Florence, Italy.

Cumberland, The. A vessel of the United States navy, sunk by the iron-clad ram *Merrimac* in Hampton Roads, Saturday, March 8, 1862, going down with her colors flying, and firing upon her impenetrable assailant as the water rose above her own gun-deck. To the last her brave commander Morris refused to surrender; and the ship sank, carrying down with her a hundred dead and wounded.

At anchor in Hampton Roads we lay,
On board of the *Cumberland*, sloop-of-war;
And at times from the fortress across the bay
The alarum of drums swept past,
Or a bugle blast
From the camp on the shore. *Longfellow.*

With decks afloat and powder gone,
The last broadside we gave
From the guns' heated iron lips
Burst out beneath the wave.
G. H. Boker.

He will think of that brave band
He sank in the *Cumberland:*
Ay, he will sink like them.
H. H Brownell.

Weep for the patriot heroes, doomed to drown;
Pledge to the sunken *Cumberland's* renown.
T. B. Read.

Cumberland Road. See NATIONAL ROAD.

Cumnor Hall. An ancient manor-house near Oxford, made memorable by the genius of Scott, in connection with the Earl of Leicester and Amy Robsart. Some remains of the building are still visible, but most of the ruins have disappeared.

The dews of summer night did fall;
The moon, sweet regent of the sky,
Silvered the walls of *Cumnor Hall,*
And many an oak that grew thereby.
. . . .
Full many a traveller oft hath sighed,
And pensive wept the countess' fall,
As wandering onward they've espied
The haunted towers of *Cumnor Hall.*
W. J. Mickle.

[Mickle's ballad of "Cumnor Hall" is supposed to have suggested to Scott the romance of "Kenilworth."]

Cupid. A statue by Michael Angelo Buonarotti (1475–1564). In the Kensington Museum.

Cupid and Danaë. See DANAË AND CUPID.

Cupid and Psyche. A celebrated ancient cameo, representing the reconciliation of Cupid and Psyche; ascribed to Tryphon, who lived in the time of Alexander's successors. It is now in the collection of the Duke of Marlborough, England.

Cupid and Psyche. See MARRIAGE OF CUPID AND PYSCHE.

Cupid catching a Butterfly. An exquisite marble sculpture by Thomas Banks (1738–1805), regarded as a model of classic grace. It was purchased by Catherine II. of Russia. In Russia.

Cupid complaining to Venus. A mythological fresco in the Vatican, Rome, designed by Raphael, but executed by his pupils.

Cupid, Education of. A well-known picture by Antonio Allegri, surnamed Correggio (1494–1534). In the National Gallery, London.

Cupid wrestling with Pan. A mythological fresco in the Vatican, Rome, designed by Raphael (1483–1520), but executed by his scholars.

Curragh of Kildare. A fine undulating down about six miles in length and two in breadth, the principal race-course in Ireland.

☞ "Unequalled perhaps in the world for the exceeding softness and elasticity of the turf, the verdure of which is 'evergreen,' and the occasional irregularities which are very attractive to the eye. The land is the property of the crown."
Mr. and Mrs. S. C. Hall.

Curraghmore. The seat of the Marquis of Waterford, in the county of Waterford, Ireland.

Curtain Theatre. A former theatre of London, conjectured to have been so called from having been the first theatre to adopt the use of a stage-curtain. It is mentioned in 1577, and is referred to by Stow and others. Aubrey (1678) speaks of it as a "kind of nursery or obscure playhouse, called the Greene Curtain, situate in the suburbs toward Shoreditch." It was afterwards used for prize-fighting.

Curule Chair. The name given to a kind of ivory chair, without arms or back, and which was one of the insignia of senatorial dignity in ancient Rome, when the Gauls under the lead of Brennus entered Rome, which had been for the most part abandoned by the citizens in terror. A few of the aged senators alone remained, clad in their purple robes and seated in their curule chairs. It is related that one of the Gauls, approaching the Senator Papirius, and supposing him to be a statue, passed his hand gently over his long beard. The patrician resented the affront by striking him with his ivory *bâton*, which was at once the signal of a general massacre. This chair was also used by successful generals in a public triumph, and was fitted to a kind of chariot (*currus*), whence its name.

The Girondists, once more united for the last time, dined together to consult upon what remained to do. They counselled each other to stand firm at their post, and to die upon their *curule chairs*, defending to the last the character with which they were invested. *Thiers.*

Than Timoleon's arms require,
And Tully's *curule chair*, and Milton's golden lyre. *Mark Akenside.*

Cuthbert. See SHRINE OF ST. CUTHBERT.

Cyclopean Towers. A singular and picturesque group of limestone towers, rising to a height of nearly 70 feet, in Augusta County, Va.

Cymon and Iphigenia. A picture by Sir Joshua Reynolds (1723-1792), the celebrated English portrait-painter.

Cypress Grove. A well-known public cemetery in New Orleans, La.

Cypress Hills. A cemetery near Brooklyn, N.Y.

Cyrus' Tomb. A ruined pyramid, but still in tolerable preservation, at Passargardæ in ancient Babylonia, believed to be the tomb of Cyrus the Great (B.C. 529).

☞ "This building is now called the tomb of Cyrus, and probably was so, though copied from a form which we have just been describing as a temple. But it must be borne in mind that the most celebrated example of this form is as often called the tomb as the temple of Belus, and among a Turanian people the tomb and the temple may be considered as one and the same thing." *Fergusson.*

D.

Dalhousie Castle. An old Scotch Castle, the seat of the Earl of Dalhousie, in the valley of the Esk, Scotland.

☞ "An avenue of near three-quarters of a mile of firs, cedars, laburnums, and larches, wound through the park to the castle, and, dipping over the edge of a deep and wild dell, I found the venerable old pile below me, its round towers and battlemented turrets frowning among the trees, and forming with the river, which swept round its base, one of the finest specimens imaginable of the feudal picturesque."
N. P. Willis.

Dalkeith Palace. The seat of the Duke of Buccleuch at Dalkeith, Scotland.

Dalmahoy Park. A mansion near Midcalder, in Scotland, the seat of the Earl of Morton. Among the curiosities here are mentioned the keys of Lochleven Castle, which, after the flight of Queen Mary, were thrown into the lake, and of which keys there are said to be seven different sets in Scottish houses, each claiming to be genuine.

Dalmeny Park. The seat of the Earl of Rosebery near the village of Dalmeny, in Scotland.

Dan. In ancient times a city in the extreme northern part of Palestine, a frontier-town or outpost of the Israelites. It was originally called Laish, and was inhabited by a people who were connected with Sidon. Its position relative to Beersheba, another ancient town on the extreme southern boundary of Palestine, some 40 miles from Jerusalem, has given rise to the familiar expression "from Dan to Beersheba," which signified the land of the Hebrews in its entirety, and which as commonly used now means to traverse the whole extent of any journey or undertaking.

I pity the man who can travel from *Dan to Beersheba*, and cry, 'Tis all barren.
Laurence Sterne: Sentimental Journey

It is sad to see an honest traveller confidently gauging all foreign objects with a measure that will not mete them; trying German Sacred Oaks by their fitness for British shipbuilding; walking from *Dan to Beersheba*, and finding so little that he did not bring with him. *Carlyle.*

Danaë. A well-known picture by Antonio Allegri, surnamed Correggio (1494-1534). In the Borghese palace, Rome.

Danaë and Cupid. An admired picture by Titian (1477-1576). In the Museum at Naples, Italy.

Dance of Death. 1. A series of wood-cuts after designs by Hans Holbein the Younger (1498-1543), the German painter. They were first published at Lyons in 41 plates, and in a subsequent edition, which also appeared at Lyons, in 1507, were increased by 12 additional plates.

2. This subject was also treated by the Swiss painter Nicolas Manuel, surnamed Deutsch (1484-1531), in a humorous way, in 46 large fresco pictures on the churchyard wall of the Dominican convent at Berne.

Dance of the Giants. A monumental structure, generally thought to be of Druidical origin, at Stonehenge, England. It consists of two circles and two ovoids, one within the other, and measuring 300 feet in circumference.

Dance of the Magdalen. A beautiful engraving by Luc Jacobsz, commonly called Lucas van Leyden (1494-1533). Now in the British Museum.

Dancing Faun. 1. An ancient statue now in the Tribune of the Uffizi Palace in Florence, Italy. It has undergone restorations by Michael Angelo.

2. There is another ancient

statue of this name, much admired, found at Pompeii in 1831, and now in the Museum at Naples, Italy. See FAUN, BARBERINI FAUN, SLEEPING FAUN, etc.

☞ "The *Dancing Faun*, a work full of spirit, and admirably restored by Michael Angelo, is a sort of connecting link between the two [the Apollino and the Wrestlers]." *Hillard.*

Daniel in the Lions' Den. A picture by Peter Paul Rubens (1577–1640), now in Hamilton Palace. "In this picture the prophet himself — a subordinate and uninteresting figure — is only the excuse for a series of studies of lions in various attitudes."

Daniel Webster. See WEBSTER.

Dante and Beatrice. A painting by Ary Scheffer (1795–1858). Now in the Museum of Fine Arts, Boston, Mass.

Dante and Virgil. A picture by Ferdinand Victor Eugène Delacroix (1799–1863), a celebrated French historical painter. This picture on its appearance in 1822 caused a great sensation.

Dante's House. [Ital. *Casa di Dante.*] A well-known house in Florence, Italy, in the Via S. Martino, in which the poet was born in 1265.

Dante's Portrait. A fresco painting by Giotto di Bondone (1276–1336) in the chapel of the Bargello, or palace of the Podestà, in Florence, Italy. After having been long hidden from view by a covering of whitewash, it was brought to light in 1840 through the exertions of three gentlemen, Mr. Richard Henry Wilde, an American, Mr. Seymour Kirkup, an Englishman, and Signor G. Aubrey Bezzi, an Italian. This is the only likeness of Dante known to have been made during his life, and is therefore regarded of the greatest value. The eye of the beautiful profile was wanting, and in its place a hole an inch deep, doubtless caused by a nail which had been driven into the plastering. Giotto's portrait of Dante has been made familiar to the public by excellent reproductions.

☞ "After all commentaries, the Book itself is mainly what we know of him. The Book; — and one might add that Portrait commonly attributed to Giotto, which, looking on it, you cannot help inclining to think genuine, whoever did it. To me it is a most touching face; perhaps, of all faces that I know, the most so. Lonely there, painted as on vacancy, with the simple laurel wound round it; the deathless sorrow and pain, the known victory which is also deathless; significant of the whole history of Dante! I think it is the mournfullest face that ever was painted from reality; an altogether tragic, heart-affecting face." *Carlyle.*

— We salute thee [Dante] who art come
Back to the old stone with a softer brow
Than Giotto drew upon the wall, for some
Good lovers of our age to track and plough
Their way to, through Time's ordures stratified,
And startle broad awake into the dull
Bargello chamber. *Mrs Browning.*

Dante's Stone. [Ital. *Sasso di Dante.*] A stone in the Piazza del Duomo, Florence, Italy, remarkable as the place where Dante is supposed to have mused while he looked upon the great cathedral.

— The stone
Called Dante's — a plain flat-stone scarce discerned
From others in the pavement, — whereupon
He used to bring his quiet chair out, turned
To Brunelleschi's church, and pour alone
The lava of his spirit when it burned.
Mrs Browning.

On that ancient seat,
The seat of stone that runs along the wall,
. . . .
Would Dante sit conversing. *Rogers.*

Dark and frowning piles of mediæval structure; a majestic dome, the prototype of St. Peter's; basilicas which enshrine the ashes of some of the mightiest of the dead; the stone where Dante stood to gaze on the *campanile.* *Edward Everett.*

Dante's Tomb. A small circular structure in Ravenna, Italy, underneath which the bones of the poet rest. Dante degli Alighieri died in 1321.

I pass each day where Dante's bones are laid:
A little cupola, more neat than solemn,
Protects his dust. *Byron.*

Bitter spirits! ye claim
Heine? Alas, he is yours!

Only a moment! I knew
Whose he was who is here
Buried. I knew he was yours!
Ah, I knew that I saw
Here no sepulchre built,
. . . no tomb
On Ravenna sands, in the shade
Of Ravenna pines, for a high
Austere Dante! *Matthew Arnold.*

Dargle, The. A beautiful and much-frequented glen in Wicklow County, Ireland.

☞ "As, in consequence of its short distance from Dublin, many travellers examine no other portions of the county, the glen has attained to greater celebrity than others, — more solemn, magnificent, and picturesque, — yet it may be a question whether, in variety, it is anywhere surpassed." *Mr. and Mrs. Hall.*

Darius and Alexander. See BATTLE OF DARIUS AND ALEXANDER and FAMILY OF DARIUS BEFORE ALEXANDER.

Darnaway Castle. The seat of the Earl of Moray, near Forres, in Scotland.

Dartmoor Prison. A noted place of confinement for prisoners of war, situated in that district of England known as Dartmoor, in the southern part of the county of Devon. Here, during the war between England and the United States, in 1812, many American prisoners were confined.

Wild *Dartmoor!* thou that midst thy mountains rude
Hast robed thyself with haughty solitude.
.
'Twas then the captives of Britannia's war
Here for their lovely southern climes afar
In bondage pined. *Felicia Hemans.*

Dartmouth College. An institution of learning in Hanover, N.H., originally founded in 1770 as a school for missionaries.

Datchet Mead. A patch of land near the village of the same name in England, immortalized by Shakespeare in his "Merry Wives of Windsor," in connection with the adventures of Sir John Falstaff.

Daughter of Titian. A picture, bearing this name, by Titian (1477-1576), representing a beautiful woman carrying with uplifted arms a plate of fruit or a casket. Of several examples, the best is in the museum at Berlin. There is one at Madrid, representing the girl as Salome carrying the head of John the Baptist. The original of these pictures is supposed to be not Titian's daughter, but Violante, the daughter of Palma Vecchio, who is known as Titian's love.

Dauphine, Place. See PLACE DAUPHINE.

Davenant's Theatre. A theatre in Lincoln's Inn Fields, London, opened in 1662. The actors were styled the "Duke of York's company of comedians."

David. A gigantic marble statue by Michael Angelo (1475-1564), which formerly stood in front of the Palazzo Vecchio, Florence, Italy, but has now been removed to the Accademia delle Belle Arti.

☞ "The erection of this David was like an occurrence in nature from which people are accustomed to reckon. We find events dated so many years after the erection of the Giant. It was mentioned in records in which there was not a line besides respecting art." *Grimm, Trans.*

☞ "As soon as the statue was set upon its pedestal the Gonfaloniere Pier Soderini came to see it, and, after expressing his great admiration for the work, suggested that the nose seemed to him too large; hearing this, Michael Angelo gravely mounted on a ladder, and after pretending to work for a few minutes, during which he constantly let fall some of the marble-dust he had taken up in his pocket, turned with a questioning, and doubtless a slightly sarcastic, expression in his face to the critic, who responded, 'Bravo! bravo! you have given it life.'" *Perkins.*

David. See ZUCCONE, LO.

David and Bathsheba. A picture by the Swiss painter, Nicolas Manuel, surnamed Deutsch (1484-1531). In the museum at Basle, Switzerland.

David and Goliath. A picture by Daniele da Volterra (1509-1566), the Italian painter, the pupil of Michael Angelo. It was, for a long time, considered to be the work of the latter. It is a double picture, representing David and Goliath in two different points of view on each side of a tablet of slate. Now in the Louvre, at Paris.

David's Well. A deep rock-cistern in the neighborhood of Bethlehem, Palestine, traditionally identified with the *Well of David*, the water of which the king coveted when hiding in the cave of Adullam. (1 Chron. xi. 15–19.)

Davidson Fountain. A magnificent fountain in Cincinnati, O. It is of bronze, cast in Munich, and presented to the city by Tyler Davidson.

Day, The. [Ital. *Il Giorno.*] One of four colossal figures by Michael Angelo Buonarotti (1475–1564). In the Church of S. Lorenzo, Florence, Italy.

☞ "They have received the names of Day and Night, Dawn and Twilight; but the subjective instinct of the master urged him here too far outside the pale of human sympathy for any terms, however vague, to define his intention." *Eastlake.*

(What word says God?) The sculptor's Night and *Day*,
And Dawn and Twilight, wait in marble scorn,
Like dogs couched on a dunghill, on the clay
From whence the Medicean stamp's outworn. *Mrs. Browning.*

2. A celebrated bas-relief by Albert Bertel Thorwaldsen (1770–1844), the Danish sculptor. It is well known through numerous reproductions. The companion piece is entitled *The Night.*

Day, The. [*Il Giorno.*] See St. Jerome.

De Soto discovering the Mississippi. A picture in one of the panels of the rotunda in the Capitol of Washington, representing the arrival of Fernando de Soto (1500?–1542), the Spanish explorer, upon the banks of the great river. This work was executed, under commission from Congress, by W. H. Powells, who received $12,000 for painting it. Previous to the engagement of Mr. Powells another artist, Henry Inman, had been commissioned to fill the vacant panel; but he died before beginning his work. This painting has been severely criticised, and pronounced "a plagiarized patchwork of generalities, absurd and incongruous, badly drawn, gaudily colored, and as destitute of historic value as an act of Congress is of poetic feeling." The picture has become very familiar to the general public from its reproduction as an engraving, upon the back of the ten-dollar notes of the national currency.

Dead Man Revived. A picture by Washington Allston (1779–1843), the American painter. It "took the prize of 200 guineas at the British Institution."

Dearborn Street. A well-known and prominent street in Chicago, Ill.

Dearborn, Fort. See Fort Dearborn.

Death. See Dance of Death; Knight, Death, and the Devil; Shadow of Death; and Triumph of Death.

Death of Ananias. One of the famous cartoons by Raphael Sanzio (1483–1520), from which the tapestries in the Vatican, at Rome, were executed.

Death of Julius Cæsar. A picture by Jean L. Gérôme (b. 1824), the French painter. In the Corcoran Gallery at Washington.

Death of Montgomery. A well-known historical picture by John Trumbull (1756–1843). In the Wadsworth Athenæum, Hartford, Conn.

☞ "Not surpassed by any similar works in the last century, and thus far stand alone in American historical painting." *Harper's Magazine.*

Death of Queen Elizabeth. A picture by Paul Delaroche (1797–1856), the celebrated French historical painter.

Death of St. Francis. A fresco picture by Giotto di Bondone (1276–1336). In the Church of Santa Croce, Florence, Italy.

Death of the Duke of Guise. An admired picture by Paul Delaroche (1797-1856), the eminent French painter.

Death of the Virgin. A picture by Jan Shoreel (1495-1562), the Dutch painter, "remarkable for its intense reality and splendor of color, and one of the great ornaments of the Boisserée Gallery." At Munich, Bavaria. There is an excellent and well-known lithograph of this picture.

Death of the Virgin. A celebrated picture by Caravaggio (1569-1609), formerly in the possession of Charles I. of England, and which has often been engraved. Now in the Louvre, Paris.

Death of the Virgin. A picture by Martin Schöngauer, commonly called Martin Schön (b. 1420 ?), a German painter, supposed to be his earliest work. It is now in the National Gallery, London.

Death of Warren. An historical picture by John Trumbull (1756-1843), the American painter. In the Wadsworth Athenæum, Hartford, Conn.

Death of Webster. A painting by Joseph Ames (1816-1872), an American painter, of which there is an engraving.

Death of Wolfe. A picture by Benjamin West (1738-1820). In the Grosvenor Gallery, London.

☞ "Just before he [Lord Nelson] went to sea for the last time, . . . he expressed his regret that he had not acquired some taste for art. 'But,' said he, turning to West, 'there is one picture whose power I do feel. I never pass a paint-shop where your *Death of Wolfe* is in the window without being stopped by it.'. . . 'But, my lord [said Mr. West], I fear your intrepidity will furnish me such another scene; and, if it should, I shall certainly avail myself of it.'—'Will you?' said Nelson, 'then I hope that I shall die in the next battle." He sailed a few days after, and the result was on the canvas before us.'" *Ticknor's Letters.*

Death on the Pale Horse. A picture by Benjamin West (1738-1820).

Décadence de Rome. [Decline of Rome.] A noted picture by Horace Vernet (1789-1863). In the palace of the Luxembourg, Paris.

☞ "In this picture is a most grand and melancholy moral lesson. The classical forms are evidently not introduced because they are classic, but in subservience to the expression of the moral. Nothing could be more exquisite than the introduction of the busts of the departed heroes of the old republic, looking down from their pedestals on the scene of debauchery below. It is a noble picture, which I wish was hung up in the Capitol of our nation to teach our haughty people that as pride, and fulness of bread, and laxness of principle, brought down the old republics, so also ours may fall." *Beecher.*

Decadence of the Romans. A well-known picture by Thomas Couture (b. 1815). In the Luxembourg, Paris.

Declaration of Independence. A large picture by John Trumbull (1756-1843), executed under commission from Congress for the rotunda of the Capitol at Washington. The picture is well known by engravings.

Decree of Canopus. See STONE OF SÂN.

Deer of Chillingham. See WILD DEER OF CHILLINGHAM.

Deer Pass. A picture by Sir Edwin Landseer (1803-1873).

Defence, The. An armor-plated ship of the British navy, launched April 24, 1861.

Deir, El. [The Convent.] A rock monument well preserved, in Petra, Arabia, being a huge monolith hewn out of the side of a cliff, and facing Mount Hor. It is of an order neither Greek nor Roman, but with something like a Doric frieze over a Corinthian capital.

☞ "The façade is nearly double the size of the Khuzneh, being 150 feet in length, by about the same in extreme height, and is in admirable preservation. Some idea may be formed of its massive proportions by the measurement of its details. The lower columns are seven feet in diameter, and over 50 in height, almost rivalling those of the great temple at Bâ'albek; the interior is one vast hall, perfectly plain. . . . The whole aspect of this singular and beautiful edifice is undoubtedly that of a heathen temple."

Murray's Handbook.

Deligny. The celebrated Imperial Swimming School, so called from the name of its director, and situated on the Quai d'Orsay, Paris.

For instance, once on the boulevard a friend tapped me on the shoulder, . . . when after taking a plunge at *Deligny's*, I came to the surface of the water blowing like a porpoise. *Taine, Trans.*

Delilah. See SAMSON AND DELILAH.

Deliverance of St. Peter. A fresco by Raphael Sanzio (1483-1520), representing the deliverance of the apostle from prison. "Peter sits asleep between his guards, his chained hands still clasped in prayer. The angel is about to strike him on the side to wake him. On the right the angel leads him through the guards who are sleeping on the steps. In both these representations, . . . the figures are illuminated by the light proceeding from the angel. On the left, the guards are roused, and seem staggering half asleep: this group receives its light from the moon and from torches. This fresco is celebrated for the picturesque effect of these lights. The subject is supposed to contain an allusion to the captivity of Leo X., who had been liberated only the year preceding his elevation to the pontificate." This picture is in the Stanza of the Heliodorus, in the Vatican, Rome.

Déliverande, La. A small Norman chapel in the neighborhood of Caen, France. It contains a shrine of the Virgin to which for 800 years the Norman sailors and peasantry have resorted. The image owes its reputation for sanctity to the miracles alleged to have been wrought by it in behalf of sailors.

Delivering the Keys to St. Peter. A well-known wall-painting by Pietro Perugino (1446-1524). In the Sistine Chapel, Rome. It is considered one of his best works.

Della Crusca. [Academy of the Sieve.] A celebrated literary association in Florence, Italy, founded by Cosimo I. for the purpose of purifying and refining the Italian language and style. It is still in existence, and continues to hold meetings. The name Della Crusca is better known, probably, to English readers, as a designation applied to a class of sentimental writers in England during the last century, distinguished by their affected style of expression.

Though *Crusca's* bards no more our journals fill,
Some stragglers skirmish round the columns still. *Byron.*

Delmonico's. A noted restaurant on Fifth Avenue, New York.

Delphic Sibyl. One of the frescos of Michael Angelo (1475-1564). In the Sistine Chapel, Rome.

Deluge, The. One of the frescos of Michael Angelo (1475-1564). In the Sistine Chapel, Rome.

Deluge in Phrygia. A picture by Peter Paul Rubens (1577-1640). Now in the gallery of Vienna, Austria.

Democritus. A picture by Salvator Rosa (1615-1673). In the Grosvenor Gallery.

Dendara, *or* **Denderah.** See TEMPLE OF DENDERAH and ZODIAC OF DENDERAH.

Denis. See PORTE ST. DENIS; ST. DENIS; and ST. DENIS, RUE.

Denis du Marais. See ST. SACRÉMENT.

Denizens of the Highlands. A picture by Rosa Bonheur (b. 1822), the celebrated French painter of animals.

Departure and the Return. A picture by Thomas Cole (1801-1848), the American painter, being scenes from feudal times. In the Corcoran Gallery, Washington.

Deposition from the Cross. 1. A well-known picture by Giotto di Bondone (1276-1336). In the Arena, at Padua, Italy.

☞ "The Descent from the Cross and the Deposition from the Cross are two separate themes. . . . The Deposition is properly that moment which succeeds the Descent from the Cross; when the dead form of Christ is deposed or laid upon the ground, resting upon the lap of his mother, and lamented by St. John, the Magdalene and others." *Mrs. Jameson.*

2. An admired picture by Tommaso di Stefano, called Giottino (1324–1356), and considered "one of the finest of the Giottesque school." In the Gallery of the Uffizi, Florence, Italy.

Derby Day. A popular picture by W. P. Frith. In the National Gallery, London.

Descent from the Cross. A very common subject of representation by the great religious painters. Of the more celebrated or familiar compositions upon this subject, may be mentioned the following: —

Descent from the Cross. A celebrated picture by Pietro Perugino (1446–1524). In the Pitti Gallery, Florence, Italy.

Descent from the Cross. A picture by Baccio della Porta, called Fra Bartolommeo (1469–1517). In the Pitti Gallery, Florence, Italy.

Descent from the Cross. A picture by Antonio Allegri, surnamed Correggio (1494–1534). In the gallery at Parma, Italy.

Descent from the Cross. A picture by Roger van der Weyden (d. 1464), the Flemish painter; described by Kugler as "a rich composition, with heads of highly pathetic expression and admirable execution." It is now in the gallery of the Hague, Holland.

Descent from the Cross. A picture by Roger van der Weyden the younger (d. 1529), the Flemish painter, and his principal work, originally executed for the Church of Our Lady "Darbuyten" at Louvain, now in the sacristy of S. Lorenzo of the Escurial, in Spain.

Descent from the Cross. A celebrated altar-piece by Peter Paul Rubens (1577–1640), in the cathedral at Antwerp, Belgium. It "represents the highest excellence attained by this master in ecclesiastical art."

☞ "In the famous 'Descent' at Antwerp, the masterpiece of Rubens, Mary stands, and supports the arm of her Son as he is let down from the cross. This is in accordance with the ancient version, but her face and figure are the least effective part of this fine picture." *Mrs. Jameson.*

Descent from the Cross. A picture by Rembrandt van Ryn (1607–1669), the Dutch painter, and regarded as one of his most admirable works. It is in the gallery at Munich, Bavaria, and there is a replica of the same in the Hermitage at St. Petersburg, Russia. There is also a picture upon this subject by Rembrandt in the National Gallery, London.

Descent from the Cross. A picture by Daniele da Volterra (1509–1566), the Italian painter, and his best work, described as "a grand impassioned work, of powerful action." It is in the Church of Trinità de' Monti, at Rome.

☞ "In the famous 'Descent from the Cross,'—the masterpiece of Daniel di Volterra, —the fainting form of the Virgin, extended on the earth, and the dying anguish in her face, have never been exceeded, and are in fact the chief merit of the picture." *Mrs. Jameson.*

Descent of the Holy Ghost. An admired picture by Taddeo di Bartolo (b. 1350?). In the Church of S. Agostino, Perugia, Italy.

Destruction of Jerusalem. A well-known painting by Wilhelm von Kaulbach (1805–1874). In the Museum at Berlin, Prussia.

☞ "The destruction of Jerusalem is dealt with in this picture as an epoch in the history of the world, as a circumstance of more than a general historic character. Thus Kaulbach has comprehended it and represented it, for he has gathered his materials from the prophets and from Josephus. At the top of the picture we see, in the clouds, the figures of Isaiah, Jeremiah, Ezekiel, and Daniel, surrounded by a glory: they prophesy the fall of Jerusalem. . . . We see the Jewish people's misery; the temple is in flames; the city is taken. . . . To the right of the

picture, a Christian family is leaving the city, accompanied by two angels; to the left is seen the Wandering Jew, chased out of the city by three demons; he is the representative of the present Judaism — a people without a home."
Hans Christian Andersen.

Destruction of the Giants. A fresco by Giulio Romano (1492–1546) in the Palazzo del Te, Mantua, Italy.

Devil Tavern. A celebrated tavern in London, between Temple Bar and the Middle Temple gate, much frequented in the time of James I. Here met the famous Apollo Club. The Devil Tavern is no longer standing. Its site is occupied by Child's Banking-house. See APOLLO CLUB.

Hence to the *Devil* —
Thus to the place where Jonson sat we climb,
Leaning on the same rail that guided him.
Prior and Montague.

☞ A *Young Devil Tavern* was established on the opposite side of the street.

Devil's Beef-tub. A singular natural curiosity in the vale of the Annan, in Scotland, in the form of a hollow or basin surrounded by high hills, so deep and so secluded as to serve in ancient times as a hiding-place for stolen cattle, whence its name. The spot is alluded to in Sir Walter Scott's tales.

Devil's Bridge. 1. A famous arch of masonry constructed in the twelfth century, and overhanging at a height of 70 feet the river Reuss, on the St. Gothard Pass, in Switzerland, in a narrow and dangerous gorge. The old bridge has been superseded by a new and secure structure, built in 1830. Here the Reuss leaps about 70 feet in a short space, while a wind created by the fall blows with such force as nearly to lift one from his feet.

Plunge with the Reuss embrowned by terror's breath,
Where danger roofs the narrow walks of Death,
By floods that, thundering from their dizzy height,
Swell more gigantic on the steadfast sight.
Wordsworth.

2. A natural curiosity in Wales, a few miles from Aberystwith. A deep rocky cleft surmounted by two arches, one above another, the lower said to have been built in the time of William Rufus, beneath which the river Mynach descends in terrific cascades.

How art thou named? In search of what strange land
From what huge height descending? Can such force
Of waters issue from a British source,
Or hath not Pindus fed thee, where the band
Of patriots scoop their freedom out, with hand
Desperate as thine? *Wordsworth.*

3. See PUENTE DEL DIABLO.

Devil's Cave. See PEAK CAVERN.

Devil's Dyke. A vast natural amphitheatre in the hills near Portslade, Sussex, England, a favorite resort of visitors.

Devil's Garden. A natural curiosity in Hardy County, W. Va.

☞ "This strange curiosity lies at the head of what is called Trout Run. . . . On the summit [of a dizzy precipice] is a natural pavement of flat rocks, and on the eastern edge stands a gigantic bust in granite, the head, neck, and shoulders clearly defined, and the whole appearance savage and terrific. Near this figure formerly stood a square granite pillar about two feet in diameter and twelve feet high, but this has been overthrown by some storm or convulsion of the earth. . . . The most singular part remains to be described. About 100 feet below the stone bust, an opening leads into deep caverns in the rock. The explorer finds himself in an apartment with a level floor and ceiling, and from this room a flight of stone steps ascends to another apartment still larger. A third flight gives access to a third cavern, and so on, until the *twelfth* apartment is reached by the eleventh flight of steps just beneath the pavement of the summit, through fissures in which a dim light enters the cavern. Such is the singular character of this natural curiosity." *Kercheval.*

Devil's Glen. A singular and romantic ravine in Wicklow County, Ireland.

☞ "Nothing astonished us or gratified us so much as the Devil's Glen; with its roaring river, its huge precipices, its circuitous paths, and the

noble and graceful fall that seems as a crown of glory to its head."
Mr. and Mrs. Hall.

Devil's Ladder. A rocky eminence near Lorch on the Rhine, crowned by a ruined castle.

Devil's Pulpit. 1. A singular granitic mass on the summit of the Brocken, in the Harz Mountains, in Germany.

2. A remarkable precipice on an island in Tupper Lake, in the Adirondack region of New York.

Devil's Punch-Bowl. A curious natural formation in Hampshire, England.

Devil's Slide. A remarkable natural curiosity in Weber Cañon, Utah Territory. It consists of two parallel lines of rock extending from the base to the top of a mountain.

☞ "Imagine a mountain 800 feet high, composed of solid dark-red sandstone. . . . From the base of the immense red mountain up to its entire height of 800 feet is what is called the 'Devil's Slide,' composed of white limestone. It consists of a smooth white stone floor from base to summit, about 15 feet wide, as straight and regular as if laid by a stone-mason, with line and plummet. On either side of this smooth white line, is what appears to the eye to be a well-laid white stone wall, varying in height from 10 to 30 feet. This white spectacle on the red mountain-side has all the appearance of being made by man or devil as a slide from the top of the mountain to the bed of Weber River."
C. C. Fulton.

There is another very similar, of the same name, in Montana.

☞ "We are now within the wild Weber Cañon, and the scene is changing every moment. On the right we pass a most wonderful sight, — the Devil's Slide. Two ridges of gray rock stand some 10 feet out of the snow and brushwood, and run parallel to each other for about 150 feet right up the mountain-side." *Smiles.*

Devil's Stone. A natural curiosity in the neighborhood of Dürkheim, Germany, in the shape of a rock bearing the print of a huge paw. It is said that the pagans used this rock for an altar of sacrifice.

Devil's Wall. 1. The old Roman wall dividing England from Scotland, so called by those living in the vicinity because they thought, from its durability, that it must have been built by the Devil. It is said that the superstitious peasantry put pieces from this wall into the foundations of their dwellings to secure an equal permanence.

2. [Ger. *Teufelsmauer* or *Pfahlgraten.*] A famous Roman rampart (now in ruins) begun by the Emperor Probus, A.D. 277, extending from Ratisbon on the Danube, across hills, valleys, rivers, and morasses, as far as to the Rhine, — a distance of nearly 200 miles. It was intended as a bulwark against the inroads of German invaders upon the soil of the empire.

☞ "Within a few years after his [Probus's] death, it was overthrown by the Alemanni. Its scattered ruins, universally ascribed to the power of the dæmon, now serve only to excite the wonder of the Swabian peasant."
Gibbon.

Devonshire House. A mansion built upon the site of Berkeley House in Piccadilly, London, the residence of the Duke of Devonshire. This house was famous, towards the close of the last century, as the headquarters of Whig politics, and for the fascinations of its beautiful duchess. It contains many artistic and bibliographical curiosities.

Diablo, Puente del. See PUENTE DEL DIABLO.

Diamond Necklace. A famous piece of jewelry which was the cause of the notorious affair of the "Diamond Necklace," in the latter part of the eighteenth century. It was made of the most beautiful diamonds, and was valued at nearly £80,000. Louis XV. commissioned the court jewellers of France to make the necklace, intending to give it to Madame du Barry, but he died before it was finished. A certain Madame La Motte, in 1785, using a forged signature of Marie Antoinette, persuaded the Cardinal de Rohan to purchase the necklace, as if for the queen. The affair created a great deal of scandal. Madame La Motte was sentenced to imprisonment for life, but managed to escape within a year, and went to England, where she was killed in trying to escape from a second-story window when pursued for debt. Cardinal de Rohan was acquitted of intentional complicity. The celebrated Count Cagliostro was also implicated in the affair. Carlyle has some chapters upon the Diamond Necklace, included in the collection of his "Critical and Miscellaneous Essays."

☞ "The great scandal of the Diamond Necklace, which to the clear vision of Goethe presaged the coming Revolution, and in which the quick-witted Talleyrand saw the overthrow of the French throne, possesses an interest akin to that of the French Revolution itself. . . . The story is one of which the world does not seem to tire, for it has been told scores upon scores of times, and more or less recently, by historians, biographers, essayists, memoir-writers, anecdotists, novelists, and dramatists, and in well-nigh every European language. . . . Whatever may have been the follies, or say the crimes even, if you please, of which Marie Antoinette was guilty, and which she more than expiated by her cruel death, complicity in any shape in this contemptible Diamond Necklace fraud is most certainly not one of them."
H. Vizetelly.

Looks dreamy to me, not self-conscious, though a black ribbon round her neck sets it off as a Marie Antoinette's *diamond necklace* could not do. *Holmes.*

Diana and Actæon. A mythological picture of great beauty by Titian (1477–1576). Now in the Bridgewater Gallery, London.

Diana and Calisto. A mythological picture by Titian (1477–1576). Now in the Bridgewater collection, London.

Diana and her Nymphs. A picture by Domenico Zampieri, surnamed Domenichino (1581–1641), and considered one of his best works. In the Borghese Gallery, Rome.

Diana, Chase of. See CHASE OF DIANA.

Diana returning from the Chase. A mythological picture by Antonio Allegri, surnamed Correggio (1494–1534). In the convent of S. Paolo, Parma, Italy.

Diana's Temple. See TEMPLE OF EPHESUS and TEMPLE OF DIANA [NÎMES].

Dice-players, The. A picture by Bartolomé Esteban Murillo (1618–1682). In the Pinacothek, Munich, Bavaria.

Dickinson College. A collegiate establishment in Carlisle, Penn. It was founded in 1783.

Dick's Coffee-house. An old house in Fleet Street, London, at first known as "Richard's," from the Christian name of its lessee (Richard Torner, or Turner) in 1680. Cowper at one time resorted to Richard's. It is no longer a coffee-house.

Dido Building Carthage. A picture by Joseph Mallord William Turner (1775–1851).

Dido's Last Moments. A large picture by Giovanni Francesco Barbieri, surnamed Guercino (1590–1666). In the Spada Gallery, at Rome.

Dieu, Hôtel. See HÔTEL DIEU.

Dighton Rock. A famous mass of granite, with rude sculptures and inscriptions upon it, near Dighton, Mass. It is by some referred to the Norsemen in the eleventh century.

Or, if letters must be written, profitable use might be made of the *Dighton Rock* hieroglyphic or the cuneiform script, every fresh decipherer of which is enabled to educe a different meaning, whereby a sculptured stone or two supplies us, and will probably continue to supply posterity, with a very vast and various body of authentic history *Lowell.*

There are inscriptions on our hearts, which, like that on *Dighton Rock*, are never to be seen except at dead-low tide. *Holmes.*

Dignity and Impudence. An admired picture of two dogs by Sir Edwin Landseer (1802–1873). In the National Gallery, London.

Digue de Cherbourg. [The Breakwater of Cherbourg.] An immense structure of masonry stretching across the roadstead of Cherbourg, in France. It was more than 50 years in building, at an expense of some $15,000,000, and was finished in 1858. The length of the breakwater is 4,120 yards, and its width at the base 310 feet.

Dilettanti. [*Literally*, lovers of the fine arts.] This society, established in 1734, owes its origin to some gentlemen who had travelled in Italy, and who wished to encourage a taste for the fine arts. The society sent an expedition to the East in 1764, the result of which appeared in volumes of "Ionian Antiquities," "Chandler's Travels in Asia Minor," "Chandler's Travels in Greece," and a volume of Greek inscriptions. Various other publications have been issued by the society at different times. Another expedition to the Levant was undertaken in 1814. The Dilettanti dine together on the first Sunday of each month from February to July. Until its removal, these dinners were held at the Thatched House Tavern, in London, in the large room of which were portraits of the Dilettanti, including three pictures by Sir Joshua Reynolds. Friendly intercourse and social enjoyment have always formed an important part in the scheme of the society. Walpole said in 1743, that the "nominal qualification [for membership] is having been in Italy, and the real one, being drunk." Sir Joshua Reynolds, Earl Fitzwilliam, C. J. Fox, Hon. Stephen Fox (Lord Holland), Charles Howard (Duke of Norfolk), Lord Robert Spencer, George Selwyn, Sir William Hamilton, David Garrick, George Colman, Joseph Windham, R. Payne Knight, Sir George Beaumont, Towneley, Sir William Gell, Henry Hallam, and many others have been members. Any use of the word Dilettanti as a term of ridicule or disparagement is comparatively recent.

☞ "We, looking back out of a graver time, can only judge from the uninterrupted course of their festive gatherings, from the names of the statesmen, the wits, the scholars, the artists, the amateurs, that fill the catalogue, from the strange mixture of dignities and accessions to wealth for which, by the rules of the society, fines were paid, — and, above all, by the pictures which they possess, — how much of the pleasantry and the hearty enjoyment must have been mixed up with the more solid pursuits of the members." *Edinburgh Review.*

Diocletian, Baths of. See BATHS OF DIOCLETIAN.

Diocletian's Palace. A splendid retreat, constructed for himself by the Emperor Diocletian on his abdication of the throne, at Salona on the Adriatic. The modern Austrian town of Spalato is chiefly built up out of the ruins of this colossal palace, and takes its name from it.

☞ "It certainly gives us a most exalted idea of what the splendor of the imperial palace at Rome must have been, when we find one emperor — certainly neither the richest, nor the most powerful — building, for his retirement, a villa in the country of almost exactly the same dimensions as the Escurial in Spain, and consequently surpassing in size, as it did in magnificence, most of the modern palaces of Europe. It is uncertain how far it resembles or was copied from that of Rome, more especially as it must be regarded as a fortified palace, which there is no reason to believe that at Rome was, while its model would seem to have been the prætorian camp rather than any habitation built within the protection of the city walls." *Fergusson.*

☞ "Spalato ought properly to be called *Diocleziano*. . . . Spalato is founded on the ruins of Diocletian's palace, the walls of which still contain the whole of the mediæval city. Every one has heard of Diocletian and his imperial cabbages, but few know how much of his imperial hermitage has been spared by time." *Bayard Taylor.*

Diogenes. A picture by Salvator Rosa (1615–1673). In the Grosvenor Gallery, London.

Dionysiac Theatre. A ruined building in Athens, Greece. There is still much obscurity in regard to these remains. The structure was not completed till the time of the orator Lycurgus, 340 B.C.; but it is thought that the general arrangement of the completed theatre was substantially the same as that of the theatre in which the dramas of Æschylus, Sophocles, Euripides, and Aristophanes were acted. The ruins of this theatre have but recently been laid bare.

Dionysius' Ear. See EAR OF DIONYSIUS.

Dionysus. See BACCHUS.

Discobolus. [Quoit-thrower.] A celebrated statue by the Greek sculptor Myron (b. 430 B.C.?). The original was in bronze, and has perished, but there are several copies in marble now existing. The best of these, discovered on the Esquiline Hill in 1782, is now in the Villa Messimi, in Rome. There are other copies in the Museums of the Vatican and of the Capitol in Rome, and in the British Museum, London.

☞ "The representation of a momentary action renders the 'Discobolus' wonderfully effective; and we feel as if we must see the throw made, and the tense muscles relaxed, before we can leave it. It is an example of the highest Greek art in the representation of the physical frame and difficult action, but it has no intellectual depth or thought."

Good plaster casts, about two feet high, copied from the antique, may now be procured for five or six shillings apiece; and such figures as the Gladiator, the *Discobolos*, and the Antinous would, to my mind, constitute a much better "finish" for the top of a bookcase than the clumsy vases and other objects usually sold for this purpose. *C. L. Eastlake.*

We may allow that a certain number of the clever children will die; but there will be enough left to carve the Niobe and the *Discobolus*. *Grant Allen.*

Dishonest Gamester. A picture by Caravaggio (1569–1609), and one of his best. In the Sciarra Palace, Rome. There are many repetitions of this picture.

Disputà della SS. Trinità. An altar-piece by Andrea Vannucchi, called Andrea del Sarto (1487–1531), the Italian painter, and regarded as one of his best works. It is a "Santa Conversazione," or discussion between six saints. In the Pitti Palace.

Dispute of the Sacrament. [*La Disputà del Sacramento.*] A celebrated fresco by Raphael Sanzio (1483–1520), representing the Almighty, the Saviour, the Virgin, with Patriarchs, Apostles, and Saints, in the glory of heaven. Below these, an assembly of the great Doctors of the Church, surrounding an altar on which is the Host. Farther off, "groups of youths and men who are pressing forward to hear the revelation of the holy mystery, some in attitudes of enthusiastic devotion, some yet doubting, and apparently in dispute." This picture is one of the series of four, — Theology, Poetry, Philosophy, and Jurisprudence, — which were intended to exhibit the lofty subjects of thought with which the human mind is occupied. They are in the Camera della Segnatura of the Vatican, Rome.

☞ "In the first of these ['Theology'], commonly but erroneously called *La Disputà del Sacramento*, Raphael has combined into one great scene the whole system of theology as set forth by the Catholic Church: it is a sort of concordance between heaven and earth, between the celestial and terrestrial witnesses of the truth." *Mrs. Jameson.*

Dispute with the Doctors. A celebrated fresco by Bernardino Luini (1480–1530). In Saronno, Italy. It has been chromo-lithographed.

Distinguished Member of the Humane Society. A picture by Sir Edwin Landseer (1803–1873), the most celebrated painter of animals. The subject is a fine dog, carrying in his mouth a basket of very bright flowers.

Ditton Park. The fine seat of Lord Montague, near Datchet, England.

Dixville Notch. A wild mountain defile in Coos Co., N.H.

Dock Square. A well-known square in Boston, Mass.

Doctors' Commons. A college of Doctors of Civil Law in London, near St. Paul's Churchyard. It includes the Court of Arches, Probate Court, High Admiralty Court, which hold, or held, their sessions in the College Hall. The name Doctors' Commons is derived from the fact that the students and lawyers lived together *in common* after the collegiate fashion. The first building was destroyed in the Great Fire of London, and was rebuilt in 1672.

☞ "Now, Doctors' Commons being familiar by name to everybody, as the place where they grant marriage-licenses to love-sick couples, and divorces to unfaithful ones; register the wills of people who have any property to leave, and punish hasty gentlemen who call ladies by unpleasant names, — we no sooner discovered that we were really within its precincts, than we felt a laudable desire to become better acquainted therewith." *Dickens.*

☞ "It's a little out-of-the-way place, where they administer what is called ecclesiastical law, and play all kinds of tricks with obsolete old monsters of acts of parliament, which three-fourths of the world know nothing about, and the other fourth supposes to have been dug up in a fossil state, in the days of the Edwards. It's a place that has an ancient monopoly in suits about people's wills and people's marriages, and disputes about ships and boats." *Dickens.*

The Earl of— Asterisk — and Lady — Blank;
Sir — Such-a-one — with those of fashion's host,
For whose blest surnames — vide "Morning Post,"
(Or if for that impartial print too late,
Search *Doctors' Commons* six months from my date). *Byron.*

Doge's Palace. [Ital. *Palazzo Ducale.*] The famous and magnificent palace of the Doges or Dukes of Venice, one of the oldest palaces in Europe, and by some regarded as, architecturally considered, the finest building in the world. The present edifice dates from the early part of the eleventh century.

☞ "There are indeed few buildings of which it is so difficult to judge calmly, situated as it is, attached to the basilica of St. Mark, and looking on the one hand into the piazza of St. Mark's, and on the other across the water to the churches and palaces that cover the islands. It is, in fact, the centre of the most beautiful architectural group that adorns any city of Europe, or of the world, — richer than almost any other building in historical associations, and in a locality hallowed especially to an Englishman by the poetry of Shakespeare. All this spreads a halo around and over the building which may furnish an excuse for those who blindly praise even its deformities. But the soberer judgment of the critic must not be led astray by such feelings; and while giving credit for the picturesque situation of this building, and a certain grandeur in its design, he is compelled wholly to condemn its execution. . . . One thing in this palace is worth remarking, — that almost all the beauty ascribed to its upper story arises from the polychromatic mode of decoration introduced by disposing pieces of different colored marbles in diaper patterns. This is better done here than in Florence, inasmuch as the slabs are built in, not stuck on. The admiration which it excites is one more testimony to the fact, that, when a building is colored, ninety-nine people in a hundred are willing to overlook all its faults, and to extol that as beautiful, which, without the adjunct of color, they would have unanimously agreed in condemning." *Fergusson.*

☞ "The Ducal Palace is so extensive a structure that the Church of St. Mark's seems nothing more than a chapel appurtenant to it. Its vast and desolate apartments, through which the visitor is carried, serve as a standard by which the ancient greatness of Venice itself may be measured. Men who could build on so gigantic a scale could have had no thought of decaying fortune or declining power." *Hillard.*

☞ "A palace more majestic and magnificent in its old age than all the buildings of the earth in the high prime and fulness of their youth. Cloisters and galleries; so light, they might be the work of fairy hands; so strong that centuries have battered them in vain; wind round and round this palace, and enfold it with a cathedral, gorgeous in the wild luxuriant fancies of the East." *Dickens.*

Dogs of St. Gothard. A picture by Sir Edwin Landseer (1803-1873).

Dolly's. A well-known tavern in Paternoster Row, London, dating from the time of Queen Anne, and still in existence.

Dolmen of Bagneux. A huge Celtic monument near Saumur, France, consisting of a house or chamber made of blocks of uncut stone. Its origin and meaning are wrapped in obscurity. It is supposed to be connected with the Druidic worship.

Dolphin, The. The ship in which Juan Verrazano crossed the Atlantic on his voyage of discovery in 1524. He entered with her Long Island Sound and New York Bay, and afterward skirted the coast of Massachusetts and of Maine.

Dome of the Rock. See MOSQUE OF OMAR.

Domes of the Yosemite. A painting by Albert Bierstadt (b. 1828). In the Athenæum at St. Johnsbury, Vt.

☞ "The 'Domes of the Yosemite' is panoramic in size: it is a wildly magnificent and unique scene, drawn with singular fidelity from the solitary heart of the Rocky Mountains." *Tuckerman.*

Domine Quo Vadis. A church upon the Via Appia, Rome, so named from the tradition, that at the time of the first persecution of the Christians, after the burning of Rome, St. Peter, fleeing from the city, was here met by a vision of the Saviour on his way to Rome. St. Peter in astonishment cried out, "Lord, whither goest thou?" (*Domine, quo vadis?*), to which Christ replied, "I go to Rome to be crucified a second time" (*Venio Romam iterum crucifigi*). Peter immediately arrested his flight, and turned back to the city. The church contains a marble slab upon which is a copy of the supposed footprint of the Saviour as left upon the pavement where he stood, the original stone being preserved in the basilica of S. Sebastiano.

☞ "On our way home we entered the Church of Domine quo Vadis, and looked at the old fragment of the Appian Way where our Saviour met St. Peter, and left the impression of his feet in one of the paving-stones. The stone has been removed; and there is now only a facsimile engraved in a block of marble, occupying the place where Jesus stood. It is a great pity they had not left the original stone; for then all its brother stones in the pavement would have seemed to confirm the truth of the legend." *Hawthorne.*

Don Saltero's Coffee-house. A house, now a tavern, in Chelsea, London, to which was formerly attached a museum, containing a collection of curiosities, the absurdity of some of which is indicated by the following remark of Steele: "He shows you a straw hat, which I know to be made by Madge Peskad, within three miles of Bedford; and tells you, 'It is Pontius Pilate's wife's chambermaid's sister's hat.'"

When I came into the coffee-house, I had not time to salute the company, before my eyes were diverted by ten thousand gimcracks round the room and on the ceiling. *Steele*

Don Saltero's Coffee-house still looks as brisk as in Steele's time. *Carlyle* (1834)

Donelson, Fort. See FORT DONELSON.

Doni, Agnolo. A well-known portrait by Raphael Sanzio (1483–1520). Now in the Uffizi Gallery, Florence, Italy.

Donington Hall. The seat of the Marquis of Hastings, near Ashby-de-la-Zouch, England.

Donnington Castle. A feudal fortress in England, near Speen, celebrated for the resistance it made to Parliament, and for having been the residence of the poet Chaucer during the latter part of his life.

Donnybrook Fair. A famous fair held annually in the village of Donnybrook, now one of the suburbs of Dublin, Ireland. The importance of the fair has of late years diminished.

☞ "Although the Irishman is no longer there 'in his glory,' tents are still annually pitched upon the sodden sward, where they have been erected for centuries; itinerant 'play-actors' continue to gather there once a year; the beggars yet make it a place of rendezvous; lads and lasses assemble even now to dance under roofs of canvas; and the din of harsh music from the 'shows,' mingled with the almost equally discordant squeakings of a score or two of bagpipes, still keep alive the memory of

'Donnybrook capers, that bother'd the
vapors,
And drove away care.'"

Mr. and Mrs. Hall.

Dorchester House. A modern mansion in London, built in 1851, on the site of the old Dorchester House, and noted for its elegance and for its fine collection of pictures.

Doria Palace. [Ital. *Palazzo Doria.*] A celebrated palace, once the residence of Andrea Doria, in Genoa, Italy.

This house was Andrea Doria's. Here he
lived —
— He left it for a better, and 'tis now
A house of trade. Yet fallen as it is,
'Tis still the noblest dwelling, even in
Genoa! *Rogers.*

The *Doria's* long pale palace striking out,
From green hills in advance of the white
town,
A marble finger dominant to ships,
Seen glimmering through the uncertain
gray of dawn *Mrs Browning.*

Doria-Pamphili Palace. [Ital. *Palazzo Doria-Pamphili.*] A palace in Rome, of immense size, having a façade upon the Corso, and containing a fine and large gallery of paintings. Among the many works in the gallery are some landscapes by Claude Lorraine, including his well-known picture of "The Mill" (*Molino*).

Dorothea, The. A vessel under command of Capt. Buchan, sent, in company with the *Trent* under Franklin, on an expedition to the Arctic regions in 1818.

Dorothea. See FORNARINA, LA.

D'Orsay, Palais. See ORSAY, PALAIS D'.

Dorset Gardens Theatre. A former theatre of London, situated at the extremity of Salisbury Court, Fleet Street, opened in 1671, and taken down about 1720.

Douglas Castle. An ancient ruined fortress near the town of the same name in Scotland. It is described by Sir Walter Scott in his "Castle Dangerous." It, as well as the modern mansion bearing the same name, belongs to the Earl of Home.

Doune Castle. An ancient baronial edifice in Doune, Scotland, associated with the romances of Sir Walter Scott. The hero of "Waverley" was imprisoned here.

Dovedale. A remarkable and far-famed chasm, in the neighborhood of Ashbourne, England, through which flows the river Dove. The scenery is of the most romantic description.

She dwelt among the untrodden ways
Beside the springs of *Dove*,
A maid whom there were none to praise,
And very few to love. *Wordsworth.*

Dover. A picture by Joseph Mallord William Turner (1775-1851), the celebrated English painter.

Dover Castle. The ancient and now modernized and greatly strengthened fortress of Dover, England, on the summit of a cliff over 300 feet in height. The foundations of the fortress are thought to be of Roman times. Dover Castle embraces an area of some 35 acres.

Dover House. A mansion in Whitehall, London, formerly belonging to the Duke of York.

Doves of Pliny. See PLINY'S DOVES.

Downing College. A foundation of the University of Cambridge, England. Established in 1800.

Downing Street. A street in London, named from Sir George Downing. The principal house in this street was given by George I. to Sir Robert Walpole, who accepted it for his office of First Lord of the Treasury. It has since been the official residence of successive prime ministers, and has given celebrity to the street in which it stands.

☞ "From all corners of the wide British Dominion there rises one complaint against the ineffectuality of what are nicknamed our 'red-tape' establishments, our Government Offices, Colonial Office, Foreign Office, and the others, in Downing Street and the neighborhood. To me individually these branches of human business are little known; but every British citizen and reflective passer-by has occasion to wonder much and inquire earnestly concerning them. . . . And, secondly, it is felt that 'reform' in that Downing-street department of affairs is precisely the reform which were worth all others; that those administrative establishments in Downing Street are really the Government of this huge ungoverned Empire." *Carlyle.*

☞ "There is a fascination in the air of this little *cul-de-sac:* an hour's inhalation of its atmosphere affects some men with giddiness, others with blindness, and very frequently with the most oblivious boastfulness." *Theodore Hook.*

Let but a hand of violence be laid upon an English subject, and the great British lion which lies couchant in *Downing Street* begins to utter menacing growls and shake his invincible locks. *Hillard.*

To call upon any judge in such a matter would be altogether out of place. . . . He had in his head some hazy idea of forcing an answer from the officials in *Downing Street;* but in his heart he did not believe he should be able to get beyond the messengers. *Anthony Trollope.*

Suave mari magno, it is pleasant sitting in the easy-chairs of *Downing Street*, to sprinkle pepper on the raw wounds of a kindred people struggling for life, and philosophical to find in self-conceit the cause of our instinctive resentment. *Lowell.*

Drachenfels. [Dragon Rock.] This castle on a mountain of the same name, 855 feet above the level of the Rhine, was built early in the twelfth century. It is about ten miles from the city of Bonn. In the Thirty Years War it was occupied by the Swedes, but was taken and destroyed by the Duke Ferdinand of Bavaria. The name is said to be derived from the dragon slain by the horned Siegfried, who figures in the "Niebelungen Lied." Stone was taken from a quarry on the Drachenfels to build the famed Cathedral of Cologne.

The castled crag of *Drachenfels*
Frowns o'er the wild and winding Rhine,
Whose breast of waters broadly swells
Between the banks which bear the vine.
Byron.

'Twas midnight as we scaled the mountain height,—
. . . .
Owls hooted, rattling sounds were heard and groans;
A furious north-wind blustered fitfully.
Such was the night, my friend, that I did pass
On the high *Drachenfels.* *Heine, Trans.*

Drapers' Hall. A well-known hall in Throgmorton Street, London, belonging to the great City Company of Drapers. The old edifice was destroyed in the great fire, but was afterwards rebuilt.

Draught of Fishes. See MIRACULOUS DRAUGHT OF FISHES.

Dreadnought, The. A celebrated ship of the British navy which fought at Trafalgar, and was afterwards moored in the Thames as a hospital for sick and diseased seamen of all nations.

Drei Gleichen. [The Three Equals.] A name given to three ruined castles of similar appearance, and all of great antiquity, in the neighborhood of Gotha, Germany.

Drei Mohren. [The Three Moors.] A famous tavern in Augsburg, Bavaria, which has existed as such for more than 500 years, and is also celebrated for its stores of rare wines.

Dresden Madonna. See MADONNA DI SAN SISTO.

Druid Hill. A beautiful and spacious park just north of Baltimore, Md. It comprises 675 acres. The trees are very ancient, and the grounds were to some extent laid out before the Revolution.

Drummond Castle. The seat of the Earls of Perth near Crieff, Scotland.

Drunken Bacchus. A statue by Michael Angelo Buonarotti (1475–1564). It is in the Uffizi Gallery, Florence, Italy.

☞ "It is a figure as large as life, of which Michael Angelo's contemporaries speak with admiration, while moderns do not accord with this unqualified appreciation." *Grimm, Trans.*

☞ "The arms are perfect in their manly beauty; the frame is powerfully modelled, and all the lines flow with boldness and truth, one into the other. As a work of art, unity alone is wanting. He should be Bacchus in every thing." *Shelley.*

☞ "The Drunken Bacchus . . . might pass for a relic of the palmiest times of Grecian art. The face, amidst its half-vacant, sensual expression.

shows traces of its immortal origin, and there is still an air of dignity preserved in the swagger of his beautiful form."
Bayard Taylor.

Drunken Faun. An admired statue, a relic of ancient sculpture. Now in the museum at Naples, Italy.

Drury Court. A court in London, formerly called May-pole Alley. See MAY-POLE and DRURY LANE.

Drury Lane. A street in London, so called from the town house of the Drury family. It was an aristocratic quarter till late in the seventeenth century. The present character of the place is implied in the lines of Gay (1688–1732), written after it had begun to deteriorate. See DRURY LANE THEATRE.

Oh, may thy virtue guard thee through the roads
Of *Drury's* mazy courts and dark abodes!
Gay.

1st May, 1667. To Westminster, in the way meeting many milkmaids with their garlands upon their pails, dancing with a fiddler before them; and saw pretty Nelly [Nell Gwynne] standing at her lodging-door, in *Drury-lane*, in her smock-sleeves and bodice, looking upon one: she seemed a mighty pretty creature *Pepys.*

Did you ever hear the like,
Or ever hear the fame,
Of five women barbers
That lived in *Drury Lane?*
Ballad.

When Calvert's butt and Parson's black champagne
Regale the drabs and bloods of *Drury Lane*;
There in a lonely room, from bailiffs snug,
The Muse found Scroggen stretched beneath a rug. *Goldsmith.*

Drury Lane Theatre. The first building of this name, situated upon the same site with the present edifice, was opened in 1663. It was subsequently burned, and was rebuilt from designs by Sir Christopher Wren. It was reopened in 1674 with a prologue and epilogue by Dryden. Many eminent actors and playwrights have at different times been connected with this theatre. It was again destroyed by fire in 1809, and the present house was opened in 1812 with a prologue by Lord Byron. This opening in 1812 is interesting from its connection with the publication of the "Rejected Addresses" of James and Horace Smith. The managers of the theatre having advertised for addresses, to be sent them, one of which was to be spoken on the first night, the brothers James and Horace wrote and published their collection of supposed *Rejected* Addresses, consisting of humorous imitations of different authors. See DRURY LANE.

This old doorway, if you are young, reader, you may not know was the identical pit entrance to old *Drury*, — Garrick's Drury, — all of it that is left. I never pass it without shaking some forty years from off my shoulders, recurring to the evening when I passed through it to see *my first play*. *Charles Lamb.*

To him [Johnson] she was as beautiful as the Gunnings, and witty as Lady Mary. Her opinion of his writings was more important to him than the voice of the pit of *Drury Lane Theatre*, or the judgment of the Monthly Review. *Macaulay.*

Then spare our stage, ye methodistic men!
Nor burn damn'd *Drury* if it rise again.
Byron.

For this world abounds in miraculous combinations, far transcending any thing they do at *Drury Lane* in the melodramatic way. *Carlyle.*

Drusus, Arch of. See ARCH OF DRUSUS.

Drusus, Tower of. A Roman ruin at Mayence, Germany, regarded by some as the tomb of Drusus, the son-in-law of Augustus. Its popular name is the *Eichelstein*.

Dryburgh Abbey. This ancient abbey of Scotland is situated on the Tweed, about 40 miles from Edinburgh. It was founded in 1144 by Hugh de Morville, and endowed by David I. and by several churches. It has long been in ruins. One of the transept aisles remains, however, and here Sir Walter Scott and his family are buried.

☞ "There is a part of the ruin that stands most picturesquely by itself, as if Old Time had intended it for a monument. It is the ruin of that part of the chapel called St. Mary's Aisle: it stands surrounded by luxuriant thickets of pine and other trees, a cluster of beautiful Gothic arches supporting a second tier of smaller and more fanciful ones, one or two of which have that light touch of the Moorish in their form which gives such a singular and poetic effect in many of the old Gothic ruins. Out of these wild arches and windows wave wreaths of ivy, and slender harebells shake their blue pendants. . . . Underneath these arches he [Scott] lies beside his wife; around him the representation of the two things he loved most, — the wild bloom and beauty of nature, and the architectural memorial of bygone history and art." *Mrs. H. B. Stowe.*

A solemn ruin, lovely in repose,
Dryburgh! thine ivied walls were grayly seen:
Thy court is now a garden, where the flowers
Expand in silent beauty, and the bird
Flitting from arch to arch alone is heard
To cheer with song the melancholy bowers. *D. M. Moir.*

Thou slumberest with the noble dead
In *Dryburgh's* solemn pile,
Amid the peers and warriors bold,
And mitred abbots stern and old,
Who sleep in sculptured aisle.
L. H. Sigourney.

Dublin Castle. The residence of the Viceroy of Ireland, in Dublin. It is an ancient stronghold, — begun in 1205, situated on very high ground nearly in the centre of the city, — but it has undergone almost entire restoration and renewal, and is now used for government offices.

Ducal Palace. See DOGE'S PALACE.

Dudley House. A mansion in London, the residence of Earl Dudley, containing a fine collection of pictures.

Dudley Observatory. An astronomical observatory in Albany, N. Y.

Duff House. The seat of the Earl of Fife, in the town of Bauff, Scotland.

Duke Humphrey's Walk. A name once popularly given to the middle aisle of the nave in St. Paul's Church, London, in which was the tomb of the duke, son of Henry IV. The young idlers of Elizabeth's time were often called "Paul's Walkers."

☞ "An open question whether 'dining with Duke Humphrey' alludes to the report that he was starved to death, or to the Elizabethan habit for poor gentility to beguile the dinner hour by a promenade near his tomb in old St. Paul's." *Yonge.*

Paul's Walk is the Land's Epitome, or you may call it the lesser Ile of Great Brittaine
Earle, Microcosmographia, 1629.

— Do you dine with Sir Humphrey to-day?
I should think with *Duke* Humphrey was more in your way. *Byron.*

Those who at Christmas do repine,
And would fain hence despatch him,
May they with old *Duke Humphrey* dine,
Or else may Squire Ketch catch 'em.

Duke of Exeter's Daughter. A name given to the rack, which was first introduced as an instrument of torture into the Tower of London by the Duke of Exeter in 1447.

Duke of Guise. See DEATH OF THE DUKE OF GUISE.

Duke of York's Column. A Scotch granite column 124 feet high, Carlton-House Gardens, London, surmounted by a statue of the Duke of York (d. 1827) in whose memory it was erected.

Duke's Theatre. A famous old London theatre, built in 1660, which took the place of the older Salisbury Court Theatre. Knight says of the Salisbury Court theatre that it was in 1583 one of the chief London playhouses. The Duke's Theatre was destroyed in the great fire, and rebuilt by Sir Christopher Wren in 1671. It lasted down to the year 1720.

"Like Nero's palace shining all with gold." *Dryden.*

Dulwich College. An educational establishment in the environs of London, founded in 1613. The present building is mostly modern.

Dulwich Gallery. A collection of paintings, founded by Sir Francis Bourgeois, now in Dulwich College, in the environs of London. It contains some fine specimens of the Dutch school.

Dumbarton Castle. An ancient and celebrated fortress on the river Clyde, in Scotland.

☞ "The rock is nearly 500 feet high, and from its position and great strength as a fortress has been called the Gibralter of Scotland."
Bayard Taylor.

☞ "All the tears we shed over Miss Porter's William Wallace seem to rise up like a many-colored mist about it. The highest peak of the rock is still called Wallace's Seat, and a part of the castle, Wallace's Tower; and in one of its apartments a huge two-handed sword of the hero is still shown. I suppose, in fact, Miss Porter's sentimental hero is about as much like the real William Wallace as Daniel Boone is like Sir Charles Grandison. Many a young lady who has cried herself sick over Wallace in the novel, would have been in perfect horror if she could have seen the real man. Still Dumbarton Castle is not a whit the less picturesque for that."
Mrs. H. B. Stowe.

Dunamase, Rock of. See ROCK OF DUNAMASE.

Dunderberg. [Thunder Mountain.] An eminence on the Hudson river at Caldwell's Landing, associated with romantic legends.

☞ "The captains of the river craft talk of a little bulbous-bottomed Dutch goblin, in trunk hose and sugar-loaf hat, with a speaking-trumpet in his hand, which they say keeps the *Donder Berg*. They declare that they have heard him in stormy weather, in the midst of the turmoil, giving orders in Low Dutch for the piping up of a fresh gust of wind, or the rattling off of another thunder-clap. . . . Several events of this kind having taken place, the regular skippers of the river for a long time did not venture to pass the *Donder Berg* without lowering their peaks, out of homage to the Heer of the mountains; and it was observed that all such as paid this tribute of respect were suffered to pass unmolested." *Washington Irving.*

Dundonald Castle. An ancient feudal mansion, now in ruins, near the town of Troon, in Scotland. King Robert II. of Scotland lived here before his accession to the throne.

☞ "Dr. Johnson, to irritate my old Scottish enthusiasm, was very jocular on the homely accommodation of King Bob, and roared and laughed till the ruins echoed." *Boswell.*

Dundrennan Abbey. An ancient and once celebrated monastic establishment near Kirkcubbright, in Scotland, and near the sea. It was built in 1140 by King David for Cistercian monks from Rievaulx. Queen Mary is said to have slept there after the battle of Langside. Only the front of the building now remains.

Dun Edin's Cross. An ancient monument, consisting of a shaft surmounted by a unicorn, standing within the enclosure of St. Giles's Church, Edinburgh, Scotland. It was taken down, and for a time removed from the city, but in 1866 was restored to its original place. The base is modern.

Dun-Edin's Cross, a pillared stone,
Rose on a turret octagon.
(But now is razed that monument
Whence royal edict rang,
And voice of Scotland's law was sent
In glorious trumpet clang);
Oh! be his tomb as lead to lead
Upon its dull destroyer's head!—
A minstrel's malison is said. *Scott.*

Dunfermline Abbey. A famous burial-place of the Scottish kings. The original edifice was founded in the eleventh century. The existing building is of the present century. The Palace of Dunfermline was a favorite residence of the kings of Scotland.

Dunloe Cave. A singular cave near the entrance to the Gap of Dunloe, in the county of Kerry, Ireland. It is remarkable for some ancient stones which it contains, inscribed with the old Ogham characters, said to have been used in Ireland long before the era of Christianity. It is conjectured that this writing may be a relic of the old Phœnician writing introduced by a colony into Ireland.

Dunloe Gap. A noted pass about four miles in length, in the county of Kerry, Ireland.

☞ "The visitor is at once convinced that he is about to visit a scene rarely paralleled for wild grandeur and stern magnificence; the singular character of the deep ravine would seem to confirm the popular tradition that it was produced by a stroke of the sword of one of the giants of old, which divided the mountains and left them apart forever. Anywhere, and under any circumstances, this rugged and gloomy pass would be a most striking object; but its interest and importance are no doubt considerably enhanced by

the position it occupies in the very centre of gentle and delicious beauty."
Mr. and Mrs. Hall.

Dunluce Castle. One of the most interesting and remarkable ruins in Ireland, in the county of Antrim, the former seat of the McDonnels. It stands on an insulated rock a hundred feet above the sea, while its base has been formed by the action of the waves into spacious and beautiful caverns.

☞ "It was the most mournful and desolate picture I ever beheld. . . . In front the breakers dashed into the entrance, flinging the spray half way to the roof, while the sound rang up through the arches like thunder. It seemed to me the haunt of the old Norsemen's sea-gods."
Bayard Taylor.

Dunmore House. The seat of the Earl of Dunmore, on the Firth of Forth, Scotland.

Dunmore House. An ancient but decaying mansion in Williamsburg, Va., the former residence of Lord Dunmore, the last of the colonial governors of Virginia. It is of brick, and was in its day a house of vice-regal splendor.

Dunnottar Castle. A ruined fortress near Stonehaven, Scotland, the seat of the Keiths, earls marischal of Scotland. It was taken by Wallace in 1296, and was dismantled in the early part of the last century. It was at one time a place of imprisonment of the Scottish Covenanters.

☞ "Bare and desolate, surrounded on all sides by the restless, moaning waves; a place justly held accursed as the scene of cruelties to the Covenanters, so appalling and brutal as to make the blood boil in the recital, even in this late day." *Mrs. H. B. Stowe.*

Dunrobin Castle. The seat of the Duke of Sutherland, a castellated mansion, and one of the finest residences in Scotland. It is situated in the parish of Golspie, in the county of Sutherland.

Dunroby Abbey. A beautiful ruined monastery in the county of Wexford, Ireland. It was founded in 1182.

Dunsinane Hill. An eminence about 1,100 feet in height, near Errol, in Scotland, famous from its associations with Shakespeare's tragedy of "Macbeth," and as having been the site of the castle mentioned in the play. See MACBETH'S CAIRN.

I pull in resolution, and begin
To doubt the equivocation of the fiend
That lies like truth: 'Fear not till Birnam Wood
Do come to *Dunsinane;*' and now a wood
Comes toward Dunsinane. *Shakespeare.*

Dunstan's, St. See ST. DUNSTAN'S.

Dunvegan Castle. An ancient mansion in the North of Scotland, the seat of Macleod of Macleod, said to be the oldest inhabited castle in the country. Sir Walter Scott composed one of his poems here.

Duomo. For names beginning with the word DUOMO (Italian for cathedral) see the next prominent word of the name; e.g., DUOMO DI PISA, see PISA, CATHEDRAL OF.

Du Quesne, Fort. See FORT DU QUESNE.

Durandal. The famous sword of Roland the Brave, said to have been brought with his body by Charlemagne from Roncesvaux, and interred in the citadel of Blaye, on the Garonne, France.

Durazzo Palace. [Ital. *Palazzo Durazzo.*] A splendid palace in Genoa, Italy, containing some fine pictures.

Dürer, Albert. See ALBERT DÜRER.

Durgah, The. A famous tomb, built for the Shekh Selim-Chisti, at Futtehpore, about 22 miles from Agra, in Hindostan.

☞ "The tomb, as well as a canopy six feet high which covers it, is made of mother-of-pearl. The floor is of jasper, and the walls of white marble inlaid with cornelian. A cloth of silk and gold was spread over it like a pall, and upon this were wreaths of fresh and withered flowers. The screens of marble surrounding the building are the most beautiful in India. They are single thin slabs about eight feet square, and wrought into such intricate open patterns that you would say they had

been woven in a loom. Bushàrat Ali informed me that the Durgah was erected in one year, and that it cost 37 lacs of rupees, — $1,750,000."
Bayard Taylor.

Durham Castle. One of the noble remains of antiquity in the North of England, different portions of which date back to different periods. A great part of it is supposed to be no older than William the Conqueror; but there must have been a fortress before that time. The old keep, which commands beautiful views, is divided into rooms which are occupied by students of the university.

Gray towers of *Durham!* there was once a time
I viewed your battlements with such vague hope
As brightens life in its first dawning prime;
. . . .
Well yet I love thy mixed and massive piles,
Half church of God, half castle 'gainst the Scot,
And long to roam these venerable aisles,
With records stored of deeds long since forgot. *Scott.*

Durham Cathedral. One of the noblest ecclesiastical edifices in England. It was founded in 1093; is 507 feet in length, 200 feet in breadth, and has a tower 214 feet in height. It is of massive Norman architecture.

Durham House. A noble mansion in London in former days, situated on the Strand. It was at one time in the possession of Sir Walter Raleigh. A part of the site is now occupied by the Adelphi Terrace.

Durham Terrace. A terrace at Quebec, Canada, 200 feet above the river, and commanding a magnificent view. The terrace, which is a favorite promenade, stands upon the platform and buttresses where was formerly the Château of St. Louis, built by Champlain in 1620.

☞ "There is not in the world a nobler outlook than that from the terrace at Quebec. You stand upon a rock overhanging city and river, and look down upon the guard-ships' masts. Acre upon acre of timber comes floating down the stream above the city, the Canadian boat-songs just reaching you upon the heights." *Sir Charles Dilke.*

Durrenstein. A famous ruined castle on the Danube, near Linz, once the prison of Richard Cœur de Lion.

Düsseldorf Gallery. A gallery of paintings in Düsseldorf, Germany, founded at the beginning of the eighteenth century. In 1805 all the finest pictures in the gallery were taken to Munich by Max. Joseph, king of Bavaria, and are now in the Pinakothek. The gallery, however, still contains many valuable sketches and drawings by celebrated artists.

Düsseldorf Madonna. A name sometimes given to a picture of a Holy Family by Raphael Sanzio (1483–1520), formerly in Düsseldorf, but now in the Pinakothek at Munich, Bavaria.

☞ "Christ and St. John attending to each other; the Virgin sitting on the ground looking at St. John; St. Joseph behind with both hands on his staff . . . altogether a very regular pyramid."
Sir Joshua Reynolds.

Dutch Church. See OLD DUTCH CHURCH.

Dying Gladiator. A famous work of ancient sculpture, representing a Gaul dying, and supposed to be one of a series of figures illustrating the incursion of the Gauls into Greece. The best authorities now regard this wonderful statue as that of a dying Gaul, and not a gladiator, though some have looked upon it as either the original work or a copy of a statue by Ctesilaus (Cresilas), a Grecian sculptor, and contemporary of Phidias. It is now preserved in the museum of the Capitol at Rome. The right arm of this statue has been restored. It is not positively known by whom this restoration was made; but the work has been credited to Michael Angelo on the ground that no one else could have done it. See BORGHESE GLADIATOR and WOUNDED GLADIATOR.

☞ "Here is a real and not an ideal statue: the figure, nevertheless, is beautiful, because men of this class devoted their lives to exercising naked."
Taine, Trans.

I must never forget the famous statue of the *Gladiator* spoken of by Pliny, so much follow'd by all the rare artists, as the many copies testify, dispersed through almost all Europe, both in stone and metal. *John Evelyn*, 1644.

I see before me the *Gladiator* lie:
He leans upon his hand — his manly brow
Consents to death, but conquers agony.
Byron.

It was that room, in the centre of which reclines the noble and most pathetic figure of the *Dying Gladiator*, just sinking into his death-swoon. *Hawthorne.*

Dying Magdalene. A well-known work of sculpture by Antonio Canova (1757-1822).

E.

Ear of Dionysius. In the neighborhood of Syracuse, in Sicily, is a cave of great depth, which is said to have been built by Dionysius the Elder, a tyrant, or usurper, who was born about B.C. 430, and died B.C. 367, in the sixty-third year of his age, and the thirty-ninth of his rule. This cave was 250 feet long and 80 feet high. It was fashioned in the form of a human ear; and the faintest sounds were carried from all parts to a central chamber, which corresponded to the tympanum, or drum, of the ear. In this remarkable whispering gallery, Dionysius imprisoned all who were the objects of his suspicions; while he himself was in the habit of passing entire days in the innermost chamber, listening to the conversation of his victims, in order that he might ascertain for himself who were really his enemies. Ancient writers tell us that the workmen who constructed the cavern were put to death to prevent them from divulging the use to which it was to be put, and that whole families were sometimes confined in it at once. Modern travellers relate that even at the present day, notwithstanding the changes which have been wrought by time, the echo is such that the tearing of a sheet of paper at the entrance can be distinctly heard in the remotest part. Pieces of iron and lead have been found in making excavations, and they are thought to be the remains of the chains and staples by which the prisoners were confined.

This serpent in the wall is arranged for hearing. It is an *Ear of Dionysius*.
George Sand, Trans.

Nevertheless, even in the height of his glory, he [Voltaire] has a strange sensitiveness to the judgment of the world: could he have contrived a *Dionysius' Ear*, in the Rue Traversière, we should have found him watching at it night and day.
Carlyle.

Earthly Love. An admired picture by Caravaggio (1569–1609). In the Berlin Museum.

East India Docks. These docks, in London, originally built for the East India Company, have been, since the opening of the trade to India, the property of the East and West India Companies. They were opened in 1806. See West India Docks.

Captain Cuttle lived on the brink of a little canal near the *India Docks*, where there was a swivel bridge, which opened now and then to let some wandering monster of a ship come roaming up the street like a stranded leviathan. *Dickens.*

East India House. The house of the East India Company, "the most celebrated commercial association of ancient or modern times." It was situated in Leadenhall Street, London, and was taken down in 1862, its celebrated museum having been removed to Fife House, Whitehall. The museum is now at the South Kensington Museum. Hoole, the translator of Tasso, Charles Lamb, and James Mill, the historian of British India, were clerks in the East India House.

☞ "My printed works were my recreations: my true works may be found on the shelves in Leadenhall Street, filling some hundred folios."
Charles Lamb.

Scandinavian Thor, who once forged his bolts in icy Hecla, and built galleys by lonely fiords, in England, has advanced with the times, has shorn his beard, enters Parliament, sits down at a desk in the *India House*, and lends Miollnir to Birmingham for a steam hammer.
Emerson.

East India Marine Hall. A building in Salem, Mass., containing collections of the Essex Institute and of the East India Marine Society. The scientific cabinets of the Essex Institute are extensive and well-arranged, and the collections of the Marine Society include many curiosities from Oriental countries and other distant nations.

☞ Among the numerous curiosities is a piece of wood-carving in the form of two hemispheres 1½ inches in diameter, in the concavities of which are carved representations on the one hemisphere of heaven and on the other of hell. There are 110 full-length figures in the carving, and the whole is very skilfully executed. It is said to be the work of an Italian monk of the fourteenth century.

East Room. A noted apartment in the White House at Washington, being a richly-decorated hall 80 feet in length by 40 feet in width, adorned with portraits of the Presidents, and used for public receptions.

Eagle's Nest. A celebrated rock about 1,200 feet in height, among the Killarney lakes in the county of Derry, Ireland. It is noted for its wonderful and exciting echoes. It derives its name from the fact, that for centuries it has been the favorite abode of eagles.

☞ "It is impossible for language to convey even a remote idea of the exceeding delight communicated by this development of a most wonderful property of nature. . . . It is not only by the louder sounds that the echoes of the hills are awakened; the clapping of a hand will call them forth; almost a whisper will be repeated, — far off, ceasing, resuming, ceasing again."
Mr. and Mrs. S. C. Hall.

☞ "It is scarcely in the power of language to convey an idea of the extraordinary effect of the echoes under this cliff, whether they repeat the dulcet notes of music or the loud, discordant report of a cannon." *Weld.*

Eastcheap. An ancient thoroughfare in London. It was the East Cheap or market, in distinction from Cheapside, which was the West Cheap. Here was the famous Boar's Head Tavern. Stowe says that Eastcheap was always famous for its "convivial doings. The cookes cried hot ribbes of beef roasted, pies well baked, and other victuals: there was clattering of pewter pots, harpe, pipe, and sawtrie." See BOAR'S HEAD TAVERN.

Then I hyed me into *Est-Chepe*,
One cryes ribbes of befe and many a pye:
Pewter pottes they clattered on a heape.
Lydgate.

Eastcheap, that ancient region of wit and wassail, where the very names of the streets relished of good cheer, as Pudding Lane bears testimony even at the present day. *Irving.*

Age, care, wisdom, reflection, begone! I give you to the winds. Let's have t'other bottle: here's to the memory of Shakespeare, Falstaff, and all the merry men of *Eastcheap*. *Goldsmith.*

Shakespeare knew . . . innumerable things: what men are, and what the world is, and how and what men aim at there, from the Dame Quickly of modern *Eastcheap* to the Cæsar of ancient Rome, over many countries, over many centuries. *Carlyle.*

Eastnor Castle. The seat of the Earl of Somers, near Ledbury, England.

Eaton Hall. A noted mansion, the seat of the Marquis of Westminster, on the banks of the Dee, near Chester, England.

Eaton Square. A well-known public square in London.

Ebernburg. A ruined castle in Bavaria, which, in the sixteenth century, afforded shelter to many of the early Reformers.

Ecce Homo. [Behold the Man.] A favorite subject of representation by the religious painters of the Middle Ages, in which Christ is exhibited as presented to the people, according to the account in John xix. 5.

☞ "The *Ecce Homo* is a comparatively late subject. It did not occur in the Greek Church, . . . it does not appear in early ivories, nor in manuscripts. . . . It was one of the aims in the Roman Church from the fifteenth century, to excite compassion for the Saviour, — an aim which has always tended to lower Art by lowering the great idea she is bound to keep in view."
Lady Eastlake.

On the freshly-stretched canvas of American landscapes plenty of *Ecce Homos* breathe and live, who hide their wounds lest they fill the eyes of beholders with a mediæval pity. *John Weiss.*

Of a great number of compositions upon this subject, a few only of the more celebrated or familiar may be named.

Ecce Homo. A picture by Fra Bartolommeo (1469–1517). In the Pitti Palace, Florence, Italy.

Ecce Homo. A celebrated picture by Antonio Allegri, surnamed Correggio (1494–1534). The Virgin is represented in front fainting—a unique incident. This picture is considered a masterwork of Correggio. Now in the National Gallery, London. There is another picture by Correggio upon the same subject, in the Museum at Berlin.

☞ "The Ecce Homo, by Correggio, in our National Gallery, is treated in a very peculiar manner in reference to the Virgin, and is, in fact, another version of *Lo Spasimo* [*q. v.*], the fourth of her ineffable sorrows. Here Christ, as exhibited to the people by Pilate, is placed in the distance, and is in all respects the least important part of the picture, of which we have the real subject in the far more prominent figure of the Virgin in the foreground."
Mrs. Jameson.

☞ "Correggio's picture in the National Gallery is a master-work, on which all praise is superfluous. The fainting Virgin in front is a novel incident in this piece, and, far from adding pathos, embarrasses the position of the Saviour, whose attention would naturally be concentrated on his mother."
Lady Eastlake.

☞ "Lastly his [Correggio's] *Ecce Homo* in the Berlin Museum, a painting in which pain and sadness and beauty are united into the most touching spectacle. Leonardo alone, beside him, could have painted it."
Grimm, Trans.

Ecce Homo. A picture by Ludovico Cardi da Cigoli (1599-1613), his *chef d'œuvre*, and a work of the highest order. It is in the Pitti Palace, Florence, Italy.

☞ "One of the most beautiful pictures of this subject was reserved for a comparatively late master to execute. Cigoli's large work in the Pitti . . . can hardly fail to touch the heart. . . . All is mournful, gentle, and loving; and the very color of the robe adds to the sadness."
Lady Eastlake.

Ecce Homo. A painting by Rembrandt van Ryn (1606-1669).

☞ "That 'inspired Dutchman,' as Mrs. Jameson has called Rembrandt, threw all his grand and uncouth soul into this subject [the Ecce Homo]. He painted it once in chiaroscuro, and treated it twice in an etching, each time historically."
Lady Eastlake.

Ecce Homo. A picture by Jan van Mabuse (1499-1562 ?), a Flemish painter. It is in the Museum at Antwerp, Belgium.

Ecce Homo. A celebrated picture by Titian (1477–1576), which includes portraits of the Emperor Charles V. in armor, of the Sultan Solyman, and of the painter himself. The picture formerly belonged to Charles I. of England, and was sold by Oliver Cromwell. Now in the Belvedere Gallery at Vienna, Austria.

Ecce Homo. An admired picture by Francesco Barbieri, called Guercino (1590–1666). In the Palazzo Corsini, Rome.

☞ "A painting which, notwithstanding the painful nature of the subject and all its hackneyed representations, is full of such deep and powerful expression, and so faultless in its execution, that it awakens our highest admiration."
Eaton.

Eccentrics, The. A convivial club in London, which first met about 1800 in a tavern in Chandos Street, Covent Garden, and afterwards removed to St. Martin's Lane, where they met till 1840. It was an offshoot of *The Brilliants.*

☞ "Amongst the members were many celebrities of the literary and political world, they were always treated with indulgence by the authorities. . . . From its commencement the Eccentrics are said to have numbered upwards of 40,000 members, many of them holding high social position: among others, Fox, Sheridan, Lord Melbourne, and Lord Brougham. On the same memorable night that Sheridan and Lord Petersham were admitted, Hook was also enrolled."
Timbs.

Echo Cañon. A remarkable and famous ravine forming a gateway through the Wahsatch range of mountains in Utah Territory. It is one of the most astonishing natural spectacles to be found in the West. The trains of the Union Pacific Railroad pass through this gorge.

Echo Lake. A picturesque little lake a short distance north of the

Profile House in the Franconia Mountains, N.H., so named from the remarkable echoes which can be heard here. "Franconia is more fortunate in its little tarn that is rimmed by the undisturbed wilderness, and watched by the grizzly peak of Lafayette, than in the Old Stone Face from which it has gained so much celebrity."

Echo River. A partly subterranean river in Kentucky. It flows for three-quarters of a mile within the Mammoth Cave, and finally empties into Green River.

Ecluse. See FORT DE L'ECLUSE.

École Polytechnique. [Polytechnic School.] A celebrated institution in Paris, founded in 1795. The pupils are admitted only on examination. The candidates must be between 16 and 20 years of age. The pupils are examined at the end of the course, which is two years in length, and are assigned to various positions in the public service, according to their proficiency. They have more than once shown themselves ardent politicians.

Ecstasy of St. Francis. A picture by Anthony van Dyck (1599–1641). In the gallery at Vienna, Austria.

Eddystone Light-house. The "Eddystone" is the name of the highest part of a perilous reef about 14 miles south-west of the harbor of Plymouth, England. The first light-house upon this dangerous rock was begun in 1696 by Henry Winstanley. Several years after the completion of this structure, which resembled a "Chinese pagoda, with open galleries and fantastic projections," it was entirely carried away. Another light-house, built of stone and timber, was completed by Mr. Rudyerd in 1709, and burned in 1755. The third and present light-house upon the Eddystone rock was begun by John Smeaton in 1756, and finished in 1759. It is built of stone, and the separate stones are securely fastened together (and the lower courses to the ledge) by an ingenious system of dovetailing. It is 100 feet in height and 26 feet in diameter. Over the door of the lantern is the inscription: "24th Aug., 1759. Laus Deo."

Eden Hall. The ancient seat of the celebrated Border clan of the Musgraves, near Penrith, in Cumberland, England. An interesting legend is connected with a curious drinking-cup, an heirloom in the family. See LUCK OF EDENHALL.

Eden Park. A pleasure-ground of 160 acres on an eminence east of Cincinnati, O.

Edgecumbe. See MOUNT EDGECUMBE.

Edinburgh Castle. A celebrated fortress in the form of an irregular pile of buildings on an eminence in the city of Edinburgh, Scotland. As a royal residence it dates back to the twelfth century. It was taken by Cromwell after the battle of Dunbar.

Edouard, Enfans d'. See ENFANS D'EDOUARD.

Edward the Confessor's Chapel. An ancient chapel in Westminster Abbey, London, in which are the tombs of many of the early kings and queens of England, with their families.

Egeria. See FOUNTAIN OF EGERIA.

Eglinton Castle. The seat of the Earl of Eglinton, near Irvine, Scotland.

Egypt. See FLIGHT INTO EGYPT and REPOSE IN EGYPT.

Egyptian Hall. **1.** The principal room in the Mansion House, London, so named from being built in accordance with the description of the Egyptian Hall given by Vitruvius.

> A playful fancy could have carried the matter further, could have depicted the feast in the *Egyptian Hall*, the ministers, chief justices, and right reverend prelates taking their seats round about his lordship, the turtle and other delicious viands.
>
> *Thackeray.*

2. An edifice known as Egyptian Hall, and containing lecture-rooms, a bazaar, and gallery of curiosities, is situated in Piccadilly, London.

Egyptian Museum. The collection of this museum, in the Vatican, Rome, was begun by Pius VII.

Ehrenberg. A fine relic of mediæval times, situated on a rocky height near the Moselle. It is thought to surpass in beauty any of the castles on the Rhine.

Ehrenbreitstein. [Broad Stone of Honor.] This fortress, called the Gibraltar of the Rhine, is situated on a precipitous rock, 377 feet above the river. During the French Revolutionary War it was besieged four times, and surrendered in 1799. The French subsequently blew it up, and deserted it in 1801. The fortress was restored at great expense by the Prussians, and is much admired. The view from the summit is one of the finest on the Rhine. Ehrenbreitstein, at first a Roman *castrum*, was a refuge for the electors of Treves in mediæval times.

☞ "Apart from its magnitude and almost impregnable situation on a perpendicular rock, it is filled by the recollections of history, and hallowed by the voice of poetry." *Bayard Taylor.*

Here *Ehrenbreitstein*, with her shattered wall
Black with the miner's blast upon her height,
Yet shows of what she was, when shell and ball
Rebounding idly on her strength did light:
A tower of victory! from whence the flight
Of baffled foes was watched along the plain;
But Peace destroyed what War could never blight,
And laid those proud roofs bare to summer's rain,
On which the iron shower for years had poured in vain. *Byron.*

Ehrenfels. [Rock of Honor.] A ruined castle of the thirteenth century, near Bingen on the Rhine.

Eichelstein. [The Acorn.] The popular name of the old Roman structure at Mayence, otherwise known as the *Tower of Drusus*. See DRUSUS, TOWER OF.

1807. A picture by Jean Louis Ernest Meissonier (b. 1813). The artist is said to have labored 15 years upon this picture, which was purchased by the late A. T. Stewart of New York for more than 300,000 francs.

1814. A picture by Jean Louis Ernest Meissonier (b. 1813), the eminent French painter.

Eildon Hall. A seat of the Duke of Buccleuch, near Newton St. Boswells, Scotland.

Einsiedeln Abbey. A famous Benedictine abbey in the town of Einsiedeln, Switzerland, after Loreto, in Italy, the most celebrated resort for pilgrims in Europe. It is estimated that more than 150,000 persons visit this shrine of the Virgin annually on the 14th of September.

☞ "I was astonished at the splendor of this church situated in a lonely and unproductive Alpine valley. The lofty arches of the ceiling, which are covered with superb fresco-paintings, rest on enormous pillars of granite, and every image and shrine is richly ornamented with gold. . . . Many of the pilgrims came from a long distance." *Bayard Taylor.*

Eiserne Jungfrau. See IRON VIRGIN.

Eleanor Crosses. A popular name of memorials, in the form of a cross, erected to Queen Eleanor of England by order of her husband, King Edward, "in every place and town where the corpse rested (on its way from Hardby to Westminster)." Fifteen crosses are believed to have been originally erected, of which only three now remain, the principal and best known being those at Northampton and at Waltham. See CHARING CROSS.

Time must destroy those crosses
Raised by the Poet-King,
But as long as the blue sea tosses,
As long as the skylarks sing,
As long as London's river
Glides stately down to the Nore,
Men shall remember ever
How he loved Queen Eleänore.
Mortimer Collins.

Electors of Treves, Castle of the. A vast mediæval palace (built

1280) near Coblenz, on the Rhine. It has been converted into a manufactory.

Elephant, The. An old London tavern in Fenchurch Street, of earlier date than the Great Fire of 1666, taken down in the first part of this century and rebuilt.

Elephanta, Cave-temples of. These celebrated remains are situated upon the island of Elephanta, about seven miles from Bombay, in India. In one of the caves is a colossal figure of the Hindoo Trinity, called the Trimurti. The largest temple-cave is 130 feet long by 123 feet in breadth.

☞ "The Portuguese, in their zeal for destroying heathen idols, planted cannon before the entrance of the cave, and destroyed many of the columns and sculptured panels, but the faces of the colossal Trinity have escaped mutilation. This, the *Trimurti*, is a grand and imposing piece of sculpture, not unworthy of the best period of Egyptian art. It is a triple bust, and with the richly adorned mitres that crown the heads, rises to the height of twelve feet." *Bayard Taylor.*

Elevation of the Cross. A colossal picture by Peter Paul Rubens (1577-1640). In the Cathedral of Antwerp, Belgium.

☞ "Rubens stands forth in all his Titanic greatness as the painter of violent and agitated scenes. The effect of this picture [the Elevation of the Cross] is something overpowering, but in all other respects it bears no comparison with the Descent from the Cross [*q. v.*]." *Handbook of Painting.*

☞ This subject has been treated by painters of the seventeenth and eighteenth centuries, by Vandyck, Lebrun, Largillière, and others.

Elgin Cathedral. This ancient cathedral, on the banks of the Lossie, was founded in 1224. It has been repeatedly injured by fire, and plundered, and rebuilt. Though not harmonious, different portions being of different styles of architecture, its remains are on the whole the most magnificent ecclesiastical ruins in Scotland.

Elgin Marbles. A collection of sculptures brought from the Parthenon at Athens by the Earl of Elgin, and now deposited in the British Museum, London. In 1801 Lord Elgin, who had gone to Athens for the purpose, received permission from the Turkish Government to take away any stones that might be interesting to him; and the result of his labors was the collection which has since borne his name. The marbles were purchased by the British Government in 1816.

☞ "Were the Elgin Marbles lost, there would be as great a gap in art as there would be in philosophy if Newton had never existed." *Haydon.*

☞ "We possess in England the most precious examples of Grecian power in the sculpture of animals. The horses of the frieze in the Elgin collection appear to live and move, to roll their eyes, to gallop, prance, and curvet; the veins of their faces and legs seem distended with circulation; in them are distinguished the hardness and decision of bony forms, from the elasticity of tendon and the softness of flesh." *Flaxman.*

☞ "Lord Elgin, at Athens, saw the imminent ruin of the Greek remains, set up his scaffoldings, in spite of epigrams, and, after five years' labor to collect them, got his marbles on shipboard. The ship struck a rock, and went to the bottom. He had them all fished up, by divers, at a vast expense, and brought to London; not knowing that Haydon, Fuseli, and Canova, and all good heads in all the world, were to be his applauders." *Emerson.*

It is 'Change time, and I am strangely among the *Elgin Marbles.*
Charles Lamb.

Elijah in the Wilderness. A picture by Washington Allston (1779-1843), the American painter. Now in England.

Eliodoro, Stanza d'. See STANZE OF RAPHAEL.

Elisius, St. See ST. ELISIUS.

Elizabeth. See ST. ELIZABETH OF HUNGARY.

Ellen's Isle. An island in Loch Katrine, Scotland, celebrated in the legendary history of Scotland, and in Sir Walter Scott's poem of "The Lady of the Lake," as the scene of the interview between Fitz James and the heroine.

☞"It is a little island, but very famous in Romance land; for Ellen, as almost everybody knows, was the Lady of the Lake. . . . A more poetic, romantic retreat could hardly be imagined: it is unique."
J. F. Hunnewell.

☞" A beautiful little turquoise in the silver setting of Loch Katrine."
Bayard Taylor.

Ellisland. A farm near Holywood on the river Nith, in Scotland, formerly rented by the poet Burns, and where he wrote some of his most-admired pieces, such as "Tam O'Shanter," and "To Mary in Heaven." "On a window in the house may still be seen, scratched by Burns upon the glass, 'An honest man's the noblest work of God.'"

Ellora, Cave-temples of. A series of remarkable and celebrated sculptured caverns or rock-temples at Ellora in the Deccan, India, which are classed among the greatest wonders of architecture.

☞" Their character is antique, but their date is uncertain: all that can be conjectured being that the more ancient portion of them belong to the ages before Christ. They are consecrated to several divinities of the Brahminic Pantheon. The hills of Ellora extend a length of two miles in the form of a crescent. Their flanks are pierced with subterranean galleries not less than two leagues in extent. Here is to be found a great hall, nearly square, which is 180 feet long, 150 feet broad, and 18 feet high. The roof is supported by 28 columns. Certain of the excavations disclose many stories which communicate with each other."
Lefèvre, Trans. Donald.

Ellsworth, Fort. See FORT ELLSWORTH.

Elmo, St. See ST. ELMO.

Elmwood. An ancient colonial house in Cambridge, Mass., near Mount Auburn Cemetery, the home of James Russell Lowell.

Eltham Castle. An ancient royal palace in England, near London, built by Edward IV. It was a frequent residence of the English sovereigns before Henry VIII., and here they held their great Christmas feasts. It is now a ruin, and used only as a barn.

Ely Cathedral. The old conventual church of Ely, near Cambridge, England, was converted into the present structure by Henry VIII. Of the existing edifice the oldest part was erected in the reign of William Rufus.

Merrily sang the monks within *Ely*
When Canute the King rowed thereby;
(Row me, Knights, the shore along,
And listen to these monks' song).
Old Ballad.

Ely House. An ancient palace in London, where "old John of Gaunt, time-honored Lancaster," died. It is alluded to in the plays of Shakespeare.

My lord of *Ely*, when I was last in Holborn,
I saw good strawberries in your garden there;
I do beseech you send for some of them.
Richard III.

Elymas the Sorcerer struck with Blindness. One of the famous cartoons by Raphael Sanzio (1483–1520), from which the tapestries in the Vatican were executed.

Elysée Bourbon. See ELYSÉE, PALAIS.

Elysées. See CHAMPS ELYSÉES.

Elysée Napoléon. See ELYSÉE, PALAIS.

Elysée, Palais. A celebrated historic house, Rue du Faubourg St. Honoré, Paris, built in 1718. Here at different times lived the Duchess of Bourbon (from whom it was called *Elysée Bourbon*), Murat, Napoleon I., the Duke of Wellington, Napoleon III. Here Napoleon I. signed his abdication, and here he passed his last night in Paris. [It was also formerly called *Elysée Napoléon.*]

Elysian Fields. A region in the neighborhood of Baiæ, in Southern Italy, covered with gardens and vineyards, and which is thought to correspond with the description of Elysium given by Virgil. See also CHAMPS ELYSÉES.

Elz Castle. A fine relic of feudal times near Carden in Rhenish Prussia, pronounced "an almost solitary example of a feudal residence spared by fire, war, and time, and remaining in nearly the same condition that it was two or three centuries ago." It is inhabited, and contains a curious collection of antiquities.

Elzevir Editions. A name applied to certain carefully printed and elegant editions of the works of Latin and Greek authors, issued by printers of the name of Elzevir in Amsterdam and Leyden, Holland, and mostly published between 1595 and 1680.

The old, dead authors thronged him round about,
And *Elzevir's* gray ghosts from leathern graves looked out. *Whittier.*

Emancipation Proclamation. A picture by Francis Bicknell Carpenter (b. 1830), and well known through the engraving by Ritchie. This painting was purchased and presented to Congress in 1877. It is now in the House of Representatives in the National Capitol, Washington.

Emanuel. See TEMPLE EMANUEL.

Emanuel College. A foundation of the University of Cambridge, England. Established in 1584.

Embarkation of St. Ursula. A picture by Vittore Carpaccio (1450-1520 ?). In the Accademia della Belle Arti at Venice, Italy.

Embarkation of the Pilgrims. A picture in one of the panels of the Rotunda in the Capitol at Washington, representing the departure of the pilgrims from Holland. It was painted by Robert Weir (b. 1803), and was completed and placed in position during the administration of President Polk. The artist is considered to have sacrificed historical truth in order that he might produce a picture full of strong effects. The sum of ten thousand dollars was paid for this work. Familiar from its reproduction upon bills of the national currency.

Embarkation of the Queen of Sheba. A celebrated picture by Claude Lorrain (1600-1682). In the National Gallery, London.

Emma Mine. A mine of precious ore in Utah Territory, south-east of Salt Lake City. The sale of this mine to a stock-company, some years ago, most of the stock being held in London, was a matter of great notoriety, and caused much sensation.

Emperor of Bells. [Russian, *Tzar Kolokol.*] A renowned bell preserved in the Kremlin at Moscow, Russia, cast by order of the Empress Anne in 1730. It was broken a few years afterward by the burning of the wooden tower in which it was suspended. It is said to be over 21 feet in height, about 22 feet in diameter at the bottom, to weigh between 100 and 200 tons, and to contain an amount of gold, silver, and copper, estimated to be worth $1,500,000. The "New Bell" of Moscow is 21 feet in height, and 18 feet in diameter.

☞ "From the time of Herodotus, the Scythians were great casters of metal, and famous for their bells. The specimens of casting of this sort in Russia reduce all the great bells of Western Europe to comparative insignificance. It of course became necessary to provide places in which to hang these bells; and as nothing in Byzantine or Armenian architecture afforded a hint for amalgamating the belfry with the church, they went to work in their own way, and constructed towers wholly independent of the churches." *Fergusson.*

Emperors, Hall of the. See HALL OF THE EMPERORS.

Empire. See COURSE OF EMPIRE and STAR OF EMPIRE.

Endowment House. A building in Salt Lake City, Utah Territory, in which many of the rites of the Mormon worship, such as "sealings," and baptisms for the dead, are performed, and where they claim to receive their "endowments" from heaven. The edifice is constructed of unburnt brick.

Enfans d'Edouard. [Edward's Children.] A picture by Paul Delaroche (1797–1856).

☞ "The 'Enfans d'Edouard' is renowned over Europe, and has appeared in a hundred different ways in print. It is properly pathetic and gloomy, and merits fully its high reputation." *Thackeray.*

Engelberg Abbey. A noted Benedictine abbey near the town of the same name in Switzerland. It was founded in the twelfth century, but the present building was erected in the early part of the last century. There is a tradition that angels chose the site of the monastery.

Whose authentic lay
Sung from that heavenly ground in middle air,
Made known the spot where Piety should raise
A holy structure to th' Almighty's praise.
Wordsworth.

Engländerhübel. [English Hillock.] A mound in Switzerland, about 11 miles from Lucerne, containing the bones of 3,000 Englishmen, followers of the Duke of Bedford, who were defeated in battle while devastating the Swiss cantons.

English Coasts. See OUR ENGLISH COASTS.

English Opera House. See LYCEUM THEATRE.

Enterprise, The. **1.** An Arctic exploring ship which sailed to the Northern seas under Sir James Ross in 1848.

2. An armor-plated ship of the British navy, launched Feb. 9, 1864.

Entombment, The. A subject very often treated by the great religious painters of the Middle Ages, exhibiting the burial of Christ in accordance with the Scriptural account of that event. Of the great number of pictures upon this subject, among the more celebrated are those given below.

Entombment, The. A picture by Giotto di Bondone (1276–1336). In the Chapel of the Arena, Padua, Italy.

Entombment, The. A magnificent picture by Taddeo Gaddi (1300–1366 ?), executed for the church of Or-San-Michele. Now in the Academy at Florence, Italy.

Entombment, The. A picture by Pietro Perugino (1446–1524). In the Palazzo Pitti, Florence, Italy.

Entombment, The. A picture by Jan Mostaert (1474–1555), the Flemish painter. It is now in the possession of Rev. Mr. Heath at Enfield, England.

Entombment, The. A famous picture by Titian (1477–1576), representing this well-known subject. It is in the Louvre, Paris. There is a copy in the Manfrin Gallery, Venice, Italy.

☞ "An instance of the manner in which all subjects ministered to his favorite forms of dignity and tranquillity. The grief of such noble beings as support the half-concealed body of the Lord is one of the most dignified and impressive things in this world. Though all intent on the sacred object they bear, the fact of their bearing it is a fiction. Such strength and strain as would actually have been needed, would have overturned all the gravity which was Titian's chief aim, and the cloth by which they sustain the great weight of a well-developed body is not even drawn tight beneath their grasp." *Eastlake.*

Entombment, The. A celebrated altar-piece by Raphael Sanzio (1483–1520), painted for the church of S. Francesco at Perugia, Italy, and now in the Borghese Gallery at Rome.

☞ "This is the first of Raphael's compositions in which a historical subject is dramatically treated; and, as is evident from the number of designs and studies he made for the picture, it tasked his powers to the utmost." *Eastlake.*

☞ "The Virgin Mother is always introduced [in an "Entombment"]. Either she swoons, which is the ancient Greek conception, or she follows with streaming eyes and clasped hands the pious disciples who bear the dead form of her Son, as in Raphael's wonderful picture in the Borghese Palace, and Titian's hardly less beautiful in the Louvre." *Mrs. Jameson.*

☞ "This picture belongs indisputably among the chief works of Raphael; and we may even assign it the preeminence over all the oil-paintings of this master in Rome, not even excepting the renowned Transfiguration and the so-called Madonna di Foligno."
Platner, Trans.

☞ "In Raphael's Entombment of Christ, we perceive the first traces of Michael Angelo's influence."
Grimm, Trans.

Entombment, The. A picture by Roger van der Weyden the Younger (d. 1529).

☞ "The picture of the Entombment by him [van der Weyden], in the National Gallery, is as much more sad to the heart than the passionate Italian conception, as a deep sigh sometimes, than a flood of tears. No finer conception of manly sorrow, sternly repressed, exists than in the heads of Nicodemus and Joseph of Arimathea."
Lady Eastlake.

Entombment, The. A picture by Paul Veronese (1530–1588), and regarded as one of his *chefs d'œuvre.* In the Hermitage, St. Petersburg, Russia.

Entombment, The. A picture by Michelangelo Amerighi, surnamed Caravaggio (1569–1609), and his most famous work. In the Vatican, Rome.

Entombment, The. A picture by Anthony van Dyck (1599–1641). In the Antwerp Museum.

Entresol, Société d'. A French club established by the Abbé Alari at Paris in 1724.

Epiphany, The. A picture by Gheerardt David (1484–1523), the Flemish painter. Now at Munich, Bavaria. A replica of the same in the gallery of Brussels, Belgium.

Epping Forest. Formerly a very large district, extending from Epping almost to London. It was known under the name of Waltham Forest. In the same neighborhood was Hainault, which contains more beautiful scenery than any other forest in England. Great inroads have been made upon Epping Forest, and it now contains not more than 4,000 acres. It is much resorted to by the inhabitants of London. In the forest, about a mile from Epping, is Queen Elizabeth's "Hunting Lodge," which commands a beautiful prospect.

The Cambridge scholars trembled [seventeenth century] when they approached *Epping Forest*, even in broad day.
Macaulay.

Erasmus. 1. A portrait by Hans Holbein the Younger (1498–1543), and considered one of his most admirable works. It is now in the possession of Lord Radnor, at Longford Castle, England. This picture is said to have been sent by Erasmus to Sir Thomas More in 1525. There is also another portrait of Erasmus by Holbein in the Louvre, Paris.

2. A bronze statue of the great scholar in Rotterdam, where he was born.

Erasmus. See MARTYRDOM OF ST. ERASMUS.

Erbach Castle. An old family mansion at Erbach in the Odenwald, containing a rare collection of antiquities.

Ercole Farnese. See FARNESE HERCULES.

Erebus, The. An Arctic exploring vessel which sailed from England under Sir John Franklin in May, 1845, and never returned. A document dated April 25, 1848, was discovered in a cairn on the shore of King William's Land by Capt. McClintock of the British expedition sent out by Lady Franklin, in which document it was stated that Sir John Franklin died June 11, 1847; that the Erebus and her companion ship, the Terror, were abandoned April 22, 1848; and that the survivors had started for the Great Fish River.

Erechtheum. ['Ερεχθειον.] This, the most venerable of the sanctuaries of Greece, and closely linked with the early legends of Attica, was situated upon the Acropolis, and was so called from being the place of interment of Erechtheus, who holds an important place in the Athenian religion. The original Erechtheum was burnt by the Persians; but the new temple, built upon the ancient site, was a very beautiful structure, and one of the chief works of Athenian architecture. It was of the Ionic order, and was situated to the north of the Parthenon, and near the northern wall of the Acropolis. The appearance of the exterior can be judged from the existing ruins, but the interior presents nothing but a heap of confusing ruins.

☞ "It contained several objects of the greatest interest to every Athenian. Here was the most ancient statue of Athena Polias, that is, Athena, the guardian of the city. This statue was made of olive-wood, and was said to have fallen down from heaven. Here was the sacred olive-tree, which Athena called forth from the earth in her contest with Poseidon for the possession of Attica; here also was the well of salt water which Poseidon produced by the stroke of his trident, the impression of which was seen upon the rock; and here, lastly, was the tomb of Cecrops as well as that of Erechtheus. . . . The form of the Erechtheium differs from every other known example of a Grecian temple. Usually a Grecian temple was an oblong figure, with two porticos, one at its eastern, and the other at its western, end. The Erechtheium, on the contrary, though oblong in shape and having a portico at the eastern front, had no portico at its western end; but from either side of the latter a portico projected to the north and south, thus forming a kind of transept. Consequently, the temple had three porticos." *Smith's Dict.*

☞ "Nowhere did the exquisite taste and skill of the Athenians show themselves to greater advantage than here; for, though every detail of the order may be traced back to Nineveh or Persepolis, all are so purified, so imbued with purely Grecian taste and feeling, that they have become essential parts of a far more beautiful order than ever existed in the land in which they had their origin. . . . Owing to the Erechtheium having been converted into a Byzantine church during the Middle Ages, almost all traces of its original internal arrangements have been obliterated; and this, with the peculiar combination of three temples in one, makes it more than usually difficult to restore." *Fergusson.*

Erectheum, The. A London club, founded in 1836, and afterwards joined with the Parthenon Club. See PARTHENON.

Eremitage. A palace in Bayreuth, Germany, erected by the margraves, in the early part of the last century.

Eremo, Sacro (*or* **Santo**). See SACRO EREMO.

Ericsson, The. A vessel built by John Ericsson (b. 1803), and named after him. She was intended to be propelled by hot air instead of steam; but, after some experimental trials, the caloric-engine was taken out in 1855, and replaced by steam-engines.

Erythræan Sibyl. A figure in one of the frescos of the Sistine Chapel, Rome, executed by Michael Angelo (1475–1564).

Esarhaddon's Palace. A celebrated Assyrian palace, commonly known as the South-West Palace at Nimroud. It was destroyed by fire; and the existing remains consist of the entrance or southern hall, the dimensions of which are 165 feet in length by 62 feet in width. It is the largest hall yet discovered in Assyria.

Esbekeeyah, The. The great square of Cairo, Egypt, containing about 450,000 square feet. On it are the principal hotels and other prominent buildings. It was formerly inundated during the annual rise of the Nile, and a canal was cut around it to prevent this disaster; but since 1866 this canal has been filled up, some of the ancient houses have been removed and replaced by new ones, and a central space has been enclosed as a public garden, with cafés, theatres, etc. [Written also *Ezbekeyieh.*]

☞ "The great square of the Ezbekeeyeh is always gay on Sundays, when the Franks walk there after church, and the Mohammedans sit smoking in groups to watch them. . . . The Eastern and Western groups, — the turbans and burnooses here, and the French bonnets and mantles there,— all among the dark acacias, or crossing the gleams of bright sunshine, make a strange picture, not to be likened to any thing I saw afterwards." *Miss Martineau.*

Eschernheim Tower. A picturesque and admired watch-tower in Frankfort-on-the-Main.

Escorial. An immense pile of buildings situated near Madrid, Spain, which has sometimes been called the eighth wonder of the world. It was built by Philip II., as a mausoleum, in accordance with the will of his father, and served at once many purposes, as a palace, convent, treasury, tomb-house, and museum. It was begun by Juan Bautista de Toledo in 1563, and finished in 1584. Its name, according to some, is derived from *Escoriæ*, the *dross* of iron-mines which still exist here. The building was begun upon the anniversary of St. Lawrence, and, according to the tradition, was made to assume the shape of a gridiron, the instrument upon which that saint is recorded to have suffered martyrdom. This story, however, is now believed to be an invention of later date. The huge and sombre structure, standing at an elevation of 2,700 feet above the level of the sea, is part and parcel of the mountain out of which it has been constructed. It is built of granite in the Doric order, and was till lately the country palace and mausoleum of the Spanish sovereigns, a part of the edifice being used for educational purposes. It is now, however, but a mere wreck, and being deprived of its monks and revenues, and exposed to the mountain storms, is constantly subject to injury. [Written also *Escurial.*]

☞ "The *Escorial* is as vulgar a name as the Tuileries. It signifies the place where scoria are thrown; and it was so called because there was an iron manufactory near that threw its scoria on the spot. Its more just name is San Lorenzo el Reale, since it is a royal convent dedicated to St. Lorenzo. It is a monument of the magnificence, the splendor, the superstition, and perhaps the personal fears, of Philip II. . . . The convent itself is worthy of the severest influences of the most monkish ages. It is the only establishment I have ever met that satisfied all the ideas I had formed of the size of a monastery such as Mrs. Radcliffe or Dennis Jasper Murphy describes, and which is here so immense that, in the space occupied by its chief staircase alone, a large house might be built." *George Ticknor.*

The romance of Tom Jones, that exquisite picture of human manners, will outlive the palace of the *Escurial* and the imperial eagle of Austria. *Gibbon.*

It [Wolfert's Roost] is said, in fact, to have been modelled after the cocked hat of Peter the Headstrong, as the *Escurial* was modelled after the gridiron of the blessed St. Lawrence. *Irving.*

No house, though it were the Tuileries, or the *Escurial*, is good for any thing without a master. *Emerson.*

Set as a challenge at the mountain's side,
Afar the dark *Escurial* is descried.
Three hundred feet from earth uplifting thus
On its colossal shoulder firmly braced,
Huge elephant, the cupola defaced,
Granite debauch of Spain's Tiberius.
T. Gautier, Trans.

Escurial. See ESCORIAL.

Esher (or Asher) Place. A lovely spot in one of the most picturesque vales of the county of Surrey, England, noted as having been the residence of Cardinal Wolsey after his fall and retirement from court. An old brick tower is still standing, which formed part of the palace when it belonged to the See of Winchester. The place is covered with fine groves of fir and beech, oaks and elms.

Esplanade, The. A magnificent promenade in Calcutta, Hindostan, being an open space of three or four miles in length and nearly a mile in breadth, extending along the banks of the Hoogly, lined with stately mansions, and crowded with fine equipages.

Esquiline Hill. [Lat. *Mons Esquilinus.*] One of the seven hills of ancient Rome, of wide extent and undefined form, and now covered with ruins. It is less a distinct hill than a projection of the Campagna. The name is derived by Varro from *excultus*, because of the ornamental groves which were planted upon it. In the later days of the republic and in the time of the empire, the Esquiline was a fashionable place for residence. The section known as the *Carinæ* was upon the slope of the hill towards the Coliseum. Consuls and emperors lived upon the Esquiline. There were the house and gardens of Mæcenas, and of Virgil, and possibly of Horace, a part of Nero's Golden House, the Baths of Titus, and many other structures, now in ruins.

Suffice it now the *Esquilian mount* to reach
With weary wing, and seek the sacred rests
Of Maro's humble tenement. *John Dyer.*

Essex, The. A noted frigate of the United States navy, in service in the war of 1812. She was built in 1812. The Essex surrendered to the British ships Phœbe and Cherub, March 28, 1814.

Our Rogers on the President
Will burn, sink, and destroy;
The Congress on the Brazil coast
Your commerce will annoy.
The *Essex* on the South Sea
Will put out all your lights:
The flag she wears at mast-head
Is "Free Trade and Sailors' Rights."
Old Song.

Essex Head. This club in London was formed in 1783 by Dr. Johnson, who writes to Sir Joshua Reynolds that "the company is numerous, and, as you will see by the list, miscellaneous. The terms are lax, and the expenses light. . . . We meet twice a week, and he who misses forfeits twopence." The club was continued for some time after Dr. Johnson's death. Boswell, describing the formation of the club, says, that, notwithstanding "the complication of disorders under which Johnson now labored, he did not resign himself to despondency and discontent, but with wisdom and spirit endeavored to console and amuse his mind with as many innocent enjoyments as he could procure. Sir John Hawkins has mentioned the cordiality with which he insisted that such of the members of the old club in Ivy Lane as survived, should meet again and dine together, which they did, twice at a tavern, and once at his house; and, in order to insure himself in the evening for three days in the week, Johnson instituted a club at the Essex Head, in Essex Street.

☞ "But, turning to Essex Street, and not many doors down on the left, at the corner of a little cross-passage leading to the pretty Temple gate with its light iron-work, we come on the Essex Head Tavern, an old, mean public house of well-grimed brick. It was here, in his decay, that Johnson set up a kind of superior club, the Ivy Lane. Boswell is angry with Hawkins for calling it an ale-house, as if in contempt; but certainly, while the Cheshire Cheese, the Mitre, and the Cock are taverns, this seems to have been more within the category of an ale or public house. It has been so re-arranged and altered to suit the intentions and purposes of the modern public, that there is no tracing its former shape."
Fitzgerald.

Essex House. A noble mansion in London, of which only a few relics now remain, the residence of the Earl of Essex, the favorite of Queen Elizabeth.

Next whereunto there standes a stately place
Where oft I gayned giftes and goodly grace
Of that great lord which therein wont to dwell. *Spenser.*

Estes Park. A picture by Albert Bierstadt (b. 1829). Now in possession of the Earl of Dunraven.

Étienne, St. See St. Étienne.

Étoile, Arc de l'. See Arc de l'Étoile.

Eton College. A famous educational establishment in the town of Eton, England. It was founded in 1440 by Henry VI. It has long been a favorite place of education for the sons of the nobility and gentry. Among the great men who have studied at Eton may be mentioned Sir Robert Walpole, the Earl of Chatham, Gray, Walpole, West, Fox, Canning, Hallam the historian, and the Duke of Wellington. The buildings form two quadrangles, and consist of towers, cloisters, and a fine Gothic chapel.

The habit of brag runs through all classes, from the *Times* newspaper through politicians and poets, through Wordsworth, Carlyle, Mill, and Sydney Smith, down to the boys of *Eton*.
Emerson.

Ye distant spires, ye antique towers,
That crown the watery glade,
Where grateful Science still adores
Her Henry's holy shade. *Gray.*

Eton Montem. A celebration held annually at first, then biennially, and at last triennially, by the boys of the school at Eton, England. They formed a procession, and marched, arrayed in military costume, to Salt Hill or Mount, where they dined, returning to their school at evening. Some of the boys, in fancy costumes, waylaid travellers upon the roads, and levied a tax for the benefit of their captain. In return they bestowed a small quantity of salt upon each contributor. The festival was abolished in 1847.

Ettrick Forest. An ancient woodland, forming part of the great Caledonian forest, situated on the borders of the river Ettrick, in Scotland. Only scanty remnants of it are now left. See CALEDONIAN FOREST.

Ettrick Forest is a fair forest,
In it grows many a seemly tree;
The hart, the hind, the doe, the roe,
And of all wild beasts great plentie.

On *Ettrick Forest's* mountains dun,
'Tis blithe to hear the sportsman's gun,
And seek the heath-frequenting brood
Far through the noonday solitude.
Scott.

Ettrick House. A farm in the parish of Ettrick, Scotland, the birthplace of James Hogg, the "Ettrick Shepherd."

Etruscan Museum (Museo Gregoriano). A splendid museum of Etruscan antiquities, collected by the efforts of Gregory XVI., in the Vatican, Rome.

Euclid Avenue. A noted street in Cleveland, O., considered one of the finest in the country.

I was going to compare the roads on these islands [near St. Petersburg] to the eastern part of *Euclid Street* in Cleveland, O.; but there the dwellings and grounds are altogether of a more stately character.
Bayard Taylor.

Eudoxian Basilica. See SAN PIETRO IN VINCOLI.

Eugubine Tables. Celebrated bronze tablets, discovered in 1444, bearing inscriptions which have given rise to much antiquarian dispute. They are preserved in the town of Gubbio, Italy, near which place they were discovered, and whence they derive their name.

Eulenspiegel. A famous engraving by Luc Jacobsz, commonly called Lucas van Leyden (1494-1533), the Flemish artist, celebrated in part for its great rarity. It is said that "not more than six original impressions are in existence, though there are many copies." One of the originals is in the British Museum. [Also called *The Peasants Travelling.*]

Europa, Rape of. See RAPE OF EUROPA.

Eustache, St. See ST. EUSTACHE.

Euston Square. A well-known public square in London, England.

Evangelists. See FOUR EVANGELISTS.

Eve. A well-known statue by Thorwaldsen (1770-1844). In Stafford House, London.

Eve. A statue by Hiram Powers (1805-1873).

☞ "His [Powers's] *Eve* is undoubtedly his masterpiece among ideal figures, although his 'Greek Slave' has attained larger popularity simply from being more widely known."
Art Journal.

☞ "The essential character of the Eve of Powers is that he so long ago imagined and proposed to embody; that is, he represents the mother of our race under the new-born sense of evil and wrong, the disturbance of that moral equilibrium that held her soul at first in tranquil self-poise . . . it is Eve, beautiful, loving, grandly maternal, tender, confiding, but tried and tempted." *Tuckerman.*

A faultless being from the marble sprung,
She stands in beauty there!
As when the grace of Eden 'round her clung,—
Fairest, where all was fair.
Bayard Taylor.

Eve. See REPENTANT EVE.

Eve of St. Agnes. A noted picture by John E. Millais (b. 1829). In London.

☞ "In the *Eve of St. Agnes* of Millais, a lady in a low-bodied evening-dress is represented through the medium of a studied effect of twilight as having the appearance of a corpse-like green; and the chamber is of the same hue." *Taine, Trans.*

Evening, The. [Ital. *Il Crepuscolo.*] One of four colossal figures executed by Michael Angelo Buonarotti (1475-1564). In the church of S. Lorenzo, Florence, Italy.

Evening School. A picture by Gerhard Dow, or Douw (1613-1680), and one of his best. In the Museum of Amsterdam, Holland.

Event in the Forest. A picture by Sir Edwin Landseer (1803-1873), the most celebrated modern painter of animals.

Exchange, Royal. See ROYAL EXCHANGE.

Exeter Cathedral. A noble church edifice in Exeter, England. It is of high antiquity, cruciform, 408 feet in length, and has one of the most beautiful façades in Europe.

Exeter Change. Situated upon the site of Exeter House, London, built as a sort of bazaar, afterwards occupied as a menagerie, and taken down in 1829.

Exeter Hall. A large proprietary establishment, situated on the Strand, London, and originally intended for religious and charitable societies, and their meetings. From April to the end of May, various religious societies hold their anniversaries here. The Great Hall is also used for the Sacred Harmonic Society's, and other concerts. The works of Handel, Haydn, and Mozart are here given with great effect.

☞ "The independent and mutually repelling bodies who congregate in Exeter Hall are one in spirit with all their differences. Without a pervading organization they are a church." *The Spectator.*

The fanaticism and hypocrisy create satire. Punch finds an inexhaustible material. Dickens writes novels on *Exeter-Hall* humanity. Thackeray exposes the heartless high life. *Emerson.*

Exeter House. A noble mansion which formerly stood in the Strand, London, the residence of the celebrated Lord Burleigh.

Exeter Street. A street in London, so named after Exeter House. See EXETER HOUSE.

He [Johnson] enters quite quietly, with some copper half-pence in his pocket; creeps into lodgings in *Exeter Street*, Strand; and has a Coronation Pontiff also, of not less peculiar equipment, whom, with all submissiveness, he must wait upon, in his Vatican of St. John's Gate. *Carlyle.*

Expulsion from Paradise. A picture by Masaccio (*Tommaso Guidi*) (1402-1429?). In the church of S. M. del Carmine, Florence, Italy.

Expulsion from Paradise. See FALL AND EXPULSION.

Expulsion of Hagar. A picture by Francesco Barbieri, called Guercino (1590-1666). In the Brera, at Milan, Italy.

Expulsion of Heliodorus. A celebrated fresco by Raphael Sanzio (1483-1520), representing the expulsion of Heliodorus from the Temple at Jerusalem, which he had attempted to plunder, and allegorically typifying the deliverance of the States of the Church from the enemies of the Pope. "The picture is a spirited development of an extended action," and is considered, together with the other works in the same room, as perhaps the finest example of the art of fresco-painting. It is in the Stanza of the Heliodorus (so called after this, the principal picture in the room) in the Vatican, Rome.

☞ "The chastisement of Heliodorus has given occasion to the sublimest composition in which human genius ever attempted to embody the conception of the supernatural, — Raphael's fresco in the Vatican." *Mrs. Jameson.*

☞ "In fine pictures the head sheds on the limbs the expression of the face. In Raphael's Angel driving Heliodorus from the Temple, the crest of the helmet is so remarkable, that, but for the extraordinary energy of the face, it would draw the eye too much; but the countenance of the celestial messenger subordinates it, and we see it not." *Emerson.*

Exton Hall. The seat of the Earl of Gainsborough near Stamford, Lincolnshire, England.

Ezbekeyieh. See ESBEKEEYAH.

Ezekiel's Tomb. A building near Bagdad, in Asiatic Turkey, traditionally held to be the tomb of the prophet. It is of much interest, and is a very striking object; but its date has not been satisfactorily determined.

Ezekiel, Vision of. See VISION OF EZEKIEL.

F.

Fagot, Le. A picture by Nikolaas (or Claes Pietersz) Berghem (1624-1683), the Dutch painter, and regarded as one of his best. In the collection of Lord Ashburton, England.

Fair, The. A picture by Peter Paul Rubens (1577-1640). In the Louvre at Paris.

Fair, The. A picture by David Teniers the Younger (1610-1694), the Belgian *genre*-painter. Of numerous pictures upon this subject, perhaps the best specimen is at Vienna, Austria.

Fair Oaks. A locality four miles from Richmond, Va., where a severe but indecisive battle took place, May 31, 1862, between the Union and Confederate forces.

Fairlop Oak. A famous tree in Hainault Forest, in Essex, England. It is said to have been 36 feet in circumference, and to have had 17 branches, each as large as an ordinary oak. For many years an annual fair, or festival, was held under and around this tree, in July, which was attended by crowds of the country people.

Fairmount Park. A vast and noble pleasure-ground in Philadelphia, Penn. It includes nearly 3,000 acres, and is larger than most, if not any, of the great parks of Europe and America. It is traversed by the river Schuylkill and by the Wissahickon Creek. In natural capabilities and in the improvements made upon them, this park must be ranked among the finest in the world. The Centennial Exhibition of 1876 was held here.

Falaise Castle. A grand old ruin in Falaise, France, the ancient seat of the dukes of Normandy, and the birthplace of William the Conqueror.

Falkenstein. 1. An imposing ruin among the Taunus Mountains, in Germany, not far from Frankfort.

2. A mediæval fortress among the Harz Mountains, in Germany.

Fall and Expulsion from Paradise. One of the frescos by Michael Angelo (1475-1564) in the Sistine Chapel, Rome.

Fall of Adam and Eve. A picture by Filippino Lippi (1460-1505). In the church of Sta. Maria del Carmine, Florence, Italy.

Fall of Schaffhausen. A picture by Joseph Mallord William Turner (1775-1851), the English landscape painter, and regarded as one of his best.

Fall of the Angels. 1. A celebrated picture by Peter Paul Rubens (1577-1640). In the gallery at Munich, Bavaria.

☞ "Though this famous picture is called the *Fall of the Angels*, I have some doubts as to whether this was the intention of the painter; whether he did not mean to express the fall of sinners, flung by the angel of judgment into the abyss of wrath and perdition."
Mrs. Jameson.

2. A picture by Frans de Vriendt, called Frans Floris (1520-1570), a Flemish painter, and considered his masterpiece. It is in the Antwerp Museum.

Fall of the Damned. A celebrated picture by Peter Paul Rubens (1577-1640). In the Pinakothek, Munich, Bavaria.

☞ "It is impossible to form an adequate idea of the powers of Rubens without having seen this picture."
Sir Joshua Reynolds.

☞ "The most surprising of Rubens's labors." *Wilkie.*

Fallen Angels. See FALL OF THE DAMNED.

Fame, Torre della. See TORRE DELLA FAME.

Family of Darius before Alexander. A picture by Paul Veronese (1530–1588), and his grandest work. Formerly in the Pisani Palace, Venice, but purchased by the British Government in 1857, and now in the National Gallery, London.

Famine. See SEVEN YEARS OF FAMINE.

Faneuil Hall. A public edifice in Boston, Mass., famous as the place where the stirring speeches of the Revolutionary orators were made, which incited the people to resist British oppression and secure their independence. The building was erected in 1742 by Peter Faneuil, a Huguenot merchant. It was destroyed by fire in 1761, but rebuilt three years later. During the siege of Boston in 1775–76, it was converted into a theatre. It has a capacious hall, containing portraits of eminent Americans.

They like to go to the theatre and be made to weep; to *Faneuil Hall*, and be taught by Otis, Webster, or Kossuth, or Phillips, what great hearts they have, what tears, what possible enlargements to their narrow horizons. *Emerson.*

Athens and the Acropolis, Rome and the Capitol, are not more associated ideas than are Boston and *Faneuil Hall*. *G. S. Hillard.*

The resistance to the Stamp Act was of the same kind as the resistance to the ship-money; and in our Revolutionary war there were as eloquent defences of our principles and course heard in the British Parliament as echoed in *Fanueil Hall*. *Mrs. H. B. Stowe.*

Let the sounds of traffic die:
Shut the mill-gate, — leave the stall, —
Fling the axe and hammer by, —
Throng to *Faneuil Hall*. *Whittier.*

Forgets she how the Bay State, in answer to the call
Of her old House of Burgesses, spoke out from *Faneuil Hall?* *Whittier.*

Farmyard, The. A celebrated picture by Paul Potter (1625–1654), the Dutch painter. It was formerly in the gallery at Cassel, Germany, but is now in that of St. Petersburg, Russia.

Farnese Bull. [Ital. *Toro Farnese*.] A celebrated work of ancient sculpture, representing the punishment of Dirce. Now in the Museo Borbonico at Naples, Italy. It is described by Pliny as one of the most remarkable monuments of antiquity. It was found in the Baths of Caracalla at Rome, in the sixteenth century, and was placed by Michael Angelo in the inner court of the Farnese Palace, whence its name. In 1786 it was removed to Naples. It is supposed to be the work of the brothers Apollonius and Tauriscus, who probably lived in the first century after Christ.

☞ "The celebrated group of the Farnese Bull is a noble work, in which the intellectual conception of the artist is not at all overlaid by the weight and bulk of the material." *Hillard.*

Farnese Cup. See TAZZA FARNESE.

Farnese Flora. See FLORA.

Farnese Hercules. A celebrated ancient statue representing Hercules resting upon his club. At the foot of the club is inscribed the name of the Greek sculptor, Glycon. This statue was found at Rome in the Baths of Caracalla, in 1540, and subsequently removed to Naples, Italy, where it is now deposited in the Museum. The right hand is modern. By some this statue is supposed to be a copy of the Hercules of Lysippus. See HERCULES.

☞ "The indication of nerves and muscles, or their absolute suppression, is what distinguishes a Hercules who is destined to fight monsters and brigands, and still be far from the end of his labors, from the Hercules who is purified of the grosser corporeal parts, and admitted to the felicity of the immortal gods. It is thus that we recognize the *man* in the Farnese Hercules, and the *god* in the Hercules of the Belvedere. It may even be said that this last approaches nearer to the sublime period in art than the Apollo itself." *Winckelmann, Trans.*

The tenor is a spasmodic buffoon, a sort of ugly *Farnese Hercules*, wearing one of those old chin-clasping casques which is only met with amongst classic rubbish. *Taine, Trans.*

Farnese Mercury. An ancient statue, now in the British Museum, London. Purchased in 1865.

Farnese Palace. [Ital. *Palazzo Farnese.*] A magnificent Roman palace of immense size, begun by Paul III., one of the Farnese family. Michael Angelo was one of its architects. The materials were taken from the Coliseum and other ruins of ancient Rome. The great hall or gallery is painted in fresco by Caracci and his scholars. The palace fell by descent to the Bourbon kings of Naples, and within the last few years the exiled court have made it their place of residence. The Farnese gallery of sculpture was formerly celebrated; but the best pieces have been removed, and are now at Naples, Italy.

☞ "The Palazzo Farnese, one of the finest palaces in Rome, is a shameless receiver of stolen goods. . . . The great hall, or gallery, is painted in fresco by Annibale and Agostino Caracci, and their scholars. . . . About half of Lempriere's Classical Dictionary is painted on the walls and ceiling of the hall." *Hillard.*

☞ "Of all these fossils, the grandest, noblest, most imposing and rigidly magnificent, is, in my opinion, the Farnese Palace. Alone, in the middle of a dark square, rises the enormous palace, lofty and massive, like a fortress capable of giving and receiving the heaviest ordnance. It belongs to the grand era. It is indeed akin to the torsos of Michael Angelo. You feel in it the inspiration of the great pagan epoch." *Taine, Trans.*

Farnesina. A beautiful villa in Rome, built in 1506 for Agostino Chigi, a great banker and patron of art. It contains some of the most beautiful frescos of Raphael. Chigi was famed for his display of princely magnificence and luxury. He gave here — the building is said to have been built expressly for the purpose — most extravagant entertainments. On the occasion of a sumptuous banquet to Leo X. and the cardinals, three fish served upon the table are said to have cost 250 crowns, and the gold and silver plate to have been thrown into the Tiber as soon as used.

☞ "The Palazzo Farnesina, the splendid monument of the taste and magnificence of Agostino Chigi, is a pilgrim-shrine in art, because it contains the finest expression of Raphael's genius, when manifesting itself in purely secular forms." *Hillard.*

☞ "Peruzzi's most beautiful building is the Farnesina. Vasari says justly that it seems not formed by masonry, but born out of the ground, so complete does it stand there in its charming solitariness. At the present day it is forsaken, its open halls are walled up, the paintings on the outer walls are faded or fallen away with the mortar. But by degrees, as we become absorbed in the paintings, the feeling of transitoriness vanishes." *Grimm, Trans.*

Note. — The Farnesina has been recently restored to an elegant and habitable condition. See GALATEA.

Farringdon Market. A market in London, erected in place of Fleet Market, opened in 1829. See FLEET MARKET.

Fast Castle. This ancient fortress in Scotland is the original of "Wolf's Crag," in Scott's novel of the "Bride of Lammermoor."

Fasti Consulares. Famous tablets containing a list of all the consuls and public officers of Rome to the time of Augustus. They are still legible, though much mutilated. In the Hall of the Conservators, Rome.

Fata Morgana. A singular atmospheric phenomenon, quite similar to the mirage, which, under certain conditions of the elements, is observed in the Straits of Messina, between the coasts of Calabria and Sicily, and which is sometimes, though rarely, seen upon other coasts. It consists of multiplied images in the air of the hills, groves, buildings, people, and other objects on the surrounding coasts. These images are inverted, and the whole forms a sort of moving spectacle. It is popularly thought to be the work of the fairy of the same name.

☞ "On Calabria's side lay Reggio, which a few weeks previously had suffered terribly from an earthquake. Now every thing lay in a warm, smiling sunlight; yet the smile of the coast here has in it something like witchcraft. My thoughts were on the millions whose hearts have beat with the fear of death and longing for life under these coasts, the millions who have sailed here, from the time Ulysses sailed past the cavern of Polyphemus, until now that our arrowy steamer glided over the watery mirror, where Fata Morgana shows her airy palace; but no colonnades of rays, no fantastic cupola and Gothic towers, arose on the blue waters. Yet the coast itself was a Fata Morgana for the eye and thought." *Hans Christian Andersen.*

But what must be thought of the female dramatist, who, for eighteen long months, can exhibit the beautifullest *Fata-morgana* to a flush cardinal, wide awake, with fifty years on his head; and so lap him in her scenic illusion that he never doubts but it is all firm earth, and the pasteboard coulisse-trees are producing Hesperides apples? *Carlyle.*

Fates. See THREE FATES.

Faubourg St. Antoine. A quarter of Paris inhabited by the working-classes, and famous in the Revolution of 1789 as the source and headquarters of the insurrectionary elements in the city. It has been since the time of the Fronde the seat of disturbances. From 1830 to 1851 many riots and bloody fights gave a disagreeable character to this quarter, but since 1854 a change has taken place in this respect. Here and in the vicinity are some of the chief manufactories of the city.

Faubourg St. Germain. A fashionable quarter of Paris in which the ancient nobility resided. Many of the houses of the old noblesse are still standing.

☞ "St. Germain is full of these princely, aristocratic mansions, mournfully beautiful, desolately grand." *C. Beecher.*

Everybody knows something of a handsome and very elegant young baron of the *Faubourg St. Germain*, who, with small fortune, very great taste, and greater credit contrived to get on very swimmingly as an adorable *roué* and *vaurien* till he was hard upon twenty-five. *N. P. Willis.*

The microscopic *Faubourg St. Germain* of the little place thought of raising the quarantine for Monsieur Madeleine, the probable relative of a bishop. *Victor Hugo, Trans.*

The strong men usually give some allowance, even to the petulances of fashion, for that affinity they find in it. Napoleon, child of the revolution, destroyer of the old noblesse, never ceased to court the *Faubourg St. Germain*, doubtless with the feeling that fashion is a homage to men of his stamp *Emerson.*

Faun, The [of Praxiteles]. A celebrated ancient statue. Now in the Capitol, Rome.

☞ "It is the marble image of a young man, leaning his right arm upon the trunk or stump of a tree. . . . It is impossible to gaze long at this stone image without conceiving a kindly sentiment towards it, as if its substance were warm to the touch, and imbued with actual life." *Hawthorne.*

The shepherd asleep on a sheltered bank under the rocks, is already a *Faun of Praxiteles*, and might be a Theseus or a Perseus. *Bayard Taylor.*

Faun. See BARBERINI FAUN, DANCING FAUN, DRUNKEN FAUN, RONDININI FAUN, SLEEPING FAUN, etc.

Favorite, The. An armor-plated ship of the British navy, launched July 5, 1864.

Fawkes's Cellar. See GUY FAWKES'S CELLAR.

Feast of Roses. A picture by Albert Dürer (1471–1528). In the monastery Strahoff at Prague, Austria.

Feast of the Gods. A large fresco in the Farnesina, Rome, representing the gods as deciding the dispute between Venus and Cupid, designed by Raphael (1483–1520), but chiefly executed by his pupil Giulio Romano.

Feast of the Gods. A noted picture begun by Giovanni Bellini (1426–1516), but completed by Titian (1477–1576), now in the collection of the Duke of Northumberland at Alnwick Castle, England. There is a copy, thought to be by Poussin, in the Scotch Academy.

Feast of the King of the Beans. A picture by Gabriel Metsu (b. 1630), a Dutch *genre*-painter. In the Gallery of Munich, Bavaria.

Feast of the Levite. A picture of great size by Paul Veronese (1530–1588). It was formerly in the refectory of SS. Giovanni e Paolo, now in the Accademia delle Belle Arti, Venice, Italy.

Fecundidad, La. [Offering to the Goddess of Fecundity.] An admired picture by Titian (1477–1576). In the gallery at Madrid, Spain.

Federal Hill. An eminence south of the centre of the city of Baltimore, Md. It was a place of much interest during the civil war, having been seized and occupied by Gen. Butler, and heavily fortified to protect the city, and to overawe internal sedition.

Feldmässer, Die. [The Land Surveyors.] See GEOMETRICIANS, THE.

Felix, The. An Arctic exploring ship which sailed to the northern seas under Sir John Ross in 1850.

Fellows Marbles. A collection of sculptures in the British Museum, London, brought from the ancient city of Xanthus.

Felsenmeer. [Sea of Rocks.] **1.** A remarkable accumulation of syenitic rocks in the Odenwald, not far from Darmstadt, Germany.

2. A natural curiosity in the form of an immense mass of detached rocks, near Hemar, in Westphalia.

Fenchurch Street. A street in London, which derives its name from a fen, or bog, caused by the overflow of a small stream which ran into the Thames.

Fernay. This château, four and one-half miles north of Geneva, was built by Voltaire, and became his residence. He also erected a church, and founded the little village about it, by promoting manufactures.

This and several subsequent appeals of the same sort are among the best points in the conduct of the Philosopher of *Fernay*. *Spalding.*

Fernihurst. A Scottish fortress of the fifteenth century, near Jedburgh.

Ferrara Castle. A noted mediæval fortress in Ferrara, Italy, once the residence of the dukes of Ferrara. It is considered one of the finest relics of feudal times.

Ferriter's Castle. An ancient ruined stronghold, situated in a wild spot, almost on the verge of the Atlantic, in the county of Kerry, Ireland.

Ferronière, La Belle. See BELLE FERRONIÈRE.

Festival of Venus in the Isle of Cytherea. A picture by Peter Paul Rubens (1577–1640). Now in the Imperial Gallery at Vienna, Austria.

Feuillant Club. A political association in Paris established during the Revolution. It was originally called the Club of 1789. It derived its name from the convent of the Feuillants in which its meetings were held.

Feuillants [Église des]. A fine church in Bordeaux, France. It contains the tomb of Montaigne.

Field Lane. A street in London which has now mostly disappeared. It was inhabited by a wretched, criminal class.

☞ "In its filthy shops are exposed for sale huge bunches of second-hand silk handkerchiefs of all sizes and patterns; for here reside the traders who purchase them from the pickpockets. Hundreds of these handkerchiefs hang dangling from pegs outside the windows, or flaunting from the door-posts; and the shelves within are piled with them. Confined as the limits of Field Lane are, it has its barber, its coffee-shop, its beer-shop, and its fried-fish warehouse. It is a commercial colony of itself, the emporium of petty larceny." *Dickens.*

Field of Blood. A tract in Italy, now occupied by the village of Canne, and still called "Campo di Sangue," Field of Blood. It is the site of the ancient battle-field of Cannæ, where Hannibal gained a great victory over the Romans, B.C. 216.

Field of Blood. See ACELDAMA.

Field of Flodden. See FLODDEN FIELD.

Field of Forty Footsteps. A region in Bloomsbury, London, formerly noted as a resort for low characters, and famous as the scene of a legendary conflict between two brothers, whose footsteps remained impressed in the soil, and over which no grass would grow. Upon this legend Jane and Anna Maria Porter based one of their popular romances.

☞ "The steps are of the size of a large human foot, about three inches deep. We counted only seventy-six, but were not exact in counting. The place where one or both of the brothers is supposed to have fallen is still bare of grass." *Southey.*

June 16, 1800. Went into the fields at the back of Montague House, and there saw, for the first time, the *forty footsteps;* the building materials are there ready to cover them from the sight of man. I counted more than forty, but they might be the footprints of the workmen.
Joseph Moser, Commonplace Book.

Field of March. See CHAMP DE MARS.

Field of Mars. See CAMPUS MARTIUS.

Field of Peterloo. The popular name of St. Peter's Field, near Manchester, England, where, Aug. 16, 1819, a riot occurred. The name was derisively imitated from Waterloo.

Bridges of Lodi, retreats of Moscow, Waterloos, *Peterloos*, ten-pound franchises, tar-barrels, and guillotines.
Carlyle.

Field of Rákos. [Hung. *Rákos Mezo.*] A celebrated plain in the immediate neighborhood of Pesth, Hungary, in which the Diet, or great national assembly, of the Hungarians, was formerly held in the open air.

Field of the Cloth of Gold. A celebrated plain near the town of Ardres in Northern France. It is known by this name in consequence of the meeting on this spot in 1520 between Henry VIII. of England and Francis I. of France with their retinues, and the cloth of gold with which the tents of the two sovereigns were covered.

I supposed you must have served as a yeoman of the guard since Bluff King Henry's time, and expected to hear something from you about the *Field of the Cloth of Gold.* *Scott.*

They [Petrarch's finer poems] differ from them [his inferior ones] as a May-day procession of chimney-sweepers differs from the *Field of the Cloth of Gold.*
Macaulay.

Fifth Avenue. A famous street in the city of New York, beginning at Washington Square and extending to Central Park. It is lined with costly edifices, the homes of wealthy citizens, and is the most splendid street of residences in America, and one of the finest in the world.

☞ "Fifth Avenue is the Belgrave Square, the Park Lane, and the Pall Mall of New York. It is certainly a very fine street. The houses in it are magnificent, not having that aristocratic look which some of our detached London residences enjoy, but an air of comfortable luxury and commercial wealth which is not excelled by the best houses of any other town that I know."
Anthony Trollope.

Fifth-Avenue Theatre. In New York. A small but elegant place of amusement.

Fighting Gladiator. A well-known Greek statue in the Louvre, Paris.

☞ "There is a left arm again, though; no, — that is from the 'Fighting Gladiator,' — the '*Jeune Héros combatant*' of the Louvre; there is the broad ring of the shield. . . . [The separate casts of the 'Gladiator's' arm look immense; but in its place the limb looks light, almost slender, — such is the perfection of that miraculous marble. I never felt as if I touched the life of the old Greeks until I looked on that statue]." *Holmes.*

Welcome, O *Fighting Gladiator*, and Recumbent Cleopatra, and Dying Warrior, whose classic outlines (reproduced in the calcined mineral of Lutetia) crown my loaded shelves! *Holmes.*

Fighting Téméraire. A picture by Joseph Mallord William Turner (1775–1851), the English landscape painter, and regarded one of his best works. In the National Gallery, London.

Fijah. A noted fountain in the vicinity of Damascus, one of the largest and most remarkable in Syria.

Filatrice, The. An admired statue by Johann Gottfried Schadow (1764–1850).

Filles du Calvaire, Boulevart des. One of the Parisian boulevards, so named from a convent. See BOULEVARDS.

Finchley Common. Formerly an open tract in the county of Middlesex, England, much frequented by highwaymen.

> His enemies affirmed . . . that he [George Porter] sometimes got on horseback late in the evening, and stole out in disguise, and that when he returned from these mysterious excursions, his appearance justified the suspicion that he had been doing business on Hounslow Heath or *Finchley Common*. *Macaulay.*

Finchley, March to. See MARCH TO FINCHLEY.

Fingal's Cave. A famous and romantic cavern in the island of Staffa, Scotland. It is 227 feet long, and 66 feet in height above the water at mean tide. It is composed of pentangular or hexagon columns of black basaltic rock, erect, inclining, and curved, and irregularly jointed.

> There all unknown its columns rose
> Where dark and undisturbed repose
> The cormorant had found,
> And the shy seal had quiet home,
> And weltered in that wondrous dome;
> Where, as to shame the temples decked
> By skill of earthly architect,
> Nature herself, it seemed, would raise
> A minster to her Maker's praise. *Scott.*

> Ye shadowy Beings, that have rights and claims
> In every cell of *Fingal's* mystic grot,
> Where are ye? *Wordsworth.*

> Not Aladdin magian
> Ever such a work began;
> Not the wizard of the Dee
> Ever such a dream could see;
> Not Saint John in Patmos' isle,
> In the passion of his toil,
> When he saw the churches seven,
> Golden-aisled, built up in heaven,
> Gazed at such a rugged wonder
> *Keats.*

Finsbury. A now populous borough of London, including the old district of Moorfields. Cunningham says that Finsbury was a popular place for Sunday walks in the times of Queen Elizabeth and James. Shadwell says that you could here see "Haberdashers walking with their whole fireside." According to tradition, the name Finsbury is derived from two daughters of one of the Crusaders, as expressed in the following extract from an old ballad:—

> Old Sir John Fines he had the name,
> Being buried in that place,
> Now, since then, called *Finsbury*,
> To his renown and grace;
> Which time to come shall not outwear,
> Nor yet the same deface.
>
> And likewise when those maidens died
> They gave those pleasant fields
> Unto our London citizens,
> Which they most bravely hield;
> And now they are made most pleasant walks,
> That great contentment yield.
> *Old Ballad.*

☞ "Moorgate opens to the moor, or fen,—hence the district name *Fin*, or Fensbury." *Athenæum.*

> And giv'st such sarcenet surety for thy oaths,
> As if thou never walk'st farther than *Finsbury*. *Shakespeare.*

Finsbury Park. A pleasure-ground in London, opened in 1869.

Finstermünz. A magnificent pass or defile in the Tyrolese Alps, second in point of grandeur only to the Via Mala.

First Lesson. A picture by Sir Edwin Landseer (1803–1873).

Fish-Street Hill. In London. Here is the monument built, from designs by Wren, in commemoration of the great fire of 1666. The Black Prince had a palace on Fish-street Hill.

> A friend of mine, who was sitting unmoved at one of the sentimental pieces, was asked how he could be so indifferent. "Why, truly," says he, "as the hero is but a tradesman, it is indifferent to me whether he be turned out of his counting-house on *Fish-street Hill*, since he will still have enough left to open shop in St. Giles's. *Goldsmith.*

> I find myself before a fine picture in the morning. Was it ever otherwise? What is become of *Fish Street Hill*. *Charles Lamb.*

> Twelve columns like the monument on *Fish Street Hill* might give the reader some idea of the vastness of these pillars [in the palace of Karnac]. *Lefèvre, Trans.*

Fisher, Fort. See FORT FISHER.

Fisher Boy. A statue by Hiram Powers (1805–1873).

☞ "Then came a lithe, graceful, immature figure of the Fisher Boy, holding a shell to his ear; the expression, the whole air and aspect, suggestive of the mystery of life that connects its outset with eternity." *Tuckerman.*

Fisherman presenting the Ring of St. Mark to the Doge of Venice. A famous picture by Paris Bordone (1500–1576). In the Accademia delle Belle Arti, Venice, Italy.

☞ "A grand piece of scenic decoration. The numerous figures, the vivid color, the luxuriant architecture, remind us of Paul Veronese, with, however, more delicacy, both in color and execution." *Mrs. Jameson.*

Fishmongers' Hall. A celebrated hall in London, belonging to one of the great city *guilds*, or companies, situated near London Bridge. This company has numbered about 50 lord mayors, and on July 10, 1864, had been incorporated 500 years.

Five Forks. A famous locality in the neighborhood of Petersburg, Va., where a last stand was made by Gen. Lee's troops, who being repulsed at this point, Lee concluded to evacuate the city of Richmond, April 2, 1865.

Five Points. A district in the city of New York near the Tombs, and at the intersection of Baxter, Park, and Worth streets, formerly noted as being one of the most wretched and dangerous quarters in the metropolis. Its character has somewhat improved of late.

There are many by-streets (in New York) almost as neutral in clean colors, and positive in dirty ones, as by-streets in London; and there is one quarter, commonly called the *Five Points*, which, in respect of filth and wretchedness, may be safely backed against Seven Dials, or any other part of famed St. Giles's. *Dickens.*

Flagellation, The. A picture by Giovanni Antonio Bazzi, called Il Sodoma (1479–1549). In the Institute of Fine Arts at Siena, Italy.

☞ "This hallowed work of genius shows what pictorial art, devoutly exercised, might effect in behalf of religious truth." *Hawthorne.*

☞ "At last we came to a picture by Sodoma, the most illustrious representative of the Sienese school. It was a fresco,—Christ bound to the pillar after having been scourged. I do believe that painting has never done any thing better, so far as expression is concerned, than this figure. In all these generations since it was painted, it must have softened thousands of hearts, drawn down rivers of tears, been more effectual than a million of sermons. Really it is a thing to stand and weep at. No other painter has done any thing that can deserve to be compared with this." *Hawthorne.*

Flagellation, Column of the. See COLUMN OF THE FLAGELLATION.

Flaminia, Porta. See PORTA FLAMINIA.

Flaminian Way. See VIA FLAMINIA.

Flavian Amphitheatre. See COLISEUM.

The *Flavian Amphitheatre* and the Baths of Caracalla enable us to realize imperial Rome more vividly than even the glowing pages of Tacitus. *James Fergusson.*

Fleece, The. Formerly a tavern in Covent Garden, London, the scene of numerous disorderly disputes, and, as Aubrey expresses it, "very unfortunate for homicides."

Fleet, The. A famous prison in London, named from the creek, or stream, of the Fleet, upon the bank of which it was erected. After an existence of nearly eight centuries, it was abolished, and removed about 1845. It has been tenanted by many distinguished victims. Pope calls it the "Haunt of the Muses," from the number of poets who have been confined here. The prisoners were subjected in many cases to most cruel and outrageous treatment. The horrors of the Fleet were brought to public notice in 1726 by the trial of the warden for murder. The prison and its immediate neighborhood were notorious for the so-called "Fleet Marriages," which were performed by clergymen imprisoned for debt. Great numbers of these marriages were solemnized, as the clergymen could of course defy the fine for performing clandestine and irregular marriages. The practice was put a stop to by act of Parliament in 1754. The day before this act went into operation, 217 marriages were recorded in one register alone. Dickens describes the latter days of the Fleet in the "Pickwick Papers." See FLETA.

Scarce had the coach discharged its trusty fare,
But gaping crowds surround th' amorous pair.
The busy plyers make a mighty stir,
And whispering, cry, "D'ye want the parson, sir?"

Humours of the Fleet.

Fleet Ditch. Formerly an open ditch in London, between Holborn and the Thames, so called from the Fleet River, the supply of water from which being diverted, the ditch became stagnant, and a receptacle for all sorts of offal and filth. Ben Jonson, Pope, Swift, and Gay have with minute detail described this pestilential nuisance. It is now arched over, and serves as the *Cloaca Maxima* of London.

To where *Fleet-ditch*, with disemboguing streams
Rolls the large tribute of dead dogs to Thames,
The king of dykes! than whom no sluice of mud
With deeper sable blots the silver flood.

Pope.

Now from all parts the swelling kennels flow,
And bear their trophies with them as they go;
Filth of all hues and odors seem to tell
What street they sail'd from by their sight and smell.
They, as each torrent drives its rapid force,
From Smithfield to St. 'Pulchre's shape their course,
And, in huge confluence joined at Snowhill ridge,
Fall from the Conduit prone to Holborn Bridge;
Sweepings from butchers' stalls, . . .
Dead cats, and turnip-tops, come tumbling down the flood.

Swift.

By what methods, by what gifts of eye and hand, does a heroic Samuel Johnson, now when cast forth into that waste chaos of authorship, maddest of things, a mingled Phlegethon and *Fleet-ditch*, with its floating lumber, and sea-krakens, and mud-spectres, — shape himself a voyage; of the *transient* driftwood, and the *enduring* iron, built him a seaworthy life-boat, and sail therein, undrowned, unpolluted, through the roaring "mother of dead dogs," onwards to an eternal landmark, and city that hath foundations? *Carlyle.*

Fleet Market. A meat and vegetable market in London, established over Fleet Ditch in 1737. Farringdon Market — occupying nearly the same place and opened in 1829 — now takes its place.

☞ "Fleet Market, at that time [No Popery Riots], was a long irregular row of wooden sheds and pent-houses, occupying the centre of what is now called Farringdon Street. They were jumbled together in a most unsightly fashion in the middle of the road, to the great obstruction of the thoroughfare and the annoyance of passengers, who were fain to make their way as best they could among carts, baskets, barrows, trucks, casks, bulks, and benches, and to jostle with porters, hucksters, waggoners, and a motley crowd of buyers, sellers, pickpockets, vagrants, and idlers. . . . It was indispensable to most public conveniences in those days that they should be public nuisances likewise, and Fleet Market maintained the principle to admiration." *Dickens.*

Fleet Street. An ancient and celebrated thoroughfare in London, so called from the stream of the same name. For centuries it has been famous for its exhibitions and processions, its printers and booksellers, its coffee-houses and taverns, and its banking-houses.

The foaming pots which the best tap of *Fleet St.* supplies. *T N. Talfourd.*

Cheapside, the Strand, *Fleet Street*, and Ludgate Hill,
Each name a very story in itself.

Robert Leighton.

Fleta. A Latinized appellation of the noted Fleet prison, formerly situated in London. John Selden (1584–1654) published a work entitled "Fleta." See FLEET, THE.

☞ "In 1647 he [Selden] published from a manuscript in the Cotton library the valuable old law treatise entitled 'Fleta,' so named from being compiled by its anonymous author while confined in the Fleet prison, most probably in the reign of Edward I." *Singer.*

Fleurs, Château des. See CHÂTEAU DES FLEURS.

Flight into Egypt. [Ital. *La Fuga in Egitto*, Fr. *La Fuite de la Sainte Famille en Egypte*] Of the compositions treating of this incident in the life of the infant Saviour, the following are among the better known. See also REPOSE IN EGYPT.

Flight into Egypt. An admired picture by Guadenzio Ferrari (1484–1550). In the church of the Minorites at Varallo, Italy.

Flight into Egypt. A beautiful fresco by Bernardin Pinturicchio (1454–1513). In the church of St. Onofrio at Rome.

Flight into Egypt. A picture by Joachim Patenier (— d. 1524), a Flemish painter. It is now in the museum at Antwerp, Belgium.

Flight into Egypt. See RETURN FROM THE FLIGHT INTO EGYPT.

Flodden Field. A locality in Scotland, in the county of Northumberland, near Cornhill, where, on the 9th of September, 1513, was fought the famous battle between the English and Scotch, which is described in Sir Walter Scott's "Marmion."

Floors Castle. The seat of the Duke of Roxburghe, near Kelso in Scotland.

Flora. A famous colossal statue, found in the Baths of Caracalla at Rome, and regarded as a masterpiece of art. It has been variously considered as representing a Venus, a Hebe, and *Hope*. By Winckelmann it was thought to be one of the Muses. Now in the museum at Naples. [Also called the *Farnese Flora*.]

☞ "I always returned to a colossal Flora, standing in the middle of the hall, draped so as to reveal her forms, but of such an austere, dignified simplicity. She is a veritable goddess." *Taine, Trans.*

Flora. A beautiful picture by Titian (1477-1576), or, as some think, by Jacopo Palma, called Palma Vecchio (1480-1528), representing a woman in white, with flowing hair, holding flowers. In the Uffizi Gallery, Florence.

Flora. A statue by Thomas Crawford (1814–1857). In Central Park, New York.

Florida, The. A Confederate privateer, built by Laird of Liverpool, and commanded by John Moffit. She was captured in San Salvador Bay, Brazil, Oct. 6, 1864, by the United States ship *Wachusett*.

☞ "The Confederates, encouraged by British favors, employed a British ship-builder (Mr. Laird, a member of Parliament) to construct vessels for them for privateering purposes. The *Oreto* was sent to sea in disguise, sailed for the British port of Nassau, and early in September appeared off the harbor of Mobile flying British colors. She ran into Mobile Harbor, eluding the blockading fleet, and escaped late in December, when she bore the name of *Florida*. She hovered most of the time on the American coast, but was closely watched by national vessels. She managed to elude them. Finally she ran into the Brazilian port of Bahia or San Salvador, after capturing a barque; and there she was captured by the *Wachusett*, Capt. Collins. This capture was a violation of neutrality, and occasioned a good deal of excitement. The captain and prize soon after appeared in Hampton Roads, and not long after the *Florida* was sunk near Newport News." *Lossing.*

Flume, The. A remarkable ravine 700 feet long in the Franconia mountains, N.H., through which flows the Flume cascade. The rocky walls which enclose the cañon are some 65 feet in height. At one point, where the passage is only ten feet in width, an enormous granite bowlder is suspended.

Foligno Madonna. See MADONNA DI FOLIGNO.

Fontaine des Innocents. A famous fountain in Paris, built in 1550 by Pierre Lescot, with statues and bas-reliefs by Jean Goujon.

Fontaine Molière. A public fountain in Paris, in the Rue de Richelieu, with the statue of Molière, and near the house where that great dramatist died.

Fontainebleau. A vast and irregularly shaped palace at Fontainebleau [fountain of beautiful water], France, about 37 miles from Paris. It is one of the most magnificent royal residences in Europe, and associated with many historical events of interest. The present palace was chiefly the work of Francis I. Large additions were made to it by Henry IV. It was here that Napoleon signed his abdication in 1814. Under Louis Philippe the palace was much improved, and restored to something like its early condition. It has a magnificent park kept with great care like a garden. The forest of Fontainebleau covers 84 English miles.

1644, 7 March. I went with some company towards *Fontainebleau*, a sumptuous palace of the King's, like ours of Hampton Court, about 14 leagues from the city. By the way, we pass through a forest so prodigiously encompassed with hideous rocks of whitish hard stone, heaped one on another in mountainous heights; but I think the like is not to be found elsewhere. It abounds with stags, wolves, boars; and not long after a lynx, or ounce, was killed amongst them, which had devoured some passengers. . . . This house is nothing so stately and uniforme as Hampton Court. *John Evelyn, Diary.*

For such it was, when long ago
I sat in my leafy studio
In the dear old Forest of *Fontainebleau*.
C. P. Cranch.

In the lone brakes of *Fontainebleau*,
Or châlets near the Alpine snow.
Matthew Arnold.

Fontana della Barcaccia. A well-known fountain in the Piazza di Spagna, Rome, designed by Bernini (1598-1680). It is in the form of a boat (barcaccia), whence the name.

Fontana di Trevi. [Fountain of Trevi.] A large and celebrated fountain in Rome, built by Clement XII., in 1735, from designs of Niccolò Salvi, with a statue of Neptune and other figures by Pietro Bracchi. The fountain is supplied by the aqueduct of the Acqua Vergine.

☞ "The Fontana di Trevi is in the heart of Rome. A mass of rocks is tumbled together at the base of the façade of an immense palace. In a large niche in the centre of the façade is a statue of Neptune in his car, the horses of which, with their attendant Tritons, are pawing and sprawling among the rocks. All this is in bad taste, an incongruous blending of fact and fable, chilled by the coldest of allegories; but it sounds worse in description than it looks to the eye. The water gushes up in sparkling and copious masses from the crevices between the rocks, spouts from the nostrils of the horses and the conchs of the Tritons, and gives to the whole scene its own dancing and glittering beauty. . . . As we look, we begin with criticism; but we end with admiration." *Hillard.*

☞ "In the daytime there is hardly a livelier scene in Rome than the neighborhood of the fountain of Trevi; . . . for the water of Trevi is in request far and wide as the most refreshing draught for feverish lips, and the wholesomest to drink that can anywhere be found. Tradition goes that a parting draught at the fountain of Trevi ensures a traveller's return to Rome whatever obstacles and improbabilities may seem to beset him." *Hawthorne.*

Till, Trajan's whispering forum passed,
We hear the waters, showering bright,
Of *Trevi's ancient fountain*, cast
Their woven music on the night.
Bayard Taylor.

Fontana Paolina. [The Pauline Fountain.] One of the largest and most imposing fountains in Rome, on the Janiculum, and built to resemble the façade of a church. It was erected by Pope Paul V. in 1612, and was designed by Fontana; so that by a whimsical coincidence both names are perpetuated in that of the fountain itself.

Fonthill Abbey. A showy monastic building, erected at great expense, at the beginning of the present century, near Salisbury, Wilts, England, by William Beckford, the celebrated author of "Vathek." The building was constructed in fantastic style, in the utmost haste and passion, shrouded with great mystery, the grounds being enclosed by a wall 12 feet high and seven miles long. At one time 500 men were employed by day and night. A wooden tower 400 feet high was capriciously built, merely to see the effect of such a structure, and, being taken down, was replaced by a tower of stone. Twenty-five years later, in 1825, this latter fell, owing to imperfect construction; and the estate being sold, the buildings were demolished. In this mansion Mr. Beckford resided for over 20 years. The property is said to have brought £350,000 at the sale.

> The mighty master waved his wand, and lo!
> On the astonished eye the glorious show
> Burst like a vision! —
> . . . . .
> Ascend the steps! the high and fretted roof
> Is woven by some elfin hand aloof:
> Whilst from the painted windows' long array
> A mellow light is shed, as not of day
> How gorgeous all! *W. L. Bowles.*

Fools, Order of. See ORDER OF FOOLS.

Force, La. A noted prison in Paris, and the principal one in the city. It is situated on the Boulevard Mazas.

> "They are," Mr Lorry whispered the words, glancing fearfully round at the locked room, "murdering the prisoners. If you are sure of what you say; if you really have the power you think you have,—as I believe you have,—make yourself known to these devils, and get taken to *La Force*." *Dickens.*

Ford's. 1. Formerly a theatre in Washington, and noted as the building within which President Lincoln was assassinated, April 19, 1865, by John Wilkes Booth. The building was purchased by the United-States Government, closed as a theatre, and appropriated to the purposes of an army medical museum, which is said to be the finest of its kind in the world.

2. A grand opera-house in Baltimore, Md. It has an elegant auditorium, and accommodates 2,500 persons.

Forefathers' Rock. See PLYMOUTH ROCK.

Forest Hills. A large cemetery in the immediate vicinity of Boston, Mass. It contains some fine monuments.

Forester's Family. A picture by Sir Edwin Landseer (1803-1873), the most celebrated modern painter of animals.

Forfarshire, The. A British steamer wrecked Sept. 6, 1838, on the voyage from Hull to Dundee. Nine persons were saved from the wreck by the heroic exertions of Grace Darling, daughter of the lighthouse-keeper on one of the Farne Islands, who rowed with her father in a small boat through the heavy sea to the sinking ship.

Forge of Vulcan. A drawing by Annibale Caracci (1560-1609). In the Louvre, Paris.

Forge of Vulcan. A celebrated picture by Diego Rodriguez de Silva y Velasquez (1599-1660), the Spanish painter. In the Museum of Madrid, Spain.

Forge of Vulcan. A picture by Jacopo Robusti, called Tintoretto (1512-1594). In the Ducal Palace, Venice, Italy.

Fornarina, La. The name given to several portraits by Raphael Sanzio (1483-1520). There is much doubt, both as to the name itself, and the person represented; but the latter is generally considered to have been Raphael's mistress. It has been surmised that the name was invented to suit a story of the painter's having attached himself to a potter's daughter, but there is no authentic evidence in the case. The portrait bearing this name, in the Barberini Palace, in Rome, is regarded as the earlier work. There is another somewhat resembling it in the Pitti Palace, Florence, which is thought to have served as a model for the Sistine Madonna. There is still another portrait, also called La Fornarina, in the Tribune of the Uffizi at Florence, which has usually been ascribed to Raphael, but is now supposed to be the work of Sebastian del Piombo (1485-1547), and has been variously adjudged to represent either the improvvisatrice Beatrice da Ferrara, or Vittoria Colonna, Marchesa di Pescara, Michael Angelo's friend. Besides the foregoing, there are several other female portraits bearing the name of La Fornarina. One in particular, which is also called Dorothea, dated 1512, and now generally ascribed to Sebastian del Piombo, is at Blenheim, England.

☞ "It is now no secret among connoisseurs that the so-called Fornarina in the Tribune of the Uffizi, and a portrait named Dorothea, at Blenheim, both supplemented with the title of Raphael's Mistress, are by the hand of Sebastian."

Eastlake, Hand-book of Painting.

☞ "The portrait of the young girl, or woman, in the Barberini Palace, is a wonderful painting. I call it so because it bears about it in a high degree the character of mysterious unfathomableness." *Grimm, Trans.*

Foro Trajano. See FORUM OF TRAJAN.

Forsyth Place. A well-known public park in Savannah, Ga.

Fort Adams. One of the strongest defences on the United-States coast, near Newport, R.I. It mounts 468 cannon, and requires a garrison of 3,000 men.

Fort Albany. A ruined earthwork south of Arlington, Va., one of the great fortifications by which Washington was defended during the civil war.

Fort Bowyer. A fortification near Mobile, Ala., taken by the British, Feb. 11, 1815, and the scene of the last encounter in the second war between England and the United States.

Fort Caroll. A strong United States fortification on an artificial island a few miles below Baltimore, Md. It commands the Patapsco River.

Fort Caswell. A fortification of brick on the Cape-Fear River, N.C. It was seized by the Confederates in 1861, and destroyed by them in 1865.

Fort Clinton. An old fortification on the Hudson, a part of the defences which were designed to close the river against the British fleet in 1777.

Fort Columbus. A United States fortification on Governor's Island in the harbor of New York.

Fort Dearborn. A stockade fort built by the United States Government in 1803 upon the site of the present city of Chicago. It was afterwards destroyed by the Indians.

Fort de l'Ecluse. A celebrated French fortress on the borders of Switzerland, not far from Geneva.

Fort Donelson. A Confederate stronghold in Kentucky during the war of the Rebellion. It was taken by Gen. Grant and Commodore Foote, Feb. 16, 1862.

The brave men who besieged *Donelson*, and who, after fighting through the day for three consecutive days, lay each night on the ground without shelter, exposed to the rain and sleet, were chiefly Illinoisans. It was there that rebellion received the heavy blow which has staggered it ever since. *L. Trumbull.*

An' how, sence *Fort Donelson*, winnin' the day
Consists in triumphantly gittin away.

Lowell, Biglow Papers.

Fort du Quesne. An old French fort and trading-post which formerly occupied the site where the city of Pittsburg, Penn., now stands. After falling into the hands of the British, another fort was built on the same spot, and named Fort Pitt.

Fort Ellsworth. A ruined earthwork near Alexandria, Va., one of the great fortifications by which Washington was defended during the civil war.

Fort Fisher. A fortification on the Cape-Fear River, and the principal defence of Wilmington, N.C., during the war of the Rebellion. It was taken by the Federal troops under Gen. Terry, Jan. 15, 1865.

Fort Frederick. A ruined fortification near Martinsburg, Va., built by the province in 1755 as a frontier fortress. It is a quadrangular structure of stone.

Fort George. A citadel in Inverness-shire, Scotland, constructed about the middle of the last century, and considered the most important fortress in Scotland.

Fort Griswold. A ruined fortification near New London, Conn. It was attacked and taken by the British in September, 1781.

Fort Hamilton. A strong fortress on the Narrows, protecting the approaches to New York.

Fort Hill. An eminence near Mystic, Conn., the seat of Sassacus, the sachem of the Pequot tribe of Indians, who had here his royal fort.

Fort Hill. An ancient fortification near Geneva, N.Y., believed to have been erected by the "mound-builders." A hundred years ago it was covered with large and ancient trees.

Fort Hill. One of the historical three hills upon which the city of Boston (Trimountain), Mass., was built. It is no longer in existence, having been levelled for building purposes.

Fort Independence. A strong granite fort, but recently finished, in the harbor of Boston, Mass. The first fortifications on this site were built in 1634. The battery was called Castle William at the time of the coronation of King William. It was strengthened by the British, who destroyed it when they evacuated Boston; but it was afterwards repaired by the Americans, and received its present name in 1798.

Fort Lafayette. A strong fortification on the Narrows, defending the approaches to New York. It was a famous prison for state criminals in the war of the Rebellion.

Fort McHenry. A United States fortification on Whetstone Point near Baltimore, Md., and commanding the harbor approaches.

Fort Mifflin. A strong fortification just below Philadelphia, and guarding the approaches to the city.

Fort Montgomery. An old fortification on the Hudson, of which some ruins still remain. It was a part of the system of defences designed to close the upper part of the river against the approach of the British fleet in 1777.

Fort Moultrie. A fortification on Sullivan's Island, protecting the approaches to Charleston, S.C. It stands on the site of an older fortress of the same name, which was built of palmetto logs, and was celebrated for its successful resistance to a British attack in 1776.

> As from *Moultrie*, close at hand,
> And the batteries on the land,
> Round its faint but fearless band
> Shot and shell
> Raining hid the doubtful light.
> *R. H. Stoddard.*

Fort Monroe. A strong United States fortification at Old Point Comfort, Va. It remained in the possession of the Federal Government at the time of the attempted secession of the State, and through the war of the Rebellion.

> Say, pilot, what this fort may be,
> Whose sentinels look down
> From moated walls that show the sea
> Their deep embrasures' frown?
> The rebel host claims all the coast;
> But these are friends, we know,
> Whose footprints spoil the "sacred soil,"
> And this is? — *Fort Monroe!*
> *O. W Holmes.*

Fort Ontario. A strong fortification at Oswego, N.Y., commanding the harbor.

Fort Pillow. 1. A Confederate fortification on the Mississippi, in the State of Tennessee, taken by Federal gun-boats, June 4, 1862.

2. A Federal fortification in Kentucky, garrisoned mainly by negroes, taken by the Confederates, April 12, 1864.

Fort Pitt. See FORT DU QUESNE.

Fort Preble. A strong fortification commanding the approaches to the harbor of Portland, Me.

Fort Richmond. A strong fortification on the Narrows, a part of the system of defences which protect the approaches to New York.

Fort St. Marks. An old Spanish fortress in St. Augustine, Fla. According to an inscription over the gateway it was finished in 1756, and is said to have been a hundred years in building. With its castellated battlements, its portcullis and drawbridge, it was more like a European mediæval stronghold than any other on this continent.

Fort Schuyler. A strong fortification commanding the entrance to New York from Long Island Sound.

Fort Sumter. A brick fortress begun in 1829, situated in the harbor of Charleston, S.C. Memorable as the scene of the first encounter in the war of the Rebellion.

☞ "The first gun that spat its iron insult at Fort Sumter, smote every loyal American full in the face. As when the foul witch used to torture her miniature image, the person it represented suffered all that she inflicted on his waxen counterpart, so every buffet that fell on the smoking fortress was felt by the sovereign nation of which that was the representative. Robbery could go no farther, for every loyal man of the North was despoiled in that single act as much as if a footpad had laid hands upon him to take from him his father's staff and his mother's Bible. Insult could go no farther; for over those battered walls waved the precious symbol of all we most value in the past and hope for in the future, — the banner under which we became a nation, and which, next to the cross of the Redeemer, is the dearest object of love and honor to all who toil or march or sail beneath its waving folds of glory."
O. W. Holmes.

For this blasted spot of earth
Where Rebellion had its birth
Is its tomb!
And when *Sumter* sinks at last
From the heavens, that shrink aghast,
Hell shall rise in grim derision and make room! *R. H. Stoddard.*

What strange, glad voice is that which calls
From Wagner's grave and *Sumter's* walls?
Whittier.

Fort Ticonderoga. A ruined fortification standing on a peninsula in Lake Champlain, memorable as one of the historic battle-grounds of North America.

Fort Trumbull. A strong fortification on the Thames, near New London, Conn.

Fort Wagner. One of the defences of Charleston, S.C., during the war of the Rebellion. It was situated on Morris Island.

Fort Warren. A modern fort (1833-1850) in the harbor of Boston, Mass., built of Quincy granite. Many Confederates were imprisoned here during the Rebellion. Here the noted Mason and Slidell were confined.

Fort Washington. **1.** The principal eminence on Manhattan Island, near High Bridge, and the site of the ancient fort which was taken by the British Nov. 16, 1776. The Americans lost 100 in killed and wounded, and 2,600 taken prisoners.

2. An old stone fort on the Potomac, a few miles below Washington. It was destroyed by the British in the war of 1812.

Fort William. An immense fortress about one mile from the city of Calcutta, India. It was erected in 1757 by Lord Clive, and has cost over $10,000,000.

Fort William Henry. A ruined fortification on Lake George, in the State of New York, near the village of Caldwell.

Fort Winthrop. A fortification on Governor's Island, in the harbor of Boston, Mass., forming one of the defences of the city.

Fort Wooster. A ruined fort near New Haven, Conn.

Fortuna Virilis, Temple of. See TEMPLE OF FORTUNA VIRILIS.

Fortune. A picture by Guido Reni (1575-1642), of which there are numerous repetitions; in the gallery of the Capitol at Rome, at Munich, in the Museum of Berlin, and elsewhere.

Fortune Theatre. A former theatre of London, opened in 1601, and so called from its sign.

The picture of Dame Fortune
Before the *Fortune playhouse.*
Heywood.

Fortune-teller, The. A picture by Michelangelo Amerighi, surnamed Caravaggio (1469-1609), and one of his masterpieces. In the gallery of the Capitol, Rome.

Forty Footsteps, Field of. See FIELD OF FORTY FOOTSTEPS.

Forum of Trajan. [Ital. *Foro Trajano.*] A magnificent forum of ancient Rome, between the Capitoline and Quirinal hills, built by the emperor Trajan after his return from the wars on the Danube. Apollodorus was the architect. A height of land connecting the two hills (the Capitoline and Quirinal) was cut away to the depth of a little more than 100 Roman feet, and the forum was placed in the valley thus formed. Portions of the buried ruins of this once magnificent forum were brought to light in the sixteenth century by Paul III., and by the French in 1812; but much still lies buried beneath the streets and houses which surround the present area of excavation. The celebrated and beautiful Column of Trajan still stands in the midst of the ruins of the forum. See TRAJAN'S COLUMN.

☞ "My feeble description can scarcely give the faintest idea of the unparalleled splendor of this forum. Besides the famous equestrian statue of Trajan in bronze, which excited the envy and admiration of Constantine, who, on viewing it, uttered the vain wish "that he had such a horse," and was told in return "that he must first build him such a stable," it was crowded with statues of marble, of bronze, and of ivory, of the great and the learned, of heroes and gods."
Eaton.

☞ "The area was adorned with numerous statues in which the figure of Trajan was frequently repeated; and among its decorations were groups in bronze or marble, representing his most illustrious actions. Here stood the great equestrian statue of the emperor; here was the triumphal arch decreed him by the Senate, adorned with sculpture, which Constantine, two centuries later, transferred without a blush to his own, a barbarous act of this first Christian emperor, to which, however, we probably owe their preservation to this day from more barbarous spoliation."
Merivale.

1644, Feb. 20. Ascending the hill, we came to the *Forum Trajanum*, where his column stands yet intire, wrought with admirable basso-rilievo recording the Dacian war . The sculpture of this stupendious pillar is thought to be the work of Apollodorus, but what is very observable is the descent to the plinth of the pedestale, shewing how this ancient Citty now lyes buried in her ruines, this monument being at first set up on a rising ground.
John Evelyn.

Forum Romanum. [Roman Forum.] An area of irregular outline at the base of the Capitoline and Palatine hills in Rome is the site of the Roman Forum, now the Campo Vaccino, q.v. The greater part of the ancient Forum is now covered by a deep accumulation of soil; and the true boundaries of the ground and the true situation of the numerous buildings said to have been erected there, have for centuries been matters of dispute and uncertainty among antiquaries. The sites of many of the edifices seem now, however, to be determined with tolerable probability.

☞ "No spot on earth is more imposing, for it is overshadowed with the power and majesty of the Roman people. . . . Nothing gives a stronger impression of the shattering blows which have fallen upon the Eternal City than the present condition of the Forum. . . . Every foot of ground has been the field of antiquarian controversy. Every ruin has changed its name two or three times. The reason of this confusion and ignorance is to be found in two circumstances: one that the buildings were very numerous in proportion to the small space which they occupied; and the other, that the original space has been covered to the depth of 12 or 15 feet by the accumulated soil of ages, so that the foundations of the structures are no longer to be seen."
G. S. Hillard.

Yes; and in yon field below,
A thousand years of silenced factions sleep,—
The *Forum*, where the immortal accents glow,
And still the eloquent air breathes — burns — with Cicero!
Byron.

It was once
And long, the centre of their Universe,
The *Forum*, — whence a mandate, eagle-winged,
Went to the ends of the earth.
Rogers.

Herds are feeding on the *Forum*, as in old Evander's time;
Tumbled from the steep Tarpeian all the towers that sprang sublime.
T. W. Parsons.

The Capitol and the *Forum* impress us with less awe than our own Westminster Hall and Westminster Abbey, the place where the great men of twenty generations have contended, the place where they sleep together!
Macaulay.

Foscari Palace. [Ital. *Palazzo Foscari.*] A splendid palace situated on the Grand Canal, in Venice, Italy. It was erected near the middle of the fifteenth century.

Fosse, The. An ancient Roman road in Britain, extending from the mouth of the Tyne to Wales. [Also called *Ryknield Street.*]

Fotheringay Castle. An ancient castle in Northamptonshire, England, belonging to the house of York, and made memorable by the confinement of Mary, Queen of Scots, who ended her life here in 1587.

Fouarre, Rue du. See STRAW STREET.

Fount of Salvation. A celebrated picture in the Museum of Madrid, representing the Almighty with the Immaculate Lamb at his feet, "whom he made an offering for the sins of the world. Below, this offering is seen in the form of a stream of water, in which the sacramental wafers are floating, flowing into a little flower-garden, where six angels are celebrating the glory of God on different instruments." The meaning of the stream of water is indicated by an inscription in Latin which refers to the passage in the Song of Solomon (iv. 15), — "A fountain of gardens, a well of living waters." There are many other symbolic representations connected with the picture, which has been attributed to one of the two brothers van Eyck, the distinguished Flemish painters. Dr. Waagen holds that it is the production of the elder, Hubert van Eyck (1366-1426); but, it is asserted, the weight of critical judgment is against this opinion. It is also called "The Triumph of the Church."

Fountain Court. A well-known court in the Middle Temple, one of the four Inns of Court in London.

> Coming through the *Fountain Court*, he [Tom Pinch] was just to glance down the steps leading into Garden Court, and to look once all round him, and if Ruth had come to meet him; there he would see her, not sauntering, you understand (on account of the clerks), but coming briskly up with the best little laugh on her face that ever played in opposition to the fountain, and beat it all to nothing.
> *Dickens.*

> It looks out upon a garden about the size of *Fountain Court*. *Thackeray.*

Fountain of Arethusa. Anciently a famous fountain in Syracuse, Sicily. Cicero speaks of it as "a fountain of fresh water, which bears the name of Arethusa, of incredible magnitude, and full of fish: this would be wholly overflowed and covered by the waves, were it not separated from the sea by a strongly-built barrier of stone." Homer's fountain of Arethusa is traditionally identified with a never-failing reservoir on the south-east part of the island of Ithaca.

> Far, far and wide along the Italian shores,
> That holy joy extends;
> Sardinian mothers pay their vows fulfilled;
> And hymns are heard beside thy banks,
> O *Fountain Arethuse!* *Southey.*

Fountain of Castalia. A fountain in Greece, falling from Parnassus down the slope where Delphi stood into the river Pleistus. A small chapel has been erected over the spring. According to Murray's Handbook, during the earthquake of 1870 a fragment of rock falling from the cliff above completely crushed the basin, and covered with rubbish and buried from sight even the water.

> ☞ "It still flows on, while the Temple of Apollo, and the Council Hall of the Amphictyons, the Treasure-house of Crœsus, and the three thousand statues which crowded the buildings and streets of Delphi, even in the time of Pliny, have all vanished as though they had never been."
> *C. Wordsworth.*

Fountain of Egeria. A name given to a vaulted chamber of brick-work in the valley of the Almo, about a mile from Rome. It derives its fame from the belief that it is the site of the grove and sacred fountain where Numa held his nightly meetings with the nymph Egeria. Modern discoveries have, however, determined that the nymphæum which has so long been regarded as the Grotto of Egeria is not the place which Numa visited, and has placed the true fountain and valley within the present walls of the city, near where the Via Appia crosses the Almo (Maranna), not far from the ancient Porta Capena.

☞ "About a mile from the Porta San Sebastiano is a pretty pastoral valley, or gorge, as quiet and secluded as if in the heart of the Apennines. On one side is a wooded hill, crowned with the ruins of a temple of Bacchus; and on the other, at some distance, a gentle elevation on which there is a graceful structure which some call a temple, and some a tomb. This is the valley of Egeria, — the spot where Numa met his shadowy counsellor. We must draw near to it in the spirit of faith, and let no clouds of doubt darken its tranquil beauty. . . . The fountain, so called, is a vaulted grotto scooped out of the hill-side, lined and floored with brick, with three niches on either side, and a larger one at the extremity containing a mutilated statue. At this extremity the water flows through a slender orifice, and is received into a small shell-like basin, from which, falling upon the floor, it glides down into the valley, and, swelled by tributes from the moist soil, forms a rivulet, takes the name of the Almo, and finally mingles with the Tiber. . . . The legend of Numa is one of the most genuine flowers of poetry that ever started from the hard rock of the Roman mind." *Hillard.*

The mosses of thy fountain still are sprinkled
With thine Elysian water-drops; the face
Of thy cave guarded spring, with years unwrinkled,
Reflects the meek-eyed genius of the place. *Byron.*

Here didst thou dwell, in this enchanted cover,
Egeria! thy all-heavenly bosom beating
For the far footsteps of thy mortal lover. *Ibid.*

A goddess, who there deigned to meet
A mortal from Rome's regal seat,
And, o'er the gushing of her fount,
Mysterious truths divine to earthly ear recount. *William Sotheby.*

The wonders of the outer world, the Tagus with the mighty fleets of England riding on its bosom, . . . the sweet Lake of Leman, the *dell of Egeria*, with its summer-birds and rustling lizards, the shapeless ruins of Rome, . . . all were mere accessories, the background to one dark and melancholy figure. *Macaulay.*

Fountain of Life. A remarkable picture by Hans Holbein the Younger (1494–1543). In the palace of the King of Portugal at Lisbon.

Fountain of the Virgin. A picturesque fountain at Jerusalem, issuing from a cave some 30 feet in depth, and associated with many legends of the Virgin. It is an intermittent spring, and by some it has been identified with the pool of Bethesda.

Fountain of Trevi. See FONTANA DI TREVI.

Fountain of Vaucluse. A celebrated fountain in the department of the same name in Southern France.

☞ "The glen seems as if struck into the mountain's depths by one blow of the enchanter's wand; and just at the end, where the rod might have rested in its downward sweep, is the fathomless well whose overbrimming fulness gives birth to the Sorgues. It was the most absolute solitude. The rocks towered above to the height of 600 feet, and the gray walls of the wild glen below shut out all appearance of life. . . . I never visted a place to which the fancy clung more suddenly and fondly." *Bayard Taylor.*

It would be the labor of a week to find in all the vast mass of Mr. Southey's poetry, a single passage indicating any sympathy with those feelings which have consecrated the shades of *Vaucluse.* *Macaulay.*

Fountain Tavern. A former house of entertainment in the Strand, London.

Fountains Abbey. The venerable remains of this abbey, said to be the most perfect monastery in England, are situated about three miles from Ripon. It was founded in 1204, and became one of the wealthiest monastic institutions in the kingdom. It originally covered ten acres, of which the ruins now occupy about two.

☞ "Travellers who can visit but one monastic relic in England should perhaps select this; for no other surpasses its combination of completeness, size, beauty of position, and architectural interest. In all Britain there is probably now no religious or benevolent institution, except the national hospital at Greenwich, that could compare in extent and grandeur with this abbey as it was during the days of its glory." *J. F. Hunnewell.*

Abbey! forever smiling pensively,
How like a thing of Nature dost thou rise,
Amid her loveliest works! as if the skies,
Clouded with grief, were arched thy roof to be,
And the tall trees were copied all from thee. *Ebenezer Elliott.*

Fountains of Moses. [Arab. *Ayoon Moosa*, or, more commonly, *Ain Moosa*.] These "Wells" in Egypt are a collection of springs, forming an oasis. They are reached from the town of Suez. There is a tradition that here Moses and Miriam and the children of Israel sang their song of triumph.

And, like the Coptic monks by *Mousa's wells*,
We dream of wonders past,
Vague as the tales the wandering Arab tells,
Each drowsier than the last. *Whittier.*

Four Elements. Celebrated pictures by Francesco Albani (1578–1660). In the Borghese palace at Rome, and also at Turin, Italy.

Four Evangelists. A celebrated picture by Peter Paul Rubens (1577–1640). In the Grosvenor Gallery, London.

☞ "As a striking instance of this mistaken style of treatment [too rigid adherence to nature], we may turn to the famous group of the *Four Evangelists* by Rubens, grand, colossal, standing, or rather moving figures, each with his emblem, if emblems they can be called, which are almost as full of reality as nature itself." *Mrs. Jameson.*

Four-in-Hand Club. The most prosperous days of this London club were in the time of George the Fourth (1820–1830). The noted Lord Onslow was a member,— ridiculed in the following epigram:—

What can Tommy Onslow do?
He can drive a coach and two.
Can Tommy Onslow do no more?
He can drive a coach and four.

☞ "The vehicles of the Club which were formerly used are described as of a hybrid class, quite as elegant as private carriages, and lighter than even the mails. They were horsed with the finest animals that money could secure. . . . The master generally drove the team, often a nobleman of high rank, who commonly copied the dress of a mail coachman. The company usually rode outside; but two footmen in rich liveries were indispensable on the back seat, nor was it at all uncommon to see some splendidly attired female on the box. A rule of the Club was, that all members should turn out three times a week; and the start was made at midday, from the neighborhood of Piccadilly, through which they passed to the Windsor-road,—the attendants of each carriage playing on their silver bugles. From 12 to 20 of these handsome vehicles often left London together." *Timbs.*

Four Marys. An admired and celebrated picture by Annibale Caracci (1560–1609). At Castle Howard, England.

☞ "On comparing this with Raphael's conception, we find more of common nature, quite as much pathos, but in the forms less of that pure poetic grace which softens at once and heightens the tragic effect." *Mrs. Jameson.*

Four Philosophers. A celebrated portrait-picture by Peter Paul Rubens (1577–1640), in the Pitti Palace, Florence, Italy.

Four Quarters of the World. A picture by Peter Paul Rubens (1577–1640), in the gallery of Vienna, and considered one of his most admirable works.

Four Seasons. **1.** A well-known picture by Francesco Albani (1578–1660). In the Palazzo Borghese, Rome.

☞ "*The Seasons*, by Francesco Albani, were beyond all others my favorite pieces." *Hans Christian Andersen.*

2. A picture by Antoine François Callet (1741–1823). In the Louvre, Paris.

Four Sibyls. A series of well-known pictures by Raphael Sanzio (1483–1520), representing the Sibyls, with angels holding tablets. They were painted for the Chigi Chapel in the church of S. Maria della Pace, Rome.

☞ "These are among the most perfect specimens of Raphael's maturer pencil, combining equal grandeur and grace. An interesting comparison may be instituted between this work and the Sibyls of Michael Angelo. In each we find the peculiar excellence of the two great masters; for while Michael Angelo's figures are sublime, profound, and entirely new, the fresco of the Pace bears the impress of Raphael's more serene and sympathetic grace." *Eastlake.*

☞ "Solemn, tranquil, elevated like antique goddesses above human action, they are truly superhuman creations: theirs is not a diffused or transitory being, but one ever existing immutably in an eternal *present*."
Taine, Trans.

Four Temperaments. The name sometimes given to pictures of the four apostles, John and Peter, Paul and Mark, by Albert Dürer (1471–1528). In the Pinakothek, at Munich, Bavaria.

Fourth Street. **1.** The fashionable promenade of Cincinnati, O.

2. The fashionable promenade of St. Louis, Mo.

Fox, The. An Arctic exploring ship which sailed for the Northern seas, under the command of Capt. M'Clintock, in the expedition fitted out by Lady Franklin in 1857 to discover traces of her husband, Sir John Franklin, the lost navigator.

Francesca da Rimini. A celebrated picture from Dante by Ary Scheffer (1795–1858), widely known through reproductions.

Francesco, San. See SAN FRANCESCO.

Franchimont. A ruined castle near Liege in Belgium, associated with legendary traditions.

The towers of *Franchimont*,
Which, like an eagle's nest in air,
Hang o'er the stream and hamlet fair.
Scott.

Francis, St. See ST. FRANCIS.

François I., Maison de. See MAISON DE FRANÇOIS I.

Franconia Notch. A picturesque and beautiful valley, or pass, in the Franconia Mountains (White Mountain range), New Hampshire. Near the head of this Notch is the famous Profile, or Old Man of the Mountain. See NOTCH, THE, and also PROFILE, THE.

☞ "The narrow district thus enclosed contains more objects of interest to the mass of travellers than any other region of equal extent within the compass of the usual White-Mountain tour. In the way of rock-sculpture and waterfalls it is a huge mass of curiosities."
Starr King.

Frankenberg. A ruined ivy-covered castle near Aix-la-Chapelle, Rhenish Prussia, in which, according to tradition, Fastrada, the wife of Charlemagne, died and was buried.

Franklin, The. A noted Boston privateer during the war of the Revolution. In May, 1776, she was grounded on Point Shirley, and attacked by 13 British man-of-war boats, but finally escaped.

Franzenburg. A modern castle, built in imitation of a mediæval fortress, containing a museum of antiquities, situated in the park of the Palace of Laxenburg, near Vienna, Austria.

Frari, Santa Maria Gloriosa dei. A noted church of the thirteenth century in Venice, Italy.

☞ "The internal effect of the church is much finer than its west front would lead one to expect. . . . The nave and aisles measure about 230 feet by 104, and the transept 160 feet by 48, — magnificent dimensions, undoubtedly. The columns are simple, cylindrical, and very lofty."
Street.

☞ "It always causes a sensation to walk from the blazing sun and laboring life into these solemn enclosures. Here are the tombs of the doges resting from their rule. They seem pondering still as they lie carved in stately marble death, contemplating the past with their calm brows and their hooked noses. The great church is piled arch upon arch, tomb upon tomb; some of these monuments hang in the nave high over the heads of the people as they kneel, above the city and its cries and its circling life, and the steps of the easy-going Venetians."
Miss Thackeray.

Frascati. A house in Paris at the corner of the Rue de Rivoli. The boulevard was called by this name until gaming was forbidden in 1837. It was the most aristocratic gambling-house of the time in Paris. Women were admitted to it.

☞ "About half-past ten I went with a couple of friends to the great gambling-house which passes under the name of Frascati. It was the first time in my life I was ever in a large establishment of this sort, or, indeed, at any, except such as are seen at watering-places: and I shall probably never see another; for it is one of the good deeds of Louis Philippe's government, that, after having abolished lotteries, it has now ordered all public gaming-houses to be closed from Jan. 1, 1838, — that is, in two days. This evening we found the rooms full, but not crowded." *George Ticknor.*

☞ "As we drove from the court, my companion, pulling the cordon, ordered to *Frascati's*. This, you know, of course, is the fashionable place of ruin; and here the heroes of all novels, and the rakes of all comedies, mar or make their fortunes. An evening dress and the look of a gentleman are the only required passport. Four large rooms, plainly but handsomely furnished, opened into each other, three of which were devoted to play and crowded with players." *N. P. Willis.*

Frauenkirche, Die. [The Church of Our Lady.] A noted church in Dresden, Saxony. Its stone dome withstood the heaviest bombs during the war with Frederick the Great.

Frederick, Fort. See FORT FREDERICK.

Frederick the Great. An equestrian statue in bronze, modelled by Christian Rauch (1777-1857), and upon which he was employed 10 years. It was erected in the Unter den Linden, Berlin, in 1851. The statue is 17 feet in height upon a pedestal of 25 feet in height, and upon the four sides of this pedestal are 31 portrait-figures of the size of life. This statue is regarded as one of the finest monuments in Europe.

Freemasons' Tavern. A noted tavern in London, used among other purposes for public meetings.

What Act of Parliament, debate at St. Stephen's, on the hustings or elsewhere, was it that brought this Shakespeare into being? Us dining at *Freemasons' Tavern*, opening subscription-lists, selling of shares, and infinite other jangling, and true or false endeavoring! *Carlyle.*

Freiburg Minster. One of the noblest Gothic churches in Germany. It is a grand and gloomy pile, dating from the eleventh century, with a tower of beautiful fretwork, rising to the height of 395 feet.

French Academy. See ACADÉMIE FRANCAISE.

Freshwater Cave. A romantic and curious cavern on the Isle of Wight, much frequented by tourists.

Friar Bacon's Brazen Head. The most famous of all brazen heads was that of Roger Bacon, a monk of the thirteenth century. According to the legend, Bacon was occupied for seven years in constructing such a head; and he expected to be told by it how he could make a wall of brass around the whole island of Great Britain. The head was warranted to speak within a month after it was finished, but no particular time was named for its doing so. Bacon's man was therefore set to watch, with orders to call his master if the head should speak. At the end of half an hour after the man was left alone with the head, he heard it say, "Time is;" at the expiration of another half-hour, "Time was;" and at the end of a third half-hour, "Time's past," when it fell down with a loud crash, and was shivered to pieces; but the stupid servant neglected to awake his master, thinking that he would be very angry to be disturbed for such trifles; and so the wall of brass has never been built.

☞ In the Middle Ages there was a pretty wide-spread belief in the existence of a talking brazen head, the invention of which was variously ascribed to persons living at different times and in different countries. William of Malmesbury, an old monkish historian, says that Gerbert, a famous French ecclesiastic, made such a head, which would speak when spoken to, and would give oracular answers to whatever questions were propounded to it. He relates, moreover, that Gerbert inquired of it whether he would ever be pope, and that the head told him he would. The prediction happened to prove true; for Gerbert afterwards became pope, under the name of Silvester the Second. In another instance, however, the oracle made a most unfortunate blunder; for it foretold that Silvester should not die until he had sung mass in Jerusalem, whereas he actually died in Rome, with the prophecy unfulfilled. Albertus Magnus, one of the greatest of the old schoolmen, is alleged to have made an entire man out of brass, which not only answered questions very readily and correctly, but was so loquacious that Thomas Aquinas, a reserved and contemplative person, — at that time a pupil to Albertus Magnus, and subsequently an illustrious doctor of the church, — knocked the image to pieces merely to stop its talking.

But the thing we meant to enforce, was this comfortable fact, that no known Head was so wooden, but there might be other heads to which it were a genius and *Friar Bacon's Oracle.* *Carlyle.*

Friedrich Strasse. [Frederick Street.] An important street and thoroughfare in Berlin, Prussia.

Frog-Pond. A small basin of water in Boston Common, regarded by the inhabitants with an esteem disproportioned to its size.

☞ "There are those who speak lightly of this small aqueous expanse, the eye of the sacred enclosure, which has looked unwinking on the happy faces of so many natives and the curious features of so many strangers. The music of its twilight minstrels has long ceased, but their memory lingers like an echo in the name it bears. . . . For art thou not the Palladium of our Troy? Didst thou not, like the Divine image which was the safeguard of Ilium, fall from the skies, and if the Trojan could look with pride upon the heaven-descended form of the Goddess of Wisdom, cannot he who dwells by thy shining oval look in that mirror and contemplate Himself, — the Native of Boston?" *Holmes.*

After a man begins to attack the State-House, when he gets bitter about the *Frog-pond*, you may be sure there is not much left of him. *Holmes.*

Frogmore. A favorite residence of members of the royal family near Windsor, England.

Frolic, The. A British war-sloop taken by the American sloop-of-war, the *Wasp*, under the command of Capt. Jacob Jones, in 1812. This victory of the latter caused great exultation throughout the United States. Congress voted Jones the thanks of the nation and a gold medal.

Frugal Meal. An admired picture by John Frederick Herring (1794-1865). In the National Gallery, London.

Fruit-venders, The. A picture by Bartolomé Esteban Murillo (1618-1682). In the Pinakothek, Munich, Bavaria.

Fuentes. A ruined fort on a rocky eminence at the head of Lake Como, Italy.

Fuentes once harbored the good and the brave,
Nor to her was the dance of soft pleasure unknown;
Her banners for festal enjoyment did wave
While the thrill of her fifes through the mountains was blown.
Wordsworth.

Fuite de Jacob. [Jacob's Flight.] A picture by Adrian van derVelde (1639-1672), the Dutch painter. In Sir R. Wallace's collection, at Bethnal Green, London.

Fulham Palace. An ancient mansion, the residence of the bishops of London.

Fuller's Field. A locality in Jerusalem mentioned in the Scriptures (Isa. vii. 3; 2 Kings, xviii. 17), and which is believed to be identified with a road, or tract, lying along the pool now called by the Arabs *Birket-el-Mamilla.*

Fulton Street. The main thoroughfare of Brooklyn, N.Y.

Fulton's Folly. See CLERMONT.

Furculæ Caudinæ. See CAUDINE FORKS.

Furlo Pass. A celebrated pass in the Apennines, in the neighborhood of Urbino, Italy.

Furness Abbey. A beautiful ruined monastery, near Ulverston, in the "Lake District" of England. It was founded by King Stephen in 1127. The remains of this once magnificent abbey are now the property of the Duke of Devonshire.

God, with a mighty and an outstretched hand,
Stays thee from sinking, and ordains to be
His witness lifted 'twixt the Irish Sea
And that still beauteous, once faith-hallowed land.
Stand as a sign, monastic prophet stand!
Aubrey de Vere.

Furnival's Inn. Formerly an Inn of Chancery in London, so called from Sir William Furnival, a former owner of the land. This Inn of Chancery was attached to Lincoln's Inn. It was rebuilt in 1818. Sir Thomas More was a "reader" here. Dickens began the "Pickwick Papers" in chambers at Furnival's Inn.

Fury, The. An Arctic exploring ship which sailed from England in 1824 under the command of Sir William Edward Parry (1790–1855). She was wrecked in the northern seas.

Fyvie Castle. An ancient and interesting mansion, with many historical associations, near Fyvie, in Aberdeenshire, Scotland.

G.

Gadshill. The residence of the late Charles Dickens (1812–1870), and the scene of Falstaff's famous exploit, at a town of the same name near Rochester, England.

Seamen who had just been paid off at Chatham were often compelled to deliver their purses on *Gadshill*, celebrated near a hundred years earlier by the greatest of poets as the scene of the depredations of Poins and Falstaff. *Macaulay.*

Gaillard. The famous castle of Richard Cœur de Lion, situated on a high rock on the bank of the Seine, near Gaillon in France. It is now an imposing ruin.

☞ "This magnificent ruin of the favorite castle of Richard I. is on the banks of the Seine, near Les Andelys, the birthplace of Poussin, and the retreat of Thomas Corneille. A single year sufficed to form its immense fosses, and to raise those walls which might seem to be the structure of a lifetime. When Cœur de Lion saw it finished, he is said to have exclaimed with exultation, 'How beautiful she is, this daughter of a year!'"

Longfellow's Poems of Places.

The two long years had passed away,
When castle *Gaillard* rose,
As built at once by elfin hands,
And scorning time or foes.
It might be thought that Merlin's imps
Were tasked to raise the wall,
That unheard axes fell the woods,
While unseen hammers fall.

W. L. Bowles.

Galatea. A beautiful fresco in the Farnesina, Rome, by Raphael Sanzio (1483–1520), representing the goddess borne over the waves in a shell drawn by dolphins, with tritons and nymphs playing around her.

☞ "This is one of the most beautiful compositions that art has produced, imbued with a sense of life and enjoyment that is perfectly enchanting." *Eastlake, Handbook of Painting.*

☞ "His 'Galatea' is a work which explains the diversity between Michael Angelo and Raphael, manifesting the exquisite refinement of the latter, and his tendency toward that pure, noble, graceful manner which constituted the beau-ideal of the ancient Greeks."

Quatremère de Quincy.

☞ "Raphael not only designed but executed this fresco; and faded as is its coloring, the mind must be dead to the highest beauties of painting that can contemplate it without admiration. The spirit and beauty of the composition, the pure and perfect design, the flowing outline, the soft and graceful contours, and the sentiment and sweetness of the expression, all remain unchanged; for time, till it totally obliterates, has no power to injure them."

C. A. Eaton.

Galatea is an image of beauty of soul united to that of the body. It is indeed a sort of glorified human nature, or rather a goddess clad in human form. *Passavant.*

I must not omit that incomparable table of *Galatea* (so I remember) carefully preserved to protect it from the air, being a most lively painting. *John Evelyn*, 1644.

On the maternal side I inherit the loveliest silver-mounted tobacco-stopper you ever saw. It is a little box-wood Triton, carved with charming liveliness and truth. I have often compared it to a figure in Raphael's *Triumph of Galatea.* *Holmes.*

Galerie d'Apollon. A magnificent and profusely decorated gallery in the Louvre, Paris. It was first built by Charles IX., burnt in the time of Louis XIV., afterwards rebuilt, and finally completed by Napoleon III. in 1851. Here is the collection of the Musée des Bijoux.

Galerie de la Colonnade. Three fine halls in the east wing of the Louvre, Paris. Here are placed the paintings of the Musée Napoléon III., bought by the Government from the Marquis Campana.

Galerie des Glaces. [*Grand Galerie de Louis XIV.*] An elegant room — one of the most magnificent in the world — in the centre of the palace of Versailles, France. It is 239 feet long, 33 feet wide, 23 feet high, and is profusely ornamented. Upon the walls are paintings in honor of the glory of Louis XIV. Balls and *fêtes* were held here until the Revolution, and on great occasions the throne was moved into this room. The last ball given here was opened by Queen Victoria (in whose honor it was held) and the emperor, in August, 1855.

☞ "'Look at this Galerie des Glaces,' cries Monsieur Vatout, staggering with surprise at the appearance of the room, two hundred and forty-two feet long, and forty high. 'Here it was that Louis displayed all the grandeur of royalty; and such was the splendor of his court, and the luxury of the times, that this immense room could hardly contain the crowd of courtiers that pressed around the monarch. Wonderful! wonderful! Eight thousand four hundred and sixty square feet of courtiers! Give a square yard to each, and you have a matter of three thousand of them. Think of three thousand courtiers per day, and all the chopping and changing of them for near forty years; some dying, some getting their wishes and retiring to their provinces to enjoy their plunder, some disgraced and going home to pine away out of the light of the sun; new ones perpetually arriving, — pushing, squeezing, for their place in the crowded Galerie des Glaces.'"
Thackeray.

Galilee Porch. The name given to an entrance vestibule of the Cathedral of Durham in England, regarded as one of the archæological and art treasures of Great Britain.

☞ "This unusual apartment, the Lady Chapel practically, was built especially as a place of worship for women, who were not admitted into the main church, on account of a violent antipathy for the sex felt by its patron saint, the reputed Anthony-like-tempted Cuthbert." *J. F. Hunnewell.*

Galileo's Tower. [Ital. *Torre del Gallo.*] A structure in the neighborhood of Florence, Italy, thought to have been the tower from which Galileo made astronomical observations.

The towering *Campanile's height*
Where *Galileo* found his starry chair.
J. E. Reade.

Galla Placidia, Mausoleum of. See MAUSOLEUM OF GALLA PLACIDIA.

Galleria Lapidaria. [Lapidary Gallery, or Gallery of Inscriptions.] A corridor in the Vatican Palace, Rome, of great length, the sides of which are covered with pagan and with early Christian inscriptions. The walls of this corridor are also lined with sarcophagi, funeral urns, and other ornaments.

Galleria Vittorio Emanuele. A beautiful and costly edifice in Milan, Italy. Used for purposes of trade.

Gallery of Gondo. This gallery, or tunnel, on the Simplon road through the Alps, is cut through a solid rock. The work was accomplished by 18 months of unintermitted labor, day and night. The gallery is 683 feet in length, and bears the inscription "Aere Italo 1805 Nap. Imp."

Gallienus, Palace of. A ruined palace, and relic of Roman times, in Bordeaux, France.

Gallows Hill. A hill near Salem, Mass., where 19 of the so-called witches were put to death in the time of the witchcraft delusion in 1692.

Ganymede and the Eagle. An admired relic of ancient sculpture. In the Museum at Naples, Italy.

Ganymede, Rape of. See RAPE OF GANYMEDE.

Garaye. A picturesque ruined château in the environs of Dinan, France. The Hon. Mrs. Norton has an admired poem, entitled "The Lady of Garaye," the story of which is associated with these ruins.

Garden of Love. A picture by Peter Paul Rubens (1577–1640), now in the gallery at Madrid, "representing various couples, elegantly dressed, and enjoying the pleasures of music and dalliance in the open air." There is a copy of this picture in the Dresden Gallery.

Garden of Plants. See JARDIN DES PLANTES.

Garden Reach. A celebrated promenade in Calcutta, India. It is laid out like a park, with fine trees and tropical plants, and is occupied by the Europeans.

Gardens of Sallust, Ruins of. See SALLUST'S HOUSE AND GARDENS.

Garisenda, La. A noted leaning tower in Bologna, Italy, which derives its name from that of its builders, the brothers Garisendi. The height of this tower is 130 feet, and the deviation from the perpendicular is eight feet towards the south and three feet towards the east. There is a companion tower called the Torre degli Asinelli. The cause of the inclination of these towers has been a subject in dispute, as in the case of the more celebrated Leaning Tower of Pisa. Eustace remarks of these in Bologna that they are "remarkable only for their unmeaning elevation and dangerous deviation from the perpendicular." See TORRE DEGLI ASINELLI.

As seems the *Garisenda*, to behold
Beneath the leaning side, when goes a cloud
Above it so that opposite it hangs;
Such did Antæus seem to me.
Dante, Inferno, Longfellow's Trans.

Garraway's. A noted coffee-house in Change Alley, Cornhill, London. Here tea was first sold in England. Garraway's was much resorted to during the time of the South-Sea Bubble, and was at all times a scene of great mercantile transactions. It was taken down in 1866.

Meanwhile, secure on *Garway's* cliffs,
A savage race by shipwrecks fed,
Lie waiting for the founder'd skiffs,
And strip the bodies of the dead.
Swift (Ballad on the South-Sea Scheme).

The Cits met to discuss the rise and fall of stocks, and to settle the rate of insurances, at *Garraway's* or Jonathan's.
National Review.

Doctor John Radcliffe, who in the year 1685 rose to the largest practice in London, came daily, at the hour when the Exchange was full, from his house in Bow Street, then a fashionable part of the capital, to *Garraway's*, and was to be found surrounded by surgeons and apothecaries, at a particular table. *Macaulay.*

Let me read the first: "*Garraway's*, twelve o'clock. Dear Mrs. B.,—Chops and tomato sauce. Yours, Pickwick." Gentlemen, what does this mean? Chops and tomato sauce. Yours, Pickwick! Chops! Gracious heavens! and tomato sauce! Gentlemen, is the happiness of a sensitive and confiding female to be trifled away by such shallow artifices as these? *Dickens.*

Garrick Club. A famous club in Covent Garden, London, founded in 1831, with the object "of bringing together the patrons of the drama and its professors, and also for offering literary men a rendezvous." The club derived its name from that of the distinguished actor; and many noted men, from James Smith ("Rejected Addresses") to Thackeray, have made it a favorite resort. The club has an interesting collection of theatrical portraits.

☞ "Among my great pleasures at the Garrick Club was the sight of the large and very interesting collection of dramatic portraits that has accumulated there in the course of many years. Almost every thing fine of this sort has gravitated there lately, as if by the operation of natural law."
Richard Grant White.

Garry Castle. A striking ruin in Kings County, Ireland.

Garter, The. An old English inn which figures in Shakespeare's comedy of "The Merry Wives of Windsor," and in which is laid the scene of the third act of that play.

Falstaff. Mine host of the *Garter.*
Shakespeare.

Gaspee, The. A British sloop-of-war captured and burned by a band of men from Providence, R. I., on the night of June 17, 1772.

Gaston de Foix. A portrait, with mirrors repeating the figure, by Girolamo Savoldo, a Brescian painter. This picture is in the Louvre, Paris; and there is an original repetition of it in Hampton Court.

Gate of Alcala. See PUERTA DE ALCALA.

Gate of the Lions. A celebrated gateway in the wall of the citadel of Mykenæ, Greece. The ruins have recently been entirely removed from around this gateway.

Pausanias says, "Among other parts of the enclosure which still remain, a gate is perceived with lions standing on it; and they report these were the works of the Cyclops, who also made for Prœtus the walls of Tiryns."

☞ "The blocks forming this [Gate of Lions] are enormous in size, quadrangular, and horizontal. They are 15 feet high and 9 feet broad; and the opening is surmounted by a huge lintel, of which the three dimensions are 15 feet long, 6 feet broad, and 3 feet thick. A bas-relief, 7 feet high, and 10 feet broad at the base, forms a sort of triangular pediment at the gate, within which are sculptured two lions standing on their hind-feet, resting their fore-paws upon a pillar placed between them so as to face each other. Their heads, which have been broken, formerly reached the height of the capital of the pillar. This pillar increases gradually in diameter from base to summit; and its capital is supported upon four disks, which are supposed to represent the billets of wood meant to maintain the sacred fire. The Gate of Lions formed the chief entrance to the Acropolis." *Lefèvre, Trans.*

Gate of the Sun. See PUERTA DEL SOL.

Gates, Iron. See IRON GATES.

Gates of Calais. A well-known picture by William Hogarth (1697–1764).

Gates of Paradise. See BRONZE GATES, etc.

Generalife. A beautiful Moorish palace, surrounded with fountains and gardens, in Granada, Spain.

Geneviève, St. See PANTHEON (2).

Genius of the Vatican. A celebrated half-figure in Parian marble, bearing this name, in the Vatican, Rome. It is supposed to be the Cupid of Praxiteles. It was found on the Via Labicana, outside of the Porta Maggiore.

We'll take, say, that most perfect of antiques,
They call the *Genius of the Vatican*,
Which seems too beauteous to endure itself
In this mixed world, and fasten it for once
Upon the torso of the Drunken Faun
(Who might limp surely, if he did not dance)
Instead of Buonarroti's mask: what then?
Mrs. Browning.

Geometricians, The. A celebrated allegorical picture by Giorgio Barbarelli, called Giorgione (1477–1511), the exact signification of which has been a matter of dispute. In the Belvedere Gallery, Vienna. [Called also sometimes *The Astrologers*, or *The Philosophers.*]

☞ "I have myself no doubt that this beautiful picture represents the 'Three wise men of the East,' watching on the Chaldean hills the appearance of the miraculous star, and that the light breaking in the far horizon, called in the German description the rising sun, is intended to express the rising of the Star of Jacob." *Mrs. Jameson.*

Geometry. A picture by Caravaggio (1569–1609), representing a ragged girl playing with a pair of compasses. In the Spada palace, Rome.

George d'Amboise. A famous bell which formerly hung in the tower of the Cathedral of Rouen. It was taken down and melted in the time of the Revolution.

George, Fort. See FORT GEORGE.

George Square. A fine park and pleasure-ground in Glasgow, Scotland, surrounded by the finest buildings in the city.

George's. **1.** An old London Club. It was accustomed to meet on St. George's Day, April 23.

2. A coffee-house in the Strand, London, famous and much frequented in this and the last century.

A certain young fellow at *George's*, whenever he had occasion to ask his friend for a guinea, used to preclude his request as if he wanted 200, and talked so familiarly of large sums, that none could ever think he wanted a small one. *Goldsmith.*

George, St. See ST. GEORGE.

George's, St. See ST. GEORGE'S.

Georgia Augusta. The name given to the University of Göttingen, Germany, from its founder, George II. of England, who established it in 1737.

Germain des Prés, St. See ST. GERMAIN DES PRÉS.

Germain l'Auxerrois, St. See ST. GERMAIN L'AUXERROIS.

Germanicus. An ancient statue called by this name, but representing a Roman orator, and supposed to be the work of the Greek sculptor Cleomenes. It is in the Louvre, Paris.

Gervais, St. See ST. GERVAIS.

Gethsemane. A small square enclosure of about 200 feet, surrounded by a high wall, a little way out of Jerusalem, below St. Stephen's Gate, and near the foot of the Mount of Olives. It is traditionally identified with the scene of the closing events in the life of Jesus as recorded in Matt. xxvi. 30-56, Mark xiv. 26-52, Luke xxii. 39-53, and John xviii. 1-14. There is no intrinsic improbability in the monastic traditions concerning it. It is now a desolate spot, containing a few very old and shattered olive-trees, the trunks of which are supported by stones, though some of the branches are flourishing. The garden belongs to the Latin Christians, and the Greek Church has fixed upon another locality as the true site of Gethsemane.

Gettysburg, Battle of. See BATTLE OF GETTYSBURG.

Gezeereh, Palace of. A modern palace at Cairo, Egypt, so called from the ground which it occupies having been formerly an island (gezeereh) between branches of the Nile.

Gherardesca, Villa. See VILLA GHERARDESCA.

Ghetto. [Jews' Quarter.] An enclosure in Rome formerly set apart for the residence of the Jews. They have, until recently, been confined to this crowded and dirty section since the time of Pope Paul IV., who first compelled them to live within the walls of the Ghetto, and forbade their appearance outside of that quarter, unless the men were distinguished from the Christians by a yellow hat, and the women by a veil of the same color. The Jews suffered much persecution, and were governed by many arbitrary regulations while confined to this crowded region; but now the limits of the Ghetto are removed, and the oppressive regulations revoked. The name Ghetto is derived by some from the Hebrew word *chat*, meaning "broken" or "destroyed." The present population of the Ghetto is estimated at 3,800.

☞ "The Ghetto, from its appearance, its filthy and narrow streets, would seem to be the very hot-bed of disease. Here we should expect to find all the plagues and pestilences which have desolated the earth in former ages preserved as in a morbid museum. But the reverse is the fact. It is in some respects the healthiest part of the city." *Hillard.*

I went to the *Ghetto*, where the Jews dwell, as in a suburb by themselves, being invited by a Jew of my acquaintance. Being invironed by walls, they are locked up every night. In this place remains yet part of a stately fabric, which my Jew told me had been a palace of theirs for the ambassador of their nation, when their country was subject to the Romans. *John Evelyn*, 1644.

'Tis called the *Ghetto;* and the pious townsman
Shuns it, unless his piety lie deep
Enough to teach him not to turn aside
From any form of human brotherhood:
Hard by the muddy Tiber's idle flow,
Beyond the shadow of the Vatican,
Yet within sound, almost, of choirs that chant
Morning and evening to a Christian organ,
Its prison-like and ragged houses rise.
Parsons.

Ghirlandina, La. [The Garland.] A noted tower in Modena, Italy, forming the campanile, or bell-tower, of the cathedral. It derives its name from the encircling sculptures which adorn it. See SECCHIA RAPITA.

Giant's Castle. A famous structure on the summit of a mountain near Cassel, Germany. On the top of the castle is a pyramid 96 feet high, supporting a statue of Hercules (a copy of the Farnese) 31 feet in height. This castle includes a system of water-works connected with the grounds of Wilhelmshöhe, which is, perhaps, unequalled. The fountain supplied by these water-works rises in a column 12 inches in diameter to the height of 190 feet.

Giant's Causeway. A celebrated mass of basaltic columns, of all forms from triangular to octagonal, on the northern coast of Ireland, extending into the sea.

☞ "I was somewhat disappointed at first, having supposed the causeway to be of great height; but I found the Giant's Loom, which is the highest part of it, to be about 50 feet from the water. The singular appearance of the columns, and the many strange forms which they assume, render it, nevertheless, an object of the greatest interest."
Bayard Taylor.

Giant's Colonnade. An interesting natural curiosity, not far from Fingal's Cave in Scotland, being a cluster of columns placed upon a row of curved pillars, and forming a little island about 30 feet high.

Giant's Column. A massive block of granite in the Odenwald, Germany, 32 feet long, and 3 or 4 feet in diameter. It still bears the mark of the chisel.

☞ "When or by whom it was made, remains a mystery. Some have supposed it was intended to be erected for the worship of the sun by the wild Teutonic tribes who inhabited this forest; it is more probably the work of the Romans. A project was once started to erect it as a monument on the battle-field of Leipsic, but it was found too difficult to carry into execution."
Bayard Taylor.

Giants, Destruction of the. See DESTRUCTION OF THE GIANTS.

Giant's Organ. The name given, from its very striking resemblance to that instrument, to a magnificent colonnade of basaltic pillars in the Giant's Causeway, Ireland. See GIANT'S CAUSEWAY.

Giant's Staircase. [Ital. *Scala dei Giganti.*] **1.** A celebrated staircase in the Doge's Palace at Venice, so called after two statues of the Greek gods, Mars and Neptune, which are of immense size.

☞ "Touching the Giant's Stairs in the court of the palace, the inexorable dates would not permit me to rest in the delusion that the head of Marin Falier had once bloodily stained them as it rolled to the ground, — at the end of Lord Byron's tragedy."
W. D. Howells.

As doge, clad in the ducal robes and cap,
Thou shalt be led hence to the *Giants' Staircase,*
Where thou and all our princes are invested;
And there, the ducal crown being first resumed
Upon the spot where it was first assumed,
Thy head shall be struck off. *Byron.*

He [Nicolo Tron] might have been present, with a countenance of pity, when Foscari, with feeble and tottering steps, descended the *Giant's Staircase*, and fainted at the sound of the bell which announced the election of a successor.
Hillard.

A poet on thy *Giant Stair* to-day
Lingers beside each wondrous balcony,
His tribute of a fruitless tear to pay.
Graf von Platen, Trans.

2. A singular freak of nature near Cork, Ireland. Fifteen or 16 huge knobs of rock rise one above another up the face of a very steep ascent, with nearly the regularity of a flight of steps.

Giant's Tower. An ancient circular building of Cyclopean architecture at Gozo, one of the Maltese islands. Human bones have been found in and about it. "Its history is lost in the mist of antiquity."

Giaour, The. A picture by Ary Scheffer (1795–1858).

Gibbon's Tennis-Court Theatre. A former theatre of London, in Gibbon's Court, Clare Market. Pepys, in 1660, wrote, "It is the finest play-house, I believe, that ever was in England."

Gibraltar. See ROCK OF GIBRALTAR, and SORTIE FROM GIBRALTAR.

Giebichenstein. A ruined castle near Halle, Germany, once a state prison of the German Emperors.

Giessbach, The. A noted waterfall near Brienz in Switzerland.

Giles's St. See ST. GILES'S.

Giltspur Street Compter. A London prison, or City House of Correction, built in 1791, closed in 1854, and since removed. About 6,000 persons were yearly imprisoned there.

Ginger-Cake Rock. A natural curiosity in Burke County, N.C. It is an inverted stone pyramid about 30 feet in height, seeming just ready to fall, but in reality perfectly secure.

Giorgio, San. See San Giorgio.

Giorno, Il. See Day and St. Jerome.

Giotto's Campanile. The famous and admired bell-tower of the cathedral, or Duomo, of Florence, Italy. It was erected by Giotto (1276–1336), about the middle of the fourteenth century.

☞ "The characteristics of Power and Beauty occur more or less in different buildings, some in one and some in another. But all together, and all in their highest possible relative degrees, they exist, as far as I know, only in one building of the world, the Campanile of Giotto. . . . Not within the walls of Florence, but among the far-away fields of her lilies, was the child trained who was to raise that head-stone of Beauty above her towers of watch and war."
Ruskin.

The mountains from without
Listen in silence for the word said next,
(What word will men say?) here where *Giotto* planted
His *campanile*, like an unperplexed
Question to Heaven, concerning the things granted
To a great people, who, being greatly vexed
In act, in aspiration keep undaunted!
Mrs. Browning.

In the old Tuscan town stands *Giotto's tower*,
The lily of Florence blossoming in stone,—
A vision, a delight, and a desire,—
The builder's perfect and centennial flower,
That in the night of ages bloomed alone,
But wanting still the glory of the spire.
Longfellow.

But behold
The graceful *tower of Giotto* there,
And Duomo's cross of freshened gold.
W. S. Landor.

That fall [Niagara] is more graceful than *Giotto's tower*, more noble than the Apollo. *Anthony Trollope.*

Giotto's Chapel. See Arena Chapel.

Giovanni, San. See San Giovanni, Baptistery of San Giovanni, and Porta San Giovanni.

Giralda, La. The tower of the Cathedral of Seville, Spain, so called from its vane *que gira* (which turns round). It is an old Moorish minaret, built in 1196, and held in great veneration.

☞ "This is a more massive tower than is, as I believe, to be found anywhere else as the work of a Moslem architect. . . . It contrasts pleasingly with the contemporary campanile at Venice, which, though very nearly of the same dimensions, is lean and bald compared with this tower at Seville. So, indeed, are most of the Italian towers of the same age. All these towers seem to have been erected for very analogous purposes; for the Giralda can never have been meant as the minaret of a mosque, to be used for the call to prayer: nor can we admit the distinction sometimes ascribed to it by those who surmise that it may have been merely meant for an observatory. Most probably it was a pillar of victory, or a tower symbolical of dominion and power, like many others. Indeed, the tradition is, that it was built by King Yousouf to celebrate his famous victory of Alarcos, gained in the year 1129, in which its construction was commenced. As such, it is superior to most of those constructed in the Middle Ages."
Fergusson.

Girandola. Celebrated fireworks formerly exhibited from the Castle of San Angelo, Rome, at Easter and at the Festival of St. Peter. This magnificent display, considered the grandest exhibition of fireworks in the world, and only surpassed by the illumination of St. Peter's, is now made upon the Monte Pincio.

☞ "The show began with a tremendous discharge of cannon; and then, for twenty minutes or half an hour, the whole castle was one incessant sheet of fire, and labyrinth of blazing wheels of every color, size, and speed; while rockets streamed into the sky, not by ones or twos or scores, but hundreds at a time. The concluding burst — the Girandola — was like the blowing up into the air of the whole massive castle without smoke or dust."
Dickens.

☞ "We did not, however, drive to the Trinità de Monti till after the exhibition of the Girandola, or great fireworks from the Castle of St. Angelo, which commenced by a tremendous explosion, which represented the raging eruption of a volcano. This was followed by an incessant and complicated display of every device that imagination could figure, one changed into another, and the beauty of the first effaced by that of the last. Hundreds of immense wheels turned round with a velocity that almost seemed as if demons were whirling them, letting fall thousands of hissing dragons and scorpions and fiery snakes, whose long convolutions, darting forward as far as the eye could reach in every direction, at length vanished into air. Fountains and jets of fire threw up their blazing cascades into the sky. The whole vault of heaven shone with the vivid fires."

Eaton.

Girard College. A grand and imposing building in Philadelphia, Penn. It is constructed of white marble in the Corinthian style of architecture. Adjoining the main building are other marble buildings used as dormitories, refectories, etc. The college was founded by Stephen Girard (1750–1831), a Philadelphia merchant, who left $2,000,000 and 45 acres for "the endowment of a college for poor white male children without fathers and between six and ten years of age." The course of instruction continues eight years. By the terms of the will, clergymen of every denomination are forbidden to enter the college grounds.

Girondists in Prison. An admired picture by Paul Delaroche (1797–1856), the celebrated French historical painter.

Giudecca, La. A broad canal in Venice which separates the principal island from the rest of the city. The island is also itself known by this name. See also CANAL OF THE GIUDECCA.

☞ "The islands near Venice are all small, except the Giudecca (which is properly a part of the city), the Lido, and Murano. The Giudecca, from being anciently the bounds in which certain factious nobles were confined, was later laid out in pleasure-gardens and built up with summer palaces. The gardens still remain to some extent, but they are now chiefly turned to practical account in raising vegetables and fruits for the Venetian market; and the palaces have been converted into warehouses and factories."

W. D. Howells.

Giulio Romano. A portrait of himself by the painter (1492–1546). In the collection of autograph portraits in the Uffizi, Florence, Italy.

Giustiniani Palace. [Ital. *Palazzo Giustiniani.*] A noted palace in Genoa, Italy.

Glaces, Galerie des. See GALERIE DES GLACES.

Glacier de Boisson. A well-known Alpine glacier in the vicinity of Chamouni, Savoy.

Gladiator. See BORGHESE GLADIATOR, DYING GLADIATOR, WOUNDED GLADIATOR.

Gladiators, The. A picture by Jean Léon Gérôme (b. 1827), the French painter.

Glamis Castle. The seat of the Earl of Strathmore, near the town of the same name in Scotland, considered one of the finest existing specimens of the old Scottish baronial castles. It is especially interesting from its associations with Shakespeare's play of "Macbeth," the "Thane of Glamis." The scene of Duncan's murder is pointed out in a room of the castle.

☞ "It is still an inhabited dwelling; though, much to the regret of antiquarians and lovers of the picturesque, the characteristic outworks and defences of the feudal ages which surrounded it have been levelled, and velvet lawns and gravel-walks carried to the very door. Scott, who passed a night there in 1793, while it was yet in its pristine condition, comments on the change mournfully, as undoubtedly a true lover of the past would. . . . Scott says in his 'Demonology,' that he never came anywhere near to being overcome with a superstitious feeling, except twice in his life, and one was on the night when he slept in Glamis Castle. . . . Scarcely ever a man had so much relish for the supernatural, and so little faith in it. One must confess, however, that the most sceptical might have been overcome at Glamis Castle; for its appearance, by all accounts, is weird and strange, and ghostly enough to start the dullest imagination."

Mrs. H. B. Stowe.

Glasgow Cathedral. An ancient church, dating from the twelfth century, and considered the finest Gothic church in Scotland.

☞ "A brave kirk, — a' solid, weel-jointed mason-wark, that will stand as lang as the world, keep hands and gunpowther aff it."

Scott.

Glastonbury Abbey. A famous ruined monastery in the town of that name in England, formerly one of the richest and most powerful institutions of the kind in the kingdom. The ashes of King Arthur, King Edgar, and many distinguished nobles are said to be contained in the ruins of this abbey. It is thought to stand on the spot where the first Christian church in England was erected.

Glastonbury Thorn. A famous hawthorn tree which once grew at Glastonbury, Somerset, England, fabled to have sprung from the staff which Joseph of Arimathea stuck into the ground. The tradition is, that it blossomed every Christmas Day; and so highly prized were the blossoms that they were exported by the merchants of Bristol to foreign parts. In the time of Queen Elizabeth one trunk of the double-bodied tree was cut down by some Puritans, and in the reign of Charles I. the other was destroyed, but slips from the tree are still flourishing. It is said to be the fact, that the shrub blossoms some months earlier than elsewhere, and occasionally as early as Christmas; which circumstance is explained by some on the supposition that the monks of Glastonbury brought the tree from Palestine, and that in its adopted soil it retained the habits of its native place.

It is the winter deep, and all
The glittering fields that morn
In Avalon's isle were oversnowed
The day the Lord was born;
And as they cross the northward brow,
See white, but not with snow,
The mystic thorn beside their path
Its holy blossoms show. *Henry Alford.*

Glen, The. The name by which is familiarly known an interesting spot in the White-Mountain region, New Hampshire, a favorite resort of tourists. It is situated at the very base of Mount Washington, with Adams, Jefferson, Clay, and Madison in full and unobstructed view. It is the point from which the carriage-road up Mount Washington begins its ascent.

Glen Almond. A lovely glen on the river Almond in Scotland, and supposed to be the burial-place of Ossian.

In this still place, remote from men,
Sleeps Ossian in the narrow glen.
Wordsworth.

Glen-Ellis Fall. A picturesque cataract in the White Mountains, New Hampshire, not far from the "Glen" and the base of Mount Washington. It is regarded as the finest cascade in the whole region.

Glen Onoko. A mountain ravine near Mauch Chunk, Penn., with attractive rock and forest scenery and many cascades. It is a place of much resort.

Glenarm Castle. The seat of the Earl of Antrim, in the county of Antrim, Ireland.

Glencoe. A celebrated glen, or pass, in the county of Argyle, Scotland.

☞ "In the Gaelic tongue, Glencoe signifies the Glen of Weeping; and, in truth, that pass is the most dreary and melancholy of all the Scottish passes, — the very Valley of the Shadow of Death. Mists and storms brood over it through the greater part of the finest summer. Huge precipices of naked stone frown on both sides. Mile after mile the only sound that indicates life is the faint cry of a bird of prey. The progress of civilization, which has turned so many wastes into fields yellow with harvest or gay with apple-blossoms, has only made Glencoe more desolate." *Macaulay.*

Globe, The. 1. A noted theatre in Southwark, London, built in the reign of Elizabeth, burnt in 1613, and rebuilt the following year. A patent was granted by James I. to Shakespeare and his companions to play "as within their then usuall house, called the Globe, in the county of Surry, as elsewhere." It is represented in an old print as resembling a high martello tower, with very narrow windows, and surmounted by a turret and a flag. Ben Jonson speaks of the Globe as the "glory of the Bank, and the fort of the whole parish." The exterior was hexagonal in shape, and the interior circular, with an open roof.

It was burned down by the accidental lighting of the thatch, occasioned by the discharge of a piece of ordnance during the representation of the play of Henry VIII., June 29, 1613. It was rebuilt during the reign of King James, and was finally taken down April 15, 1644.

Alas! Shakespeare had to write for the *Globe Playhouse*, — his great soul had to crush itself, as it could, into that and no other mould. It was with him then, as it is with us all. No man works save under conditions. *Carlyle.*

2. A theatre in Boston, Mass.

Globe Tavern. A house of entertainment, now closed, in Fleet Street, London, frequented in the last century.

Gloom. See CASTLE CAMPBELL.

Gloriette. An open pillared hall, 300 feet long, and commanding a magnificent view, in the gardens of Schönbrunn, near Vienna.

Gloucester Cathedral. One of the finest ecclesiastical structures in England, in Gloucester, the capital of the county of the same name. It was built in 1047, and was formerly a rich Benedictine abbey.

Gloucester House. A noble house in Piccadilly, London, belonging to the Duke of Cambridge.

Glyptothek. [Gr. γλυπτός, carved, θήκη, collection.] A famous gallery of sculpture in Munich, Bavaria, regarded as the finest collection, with the exception of that in the British Museum, north of the Alps. The building, which forms a hollow square, lighted entirely from the inner side, with an Ionic portico of white marble, was finished by Klenze in 1830.

☞ "The Glyptothek — an affected name for a statue-gallery — is, on the whole, the most beautiful, merely *beautiful* building I ever saw; and there is a school of painting there, which for the wideness and boldness of its range, and the number of artists attached to it, is a phenomenon the world has not seen since the days of Raffaelle and Michael Angelo." *George Ticknor.*

☞ "In the Glyptothek we wander amongst the most beautiful productions of art, brought together from the four corners of the world. In the Glyptothek stand the immortal figures by Scopas, Thorwaldsen, and Canova; and the walls are resplendent with colors that will tell posterity of Cornelius, Zimmermann, and Schlotthauer." *Hans Christian Andersen.*

Nowhere, not even on a gala-day in the Pope's Church of St. Peter, is there such an explosion of intolerable hypocrisy, on the part of poor mankind, as when you admit them into their Royal Picture gallery, *Glyptothek*, museum, or other divine temple of the fine arts. *Carlyle.*

Gobelins. A famous carpet manufactory in Paris, so called from its founder, Jean Gobelin (1450). The state purchased the present site in 1662. Here are executed with the needle splendid specimens of carpets and tapestry. Some of the pieces of work have cost as much as £6,000, requiring the labor of 5 or 10 years. The building, looms, and many pieces of tapestry were destroyed by the Commune in 1871. Here were made the tapestries and carpets which adorn the various palaces, or have been presented to royal foreigners.

☞ "The famous manufactory of the Gobelins was established by Louis XIV., who purchased the premises of some clever dyers of that name (Gobelin) about 1666; and the productions of the Hôtel Royal des Gobelins are said to have attained the highest degree of perfection in the time of Louis's great minister, Colbert, and his successor, Louvois." *L. Jewitt.*

God appearing to Noah. A fresco by Raphael Sanzio (1483-1520). In the Stanza of the Heliodorus, in the Vatican, Rome.

Godolphin Park. The seat of the Duke of Leeds, near St. Breague, England.

Gods, Feast of the. See FEAST OF THE GODS.

God's Gift. A name given to Dulwich College, in England. The college was founded by Edward Alleyne, an actor in the age of Elizabeth.

Goethe Monument. A magnificent bronze monument to the poet, modelled by the sculptor Schwanthaler (1802–1848), and standing in an open square in the city of Frankfort-on-the-Main. The bronze pedestal contains bas-reliefs representing scenes in Goethe's poems.

Gog and Magog. Names applied to two huge figures of wood, about 14 feet in height, in the Guildhall, London. These celebrated statues are thought to be connected with the Gotmagot and Corinæus of the Armorican chronicle which Geoffrey of Monmouth quotes, from the former of which names both the modern appellations are supposed to be derived. Hawthorne says that they look like enormous playthings for the children of giants. Mother Shipton has a prophecy that when these statues fall, London will also fall.

☞ "Our Guildhall giants boast of almost as high an antiquity as the Gog and Magog of the Scriptures; as they, or their living prototypes, are said to have been found in Britain by Brute, a younger son of Anthenor of Troy, who invaded Albion, and founded the city of London (at first called Troy-novant), 3,000 years ago. However the fact may have been, the two giants have been the pride of London from time immemorial. . . . There can be little doubt that these civic giants are exaggerated representatives of real persons and events." *Chambers.*

☞ "These absurd monsters look like painted and gilded toys, made to please the boys of Brobdignag. Words can hardly express their gigantic childishness. Why they are retained in their present position, and how they ever came there, seem to be beyond conjecture. They have not even the glamour of antiquity upon them. . . . They stand there, wonderful and ridiculous witnesses to the immobility of British Philistinism." *Richard Grant White.*

Nor had Fancy fed
With less delight upon that other class
Of marvels, broad-day wonders permanent:
The river proudly bridged; the dizzy top
And Whispering Gallery of St. Paul's; the tombs
Of Westminster; the *giants of Guildhall.*
Wordsworth.

Going to Market. A large landscape picture, so called, by Peter Paul Rubens (1577–1640), now in Windsor Castle, England.

Golden Gate. An ancient gate in Constantinople (Byzantium), much celebrated by the Byzantine writers, but which is now "sought for in vain; though a gate, now wholly blocked up, with two mean pillars supporting a low arch, is sometimes shown to travellers for it."

Golden Gate. An ancient portal bearing this name, in the Haram at Jerusalem occupying the site of the Jewish Temple.

Golden Gate. A portal in the Mosque of Omar at Jerusalem.

☞ "Well walled up, and constantly guarded; the Mohammedans having a tradition that if ever they are driven out from possession, it will be by the Jews or Christians entering at this gate." *Miss Martineau.*

Golden Gate. A celebrated strait connecting the harbor of San Francisco, Cal., with the ocean.

Up the long western steppes the blighting steals;
Down the Pacific slope the evil Fate
Glides like a shadow to the *Golden Gate:*
From sea to sea the drear eclipse is thrown.
Whittier.

The air is chill, and the day grows late,
And the clouds come in through the *Golden Gate:*
Phantom fleets they seem to me,
From a shoreless and unsounded sea.
E. Pollock.

Within this *Golden Gate*, the noblest, surely,
Of all the entrances of all the seas,
The Asian barks-of-hope float in securely,
And furl their lateen sails, and ride at ease. *H. Morford.*

A truce to moralizing, for we are approaching the *Golden Gate.* *Smiles.*

Golden Grove. The seat of the Earl of Cawdor in Caermarthenshire, Wales. The present building is modern; but the former house was memorable from its associations with Jeremy Taylor, who resided here for a time, and composed some of his chief works, one of which was entitled the "Golden Grove."

Golden Hind. The vessel in which Sir Francis Drake (1540?–1595) circumnavigated the globe, reaching home in 1579.

Golden Horn. A famous inlet of the Bosporus at Constantinople, Turkey. The city lies between the Sea of Marmora and the Bosporus on the south and east, and the Golden Horn on the north.

We swept around the *Golden Horn*, . . . and now lay in the harbor which extends into the sweet waters.
Hans Christian Andersen.

Golden House. [Lat. *Aurea Domus.*] The celebrated palace of Nero upon the Palatine, Esquiline, and Cœlian Hills, at Rome. Merivale says that it was the old mansion of Augustus and the house of Mæcenas, connected by a long series of arches and columns. Titus and Trajan erected baths upon a part of the same site, and the ruins of these and other buildings are now mingled in inextricable confusion. We are told by Suetonius and others of the great magnificence of Nero's palace: that its whole interior was covered with gold and with gems; that it was adorned with the finest paintings and statues the world could furnish; that it had triple porticos a mile in length, and a circular banquet-hall which perpetually revolved in imitation of the motion of the sun. We read, also, of vaulted ivory ceilings which opened and scattered flowers upon the guests, and of golden pipes that poured over them showers of soft perfumes. It is related that when Nero surveyed its costliness and immense extent he declared that he should now "be lodged like a man." See PALACE OF THE CÆSARS.

☞ "To give an idea of the extent and beauty of this edifice, it is sufficient to mention that in its vestibule was placed his [Nero's] colossal statue, one hundred and twenty feet in height. It has a triple portico, supported by a thousand columns, with a lake like a little sea, surrounded by buildings which resemble cities. It contained pasture-grounds and groves in which were all descriptions of animals, wild and tame." *Suetonius, Trans.*

Without it, proud Versailles! thy glory falls;
And *Nero's* terraces desert their walls.
Pope.

Hark! the owlet's cry,
That, like a muttering sibyl, makes her cell
Mid *Nero's house of gold*, with clustering bats
And gliding lizards. *L. H. Sigourney.*

Golden Rose. In former times the golden rose was sent annually from Rome by the popes to sovereign princes. The consecration of it took place in the Basilica of Sta. Croce in Gerusalemme, Rome. It was regarded as a gift of peculiar mystery and sanctity, "representing by its gold, its odor, and its balm, the godhead, the body and the soul of the Redeemer, and was only bestowed by the popes upon sovereigns who were the most loyal servants of the church." Leo the Ninth, who was elected pope in 1048, is said to have entered into a compact with the monastery of Sainte Croix in Alsace, by which the monastery was bound to send a golden rose every year to the head of the Roman Church. The ceremony of the benediction of the rose takes place on the fourth Sunday in Lent.

Golden Square. A district in London made famous by Charles Dickens in his novel of "Nicholas Nickleby."

☞ "It is one of the squares that have been, — a quarter of the town that has gone down in the world, and taken to letting lodgings." *Dickens.*

Golden Staircase. [Ital. *Scala d'Oro.*] A celebrated staircase in the Doge's Palace, Venice, Italy. It derives its name from the elaborate way in which it is adorned.

Golden Tree. See ALBERO D'ORO.

Goldene Aue. [The Golden Meadow.] A beautiful valley, so called, not far from Nordhausen in Germany. It is watered by the river Helme.

Goldsmiths' Hall. A building in Cheapside, London, belonging to the Company of Goldsmiths, one of the ancient city guilds. It was built after a design by Philip Hardwick, and was opened for use in July, 1835.

Golgotha. See CALVARY.

Goliath's Castle. The foundations of a ruined tower in Jerusalem, now called Kul' at-el-Jâlûd, the castle of Goliath.

Gondo. See GALLERY OF GONDO and GORGE OF GONDO.

Good Samaritan. A picture by Rembrandt van Ryn (1606-1669), the Dutch painter. It is now in the Louvre, Paris.

Goodman's Fields Theatre. A theatre in London, first opened in 1729, and taken down about 1746. Garrick first appeared in London at this theatre, in 1741, as Richard III.

> Did I tell you about Mr. Garrick, that the town are horn mad after? There are a dozen dukes of a night in *Goodman's Fields* sometimes. *Gray.*

> His [Johnson's] pupil, David Garrick, had, in 1741, made his appearance on a humble stage in *Goodman's Fields*, had at once risen to the first place among actors, and was now, after several years of almost uninterrupted success, manager of Drury Lane Theatre. *Macaulay.*

Goodwood. The splendid seat of the Duke of Richmond, near Chichester, England.

Goosetree's Club. See ALMACK'S CLUB.

Gordon Castle. The seat of the Duke of Richmond, near Fochabers, Scotland. It is the chief mansion in that part of the country.

Gore Hall. A granite building containing the library of Harvard University, Cambridge, Mass. It was designed to be a copy of the famous King's College Chapel in Cambridge, England; but the recent addition of a wing, for the purpose of increasing the capacity of the building, has impaired the resemblance.

Gorge of Gondo. On the route of the Simplon pass, Switzerland. This is one of the wildest and grandest ravines among the Alps. Its precipitous walls completely overhang the road.

☞ "Few scenes in Europe are more impressive than the Gorge of Gondo. The dizzy plunge of the snow-white torrent, the steep, dark rocks of slate, crested with trees, and the thread-like stream winding away far below over its pebbly bed, derive new beauty and significance from the work of human skill which enables the traveller to observe them so safely and so completely." *Hillard.*

Gorge of Pfäffers. An extraordinary chasm or ravine near Ragatz, Switzerland.

Gorges du Trient. A remarkable chasm in the neighborhood of Martigny, Switzerland, somewhat resembling the Gorge of Pfäffers.

Gorner Glacier. A famous Alpine glacier in Switzerland. This glacier is more extensive than the Mer de Glace at Chamouni, and is joined in its course by ten other glaciers.

Gorner Grat. A rocky ridge in Switzerland. It commands a most magnificent prospect. Monte Rosa and the Matterhorn are in full view, and the spectator is surrounded by glaciers and snow-peaks.

Gosford House. The seat of the Earl of Wemyss, near Berwick, Scotland.

Goswell Street. A street in London. Dickens, in the "Pickwick Papers," places here the house of Mrs. Bardell.

> *Goswell Street* was at his [Pickwick's] feet, *Goswell Street* was on his right hand, as far as the eye could reach *Goswell Street* extended on his left, and the opposite side of *Goswell Street* was over the way. *Dickens.*

> With this little boy, the only pledge of her departed exciseman, Mrs. Bardell shrunk from the world, and courted the retirement and tranquillity of *Goswell Street;* and here she placed in her front-parlor window a written placard, bearing this inscription, "Apartments furnished for a single gentleman. Enquire within." *Dickens.*

Gothard. See DOGS OF ST. GOTHARD, and HOSPICE OF THE ST. GOTHARD.

Gough Square. See note under JOHNSON'S COURT.

☞ "It is, perhaps, Gough Square, to which one of the little passages out of Fleet Street leads, that most faithfully preserves the memory of Johnson. It is rather a court than a square;

so small is it that carriages could never have entered, and it is surrounded with good old brick houses that in their day were of some pretensions. A worthy society has fixed a tablet in the wall, recording that here lived Samuel Johnson. There is a pleasant flavor of grave old fashion and retirement about the place; and little has, as yet, been touched or pulled down. Johnson's house faces us, and is about the most conspicuous. He had, of course, merely rooms; as it is a rather large mansion, a little shaken and awry, queerly shaped about the upper story, but snug and compact." *Fitzgerald.*

Goumont. See HOUGOUMONT.

Government Street. The principal avenue and favorite promenade in Mobile, Ala.

Graben. A noted street in Vienna, Austria.

Grace Church. This church, with its rectory, on Broadway, New York, is built of marble in a florid Gothic style. It has a tall and graceful spire.

Grace, Val de. See VAL DE GRACE.

Graces. See THREE GRACES.

Gräfenburg. A castle in Rhenish Prussia, near Trarbach, once one of the strongest fortresses on the Moselle.

Grafton House. An ancient manor house, and historically one of the most interesting of the English halls; the seat of the Duke of Grafton, near Towcester.

Graham's Dike. The name popularly given in Scotland to the remains of the old Roman Wall of Antoninus. See WALL OF ANTONINUS.

Gran Duca, Piazza del. See PIAZZA DELLA SIGNORIA.

Granary, The. An ancient burial-ground in Boston, Mass., situated on Tremont Street, adjoining Park-street Church. Here are buried Peter Faneuil, Paul Revere, Chief Justice Sewall, John Hancock, and Samuel Adams, as well as several of the old colonial governors of Massachusetts. On the street bordering this cemetery formerly stood the Paddock elms, transplanted from England and placed here in 1762, but lately removed.

Grand Canal. [Ital. *Canale Grande.*] The principal canal and main water-thoroughfare of Venice, Italy.

☞ "Nay, what potenter magic needs my Venice to revivify her past whenever she will, than the serpent cunning of her Grand Canal. Launched upon this great S, have I not seen hardened travellers grow sentimental, and has not this prodigious sibilant, in my hearing, inspired white-haired Puritan ministers of the gospel to quote out of the guide-book 'that line from Byron.' For myself I must count as half-lost the year spent in Venice before I took a house upon the Grand Canal. There alone can existence have the perfect local flavor. But by what witchery touched, one's being suffers the common sea-change till life at last seems to ebb and flow with the tide in that wonder-avenue of palaces, it would be idle to attempt to tell." *W. D. Howells.*

☞ "As we are borne along the Grand Canal the attention is every moment attracted by the splendid show on either side. The long wave which the prow turns over is dashed against a wall of marble-fronted palaces, the names of which, carelessly mentioned by the gondolier, awaken trails of golden memories in the mind."
Hillard.

☞ "We procured four or five gondoliers, and, embarking just at dark, rowed down the Grand Canal towards the Lagune. As soon as we were fairly in motion they began to sing. They took at first Tasso, and began in a sort of recitative, and in their soft Venetian dialect to chant the Episode of Armida. At first it did not produce much effect; but the recurrence of the same melody in the recitative soon got the command of our feelings, and it became striking. Wordsworth, who was with us, enjoyed it very much." *George Ticknor.*

Grand Canal at Venice. A fine picture by Antonio Canaletto (1697–1768). Now in the Soane Museum, London.

Grand Cañon of the Yellowstone. A picture by Thomas Moran (b. 1837). Purchased by Congress, and now in the Capitol at Washington.

Grand Galerie de Louis XIV. See GALERIE DES GLACES.

Grand Trianon. A charming residence near the palace of Versailles, built in 1688 by Louis XIV. It contains valuable paintings and portraits of several of the kings and queens of France. It has been occupied by Madame de Maintenon, Louis XIV., Louis XV., and Louis XVI., and by Napoleon. It is like an Italian palace, with the rooms all on one floor. There was also another château in the park of Versailles, called *Trianon de porcelaine.* This was demolished in 1687. See PETIT TRIANON.

☞ "The Grand Trianon built for Madame Maintenon is a very lovely spot, made more interesting by the preference given to it over all other places by Marie Antoinette. Here she amused herself with her Swiss village. The cottages and artificial 'mountains' (10 feet high, perhaps) are exceedingly pretty models in miniature, and probably illustrate very fairly the ideas of a palace-bred fancy upon natural scenery. There are glens and grottos and rocky beds for brooks that run at will ('*les rivieres à volonté*', the guide calls them), and trees set out upon the crags at most uncomfortable angles, and every contrivance to make a lovely lawn as inconveniently like nature as possible. The Swiss families, however, must have been very amusing. Brought fresh from their wild country, and set down in these pretty mock cottages with orders to live just as they did in their own mountains, they must have been charmingly puzzled."
N. P. Willis.

Behold him [Rohan] even, with his red stockings, at dusk, in the Garden of *Trianon:* he has bribed the Concierge; will see her Majesty in spite of Etiquette and Fate; peradventure, pitying his long sad king's-evil, she will touch him, and heal him.
Carlyle.

She [Marie Antoinette] indeed discarded Etiquette; once, when her carriage broke down, she even entered a hackney-coach. She would walk, too, at *Trianon*, in mere straw hat, and, perhaps, muslin gown!
Carlyle.

Grande Chartreuse. A celebrated monastery, founded in 1137, situated in a wild mountain region on the borders of Savoy. The buildings consist of an immense mass of masonry, towers, and roofs, surrounded by a wall extending more than a mile in circumference. The monks are of the order of La Trappe, and the discipline which enjoins silence is of the severest kind.

☞ "On my way from the Pyrenees to Germany, I turned aside from the Rhone highway of travel to make acquaintance with a place of which everybody has heard, yet which seems to have been partly dropped from the rapid itineraries which have come into fashion with railways. This is the celebrated monastery called the 'Grande Chartreuse.' . . . During the last century, when Gray and Horace Walpole penetrated into those solitudes, it was a well-known point of interest in the 'grand tour;' but it seems to have been neglected during and since the great upheaval of the French Revolution and the Napoleonic empire. The name, however, is kept alive on the tongues of gourmands by a certain greenish, pungent, perfumed liquor, which comes upon their tables at the end of dinner." *Bayard Taylor.*

And now, emerging from the forest's gloom,
I greet thee, *Chartreuse*, while I mourn thy doom.
Whither is fled that power whose frown severe
Awed sober Reason till she crouched in fear? *Wordsworth.*

Grandes Reliques. [The Grand Relics.] A name of general application, but commonly and familiarly applied to the sacred relics preserved in the treasury, or sacristy, of the Cathedral of Aix-la-Chapelle, in Rhenish Prussia. These relics are publicly exhibited once in seven years. So great is the curiosity to see them that it is said more than 180,000 visitors flocked to the spot in a single year. They comprise, among other things, the skull of Charlemagne, and his hunting-horn, the leathern girdle of Christ, a nail of the cross, the sponge that was dipped in vinegar, the cotton robe worn by the Virgin Mary at the Nativity, the swaddling-clothes of the infant Saviour, the cloth on which the head of John the Baptist was laid, and so forth. These relics, with the exception of the first two, are said to have been presented to Charlemagne by the Patriarch of Jerusalem and by the celebrated Haroun-al-Raschid.

Grands Mulets. The name given to a mass of black rocks on the side of Mont Blanc, well known to Alpine travellers, who, when making the ascent of the mountain, are accustomed to pass the night here.

Granja, La. [The Grange.] A royal palace in Spain, near Madrid, built by Philip V. in the style of a French château. It stands at an elevation of 3,840 feet above the level of the sea, amid wild mountain scenery. It derives its name from a grange, or farmhouse, of monks which formerly occupied the site. [Also called *San Ildefonso.*]

☞ "St. Ildefonso, or, as it is commonly called here, *La Granja*, is situated where no other monarch's palace is, in the region of the clouds; since it is higher up than the crater of Vesuvius, and precisely at that elevation where the great clouds are commonly formed in summer. . . . Philip was a Frenchman, who knew of nothing and conceived of nothing more beautiful than Versailles. *La Granja*, therefore, is its miniature." *George Ticknor.*

And in the vale below,
Where yonder steeples flash like lifted halberds,
San Ildefonso, from its noisy belfries,
Sends up a salutation to the morn,
As if an army smote their brazen shields,
And shouted victory! *Longfellow.*

Grange, The. An old mansion — the home of Alexander Hamilton — near High Bridge, on the Harlem River, N.Y. Near the house is a cluster of thirteen trees which he planted, and named after the thirteen original States. It is said that the South-Carolina tree is the only one that grew up crooked.

Grange, New. See New Grange.

Granville, Grotto of. See Grotto of Granville.

Gray's Inn. One of the Inns of Court in London. Lord Bacon was a member of Gray's Inn, and here sketched his great work, the "Organum," though law was his principal study. He dedicated his essays "from my chamber at Graie's Inn, this 30 of Januarie, 1597." This inn, which Stow says has been "a goodly house since Edward III.'s time," was so called from Edmund, Lord Gray of Wilton (time of Henry VII.). The Hall was finished in 1560. The men of Gray's Inn had their revels, masques, and interludes. The Society of Gray's Inn drink publicly only one toast, —"to the glorious, pious, and immortal memory of Queen Elizabeth." Dickens, in his "Uncommercial Traveller," gives a description of Gray's Inn. See Inner Temple.

☞ "Gray's Inn is a great quiet domain, quadrangle beyond quadrangle, close beside Holborn, and a large space of greensward enclosed within it. . . . Nothing else in London is so like the effect of a spell, as to pass under one of these archways, and find yourself transported from the jumble, rush, tumult, uproar, as of an age of week-days condensed into the present hour, into what seems an eternal Sabbath." *Hawthorne.*

Gray's-Inn Gardens. A fashionable promenade in London in the time of Charles II. Lord Bacon originally planted the trees in Gray's-Inn Gardens, though the same trees are not now standing.

When church was done, my wife and I walked to *Graye's Inne*, to observe the fashions of the ladies, because of my wife's making some clothes. *Pepys, May*, 1662.

Gray's Inn for walks, Lincoln's Inn for wall,
The Inner Temple for a garden, and the Middle for a hall.

Grazie, Ponte alle. See Ponte alle Grazie.

Great Bed of Ware. In Shakespeare's comedy of "Twelfth Night," the jolly Sir Toby Belch says to that charming simpleton Sir Andrew Ague-cheek, who is about to write a challenge, "As many lies as will lie in thy sheet of paper, although the sheet were big enough for *the bed of Ware* in England, set 'em down." The piece of furniture here alluded to is a very curious, carved, oaken bedstead, still preserved in an inn called the "Saracen's Head," at Ware. It bears the date 1460, but is said by antiquarians to be not older than the time of Queen Elizabeth (1558–1603); so that it must have been comparatively new in 1601, when Shakespeare is supposed to have written the "Twelfth Night." It measures twelve feet square, and is surmounted by a heavy roof, or canopy, supported by a very high head-board, and by elaborately turned and carved posts at the foot. A few years ago it was put up for sale by auction, and Charles Dickens offered 100 guineas ($500) for it; but it was valued at a higher sum, and was consequently bid in by the owner.

Great Bell of Moscow. See EMPEROR OF BELLS.

Great Bell of St. Paul's. This bell of London is only used at the death and funeral of members of the royal family, the bishop of the diocese, the dean of the cathedral, and the lord-mayor of London (while holding office). It was cast in 1716, weighs 5 tons 4 cwt., and is 6 feet 10½ inches in diameter at the mouth.

Little Britain has its long catalogue of city wonders, which its inhabitants consider the wonders of the world; such as the *Great Bell of St. Paul's*, which sours all the beer when it tolls. *Irving.*

Great Comstock Lode. See COMSTOCK LODE.

Great Conception of Seville. A celebrated picture by Bartolomé Esteban Murillo (1617–1682), representing the Immaculate Conception of the Virgin, called "the Great Conception," from its colossal size. In the gallery at Seville, Spain.

Great Eastern. A well-known mammoth steamship, without doubt the largest vessel ever built, originally designed for the Australian trade around the Cape of Good Hope. The vessel was intended to transport 1,000 passengers, 5,000 tons of merchandise, and 15,000 tons of coal for fuel. She was several years building, and was launched in 1857–58 with the broadside toward the river, but not until after various unsuccessful efforts had been made, with an expenditure of some $300,000. For a year she plied between England and the United States, but without earning sufficient to pay the running expenses. In 1861 she was employed to convey 2,000 troops from England to Canada. In 1864 she was employed to lay the Atlantic cable, and has since been repeatedly used for the same purpose. For ordinary traffic she has proved an expensive luxury, having cost, so far, it is said, some $25,000,000, including repairs, and has never returned a quarter of that sum.

What must be the natural excellence of the harbor of Portland will be understood when it is borne in mind that the *Great Eastern* can enter it at all times, and that it can lay along the wharves at any hour of the tide. *Anthony Trollope.*

Great Gun of Moscow. A famous piece of ordnance preserved in the Kremlin at Moscow, Russia, and popularly called the "pocket-piece" of the Empress Anne. The diameter of the bore is three feet, but the gun is said never to have been used.

Great Harry. This was the first double-decked vessel, and the first war-vessel of any size, built in England. She was constructed in 1509, by order of King Henry the Seventh, in honor of whom she was named. She was of 1,000 tons' burden, measured 138 feet in length and 38 feet in breadth, from outside to outside, carried 80 guns, and cost upwards of £14,000. Her stem and stern were very lofty; and she carried four masts, according to the fashion of the time. She had three flush-decks, a forecastle, half-deck, quarter-deck, and round-house. Down to the year 1545, the *Great Harry* was the only vessel of her kind in the British service. She was accidentally burned at Woolwich in 1553, in her forty-fifth year.

And above them all, and strangest of all,
Towered the *Great Harry*, crank and tall,
Whose picture was hanging on the wall,
With bows and stern raised high in air,
And balconies hanging here and there,

And signal-lanterns and flags afloat,
And eight round towers, like those that
frown
From some old castle, looking down
Upon the drawbridge and the moat.
Longfellow.

Great Mogul, Court of the. See COURT OF THE GREAT MOGUL.

Great Peter. **1.** The oldest of the existing great bells in England is Great Peter of Exeter. Its predecessor was of the date of 1484. The present bell was cast in 1676, weighs 6 tons 5 cwt., and is 6 feet 4 inches in diameter at the mouth.

2. Great "Peter of York" was cast in 1845, weighs 12 tons 10 cwt., and is 8 feet 4 inches in diameter at the mouth.

Great Pyramid. This oldest monument of Egypt and of the world, near Gheezeh and Cairo, was founded about 5,000 years ago by Cheops, or Suphis, who is said to have employed 100,000 men at a time on the work, who were relieved by the same number every three months. The work occupied twenty years, besides ten for constructing the causeway by which the immense stones were conveyed from the Arabian hills. It was undoubtedly designed for a tomb as well as for astronomical purposes. It covers an area of 577,600 square feet, and is 484 feet in perpendicular height. The view from the summit is extensive and interesting, including as it does the Nile, the minarets of Cairo, the pyramids of Abooseer, Sakkára and Dashoor, and a wide expanse of desert. The principal apartment in the pyramid is called the King's Chamber: in it is a sarcophagus, which is without sculptures or hieroglyphics. There are also many other apartments, one of which is called the Queen's Chamber. It is said that the pyramid was first opened by the Caliph Mamoon, about the year 820 A.D.; but it is quite probable that it had been previously opened. Arab historians relate that a statue enclosing a body supposed to be that of the king, was found in the sarcophagus; but this statement is not wholly trustworthy. The second pyramid, as it is called, near the Great Pyramid, contains one main chamber in which is a sarcophagus. The third pyramid, though much smaller than the others, excels them by having a coating of beautiful red granite from Syene.

☞ "The area of the Great Pyramid is more than twice the extent of that at St. Peter's at Rome, or of any other building in the world. Its height is equal to the highest spire of any cathedral in Europe; for though it has been attempted to erect higher buildings, in no instance has this yet been successfully achieved. Even the third pyramid covers more ground than any Gothic cathedral, and the mass of materials it contains far surpasses that of any erection we possess in Europe."
Fergusson.

☞ "Profound as is the impression created at the foot of the pyramid,—where the spectator, face to face with the enormous mass, loses the full view of the angles and the summit,—it is only after ascending to the top that he obtains a just idea of the whole, and finds expectation eclipsed by reality. From the summit the eye might traverse a distance of 36 miles were the human vision capable of distinguishing objects so far away. A stone thrown with the greatest possible force does not clear the base, but usually falls upon some of the lower steps. Owing to a common optical illusion, he who casts the stone imagines that he has sent his missile to a great distance: but as the eye follows it, the stone seems to turn back; and it falls only at the foot of the vast structure."
Lefèvre, Trans.

A man shall sit down with his friend at the foot of the *Great Pyramid;* and they will take up the question they had been talking about under "the great elm," and forget all about Egypt. *Holmes.*

At last, our short noon-shadows hid
The top-stone, bare and brown,
From whence, like *Gizeh's pyramid,*
The rough mass slanted down.
Whittier.

Great Seal (of England). A pair of dies made of silver into which, when closed, melted wax is poured. "The impression of the seal is six inches in diameter and three-quarters of an inch thick.

On every accession to the throne a new seal is struck; and the old one is cut into four pieces, and deposited in the Tower of London."

Nay, more; I can say and will say, that, as a Peer of Parliament, as a Speaker of this right honorable House, as Keeper of the *Great Seal*, as Guardian of his Majesty's conscience, as Lord High Chancellor of England, — nay, even in that character alone, in which the noble Duke would think it an affront to be considered, but which character none can deny me, — as a MAN, — I am, at this moment, as respectable — I beg leave to add, I am as much respected — as the proudest peer I now look down upon. *Lord Thurlow.*

Great Square. See PLACE MÉHÉMET ALI and PLAZA MAYOR.

Great Stone Face. See PROFILE, THE.

Great Tom. **1.** A famous bell in the tower of Christ Church College, Oxford, England. It was cast in 1681, weighs 17,000 pounds, and is seven feet in diameter at the mouth. The original bell belonged to Osney Abbey, and was inscribed, "In Thomæ laude resono Bim Bom sine fraude."

One hundred and one times the mighty sound,
Such as when Vulcan forged the war-god's shield,
Startled the Lemnian shepherd in his field,
Hath Christ-church giant bell swung out around,
And the night songster's voice melodious drowned. *J. B. Norton.*

2. A famous bell, formerly in Westminster Palace, London, afterwards given or sold by William III. to dean and chapter of St. Paul's, and then broken and recast. See BIG BEN.

☞ "There was formerly a 'Great Tom of Westminster,' which was sold for St. Paul's Cathedral in 1698; but, as though he determined never to give out a sound of his voice away from his own place, as he was being conveyed by Temple Bar — the boundary of Westminster and London — he rolled off the carriage and was broken. In 1708 he was recast by Philip Wightman." *L. Jewitt.*

3. [of Lincoln.] The celebrated bell of this name was cast, with additional material, from a still older bell, in 1610. This "Tom" was the predecessor of the present bell, which was cast in 1834, weighs 5 tons 8 cwt., and is 6 feet 10½ inches in diameter at the mouth.

4. A celebrated bell in the tower of St. Peter's Cathedral, in Exeter, England. This bell weighs 12,500 pounds.

Great Tun of Heidelberg. See TUN OF HEIDELBERG.

Great Wall of China. A famous structure traversing the northern boundary of the Chinese empire, carried over hills, valleys, and rivers. Its length is over 1,200 miles, its height 20 feet, its thickness 25 feet at the base, and 15 feet at the top. At intervals of 100 feet are towers. For a good part of its length, the wall is now but a heap of rubbish. This great structure was built about 200 B.C. as a defence against the Tartars.

There standeth a building which ages have tried:
It is not a dwelling, it is not a fane.
A hundred days round it the rider may ride,
And ride, if to compass its measure, in vain;
And years told in hundreds against it have striven.
By time never sapped, and by storm never bowed,
Still sublimely it stands in the rainbow of heaven,
Reaching now to the ocean and now to the cloud.
Not constructed a boast to vainglory to yield,
It serves as defender, to save and to shield;
And nowhere its like on the earth is surveyed;
And yet by the labors of man it was made! *Schiller, Trans.*

Mr. Huc, I think it is, who tells us some very good stories about the way in which two Chinese gentlemen contrive to keep up a long talk without saying a word which has any meaning in it. Something like this is occasionally heard on this side of the *Great Wall.* *Holmes.*

Great Western. One of the early steam-propelled vessels of the British merchant-marine. She left Bristol April 7, 1838, and reached New York in 15 days.

Greater and the Lesser Passion. See PASSION, etc.

Grecian, The. A former coffee-house of London, in Devereux

Court, Strand, so called after the "Grecian" (one Constantine) by whom it was kept. The Grecian figures in "The Tatler" and "Spectator," and was resorted to by Goldsmith, Foote, and by Fellows of the Royal Society. It was closed in 1843.

The coffee-house was the Londoner's house; and those who wished to find a gentleman, commonly asked, not whether he lived in Fleet Street or Chancery Lane, but whether he frequented "the *Grecian*" or "the Rainbow." *Macaulay.*

Grecian Theatre. A theatre near the garden of the Eagle Tavern, City Road, London, devoted to the melo-drama, farce, and ballet.

Greek Cross, Hall of the. See SALA A CROCE GRECA.

Greek Slave. A celebrated statue by Hiram Powers (1805-1873). It was finished in 1873, and several copies came from the artist's studio. One is now in the gallery of the Duke of Cleveland, England, another in the Corcoran Gallery, Washington, a third in the possession of Earl Dudley, and others elsewhere.

They say Ideal Beauty cannot enter
The house of anguish. On the threshold stands
An alien Image with the shackled hands,
Called the *Greek Slave:* as if the artist meant her
(That passionless perfection which he lent her,
Shadowed, not darkened, where the sill expands)
To so confront man's crimes in different lands
With man's ideal sense. Pierce to the centre,
Art's fiery finger!—and break up ere long
The serfdom of this world! Appeal, fair stone,
From God's pure heights of beauty, against man's wrong!
Catch up in thy divine face, not alone
East griefs but west, and strike and shame the strong,
By thunders of white silence overthrown.
Mrs. Browning.

I mean no disrespect to Gibson or Powers; . . . but I think the world would be all the richer if their Venuses, their *Greek Slaves*, their Eves, were burnt into quicklime, leaving us only this statue [the Venus de Medici] as our image of the beautiful. *Hawthorne.*

Green, The. A central square in the city of New Haven, Conn., generally known by this name. It was laid out in 1638 by John Davenport of London, the founder of the city and colony.

Green Gallery. [Ger. *Das grüne Gewölbe.*] A collection of jewels and costly articles in the palace of the elector of Saxony, at Dresden, Germany. This collection is unsurpassed in Europe.

Green Grotto. A celebrated cavern in the isle of Capri, near Naples.

☞ "Under these amazing crags, over a smooth, sunny sea, we sped along towards a point where the boatman said we should find the Green Grotto. It lies inside a short projecting cape of the perpendicular shore, and our approach to it was denoted by a streak of emerald fire flashing along the shaded water at the base of the rocks. A few more strokes on the oars carried us under an arch twenty feet high, which opened into a rocky cave beyond. The water being shallow, the white bottom shone like silver; and the pure green hue of the waves, filled and flooded with the splendor of the sun, was thrown upon the interior facings of the rocks, making the cavern gleam like transparent glass. It was a marvellous surprise. . . . The brightness of the day increased the illusion, and made the incredible beauty of the cavern all the more startling, because devoid of gloom and mystery. It was an idyl of the sea, born of the god-lore of Greece." *Bayard Taylor.*

☞ "The so-called Green Grotto has the beauty of moss-agate in its liquid floor; . . . and where there is no other charm to notice, endless beauty may be found in the play of sunlight upon roofs of limestone . . . mossed over, hung with fern, and catching tones of blue or green from the still deeps beneath." *J. A. Symonds.*

Green Park. An area of 60 acres in London, situated between Piccadilly and St. James's Park, Constitution Hill, and the houses of Arlington Street and St. James's Place. It was formerly called Little St. James's Park. Stafford House, Bridgewater House, and Spencer House are upon the east side of the park.

Greenmount. A cemetery near Baltimore, Md., established in 1838. The grounds are laid out with much taste and skill, and contain many fine monuments.

Greenway Court. A decayed mansion near Berryville, Va., once the residence of Lord Fairfax.

Greenwich Hospital. An asylum for old and disabled seamen on the Thames, a few miles below London. It was opened in 1705.

☞ Macaulay says in his sketch of the death of Mary II., "The affection with which her husband cherished her memory was attested by a monument the most superb that was ever erected to any sovereign. No scheme had been so much her own, none had been so near her heart, as that of converting the palace at Greenwich into a retreat for seamen. It had occurred to her when she had found it difficult to provide good shelter and good attendance for the thousands of brave men who had come back to England wounded after the battle of La Hogue. While she lived, scarcely any step was taken towards the accomplishing of her favorite design. But it should seem, that, as soon as her husband had lost her, he began to reproach himself for having neglected her wishes. No time was lost. A plan was furnished by Wren; and soon an edifice, surpassing that asylum which the magnificent Lewis had provided for his soldiers, rose on the margin of the Thames. . . . Few of those who now gaze on the noblest of European hospitals, are aware that it is a memorial of the virtues of the good Queen Mary, of the love and sorrow of William, and of the great victory of La Hogue."

Greenwich Park. A royal demesne at Greenwich, near London, much resorted to by the inhabitants of the metropolis. It was enclosed as a park by Duke Humphrey of Gloucester in the reign of Henry VI.

Greenwood. A beautiful cemetery three miles from Fulton Ferry, Brooklyn, N.Y., containing 242 acres of land, and ornamented with winding paths, forests, and lakes.

Gregorio, San. See SAN GREGORIO.

Greifenstein. A picturesque mediæval stronghold, now in ruins, near Rudolstadt in Germany.

Grenan, Temple of. See TEMPLE OF GRENAN.

Gresham College. This institution in London stood on Bishopsgate Street, and was so called after Sir Thomas Gresham, in whose honor it was established. The Royal Society originated here in 1645. After 1710 the college fell into decay, and in 1768 the building was sold. A handsome stone structure, Basinghall Street, was opened in 1843 for the Gresham Lectures.

Greta Hall. The former residence of the poet Southey, situated on a slight eminence near the town of Keswick, in what is called the Lake District of England.

Gretna Green. A little village in Scotland much resorted to formerly by runaway couples from England. Marriages were here celebrated with very little ceremony, but of late they have been prohibited by Act of Parliament.

Once in my life I married a wife,
  And where do you think I found her?
On *Gretna Green*, in a velvet sheen,
  And I took up a stick to pound her.
She jumped over a barberry-bush,
  And I jumped over a timber;
I showed her a gay gold ring,
  And she showed me her finger.
Mother Goose.

Grève, Place de. See PLACE DE L'HÔTEL DE VILLE.

Grey Abbey. A picturesque ruined monastery in the county of Down, Ireland.

Grey Friars. This important monastery in London was established by the early Franciscans who came to England in the time of Henry III. It was a favorite place of interment for royal personages. Nothing but a few arches now remains of the monastery, upon the site of which was founded Christ's Hospital.

How often have I seen the casual passer through the cloisters stand still, entranced with admiration . . . to hear thee [Coleridge] unfold, in thy deep and sweet intonations, the mysteries of Jamblicus or Plotinus, . . . while the walls of the old *Grey Friars* re-echoed to the accents of the inspired charity boy! *Charles Lamb.*

Grey Mare's Tail. A cataract issuing from the Loch Skene in Scotland. It is one of the loftiest cascades in the country.

Where deep, deep down, and far within,
Toils with the rocks the roaring linn;
Then issuing forth one foaming wave,
And wheeling round the Giant's Grave
White as the snowy charger's tail,
Drives down the pass of Moffatdale.
Scott.

☞ "A rather narrow stream, whitened in plunges over rough rocks, pours, in one broad broken sheet, over a precipitous crag of jagged, eccentrically stratified, gray rock. . . . The entire height of the fall is about 350 feet. It is part of a capital example of peculiarly Scottish scenery." *J. F. Hunnewell.*

Grillo, Torre del. See TORRE DEL GRILLO.

Grimani Breviary. A celebrated illuminated service-book, containing beautiful miniatures. In the library of the Ducal Palace, Venice.

Grimani Palace. [Ital. *Palazzo Grimani.*] A noble palace in Venice, Italy, fronting on the Grand Canal. It was built in the sixteenth century, and is now used as the post-office. It was formerly decorated with frescos of Tintoretto which have disappeared.

☞ "San Micheli's masterpiece is the design of the Grimani Palace. The proportions of the whole façade are good, and its dimensions give it a dignity which renders it one of the most striking façades on the Grand Canal; while the judgment displayed in the design elevates it into being one of the best buildings of the age in which it was erected." *Fergusson.*

Grimes's Dike. See GRAHAM'S DIKE.

Grimsel. See HOSPICE OF THE GRIMSEL.

Griper, The. An Arctic exploring ship which sailed from England under Commander Lyon in 1824.

Griswold, Fort. See FORT GRISWOLD.

Grizzly Giant. A famous tree in Mariposa County, Cal., the largest of a remarkable grove of trees of the *Sequoia gigantea* species. This tree is 107 feet in circumference, and in one place is 34 feet in diameter. It reaches a height of 200 feet before throwing out a branch, and the first branch is eight feet in diameter.

Grocers' Hall. A building in London belonging to the Company of Grocers, one of the great city guilds. The original hall was built in 1427, but was seriously damaged by the great fire of 1666. It was restored in 1668–69, but in 1681 was again in ruins. The present building was erected in 1802, and repaired in 1827.

Gros Bourdon. The largest bell in America, hung in one of the towers of the church of Notre Dame at Montreal, Canada. Its weight is nearly fifteen tons.

Grosse Garten. [The Great Garden.] A fine public park in the neighborhood of Dresden, Germany. It is five miles in circumference.

Grosvenor Gallery. See GROSVENOR HOUSE.

Grosvenor House. The city residence of the Marquis of Westminster, London. Formerly, as Gloucester House, it was inhabited by the Duke of Gloucester, brother of George III. It contains a fine collection of paintings, — the celebrated Grosvenor Gallery, — including some of the best works of Claude and Rubens.

Grosvenor Square. An area of six acres in London, built 1723–1730, and so called from Sir Richard Grosvenor (d. 1732). One of the most aristocratic quarters in London.

They [certain writers] conceived of liberty as monks conceive of love, as cockneys conceive of the happiness and innocence of rural life, as novel-reading sempstresses conceive of Almack's and *Grosvenor Square*, accomplished marquesses and handsome colonels of the Guards. *Macaulay.*

Let Stott, Carlisle, Matilda, and the rest
Of Grub Street, and of *Grosvenor-place* the best,
Scrawl on, 'till death release us from the strain,
Or Common Sense assert her rights again.
Byron.

Grotta Azzura. See BLUE GROTTO.

Grotta del Cane. [Grotto of the Dog.] A celebrated but small cave at the base of a rocky hill on the southern bank of the Lake Agnano near Naples. The cavern is constantly emitting from its sides and floor quantities of vapor mingled with carbonic-acid gas. The latter, being the heavier, accumulates at the bottom, leaving the upper part of the cave free from gas. The cave derives its name from the common experiment of subjecting a dog to the effects of the gas, and afterwards restoring him by exposure to the air.

We tried the old experiment of a dog in the *Grotto del Cane*, or Charon's Cave; it is not above three or four paces deepe, and about the height of a man, nor very broad. Whatever having life enters it presently expires. . . . This experiment has been tried on men, as on that poor creature whom Peter of Toledo caus'd to go in; likewise on some Turkish slaves, two soldiers, and other foole-hardy persons, who all perished, and could never be recovered by the water of the lake, as are doggs; for which many learned reasons have been offered, as Simon Majolus in his booke of the Canicular days has mentioned.
John Evelyn, 1644.

Grotta della Sibylla. See SIBYL'S CAVE.

Grotta di Posilipo. [Grotto of Posilipo.] An excavation in the volcanic soil near Naples, at the extremity of the street called the Chiaja. The earliest mention of it was in the time of Nero. It was enlarged in the fifteenth century by Alfonso I. In the centre of the tunnel is a recess, forming the chapel of the Virgin, before which a lamp is always burning. Near the top of the east entrance to the grotto is the Roman *columbarium*, or sepulchre, known as the tomb of Virgil. See VIRGIL'S TOMB.

☞ "Above the grotto are the remains of a columbarium, which, time out of mind, has enjoyed the honor of being called the tomb of Virgil. Nor is it by any means impossible that it is so, though it must be admitted that the weight of evidence is against the claim. But there is quite enough of interest clinging round it from the fact that a long line of poets and scholars, beginning with Petrarch and Boccaccio, have visited the spot more in the spirit of faith than of scepticism. There is nothing at all remarkable in the structure itself, which is of brick, shattered by time, and overgrown with myrtle, wild vines, and grass. Whether Virgil were really buried here or not, it is certainly a spot which a poet might well choose for his last repose."
Hillard.

Ah! precious every drape of myrtle bloom
And leaf of laurel crowning *Virgil's tomb!*
. . . .
Through the steep
Is hewn *Posilipo's* most marvellous *grot;*
And to the prince of Roman bards, whose sleep
Is in this singular and lonely spot,
Doth a wild rumor give a wizard's name,
Linking a tunnelled road to Maro's fame!
W. Gibson.

Grotto de la Vierge. [Grotto of the Virgin.] A noted place of pilgrimage in the present century at Lourdes, France. Its celebrity began in 1858 through the declarations of a girl who affirmed that the Holy Virgin had appeared to her. In the following year over 200,000 persons visited the spot. In the cavern is a spring which is believed to possess miraculous properties of healing.

Grotto of Adelsberg. A celebrated grotto, or cave, in the limestone rock near Adelsberg in Styria, Southern Austria. It is one of the most interesting and extensive in the world, and is hung with the most beautiful stalactites.

Grotto of Antiparos. A celebrated stalactitic cavern on the island of Oliaros (Antiparo), in the Ægean Sea.

Grotto of Egeria. See FOUNTAIN OF EGERIA.

Grotto of Granville. A natural curiosity in Southern France, near Le Bugue. It is a cavern extending a mile in a straight line, and, with its branches, measuring some two or three miles.

Grotto of Jeremiah. A spacious cave near the Damascus Gate of Jerusalem.

Grotto of St. John. A cavern, or grotto, belonging to the monastery of St. John in the island of

Patmos, off the west coast of Asia Minor. It is the supposed abode of the apostle John, who had been banished to this island, A.D. 94, by the Roman emperor, Domitian, and who is reported to here have had the visions recorded in the Book of Revelation.

Grottos of Beni Hassan. See BENI HASSAN.

Growler, The. A United States vessel of war captured by the British, June 3, 1813.

Grub Street. The former title of Milton Street, Cripplegate, London, which was once the residence of authors of the less fortunate class, and the jest of the more favored. From its being inhabited by these literary hacks, the name was familiarly used to characterize any worthless author or any poor production. This character it seems to have obtained as far back as the time of Cromwell, when the street consisted of low and mean houses, which were let out in lodgings, in many instances to persons whose occupation was publishing anonymously what were then deemed libellous or treasonable works. John Foxe the martyrologist, Speed the historian, and other authors, resided in Grub Street. Memoirs of the Society of Grub Street appeared in 1737. Its name was changed to Milton Street in 1830. The name Grub Street, as a term of reproach or contempt, is said to have been first used with reference to the works of Foxe. The present designation of the street is taken from the name of one Milton, a builder, and not, as might naturally be conjectured, from that of the poet.

☞ "Pope's arrows are so sharp, and his slaughter so wholesale, that the reader's sympathies are often enlisted on the side of the devoted inhabitants of Grub Street. He it was who brought the notion of a vile Grub Street before the minds of the general public; he it was who created such associations as author and rags, author and dirt, author and gin. The occupation of authorship became ignoble through his graphic description of misery, and the literary profession was for a long time destroyed."

Thackeray.

Our theatres are now open, and all *Grub-street* is preparing its advice to the managers. We shall undoubtedly hear learned disquisitions on the structure of one actor's legs, and another's eyebrows. We shall be told much of enunciations, tones, and attitudes, and shall have our lightest pleasures commented upon by didactic dulness. *Goldsmith*

When we first visited *Grub-street*, and with bared head did reverence to the genius of the place, with a "Salve, magna parens!" we were astonished to learn, on inquiry, that the authors did not dwell there now, but had all removed, years ago, to a sort of "High Life below Stairs," far in the west. *Carlyle.*

Let Budgel charge low *Grub-street* with his quill,
And write whate'er he please, — except my will. *Pope.*

Not with less glory mighty Dulness crown'd,
Shall take through *Grub-street* her triumphant round,
And her Parnassus glancing o'er at once,
Behold a hundred sons, and each a dunce.
Pope.

I'd sooner ballads write, and *Grub-street* lays. *Gay.*

Grüne Gewölbe. See GREEN GALLERY.

Grütli. A meadow on the shore of the Lake of Lucerne, Switzerland, famous as the meeting-place of the three mythical heroes of Switzerland, Werner Stauffacher, Erni of Melchthal, and Walter Fürst of Uri, who are said to have assembled here in the night, and formed plans for the deliverance of their country from the Austrian yoke. This spot is now the property of the Swiss Republic, having been purchased in 1859 by subscriptions.

Guards. See HORSE GUARDS.

Guards' Club. A London club, founded in 1810, and confined to officers of the regiments of Foot-Guards who distinguished themselves at Waterloo and in the Crimea. The club-house is in Pall Mall.

Guelfa, Torre. See TORRE GUELFA.

Guernica, Oak of. See OAK OF GUERNICA.

Guerrière, La. A British frigate captured during the war of 1812 by the United States vessel *Constitution*.

Long the tyrant of our coast
  Reigned the famous *Guerrière*.
Our little navy she defied,
  Public ship and privateer.
On her sails in letters red
  To our captains were displayed
Words of warning, words of dread, —
  "All who meet me have a care,
I am England's *Guerrière*."

Old Song.

"The wand of British invincibility was broken when the flag of the *Guerrière* came down. That one event was worth more to the Republic than all the money which has ever been expended for the navy. *R. F. Stockton.*

Guildhall, The. A name of general application, but specially used to designate the Town-Hall of the city of London, where the principal corporation business is transacted, and its hospitality exercised. The Guildhall will contain between 6,000 and 7,000 persons. The inauguration dinners of the lord-mayors have been held here since 1501. It is magnificently decorated upon the occasion of royal entertainments. The present, or third Guildhall, was first built in 1411, though but little more than the walls of the original building now remain. See GOG AND MAGOG.

☞ "The building itself is a strange architectural medley. . . . The great hall, however, has the grandeur which, in architecture, is always given, in a certain degree, by size. It is 150 feet long. The building has its name from the fact that it was erected by the united efforts of the various guilds of the city, — associations, or rather trading and social institutions, of which the very germ seems not to have crossed the ocean." *Richard Grant White.*

Our great fault with writers used to be, not that they were intrinsically more or less completed Dolts, with no eye or ear for the "open secret" of the world, or for any thing save the "open display" of the world, — for its gilt ceilings, marketable pleasures, war-chariots, and all manner, to the highest manner, of Lord-Mayor shows and *Guildhall* dinners, and their own small part and lot therein: but the head and front of their offence lay in this, that they had not "frequented the society of the upper classes." *Carlyle.*

Gloster. Go after, after, Cousin Buckingham.
The Mayor towards *Guildhall* hies him in all post:
There, at your meetest vantage of the time,
Infer the bastardy of Edward's children:
Tell them how Edward put to death a citizen,
Only for saying he would make his son
Heir to the crown; meaning, indeed, his house,
Which, by the sign thereof, was termed so.
. . . .
Buck. I go; and, towards three or four o'clock,
Look for the news that the *Guildhall* affords.

Shakespeare.

Gutenberg. A bronze statue of the inventor, modelled by Albert Bertel Thorwaldsen (1770–1844), erected in 1837 at Mayence, the expense being defrayed by subscriptions from all parts of Europe.

Gutenfels. A well-known stately castle on the banks of the Rhine, near the town of Caub. It is alluded to as early as 1257. In 1504 it was besieged for six weeks by the Landgrave William of Hessen, but without success. It remained in a habitable condition till the beginning of the present century, when, in 1805, it was demolished by order of Napoleon, and is now but a picturesque ruin.

Guy Fawkes's Cellar. An underground apartment, which formerly served as a kitchen, in the old palace at Westminster, and into which the conspirators obtained entrance from an adjoining house. The Parliament chamber above this vault was taken down about the year 1823.

Guy's Cliff. A noted spot, the retreat of the famous Earl Guy of Warwick, where he and his countess are supposed to be buried, about a mile from Warwick Castle, in England. It has a fine mansion and a romantic cavern, and is one of the places generally visited by tourists.

Guy's Hospital. An institution for the sick and lame, near London Bridge, in Southwark, London, founded by Thomas Guy (b. 1645).

Gymnasium of Ptolemy, or Stoa of Attalus. A marble building in ancient Athens. Pausanias says, that in the Gymnasium, "which is not far from the Agora, and is called Ptolemæum from him who built it, are Hermæ of stone worth inspection." See HERMÆ.

Gyzen George. A remarkable portrait by Hans Holbein the Younger (1498?-1543), pronounced by Ruskin "inexhaustible." Now in Berlin, Prussia.

H.

Habsburg Castle. [Habichtsburg, Hawk's Castle.] An ancient ruined castle of which little now remains, the old seat of the Imperial House of Austria, near Brugg, in Switzerland.

Hackney. A thickly populated district in London.

☞ Hackney coaches were not so called, as sometimes stated, after this district.

Haddon Hall. An ancient mansion, the seat of the Duke of Rutland, near Ashbourne and Bakewell, in Derbyshire, England. The various portions are of different orders of architecture, — pointed Gothic, Tudor, and Elizabethan. No part of the building is of later date than the sixteenth century. It is in good preservation, and is one of the curiosities of the Peak Country.

Not fond displays of cost, nor pampered train
Of idle menials, me so much delight,
As these time-honored walls crowning the plain
With their gray battlements; within bedight
With ancient trophies of baronial might.
Henry Alford.

Hadrian's Gate, *or* Arch. See Arch of Hadrian.

Hadrian's Mausoleum (Mole, *or* Tomb). See St. Angelo.

The highest part [of a monument at St. Rémi] is a circular colonnade, a miniature copy of that which we know to have once encircled *Hadrian's Mole.* *Fergusson.*

Hadrian's Villa. [Ital. *Villa Adriana.*] A famous and wonderful relic of imperial times on a plain at the foot of the hill of Tivoli, in the neighborhood of Rome. The emperor Hadrian having resolved to reproduce all the most striking objects which he had seen in his extensive travels, chose for the purpose a spot singularly favorable by its natural advantages; and in a short time, with the immense resources at his command, he covered the ground with a vast number of costly and extensive structures. He is said to have enclosed in this way a space eight or ten miles in circuit. At the present day the ruins present the appearance of a confused mass of buildings going to decay. Within seventy years after the death of Hadrian, many of the precious marbles used in the construction of these buildings were carried by Caracalla to Rome to decorate the Baths which he had then begun.

☞ "It rather resembled a city in itself than a single mansion. . . . These proud imperial ruins are now lost among thick olive-groves; their floors, instead of being paved with pictured mosaics, are overgrown with grass; their once magnificent halls are filled with thickets of aged ilex; yet enough still remains to attest their former extent and splendor." *Eaton.*

☞ "Before quitting the Villa Adriana, I filled my pockets with bits of porphyry, alabaster, verd antique, and pieces of stucco and mosaic, all which I afterwards threw away. Many travellers who have gone before me have written their names on the marbles of the Villa Adriana. They have hoped to prolong their existence by attaching a memorial of their fleeting presence to celebrated spots; but they have been deceived. While I was attempting to decipher a name newly written in pencil, a bird started from a tuft of ivy, and a few drops of the recent shower were shaken from its leaves, and, falling upon the name, blotted it out forever. *Châteaubriand, Trans.*

Hadrian's Wall. This wall extended from Bowness (*Tunnocelum*) on the Solway Firth, a distance of nearly 70 miles, to Wallsend (*Segedunum*) on the Tyne. There were 23 towns on its line; and between these towns, at intervals of a Roman mile, were fortresses, or "mile-castles." The common opinion tends to the belief that Hadrian built (A. D. 121) an earthen rampart, and that Severus, to strengthen it, constructed a stone wall (A.D. 208). [Also called the *Picts' Wall.*]

☞ "Of the wall itself (which was a huge work of masonry varying from 18 to 20 feet in height, and from 6 to 10 feet in thickness, with fosse and vallum on either side), and of these towers, etc., extensive and wonderful remains exist at the present day, and have, from the inscribed stones and other relics they have furnished, proved a rich storehouse of valuable knowledge."
L. Jewitt.

Hagar and Ishmael. A picture by Giovanni Francesco Barbieri, surnamed Guercino (1590–1666). In the Brera at Milan, Italy.

☞ "The severity of the patriarch, the half-concealed triumph of Sarah, and the broken-hearted expression of the beautiful victim, produce altogether an effect which places it among the very first pictures in the world."
George Ticknor.

"The famous Guercino is at Milan, however, the 'Hagar' which Byron talks of so enthusiastically. The picture catches your eye on your first entrance. There is that harmony and effect in the color that mark a masterpiece even in a passing glance. It is a piece of powerful and passionate poetry. The eyes get warm and the heart beats quick; and, as you walk away, you feel as if a load of oppressive sympathy was lifting from your heart."
N. P. Willis.

Hagar, Expulsion of. See EXPULSION OF HAGAR.

Hagley Park. A noble mansion, the seat of Lord Lyttelton, in Worcestershire, England. It is especially memorable as having been the favorite resort of the English poets, Thomson, Shenstone, and Pope.

Courting the Muse, through *Hagley Park* you stray:
Thy British Tempe! there along the dale,
With woods o'erhung, and shagged with mossy rocks
Whence on each hand the gushing waters play,
And down the rough cascade white-dashing fall,
You silent steal. *James Thomson.*

Hákem. See MOSQUE OF SULTAN EL HÁKEM.

Half-Moon, The. The ship in which Henry Hudson sailed for America in the service of the Dutch East India Company, in 1609. In this ship he began to explore the coast of New England for an open channel to the South Sea, and ascended the river afterwards called by his name.

☞ "In the ever-memorable year of our Lord, 1609, on a Saturday morning, the five-and-twentieth day of March, old style, did that 'worthy and irrecoverable discoverer (as he has justly been called), Master Henry Hudson,' set sail from Holland in a stout vessel called the *Half-Moon*, being employed by the Dutch East India Company, to seek a north-west passage to China."
Irving.

While drinking in the scene,
My mind goes back upon the tide of years,
And lo, a vision! On its upward path
The *Half-Moon* glides. *A. B. Street.*

Others held that it was Hendrick Hudson and the shadowy crew of the *Half-Moon* sailing to their weird revels in the Catskills. *Washington Irving.*

Half-Moon Tavern. See SHAKESPEARE'S HOUSE.

Halidon Hill. An eminence near Berwick, in Scotland, memorable for a sanguinary battle between the English and Scotch forces in 1333, when the former, under Edward III., defeated the Scotch army under the regent Archibald Douglas. Sir Walter Scott published in 1822 a dramatic tale called "Halidon Hill."

Aye, but King Edward sent a haughty message,
Defying us to battle on this field,
This very hill of *Halidon.* *Scott.*

Halifax Gibbet. See MAIDEN.

Hall of Animals. See SALA DEGLI ANIMALI.

Hall of Columns. A magnificent colonnade in the palace of Karnac, on the Nile, Egypt.

☞ "A symmetrical forest of oaks and beeches ten centuries old would not give an adequate idea of its thirty parallel ranks of columns. No tree, for instance, could attain the diameter, or the height even, of the twelve great columns that form the axis of the hall. . . . The enormous monolith capitals —heavy enough, one would think, to crush any pillar — oppress the imagination with their size. A hundred men could stand on one of them without crowding. Never have greater masses of stone been laid than these. . . . The hall itself is 422 feet long by 165 feet broad. The stones of the ceiling rest upon architraves supported by 134 columns which are still standing, and of which the largest measures 10 feet in diameter, and more than 72 feet in height. Sesostris and his two predecessors constructed the hall of columns, and the date of its construction was about the fourteenth and thirteenth centuries before Christ."

Lefèvre, Trans. Donald.

Hall of Fame, The Bavarian. [Ger. *Die baierische Ruhmeshalle.*] A famous structure in the immediate neighborhood of Munich, the capital of Bavaria, consisting of "a Doric portico forming three sides of a quadrangle, in the centre of whose open side rises the colossal statue of Bavaria," *q.v.* The building contains the statues of distinguished Bavarians.

Hall of the Biga. See SALA DELLA BIGA.

Hall of the Emperors. A hall in the Museum of the Capitol, Rome, so called because around the room is arranged a very valuable collection of 83 busts of Roman emperors, their wives and relations.

Hall of the Greek Cross. See SALA A CROCE GRECA.

Hall of the Vase. An apartment in the Museum of the Capitol, Rome, so called from a fine vase of white marble in the middle of the room.

Hall of Xerxes. See XERXES.

Halles, Les. A building of the fourteenth century in the market-place of Bruges, Belgium, with a lofty belfry-tower containing the finest chimes in Europe, which are played four times an hour by machinery.

In the market-place of Bruges stands the belfry old and brown,
Thrice consumed and thrice rebuilded, still it watches o'er the town.

Longfellow.

Halloren, The. A name applied to a cluster of families, some fifty in number, in Halle, Germany, who herd together, and gain a poor subsistence in the salt-mines by teaching swimming and by catching larks. They are curious as being probably the last remnant of the ancient Wendish people, who have retained their peculiar dress and customs from the time of Charlemagne to the present.

Ham Citadel. A celebrated political prison in the little town of Ham, France. It was built in 1470. The central tower is 100 feet high, and the walls are 36 feet thick. Many noted prisoners have been confined here, among others Louis Napoleon, who, after his failure at Boulogne in 1840, remained here for six years until he succeeded in making his escape.

Even now, when the other accusations against her [Marie Antoinette] have sunk down to oblivion and the Father of Lies, this of wanting etiquette survives her. In the *Castle of Ham*, at this hour [1831], M de Polignac and Company may be wringing their hands, not without an oblique glance at *her* for bringing them thither.

Carlyle.

Ham House. The seat of the Earl of Dysart. A residence of the time of James I. at Twickenham near London, where the "Cabal" ministers of Charles II. used to meet.

The more than Italian luxury of *Ham*, with its busts, fountains, and aviaries, were among the many signs which indicated what was the shortest road to boundless wealth.

Macaulay.

Hambye. A beautiful ruined monastery near Coutances, France. It was founded in 1145.

Hamilton, Fort. See FORT HAMILTON.

Hamilton Palace. An old feudal mansion of much historic interest, the seat of the Duke of Hamilton, in the town of the same name in Scotland. The old palace was rebuilt in the seventeenth century, and has received large additions in the present century. It contains one of the most valuable private collections of paintings and other works of art in Great Britain.

Hamlet and Ophelia. A picture by Benjamin West (1738-1820). In the collection of Mr. Longworth, at Cincinnati, O.

Hampton Court Palace. The renowned palace built in the parish of Hampton, near London, by Cardinal Wolsey, and by him resigned to his sovereign, Henry VIII. Two of the original quadrangles still remain. The later buildings erected by Sir Christopher Wren for William III. contain the famous state-rooms, portrait-galleries, and cartoons of Raphael.

☞ "Hampton Court is a large garden in the French style, laid out in the time of William III. Our style was then the reigning one in Europe."
Taine, Trans.

It was idle to expect that old sailors, familiar with the hurricanes of the tropics and with the icebergs of the Arctic Circle, would pay prompt and respectful obedience to a chief who knew no more of winds and waves than could be learned in a gilded barge between Whitehall Stairs and *Hampton Court.* *Macaulay.*

For ever curs'd be this detested day,
Which snatch'd my best, my favourite curl away;
Happy! ah ten times happy had I been,
If *Hampton Court* these eyes had never seen! *Pope.*

Hancock House. A famous old mansion which stood until within a few years in Boston, Mass. It was erected in 1737, and was the residence of Governor John Hancock (1737-1793). The governors of Massachusetts with the council were for a long period of years in the habit of dining in this mansion annually on Election Day. It was taken down in 1863.

Haram, The. [Arab. *el Haram esh-Sherif.*] A pile of walls and buildings occupying the site of the ancient Temple on Mount Moriah in Jerusalem, and extending beyond the ancient limits. In extent it is almost equal to a quarter part of the city. It contains the celebrated mosques el-Aksa, and Kubbet es-Sukhrah. The interior of the enclosure, with its green grass, its olive-trees and cypresses, and marble fountains, is beautiful. The Haram is of an oblong shape, measuring on its eastern side 1,580 feet, and on its southern 920 feet.

Harcourt House. The city residence of the Duke of Portland, London. It was originally called Bingley House, from its builder, Lord Bingley.

Hardwick Hall. An Elizabethan mansion, a seat of the Duke of Devonshire, near Glapwell, England.

Harleian Library. A collection of manuscripts made by Mr. Harley, subsequently the Earl of Oxford (d. 1724). The collection was purchased by the Government, and is now in the British Museum. The most important documents in this collection have appeared in the publication known as the Harleian Miscellany, the first edition of which came out in 1744.

Harlot's Progress. A series of famous dramatic and satirical pictures by William Hogarth (1697-1764).

☞ "It would be suppressing the merits of his heart to consider him only a promoter of laughter. . . . Mirth colored his pictures, but benevolence designed them. He smiled like Socrates, that men might not be offended at his lectures, and might learn to laugh at their own follies." *Lord Orford.*

Harpers' Tomb, The. This tomb of Rameses III. at Thebes, Egypt, is commonly known as The Harpers' Tomb, from a picture in one of the chambers, or as Bruce's Tomb, from its discoverer. It contains some interesting sculptures.

☞ "One of the most celebrated is the Harpers' Tomb, first mentioned by Bruce, and therefore often called by his name. This is the work of two of the Rameses; and a vast work it is, — extending 405 feet into the hill."
Miss Martineau.

Harrow. A famous grammar-school in the town of the same name, in the county of Middlesex, England. The school was founded by John Lyon in 1571.

Harry, The Great. See GREAT HARRY.

Hart, White. See WHITE HART.

Hartford, The. The flagship of Admiral Farragut in the attack upon the defences of New Orleans, in April, 1862, and subsequently in the attack upon Mobile.

☞ "On the evening of the 23d, Farragut was ready for his perilous forward movement. The mortar-vessels covered the advance by a terrible shower of shells. Farragut in the forechains of the *Hartford* watched the movements with intense interest through his night-glass. Just at the waning moon, when he was a mile from Fort Jackson, that fortress opened a heavy fire upon the *Hartford* with great precision. Very soon she returned such a tremendous broadside of grape and canister that the garrison were driven from their barbette guns. Before the fleet had fairly passed the forts, the Confederate gunboats and rams took part in the conflict. The scene was awful and grand. The noise of 20 mortars and 260 great guns afloat and ashore was terrific. And all this noise and destructive energy — blazing fire-rafts; floating volcanoes, belching out fire and smoke with bolts of death; the fierce rams pushing here and there with deadly force, and the thundering forts — were all crowded in the darkness, within the space of a narrow river." *Lossing.*

Came the word of our grand old chief, —
"Go on!" 'twas all he said.
Our helm was put to the starboard,
And the *Hartford* passed ahead.
H. H. Brownell.

Harvard College. The oldest and most richly endowed institution of learning in the United States, situated in Cambridge, Mass. It was founded in 1638, and named after Rev. John Harvard, who bequeathed it a legacy of £780. The university comprises some 28 buildings, three of which are in Boston.

Hassan, Mosque of Sultan. See MOSQUE OF SULTAN HASSAN.

Hastings. A picture by Joseph Mallord William Turner (1775-1851), the celebrated English painter.

Hatfield House. A palace in the county of Hertford, England, celebrated as being the place of Elizabeth Tudor's imprisonment previous to her accession to the throne of England. It is one of the noblest old places in the country. The hall of the old palace remains; and an old oak is still standing under which Elizabeth was sitting when the news of Queen Mary's death arrived, and she was saluted as queen. The river Lea runs through the park. The present building was erected at the beginning of the seventeenth century, and was partially destroyed by fire in 1835. Charles I. was a prisoner here. Hatfield House is the seat of the Marquis of Salisbury, and is extremely interesting for its historical documents, pictures, and other valuable relics. The castle has been restored to its original magnificence. It is within 20 miles of London.

1643, 11 March. I went to see my Lord of Salisbury's palace at *Hatfield*, where the most considerable rarity beside the house was the garden and vineyard.
John Evelyn, Diary.

Hattin. See HORNS OF HATTIN.

Haussman, Boulevart de. A splendid avenue in Paris. It is one of the modern boulevards of the city, and has a number of palatial residences. See BOULEVARDS.

Haute Vieille Tour. A singular old edifice in Rouen, France, supposed to be a part of the ancient palace in which King John murdered his nephew Prince Arthur.

Hawk's Nest. See MARSHALL'S PILLAR.

Hawthornden. An ancient cottage on the banks of the Esk near Dalkeith, where the poet Drummond once lived.

☞ "I know in my childhood I often used to wish that I could live in a ruined castle; and this Hawthornden would be the very *beau-ideal* of one as a romantic dwelling-place. It is an old castellated house, perched on the airy verge of a precipice, directly over the beautiful river Esk, looking down one of the most romantic glens in Scotland. The house itself, with its quaint high gables and gray antique walls, appears old enough to take you back to the times of William Wallace."

Mrs. H. B. Stowe.

Who knows not Melville's beechy grove,
And Roslin's rocky glen,
Dalkeith, which all the virtues love,
And classic *Hawthornden?* *Scott.*

—here's the hawthorn-broidered nook,
Where Drummond, not in vain,
Awaited his inspiring muse,
And wooed her dulcet strain.
And there's the oak, beneath whose shade
He welcomed tuneful Ben;
And still the memory of their words
Is nursed in *Hawthornden.*

L. H. Sigourney.

Haymarket, The. "A very spacious and public street [in London], where is a great market for hay and straw" (Hatton, 1708). Here are situated the "Haymarket Theatre," and "Her Majesty's Theatre," or the "Italian Opera House." The market was not finally abolished until 1830. Addison wrote his poem "The Campaign" in the Haymarket where he then lived.

Haymarket Theatre. A celebrated playhouse in London devoted to the regular drama. The first building was opened to the public in 1720, and was called the New French Theatre. This was taken down, and the present theatre was opened July 14, 1821.

Calculate how far it is from Sophocles and Æschylus to Knowles and Scribe; how Homer has gradually changed into Sir Harris Nicolas; or what roads the human species must have travelled before a Psalm of David could become an Opera at the *Haymarket.* *Carlyle.*

Healing of the Lame Man. See Peter and John at the Beautiful Gate of the Temple.

Heart of Mid-Lothian. See Tolbooth.

Heart of the Andes. A picture by Frederick E. Church (b. 1826).

☞ "In the Heart of the Andes, philosophically as well as poetically so called, the characteristics of their fertile belt are, as it were, condensed; it is at once descriptive and dramatic; all the tints of tropical atmosphere and all the traits of tropical vegetation combine 'to conform the show of things to the desire of the mind,' and to place before it the spectacle of a phase of nature which to northern vision is full of enchantment." *Tuckerman.*

Hecla, The. An Arctic exploring ship which sailed from England under Sir James Parry in 1824.

Hector, The. An armor-plated ship of the British navy, launched Sept. 26, 1862.

Heidelberg. A picture by Joseph Mallord William Turner (1775-1851), the celebrated English painter.

Heidelberg Castle. An imposing ruin on a height adjacent to the city of Heidelberg, Germany. It was both a palace (of the Elector's Palatine) and a fortress. In the last century it had been restored to something like its former splendor; but, having been struck by lightning in 1764 and burned, it has never been rebuilt. The fortress was built in the thirteenth century.

☞ "Some idea of the strength of the castle may be obtained when I state that the walls of this tower [one of the round towers] are twenty-two feet thick." *Bayard Taylor.*

☞ "Heidelberg Castle is of vast extent and various architecture; parts of it, a guide-book says, were designed by Michael Angelo. Over one door was a Hebrew inscription. Marshalled in niches in the wall stood statues of electors and knights in armor,—silent, lonely. The effect was quite different from the old Gothic ruins I had seen. This spoke of courts, of princes; and the pride and grandeur of the past contrasted with the silence and desertion, reminded me of the fable of the city of enchantment, where king and court were smitten to stone as they stood."

C. Beecher.

Heidelberg Tun. See Tun of Heidelberg.

Heidenmauer. [Pagan's Wall.] An old Roman relic, on a height near the town of Dürkheim, in Rhenish Bavaria, consisting of a rampart, said to have been built as a defence against the barbarians, and enclosing a space some two miles in circuit. Attila the Hun is said to have wintered here; and James Fenimore Cooper, the novelist, has taken from it the title of one of his stories, the scene of which he lays in the Vosges mountains in the Middle Ages.

Heights of Abraham. See ABRAHAM.

Helena's Tomb. A remarkable catacomb at Jerusalem. It is alluded to by Josephus, and by Pausanias, the Greek historian; and by the latter it is coupled with the tomb of Mausolus in Caria as deserving of special admiration. The locality is thought to be identified beyond doubt, and some curious features of the mechanism of the tomb correspond closely with the description of Pausanias. [Called also *Tomb of the Kings.*]

Helen's, St. See ST. HELEN'S.

Heliodorus. See EXPULSION OF HELIODORUS and STANZE OF RAPHAEL.

Heliopolis, Obelisk of. See OBELISK OF HELIOPOLIS.

Hell. See INFERNO.

Hell Gate. A part of the East River, about a mile from Central Park, New York, which formerly abounded in rocks very dangerous to navigation; but these have for the most part been removed.

☞ "It is certain, however, that to the accounts of Oloffe and his followers may be traced the various traditions handed down of this marvellous strait: as how the devil has been seen there, sitting astride of the Hog's Back and playing on the fiddle; how he broils fish there before a storm; and many other stories in which we must be cautious of putting too much faith. In consequence of all these terrific circumstances, the Pavonian commander gave this pass the name of *Helle-gat*, or, as it has been interpreted, *Hell-Gate;* which it continues to bear at the present day." *Irving's Knickerbocker.*

Hurl-Gate is at least as terrible as this fabled monster [Charybdis]. *T. Chase.*

Hemicycle, The. A picture by Paul Delaroche (1797–1856). "It contains 75 life-size figures, and employed him three years. It represents the arts of different countries and times by groups of portraits of the artists of those times and nations." In the theatre of L'École des Beaux Arts at Paris.

Henham Oak. A noted tree in Suffolk County, England, of great age and size. It is still standing, though shorn of much of its beauty.

☞ "The oak was a noted resort for select Jacobite meetings of a convivial nature, when Sir Robert Rous and two or three stanch adherents of the exiled house of Stuart were accustomed to drink deep healths 'to the king, over the water,' on bended knees." *Agnes Strickland.*

Henrietta, The. A noted yacht which crossed the Atlantic in 14 days, 4 hours, reaching Cowes, England, Dec. 25, 1866, and winning a prize of $90,000 for superior speed.

Henry-Grace-à-Dieu. A noted man-of-war belonging to the British navy, built by Henry VIII. in 1515.

Henry VII.'s Chapel. A chapel in Westminster Abbey, London, richly ornamened with panelling, its entrance-gates overlaid with brass, gilt, wrought into various devices, and containing many monuments and tombs of royal and distinguished persons.

☞ "The Chapel of Henry VII. is indeed well called by his name, for it breathes of himself through every part. It is the most signal example of the contrast between his closeness in life and his magnificence in the structures he hath left to posterity, — King's College Chapel, the Savoy, Westminster." *Dean Stanley.*

☞ "The Chapel of Henry VII. is one of the most elaborate specimens of Gothic workmanship in the world. If the first idea of the Gothic arch sprung from observing the forms of trees, this chapel must resemble the first conceptions of that order; for the fluted columns rise up like tall trees, branching out at the top into spreading capitals covered with leaves and supporting arches of the ceiling resembling a leafy roof." *Bayard Taylor.*

☞ "The very walls are wrought into universal ornament, incrusted with tracery, and scooped into niches crowded with statues of saints and martyrs." *Washington Irving.*

I may mention the frieze of angels in *Henry the Seventh's Chapel*, merely as an example at hand, and which can be referred to at any moment. *Mrs Jameson.*

In the *Chapel of Henry the Seventh*,
Where the sculptured ceilings rare
Show the conquered stone-work, hanging
Like cobweb-films in air,
There are held two shrines in keeping,
Whose memories closely press,—
The tomb of the Rose of Scotland,
And that of stout Queen Bess.
Henry Morford.

The gentle queen [Mary II.] sleeps among her illustrious kindred in the southern isle of the *Chapel of Henry the Seventh.* *Macaulay*

Heptastadium. The grand causeway which connected the island of Pharos with Alexandria, in Egypt. It was so called from its length, which was seven stadia, or about three-fourths of a mile. It now forms the base of a portion of the modern city; but, owing to the ruins of ancient, and the encroachments of modern, buildings, its precise position can hardly be discerned.

Heraclean Tables. Two bronze plates of an oblong shape discovered in 1832 on the site of the ancient city of Heracleia, in Calabria, Italy, and now preserved in the Museum at Naples. These plates contain interesting inscriptions in Greek.

Heralds' College. An edifice in Doctors' Commons, now removed to Queen Victoria Street, London, erected by Sir Christopher Wren in 1683, belonging to the institution of the same name which was incorporated by letters-patent of Richard III. The college consists of three kings-at-arms, namely, "Garter," "Clarencieux," and "Norroy," and also includes six heralds and four pursuivants.

Few things illustrate more strikingly the peculiar character of the English Government and people than the circumstance that the House of Commons, a popular assembly, should, even in a moment of joyous enthusiasm, have adhered to ancient forms with the punctilious accuracy of a *College of Heralds.* *Macaulay.*

Bob has done more to set the public right on this important point of blazonry than the whole *College of Heralds.*
Charles Lamb.

Hercules. An ancient statue in the British Museum, London. It is supposed by some to be the work of Lysippus, the Greek sculptor.

Hercules. A colossal statue, made of copper, in the grounds of the famous palace of Wilhelmshöhe, Germany. "Eight persons can stand at a time in the hollow of the club, and out of a little window formed in it enjoy a prospect extending nearly as far as the Brocken." See WILHELMSHÖHE.

Hercules killing Cacus. A well-known marble group by Baccio Bandinelli (1487–1559). Near the entrance of the Palazzo Vecchio, Florence, Italy.

Hercules. See FARNESE HERCULES and TORSO.

Hercules and Nessus. A group of statuary by Giovanni da Bologna, called Il Fiammingo (1530?–1608). In the Loggia de' Lanzi, Florence, Italy.

Hercules and the Centaurs. See BATTLE OF HERCULES WITH THE CENTAURS.

Hercules, Apotheosis of. See APOTHEOSIS OF HERCULES.

Hercules attacking the Harpies. A painting in distemper by Albert Dürer (1471–1528). In the collection of the Landauer Brüderhaus, at Nuremberg, Bavaria.

Hercules' Pillars. An ancient tavern which was situated in Fleet Street, London.

After the play was done . . . we all supped at *Hercules Pillars*; and there I did give the best supper I could, and pretty merry; and so home between eleven and twelve at night. *Pepys.*

☞ Another house of the same name was at Hyde-park Corner, London.

Hercules strangling the Serpents. See INFANT HERCULES.

Hermæ. The name given in ancient Athens, as a technical term, to any four-cornered posts terminating in a head or bust, such as were very common in the public places of that city. The name is derived from the Greek Ἑρμης, Mercury.

Hermannsdenkmal. [Monument to Hermann, or Arminius.] A statue of colossal size, erected in the present century by general subscription throughout Germany, on the Grotenberg, the highest peak in the Teutoburger Forest, Germany, to the memory of the old German hero, Hermann, who defeated the Roman army under Varus, as it is supposed, upon this spot, A.D. 9.

Hermes. See MERCURY.

Hermin Street. An old Roman road extending from Pevensey, England, to the south-east of Scotland. It derives its name from one of the Saxon divinities.

Hermitage, The. An imperial palace in St. Petersburg, Russia, connected with the Winter Palace by covered galleries, and forming a sort of continuation of that vast building. It was built by the Empress Catherine in 1804, as a sort of *Sans Souci*, and a place of escape from the fatigue of court-life. The principal façade of the palace faces the Neva. It contains a renowned gallery of paintings, embracing some of the choicest productions of the various schools.

☞ "The name seems to have been jestingly or ironically given. Who would not be a hermit in this immense pile, whose walls are of marble, blazing with gold, whose floors are of the choicest inlaid woods, and whose furniture is of the rarest and most costly workmanship in porphyry, jasper, lapis-lazuli, and malachite. Such splendor is now out of place since the palace has been given up to the arts. The vast collection of pictures accumulated by the Russian emperors is here displayed, together with a gallery of sculpture, one of the finest assortments of antique gems in the world, a collection of Grecian and Etruscan antiquities, and a library of rare books and manuscripts. The picture-gallery is particularly rich in the works of Rubens, Vandyke, Rembrandt, Murillo, and the Dutch school."

Bayard Taylor.

Hermitage, The. A picturesque garden and fashionable resort in Moscow, Russia.

☞ "It lies upon the side of a hill, at the foot of which is a little lake embowered in trees. Beyond the water rise massive zigzag walls, the fortifications of a Tartar city, whose peaked roofs climb an opposite hill, and stretch far away into the distance; and yet the whole thing is a scenic illusion. Three canvas frames, not a hundred yards from your eye, contain the whole of it. Thousands of crimson lamps illuminate the embowered walks, and on the top of the hill is a spacious auditorium, enclosed by lamp-lit arches."

Bayard Taylor.

Hermitage, The. A palace in the neighborhood of Baireuth, Bavaria, once occupied by Frederick the Great.

Hermitage, The. A venerable retreat at Warkworth, Northumberland, England, the most perfect work of its kind in the kingdom. It is a romantic solitude excavated out of the solid rock.

The lonely cavern, like a chapel carved,
Is situate amid the lonely hills.
The scutcheon, cross, and altar hewn in rock,
And by the altar is a cenotaph. . . .
Such must have been his history, who first
Cut this sad hermitage within the rock,
Some spirit-broken and world-weary man.

Anonymous

Hermitage, The. The residence of a hermit of the seventh century on St. Herbert's Island, in Derwent-Water, near Keswick, England. The ruins are still visible.

Stranger! not unmoved
Wilt thou behold this shapeless heap of stones,
The desolate ruins of St. Herbert's cell.

Wordsworth.

Hermitage, The. An interesting Border mansion in Scotland, near the town of Castelton, a stronghold of the Douglas family, supposed to have been built 1244, and regarded as the oldest baronial edifice in Scotland.

Hermitage, The. A mansion near Nashville, Tenn., the home for many years of Andrew Jackson, the seventh President of the United States.

Hermitage. See SACRO EREMO and SAN FRANCESCO.

Herne's Oak. A famous tree in Windsor Park, near London, immortalized by Shakespeare.

There is an old tale goes, that Herne the hunter,
Sometime a keeper here in Windsor Forest,
Doth all the winter time, at still midnight,
Walk round about an oak, with great ragg'd horns;
And there he blasts the tree, and takes the cattle;
And makes milch-kine yield blood, and shakes a chain
In a most hideous and dreadful manner.
Shakespeare.

And, 'neath *Herne's oak*, for Shakespeare's sight,
Strewed moss and grass with diamonds bright. *Lowell.*

Herod's Temple. The old temple at Jerusalem, rebuilt by Herod the Great (b. 72 B.C.) on a magnificent scale in the first century before Christ.

☞ "In the last Temple we have a perfect illustration of the mode in which the architectural enterprises of that country [Judea] were carried out. The priests restored the Temple itself, not venturing to alter a single one of its sacred dimensions, only adding wings to the façade. At this period, however, Judea was under the sway of the Romans and under the influence of their ideas; and the outer courts were added with a magnificence of which former builders had no conception, but bore strongly the impress of the architectural magnificence of the Romans. An area, measuring 600 feet each way, was enclosed by terraced walls of the utmost lithic grandeur. On these were erected porticos unsurpassed by any we know of. One, the Stoa Basilica, had a section equal to that of our largest cathedrals, and surpassed them all in length; and within this colonnaded enclosure were 10 gateways, two of which were of surpassing magnificence; the whole making up a rich and varied pile worthy of the Roman love of architectural display, but in singular contrast with the modest aspirations of a purely Semitic people." *Fergusson.*

Herrenhausen. A royal palace in Hanover, Prussia, once a favorite residence of George I. and George II. of England.

Hertford House. A city residence built by the Marquis of Hertford, Piccadilly, London, now occupied by Sir Richard Wallace. It contains a picture-gallery.

Hertha See. [The lake of Hertha, the Scandinavian goddess.] A small lake in the island of Rügen, in the Baltic, held in veneration by the inhabitants from its associations with the old Norse religion and mythology.

Hever Castle. An historical mansion and private fortress in Kent, England, interesting from its associations with Anne Boleyn, of whom it was the ancestral abode.

High Bridge. The structure which serves to carry the Croton Aqueduct across Harlem River at New York City. It is built of granite, cost $900,000, and is 1,450 feet long and 114 feet high, with 14 piers.

High Life. See LOW LIFE AND HIGH LIFE.

High Street. The main avenue and thoroughfare of the Old Town of Edinburgh, Scotland. In some parts of its course it is called by other names. See CANONGATE.

But neither the ignominious procession up the *High Street*, nor the near view of death, had power to disturb the gentle and majestic patience of Argyle. *Macaulay.*

Highland Music. A picture by Sir Edwin Landseer (1802-1873). In the National Gallery, London.

Highland Shepherd's Home. A picture by Sir Edwin Landseer (1802-1873), the most celebrated modern painter of animals.

Hilda's Tower. See TORRE DELLA SCIMIA.

Hills of Rome. See SEVEN HILLS [OF ROME].

Hinnom. A valley near Jerusalem, Palestine, beginning on the west side of the city. It is referred to in the Hebrew and Christian scriptures. Its present name is Wady Jehennam.

Hippicus. See TOWER OF DAVID.

Hippolitus. See MARTYRDOM OF ST. HIPPOLITUS.

Hiram's Tomb. A remarkable and quite perfect sepulchral monument in Northern Palestine, not far from ancient Tyre, and believed, not without good reason, to be the mausoleum of Hiram, the friend and ally of

Solomon. It is a colossal sarcophagus with a cover, and rests upon a massive pedestal.

History of Painting. A well-known picture by Peter von Cornelius (1787-1866). In the Pinakothek, at Munich, Bavaria

Hockley in the Hole. A region in London, of ill-repute a hundred years ago, but which has now passed out of existence. It is alluded to by Fielding and by Gay.

> You should go to *Hockley-in-the-Hole* to learn valor. *Gay.*

Hogue, La. A British frigate, which, in the war of 1812, committed great havoc on Long Island Sound, and in Connecticut, destroying many vessels.

Hohen-Rhoetien. This is the oldest castle in Switzerland, supposed to have been founded 587 years before Christ.

Hohenschwangau. A famous toy-castle built in 1809 by the King of Bavaria on the top of a high hill, near Füssen, in Bavaria.

Hohenstein. A feudal stronghold near Schwalbach, Nassau, Germany. It is now an imposing ruin.

Hohenzollern. A celebrated castle near Hechingen in Germany, the "cradle of the royal family of Prussia." It has been almost completely rebuilt in this century.

Holborn. A thoroughfare in London of varying widths. It was anciently called Old-bourne, from being built on the side of a brook, or bourne (Oldbourne or Hilbourne), which emptied into Fleet Ditch. By this road criminals were formerly conveyed from Newgate and the Tower to the gallows at St. Giles's and Tyburn. Milton lived in Holborn in 1647-49.

> As clever Tom Clinch, while the rabble was bawling,
> Rode stately through *Holborn* to die of his calling,
> He stopped at the George for a bottle of sack,
> And promised to pay for it when he came back. *Swift.*

> Methinks I see him already in the cart, sweeter and more lovely than the nosegay in his hand! . . . What volleys of sighs are sent from the windows of *Holborn* that so comely a youth should be brought to the sack!
> *Gay (Beggar's Opera).*

> An old counsellor in *Holborn* used every execution-day to turn out his clerks with this compliment: Go, ye young rogues; go to school and improve.
> *Tom Brown.*

> My Lord of Ely, when I was last in *Holborn*,
> I saw good strawberries in your garden there.
> I do beseech you send for some of them.
> *Shakespeare.*

Holdernesse House. The city residence of Earl Vane in London. It contains a fine sculpture-gallery, in which are several works by Canova and other great sculptors.

Holkham Hall. A splendid pile of buildings in the county of Norfolk, England, situated near the sea-coast, built by the Earl of Leicester in the middle of the last century. It contains a rare and celebrated collection of pictures and statues, and also some ancient and valuable manuscripts.

Holland House. A picturesque Elizabethan mansion about two miles from London. It was built in 1607, and descended to Henry Rich, first Earl of Holland, whence it was named Holland House. It was next occupied by Sir Thomas Fairfax, the Parliamentary General. Subsequently the estate passed to Addison the essayist, who died here. About 1762 it was sold to Henry Fox, the first Lord Holland of that name, whose second son, Charles James Fox, passed his early years here, and whose descendants still hold the estate. Holland House for nearly two centuries and a half was the favorite resort of wits and beauties, of painters and poets, of scholars, philosophers, and statesmen. It can boast, says Macaulay, of a greater number of inmates distinguished in political and literary history than any other private dwelling in England.

☞ "Two circles of rare social enjoyment — differing as widely as possible in all external circumstances, but each superior in its kind to all others — may without offence be placed side by side in grateful recollection: they are the dinners at Holland House, and the suppers of 'the Lambs' at the Temple, Great Russell Street, and Islington." *T. N. Talfourd.*

☞ "In what language shall we speak of that house, once celebrated for its rare attractions to the farthest ends of the civilized world. . . . The wonderful city . . . may soon displace those turrets and gardens which are associated with so much that is interesting and noble, with the courtly magnificence of Rich, with the loves of Ormond, with the counsels of Cromwell, with the death of Addison. . . . They [the last survivors of Macaulay's generation] will recollect how many men who have guided the politics of Europe, who have moved great assemblies by reason and eloquence, who have put life into bronze and canvas, or who have left to posterity things so written as it shall not willingly let them die, were there mixed with all that was loveliest and gayest in the society of the most splendid of capitals. These will remember the peculiar character which belonged to that circle, in which every talent and accomplishment, every art and science, had its place. They will remember how the last debate was discussed in one corner, and the last comedy of Scribe in another, while Wilkie gazed with modest admiration on Sir Joshua's Baretti; while Mackintosh turned over Thomas Aquinas to verify a quotation; while Talleyrand related his conversations with Barras at the Luxembourg, or his ride with Lannes over the field of Austerlitz. They will remember, above all, the grace, and the kindness, far more admirable than grace, with which the princely hospitality of that ancient mansion was dispensed." *Macaulay.*

Thou hill, whose brow the antique structures grace,
Reared by bold chiefs of Warwick's noble race,
How sweet were once thy prospects fresh and fair,
Thy sloping walks and unpolluted air!
How sweet the glooms beneath thy aged trees,
Thy noontide shadow and the evening breeze! *Tickell.*

Blest be the banquets spread at *Holland House*,
Where Scotchmen feed, and critics may carouse! *Byron.*

Hollenthal. [Valley of Hell.] A name given to several glens in North and South Germany. The most celebrated is near Gloggnitz, in Austria, being a deep and gloomy ravine surrounded with scenery of the wildest character. There is another near Freiburg.

Hollywood. A cemetery in Richmond, Va., a place of much natural beauty, and containing the monuments of many persons of note.

Holofernes. See JUDITH AND HOLOFERNES.

Holy and Apostolical Crown. The ancient crown of the Hungarian kings. It is surmounted by two ribs of gold, which belonged to a crown presented by Pope Sylvester II. to St. Stephen in the year 1000, and believed by the faithful to have been made by angels. It is kept in the royal palace at Buda, Hungary.

Holy Coat (of Treves). A famous relic preserved in the church of St. Peter and St Helen in Treves, in Germany, devoutly believed by Catholics to be the coat without seam worn by the Saviour. In 1844, within the space of eight weeks, over one million pilgrims visited this church to behold this relic. It is mentioned as far back as 1190.

Holy Cross. An imposing Roman Catholic church-edifice in Boston, Mass. It is larger than very many of the Old-World cathedrals, and there are but two in America (those at New York and Montreal) which can be compared with it. It covers more than an acre of ground, and is to have two spires, respectively 300 and 200 feet in height. Also a Catholic college of this name in Worcester, Mass.

Holy Cross. See VISION OF THE HOLY CROSS.

Holy-Cross Abbey. A noted and picturesque ruin in Tipperary County, Ireland.

☞ "As a monastic ruin, the abbey of Holy Cross ranks in popular esteem as one of the first, if not the very first, in Ireland." *Petrie.*

Holy Family, The. [Ital. *Sacra Famiglia.*] A name applied to a numerous class of compositions by the great mediæval painters of Europe, in which are portrayed the domestic life of the Virgin and the infancy of the Saviour. Of the great number of pictures which are designated by this title, apart from those generally called by the name Madonna, or the French equivalent *La Vierge*, the following may be mentioned as among the more celebrated and familiar. See also MADONNA and VIRGIN.

☞ "It is towards the end of the fifteenth century, or a little later, that we first meet with that charming domestic group called the *Holy Family*, afterwards so popular, so widely diffused, and treated with such an infinite variety." *Mrs. Jameson.*

Holy Family. A picture by Fra Bartolommeo (1469-1517), regarded as a fine specimen of this artist's work.

Holy Family. A picture by Rembrandt van Ryn (1606-1669), the Dutch painter. Now in the Louvre, Paris. There is another upon the same subject at the Hermitage in St. Petersburg.

Holy Family. A celebrated painting by Michael Angelo (1474-1564), in the Tribune of the Uffizi, Florence. It is the only finished picture by his hand known to be in existence.

☞ "The composition by Michael Angelo, styled a 'Holy Family,' is, though singular in treatment, certainly devotional in character. The grand, mannered, symmetrical treatment is very remarkable and characteristic. There are many engravings of this celebrated composition." *Mrs. Jameson.*

☞ "The picture altogether is a work which we study with admiration, rather than one which irresistibly attracts and fascinates us." *Grimm, Trans.*

Holy Family. A picture by Michael Angelo Amerighi, surnamed Caravaggio (1569-1609). In the Palazzo Borghese, Rome.

Holy Family. A picture by Peter Paul Rubens (1577-1640). In the Palazzo Pitti, Florence, Italy.

☞ "Mary, seated on the ground, holds the Child with a charming maternal expression a little from her, gazing on him with rapturous earnestness, while he looks up with responsive tenderness in her face. . . . Wonderful for the intensely natural and domestic expression and the beauty of execution." *Mrs. Jameson.*

Holy Family. A picture by Peter Paul Rubens (1577-1640), representing the Virgin holding the Infant, who is adored by St. John, with Elizabeth and Joseph. This picture was formerly in the gallery of Vienna, afterwards in the collection of the Marquis of Hertford, and is now in the Bethnal-Green Museum, London.

Holy Family. A picture by Andrea del Sarto (1488-1530). In the Louvre, Paris. There is another upon the same subject in the National Gallery, London. and a third in the collection of Lord Lansdowne. In the Pitti Gallery, Florence, Italy, is a picture upon the same subject by this artist, and another still is in the Pinakothek, Munich, Bavaria.

Holy Family. A picture by Giulio Romano (1492-1546), the pupil of Raphael, and often ascribed to that master, representing the Virgin as preparing to wash the child, who is standing in a vase, while the little St. John is pouring in the water. In the Dresden Gallery.

Holy Family. A noted picture by Bernardino Pinturicchio (1454-1513). In the Academy at Siena.

☞ "Mary and Joseph are seated together; near them are some loaves and a small cask of wine. More in front the two children, Jesus and St. John, are walking arm in arm. Jesus holds a book, and John a pitcher, as if they were going to a well." *Mrs. Jameson.*

Holy Family. A picture by Anthony van Dyck (1599-1641). In the Pinakothek at Munich, Bavaria.

Holy Family. A noted picture by Leonardo da Vinci (1452-1519), "in which St. Anna is seated on a sort of chair; and the Virgin on her knees bends down toward the infant Christ, who is sporting with a lamb." In the gallery of the Louvre, Paris.

Holy Family. A celebrated picture by Raphael Sanzio (1483–1520). See BRIDGEWATER MADONNA.

Holy Family under the Oak. A picture executed chiefly by Giulio Romano (1492–1546), but in parts, it is supposed, by Raphael, and deriving its name from the oak under which the figures are standing. It is in the Museum at Madrid. There is a copy in the Pitti Palace, Florence, which is known as the *Madonna della Lucertola*, q.v.

Holy Family with the Palm-tree. A circular picture by Raphael Sanzio (1483–1520), representing the Virgin seated under a palm, holding the Child in her lap; while Joseph, kneeling, presents flowers to him. This picture was formerly in the Orleans collection, but is now in the collection of the Earl of Ellesmere, London.

☞ "The following anecdote of this picture was related to the Marquis of Stafford by the Duke of Orleans when on a visit to England. It happened once . . . that this picture fell to the portion of two old maids. Both having an equal right, and neither choosing to yield, they compromised the matter by cutting it in two. In this state the two halves were sold to one purchaser, who tacked them together as well as he could, and sent them further into the world. The transfer from canvas to wood has obliterated every trace by which the truth of this tale might be corroborated." *Passavant*.

Holy Ghost, Descent of the. See DESCENT OF THE HOLY GHOST.

Holy Grotto. A sacred shrine in the Latin Convent of Nazareth, in Northern Palestine, believed to be the spot in which the annunciation by the angel to the Virgin Mary took place. Over the vestibule in front of this grotto once stood, according to the Catholic legends, the famous house in which Mary was born, and which was afterwards miraculously transported to Loreto in Italy. See SANTA CASA.

Holy Island Castle. A fortress upon the so-called Holy Island, on the coast of Northumberland, England, the scene of much legendary and poetical narrative.

Holy Mountain. See MOUNT ATHOS.

Holy of Holies. The name given to the innermost apartment in the Temple at Jerusalem, which was held peculiarly sacred, and into which the high priest only was allowed to enter once a year. See SANCTA SANCTORUM.

☞ "In the Temple, the only light that could penetrate to the Holy of Holies was from the front; and though the holy place was partially lighted from the sides, its principal source of light must have been through the eastern façade." *Fergusson*.

The spirit of Mammon has a wide empire; but it cannot, and must not, be worshipped in the *Holy of Holies*.
Carlyle.

Holy Oil. [Mir.] The oil of baptism with which all Russian children throughout the whole extent of the empire are anointed. It is preserved in 33 jars of massive silver in the Kremlin, Moscow; and it is said that about two gallons a year are necessary to supply Russia.

Holy Pillar. See CAPELLA DELLA COLONNA SANTA.

Holy Sepulchre. This church of Jerusalem purports to be built, as the name indicates, over the garden-tomb of Jesus. It is showy and gorgeous, and contains chapels for Latins, Greeks, and Armenians. The visitor is shown the tomb, the place of the cross, the pillar of scourging, and various other sacred places, whose genuineness is, however, more than questionable. The church is a Byzantine edifice, and was erected by the Empress Helena, mother of Constantine the Great. The Holy Sepulchre stands in the centre of the rotunda of the church.

Holy Staircase. See SANTA SCALA.

Holy Stone. A famous stone preserved at Ardmore, in the county of Waterford, Ireland, sacred to St. Patrick, and believed to have floated over the ocean from Rome with the vestments of the saint, a bell for his tower, and a lighted candle for the celebration of mass.

☞ "The people crowd to the Holy Stone, and, having gone on their bare knees several times round it, creep under it, lying flat. The painful contortions of some of these poor people it is distressing to witness, as they force themselves through the narrow passage. It is only at low water that this part of the ceremony can be performed. The stone, which weighs perhaps four or five tons, rests upon two small rocks, leaving a passage under it."
Mr. and Mrs. Hall.

Holy Synod, House of the. A celebrated structure in the Kremlin, Moscow, Russia. It derives its name from the council-hall of the Holy Synod, which is in the building. It contains the robes worn by the Russian patriarchs during the last 600 years, as well as the silver jars containing the holy oil of baptism used throughout the whole empire.

Holyrood Abbey. [i. e., Abbey of the Holy Rood or Cross.] A ruined monastery in Edinburgh, Scotland, the foundation of which dates from the twelfth century. At the time of the Reformation the church was plundered and burned. Attempts were made to restore it in the last century, but the undertaking was relinquished.

Holyrood Palace. An ancient and famous royal palace in Edinburgh, Scotland. It stands on the summit of a huge rock, 443 feet above the sea, and is built in the shape of a quadrangle, with a court in the centre. The palace was begun in the reign of James IV., was nearly destroyed by the soldiers of Cromwell in 1650, and was rebuilt in the reign of Charles II. The apartments occupied by Mary Queen of Scots are preserved almost in their original condition. The palace has in recent times been very seldom used as a place of residence.

☞ "Dark old Holyrood, where the memory of lovely Mary lingers like a stray beam in her cold halls, and the fair, boyish face of Rizzio looks down from the canvas on the armor of his murderer." *Bayard Taylor.*

The truth of the record has been called in question, but I regarded it with the same determined faith with which I contemplated the stains of Rizzio's blood on the floor of the palace of *Holyrood.*
Irving.

Old *Holyrood* rung merrily
That night with wassail, mirth, and glee:
King James, within her princely bower,
Feasted the chief of Scotland's power.
Scott.

Or should some cankered biting shower
The day and a' her sweets deflower,
To *Holyrood*-house let me stray,
And gie to musing a' the day.
Robert Fergusson.

Homer and the Greeks. A picture by Wilhelm Kaulbach (b. 1805), the eminent German painter.

Honoré, Rue St. See St. Honoré.

Hope, The. One of the principal theatres in London in Shakespeare's time.

Scenery, dresses, and decorations such as would now be thought mean and absurd, but such as would have been esteemed incredibly magnificent by those who, early in the seventeenth century, sate on the filthy benches of the *Hope*, or under the thatched roof of the Rose, dazzled the eyes of the multitude.
Macaulay.

Hope House. A modern mansion in London, built in 1849, and noted for its rich and elaborate ornamentation, and collections of art.

Hope, Mount. See Mount Hope.

Hore Abbey. An interesting and well-preserved ruined monastery in Tipperary County, Ireland.

Hornberg. A castle on the Neckar in Germany, once the fortress of Goetz of the Iron Hand. His armor is kept here, and the castle was inhabited nearly to the beginning of the present century.

Hornet, The. An American war-ship, which, under Capt. James Lawrence, captured, in January, 1813, the British ship *Peacock.*

Horns of Hattin. A singularly shaped hill in Northern Palestine, not far from Nazareth. According to the tradition of the Latin Church, this is the Hill of the Beatitudes from which the "Sermon on the Mount" was delivered. According to the tradition of the Greek Church, it is the scene of the miracle of the multiplication of the loaves and the fishes (Matt. xiv. 15 *et seq.*). In the neighborhood of this hill took place the great battle in which Saladin overthrew the Christian power in Syria.

Horologe of Petrus Lombardus. [Ital. *Torre del Orologio.*] A celebrated clock-tower in Venice, Italy, erected 1466. It has a blue-and-gold dial, and is surmounted by two Moorish figures in bronze, which, swinging round, strike the hours upon a bell with a hammer.

☞ "Over this Porch stands that admirable Clock celebrated next to that of Strasburg for its many movements; amongst which, about 12 and 6, which are their hours of Ave Maria, when all the towne are on their knees, come forth the three kings led by a starr, and, passing by the image of Christ in his Mother's arms, do their reverence, and enter into the clock by another door. At the top of this turret another automaton strikes the quarters. An honest merchant told me, that one day, walking in the Piazza, he saw the fellow who kept the Clock struck with this hammer so forceably as he was stooping his head neere the bell to mend something amisse at the minute of striking, that, being stunn'd, he reel'd over the battlements and broke his neck."
John Evelyn, 1645.

Horse Armory. A celebrated collection of equestrian figures clothed in the armor of various reigns from the time of Edward I. to James II., contained in a gallery of the Tower of London.

Horse-fair, The. A well-known picture by Rosa Bonheur (b. 1822).

Horse Guards. A building used for military purposes in London, and comprising the offices of the secretary-at-war, the commander-in-chief, the adjutant-general, and quartermaster-general. In the rear is a parade-ground for the inspection of troops. In two stone alcoves, flanking the gates, is stationed a guard of two mounted cavalry soldiers from ten to four o'clock, relieved every two hours. Orders concerning all the guards are given out by the field-officer on duty. The marching and countermarching of the Guards, who are considered the finest "Household Troops" in Europe, make one of the most picturesque sights of London.

Let no man despair of Governments who looks on these two sentries at the *Horse-Guards*, and our United Service Clubs! *Carlyle.*

Horse of Berkshire. See White Horse of Berkshire.

Horse-Shoe Bend. A celebrated curve on the Pennsylvania Railroad, near Kittanning Point. The curve is so short that the front of the train may be seen going in a direction just opposite to that of the rear portion.

Horse-Shoe Fall. This fall at Niagara is 158 feet in height and nearly 2,400 feet in width. The river is divided above the falls into two branches by Goat Island; and the larger volume of water, which flows on the Canada side, forms the Horse-Shoe Fall. [Called also the *Canadian Fall.*]

Horses, Bronze. See Bronze Horses.

Horticultural Hall. 1. A fine edifice in Boston, Mass., of composite architecture, designed for floral exhibitions, fairs, and other purposes.

2. A building on Broad Street, Philadelphia, Penn., devoted to exhibitions of flowers and fruit.

Hospice of St. Bernard. A celebrated stone building, serving both as a monastery and as an inn for the accommodation of travellers, at the summit of the St. Bernard Pass, in Switzerland. It is supposed to have been founded by St. Bernard in 962, hence the name of both Hospice and Pass. Everybody has heard of the St. Bernard dogs which render such efficient aid to travellers: their number has now become very small. This is the highest winter habitation in the Alps.

Hospice of the Grimsel. A celebrated inn, once a monastery, near the summit of the Grimsel pass in Switzerland.

Hospice of the St. Gothard. A well-known inn near the summit of the St. Gothard pass in Switzerland.

Hôtel Cluny. This beautiful building in Paris derives its name from the Abbé of Cluny, who bought an ancient palace which stood on the spot now occupied by the present one. This was built in 1490. It was once used as a theatre, afterwards as a convent, and during the Revolution Marat held his meetings there. Subsequently it became a museum, and passed into the hands of the government. It contains many treasures of art, mosaics, reliefs, stained glass windows, ivory cabinets, vases, and paintings. The building itself is much admired for the grace and delicacy of its sculptures. See PALAIS DES THERMES.

Hôtel de Pimodan. A noted mansion in Paris of the time of Louis XIV.

Hôtel de Rambouillet. A palace in Paris — the residence of the Marquis de Rambouillet — very famous in the seventeenth century, and subsequently, as the centre of a literary and political *coterie*. According to Roederer, the opening of the *salon* of the Hôtel de Rambouillet took place in the year 1600, under the reign of Henry IV. The marquis was an enemy of Sully; and his house became the headquarters of the opposition party, where the barbarism and immoralities of the court were offset by purity of language and of manners. The most celebrated wits of the period, and the finest ladies of the realm, sought admission to these *réunions*. Through the indifference to literature manifested by Louis XIII. and the various ministries which succeeded each other down to the time of Richelieu, the Hôtel de Rambouillet soon had the exclusive patronage and direction of letters, and exerted an influence which was for a long time without a rival. But notwithstanding the excellence of its motives, it could not escape the law which governs all literary *coteries*. In time it engendered mannerism and affectation. The discussions turned upon idle and frivolous questions, upon the merits of roundelays, madrigals, enigmas, and acrostics. The women who frequented the Hôtel de Rambouillet took the name of *Précieuses*. It was a title of honor and a sort of diploma of talent and purity; but when pedantry and affectation had begun to draw down upon them the shafts of the satirists, it lost its original meaning, the epithet *ridicules* was appended to it, and Molière, with his pungent irony, gave the fatal blow to the literary fame of the celebrated *salon* by holding it up to public laughter in his "Précieuses Ridicules" and his "Femmes Savantes." The name Hôtel de Rambouillet is at present only a derisive *sobriquet*.

> The house of Mlle. de L'Enclos was a branch establishment of the *Hôtel de Rambouillet*. — *J. Janin.*

> The great *comédienne* [Contat] had her court and her *Hôtel Rambouillet* — *Roger de Beauvoir.*

Hôtel de Ville. [City-Hall.] A general term applied in France and Belgium to the buildings used for municipal offices, some of which are among the finest existing specimens of architecture. See *infra*.

Hôtel de Ville. A large and beautiful building in Paris, the official residence of the Prefect of the Seine. It contained also rooms for the public festivals of the city, the sittings of the council, and meetings of learned and scientific societies. It was adorned by sculptures which were chiefly from the hand of Jean Goujon. The building had many interesting historical associations; the insurrection of the Maillotins, in 1358, broke out here; here met societies of the Fronde; here Robespierre held his council; and here Louis Philippe was presented to the French nation by La Fayette in 1830. The Hôtel de Ville was destroyed by the leaders of the Commune prior to the entrance of the German army, May 28, 1871, and has not been rebuilt. Among the finer examples of architecture bearing this name may be mentioned the town-halls of Brussels, Bruges, Louvain, Ypres, etc.

And for about four months all France, and to a great degree all Europe, rough-ridden by every species of delirium, except happily the murderous for most part, was a weltering mob, presided over by M. de Lamartine at the *Hôtel de Ville*. *Carlyle.*

Hôtel de Ville. [Bruges.] The municipal building of Bruges, Belgium, the oldest edifice of the kind in the country, having been erected in 1377.

☞ "It is a small building, being only 88 feet in front by 65 in depth, and of a singularly pure and elegant design. . . . The belfry is one of the most picturesque towers in the country." *Fergusson.*

Hôtel de Ville. [Brussels.] A noble Gothic edifice, the municipal hall of Brussels, Belgium. In the grand hall of this building the abdication of Charles V. took place in 1555. It is considered the finest of the town-halls of Belgium. It was begun in 1401, and finished in 1455. It has a spire of open stone-work 364 feet in height.

☞ "The spire that surmounts its centre is unrivalled for beauty of outline and design by any spire in Belgium, and is entitled to take rank amongst the noblest examples of its class in Europe." *Fergusson.*

Hôtel de Ville. [Louvain.] A splendid edifice in Louvain, Belgium, used for municipal purposes, and one of the finest Gothic buildings in the world.

☞ "The well-known and beautiful town-hall at Louvain is certainly the most elaborately decorated piece of Gothic architecture in existence. Though perhaps a little overdone in some parts, the whole is so consistent, and the outline and general scheme of decoration so good, that little fault can be found with it. In design it follows very closely the hall at Bruges, but wants the tower which gives such dignity to those at Brussels and at Ypres." *Fergusson.*

Hôtel de Ville. [Ypres.] A noted building in Ypres, Belgium, restored in 1860, and now used for municipal purposes. It was originally called the Halle, or Cloth-Hall, cloth having been the great staple manufacture of Belgium during the Middle Ages.

☞ "The cloth-hall at Ypres is by far the most magnificent and beautiful of these [trade-halls], as also the earliest. The foundation-stone was laid in 1200 by Baldwin of Constantinople, but it was not finished till 104 years afterwards. The façade is 440 feet in length, and of the simplest possible design, being perfectly straight and unbroken from end to end. . . . Its height is varied by the noble belfry which rises from its centre, and by a bold and beautiful pinnacle at each end. The whole is of the pure architecture of the thirteenth century, and is one of the most majestic edifices of its class to be seen anywhere." *Fergusson.*

Hôtel de Ville, Place de l'. See PLACE DE L' HÔTEL DE VILLE.

Hôtel des Invalides. See INVALIDES.

Hôtel des Monnaies. A handsome classical edifice near the Pont Neuf, Paris, built in 1775. The mint of Paris is the principal one in France. The rate at which coins can be struck off is about 1,500,000 per day. In the Museum are interesting collections of coins, medals, models, etc. The establishment also contains, besides the workshops for coining, laboratories for assaying.

Hôtel Dieu. A magnificent hospital in Paris, on the river Seine. Its wards are on both sides of the river. It was established as early as the seventh century, and has been richly endowed by various kings, nobles, and wealthy men. All the arrangements are on the most liberal scale. This name is given to the chief hospital of many places.

Hôtel Lambert. A handsome structure on the Ile St. Louis, Paris, of the style of architecture under Louis XIV. Voltaire lived here; and here, in 1815, Napoleon held one of his last conferences.

Hôtel St. Aignan. An old aristocratic hotel of Paris, where lived the Duc d' Avaux, and later the Duc de St. Aignan. The gateway and court, with Corinthian pilasters, are left.

Hôtel St. Paul. A former palace of Paris, built by Charles V. about 1364. Nothing now remains of it.

Hotoie, La. A fine promenade in the city of Amiens, France. It covers 52 acres.

Houghton Hall. A splendid mansion in the county of Norfolk, England, formerly the residence of Sir Robert Walpole, and famous for the rare collection of pictures which it contained. Most of the pictures are now dispersed; the greater part, having been sold to the Empress of Russia, are now at St. Petersburg. The estate now belongs to the Marquis of Cholmondeley.

Hougoumont. A mansion in the neighborhood of Waterloo, noted for its importance in connection with the battle upon that field. [Written also *Goumont*.]

Nor wood, nor tree, nor bush, are there,
Her course to intercept or scare,
Nor fosse nor fence are found,
Save where, from out her shatter'd bowers,
Rise *Hougoumont's* dismantled towers.
Scott.

Hounsditch *or* **Houndsditch.** This is the centre of the Jews' quarter in London, so called from the ancient foss around the city, once a receptacle for dead dogs.

☞ "From Aldgate, north-west to Bishopsgate, lieth the ditch of the city, called Houndsditch; for that in old time, when the same lay open, much filth (conveyed from the city), especially dead dogs, were there laid or cast." *Stow.*

More knavery and usury,
And foolery and trickery, than *Dogsditch*.
Beaumont and Fletcher.

If it please Heaven, we shall all yet make our Exodus from *Houndsditch*, and bid the sordid continents, of once rich apparel now grown poisonous *Ou'-clo'*, a mild farewell! *Carlyle.*

Hounslow Heath. A region once open and infested by highwaymen, but now enclosed, adjacent to Hounslow, in Middlesex County, England.

☞ "The waste tracts which lay on the great routes near London were especially haunted by plunderers of this class. Hounslow Heath, on the great Western road, and Finchley Common, on the great Northern road, were perhaps the most celebrated of these spots." *Macaulay.*

House. For names beginning with HOUSE, see the next prominent word. See also *infra.*

House of Commons. One of the houses of Parliament in the New Palace at Westminster, London.

☞ "The principal chamber of the manufactory of statute law."
Quarterly Review.

House of Lords, *or* **House of Peers.** One of the houses of Parliament, magnificently and richly fitted up, in the New Palace at Westminster, London.

Houses of Parliament. See WESTMINSTER PALACE.

Howard. See CASTLE HOWARD.

Howe's Cave. A natural curiosity in Schoharie County, N.Y. The cave has been penetrated a distance of eight or ten miles, and visitors usually go as far as three or four miles. It was discovered in 1842, and is thought to be hardly surpassed by any cavern except the Mammoth Cave in Kentucky. [Sometimes called also the *Otsgaragee Cavern.*]

Hoy, Old Man of. See OLD MAN OF HOY.

Hradschin, The. The ancient palace of the Bohemian kings, in Prague, Austria. This imposing pile was begun in 1541, but not completed till 200 years later. There are said to be 440 apartments in it. It commands a noble view.

Aloft on the mountain, with prospect over city, river, and wood-grown isles, his old *Hradschin* beaming in the sun.
Hans Christian Andersen.

Huguenot, The. A well-known picture by J. E. Millais (b. 1829).

☞ "The incident of the 'Huguenot' picture is founded on the order of the Duc de Guise, that each good Catholic should, on the eve of St. Bartholomew, bind a strip of white linen round his arm, as a badge to be known by." *Sarah Tytler.*

Huis in 't Bosch. [House in the Wood.] A palace in a wooded park in the environs of the Hague, Holland.

Human Life. See REPRESENTATION OF HUMAN LIFE.

Humane Society. See DISTINGUISHED MEMBER OF THE HUMANE SOCIETY.

Hume Castle. A picturesque ruined castle near Kelso in Scotland, once the residence of the Earls of Home.

Humphrey's Walk. See DUKE HUMPHREY'S WALK.

Hungerford Market. A well-known London market.

He [Charles Dickens] informed me as he walked through it, that he knew *Hunger*ford market well. *Payne Collier.*

Hünnengräber. [Graves of the Huns.] Curious sepulchral mounds and stone monuments in which ashes and bones have been found, in the island of Rügen in the Baltic.

Hunnenschlacht. See BATTLE OF THE HUNS.

Hunted Stag. A picture by Sir Edwin Landseer (1802-1873). In the National Gallery, London.

Huss before the Council of Constance. A noted and elaborately finished picture by Karl Friedrich Lessing (b. 1808). In the Städel Institute at Frankfort-on-the-Main, Germany.

☞ "It is said that this picture has had a great effect upon Catholics who have seen it, in softening the bigotry with which they regarded the early reformers; and if so, it is a triumphant proof how much art can effect in the cause of truth and humanity."
Bayard Taylor.

☞ "A most glorious picture here. The Trial of John Huss before the Council of Constance, by Lessing. . . . The painter has arrayed with consummate ability in the foreground a representation of the religious respectability of the age: Italian cardinals in their scarlet robes . . . men whom it were no play to meet in an argument, — all that expressed the stateliness and grandeur of what Huss had been educated to consider the true church. In the midst of them stands Huss in a simple dark robe: his sharpened features tell of prison and of suffering. He is defending himself, and there is a trembling earnestness in the manner with which his hand grasps the Bible. With a passionate agony he seems to say, Am I not right? Does not this Word say it? and is it not the word of God?"
Beecher.

Hyde Park. A large pleasure-ground in London, extending from Piccadilly westward to Kensington Gardens. It is the site of the ancient manor of Hyde. For nearly two centuries it has been the scene of military reviews and spectacles. Hyde Park was enclosed about the middle of the sixteenth century. It was opened to the public during the time of Charles I. Reform meetings and other turbulent gatherings have frequently been held here, which have been sometimes attended with violence.

☞ "In this Park, in the London season, from May to August (between 11 and 1, and 5½ and 7), may be seen all the wealth and fashion and splendid equipages of the nobility and gentry of Great Britain. As many as 800 equestrians, including the Knot at the music, have been seen assembled at Hyde Park in the height of the season."
Murray's Handbook.

☞ "Hyde Park . . . with its small rivulet, its wide greensward, its sheep, its shady walks, resembling a pleasure-park suddenly transported to the centre of a capital." *Taine, Trans.*

Now, at *Hyde Park*, if fair it be,
A show of ladies you may see.
Poor Robin's Almanack (*May*, 1698).

At fourscore he [the Duke of Schomberg] retained a strong relish for innocent pleasures; he conversed with great courtesy and sprightliness; nothing could be in better taste than his equipages and his table; and every cornet of cavalry envied the grace and dignity with which the veteran appeared in *Hyde Park* on his charger at the head of his regiment.

Macaulay.

Sooner shall grass in *Hyde-park* circus grow,
And wits take lodgings in the sound of Bow!
Sooner let air, earth, sea, to chaos fall,
Men, monkeys, lap-dogs, parrots, perish all! *Pope.*

2. A public pleasure-ground in St. Louis, Mo.

Hyder Ali. A vessel belonging to the State of Pennsylvania, which, in 1782, captured the British ship *General Monk*, in Delaware Bay, an exploit pronounced by Cooper "one of the most brilliant actions that ever occurred under the American flag." See MONK, THE.

I.

Iberian Madonna. The name given to a miraculous picture of the Virgin and Child, placed in a niche lighted with silver lamps, in the Kremlin at Moscow, Russia. The picture was originally brought from Mt. Athos.

☞ "For the last 200 years, the protectress of the Muscovites. Her aid is invoked by high and low, in all the circumstances of life; and I doubt whether any other shrine in the world is the witness of such general and so much real devotion." *Bayard Taylor.*

Ice Palace. The Empress Anne of Russia, who reigned from 1730 to 1740, took into her head a "most magnificent and mighty freak." One of her nobles, Prince Galitzin, having changed his religion, was punished by being made a court page and buffoon. His wife being dead, the empress required him to marry again, agreeing to defray the expense of the wedding herself. The prince, true to his new character, selected a girl of low birth. This was in the winter of 1739–40, which was one of extraordinary severity. By her majesty's command, a house was built entirely of ice. It consisted of two rooms; and all the furniture, even to the bedstead, was made of the same material. Four small cannons and two mortars, also of ice, were placed in front of the house, and were fired several times without bursting, small wooden grenades being thrown from the mortars. On the wedding-day a procession was formed, composed of more than 300 persons of both sexes, whom the empress — desirous of of seeing how many different kinds of inhabitants there were in her vast dominions — had caused the governors of the various provinces to send to St. Petersburg. The bride and bridegroom were conspicuously placed in a great iron cage on the back of an elephant. Of the guests (all of whom were dressed in the costume of their respective countries), some were mounted on camels; others were in sledges — a man and a woman in each — drawn by beasts of all descriptions, as reindeer, oxen, goats, dogs, hogs, and the like. After passing before the imperial palace, and marching through the principal streets of the city, the motley cavalcade proceeded to the Duke of Courland's riding-house, where dinner was served to each after the manner of cookery in his own country. The feast over, there was a ball, those from each nation having their own music and their own style of dancing. When the ball was ended, the newly-married pair were conducted to their palace of ice, and guards were stationed at the door to prevent their going out until morning. The building is said to have lasted uninjured, in that cold climate, for several months.

No forest fell
When thou wouldst build, no quarry sent its stores
To enrich thy walls; but thou didst hew the floods,
And make thy marble of the glassy wave.
Cowper.

Icebergs, The. A noted picture by Frederic Edwin Church (b. 1826), the American landscape painter.

Idle and Industrious Apprentices. A series of pictures by William Hogarth (1697–1764).

☞ "What a living and breathing gallery of old English life we have in Hogarth's series of the 'Idle and Industrious Apprentices,' and how perfect it is as far as it goes. It is complete and self-consistent, from the first picture where the ill-conditioned, ill-looking lad sits dozing, neglecting his work, with the evil ballad of 'Moll Flanders' hung up on his loom; while the pleasant, comely-faced youth is sedulously minding his business, with the volume of the 'Apprentices' Guide' lying open before him, through each intervening stage of the rise and fall . . . on to the noble pathos of the last meeting of the early companions, when the justice on the bench hides his face after pronouncing condemnation on the felon at the bar." *Sarah Tytler.*

Idle Servant Maid. A picture by Nicolas Maas (1632–1693), the Dutch *genre*-painter, and one of his principal works. In the National Gallery, London.

Idlewild. An estate on the Hudson River, near the village of Cornwall, N. Y., formerly the home of N. P. Willis.

Idolino, L'. [The Little Image.] An ancient statue. Now in the Uffizi, Florence, Italy.

If. A famous castle, used as a state prison in part for political offenders, situated upon a small island of the same name in the Mediterranean, near Marseilles. The name is said to signify a yew-tree.

Happily, the old marquis himself, in periods of leisure, or forced leisure, whereof he had many, drew up certain "unpublished memoirs" of his father and progenitors; out of which memoirs young Mirabeau, also in forced leisure (still more forced, in the Castle of *If!*), redacted one memoir of a very readable sort: by the light of this latter, so far as it will last, we walk with convenience. *Carlyle.*

Igel Säule. [The Igel-column.] A monumental structure of Roman times near Treves, in Rhenish Prussia. It is a sandstone obelisk, 70 feet in height, with inscriptions and bas-reliefs. It is of uncertain date and origin.

Ikenild Street. An ancient Roman road in Britain. It extended from the coast of Norfolk to the south-west of Cornwall. The name is of uncertain origin.

Ildefonso Group, The. A celebrated marble group in the Museum at Madrid, Spain.

☞ "F. Tieck, the sculptor and brother of the poet, was the first to suggest that we have here Antinous, the Genius of Hadrian, and Persephone. . . . Charles Bötticher started a new solution of the principal problem. According to him it was executed in the lifetime of Antinous, and it represents . . . a sacrifice of fidelity on the part of the two friends Hadrian and Antinous, who have met together before Persephone to ratify a vow of love till death. . . . After all is said, the Ildefonso marble, like the legend of Antinous, remains a mystery." *J. A. Symonds.*

Ildefonso, San. See GRANJA, LA.

Ile de la Cité. [Island of the City.] An island, in Paris, which, previous to 1608, was divided into two parts. On this island, which is formed by two arms of the Seine, are situated Sainte Chapelle, Notre Dame, the Palais de Justice, the Préfecture de Police, the Tribunal de Commerce, the Morgue, Caserne de Gendarmerie, the Hôtel Dieu. Here is the legal quarter of Paris, — the civil, criminal, and commercial law-courts. Here was the principal part of mediæval Paris.

From the centre of the Pont Neuf we could see for a long distance up and down the river. The different bridges traced on either side a dozen starry lines through the dark air, and a continued blaze lighted the two shores in their whole length, revealing the outline of the *Isle de la Cité.* *Bayard Taylor.*

Ile de Paix. [Isle of Peace.] A little island in Lake Geneva, commanding a lovely view. It is referred to by Byron in the "Prisoner of Chillon."

And then there was a little isle,
Which in my very face did smile,
The only one in view.

Ile St. Louis. An island in the Seine at Paris, France.

Ilioneus. An admired antique kneeling figure in the Glyptothek, or gallery of sculptures, at Munich, Bavaria.

☞ "The head and arms are wanting; but the supplicatory expression of the attitude, the turn of the body, the bloom of adolescence, which seems absolutely shed over the cold marble, the unequalled delicacy and elegance of the whole, touched me deeply." *Mrs. Jameson.*

Immaculate Conception [of the Virgin Mary]. A picture by Giuseppe Ribera, called Lo Spagnoletto (1588-1656), and one of his chief works. In the gallery of Madrid, Spain.

Immaculate Conception. See GREAT CONCEPTION OF SEVILLE.

Inarimé. A ruined castle at Ischia, once occupied by Vittoria Colonna.

High o'er the sea-surge and the sands,
Like a great galleon wrecked and cast
Ashore by storms, thy castle stands
A mouldering landmark of the Past.

Inarimé! Inarimé!
Thy castle on the crags above
In dust shall crumble and decay,
But not the memory of her love.
Longfellow.

Incendio del Borgo. [Burning of the Borgo.] A celebrated fresco by Raphael Sanzio (1483–1520), representing the fire in the Borgo, or suburb, of Rome, which was miraculously extinguished by the Pope. It is in a chamber of the Vatican, Rome, called, after this picture, the Stanza del Incendio.

Incendio del Borgo. See STANZE OF RAPHAEL.

Inchcape, or Bell Rock. The celebrated and dangerous sunken reef known as the Inch Cape, or Bell Rock, is in the German Ocean, on the northern side of the entrance of the Firth of Forth, and about twelve miles from land. An abbot of Aberbrothock (Arbroath) is said to have placed a bell here, as a warning to sailors, which was cut loose by a Dutch rover, who, as a retribution for this mischievous act, was subsequently wrecked upon the very same rock. This story, which is an old tradition, is told by Southey in his well-known ballad of "The Inchcape Rock." See BELL ROCK LIGHT-HOUSE.

☞ "In old times upon the saide rock there was a bell fixed upon a timber, which rang continually, being moved by the sea, giving notice to saylers of the danger. This bell was put there and maintained by the abbot of Aberbrothock; but, being taken down by a sea-pirate, a yeare thereafter he perished upon the same rocke, with ship and goodes, in the righteous judgement of God."
Stoddart, Remarks on Scotland.

The Abbot of Aberbrothock
Had placed that bell on the *Inchcape rock*.
On a buoy in the storm it floated and swung,
And over the waves its warning rung.
When the rock was hid by the surge's swell
The mariners heard the warning bell;
And then they knew the perilous rock,
And blessed the Abbot of Aberbrothock.
Southey.

Incredulity of St. Thomas. A picture by Giovanni Battista Cima, called le Conegliano (b. about 1460). Now in the National Gallery, London. There is another work of a similar character in the Brera, Milan, Italy.

Incredulity of St. Thomas. A distinguished picture by Giovanni Francesco Barbieri, surnamed Guercino (1590–1666). In the Vatican, Rome.

Independence, Fort. See FORT INDEPENDENCE.

Independence Hall. A building on Chestnut Street, Philadelphia, rich in historical associations, and regarded as the birthplace of the American Republic. Here the Continental Congress assembled. Here in June, 1775, George Washington was chosen commander of the American forces. Here on July 4, 1776, the Declaration of Independence was adopted by Congress, and read to a great multitude assembled in front of the building amidst the ringing of bells and prodigious enthusiasm. It is from this circumstance that the edifice derived its name. The halls are now used as a museum and a receptacle for curiosities and relics connected with the history of the country. It contains portraits of the Revolutionary patriots, specimens of old furniture, autographs, and other *souvenirs* of the past, including the famous Liberty Bell.

Independence Square. A public ground in Philadelphia, Penn., contiguous to Independence Hall, from which the Declaration of Independence was read to the people assembled in the square.

India Docks. See EAST INDIA DOCKS and WEST INDIA DOCKS.

India House. See EAST INDIA HOUSE.

India Museum. A celebrated collection of curiosities formerly in the East India House (*q.v.*), afterwards in Fife House, Whitehall, and now at the South Kensington Museum. Large additions have been made to the old collection, exhibiting the riches and resources of British India. It contains, besides historical relics and antiquities, specimens of the natural productions, arts, manufactures, etc., of India.

Indian Chief. A statue by Thomas Crawford (1818-1857). In the hall of the New York Historical Society.

Indian Hill. An old mansion near Newburyport, Mass., the residence of Ben: Perley Poore. It is noted for the historical curiosities which it contains.

Indianola, The. A powerful ironclad steamer of the United States navy in the civil war in 1861-65. She ran safely the batteries at Vicksburg, but was finally captured by a Confederate "ram."

Industrie, Palais de l'. See PALAIS DE L'INDUSTRIE.

Infant Hercules strangling the Serpents. A mythological picture by Sir Joshua Reynolds (1723-1792), the celebrated English portrait-painter. It was painted for the Empress of Russia, and is regarded as one of his best works.

Inferno. [Hell.] A celebrated fresco by Andrea di Cioni, called Orcagna (1325?-1385?). In the Campo Santo, Pisa, Italy.

Influence of Christianity in the Arts. A large and noted picture by Friedrich Overbeck (1789-1869). In the Städel Institut, Frankfort-on-the-Main.

☞ "Among the oil-paintings by Overbeck, the Triumph of Religion in the Arts, one of the choicest treasures in the Städel Institute, is certainly the most elaborate and ambitious. This grand composition, which may be likened in its intent to Raphael's 'School of Athens,' or to the 'Hemicycle' by Delaroche, has been aptly termed by German critics the 'Christian Parnassus,' the dawn of light in Europe."

I. B. Atkinson.

Inghirami, Fedra. A portrait by Raphael Sanzio (1483-1520). In the Pitti palace, Florence, Italy.

Iniscealtra. [Holy Island.] An islet in the Shannon, in the county of Clare, Ireland, famous from very early ages for its reputed sanctity.

☞ "It possesses structures belonging to the Pagan as well as Christian periods, — a round tower, and seven small churches, or rather cells, or oratories. The round tower is about 70 feet high, and is in good preservation. . . . Holy Island continues a favorite burial-place with the peasantry; and although its religious establishments are ruined and desecrated, the ancient sanctity of its character still endures, and pilgrims from remote distances seek its shores. On the *patron*, or festival, day of St. Camin (12th of March), the crowd of these devotees is very great."

Mr. and Mrs. Hall.

Inner Temple. One of the four Inns of Court in London which have the exclusive privilege of conferring the degree of barrister-at-law requisite for practising as an advocate or counsel in the superior courts. The gentlemen of the Inner Temple were of old famed for their plays, masques, revels, and other sumptuous entertainments. Among the eminent members were Littleton and Coke, Sir Christopher Hatton, Selden, Judge Jeffreys, and the poets Beaumont and Cowper. The Inns of Court have always been celebrated for the beauty of their gardens. In the "Temple Garden," Shakespeare has laid the scene of the origin of the red and white roses as the cognizances of the houses of York and Lancaster. The red and white Provence rose no longer blossoms here; but the gardens are carefully kept, and are very attractive.

In signal of my love to thee,
Against proud Somerset and William Poole,
Will I upon thy party wear this rose:
And here I prophesy, — this brawl to-day,
Grown to this faction, in the *Temple Garden*,

Shall send, between the red rose and the white,
A thousand souls to death and deadly night.

Shakespeare, Henry VI., Pt. 1.

☞ "I was born, and passed the first seven years of my life, in the Temple. Its church, its halls, its gardens, its fountain, its river I had almost said, — for in those young years, what was this king of rivers to me but a stream that watered our pleasant places? — these are of my oldest recollections. I repeat, to this day, no verses to myself more frequently, or with kindlier emotion, than those of Spenser, where he speaks of this spot.

There when they came, whereas those bricky towers,
The which on Themmes brode aged back doth ride,
Where now the studious lawyers have their bowers,
There whylome wont the Templer knights to bide
Till they decayed through pride.

Indeed, it is the most elegant spot in the metropolis. What a transition for a countryman visiting London for the first time, — the passing from the crowded Strand or Fleet Street, by unexpected avenues, into its ample squares, its classic green recesses! What a cheerful, liberal look hath that portion of it which, from three sides, overlooks the greater garden;

That goodly pile
Of building strong, albeit of Paper hight,

confronting, with massy contrast, the lighter, older, more fantastically shrouded one, named of Harcourt, with the cheerful Crown-office Row (place of my kindly engendure), right opposite the stately stream which washes the garden-foot with her yet scarcely trade-polluted waters, and seems but just weaned from her Twickenham Naiads! a man would give something to have been born in such places."

Charles Lamb.

Innocents. See FONTAINE DES INNOCENTS and MASSACRE OF THE INNOCENTS.

Inns of Court. The name given to the celebrated law-colleges in London, known respectively as the Inner Temple, Middle Temple, Lincoln's Inn, and Gray's Inn. The Inns of Court were so called because the students of the law belonged to the "King's Court." James I. is said to have declared that there were only three classes of persons who had any right to settle in London, — "the courtiers, the citizens, and the gentlemen of the Inns of Court." The lawyers were unpopular in the time of Jack Cade's rebellion; and Shakespeare, in "Henry VI.," represents Jack Cade as saying, "Now go some and pull down the Savoy; others the Inns of Court; down with them all!" See INNER TEMPLE, MIDDLE TEMPLE, LINCOLN'S INN, and GRAY'S INN.

"The Inns of Court are interesting to others besides lawyers, for they are the last working institutions in the nature of the old trade-guilds. It is no longer necessary that a shoemaker should be approved by the company of the craft before he can apply himself to making shoes for his customers; and a man may keep an oyster-stall without being forced to serve an apprenticeship, and be admitted to the Livery of the great Whig Company; but the lawyers' guilds guard the entrance to the law, and prescribe the rules under which it shall be practised."

Times Journal.

The lawyers discussed law or literature, criticised the last new play, or retailed the freshest Westminster Hall "bite" at Nando's or the Grecian, both close on the purlieus of the Temple. Here the young bloods of the *Inns of Court* paraded their Indian gowns and lace caps of a morning, and swaggered in their lace coats and Mechlin ruffles at night, after the theatre.

National Review.

They [Christ-Churchmen] were dominant at Oxford, powerful in the *Inns of Court* and in the College of Physicians, conspicuous in parliament and in the literary and fashionable circles of London.

Macaulay.

Institut, Palais de l'. See PALAIS DE L'INSTITUT.

Insurgente, L'. [The Insurgent.] A famous French frigate of 40 guns, captured by the United States vessel of war *Constellation*, in 1798. The *Insurgente* was at that time one of the fastest sailing vessels in the world.

Intermontium. The ancient Latin name of the place in Rome now occupied by the Piazza del Campidoglio. See PIAZZA DEL CAMPIDOGLIO.

Intrepid, The. 1. A famous vessel, originally a Tripolitan ketch, captured by Stephen Decatur, and in which he accomplished his brilliant naval exploit of destroying vessels in the harbor of Tripoli, Feb. 16, 1804. Later, the *Intrepid* was used as a floating mine to destroy the Tripolitan cruisers in the harbor. The ship was exploded with a terrible concussion, but the brave men who went on the expedition never returned.

☞ "Nearly fourscore years their fate has been an impenetrable secret. At the front of the midshipmen's quarters at Annapolis [Md.] stands a fine monument erected to their memory, and of those who perished on the 7th of August, by the officers of the navy. The monument is of white marble, and is about 40 feet in height." *Lossing.*

2. An Arctic exploring ship which set sail from England under Commander Austin in 1850.

Invalides, Hôtel des. One of the chief public monuments of Paris. It was begun by Louis XIV. in 1671, as an asylum for the soldiers wounded and maimed in his numerous wars. At the revolution of 1793 it was called the Temple of Humanity; under the reign of Napoleon, the Temple of Mars. The building is capable of containing 5,000 persons. Its library and council chamber contain some interesting objects, but the church is the most attractive part of the institution. The portico and dome are exceedingly beautiful, as is also the interior of the church. It contains the grand mausoleum of Napoleon, and his remains as they were brought from St. Helena. Bertrand and Duroc, the near friends and companions of Napoleon, lie on each side of the entrance of the crypt that leads to his tomb.

☞ "In the afternoon we went to the Hôtel des Invalides, which contains 3,000 old soldiers. Those who were wounded in the Crimean campaign are, however, nearly all sent to their own homes with an allowance of six hundred francs." *Count Moltke, Trans.*

☞ "The dome of the Invalides rises upon the eye from all parts of Paris, a perfect model of proportion and beauty. It was this which Bonaparte ordered to be gilded, to divert the people from thinking too much upon his defeat. . . . The interior of the dome is vast, and of a splendid style of architecture; and out from one of its sides extends a superb chapel hung all round with the tattered flags taken in his victories alone." *N. P. Willis.*

The Lion [of St. Mark's] has lost nothing by his journey to the *Invalides* but the Gospel which supported the paw that is now on a level with the other foot. *Byron.*

The beautiful sarcophagus of Scipio, the silent soldier of the *Invalides*, yet speaks in graceful epitaphs. *H. T. Tuckerman.*

I walked the day out, listening to the chink
Of the first Napoleon's dry bones, as they lay
In his second grave beneath the golden dome
That caps all Paris like a bubble.
Mrs. Browning.

Inverary Castle. A baronial mansion near Inverary, Scotland, the seat of the Duke of Argyle.

Inverleithen. A watering-place at the junction of the Leithen Water and Tweed, somewhat celebrated for its mineral springs. This spot is the scene of "St. Ronan's Well."

Inverna. The name given in some parts of Italy to a wind blowing from the south.

Investigator, The. An Arctic exploring ship, the companion ship to the *Enterprise*, in Sir James Ross's expedition, set sail from England in 1848.

Invincible Armada. See Armada, The Invincible.

Io and Jupiter. A picture by Antonio Allegri, surnamed Correggio (1494–1534). In the Museum of Berlin, Prussia. The head of this picture, which was formerly in the Orleans Gallery, was cut out by the son of its owner, the Duke of Orleans, "because it was too voluptuous in expression." Another was substituted by Prud'hon. A replica of this picture, or what is believed to be such, is in the gallery at Vienna, Austria.

Ireland Yard. A locality in London, England. So called from one William Ireland. His name occurs in a deed by which a house on this site was conveyed to Shakespeare.

Iron Crown (of Lombardy). A famous crown, consisting of "a broad fillet of gold, within which runs a thin circlet or hoop of iron, formed of one of the nails of the Holy Cross beaten out." It is said to have been brought from the Holy Land by the Empress Helena. As many as 34 kings, including the emperors Charles V. and Napoleon Bonaparte, have been crowned with it. Until the year 1859 it was kept in the Chapel of the Holy Nail (Santo Chiodo) in the Cathedral of St. John, in Monza, Italy; but it is now preserved in the Belvedere Museum at Vienna, Austria, the model alone being shown at Monza.

Iron Gates. A celebrated pass on the Lower Danube, near Gladova, where a spur of the Transylvanian Alps nearly barricades the river.

☞ "A mile and a half of slow, trembling, exciting progress, and we have mounted the heaviest grade; but six hours of the same tremendous scenery awaits us. We pierce yet sublimer solitudes, and look on pictures of precipice and piled rock, of cavern and yawning gorge, and mountain walls, almost shutting out the day, such as no other river in Europe can show."
Bayard Taylor.

Iron Mask. A black mask, not of iron, as the popular name would imply, but of black velvet, stiffened with whalebone, and fastened behind the head with a padlock or by steel springs. It owes its celebrity to the fact that in the reign of Louis XIV. it served to conceal the features of the mysterious state prisoner of France, known in consequence as the Man with the Iron Mask (L'Homme au Masque de Fer), about whom there has been much difference of opinion, and whose identity has never been satisfactorily determined. He was secretly conveyed, about 1679, wearing this mask as a disguise, to the castle of Pignerol. In 1686 he was removed to the isle of Sainte Marguerite, and in 1698 was carried to the Bastille, where he died in 1703. He was always treated with great respect and courtesy, but was continually watched, and during all these years of imprisonment was never seen without the concealment of the Iron Mask.

☞ He has been variously conjectured to have been a son of Anne of Austria and Cardinal Mazarin (Gibbon argues in favor of this theory); a twin brother of Louis XIV. (Voltaire, among others, adopts this view); the Duke of Monmouth; and Fouquet. Among these and other suppositions, the one now generally received is, that the disguised prisoner was a Count Matthioli, a minister of Charles III., Duke of Mantua. Delort and Lord Dover adopted this explanation, which is favored in Topin's "Man with the Iron Mask," 1869, but disputed by other recent writers. Another theory is, that he was a conspirator against Louis XIV., known as Lefroid. Iung holds this view in his "La Vérité sur le Masque de Fer," Paris, 1873; but the whole matter is involved in entire uncertainty. Dumas has a story concerning this famous prisoner, entitled "The Iron Mask."

It varied, till I don't think his own mother
(If that he had a mother) would her son
Have known, he shifted so from one to
t'other;
Till guessing from a pleasure grew a task,
At this epistolary "*Iron Mask.*" *Byron.*

Iron Virgin. [Ger. *Die Eiserne Jungfrau.*] A famous instrument of torture, of a kind not uncommon in the Middle Ages, still existing in Nuremberg, Germany. It represents a girl of the fifteenth century. The front, when opened by a spring, discloses the interior lined with pointed spikes which pierced the victim who was forced into it. Beneath is a trap-door into which the body fell.

Ironmongers' Hall. The building of the Ironmongers' Company, one of the old London city companies. In Fenchurch Street.

Isaac of York. A painting by Washington Allston (1779–1843).

Now in the Museum of Fine Arts, Boston, Mass.

Isaac, Sacrifice of. See SACRIFICE OF ISAAC.

Isabella. A portrait of Isabella, Governess of the Low Countries, by Anthony van Dyck (1599-1641). There are several portraits of this princess by this painter, the best being the one now in the Vienna Gallery.

Isaiah. A picture of the prophet on a pillar of the church of S. Augustine, Rome.

☞ "In the church of the Augustines is Raphael's inimitable fresco of Isaiah, — a work sufficient of itself to have crowned his name with immortality. The fire and fervor of the prophet beam from that inspired and holy countenance. Even in force and sublimity it will bear a comparison with the Prophets and Sibyls which Michael Angelo has left in the Sistine Chapel." *Eaton.*

Isaiah's Tree. An ancient and venerable mulberry tree in Jerusalem, its trunk propped up by a pile of stones, and deriving its name from the circumstance that it, according to tradition, marks the spot where Manasseh caused the prophet Isaiah to be sawn in two.

Isis, Temple of. See TEMPLE OF ISIS.

Isle of Dogs. An island — formerly a peninsula, but made an island by a canal cut in 1800 — lying in the river Thames, and constituting a part of London. The name is said by some to be a corruption from the Isle of Ducks, from the numbers of wild fowl formerly upon it.

Granted, the ship comes into harbor with shrouds and tackle damaged; and the pilot is therefore blame-worthy, for he has not been all-wise and all-powerful: but to know *how* blameworthy, tell us first whether his voyage has been round the Globe, or only to Ramsgate and the *Isle of Dogs*. *Carlyle.*

Isle. See ILE.

Islington. Now a part of London, but originally two miles north of the town. Said to be so called from Isheldun, the Lower Fortress. Before the reign of James I. it was a favorite place for the practise of archery. Macaulay, speaking of this now populated district, says, that in the time of Charles I. Islington was almost a solitude; and poets loved to contrast its silence and repose with the din and turmoil of the monster London. [Also called *Iseldon, Yseldon, Eyseldon, Isondon, Isendune.*]

Hogsdone, *Islington*, and Tothnam Court,
For cakes and creame had then no small
resort. *Wither* (1628).

Let but thy wicked men from out thee
[London] go,
And all the fools that crowd thee so,
Ev'n thou, who dost thy millions boast,
A village less than *Islington* will grow,
A solitude almost. *Cowley.*

London has got a great way from the
streame.
I think she means to go to *Islington*.
To eat a dish of strawberries and creame.
Thomas Freeman's Epigrams (1614).

"It used to be called *Merry Islington* once upon a time. Perhaps it's merry now, if so, it's all the better." — *Tom Pinch.* *Dickens.*

Tom, Tom, of *Islington*,
Married a wife on Sunday;
Brought her home on Monday;
Hired a house on Tuesday;
Fed her well on Wednesday;
Sick was she on Thursday;
Dead was she on Friday;
Sad was Tom on Saturday,
To bury his wife on Sunday.
Mother Goose.

Isly, Battle of. See BATTLE OF ISLY.

Isnah, Temple of. See TEMPLE OF ISNAH.

Isola Bella. [The beautiful island.] An island (one of the so-called Borromean Isles) upon Lago Maggiore, famed for its beauty.

O fairy island of a fairy sea,
Wherein Calypso might have spelled the
Greek,
Or Flora piled her fragrant treasury.
Lord Lytton.

Isola Bella, Palace and Gardens of. A famous show-palace, with a delightful prospect and elaborate pleasure-grounds, on the island of Isola Bella (one of the so-called Borromean Isles) in Lago Maggiore, Italy.

☞ "Isola Bella looks like a gentleman's villa afloat. A boy would throw a stone entirely over it in any direction. It strikes you as a kind of toy, as you look at it from a distance: and, getting nearer, the illusion scarcely dissipates; for, from the water's edge, the orange-laden terraces are piled, one above another, like a pyramidal fruit-basket, the villa itself peers above like a sugar castle; and it scarce seems real enough to land upon." *N. P. Willis.*

Isola Madre. [The Mother Island.] A celebrated island in the Lago Maggiore, one of the four called the Borromean Islands.

Issus, Battle of the. See BATTLE OF THE ISSUS.

Italiens, Boulevart des. The gayest and most frequented of the boulevards of Paris. A modern enthusiast of Paris says, "France is the centre of civilized nations, Paris is the centre of France, the *boulevard des Italiens* is the centre of Paris." See BOULEVARDS.

Italy. See ANCIENT ITALY and MODERN ITALY.

Itaska, The. A noted vessel of the United States Navy in the civil war of 1861-65. She was one of Admiral Farragut's flotilla at the attack upon the defences of Mobile, Aug. 5, 1864.

Ivan Veliki. [Tower of John the Great.] A famous tower in the Kremlin at Moscow, Russia. This tower rises to the height of 209 feet, and is surmounted by a gided dome.

☞ "Before us rises the tower of Ivan Veliki, whose massive sturdy walls seem to groan under its load of monster bells. At the foot of the tower stands on a granite pedestal the *Tzar Kolokol*, or Emperor of Bells, whose renown is world-wide. [See EMPEROR OF BELLS.] In one of the lower stories of the tower hangs another bell cast more than a century before the Tzar Kolokol, and weighing 64 tons. Its iron tongue is swung from side to side by the united exertions of three men. It is only rung thrice a year; and when it speaks, all other bells are silent. To those who stand near the tower, the vibration of the air is said to be like that which follows the simultaneous discharge of a hundred cannon. In the other stories hang at least 40 or 50 bells, varying in weight from 36 tons to 1,000 pounds: some of them are one-third silver. When they all sound at once, as on an Easter morn, the very tower must rock on its foundation." *Bayard Taylor.*

Ivy-Lane Club. This London club, founded by Dr. Johnson in 1749, met on Tuesday evenings at the King's Head, Ivy Lane, Paternoster Row. See ESSEX-HEAD CLUB.

I remember to have read in some philosopher, — I believe in Tom Brown's works, — that, let a man's character, sentiments, or complexion be what they will, he can find company in London to match them. . . . If he be phlegmatic, he may sit in silence in the hum-drum club in *Ivy-Lane;* and if actually mad, he may find very good company in Moorfields, either at Bedlam or the Foundery, ready to cultivate a nearer acquaintance. *Goldsmith.*

Izaak Church. A church in St. Petersburg, Russia, begun by the Empress Catherine, and completed by Nicholas I. It is a magnificent structure, with a gilded dome, and one of the most remarkable sights of the Russian capital. The foundation alone, of piles, is said to have cost $1,000,000.

☞ "The finest building in Russia — in all Northern Europe, indeed — is the Cathedral of St. Izaak. Thirty-two years of uninterrupted labor, backed by the unlimited resources of the Empire, were required to complete this gigantic work. Its cost is estimated at 90,000,000 rubles, or $67,500,-000. The design is simple and majestic; and the various parts are so nicely balanced and harmonized, that at first sight the cathedral appears smaller than is really the case. It grows upon the eye with each visit. . . . Crowning this sublime pile is the golden hemisphere of the dome, which so flashes in the sunlight that the eye can scarcely bear its splendor. Far out over the Gulf of Finland, it glitters over the evening horizon like a rising star." *Bayard Taylor.*

See! From the Finland marshes there
'Tis proud *St. Isaac's* rears in air,
Pillar on pillar, that shining dome!
E. D. Proctor.

J.

Jacinto, San. See SAN JACINTO.

Jackson Square. A well-known public square and pleasure resort in New Orleans, La. Formerly called the Place d' Armes.

Jacob and Rachel. A well-known picture ascribed to Giorgio Barbarelli, commonly called Giorgione (1477-1511), in the Dresden Gallery. This picture has also been attributed to Palma Vecchio, and of late, by some, to Cariani, of Bergamo, Italy.

Jacob blessing the Sons of Joseph. A picture by Rembrandt van Ryn (1606-1669), the Dutch painter. It bears date 1656, and is now in the gallery of Cassel, Germany.

Jacob. See FUITE DE JACOB and VISION OF JACOB.

Jacobin Club. A famous political association organized in Paris, France, shortly before the Revolution of 1789. It derives its name from the monastery of Jacobin friars, where its meetings were held.

Jacob's Dream. A fresco by Raphael Sanzio (1483-1520). In the Stanza of the Heliodorus, in the Vatican, Rome.

Jacob's Dream. A picture by Rembrandt van Ryn (1606-1669), the Dutch painter. Now in the Dulwich Gallery, England.

☞ "Strange to say, the most poetical painter of angels in the seventeenth century is that inspired Dutchman, Rembrandt. For instance, look at his Jacob's Dream, at Dulwich."
Mrs. Jameson.

Jacob's Dream. A picture by Washington Allston (1779-1843), the American painter. Now at Petworth, England.

Jacob's Flight. See FUITE DE JACOB.

Jacob's Ladder. A picture by Giuseppe Ribera, called Lo Spagnoletto (1588-1656), and one of his best. In the gallery of Madrid, Spain.

Jacob's Well. A rock-hewn well, 9 feet in diameter, 75 feet or more "deep," at the foot of Mount Gerizim in Northern Palestine, traditionally held to be the ancient well of the patriarch Jacob, and the same by which Jesus sat wearied at noon, and conversed with the woman of Samaria. Over this well a church was built in very ancient times. It is alluded to by Jerome in the fourth century; and, though destroyed during the wars of the Crusades, the ruins are still traceable. All circumstances concur with the universal tradition shared in by Jews and Samaritans, by Mohammedans and Christians, to identify this well as the one spoken of in the sacred history. The water in it is at present quite variable, sometimes there being a depth of several feet, and at another time the well being entirely dry.

☞ "No scene of these ancient incidents is more clear and interesting than this. It is impossible not to see his very gestures when he spoke of 'this mountain,'—the Gerizim which rose above him,—and when he bade his hearers lift up their eyes and look on the fields, already 'white unto the harvest,' the tilled lands of Jacob's plain which stretched before him."
Miss Martineau.

Jacques, St. See ST. JACQUES.

Jama (Gama) Tooloon. See MOSQUE OF AHMED EBN TOOLOON.

James, Shrine of St. See SHRINE.

James the Apostle. A picture by Albert Dürer (1471-1528), the German painter. Presented by the Emperor Ferdinand III. to the Duke of Tuscany. Now in the Uffizi Gallery, in Florence, Italy.

James's, St. See St. James's

Janiculum, *or* **Janiculan, The.** [Lat. *Mons Janiculus.*] A hill rising abruptly on the west bank of the Tiber, at Rome. It derives its name, according to the tradition generally believed by the ancients, from Janus, the sun-god of the Latins. Numa Pompilius is said to have been buried upon Mons Janiculus. Ancus Martius, fourth king of Rome, fortified the Janiculan, and connected it with the city by the first bridge of Rome, the Pons Sublicius, celebrated in the old Roman lays as the bridge which Horatius Cocles defended against the whole Etruscan army under Porsena. The Janiculan is connected with numerous other stories of early Roman history, — with that of Caius Mucius Scævola, the young Roman patrician, who, having made his way into the camp of Porsena, with the purpose of killing him, and his intention being discovered, burned off his own right hand, to show that he feared neither torture nor death, — with that of the hostage Clœlia, who escaped from the power of Porsena by swimming across the Tiber.

Januarius, Blood of St. See Blood of St. Januarius.

Janus, Arch of. See Arch of Janus.

Japanese Palace. See Augusteum.

Jardin, Le. [The Garden.] A well-known spot in the Alps, on the Glacier de Talèfre, near Chamonix.

Jardin des Plantes. [Garden of Plants.] This garden in Paris was established by Louis XIII. in 1635. Buffon was made superintendent of it in 1729, and greatly enriched it, besides establishing its museums, galleries, and hot-houses. It has been greatly improved under recent governments; and almost every known flower, shrub, or tree may be seen here, besides a great variety of birds, beasts, and fishes. Much damage was done to it during the bombardment of 1871 by the Prussians.

☞ "This establishment combines large botanical and zoölogical gardens, connected with which are most interesting collections of natural history in every department, and comparative anatomy. The botanical garden is not to be compared to that at Kew, either in arrangement, number, or luxuriant growth of the plants; and the zoölogical one is far surpassed by that in the Regent's Park." *Murray's Handbook.*

He [Diderot] cannot work; he hopes to dissipate his melancholy by a walk; goes to the Invalides, to the Courts, to the Bibliothèque du Roi, to the *Jardin des Plantes* *Mademoiselle Diderot.*

These people all look like the doleful birds of the *Jardin des Plantes*, begilded, striped, befeathered, and sad, but roosting on a suitable perch. *Taine, Trans.*

Jardin Mabille. A famous garden in Paris (Avenue Montaigne, Champs Elysées), which is open in the evening, brilliantly illuminated, and much frequented by the populace for dancing and other amusements. It is much resorted to by "strangers and the women of the demi-monde." The Château des Fleurs is now combined with this garden.

☞ "At *Mabille.* How often I had heard it spoken of! Young men dream of it. Strangers take their wives to see it. Historians will some day speak of it. . . . At ten o'clock in the evening, I go to Mabille. It is a grand ball-night. . . . The men are said to be hired; the women exhibit themselves gratis, though they feel that they are despised. . . . A great moving circle floats around the dancers."

Taine, Trans.

☞ "There are bowers and refreshment-rooms around it, and a large saloon for wet weather; in fact, it is a Parisian Cremorne without the fireworks and amusements; smaller, but brighter and gayer. This is the best appointed and best attended of all the summer balls." *Murray's Handbook.*

I was never more surprised in my life than to see that staid, solemn, meditative, melancholy beast suddenly perk up both his long ears, and hop about over the steep paths like a goat. Not more surprised should I be to see some venerable D.D. of Princeton leading off a dance in the *Jardin Mabille.* *Beecher.*

Whether they inhabit princely houses in fashionable streets (which they often do), or not; whether their sons have graduated at the *Jardin Mabille*, or have been taken from their father's shops.
G. W. Curtis.

Jardinière, La Belle. See BELLE JARDINIÈRE.

Jarvis Gallery. A collection of early Italian pictures in the Art School of Yale College, New Haven, Conn.

Jason. A statue by Albert Bertel Thorwaldsen (1770–1844), the Danish sculptor.

Jasper Park. A public square in Savannah, Ga., named after Sergeant Jasper, a hero of the war of the Revolution.

Java, The. A British frigate captured during the war of 1812 by the United States frigate *Constitution.*

Jean Arnolfini. Portrait of, and of Jeanne de Chenany his wife, by the Flemish painter, Jan van Eyck (1370–1441). It is related that the Princess Mary, sister of Charles V., bestowed a post of 100 guldens a year upon the barber to whom it belonged. The picture is now in the National Gallery, London.

Jeanne de Chenany. See JEAN ARNOLFINI.

Jebel-er-Rahm. A sacred hill in Arabia, not far from Mecca, and a famous resort of Mohammedan pilgrims. The tradition is that it is the place where Adam received his wife after their expulsion from Paradise, and a separation of 120 years.

Jedburgh Abbey. A well-known ruined monastery in the town of Jedburgh, Scotland.

☞ "The abbey churches of Kelso and Jedburgh, as we now find them, belong either to the very end of the twelfth, or the beginning of the thirteenth, century. They display all the rude magnificence of the Norman period used in this instance not experimentally, as was too often the case in England, but as a well-understood style, whose features were fully perfected. The whole was used with a Doric simplicity and boldness which is very remarkable." *Fergusson.*

Jehoshaphat. See VALLEY OF JEHOSHAPHAT.

Jenny's Whim. A noted place of entertainment in London, said to have been established in the time of George I., and characterized in 1775 as the Vauxhall of the lower class of people. It is no longer in existence.

Jephthah and his Daughter. A work of sculpture by Hezekiah Augur (1791–1858). At Yale College, New Haven, Conn.

Jeremiah. A picture by Washington Allston (1779–1843). Now in the possession of Yale College, New Haven, Conn.

Jeremiah's Cave. See CAVE OF JEREMIAH.

Jerome Park. A park in the neighborhood of the city of New York, a mile from Fordham, "the most aristocratic race-course in America."

Jerome, St. See ST. JEROME and COMMUNION OF ST. JEROME.

Jerpoint Abbey. An ancient and impressive ruined monastery near Kilkenny, in the county of Leinster, Ireland. It was founded in 1180.

I gaze where *Jerpoint's* venerable pile
Majestic in its ruins o'er me lowers.
S. C. Hall.

Jersey, The. A vessel of the British navy used as a prison-ship, in which many Americans were confined during the Revolutionary war.

Jerusalem Chamber. An apartment in the cloisters of Westminster Abbey, London, in which the upper House of Convocation meets, and where King Henry IV. died. It is said to have derived its name from having been hung with tapestries representing the history of Jerusalem.

King Henry. Doth any name particular belong
Unto the lodging where I first did swoon?
Warwick. 'Tis called Jerusalem, my noble lord.
King Henry. Laud be to God! even there my life must end.
It hath been prophesied to me many years,
I should not die but in Jerusalem;
Which vainly I supposed the Holy Land:

But bear me to that chamber; there I'll lie;
In that Jerusalem shall Harry die.
Shakespeare, King Henry IV., Part II.

☞ "Out of these walls came the Directory, the Longer and Shorter Catechism, and that famous Confession of Faith which, alone within these islands, was imposed by law on the whole kingdom." *Dean Stanley.*

Jerusalem Coffee-house. An old house in Cornhill, London, resorted to by captains and merchants interested in eastern commerce.

Jerusalem Delivered. A series of five large frescos, taken from Tasso's poem "La Gerusalemme Liberata," by Friedrich Overbeck (1789–1869). In the Villa Massimi, Rome.

Jerusalem, Destruction of. See DESTRUCTION OF JERUSALEM.

Jerusalem Road. A road leading from Nantasket to Cohasset, Mass., following the line of the coast, with grand ocean scenery, and adorned with many fine villas.

Jerusalem Taverns. Houses in Clerkenwell, London, so called from the ancient priory of the Knights of St. John of Jerusalem.

Jesus College. A foundation of the University of Cambridge, England. Established in 1496.

Jeux Floraux, Société des. A society in Toulouse, France, claiming to be the oldest literary institution in Europe, founded in the fourteenth century, and to be derived from the ancient troubadours. It distributes annually prizes of golden and silver flowers for the best essays in prose and verse upon prescribed subjects.

Jewish Cemetery. A picture by Jacob Ruysdael (1625?–1682), the Dutch landscape painter. In the Dresden Gallery.

Jewry, Old. See OLD JEWRY.

Jews' Quarter. See GHETTO and JUDENSTADT.

☞ In the Middle Ages the Jews were commonly confined to a certain prescribed quarter of the cities in which they lived, and, as a rule, were locked in at night. Among better known districts occupied by them in European cities are the famous "Jews' Quarter" in Rome and that in Prague.

Joachim, St. See ST. JOSEPH AND ST. JOACHIM.

Joan of Arc. An admired picture by Paul Delaroche (1797–1856), the celebrated French historical painter.

Joanna of Aragon. A portrait of this famous beauty, who was the wife of Ferdinand of Aragon, by Raphael Sanzio (1483–1520), of which there are numerous repetitions. One is in the collection of Baron Speck, of Lutschena, near Leipzig; another in Warwick Castle; another in the Louvre Gallery, Paris. The larger part of this last picture is said to have been executed by Giulio Romano. There is a copy which has sometimes been ascribed, but wrongly, to Leonardo da Vinci, in the Palazzo Doria, Rome. There are still other existing copies.

Job, Misfortunes of. A well-known fresco by Francesco da Volterra in the Campo Santo, Pisa, Italy.

Joconde, La. See BELLE JOCONDE.

Johanneum, The. An institution in Grätz, Styria, the "pride of Styria," founded in 1812, and containing fine collections of art, and museums of antiquities and of natural science.

John and Peter. A picture of the two apostles, the figures the size of life, by Albert Dürer (1471–1528), the German painter and engraver. Another picture corresponding with this represents the apostles Mark and Paul. These are considered to be the grandest works of this master, and the last executed by him. They are now in the Munich Gallery.

☞ "These pictures are the fruit of the deepest thought which then stirred the mind of Albert Dürer, and are executed with overpowering force. Finished as they are, they form the first complete work of art produced by

Protestantism. Well might the artist now close his eyes. He had in this picture attained the summit of art: here he stands side by side with the greatest masters known in history."
Kugler. Handbook of Painting.

John Brown's Farm. An estate near North Elba, in Essex County, N.Y., the former home of the famous abolitionist John Brown (1800–1859), the invader of Virginia, and leader of the expedition against the national arsenal at Harper's Ferry. The house and farm are now the property of an association organized for its purchase.

John O'Groat's House. This house is celebrated as having been considered the most northerly dwelling in Great Britain. Nothing remains of it but a turf-covered mound. It is related that John O'Groat and his cousins used to meet here once a year to celebrate the memory of their ancestor De Groot, a Dutchman who had settled here long previous. They fell into a dispute as to which should preside at table; and John settled the difficulty by building a room with as many sides as there were cousins, and with a corresponding number of doors, and sides to the table, so that each, or neither, might be considered as presiding.

Hear, land o' cakes, and brither Scots,
Frae Maidenkirk to *John o' Groat's*,
If there's a hole in a' your coats,
I rede ye tent it:
A chiel's amang you takin' notes,
And, faith, he'll prent it. *Burns.*

I was with a commercial friend at the hour of the mid-day meal; and he proposed luncheon, adding, "Let's go to Crosby Hall." I did not quite apprehend his meaning. It was much as if he had proposed to me to take luncheon with him in Stonehenge or *John O' Groat's house.*
Richard Grant White.

John, St. See St. John.

John the Baptist. An altar-piece representing three scenes in his life, by the Flemish painter Roger van der Weyden (d. 1464). These pictures were formerly in Spain, but are now in the Museum of Berlin, Prussia.

John the Baptist in the Wilderness. A well-known picture by Raphael Sanzio (1483–1520), in the Uffizi Gallery, Florence, Italy. It is supposed that this picture was executed in part by other hands. Similar pictures in the Louvre, Paris, at Bologna, and elsewhere, are thought to have been taken from it.

John the Baptist. See Beheading of St. John.

John's, St. See St. John's.

Johnson's Court. A place in London near Fleet Street, known as one of the residences of Dr. Johnson. It did not, however, derive its name from him.

We ourselves, not without labor and risk, lately discovered Gough Square, between Fleet Street and Holborn (adjoining both to Bolt Court and *Johnson's Court*), and on the second day of search the very house there, wherein the English Dictionary was composed. *Carlyle.*

Jonah. A statue executed by Raphael (1483–1520), the Italian painter, and pronounced "a remarkable work of sculpture." It is in the Chigi Chapel, S. Maria Novella, Florence, Italy.

☞ "Raphael, who handled the myth of Cupid and Psyche so magnificently in the Villa Farnesina of his patron Agostino Chigi, dedicated a statue of Antinous, — the only statue he ever executed in marble, — under the title of a Hebrew prophet in a Christian sanctuary. The fact is no less significant than strange. During the early centuries of Christianity . . . Jonah symbolized self-sacrifice and immortality. During those same centuries Antinous represented those same ideas, however inadequately, and for the unlettered laity of Paganism. It could scarcely have been by accident, or by mere admiration for the features of Antinous, that Raphael, in his marble, blent the Christian and the Pagan traditions. To unify and to transcend the double views of Christianity and Paganism in a work of pure art was Raphael's instinctive, if not his conscious, aim." *J. A. Symonds.*

Jonathan's. A former coffee-house and resort of stock-jobbers in Change Alley, London.

The Cits met to discuss the rise and fall of stocks, and to settle the rate of insurance, at Garraway's or *Jonathan's.*
National Review.

Joseph. See St. Joseph and Potiphar's Wife accusing Joseph.

Joseph sold into Captivity. A fresco-painting by Friedrich Overbeck (1789–1869). Executed for the villa of the consul-general Bartholdy, in Rome.

Joseph's Coat. A celebrated picture by Diego Rodriguez de Silva y Velasquez (1599–1660), the Spanish painter. In the Museum of Madrid, Spain.

Joseph's Tomb. A burial-place near Mount Gerizim and Jacob's Well in Northern Palestine, traditionally held to be the tomb of the patriarch Joseph. It is believed to be genuine.

Joseph's Well. A well of a total depth of 290 feet on the citadel hill at Cairo, Egypt, supposed to be so called from Yoosef, the other name of Saladin, by whom it was cleared of the sand which had filled it. It is thought to have been cut in the rock by the ancient Egyptians. It is built in two stages, the water being raised from the bottom to the first stage by donkeys or bullocks, and from the first stage to the top in the same manner.

Joux, Château de. A noted castle near Pontarlier in France, situated on a lofty hill, and memorable as having been the place of confinement of Toussaint L' Ouverture, who died here, and also of Mirabeau.

Solely by way of variation, not of alleviation (especially as the If Cerberus too has been bewitched), he has this sinner [Mirabeau] removed in May next, after some nine months space, to the *Castle of Joux*; an "old Owl's nest, with a few invalids," among the Jura Mountains.
Carlyle.

Joux, Colonne de. See Colonne de Joux.

Joyeuse, La. The sword of Charlemagne. It was found lying by the side of the emperor when his tomb at Aix-la-Chapelle was opened in 997 by Otho III. Most of the relics there found were subsequently removed to Vienna, Austria.

Joys and Sorrows of the Virgin. See Virgin.

Judenstadt. [Jews'-town]. A famous quarter in Prague, Bohemia, occupied by Jews, and one of the most widely known *Ghettos*, or Jews' quarters, of those existing in any city. The Jews were formerly confined here, and the gates locked at eight o'clock in the evening; but all restrictions are now removed. In this close quarter of narrow labyrinthine streets are huddled together some 8,000 Jews. It is supposed to be the oldest Jewish settlement in Europe, the colony having existed, according to tradition, before the downfall of Jerusalem. In another quarter of the city is a celebrated Jewish cemetery of great antiquity, but no longer used.

Judge's Cave. A cleft in a group of rocks near New Haven, Conn., where the famous regicides Goffe and Whalley were secreted for a time in 1661.

Judgment, Last. See Last Judgment.

Judgment of Paris. A picture by Peter Paul Rubens (1577–1640). It is in the National Gallery in London.

2. A picture by Angelica Kauffman (1741–1807).

Judgment of Solomon. 1. A picture by Giorgio Barbarelli, commonly called Giorgione (1477–1511). In the Uffizi Palace, Florence, Italy.

2. A noted picture by Benjamin Robert Haydon (1786–1846).

Judgment of the Gods. See Feast of the Gods.

Judith and Holofernes. A well-known bronze statue by Donato di Betto Bardi, called Donatello (1383–1466). In the Loggia de' Lanzi, Florence, Italy.

☞ "The Judith — a strange rather than an attractive work — was removed from the Medici Palace in the year 1495, and set up at the entrance of the palace of the Government."
Grimm, Trans.

Judith and Holofernes. A picture by Andrea Mantegna (1430–1506). In the Museum at Florence, Italy.

Judith and Holofernes. One of the frescos of Michael Angelo (1474–1564). In the Sistine Chapel, Rome.

Judith and Holofernes. An admired picture by Cristofano Allori (1577–1621). In the Pitti Palace, Florence, Italy. There are repetitions of this picture, one in the Belvedere, Vienna, another in the Uffizi, Florence.

Juggernaut. A celebrated temple at Juggernaut, in India. It is the most famous place of pilgrimage in Hindostan. The name Juggernaut signifies the Lord of the World. In this temple is an image gorgeously decorated, which is carried on festal days upon a car moving upon wheels, and is drawn by people. The old belief, that while this car was moving along the crowded streets numbers of devout worshippers would throw themselves upon the ground in order to be crushed by the wheels, as an act of sacrifice to the idol deity, is now understood to be a gross exaggeration, the loss of life which occasionally attends the moving vehicle being the result of accident rather than intention. [Written also *Juggernath.*]

☞ "The Asiatic Society has presented the French Government with a model of the temple and the processional car of Juggernaut. This precious specimen of art of the Middle Ages (1198) is placed in the Louvre, at Paris." *Lefèvre. Tr. Donald.*

A thousand pilgrims strain
Arm, shoulder, breast, and thigh, with might and main,
To drag that sacred wain,
And scarce can draw along the enormous load.
Prone fall the frantic votaries in its road,
And, calling on the god,
Their self-devoted bodies there they lay
To pave his chariot-way.
On *Jaga-Naut* they call,
The ponderous car rolls on, and crushes all.
Through flesh and bones it ploughs its dreadful path.
Groans rise unheard; the dying cry,
And death and agony
Are trodden under foot by yon mad throng
Who follow close, and thrust the deadly wheels along. *Southey.*

Juillet, Colonne de. See COLONNE DE JUILLET.

Julian, St. See ST. JULIAN.

Julius Cæsar. See DEATH OF JULIUS CÆSAR and TRIUMPHS OF JULIUS CÆSAR.

Julius II. A celebrated portrait of this pope by Raphael Sanzio (1483–1520), representing him as seated in an arm-chair, wrapt in meditation. It is adjudged one of Raphael's best portraits. Among the well-known copies of this picture are one in the Uffizi Gallery, Florence, one in the National Gallery, London, and another in the Berlin Museum.

Jumma Musjeed. A famous Mohammedan temple or mosque at Delhi, Hindostan. It is built of sandstone and white marble.

Jungfernstieg. [The Maiden's Walk.] A fashionable promenade in the city of Hamburg, Germany. It is a broad walk around the sides of a basin of water formed by damming up the small river Alster. It is a scene of much animation on summer evenings when the surface of the water is covered with gayly-painted boats.

Junior United Service Club. A London club, founded in 1826. See UNITED SERVICE CLUB.

Some of our party . . . made choice of the club-house in Commercial Square [Gibraltar], . . . rather, perhaps, resembling the *Junior United Service Club* in Charles Street, by which every Londoner has passed ere this with respectful pleasure, catching glimpses of magnificent blazing candelabras, under which sit neat half-pay officers, drinking half-pints of port. *Thackeray.*

Juno. A celebrated head of the goddess in the Villa Ludovisi, Rome, and hence generally known as the Ludovisi Juno. It has been ascribed to the Greek sculptor, Polycleitus the Elder (452?–412? B.C.). See BARBERINI JUNO.

☞ "There is a head of 'Juno, Queen,' possessing a grandeur and seriousness altogether sublime. I do not believe there is any thing superior to it in Rome." *Taine, Trans.*

Juno. See JUPITER AND JUNO.

Jupiter [of Phidias]. See OLYMPIAN JUPITER.

Jupiter and Antiope. A well-known picture by Antonio Allegri, surnamed Correggio (1494–1534), pronounced "the *chef d'œuvre* of the master in the mythological class" of subjects. It is now in the tribune of the Louvre, Paris.

Jupiter and Io. See IO AND JUPITER.

Jupiter and Juno. A fresco by Annibale Caracci (1560–1609). In the Farnese Palace, Rome.

Jupiter, Education of. A picture by Giulio Romano (1492–1546). Now in the National Gallery, London.

Jupiter Latialis. See TEMPLE OF JUPITER LATIALIS.

Jupiter Stator, Temple of. See TEMPLE OF JUPITER STATOR.

Jurisprudence. A celebrated fresco by Raphael Sanzio (1483–1520), representing the science of jurisprudence in its two divisions of ecclesiastical and civil law, with female figures personifying Prudence, Fortitude, and Temperance, and the figures of Pope Gregory XI., and the Emperor Justinian. This picture forms one of the series of four, entitled respectively, Theology, Poetry, Philosophy, and Jurisprudence, which were intended to exhibit the lofty subjects of thought with which the human mind is occupied. They are all in the Camera della Segnatura of the Vatican, Rome.

Justice and Divine Vengeance pursuing Crime. An admired picture by Pierre Prud'hon (1758–1823). In the Louvre, Paris.

Justice. See BED OF JUSTICE and PALAIS DE JUSTICE.

Justina, St. See ST. JUSTINA AND THE DUKE OF FERRARA.

Juvenis Adorans. See BOY PRAYING.

K.

Kaabah. See CAABA.

Kailasa. A famous cave-temple at Elora, in the Deccan, India.

☞ "A magnificent jewel in stone, as large as the Royal Exchange of London, made of a single isolated rock, hollowed within and magnificently carved without. Nothing is wanting to render its proportions, its grace, and its beauty perfect. The hand of a master must have fashioned this gorgeous structure which comprises chapels, porticos, colonnades supported by figures of elephants, two basilisks 39 feet high, a pagoda 100 feet high, flights of stairs, and galleries made solemn with a dim and almost a religious light. The whole structure covers a space of 340 feet in length by 190 feet in breadth, and the exterior walls are separated from the cliff to which the rock originally belonged by an excavated passage 26 to 32 feet in width; so that this wonderful rock-temple is completely isolated in the centre of a court hollowed out in the flank of the hill. Time, passing over the walls covered with innumerable statues, has blackened them; but in robbing them of much it has also imparted to them a real beauty. And here it may be remarked that the strange sculptures of Elora are only to be compared to the shapeless works of our middle ages; and though they are wanting in the repose of the Egyptian sculptures, they seem to live and breathe with a monstrous life." *Lefèvre, Tr. Donald.*

Kaiserstuhl. [Cæsar's Seat.] An eminence rising above Heidelberg, in Germany, and affording a magnificent view.

Karlstein. [Charles's Stone.] A famous feudal castle, the residence of the Bohemian kings, built in the middle of the fourteenth century, and still in a good state of preservation, not far from Prague.

Karnak, Temple of. See TEMPLE OF KARNAK.

Kasr. A ruin in ancient Babylon on the supposed site of the palace of Nebuchadnezzar.

Katherine Docks. See ST. KATHERINE DOCKS.

Kazan Cathedral. The metropolitan church of St. Petersburg, dedicated to our Lady of Kazan, standing upon the Nevskoi Prospekt. It is built of gray Finland granite, and was intended to be a copy of St. Peter's at Rome, having a circular colonnade in front like the latter, but is, however, only a feeble imitation of it.

Where are our shallow fords? and where
The power of *Kazan* with its fourfold gates?
From the prison windows our maidens fair
Talk of us still through the iron grates.
Longfellow, Adaptation.

Kazan looks down from the Volga wall,
Bright in the darkest weather;
And the Christian chime and the Moslem call
Sound from her towers together.
E. D. Proctor.

Kazan, Defile of. An extraordinary pass in the Lower Danube, through which the river rushes. A road is carried along the bank by tunnelling through the perpendicular cliffs.

Kearsarge, The. A Union ship of war, commanded by Capt. Winslow, which, on the 19th of June, 1864, destroyed the Confederate privateer *Alabama*, off the coast of France, near Cherbourg.

Kelso Abbey. An ancient ruined monastery in the town of Kelso, Scotland.

Kenilworth Castle. A magnificent ruined mansion, one of the most interesting and picturesque feudal remains in England, at Kenilworth, near Leamington. It is familiar to readers through the description of Sir Walter Scott in his novel of the same name. Kenilworth Castle was one of the strongholds of Simon de Montfort, Earl of Leicester, in his insurrection against Henry

III. John of Gaunt, coming into possession of the castle, enlarged it by magnificent buildings. Queen Elizabeth bestowed it upon Robert Dudley, Earl of Leicester, who also made important additions. It was dismantled after the civil war of Charles I.

☞ "Of this lordly palace, where princes feasted and heroes fought, now in the bloody earnest of storm and siege, now in the games of chivalry, where beauty dealt the prize which valor won, all is now desolate. The massy ruins of the castle only serve to show what their splendor once was, and to impress on the musing visitor the transitory value of human possessions." *Sir Walter Scott.*

☞ "Some of the ivy that mantles this building has a trunk as large as a man's body, and throws out numberless strong arms, which, interweaving, embrace and interlace half-falling towers, and hold them up in a living, growing mass of green. The walls of one of the oldest towers are sixteen feet thick. The former moat presents only a grassy hollow. What was formerly the gate-house is still inhabited by the family who have the care of the building. The land around is choicely and carefully laid out." *Mrs. H. B. Stowe.*

Heards't thou what the Ivy sighed,
Waving where all else hath died,
In the place of regal mirth,
Now the silent *Kenilworth.*
Felicia Hemans.

Kennedy. See CASTLE KENNEDY.

Kennington Common. An enclosure (comprising some 20 acres) in Lambeth, London, once celebrated as a place of gathering for pugilists and also itinerant preachers, and memorable as the scene of the great Chartist meeting in 1848. It has now been converted into a park. Whitefield used to preach here to great crowds of people.

☞ "Sunday, May 6, 1731. At six in the evening went and preached at Kennington, but such a sight I never saw before. Some supposed there were above 30,000 or 40,000 people, and near fourscore coaches, besides great numbers of horses; and there was such an awful silence amongst them, and the word of God came with such power, that all seemed pleasingly surprised. I continued my discourse for an hour and a half." *George Whitefield's Diary.*

Kennington Park. A modern park in London, formerly known as Kennington Common. See *supra.*

Kensal-Green Cemetery. On the Harrow Road, two and a half miles beyond Paddington, London. It occupies eighteen acres.

Kensington. A parish of London, containing several hamlets. The palace of Kensington is in St. Margaret's parish, Westminster.

Kensington Gardens. Extensive pleasure-grounds attached to Kensington Palace, London, England, much frequented during the London season. The gardens were laid out in the time of William III., and at first consisted of only 26 acres.

Where *Kensington* high o'er the neighboring lands
Midst greens and sweets a regal fabric stands,
And sees each spring, luxuriant in her bowers,
A snow of blossoms and a wild of flowers,
The dames of Britain oft in crowds repair
To groves and lawns and unpolluted air.
Thomas Tickell.

Wise and Loudon are our heroic poets; and if, as a critic, I may single out any passage of their works to commend, I shall take notice of that part in the upper garden at *Kensington*, which at first was nothing but a gravel-pit. *Spectator.*

Here in *Kensington* are some of the most poetical bits of tree and stump and sunny brown and green glen, and tawny earth. *Haydon.*

Kensington Museum. See SOUTH KENSINGTON MUSEUM.

Kensington Palace. A royal residence of the English sovereigns, situated about two miles west of London. William and Mary lived here, and here Mary died in 1694, and William in 1702. After the death of William III., Anne and Prince George of Denmark lived at Kensington Palace, the latter dying here in 1708, and the former in 1714. Queen Victoria was born here May 24, 1819. It formerly contained the collection of pictures known as the Kensington Collection.

Kent's Hole. A cavern near Torquay, England, celebrated for its ossiferous remains.

Kevin's Kitchen. See St. Kevin's Kitchen.

Kew Botanical Gardens. An enclosure, 270 acres in extent, at Kew, near London, containing the plants, flowers, and vegetable curiosities of all countries.

Keyne's Well. See St. Keyne's Well.

Keys of St. Peter. See Delivering the Keys.

Khasne, The. The great temple of Petra, occupying an unrivalled situation opposite the opening of the Sîk, and in full view of every one entering the city. Almost the entire structure is hewn in the rock; and the age, and even the purpose of the monument, are matters of controversy. Its name, meaning "the Treasure," was given to it by the Arabs, who have a tradition that vast treasures of jewels and money were once placed in the urn upon the top of the façade, where they are still carefully guarded by jealous genii.

☞ "With consummate skill have the architects of Petra availed themselves of remarkable natural formation to dazzle the stranger, as he emerges from an all but subterranean defile, by the enchanting prospect of one of their noblest monuments. Most fortunate, too, were they in the material out of which it is hewn; for the rosy tint of the portico, sculptured pediment, and statues overhead, contrasts finely with the darker masses of rugged cliff above and around, and the deep green of the vegetation at its base. The monument is in wonderful preservation; some of the most delicate details of the carving are as fresh and sharp as if executed yesterday."
Murray's Handbook.

☞ "Its position is wonderfully fine, and its material and preservation very striking; but it is inconceivable how any one can praise its architecture. This temple, called by the Arabs 'Pharaoh's Treasury,' is absolutely set in a niche."
Miss Martineau.

☞ "One of the most elegant remains of antiquity existing in Syria."
Burckhardt.

☞ "The typical and most beautiful tomb of this place [Petra] is that called the Khasne, or Treasury of Pharaoh. . . . Though all the forms of the architecture are Roman, the details are so elegant and generally so well designed, that there must have been some Grecian influence brought to bear upon the work."
Fergusson.

Khuttub Minar. A famous pillar in the neighborhood of Delhi, India. It is of a circular form, 240 feet in height, with a base of 35 feet, diminishing to less than 10 feet at the top. It consists of five stories, the three lower being of red sandstone, and the two upper of white marble.

"As I stood a short distance from the base, my gaze travelling slowly from bottom to top, and from top to bottom, Mr. Place declared it to be the finest single tower in the world, and asked me whether I did not think so. I said 'no,' for just then I had Giotto's Florentine Campanile and the Giralda of Seville in mind, and could not venture to place it above them; but the longer I looked, the more its beauty grew upon me; and after spending three or four hours in its vicinity, I no longer doubted. It *is*, beyond question, the finest shaft in the world."
Bayard Taylor.

Kidron. A brook in the vicinity of Jerusalem, Palestine, alluded to in the Bible, and associated with the later scenes in the life of Christ.

Kieran's Chair. See St. Kieran's Chair.

Kilchurn Castle. A massive stronghold of the fifteenth century near Dalmally, Argyle, Scotland. It is now an imposing ruin.

Abandoned by thy rugged sire
Nor by soft peace adopted, though in place
And in dimension such that thou might'st seem
But a mere footstool to yon sovereign lord,
Huge Cruachan.
Wordsworth.

Kildare, Curragh of. See Curragh of Kildare.

Kilkenny Castle. The seat of the Marquis of Ormonde in Kilkenny, Leinster County, Ireland. It dates from the twelfth century.

Kilcoleman. A picturesque ruined castle in the county of Cork, Ireland. It was once the home of Edmund Spenser, the poet.

☞ "Four years of happy tranquillity here passed away, bearing for the world the glorious fruit of the first three books of the Fairy Queen. These he conveyed to London in company with his friend, Sir Walter Raleigh, and there published them. . . . A dreadful calamity now awaited him. The Tyrone rebellion broke out (in 1598); his estate was plundered; Kilcoleman was burned by the Irish; in the flames his youngest child perished; and he was driven into England with his wife and remaining children, — a poor and wretched exile. From this affliction he never recovered, dying a year after in an obscure lodging in London in extreme indigence." *Mr. and Mrs. Hall.*

Kilcrea. A beautiful ruined friary or abbey in the county of Cork, Ireland.

Kilmallock Abbey. An interesting monastic abbey in the county of Limerick, Ireland.

Kimbolton Castle. The seat of the Duke of Manchester, near Huntingdon, England.

☞ "Though pulled about, and rebuilt by Sir John Vanbrugh, the castle has still a grand antique and feudal air. The memories which hang about it are in the last degree romantic and imposing. There Queen Katherine of Aragon died. There the Civil Wars took shape. . . . Kimbolton is perhaps the only house now left in England in which you still live and move, distinguished as the scene of an act in one of Shakespeare's plays. . . . For a genuine Shakesperian house, in which men still live and love, still dress and dine, to which guests come and go, in which children frisk and sport, where shall we look beyond the walls of Kimbolton Castle?" *Hepworth Dixon.*

King Arthur's Palace. The name given to the vast intrenchments of an ancient Roman or British camp, still existing in a ruined state, in the ancient Camelot, or, as it is now called, Queen's Camel, England.

King Arthur's Round Table. A singular and very ancient circular area, surrounded by a fosse and mound, and supposed to have been intended for the practice of the feats of chivalry, near Penrith, in the county of Cumberland, England.

He passed red Penrith's *Table Round*
For feats of chivalry renowned.
Sir Walter Scott.

☞ "A circular intrenchment, about half a mile from Penrith, is thus popularly termed. The circle within the ditch is about 160 paces in circumference, with openings, or approaches, directly opposite to each other. As the ditch is on the inner side, it could not be intended for the purpose of defence; and it has reasonably been conjectured that the enclosure was designed for the solemn exercise of feats of chivalry, and the embankment around for the convenience of the spectators." *Scott.*

King Arthur's Round Table. See Round Table.

King Club, *or* **Club of Kings.** A club which was in existence in London in the time of Charles II. (1660-1685). The name of "King" was applied to all the members, and Charles was himself an honorary member.

King John's Castle. 1. This fortress, built in the thirteenth century upon a rock overlooking the sea, in the town of Carlingford, Ireland, commands charming views of the Mourne Mountains. Near this castle is an ancient abbey, now in ruins, which was built in the fourteenth century.

2. An ancient royal residence and fortress at Limerick, Ireland.

☞ "The castle has endured for above six centuries; in all the 'battles, sieges, fortunes,' that have since occurred, it has been the object most coveted, perhaps, in Ireland, by the contending parties; and it still frowns, a dark mass, upon the waters of the mighty Shannon." *Mr. and Mrs. Hall.*

King of Clubs. A club in London, founded about 1801, and at first composed of a few lawyers and literary men. The meetings of the club were held at the Crown and Anchor Tavern, in the Strand. Richard Sharp ("Conversation Sharp") was regarded as the first of the club; and the poet Rogers, Sir James Mackintosh, Lady Mackintosh, and others were frequent attendants.

King of the Beans. See FEAST OF THE KING OF THE BEANS.

King of the Forest. A picture by Sir Edwin Landseer (1803-1873), the most celebrated modern painter of animals.

Kings, Adoration of the. See ADORATION OF THE MAGI

King's Bench and Queen's Bench. An old prison in London, more recently known as the Queen's Prison, Southwark. Stow relates that the rebels under Wat Tyler "brake down the houses of the Marshalsey and King's Bench, in Southwarke." The Prince of Wales, afterwards Henry V., was committed to this prison. It was known as the Upper Bench Prison during the Commonwealth. The King's Bench Prison figures in the works of Dickens.

Micawber. — "And this is the *Bench!* Where for the first time in many revolving years the overwhelming pressure of pecuniary liabilities was not proclaimed from day to day by importunate voices declining to vacate the passage; where there was no knocker on the door for any creditor to appeal to; where personal service of process was not required, and detainers were merely lodged at the gate!"
Dickens.

King's Cave. A cavern near Tormore, in Scotland. It derives its name from the tradition that it was occupied by Fingal, Bruce, and other Scottish heroes. The interior is carved with rude devices. This cave, the largest of a line of caves on the Scottish coast, is hollowed out under the cliffs, and is supported partly by a natural pillar that divides the upper portion into two chambers.

King's Chapel. A religious edifice on Tremont Street, Boston, Mass. It was built in 1754 on the site of an older church edifice. During the war of the Revolution it was for a time forsaken by its loyalist congregation. In the adjacent burial-ground, which has been used from 1630, many of the early Puritans, including Gov. Winthrop, are interred.

☞ "The edifice, its records and the worshippers in it, are illustrative of the court-epoch of life in Boston, under the royal governors. A state pew, with canopy and drapery, was fitted up in the chapel for the Earl of Bellomont; and the royal governor and his deputy were always to be of the vestry. When Joseph Dudley came home as governor, he seems, at least in part, to have turned his back upon his own place for worship and communion. His own armorial bearings and escutcheon were hung on one of the pillars of the chapel, as were those of other gentry. Gov. Hutchinson after him did the same. The edifice, in fact, and all that was done within its walls, and its objects and purposes, was a type and obtrusion of royal interference with the usages, the traditions, and the dearest attachments of the people. Men of note sat and worshipped in that first royal chapel. Among its worshippers were true Episcopalians by birth and conviction, and others who, without any special convictions, might reasonably seek there a substitute for that espionage and unwelcome form of religious dispensation found in the meeting-houses. Suspended from the pillars were the escutcheons of Sir Edmund Andros, Francis Nicholson, Capt. Hamilton, and Govs. Dudley, Shute, Burnet, Belcher, and Shirley. The altar-piece, with the gilded Gloria, the Creed, the Commandments, the Lord's Prayer, the organ, the surpliced priest, and, above all, the green boughs of Christmas, composed altogether a sight which some young Puritan eyes longed, and some older ones were shocked, to see."
George E. Ellis.

The *Chapel*, last of sublunary things
That shocks our echoes with the name of *Kings*,
Whose bell, just glistening from the font and forge,
Rolled its proud requiem for the second George,
Solemn and swelling, as of old it rang,
Flings to the wind its deep, sonorous clang.
Holmes.

King's Coffee-house. A rude structure in Covent Garden, London, formerly much frequented by persons from various ranks of society.

What rake is ignorant of *King's Coffee-house?*
Fielding.

King's College. **1.** An ancient college in Cambridge, England, one of the 13 colleges of the university, founded in 1441, enjoying some peculiar privileges, and noted for its beautiful chapel.

The groves of Granta, and her gothic halls,
King's Coll., Cam's stream, stain'd windows, and old walls.
Byron.

2. An ancient college in Aberdeen, Scotland, founded in 1494, by a bull of Pope Alexander VI. The building is noticeable for the fine carving in the chapel and library. The college now forms a part of the new University of Aberdeen.

☞ "The tower of it [King's College] is surmounted by a massive stone crown, which forms a very singular feature in every view of Aberdeen, and is said to be a perfectly unique specimen of architecture."
Mrs. H. B. Stowe.

3. A college in London, founded in 1828, and occupying the east wing of Somerset House.

King's College Chapel. A magnificent pile, connected with King's College, Cambridge, England. It is regarded as one of the finest specimens in existence of the perpendicular Gothic.

☞ "The interior is imposing from its great height, from the solemn beauty and splendor of the stained glass, and from the magnificent fan-tracery of the vaulting, which extends, bay after bay, in unbroken and unchanged succession, from one end of the chapel to the other." *Fergusson.*

—nothing cheered our way till first we saw
The long-roofed chapel of King's College lift
Turrets and pinnacles in answering files,
Extended high above a dusky grove.
Wordsworth.

Tax not the royal saint with vain expense,
With ill-matched aims the architect who planned—
Albeit laboring for a scanty band
Of white-robed scholars only—this immense
And glorious work of fine intelligence!
Ibid.

King's College Hospital. Established in London for the sick poor, to afford instruction to the students of King's College, in 1839. The first stone of the present building was laid in 1852.

King's Head. A club in London, of the time of Charles II., also known as the Green-Ribbon Club, from the distinguishing mark of a green ribbon to be worn in the hat, founded by Lord Shaftesbury, with the object of affording support to the court and government, and of influencing Protestant zeal. The members, who were popularly known as "hogs in armour," from the peculiar dress which they wore, carried the weapon known as the Protestant Flail. According to Roger North, at the time of the pope-burning procession of November, 1680, "the Rabble first changed their title, and were called *the Mob* in the assemblies of this club. It was their Beast of Burden, and called first *mobile vulgus*, but fell naturally into the contraction of one syllable, and ever since is become proper English." The club declined after these celebrations were suppressed in 1683.

☞ "The gentlemen of that worthy society held their evening sessions continually at the King's Head Tavern, over against the Inner Temple Gate. . . . They admitted all strangers that were confidingly introduced; for it was a main end of their institution to make proselytes, especially of the raw estated youth, newly come to town. This copious society were to the faction in and about London a sort of executive power, and, by correspondence, all over England. The resolves of the more retired councils of the ministry of the Faction were brought in here, and orally insinuated to the company, whether it were lyes, defamations, commendations, projects, etc., and so, like water diffused, spread all over the town; whereby that which was digested at the club over night, was, like nourishment, at every assembly, male and female, the next day; and thus the younglings tasted of political administration, and took themselves for notable counsellors."
Roger North.

King's Head. A tavern, now closed, in the Poultry, London. It was burnt in the great fire of 1666, and rebuilt. It was at first known by the sign of the Rose. Also a *King's Head* in Fenchurch Street, London, and many other public houses of this name, which was a common appellation.

King's Market. [Dan. *Kongen's Nytorv.*] The principal square in Copenhagen, Denmark.

Kings of Cologne. See SHRINE OF THE THREE KINGS OF COLOGNE

Kings, Tombs of the. See TOMBS OF THE KINGS.

Kirkconnell. A ruined church in Scotland, near Kirkpatrick. The adjoining churchyard is the scene of the ballad of "Fair Helen of Kirkconnell."

> I wish I were where Helen lies!
> Night and day on me she cries.
> Oh that I were where Helen lies
> On fair *Kirkconnell* Lee!

Kit-Kat Club. A celebrated association in London, founded about the year 1700, and said to have derived its name from a certain Christopher Katt, a mutton-pieman or pastry-cook, at whose house in Shire Lane the meetings of the club are supposed to have been first held. It was the chief society for the leaders among the Whigs, and originally consisted of 39 noblemen and gentlemen known for their warm attachment to the house of Hanover. The Duke of Marlborough, Sir Robert Walpole, Addison, Steele, and many other noted men of the time were members; and the reputation of the club is literary and artistic as well as political. Here "used to meet many of the finest gentlemen and choicest wits of the days of Queen Anne and the first George. Halifax has conversed and Somers unbent, Addison mellowed over a bottle, Congreve flashed his wit, Vanbrugh let loose his easy humor, Garth talked and rhymed." Ward, who claims that the pieman was named Christopher, and that he lived at the sign of the Cat and Fiddle, in Gray's-Inn Lane, says, "the cook's name being Christopher, for brevity called Kit, and his sign being the Cat and Fiddle, they very merrily derived a quaint denomination from puss and her master, and from thence called themselves of the Kit-Kat Club." Others say that the club derived its name from the pie itself and not from the maker of the pie, the pies being a regular dish at the suppers of the club.

> Whence deathless *Kit-Kat* took his name,
> Few critics can unriddle;
> Some say from pastry-cook it came,
> And some from Cat and Fiddle.
> From no trim beaus its name it boasts,
> Gray statesmen or green wits,
> But from this pell-mell pack of toasts
> Of old Kats and young Kits.
>
> *Arbuthnot.*

Kits Coity-House. A famous cromlech near Aylesford, Kent, England. By some thought to have been a sepulchral monument to the memory of Catigern, who, with Horsa, was killed here in battle A.D. 455. The monument is now destroyed.

Knife-grinder. See ARROTINO, L'.

Knight, Death, and the Devil. A celebrated engraving by Albert Dürer (1471–1528), the German painter and engraver. It has been pronounced "the most important work which the fantastic spirit of German art has ever produced. . . . We see a solitary knight riding through a dark glen; two demons rise up before him, . . . the horrible figure of Death on the lame horse, and the bewildering apparition of the Devil. But the knight, prepared for combat wherever resistance can avail, . . . looks steadily forward on the path he has chosen, and allows these creations of a delusive dream to sink again into their visionary kingdom. The masterly execution of the engraving is well known." The print bears date 1513.

Knight. See VISION OF A KNIGHT.

Knockgraffon, Moat of. See MOAT OF KNOCKGRAFFON.

Knowle Park. A fine old castellated mansion near London, in the county of Kent.

> ☞ "Parts of it date from the time of King John, and none of it is more recent than the time of Henry VIII. It is very extensive, few old castles being so large; and it has an awful hard, grim, feudal look, so slight have been the changes made in it."
>
> *George Ticknor.*

Knowsley Hall (Park). A splendid baronial mansion, the seat of the Earl of Derby, in Lancashire, England. It contains some celebrated art-treasures.

Kohinoor, The. [Mountain of Light.] A celebrated diamond found in the mines of Golconda, India. Its original weight was 793 carats, which by unskilful cutting was reduced to 186. Having been recut in Amsterdam, 1852, it was still further reduced to $106\frac{1}{16}$ carats, which is its present weight. This diamond, which for a long time was a chief feature in the treasury of Delhi, passed into the hands of the British in 1849, and was presented to Queen Victoria, June 3, 1850.

More than the diamond *Koh-i-noor*, which glitters among their crown-jewels, they [the English] prize that dull pebble which is wiser than a man, whose poles turn themselves to the poles of the world, and whose axis is parallel to the axis of the world. *Emerson.*

To have and to hold for one's own property one of the largest diamonds ever discovered, is no doubt a magnificent possession: but in a purely artistic sense I prefer the original *Koh-i-noor*, worn on the arm of Runjeet Sing as he sat "cross-legged in his golden chair, dressed in simple white, with a single string of huge pearls round his waist," to the Koh-i-noor cut and pared down to mathematical symmetry by English lapidaries, with a loss of one-third of its weight. *C. L. Eastlake.*

Cracking up Boston folks, — said the gentleman with the *diamond*-pin, whom, for convenience' sake, I shall hereafter call the *Koh-i-noor*. *Holmes.*

Kohlmarkt, The. [The Cabbage Market.] A well-known and fine street in Vienna, Austria.

The Toledo of Naples, the Corso of Rome, the *Kohl-market* of Vienna, the Rue de la Paix and Boulevards of Paris, have each impressed me strongly with their magnificence; but they are really nothing to Regent Street. *N. P. Willis.*

Königgrätz Strasse. [Königgrätz Street.] A well-known street in Berlin, Prussia.

Königsbau. See NEW PALACE.

Königsstuhl. [King's Seat.] A vaulted hall near the town of Rhense on the Rhine, once the place of assembly for the electors of the German empire. The building now standing is chiefly modern.

Königsstein. [King's Stone.] 1. A celebrated fortress in Saxony, situated at a height of about 780 feet above the river Elbe. It has been regarded as impregnable, both on account of its isolated position with regard to other commanding heights (the Lilienstein and Pfaffenstein are about $1\frac{3}{4}$ miles distant), and from the extreme steepness of the escarpments by which it is surrounded. It is approached by a sloping path cut in the rock, and by a slanting wooden bridge which can be removed in time of war. Water for the fortress is obtained from a well 613 feet deep, cut in the solid rock. The valuable works of art of Saxony owe their preservation to the fortress of Königstein, and treasures of various kinds have often been placed here for safe keeping. Frederick Augustus II. made the fortress a retreat in the time of the Seven Years' War.

2. A ruined fortress which stands high above the banks of the Rhine. The castle was demolished by the French in 1796.

Kratzer, Nicholas. A picture by Hans Holbein the Younger (1498–1543), the German painter. It is in the Louvre, Paris.

Kremlin, The. A hill and quarter in Moscow, Russia, containing an imposing collection of buildings, palaces, churches, and towers, surrounded by a wall sixty feet in height and nearly a mile in circumference. Among the principal buildings are the old and new palaces of the czars, the Cathedral of St. Michael, the Church of the Assumption, the tower of Ivan Veliki, and the Church of St. Basil. The old palace of the czars, the *Terema*, or balcony, forms the rear wing of the new palace [Granovitaya Palata]. The former was mainly destroyed in the fire of 1812 during the French occupation of the city, the latter was built in 1816. See IVAN VELIKI, ST. BASIL, etc.

☞ "If Moscow is the Mecca of the Russians, the *Kremlin* is its Kaaba. Within its ancient walls is gathered all that is holiest in religion or most cherished in historical tradition. . . . Its very gates are protected by miracles, and the peasant from a distant province enters them with much the same feeling as a Jewish pilgrim enters the long-lost city of Zion." *Bayard Taylor.*

☞ "Every city in Russia had its Kremlin, as every one in Spain had its Alcazar; and all were adorned with walls deeply machicolated, and interspersed with towers. Within were enclosed five-domed churches and belfries, just as at Moscow, though on a scale proportionate to the importance of the city." *Fergusson.*

Mind that I gild the Invalides
To match the *Kremlin* Dome.
Walter Thornbury.

The bells that rock the *Kremlin* tower
Like a strong wind, to and fro, —
Silver sweet in its topmost bower,
And the thunder's boom below.
E. D. Proctor.

Kubbet es Sukhrah. [The Dome of the Rock.] See MOSQUE OF OMAR.

Kuhstall. A remarkable natural arch through a rocky wall or rampart 150 feet thick, in the region known as the Saxon Switzerland, near its capital, Schandau. The place is said to derive its name from having been used by the mountaineers as a hiding-place for their cattle in time of war.

Kyburg Castle. An ancient Austrian stronghold near Winterthur, Switzerland. The regalia of the empire was formerly kept here.

Kyffhäuser, The. A famous ruined castle, crowning an eminence in Thuringia, underneath which, in a vault, the Emperor Frederic Barbarossa is fabled to lie enchanted

The ancient Barbarossa,
Friedrich, the Kaiser great,
Within the castle-cavern
Sits in enchanted state.

He did not die; but ever
Waits in the chamber deep,
Where, hidden under the castle,
He sat himself, to sleep.

The splendor of the empire
He took with him away,
And back to earth will bring it
When dawns the chosen day.
Rückert, Trans.

Far within the lone *Kyffhäuser*,
With a lamp red glimmering by,
Sits the aged Emperor Frederick,
At a marble table nigh.
Emanuel Geibel, Trans.

Full darkly loomed *Kyffhäuser*
Through fog which slowly broke,
When first the spellbound Kaiser
From his long sleep awoke.
Ferdinand Freiligrath, Trans.

L.

Labourage Nivernais. See PLOUGHING IN NIVERNAIS.

Labyrinth. 1. One of the most remarkable and mysterious monuments of ancient Egypt, near Lake Mœris. According to Manetho, the Egyptian historian, it was built by Mœris as a sepulchre for himself. In 1843 the site of this monument was excavated and explored by a Prussian expedition under Lepsius, but without fully satisfactory results. It was described and greatly admired by Herodotus, who says that it surpassed the Pyramids, and consisted of 3,000 chambers, half of which were below ground, and contained "the sepulchres of the kings who built the Labyrinth; and also those of the sacred crocodiles." Ancient authors differ as to the founder of this Labyrinth; but the earliest name discovered among the ruins is that of Amenemha III., of the twelfth dynasty, and it is thought that he was the builder of the Labyrinth, as well as of Lake Mœris.

"I visited this place, and found it to surpass description; for if all the walls and other great works of the Greeks were put together in one, they would not equal, either for labor or expense, this Labyrinth." *Herodotus.*

☞ "From such data as have been given to the public, we learn that the Labyrinth was a building measuring about 1,150 feet east and west, by 850 feet north and south, surrounding three sides of a court-yard. . . . In the Labyrinth itself a number of small chambers were found, two stories in height, as the account of Herodotus leads us to expect, but so small, being only four feet in width at most, that we cannot understand the admiration they excited in his mind. As there are no hieroglyphics upon them, it is difficult to determine whether they belong to the old Labyrinth, or to that which Herodotus writes of as erected by Psammeticus and the kings of his day." *Fergusson.*

— within the brazen doors
Of the great *Labyrinth*, slept both boy and beast,
Tired with the pomp of their Osirian feast.
Shelley.

2. Dædalus is said to have built a Labyrinth near Cnossus in Crete, for the confinement of the fabled monster the Minotaur, but nothing of this structure can be found. Remains of a labyrinth were extant in the time of Pliny on the isle of Lemnos. Others, the existence of which is doubtful, are said to have been built on the island of Samos, and in Clusium, near Etruria. A remarkable example of a natural labyrinth is found in the Adersbach Rocks.

Mausolus worke will be the Carians glorie
And Crete will boast the *Labyrinth*, now raced.
Spenser.

Lackawanna, The. A noted iron-clad of the Confederate navy in the civil war of 1861–65.

The great *Lackawana* came down
Full tilt for another blow:
We were forging ahead,
She reversed; but, for all our pains,
Rammed the old Hartford instead,
Just for'ard the mizzen-chains!
H. H. Brownell.

Lacryma Christi. [The Tear of Christ.] A celebrated wine, distinguished for the delicacy of its flavor, produced upon the slopes of Mount Vesuvius, Italy.

Lady Franklin. An Arctic exploring ship which sailed from England under Capt. Penny in 1850.

Lady of Aboshek. This smaller temple at Aboo-Simbil, Egypt, dedicated to Athor, who is called the "Lady of Aboshek," "Lady of the West," etc., is like the other, very old, having been excavated from the solid rock in the time of Rameses the Great, 1400 B.C. The temple is 90 feet in depth. It contains statues of Athor and of other deities. See TEMPLE OF ABOO-SIMBEL.

☞ "The smaller temple of 'the Lady of Aboshek,' — Athor, — beside the large one, is very striking, as seen from the river. The six statues on the façade stand out boldly between buttresses; and their reclining backwards against the rock has a curious effect."
Miss Martineau.

Lady with the Lute. An admired picture in Alnwick Castle, England. It was formerly ascribed to Giorgione, but is now attributed to Jacopo Palma, called Palma Vecchio (1480–1528).

Lafayette. A well-known bust of the marquis, executed by the French sculptor Jean Antoine Houdon (1741–1828) for the Capitol at Richmond, Va.

Lafayette College. A collegiate establishment in Easton, Penn. It was founded in 1826, and is well endowed.

Lafayette, Fort. See FORT LAFAYETTE.

Lafayette Park. A public square in St. Louis, Mo.

Lafayette Square. A beautiful park in Washington. It contains a colossal equestrian statue of Gen. Jackson.

Lafitte. A farmhouse or small château in the vine district of Médoc, on the Garonne, below Bordeaux. Here is produced the celebrated wine known as *Château Lafitte*, which is sometimes sold as high as $25 a bottle. The estate is the property of Baron Rothschild. The annual yield of the vineyard does not exceed 400 hogsheads.

Lafitte, Rue. A street in Paris, so called from M. Lafitte, once a well-known banker and politician. It was formerly known as the Rue d'Artois. Here some of the richest bankers live; and here the Rothschilds have two hôtels, which are among the finest private residences in the city.

Lahneck. A well-known ruined fortress of mediæval times in the neighborhood of Coblenz, on the Rhine. The poet Goethe has commemorated it in his "Geister Gruss."

Lais Corinthiaca. [The Corinthian Lais.] A picture by Hans Holbein the Younger (1498–1543), the German painter, representing a beautiful young girl in elegant dress, professedly the portrait of a member of the Offenburg family. It is in the Basle Gallery.

Lake Country *or* **District.** The general name by which the counties of Cumberland and Westmoreland in England are often known from the picturesque lakes with which they are interspersed, and also familiar from their association with the so-called Lake School of poets and writers, of which Wordsworth, Southey, Coleridge, Lamb, and Wilson may be taken as representatives.

Those who travel much in the "*Lake District*" can readily trace the course of the chivalrous Baron. *J. F. Hunnewell.*

Lake Mœris. A celebrated reservoir which was situated in the centre of the plateau of the Fyoóm, Egypt, serving to store up the water of the Nile during the inundation, and to afterwards distribute it through canals over the land during the dry season.

☞ Herodotus, who speaks of it as being "in the neighborhood of Crocodilopolis," says: "Wonderful as is the labyrinth, the work called the Lake of Mœris, which is close by the labyrinth, is yet more astonishing. The measure of its circumference is 3,600 furlongs, which is equal to the entire length of Egypt along the sea-coast. The lake stretches in its longest direction from north to south, and in its deepest parts is of the depth of 50 fathoms. It is manifestly an artificial excavation; for nearly in the centre stand two pyramids, rising to the height of 300 feet above the surface of the water, and extending as far beneath, each crowned with a colossal statue sitting upon a throne. The water of the lake does not come out of the ground, which is here excessively dry, but is introduced by a canal from the Nile. The current sets for six months into the lake from the river, and for the next six months into the river from the lake." This great work was built by Amenemha III. of the twelfth dynasty, who is thought to have also built the labyrinth. Lake Mœris is not to be confounded with the natural lake Birket el Korn, with which it probably communicated during the inundation.

By *Mœris* and the Mareotid lakes,
Strewn with faint blooms like bridal-chamber floors;
Where naked boys bridling tame water-snakes,
Or charioteering ghastly alligators,
Had left on the sweet waters mighty wakes
Of those huge forms. *Shelley.*

He lifts his head and roars amain;
So wild and hollow is the strain,
It booms along the desert sand,
And shakes the flood on *Mœris'* strand.
F. Freiligrath, Trans.

Lamb, Adoration of the. See ADORATION OF THE LAMB.

Lambert, Hôtel. See HÔTEL LAMBERT.

Lambeth. A metropolitan borough of London. The name of this now densely populated district, once a swamp, is said, but not with certainty, to be derived from Lamb-hithe, that is, a landing-place for sheep.

Yonder fish-wipe
Will not away. And there's your giantess,
The bawd of *Lambeth.* *Ben Jonson.*

Lambeth Bridge. An iron-wire suspension bridge across the Thames at London.

Lambeth Palace. An episcopal mansion in London, and for six and a half centuries the residence of the Archbishops of Canterbury. Lambeth House has at various times proved an asylum for learned foreigners who have been compelled to flee from the intolerance of their countrymen.

☞ "Lambeth is a stately pile of quaint antique buildings, rising most magnificently on the banks of the Thames. It is surrounded by beautiful grounds laid out with choice gardening." *Mrs. H. B. Stowe.*

Such *Lambeth*, envy of each band and gown. *Pope.*

The grand hospitalities of *Lambeth* have perished, but its charities live.
Douglas Jerrold.

Landing of Columbus. A picture in one of the panels of the Rotunda in the Capitol at Washington, representing the debarkation of the great discoverer with his companions upon the soil of the New World in 1492. This painting was executed under commission from Congress by John Vanderlyn (1776–1852), who employed a French artist to do a good part of the work. It has been severely criticised for its inaccuracy and marks of haste; in proof of which, among other things, it is noted that the three flags borne by the three vessels of the original discoverers are represented in the picture as blown outward in three different directions. This work of art has become very familiar to the general public by its reproduction in the form of an engraving upon the back of the five-dollar notes of the national currency.

Landing of the Pilgrims. A well-known painting by Sargent, in the Pilgrim Hall at Plymouth, Mass.

Landing of Venus at Cytherea. A picture by Francesco Albani (1578–1660), and one of his best works. In the Chigi Palace, Rome.

Landore, Villa. See VILLA GHERARDESCA.

Land's End. The famous headland in which the western coast of England terminates at the extremity of the county of Cornwall.

Let any social or physical convulsion visit the United States, and England would feel the shock from *Land's End* to John o' Groat's. *Charles Dickens.*

Langton Elm. A famous elm of great age in what was Sherwood Forest. It was for a long time so remarkable as to have a special keeper.

Lanleff Temple. A remarkable structure of unknown origin and antiquity, near St. Briene, in France. It is thought by some to be a pagan temple, but is probably a Christian church of the eleventh or twelfth century. It is of a circular form, like some of the English and Dutch churches, and built in imitation of the Church of the Holy Sepulchre.

Lansdowne. A noted house, formerly standing in what is now Fairmount Park, Philadelphia. It was the residence of Joseph

Bonaparte, and later of Lord Ashburton. It was destroyed by fire in 1854.

Lansdowne House. A noble house in London, situated on the south side of Berkeley Square, originally built for the Marquis of Bute, and subsequently sold to the Marquis of Lansdowne. It contains a gallery of paintings and sculptures.

Lantern of Diogenes. A popular name for the Choragic Monument of Lysicrates at Athens. A structure in imitation of the Greek monument formerly stood at St. Cloud [France], but was destroyed in 1870 by the Prussians. [Also called the *Lantern of Demosthenes*.] See CHORAGIC MONUMENT OF LYSICRATES.

☞ "A little monument, formerly known under the name of the Lantern of Demosthenes, and of which a copy occupies at St. Cloud [France] the summit of a tower well known to the Parisians, deserves attention as one of the rare specimens of the Corinthian order to be seen in Greece. It formed one of those small houses which were used to contain the tripods received by the victors in the scenic games." *Lefèvre, Trans.*

Lantern of Ireland. The popular name of the beautiful ruined Priory of St. John, in Kilkenny, Ireland. It is so called from the number of its windows.

☞ "For about fifty-four feet of the south side of the choir, it seems to be almost one window." *Grose.*

Lanti Vase. An antique vase brought from England by Lord Cawdor, and now in Woburn Abbey, the seat of the Duke of Bedford.

Lanzi, Loggia de'. See LOGGIA DE' LANZI.

Laocoon, The. A celebrated work of sculpture, now in the Belvidere of the Vatican at Rome, discovered in 1506. It represents the death of Laocoon, a mythical priest of Apollo or of Neptune, and his two sons, who are crushed in the folds of two monstrous serpents. The group is probably the same as that referred to by Pliny as standing in the palace of the Emperor Titus. Virgil gives a vivid description of the death of Laocoon in the second book of the Æneid (line 263 *et seq.*).

☞ "The fame of many sculptors is less diffused, because the number employed upon great works prevented their celebrity; for there is no one artist to receive the honor of the work, and, where there are more than one, they cannot all obtain an equal fame. Of this the *Laocoon* is an example, which stands in the palace of the Emperor Titus, — a work which may be considered superior to all others, both in painting and statuary. The whole group — the father, the boys, and the awful folds of the serpents — were formed out of a single block, in accordance with a vote of the Senate, by Agesander, Polydorus, and Athenodorus, Rhodian sculptors of the highest merit." *Pliny, Trans.*

☞ "I felt the Laocoon very powerfully, though very quietly; an immortal agony, with a strange calmness diffused through it, so that it resembles the vast rage of the sea, calm on account of its immensity, or the tumult of Niagara, which does not seem to be tumult, because it keeps pouring on for ever and ever. It is a type of human beings struggling with an inexplicable trouble, and entangled in a complication which they cannot free themselves from by their own efforts, and out of which Heaven alone can help them." *Hawthorne.*

☞ "This work is a compromise between two styles and two epochs, similar to one of Euripides' tragedies. . . . Aristophanes would say of this group, as he said of the Hippolytus or Iphigenia of Euripides, that it makes us weep and does not fortify us; instead of changing women into men, it transforms men into women." *Taine, Trans.*

Turning to the Vatican, go see
Laocoon's torture dignifying pain —
A father's love and mortal's agony
With an immortal's patience blending.
Lord Byron.

Lapidary Gallery. See GALLERIA LAPIDARIA.

Larissa. See ACROPOLIS [of Argos].

Last Judgment. A favorite subject of representation by the great religious painters of the Middle

Ages. Of the many compositions upon this theme, a few of the more celebrated and familiar examples are mentioned below. Concerning the treatment of this subject, Lady Eastlake writes: "The 'Last Judgment' has tested the powers of some of the greatest and most opposite masters, both north and south of the Alps. Giotto appropriately led the way with the now ruined wall-painting in the Chapel of the Arena at Padua. The solemn Orcagna followed in the Campo Santo. . . . Fra Angelico has left several versions of the subject. . . . Michael Angelo stands alone here, as in every subject on which he set the stamp of his paganized time, and his *maniera terribile*. Roger van der Weyden, the mournful painter of Brussels, treated the subject with great dignity and reticence; . . . while Rubens, like Michael Angelo, has made the subject rather an occasion for displaying his peculiar powers, than an illustration of the most awful chapter in Christian art."

Last Judgment. An admired picture by Fra Angelico (1387–1455). In the Academy at Florence, Italy.

Last Judgment and Hell. A celebrated fresco in the Campo Santo, Pisa, Italy, which has usually been ascribed to Andrea Orcagna (d. 1389), but has of late been referred by some to the Sienese painter, Pietro Lorenzetti.

☞ "In the *Last Judgment* of Orcagna, in the Campo Santo at Pisa, the Seven Angels [archangels] are important personages. They have the garb of princes and warriors, with breastplates of gold, jewelled sword-belts and tiaras, . . . while other angels hover above, bearing the instruments of the Passion." *Mrs. Jameson.*

Last Judgment. A celebrated picture by the Flemish painter, Roger van der Weyden (d. 1464). It was executed for the Burgundian Chancellor Rollin, between 1443 and 1447, and is now in the Hospital of Beaune, France. It is pronounced by Kugler the most comprehensive example of this master that is left to us.

Last Judgment. A picture by the Flemish painter, Petrus Cristus, executed (1452) for a convent at Burgos. Now in the Museum of Berlin, Prussia.

Last Judgment. A celebrated altar-picture by Hans Memling (d. 1495), the Flemish painter, and pronounced not only his most important work, but one of the *chefs-d'œuvre* of the whole Flemish school. From an inscription upon the picture, it is probable that it was painted in 1467. It is now in the Church of Our Lady at Dantzic, Prussia.

☞ "In Memling's Last Judgment the redeemed are passing into a regular church, with angel musicians hymning their welcome from seats in the architecture above the porch." *Lady Eastlake.*

Last Judgment. A fresco by Fra Bartolommeo (1477–1517), the Italian painter. In the Church of S. Maria Novella, Florence, Italy.

Last Judgment. A picture by Peter Paul Rubens (1577–1640). Now in the gallery of Munich, Bavaria.

Last Judgment. A fresco painting of great size, 60 feet high by 30 feet broad, occupying the end wall opposite to the entrance of the Sistine Chapel, in the Vatican Palace at Rome. It is the work of Michael Angelo (1475–1564), who designed it in his sixtieth year, and completed it after eight years of labor, in 1541. It comprises nearly 300 figures, and presents "a confused mass of naked bodies in the most violent attitudes and most admired disorder, and excels chiefly in energy of expression." This picture is seen now under many disadvantages, having suffered from neglect and from alterations, and being obscured by the dampness, the smoke of candles and incense, but is still regarded as a masterpiece in painting of the great artist. It was undertaken by desire of Pope Clement VII., and finished in the pontificate of Paul III. A copy on a small scale by

Marcello Venusti, seven and a half feet high, is in the Gallery at Naples, and another by Sigalon in the Beaux Arts at Paris.

☞ "Many fresco paintings belonging to the sixteenth century are at the present day in a sad state; few, however, have been more cruelly trifled with than the *Last Judgment* of Michael Angelo. The smoke of the altar-candles has had a fatal effect in the course of centuries. The lower part of the painting is most damaged. . . . The greatest evil, however, has been intentionally done to the work; the nakedness of the figures has been considered offensive; and they have been covered with painted, and often glaringly bright, drapery. . . . From all this, the work appears in such a condition, that only after long study is it possible to form an idea of what it was in the year 1541." *Grimm, Trans.*

☞ "While in Raphael's angels we do not feel the want of wings, we feel, while looking at those of Michael Angelo, that not even the 'sail-broad vans' with which Satan labored through the surging abyss of Chaos could suffice to lift those Titanic forms from earth, and sustain them in mid-air. The group of angels over the *Last Judgment*, flinging their mighty limbs about, . . . may be referred to as characteristic examples." *Mrs. Jameson.*

Or hues of Hell be by his pencil pour'd
Over the damn'd before the Judgment throne,
Such as I saw them, such as all shall see.
Byron.

Last Judgment. A picture by Luca Signorelli (1441–1523?), and his masterpiece. In the Cathedral of Orvieto, Italy.

Last Judgment. A picture by Hieronymus van Aeken, commonly known as Jerom Bosch (1460–1516), the Flemish painter. It is now in the Museum at Berlin, Prussia.

Last Judgment. A picture by Luc Jacobsz, called Lucas van Leyden (1494–1533), a Flemish painter, and one of his most important works. It is now in the Town-house of Leyden, Holland.

Last Judgment. A famous fresco painting by Peter von Cornelius (1787–1867). In the Ludwig's Kirche, Munich, Bavaria. It occupies the whole end of the church behind the high altar, and is perhaps the largest painting in the world. The circular dome in the centre contains groups of martyrs, prophets, and saints, painted in fresco on a ground of gold.

Last Supper. [Ital. *Il Cenacolo*, or *La Cena*; Fr. *La Cène*.] A favorite subject of representation by the great painters of the Middle Ages. This incident in the life of Christ is depicted both historically and as a religious mystery. Among the more noted and familiar paintings which illustrate this theme, the following may be mentioned.

Last Supper. A picture by Giotto di Bordone (1276–1336). In the refectory of the convent of Santa Croce at Florence, Italy. The earliest representation of this subject in Western art.

☞ "The arrangement of the table and figures, so peculiarly fitted for a refectory, has been generally adopted since the time of Giotto in pictures painted for this especial purpose." *Mrs. Jameson.*

Last Supper. A fresco painting by Cosimo Rosselli (1439–1506). In the Sistine Chapel, Rome.

Last Supper. A composition by Ghirlandaio (1449–1494). Executed for the refectory of San Marco in Florence, Italy. "The arrangement is ingenious: the table is what we call of the horse-shoe form, which allows all the figures to face the spectator."

Last Supper. A fresco discovered in 1845, in what was formerly the refectory of the convent of S. Onofrio, Florence, Italy. It bears in one place the name of Raphael and the date 1505, which circumstance has given rise to much discussion concerning its authorship. It is now generally agreed that it is the work of some other painter — perhaps Pinturicchio.

☞ "The authenticity of this picture has been vehemently disputed; for myself — as far as my opinion is worth any thing — I never, after the first five minutes, had a doubt on the subject." *Mrs. Jameson.*

Last Supper. A picture by Andrea del Sarto (1487–1531), generally considered as taking rank next after the representations of this subject by Leonardo da Vinci and Raphael. In the convent of the Salvi, near Florence, Italy.

Last Supper. A famous picture by Hans Holbein (1494-1543). At Basle, Switzerland. There is another and smaller work on this subject by the same artist in the Louvre at Paris.

Last Supper. A famous picture by Leonardo da Vinci (1452–1520), painted by order of the Duke of Milan, Ludovico Sforza, on the walls of the refectory in the Dominican convent of the Madonna delle Grazie. The figures, being above the eye, and to be viewed from a distance, are colossal. The picture is now in a state of great decay, but it is very familiar through the engraving of Raphael Morghen. There are many good old copies of this celebrated picture; one of the best being by Marco d'Oggione, about 1510, and now in the Royal Academy, London.

☞ "When Leonardo da Vinci, the greatest thinker as well as the greatest painter of his age, brought all the resources of his mind to bear on the subject, there sprang forth a creation so consummate, that since that time it has been at once the wonder and the despair of those who have followed in the same path. True, the work of his hand is perishing — will soon have perished utterly. Fortunately for us, multiplied copies have preserved, at least the intention of the artist in his work." *Mrs. Jameson.*

☞ "It is probably the most celebrated picture in the world; that is, the most talked of and written about, . . . a work full of melancholy interest, — a picture in ruins; and the imagination peoples the denuded walls with forms not inferior to those which time has effaced." *G. S. Hillard.*

☞ "At the present day, when the work has almost disappeared, it still produces an irresistible effect from the attitude of the figures and the art with which they are formed into groups. . . . It is certainly the earliest work of that magnificent new style in which Michael Angelo and Raphael subsequently painted." *Grimm, Trans.*

Though searching damps and many an envious flaw
Have marr'd this work, the calm, ethereal grace,
The love deep seated in the Saviour's face,
The mercy, goodness, have not failed to awe
The elements; as they do melt and thaw
The heart of the beholder — and erase
(At least for one rapt moment) every trace
Of disobedience to the primal law.
The annunciation of the dreadful truth
Made to the twelve survives; the brow, the cheek,
And hand reposing on the board in ruth
Of what it utters, while the unguilty seek
Unquestionable meanings, still bespeak
A labor worthy of eternal youth.
Wordsworth.

Time hath done
His work on this fair picture; but that face
His outrage awes. Stranger! the mist of years
Between thee hung and half its heavenly grace,
Hangs there, a fitting veil; nor that alone —
Gaze on it also through a veil of tears!
Aubrey de Vere.

Last Supper. A picture by Domenico Ghirlandajo (1449–1498?). In the museum of St. Mark, Florence, Italy.

Last Supper. A picture by Jacopo Robusti, called Il Tintoretto (1512–1594).

Last Supper. An altar-piece by Dierick Steuerbout (d 1475), the Flemish painter. In the Church of St. Peter's at Louvain, Belgium.

Lateran, Palace of the. The old palace was the residence of the popes in Rome for nearly a thousand years, from the time of Constantine to the return of the Holy See from Avignon. It was finally destroyed by Sixtus V. The private chapel of the popes, and a portion of the dining-hall, are all that now remain of this famous building. The new or modern Palace of the Lateran was built by Sixtus V. In 1693 it was turned into a hospital; in 1843 it was converted by Gregory XVI. into a museum; and it is now the principal depository for antiquities found at Rome within the last few years.

Lateran. See OBELISK OF THE LATERAN and ST. JOHN LATERAN.

Latin Convent, Nazareth. This convent is the largest building in Nazareth, and contains the Church of the Annunciation. This church is built, according to tradition, over the grottos which formed the lower part of the house of Joseph and Mary. The church is plain but handsome, and the music is very fine. The monks show the granite pillars which stand where the angel Gabriel and Mary stood at the annunciation, the workshop of Joseph, the house where "Jesus gave a supper to his friends before and after his resurrection, and the table 'Mensa Christi,' which they seem to value most of all."

Latin Quarter. See QUARTIER LATIN.

Latin School [of Boston]. An ancient school foundation in Boston, Mass., the oldest institution of the kind in America. It originated in 1634. Benjamin Franklin, Sam Adams, John Hancock, Cotton Mather, Sir William Pepperell, and other celebrities of early days, as well as many eminent men of later times, have been pupils of this school. The school building was originally on School Street, to which it gave its name.

Latour. A farmhouse, or small château, in the wine district of Médoc, on the Garonne, below Bordeaux, France. Here is produced the celebrated wine known as the *Château Latour*.

Laurel Hill. A large and beautiful cemetery adjoining Fairmount Park, Philadelphia. It has fine views of the Schuylkill, and noted collections of trees, including some cedars of Lebanon.

Laval University. An institution of learning, with fine buildings, a library, museum, etc., in Quebec, Can.

Lawrence, The. The flag-ship of Commodore Perry's squadron on Lake Erie in 1813.

Laxenburg. A palace near Vienna, which has been a favorite residence of the royal house of Austria. It is generally known as the Blue House.

Laying down the Law. A picture by Sir Edwin Landseer (1803–1873), the most celebrated modern painter of animals.

Lazare, St. See ST. LAZARE.

Lazarus, Raising of. See RAISING OF LAZARUS.

Leadenhall Market. The largest and best poultry-market in London, formerly celebrated for its beef. It derives its name from the manor-house of Sir Hugh Neville.

> Wouldst thou with mighty beef augment
> thy meal,
> Seek *Leadenhall*. *Gay*.

Leadenhall Street. A well-known street in London, formerly a great meat-market. The East India House stood in this street.

> Further on, through *Leadenhall Street* and Fleet Street — what a world! Here come the ever-thronging, ever-rolling waves of life, pressing and whirling on in their tumultuous career.
> *Bayard Taylor*.

Leads, The. [Ital. *I Piombi*.] The celebrated prison-cells in the Doge's Palace, Venice, Italy, so called from their situation under the roof.

> But let us to the roof,
> And when thou hast surveyed the sea, the land,
> Visit the narrow cells that cluster there,
> As in a place of tombs. There burning suns
> Day after day, beat unrelentingly;
> Turning all things to dust, and scorching up
> The brain, till Reason fled, and the wild yell
> And wilder laugh burst out on every side,
> Answering each other as in mockery!
> *Rogers*.

> I have betray'd myself;
> But there's no torture in the mystic wells
> Which undermine your palace, nor in those
> Not less appalling cells, the "leaden roofs,"
> To force a single name from me of others.
> The Pozzi and the *Piombi* were in vain;
> They might wring blood from me, but treachery never. *Byron*.

League House. See UNION LEAGUE HOUSE.

Leander's Tower. An ancient structure near the Golden Horn at Constantinople, so called after the Leander of classic story, a youth of Abydos, who swam nightly across the Hellespont to visit his love, Hero, a priestess of Sestos. The Turks call this tower the "Maiden's Tower," and connect with it a story of a Greek princess, who was kept imprisoned here by her father, but was liberated by the Arabian hero Heschan. It is now used as a light-house.

We swept round the Golden Horn, past *Leander's tower*, and now lay in the harbor which extends into the sweet waters. *Hans Christian Andersen.*

Leaning Tower [of Pisa]. The name by which the Campanile, or Bell-tower, of the Cathedral of Pisa, Italy, is popularly designated. The deviation of about 13 feet from the perpendicular is doubtless owing to an imperfect foundation. The same peculiarity is observed in many other Italian towers, but nowhere to the same extent as here. That the inclination of the tower was not intentional, but the result of a defective foundation, is said by competent judges to be very evident. It was begun in 1174, is built of white marble, and is 178 feet in height, and 50 feet in diameter. See CAMPANILE.

☞ "Sismondi compares the Tower to the usual pictorial representations in children's books of the Tower of Babel. It is a happy simile, and conveys a better idea of the building than chapters of labored description. Nothing can exceed the grace and lightness of the structure; nothing can be more remarkable than its general appearance. In the course of the ascent to the top (which is by an easy staircase), the inclination is not very apparent; but at the summit it becomes so, and gives one the sensation of being in a ship that has heeled over, through the action of an ebb-tide. The effect *upon the low side*, so to speak, — looking over from the gallery, and seeing the shaft recede to its base, — is very startling; and I saw a nervous traveller hold on to the Tower involuntarily, after glancing down, as if he had some idea of propping it up. The view within, from the ground, — looking up, as through a slanted tube, — is also very curious. It certainly inclines as much as the most sanguine tourist could desire. The natural impulse of ninety-nine people out of a hundred, who were about to recline upon the grass below it, to rest, and contemplate the adjacent buildings, would probably be, not to take up their position under the leaning side; it is so very much aslant." *Dickens.*

☞ "This piece of architectural eccentricity was, and I suppose is, one of the commonplaces of geography, and is put in the same educational stateroom with the Wall of China, the Great Tun of Heidelberg, and the Natural Bridge of Virginia. . . . This singular structure is simply a campanile, or bell-tower, appurtenant to the cathedral, as is the general custom in Italy. It is not merely quaint, but beautiful; that is, take away the quaintness, and the beauty will remain. It is built of white marble, wonderfully fresh and pure when we remember that nearly seven centuries have swept over it." *Hillard.*

☞ "In any event, there are other leaning towers in Italy, at Bologna for example: voluntarily, or involuntarily, this feeling for oddness, this love of paradox, this yielding to fancy, is one of the characteristics of the Middle Ages." *Taine, Trans.*

☞ "The Tower of Pisa may claim to be the noblest tower of Southern Romanesque. The round form doubtless comes from Ravenna; but the Pisan tower is a Ravenna tower glorified." *Freeman.*

The well-curb had a Chinese roof;
And even the long sweep, high aloof,
In its slant splendor, seemed to tell
Of *Pisa's leaning miracle.* *Whittier.*

Lear. A picture by Benjamin West (1738–1820). Now in the Boston Athenæum.

Leda. 1. A mythological picture by Leonardo da Vinci (1452-1519), sometimes called a Carità, or Charity. It is in the possession of Prince Frederic of Holland, at the Hague. A picture by Michael Angelo (1475–1564) upon this subject, executed for the Duke of Ferrara, is lost; but an early copy — a cartoon — is in the Royal Academy, London.

2. A picture by Antonio Allegri, surnamed Correggio (1494–1534). In the Museum at Berlin, Prussia.

Leeds Castle. An ancient ruined fortress near Maidstone, Kent, England.

Lehigh University. A collegiate establishment in Bethlehem, Penn., founded in 1865 by Asa Packer.

Leicester House. A mansion built about 1650 in Leicester Square, London, for the Earl of Leicester. It was occupied at various times by royal personages, among others by Elizabeth, Queen of Bohemia, who lived there, and died there in 1662. George II. resided in Leicester House from 1717 to 1720.

Leicester Square. A well-known square in London, built between 1630 and 1731, noted as a resort and place of residence for foreigners.

☞ "Come through this narrow lane into Leicester Square. You cross here the first limit of the fashionable quarter. This is the home of that most miserable fish out of water — a Frenchman in London." *N. P. Willis.*

They dined at a miserable cheap French *restaurateur* in the neighborhood of *Leicester Square*, where they were served with a caricature of French cookery. *Irving.*

Lemon Hill. An eminence in Fairmount Park, Philadelphia, surmounted by an old mansion, once the residence of Robert Morris, the great financier of the Revolution.

Lenox Library. A marble building in New York City, fronting on Central Park, built at a cost of $500,000, to contain a museum, art-gallery, library, and lecture-hall. It derives its name from its founder, James Lenox, a wealthy citizen of New York.

Leo X. A celebrated portrait of this Pope by Raphael Sanzio (1483–1520), representing him as seated at a table, with the Cardinals de' Medici and de' Rossi behind him on each side. This is regarded as one of Raphael's best portraits. It is now in the Pitti Palace, Florence, Italy. There is a repetition of this picture by Andrea del Sarto (1488-1530), who was employed by Ottaviano de' Medici, the possessor of it, to copy it for the Duke of Mantua. This repetition is so well executed that it deceived even Giulio Romano, who had taken part in the execution of the original. This copy is in the Gallery of Naples, and there has been much discussion as to which was the original picture.

Leonardo da Vinci. A portrait of himself by the painter (1452–1520). In the collection of autograph portraits of the painters, in the Uffizi, Florence, Italy.

Leonard's Crags. See St. Leonard's Crags.

Leonine City. [Ital. *Città Leonina.*] The northern district or quarter of modern Rome, founded in the ninth century by Leo IV., who enclosed it in walls to protect it from the devastation of the Moorish pirates. It is the most interesting quarter of the modern city, as it includes the Castle of St. Angelo, the Vatican, and St. Peter's. At the Italian invasion of September, 1870, it was promised to the Pope, as the sanctuary of the Holy See, the last relic of its temporal sovereignty. This quarter of the city is known as the Borgo. Dyer says, that, when it was enclosed by Leo IV., it obtained the name of Borgo from the Saxon settlement called "Burgus Saxonum."

Leopard, The. A British ship of war which attacked and captured the American vessel *Chesapeake*, in a naval duel in 1813.

Lepanto, Battle of. See Battle of Lepanto.

Lethe Lake. A well-known subterranean lake in the Mammoth Cave, Kentucky. It is crossed in boats.

Levant, The. A vessel of the United States navy. See Portsmouth, The.

Levee, The. A famous dike or

embankment of earth constructed for a great distance along the Mississippi River at and near New Orleans, La. It is 15 feet wide and four feet high, and is used in the fall and winter as a promenade. Crevasses have frequently occurred to damage it, but it has been much strengthened of late. The scene of bustle and activity which the levee presents at times is unequalled in America.

Levite, Feast of the. See FEAST OF THE LEVITE.

Lia Fail. A singular pillar-stone on the summit of the Hill of Tara, in the county of Meath, Ireland.

☞ "This is the celebrated 'coronation stone' of the ancient Irish kings. It is composed of granular limestone, and is at present about six feet above ground, but its real height is said to be 12 feet. At its base it is, perhaps, four feet in circumference; but it tapers somewhat towards the top, not unlike the Round Towers."
Mr. and Mrs. Hall.

See HILL OF TARA and also STONE OF SCONE.

Libby Prison. In Richmond, Va. A noted and notorious place of confinement for military prisoners during the war of the Rebellion. Here the Federal soldiers were subjected to the greatest cruelty and hardships. The building was simply a warehouse converted to the purposes of a jail.

Liber Studiorum. [Book of Studies.] A famous series of prints or drawings by Joseph Mallord William Turner (1775-1851), the English landscape-painter.

Liber Veritatis. [Book of Truth.] A book of original drawings by Claude Lorraine (1600-1682), the French landscape-painter, kept to identify his pictures which were being constantly imitated by other artists. There are six copies of this work, one of which is at Chatsworth, England.

Liberian Basilica. See SANTA MARIA MAGGIORE.

Liberties, The. A district of Dublin, Ireland, in the most elevated and airy part of the city, so called from certain privileges and immunities possessed by the inhabitants, having manor courts of their own with seneschals to preside over them. Some 40 streets and lanes, containing a population estimated at 40,000 souls, are embraced within its precincts.

☞ "The present state of this once flourishing region forms a strong contrast to its former, but it still retains many evidences of what it has been. In passing along its desolate streets, large houses of costly structure everywhere present themselves. Lofty façades adorned with architraves, and mouldings to windows, and door-cases of sculptured stone or marble; grand staircases with carved and gilded balustrades; panelled doors opening into spacious suits of corniced and stuccoed apartments — all attest the opulence of its former inhabitants. They are now the abode only of the most miserable."
Mr. and Mrs. Hall.

Liberty. A colossal statue designed by Thomas Crawford (1814-57), surmounting the dome of the Capitol at Washington. It is undoubtedly the best known of his works. The statue is executed in bronze, and is 19½ feet in height. It was cast at Bladensburg, Md., by Clark Mills.

Liberty Bell. A famous bell now preserved in Independence Hall, Philadelphia, Penn. It was originally cast in London in 1752, and bore the motto, "Proclaim liberty throughout the land unto all the inhabitants thereof." It was subsequently re-cast in Philadelphia, retaining the same inscription, and was rung on the occasion of the adoption by Congress of the Declaration of Independence.

☞ "The bell which rang out the Declaration of Independence has found at last a voice articulate, to 'proclaim liberty throughout all the land unto all the inhabitants thereof.' It has been heard across oceans, and has modified the sentiments of cabinets and kings. The people of the Old World have heard it, and their hearts stop to catch the last whisper of its echoes. The poor slave has heard it, and with bounding joy, tempered by the mystery of religion, he worships and adores. The waiting Continent has heard it, and already foresees the fulfilled prophecy, when she will sit 'redeemed, regenerated, and disinthralled by the irresistible Genius of Universal Emancipation.'" *J. A. Andrew.*

Liberty-Cap. This symbol of liberty is very ancient. According to the Roman legend, when Saturninus seized the Capitol at Rome, in the first century before Christ, he raised a cap on the point of a spear as a sign of freedom to all slaves who should join him. A similar expedient was often adopted subsequently, and in modern times the crowning of a liberty-pole with a cap is a relic of the old custom.

Liberty Club. See RUMP-STEAK CLUB.

Liberty Tree. A large elm in Boston, Mass., used to hang effigies of obnoxious persons upon at the time of the disturbances caused by the Stamp Act. The site of this tree is commemorated by a device upon the building which now occupies its place upon Washington Street. Lafayette said, "The world should never forget the spot where once stood *Liberty Tree.*"

Libyan Sibyl. A statue by W. W. Story (b. 1819).

☞ "The two conceptions, 'Cleopatra' and the 'Libyan Sibyl,' have placed Mr. Story in European estimation at the head of American sculptors." *Jarves.*

Lichfield Cathedral. One of the most interesting ecclesiastical structures in England, in the town of Lichfield. It was erected in the twelfth and thirteenth centuries.

Lichtenstein. A mimic castle near Reutlingen, Germany, on the summit of a lofty rock, with precipices of 800 feet, and accessible only by a drawbridge. Built in 1842.

Lido, The. The name by which the sea-shore in the immediate neighborhood of Venice is commonly known, and still as formerly a favorite resort and bathing-place.

☞ "Thither in more cheerful days the Venetians used to resort in great numbers on certain holidays, called the Mondays of the Lido, to enjoy the sea-breeze and the country scenery, and to lunch upon the flat tombs of the Hebrews, buried there in exile from the consecrated Christian ground." *W. D. Howells.*

Through all the music ringing in my ears
A knell was sounding as distinct and clear,
Though low and far, as e'er the Adrian wave
Rose o'er the city's murmur in the night,
Dashing against the outward *Lido's* bulwark. *Byron.*

Liebenstein. A well-known ruined castle on the Rhine, near St. Goar. It is one of two which go by the name of the Brothers, and which are associated with a romantic legend.

Liechtenstein, Das alte Schloss. An ancient castle, now in ruins, in the neighborhood of Vienna, Austria.

Life, Fountain of. See FOUNTAIN OF LIFE.

Life of the Virgin. See VIRGIN.

Light of the World. A picture by William Holman Hunt (b. 1827), and regarded as one of his masterpieces. It is a symbolic figure of Christ.

☞ "Hunt's *Light of the World* is, I believe, the most perfect instance of expressional purpose with technical power which the world has yet produced" *Ruskin: Modern Painters.*

☞ "*Christ the Light of the World* is set in a greenish-yellow atmosphere, resembling that perceived on ascending to the surface of turbid water after a plunge." *Taine, Trans.*

Limbo, The. A picture by Angiolo Bronzino (1502–1572). In the Uffizi, Florence, Italy.

Lincei, Accademia de'. A scientific society, the oldest of the kind in Italy, founded in 1603 by a number of philosophers, including Galileo. It was re-organized in

1849 by Pius IX. Its meetings are held on Sunday in the Palace of the Senator at Rome. Its name is taken from its symbol, the lynx, the emblem of watchfulness.

Lincluden Abbey. An ancient and picturesque ruined monastery near Dumfries, Scotland.

> Ye holy walls, that, still sublime,
> Resist the crumbling touch of Time,
> How strongly still your form displays
> The piety of ancient days!
> As through your ruins, hoar and gray —
> Ruins yet beauteous in decay —
> The silvery moonbeams trembling fly.
> *Burns.*

Lincoln College. One of the colleges included in the University of Oxford, England. It was founded about 1427.

Lincoln Park. 1. A public pleasure-ground in Chicago, Ill., laid out on the lake-shore. It includes 250 acres.

2. A public pleasure-ground in Cincinnati, O.

Lincoln's Inn. One of the four Inns of Court, London, built upon the site of the town-house of Henry de Lacy, earl of Lincoln (d. 1312), from whom its name is derived. See INNS OF COURT, INNER TEMPLE, MIDDLE TEMPLE, GRAY'S INN.

> Will any man, for instance, tell us which *bricks* it was in *Lincoln's Inn Buildings*, that Ben Jonson's hand and trowel laid? No man, it is to be feared, — and also grumbled at. *Carlyle.*

Lincoln's Inn Fields. A fine square in London, laid out by Inigo Jones, and built in 1619-36. Lincoln's Inn Fields were long the resort of vagrants. Gay in his "Trivia" says: —

> Where Lincoln Inn's wide space is rail'd around,
> Cross not with vent'rous step; there oft is found
> The lurking thief, who, while the daylight shone,
> Made the walls echo with his begging tone:
> That wretch, which late compassion moved, shall wound
> Thy bleeding head, and fell thee to the ground.

> Perhaps he remembered that one of them [the Pyramids] was as big as *Lincoln's Inn Fields.* *Thackeray.*

Linden, Unter den. See UNTER DEN LINDEN.

Lindenwald. The country-seat of Martin Van Buren (1782–1862), the eighth president of the United States, situated near Kinderhook, N.Y.

Lindsey House. A noble mansion on the west of Lincoln's Inn Fields in London, built by the Earl of Lindsey, the general of Charles I. Afterwards called Ancaster House.

Linlithgow Palace. One of the most ancient royal residences in Scotland, situated in the town of Linlithgow. The present building was begun by Edward I., about the year 1300, and is memorable as having been the birthplace of Mary Queen of Scots. It is now a magnificent ruin. The situation is remarkably lovely.

> Of all the palaces so fair,
> Built for the royal dwelling,
> In Scotland, far beyond compare,
> *Linlithgow* is excelling. *Scott.*

☞ "The castle has a very sad and romantic appearance, standing there all alone as it does, looking down into the quiet lake. It is said that the internal architectural decorations are exceedingly rich and beautiful, and a resemblance has been traced between its style of ornament and that of Heidelberg Castle, which has been accounted for by the fact that the princess Elizabeth, who was the sovereign lady of Heidelberg, spent many of the earlier years of her life in this place." *Mrs. H. B. Stowe.*

Lion House. A building in Salt Lake City, Utah Territory, used as a sort of seraglio of the Mormon leaders. It derives its name from the image of a lion over the entrance.

Lion Hunt. A noted picture by Peter Paul Rubens (1577–1640), and one of his finest works. In the Pinakothek at Munich, Bavaria. Also at Dresden, Saxony.

Lion [of Bastia], The. A natural curiosity at the entrance of the harbor of Bastia in Corsica. It is a rock bearing an extraordinary likeness to a lion couchant, the resemblance being striking in all details even to the bushy mane, which is formed by a growth of creeping plants.

Lion of Lucerne. A celebrated work of sculpture at Lucerne, Switzerland, modelled by Albert Bertel Thorwaldsen (1770–1844). It was erected in 1821, in memory of 21 officers and about 760 soldiers of the Swiss guard, who were slain in defending the Tuileries on Aug. 10, 1792. The lion, which is of colossal size, is represented as dying, a broken spear transfixes his body, and with his paw he tries to protect the Bourbon lily. The figure is of sandstone rock, 28 feet long and 18 high, and upon it are inscribed the names of the officers.

☞ "In a sequestered spot the rocky hill-side is cut away, and in the living strata is sculptured the colossal figure of a dying lion. A spear is broken off in his side, but in his last struggle he still defends a shield marked with the fleur-de-lis of France. Below are inscribed in red letters, as if charactered in blood, the names of the brave officers of that devoted band." *Beecher.*

Lion of St. Mark. A winged lion, the heraldic device of the ancient republic of Venice, whose patron saint is St. Mark. One of the noted columns in the Piazzetta at Venice is surmounted by the image of a winged lion.

And every monument the stranger meets,
Church, palace, pillar, as a mourner greets;
And even the *Lion* all subdued appears.
Byron.

Lone seated on the strand,
Uplifts the *lion* grand
His foot of bronze on high
Against the sky.
Alfred de Musset, Trans.

Sullen old *lion* of grand *St. Mark*
Lordeth and lifteth his front from the dark.
Joaquin Miller.

Lions. See Court of Lions and Gate of the Lions.

Lion's Mouth. [Ital. *Bocca di Leone.*] A famous hole or opening in the wall, in the ante-chamber of the Great Council, in the Doge's Palace, Venice, through which anonymous accusations were passed in against individuals who had incurred suspicion or enmity.

And in the palace of St. Mark
Unnamed accusers in the dark
Within the "*Lion's mouth*" had placed
A charge against him uneffaced.
Byron.

Liparata, Santa. See Santa Maria del Fiore.

Lippi, Fra Filippo. A portrait of himself by the painter (1412–1469). In the Museum at Berlin, Prussia.

Lismore Castle. A seat of the Duke of Devonshire in the county of Waterford, Ireland.

Lit de Justice. See Bed of Justice.

Literary Club. See Club, The.

Literary Fund. A society established in London, in 1790, by David Williams, the object of which is to furnish aid to authors who may be in distress, and to render assistance to their widows and children.

☞ "Some of the brightest names in contemporary literature have been beholden to the bounty of this institution, and in numerous instances its interference has shielded friendless merit from utter ruin." *Quarterly Review.*

☞ The permanent fund of the Literary Fund on the 1st of January, 1880, consisted of £6,200 in consols. The actual number of grants paid by the society from its foundation up to 1880 was 3,796, amounting to £90,617.

Little Bengal. A name applied to Cavendish and Portman Squares, and adjoining streets, in London, — a district inhabited by retired Indians.

Little Britain. This quarter in London, so called from having been in old times the residence of the Dukes of Brittany, was, in the reigns of the Stuarts, remarkable as a great centre for booksellers — a sort of Paternoster Row.

"*Little Britain* was a plentiful and perpetual emporium of learned authors, and men went thither as to a market. . . . But now this emporium has vanished, and the trade contracted into the hands of two or three persons." *Roger North.*

☞ "In the centre of the great City of London lies a small neighborhood, consisting of a cluster of narrow streets and courts, of very venerable and debilitated houses, which goes by name of *Little Britain*. Little Britain may truly be called the heart's core of the city, the stronghold of true John Bullism. It is a fragment of London as it was in its better days, with its antiquated folks and fashions." *Irving.*

The race of booksellers in *Little Britain* is now [1731] almost extinct.
Gentleman's Magazine.

Little Messenger, The. An admired picture by Jean Louis Ernest Meissonier (b. 1811).

Little Round Top. A rugged eminence in the vicinity of Gettysburg, Penn., famous as the scene of a desperate struggle between the Union forces and the Confederate troops on the 2d of July, 1863, which led to the greater battle of Cemetery Hill on the next day.

Little Trianon. See PETIT TRIANON.

Lizard Point. A famous headland, the southernmost promontory of England, — the *Ocrinum* of Ptolemy, the ancient geographer. There are two large light-houses here.

May never saw dismember thee,
Nor wielded axe disjoint;
Thou art the fairest spoken tree
From here to *Lizard Point*.
Tennyson.

Lloyd's. The name given to a series of rooms in the Royal Exchange, London, — the rendezvous of the most eminent merchants, shipowners (and those who seek shipping news), underwriters, insurance, stock and exchange brokers, etc. The name originated with one Lloyd, a coffee-house keeper in Lombard Street, at whose house merchants were in the habit of congregating in the early part of the eighteenth century for the transaction of the business. The subscribers to Lloyd's represent the greater part of the mercantile wealth of England. A similar institution was established at Trieste, Austria, in 1833, and is known as the Austrian-Lloyds.

Loch Inch Castle. The seat of the Earl of Stair, near Stranraer, Scotland.

Lochleven Castle. An ancient castle on an island in the lake of Lochleven, Scotland, memorable as the scene of the imprisonment of Mary Queen of Scots. Her escape from this fortress is related in Sir Walter Scott's novel entitled "The Abbot."

Put off, put off, and row with speed,
For now's the time and the hour of need!
To oars, to oars, and trim the bark,
Nor Scotland's queen be a warder's mark!

Those ponderous keys shall the kelpies keep,
And lodge in their caverns dark and deep;
Nor shall *Lochleven's* towers or hall
Hold thee, our lovely lady, in thrall.
Robert Allan.

Locum Abbey. A fine monastic ruin near Wunstorf in Prussia. The abbey dates from the thirteenth century.

Lodi, Bridge of. See BRIDGE OF LODI.

Lodore. A noted waterfall in the lake district of England, near Keswick. The effect of the cascade is dependent in a good measure upon the state of the weather, and the quantity of water.

How does the water
Come down at *Lodore?*

. . . .

All at once and all o'er, with a mighty uproar;
And this way the water comes down at *Lodore.* *Southey.*

Logan Stone. A famous rocking-stone near the Gap of Dunloe in the county of Kerry, Ireland. It is thought to be a Druidical remain of remote antiquity. The poet Moore likens it to the poet's heart, which

"The slightest touch alone sets moving,
But all earth's power could not shake from its base."

Loggia de' Lanzi. A well-known arcade in Florence, Italy, built in the fourteenth century, and containing famous works of sculpture. The name is derived from the Swiss lancers in the employ of Cosimo de' Medici (1389–1464).

No! the people sought no wings
From Perseus in the *Loggia*, nor implored
An inspiration in the place beside,

From that dim bust of Brutus, jagged and grand,
Where Buonarotti passionately tried
Out of the clenched marble to demand
The head of Rome's sublimest homicide.
Mrs. Browning.

Loggie of Raphael. A celebrated portico (the Loggie form a series of three corridors, or a triple portico, round three sides of an open court) in the Vatican Palace at Rome, deriving its name from the frescos of that master and his pupils which it contains.

☞ "From the Sistine Chapel we went to Raphael's *Loggie*, and I hardly venture to say that we could scarcely bear to look at them. The eye was so educated and so enlarged by those grand forms and the glorious completeness of all their parts, that it could take no pleasure in the imaginative play of arabesques, and the scenes from Scripture, beautiful as they are, had lost their charm. To see these works *often* alternately, and to compare them at leisure and without prejudice, must be a great pleasure; but all sympathy is at first one-sided."
Goethe, Trans.

Lollards' Prison. A celebrated prison-room in the tower of Lambeth Palace, London, in which many followers of Wickliffe (known as Lollards), as well as others, were confined. The apartment is some 12 feet square and 8 feet high. The walls, ceiling, and floor are laid with rough-hewn boards upon which are numerous fragments of inscriptions, and notches to mark the passage of time, cut by those imprisoned here.

☞ "In order to get to the tower, we had to go through a great many apartments, passages, and corridors, and terminate all by climbing a winding staircase, steeper and narrower than was at all desirable for any but wicked heretics. The room is 13 feet by 12, and about 8 feet high, wainscoted with oak, which is scrawled over with names and inscriptions. There are eight large iron rings in the wall, to which the prisoners were chained; for aught we know, Wickliffe himself may have been one. . . . We all agreed, however, that, considering the very beautiful prospect this tower commands up and down the Thames, the poor Lollards in some respects might have been worse lodged."
Mrs. H. B. Stowe.

Lollards' Tower. A famous tower in London. See LOLLARDS' PRISON.

Lombard Street. A celebrated street in London, the centre of the "banking world." It derives its name from the Longobards, a family of whom, in early times, settled here, and established a bank. The poet Pope was born in this street.

☞ "Lombard Street and Threadneedle Street are merely places where men toil and accumulate. They go elsewhere to enjoy and to expend."
Macaulay.

London Bridge. The last bridge on the Thames, or the one nearest the sea, built of granite, and first opened to the public by William IV., Aug. 1, 1831. It was built at an outlay of £2,566,268, from designs of John Rennie and his sons John and George. In Saxon times there was a bridge at this spot, and in 1176 the first stone bridge was built here. The old London Bridge had houses upon each side. At one time it was noted for its booksellers' shops, and at a later period was famous for its many pin-makers. Pennant says that the street on Old London Bridge was "narrow, darksome, and dangerous to passengers from the multitude of carriages: frequent arches of strong timbers crossing the street from the tops of the houses, to keep them together and from falling into the river. Nothing but use could preserve the repose of the inmates, who soon grew deaf to the noise of falling waters, the clamors of watermen, or the frequent shrieks of drowning wretches." London Bridge, in the time of Shakespeare and for years afterwards, was built of wood and lined with houses on either side. In the second part of King Henry VI., Cade says, "Come, then, let's go fight with them. But, first, go and set *London-bridge* on fire; and, if you can, burn down the Tower too."

☞ "It has been ascertained that the number of carriages of all descriptions, and equestrians, who daily pass along London Bridge in the course of 24 hours, exceeds 20,000; and that the number of pedestrians who pass across the bridge daily during the same space of time is no fewer than 107,000."

Murray's Handbook.

☞ "Such who only see it [the *old* bridge] *beneath*, where it is a bridge, cannot suspect that it should be a street; and such who behold it *above*, where it is a street, cannot believe it is a bridge." *Fuller.*

Stopp'd by the houses of that wondrous street,
Which rides o'er the broad river like a fleet. *Cowley.*

London bridge is broken down,
Dance o'er my lady Lee;
London bridge is broken down,
With a gay lady. *Mother Goose.*

As I was going o'er *London Bridge*,
And peeped through a nick,
I saw four and twenty ladies
Riding on a stick! *Mother Goose.*

London Coffee-house. **1.** Formerly an establishment on Ludgate Hill, London, now a tavern. It was opened before 1731.

Yesterday morning I came early to Bath, . . . and at five in the evening took my seat in the mail-coach, which, this morning at eight, landed me safely in the *London Coffee-House*, Ludgate Hill.

George Ticknor.

2. A noted old building in Philadelphia, Penn., on Market Street, erected in 1702, and a place of much resort before the Revolution.

London Docks. An immense establishment, in London, on the left bank of the Thames, covering an area of 90 acres, and including 20 warehouses, 18 sheds, 17 vaults, and six quays. The first dock was opened in 1805. The Western and Eastern Docks embrace respectively 20 and 7 acres; and the Wapping Basin, 3 acres. The cost of the whole structure has exceeded £4,000,000, and the number of laborers employed to carry on the business of the docks varies from 1,000 to 3,000.

☞ "As you enter the dock, the sight of the forest of masts in the distance and the tall chimneys vomiting clouds of black smoke, and the many-colored flags flying in the air, has a most peculiar effect; while the sheds, with the monster wheels arching through the roofs, look like paddle-boxes of huge steamers."

Henry Mayhew.

☞ "These docks are prodigious, overpowering. . . . There are ships everywhere, and ships upon ships in rows show their heads and their swelling bosoms, like beautiful fish under their cuirass of copper."

Taine, Trans.

London House. Once the town residence of the Bishop of London.

London Monument. See MONUMENT, THE.

London Stone. An ancient relic, supposed to be a fragment of the *milliarium*, or mile-stone of the Romans, now preserved in Cannon Street, London. There is evidence that it was placed there a thousand years ago; and Camden considers it to have been the great central mile-stone, from which the British high roads radiated, similar to that in the Forum at Rome. Tradition declares that the stone was brought from Troy by Brutus, and laid by his own hand as the foundation-stone of London, and its palladium. It is referred to in the ancient Saxon charters as a local mark of immemorial antiquity. The stone before the Great Fire [1666] was much worn away: it was then cased over with new stone, admitting the ancient stone to be seen through a large aperture at the top. It is now placed against the south wall of St. Swithin's Church. It has been from the earliest ages jealously guarded and embedded, perhaps from a superstitious belief in the identity of the fate of London with its palladium. Jack Cade struck London Stone, exclaiming, "Now is Mortimer lord of this city."

☞ "On the south side of this high street, neere unto the channell, is pitched upright a great stone, called London Stone, fixed in the ground very deep, fastened with bars of iron, and otherwise so stronglie set that if cartes do runne against it through negligence, the wheeles be broken and the stone itselfe unshaken. The cause why this stone was there set, the verie time when, or other memory hereof, is there none; but that the same hath long continued there, is manifest, namely since, or rather before the time of the Conquest." *Stow.*

Cade. And here, sitting upon *London Stone*, I charge and command, that, of the city's cost, the conduit run nothing but claret wine this first year of our reign.
King Henry VI., Part II.

Jack Straw at *London Stone* with all his rout
Struck not the city with so loud a shout.
Dryden.

London Stone Tavern. A house near the famous London Stone, in London, which has been incorrectly called the oldest tavern in the metropolis. The celebrated Robin Hood society originated here.

London Tavern. A well-known place of entertainment in London, where are held many meetings, banquets, and other gatherings. It is situated in Bishopsgate Street Within. Dickens in "Nicholas Nickleby" describes a meeting of the "United Metropolitan Improved Hot Muffin and Crumpet Baking and Punctual Delivery Company," holden at the London Tavern.

London University. The University of London, Burlington Gardens, was established in 1837 for the sole purpose of examining candidates for academical honors, and for conferring degrees on college graduates, previously matriculated at this university. The university has nothing to do with the ordinary business of education, and the board of examiners is paid by Government.

London Wall. This name is now applied to a street in London, the north side of which occupies the site of part of the old City wall. The wall, thought to be the work of the later Roman period, extended "from the Tower through the Minories to Aldgate, Houndsditch, Bishopsgate, *along London Wall* to Fore-street, through Cripplegate and Castle-street to Aldersgate, and so through Christ's Hospital by Newgate and Ludgate towards the Thames" (*Timbs*).

And when we come to *London Wall*,
A pleasant sight to view,
Come forth! come forth, ye cowards all,
Here's men as good as you.
R. S. Hawker.

Lone Mountain. A well-known cemetery, or cluster of cemeteries, in the neighborhood of San Francisco, Cal. Around the conical peak called the Lone Mountain a number of burial-places have been laid out.

Long Acre. A well-known street in London, between Covent Garden and St. Giles's.

Dick Swiveller. This dinner to-day closes *Long Acre* . . . There's only one avenue to the Strand left open now, and I shall have to stop up that to-night with a pair of gloves. *Dickens.*

Make his acquaintance by chance, and he takes you home to supper in a plain chariot on the best springs *Long Acre* can turn out. *N. P. Willis.*

Long Bridge. A structure about a mile in length, crossing the Potomac River at Washington. This bridge was famous during the civil war, being strongly fortified, and the great thoroughfare for troops and supplies, and the main avenue of communication with the Army of the Potomac.

Long Meg. A singular relic, supposed to be a part of a Druidical temple, near Penrith, in the county of Cumberland, England. It is a square unhewn column of red freestone, 15 feet in circumference, and 18 feet high. Sixty-seven stones arranged in a circle near by are known as Long Meg's Daughters.

☞ "When I first saw this monument, as I came upon it by surprise, I might overrate its importance as an object; but, though it will not bear a comparison with Stonehenge, I have not seen any other relic of those dark ages which can pretend to rival it in singularity and dignity of appearance."
Wordsworth.

A weight of awe, not easy to be borne,
Fell suddenly upon my spirit —
When first I saw that family forlorn —
That sisterhood, in hieroglyphic round.
Wordsworth.

Long Walk. A famous avenue in Windsor Park, near London, nearly three miles in length, in a perfectly straight line, lined with trees, and terminated by the colossal equestrian statue of George III., in bronze, by Westmacott (1775–1856). It is considered the finest avenue of the kind in Europe.

Long Walls. The name given to the walls which in ancient times connected Athens with the sea. There were three "Long Walls;" but the name appears to have been applied to those two which connected the city with the Piræus, that leading to Phalerum being called the Phalerian Wall. These two walls (to the Piræus) were but a short distance apart. The foundations of the Long Walls may still be traced in part, though they were in ruins in the time of Pausanias. They were built during the administrations of Themistocles and of Pericles, in the fifth century B.C. A railway seven miles in length now extends from Athens to Piræus, and follows the course of one of these famous walls.

Longford Castle. The seat of the Earl of Radnor, near Salisbury, England. The mansion contains a fine collection of pictures.

Longleat. The seat of the Marquis of Bath, on the borders of Wiltshire, England. A beautiful mansion of the Elizabethan age.

We should see the keeps where nobles, insecure themselves, spread insecurity around them, giving place to the halls of peaceful opulence, to the oriels of *Longleat*, and the stately pinnacles of Burleigh.
Macaulay.

O'er *Longleat's* towers, o'er Cranbourne's oaks,
The fiery herald flew;
He roused the shepherds of Stonehenge,
The rangers of Beaulieu. *Macaulay.*

Longwood. Napoleon Bonaparte's villa, on the island of St. Helena, occupied by the emperor during his exile. It was here that he died May 5, 1821.

Our age has indeed been fruitful of warnings to the eminent, and of consolation to the obscure. Two men have died within our recollection, who, at a time of life at which few people have completed their education, have raised themselves, each in his own department, to the height of glory. One of them died at *Longwood;* the other at Missolonghi. *Macaulay.*

Lord Clyde. An armor-plated ship of the British navy, launched Oct. 13, 1864.

Lord Mayor's Coach. The carriage in which, on state occasions, the Lord Mayor of London rides forth. It is a great lumbering vehicle, carved and gilded, said to have been designed and painted by Cipriani in 1757, built at an original cost of £1,065, and kept in repair at an annual expediture of £100. See CORONATION COACH.

☞ "It seemed to me that a man of any sense must be very glad to get out of such a vehicular gimcrack as that. . . . Nothing could be more out of place, more incongruous, than this childish masquerading seemed to be with English common-sense, and with the sobriety and true dignity befitting such an official person as the mayor of the city of London."
Richard Grant White.

Lord Warden. An armor-plated ship of the British navy, launched May 27, 1865.

Lords, House of. See HOUSE OF LORDS.

Lorelei, The. [Ger. *Lurleiberg.*] Rugged and precipitous rocks, rising 420 feet from the river Rhine. The old legend of a siren who lived on the summit of the rock, and enticed sailors and fishermen to their destruction in the rapids at the base of the rock, has formed a subject for poets and painters. Goethe's pretty little ballad is perhaps most familiar. Heinrich Heine, the German poet (1799?–1856), has a well-known lyric entitled the "Lorelei." [Written also *Lurlei* and *Loreley.*]

Yonder we see it from the steamer's deck,
The haunted mountain of the *Lorelei.*
The o'erhanging crags sharp-cut against a sky
Clear as a sapphire without flaw or rack.
T. B. Aldrich.

Loreley. A popular picture illustrating the well-known legend upon the subject of the Loreley, by W. Kray. The same subject has also been treated by others. See LORELEI.

Lorenzo de' Medici. A famous statue by Michael Angelo Buonarotti (1475–1564). In the Church of S. Lorenzo, Florence, Italy. Called "Il Pensoso," "the thinker."

☞ "From its character of profound reflection, the figure of Lorenzo has acquired the distinctive appellation of 'La Pensée de Michel Ange.' It is, in fact, the personification of contemplative thought." *J. S. Harford.*

☞ "Of a still higher order of art is the statue of Lorenzo. . . . The air of the figure is thoughtful and contemplative. It is that of a man meditating and absorbed by some great design, and not without a dash of the formidable. There is something dangerous in that deep, solemn stillness and intense self-involution. Deadly will be the spring that follows the uncoiling of those folds. I recall no work in marble which leaves the same impression as this remarkable statue. Its power is like that of a magician's spell, . . . such a work as would have been pronounced impossible to be executed in marble, had it not been done." *Hillard.*

☞ "I observe that the costume of the figure, instead of being mediæval, is Roman; but, be it what it may, the grand and simple character of the figure imbues the robes with its individual propriety. I still think it the greatest miracle ever wrought in marble." *Hawthorne.*

☞ "It really is not worthy of Mr. Powers to say that the whole effect of this mighty statue depends, not on the positive efforts of Michael Angelo's chisel, but on the absence of light in the space of a few inches. He wrought the whole statue in harmony with that small part of it which he leaves to the spectator's imagination, and, if he had erred at any point, the miracle would have been a failure; so that, working in marble, he has positively reached a degree of excellence above the capability of marble, sculpturing his highest touches upon air and duskiness." *Hawthorne.*

Lorenzo, San. See SAN LORENZO.

Loreto. See SANTA CASA.

Lorsch, Abbey of. A ruined monastery near Bensheim, Germany. It is considered one of the oldest Gothic edifices in Germany, parts of the existing building dating from the year 774.

Lost Pleiad. An admired picture by Thomas Buchanan Read (1822–1872).

Lost River. A natural curiosity in Hampshire County, W. Va. A stream disappears abruptly at the base of a mountain, through which it finds its way by underground channels.

Lothbury. A district in London where live many candlestick-makers and pewterers. According to Stow the name is derived from the loathsome noise proceeding from the shops of these metal-workers.

And, early in the morning, will I send
To all the plumbers and the pewterers,
And buy their tin and lead up; and to *Lothbury*
For all the copper. *Ben Jonson.*

'Tis a note of enchantment; what ails her? she sees
A mountain ascending, a vision of trees;
Bright volumes of vapor through *Lothbury* glide,
And a river flows on through the vale of Cheapside. *Wordsworth.*

Lot's Wife. The name given to a pillar covered with asphaltum, which stands in a region adjacent to the Dead Sea, Palestine. The allusion is to the account given in Gen. xix. 26.

Lottatori, I. See WRESTLERS, THE.

Loudon Castle. An ancient feudal mansion near Galston, Scotland, belonging to Lord Bute, who purchased it in 1868 for $300,000.

Loudon Park. A fine cemetery near Baltimore, Md. The grounds cover 100 acres.

Louis-le-Grand, Collége. A famous school of the seventeenth century, in Paris. It was the great school, the Eton, of France, attended by thousands of the children of the most distinguished families in the kingdom. Voltaire was at one time a member of this school. It was under the control of the Jesuits, and was originally known as the College of Clermont, but was afterwards named in honor of Louis XIV.

The school still exists upon its old site in Paris.

Louis, St. See St. Louis.

Louisa, Queen of Prussia. A work of sculpture by Christian Rauch (1777-1857), and regarded as one of his masterpieces. At Charlottenburg, Prussia.

Louise Home. A fine building in Washington, erected by W. W. Corcoran, and intended as a home for indigent ladies of culture.

Louisiana, The. 1. A gunboat of the United States navy during the war of the Rebellion. Having been laden with 250 tons of powder, she was towed close under the walls of Fort Fisher, in North Carolina, when the powder was exploded on the 24th of December, 1864, but without doing any serious injury to the fortifications.

☞ "A capital feature in the plan of the expedition was the explosion of an enormous floating-mine as near the fort as possible, with the intention of demolishing the work, or so paralyzing the garrison that the seizure of the fort might be an easy task for the troops that were to debark immediately after the explosion. A captured blockade-runner was converted into a monster torpedo, charged with 430,000 pounds of gunpowder, and placed under command of Capt. Rhind. The powder was in barrels and bags, and penetrated by Gomez fuses for ignition. It was intended to have her towed near the fort by a tug, in which the crew, after firing combustibles which were placed on board the torpedo-vessel, might escape. . . . Before their [the transports'] return with the troops that were to play an important part with the torpedo-vessel, Porter had exploded that mine without any visible effect on the fort or garrison." *Lossing.*

2. A Confederate steam-battery used in the defence of the approaches to New Orleans, La. She was destroyed by the vessels of Admiral Farragut's fleet, April 24, 1862.

Lourdes, Virgin of. See Grotto de la Vierge.

Louvre, The. This palace in Paris, France, is connected with the Tuileries by a long gallery which contains the French national collection of pictures. On the site of the present palace once stood a castle, the hunting-seat of King Dagobert, which was called Louveterie, or wolf-hunting establishment, whence the name Louvre is said to be derived. The building was completed by Napoleon 250 years after the first foundations were laid. It was occupied as a residence by several monarchs of France, but since the time of Louis XV. it has been devoted to the exhibition of works of art. Its galleries are filled with paintings by the best masters, such as Raphael, Murillo, Guido, Domenichino, and others, also splendid vases, mosaics, and sculptures, with many valuable and magnificent reliques of the kings and queens of France.

☞ "I must confess that the vast and beautiful edifice struck me far more than the pictures, sculpture, and curiosities which it contains, — the shell more than the kernel inside; such noble suites of rooms and halls were those through which we first passed, containing Egyptian, and, farther onward, Greek and Roman antiquities; the walls cased in variegated marbles, the ceilings glowing with beautiful frescos; the whole extended into infinite vistas by mirrors that seemed like vacancy, and multiplied every thing forever. . . . From the pictures we went into a suite of rooms where are preserved many relics of the ancient and later kings of France. . . . If each monarch could have been summoned from Hades to claim his own relics, we should have had the halls full of the old Childerics, Charleses, Bourbons and Capets, Henrys and Louises, snatching with ghostly hands at sceptres, swords, armor, and mantles; and Napoleon would have seen, apparently, almost every thing that personally belonged to him, — his coat, his cocked hats, his camp-desk, his field-bed, his knives, forks, and plates, and even a lock of his hair." *Hawthorne.*

☞ "What a paradise this gallery is for French students, or foreigners who sojourn in the capital! It is hardly necessary to say that the brethren of the brush are not usually supplied by Fortune with any extraordinary wealth or means of enjoying the luxuries with which Paris, more than any other city, abounds. But here they have a luxury which surpasses all others, and spend their days in a palace which all the money of all the Rothschilds could not buy. They sleep, perhaps, in a garret, and dine in a cellar; but no grandee in Europe has such a drawing-room. Kings' houses have at best but damask hangings and gilt cornices. What are those to a wall covered with canvas by Paul Veronese, or a hundred yards of Rubens? . . . Here is a room half a mile long, with as many windows as Aladdin's palace, open from sunrise till evening, and free to all manners and varieties of study." *Thackeray.*

The next day I went to see the *Louvre* with more attention, its severall courts and Pavilions. One of the quadrangles, begun by Hen. IV. and finished by his son and grandson, is a superb but mix'd structure. The cornices, mouldings, and compartments, with the insertion of several colored marbles have been of great expence. We went through the long gallery, pav'd with white and black marble, richly fretted and painted *a fresca.* The front looking to the river, tho' of rare work for the carving, yet wants of that magnificence which a plainer and truer designe would have contributed to it.
John Evelyn, Diary, 3 Feb., 1644.

It was thy Pleasure House, thy Palace of Dainty Devices; thy *Louvre,* or thy White-Hall. *Charles Lamb.*

Louvre, Musée du. See MUSÉE DU LOUVRE.

Love. See EARTHLY LOVE, GARDEN OF LOVE, and SACRED AND PROFANE LOVE.

Lovell's Pond. See LOVEWELL'S POND.

Lovers' Leap. See SAPPHO'S LEAP.

Lovewell's Pond. A small lake near the village of Fryeburg, in Maine, noted as being the scene of a desperate fight with the Indians in the old colonial days. It was one of the most fierce and sanguinary of the many encounters between the early settlers and the savages; and the fame of the heroism there displayed by the brave colonists, under the lead of Capt. John Lovewell (from whom the pond takes its name), still survives in ballad and tradition. [Also *Lovell's Pond.*]

"What time the noble Lovewell came
With fifty men from Dunstable,
The cruel Pequot tribe to tame,
With arms and bloodshed terrible.
With footsteps low shall travellers go
Where *Lovewell's Pond* shines clear and bright,
And mark the place where those are laid
Who fell in Lovewell's bloody fight."

Loving Cup. The name given to a goblet, usually of silver, which on ceremonial occasions, like the Lord Mayor's feast, is passed from one guest to another at the table, each raising it to his lips and tasting of its contents.

A playful fancy could have carried the matter farther, could have depicted the feast in the Egyptian Hall, . . . and Mr. Toole behind the central throne, bawling out to the assembled guests and dignitaries: "My Lord So-and-so, my Lord What-d'ye-call-'im, my Lord Etcætera, the Lord Mayor pledges you all in a *Loving-Cup.*" *Thackeray.*

Low Life and High Life. A picture of two dogs by Sir Edwin Landseer (1802–1873). In the National Gallery, London. The subject of High Life is a slender and delicate deerhound, long supposed to have been a portrait of Sir Walter Scott's "Maida," at home in the luxurious chamber of its master. The picture was painted in 1829. The subject of Low Life is a massive bull-dog, sitting in a rude doorway, keeping guard with one eye over the hat, boots, and pint-pot of his master the butcher, and with the other lazily blinking in the warm sunshine.

Löwenburg. An *artificial* ruined castle near Cassel, Germany, fitted in every respect to correspond with the description of a Middle-Age fortress, "with moat, drawbridge, chapel, and garden of pyramidal trees."

Löwendenkmal. See LION OF LUCERNE.

Lowther Arcades. One of the principal arcades in London.

Lowther Castle. The seat of the Earl of Lonsdale, near Carlisle, England.

Luca, Accademia di San. See ST. LUKE.

Luccombe Chine. A curious and celebrated ravine on the Isle of Wight, not far from Ventnor, much visited by tourists.

Lucerne, Lion of. See LION OF LUCERNE.

Luchsberg. [Lynx Mountain.] A remarkable natural curiosity in the shape of a disintegrated and phosphorescent mountain near Alexandersbad, on the route between Frankfurt and Carlsbad in Germany. The phenomenon is probably owing either to an earthquake, or to the peculiar structure of the rocks, and the action of the atmosphere upon them.

Luck of Edenhall. This name is given to a drinking-vessel long and carefully preserved at Edenhall, in Cumberland, England. It is traditionally said to have been stolen from the elves at one of their banquets, by a member of the ancient family of Musgrave, or, according to some accounts, by one of their domestics. The fortunes of the house are, or at least were, believed to depend upon its preservation.

> "If that glass do break or fall,
> Farewell to the luck of Edenhall."

It is described as a tall enamelled glass, apparently of Venetian workmanship of the tenth century; and it is supposed to have been a chalice belonging to St. Cuthbert's ruined chapel, in the neighborhood of the hall. Longfellow has translated from the German poet Uhland a pretty ballad about the "Luck of Edenhall."

☞ One legend connected with this curious heirloom relates that the butler having gone to the well of St. Cuthbert found there a group of fairies, and this remarkable goblet standing on the brink of the well. He seized it; and the fairies, having tried in vain to recover it, fled, exclaiming,—

> "If this glass do break or fall,
> Farewell the luck of Edenhall."

The letters I. H. S. are inscribed on the case containing the cup, hence the surmise that it was originally a chalice.

> For its keeper takes a race of might,
> The fragile goblet of crystal tall;
> It has lasted longer than is right;
> Kling! klang! — with a harder blow than all
> Will I try the Luck of Edenhall!
> As the goblet ringing flies apart,
> Suddenly cracks the vaulted hall;
> And through the rift, the wild flames start;
> The guests in dust are scattered all,
> With the breaking Luck of Edenhall!

Lucretia. A picture by Albert Dürer (1471–1528), the German painter. In the Gallery of Munich, Bavaria.

Lucretia. A picture by Jacopo Palma, called Palma Vecchio (1480?–1548?). In the Belvedere Gallery, Vienna, Austria.

Lucretia. A picture by Rembrandt van Ryn (1607–1669), the Dutch painter. Now in possession of Mrs. Butler Johnstone, London.

Ludgate. Anciently one of the principal gates of the city of London. Its traditional name is derived from the mythical British king Lud (66 B.C.), who is said by Geoffrey of Monmouth to have built it. Ludgate Hill is the name of the great street, one of the most crowded thoroughfares in London, extending from Bridge Street to St. Paul's.

Ludgate Hill. See LUDGATE.

> Cheapside, the Strand, Fleet Street, and *Ludgate Hill*,
> Each name a very story in itself.
> *Robert Leighton.*

Ludgate Prison. A celebrated prison for poor debtors in London, taken down in 1760–62.

Ludlow Castle. An ancient castle in Ludlow, county of Salop, England, of which fine remains exist.

☞ "Sir Philip Sidney, the *preux chevalier* of his age, the poet, and lover of letters and men of letters, was no doubt a frequent resident in Ludlow Castle, and probably there collected at times around him the Spensers and the Raleighs and the other literary stars of the day." *Thomas Wright.*

I must hold *Ludlow Castle* an honest house, for which Milton's "Comus" was written, and the company nobly bred, which performed it with knowledge and sympathy. *Emerson.*

Ludovisi Juno. See JUNO, and also VILLA LUDOVISI.

Ludovisi, Villa. See VILLA LUDOVISI.

Ludwigstrasse. [Louis Street.] A noted street in Munich, Bavaria, with magnificent buildings.

Lueg Castle. A remarkable castle constructed in a *cavern* near the grotto of Adelsberg, in Southern Austria. It was built in 1570. It can only be approached by steps cut in the rock, by ladders and drawbridges. It has served as a mysterious place of retreat for centuries.

Luke, St. See ST. LUKE.

Lumley Castle. A seat of the Earl of Scarborough, near Durham, England.

Lundy's Lane. A locality in the province of Ontario, Canada. It was the scene of a battle between the United States forces and the British in 1814, resulting in the defeat of the latter.

The courage which girls exhibit is like a battle of *Lundy's Lane*, or a sea-fight. *Emerson.*

Lung' Arno. [Along the Arno.] The celebrated street and thoroughfare of Florence, Italy, extending along the right bank of the river, the Arno, which divides the city. Also the principal street in Pisa, Italy.

Who, that remembers Florence, does not remember well the San Miniato in Monte, towering on its lofty eminence above the city, and visible along the *Lung' Arno* from the Ponte alle Grazie to the Ponte alla Carraja? *Mrs. Jameson.*

Lurlei. See LORELEI.

Lute Player. A picture by Michelangelo Amerighi, called Caravaggio (1569–1609). In the Lichtenstein Collection, Vienna, Austria. See LADY WITH THE LUTE.

Luther's Beech. A magnificent tree which formerly stood near Liebenstein, Germany, on the borders of the Thuringian forest, and was celebrated as the tree under which the reformer was seized on his return from Worms, and carried to the prison of the Wartburg.

Luther's Cell. A room in the Augustine convent in Erfurt, Germany, memorable as the apartment in which the great reformer lived while a monk, and which contains his Bible and other interesting relics.

Luther's Elm Tree. A tree near Worms, Germany, famous from the tradition that the great reformer rested under it on his memorable journey to the city.

Luther's House. A mansion in Wittenberg, Germany, where the reformer lived after his marriage, and which is carefully preserved in an almost unaltered condition. It contains various interesting relics.

Luton-Hoo. Formerly the seat of the Marquis of Bute, near Bedford, England. It was destroyed by fire in 1843.

☞ "This is one of the places I do not regret having come to see. It is a very stately palace indeed. The dignity of the rooms is very great, and the quantity of the pictures is beyond expectation — beyond hope." *Dr. Johnson.*

Luxembourg. See MUSÉE DU LUXEMBOURG and PALAIS DE LUXEMBOURG.

Luxor. See OBELISK OF LUXOR and TEMPLE OF LUXOR.

Lycabettus. A rocky conical hill of considerable height, about one mile north-east of the Acropolis, and forming a striking feature in the scenery of Athens, Greece. This hill is said to have been dropped here, that it might serve as a bulwark of Athens, by Pallas Minerva, who, at the birth of Erichthonius, the ancient king of Attica, came from her temple at Pallené, and bore this hill through the air in her arms as a birthday gift. It is now known as the mountain of ST. GEORGE.

☞ "This hill is to the Grecian capital what Vesuvius is to Naples, or Arthur's Seat to Edinburgh; from its summit Athens and its neighborhood lie unrolled before the eye as in a map." *Murray.*

Lyceum. A famous school in ancient Athens, where the philosopher Aristotle taught his pupils while walking about with them, from which circumstance his school is known as the Peripatetic (from Gr. περιπατεῖν, to walk about). The Lyceum derived its name from Lyceius, a surname of Apollo to whom it was dedicated, and has bequeathed the name to similar modern institutions of learning.

> The schools of ancient sages; his who bred
> Great Alexander to subdue the world,
> *Lyceum* there, and painted Stoa next.
> *Milton.*

Lyceum Theatre. The Royal Lyceum Theatre, Strand, London, was built in 1834, and so called from a former academy or exhibition-room, which was converted into a theatre in 1790, and burnt in 1830.

Lycian Gallery. A collection of Greek works of sculpture, consisting of reliefs, tombs, and sarcophagi brought to England by Sir Charles Fellows from Xanthus, in Lycia, Asia Minor, in 1841, and now deposited in a room specially devoted to the purpose in the British Museum, London. [Called also the *Lycian Marbles.*]

Lyon's Inn. A seminary of legal learning in London — one of the nine inns of chancery. Lyon's Inn, once a hostelry, was destroyed in 1863.

> They cut his throat from ear to ear,
> His brains they battered in;
> His name was Mr. William Weare,
> He dwelt in *Lyon's Inn.*

Lysicrates. See CHORAGIC MONUMENT OF LYSICRATES.

Lyversberg Passion. A painting of the Passion, or suffering of Christ, attributed to Israel von Meckenen (1440-1503), but really by an unknown master. It derives its name from having been owned by Herr Lyversberg. At Cologne, Germany.

M.

Mabille. See JARDIN MABILLE.

Macaroni Club. A company of eccentric fops who flourished in England in the eighteenth century. They dressed in the most fantastic manner. One of their most noticeable peculiarities was wearing a large knot of hair upon the back of the head. Their name was derived from their having always upon the dinner-table a dish of macaroni, then a novelty in England. For a time these eccentric young men were the leaders of fashion in London. Every thing, from the costume of the clergy to the music at public entertainments, was *à la Macaroni.*

☞ "A winter without politics—even our Macaronis entertain the town with nothing but new dresses, and the size of their nosegays. They have lost all their money, and exhausted their credit, and can no longer game for £20,000 a night." *Horace Walpole.*

Macbeth's Cairn. This is supposed to be on the spot where Macbeth, flying from his castle at Dunsinane, was slain by Macduff. See DUNSINANE HILL.

Macedonian, The. A British frigate captured in the war of 1812 by the United States frigate *Constitution.*

McGill Street. A main thoroughfare in Montreal, Can.

McHenry, Fort. See FORT MCHENRY.

M'Swine's Gun. A natural curiosity in the county of Donegal, Ireland. It is a prodigious cavity into which the tide rushes with such force as to produce a sound capable, it is said, of being heard distinctly a distance of between 20 and 30 miles, and shooting up a shaft of water some hundreds of feet into the air.

☞ "Altogether, perhaps, so extraordinary a natural marvel does not exist in the British dominions." *Mr. and Mrs. Hall.*

Machpelah, Cave of. See CAVE OF MACHPELAH.

Mad Margery. [Dutch, *De dulle Griete.*] An enormous piece of ordnance preserved at Ghent, Belgium. It is made of wrought iron, and was used by the citizens of Ghent at the siege of Oudenarde in 1382.

Madama, Villa. See VILLA MADAMA.

Madame Tussaud's Exhibition. A famous exhibition of waxwork figures in London. It is situated in Baker Street.

☞ "Many of these, especially those relating to the French Revolution, were modelled from life, or death, by Madame Tussaud, who was herself imprisoned and in danger of the guillotine, with Madame Beauharnais and her child Hortense as her associates." *Hare.*

Madeleine, The. This church is one of the most beautiful buildings in Paris. It was begun by Louis XV., and completed in the reign of Louis Philippe. It is of Grecian architecture. The principal façade looks upon the Rue Royale and the Place de la Concorde, and is very magnificent. The interior of the church is richly decorated in gilt and marble. It contains many paintings and sculptures illustrative of the life of the Magdalene. In May, 1871, 300 insurgents were driven by the Versailles troops into this church and there killed.

☞ "The most sumptuous fane ever erected to her [the Magdalen's] special honor is that which, of late years, has arisen in the city of Paris. The church, or rather temple, of *La Madeleine* stands an excelling monument, if not of modern piety at least of modern art. That which is now the temple of the lowly penitent was, a few years ago, *Le Temple de la Gloire*."

Mrs. Jameson.

☞ "A Grecian temple requires to be seen against the sky, and loses all its dignity when surrounded by lofty buildings." *Fergusson.*

The Attic temple whose majestic room
Contained the presence of Olympian Jove,
With smooth Hymettus round it and above
Softening the splendor by a sober bloom,
Is yielding fast to Time's irreverent doom;
While on the then barbarian banks of Seine
That nobler type is realized again
In perfect form, and dedicate — to whom?
To a poor Syrian girl of lowest name,
A hapless creature, pitiful and frail
As ever wore her life in sin and shame;
Of whom all history has this single tale, —
"She loved the Christ, she wept beside his grave,
And He, for that love's sake, all else forgave." *Lord Houghton.*

Madeleine, Boulevart de la. One of the boulevards of Paris, extending only about 600 feet from the church of the Madeleine. See BOULEVARDS.

Madem's Well. See ST. MADEM'S WELL.

Madison Square. A fashionable park in the city of New York, some six acres in extent, three miles from the Battery. It is bordered by magnificent hotels, and contains a monument erected to the memory of Gen. Worth.

Miss Flora M'Flimsey, of *Madison Square.*
W. A. Butler.

Madison's Cave. A natural curiosity in Augusta County, Va.

☞ "It extends into the earth about 300 feet, branching into subordinate caverns, and at length terminates in two different places at basins of water of unknown extent. The vault of this cave is of solid limestone from 20 to 40 or 50 feet high, through which water is continually percolating. This trickling down the sides of the cave has incrusted them over in the form of elegant drapery." *Jefferson.*

Madness. One of two celebrated statues by Caius Gabriel Cibber (d. 1700?), which formerly adorned the principal gate of the old Bethlehem Hospital, London, and are now in the entrance-hall of the new Bethlem Hospital. The companion figure is called Melancholy. See MELANCHOLY.

☞ "These are the earliest indications of the appearance of a distinct and natural spirit in sculpture. . . . Those who see them for the first time are fixed to the spot with terror and awe. . . . From the degradation of the actual madhouse we turn overpowered and disgusted, but from these magnificent creations we retire in mingled awe and admiration." *Cunningham.*

Madonna. [My Lady, i.e. the Virgin Mary.] The favorite subject of pictorial representation by the great religious painters of the Middle Ages.

☞ "Of the pictures in our galleries, public or private, . . . the largest and most beautiful portion have reference to the Madonna, — her character, her person, her history. It was a theme which never tired her votaries, whether, as in the hands of great and sincere artists, it became one of the noblest and loveliest, or, as in the hands of superficial, unbelieving, time-serving artists, one of the most degraded. All that human genius, inspired by faith, could achieve of best; all that fanaticism, sensualism, atheism, could perpetrate of worst, — do we find in the cycle of those representations which have been dedicated to the glory of the Virgin."

Mrs. Jameson.

Of the almost innumerable compositions upon this theme, a few of the more celebrated and familiar, especially those which bear a distinctive title, are given below. See also, for pictures relating to this subject, HOLY FAMILY and VIRGIN.

Madonna. An altar-piece by Giovanni Cimabue (1240-1302?). In the church of S. Maria Novella, Florence, Italy.

☞ "In spite of its colossal size, and formal attitude and severe style, the face of this Madonna is very striking, and has been well described as 'sweet and unearthly, reminding you of a sibyl.'" *Mrs. Jameson.*

☞ "It happened that this work was so much an object of admiration to the people of that day, they having then never seen any thing better, that it was carried in solemn procession, with the sound of trumpets and other festal demonstrations, from the house of

Cimabue to the church. . . . All the men and women of Florence hastened in crowds to admire it, making all possible demonstrations of delight."
Vasari, Trans.

☞ "We next saw the famous picture of the Virgin by Cimabue, which was deemed a miracle in its day, and still brightens the sombre walls with the lustre of its gold ground."
Hawthorne.

Bright and brave,
That picture was accounted, mark, of old!
A king stood bare before its sovran grace;
A reverent people shouted to behold
The picture, not the king; and even the place
Containing such a miracle, grew bold,
Named the glad Borgo from that beauteous face.
. . . .
A noble picture! worthy of the shout
Wherewith along the streets the people bore
Its cherub faces, which the sun threw out
Until they stooped and entered the church door! *Mrs. Browning.*

Madonna. A marble statue of the Virgin by Michael Angelo Buonarotti (1474–1564). In the Church of Notre Dame at Bruges, Belgium.

☞ "This Madonna is one of Michael Angelo's finest works. She is looking straight forward; a handkerchief is placed across her hair, and falls softly, on both sides, on her neck and shoulders. In her countenance, in her look, there is a wonderful majesty, a queenly gravity, as if she felt the thousand pious glances of the people who look up to her on the altar."
Grimm, Trans.

Madonna Aldobrandini. A well-known picture of the Virgin and Child by Raphael Sanzio (1483-1520), representing her as "seated upon a bench, and bending tenderly toward the little St. John, her left arm around him; he reaches up playfully for a flower offered to him by the Infant Christ who rests on his mother's lap." This picture is now in the National Gallery, London.

Madonna Ancajani. A picture of the Holy Family by Raphael Sanzio (1483-1520), so called from a family of that name at Spoleto, Italy, to whom it formerly belonged. It is said to be the largest picture by Raphael in Germany, after the Sistine Madonna, but it has suffered much from injury. In the Museum at Berlin, Prussia.

Madonna and Child with a Lily. An admired picture by Carlo Dolce (1616-1686), one of his best works. In the Pinakothek at Munich, Bavaria.

Madonna and Child with S. Anne. A group of figures executed by Andrea Sansovino (1460-1529), the Italian sculptor, for the church of S. Agostino, Florence, Italy.

☞ "One of the most beautiful detached groups of modern art."
Lübke, Trans.

Madonna at the Well. A picture by Giuliano Bugiardini (1481–1556). Formerly attributed to Raphael. In the Uffizi, Florence, Italy.

Madonna col Divino Amore. [Madonna with the Divine Love.] A picture of the Holy Family by Raphael Sanzio (1483-1520), or, as some think, by Giulio Romano (1492–1546). Now in the Museum of Naples, Italy.

Madonna dei Ansidei. A picture by Raphael Sanzio (1483–1520). Now at Blenheim, England.

Madonna del Bacino. [Madonna of the Basin.] A well-known picture by Giulio Romano (1492–1546). In the gallery at Dresden, Saxony.

☞ "The Child stands in a basin, and the young St. John pours water upon him from a vase, while Mary washes him. St. Elisabeth stands by, holding a napkin; St. Joseph behind is looking on. Notwithstanding the homeliness of the action, there is here a religious and mysterious significance, prefiguring the Baptism." *Mrs. Jameson.*

Madonna del Baldacchino. [Madonna of the Canopy.] 1. A celebrated altar-piece by Raphael Sanzio (1483–1520), in which the Virgin and the Child are represented as seated on a throne over which is a canopy (baldacchino), the curtains of which are held by two angels. This picture was left unfinished by Raphael. It is in the Pitti Palace, Florence, Italy.

☞ "The picture is not deficient in the solemnity suited to a church subject, . . . in other respects, however, the taste of the *naturalisti* prevails, and the heads are in general devoid of nobleness and real dignity." *Eastlake.*

2. A large picture by Fra Bartolommeo (1469-1517), the Italian painter. In the Pitti Palace, Florence, Italy.

Madonna del Cardellino. [Madonna of the Goldfinch.] A beautiful painting of the Virgin by Raphael Sanzio (1483-1520). Now in the Tribune of the Uffizi Palace in Florence, Italy. The little St. John is represented as offering a goldfinch to the Infant Christ, whence the name of the picture.

☞ "The form and countenance of the Madonna are here of the purest beauty; the little Baptist also is extremely sweet; but the conception of the Infant Christ does not fulfil the master's intention, which appears to have been to represent the dignity of a divine being in a childlike form; both the figure and expression are rather stiff and affected." *Eastlake.*

☞ "Perhaps the most perfect example [of the domestic style of treatment] which could be cited from the whole range of art is Raphael's *Madonna del Cardellino.*" *Mrs. Jameson.*

☞ "The divine goodness expressed in the countenance of the Child Jesus whilst he holds his hands over the little bird, and seems to say, 'Not one of these is forgotten by my Father,' is beyond all description." *Frederika Bremer.*

Madonna del Donatore. See MADONNA DI FOLIGNO.

Madonna del Giglio. [Madonna of the Lily.] A picture by Raphael Sanzio (1483-1520). In the collection of Lord Garvagh.

Madonna del Gran Duca [of the Grand Duke]. A well-known picture by Raphael Sanzio (1483-1520), representing the Mother holding the Child tranquilly in her arms, and looking down in deep thought. In the Palazzo Pitti, Florence, Italy.

☞ "The *Madonna Gran Duca* marks the growing transition from the first to the second manner of Raphael." *J. S. Harford.*

Madonna del Orto. A celebrated church of the fourteenth century in Venice, Italy. It contains among other pictures the famous Last Judgment of Tintoretto.

Madonna del Passegio. [Madonna of the Walking-place.] A picture of the Holy Family, consisting of four figures, — the Virgin, the Child, the infant St. John, with St. Joseph standing by, — commonly attributed to Raphael Sanzio (1483-1520), but which some suppose to have been painted by Francesco Penni. It was formerly in the Orleans Gallery, but is now in the Bridgewater Collection, in London. Copies of this picture are in the Museum of Naples, and elsewhere.

☞ "In a Holy Family of four figures, we have frequently the Virgin, the Child, and the infant St. John, with St. Joseph standing by. Raphael's *Madonna del Passegio* is an example." *Mrs. Jameson.*

Madonna del Pesce. [Madonna of the Fish.] A celebrated picture by Raphael Sanzio (1483-1520), representing the Virgin and Child enthroned, with St. Jerome on one side, and on the other an archangel with the young Tobit who carries a fish. The picture derives its name from this last circumstance. It is considered one of the finest of Raphael's Madonnas. This picture is now in the Gallery of Madrid, Spain.

☞ "Tobias with the fish was an early type of baptism. In Raphael's Madonna dell' Pesce, he is introduced as the patron saint of the painter, but not without a reference to a more sacred meaning, that of the guardian spirit of all humanity." *Mrs. Jameson.*

Madonna del Pozzo. [Madonna of the Well.] A picture attributed to Raphael (1483-1520), but thought by some to be the work of Giulio Romano (1492-1546). In the Tribune of the Uffizi, Florence, Italy.

Madonna del Rosario. [Madonna of the Rosary.] A picture of the Virgin and Child by Giovanni Battista Salvi, surnamed Sassoferrato (1605–1685), and his most celebrated work. In the church of S. Sabina, at Rome.

☞ "When the Virgin or the Child holds the rosary, it [the picture] is then a *Madonna del Rosario*, and painted for the Dominicans."
Mrs. Jameson.

☞ "Domenichino, who died of a broken heart at Rome, because his productions were neglected, is a painter who always touches one nearly. His Madonna del Rosario is crowded with beauty. Such children I never saw in painting, — the very ideals of infantine grace and innocence." *N. P. Willis.*

Madonna del Sacco. [Madonna of the Sack.] A picture by Andrea Vanucchi, called Andrea del Sarto (1487–1531), the Italian painter, and regarded as one of his masterpieces. "A lunette fresco, known and praised the world over." It derives its name from the sack on which Joseph leans. It is painted over a door in the court of the Convent of SS. Annunziata, Florence, Italy.

☞ "1645, 21 May. We went to see the famous piece of Andrea del Sarto in the Annunciata; the storie is that the Painter in a time of dearth borrow'd a sack of corne of the religious of that convent, and repayment being demanded, he wrought it out in this picture, which represents Joseph sitting on a sack of corne, and reading to the B. Virgin; a piece infinitely valued."
John Evelyn.

☞ "Michael Angelo and Raphael are said to have 'gazed at it unceasingly.' It is much defaced, and preserves only its graceful drawing. The countenance of Mary has the *beau reste* of singular loveliness." *N. P. Willis.*

Madonna del Tempi. A well-known picture of the Virgin and Child by Raphael Sanzio (1483–1520), so called from the Palazzo Tempi at Florence, Italy, where it was formerly situated. It is now in the Pinakothek, at Munich, Bavaria.

Madonna del Trono. [Madonna of the Throne.] A famous picture by Fra Bartolommeo (1469–1517). In the Uffizi Gallery, Florence, Italy.

"The perfect architectonic idea is not only everywhere set forth in a lively manner, but also filled with the noblest individual life." *Burckhardt.*

Madonna del Viaggio. See MADONNA DEL GRAN DUCA.

Madonna della Candelabra. [Madonna of the Candlestick.] A well-known circular picture of the Virgin and Child by Raphael Sanzio (1483–1520), in which the Madonna is represented seated, with an angel on each side bearing a torch. This picture is now the property of Hon. H. Butler Johnstone, England. [Called also *La Vierge aux Candélabres.*]

Madonna della Casa Colonna. A picture by Raphael Sanzio (1483–1520). In the Museum at Berlin, Prussia.

Madonna della Casa d'Alba. [Madonna of the House of Alva, called also Madonna della Famiglia d'Alva.] A beautiful and well-known circular picture of the Virgin and Child by Raphael Sanzio (1483 1520), representing the Madonna, "a full-length figure seated in a quiet landscape; the Child on her lap, she holds a book in her hand; the little St. John, kneeling before his divine companion, offers him a cross, which he receives with looks of unutterable love." This picture, which was formerly in London, is now in the Hermitage, St. Petersburg. There is a copy of it in the Palazzo della Torre, Ravenna, Italy.

Madonna della Casa Tempi. A picture by Raphael Sanzio (1483–1520), in which the Virgin is represented standing and pressing the Child closely to her. This picture was formerly in Florence, Italy, but is now in the Gallery of Munich, Bavaria.

Madonna della Cintola. [Madonna of the Girdle.] A legendary subject frequently treated by the Middle-Age artists.

☞ "The legend relates that when

the Madonna ascended into heaven, in the sight of the apostles, Thomas was absent; but after three days he returned, and, doubting the truth of her glorious translation, he desired that her tomb should be opened, which was done, and lo! it was found empty. Then the Virgin, taking pity on his weakness and want of faith, threw down to him her girdle, that this tangible proof might remove all doubts forever from his mind. Hence, in many pictures, St. Thomas is seen below, holding the girdle in his hand."

Mrs. Jameson.

Madonna della Famiglia Bentivoglio. [Madonna of the Bentivoglio Family.] A picture of the Virgin and Child, by Lorenzo Costa (—— 1530?). It was painted for Giovanni II., lord of Bologna from 1462 to 1506. In the church of San Giacomo at Bologna, Italy.

Madonna della Famiglia d'Alva. See MADONNA DELLA CASA D'ALBA.

Madonna della Famiglia Pesaro. A picture by Titian (1477-1576). In the church of S. Maria dei Frari, at Venice, Italy.

Madonna della Gatta. [Madonna of the Cat.] A picture of the Holy Family, much resembling the so-called "Pearl" by Raphael, executed by Giulio Romano (1492-1546). The picture, which derives its name from a cat that appears in it, crouching in a corner, is in the Museum at Naples, Italy.

☞ There is another picture bearing this name, the work of Federigo Baroccio (1528-1612). In the National Gallery, London.

Madonna dell' Impannata [of the Paper Window]. A well-known picture of the Virgin and Child by Raphael Sanzio (1483-1520), deriving its name from the oiled-paper window in the background. It is in the Pitti Palace, in Florence, Italy.

☞ "The incident is most charming. Two women have brought the Child, and hand it to the Mother; and while the boy turns, still laughing, after them, he takes fast hold of the Mother's dress, who seems to say, 'Look, he likes best to come to me.'"

Burckhardt.

Madonna dell' Impruneta. A celebrated church and pilgrim-shrine in the neighborhood of Florence, Italy.

Madonna della Lucertola. [Madonna of the Lizard.] A copy in the Pitti Palace, Florence, of a Holy Family now in the gallery at Madrid, Spain. This copy derives its name from the lizard which appears in the picture. See HOLY FAMILY UNDER THE OAK.

Madonna della Misericordia. A celebrated picture by Fra Bartolommeo (1469-1517), the Italian painter; his largest, and by many considered his most important, work. It has suffered from injuries and restorations. It is in the church of S. Romano, Lucca, Italy.

Madonna della Rosa. [Madonna with the Rose.] A well-known picture by Francesco Maria Mazzuoli, called Il Parmigiano (1503-1540). In the Gallery of Dresden, Germany.

Madonna della Scodella. [Madonna of the Cup.] A picture of the Holy Family by Antonio Allegri, surnamed Correggio (1494-1534), representing the Virgin as holding in her hand a cup (whence the name), and Joseph as bending down the branches of a palm-tree to gather dates. This Madonna belongs to the class of pictures called *Il Riposo*, or the Repose in Egypt, *q.v.* This picture is in the Gallery of Parma, Italy.

☞ "This entirely realistic composition, — the infant Saviour is dressed like a little Italian boy, — though much injured, is still one of the most transparently beautiful of his [Correggio's] works."

Eastlake, Handbook of Painting.

Madonna della Sedia. [Madonna of the Chair.] See MADONNA DELLA SEGGIOLA.

Madonna della Seggiola [of the low Chair]. A celebrated picture of the Virgin and Child by Raphael Sanzio (1483-1520), and perhaps the most familiar of all his Madonnas from the numerous engravings and other reproductions of it. It is a circular picture, representing the Mother seated on a low chair, holding the Child in her arms. The little St. John stands by her side with folded hands. "The Madonna wears a gay striped handkerchief on her shoulders, and another on her head, after the manner of the Italian women. She appears as a beautiful and blooming woman, looking out of the picture in the tranquil enjoyment of maternal love; the Child, full and strong in form, has an ingenuous and grand expression." The picture is in the Pitti Palace, Florence, Itay. It is well known through the engravings of Raphael Morghen (1758-1833) and John Gottfried Müller (1747-1830).

☞ "The most beautiful picture in the world, I am convinced, is the Madonna della Seggiola. I was familiar with it in a hundred engravings and copies, and therefore it shone upon me as with a familiar beauty, though infinitely more divine than I had ever seen it before. . . . Miss ——, whom I met in the gallery, told me that to copy the 'Madonna della Seggiola,' application must be made five years beforehand, so many are the artists who aspire to copy it." *Hawthorne.*

The crowned Queen-Virgin of Perugino sank into a simple Italian mother in Raffaelle's "*Madonna of the Chair.*" *Ruskin.*

Created by Raphael in one of his poetical inspirations, it is of magical and fascinating beauty. Perhaps no picture has ever been rendered so popular by copies and imitations of every sort. *Passavant.*

Madonna della Stella. [Madonna of the Star.] A picture by Giovanni da Fiesole, called Fra Angelico (1387-1455). In the Museum of St. Mark, Florence, Italy.

Madonna della Tenda. [Madonna of the Curtain.] A picture of the Virgin and Child by Raphael Sanzio (1483-1520), somewhat resembling the celebrated Madonna della Seggiola, of the Pitti in Florence. The picture derives its name from a curtain in the background. Now at Munich, Bavaria. There is a repetition of this picture, also said to be an original, at Turin, Italy.

Madonna della Vittoria. [Madonna of the Victory.] A large altar-piece by Andrea Mantegna (1431-1506), the Italian painter. It was painted in commemoration of a victory supposed to have been obtained by Gonzaga over Charles VIII. of France. It is now in the Louvre, Paris.

☞ "Another class of votive pictures are especial acts of thanksgiving; first, for victory, as La Madonna della Vittoria, Notre Dame des Victoires. The Virgin on her throne is then attended by one or more of the warrior saints, together with the patron or patroness of the victors. She is then Our Lady of Victory. A very perfect example of these victorious Madonnas exists in a celebrated picture by Andrea Mantegna." *Mrs. Jameson.*

He [St. Maurice] stands on the left of the Madonna in Mantegna's famous *Madonna della Vittoria*, in the Louvre. *Mrs. Jameson.*

Madonna dell'Lungo Collo. [Madonna of the Long Neck.] A well-known picture by Francesco Maria Mazzuoli, called Il Parmigiano (1503-1540). In the Palazzo Pitti, Florence, Italy.

☞ "The Madonna dell'Lungo Collo of Parmigiano might be cited as a favorable example of artificial and wholly mistaken grace." *Mrs. Jameson.*

Madonna dello Spasimo. See SPASIMO, LO.

Madonna di Foligno. A noted altar-picture by Raphael Sanzio (1483-1520), in the Vatican Gallery at Rome, originally painted for the Church of Ara Cœli. In 1565 it was removed to Foligno, and later to Paris where it was transferred to canvas from the wood on which it was originally painted. It derives its name from the city of Foligno, which is represented in the background with a bomb falling upon it — in allusion probably to its escape from some calamity. A tablet in the foreground gives color to the supposition that this was designed to be a votive picture. [Called also *La Vierge au Donataire.*]

☞ "The whole picture glows throughout with life and beauty, hallowed by that profound religious sentiment which suggested the offering, and which the sympathetic artist seems to have caught from the grateful donor."
Mrs. Jameson.

Madonna di Loreto. A picture by Raphael Sanzio (1483-1520), representing the Virgin as lifting the veil from the Child who is just waking. The original of this picture is thought to be lost; but there is a picture at Florence, belonging to Mr. Lawrie, which is pronounced by Sir Charles Eastlake "the best of the many editions of the Loreto Raphael," and "partly by his hand."

Madonna di Lucca. A picture by the Flemish painter Jan van Eyck (1370-1441), representing the Virgin enthroned, giving her breast to the Child. It was so called from having been in the possession of the Duke of Lucca, but is now in the Städel Institute in Frankfort-on-the-Main, Germany.

Madonna di Misericordia. [Madonna of Mercy.] A common subject of representation by the great mediæval painters. As an example, see MISERICORDIA DI LUCCA.

Madonna di San Brizio. An old Greek representation of the Virgin and Child, "venerated as miraculous, and to which is attributed a fabulous antiquity." In the cathedral of Orvieto, Italy.

Madonna di San Francesco. [Madonna of St. Francis.] A picture by Andrea Vanucchi, called Andrea del Sarto (1487-1531), the Italian painter, and regarded as one of his most beautiful compositions. It is in the Tribune of the Uffizi at Florence, Italy.

☞ "Andrea del Sarto has placed harpies at the corner of the pedestal of the throne, in his famous *Madonna di San Francesco,*—a gross fault in that otherwise grand and faultless picture."
Mrs. Jameson.

Madonna di San Giorgio. [Madonna of St. George.] A celebrated picture by Antonio Allegri, called Correggio (1494-1534). In the Gallery of Dresden, Germany.

☞ "The Madonna di San Giorgio of Correggio is a votive altar-piece dedicated on the occasion of a great inundation of the river Secchia. The Virgin is seated on her throne, and the Child looks down on her worshippers and votaries. St. George stands in front victorious, his foot on the head of the dragon."
Mrs. Jameson.

Madonna di San Sebastiano. See ST. SEBASTIAN.

Madonna di San Sisto. A large altar-picture of the Virgin and Child by Raphael Sanzio (1483-1520), perhaps the most widely known of all his works through the numerous reproductions of it, and universally regarded as one of the supreme and most wonderful works of art. Vasari relates that Raphael painted this picture for the church of St. Sixtus at Piacenza. It is now in the Gallery of Dresden, Germany.

☞ "The Madonna, in a glory of cherubim, standing on the clouds, with the eternal Son in her arms, appears truly as the Queen of Heaven; St. Sixtus and St. Barbara kneel at the sides. These two figures help to connect the composition with the real spectators. A curtain drawn back encloses the picture on each side; below is a light parapet on which two beautiful boy angels lean. The Madonna is one of the most wonderful creations of Raphael's pencil. . . . The Child rests naturally, but not listlessly, in her arms, and looks down upon the world with the grandest expression. Never has the loveliness of childhood been blended so marvellously with the solemn consciousness of a high calling, as in the features and countenance of this Child."
Eastlake, Handbook of Painting.

This picture is entirely by the hand of Raphael. It was painted upon wood, and has been transferred to canvas. The best engraving is that by Steinla (1791-1858). There is also one by Christian Friedrich von Müller (1783-1816).

☞ "For myself, I have seen my ideal once and only once attained, there where Raphael — inspired if ever a painter was inspired — projected on the space before him that wonderful creation which we style the *Madonna di San Sisto*." *Mrs. Jameson.*

☞ "The head of the Virgin is perhaps nearer the perfection of female beauty and elegance than any thing in painting." *Wilkie.*

Madonna di Terranuova. A picture by Raphael Sanzio (1483–1520). In the Museum at Berlin, Prussia.

Madonna Enthroned. A picture by Fra Bartolommeo (*Della Porta*) (1469–1517). At Lucca, Italy.

Madonna Incoronata. [The Virgin Crowned.] A picture by Sandro Botticelli (1448–1505). In the Uffizi, Florence, Italy.

Madonna, Düsseldorf. See DÜSSELDORF MADONNA.

Madonna, Iberian. See IBERIAN MADONNA.

Madonna Litta. A picture by Leonardo da Vinci (1452–1519). In the Hermitage, St. Petersburg.

Madonna, Medica. See MEDICI MADONNA.

Madonna of Francis I. A picture of the Holy Family by Raphael Sanzio (1483–1520), painted by him for the Duke of Urbino, as a present from the latter to Francis I. Parts of this picture were executed by Giulio Romano. It is now in the Louvre, Paris.

☞ "Mary, a noble queenly creature, is seated, and bends towards her Child, who is springing from his cradle to meet her embrace. Elizabeth presents St. John, and Joseph, leaning on his hand, contemplates the group; two beautiful angels scatter flowers from above." *Mrs. Jameson.*

Madonna of Mercy. See MADONNA DI MISERICORDIA.

Madonna of the Basin. See MADONNA DEL BACINO.

Madonna of the Bridgewater Gallery. A picture of the Virgin and Child by Raphael Sanzio (1483–1520), belonging to Lord Ellesmere, and forming part of the Bridgewater Gallery. Copies of this picture are in the museums at Berlin, Naples, and elsewhere.

Madonna of the Burgomaster Meyer. A celebrated picture by Hans Holbein the Younger (1498–1543). In the Gallery of Dresden, Germany. It was painted for the burgomaster, Jacob Meyer, of Basle. There is another beautiful picture in the possession of Princess Charles of Hesse at Darmstadt, very similar to this, respecting the priority of which there has been much discussion, many inclining to the opinion that the Darmstadt Madonna is the original, and the Dresden picture a copy. The engraving of this picture by Steinla is very celebrated.

☞ "In purity, dignity, humility, and intellectual grace, this exquisite Madonna has never been surpassed, not even by Raphael; the face once seen haunts the memory." *Mrs. Jameson.*

Madonna of the Candlestick. See MADONNA DELLA CANDELABRA.

Madonna of the Canopy. See MADONNA DEL BALDACCHINO.

Madonna of the Cat. See MADONNA DEL GATTA.

Madonna of the Certosa at Pavia. A celebrated picture by Pietro Perugino (1446–1524), the Italian painter, and regarded as his masterpiece. It is now in the National Gallery, London.

Madonna of the Chair. See MADONNA DELLA SEGGIOLA.

Madonna of the Cup. See MADONNA DELLA SCODELLA.

Madonna of the Curtain. See MADONNA DELLA TENDA.

Madonna of the Fish. See MADONNA DEL PESCE.

Madonna of the Girdle. See MADONNA DELLA CINTOLA.

Madonna of the Goldfinch. See MADONNA DEL CARDELLINO.

Madonna of the Grand Duke. See MADONNA DEL GRAN DUCA.

Madonna of the Lily. See MADONNA DEL GIGLIO and MADONNA AND CHILD WITH A LILY.

Madonna of the Lizard. See MADONNA DELLA LUCERTOLA.

Madonna of the Long Neck. See MADONNA DELL' LUNGO COLLO.

Madonna of the Meadow. A picture by Raphael Sanzio (1483–1520). In Vienna, Austria.

Madonna of the Napkin. See VIRGEN DE LA SERVILETTA.

Madonna of the Paper Window. See MADONNA DELL' IMPANNATA.

Madonna of the Pearl. See PEARL, THE.

Madonna of the Rose. See MADONNA DELLA ROSA.

Madonna of the Rosary. See MADONNA DEL ROSARIO.

Madonna of the Sack. See MADONNA DEL SACCO.

Madonna of the Star. See MADONNA DELLA STELLA.

Madonna of the Tempi Family. See MADONNA DELLA CASA TEMPI.

Madonna of the Victory. See MADONNA DELLA VITTORIA.

Madonna of the Walking Place. See MADONNA DEL PASSEGIO.

Madonna of the Well. See MADONNA DEL POZZO.

Madonna, Staffa. See STAFFA MADONNA.

Madonna with the Pink. A picture representing the Virgin with the Child in her lap, who is reaching gayly towards the pink which she is giving him. The original of this picture is unknown. There is a repetition of it, said to be probably by Sassoferrato, at Basle.

Madracen. A remarkable and elegant Mauritanian sepulchral monument in Algeria. It has a Doric peristyle, surmounted by an Egyptian cornice, and is undoubtedly a work of ante-Christian times.

Mafra Palace *and* **Convent.** A superb pile of buildings at Mafra, near Lisbon, Portugal, built in 1717 by John V., in imitation of the Escurial at Madrid.

> But here the Babylonian whore hath built
> A dome, where flaunts she in such glorious sheen,
> That men forget the blood which she hath spilt,
> And bow the knee to Pomp that loves to varnish guilt. *Byron.*

Magdalene, The. A famous statue carved in wood by Donatello (1383–1466). In the Baptistery at Florence, Italy.

Magdalen, The. A celebrated picture by Titian (1477–1576), so famous in its day that he painted five or six copies of it, and there have been since numerous copies and engravings. It is said that his model for this picture was "a young girl, who being fatigued with long standing, the tears ran down her face."

Magdalen, The. A picture by Titian (1477–1576). In the Manfrini Palace, Venice, representing the Magdalen as *standing* at the entrance of her cave.

> ☞ "I do not know why this lovely Manfrini picture should be so much less celebrated than the Dresden Magdalen." *Mrs. Jameson.*

Magdalen, The. A picture by Titian (1477–1576). In the Palazzo Pitti, Florence, Italy.

Magdalen, The. A famous and often-repeated picture by Antonio Allegri, surnamed Correggio (1494–1534), representing the Magdalene as penitent, reclining, and reading from a book. It is in the gallery at Dresden, Germany, having been purchased by Augustus III., the Elector of Saxony, from the Duke of Modena, in 1745. This picture was painted on copper over a wash of gold in 1533. It was formerly kept in the Golden Chamber of the Castle of Modena, in a costly silver frame ornamented with precious stones.

☞ "The earliest example I can remember of the Penitent Magdalene, *dramatically* treated, remains as yet unsurpassed, — the Reading *Magdalene* of Correggio, in the Dresden Gallery. This lovely creation has only one fault, — the virginal beauty is that of a Psyche or a seraph. In Oëlenschläger's drama of 'Correggio' there is a beautiful description of this far-famed picture: he calls it 'Die Gottinn des Waldes Frommigkeit,' — the goddess of the religious solitude. And, in truth, if we could imagine Diana reading instead of hunting, she might have looked thus." *Mrs. Jameson.*

☞ "Correggio's other pictures are excellent, but this one is wonderful." *Mengs.*

Magdalen. A picture by Jacopo Robusti Tintoretto (1512–1594). In the Museum of the Capitol, Rome.

☞ "A 'Magdalen' by Tintoretto, on a heap of straw, dark, haggard, with hair dishevelled, and profoundly penitent. . . . Through the entrance of the cavern gleams the mournful crescent moon; that glimpse of the desert, with the terrors of night above the poor sobbing creature, is heart-rending." *Taine, Trans.*

Magdalen. A noted picture by Francesco Barbieri Guercino (1590-1666), representing the Magdalen in prayer. In the Museum at Naples, Italy.

☞ "His [Guercino's] charming Magdalen. How remote from the simplicity and vigor of the preceding age. The reign of pastorals, sigisbes, and devout sentimentality, has commenced; this Magdalen is related to the Herminias and Sophronias and the gentle heroines of Tasso, and, with them, is born out of the Jesuitical reformation." *Taine, Trans.*

Magdalen. A picture by Carlo Dolce (1616-1686). In the Uffizi, Florence, Italy.

Magdalen. An admired picture by Pompeo Girolamo Batoni (1708-1787). In the Gallery of Dresden, Germany.

Magdalen clinging to the foot of the Cross. A picture by Ary Scheffer (1795-1858). Very familiar by reproductions.

Magdalen College. A noted college in Oxford, England, one of the nineteen colleges included in the university. Founded in the year 1457.

☞ "A walk in *Magdalen College.* I never weary with admiring these old edifices festooned with ivy and blackened by age; . . . above all these vast square courts, of which the arcades form a promenade like the Italian convents." *Taine, Trans.*

Greek erudition exists on the Isis and Cam, whether the *Maud* man or the Brasen Nose man be properly ranked or not; the atmosphere is loaded with Greek learning; the whole river has reached a certain height, and kills all that growth of weeds, which this Castalian water kills. *Emerson.*

My chums will burn their Indian weeds
The very night I pass away,
And cloud-propelling puff and puff,
As white the thin smoke melts away;
Then Jones of Wadham, eyes half closed,
Rubbing the ten hairs on his chin,
Will say, "This very pipe I use
Was poor old Smith's of *Maudlin.*"
Walter Thornbury.

Magdalene College. A foundation of the University of Cambridge, England. Established in 1519.

Magdalen, Dance of the. See DANCE OF THE MAGDALEN.

Magdalene, Dying. See DYING MAGDALENE.

Magdalen Hospital. A hospital in London, instituted in 1758. The building in Leigham Court Road, Streatham, was opened in 1869.

Magdalen, Penitent. See PENITENT MAGDALEN.

Magdalen washing the feet of Christ. A picture by Paolo Cagliari, called Paul Veronese (1530?-1588). In the Louvre, Paris.

Magdalenen-Grotto. A celebrated cavern in the limestone rock, near the Grotto of Adelsberg, in Southern Austria.

Magenta, Boulevard de. A fine avenue in Paris, France. See BOULEVARDS.

Magi, Adoration of the. See ADORATION OF THE MAGI.

Magliabecchian Library. A celebrated library in Florence, Italy, so-called after its founder, Antonio Magliabecchia (d. 1714). It is now incorporated with the National Library.

Magna Charta Island. An island in the river Thames, near Egham, England, on which the Great Charter was signed in 1215.

Magnolia. A well-known cemetery in Charleston, S.C.

Magog. See GOG AND MAGOG.

Maid and the Magpie. A picture by Sir Edwin Landseer (1802–1873). In the National Gallery, London.

Maid of the Mist. A little steamer formerly accustomed to ply on the Niagara River below the falls, and used to take adventurous tourists up amid the spray as near to the cataract as possible. She is celebrated for having "shot" the famous Whirlpool Rapids, June 15, 1867, with only slight injury, successfully reaching the calm water below Lewiston. It is said that the chances are fifty to one against any vessel which should undertake to repeat this marvellous and unprecedented adventure. See WHIRLPOOL RAPIDS.

☞ "The story of that wondrous voyage was as follows. . . . The Maid of the Mist got into debt, or her owner had embarked in other and less profitable speculations: at any rate, he became subject to the law, and tidings reached him that the sheriff would seize the Maid. . . . There was but a mile or two on which she could ply: the sheriff's prey, therefore, was easy, and the Maid was doomed. . . . He [the captain] concluded to run the rapids, and he procured two others to accompany him in the risk. . . . I was told by a man who saw the boat pass under the bridge, that she made one long leap down as she came thither; that her funnel was at once knocked flat on the deck by the force of the blow; that the waters covered her from stem to stern; and that then she rose again, and skimmed into the whirlpool a mile below. When there she rode with comparative ease upon the waters, and took the sharp turn round into the river below without a struggle. The feat was done, and the Maid was rescued from the sheriff." *Anthony Trollope.*

Maidan. A magnificent bazaar in Ispahan, Persia. It was built by Shah Abbas the Great (1585–1629), whose great works rendered Ispahan one of the most splendid cities of the East.

☞ "The Maidan Shah, and its accompanying gates and mosques, — the whole the work of one king and on one design, — present a scene of gorgeous, though it may be somewhat barbarous, splendor, almost unequalled in the whole world. Even now in its premature decay, it strikes almost every traveller with astonishment, though the style is not one that looks well in ruin, owing to the perishable nature of the materials employed, and the tawdry effect of glazed tiles when attention is drawn to the fact that they are a mere surface ornament to the walls." *Fergusson.*

Maiden, Halifax Gibbet, *or* **Widow.** An ancient instrument of execution, similar to the guillotine, used in both England and Scotland during the Middle Ages.

He [Argyle] mounted the scaffold, where the rude old guillotine of Scotland, called the *Maiden*, awaited him, and addressed the people in a speech, tinctured with the peculiar phraseology of his sect, but breathing the spirit of serene piety. *Macaulay.*

Maiden Bower. An ancient British fortification near Dunstable, England.

Maiden Castle. A famous earthwork near Monkton, in England, of great antiquity, supposed to belong to a period earlier even than that of the Britons and Romans. The works are a mile in extent, and in some portions 60 feet high. It had four stone gateways, and occupied the summit of a hill.

Maiden Lane. Situated to the south of Covent Garden, London. Here Turner, the artist, was born in 1775.

Maiden Stone. A curious sculptured stone near Inveramsay, Scotland, supposed to be an early Christian monument.

Maids of Honor. [Span. *Las Meniñas.*] A celebrated picture by Diego Rodriguez de Silva y Velasquez (1599–1660), the Spanish painter. In the Museum of Madrid, Spain. "This wonderful picture is alike a masterpiece in local color and in aërial lineal perfection."

Maison Anseatic. [Hanseatic House.] A public building in Antwerp, Belgium.

Maison Carrée. [Square House.] A celebrated Roman ruin at Nîmes, in Southern France.

☞ "France, which was under the dominion of Rome for more than 500 years, still preserves some antique temples reared under the influence of the Romans. Undoubtedly the best preserved and most important of these ancient structures which have escaped the devastations of barbarians and the hostile zeal of early Christians, is situated at Nîmes. It is called the Maison Carrée, owing doubtless to its rectangular form. At the present day its interior is used as a museum. This beautiful edifice was attributed to Augustus; but the exaggerated richness of the frieze and the Corinthian cornices, and an inscription on the façade, fix the period of its construction in the time of the Antonines."

Lefèvre, Trans.

☞ "The finest specimen [of the pseudo-peripteral temples] now remaing to us is the so-called Maison Carrée at Nîmes, which is indeed one of the most elegant temples of the Roman world, owing probably a great deal of its beauty to the taste of the Grecian colonists long settled in the neighborhood. . . . The temple is small, only 45 by 85 feet; but such is the beauty of its proportions and the elegance of its details that it strikes every beholder with admiration. The date of this temple has not been satisfactorily ascertained. From the nail-holes of the inscription on the frieze, it has been attempted to make out the names of Caius and Julius Cæsar, and there is nothing in the style of architecture to contradict this hypothesis. . . . But for their evidence we might almost be inclined to fancy its style represented the age of Trajan." *Fergusson.*

Remains of giant old whose magnitude
Can show the scale of Nîmes as once she stood,
The stranger's being thrills with feeling deep,
When thy vast outlines stretch before his eyes;
No stirring reveries in me arise,
For here did boyhood sleep.

Jean Reboul, Trans.

Maison de François I. [House of Francis I.] A house in Paris, copied from one built in 1520 for his sister by Francis I. at Moret near Fontainebleau, and ornamented with sculptured work by Jean Goujon, removed from Moret.

Maison Dorée. [The Golden House.] One of the most celebrated cafés in Paris, on the Boulevard des Italiens. Its architecture is very fine, and it is highly ornamented with gold.

Maison Pompeian. [Pompeian House.] This building in Paris was built for Prince Napoleon, and is profusely ornamented with statues and paintings.

☞ "An imitation of a Pompeian house, familiar to our readers from that at the Crystal Palace."

Murray's Handbook.

Majorat's Haus. A grand palace in Vienna, Austria, the residence of Prince Liechtenstein.

Mala, Via. See VIA MALA.

Malahide. One of the most venerable and interesting castles of Ireland, in the neighborhood of Dublin, the ancient fortified mansion of the "Talbots," and still held by that family.

☞ "The hall is perhaps one of the purest examples of Norman architecture to be found in the kingdom. The mansion is beautifully furnished, and the collection of paintings, though not extensive, is unsurpassed in value. Among them are choice specimens of the old Dutch and Italian masters in excellent preservation."

Mr. and Mrs. Hall.

Malakhoff. A stone tower forming one of the defences of Sebastopol in the Crimea, during the war between the Russians and the Allies in 1854. It was of immense strength, and believed to be impregnable, but was taken by assault, Sept. 8, 1855, by the combined French and Sardinian forces.

Malesherbes, Boulevart de. A splendid street in Paris, one of the new boulevards, lined with grand hotels, extending from the Church of the Madeleine to the

Park of Monçeau. See BOULEVARDS.

Malick é Meidan. An immense piece of ordnance cast in 1686 at Bejapore, India, to commemorate the capture of the city in that year by Aurungzebe. It is said to be the largest brass cannon in existence, sending a shot weighing 1,600 pounds.

Mall, The. 1. A well-known promenade, and once the most fashionable public resort in London, in St. James's Park. For the origin of the name see PALL MALL.

The ladies, gayly drest, the *Mall* adorn
With various dyes, and paint the sunny morn. *Gay.*

When late their miry sides stage-coaches show,
And their stiff horses through the town move slow;
When all the *Mall* in leafy ruin lies,
And damsels first renew their oyster-cries. *Gay.*

2. A beautiful esplanade in Central Park, New York, ornamented with fine groups of statuary. It is over 1,200 feet in length and some 200 feet in width, lined with trees. It is one of the principal attractions of the park.

Malmaison. A noted villa or château in France, the favorite residence of the Empress Josephine, wife of Napoleon I., near Paris, on the road to St. Germain. It was owned for a time by Queen Christina of Spain, but purchased by Napoleon III. in 1861, and partially restored by the Empress. The attractions of the place are due to art rather than to nature.

At last he [Napoleon] spoke, and slowly turned
(A moisture in his eyes), —
Massena gave a shrug that showed
A cynical surprise:
"Long years ago, at *Malmaison*,
When all unknown of men,
I heard just such a laughing peal,
And I was happy then."
Walter Thornbury.

Malvern, The. A vessel of war of the United States navy in the Civil War in 1861–1865. She was the flag-ship of Admiral Porter. It was on this vessel that on the 4th of April, 1865, President Lincoln went up to Richmond from City Point.

Malvern Hill. A hill about 11 miles from Richmond, Va., and one mile from the James River, where on the 1st of July, 1862, took place a severe battle between the Union and Confederate troops, resulting in the defeat of the latter.

Mamelon. A fortified hill forming one of the defences of Sebastopol. It was captured by the French, June 8, 1855.

Mamertine Prisons. A celebrated state prison on the slope of the Capitoline in Rome. It is one of the few remaining works of the time of the kings, begun, according to tradition, by Ancus Martius, and said to have been enlarged by Servius Tullius, from whom (or from a spring, *tullius*, issuing from the floor of the dungeon) it took the name of Tullian. Here Jugurtha is said to have been starved to death, the accomplices of Catiline strangled by command of Cicero, and Sejanus, the minister and favorite of Tiberius, executed. According to the tradition of the Church, this prison has been consecrated as the place where St. Peter and St. Paul were confined by order of Nero. It is entered through the Church of San Pietro in Carcere.

☞ "The Mamertine Prison is a hideous vault divided into an upper and lower portion, scooped out of the solid rock . . . and lined with massive blocks in the Etruscan style of architecture. A more heart-breaking place of confinement it is not easy to imagine. According to the traditions of the Church, St. Peter was imprisoned here by order of Nero; and the pillar to which he was bound, and a fountain which sprang up miraculously to furnish the water of baptism to his jailers whom he converted, are shown to the visitor. There is no reason to doubt that Jugurtha was starved to death in these pitiless vaults. . . . Here, too, the companions of Catiline were strangled. It is a curious fact that the chances of literature and history should have carved two such names as those of Sallust and Cicero on these Cyclopean walls." *G. S. Hillard.*

Mammoth Cave. A celebrated cavern in Kentucky, near Green River, about 28 miles from Bowling Green. It is unequalled, probably, in the world, in point of extent, and in the variety of interesting objects. It has been explored a distance of more than 10 miles, and is thought to include as many as 40 miles of tortuous passages. It comprises large and lofty galleries and halls, with curious limestone formations in the shape of huge stalactites and stalagmites; and also streams and ponds inhabited by sightless fishes. One room in this cavern is said to occupy two acres, and to be surmounted by a dome of solid rock 120 feet in height. This natural curiosity is a great resort of tourists.

In the *Mammoth Cave* in Kentucky, the torches which each traveller carries make a dismal funeral procession, and serve no purpose but to see the ground. . . . But the guide kindled a Roman candle, and held it here and there, shooting its fireballs successively into each crypt of the groined roof, disclosing its starry splendor, and showing for the first time what that plaything was good for.
Emerson.

Then, again, some kinds of thought breed in the dark of one's mind like the blind fishes in the *Mammoth Cave*.
Holmes.

Mammoth Mound. A noted Indian relic in Marshall County, Va. The mound is 75 feet in height, and is thought to be a sepulchral monument to some personage of high rank among the aborigines.

Mammoth Trees of California. See CALAVERAS.

Man with the Pinks. The portrait of a beardless and weather-beaten old man by the Flemish painter Jan van Eyck (1370–1441). It is now in the Suermondt Collection, at Aix-la-Chapelle, Germany.

Manassas, The. A powerful Confederate iron-plated ram, used in the defence of the approaches to New Orleans. She was destroyed by the vessels of Admiral Farragut's fleet, who forced the passage of the river, April 24, 1862.

Manchester House. The city mansion of Sir Richard Wallace in London, recently belonging to the late Marquis of Hertford, and containing one of the finest collections of paintings in the city.

Manchester Square. A well-known square in London.

Oh, who will repair to *Manchester Square*,
And see if the lovely Marchesa be there?
Moore.

Manco Capac's House. An ancient ruin in Peru, situated on an island in Lake Titicaca, and believed to be the oldest building of the Incas.

☞ "At about that period [three or four centuries before the Spanish conquest], it is fabled that a godlike man, Manco Capac, appeared with a divine consort, on an island in the Lake of Titicaca, journeying from whence they taught the rude and uncivilized inhabitants of the country to till the ground, to build houses and towns, and to live together in communities. Like the Indian Bacchus, Manco Capac was after his death reverenced as a god, and his descendants, the Incas, were considered as of divine origin, and worshipped as children of the Sun, which was the great object of Peruvian adoration." *Fergusson.*

Manfrini Palace. [Ital. *Palazzo Manfrini.*] A noted palace of the seventeenth century in Venice, Italy. It contains a gallery of pictures.

And when you to *Manfrini's Palace* go,
That picture (howsoever fine the rest)
Is loveliest, to my mind, of all the show.
Byron.

Manse, The Old. See OLD MANSE.

Mansion House. The official residence of the Lord Mayor of London, built in 1739-41. It occupies the site of the Stocks Market, nearly facing the Royal Exchange. The grand banquet-room is called the Egyptian Hall. Here the Lord Mayor gives his state banquets.

Cornhill is accustomed to grandeur and greatness, and has witnessed every 9th of November, for I don't know how many centuries, a prodigious annual pageant, chariot, progress, and flourish of trumpetry, and, being so very near the *Mansion House*, I am sure the reader will understand how the idea of pageant and procession came naturally to my mind.
Thackeray.

Mar Sâba. See SANTA SABA.

Marbles, Ægina. See ÆGINA MARBLES; and for ARUNDELIAN MARBLES, ELGIN MARBLES, and the like, see the various adjectives ARUNDELIAN, ELGIN, etc.

Marcellus, Theatre of. See THEATRE OF MARCELLUS.

March Club. See OCTOBER CLUB.

March to Finchley. A celebrated picture by William Hogarth (1697–1764). Now in the Foundling Hospital, London.

Marco, San. See SAN MARCO and ST. MARK'S SQUARE.

Marcus Aurelius. A celebrated bronze equestrian statue now in the centre of the Piazza del Campidoglio upon the Capitoline Hill, Rome. It is the only entire bronze equestrian statue which has come down to us from antiquity, and is regarded as a magnificent specimen of ancient art. Michael Angelo had great admiration for this work, and is said to have exclaimed to the horse, "*Cammina!*" "Go along!"

☞ "It is the most majestic representation of the kingly character that the world has ever seen. A sight of the old heathen emperor is enough to create an evanescent sentiment of loyalty, even in a democratic bosom, so august does he look, so fit to rule." *Hawthorne.*

☞ "The proportions of the horse are not such as would satisfy a Newmarket jockey; but the animation and spirit of the attitude, and the air of life which informs the limbs and seems actually to distend the nostrils, cannot be too much praised. The face and figure of the rider are worthy of the noble animal on which he is seated, and worthy of the good name which he has left in history." *G. S. Hillard.*

☞ "The attitude is perfectly easy and natural: he is making a sign with his right hand, a simple action, that leaves him calm, while it gives life to the entire person. He is going to address his soldiery, and certainly because he has something important to say to them. He does not parade himself, he is not a riding-master like most of our modern equestrian figures, nor a prince in state, displaying his rank: the antique is always simple." *Taine, Trans.*

Marcus Aurelius Antoninus, Column of. See ANTONINE COLUMN.

Maremma. A pestilential and fatal tract of country in Western Italy in the southern part of Tuscany.

"Farther south is the Maremma, a region, which, though now worse than a desert, is supposed to have been anciently both fertile and healthy. The Maremma certainly formed part of that Etruria which was called from its harvests the *annonaria*. . . . Yet both nature and man seem to have conspired against it." *Forsyth.*

Marforio. A colossal recumbent statue of Oceanus, or some river-god, but now known by the name of Marforio, probably from its having stood in the Forum of Mars, and famous for the witty and caustic replies to the satire of Pasquino, which were affixed to it. This statue formerly stood near the entrance to the Museo Capitolino, in Rome, but has lately been placed in the Capitol. See PASQUINO.

Margaret at Church. A picture by Ary Scheffer (1795–1858).

Margaret at the Spinning-wheel. A picture by Ary Scheffer (1795–1858).

Margaret, St. See ST. MARGARET.

Margaux. An Italian villa on the Garonne below Bordeaux, France, in the midst of vineyards noted for the wine they produce, called the *Château Margaux*.

Marguerite. A well-known picture by Alexandre Cabanel (b. 1823), a French painter.

Marguérite, St. See ST. MARGUÉRITE.

Marguerites, The. A picture by William Morris Hunt. There is a popular lithograph of this picture.

☞ "A beautiful girl slowly testing her love, by nipping leaf after leaf from the flower of that name, — simple in action, but naïvely true." *Tuckerman.*

Maria, Santa. See SANTA MARIA.

Marie de Medicis. A series of twenty-one large pictures, representing scenes in the life of Mary of Medicis, by Peter Paul Rubens (1577-1640). They are in the Louvre Gallery in Paris.

Marienburg. A ruined fortress on the Moselle, near the village of Pünderich.

Mario, Monte. See MONTE MARIO.

Mariposa. See CALAVERAS PINES.

Marischal College. A fine building in Aberdeen, Scotland. The college, which was founded in 1593, now forms a part of the new University of Aberdeen.

The general idea of the character [Dugald Dalgetty] is familiar to our comic dramatists after the Restoration, and may be said in some measure to be compounded of Captain Fluellen and Bobadil; but the ludicrous combination of the soldado with the divinity student of *Marischal College* is entirely original. *Jeffrey.*

Märjelen See. A small mountain lake in Switzerland, bordering on the Aletsch glacier, formed by the drainage from the mountains in the summer.

Mark and Paul. A picture of the two apostles, the figures the size of life, by Albert Dürer (1471-1528), the German painter and engraver, and considered to be one of his grandest works. It is now in the gallery at Munich, Bavaria. A companion picture to this is that of *John and Peter* (*q.v.*), which is also in the same gallery.

Mark-Lane. A street in London which is widely known as the seat of the great Corn Market, and a scene of busy traffic. It was originally called "Mart Lane from the privilege of fair accorded by Edward I. to Sir Thomas Ross of Hamlake."

Mark, St. See ST. MARK.

Market Street. A great thoroughfare in Philadelphia, Penn. It is 100 feet wide.

Marksburg. An imposing ruin on the Rhine near Boppart. The emperor Henry IV. was imprisoned in this castle.

Marlborough House. A palace in London, built by Wren in 1709-10 for the great Duke of Marlborough. It was purchased in 1817 by the Crown, and has been since enlarged and fitted up for the residence of the Prince and Princess of Wales.

Playing the part of artists they prompt the setting up of drawing schools, provide masters and models, and at *Marlborough House* enact what shall be considered good taste and what bad. *Herbert Spencer.*

Marriage à la Mode. A famous dramatic and satirical picture by William Hogarth (1697-1764). In the National Gallery, London.

☞ "If catching the manners and follies of an age . . . be comedy, Hogarth composed comedies as much as Molière; in his *Marriage à la Mode* there is even an intrigue carried on throughout the piece. Hogarth had no model to follow and improve upon. He created his art, and used colors instead of language." *Walpole.*

☞ "His [Hogarth's] series of six scenes known as 'Marriage à la Mode' were sold by auction in 1750, when the painter was at the height of his power, in his forty-seventh year; but only one bidder appeared, and the whole series were knocked down to him at a hundred and ten guineas, while the frames alone had cost the painter twenty-four guineas." *Sarah Tytler.*

☞ "Note in the *Marriage à la Mode* the sorrowing gesture of the old steward who foresees the ruin of the house, and deprecates with uplifted hands the gross and sensual folly of the bridegroom." *Taine, Trans.*

Marriage at Cana. [Ital. *Le Nozze di Cana*, Fr. *Les Noces de Cana.*] A very frequent subject of representation by the mediæval painters. Of the more celebrated pictures treating of this theme, the following may be named.

Marriage at Cana. A colossal picture, 30 feet wide by 20 feet high, executed by Paul Veronese (1530?-1588). It was formerly in the refectory of S. Giorgio Maggiore, at Venice, Italy, but is now in the gallery of the Louvre, at Paris. "The most remarkable feature is a group of musicians in the centre, in front, round a table; also portraits, — Paul Veronese himself is playing the violoncello, Tintoret a similar instrument, the gray-haired Titian, in a red-damask robe, the contrabass." There is a smaller repetition of this picture in the Brera at Milan, and another in the Dresden Gallery.

☞ "The chief action to be represented, the astonishing miracle performed by him at whose command 'the fountain blushed into wine,' is here quite a secondary matter; and the value of the picture lies in its magnitude and variety as a composition, and the portraits of the historical characters and remarkable personages introduced."

Mrs. Jameson.

Marriage at Cana. A fine picture by Jacopo Robusti, called Il Tintoretto (1512-1594), in the church of Della Salute in Venice, Italy.

☞ "Taken as a whole, the picture is perhaps the most perfect example which human art has produced of the utmost possible force and sharpness of shadow united with richness of local color. This picture unites color as rich as Titian's with light and shade as forcible as Rembrandt's, and far more decisive." *Ruskin.*

Marriage at Cana. A picture by Gheerardt David (1484-1523), the Flemish painter. It was formerly in the church of St. Basile at Bruges, Belgium, but is now in the Louvre at Paris.

Marriage of Alexander and Roxana. A celebrated picture by the Greek painter Aëtion, the precise date of whose life is unknown. The picture was carried to Rome, and has been described by Lucian.

Marriage of Alexander and Roxana. A mythological fresco designed by Raphael, but executed by one of his scholars, probably Perino del Vaga. Now in the Borghese Palace, Rome.

Marriage of Alexander and Roxana. A fresco painting by Gianantonio Bazzi, called Il Sodoma (1479-1554). In the Farnesina, Rome.

Marriage of Cupid and Psyche. A large fresco in the Farnesina, Rome, designed by Raphael, but executed wholly or chiefly by his pupil Giulio Romano (1492-1546).

Marriage of St. Catherine. A celebrated and often repeated picture by Antonio Allegri, surnamed Correggio (1494-1534), representing the saint as betrothed to the infant Saviour in the presence of the Virgin and St. Sebastian. It is supposed to be connected with "a domestic incident in the life of the painter, viz., the marriage of his sister, Caterina Allegri, in 1519, for whom it was painted." The picture is now in the gallery of the Louvre, Paris. There is another upon the same subject, but different in some particulars, at Naples, Italy. Other early copies are now at St. Petersburg, Russia, in the Capitol at Rome, and elsewhere.

☞ "St. Catherine bends down with the softest, meekest tenderness and submission, and the Virgin unites her hand to that of the infant Christ, who looks up in his mother's face with a divine yet infantine expression. St. Sebastian stands by holding his arrows. It is of this picture that Vasari truly says that the heads appeared to have been painted in Paradise."

Mrs. Jameson.

Marriage of St. Catherine. A picture by Fra Bartolommeo (1469-1517). Now in the Louvre, Paris.

Marriage of St. Catherine. A picture by Bartolomé Esteban Murillo (1618-1682). In the Vatican, Rome.

Marriage of St. Catherine. A picture by Jacopo Robusti, called Tintoretto (1512-1594). In the Ducal Palace, Venice, Italy.

Marriage of St. Catherine. A picture by Bartolomé Esteban Murillo (1618-1682), the Spanish painter. Now at Cadiz, Spain.

Marriage of St. Catherine. A picture by Hans Memling (d. 1495), the Flemish painter, in the Gallery of Strasburg. This picture was destroyed by fire during the bombardment of Strasburg in 1870. There is another upon the same subject by this artist in St. John's Hospital at Bruges, Belgium.

Marriage of the two SS. Catherine. A picture by Fra Bartolommeo (1469-1517), the Italian painter, and regarded as his grandest work. It is now in the Pitti Palace, Florence, Italy. He was assisted in the composition of this picture by Mariotto.

Marriage of the Virgin. [Ital. *Lo Sposalizio.*] A celebrated picture by Raphael Sanzio (1483-1520), well known by the engraving of Longhi. The painting has undergone, within a few years, a very careful restoration, which will insure its continuance for a long time. It is now in the Brera at Milan, Italy.

☞ "Every one knows the famous Sposalizio of the Brera. It was painted by Raphael in his twenty-first year, for the church of S. Francesco, in Città di Castello, and though he has closely followed the conception of his master, it is modified by that ethereal grace which even then distinguished him. . . . In fact, the whole scene is here idealized; it is like a lyric poem." *Mrs. Jameson.*

☞ "Raphael's 'Sposalizio' leaves no recollections but those of unmingled pleasure. It is well known by engravings, and, as its prominent merits are in the drawing and expression, it loses little in this interpretation. It was an old friend in a richer and more becoming costume." *G. S. Hillard.*

Marriage of the Virgin. A celebrated fresco by Bernardin Luini (—aft. 1530). In Saronno, Italy. It has been chromo-lithographed.

Mars, Field of. See CAMPUS MARTIUS.

Mars Hill. See AREOPAGUS.

Mars Ultor, Temple of. See TEMPLE OF MARS ULTOR.

Marshall's Pillar. An imposing mass of rock rising in columnar form to a height of 1,000 feet. It is situated in Fayette county, Va., and is regarded as a striking natural curiosity.

Marshalsea, The. An old prison in London, so called, as "pertaining to the Marshalles of England." It is not now standing. Here were imprisoned many of the martyrs who were persecuted for their religion in the bloody reign of Mary. George Wither was here imprisoned for writing his "Abuses Stript and Whipt," and while confined here wrote his "Shepheard's Hunting." The Marshalsea figures prominently in Dickens's novel of "Little Dorrit."

Marston Moor. A place in the county of York, England, famous for the battle fought in 1644, in which King Charles I. was defeated.

Martin, St. See ST. MARTIN, PORTE ST. MARTIN, and ST. MARTIN RUE.

Martinella. A famous bell which, in the old days of Florence, was used to signalize the outbreak of war.

☞ "Besides the Caroccio, the Florentine army was accompanied by a great bell called Martinella, or Campana degli Asini, which, for thirty days before hostilities began, tolled continually day and night from the arch of Porta Santa Maria, as a public declaration of war, and, as the ancient chronicle hath it, 'for greatness of mind that the enemy might have full time to prepare himself.'" *Napier.*

See CAROCCIO.

Martin's, St. See ST. MARTIN'S IN THE FIELDS, ST. MARTIN'S LE GRAND, ST. MARTIN'S LUDGATE.

Martyrdom of St. Agnes. A well-known picture by Domenichino (1581-1641), and reckoned among the most celebrated productions of the Bologna school. Now in the gallery at Bologna, Italy. See ST. AGNES.

Martyrdom of St. Catherine. 1. A picture by Giuliano Bugiardini (1480-1552), and his most important work. In the Capella Rucelai, in S. Maria Novella, Florence, Italy.

☞ "The subject usually called the *Martyrdom of St. Catherine*, her exposure to the torture of the wheels, should rather be called the Deliverance of St. Catherine. It is one of the most frequent subjects in early art." *Mrs. Jameson.*

2. A grand picture by Gaudenzio Ferrari (1484-1550). In the Brera at Milan, Italy.

Martyrdom of St. Erasmus. An altar-piece by Dierick Stuerbout (d. 1475), a Flemish painter. In the church of St. Peter's at Louvain, Belgium.

Martyrdom of St. Hippolitus. An altar-piece by Dierick Stuerbout (d. 1475), a Flemish painter. In the cathedral of Bruges, Belgium.

Martyrdom of St. Sebastian. 1. A picture by Hans Holbein the Younger (1498?-1543). In the Pinakothek at Munich, Bavaria. See also ST. SEBASTIAN.

2. A picture by Il Sodoma (1479-1554). In the Uffizi Palace, Florence, Italy.

Martyrdom of St. Stephen. 1. An altar-piece by Giulio Romano (1492-1546), the pupil of Raphael, and painted immediately after the death of the latter, for the church of S. Stephano at Genoa, Italy.

2. A picture by Giorgio Barbarelli, called Giorgione (1477-1511). In Verona, Italy.

Martyrdom of San Lorenzo. A celebrated picture by Titian (1477-1576). In the Jesuits' church at Venice, Italy.

Martyrdom of San Placido and Santa Flavia. A picture by Antonio Allegri, surnamed Correggio (1494-1534). In the Gallery of Parma, Italy.

Martyrdom of Santa Felicità. A fresco by Raphael Sanzio (1483-1520), or by one of his best pupils, painted for the chapel of the castle of La Magliana, a residence of Leo X. It has been transferred to canvas, and is now in the Monte di Pietà, Rome.

☞ "There can be no doubt that we have here the death of St. Cecilia, and not the death of St. Felicitas; that this was the subject designed by Raphael, probably about the time that he painted the St. Cecilia at Bologna, and that the print was afterwards misnamed." *Mrs. Jameson.*

Martyrdom of Santa Petronilla. A mosaic in St. Peter's Church, Rome. The work of Francesco Barbieri, called Guercino (1590-1666). It is a copy of the picture by the same master in the Museum of the Capitol.

☞ "The finest mosaic in St. Peter's (and consequently in the world), is generally, and I think justly, said to be Guercino's famous Martyrdom of Santa Petronilla; though why called a martyrdom, I cannot imagine, since it only represents below the lifeless body of the saint raised from the grave at the request of her mourning lover, and found to be miraculously preserved in all the charms of youth and beauty." *Eaton.*

Martyrdom of the Ten Thousand Saints. A picture by Albert Dürer (1471-1528), the celebrated German painter and engraver. It bears the date of 1508, and was painted for Duke Frederic of Saxony. It is now in the Belvedere Gallery at Vienna, Austria. There is also a copy in the Schleissheim Gallery.

Martyrs. See CHRISTIAN MARTYRS (IN THE COLISEUM).

Mary and Elizabeth, Meeting of. A picture by Domenico Ghirlandajo (1449-1498?). In the gallery of the Louvre, Paris.

Mary. See SEVEN JOYS OF MARY.

Mary Rose. A British man-of-war which sunk off the coast of France in 1545, owing to the weight of the artillery she carried. It is said that breech-loading cannon have been recovered from the wreck.

Maryland Avenue. One of the principal streets in Washington, leading from the Capitol to the Long Bridge.

Maryland Institute. A large building in Baltimore, Md., erected in 1854, used for a market, industrial exhibitions, etc., with a library and school of art. In the hall of the Institute, which is capable of holding 5,000 persons, the Southern Democratic Convention held its sessions in 1860.

Mary-le-Bow, St. See BOW CHURCH.

Mary-le-Strand, St. See ST. MARY-LE-STRAND.

Marylebone. A parliamentary borough of London, originally called Tyburn, or Tybourne. See TYBURN.

Marylebone Gardens. A popular place of resort in the north-west part of London. It was famous for its bowling-alleys, and for its illuminations, balls, and concerts. The poet Gay alludes to it more than once in his "Beggar's Opera."

At the Groom-porter's batter'd bullies play,
Some dukes at *Marybone* bowl time away.
Pope.

Marys. See FOUR MARYS and THREE MARYS.

Marzocco. The name given to a celebrated statue of a recumbent lion, the work of Donatello (1383–1466), standing at the corner of the Palazzo Vecchio in Florence, Italy.

Masaccio, Tommaso Guidi. (1402–1443.) A portrait of himself by the painter in the collection of autograph portraits in the Uffizi, Florence, Italy.

Masada. A remarkable desert fortress in Palestine, now in ruins. It was placed upon a rock which overlooks the Dead Sea, was surrounded by very deep valleys, and was only accessible by two paths hewn in the rock. It was first built by Jonathan Maccabæus in the second century B.C., and afterwards enlarged and strengthened by Herod the Great. Before the siege of Jerusalem by Titus, the Sicarii obtained possession of Masada and its treasures. These Jews, who loved freedom and their country, used every means to revenge themselves for their wrongs against the Romans, and became a terror to the whole country. The fortress of Masada held out against the Romans after the destruction of Jerusalem and was only taken after a fierce siege. The garrison, consisting of 967 men, women, and children, finding defence hopeless, resolved to perish by their own hands rather than be taken by the Romans; and when the latter, making the final attack and expecting fierce resistance, reached the summit, they found only two women and a few children alive to tell the story of the tragedy. All trace of this ancient fortress was for a long period lost; but within the present century its site has been discovered and identified by the American traveller, Dr. Robinson.

Maschere, Stanza delle. See STANZA DELLE MASCHERE.

Mashita, Palace of. A celebrated ruined palace of the Sassamian kings in Mesopotamia.

☞ "The great defect of the palace at Mashita as an illustration of Sassamian art arises from the fact, that, as a matter of course, Chosroes did not bring with him architects or sculptors to erect this building. He employed the artists of Antioch, or Damascus, or those of Syria, as he found them. He traced the form and design of what he wanted, and left them to execute it, and they introduced the vine and other details of Byzantine art with which Justinian had made them familiar. . . . Though it stands thus alone, the discovery of this palace fills a gap in our history such as no other building occupies up to the present time. . . . Its greatest interest, however, lies in the fact that all the Persian and Indian mosques were derived from buildings of this class." *Fergusson.*

Mason and Dixon's Line. A celebrated boundary line between the State of Pennsylvania and the States of Maryland and Virginia. It was so called after the surveyors, Charles Mason and Jeremiah Dixon, by whom it was mainly run, about the year 1765. The name acquired great celebrity through the speeches of John Randolph of Virginia, who in the Congressional debates in the year 1820, in regard to the exclusion of slavery from the Territories, made frequent reference to it, Pennsylvania being a free State, and Maryland and Virginia at that time slave States. Though the name has lost its old importance and significance, it is still often alluded to. The line was originally over 300 miles long, and was marked by stone posts at intervals of one mile.

Mason and Dixon's line, of which we hear so often, and which was first established as the division between slave soil and free soil, runs between Pennsylvania and Maryland. *Anthony Trollope.*

He [Davis] is a wise man. He knows what he wants, and he wants it with a will, like Julius Cæsar of old. He has gathered every dollar and every missile south of *Mason and Dixon's line* to hurl a thunderbolt that shall serve his purpose. *W. Phillips.*

Mass of Bolsena. A well-known fresco by Raphael Sanzio (1483-1520), representing a miracle wrought in 1263, by which a priest who doubted the doctrine of transubstantiation was convinced by the blood which flowed from the Host he was consecrating. It is in the stanza of the Heliodorus, in the Vatican, Rome.

Massachusetts, The. A royal frigate which took part in the attack upon Louisbourg in 1745, capturing the French frigate *Vigilant.*

Massachusetts Avenue. One of the principal streets and thoroughfares in the city of Washington.

Massacre of Scio. A picture by Ferdinand Victor Eugène Delacroix (1799-1863), the celebrated French historical painter.

Massacre of the Innocents. A celebrated picture by Guido Reni (1575-1642). In the Gallery of Bologna, Italy.

☞ "Guido's celebrated picture of the Massacre of the Innocents is a powerful and painful thing. The marvel of it to me is the simplicity with which its wonderful effects are produced, both of expression and color. The kneeling mother in the foreground, with her dead children before her, is the most intense representation of agony I ever saw. Yet the face is calm, her eyes thrown up to heaven, but her lips undistorted. It is the look of a soul overwhelmed, — that has ceased to struggle because it is full." *N. P. Willis.*

Massacre of the Innocents. A celebrated picture by Daniele da Volterra (1509-1566), the Italian painter, containing more than 70 figures. It is now in the Tribune of the Uffizi, at Florence, Italy.

Massacre of the Innocents. A picture by Giotto di Bondone (1276-1336). In the Arena Chapel, Padua, Italy.

Massacre of the Mamelukes. A noted picture by Horace Vernet (1789-1863). In the Luxembourg, Paris.

Massimo delle Colonne Palace. [Ital. *Palazzo Massimo delle Colonne.*] A well-known palace in Rome, begun in 1526, and containing the celebrated Discobolus found upon the Esquiline Hill.

Massimo, Villa. See VILLA MASSIMO.

Mater Dolorosa. [The Mourning Mother; Ital. *La Madre di Dolore, L'Addolorata;* Fr. *Notre Dame de Pitié.*] A very familiar subject of representation by the great painters of the Middle Ages, exhibiting the Virgin in the character of the mother of the crucified Redeemer, and "queen of martyrs." See also PIETÀ, LA. Among the more celebrated pictures which treat of this subject the following may be named.

Mater Dolorosa. A picture by Jan Mostaert (1499-1555), a Flemish painter, and regarded as his most important work. It is now in the church of Notre Dame at Bruges, Belgium.

Mater Dolorosa. A picture by Albert Dürer (1471-1528), the German painter and engraver. Now in the gallery at Munich, Bavaria.

Maud. See MAGDALEN COLLEGE.

Maurice, St. See ST. MAURICE and CONVERSION OF ST. MAURICE BY ERASMUS.

Mäusethurm. See MOUSE TOWER.

Mausoleum, The (of Halicarnassus). A famous edifice, built of marble, erected as a monument or mausoleum to the memory of her husband by Artemisia, the Princess of Caria, frequently alluded to by Greek and Latin writers, and reckoned one of the seven wonders of the world. It gave its name to all monumental structures of the same kind. Some of the relics of this celebrated monument were brought to England in 1846, and are now preserved in the British Museum, in a room devoted to the purpose.

☞ "Till Mr. Newton's visit to Halicarnassus in 1856, the very site of this seventh wonder of the world was a matter of dispute. We now know enough to be able to restore the principal parts with absolute certainty, and to ascertain its dimensions and general appearance within very insignificant limits of error. . . . The building consisted internally of two chambers, superimposed the one on the other. . . . Though its height was unusually great for a Greek building, its other dimensions were small. It covered only 13,230 feet. The admiration, therefore, which the Greeks expressed regarding it must have arisen, first, from the unusual nature of the design, and of the purpose to which it was applied, or perhaps still more from the extent and richness of its sculptured decorations, of the beauty of which we are now enabled to judge, and can fully share with them in admiring." *Fergusson.*

Mausolus worke will be the Carians glorie. *Spenser.*

Her power, her fame,
Thus pass away, a shade, a name!
The *Mausoleum* murmured as I spoke;
A spectre seemed to rise, like towering smoke;
It answered not, but pointed as it fled
To the black carcass of the sightless dead.
W. L. Bowles.

Mausoleum of Augustus. A magnificent structure, now a ruin, erected on the banks of the Tiber, in the Campus Martius, Rome. This huge circular monument built by the Emperor Augustus, was designed to contain his own ashes and those of the whole imperial family and dependents. The first member of the family buried here was Marcellus; and the mausoleum is alluded to by Virgil in these famous lines: —

What groans of men shall fill the Martian field!
How fierce a blaze his flaming pile shall yield!
What fun'ral pomp shall floating Tyber see,
When, rising from his bed, he views the sad solemnity!
No youth shall equal hopes of glory give,
No youth afford so great a cause to grieve,
The Trojan honor and the Roman boast,
Admir'd when living, and ador'd when lost!
Mirror of ancient faith in early youth!
Undaunted worth, inviolable truth!
Ah! could'st thou break through Fate's severe decree,
A new Marcellus shall arise in thee!
Æneid, VI. (Dryden's Translation).

☞ "In the centre of that massive mound, the great founder of the empire was to sleep his last sleep; while his statue was ordained to rise conspicuous on its summit, and satiate its everlasting gaze with the view of his beloved city." *Merivale.*

Mausoleum of Galla Placidia. A celebrated sepulchral monument in Ravenna, Italy, erected to the memory of the Empress Gallia Placidia, daughter of Theodosius the Great. This tomb is interesting on account of its architecture and mosaics, and rich decoration.

Mausoleum of Hadrian. See St. Angelo.

Maximilian. A portrait of the emperor by Albert Dürer (1471–1528), the German painter. It is in the gallery of the Belvedere in Vienna, Austria. A replica of the same was in the collection of Lord Northwick at Thirlestain Hall, England.

Maximilian's Triumphal Car. A series of wood-cuts by Albert Dürer (1471–1528), the celebrated German painter and engraver. They are in the British Museum.

Max-Joseph-Platz. A large public square in Munich, Bavaria, one of the finest in Europe.

May Fair. A district in London so called from the fair which was formerly held there in the month of May.

☞ "*May Fair!* What a name for the core of dissipated and exclusive London! A name that brings with it only the scent of crushed flowers in a green field, of a pole wreathed with roses, booths crowded with dancing peasant-girls, and nature in its holyday! This — to express the costly, the court-like, the *so called* 'heartless' precinct of fashion and art in their most authentic and envied perfection. *Mais les extrêmes se touchent;* and perhaps there

is more nature in May Fair than in Rose Cottage or Honeysuckle Lodge."
N. P. Willis.

But the ordinary residences of fashionable life — the mansions of Belgravia, Tyburnia, and *Mayfair* — are mere shells of brick and stucco, which present such a dreary appearance outside that one is surprised sometimes to find them palaces of comfort within. *C. L. Eastlake.*

She puts off her patched petticoat to-day,
And puts on *May-fair* manners, so begins
By setting us to wait. *Mrs. Browning.*

Mayflower, The. A famous vessel of 180 tons, chartered by the "Pilgrim Fathers," or first settlers of Massachusetts, and in which a portion of them embarked in the summer of 1620 for the New World. The Mayflower set sail from Southampton, England, in company with the *Speedwell*, on the 5th of August; but, the courage of the captain and crew of the latter failing, both vessels put back to port. Finally, on the 6th of September, the Mayflower again spread her sails, and with 41 men and their families (101 in all) crossed the Atlantic, reaching anchorage within Cape Cod after a stormy passage of 63 days.

Methinks I see it now, that one, solitary, adventurous vessel, the *Mayflower*, of a forlorn hope, freighted with the prospects of a future state, and bound across the unknown sea. . . . Suns rise and set, and weeks and months pass, and winter surprises them on the deep, but brings them not the sight of the wished-for shore. . . . I see them, escaped from these perils, pursuing their all but desperate undertaking, and landed at last after a five months' passage on the ice-clad rocks of Plymouth, weak and weary from the voyage, poorly armed, . . . without shelter, without means, surrounded by hostile tribes.
Edward Everett.

Give a thing time, — if it can succeed, it is a right thing. Look now at American Saxondom; and at that little Fact of the sailing of the *Mayflower*, two hundred years ago, from Delft Haven in Holland! Were we of open sense as the Greeks were, we had found a Poem here; one of Nature's own Poems, such as she writes in broad facts over great continents.
Carlyle.

Or if we shrink, better remount our ships,
And, fleeing God's express design, trace back
The hero-freighted *Mayflower's* prophet-track
To Europe, entering her blood-red eclipse.
Lowell.

Sad *Mayflower!* watched by winter stars,
And nursed by winter gales,
With petals of the sleeted spars,
And leaves of frozen sails! *Whittier.*

O Mother State, how quenched thy Sinai fires!
Is there none left of thy stanch *Mayflower* breed? *Lowell.*

Mayor's Coach. See LORD MAYOR'S COACH.

Maypole, The. A famous pole 134 feet high, which formerly stood in the Strand, London, was taken down in the time of Cromwell as "a last remnant of vile heathenism, an idol of the people," re-erected with great ceremony under Charles II., and finally taken down in 1717 and presented to Sir Isaac Newton.

Amidst that area wide they took their stand,
Where the tall *Maypole* once o'erlooked the Strand. *Pope.*

Mazarin Library. See BIBLIOTHÈQUE MAZARINE.

Mazas. A prison and house of detention in the Boulevard de l'Hôpital, Paris. Here on the night of Dec. 2, 1851, Napoleon III. imprisoned for two days 18 deputies, including MM. Thiers, Baze, Roger Charras, Greppo, Miot, Lagrange, and Gens. Changarnier, Lamoricière, Cavaignac, etc., with 60 chiefs of barricades.

My neighbor said to a vulgar creature who was dancing: "Has the Saltpetrière come down to the bal du Trône to-day?" "No; but *Mazas* has emptied itself to-day into the bal du Trone." A distinction is made between them. *Taine, Trans.*

Meadows, The. A large public park and pleasure-ground in Edinburgh, Scotland.

Meal, The. See FRUGAL MEAL.

Médard, St. See ST. MÉDARD.

Medea. A picture by Ferdinand Victor Eugène Delacroix (1799–1863), the celebrated French historical painter.

☞ "Delacroix is a man of a very different genius, and his 'Medea' is a genuine creation of a noble fancy."
Thackeray.

Medicean Venus. See VENUS DE' MEDICI.

Mediceo-Laurentian Library. A famous library in Florence, Italy, containing many rare and precious manuscripts and early copies of books.

Medici Chapel. **1.** A chapel in the church of Santa Croce in Florence, Italy. It contains some fine works of Luca della Robbia.

2. A chapel built as a mausoleum in the church of S. Lorenzo, Florence. It contains the cenotaphs of the Medici family.

Medici, Lorenzo de'. See LORENZO DE' MEDICI.

Medici Madonna. The name sometimes given to a picture of the Virgin and Child by Roger van der Weyden (— d. 1464), the Flemish painter. Now in the Städel Institute in Frankfort, Germany.

Medici, Tombs of. See SAN LORENZO.

Medici, Villa. See VILLA MEDICI.

Medicis. See MARIE DE MEDICIS.

Medora. An admired statue by Horatio Greenough (1805–1852).

☞ "Among the beautiful ideal works he [Greenough] executed, within the few succeeding years, was Medora — illustrative of Byron's memorable description of the Corsair's bride after death, of which the greatest praise is to say that the marble embodies the verse." *Tuckerman.*

Medusa. A celebrated painting by Leonardo da Vinci (1452–1519). In the Uffizi Gallery, Florence, Italy. Grimm says, "Leonardo collected a brood of venomous swelling toads; he put them in his house, provoked them to rage, and observed them until his imagination had absorbed enough for his painting. When completed, he brought the picture into a darkened room, cut a hole in the window-shutter, so that the ray of light exactly fell upon the head of the Medusa, and beamed upon it with lustrous brightness. With this the curious, who were mysteriously brought in, were filled with fright."

☞ "The *Medusa's Head*, by Leonardo da Vinci, is a very curious work, elaborately painted, as all his pictures were, and attracting the gaze by a strange species of fascination. . . . What could have induced a man of such various and wonderful powers, with an organization so sensitive to beauty and all pleasurable sensations, to give so much time to a picture which we are afraid to look at steadily, lest it should start into life in our next troubled dream." *Hillard.*

Upon its lips and eyelids seems to lie
Loveliness like a shadow, from which shine
Fiery and lurid, struggling underneath,
The agonies of anguish and of death.
Shelley.

Medusa. See RONDININI MEDUSA.

Méduse, La. See SHIPWRECK OF THE MEDUSA.

Meg. See LONG MEG, MONS MEG, ROARING MEG.

Megaspelion. A picturesque and irregular structure of large size upon a steep and narrow ridge at the mouth of a large cavern, in which much of the building is contained. It is overhung by a precipice several hundred feet in height rising above the cavern. The present front is modern, but the convent is traditionally one of the oldest monastic foundations in Greece. [Correctly *Megaspelæon*; Gr. Μεγασπήλαιον.]

Meier Madonna. See MADONNA OF THE BURGOMASTER MEYER.

Melancholy. One of two celebrated statues by Caius Gabriel Cibber (d. 1700?), which formerly adorned the principal gate of old Bethlehem Hospital, London, and are now in the entrance hall of the new Bethlem Hospital. The companion figure is called Madness. See MADNESS.

☞ "Cibber, whose pathetic emblems of Fury and Melancholy still adorn Bedlam, was a Dane." *Macaulay.*

Where o'er the gates by his famed father's hand,
Great Cibber's brazen brainless brothers stand. *Pope.*

Bedlam, and those carved maniacs at the gates,
Perpetually recumbent. *Wordsworth.*

Melancholy. See MELENCOLIA.

Meleager. A celebrated Greek statue of Meleager with boar's head and dog, now in the Vatican, Rome. It was found near the Porta Portese in a nearly perfect state, the left hand, which is supposed to have held a spear, being alone wanting.

☞ "This is simply a body, but one of the finest I ever saw. The head, almost square, modelled in solid sections, like that of Napoleon, has only a mediocre brow, and the expression seems to be that of an obstinate man. The beauty of the figure consists in a powerful neck and a torso admirably continued by the thigh. He is a hunter and nothing more."

Taine, Trans.

Melencolia. A celebrated print by Albert Dürer (1471-1528), the German painter and engraver.

☞ "In the seated figure of this grand winged woman, absorbed in thought, he has expressed, in a highly original and intellectual manner, the insufficiency of the human reason, either to explore the secrets of life, fortune, and science, or to unravel those of the past. Symbolical allusions of various kinds lie around, in the shape of the sphere, the book, the crystal polygon, the crucible, the bell, the hour-glass, etc., with many implements of human activity, such as the plane, the hammer, and the rule. The intention of the plate is greatly enhanced by the grandly melancholy character of the landscape background."

Kugler's Handbook of Painting.

Mellifont. A beautiful ruined monastery on the river Mattock, near the banks of the Boyne, on the borders of Meath County, Ireland, regarded as one of the finest architectural remains in the island.

Melon-Eaters, The. A picture by Bartolomé Esteban Murillo (1618-1682). In the Pinakothek, Munich, Bavaria.

Melrose Abbey. A beautiful and far-famed ruined monastery in the little town of the same name in Scotland. The existing ruin is the relic of the third building which has occupied the site. There is probably no part of the present structure older than the year 1400. It is greatly admired for its picturesque beauty, and the fine tracery of its windows. This venerable building is similar, in the stone of which it is built, and in the style of its architecture and ornament, to Strasburg Cathedral. It has been twice rebuilt, once by Robert Bruce. In the chancel is an exquisitely beautiful window, which Sir Walter Scott thus describes, —

"The moon on the east oriel shone
Through slender shafts of shapely stone,
By foliaged tracery combined;
Thou wouldst have thought some fairy's hand
'Twixt poplars straight the osier wand
In many a freakish knot had twined;
Then framed a spell when the work was done,
And changed the willow wreaths to stone."

The scene of Scott's novel of "The Monastery" is laid at Melrose Abbey, in the sixteenth century.

☞ "The most beautiful not only of the Scottish Second Pointed churches, but of all the northern fanes of whatever age. The splendor of middle-age romance which Scott has thrown around the place has almost obliterated its older and holier renown, when it was described by Bede as the home of the meek Eata, the prophetic Boisil, the austere Cuthbert; when . . . it was the lamp of that Anglo-Saxon Lothian, which, deriving its own faith from Iona, sped the glad gift to many an English province, and even sent a missionary across the seas to become the apostle of the Austrasian tribes on the Meuse, the Waal, and the Rhine."

Quarterly Review.

☞ "Melrose is the finest remaining specimen of Gothic architecture in Scotland. . . . The heart of Bruce is supposed to have been buried beneath the high altar. The chancel is all open to the sky, and rooks build their nests among the wild ivy that climbs over the crumbling arches."

Bayard Taylor.

☞ "Here is this Melrose, now, which has been berhymed, bedraggled through infinite guide-books, and been gaped at and smoked at by dandies, and been called a 'dear love' by pretty young ladies, and been hawked about as a trade article in all neighboring shops, and you know perfectly well that all your raptures are spoken for and expected at the door, and your going off in ecstacy is a regular part of the programme: and yet, after all, the sad, wild, sweet beauty of the thing comes down on one like a cloud; even for the sake of being original you could not in conscience declare you did not admire it." *Mrs. H. B. Stowe.*

Oh, the monks of *Melrose*, they made good kail
  On Fridays when they fasted;
They never wanted beef or ale
  As long as their neighbors' lasted.
Ballad.

If thou wouldst view fair *Melrose* aright,
Go visit it by the pale moonlight;
For the gay beams of lightsome day
Gild but to flout the ruins gray;
When the broken arches are black in night,
And each shafted oriel glimmers white;
When the cold light's uncertain shower
Streams on the ruin's central tower,

. . . .

Then go, — but go alone the while, —
Then view St. David's ruined pile;
And, home returning, soothly swear,
Was never scene so sad and fair. *Scott.*

So perished Albion's "glammarye,"
  With him in *Melrose Abbey* sleeping,
His charmed torch beside his knee,
That even the dead himself might see
  The magic scroll within his keeping.
Whittier.

Member of the Humane Society. See DISTINGUISHED MEMBER OF THE HUMANE SOCIETY.

Memnon. This celebrated vocal statue at Thebes, in Egypt, is of great antiquity, and is supposed to have uttered at sunrise a sound like a metallic ring or the breaking of a harp-string. It was greatly shattered, probably by Cambyses or by the earthquake of 27 B.C., but has been repaired. This and the companion colossus (called "The Pair") are about 60 feet in height, sitting with their hands on their knees, apparently looking across the river. They are inexpressibly grand and impressive.

☞ "No record exists of the sound which made the statue so famous having been heard while it was entire. Strabo, who visited it with Ælius Gallus, the governor of Egypt, speaks of the 'upper part' having been 'broken and hurled down,' as he was told, 'by the shock of an earthquake,' and says that he heard the sound, but could 'not affirm whether it proceeded from the pedestal or from the statue itself, or even from some of those who stood near its base;' and it appears, from his not mentioning the name of Memnon, that it was not yet supposed to be the statue of that doubtful personage. But it was not long before the Roman visitors ascribed it to the 'Son of Tithonus,' and a multitude of inscriptions, the earliest in the reign of Nero, and the most recent in the reign of Septimius Severus, testify to his miraculous powers, and the credulity of the writers. Pliny calls it the statue of Memnon; and Juvenal thus refers to it. —

'Dimidio magicæ resonant ubi Memnone chordæ.'

Various opinions exist among modern critics as to whether the sound this statue was said to emit, and which is described as resembling either the breaking of a harp-string or the ring of metal, was the result of a natural phenomenon or of priestly craft. Some say that the action of the rising sun upon the cracks in the stone moist with dew caused the peculiar sound produced; while others declare that it was a trick of the priests, one of whom hid himself in the statue, and struck a metallic-sounding stone there concealed. The chief arguments in favor of this last view are, that such a stone still exists in the lap of the statue, with a recess cut in the block immediately behind it, capable of holding a person completely screened from view below; and, above all, the suspicious circumstance that the sound was heard twice or thrice by important personages, like the Emperor Hadrian, — '*Χαιρων και τριτον αχον ιη*,' rejoicing (at the presence of the emperor), it 'uttered a sound' a third time,' — while ordinary people only heard it once, and that sometimes not until after two or three visits."
Murray's Handbook for Egypt.

☞ "And next appeared — and my heart stood still at the sight the Pair. There they sat, together yet apart, in the midst of the plain, serene and vigilant, still keeping their untired watch over the lapse of ages and the eclipse of Egypt. I can never believe that any thing else so majestic as this Pair has been conceived of by the imagination of Art. Nothing even in nature certainly ever affected me so unspeakably; no thunder-storm in my childhood, nor any aspect of Niagara, or the Great Lakes of America, or the Alps, or the Desert, in my later years."
Miss Martineau.

☞ "The impression of sublime tranquillity which they convey when seen from distant points is confirmed by

a near approach. There they sit, keeping watch, — hands on knees, gazing straight forward, seeming, though so much of the faces is gone, to be looking over to the monumental piles on the other side of the river, which became gorgeous temples after these throne seats were placed here — the most immovable thrones that have ever been established on this earth."
Miss Martineau.

Then say, what secret melody was hidden
In *Memnon's statue*, which at sunrise played?
Perhaps thou wert a priest: if so, my struggles
Are vain, for priestcraft never owns its juggles! *Horace Smith.*

I thank no one for enlightening my credulity on points of poetical belief. It is like robbing the statue of *Memnon* of its mysterious music. *Washington Irving.*

But what is the song they sing? Is it a tone of the *Memnon Statue*, breathing music as the *light* first touches it? a "liquid wisdom," disclosing to our sense the deep, infinite harmonies of Nature and man's soul? *Carlyle.*

Of a more glorious sunrise than of old
Drew wondrous melodies from *Memnon* huge,
Yea, draws them still, though now he sits waist-deep
In the ingulfing flood of whirling sand.
Lowell.

'Twas close beside him there,
Sunrise whose *Memnon* is the soul of man.
Lowell.

And morning-smitten *Memnon*, singing, wakes;
And, listening by his Nile,
O'er Ammon's grave and awful visage breaks
A sweet and human smile. *Whittier.*

Memnonium. See RAMASEUM.

Memorial Hall. An imposing collegiate building, connected with Harvard University, in Cambridge, Mass. It contains a dining-hall, a theatre, and a monumental hall in memory of the graduates who fell in the war of the Rebellion. The dining-hall, which is one of the largest university halls in the world, will seat 1,000 persons, and is adorned with portraits and busts of eminent men and benefactors of the college. The building is of brick and stone, over 300 feet in length, with a lofty tower. It was dedicated in 1874.

Ménage du Menuisier. [The Joiner's House.] A famous picture by Rembrandt van Ryn (1607–1669), exhibiting a rustic interior; the Virgin, seated with the volume of the Scriptures open on her knees, contemplates the Infant asleep; in the background Joseph is seen at his work, while angels hover above keeping watch over the Holy Family. Exquisite for the homely natural sentiment and the depth of the color and chiaroscuro. Now in the gallery at St. Petersburg, Russia.

Menai Bridge. A famous suspension bridge across Menai Strait, which separates the island of Anglesea from Wales. It was erected at a cost of over £200,000.

Menelaus, The. A British frigate which blockaded the Chesapeake in 1814, and landed an attacking force.

Menhir of Lochmariaker. A large Druidic or ante-Druidic monument of unknown antiquity, in the Department of Morbihan, France. Its origin and purpose are involved in complete obscurity.

Menhir of Plonarzel. A lofty Celtic monument of unknown antiquity about ten miles from Brest, France. It stands on an elevation in the midst of a wild region, and is regarded with superstitious awe by the peasantry.

Meniñas, Las. See MAIDS OF HONOR.

Menuisier. See MÉNAGE DU MENUISIER.

Mephistopheles appearing to Faust. A picture by Ferdinand Victor Eugène Delacroix (1799–1863), the celebrated French historical painter.

Mer de Glace. [Ger. *Eismeer*, The Sea of Ice.] A general name for a glacier, but more particularly applied to an immense sea of ice, which fills the highest gorges of the chain of Mont Blanc, and extends over a distance of 12 miles into the valley of Chamouni. From the lower part of this glacier springs the river Arveiron. De Saussure says that its surface resembles that of "a sea which has become suddenly frozen, not in the moment of a tempest, but at the instant when the wind has calmed, and the waves, although very high, have become blunted and rounded." There are other seas of ice among the Alps, but this is the Mer de Glace *par eminence*.

Merceria. A street of busy traffic in Venice, Italy, leading out of the Piazza of S. Mark.

☞ "Hence I passed thro' the Merceria, which is one of the most delicious streets in the world for the sweetnesse of it, and is all the way on both sides tapistred as it were with cloth of gold, rich damasks and other silks, which the shops expose and hang before their houses from the first floore, and with that varietie that for neere halfe the yeare spente chiefly in this Citty, I hardly remember to have seen the same piece twice exposed; to this add the perfumes, the apothecaries' shops, and innumerable cages of nightingales which they keepe that entertaine you with their melodie, so that shutting your eyes you would imagine yourselfe in the countrie, when indeed you are in the middle of the Sea. This street paved with brick and exceedingly cleane brought us thro' an arch into the famous piazza of St. Mark." *John Evelyn*, 1645.

Mercers' Hall. A building situated in Cheapside, London, belonging to the Company of Mercers, the oldest of the great City guilds or companies.

Merchant Taylors' Hall. In Threadneedle Street, London, built after the Great Fire. It is the largest of the companies' halls. The Merchant Taylors' Company, the great Tory company, was incorporated in 1466, and has counted among its members several kings of England, and many of the nobility.

Merchants' Tables. A celebrated dolmen or burial grotto at Lochmariaker, in the little island of Gavrinnis, France. Upon the stones the form of a hatchet or mason's trowel can still be distinctly traced. This was a very common symbol in ancient times, intended to indicate that the monument was still under the trowel, that is, devoted to the purposes of a tomb; this device, it is supposed, being had recourse to in order to protect the empty tombs from mutilation.

Mercury. A well-known and admired statue by Giovanni da Bologna, called Il Fiammingo (1524–1608). In the Bargello, Florence, Italy.

☞ "Who does not know the *Mercury* of Gian Bologna, that airy youth with winged feet and cap, who, with the caduceus in his hand, and borne aloft upon a head of Æolus, seems bound upon some Jove-commissioned errand? Who has not admired its lightness and truth of momentary action, . . . since, Mercury-like, it has winged its way to the museums and houses of every quarter of the globe?" *Perkins's Tuscan Sculptors.*

☞ "The unrivalled Mercury of John of Bologna — aërial, spirited, designing, full of art and purpose — quick in intellect, invention, and rare device — it is Hermes himself, the winged messenger of the gods. His foot rests on the head of a Zephyr — a beautiful, poetic thought. . . . This exquisite statue is excelled only by a few masterpieces of ancient art." *Eaton.*

☞ "The first object that attracted us was John of Bologna's *Mercury*, poising himself on tiptoe, and looking not merely buoyant enough to float, but as if he possessed more than the eagle's power of lofty flight. . . . No bolder work was ever achieved; nothing so full of life has been done since." *Hawthorne.*

Mercury. A beautiful work of ancient sculpture. Now in Lansdowne House, London.

Mercury. See ANTINOUS, THE.

Mercury and Argus. A picture by Joseph Mallord William Turner (1775–1851), the eminent English painter.

Mercury teaching Cupid. A noted picture by Antonio Allegri, called Correggio (1493–1534). In the National Gallery, London.

Mercy. See SEVEN WORKS OF MERCY.

Mercy's Dream. A picture by Daniel Huntington (b. 1816). In the Corcoran Gallery, Washington.

Merlin's Hill. A noted eminence near Caermarthen, Wales. Upon it is a natural seat called Merlin's Chair, where the famous prophet is reputed to have sat when he uttered his prophecies.

Mermaid, The. (Tavern and Club.) A celebrated tavern formerly situated in Bread Street, London, the favorite resort of actors and literary men in the time of Elizabeth. The famous Mermaid Club, said to have been founded by Sir Walter Raleigh, and including as members Jonson, Beaumont, Fletcher, Selden, Carew, Donne, and probably Shakespeare, met here for social and convivial enjoyment. Fuller makes this tavern the scene of the wit combats between Shakespeare and Jonson; although there is no positive evidence that Shakespeare was one of the club, or that he frequented the *Mermaid*, our confidence that this was the case resting, as has been said, "upon the moral impossibility that he should have been absent." Knight remarks, that the circumstance that Fuller was only eight years old when Shakespeare died appears to have been forgotten by some who have written of these matters. Mr. Burn, in reference to the situation of the Mermaid Tavern (destroyed in the Great Fire), where the meetings of this famous club were held, says, "The Mermaid in Bread Street, the Mermaid in Friday Street, and the Mermaid in Cheap, were all one and the same. The tavern, situated behind, had a way to it from these thoroughfares, but was nearer to Bread Street than Friday Street." Ben Jonson also writes, —

At *Bread-street's Mermaid* having dined and merry,
Proposed to go to Holborn in a wherry.

The origin of the Mermaid Club is traditionally ascribed to Sir Walter Raleigh. Gifford says: "Sir Walter Raleigh, previously to his unfortunate engagement with the wretched Cobham and others, had instituted a meeting of *beaux esprits* at the Mermaid, a celebrated tavern in Friday Street. Of this club, which combined more talent and genius than ever met together before or since, our author [Jonson] was a member; and here for many years he regularly repaired, with Shakespeare, Beaumont, Fletcher, Selden, Cotton, Carew, Martin, Donne, and many others, whose names, even at this distant period, call up a mingled feeling of reverence and respect." But whether Raleigh really founded the club must be considered a matter of doubt.

What things have we seen
Done at the *Mermaid!* heard words that have been
So nimble, and so full of subtle flame,
As if that every one from whom they came
Had meant to put his whole wit in a jest,
And had resolved to live a fool the rest
Of his dull life.

Beaumont, Letter to Ben Jonson.

Souls of poets dead and gone,
What Elysium have ye known,
Happy field or mossy cavern,
Choicer than the *Mermaid Tavern?*
Have ye tippled drink more fine
Than mine host's canary wine?
Or are fruits of Paradise
Sweeter than those dainty pies
Of venison?

Keats, Lines on the Mermaid Tavern.

The poet only is not bound, when it is inconvenient, to what may be called the accidents of facts. It was enough for Shakespeare to know that Prince Hal in his youth had lived among loose companions, and the tavern in Eastcheap came in to fill out his picture; although Mrs. Quickly and Falstaff and Poins and Bardolph were more likely to have been fallen in with by Shakespeare himself at the *Mermaid* than to have been comrades of the true Prince Henry. *Froude.*

☞ There were other Mermaid Taverns, one in Cheapside and another in Cornhill.

Merode Castle. An ancient, now ruined, stronghold in Rhenish Prussia, once the residence of a family one of whose members is said to have been conspicuous in the Thirty Years' War as a freebooter, and interesting from the fact that this circumstance, together with the name of the castle, has, according to some authorities, given to our language the term *marauder*. There are, however, other etymologies of the word.

Merri, St. See St. Merri.

Merrimack, The. A noted vessel of the Confederate navy during the Civil War. When the rebels seized the United States navy-yard at Norfolk, they had sunk this vessel, which was formerly a fine ship of war, in the harbor; but on reflection they concluded to raise her. After so doing, they covered the deck with a shelving iron roof, plated the sides with iron to below the water-level, and fitted up on her bow a pointed "beak" of oak and iron, thus converting the vessel into a most formidable ram. Thus armed, on the 8th of March, 1862, she bore down upon the *Cumberland* and the *Congress*, lying in Hampton Roads, and destroyed them both. The following day she encountered the iron-clad *Monitor*, just built in New York by John Ericsson, and was compelled to retire, leaving the victory to the latter.

☞ "Before sunrise the dreaded Merrimac was seen coming down from Norfolk with attendants to renew her savage work on the Minnesota. As she approached, the latter opened her stern guns on the assailant, when the *Monitor*, to the astonishment of friend and foe, ran out and placed herself alongside the giant warrior, — a little David defying a lofty Goliath. The faith of her commander in her strength and invulnerability was amply justified. The turret of the *Monitor* began to move, and from her guns were hurled ponderous shots in quick succession. The Merrimac responded with two-hundred-pound shots, moving at the rate of two thousand feet in a second. These, with solid round shots and conical bolts, glanced from the deck and citadel of the *Monitor* like pebbles, scarcely leaving a mark behind. Neither of these mailed gladiators was much bruised in this terrible encounter. . . . The Merrimac now [later] was more injured than her antagonist, and after a short and sharp combat they both withdrew. The commander of the former was so impressed with profound respect for the *Monitor* that he did not again invite his little antagonist to combat."
Lossing.

A frown came over Morris's face;
The strange, dark craft he knew:
"That is the iron *Merrimac*,
Manned by a rebel crew."
G. H. Boker.

Merry Maidens. A Druidical circle, so called, near Penzance, Cornwall, England.

Merry Mount. A district which in the early colonial days of New England bore this name was situated in the neighborhood of what is now the town of Quincy, Mass. It was occupied by a party of Church-of-England men, who paid little respect to the rigid and austere habits of the Puritans, whom they greatly offended by the laxity of their manners. An attack was made upon this settlement by the forces of the Plymouth colony in 1630. John Lothrop Motley, the American historian, produced in 1849 a romance entitled "Merry Mount."

Merton College. A noted college in Oxford, England; founded about 1264, one of the 19 colleges included in the university. Its chapel is much admired, and its library is the oldest in Great Britain.

My new friends showed me their cloisters, the Bodleian Library, the Randolph Gallery, *Merton Hall*, and the rest.
Emerson.

Mesjid Shah. The great mosque at Ispahan, Persia. It is a rectangular building surmounted by a dome, the external height of which is 165 feet.

☞ "On three sides the mosque is surrounded by court-yards, richly ornamented and containing fountains and basins of water for the ablutions of the faithful. The principal court, surrounded as it is on all sides by façades in the richest style of Persian polychromatic decoration, in the brilliancy of its architectural effect, is almost unrivalled by any other example of its class."
Fergusson.

Meta Sudans. A famous fountain, now a ruin, near the Coliseum, in Rome. It was built in a conical form, of brick, was placed in the centre of a basin, also of brick, 75 feet in diameter, and is supposed to have been used by the gladiators after their contests in the amphitheatre. In one of Seneca's epistles he speaks of the noise made by a showman blowing his trumpet in the vicinity of this fountain.

Metella, Tomb of Cecilia. See TOMB OF CECILIA METELLA.

Meteora, Monasteries of. A group of monastic establishments in Greece, formerly 24 in number, but of which only ten now remain. They derive their name from their situation "high up in the air" (Τὰ Μετέωρα, sc. Μοναστήρεα, i.e., the Meteor-Monasteries), being placed upon the summit of a cluster of detached rocks divided by deep chasms. The mode of communication between this abode

"Of the monastic brotherhood upon rock Aërial"—

and the earth 300 feet below is by a suspended rope. The person wishing to visit the monastery takes his seat in a net fastened to the end of a rope lowered from the rock, and, after an ascent lasting about four minutes and a half, reaches the landing-place of the monastery. The ascent can also be made by suspended ladders.

☞ "They [the monks] cast their net into the world below; sometimes these monastic fishermen draw up an inquisitive traveller, sometimes a brother Cœnobite from Mount Athos, sometimes a Neophyte, yearning for ascetic solitude: once they received in this manner an Emperor, who came here, as is said, to exchange the purple of Constantine for the cowl of St. Basil." *C. Wordsworth.*

Metropolitan Museum. A building near Union Square, in the city of New York, containing a picture-gallery, and gallery of statuary, and valuable collections of manuscripts, Egyptian and Greek antiquities, etc.

Michael Angelo. A portrait of himself by the painter (1474–1564). In the collection of autograph portraits in the Uffizi, Florence, Italy.

Michael Angelo's House. In the Via Ghibellina, Florence, Italy. It remains in the possession of the sculptor's family, and is exhibited to visitors.

Michael, St. See ST. MICHAEL, ST. MICHAEL'S CHAIR, ST. MICHAEL'S MOUNT, etc.

Michele, San. See SAN MICHELE and OR SAN MICHELE.

Michigan Avenue. A well-known street in Chicago, Ill.

Middle Temple. One of the Inns of Court in London. The poet Chaucer was a student here; and here lived Blackstone, the lawyer, and also Oliver Goldsmith, who died here in 1774. See INNS OF COURT, INNER TEMPLE, LINCOLN'S INN, GRAY'S INN.

1636, 13 Feb. I was admitted into the *Middle Temple*, London, though absent and yet at schoole. *John Evelyn, Diary.*

Middle Temple Hall. An Elizabethan structure of the Temple, London. "Twelfth Night" was performed here in 1601.

☞ "Truly it is a most magnificent apartment; very lofty, so lofty, indeed, that the antique oak roof is quite hidden, as regards all its details, in the sombre gloom that broods under its rafters." *Hawthorne.*

Mid-Lothian, Heart of. See TOLBOOTH.

Mifflin, Fort. See FORT MIFFLIN.

Mignon. A picture by Ary Scheffer (1795–1858), which is well known through reproductions.

Milan Cathedral. A magnificent and celebrated marble church. Its erection was begun in the latter part of the fourteenth century.

☞ "The stranger in Milan naturally hurries to the cathedral, a structure the merits and demerits of which require an architectural eye to comprehend and interpret. I can only say that its exterior was somewhat disappointing. . . . The interior, always excepting the disingenuous trick of the painted ceiling, called forth unqualified admiration. . . . The most striking part of the Milan Cathedral is the outside of the roof. The great extent of the building is more justly estimated there than from any part of the interior, and the eye and mind are overpowered by the multitude of architectural details, the rich ornaments, the delicately carved flying buttresses, the wilderness of pinnacles." *Hillard.*

☞ "The design of the Duomo is said to be taken from Monte Rosa, one of the loftiest peaks of the Alps. Its hundred of sculptured pinnacles rising from every part of the body of the church certainly bear a striking resemblance to the splintered ice-crags of Savoy. Thus we see how Art, mighty and endless in her forms though she be, is in every thing but the child of Nature." *Bayard Taylor.*

☞ "Gothic art attains at once its triumph and its extravagance. Never had it been so pointed, so highly embroidered, so complex, so overcharged, so strongly resembling a piece of jewelry; and as, instead of course and lifeless stone, it here takes for its material the beautiful lustrous Italian marble, it becomes a pure chased gem, as precious through its substance as through the labor bestowed on it."
Taine, Trans.

O *Milan*, O the chanting quires,
The giant windows' blazoned fires,
The height, the space, the gloom, the glory!
A mount of marble, a hundred spires!
Tennyson.

O peerless church of old Milan,
How brightly thou com'st back to me,
With all thy minarets and towers,
And sculptured marbles fair to see!
Henry G. Bell.

Mile End. A locality in London, England, at the head of Whitechapel Road.

I remember at *Mile-end* green (when I lay at Clement's Inn). I was then Sir Dagonet in Arthur's show. *Shakespeare.*

He found Wat holding his ragged court at *Mile End*. The king, despairing of immediate assistance, had conceded every request that was presented to him.
J. A. Froude.

Military Academy. See UNITED STATES MILITARY ACADEMY.

Milk Grotto. A cave, or grotto, in the neighborhood of Bethlehem, in which, according to monastic legend, Mary and the Child secreted themselves from the rage of Herod before they took their flight to Egypt. The spot is a great resort of pious pilgrims, drawn hither by the superstitious belief that the stone of which the cave is composed has the miraculous power of increasing woman's milk. It is stated to be a fact, that portions of this stone are continually broken off by the pilgrims, and sent all over Europe and the East, wherever a belief in its efficacy prevails.

Milking-time at Dort. An admired picture by Albert Cuyp (1605-1691). In the National Gallery, London.

Mill, The. A celebrated picture by Claude Lorraine (1600-1682). In the Palazzo Doria, Rome.

☞ "A fair example of what is called an 'ideal' landscape, i.e., a group of the artist's studies from nature individually spoiled, selected with such opposition of character as may insure their neutralizing each other's effect and producing a general sensation of the impossible." *Ruskin.*

Millbank Prison. A prison in the parish of Westminster, London, and said to be "the largest penal establishment in England." It was begun in 1812, and has sometimes been called the English Bastille.

Milliarium Aureum. [The Golden Mile-stone.] A mile-stone of ancient Rome, in the Forum, and said to have been set up by Augustus, upon which distances, beyond the walls of the city, upon the great Roman roads, were inscribed. The Milliarium Aureum formed one extremity of a semicircular wall, which terminated at the other end in a conical pyramid, called Umbilicus Romæ, upon which were inscribed all distances within the walls.

Milton at Home. An admired picture by Emanuel Leutze (1816-1868). In the Corcoran Gallery, Washington.

Milvian Bridge. See PONTE MOLLE.

Mincing Lane. A street in London, so called from buildings which formerly belonged to the Minchuns or nuns of St. Helen's. Mincing Lane figures in Dickens's novel of "Our Mutual Friend."

Stones of old *Mincing Lane*, which I have worn with my daily pilgrimage for six-and-thirty years, to the footsteps of what toil-worn clerk are your everlasting flints now vocal? *Charles Lamb*

Minerva. A famous statue of antiquity, executed by Phidias (500 B.C.?), the Greek sculptor, for the Parthenon at Athens.

Minerva Medica. A celebrated Greek statue which derives its name from the Temple of Minerva Medica, where it was discovered. Now in the Vatican, Rome.

☞ "In the Giustiniani palace [since removed] is a statue of Minerva which fills me with admiration. Winckelmann scarcely thinks any thing of it, or at any rate does not give it its proper position, but I cannot praise it sufficiently." *Goethe, Trans.*

That's you, Miss Leigh: I've watched you
half an hour,
Precisely as I watched the statue called
A Pallas in the Vatican. *Mrs. Browning.*

Minerva Medica, Temple of. See TEMPLE OF MINERVA MEDICA.

Minerva Press. The name applied to a printing-house in Leadenhall Street, London. In the latter part of the eighteenth century and the early part of the nineteenth century, numbers of popular but trashy novels were issued from this establishment. Lamb speaks of these works, which had a wide circulation, as having heroes which are neither of this nor of any conceivable world.

Hesperus and Titan themselves, though in form nothing more than "novels of real life," as the *Minerva Press* would say, have solid metal enough in them to furnish whole circulating libraries, were it beaten into the usual filigree. *Carlyle.*

In this respect, Burns, though not perhaps absolutely a great poet, better manifests his capability, better proves the truth of his genius, than if he had, by his own strength, kept the whole *Minerva Press* going, to the end of his literary course. *Carlyle.*

Miniato, San. See SAN MINIATO AL MONTE.

Minories, The. A parish in London, named from the Sorores Minores, or nuns of the order of St. Clare, founded 1293, whose convent stood in this street. The street has long been noted for its gunsmiths.

The Mulcibers who in the *Minories* sweat. *Congreve.*

Minotaur, The. A very formidable iron-clad ship of the British navy, launched Dec. 12, 1863.

Minot's Ledge Light. A well-known light-house on Cohasset reefs, in Massachusetts Bay.

The lonely ledge of *Minot*,
Where the watchman tends his light,
And sets his perilous beacon,
A star in the stormiest night.
Mary Clemmer.

And naked in the howling night
The red-eyed light-house lifts its form.
The waves with slippery fingers clutch
The massive tower, and climb and fall,
And, muttering, growl with baffled rage
Their curses on the sturdy wall.
Fitz-James O'Brien.

Mir. See HOLY OIL.

Miracle of Bolsena. See MASS OF BOLSENA.

Miracle of Roses of St. Francis. A large fresco-painting by Friedrich Overbeck (1789–1869), and considered his masterpiece in that department of art. At Assisi, Italy.

Miracle of St. Mark. A celebrated picture attributed to Giorgio Barbarelli, called Giorgione (1477–1511), based upon a famous legend connected with the history of Venice. In the Accademia delle Belle Arti, in Venice, Italy.

☞ "No painting, in my judgment, surpasses or perhaps equals his [Tintoret's] St. Mark. No one, save Rubens, has so caught the instantaneousness of motion, the fury of flight; alongside of this vehemence and this truthfulness, classic figures seem stiff, as if copied after Academy models whose arms are upheld by strings: we are borne along with him, and follow him to the ground, as yet unreached." *Taine, Trans.*

Miracle of the Cross. A picture by Gentile Bellini (1421–1507). In the Accademia delle Belle Arti, at Venice, Italy.

Miraculous Draught of Fishes. The subject of one of the famous cartoons of Raphael Sanzio (1483–1520), from which the tapestries in the Vatican at Rome were executed.

☞ "The composition of Raphael [the cartoon of the *Miraculous Draught of Fishes*] is just what we should seek for in Raphael, a masterpiece of dramatic expression — the significant, the poetical, the miraculous predominating." *Mrs. Jameson.*

Miraculous Wafers. A Catholic holy relic preserved in the chapel of St. Sacrament des Miracles in the Cathedral of Brussels, Belgium. The wafers when scoffingly pierced with knives by Jews, who in the fourteenth century had stolen them from the altar, are said to have emitted jets of blood. The miracle is the occasion of an annual religious ceremony.

Miramar. A well-known Gothic castle on a point of land extending into the sea, near Trieste, Austria. It was the residence of Maximilian, the Emperor of Mexico, and Carlotta, his wife.

Miriam singing the Song of Triumph. A picture by Washington Allston (1779-1843). Formerly in possession of Hon. David Sears, Boston, Mass.

Misericordia di Lucca. A celebrated picture by Baccio del Porta, called Fra Bartolommeo (1469-1517), and his most important work. At Lucca, Italy.

☞ "Famous in the history of art. The expression in the heads, the dignified beneficence of the Virgin, the dramatic feeling in the groups, particularly the women and children, justify the fame of this picture as one of the greatest of the productions of mind." *Mrs. Jameson.*

Misers, The. See Two Misers.

Misfortunes of Job. See Job.

Miss Kelley's Theatre. See Soho Theatre.

Mission Dolores. An interesting old Spanish mission station and church about three miles from San Francisco, Cal. It was founded by Jesuit missionaries upwards of a hundred years ago. The church has been partly enclosed with wood in order to preserve it.

Mitre, The. 1. A noted tavern in Fleet Street, London, deriving its fame chiefly from the fact that it was a favorite resort of Dr. Johnson. It is no longer standing. Here Johnson and Boswell determined to make a tour to the Hebrides.

☞ "The Mitre Tavern still stands in Fleet Street; but where now is its scot-and-lot paying, beef-and-ale loving, cocked-hatted, pot-bellied Landlord; its rosy-faced, assiduous Landlady, with all her shining brass pans, waxed tables, well-filled larder-shelves; her cooks, and bootjacks, and errand-boys, and watery-mouthed hangers-on? Gone! Gone! The becking waiter, that with wreathed smiles, wont to spread for Samuel and Bozzy their 'supper of the gods,' has long since pocketed his last sixpence; and vanished, sixpences and all, like a ghost at cock-crowing. The Bottles they drank out of are all broken, the Chairs they sat on all rotted and burnt; the very Knives and Forks they ate with have rusted to the heart." *Carlyle.*

☞ "The orthodox high-church sound of *The Mitre* — the figure and manner of the celebrated Samuel Johnson — the extraordinary power and precision of his conversation, and the pride arising from finding myself admitted as his companion, produced a variety of sensations and a pleasing elevation of mind, beyond what I had ever experienced." *Boswell.*

☞ "On the other side of Fleet Street we can see the 'Mitre Tavern,' closing up the end of a court — but not the old original 'Mitre' where Johnson sat with Boswell. It was pulled down within living memory, and with it the corner in which the sage used to sit, and which was religiously marked by his bust. Yet even as it stands in its restoration, there is something quaint in the feeling, as you enter through a low covered passage from Fleet Street, and see its cheerful open door at the end. The passage to the 'Mitre' is as it was in Johnson's day, and his eyes must have been often raised to the old beams that support its roof. Even in its modern shape, it retains much that is old-fashioned and rococo." *Fitzgerald.*

2. A London tavern, in Wood Street, destroyed in the Great Fire of 1666, and spoken of by Pepys a few years before that time as being "a house of the greatest note in London."

3. An old London tavern in Fenchurch Street, destroyed in

the Great Fire (1666), but soon afterwards rebuilt.

Moat of Knockgraffon. A very singular artificial mound in Tipperary county, Ireland, built, according to tradition, in 1108, and invested with much legendary lore.

Mock Election. A noted picture by Benjamin Robert Haydon (1786-1846).

Modern Italy. A picture by Joseph Mallord William Turner (1775-1851), the celebrated English painter.

Modesty and Vanity. A celebrated picture by Leonardo da Vinci (1452-1519). In the Palazzo Sciarra, Rome.

☞ "One of Leonardo's most beautiful pictures, . . . remarkably powerful in coloring and wonderfully finished." *Kugler.*

☞ "'Mary Magdalene rebuked by her sister Martha for her vanity and luxury.' I believe I am the first to suggest that the famous picture in the Sciarra Palace, by Leonardo da Vinci, known as '*Modesty and Vanity*,' is a version of this subject." *Mrs. Jameson.*

☞ "One of the masterpieces of this gallery [in the Sciarra Palace], and perhaps the greatest, I find to be the *Modesty and Vanity* of Leonardo da Vinci. It is simply two female figures on a dark background. . . . The expression of the face representing Vanity is extraordinary. We can never know the research, the combinations, the internal spontaneous reflective labor, the ground traversed by his spirit and intellect in order to evolve a head like this. She is much more delicately formed and more noble and elegant than Mona Lisa. The luxuriance and taste of the coiffure are remarkable. She has a strange, melancholy smile, one peculiar to Da Vinci, combining the sadness and irony of a superior nature." *Taine, Trans.*

Mœris, Lake. See Lake Mœris.

Mogul. See Court of the Great Mogul.

Mohammed Ali, Mosque of. See Mosque of Mohammed Ali.

Mohocks, The. A name under which ruffians and villians committed dastardly assaults and various cruelties in London. This fraternity assembled in the time of Queen Anne, and was not broken up till nearly the end of George the First's reign. A royal proclamation was issued against them in 1712, but with little result.

☞ "Here is the devil and all to do with these Mohocks. Grub-street papers about them fly like lightning, and a list printed of near eighty put into several prisons, and all a lie; and I begin to think there is no truth, or very little, in the whole story. . . . My man tells me that one of the lodgers heard in a coffee-house, publicly, that one design of the Mohocks was upon me, if they could catch me; and though I believe nothing of it, I forbear walking late."

Dean Swift (*Journal to Stella*, 1712).

Who has not trembled at the *Mohock's* name?
Was there a watchman took his hourly rounds
Safe from their blows or new-invented wounds?
I pass their desperate deeds and mischiefs, done
Where from Snow-hill black steepy torrents run;
How matrons, hooped within the hogshead's womb,
Were tumbled furious thence; the rolling tomb
O'er the stones thunders, bounds from side to side:
So Regulus, to save his country, died.

Gay.

Molière, Fontaine. See Fontaine Molière.

Molle, Ponte. See Ponte Molle.

Momba Devi. A famous Hindoo temple in Bombay, India.

Mona Lisa. See Belle Joconde.

"Monaco di Leonardo." A picture by Leonardo da Vinci (1452-1519). In the Palazzo Pitti, Florence, Italy.

Monadnock, The. A formidable armor-plated vessel of the United States navy in the Civil War of 1861-65. She was one of the vessels of Admiral Porter's flotilla in the attack upon Fort Fisher, Dec. 14, 1864.

Monarch of the Glen. A well-known picture by Sir Edwin Landseer (1803-1873), the most celebrated modern painter of animals.

Monastery, The. A picture by Jacob Ruysdael (1625?-1681), and considered one of his masterpieces. In the Dresden Gallery.

Monboddo. A country-seat in Scotland, near Fordoun, formerly the seat of Lord Monboddo, distinguished for the remarkable speculations upon the origin of man, contained in his "Dissertations upon the Origin and Progress of Language."

Monceaux, Parc de. A promenade and garden in Paris, tastefully laid out, containing flowers, shrubs, some fine ancient trees, and various artificial adornments. Here is a small lake surrounded by a partly ruined portico of Corinthian columns. It was originally laid out in 1778 with grottos, bowers, fountains, etc., by Carmontel, for Philippe Egalité. It is now the property of the municipality of Paris, and is open to the public.

Monitor, The. A novel American gunboat, built in New York by John Ericsson (b. 1803), a Swedish engineer, during the war of the Rebellion. Her first engagement was with the Confederate ram *Merrimack*, in Hampton Roads, on the 9th of March, 1862. The *Merrimack* was quickly put to flight. The *Monitor* was a sort of flat iron raft with a heavy-plated revolving turret containing two powerful guns. The name Monitor has since been applied to iron-clad vessels of similar construction.

☞ "The *Monitor* was built almost wholly of three-inch iron, pointed at both ends like a whale-boat, her deck only a few inches above the water. It was 124 feet in length, 34 in width, and six in depth, with a flat bottom. Over this hull was another that extended over the lower one three feet all round, excepting at the ends, where the projection was 25 feet, for the protection of the anchor, propeller, and rudder. On her deck was a revolving turret made of eight thicknesses of one-inch wrought-iron plates, round, 20 feet in diameter, and 10 feet high. The smoke-stack was telescopic in construction, so so as to be lowered in battle. Within this revolving turret or citadel (which was easily turned by a contrivance) were two heavy Dahlgren cannons. By turning the turret these 'bull-dogs' might look straight into the face of an attacking enemy, wherever he might be, without changing the position of the vessel. The *Monitor* was propelled by a powerful steam-engine."
Lossing.

Monmouth Street. A well-known London street, called by Dickens, from its shops for old clothes, "the burial-place of the fashions." It is now Dudley Street.

☞ "If Field Lane, with its long fluttering rows of yellow handkerchiefs, be a Dionysius' Ear, where, in stifled jarring hubbub, we hear the Indictment which Poverty and Vice bring against lazy Wealth, that it has left them there cast-out and trodden under foot of Want, Darkness, and the Devil, — then is Monmouth Street a Mirza's Hill, where, in motley vision, the whole Pageant of Existence passes awfully before us; with its wail and jubilee, mad loves and mad hatreds, church-bells and gallows-ropes, farce-tragedy, beast-godhood, — the Bedlam of Creation!"
Carlyle (Sartor Resartus).

The long tables had disappeared, and, in place of the sage magi, I beheld a ragged, threadbare throng, such as may be seen plying about the great repository of cast-off clothes, *Monmouth Street*.
Irving.

With awe-struck heart I walk through that *Monmouth Street*, with its empty Suits, as through a Sanhedrim of stainless Ghosts. *Carlyle.*

Monongahela, The. A noted vessel of the United States navy, in service in the War of the Rebellion, 1861-65.

Quickly breasting the wave,
Eager the prize to win,
First of us all the brave
Monongahela went in,
Under full head of steam.
H. H. Brownell.

Mons Aventinus. See AVENTINE MOUNT; and for MONS CAPITOLINUS, MONS CŒLIUS, MONS ESQUILINUS, MONS PALATINUS, MONS QUIRINUS, MONS VIMINALIS, and the like names, see CAPITOLINE HILL, CŒLIAN HILL, ESQUILINE HILL, PALATINE MOUNT, QUIRINAL HILL, VIMINAL HILL, etc.

Mons Meg. A famous piece of ancient ordnance in Edinburgh Castle, Scotland, supposed to have been forged at Mons, in Flanders, in the fifteenth century.

Mons Sacer. [Ital. *Monte Sacro*, The Sacred Mount.] A hill three miles from Rome, and beyond the Anio, to which the plebeians withdrew at the time of their famous secession under Menenius Agrippa, B.C. 494. A second secession took place, after the death of Virginia, when the plebeians revolted against Appius Claudius, and retired again to Mons Sacer. The epithet Sacer is derived, according to Dionysius, from an altar erected to Ζεὺς Δειμάτιος. According to others it was from the Lex *Sacrata* decreed upon the occasion of the first secession.

Monserrat. [From *Mons Serratus*, the jagged mountain.] This famous Benedictine convent, near Barcelona, Spain, was founded A.D. 976. It owes its origin, according to the Catholic legend, to the miraculous image of the Virgin, which was brought to Barcelona by St. Peter himself, A.D. 50. Upon reaching the summit of the Mons Serratus, where the convent now stands, the Virgin refused to proceed any farther; upon which a chapel with a cross was built over her, where she remained 100 years. It is said that not less than 100,000 persons, including tourists and pilgrims, visit this convent yearly.

Mont Brilliant. A royal country residence, with a fine picture-gallery, near Hanover, Germany.

Mont de Piété. The great pawnbroking concern of Paris, established in 1777.

☞ "The name *Mons Pietatis* came with the invention from Italy. In the first century of the Christian era, free gifts were collected, and preserved in churches, to defray the expenses of divine service, and for the relief of the poor. The collections thus made were called *Montes* or *Mounts*, a name originally applied to all moneys procured or heaped together; and it has appeared that the inventor added the word *Pietas* to give to his institution a sacred or religious character, and to procure for it universal approbation and support. In Italy their establishment is of very early date, and in the fifteenth and sixteenth centuries the plan had spread to nearly all the cities. In 1777 a Mont de Piété was established in Paris by a royal ordinance of Louis XVI." *Mr. and Mrs. Hall.*

☞ "Pawnbroking in France, as in most parts of the Continent, is a municipal monopoly. It was established in 1777, but is now regulated by the law of June, 1851, and the necessary capital taken from the general hospital fund, which also receives the net profits for charitable purposes. About 1,000,000*l.* is usually lent out. The average of articles pledged is 17*f.*; the lowest value rate of interest is about six per cent. The articles pledged, if not redeemed, are sold at the expiration of 14 months; and the surplus money, if any, is paid to the owner if application is made within three years. There are two large branch establishments in the Rue Bonaparte and Rue de la Roquette, and about 20 branches (*Commissionaires*) in different parts of Paris. The profit annually to the institution is about 233,000*f.*" *Murray's Handbook.*

☞ "I must own, however, that although the interior of the Mont de Piété was repulsive to witness, I left its central office with an impression which reflection has strengthened rather than removed. — that that portion of the community of any country, whose necessities force them occasionally to pawn their effects, have infinitely less to fear from an establishment guided by fixed principles, and open every day from nine till four to the public, than they would be, — and in England are, — in transacting the same business in private, cooped with an individual who, to say the least, may encourage the act which nothing but cruel necessity can authorize."

Sir Francis B. Head.

Mont Parnasse, Boulevard du. This quarter of Paris is said to have been so called because the students were accustomed to declaim verses here.

Mont Valérien. [*Mount Valérien.*] An eminence near Paris, rising 343 feet above the Seine, on the route to St. Germain, converted into a citadel, which is considered one of the strongest of the fortifications of Paris.

In *Mount Valérien's* chestnut wood
The Chapel of the Hermits stood;
And thither at the close of day
Came two old pilgrims, worn and gray.

. . . .

Forth from the city's noise and throng,
Its pomp and shame, its sin and wrong,
The twain that summer day had strayed
To *Mount Valérien's* chestnut shade.
Whittier.

Montague House. 1. The city residence of the Duke of Buccleuch, London, who inherits it from the family of Montague. The mansion contains some fine pictures by Vandyke, and a valuable collection of historical miniatures. The present house is modern.

2. A former mansion situated in Bloomsbury, London. Its site is now occupied by the British Museum.

3. A London mansion, noted as the residence of Mrs. Elizabeth Montague.

Montauk. A noted armor-plated vessel of the United States navy — of the "Monitor" class — in the Civil War of 1861–65. She was commanded by Capt. Worden, and among other achievements captured the Confederate steamer *Nashville.*

Monte Beni. A hill in the immediate neighborhood of Florence, Italy. Hawthorne has made its scenery familiar in his "Romance of Monte Beni."

Monte Caprino. [Goat Hill.] A hill in Rome, being the southeastern summit of the Capitoline. In a garden on this hill may be seen what remains of the Tarpeian Rock.

Monte Casino. A famous monastic establishment, of the Benedictine order, near San Germano, on the route between Rome and Naples, Italy. The monastery was founded by St. Benedict in 529, and is the parent of all the greatest Benedictine monasteries in the world. It was rebuilt towards the end of the sixteenth century. The interior of the abbey church is one of the most splendid in Europe.

☞ "There is scarcely a Pope or Emperor of importance who has not been personally connected with its history. From its mountain crag it has seen Goths, Lombards, Saracens, Normans, Frenchmen, Spaniards, Germans, scour and devastate the land which, through all modern history, has attracted every invader."
London Daily News, 1866.

☞ "From this centre monastic life spread over barbarous Europe in the darkest period of the Middle Ages. Whatever remained of ancient civilization reposed thus in remote corners, within a monastic shell, like a chrysalis within its covering. You have every thing here, not only the arts and the sciences, but the grand spectacles of nature. This is what the old feudal and religious society provided for its pensive, solitary spirits; for minds which, repelled by the bitterness of life, reverted to speculation and self-culture. The race still subsists: only they no longer possess an asylum; they live in Paris and in Berlin in garrets. I know of many that are dead, of others saddened and chilled, others again worn out and disgusted. Will science ever do for its faithful servants what religion has done for hers? Will there ever be a laic *Monte Casino?*" *Taine, Trans.*

That mountain on whose slope *Cassino* stands
Was frequented of old upon its summit
By a deluded folk and ill-disposed;
And I am he who first up thither bore
The name of Him who brought upon the earth
The truth that so much sublimateth us.
Dante.

And there, uplifted, like a passing cloud
That pauses on a mountain summit high,
Monte Cassino's convent rears its proud
And venerable walls against the sky.
Longfellow.

Monte Cavallo, *and* **Piazza di Monte Cavallo.** See QUIRINAL HILL. See also OBELISK OF THE MONTE CAVALLO.

Monte Mario. [Mount Mario.] An eminence in the neighborhood of Rome, deriving its name from Mario Mellini, who owned it in the time of Sixtus V. In ancient times it was called *Clivus Cinnæ,* the hill of Cinna. In the Middle Ages it was known as Monte Malo. It is crowned with cypresses, and commands a beautiful and extensive view.

☞ "The Monte Mario, like Cooper's Hill, is the highest, boldest, and most prominent part of the line; it is about the height and steepness, too, of Cooper's Hill, and has the Tiber at the foot of it, like the Thames at Anchorwick. Here we stood, on a most delicious evening, and before our eyes all that one has read of in Roman history, —the course of the Tiber between the hills that bound it, . . . beyond the Apennines, the distant and higher summits still white with snow; in front the Alban Hills; on the right, the Campagna to the sea; and just beneath us the whole length of Rome, ancient and modern. . . . One may safely say that the world cannot contain many views of such mingled beauty and interest as this." *Arnold.*

The purple day
O'er *Monte Mario* dies from off the dome,
And, lo! the first star leads us into Rome.
T. B. Read.

Monte Oliveto. 1. An ancient and celebrated Benedictine monastery in Naples, Italy. It was founded in the early part of the fifteenth century. It is now occupied for city offices.

2. A celebrated monastic establishment in the neighborhood of Siena, Italy. It contains some fine frescos.

Monte Pincio. See PINCIAN HILL.

Monte Sacro. [The sacred mountain.] A celebrated hill and sanctuary — the latter called La Nuova Gerusalemme — near Varallo, in Piedmont. The hill is covered with some 50 chapels, containing groups of life-sized figures representing the chief scenes in the history of Christ. This sanctuary was founded in the fifteenth century, and was much extended and enriched in the following century.

Monte Sacro. See MONS SACER.

Monte Testaccio. An eminence, 160 feet in height, just outside the walls of Rome. It is composed entirely of broken pieces of pottery, and its extraordinary formation has never been satisfactorily explained.

☞ "From its loose and porous composition it acts, as if formed by Wedgwood, for a great wine-cooler, and serves as the cellar of all Rome. The wine-merchants have excavated vaults in it to keep their stores cool, and every morning a quantity sufficient for the daily demand is brought into the city." *Eaton.*

Montereggione. A picturesque old castle on an eminence near Siena, Italy.

☞ "This fortress, as the commentators say, was furnished with towers all round about, and had none in the centre. In its present state it is still very faithfully described by the verse [of Dante], —

'Montereggion di torri si corona.'"
Ampère.

Montfaucon. A slight eminence in the northern suburbs of Paris. Here in 885 A.D. the Normans were defeated, and 20,000 of their number killed. Here was the gibbet (*Fourches Patibulaires*), where criminals were executed. Montfaucon was afterwards the central station for the slaughter of horses, dogs, etc. A Protestant church for poor Germans, to which ragged and infant schools are attached, now occupies the summit.

Montgomery. See FORT MONTGOMERY, DEATH OF MONTGOMERY, and TOUR DE MONTGOMERY.

Montgomery Street. The leading thoroughfare of San Francisco, Cal.

The money-brokers' shops are very numerous in the two finest streets, — *Montgomery* and California Streets. Nearly every shop there belongs to a money-broker or money-changer. *Samuel Smiles.*

Monticello. The country-seat of Thomas Jefferson (1743–1826), the third president of the United States, near Charlottesville, Albemarle County, Va. It has a beautiful situation, with an extensive prospect.

☞ "He [Jefferson] lives, you know, on a mountain, which he has named *Monticello*, and which, perhaps you do not know, is a synonyme for Carter's Mountain. The ascent of this steep, savage hill, was as pensive and slow as Satan's ascent to Paradise. We were obliged to wind two-thirds round its sides before we reached the artificial lawn on which the house stands; and, when we had arrived there, we were about 600 feet, I understand, above the stream which flows at its foot. . . . In the centre of the lawn, and facing the south-east, Mr. Jefferson has placed his house, which is of brick, two stories high in the wings, with a piazza in front of a receding centre." *George Ticknor* (*in* 1815).

☞ "This venerated mansion is yet standing, though somewhat dilapidated, and deprived of its former beauty by neglect. The furniture of the distinguished owner is nearly all gone, except a few pictures and mirrors; otherwise the interior of the house is the same as when Jefferson died. It is upon an eminence, with many aspen trees around it, and commands a view of the Blue Ridge for 150 miles on one side, and on the other one of the most beautiful and extensive landscapes in the world." *Lossing.*

As from the grave where Henry sleeps,
From Vernon's weeping willow,
And from the grassy pall which hides
The Sage of *Monticello*. *Whittier.*

The nursling growth of *Monticello's* crest
Is now the glory of the free North-west.
Whittier.

Montmartre. A hill on the north of Paris, rising 320 feet above the Seine, and said to have been so called because St. Denis suffered martyrdom here. A nunnery was formerly situated on the summit; and here was the Chapelle des Martyrs, where in 1534 Ignatius Loyola and followers took the vow in which the Order of the Jesuits had its origin. The cemetery on the south slope of the hill is the oldest in Paris, though smaller and less important than Père-la-Chaise. The outbreak and civil war of 1871 took its rise at Montmartre. Gypsum, or plaster of Paris, has long been quarried at Montmartre.

Through Paris lay my readiest course; and there
Sojourning a few days, I visited
In haste, each spot of old or recent fame,
The latter chiefly, from the field of Mars
Down to the suburbs of St. Antony,
And from *Mont Martyr* southward to the dome
Of Geneviève. *Wordsworth.*

Disputed foot by foot, till treason, still
His only victor, from *Montmartre's* hill
Look'd down o'er trampled Paris!
Byron.

Montmartre, Boulevard de. A well-known avenue in Paris, France. See BOULEVARDS.

Montrouge Club. A political club in Paris at the time of the French Revolution of 1789, of which Mirabeau and other noted men were members. It was named from the place, near Paris, where its meetings were held.

Montserrat. See MONSERRAT.

Monument, The. A stone column, 202 feet in height, Fish Street Hill, London, erected by Sir Christopher Wren (1671–1680) to commemorate the Great Fire of 1666, and the rebuilding of the city. The following inscription, now effaced, was cut in 1681 upon the pedestal: "This pillar was set up in perpetual remembrance of that most dreadful burning of this Protestant city, begun and carried on by ye treachery and malice of ye popish factio, in ye beginning of Septem, in ye year of our Lord 1666, in order to ye carrying on of their horrid plott for extirpating the Protestant religion and old English liberty, and the introducing popery and slavery."

☞ "Six persons have thrown themselves off the Monument. This kind of death becoming popular, it was deemed advisable to encage and disfigure the Monument as we now see it." *Murray's Handbook.*

Where London's column, pointing at the skies,
Like a tall bully, lifts the head and lies.
Pope.

Electricity cannot be made fast, mortared up and ended, like *London Monument*, or the Tower, so that you shall know where to find it, and keep it fixed, as the English do with their things, forevermore. *Emerson.*

Nor had Fancy fed
With less delight upon that other class
Of marvels, broad-day wonders permanent:
. . . .
The *Monument*, and that chamber of the Tower,
Where England's sovereigns sit in long array,
Their steeds bestriding. *Wordsworth.*

Above the wilderness of buildings stood a dim, gigantic dome in the sky. . . . And the tall pillar that stood near it — I did not need a second glance to recognize the *Monument*. *Bayard Taylor.*

Monumental Church. A religious edifice in Richmond, Va., erected on the site of the old Richmond Theatre, and built to commemorate the destruction of the latter by fire in 1811, on which occasion the Governor of Virginia and over 60 persons, including many of the most eminent men and women in the State, lost their lives.

Moonrise at Madeira. A picture by Ferdinand T. Hildebrandt (b. 1804). In the Corcoran Gallery, Washington.

Moorfields. A part of old London, now covered by Finsbury Square and adjoining streets, so called from the great fen or moor which bordered the walls of the city on the north side. It was a place for walking and recreation. See FINSBURY.

Through famed *Moorfields* extends a spacious seat. *Gay.*

Moors, Three. See DREI MOHREN.

Moot of Urr. A curious monument of antiquity, near Dalbeattie, Scotland, in the form of a circular mound enclosed by a moat. It is supposed to have been used as a council-place and tribunal of justice by the Celts in ancient times.

Moothill. An eminence near Scone, Scotland, where the Scottish kings sat to hold parliaments and law courts.

Mora Stone. [*Mora stena.*] A place about one mile from the city of Upsala, in Sweden, celebrated as the spot where the Swedish kings were formerly elected, and where they received the homage of their subjects. The Mora Stone is composed, in fact, of eleven stones of various sizes, bearing the names and dates of the kings elected here. A house was built by Gustavus III., in 1780, to enclose this interesting national monument.

"Morett," The. A celebrated portrait by Hans Holbein the Younger (1498-1543), in the Gallery of Dresden, Saxony, and regarded as one of the finest of his works. "It is not known whom it represents. Thomas Morett was a distinguished jeweller who served Henry VIII., and was a friend of Holbein."

Morgue. [Fr. *La Morgue.*] In Paris and other cities of France a place where dead bodies that have been found are deposited for purposes of recognition by the relatives or friends of the deceased. The name is also used in other countries. The morgue in Paris is a small, low building, within which the bodies are laid upon a stone platform until they are identified or claimed by friends. Strange as it may seem, it is visited by crowds of people.

☞ "On the whole, I left my position in the corner impressed with an opinion, since strengthened by reflection, that La Morgue at Paris is a plague-spot that must inevitably, more or less, demoralize every person who views it." *Sir Francis B. Head.*

Only the Doric little *Morgue*,
The dead-house where you show your drowned,
Petrarch's Vaucluse makes proud the Sorgue,
Your *Morgue* has made the Seine renowned. *Robert Browning.*

Moriah. A hill in Jerusalem, Palestine, the position of which is beyond dispute. It was the site of the great Jewish Temple, and is associated with many sacred events in the history of the Hebrew nation. Upon this hill now stands the great structure of the Haram, with its mosques. See HARAM.

Mormon Temple. 1. A building of polished limestone, about 130 feet in length, by 90 feet in breadth, which formerly stood in Nauvoo City, Ill. It was the chief religious edifice of the Mormons, who had settled in the place in 1840, and was built at a cost of over $500,000. In the basement was a huge stone baptistery or basin, resting upon 12 oxen of colossal size. The Mormons afterwards made their way to Utah, and settled there. The building is now in ruins.

2. An unfinished building in Salt Lake City, Utah Territory. It is designed to be the magnificent seat of Mormon worship. The foundation was laid some 25 years ago, and immense sums of money have been raised to defray the cost of its erection; but whether it will ever be completed, is extremely doubtful.

Morning, The. One of four colossal figures executed by Michael Angelo Buonarotti (1475–1564). In the church of S. Lorenzo, Florence, Italy.

☞ "This figure [The Morning] is the most beautiful of all. It is also the most finished. Whilst in the others the heads are only roughly designed, every line of the face in this possesses a spiritual meaning." *Grimm, Trans.*

Morning. A picture by Sir Edwin Landseer (1803–1873), the eminent English painter.

Morrin College. A collegiate establishment in Quebec, Canada.

Morris House. An old colonial mansion near High Bridge, N.Y. It was the headquarters of Washington in 1776.

Morrison's Cove. A valley in Pennsylvania, near Petersburgh, settled about the middle of the last century by a peculiar German sect called the Dunkards, who professed the principles of non-resistance. When in 1777 the community was attacked by the Indians, the settlers faithfully carried out their doctrine in practice, and most of them were put to death.

Morton Castle. A feudal mansion, said to have been founded in the eleventh century, near Thornhill, Scotland, now belonging to the Duke of Buccleuch.

Moses. A celebrated statue by Michael Angelo, in the church of San Pietro in Vincoli in Rome,—intended to form a part of the unfinished monument of Julius II. "This statue, as is well known, has the hair so disposed in front as to resemble horns projecting from the top of the forehead. This was a common representation of Moses in early and mediæval art, and was founded upon an erroneous translation in the Vulgate Bible of the twenty-ninth verse of the thirty-fourth chapter of Exodus. In the Vulgate it reads, 'Ignorabat quod cornuta esset facies sua,' 'He knew not that his face was horned.' The received version, 'He wist not that the skin of his face shone,' is the correct translation of the passage."

☞ "The eye does not know where to rest in this, the masterpiece of sculpture since the time of the Greeks. . . . Yes! there is something infinite which lies in the *Moses* of Michael Angelo. . . . This statue might take its place in the cell of a colossal temple, as that of Jupiter Ammon; but the tomb where it is placed is so little suited to it that regarded even only as its frame it is too small." *Gregorovius.*

☞ "Whoever has once seen this statue must retain the impression of it forever. The Moses is the crown of modern sculpture, not only in idea, but also with regard to the work. All the power which Michael Angelo possessed, and which the world did not understand, was exhibited in those limbs, and the demon-like, passionate violence of the pope [Julius II.] in that countenance." *Grimm, Trans.*

☞ "Here sits the *Moses* of Michael Angelo, frowning with the terrific eyebrows of Olympian Jove. Much wit has been levelled of late at his flowing beard and flaming horns. But the true sublime resists all ridicule; the offended lawgiver frowns on unrepressed, and awes you with inherent authority." *Forsyth.*

☞ "We went as far as San Pietro in Vincoli to see the '*Moses*' of Michael Angelo. The first sight of the statue is less surprising than one would suppose. We are familiar with it engraved and reduced; the imagination, as is always the case, has exaggerated it; moreover, it is polished and finished with extreme perfection. It is in a brilliantly decorated church, and is framed in by a handsome chapel. As you dwell on it, however, the colossal mass produces its effect. You feel the imperious will, the ascendancy, the tragic energy, of the legislator and exterminator; his heroic muscles and virile beard indicate the primitive barbarian, the subduer of men, while the long head and the projections of the temple denote the ascetic. Were he to arise, what action and what a lion's voice!" *Taine, Trans.*

There is the *Moses*, the grandest figure that was ever carved in stone. It has about it something frightfully majestic, if one may so speak. *Thackeray.*

Moses. A fresco by Francesco Mazzuoli, surnamed Il Parmigiano (1503-1540). In the church of Della Steccata, Parma, Italy.

Moses and the Burning Bush. A fresco by Raphael Sanzio (1483-1520). In the Stanza of the Heliodorus, in the Vatican, Rome.

Moses and the Israelites. A fresco painting by Cosimo Rosselli (1439-1506). In the Sistine Chapel, Rome.

Moses and Zipporah. A fresco by Luca Signorelli (da Cortona) (1441-1521). In the Sistine Chapel, Rome.

Moses, Choice of. A picture by Giorgio Barbarelli, commonly called Giorgione (1477-1511). In the Uffizi Palace, Florence, Italy.

Moses, Fountains of. See FOUNTAINS OF MOSES.

Moses Striking the Rock. A picture by Bartolomé Esteban Murillo (1618-1682), considered one of his masterpieces. In Seville, Spain.

☞ "No man ever stood before the works of Murillo here [in Seville], . . . his Moses opening the Rock, — and yet could be guilty of breathing a single regret at the recollections of Italy. The wonderful genius of Murillo can be studied and felt nowhere but at Seville, where he lived and died, and whose cathedral, convents and houses are full of his works." *George Ticknor.*

Mosque el-Aksa. This structure, situated within the enclosure of the Haram at Jerusalem, is supposed to be of the same outline and to occupy the same site as a magnificent basilica built in the sixth century in honor of the Virgin by the emperor Justinian. De Vogüé says that the present edifice is of Arabian construction, built upon the ruins of a Christian church as substructure. Mr. Fergusson declares that it is entirely a Mohammedan structure, and not the Mary Church of Justinian. This mosque is in the form of a basilica, consisting of seven aisles, and covering in all an area of about 50,000 square feet.

Mosque of Ahmed ebn Tooloon. This mosque, usually called the Jama (Gama) Tooloon, is the oldest in Cairo, Egypt, dating from 879 A.D. It is architecturally interesting because it shows that the pointed arch was used in Egypt about 300 years before it was introduced into Europe.

Mosque of Amer. An interesting mosque at Old Cairo, Egypt, now in a state of partial decay.

Mosque of Azhar. A large mosque at Cairo, Egypt, founded about 970, and afterwards rebuilt and enlarged. Here is the chief university of the East, containing about 300 professors, and nearly 10,000 students.

Mosque (*or* Cathedral) of Cordova. A grand church, formerly a Moorish mosque, in Cordova, Spain. It was begun by Abderrahman I. in 786, and until 1528 remained precisely as the Moors left it; and even now the alterations are inconsiderable. It is still called the Mezquita, the mosque. It is now converted into the Catholic church of the city.

☞ "The grandest of all the monuments of Arabic architecture, for between Bagdad and the Pillars of Hercules nothing to be compared to it is to be found. It is one of the largest churches in the world. The *coup d'œil* on entering is magnificent. Nothing but St. Peter's equals it; not even the vast Gothic churches of the North, or the Cathedral of Milan, besides that it has the charm of entire novelty in its form, style, and tone." *George Ticknor.*

☞ "As far as the history of architecture is concerned, by far the most interesting building in Spain is this Mosque of Cordoba. It was the first important building commenced by the Moors, and was enlarged and ornamented by successive rulers, so that it contains specimens of all the styles current in Spain from the earliest times till the building of the Alhambra, which was in the latest age of Moorish art. This celebrated mosque was commenced by Caliph Abd-el-Rahman, in the year 786, and completed by his son Hesham, who died 796. . . . It covers 157,500 square feet, being a larger superficies than that of any Christian church except that of St. Peter's at Rome. It is, however, sadly deficient in height, being only about 30 feet high to the roofs, and also wants subordination of parts." *Fergusson.*

In *Cordova's grand cathedral*
Stand the pillars thirteen hundred;
Thirteen hundred giant pillars
Bear the cupola, — that wonder.

Moorish monarchs once erected
This fair pile to Allah's glory;
But in the wild, dark whirl of ages
Many a change has stolen o'er it.
Heine, Trans.

And in whose mosque Almanzor hung
As lamps the bells that once had rung
At Compostella's shrine.
Longfellow.

Mosque of Kaitbey. A beautiful Mohammedan temple in Cairo, Egypt.

☞ "Looked at externally or internally, nothing can exceed the grace of every part of this building. Its small dimensions exclude it from any claim to grandeur, nor does it pretend to the purity of the Greek and some other styles; but as a perfect model of the elegance we generally associate with the architecture of this people, it is perhaps unrivalled by any thing in Egypt, and far surpasses the Alhambra or the other western buildings of its age." *Fergusson.*

Mosque of Mohammed Ali. This mosque at Cairo, Egypt, was begun by Mohammed Ali, and finished after his death. It is not admired for its architecture; but a good effect is however produced by the richness of the materials used, and by the vast size of the structure. It is of Oriental alabaster, with the exception of the outer walls. A fine view can be obtained from this mosque.

☞ Miss Martineau says of the view from the mosque: "In the evening the beauty is beyond description. The vastness of the city, as it lies stretched below, surprises every one." After speaking of the more distant objects to be seen — the Pyramids, etc., — she adds: "This view is the great sight of Cairo, and that which the stranger contrives to bring into his plan for almost every day."

The great lion of the place. . . . It is built of alabaster of a fair white, with a delicate blushing tinge; but the ornaments are European — the noble, fantastic, beautiful Oriental art is forgotten. *Thackeray.*

Mosque of Omar. This mosque (Kubbet es-Sukhrah, "the Dome of the Rock") covers the site long occupied by the great Jewish temples on the heights of Mount Moriah, in Jerusalem. It is very beautiful, being built of variegated marbles, with a splendid dome, fine arches and arcades, surrounded by green lawns dotted by cypress-trees. On the Mohammedan Sabbath it presents a very cheerful spectacle, worshippers being at prayers under the cypress-trees, women, Mohammedan nuns, sitting about the lawns, and children sitting upon the grass. Any Christian who should enter even the outermost court of the mosque would be liable to immediate death by stoning, and even an approach to it subjects him to insult. The Caliph Omar built this mosque, according to the common tradition, over the celebrated rock *es-Sukhrah.* The Arab historians say, however, that the mosque was rebuilt by the Caliph Abd el-Melek, the work being begun in 686 A.D. Upon the sacred rock, directly under the dome, is shown the "Footprint of Mohammed," where the foot of that prophet left the earth on his journey to heaven; and near by the "Handprint of Gabriel," where that angel seized the rock and held it down when it was rising with Mohammed.

☞ "According to the treaty of capitulation, in virtue of which the city [Jerusalem] was ceded to the Moslems . . . it was agreed that a spot of ground should be ceded to Omar, in which he might establish a place of prayer. For this purpose the site of the old Temple of the Jews was assigned him, that spot being considered sacred by the Moslems on account of the nocturnal visit of the prophet, and because they then wished to conciliate the Jews, while at the same time the spot was held accursed by the Christians on account of the Lord's denunciation, and

Julian's attempt to rebuild it. Here Omar built a small mosque which still exists, but all the traditions of the place have become so confused by subsequent interchanges between the Christians and themselves that it is difficult to say whether it is the chamber bearing the name on the east of the Mosque of the Monegrins, or to the west. As might be expected from the simplicity of Omar's character, his poverty, and his hatred of every thing like ostentation, his mosque is a very simple building." *Fergusson.*

☞ "The Dome of the Rock, now known to European travellers as the 'Mosque of Omar,' — which was undoubtedly the church which Constantine erected over what he believed to have been the sepulchre of Christ, — was throughout the twelfth century considered equal in sanctity with the Church of the Sepulchre; and the veneration with which it was regarded had, no doubt, considerable influence upon the architecture of the age." *Fergusson.*

The *Mosque of Omar* is the St. Peter's of Turkey. *Sir Frederick Henniker.*

Mosque of Sultan el Hákem. The oldest mosque but one at Cairo, Egypt. It affords an example of the early use of the pointed arch in Saracenic buildings, the time of its erection being nearly two centuries earlier than the general adoption of that style of architecture in England.

Mosque of Sultan Hassan. [*Jáma-t-es Soltán Hassan.*] This mosque at Cairo, Egypt, the finest in the city, was begun in 1357, and finished three years later. It is much admired for its architecture.

Motee Musjeed. See PEARL MOSQUE.

Moultrie, Fort. See FORT MOULTRIE.

Mount Athos, Monasteries of. The sides of this mountain, Mount Athos, in Turkey, are occupied by 22 convents, together with many cells, grottos, etc., affording a habitation to more than 3,000 monks. Most of these convents were founded in the time of the Byzantine Empire, some in the time of Constantine the Great. From the multitude of these ascetic retreats, Mount Athos, together with the peninsula upon which it stands, is known in the Levant as the *Holy Mountain* (Ἅγιον Ὄρος, *Monto Santo*).

Mount Auburn. An extensive and beautiful cemetery in Cambridge, Mass., the first of the large country cemeteries of the United States. It was consecrated in 1831. The grounds are laid out with great taste, and contain many fine and costly monuments. The place was formerly known as "Sweet Auburn."

☞ "What parent, as he conducts his son to Mount Auburn or to Bunker Hill, will not, as he pauses before their monumental statues, seek to heighten his reverence for virtue, for patriotism, for science, for learning, for devotion to the public good, as he bids him contemplate the form of that grave and venerable Winthrop, who left his pleasant home in England to come and found a new republic in this untrodden wilderness; of that ardent and intrepid Otis, who first struck out the spark of American independence; of that noble Adams, its most eloquent champion on the floor of Congress; of that martyr Warren, who laid down his life in its defence; of that self-taught Bowditch, who, without a guide, threaded the starry mazes of the heavens; of that Story, honored at home and abroad as one of the brightest luminaries of the law, and by a felicity of which I believe there is no other example, admirably portrayed in marble by his son?" *Edward Everett.*

I thought of a mound in sweet *Auburn*,
  Where a little headstone stood;
How the flakes were folding it gently,
  As did robins the babes in the wood.
Lowell.

Mount Calvary. See CALVARY.

Mount Carmel, Convent of. A noble monastic establishment, belonging to the order of Carmelites, on Mount Carmel, in northern Palestine. The spot is associated with many interesting events, not only in sacred story, but in modern history. During the siege of Acre by Napoleon, the convent was used as a hospital for French soldiers. The buildings were afterwards burned by the Turks, but have been rebuilt in this century, and are the finest of the kind in Palestine.

Mount Edgecumbe. A castellated mansion, dating from the time of Henry VIII., the seat of the Edgecumbe family, near Plymouth, England. The grounds are famous for their beautiful views of land and sea.

> Forthwith, a guard at every gun
> Was placed along the wall;
> The beacon blazed upon the roof
> Of *Edgecombe's* lofty hall.
> *Macaulay.*

Mount Holyoke Seminary. A well-known school for young women, founded in 1836. It is situated in South Hadley, Mass.

Mount Hood. A well-known picture by Albert Bierstadt (b. 1829).

Mount Hope. An eminence in Bristol County, R.I., nearly opposite what is now called Fall River, Mass., and celebrated as the residence of King Philip, the chief of the Indian tribe of the Wampanoags, who carried on the long and destructive war with the early settlers of New England, which broke out in 1675, and is known as "King Philip's War."

☞ "Near the brow of the hill, Philip fixed his wigwam and held his dusky court. He has had Irving for his biographer, Southey for his bard, and Forrest for his ideal representative. In his own time he was the public enemy whom any should slay: in ours he is considered a martyr to the idea of liberty — his idea of liberty not differing from that of Tell and Toussaint, whom we call heroes." *Drake.*

☞ "As Philip looked down from his seat on Mount Hope, that glorious eminence, that —

> — 'throne of royal state, which far
> Outshone the wealth of Ormus and of Ind,
> Or where the gorgeous East, with richest hand,
> Showers on her kings barbaric pearl and gold.' —

as he looked down, and beheld the lovely scene which spread beneath, at a summer sunset, the distant hill-tops glittering as with fire, the slanting beams streaming across the waters, the broad plains, the island groups, the majestic forest, — could he be blamed if his heart burned within him, as he beheld it all passing, by no tardy process, from beneath his control, into the hands of the stranger?" *Edward Everett.*

Mount Lander. A well-known picture by Albert Bierstadt (b. 1829).

Mount Mario. See MONTE MARIO.

Mount of Precipitation. A locality fixed upon by monastic tradition in the immediate vicinity of Nazareth in northern Palestine, as the spot to which Jesus was taken by the Jews, with a design to cast him down "from the brow of the hill."

Mount Pleasant. An old colonial house in what is now Fairmount Park, Philadelphia, Penn. It was built in 1761, and was owned for a time by Benedict Arnold, having been confiscated after his act of treason.

Mount St. Michael. A renowned castle-convent, situated upon the summit of a picturesque isolated rock of the same name rising out of a wide expanse of sands in Normandy, France. This shrine of the Archangel Michael has been for centuries the resort of thousands of pious worshippers including many royal pilgrims. The convent bore the name of the Marvel, from the immense size and strength of its walls. During the Revolution it was turned into a prison. St. Michael's Mount in Cornwall was a dependency of this monastery.

> From various letters which my friend had written me from this proud eminence, I had formed a very distinct idea of the place. I had imagined a hill not unlike *Mount St. Michel*, my friend's house answering to the monastery on the top. *Harper's Magazine.*

Mount Sinai (Convent). See ST. CATHERINE.

Mount Valerien. See MONT VALÉRIEN.

Mount Vernon. The estate and home of George Washington, in Fairfax County, Va., about 15 miles below the city of Washington. It was named after Admiral

Vernon of the British navy. The mansion contains many interesting relics connected with Washington, and among others the key of the Bastille which was presented to him by Lafayette. In 1856 the house with six acres of land was purchased by the Ladies' Mount Vernon Association, and is now the property of the nation.

Tell me, ye who make your pious pilgrimage to the shades of *Vernon*, is Washington indeed shut up in that cold and narrow house? That which made these men, and men like these, cannot die.
Edward Everett.

The tree whose branches in your north winds wave
Dropped its young blossoms on *Mount Vernon's* grave. *Whittier.*

As from the grave where Henry sleeps,
From *Vernon's* weeping willow,
And from the grassy pall which hides
The Sage of Monticello. *Whittier.*

Mount Zion. The chief and most interesting of the hills upon which Jerusalem is built. It is the oldest part of the city, the first upon which buildings were erected.

Sing, heavenly Muse, that on the secret top
Of Oreb, or of Sinai, didst inspire
That shepherd, who first taught the chosen seed
In the beginning how the heavens and earth
Rose out of Chaos; or if *Sion* hill
Delight thee more, and Siloa's brook that flowed
Fast by the oracle of God, I thence
Invoke thy aid to my adventurous song.
Milton.

Mountain of Light. See KOHI-NOOR.

Mourning Bush. An ancient and celebrated tavern in Aldersgate, London.

Mousa Castle. A Pictish castle on one of the Orkney Islands, said to be "perhaps the most perfect Teutonic fortress now extant in Europe."

Mouse-tower, The. [Ger. *Mäusethurm.*] A tower on an island in the Rhine, supposed to have been erected in the Middle Ages by some of the robber-knights of the Rhine. The ruins have been covered with stucco, and converted into a watch-tower. It derives its name from the legend of the cruel Archbishop Hatto of Mayence. According to the story, as told by Southey in his familiar ballad, the Bishop, having burned alive a barnful of starving poor in order to rid himself of their importunities for food from his well-furnished granaries, was punished for his cruel act by being devoured by a whole army of rats in his tower on the Rhine, to which he had fled for safety.

"Fly! my Lord Bishop, fly," quoth he,
"Ten thousand rats are coming this way —
The Lord forgive you for yesterday!"

"I'll go to my tower on the Rhine," replied he,
"Tis the safest place in Germany;
The walls are high, and the shores are steep,
And the stream is strong, and the water deep!" *Southey.*

☞ "It appears to have been built in the thirteenth century by a Bishop Siegfried (full 200 years after the death of Bishop Hatto), along with the opposite castle of Ehrenfels, as a watch-tower and toll-house for collecting the duties upon all goods which passed the spot. The word *maus* is probably only an older form of *mauth*, duty or toll: and this name, together with the very unpopular object for which the tower was erected, perhaps gave rise to the dolorous story of Bishop Hatto and the rats." *Murray's Handbook.*

From my study I see in the lamp-light,
Descending the broad hall-stair,
Grave Alice, and laughing Allegra,
And Edith with golden hair.

. . . .

They almost devour me with kisses;
Their arms about me intwine,
Till I think of the Bishop of Bingen
In his *Mouse-Tower* on the Rhine.
Longfellow.

Moyamensing Prison. A massive prison in Philadelphia, Penn.

Mozart Hall. A building in Cincinnati, O., devoted to lectures and concerts.

Mozzi, Villa. See VILLA MOZZI.

Mucross Abbey. A beautiful and famed monastery, now in ruins, situated in the county of Kerry, Ireland. It is of the fourteenth century. The best-preserved portion is the cloister, which consists of 22 arches. The whole area is covered by a magnificent yew-tree of a growth of centuries.

Muezzin, The. A picture by Jean Léon Gérôme (b. 1824), the French painter.

Mug-house Clubs. The Mug-house club was one of the most popular clubs in London early in the eighteenth century. The house in Long Acre derived its name from the fact that each member drank his ale from a separate mug. After a time other similar clubs were formed, and they became intimately connected with political events. Their tumults and struggles with the Jacobites culminated in the serious Mug-house riots of the year 1716. The Mug-house club in Long Acre, though subsequently a political rendezvous, was not such at first, and is said to have consisted of gentlemen, lawyers, and statesmen. The Club in its early days is thus described: "They have a grave old Gentleman, in his own gray Hairs, now within a few months of Ninety years old, who is their President, and sits in an arm'd chair some steps higher than the rest of the company to keep the whole Room in order. A Harp plays all the time at the lower end of the Room; and every now and then one or other of the Company rises and entertains the rest with a song, and (by the by) some are good Masters. Here is nothing drunk but ale; and every Gentleman hath his separate Mug, which he chalks on the Table where he sits as it is brought in; and every one retires when he pleases as from a Coffee-house. The Room is always so diverted with Songs, and drinking from one Table to another to one another's Healths, that there is no room for Politicks, or any thing that can sow'r conversation."

Mulberry Garden. A celebrated place of resort and entertainment in London in the seventeenth century, now included in the gardens of Buckingham Palace.

Muleteer, The. A picture by Antonio Allegri, surnamed Correggio (1494–1534). In the gallery of Stafford House, London.

Mulets, Grands. See GRANDS MULETS.

Mulino, Il. See MILL, THE.

Mungret Priory. An interesting monastic ruin in the county of Limerick, Ireland. It is said to have been founded by St. Patrick, and is undoubtedly of high antiquity.

Münster Congress. A picture by Gerard Terburg (1608–1681), the Dutch *genre*-painter, and considered one of his masterpieces. It was sold at the Demidoff sale for 182,000 francs, and is now in the National Gallery, London.

Murder of the Innocents. See MASSACRE OF THE INNOCENTS.

Muro Torto. A piece of broken wall in the garden of the Pincian Hill.

☞ "At the farthest point of the Pincio you look down from the parapet upon the *Muro Torto*, a massive fragment of the oldest Roman wall, which juts over, as if ready to tumble down by its own weight, yet seems still the most indestructible piece of work that men's hands have ever piled together."
Hawthorne, The Marble Faun.

Hence turning to the right out of the Porto del Popolo, we came to Justinian's garden neere the *Muro Torto*, so prominently built as threatening every moment to fall, yet standing so for these thousand years. *John Evelyn*, 1644.

☞ "Vainly have the antiquaries puzzled themselves to conceive them with what intention, or by whom, this piece of deformity was made, whether originally built in this strange shape, or whether fallen into it by time or accident." *Eaton.*

Musée du Louvre. A vast collection of works of art in Paris, occupying almost the whole of the Louvre Palace and Louvre Gallery. See LOUVRE.

☞ "As a whole it is perhaps the finest, and as regards numbers the largest in Europe, although it must yield in Italian art to those of the Vatican and Florence; in Dutch, to those of the

Hague, Amsterdam, and Antwerp; in Roman antiquities, to the Museums of the Capitol and Vatican at Rome, and to that of Naples; and in Greek sculpture, to the British Museum. Most of the objects are set out and exhibited to the best advantage in splendid rooms. Under Napoleon III. the whole was re-arranged, whilst very great additions were made in every department, especially in the Egyptian, Assyrian, and Etruscan, — among them the magnificent collections of the Marquis Campana, of Rome, purchased in 1861 for nearly 200,000*l.*, which form the most important portion of the Musée Napoléon III." *Murray's Handbook.*

Musée du Luxembourg. [Museum of the Luxembourg.] A gallery of paintings in the Luxembourg Palace, Paris.

☞ "This gallery contains what are considered to be the best works of living French painters; at the expiration of ten years from the death of an artist, his works may be transferred to the Louvre. This gallery dates from 1818, and the works have been mostly purchased after the annual exhibitions under the selection of a jury composed chiefly of members of the Institute. Until lately the pictures selected were almost entirely of the school of the Empire and Restoration — enormous classical or academic subjects. Of late, however, this system has been departed from, and the collection is now a fairer representation of the French school of the day." *Murray's Handbook.*

Museo, El. [The Museum.] The royal picture-gallery of Madrid, Spain, and one of the richest collections in the world. Of the building, Fergusson says, "If not quite successful in design, it has so many good points about it as to be well worthy of study." The gallery contains a vast number of pictures by Spanish and Italian artists.

Museo Borbonico. [Bourbon Museum.] A celebrated museum of antiquities, sculptures, paintings, gems, etc., in Naples, Italy. It received its name from Ferdinand I., in 1816, who placed in it the royal collections of antiquities and pictures. The greater part of the relics found at Herculaneum and Pompeii are deposited here. This museum is now called *Museo Nazionale.*

Museo Capitolino. [Capitoline Museum.] A gallery of sculpture, — the Museum of the Capitol, — at Rome. It was begun by Pope Clement XII., and, though not so extensive as that of the Vatican, is a most interesting collection.

Museo Chiaramonti. An apartment in the Vatican, Rome, filled with sculptures, arranged by Canova. It was founded by Pope Pius VIII., and derives its name from that of his family.

☞ "Here are some seven hundred pieces of sculpture, — all worthy of examination, many of them curious, and some of them of great merit." *Hillard.*

Museo Gregoriano. See ETRUSCAN MUSEUM.

Museo Nazionale. See MUSEO BORBONICO.

Museo Pio-Clementino. A museum in the Vatican Palace at Rome, so called from the two popes Clement XIV. and Pius VI., who made large donations to it. It contains the most magnificent collection of ancient sculpture in the world, among which may be mentioned the Torso Belvedere, the Meleager, the Antinous, the Laocoon, and the Apollo Belvedere.

☞ "This is by far the most extensive collection in the Vatican. Besides the Cortile of the Belvidere . . . it comprises the Hall of Animals, the Gallery of the Muses, the Circular Hall, the Hall of the Greek Cross, the Hall of the Biga, and the Grand Staircase. In point of architecture, these are the most splendid portions of the whole Vatican, and the visitor knows not which most to admire, the innumerable works of art which solicit his attention, or the spacious courts, and the noble apartments around and in which they are distributed." *Hillard.*

Museum, The. 1. This renowned institution at Alexandria, Egypt, was founded by Ptolemy Soter. Alexandria was a famous seat of learning, where for a long time flourished literature, science, and all branches of philosphy. According to Strabo, the Museum was a large structure surrounded by a corridor, and the famous Library of Alexandria was attached to it.

2. A hill in Athens, Greece, south-west of the Acropolis.

3. A well-known edifice on Tremont Street, Boston, Mass., used for theatrical purposes, and containing a museum of curiosities and antiquities.

Tickets to the *Múseum*, — said the landlady. — There is them that's glad enough to go to the *Múseum*, when tickets is given 'em; but some of 'em ha'n't had a ticket sence Cenderilla was played. *Holmes.*

4. See British Museum, India Museum, Sloane Museum, Soane Museum, etc.

Music Hall. A plain edifice in Boston, Mass., containing a noble hall, used for concerts and other purposes, and the largest organ in America.

Music Master. A picture by Jan Steen (1626-1679), the Dutch *genre* painter. In the National Gallery, London.

Musidora. An admired picture by Thomas Gainsborough (1727-1788). In the National Gallery, London.

☞ "His [Gainsborough's] *Musidora* has such delicate feet and so intelligent a head that she is no simple girl bathing, but a lady."

Taine, Trans.

Myrtle Grove. A mansion near Youghall, Ireland, near Cork, once the home of Sir Walter Raleigh. It derives its name from the luxuriant growth of the myrtles by which it is nearly covered, and some of which are nearly 30 feet high.

N.

Nag's Head. A former tavern in London.

Namur, Siege of. See SIEGE OF NAMUR.

Nando's. A coffee-house in Fleet Street, London, formerly much frequented by professional loungers. It is no longer a coffee-house.

☞ "The lawyers discussed law or literature; criticised the last new play, or retailed the freshest Westminster Hall 'bite' at *Nando's* or the Grecian, both close on the purlieus of the Temple. Here the young bloods of the Inns-of-Court paraded their Indian gowns and lace caps of a morning; and swaggered in their lace coats and Mechlin ruffles at night, after the theatre." *National Review.*

Napoleon at Fontainebleau. A picture by Paul Delaroche (1797–1856), the eminent French historical painter.

Napoleon at St. Helena. An admired picture by Benjamin Robert Haydon (1786–1846).

Narcissus. An ancient marble statue supposed to be the copy of a work by Praxiteles, the Greek sculptor (b. 392? B.C.). It is in the Museum at Naples, Italy. [Called also *Pan*, and *Bacchus.*]

Narcissus and Echo. A picture by Joseph Mallord William Turner (1775–1851), the English landscape-painter, and regarded one of his best works.

Narragansett Fort. A ruined Indian fortress near Kingston, R.I., the scene of one of the most desperate conflicts between the early colonists of New England and the Indian tribes during "King Philip's War." The fort, of which a few remains still exist, was taken by the Massachusetts and Connecticut men in December, 1675.

Nashville, The. A noted privateer of the Confederate navy in the war of the Rebellion. She was one of the most active and formidable vessels afloat, but was finally destroyed by the *Montauk*, under command of Capt. Worden.

Nassau, John, Duke of, and his Family. A family picture by Anthony van Dyck (1599–1641), and one of his grandest compositions. Now at Panshanger.

National Academy of Design. A fine building on Fourth Avenue, New York, devoted to the exhibition of works of American art.

National Cemetery. A national burying-ground in Arlington, Va., containing the bodies of 16,000 soldiers, who fell in the war of the Rebellion.

National Gallery. A collection of paintings and works of art in London. It originated under the auspices of the British government, and was founded in 1824. The building of the National Gallery was erected 1832–38.

☞ "It possesses windows without glass, a cupola without size, a portico without height, pepper-boxes without pepper, and the finest site in Europe, without any thing to show upon it." *All the Year Round.*

National Gallery of Statuary. A semicircular chamber in the Capitol at Washington, formerly the hall of the House of Representatives, in which that body sat for 32 years. In 1864 the room was set apart as a hall of statuary. It contains statues of some of the most eminent men of the republic, and of the colonial period, contributed by the different States.

National Monument. A memorial structure in Edinburgh, Scotland, begun in 1822, in honor of those British soldiers who fell in the Napoleonic wars. It was designed to be a copy of the Parthenon at Athens, but for want of funds the building is still in an unfinished state.

National Monument. An imposing memorial structure of granite, erected on Cemetery Hill, Gettysburg, Penn., in honor of the Union soldiers who gave their lives for their country at this place in the great battle of July 3, 1863. It stands in the centre of the enclosure, which contains the bodies of some 3,500 soldiers, representing eighteen Northern States. The monument bears upon its base the famous words of President Lincoln, delivered at the consecration of the cemetery in November, 1863.

National Portrait Gallery. An interesting gallery in the South Kensington Museum, London, founded in 1858.

National Road. An ancient national highway, established by Thomas Jefferson, and once a great thoroughfare. It extended from Baltimore, Md., through Frederick, Cumberland, and Wheeling, to Columbus, O. Sometimes called the old Cumberland Road.

Nativity, The. [Ital. *Il Presepio*, Fr. *La Nativité*.] A very common subject of representation by the great mediæval painters, exhibiting, under various aspects and circumstances, the birth of Christ. Of the numerous pictures treating of this subject, the following may be mentioned as among the more noted.

> But for the occasion and the appellation it would be quite impossible to distinguish the loves that sport round Venus and Adonis from the Cherubim, so called, that hover above a *Nativity*, or a Riposo.
>
> *Mrs. Jameson.*

Nativity, The. A celebrated picture by Correggio. See NOTTE, LA.

Nativity, The. An admired picture by Mariotto Albertinelli (1474-1515). In the Pitti Gallery, Florence, Italy.

Nativity, The. A well-known picture by Giulio Romano (1492-1546), which formerly belonged to Charles I. of England. Now in the Louvre, Paris.

Nativity, The. A picture by Albert Dürer (1471-1528), the German painter and engraver, erroneously ascribed to Herri de Bles. It is in the collection of the Marquis of Exeter at Burleigh House, England.

Nativity, The. An altar-piece with wings, executed by Hugo van der Goes (d. 1482), the Flemish painter, for the church of the Hospital of Santa Maria Nuova at Florence, Italy, where it is still preserved.

Nativity, The. A small triptych altar-piece, representing the Nativity, a Dead Christ in the lap of the Virgin, and Christ appearing to his mother after the Resurrection, by Roger van der Weyden, (d. 1464). It was presented by Pope Martin V. to the King of Spain, afterwards was brought to France, and is now in the Berlin Museum.

Nativity, The. A wall-painting by Nabor Martin (1404-1453), a Flemish painter. In the "Grande Boucherie" at Ghent, Belgium.

Nativity, The. A picture by Gheerardt David (1484-1523), a Flemish painter. Now in the National Gallery at Madrid, Spain.

Nativity, Cave of the. See CAVE OF THE NATIVITY.

Nativity, Church of the. This splendid basilica at Bethlehem, the oldest specimen of Christian architecture in the world, was built by the Empress Helena in 327 A.D. In consequence of its being used by all sects alike, the church is now in a state of neglect. Connected with it is a chamber which was formerly the study of Jerome. In the church is an altar reputed to be upon the spot where were buried the 20,000 children massacred by order of Herod. There is also here a low vault known as the *Chapel of the Nativity*, within which is a marble slab bearing the inscription, "Hic de Virgine Maria Jesus Christus natus est" ("Here Jesus Christ was born of the Virgin Mary"). Here is also the small chapel of the *Præsepium*, or "Manger," the manger being represented by a marble trough. Attached to the church are large convents belonging to Roman Catholics, the Greek Church, and the Armenians.

Natural Bridge. 1. A remarkable natural curiosity near the James River in Virginia, about 125 miles west of Richmond. It is an arch more than 200 feet in height spanning Cedar Creek.

This scene [the passage of the Potomac through the valley of the Blue Ridge] is worth a journey across the Atlantic; yet here, as in the neighborhood of the *Natural Bridge*, are people who have passed their lives within a dozen miles, and have never been to survey these monuments of a war between rivers and mountains, which must have shaken the earth itself to its centre. *Thomas Jefferson.*

2. A curiosity of nature in Walker County, Ala., considered by many as remarkable as the celebrated bridge in Virginia.

Naval Academy. See UNITED STATES NAVAL ACADEMY.

Naval Club. See ROYAL NAVAL CLUB.

Navicella, La. [The boat or barge.] A celebrated mosaic now in the vestibule of St. Peter's Church in Rome, executed by Giotto (1276-1336), with the help of his pupil Pietro Cavallini, and representing a ship (symbolizing the Church) with the disciples upon an agitated sea, and the Saviour raising Peter from the waves. On the shore opposite is a fisherman. Several figures of Fathers are seen in the sky manifesting sympathy with those in the ship. The winds are represented below on each side in the form of a demon. The picture has undergone such injuries and repairs as to make any critical estimate difficult.

☞ "'Christ walking on the Sea' is a familiar and picturesque subject, not to be mistaken. The most ancient and most celebrated representation is Giotto's mosaic (A.D. 1298), now placed in the portico of St. Peter's over the arch opposite to the principal door. The sentiment in the composition of this subject is, generally, 'Lord, help me; or I perish.' St. Peter is sinking, and Christ is stretching out his hand to save him. It is considered as a type of the Church in danger, assailed by enemies, and saved by the miraculous interposition of the Redeemer; and in this sense must the frequent representations in churches be understood." *Mrs. Jameson.*

Navona, Piazza. See PIAZZA NAVONA.

Naworth Castle. The seat of the Earl of Carlisle, near Gilsland, Scotland.

Nazionale, Villa. See VILLA REALE.

Necessidades. A palace of vast size in Lisbon, Portugal, used for the meetings of the Cortes.

☞ "Hence we were driven to the huge palace of Necessidades, which is but a wing of a building that no King of Portugal ought ever to be rich enough to complete, and which, if perfect, might outvie the Tower of Babel. The mines of Brazil must have been productive of gold and silver indeed when the founder imagined this enormous edifice. . . . Although the palace has not attained any thing like its full growth, yet what exists is quite big enough for the monarch of such a little country. . . . The Necessidades are only used for grand galas, receptions of ambassadors, and ceremonies of state. . . . Of all the undignified objects in the world, a palace out at elbows is surely the meanest." *Thackeray.*

Necklace, The Diamond. See DIAMOND NECKLACE.

Negroni, Villa. See VILLA MASSIMO.

Nelson Column. A monument erected in 1843 to the memory of Lord Nelson in Trafalgar Square, London, and supporting a statue of that great admiral.

I wish they would offer the *Trafalgar-square Pillar* to the Egyptians; and that both of the huge, ugly monsters were lying in the dirt there [Egypt], side by side. *Thackeray.*

Nelson's Pillar. A fine Ionic column in Sackville Street, Dublin, Ireland. It is 134 feet in height, and is surmounted by a statue of Lord Nelson, leaning upon the capstan of a ship. The pillar commands a fine view of the city.

Nepomuck. See ST. JOHN NEPOMUCK and SHRINE OF ST. JOHN NEPOMUCK.

Neptune, Temple of. See TEMPLE OF NEPTUNE.

Nero's Golden House. See GOLDEN HOUSE.

Nesle, Tour de. See TOUR DE NESLE.

Neutral Ground. 1. The name given to a space near the northern extremity of the isthmus which connects the fortress of Gibraltar with the mainland. It is between the "Spanish lines" and the English "Rock" of Gibraltar.

2. A name formerly applied to Westchester County, N.Y., which was for five years or more during the Revolutionary War the scene of constant skirmishing between the Loyalists and Queen's Rangers on the one side, and the patriot soldiery of New York and New England on the other. Cooper's well-known "Spy" is a "Tale of the Neutral Ground."

Nevskoi Prospekt. [The New Prospect.] The principal street and public promenade in St. Petersburg, Russia. It is four miles in length, nearly in a right line, and 150 feet in breadth, with a double carriage-way. The houses facing upon it are magnificent, and some of the finest churches in the city are here located. In winter the display of sledges and costumes which crowd this street affords one of the finest spectacles to be seen in Europe.

A walk in Broadway or Fifth Avenue will show you damsels and dames who will remind you of those you have met in Piccadilly or the Boulevards . . . in the Prater or *Nevskoi Prospekt.* *Galaxy.*

The days came and went; fashionable equipages forsook their summer ground of the Islands and crowded the *Nevskoi Prospekt;* the nights were cold and raw, the sun's lessening declination was visible from day to day, and still Winter delayed to make his appearance. *Bayard Taylor.*

New Abbey. An interesting ruined monastery, founded in the thirteenth century, near Dumfries, Scotland. Its last abbot is said to have been the original of Sir Walter Scott's Abbot of St. Mary's.

New Forest. A large tract of woodland, the greater part of which belongs to the Crown, in the neighborhood of Southampton, England, about 50 miles in circumference, originally set apart by William the Conqueror, and of much historical interest.

This is the place where William's kingly power
Did from their poor and peaceful homes expel,
Unfriended, desolate, and shelterless,
The inhabitants of all the fertile tract
Far as these wilds extend.
Robert Southey.

I have read somewhere that the lineal descendants of the man who carted off the body of William Rufus, with Walter Tyrrel's arrow sticking in it, have driven a cart (not absolutely the same one, I suppose) in the *New Forest*, from that day to this. *Holmes.*

New Grange. A remarkable Druidical tumulus on the banks of the Boyne, between Drogheda and Slane, Ireland. One or two others of a similar character are in the neighborhood. The interior was first explored in 1699. A long gallery opens into a wonderful cave or sacrificial chamber, where more than 2,000 years ago the Druids held their solemn meetings.

☞ "Of their Druidical character no one can entertain the remotest doubt; they would carry conviction to the most sceptical, even if ample corroborative testimony did not exist." *Mr. and Mrs. Hall.*

New Hall. An historical mansion near Chelmsford, England, once belonging to the Duke of Buckingham, and the scene of many interesting incidents. Only a part of the building now remains.

New Harmony. A celebrated socialist community established in 1825, in a place bearing this name in Indiana, purchased by Robert Owen (1771-1858) for the purpose of testing his theory of society. The experiment proved entirely unsuccessful.

New Inn. A law seminary in London, one of the inns of Chancery.

New Ironsides. A noted vessel in the United States navy in the Civil War of 1861-65. She was the flag-ship of Admiral Dupont's flotilla in the attack upon the defences of Charleston, S.C.

New Palace. [Ger. *der Königsbau.*] A splendid palace in Munich, Bavaria, imitated in part from the Palazzo Pitti in Florence, Italy, built in 1835.

☞ "The New Residence is not only one of the wonders of Munich, but of the world." *Bayard Taylor.*

New Palace (at Westminster). See WESTMINSTER PALACE.

New Place. The name of the house which Shakespeare purchased at Stratford-on-Avon, after his return to his native town, and in which he died. The foundations of the house are all that now remain. The site, purchased by public subscription, has been converted into a pleasure-ground.

☞ "It cost Shakespeare sixty pounds sterling (equal to about $1,500); a small outlay for the dwelling of a man of its new possessor's means and capacity of enjoyment. No representation of the house as it was in Shakespeare's time is known to exist, it having been altered after his death; yet its size was not enlarged, and an existing representation of it in its last condition shows that it was a goodly mansion." *Richard Grant White.*

☞ "After that we were taken to see New Place. 'And what is New Place,' you say, — 'the house where Shakespeare lived?' Not exactly, but a house built where his house was. . . . We went out into Shakespeare's garden, where we were shown his mulberry, — not the one that he planted, though, but a veritable mulberry planted on the same spot." *Mrs. H. B. Stowe.*

New York University. See UNIVERSITY OF THE CITY OF NEW YORK.

Newark Castle. This Scottish castle on the river Yarrow was formerly a royal residence. The Duchess of Buccleuch is supposed to have been here, listening to the "Lay of the Last Minstrel," who

"Passed where Newark's stately tower
Looks out from Yarrow's birken bower."

Rising from those lofty groves,
Behold a ruin hoary,
The shattered front of *Newark's tower*,
Renown'd in Border story.
Wordsworth.

Newbattle Abbey. The seat of the Marquis of Midlothian, near Dalhousie, Scotland.

Newcastle House. A famous mansion in London, the residence of the Duke of Newcastle. It is no longer standing, its site being occupied by Newcastle Place.

Newgate. A celebrated prison in London, and the oldest in the city, formerly used for felons and debtors, now as a jail for the confinement of prisoners before and after trial at the Old Bailey. Many distinguished persons have been imprisoned within the walls of Newgate, and many famous criminals have here been executed. It was rebuilt in 1770-80. Among those who have been imprisoned here are, Sackville the poet, George Wither, Penn, De Foe, Jack Sheppard, Dr. Dodd, Lord George Gordon. Newgate prison had its origin in the gate-house of New-Gate, which was one of the principal gates of the City. The executions which formerly were carried out at Tyburn now take place here.

☞ "It has a most imposing exterior, which is perhaps its greatest use as a deterrer from crime, and the worst possible interior." *Capt. Williams.*

☞ "There, at the very core of London, in the heart of its business and animation, in the midst of a whirl of noise and motion: stemming, as it were, the giant currents of life that flow ceaselessly on from different quarters, and meet beneath its walls, stands Newgate." *Dickens.*

☞ "Newgate, though only a prison, and pretending to be nothing else, is still one of the best public buildings in the metropolis. . . . There is nothing in it but two great windowless blocks, each 90 feet square, and between them a very commonplace gaoler's residence." *Fergusson.*

Newgate he builded faire
For prisoners to live in;
Christs-church he did repaire
Christian love for to win.
Many more such like deedes
Were done by Whittington;
Which joy and comfort breedes,
To such as looke thereon.
Anonymous.

For what is history, in fact, but a kind of *Newgate* calendar, a register of the crimes and miseries that man has inflicted on his fellow-man? *Irving.*

Nay, look at *Newgate:* do not the offscourings of Creation, when condemned to the gallows, as if they were not men but vermin, walk thither with decency, and even to the scowls and hootings of the whole Universe give their stern good-night in silence? *Carlyle.*

The drop on the stones, of the blind man's staff,
As he trades in his own grief's sacredness;
The brothel's shriek, and the *Newgate* laugh. *Mrs. Browning.*

Newstead Abbey. An antique building near Nottingham, England, originally a monastery, founded by Henry II., celebrated as having been once the residence of Lord Byron, and in which numerous relics of the poet are still preserved. The building is now the property of Col. Wildman.

☞ "Newstead Abbey is one of the finest specimens in existence of those quaint and romantic piles, half castle, half convent, which remain as monuments of the olden times of England. It stands, too, in the midst of a legendary neighborhood; being in the heart of Sherwood Forest, and surrounded by the haunts of Robin Hood and his band of outlaws, so famous in ancient ballad and nursery tale." *Irving.*

Newstead! fast falling, once resplendent dome!
Religion's shrine! repentant Henry's pride! *Byron.*

Through thy battlements, *Newstead*, the hollow winds whistle;
Thou, the hall of my fathers, art gone to decay;
In thy once smiling garden the hemlock and thistle
Have choked up the rose which late bloomed in the way. *Ibid.*

What made my heart, at *Newstead*, fullest swell?
'Twas not the thought of Byron, of his cry
Stormily sweet, his Titan agony.
Matthew Arnold.

Newtown Abbey. A picturesque ruined monastery near Trim, in the county of Meath, Ireland.

Niagara. A picture by Frederick E. Church (b. 1826), well known through frequent reproductions. Now in the Corcoran Gallery, Washington.

☞ "Church's *Niagara* was immediately recognized as the first satisfactory delineation by art of one of the greatest natural wonders of the Western world, and this is in itself extraordinary praise." *Tuckerman.*

☞ "Mr. Ruskin, when looking at Church's 'Niagara,' pointed out an effect of light upon water, which he declared he had often seen in nature, especially among the Swiss waterfalls, but never before on canvas." *Tuckerman.*

Niagara, The. 1. A ship of Commodore Perry's squadron, which did great service in the naval battle with the British on Lake Erie in 1813.

2. An American man-of-war employed, in connection with the English steamer *Agamemnon*, in laying the first Atlantic cable in 1857 and 1858.

Niblo's Garden. A theatre on Broadway, New York, chiefly used for spectacular plays.

Nickajack Cave. A natural curiosity in Alabama on the borders of Georgia. The name is a corruption or improvement upon "Nigger Jack," the leader of a band of negroes who frequented this cave.

Nicolas des Champs. See St. Nicolas des Champs.

Nicolas du Chardonnet. A church in Paris, rebuilt in 1656-1709 in the Italian style of that time.

Niddrie Castle. A ruined feudal stronghold in Scotland not far from Linlithgow. Here Mary Queen of Scots tarried for a time after her escape from Lochleven.

Niederwald. The name given to a series of heights and also to a forest near Bingen on the Rhine.

Night, The. One of four colossal figures executed by Michael Angelo Buonarotti (1475-1564). In the church of S. Lorenzo, Florence, Italy.

☞ "The famous statue of the Night, *La Notte di Michelagnolo*, that work known by name to all who have heard of Michael Angelo. Of none can it be asserted with so much justice that he alone could have produced it."
Grimm, Trans.

Michel's *Night* and Day
And Dawn and Twilight wait in marble scorn. *Mrs. Browning.*

Night, The. A celebrated bas-relief by Albert Bertel Thorwaldsen (1770-1844), the Danish sculptor. It is well known by engravings.

Night. A picture by Sir Edwin Landseer (1803-1873), the celebrated English painter.

Night-Watch, The. A celebrated picture by Rembrandt van Ryn (1607-1669), the Dutch painter, the largest he ever painted, and regarded as his chief work, It is in the Amsterdam Gallery.

Nile, The. A colossal marble statue discovered during the pontificate of Leo X., and now in the Vatican, Rome.

☞ "A grand reclining statue called 'The Nile,' a copy of which is in the Tuileries. Nothing could be more graceful, more fluid, than these infantile diminutive creatures playing around this large body; nothing could better express the fulness, the repose, the indefinable, the almost divine life of a river." *Taine, Trans.*

Nilometer. [Arab. *Mekkeeás.*] This celebrated structure, situated on the island of Roda, near Cairo, Egypt, serves, as its name indicates, to measure the height of the water in the Nile. It consists of a square well or chamber, within which is a pillar graduated into cubits (each 21 7-16 inches long), those in the upper part of the pillar being subdivided into 24 digits each. Every day during the period of the inundation criers proclaim through the streets of Cairo the height to which the water has risen, as indicated by the Nilometer; and when it has reached a certain height the canals are opened, and the water flows over the land. The usual height to which the water rises (during the inundation) at Cairo is from 24 to 26 feet. The date of construction of the Nilometer at Roda is assigned to the ninth century.

☞ Among other Nilometers was one at Memphis in the time of the Pharaohs, one at Ilithyia in the time of the Ptolemies, and one at Elephantiné during the reigns of the early Roman emperors.

☞ "We crossed by a ferry-boat to the island of Roda, to see the Nilometer, which I was surprised to find a very pretty place; a damp, dim chamber, tufted with water-weeds, steep stairs down into it, and a green pool and mud at the bottom; in the centre, a graduated pillar; in the four sides of the chamber, four pointed arches, — one filled in with an elegant grating; round the cornice, and over the arches, Cufic inscriptions; and in two of the niches, within the arches, similar inscriptions. The crypt-like aspect of the chamber, with its aquatic adornments of weeds and mosses, — so perfectly in accordance with its purpose, — was charming." *Miss Martineau.*

Nîmes Arena. See ARENA.

Nina, The. One of the three vessels with which Columbus set sail for America from Palos, Spain, on the 3d of August, 1492. The *Nina* was commanded by Vincente Yanez Pinzon.

Nine Ladies. The name given to a so-called Druidical circle at Stanton Moor, England. It is formed of a circular mound of earth, about 36 feet in diameter, on which the upright stones are placed at irregular distances. In the centre are the remains of a sepulchral mound.

Niobe. A celebrated group of ancient sculpture, now in the gallery of the Uffizi Palace in Florence, Italy, representing Niobe mourning the death of her children slain by Apollo and Diana. It was found at Rome in 1583.

☞ "I saw nothing here so grand as the group of Niobe; if statues which are now disjointed and placed equi-distantly round a room may be so called. Niobe herself, clasped by the arm of her terrified child, is certainly a group, and, whether the head be original or not, the contrast of passion, of beauty, and even of dress, is admirable." *Forsyth.*

"The *Niobe* of nations! there she stands,
Childless and crownless in her voiceless woe." *Byron (on Rome).*

☞ "Niobe . . . is true tragedy. She is bending over her youngest child, who clings to her knees; and while in an agony of maternal love she encircles with her arm the most helpless of her devoted progeny, conscious despairing inability to save is expressed in every lineament of the living marble. The powerful pathos, and the deep-seated expression of agonizing grief, which speaks in her countenance and gesture, find their way at once to the heart." *Eaton.*

☞ "I seemed to be in the presence of a touching domestic tragedy, told in marble. The artist appeared to be swallowed up in his work. . . . The majesty of the subject seemed to brood over the chisel and guide its edge. . . . The grief of Niobe is feminine, deep, overwhelming, and hopeless, but not fierce or struggling. This exquisite group is not very happily placed: the figures are arranged in the form of an oval, the Niobe making the central point of interest, — a disposition which seems formal and unnatural." *Hillard.*

☞ "No wonder the strength of that woe depicted on her countenance should change her into stone. One of her sons — a beautiful, boyish form — is lying on his back, just expiring, with the chill languor of death creeping over his limbs. We seem to hear the quick whistling of the arrows, and look involuntarily into the air to see the hovering figure of the avenging god." *Bayard Taylor.*

Nivernais Ploughing. See PLOUGHING IN NIVERNAIS.

Noli me tangere. [Touch me not.] These words of Christ, spoken in the garden to Mary Magdalene (John xx. 17), make the subject of many pictures by the great painters of the Middle Ages. Of these compositions it will be sufficient to name as among the more celebrated, the following.

Noli me tangere. A great altar-piece by Federigo Baroccio (1528-1612), once very celebrated and well-known from the fine engraving by Raphael Morghen. Now in England.

Noli me tangere. A picture by Titian (1477-1576), representing the Magdalene as kneeling, and bending forward with one hand extended to touch the Saviour, who, "drawing his linen garment round him, shrinks back from her touch — yet with the softest expression of pity." Formerly in the collection of Rogers, the poet. Now in the National Gallery, London.

Noli me tangere. A picture by Rembrandt (1607-1669). In the Queen's Gallery, London.

Noli me tangere. A small picture by Mariotto Albertinelli (1474-1515), the Italian painter, and long attributed to Perugino. It is in the Louvre, Paris.

Nonantum Hill. An eminence — so called in colonial times — near Newton Corner, Mass. Here the Apostle Eliot preached to the Indians.

Nonnenwerth. An old Benedictine nunnery on an island of the same name in the Rhine.

Nonsuch House. A curious building that once stood upon London Bridge. According to Timbs, it was "so called because it was constructed in Holland entirely of wood, and, being brought over in pieces, was erected in this place with wooden pegs only, not a single nail being used in the whole structure. Its situation is even yet pointed out by the seventh and eighth arches of the bridge being still called the Draw Lock and the Nonsuch Lock."

Nonsuch Palace. A royal mansion erected by Henry VIII. in a little place called Codintone. The palace was so named in consequence of its then unequalled beauty. It was taken down in the seventeenth century.

Norfolk House. A noble house in St. James's Square, London, so called from the seventh Duke of Norfolk, who died here in 1701. George III. was born here in 1738.

Norfolk Street. A London street associated with Sir Roger de Coverley, and in which William Penn formerly lived.

Norman's Woe. A mass of rocks near the entrance of the harbor of Gloucester, Mass., familiar to many through Longfellow's ballad of "The Wreck of the Hesperus."

It was the schooner Hesperus
That sailed the wintry sea.

. . . .

And fast through the midnight dark and drear,
Through the whistling sleet and snow,
Like a sheeted ghost the vessel swept
Towards the reef of *Norman's Woe*.
Longfellow.

North Star. An Arctic exploring ship employed in the expedition of Capt. Saunders in 1849, and in that of Capt. Pullen in 1852-54.

Northumberland House. The city residence of the Duke of Northumberland, Strand, London. It was built by Henry Howard, the Earl of Northampton, who left it in 1614 to his nephew, Thomas Howard, Earl of Suffolk, when it received the name of *Suffolk House*. It was afterwards bought by Algernon Percy, Earl of Northumberland, from whom it received its present name. This mansion, called the finest great historical house in London, "commenced by a Howard, continued by a Percy, and completed by a Seymour," has been recently destroyed.

☞ "One only of the great Strand palaces has survived entire to our own time. We have all of us seen and mourned over Northumberland House, one of the noblest Jacobean buildings in England, and the most picturesque feature of London. . . . Of all the barbarous and ridiculous injuries by which London has been wantonly mutilated within the last few years, the destruction of Northumberland House has been the greatest." *Hare.*

Notch, The. [Known also as the *Crawford* Notch in distinction from the *Pinkham* and *Franconia* Notches.] A grand and impressive valley between Willey Mountain and Mount Webster in the White Mountains, New Hampshire. It contains the famous Willey House. Bayard Taylor, speaking of the view looking down upon the tremendous gulf of the Notch from the top of Mount Willard (at the head of the Notch), says, "As a simple mountain pass, seen from above, it cannot be surpassed in Switzerland. Something like it I have seen in the Taurus, otherwise I can recall no view with which to compare it." See WILLEY HOUSE.

☞ "I know nothing on the Rhine equal to the view from Mount Willard down the mountain pass called the Notch." *Anthony Trollope.*

He hears the echoes of a horn in a hill country, in the *Notch* mountains, for example, which converts the mountains into an Æolian harp, and this supernatural *tiralira* restores to him the Dorian mythology, Apollo, Diana, and all divine hunters and huntresses. *R. W. Emerson.*

Notre Dame. [Our Lady.] A name commonly applied in France to churches dedicated to the Virgin Mary. When the name is used in literature, unaccompanied by any designation of place, reference is usually intended to the metropolitan cathedral of Paris. See *infra.*

Notre Dame. [Our Lady.] The most celebrated church in Paris. It was begun by Pope Alexander the Third, but was not completed for nearly 300 years (not until 1420). It is built in the form of a Latin cross. The exterior is more imposing than the interior. The principal entrance is ornamented by bas-reliefs illustrative of the resurrection, and the seven cardinal virtues with their opposite vices. The interior is richly adorned with bas-reliefs, paintings, and sculptures, and magnificent rose-windows of stained glass, illustrating sacred history. The church is surrounded by 24 chapels. In one of the towers is a famous bell, weighing 32,000 pounds, which is rung only on very great occasions. This church has been often referred to of late years in connection with Père Hyacinthe, the distinguished monk and preacher, whose eloquence drew crowds within its walls until his independence and freedom of speech brought upon him the interdict of his superiors. The church has suffered from various alterations, and, in the time of the Revolution, from wanton desecration. It has, however, since 1845, been restored as nearly as possible in accordance with the old design.

☞ "We had been much disappointed at first by the apparently narrow limits of the interior of this famous church; but now, as we made our way round the choir, gazing into chapel after chapel, each with its painted window, its crucifix, its pictures, its confessional, and afterwards came back into the nave, where arch rises above arch to the lofty roof, we came to the conclusion that it was very sumptuous." *Hawthorne.*

☞ "The cathedral of Paris was designed at a time when the architects had not obtained that confidence in their own skill which made them afterwards complete masters of the constructive difficulties of the design. . . . The cathedral has not internally the same grandeur as the other three [those at Amiens, Chartres, and Rheims], though externally there is a very noble simplicity of outline and appearance of solidity in the whole design." *Fergusson.*

On Christmas day I went to see the Cathedrall of *Notre Dame*. . . This is the prime church of France for dignity, having Archdeacons, Vicars, Canons, Priests, and Chaplaines in good store to the number of 127. It is also the palace of the Archbishop. The young king (Louis XIV.) was there with a great and martial guard, who entered the Nave of the Church with drums and fifes, at the ceasing of which I was entertained with the church musiq. *John Evelyn, Diary.*

In these far climes it was my lot
To meet the wondrous Michael Scott;
A wizard of such dreaded fame
That when, in Salamanca's cave,
Him listed his magic wand to wave,
The bells would ring in *Notre Dame!*
Scott.

Next year as I, poor soul, by chance,
Through Paris strolled one day,
I saw him go to *Notre Dame*,
With all his court so gay.
Béranger, Trans.

And when the morning sun was bright,
When wind and wave were calm,
And flamed in thousand-tinted light
The rose of *Notre Dame*. *Holmes.*

The very youth of the schools gave up their pipes and billiards for some time and flocked in crowds to *Notre Dame*. *Thackeray.*

Notre Dame [d'Amiens]. A magnificent Gothic church in Amiens, France, one of the finest church edifices in Europe. It was founded in 1220. It is larger than any cathedral in Europe except St. Peter's and Cologne. Its length is 469 feet, and the height of its spire 422 feet. It is dedicated to the Virgin.

☞ "The interior is one of the most magnificent spectacles that architectural skill can ever have produced. The mind is filled and elevated by its enormous height, its lofty and many-colored clerestory, its grand proportions, its noble simplicity. . . . Such terms will not be considered extravagant when it is recollected that the vault is half as high again as Westminster Abbey." *Whewell.*

Notre Dame [de Rouen]. A fine Gothic church of the thirteenth century, in Rouen, France, dedicated to the Virgin. It abounds in profuse and elaborate ornamentation.

Notre Dame. An immense church in Montreal, Can., the largest in America. It was built in 1824. It is 255 feet long and 145 feet wide, with a seating capacity of 10,000. It has two towers, in one of which hangs the largest bell on the continent. See GROS BOURDON.

Notre Dame de Lorette. A gorgeously decorated modern church in Paris, begun in 1823, and built in imitation of the smaller Roman basilicas.

Notre Dame du Spasme [*or* du Pâmoison]. See SPASIMO, LO.

Notre Dame des Victoires. [*or* Church of Petits Pères.] A church of the Austin friars in Paris, completed in 1739.

Notre Dame, Parvis. See PARVIS NOTRE DAME.

Notte, La. [The Night.] A celebrated picture of the Nativity by Antonio Allegri, surnamed Correggio (1494–1534), remarkable for the striking effect produced by the light proceeding from the infant Saviour. This picture is in the Dresden Gallery.

☞ "Correggio has been much admired for representing in his famous Nativity the whole picture as lighted by the glory which proceeds from the divine Infant, as if the idea had been new and original. It occurs frequently before and since his time, and is founded upon the legendary story . . . which describes the cave or stable filled with dazzling and supernatural light."
Mrs. Jameson.

☞ "All the powers of art are here united to make a perfect work. Here the simplicity of the drawing of the Virgin and Child is shown in contrast with the foreshortening of the group of angels. The emitting the light from the body of the child, though a supernatural illusion, is eminently successful. The matchless beauty of the Virgin and Child, the group of angels overhead, the daybreak in the sky, and the whole arrangement of light and shade, give it a right to be considered, in conception at least, the greatest of his [Correggio's] works. . . . I consider it one of the first works the art of painting has to boast of."
Wilkie.

Nozze Aldobrandini. See ALDOBRANDINI MARRIAGE.

Nozze di Cana. See MARRIAGE AT CANA.

Nuova Gerusalemme. See MONTE SACRO.

Nuremberg Eggs. The name by which are known two curious old watches in the Green Vault (Grüne Gewölbe) in Dresden. They are so called from their form and from the place in which they were made, in 1500.

Nursery, The. A building in Golding Lane, London, erected during the reign of Charles II. as a school for the training of children for the stage. It was standing till the present century.

Near these a *Nursery* erects its head,
Where queens are formed, and future heroes bred,
Where unfledged actors learn to laugh and cry,
Where infant punks their tender voices try,
And little Maximins the gods defy.
Dryden.

Nymphenburg. A royal palace in the immediate neighborhood of Munich, Bavaria.

O.

Oak Hill. A beautiful cemetery in Georgetown, D.C. It contains the tombs of many eminent men.

Oak of Guernica. A venerable tree of Guernica, Spain, cut down by the French in 1808. According to Laborde, it was a very ancient natural monument. Under this oak Ferdinand and Isabella, in 1476, swore to maintain the municipal laws (*fueros*) of the Biscayans.

Oak of Guernica! Tree of holier power
Than that which in Dodona did enshrine
(So faith too fondly deemed) a voice divine,
Heard from the depths of its aërial bower,
How canst thou flourish at this blighting hour? *Wordsworth.*

Oak of Reformation. A tree in Norfolk County, England, associated with an insurrection in 1549, called Kett's Rebellion. Kett held a court, and assemblies of his adherents, around this tree; and after the rebellion was finally subdued, many of the insurgents were hung upon its branches.

Oatlands. An ancient royal residence near Hampton Court, in England. It was built by Henry VIII., but is no longer standing.

Obelisk of Axum. A remarkable monument at Axum in Nubia, Africa. It is the only one now standing of a group said to have consisted of 55.

☞ "The most exceptional monuments in the world,—the obelisks at Axum. . . . Its height [that of the one now standing] is 60 feet, its width at base nearly 10, and it is of one stone. The idea is evidently Egyptian, but the details are Indian. It is, in fact, an Indian nine-storied pagoda, translated in Egyptian in the first century of the Christian era!" *Fergusson.*

Obelisk of Heliopolis. This obelisk—the oldest in Egypt—which with some mounds is about all that remains of Heliopolis (that great seat of learning where Plato and Eudoxus lived and studied), is between 60 and 70 feet in height. Tradition speaks of another similar obelisk which stood opposite this, according to the Egyptian custom of placing them in pairs at the entrances of their temples.

☞ "A class of monuments almost exclusively Egyptian, are the obelisks, which form such striking objects in front of almost all the old temples of the country. . . . The two finest known to exist are, that now in the piazza of the Lateran, originally set up by Thotmes III., 105 feet in height, and that still existing at Karnac, erected by Thotmes I., 93 feet. Those of Luxor, erected by Rhamses the Great, one of which is now in Paris, are above 77 feet in height; and there are two others in Rome, each above 80 feet. Rome, indeed, has 12 of these monuments within her walls,—a greater number than exist, erect at least, in the country whence they came. Their use seems to have been wholly that of monumental pillars recording the style and title of the king who erected them, his piety, and the proof he gave of it in dedicating these monoliths to the deity whom he especially wished to honor. With scarcely an exception all the pyramids are on the west side of the Nile, all the obelisks on the east. With regard to the former, this probably arose from a law of their existence, the western side of the Nile being in all ages preferred for sepulture; but with regard to the latter it seems to be accidental." *Fergusson.*

Obelisk of Luxor. A magnificent monolith of red Egyptian granite in the Place de la Concorde, Paris. It was one of two obelisks of the same shape and size, erected in 1350 B.C., by Rameses the Great, at the entrance of the temple of Thebes (now Luxor). It was a gift to the French Government from Mohammed Ali, Pasha of Egypt; was removed with much difficulty, at a great cost; and was raised in its present position in 1836, by a very skilful feat of engineering, in the presence of Louis Philippe and 150,000 persons. The removal of this obelisk, which is 74 feet high and weighs 500,000 pounds, employed 800 men, and cost, including its elevation, £80,000. It was brought to France in a vessel especially built for the purpose.

Obelisk of Orsotasen. One of the earliest and finest of the Egyptian obelisks, still standing at Heliopolis. It is inscribed with the name of Orsotasen, one of the greatest rulers of the twelfth dynasty.

☞ "It is 67 feet 4 inches in height, without the pyramidion which crowns it, and is a splendid block of granite, weighing 217 tons. It must have required immense skill to quarry it, to transport it from Syene, and finally, after finishing it, to erect it where it now stands and has stood for 4,500 years." *Fergusson.*

Obelisk of St. Peter's, *or* **of the Vatican.** A celebrated Egyptian column of red granite, brought from Heliopolis to Rome by the Emperor Caligula, and now standing in front of St. Peter's Church. It is 132 feet in height, and its weight is 360 tons. Pliny says that the ship which brought the obelisk from Heliopolis was almost as long as "the left side of the port of Ostia." It was successfully set up in its present position by Domenico Fontana, and it is about the raising of this obelisk that the following familiar story is told. The ceremony having been preceded by high mass in St. Peter's, and solemn benediction having been pronounced upon Fontana and the workmen, the Pope ordered that no one should speak, under penalty of death, while the obelisk was being raised. But, owing to the stretching of the ropes, the immense mass did not quite reach the required position, and the operation would have failed, had not a man in the crowd broken over the order of the Pope, and called to the workmen to "wet the ropes." This suggestion was immediately acted upon, and the huge column slowly rose to its destined place. This story is not found in any writer of that period; and it is, according to Platner, one of those inventions which spring from a wish to disparage the triumphs of genius, and to lower its claims.

Obelisk of the Lateran. An Egyptian monument of red granite, nearly 150 feet in height, originally belonging to the Temple of the Sun at Heliopolis, removed thence to Alexandria by Constantine, and subsequently brought to Rome, where it now stands in the centre of the Piazza di San Giovanni. It is the oldest object in Rome, being referred by antiquaries to the year 1740 B.C., when it was erected to the memory of Thotmes IV.

Obelisk of the Monte Cavallo. A famous Egyptian monument of red granite, being a plain shaft without hieroglyphics, which formerly stood in front of the Mausoleum of Augustus, and is now in the Piazza di Monte Cavallo, Rome. It was brought from Egypt by the Emperor Claudius, A.D. 57.

Obelisk of the Piazza del Popolo. An ancient Egyptian column, brought from Heliopolis to Rome by the Emperor Augustus, and set up in the Piazza of the People in 1589. It is of the age of Moses.

☞ "This red granite obelisk, oldest of things even in Rome, . . . with hardly a trace of decay upon it, is the first thing the traveller sees after entering the Flaminian Gate." *Hawthorne.*

Obelisk of the Vatican. See OBELISK OF ST. PETER'S.

Ocean, The. An armor-plated ship of the British navy, launched March 19, 1863.

Ocean Monarch. An American emigrant ship, burned off Liverpool, Aug. 24, 1848, with a loss of nearly 200 lives.

October Club. A Parliamentary club in London, first formed about 1690, in the reign of William III. and Mary. Its meetings were first held at the Bell Tavern, and afterwards at the Crown, in King Street, Westminster. The influence of Swift had much to do with the final breaking up of the October Club; the more violent Jacobites seceding, and forming the "March Club." A writer in "The National Review" thus describes the October Club: "The high-flying Tory country gentleman and country member drank the health of the king, — sometimes over the water-decanter, — and flustered himself with bumpers in honor of Dr. Sacheverell and the Church of England, with true-blue spirits of his own kidney, at the October Club, which, like the Beef-Steak Club, was named after the cheer for which it was famed, — *October ale;* or rather, on account of the quantities of the ale which the members drank. The 150 squires, Tories to the backbone, who, under the above name, met at the Bell Tavern in King Street, Westminster, were of opinion that the party to which they belonged were too backward in punishing and turning out the Whigs; and they gave infinite trouble to the Tory administration which came into office under the leadership of Harley, St. John, and Harcourt, in 1710. The Administration were for proceeding moderately with their rivals, and for generally replacing opponents with partisans. The October Club were for immediately impeaching every member of the Whig party, and for turning out, without a day's grace, every placeman who did not wear their colors, and shout their cries."

☞ "We are plagued here with an October Club; that is, a set of above a hundred Parliament men of the country, who drink October beer at home, and meet every evening at a tavern near the Parliament, to consult affairs, and drive things on to extremes against the Whigs, to call the old ministry to account, and get off five or six heads."

Swift (*to Stella*, February, 1710-11).

Odeon, L'. A well-known theatre in Paris, originally intended, as the name indicates, for music only, but used for regular dramatic performances. It has been several times destroyed by fire. Beaumarchais' "Marriage of Figaro" (Mariage de Figaro) was first produced here in 1784.

Odeum. A structure in ancient Athens, Greece, built by Pericles, and designed (as the name implies, ᾠδή) for musical performances. It was surmounted by a circular roof, constructed with the masts and yards of the Persian ships which were captured at Salamis. Nothing remains of the Odeum, but it has given its name to buildings in modern times designed for similar uses.

Œil de Bœuf. A famous anteroom in the palace at Versailles, the scene of many quarrels, intrigues, *bon mots*. Here waited the courtiers in attendance upon Louis XIV.

Versailles, the *Œil de Bœuf*, and all men and things, are drowned in a sea of Light; Monseigneur and that high beckoning Head are alone, with each other, in the universe. *Carlyle.*

As experience in the river is indispensable to the ferryman, so is knowledge of his Parliament to the British Peel or Chatham; so was knowledge of the *Œil-de-Bœuf* to the French Choiseul. *Ibid.*

Œnone. A life-size statue by Harriet Hosmer (b. 1831). In the Mercantile Library building, St. Louis, Mo.

Olave's, St. See St. Olave's.

Old Bailey, The. 1. A street in London extending from Ludgate-hill to Newgate Street. It has been the scene of many memorable executions.

2. The Old Bailey Sessions Court, or Central Criminal Court, at the bar of which upwards of 2,000 persons are annually tried, is located here, immediately adjoining the prison called Newgate.

☞ "But the jail was a vile place, in which most kinds of debauchery and villany were practised, and where dire diseases were bred, that came into court with the prisoners, and sometimes rushed straight from the dock at my Lord Chief Justice himself, and pulled him off the bench. . . . For the rest, the Old Bailey was famous as a kind of deadly inn-yard, from which pale travellers set out continually, in carts and coaches, on a violent passage into the other world: traversing some two miles and a half of public street and road, and shaming few good citizens, if any. . . . It was famous, too, for the pillory, a wise old institution, that inflicted a punishment of which no one could foresee the extent; also, for the whipping-post, another dear old institution, very humanizing and softening to behold in action; also, for extensive transactions in blood-money, another fragment of ancestral wisdom, systematically leading to the most frightful mercenary crimes that could be committed under Heaven. . . . For, people then paid to see the play at the Old Bailey, just as they paid to see the play in Bedlam — only the former entertainment was much the dearer. Therefore, all the Old Bailey doors were well guarded — except, indeed, the social doors by which the criminals got there, and they were always left wide open." *Dickens.*

In short, Jane Rouse was accused of witchcraft; and though she made the best defence she could, it was all to no purpose: she was taken from her own bar to the bar of the *Old Bailey*, condemned and executed accordingly. These were times, indeed, when even women could not scold in safety. *Goldsmith.*

When will you pay me?
Say the bells at *Old Bailey*.
Mother Goose.

Old Cumberland Road. See NATIONAL ROAD.

Old Dutch Church. An ancient church-edifice in New York City, built in 1723. It served as a prison for Americans during the British occupation of the city in the Revolution, and was used by the British cavalry as a riding-school.

Old Elm, The. A venerable tree which stood on the Common in Boston, Mass., until Feb. 15, 1876, when it was overthrown by a high wind. It is believed to have been standing before the settlement of the town. It is supposed to have been the oldest tree in New England. It was laid down upon a map engraved in 1722, and a computation of the rings of the branch broken off in 1860 would carry the age of that limb to 1670.

Old Ironsides. See CONSTITUTION.

Old Jewry. A street in London so named from the Jews who dwelt in and near it.

I am sent for this morning by a friend in the *Old Jewry* to come to him. *Ben Jonson.*

Old Lady of Threadneedle Street. See BANK OF ENGLAND.

Old Man of Hoy. A natural curiosity in the Orkney Islands, in the shape of a solitary pillar, rising perpendicularly to the height of 300 feet, and bearing the likeness of the human form.

"See *Hoy's Old Man* whose summit bare
Pierces the dark blue fields of air;
Based in the sea, his fearful form
Glows like the spirit of the storm."

Old Man of Storr. A natural curiosity in the North of Scotland, near the town of Portree. It consists of a solitary black pillar of trap rock, 160 feet in height.

Old Man of the Mountain. See PROFILE, THE.

Old Manse. An ancient house in Concord, Mass., built before the Revolution, which derives its present name from the celebrity given to it by Hawthorne's tales, the "Mosses from an Old Manse." Here he lived and wrote, and in this house also Emerson was born and lived.

Old Protestant Cemetery. See PROTESTANT CEMETERY.

Old Shepherd's Chief Mourner. A picture by Sir Edwin Landseer (1804–1873).

☞ "One of the most perfect poems or pictures (I use the words as synonymous) which modern times have seen. The close pressure of the dog's breast against the wood, the convulsive clinging of the paws, which has dragged the blanket off the trestle, the total powerlessness of the head, laid close and motionless upon its folds, the fixed and tearful fall of the eye in its utter hopelessness; . . . these are all thoughts by which the picture is separated at once from hundreds of equal merit, so far as mere painting goes, by which it ranks as a work of high art, and stamps its author not as the neat imitator of the texture of a skin, or the fold of a drapery, but as the Man of Mind." *Ruskin.*

Old South. An historic church in Boston, Mass., identified with the early struggles for independence, and associated with many interesting persons and events. The present edifice was built in 1729 on the site of an older church, in which Benjamin Franklin had been baptized. The famous assemblage of citizens known as the Boston Tea Party marched from this church to the attack upon the ships in the harbor. During the British occupation of Boston, in 1775, the pews were removed, and the church was turned into a riding-school for the cavalry. In 1876 the church was sold, and passed into the hands of an association which aims to preserve it as an historical relic, and has converted it into a museum of antiquities and curiosities. The society upon leaving their former place of worship built a new and fine church edifice at the corner of Boylston and Dartmouth Streets, costing about $500,000.

So long as Boston shall Boston be,
And her bay-tides rise and fall,
Shall freedom stand in the *Old South Church*,
And plead for the rights of all.
Whittier.

On the cross-beam under the *Old South* bell,
The nest of a pigeon is builded well.
In summer and winter that bird is there,
Out and in with the morning air.
N. P. Willis.

And while from mouth to mouth
Spread the tidings of dismay,
I stood in the *Old South*,
Saying humbly, "Let us pray!"
Longfellow.

Old State House. An ancient edifice in Boston, Mass., originally used for the sessions of the colonial legislature. It was built in 1748. In 1770 occurred the affair between the British guard stationed in this building and the citizens, which is known as the "Boston Massacre." The building is now used for business purposes.

Old Stone Face. See Profile.

Old Stone Mill. A circular stone tower at Newport, R.I., supported on round arches and overgrown with ivy. There has been much dispute among antiquarians with regard to the origin and purpose of this ancient tower. Some think it was built in the eleventh century by the Norsemen; others, that it was erected for a windmill, in the seventeenth century, by some colonial governor. It is not mentioned by Verrazzani, who, in 1524, spent 15 days in the harbor, and explored the land. It is, on the other hand, different in architecture and construction from other works of the early colonists. Gov. Benedict Arnold (d. 1678) bequeathed the structure in his will, calling it "my stone-built windmill." Cooper has laid the opening scenes of "The Spy" in this vicinity, and Longfellow has connected with it his poem of "The Skeleton in Armor."

☞ "On the ancient structure in Newport there are no ornaments remaining, which might possibly have served to guide us in assigning the probable date of its erection. . . . From such characteristics as remain, however, we can scarcely form any other inference than one in which I am persuaded that all who are familiar with old Northern architecture will concur, — that this building was erected at a period decidedly not later than the twelfth century. . . . That this building could not have been erected for a windmill, is what an architect will easily discern." *Professor Rafn.*

☞ "Some thirty-five years ago, Professor Rafn, of the Royal Society of Northern Antiquaries at Copenhagen, published a book showing that the Northmen, or Scandinavians, undoubtedly visited the shores of North America about A.D. 1000, and that they probably entered Narragansett Bay. It then occurred to some American antiquaries that this old building at Newport might have been erected by those early voyagers. . . . As for the Old Stone Mill, it is found to be very much like some still standing in that very county of England from which Gov. Arnold came. So it is not at all likely that any of these memorials could date back as far as the time of the Northmen; and yet it is altogether probable that the Northmen visited America at a very early time." *T. W. Higginson.*

☞ "I will not enter into a discussion of the point. It is sufficiently well established for the purpose of a ballad; though doubtless many an honest citizen of Newport, who has passed his days within sight of the Round Tower, will be ready to exclaim with Sancho, 'God bless me! did I not warn you to have a care of what you were doing, for that it was nothing but a windmill; and nobody could mistake it, but one who had the like in his head.'" *Longfellow.*

And who has not seen, 'mid the summer's gay crowd,
That old pillared tower of their fortalice proud,
How it stands solid proof of the sea chieftains' reign
Ere came with Columbus those galleys of Spain? *A. C. Coxe.*

Old Swan. An old London tavern, Thames Street, in existence as early as 1323, burnt in the Great Fire of 1666, and afterwards rebuilt.

Old Swedes' Church. An ancient and quaint church edifice in Wilmington, Del., founded in 1698, with contributions from William Penn, Queen Anne, and others.

Old Swedes' Church. An ancient and venerable church edifice in Philadelphia, Penn. It was built in 1700, occupying the site of a still older log church, and was the place of worship of the Swedes prior to the arrival of William Penn.

Old Téméraire. See FIGHTING TÉMÉRAIRE.

Old Wagon. See UNITED STATES.

Old Witch House. See WITCH HOUSE.

Oliveto, Monte. See MONTE OLIVETO.

Oltr' Arno. A quarter in Florence, Italy, on the southern side of the river, the Arno, which divides the city.

Olympian Jupiter. A famous statue of antiquity, executed by Phidias (500 B.C.?), the Greek sculptor, for the Temple of Jupiter at Elis.

Olympic, The. 1. A theatre near the Strand, London.

2. A vaudeville and varieties theatre in New York City.

Olympieum. A magnificent temple to the Olympian Zeus in Athens, Greece. The Athenians began this temple in the first period of their greatness, the Greek princes of Asia continued it, Augustus left it unfinished, and, 650 years after it was begun, Hadrian completed and dedicated it. During the Dark Ages it served as a quarry of building-stone for the Athenians. Fifteen lofty Corinthian columns of Pentelic marble, rising to a height of more than 60 feet, are now standing as the remains of this colossal temple. Livy speaks of this temple as the only one in the world undertaken "upon a scale commensurate with the majesty of the god."

☞ "The charm of this stately group of columns is all their own, for they boast no such fascinating associations as those which cluster around the ruins on the Acropolis. Begun by the tyrant Pisistratus, and finished 700 years afterwards by the Roman Emperor Hadrian, the Olympieum, though one of the grandest temples in the world, seems hardly a part of the glory of Athens, — breathes not her peculiar spirit, nor is redolent with the aroma of her soil." *T. Chase.*

Onoko, Glen. See GLEN ONOKO.

Ontario, Fort. See FORT ONTARIO.

Ophelia. A picture by John Everett Millais (b. 1827), the English painter.

Or San Michele. A celebrated church in Florence, Italy, erected towards the close of the fourteenth century. The name is derived from the Horreum, or granary of St. Michael, the first building on the site having been used as a storehouse for corn.

☞ "Or San Michele would have been a world's wonder, had it stood alone, and not been companioned with such wondrous rivals that its own exceeding beauty scarce ever receives full justice. Surely that square-set strength, as of a fortress towering against the clouds, and catching the last light always on its fretted parapet, and everywhere embossed 'and enriched with foliage and tracery and figures of saints, and the shadows of vast arches, and the light of niches gold-starred and filled with divine forms, is a gift so perfect to the whole world, that, passing it, one should need say a prayer for the great Taddeo's soul."

Pascarel, Trans.

Here and there an unmistakable antiquity stands in its own impressive shadow; the church of *Or San Michele*, for instance, once a market, but which grew to be a church by some inherent fitness and inevitable consecration. *Hawthorne.*

Oratoire. A French Protestant church in the Rue St. Honoré and Rue de Rivoli, Paris, originally erected in 1630 for the priests of the Oratory.

Order of Fools. An association founded in 1381 by Adolphus, Count of Cleves. It consisted of gentlemen of the highest rank and character, and their object was the promotion of benevolence and charity.

Ordinance, The. A picture by Jean Louis Ernest Meissonier (b. 1811), the French painter.

Ordre, Tour d'. See TOUR D'ORDRE.

Oread, The. A seminary in Worcester, Mass. The buildings are of stone.

Oriel College. A noted college in Oxford, England, founded about 1326, one of the 19 colleges included in the University.

Orient, L'. A French vessel, the blowing-up of which formed a decisive point in the Battle of the Nile. An incident connected with the destruction of the vessel is commemorated by Mrs. Hemans in her well-known poem of "Casabianca," which begins: —

"The boy stood on the burning deck."

Young Casabianca, a boy 13 years old, son of the commander, remained at his post after the ship had taken fire and all the guns had been abandoned, and was blown up with the vessel when the flames reached the magazine.

Oriental Club. A London club, established in 1824 by Sir John Malcolm. The Alfred Club joined the Oriental in 1855.

Oriente, Plaza de. See PLAZA DE ORIENTE.

Orleans House. The former residence of Louis Philippe, and afterwards of his son, the Duc d'Aumale, at Twickenham, near London.

Orloff Diamond. This great diamond of the sceptre of Russia is said to weigh 193 carats. It was once the eye of an Indian idol. Catherine II. bought it, in 1775, for £90,000, with the addition of an annuity of £4,000, and a patent of nobility.

☞ "For a time supposed to be the largest in the world. It turns out to be smaller than the Koh-i-nor, though (to my eyes at least) of a purer water."

Bayard Taylor.

Eye of a god was this blazing stone,
Beyond the snows of the Himalaya.

E. D. Proctor.

Orpheus. A statue by Thomas Crawford (1814–1857). In the Museum of Fine Arts, Boston, Mass.

Orpheus, The. A British steam corvette which foundered off the coast of New Zealand, Feb. 7, 1863, with a loss of nearly two hundred lives.

Orpheus charming the Animal World. A picture by Paul Potter (1625–1654), the Dutch painter, and one of his most admired works. It is now in the Amsterdam Museum.

Orr's Island. A small island in Casco Bay, near Harpswell, Me., made familiar by Mrs. H. B. Stowe's story, "The Pearl of Orr's Island."

Orsay, Palais d'. This palace, opposite the Tuileries Gardens, one of the most imposing in Paris, was begun by Napoleon I., and completed by Louis Philippe. It cost more than half a million sterling, and the interior is adorned with beautiful frescos and paintings. The building was designed for exhibiting the works of industry of France, but under the Republic it was used for the sittings of the Cours des Comptes and the Conseil d'Etat.

Orsotasen. See OBELISK OF ORSOTASEN.

Orto del Paradiso. [Garden of Paradise.] A chapel, so called from its remarkable splendor, in the Church of Santa Prassede in Rome. It contains the famous relic — one of chief objects of pilgrimage in Rome — the column to which the Saviour is said to have been bound. The column, which is of blood jasper, is said to have been obtained from the Saracens by Giovanni Colonna, cardinal of this church. The present name of the chapel (Colonna Santa) is derived from this relic.

Osborne House. The sea-shore residence of Queen Victoria, situated in the Isle of Wight, in the immediate neighborhood of East Cowes. At the corner of the palace is a massive tower which is a conspicuous object for miles around, and affords a magnificent view.

Osgoode Hall. A fine structure in Toronto, the capital of Ontario, Can. It contains the superior law courts of the province.

☞ "The Osgoode Hall is to Upper Canada what the Four Courts are to Ireland. The law courts are all held there." *Anthony Trollope.*

Ostiensis, Porta. See PORTA OSTIENSIS.

Otsego Hall. The old mansion of the Cooper family in Cooperstown, N.Y. It was destroyed by fire in 1854.

Otsgaragee Cavern. See HOWE'S CAVE.

Ouen, St. See ST. OUEN.

Our English Coasts. A picture by William Holman Hunt (b. 1827), and regarded as one of his master-pieces. Painted in 1853.

Our Lady of Loreto. See SANTA CASA.

Our Lady of Walsingham. See SHRINE OF OUR LADY OF WALSINGHAM.

Outer House. The name by which the Parliament House in Edinburgh, Scotland, is now known. See PARLIAMENT HOUSE.

Overland Route. A name frequently applied to the new and shorter route between England and India *via* the Suez Canal. A mail-route by the way of the Isthmus of Suez was established by Lieut. Waghorn, in 1847, effecting a saving in time of 13 days. The term was also formerly applied to the direct route from the Eastern States to California.

Oxford and Cambridge Club. A club in London, for members of these two universities. The club-house in Pall Mall was finished in 1838. There are 500 members from each university.

Oxford Arms. A quaint and celebrated old London inn in Warwick Lane. It was destroyed in 1877.

These are to notify that Edward Bartlett . . has removed his inn in London . . . to the *Oxford Arms*, in Warwick Lane, where he did inn before the Fire. *London Gazette*, 1672-73.

Oxford Marbles. See ARUNDELIAN MARBLES.

Oxford Street. A well-known street in London, a mile and a half in length, and extending westward to Hyde Park corner.

☞ "It is the longest, broadest, and in a certain sense the most important thoroughfare in London. . . . It is, however, really the continuation of a great street, which runs very directly through London from east to west, and which is called successively, beginning at the east, Mile End, Whitechapel Road, Aldgate High Street, Leadenhall Street, Cornhill, Cheapside, Newgate Street, Skinner Street, Holborn, Oxford Street."

Richard Grant White.

☞ "The various, shifting, motley group that belong to Oxford Street, and to Oxford Street alone! What thoroughfares equal thee in the variety of human specimens! in the choice of objects for remark, satire, admiration! Besides, the other streets seem chalked out for a sect, narrow-minded and devoted to a *coterie*. Thou alone art catholic — all receiving." *N. P. Willis.*

My good people, I hardly see you. You no more interest me than a dozen orange-women in Covent Garden, or a shop book-keeper in *Oxford Street*. *Thackeray.*

Yet my creature said
She saw her stop to speak in *Oxford Street*
To one . . . no matter! *Mrs. Browning.*

Ozinda's. A coffee-house which was situated in St. James's Street, London.

A Whig will no more go to the Cocoa-tree or *Ozinda's* than a Tory will be seen at the Coffee-house, St. James's.

Journey through England, 1714.

P.

Pacific, The. A steamer belonging to the Collins line, plying between New York and Liverpool. She left the latter port Jan. 23, 1856, with nearly 200 persons on board, and was never heard from afterwards.

Paddington. A now populous district of London.

> Pitt is to Addington,
> As London is to *Paddington*.
> *Canning.*

Paddock Elms. A row of stately elms which, until recently, stood before the Old Granary Burying-ground in Boston, Mass. They were brought from England and planted by Capt. Adino Paddock, a loyalist, about 1762. During the British occupation of the city they were well cared for and protected, but within a few years have been cut down.

> We walked under Mr. Paddock's row of English elms. The gray squirrels were out looking for their breakfasts; and one of them came toward us in light, soft, intermittent leaps, until he was close to the rail of the burial-ground. *Holmes.*

Pæstum, Roses of. See ROSES OF PÆSTUM.

Painted Chamber. A room of historical interest in the Old Palace at Westminster, so called from its having been painted by order of Henry III. It was hung with tapestries representing the siege of Troy. In this room Parliament sat for a time. The building was taken down in 1852.

Painter in his Studio. An admired picture by Jean Louis Ernest Meissonier (b. 1811).

Painting. See HISTORY OF PAINTING.

Pair, The. See MEMNON.

Paix, Ile de. See ILE DE PAIX.

Paix, Rue de la. One of the principal streets of Paris, extending from the Place Vendôme to the Boulevart des Capucines. Here are some of the most elegant shops in Paris, over which are fashionable residences and hotels.

> Nay, it was said that his victories were not confined to the left bank of the Seine; reports did occasionally come to us of fabulous adventures by him, accomplished in the far regions of the *Rue de la Paix*. *Thackeray.*

> There is a little Jewess hanging about the Louvre, who begs with her dark eyes very eloquently; and in the *Rue de la Paix* there may be found at all hours a melancholy, sick-looking, Italian boy, with his hand in his bosom, whose native language and picture-like face are a diurnal pleasure to me. *N. P. Willis.*

Palace of Augustus. See PALACE OF THE CÆSARS.

Palace of Justice. See PALAIS DE JUSTICE.

Palace of the Cæsars. A mass of ruins upon the Palatine Hill, in Rome, being all that now remains of the extensive buildings erected by Augustus Cæsar and succeeding emperors for the imperial residence. The palace of Augustus, built upon the site of the houses of Hortensius, Cicero, Catiline, and Claudius, was the first Palace of the Cæsars. It was enlarged in different directions by Tiberius and by Caligula, and the Golden House of Nero with its grounds spread over the Esquiline and Cœlian hills, as well as the Palatine. Vespasian afterward contracted the limits of the immense edifice, and Titus made use of part of the foundations upon the Esquiline in building his Baths. The Palace of the Cæsars was repeatedly altered and rebuilt by the different succeeding emperors, and these various changes have all combined to make a most confused mass of ruins. See GOLDEN HOUSE.

☞ "In Rome itself no ancient house — indeed, no trace of a domestic edifice — exists, except the Palace of the Cæsars on the Palatine Mount; and this, even, is now merely a congeries of shapeless ruins, so completely destroyed as to have defied even the most imaginative of restorers to make much of it except a vehicle for the display of his own ingenuity. The extent of these ruins, coupled with the descriptions that have been preserved, suffice to convince us that of all the palaces ever built, either in the East or the West, this was probably the most magnificent and the most gorgeously adorned. Never in the world's history does it appear that so much wealth and power were at the command of one man as was the case with the Cæsars, and never could the world's wealth have fallen into the hands of men more inclined to lavish it for their own personal gratification than those emperors were. They could, moreover, ransack the whole world for plunder to adorn their dwellings, and could command the best artists of Greece, and of all the subject kingdoms, to assist in rendering their golden palaces the most gorgeous that the world had then seen, or is likely soon to see again. The whole area of the palace may roughly be described as a square platform, measuring 1,500 feet east and west, with a mean breadth of 1,300 feet in the opposite direction. Owing, however, to its deeply-indented and irregular outline, it hardly covers more ground than the Baths of Caracalla. . . . Notwithstanding all its splendor, this palace was probably, as an architectural object, inferior to the Thermæ. In its glory the Palace of the Cæsars must have been the world's wonder; but as a ruin, deprived of its furniture and ephemeral splendor, it loses much that would tend to make it either pleasing or instructive." *Fergusson.*

☞ "Imagine a hill, upwards of a mile in circuit, and less than 200 feet high, strewn with shapeless ruins and yawning with excavations to such an extent that the original soil is almost displaced by fragments of brick and mortar; intersperse it with kitchen gardens for the growing of such matter-of-fact vegetables as cauliflower, artichokes, and lettuce; throw in occasionally the vine, the laurel, the cypress, and the ivy; overshadow it with here and there a stately oak; crown the whole with a smart modern villa, — and you will have some notion of the Palace of the Cæsars." *Hillard.*

Where the Cæsars dwelt,
And dwell the tuneless birds of night, amidst
A grove which springs through levell'd battlements,
And twines its roots with the imperial hearths,
Ivy usurps the laurel's place of growth;
But the gladiators' bloody Circus stands,
A noble wreck in ruinous perfection!
While Cæsar's chambers, and the Augustan halls;
Grovel on earth in indistinct decay.

Byron.

Palace of the Conservators. See PIAZZA DEL CAMPIDOGLIO.

Palace of the Lateran. See LATERAN, PALACE OF THE.

Palace of the Luxembourg. See PALAIS DE LUXEMBOURG.

Palace of the Senator. See PIAZZA DEL CAMPIDOGLIO.

Palace. For names beginning with the word PALACE, see the next prominent word of the title. See also *supra.*

Palais Bourbon. See PALAIS DU CORPS LÉGISLATIF.

Palais de Justice. This ancient palace in Paris is very interesting from its associations. It was built by one of the Capets, and was the residence of several of the ancient kings. It was originally small, but has been enlarged at various times, and of late has been greatly improved and adorned. The square tower, known as the "Tour de l'Horloge," was built in the time of Philippe Augustus. This tower contains a famous clock which was made by a German and presented to Charles V. The tocsin, or alarm-bell, which was rung at the death of a king or the birth of a dauphin, hung in this tower. This bell also, in response to the alarm from the bell of St. Germain l'Auxerrois, sounded the death-signal for the massacre of the Huguenots. The steps approaching the palace are adorned by figures representing Justice, Prudence, and Force. Since the reign of Charles V. the palace has served for the Parliament of Paris, courts of justice, and a prison. A Roman palace or castle is supposed to have been built upon this site. The Sainte Chapelle, the clock-tower, the kitchen of St. Louis, two circular towers, and some vaults, are all that remain of the ancient palace, the rest having been destroyed by fire. Here is the famous Conciergerie, or ancient prison, where so many victims were confined during the Reign of Terror.

Palais de l'Industrie. A building of stone and glass in the Champs Elysées, Paris, built in 1852 for the exhibition of objects of national industry. Here was held the exhibition of 1855, for the accommodation of which extensive additions were made to the permanent building.

Palais de l'Institut. A massive classical structure on the south bank of the Seine, opposite the Louvre, Paris. It was begun in 1662, and since 1795 has been occupied by the Institut and the Bibliothèque Mazarine. See INSTITUT and also BIBLIOTHÈQUE MAZARINE.

Palais de Luxembourg, *or* du Senat. [Palace of Luxembourg, *or* of the Senate.] A magnificent palace in Paris, whose architecture is particularly admired. It was built by Marie de Medicis, occupied successively by several Dukes of France, and during the Revolution it was converted into a prison. Bonaparte made it the Palace of the Senate, afterwards the peers of the realm met there, and after the restoration the Senate again held its meetings there. It contains a very valuable library, and fine works of art, paintings, sculptures, Gobelin tapestry, etc. A palace was begun on the same site in the fifteenth century, and completed by the Duke de Luxembourg, hence the name of the present palace.

He had Versailles and St. Cloud for his country resorts, and the shady alleys of the Tuileries and the *Luxembourg* for his town recreation. *Irving.*

Sir, — said he, — I am proud to say, that Nature has so far enriched me, that I cannot own so much as a *duck* without seeing in it as pretty a swan as ever swam the basin in the garden of the *Luxembourg*. *Holmes.*

Palais des Tournelles. A former large castle or palace of Paris, enlarged by the recent Duke of Bedford, inhabited by Charles VII. and a number of his successors. Nothing is now left of this palace, the destruction of which was begun by Catherine de Médicis. Its site is now occupied by the Place Royale and adjoining streets extending to the Rue St. Antoine.

Palais des Beaux Arts. A building in Paris, France, devoted to the Fine Arts.

☞ "A word for the building of the Palais des Beaux Arts. It is beautiful and as well finished and convenient as beautiful. With its light and elegant fabric, its pretty fountain, its archway of the Renaissance and fragments of sculpture, you can hardly see, on a fine day, a place more *riant* and pleasing." *Thackeray.*

Palais des Thermes. Ruins near the Hôtel de Cluny, Paris, the chief part of which is thought to have belonged to the baths built by the Emperor Constantius Chlorus (250 ?-306).

Palais d'Orsay. See ORSAY, PALAIS D'.

Palais du Corps Législatif. [Palace of the Legislative Assembly.] A handsome building in Paris, begun in 1622 by the Duchess de Bourbon, completed in 1789 by the Prince of Condé, and called at that time Palais Bourbon. Here the Council of Five Hundred held their sittings, after the confiscation of the building in 1792. Part of the palace was afterwards used by Napoleon's Corps Législatif. The palace was restored to the Prince de Condé at the Restoration, but finally became the property of the state. Here sat the Chamber of Deputies (1814 to 1848), the Constituent Assembly of 1848, the Corps Législatif of the Second Empire. A fine portico was added to the building in 1807. The halls within are adorned with paintings and statuary.

In vain wilt thou go to Schönbrunn, to Downing Street, to the *Palais Bourbon:* thou findest nothing there but brick or stone houses, and some bundles of Papers tied with tape. *Carlyle.*

Palais Elysée. See ELYSÉE, PALAIS.

Palais Royal. This palace, in Paris, was built by Cardinal Richelieu. It is associated with the political intrigues of France from the time of its founder down to the accession of Louis Philippe. Many of the most dramatic scenes of the party of the Fronde occurred here. Here many of the extreme measures of the Red Republicans were taken. In a café of the gardens belonging to the palace the Dantonists met, and in another the Girondists. It is now used as a royal residence. The gardens are prettily ornamented, and much frequented by men, women, and children during the warm weather. The Boulevards have now diminished the attractions of the Palais Royal—once the centre of life, gayety, and splendor in Paris.

From that first necessary assertion of Luther's, "You, self-styled *Papa*, you are no Father in God at all; you are—a Chimera, whom I know not how to name in polite language!"—from that onwards to the shout which rose round Camille Desmoulins in the *Palais-Royal*, "Aux armes!" when the people had burst up against *all* manner of Chimeras,—I find a natural historical sequence. *Carlyle.*

John to the *Palais-Royal* came,
Its splendor almost struck him dumb.
"I say, whose house is that there here?"
"House! Je vous n'entends pas, Monsieur." *C. Dibdin.*

Palais Royal. A small theatre, noted for its light comedy and farces, in the Montpensier Gallery of the Palais Royal, Paris. It was opened in 1831, and has been called "la Parapluie des dîneurs du Palais Royal."

Twice a week he goes to the theatre; he prefers the *Palais Royal;* perhaps twice more he takes upon his arm one of the figurantes of the Théâtre Lyrique. *Taine, Trans.*

Palais Royal, Place du. See PLACE DU PALAIS ROYAL.

Palatine Library. A celebrated collection of ancient books and manuscripts, formerly in Heidelberg, Germany, afterwards carried to Rome and deposited in the Vatican, and during the present century in part restored to its original place.

Palatine Mount *or* **Hill.** [Lat. *Mons Palatinus.*] One of the original seven hills of Rome, and the seat of the earliest settlement of the city. It is now covered with the ruins of the Palace of the Cæsars. The history of the Palatine is an epitome of that of Rome. From the time when Romulus encircled it with a furrow, and raised his straw-roofed cottage, it was the site of the mansions of the highest nobility. These structures and palaces became successively more and more splendid and luxurious till they reached their limit of magnificence in the Golden House of Nero. From that time the buildings of the Palatine have degenerated to their present state of ruin.

☞ "The Palatine formed a trapezium of solid rock, two sides of which were about 300 yards in length, and others about 400; the area of its summit, to compare it with a familiar object, was nearly equal to the space between Pall-Mall and Piccadilly in London. . . . After the Etruscan fashion, he [Romulus] traced round the foot of the hill with a plough drawn by a bull and heifer, the furrow being carefully made to fall inwards, and the heifer yoked to the near side, to signify that strength and courage were required without, obedience and fertility within, the city. . . . The locality thus enclosed was reserved for the temples of the gods, and the residence of the ruling class, the class of patricians or burghers, as Niebuhr has taught us to entitle them, which predominated over the dependent commons, and only suffered them to crouch for security under the walls of Romulus. The Palatine was never occupied by the plebs. In the last age of the republic, long after the removal of this partition, or of the civil distinction between the great classes of the state, here was still the chosen site of the mansions of the highest nobility." *Merivale.*

☞ "Every step we tread here is

big with recollections — for it was the scene of early glory, the spot where Rome grew into greatness and fell into decay. . . . That spot which once comprised the whole of Rome; which, till the extinction of the republic, contained the dwellings of her senators and the temples of her gods, but which, during the Empire, was found to be too circumscribed for the wants of one individual, — is now heaped with the wide-spreading ruins of that magnificent edifice, which was the abode of her tyrants, and the tomb of her liberties. Over the wide expanse of the Palatine, no human dwelling or habitation is now to be seen, except where one solitary convent shelters a few barefooted friars, and where, amid the ruined arches and buried halls of the Palace of the Cæsars, the laborers of the vineyards and cabbage-gardens that now flourish over them have made their wretched abodes." *C. A. Eaton.*

The *Palatine*, proud Rome's imperial seat,
(An awful pile!) stands venerably great;
Thither the kingdoms and the nations come,
In supplicating crowds to learn their doom:
To Delphi less th' inquiring worlds repair,
Nor does a greater god inhabit there;
This sure the pompous mansion was design'd
To please the mighty rulers of mankind;
Inferior temples rise on either hand,
And on the borders of the palace stand,
While o'er the rest her head She proudly rears,
And lodged amidst her guardian gods appears.
Claudian (Addison's Translation).

Cypress and ivy, weed and wall-flower grown
Matted and mass'd together, hillocks heap'd
On what were chambers, arch crush'd, columns strewn
In fragments, choked-up vaults, and frescos steep'd
In subterranean damps, where the owl peep'd,
Deeming it midnight: —
Temples, baths, or halls?
Pronounce who can; for all that Learning reap'd
From her research has been that these are walls.
Behold the Imperial Mount! 'Tis thus the mighty falls. *Byron.*

There the Capitol thou seest,
Above the rest lifting his stately head
On the Tarpeian rock, her citadel
Impregnable; and there *Mount Palatine*,
The imperial palace, compass huge, and high
The structure, skill of noblest architects,
With gilded battlements conspicuous far,
Turrets, and terraces, and glittering spires.
Milton.

Palazzo. For most names beginning with PALAZZO, see the next prominent word. For example, PALAZZO PITTI, see PITTI PALACE; PALAZZO DEGLI UFFIZI, see UFFIZI, etc. See also *infra.*

Palazzo del Podestà. See BARGELLO.

Palazzo della Signoria. See PALAZZO VECCHIO.

Palazzo Ducale. See DOGE'S PALACE.

Palazzo Rosso. See BRIGNOLE SALE PALACE.

Palazzo Vecchio (della Signoria). [The Old Palace (of the Signory).] The ancient residence of the Gonfaloniere, or superior magistracy of Florence, now used for government offices, and containing many works of art. It was erected in 1298.

☞ "The prominent and central object is the Palazzo Vecchio, a massive and imposing structure, with enormous projecting battlements, and a lofty bell-tower stuck upon the walls in defiance of proportion, partly overhanging them, and disturbing the passers-by with a constant sense of insecurity." *Hillard.*

Palisades, The. A lofty columnar mass of basalt or trap-rock, nearly 500 feet in height and some 18 miles in length, extending along the right or western bank of the Hudson River in New York and New Jersey.

Pall Mall. A street in London, named from the French game of *paille-maille*, formerly played there. During the last century it contained many taverns, which are now replaced by club-houses. The street, at one time known as Catherine Street, was enclosed about 1690, and was a fashionable promenade. Palle-malle (from *Palla*, a ball, and *Maglia*, a mallet) is still played in old Italian cities.

We went to Wood's at the *Pell Mell* (our old house for clubbing), and there we spent till ten at night.
Pepys (26 July, 1660).

O bear me to the paths of fair *Pall Mall!*
Safe are thy pavements, grateful is thy smell!

At distance rolls along the gilded coach,
Nor sturdy carmen on thy walks encroach;
No lets would bar thy ways were chairs deny'd,
The soft supports of laziness and pride;
Shops breathe perfumes, through sashes ribbons glow,
The mutual arms of ladies and the beau.
Gay.

In town let me live, then, in town let me die;
For in truth I can't relish the country, not I.
If one must have a villa in summer to dwell,
Oh! give me the sweet shady side of *Pall Mall.* *Charles Morris.*

I am lodged in the street called *Pall Mall*, the ordinary residence of all strangers, because of its vicinity to the Queen's Palace, the Park, the Parliament House, the Theatres, and the Chocolate and Coffee-houses, where the best company frequent. *Journey through England*, 1714.

I indent the gayer flags of *Pall Mall.* It is 'change time, and I am strangely among the Elgin marbles. *Charles Lamb.*

Have society, *Pall Mall* clubs, and a habit of sneering, so withered up our organs of veneration that we can admire no more? *Thackeray.*

My little friend, so small and neat,
Whom years ago I used to meet
In *Pall Mall* daily;
How cheerily you tript away
To work — it might have been to play,
You tript so gayly. *Frederick Locker.*

Palladium. A celebrated statue of antiquity representing the goddess Pallas as seated, holding in one hand a spear, in the other a distaff. This statue, which was said to have fallen from heaven on the plain of Troy, was believed to have been the guardian or preserving genius of the city. Hence the modern signification of the word as a security or protection.

Pallas, The. An armor-plated ship of the British navy, launched March 14, 1865.

Pallas. See MINERVA.

Pallione, Il. [The Church Standard.] A celebrated votive picture by Guido Reni (1575-1642), painted by command of the Senate of Bologna after the cessation of the plague in 1630. It represents "the Madonna in a glory of angels, with the patron saints of Bologna underneath." The picture derives its name from having been originally used in processions. Now in the Gallery of Bologna, Italy.

☞ "Guido, it is said, had no time to prepare a canvas or cartoons, and painted the whole on a piece of white silk. It was carried in grand procession, and solemnly dedicated by the Senate, whence it obtained the title by which it is celebrated in the history of art, 'Il Pallione del Voto.'" *Mrs. Jameson.*

Palsgrave Head. A former noted tavern near Temple Bar, London.

But now at Piccadilly they arrive,
And taking coach, t'wards Temple Bar they drive,
But at St. Clement's eat out the back,
And slipping through the *Palsgrave*, bilkt poor hack. *Prior and Montague.*

Pamfili-Doria, Villa. See VILLA PAMFILI-DORIA.

Pamfili Palace. [Ital. *Palazzo Pamfili.*] A palace built in 1650 for Innocent X., in Piazza Navona, Rome. Here lived Olimpia Maldalchini Pamfili, notorious for her ambition, vices, and political influence.

Pan. See NARCISSUS.

Panathenaic Frieze. The name often given to the frieze of the Parthenon at Athens, now among the Elgin marbles in the British Museum, London. It is so called from the subject represented, which is the procession which took place every five years in honor of the goddess Minerva, to whom the temple was dedicated, and which was participated in by all the Athenian colonies.

☞ "We possess in England the most precious examples of Athenian power in the sculpture of animals. The horses of the frieze, in the Elgin collection, appear to live and move, to roll their eyes, to gallop, prance, and curvet; the veins of their faces and legs seem distended with circulation; in them are distinguished the hardness and decision of bony forms from the elasticity of tendon and the softness of flesh. The beholder is charmed with the deer-like lightness and elegance of their make, and although the relief is not above an inch from the background, and they are so much smaller than nature, we can scarcely suffer reason to persuade us they are not alive." *Flaxman.*

Pancras, St. See ST. PANCRAS.

Pancrazio, San. See SAN PANCRAZIO.

Panshanger House. The seat of Earl Cowper, in the county of Hertford, England. It contains a fine collection of paintings.

Pantheon. 1. [*La Rotonda, Santa Maria di Rotonda, Santa Maria ad Martyres.*] The best preserved monument of ancient Rome. It was built by Marcus Agrippa, B.C. 27, as shown by the inscription upon the frieze. In A.D. 608 it was consecrated as a Christian church by Pope Boniface IV. under the name of *Santa Maria ad Martyres.* The proportions of the beautiful portico have long been regarded as faultless. The interior is a rotunda surmounted by a dome, and lighted by a circular opening 28 feet in diameter in the centre of the dome. The inside diameter of the rotunda is 142 feet. The Pantheon has been used as the burial-place of painters, Raphael, Annibale Caracci, and others being interred here beneath the pavement.

☞ "The world has nothing else like the Pantheon. So grand it is, that the pasteboard statues over the lofty cornice do not disturb the effect, any more than the tin crowns and hearts, the dusty artificial flowers, and all manner of trumpery gewgaws hanging at the saintly shrines. The rust and dinginess that have dimmed the precious marbles on the walls; the pavement, with its great squares and rounds of porphyry and granite, cracked crosswise, and in a hundred directions, showing how roughly the troublesome ages have trampled here; the gray dome above, with its opening to the sky, as if heaven were looking down into the interior of this place of worship; . . . all these things make an impression of solemnity which St. Peter's itself fails to produce."
Hawthorne.

☞ "Though plundered of all its brass, except the ring which was necessary to preserve the aperture above; though exposed to repeated fires; though sometimes flooded by the river, and always open to the rain, no monument of equal antiquity is so well preserved as this rotunda. It passed with little alteration from the Pagan into the present worship; and so convenient were its niches for the Christian altar, that Michael Angelo, ever studious of ancient beauty, introduced their design as a model in the Catholic church."
Forsyth's Italy.

☞ "Our Pantheon [at Paris] compared with this seems mean; and when, after a half-hour's contemplation of it, you abstract its mouldiness and degradation, and divorce it from its modern dilapidated surroundings, when the imagination pictures to itself the white glittering edifice with its fresh marble, as it appeared in the time of Agrippa, when, after the establishment of universal peace, he dedicated it to all the gods, then do you figure to yourself with admiration the triumph of Augustus which this fête completed, a reconciled, submissive universe, the splendor of a perfected empire."
Taine, Trans.

☞ "The preservation and embellishment of the Pantheon have seemed to be dear to every mind of genius in every age. Raphael bequeathed a sum of money for its repair; so did Annibal Caracci, and many other distinguished artists; but it appears to have all gone to the Madonna and the martyrs, to priests and masses."
C. A. Eaton.

☞ "The character of the architecture, and the sense of satisfaction which it leaves upon the mind, are proofs of the enduring charm of simplicity. . . . This charm is the result of form and proportion, and cannot be lost except by entire destruction." *Hillard.*

Simple, erect, severe, austere, sublime —
Shrine of all saints and temple of all gods
From Jove to Jesus — spared and bless'd by time,
Looking tranquillity, while falls or nods
Arch, empire, each thing round thee, and man plods
His way through thorns to ashes — glorious dome!
Shalt thou not last? Time's scythe and tyrants' rods
Shiver upon thee, — sanctuary and home
Of art and piety, — *Pantheon!* pride of Rome!
Relic of nobler days, and noblest arts!
Despoil'd yet perfect, with thy circle spreads
A holiness appealing to all hearts —
To art a model; and to him who treads
Rome for the sake of ages, Glory sheds
Her light through thy sole aperture; to those
Who worship, here are altars for their beads;
And they who feel for genius may repose
Their eyes on honor'd forms, whose busts around them close. *Byron,*

Well speed thy mission, bold Iconoclast!
Yet all unworthy of its trust thou art,
If, with dry eye, and cold, unloving heart,
Thou tread'st the solemn *Pantheon* of the past,
By the great Future's dazzling hope made blind
To all the beauty, power, and truth behind. *Whittier.*

No, great Dome of Agrippa, thou art not Christian. Canst not,
Strip and replaster and daub and do what they will with thee, be so. *Clough.*

2. A church in Paris now called St. Geneviève. The corner-stone of this building was laid by Louis XV. in 1764. In 1791 the Assembly decreed that it should be used as a place of sepulture for the illustrious dead of France. Mirabeau, Voltaire, and Rousseau were interred here, and also many distinguished generals of Napoleon's army. In 1851 the temple was presented to the Roman Catholic Church. The church is in the form of a Greek cross, and is very imposing from its great size and the magnificence of its dome. It is adorned with statues and paintings of the great kings and queens, military heroes, and literary men of France. It is situated on the south of the river, upon the highest ground in Paris. It is called the largest and finest church of the Italian style in the city. It was changed into a pantheon, in 1792, inscribed "Aux Grands Hommes la Patrie reconnaissante," restored to a church in 1822, in 1831 again changed to a pantheon, and in 1853 re-converted into a church.

☞ "The object of this splendid pile — for it is not a church — is sufficiently explained by a series of figures in relief by David, representing, on the triangular pediment of the portico, France, a figure 15 feet high, attended by Liberty and History, surrounded by, and dispensing honor to, Voltaire, Lafayette, Fénelon, Rousseau, Mirabeau, Manuel, Carnot, David, and, of course, Napoleon, and the principal heroes of the republican and imperial armies." *Sir Francis B. Head.*

☞ "Begun as a church, in the Revolution its destination was altered, and it was to be a temple to the manes of great men; and accordingly Rousseau, Voltaire, and many more are buried here. Well, after the Revolution, the Bourbons said it should not be a temple for great men, it should be a church. The next popular upset tipped it back to the great men, and it stayed under their jurisdiction until Louis Napoleon, who is very pious, restored it to the Church. . . . This Pantheon is, as one might suppose from its history, a hybrid between a church and a theatre, and of course good for neither — purposeless and aimless." *C. Beecher.*

☞ "The present superb church of St. Geneviève was the Pantheon of the Revolution. The painting of the dome, which is in the worst possible taste, represents St. Geneviève in glory, receiving the homage of Clovis, Charlemagne, St. Louis, and Louis XVIII. *Au reste*, the classic magnificence of the whole structure is as little in harmony with the character of the peasant patroness, as the church of the Madeleine with that of the Syrian penitent and castaway." *Mrs. Jameson.*

☞ "On arriving at the object of our ambition — the small balustrade surrounding the lantern which forms the summit of the Pantheon — there burst upon us all a magnificent panorama it would be utterly impossible to describe. The whole of Paris — every window, every chimney, were distinguishable." *Sir Francis B. Head.*

The church of *St. Geneviève* is a place of greate devotion, dedicate to another of their Amazons sayd to have delivered the City from the English, for which she is esteemed the tutelary saint of Paris. It stands on a steepe eminence, having a very high spire, and is governed by Canons Regular.
John Evelyn, Diary, Feb. 7, 1644.

Alike the better-seeing shade will smile
On the rude cavern of the rocky isle,
As if his ashes found their latest home
In Rome's Pantheon or Gaul's mimic dome. *Byron.*

3. A well-known building in London, at first built for a theatre and public promenade, and opened in 1772. The Pantheon was burned in 1792, and rebuilt; afterwards taken down and reconstructed in 1812, and in 1834 turned into a bazaar.

I saw Hood once as a young man, at a dinner which seems almost as ghostly now as that masquerade at the *Pantheon* of which we were speaking anon. *Thackeray.*

Paoli, San. See SAN PAOLI FUORI LE MURA.

Paoline Chapel. See CAPELLA PAOLINA.

Paolo, San. See Porta di San Paolo.

Paraclete. This celebrated abbey, founded by Abelard, stood at the village of St. Aubin, on the stream Ardusson, in France. Here was the retreat of Heloïse, and her final resting-place as well as that of Abelard.

Sometimes I grieve for the loss of the house of *Paraclete*, and wish to see it again. Ah, Philintus, does not the love of Heloïse still burn in my heart?
Abelard, Letters of Abelard and Heloise.

To the gray walls of fallen *Paraclete*,
To Juliet's urn,
Fair Arno and Sorrento's orange-grove,
Where Tasso sang, let young Romance and Love
Like brother pilgrims turn. *Whittier.*

God's love, — unchanging, pure, and true, —
The *Paraclete* white-shining through
His peace, — the fall of Hermon's dew!
Whittier.

With all my sorrows trembling still,
Fate, vainly lenient, bade us meet,
Resistless victims of its will!
And led my steps to *Paraclete*.
L. S. Costello.

Paradiso, Il. A famous picture by Jacopo Robusti, called Il Tintoretto (1512–1594). It is an oil-painting, 84 feet long and 34 feet high. In the Doge's Palace, at Venice, Italy.

☞ "In the *Paradise* of Tintoret, the angel is seen in the distance driving Adam and Eve out of the Garden. . . . Full speed they fly, the angel and the human creatures; the angel wrapt in an orb of light floats on, and does not touch the ground; the chastised creatures rush before him in abandoned terror. All this might have been invented by another, . . . but one circumstance which completes the story could have been thought of by none but Tintoret. The angel casts a *shadow* before him towards Adam and Eve."
Ruskin (*Modern Painters*).

☞ "At first this *Paradise* of Tintoret is so strange that no wonder the lovely world outside, the beautiful court-yard, the flying birds, and drifting Venetians seem more like Heaven to those who are basking in their sweetness. But it is well worth while by degrees, with some pain and self-denial, to climb in spirit to that strange crowded place towards which old Tintoret's mighty soul was bent."
Miss Thackeray.

Paradiso, Orto del. See Orto del Paradiso.

Parcæ. See Three Fates.

Parc-aux-Cerfs. [Deer-park.] A park or preserve at Versailles, France.

The true conduct and position for a French Sovereign towards French Literature, in that country, might have been, though perhaps of all things the most important, one of the most difficult to discover and accomplish. What chance was there that a thick-blooded Louis Quinze, from his *Parc aux Cerfs*, should discover it, should have the faintest inkling of it?
Carlyle.

Meanwhile Louis the well-beloved has left (forever) his *Parc-aux-cerfs*, and, amid the scarce-suppressed hootings of the world, taken up his last lodging at St. Denis. *Carlyle.*

Parian Chronicle. One of the so-called Arundelian marbles at Oxford, England. It is a chronological register or compendium of the history of Greece from B.C. 1582 to B.C. 355. It is so called because thought to have been made in the island of Paros. See Arundelian Marbles.

Paris Garden. A region in London, so called from Robert de Paris, who had a house and grounds there in the reign of Richard II., now built upon and occupied with public works.

Paris, Judgment of. See Judgment of Paris.

Park Lane. A street of aristocratic residences in London, England.

Fifth Avenue is the Belgrave Square, the *Park Lane*, and the Pall Mall of New York. *Anthony Trollope.*

Park Square. A well-known public square in London, England.

Park-Street Church. A well-known religious edifice in Boston, Mass. It has a lofty spire.

I tell you what, — the idea of the professions' digging a moat round their close corporations, like that Japanese one at Jeddo, which you could put *Park-Street Church* on the bottom of and look over the vane from its side, and try to stretch another such spire across it without spanning the chasm, — that idea, I say, is pretty nearly worn out. *Holmes.*

Parliament House. 1. A building in Edinburgh, Scotland, of the Italian style of architecture, used for Courts of Justice. The old Parliament House, of which only a portion remains, is used by lawyers and their clients.

2. An imposing pile of buildings in Ottawa, Can., containing the halls of Parliament of the Dominion of Canada, and the Department offices. It was begun in 1860.

Parliament Houses. See WESTMINSTER PALACE.

Parliament Oak. An ancient and famous tree in what was once Sherwood Forest. It derived its name from the tradition of a parliament having been held there by Edward the First.

Parnasse, Boulevard du Mont. See MONT PARNASSE.

Parnassus. A celebrated fresco by Raphael Sanzio (1483-1520), representing Apollo and the Muses, under laurel-trees, on the heights of Parnassus. On either side and below are ranged the poets of antiquity and of modern Italy. This picture is one of the series of four, entitled respectively, Theology, Poetry (or the Parnassus), Philosophy, and Jurisprudence, which were intended to exhibit the lofty subjects of thought with which the human mind is occupied. They are all in the Camera della Segnatura of the Vatican, Rome.

Parnassus. An allegorical picture by Andrea Mantegna (1431-1506), the Italian painter. In the Gallery of the Louvre, Paris.

Parnassus. A celebrated fresco in the Villa Albani, Rome, by Anton Rafael Mengs (1728-1779). It has been engraved by Raphael Morghen. [Called also *Apollo and the Muses.*]

Parthenon, The. This structure, — the glory of the Acropolis at Athens, Greece, — "the finest edifice on the finest site in the world, hallowed by the noblest recollections that can stimulate the human heart," — was so called from being the temple of Athena Parthenos (Ἀθηνᾶ Παρθένος). The time at which the Parthenon was begun is not definitely known; but it was built under the administration of Pericles, and finished 438 B.C. The architects were Ictinus and Callicrates, and the general supervision of the work was intrusted to Phidias. This most perfect product of Grecian architecture was of the Doric order, was built of Pentelic marble, and stood upon the highest part of the Acropolis. The Parthenon was beautifully adorned, both without and within, with exquisite works of sculpture, some of which have been removed and deposited in the British Museum. The Parthenon was sometimes called *Hecatompedos* or *Hecatompedon* (i.e., the Temple of One Hundred Feet), a name derived from its breadth. This temple beautifully illustrates the architectural principle known to the ancient Greeks by which they prevented the *apparent* sagging of horizontal and the bending of perpendicular lines in a structure. By substituting very slight and delicate curves for the ordinary right lines, this common optical illusion was entirely avoided. The perpendicular lines also slightly incline inwards, thus preventing any appearance — as for example in the columns, which incline three inches in their height — of leaning outwards. The most celebrated of the sculptures of the Parthenon was a colossal statue of the Virgin Goddess, by Phidias. It was made of ivory for the undraped parts, while solid gold was used for the dress and ornaments, — a kind of work which the Greeks called *chryselephantine*. The Parthenon was turned into a Greek church dedicated to the Virgin Mother, probably in the sixth century. It was badly damaged by a shell during the siege of Athens by the Venetians in 1687, and also received additional injury during the bombardment of the city in 1827.

☞ "Such was the simple structure of this magnificent building, which, by its united excellences of materials, design, and decorations, was the most perfect ever executed. Its dimensions of 228 feet by 101, with a height of 66 feet to the top of the pediment, were sufficiently great to give an appearance of grandeur and sublimity; and this impression was not disturbed by any obtrusive subdivision of parts, such as is found to diminish the effect of many larger modern buildings, where the same singleness of design is not apparent. In the Parthenon there was nothing to divert the spectator's contemplation from the simplicity and majesty of mass and outline, which forms the first and most remarkable object of admiration in a Greek temple." *Leake.*

☞ "Down to the year 1637, the Parthenon remained entire. The Christians converted it first into a church, and the Turks, jealous of the Christians, afterward converted it into a mosque. Then came the Venetians in the highly civilized seventeenth century, and cannonaded the monuments of Pericles. They shot their balls upon the Propylæum and the Temple of Minerva; a bomb sunk into the roof set fire to a number of barrels of gunpowder inside, and demolished in part a building that did less honor to the false gods of Greece than to the genius of man. The town being taken, Morosini, with the design of embellishing Venice with the spoils of Athens, wished to take down the statues of the pediment of the Parthenon, and broke them. A modern succeeded in achieving (in the interest of the arts) the destruction which the Venetians had begun. Lord Elgin lost the merits of his commendable enterprises in ravaging the Parthenon. He wished to take away the bassi-relievi of the frieze; in order to do so, he employed Turkish workmen, who broke the architrave, threw down the capitals, and smashed the cornice." *Chateaubriand, Trans.*

☞ "The last of the portals is passed: you are on the summit alone with the *Parthenon*. Over heaps of ruin, over a plain buried under huge fragments of hewn and sculptured marble — drums of pillars, pedestals, capitals, cornices, friezes, triglyphs, and sunken panel-work — a wilderness of mutilated art — it rises between you and the sky, which forms its only background, and against which every scar left by the infidel generations shows its gash. Broken down in the middle, like a ship which has struck and parted, with the roof, cornices, and friezes mostly gone, and not a column unmutilated, and yet with the tawny gold of 2,000 years staining its once spotless marble, sparkling with snow-white marks of shot and shell, and with its soaring pillars embedded in the dark-blue ether (and here the sky seems blue only because they need such a background), you doubt for a moment whether the melancholy of its ruin, or the perfect and majestic loveliness which shines through that ruin, is the most powerful." *Bayard Taylor.*

☞ "The appearance of the Parthenon testifies more loudly than history itself to the greatness of this people [the Greeks]. Pericles will never die. What a civilization was that which found a great man to decree, an architect to conceive, a sculptor to adorn, statuaries to execute, workmen to carve, and a people to pay for and maintain, such an edifice! In the midst of the ruins which once were Athens, and which the cannon of the Greeks and Turks have pulverized and scattered throughout the valley, and upon the two hills upon which extends the city of Minerva, a mountain is seen towering up perpendicularly upon all sides. Enormous ramparts surround it; built at their base with fragments of white marble, higher up with the *débris* of friezes and antique columns, they terminate in some parts with Venetian battlements. This mountain seems to be a magnificent pedestal cut by the gods themselves whereon to seat their altars." *Lamartine, Trans.*

☞ "Of all the great temples, the best and most celebrated is the Parthenon, the only octastyle Doric temple in Greece, and in its own class undoubtedly the most beautiful building in the world. It is true, it has neither the dimensions nor the wondrous expression of power and eternity inherent in Egyptian temples, nor has it the variety and poetry of the Gothic cathedral; but for intellectual beauty, for perfection of proportion, for beauty of detail, and for the exquisite perception of the highest and most recondite principles of art ever applied to architecture, it stands utterly and entirely alone and unrivalled — the glory of Greece and a reproach to the rest of the world." *Fergusson.*

Earth proudly wears the *Parthenon*,
As the best gem upon her zone.
Emerson.

Parthenon, The. A London club, dissolved in 1862. The Erectheum Club was joined with it in 1854.

Parvis Notre Dame. This name, a corruption of Paradisus, is applied to the open space in front of the cathedral of Notre Dame, Paris.

Pas Perdus, Salle des. A large hall, from which open different law-courts, in the Palais de Justice, Paris.

Pasquino. A celebrated mutilated statue in Rome, so called from a witty tailor of that name who kept a shop near by, and was given to entertaining his customers with the gossip and scandal of the day. Upon the pedestal of this statue were affixed pungent criticisms on passing events, squibs, and sarcasms, from which the term *Pasquinade* is derived.

☞ "The public opinion of Rome has only one traditional organ. It is that mutilated block of marble called Pasquin's statue, on which are mysteriously affixed by unknown hands the frequent squibs of Roman motherwit on the events of the day."
The Times, 1870.

Passaic, The. A United States monitor in the war of the Rebellion (1861-65). She took part, in connection with the land batteries, in the attack upon Fort Sumter, July 11, 1863. On the 24th, Gen. Gilmore wrote to Gen. Halleck, "Fort Sumter is to-day a shapeless mass of ruins."

Passion, The. A picture by Hans Memling (d. 1495), the Flemish painter, representing all the scenes of the Passion of Christ in a number of separate groups with figures of small size. It is now in the Royal Gallery at Turin, Italy.

Passion, The Greater and the Lesser. A series of wood-cuts by Albert Dürer (1471-1528), the German painter and engraver, and considered to be among the best of his works which have descended to us.

Passion. See LYVERSBURG PASSION.

Passion Play. See PASSIONSPIEL.

Passionspiel. [Passion Play.] A famous dramatic representation of the scenes of the Passion and Death of Christ, exhibited at the village of Ober-Ammergau, in Bavaria. The acting takes place in the day-time, and under the open sky. The play was first performed in 1633, under a religious vow offered by the inhabitants of the village, that they would enact it at regular periods, if delivered from the infliction of the plague.

☞ "The decadal period was chosen for 1680, and the Passion Play has been enacted, with various interruptions, every tenth year since that time. The Passion Play is, however, of much older date than this. It is not probable that simple villagers would make a vow to perform a play totally unknown to them, and, even in its rudest form, demanding such capacity and preparatory study. The vow speaks of the Passion Tragedy as something already well known; only the period of performing the play every ten years is positively stated. The oldest known text-book of the play bears the date 1662, and it refers to a still older book. Since the year 1634 the Passion Play has undergone great change and improvements. Such figures as Lucifer, Prince of Hell, who, with his retinue used to play a great part in the Ammergau performance, have been banished. Up to the year 1830, the play was performed in the village churchyard in the open air. In the first decades of the present century the text of the play was thoroughly revised by Father Ottmar Weiss of Jesewang (d. 1843), who removed unsuitable and inharmonious passages, substituting prose for doggerel verse. The improvements then commenced have been carried on up to the present time by the former pastor of the village, the Geistlicher-Rath Daisenberger, who is still active in promoting the success of the play."
J. P. Jackson.

Patapsco, The. A United States monitor in the war of the Rebellion (1861-65). She took part, in connection with the land batteries, in the attack upon Fort Sumter, July 11, 1863, and within a few days it was reduced to a shapeless mass of ruins.

Paternoster Row. A street in London said to be so named from the turners of rosaries, or Pater Nosters, who formerly dwelt there. It is noted as the locality of stationers, printers, and booksellers.

☞ "Paternoster Row was for many years sacred to publishers. It is a narrow flagged street, lying under the shadow of St. Paul's; at each end there are posts placed, so as to prevent the passage of carriages, and thus preserve a solemn silence for the deliberations of the 'fathers of the Row.' The dull warehouses on each side are mostly occupied at present by wholesale stationers; if they be publishers' shops, they show no attractive front to the dark and narrow street."
Mrs. Gaskell (*in* 1848).

I have been told of a critic who was crucified at the command of another to the reputation of Homer. That, no doubt, was more than poetical justice, and I shall be perfectly content if those who criticise me are only clapped in the pillory, kept fifteen days upon bread and water, and obliged to run the gantlope through *Paternoster-row*. *Goldsmith.*

At the time of Johnson's appearance, there were still two ways, on which an Author might attempt proceeding: these were the Mæcenases proper in the West End of London; and the Mæcenases virtual of St. John's Gate and *Paternoster Row*. *Carlyle.*

For him reviews shall smile, for him o'erflow
The patronage of *Paternoster-row*. *Byron.*

Fraught with invective they ne'er go
To folks at *Paternoster-row*. *Goldsmith.*

Having a little "Grub-street" business, I made my way to the purlieus of publishers, *Paternoster Row*. *N. P. Willis.*

Patrick's, St. See ST. PATRICK'S.

Paul and Barnabas at Lystra. One of the famous cartoons by Raphael Sanzio (1483–1520), from which the tapestries in the Vatican at Rome were executed.

Paul in the Prison at Philippi. The subject of a tapestry picture in the Vatican, Rome, after a cartoon by Raphael. This cartoon is no longer in existence.

Paul preaching at Athens. One of the famous cartoons by Raphael Sanzio (1483–1520), from which the tapestries in the Vatican, at Rome, were executed.

☞ "In Raphael's cartoon of *Paul preaching at Athens*, the figure of the man in front, who, as Sir Joshua says, 'appears to be thinking all over,' is probably Dionysus." *Mrs. Jameson.*

Paul, St. See ST. PAUL.

Pauline Borghese. See VENUS VICTRIX.

Pauline Chapel. See CAPELLA PAOLINA.

Pauline Fountain. See FONTANA PAOLINA.

Paulovsk. A palace and summer residence of the imperial family of Russia, near St. Petersburg. The park is of great extent, the estimated aggregate length of the walks being 100 miles. It is at all times open to the public, and a favorite pleasure resort of the inhabitants of the capital.

Paul's, St. See ST. PAUL'S.

Paul's Walk. See DUKE HUMPHREY'S WALK.

Pavilion. A royal palace in Brighton, England, built in the Oriental style by George IV.

Pays Latin. See QUARTIER LATIN.

Peabody Institute. 1. A marble building in Baltimore, Md., containing a library, a gallery of art, a conservatory of music, and a fine lecture-hall. The Institute was founded by George Peabody (1795–1869), the London banker, and is designed for the promotion of education, and the diffusion of useful knowledge among the masses.

2. A building in Peabody, Mass., provided with a library and lecture-room, founded and endowed by the well-known London banker of the same name. See *supra*.

Peabody Museum. A large Gothic building connected with Yale College, New Haven, Conn., containing large collections in natural history, mineralogy, etc. It was built with proceeds of the endowment made by George Peabody of London. See *supra*.

Peacock, The. A British warship captured in 1813 by the American ship *Hornet*.

Peacock Island. [Ger. *Pfauen-Insel.*] A small island in the river Havel, near Potsdam, Germany. It has been at times the favorite resort of the royal family of Prussia, and contains a summer-house, menagerie, palm-house, and pleasure-grounds.

Peak Cavern. A series of subterranean chambers near Castleton, England, forming the largest cave in Britain. [Called also the *Devil's Cave.*]

Pearl, The. A celebrated picture by Raphael Sanzio (1483-1520), parts of which are supposed to have been executed by Giulio Romano (1492-1546). "This picture has derived a fictitious importance from the supposed words of Philip IV. of Spain, who, having purchased the picture from the gallery of Charles I., is said to have exclaimed on seeing it, 'This is my pearl!'" It is now in the Gallery at Madrid, Spain.

Pearl Mosque. [*Motee Musjeed.*] A famous Mohammedan temple or mosque in the city of Agra, Hindostan. It is a small but very perfect building. It has three domes of white marble with gilded spires.

☞ "The Motee Musjeed can be compared to no other edifice that I have ever seen. To my eye, it is a perfect type of its class. While its architecture is the purest Saracenic, which some suppose cannot exist without ornament, it shows the severe simplicity of Doric art. It has, in fact, nothing which can properly be termed ornament. It is a sanctuary so pure and stainless, revealing so exalted a spirit of worship, that I felt humbled as a Christian, to think that our nobler religion has so rarely inspired architects to surpass this temple to God and Mohammed." *Bayard Taylor.*

Peasant Feast. A picture by David Teniers the Younger (1610-1694), the Belgian *genre*-painter. In the Louvre, at Paris.

Peasant Wedding. A picture by David Teniers the Younger (1610-1694), the Belgian *genre*-painter. In the Gallery of Munich, Bavaria. There is another upon the same subject at Vienna, Austria.

Peasants Travelling. See EULENSPIEGEL.

Peele Castle. A venerable and famous fortress on the Isle of Man, familiar to the readers of Scott by having been the place where some of the most interesting scenes in "Peveril of the Peak" are laid. It was formerly used as a place of confinement for prisoners of state.

I was thy neighbor once, thou rugged pile!
Four summer weeks I dwelt in sight of thee:
I saw thee every day; and all the while
Thy form was sleeping on a glassy sea.
Wordsworth (Elegiac Stanzas, suggested by a picture of Peele Castle in a storm, painted by Sir George Beaumont).

Pembroke College. A foundation of the University of Cambridge, England. Established in 1347.

Pembroke Family. A grand family picture, including ten figures, by Anthony van Dyck (1599-1641), and regarded as one of his principal works. In Wilton House, England.

Pendennis Castle. An ancient fortress at Falmouth, England.

Penitent Magdalen. A well-known work of sculpture by Antonio Canova (1757-1828).

Penn Cottage. An old and interesting house in Philadelphia, Penn., on Letitia Street, occupied by William Penn in 1682, and said to be the first brick building erected in the town.

Pennsylvania Avenue. The chief thoroughfare of the city of Washington. It extends from the Capitol across the level tract where it was intended the city should be built towards Georgetown. On the line of its course are the Treasury building, the Executive Mansion or White House, and the building of the Department of State.

Penseroso, Il. A statue by Hiram Powers (1805-1873). In the Lenox Library, New York.

Penshurst Place *and* **Oak.** A noted mansion near Tunbridge, England, in which Sir Philip and Algernon Sidney were born. It is now in possession of Lord de Lisle and Dudley, one of their descendants. Near by is the famous oak which was planted at the birth of Sir Philip Sidney. It is now 22 feet in girth.

Thou art not, *Penshurst*, built to envious show
Of touch or marble; nor canst boast a row
Of polish'd pillars or a roofe of gold;
Thou hast no lantherne, whereof tales are told;
Or stayre, or courts; but standst an ancient pile,
And these grudged at, art reverenc'd the while,
Thou joy'st in better marks, of soile, of ayre,
Of wood, of water: therein thou art faire.
Ben Jonson.

Genius of *Penshurst* old!
Who saw'st the birth of each immortal oak,
Here sacred from the stroke;
Where Sidney his Arcadian landscape drew,
Genuine from thy Doric view!
And patriot Algernon unshaken rose
Above insulting foes;
And Sacharissa nursed her angel charms.
Francis Coventry.

Penshurst still shines for us, and its Christmas revels, "where logs not burn, but men." *Emerson.*

That tall tree, too, which of a nut was set,
At his great birth, where all the Muses met.
Ben Jonson.

Go, boy, and carve this passion on the bark
Of yonder tree, which stands the sacred mark
Of noble Sidney's birth.
Waller.

Pensoso, Il. See LORENZO DE' MEDICI.

Pentinger Tables. An ancient itinerary discovered at Spires in 1508. A copy was published by Pentinger in 1591, and since then many editions of the original have appeared. The tablet is a map of the world as known to the ancients, and is about 20 feet in length by a foot in breadth.

Pepysian Library. The valuable collection of manuscripts and early English books belonging to Samuel Pepys (1632–1703), the celbrated gossip and diarist. It is now in Magdalen College, Cambridge, England.

Pequot Hill. An elevation near Mystic, Conn., the scene of one of the most desperate and sanguinary engagements between the Indian tribe of the Pequots and the New England colonists, in May, 1637.

Père-la-Chaise. A cemetery near Paris, so called because that on the ground it occupies formerly stood the dwelling of Père-la-Chaise, the confessor of Louis XIV. It was consecrated in 1804, and now covers more than 200 acres. It is laid out and ornamented with much taste and elegance, and commands a fine view of Paris and the surrounding country. One of the principal objects of interest is the tomb of Abelard and Heloise, which consists of a chapel built of materials brought from the Abbey of the Holy Ghost, which Abelard founded, and of which Heloise was abbess. Père-la-Chaise was made a final place of refuge for the insurgents of the Commune in 1871, and here were two graves, in one of which were thrown 200 bodies of Communists, and in the other more than 700. About 50 burials a day take place here. There are about 16,000 stone monuments, which have cost nearly £5,000,000.

The dead of distant lands
Are gathered here. In pomp of sculpture sleeps
The Russian Demidoff, and Britain's sons
Have crossed the foaming sea, to leave their dust
In a strange soil. Yea, from my own far land
They've wandered here, to die.
Mrs. L. H. Sigourney.

I see grand tombs to France's lesser dead;
Colossal steeds, white pyramids, still red
At base with blood, still torn with shot and shell,
To testify that here the Commune fell;
And yet I turn once more from all of these,
And stand before the tomb of Eloise.
Joaquin Miller.

When years have clothed the line in moss
That tells thy name and days,
And withered, on thy simple cross,
The wreaths of *Père-la-Chaise!*
Holmes.

Perla, La. See PEARL, THE.

Perseus, The. A well-known bronze statue by Benvenuto Cellini (1500–1570), and his *chef d'œuvre*. In the Loggia de' Lanzi, Florence.

☞ "When one recalls the details of its casting, the intrepidity with which the artist, exhausted with fatigue, devoured by fever, leaped from his bed to hasten the liquidation of the bronze into which he cast all the pewter vessels of his house, his fervent and devout prayers, his sudden recovery, and his joyous meal with his family and friends, this statue becomes a sort of action which paints the manners of the time and the character of the extraordinary man who executed it."
Valery, Trans.

In the Loggia? where is set
Cellini's god-like *Perseus*, bronze — or gold —
(How name the metal, when the statue flings
Its soul so in your eyes?) with brow and sword
Superbly calm, as all opposing things
Slain with the Gorgon, were no more abhorred
Since ended? *Mrs. Browning.*

Perseus and Andromeda. A picture by Peter Paul Rubens (1577–1640). In Berlin, Prussia.

Perseus with the Head of Medusa. A statue by Antonio Canova (1757–1822). In the Vatican, Rome.

☞ "During the absence of the Apollo [Belvidere] in Paris, under the rule of Napoleon, the Perseus was placed on its pedestal; an honor of which it was hardly worthy, as it is rather a fine than a beautiful statue, and is deficient in beauty and expression." *Hillard.*

Persian Sibyl. A noted picture by Guido Reni (1575–1642). In the Museum of the Capitol, Rome.

☞ "His [Guercino's] *Sibyl Persica*, under her peculiar head-dress, is already quite modern. She has one of those pensive, complicated, indefinable expressions which pleases us so greatly, a spirit of infinite delicacy, whose mysterious fascinations will never end."
Taine, Trans.

There is another picture known by this name, by Guido Reni (1575-1642). In the Uffizi Gallery, Florence, Italy.

Perte du Rhone. A remarkable spot not far from Geneva, Switzerland, where the river Rhone plunges into a mass of broken rocks, and disappears completely from sight for a space of 120 yards.

Pesaro Palace. [Ital. *Palazzo Pesaro.*] A fine palace of the seventeenth century in Venice, Italy.

Peter. See GREAT PETER and JOHN AND PETER.

Peter and John at the Beautiful Gate of the Temple. One of the famous cartoons by Raphael Sanzio (1483–1520), from which the tapestries in the Vatican at Rome were executed.

Peter and Paul in Discussion about the Gentiles. A picture by Guido Reni (1575–1642). In the Brera at Milan, Italy.

☞ "A grand picture, full of deep meaning." *Ticknor.*

Peter denying Christ. A picture by David Teniers the Younger (1610-1694), the Belgian *genre*-painter. It is now in the Louvre, in Paris.

Peter, St. See ST. PETER.

Peter the Great teaching the art of Ship-building. A picture by Sir William Allan (1782–1850). In the Winter Palace, St. Petersburg, Russia.

Peterhouse. The most ancient collegiate foundation in the University of Cambridge, England. It was founded near the close of the thirteenth century.

Peterloo, Field of. See FIELD OF PETERLOO.

Peter's Chains. See SAN PIETRO IN VINCOLI.

Peter's Chair. See CHAIR OF ST. PETER.

Peter's College, St. See WESTMINSTER SCHOOL.

Peter's, St. See ST. PETER'S.

Petit Château. [The Little Castle.] A castle in Chantilly, France, built by the Montmorencys, and considered one of the most beautiful monuments of the Renaissance style of architecture in France. The estate, which belonged to the Orleans family, was confiscated by Napoleon III., and sold in 1853 to the English bankers Coutts & Co.

Petit Trianon. [The Little Trianon.] A pleasant little residence near the royal palace of Versailles, France, which was occupied by the Duchess of Orleans. It is exquisitely fitted up, and embellished by paintings. Petit Trianon was built in 1766 by Louis XV. for Madame Dubarry. Louis XVI. gave it to Marie Antoinette, who laid out the gardens with rock-work, lakes, Swiss cottages, etc., and who here with her court played at shepherds and shepherdesses. See GRAND TRIANON.

☞ "A walk to the Little Trianon is both pleasing and moral: no doubt the reader has seen the pretty fantastical gardens which environ it; the groves and temples, the streams and caverns, (whither, as the guide tells you, during the heat of summer, it was the custom of Marie Antoinette to retire with her favorite, Madame de Lamballe); the lake and Swiss village are pretty little toys, moreover; and the cicerone of the place does not fail to point out the different cottages which surround the piece of water, and tell the names of the royal masqueraders who inhabited each. . . . Yonder is the pretty little dairy which was under the charge of the fair Marie Antoinette herself."
Thackeray.

☞ "The little marble palace, called 'Petit Trianon,' built for Madame Pompadour in the garden grounds, is a beautiful affair, full of what somebody calls 'affectionate-looking rooms.' . . . It was in the litttle palace of Trianon that Napoleon signed his divorce from Josephine." *N. P. Willis.*

Petits Pères. See NOTRE DAME DES VICTOIRES.

Petrarch's House *and* Tomb. At Arqua, Italy. Both are still preserved. The latter is of marble.

There is a tomb in Arqua; rear'd in air,
Pillar'd in their sarcophagus, repose
The bones of Laura's lover. *Byron.*

☞ "On the little square before the church door, where the peasants congregate at mass time, . . . is Petrarch's sepulchre. Fit resting-place of what remains to earth of such a poet's clay. . . . A simple rectilinear coffin, of smooth Verona *mandorlato*, raised on four thick columns, and closed by a heavy cippus-cover. Without emblems, allegories, lamenting genii, this tomb of the great poet, the great awakener of Europe from mental lethargy, encircled by the hills, beneath the canopy of heaven is impressive beyond the power of words." *J. A. Symonds.*

Petrella. A noted fortress, now in ruins, in the village of the same name in Southern Italy, celebrated by its connection with the tragic history of the Cenci family.

That savage rock, the castle of *Petrella*,
'Tis safely wall'd, and moated round about:
Its dungeons underground and its thick towers
Never told tales; though they have heard and seen
What might make dumb things speak.
Shelley.

Petrified Forest. A collection of petrified fragments of trees, scattered about in the sand at a distance of three or four hours' journey from Cairo, Egypt. These fragments of silicified wood are said not to correspond with any vegetation now existing in Egypt.

Petrified Forest. A natural curiosity in California, situated about five miles from Calistoga Hot Springs. It was discovered in July, 1870.

☞ "All the trees discovered were prostrate, and most of them after their petrifaction had been broken transversely into several sections. . . . All the fossil wood observed was silicified, probably by means of hot alkaline waters containing silica in solution, a natural result of volcanic action, especially when occurring in connection with water, as was evidently the case in the present instance."
C. H. Denison.

Petroffskoi. A famous palace in the immediate neighborhood of Moscow, Russia, built after a fantastic style, apparently borrowed from that of the Kremlin. After the burning of Moscow, Napoleon took up his residence here. The park is always open to the public, and is a great popular resort.

Petronilla, Santa. See SANTA PETRONILLA.

Petrus Lombardus, Horologe of. See HOROLOGE OF PETRUS LOMBARDUS.

Pevensey Castle. A very ancient Roman castle in the town of

Pevensey, Sussex, England, famous as having been occupied by William, Duke of Normandy, when he invaded England. It is now in ruins. Its walls were of great strength, and resisted many attacks. It remained a fortress till the reign of Elizabeth. The castle is now in the possession of the Cavendish family.

Pfäffers, Gorge of. See GORGE OF PFÄFFERS.

Pfalz, Die. [The Palatinate.] A castle on an island in the Rhine, opposite the village of Caub, a familiar object to travellers. It dates from the early part of the fourteenth century.

Pfauen-Insel. See PEACOCK ISLAND.

Phalaris, Bull of. See BULL OF PHALARIS.

Pharaoh's Bed. A hypæthral temple at Philæ, built by the Ptolemies and Cæsars. It seems to have been designed with special reference to its appearance from the river, which is fine and impressive.

Pharaoh's Palace. One of the two remaining edifices in Petra, the ruined city of Arabia Petræa.

☞ "The only remaining edifice in Petra is that called Pharaoh's Palace,— a rather vulgar building, Roman in its style, and adorned with stucco garlands. It is cracked and mouldering, and will not last long."

Miss Martineau.

Pharos [*or* Pharos of Ptolemy]. This tower or light-house, one of the seven wonders of the world, stood on a rock at the north-east extremity of the island of the same name, opposite Alexandria, in Egypt. It was a square building of white marble and very costly, surmounted by a fire or lantern which was kept burning continually, and which could be seen for many miles at sea, and along the coast. It is supposed to have been built by order of Ptolemy Philadelphus, and the name Pharos has been applied to light-houses ever since. The structure was several stories in height, each diminishing in size towards the top. No remains of the Pharos can now be found, though according to Arabian records it was in existence in the thirteenth century. Its site is still occupied by the more modern light-house of Alexandria. Sostrates, the architect of the Pharos, according to an anecdote of very doubtful authenticity, immortalized his name in the following manner. He caused this inscription to be cut in the wall of the tower: "Sostrates of Cnidos, son of Dexiphanes, to the Gods who Protect those who are upon the Sea." Then, thinking it would not do to ignore Ptolemæus in such a manner, he covered over the inscription with a coating of cement, upon which he carved the name of Ptolemæus. The cement, with the name upon it, disappeared after some years, leaving only the original inscription, which gave all the credit to Sostrates. Another story is that Ptolemæus, out of modesty, perferred to perpetuate the name of the architect rather than his own. Extraordinary statements, undoubtedly fictitious, have been made of the distance at which the light could be seen. Even Josephus, who perhaps makes the most reasonable assertion, states that it could be discerned for 34 English miles, which, it is said, would require a height of about 500 feet. It is not certain whether the light was from a common fire or from some more complete system of illuminating apparatus.

☞ "This pharos has not its like in the world for skill of construction or for its solidity; since, to say nothing of the fact that it is built of excellent stone of the kind called *kedan*, the layers of these stones are united by molten lead, and the joints are so adherent that the whole is indissoluble, though the waves of the sea from the north incessantly beat against it. From the ground to the middle gallery or stage the measurement is exactly 70 fathoms, and from this gallery to the summit, 26. We ascend to the summit by a staircase constructed in the interior, which is as broad as those ordinarily erected in towers. This staircase terminates at about half-way, and thence the building becomes much narrower. In the interior, and under the staircase, some chambers have been built. Starting from the gallery, the pharos rises to its summit with a continually increasing contraction, until at last it may be folded round by a man's arms. From this same gallery we recommence our ascent by a flight of steps of much narrower dimensions than the lower staircase: in every part it is pierced with windows to give light to persons making use of it, and to assist them in gaining a proper footing as they ascend. This edifice is singularly remarkable, as much on account of its height as of its massiveness; it is of exceeding utility, because its fire burns night and day for the guidance of navigators: they are well acquainted with the fire, and steer their course by it, for it is visible at the distance of a day's sail. During the night it shines like a star; by day you may distinguish its smoke."

Edrisi (the Arabian geographer, who lived in the twelfth century).

Phi Beta Kappa. [Φ Β Κ.] A well-known literary society founded in 1776 at the College of William and Mary in Virginia. Chapters were afterwards chartered at Harvard, Yale, and other prominent colleges. It was originally a secret fraternity; but of late its existence as a society has been merely nominal, though meetings are still held at the various colleges about Commencement time. Election to the Φ Β Κ is a mark of scholarship, the students of highest rank in each class being elected as a matter of course. The total membership at the present time is thought to be between 6,000 and 7,000.

Phidian Jove. See OLYMPIAN JUPITER.

Phigalian Marbles. A collection of groups of sculpture found in the ruins of a temple of Apollo near Phigalia, in Arcadia, Greece, and now deposited in the British Museum, London.

Philadelphia. An American ship captured by the Algerine pirates, and carried to Tripoli, where she was surprised and burned by Stephen Decatur, an officer on Commodore Preble's ship, who volunteered to destroy her that she might not be used by the pirates in the war against the United States.

Philæ. An island in the Nile, about seven miles from the first cataract. It is the "Holy Island" of the Egyptians, since they believed their god Osiris to be buried there. It contains very interesting ruins. The principal building here is the Temple of Isis. See TEMPLE OF ISIS.

Philharmonic Hall. A concert-hall of colossal dimensions in Liverpool, England, one of the finest structures of the kind in the world.

Philip IV. A grand bronze equestrian statue, regarded as one of the finest in the world, now in the Plaza de Oriente, Madrid, Spain. It was formerly in the Buen Retiro gardens, but was moved to its present location in 1844. It was cast at Florence, Italy, in 1640. The statue is 19 feet in height, and weighs 180 cwt. The means by which the equilibrium in the figure of the prancing horse is preserved are said to have been suggested by Galileo.

Philip IV. A picture by Diego Rodriguez de Silva y Velasquez (1599-1660), pronounced "the finest equestrian portrait in the world." In the Gallery at Madrid, Spain.

Philip the Apostle. A picture by Albert Dürer (1471-1528), the German painter. Presented by the Emperor Ferdinand III. to the Duke of Tuscany. Now in the Uffizi Gallery in Florence, Italy.

Philippe, St. See ST. PHILIPPE.

Philipse Manor-House. A stone mansion in Yonkers, N.Y., a part of which was built in 1682, and the remainder in 1745. It is an interesting relic by reason of its wide halls and antique wainscoting, and its associations with

Mary Philipse, the first love of George Washington.

Phillips Academy. 1. A well-known school at Exeter, N.H., founded in 1781 by John Phillips, and richly endowed. Some of the most distinguished men in the country have received a preparatory education here.

2. A school in Andover, Mass., endowed by the Phillips family in 1778.

Philosophers, The. See GEOMETRICIANS, TWO PHILOSOPHERS, and FOUR PHILOSOPHERS.

Philosophy. See SCHOOL OF ATHENS.

Phocas, Column of. A column in the Forum, Rome, and the one referred to by Byron as

"The nameless column with the buried base."

The earth which had accumulated around the pedestal was removed in 1813, when the inscription showed that the column was raised to the Emperor Phocas, in 608, by the Exarch Smaragdus.

☞ "Has not the column lost something of its charm? Before, there was a beauty and a mystery around it — it was a voice that sounded from a dim and distant past, and therefore all the more impressive. But now the ideal light has vanished, and the column loses half its grace, since it speaks to us of the wickedness of tyrants and the weakness of slaves." *G. S. Hillard.*

Tully was not so eloquent as thou,
Thou nameless column with the buried base! *Byron.*

Phœbus and Aurora. See AURORA.

Phœnix, The. An Arctic exploring ship which sailed from England under the command of Capt. Inglefield, May 19, 1853.

Phœnix Park. A fine pleasure-ground and favorite resort in Dublin, Ireland.

Phœnix Theatre. See COCKPIT.

Phoul-a-Phouka. A beautiful and noted waterfall in the county of Wicklow, Ireland.

Phthah. See TEMPLE OF PHTHAH.

Physicians, College of. See COLLEGE OF PHYSICIANS.

Pianto di Maria. See SPASIMO, LO.

Piazetta. [The Small Square.] A public square in Venice, connecting with the Piazza di San Marco, and opening out upon the water of the harbor. At the foot of this enclosure are the two columns of St. Mark and St. Theodore.

The splendid approach to the *Piazetta;* the transfer to the gondola and its soft motion; the swift and still glide beneath the balconies of palaces — made up altogether a moment of high happiness. *N. P. Willis.*

Piazza, The. A name given to a row of lofty houses in Covent Garden, London, built by Inigo Jones, from the resemblance it bore to the arcades common in Italian towns. The popularity of this odd name may be inferred from the frequency in the baptismal registers of the time of such names as Paul Piazza, Mary Piazza, etc.

Unfortunately for the fishmongers of London, the Dory only resides in the Devonshire seas; for could any of this company only convey one to the Temple of luxury under the *Piazza*, where Mecklin, the high priest, daily serves up his rich offerings, great would be the reward of that fishmonger. *Fielding.*

And even in Italy such places are
With prettier name in softer accents spoke,
For, bating Covent Garden, I can hit on
No place that's called "*Piazza*" in Great Britain. *Byron.*

Piazza, The. A coffee-house, no longer standing, in Covent Garden, London. Sheridan often visited the Piazza.

☞ "'Twas when the cup was sparkling before us, and heaven gave a portion of its blue, boys, blue, that I remember the song of Roland at the Old Piazza Coffee House. And now where is the Old Piazza Coffee House? Where is Thebes? Where is Troy?" *Thackeray.*

Piazza Barberini. [Barberini Square.] A well-known public square in Rome, Italy, near the Via Felice.

☞ "Whoever has been in Rome is well acquainted with the *Piazza Bar-*

berini, in the great square, with the beautiful fountain where the Tritons empty the spouting conch-shell, from which the water springs upwards many feet." *H. C. Andersen, Trans.*

☞ "The Piazza Barberini, where I lodge, is like a catafalque of stone with a few forgotten tapers burning on it; the feeble little lights seem to be swallowed up in a lugubrious shroud of shadow, and the indistinct murmur of the fountain in the silence is like the rustling of phantoms." *Taine, Trans.*

Piazza Colonna. A square, facing the Corso, in Rome, and having in its centre the Antonine Column.

Piazza del Campidoglio. [Square of the Capitol.] A square upon the Capitoline Hill, Rome, having upon one side the Palace of the Conservators, upon the other the Museum of the Capitol, at the back the Palace of the Senator, and in the centre the bronze equestrian statue of Marcus Aurelius. This square, with the group of buildings upon it, taken collectively, is often referred to as the Capitol. See also CAPITOLINE HILL.

☞ "The central building in front is called the Palace of the Senator; for there is still a Roman Senator, a harmless puppet created by the pope, and resembling one of his namesakes of antiquity as a chattering cicerone resembles Cicero. The palace is not his residence, but a place where he sometimes comes to amuse himself and the public by holding a court." *Hillard.*

☞ "The building on the south side of the square to the right as we face the Palace of the Senator is called the Palace of the Conservatori. . . . The Conservatori were originally administrative officers, the senator being a judicial magistrate. Their functions have long since become merely nominal." *Hillard.*

☞ "Who has not silently wondered on thinking of the *Capitol*? This mighty word agitates you beforehand, and you are disappointed on finding a moderately grand square flanked by three palaces not at all grand. Nevertheless, it is imposing: a grand stone staircase leading up to it gives it a monumental entrance. *Taine, Trans.*

Then none have I offended. I have done no more to Cæsar than you shall do to Brutus. The question of his death is enrolled in the *Capitol;* his glory not extenuated, wherein he was worthy; nor his offences enforced, for which he suffered death. *Shakespeare.*

Ages on ages shall your fate admire,
No future day shall see your names expire,
While stands the *Capitol*, immortal dome!
Byron.

Piazza del Duomo. [The Cathedral Square.] A well-known public square in Florence, Italy, in which some of the most interesting events in the history of the city have taken place.

Piazza del Gran Duca. See PIAZZA DELLA SIGNORIA.

Piazza del Popolo. [Square of the People.] A square, near the Porta del Popolo, in Rome, from which three streets radiate into the city — the Babuino, the Corso, and the Ripetta. See OBELISK OF THE PIAZZA DEL POPOLO.

Piazza della Annunziata. [Square of the Annunziata.] A well-known public square in Florence, Italy. It is surrounded by arcades and adorned with an equestrian statue, fountains, and busts of the Medici family.

Piazza della Signoria. [Square of the Signory.] The great public square of Florence, Italy, and the scene of all the principal events in its history. It was long called the Piazza di Gran Duca, Square of the Grand Duke [of Tuscany], but now bears again the still more ancient name of the Piazza della Signoria.

☞ "One of the first places which a traveller visits in Florence is the Piazza del Gran Duca, a place not imposing from its size, but interesting from its historical associations, and the works of art which are here assembled." *Hillard.*

Piazza di Gran Duca. See PIAZZA DELLA SIGNORIA.

Piazza di Spagna. [Spanish Square.] A square of a triangular form in Rome, so called from the residence (Palazzo di Spagna) of the Spanish ambassador which is situated upon it. The square is terminated at one end by the buildings of the Propaganda, and above it, and connected by a magnificent flight of steps, is the church of La Trinità de' Monti.

☞ "This flight of steps leads from the *Piazza di Spagna* to the promenade on the Pincio, and, crowned as it is with the façade of the church of the Trinità de' Monti, and the Egyptian obelisk in front of the church, it forms one of the noblest architectural combinations to be seen in Rome or anywhere else." *Hillard.*

And, veiling thus my discontent,
This missive o'er the main
Unto my friend at Rome I sent,
In the sunny "*Square of Spain.*"
T. W. Parsons.

Piazza Navona. A large square in Rome, ornamented with three fountains. It has served as a market since 1447.

☞ "The Piazza Navona is an irregular area of an oblong shape about 850 feet in length and 180 in breadth. The most conspicuous object in it is an immense fountain in the centre, which is one of the heaviest sins against good taste that was ever laid upon the much-enduring earth. . . . On Saturdays and Sundays in the month of August, the sluices which carry off the waters of the great fountain are stopped, and all the central portions of the Piazza are overflowed to the depth of one or two feet. The populace then, obeying that impulse which draws all living things towards water in hot weather, rush to the temporary lake in eager crowds. Horses, oxen, and donkeys are driven into the cooling water; vehicles of all kinds, from the stately coach of a Roman principe to the clumsy wagon of a contadino, roll through them. . . . On these occasions the outer margin of the Piazza not reached by the water, and especially the capacious steps of the church of St. Agnes, are occupied by crowds of idlers. . . . And the whole spectacle is described by those who have witnessed it as one of the most agreeable in Rome."

I went (as was my usual costome) and spent an afternoone in *Piazza Navona*, as well to see what antiquities I could purchase among the people who held mercat there, as to heare the montebanks prate and distribute their medicines. This was formerly the Circus or *Agonales*, dedicated to sports and pastimes, and is now the greatest mercat of the Citty, having three most noble fountaines, and the stately palaces of the Pamfilij, to which add two convents for friars and nuns all Spanish. *John Evelyn*, 1644.

Piazza S. Marco. See St. Mark's Square.

Picador. A picture by Jean Léon Gérôme (b. 1824), the French painter.

Piccadilly. A leading street in London, consisting of shops and fashionable dwelling-houses, said to be so called from the ruffs, or "pickadils," worn by the gallants of James I. and Charles I., the stiffened points of which resembled spear-heads or picardills, a diminutive of *pica*, the Italian and Spanish name for spear. "Piccadille" is however referred to some years before the introduction of these collars, and it is surmised by Jesse that the collar may have been so called from being worn by the frequenters of Piccadilla House, which in turn may have taken its name from the Spanish *peccadillo* (a venial fault).

Will spear, or sword-stick, thrust at him [the Sieur de Lamotte], (or supposed to be thrust), through window of hackney-coach, in *Piccadilly* of the Babylon of Fog, where he jolts disconsolate, not let out the imprisoned animal existence? *Carlyle.*

I returned on foot to *Piccadilly*; again the London weather begins — the small and constant rain, the dissolving mud. *Taine, Trans.*

Picpus, Rue de. A street near the Barrière du Trône, Paris.

Picts' Wall. See Hadrian's Wall.

Pictured Rocks. A series of sandstone bluffs extending for about five miles along the shore of Lake Superior, and rising vertically from the water to a height of from 50 to nearly 200 feet. They derive their name from the very curious manner in which large portions of the surface have been colored by bands of brilliant hues. The French voyageurs call these cliffs *Les Portails*, from the strange forms into which they have been excavated and worn by the surf which the lake has for centuries dashed against their base.

Westward by the Big-Sea-Water,
Came unto the rocky headlands,
To the *Pictured Rocks* of sandstone,
Looking over lake and landscape.
Longfellow.

He's whittling by St. Mary's Falls,
 Upon his loaded wain;
He's measuring o'er the *Pictured Rocks*,
 With eager eyes of gain. *Whittier.*

Pierre aux Dames. A remarkable stone block with female figures in relief, thought to be of Celtic origin, formerly standing on a little hill near Geneva, Switzerland, but now transferred to the city. [Called also *Pierre aux Fées*.]

Pierre de Sân. See STONE OF SÂN.

Pierre Levée. A Druidic monument near Poitiers, France, consisting of several blocks of sandstone. It is alluded to by Rabelais, who ascribes the erection of it to Pantagruel.

Pietà, La. [Pity, compassionate sorrow.] A very common subject of representation by the great artists of the Middle Ages, in which the Virgin as the Mourning Mother (Mater Dolorosa) is exhibited holding her dead Son in her arms, or in her lap, or lying at her feet, and lamenting over him.

☞ "This incident has no mention in the Gospels; but Art would have been cold in feeling and barren in invention if she had not perceived a vacant place here, waiting to be filled with one of the most touching scenes that Nature presents. For it was the old as it is the ever-new story, that Lamentation over the Dead. . . . Thus the *Pietà*, to those who consider some of its finest examples, has a twofold sense, — the sorrow of a mother weeping for her son, and also the last strong cry of our humanity. . . . Yet natural as this subject appears, it was not of early invention. The very word Pietà would have found no place in early art, where Faith and not Pity was the paramount object. It may be doubted whether this subject arose in Italy before the thirteenth century, when Art and Nature began to recognize what each could do for the other; and it would be difficult to determine whether the pen of the the writer or the pencil of the painter took the initiative." *Lady Eastlake.*

Of the numerous compositions upon this theme, the following may be named as among the more celebrated and better known.

Pietà. A small picture by Anthony van Dyck (1599-1641), and one of his admired works. In the Munich Gallery. There is also a larger picture upon this subject by the same painter in the Museum of Berlin, Prussia.

Pietà. A picture by Giovanni Bellini (1426-1516). In the Brera at Milan, Italy. Other examples of this subject by this master are in the Lochis-Carrara Gallery, Bergamo, in the Vatican, at Toledo, in the Stuttgardt Gallery, and elsewhere.

Pietà. A picture ascribed to Andrea Mantegna (1431-1506), the Italian painter. Now in the Berlin Museum.

Pietà. A picture by Antonio Allegri, surnamed Correggio (1494-1534). In the Gallery of Parma, Italy.

Pietà. A celebrated marble group by Michael Angelo (1474-1564) in one of the chapels of St. Peter's, at Rome, representing the Virgin with the dead body of Christ upon her knees. It was one of Michael Angelo's earliest works, executed in his 24th year, and said to be the only one upon which he has inscribed his name.

☞ "Michael Angelo's principal work, however, — that work by which he suddenly passed from being an esteemed artist to be the most famous sculptor in Italy, — is at the present day as good as veiled; the mourning Mary with her dead Son in her lap, — 'la Pietà,' as the Italians call the group. Placed at first in a side chapel in the old Basilica of St. Peter, it received another place on the rebuilding of the church, and now again stands in a side chapel of St. Peter's, so high, however, and in such a fatal light, that it is for the most part impossible to obtain a sight of it, either near or at a distance." *Grimm, Trans.*

☞ "In none of his works has he displayed more perfect knowledge of design and anatomy, or more profound truth of expression." *Ernest Breton.*

☞ "His [Michael Angelo's] Virgin's head, generally of an unsympathetic type, is here appropriate in its grandly abstract and solemn character, a grief locked within, stony as the material in which it is rendered. . . . The curious flatness of the Saviour's face is

supposed to have been owing to a miscalculation of the size of the marble."
Lady Eastlake.

Pietà. A picture by Fra Bartolommeo (1469–1517). In the Pitti Palace, Florence, Italy.

Pietà. An admired picture by Francesco Francia (1450–1518). Now in the National Gallery, London.

Pietà. An admired picture by Pietro Perugino (1446–1524). In the Palazzo Pitti, Florence, Italy.

☞ "Perugino's exquisite picture in the Pitti, a work in which there are more beautiful heads than perhaps in any other in the world."
Lady Eastlake.

Pietà. A picture by Raphael Sanzio (1483–1520), usually styled a Pietà, but properly a "Deposition from the Cross."

☞ "This wonderful drawing (there is no *finished* picture) was in the collection of Count Fries, and then belonged to Sir T. Lawrence. There is a good engraving." *Mrs. Jameson.*

Pietà. A picture by Andrea Vannucchi, called Andrea del Sarto (1487–1531), the Italian painter, and considered one of his best works. In the Belvedere Gallery, Vienna, Austria. There is another upon the same subject in the Pitti Palace, Florence, Italy.

Pietà. A celebrated picture by Guido Reni (1575-1642), representing the body of Christ on a bier, with the weeping mother and two angels at the sides, and below the patron saints of Bologna. In the Gallery at Bologna, Italy.

☞ "This wonderful picture was dedicated as an act of penance and piety, by the magistrates of Bologna, 1616, and placed in their chapel in the church of the 'Mendicanti,' otherwise S. Maria-della-Pietà. It hung there for two centuries for the consolation of the afflicted. It is now placed in the Academy of Bologna for the admiration of connoisseurs."
Mrs. Jameson.

Pietà. A small altar-piece by Hans Memling (d. 1495), the Flemish painter. Now in the St. John's Hospital at Bruges, Belgium.

Piété, Mont de. See MONT DE PIÉTÉ.

Pietra del Bando. [Stone of Proclamation.] A porphyry pillar standing near St. Mark's Church in Venice, Italy, from which, according to tradition, the ancient laws of the Republic of Venice were proclaimed.

Pietro, San. See SAN PIETRO IN MONTORIO and SAN PIETRO IN VINCOLI.

Pigna. A gigantic finial, in imitation of a fir-cone, which once crowned the summit of Hadrian's Mausoleum. Now in the garden of the Vatican, Rome.

☞ "This pine cone, of bronze, was set originally upon the summit of the Mausoleum of Hadrian. After this imperial sepulchre had undergone many evil fates, and as its ornaments were stripped one by one from it, the cone was in the sixth century taken down and carried off to adorn a fountain, which had been constructed for the use of dusty and thirsty pilgrims, in a pillared enclosure, called the *Paradiso*, in front of the old basilica of St. Peter. Here it remained for centuries; and when the old church gave way to the new, it was put where it now stands, useless and out of place, in the trim and formal gardens of the Papal Palace. . . . At the present day it serves the bronze-workers of Rome as a model for an inkstand, such as is seen in the shop windows every winter, and is sold to travellers, few of whom know the history and poetry belonging to the original." *C. E. Norton.*

☞ "I have looked daily over the lonely, sunny gardens, where the wide sweeping orange-walks end in some distant view of the sad and distant Campagna; . . . and where the huge bronze pine by which Dante measured his great giant yet stands in the midst of graceful vases and bas-reliefs wrought in former ages, and the more graceful blossoms blown within the very hour." *Mrs. Kemble.*

His face appeared to me as long and large
As is at Rome the pine cone of St. Peter's,
And in proportion were the other bones.
Dante, Inferno, XXXI., Longfellow's Translation.

Pigott Diamond. A diamond, weighing 49 carats, and estimated to be worth £40,000, brought to England by Earl Pigott, and sold in 1801.

Pilate's House. See RIENZI'S HOUSE.

Pilgrim Hall. An edifice in Plymouth, Mass., containing many interesting relics of the Pilgrim Fathers and of the old colonial days. Among the more noted curiosities here preserved are the chair of Gov. Carver, the sword of Miles Standish, the gun-barrel with which King Philip, the brave chief of the Wampanoags, was killed, and many original documents of the Plymouth colony.

Pilgrim Oak. A tree in front of Newstead Park, England, known throughout that region of country as the Pilgrim Oak.

☞ "It is a venerable tree, of great size, overshadowing a wide area of the road. Under its shade the rustics of the neighborhood have been accustomed to assemble on certain holidays, and celebrate their rural festivals. This custom had been handed down from father to son for several generations, until the oak had acquired a kind of sacred character. The 'old Lord Byron,' however, in whose eyes nothing was sacred, when he laid his desolating hand on the groves and forests of Newstead, doomed likewise this traditional tree to the axe. Fortunately the good people of Nottingham heard of the danger of their favorite oak, and hastened to ransom it from destruction. They afterwards made a present of it to the poet, when he came to the estate." *Irving.*

Pilgrims. See EMBARKATION OF THE PILGRIMS, LANDING OF THE PILGRIMS, and SUPPER AT EMMAUS.

Pillar of Trajan. See TRAJAN'S COLUMN.

Pillars of Hercules. The name given in ancient times to the mountains of Calpe and Abyla, standing opposite to each other, the one on the European, the other on the African, shore of the straits which connect the Mediterranean with the Atlantic. The present names of these mountains are the Rock of Gibraltar and Jebel Zatout.

Pillow, Fort. See FORT PILLOW.

Pilot Butte. A natural curiosity in Wyoming Territory, being a mound of rock and earth standing on the level plain, one of the more celebrated of the huge monumental and often fantastically shaped mountains which are found along the line of the Union Pacific Railroad in this part of its course.

Pimento, Accademia del. A Florentine academy founded in 1657.

Pimlico. A district in London, formerly noted for its public gardens, which were often mentioned by the early English dramatists.

Gallants, men and women,
And of all sorts, tag-rag, been seen to flock here
In threaves, these ten weeks, as to a second Hogsden,
In days of *Pimlico* and Eye-bright.
Ben Jonson.

Of course the people came in uncompelled,
Lame, blind, and worse, — sick, sorrowful, and worse,
The humors of the peccant social wound
All pressed out, poured out upon *Pimlico.*
Mrs. Browning.

Pin, Society of the. See SOCIETY OF THE PIN.

Pinacotheca. [Gr. Πινακοθήκη, a collection of pictures.] **1.** The name given to a gallery of paintings in the Vatican at Rome, which, though not containing more than 50 pictures, includes some of the richest treasures of art, among which are the Transfiguration, the Madonna di Foligno, and the Communion of St. Jerome. The name is also applied to other picture galleries, notably to the fine collection in Munich. See PINAKOTHEK.

2. A chamber of the Propylæa, at Athens, so called from its walls being covered with paintings.

Pinakothek. [Gr. πίναξ, a picture, θήκη, a collection.] A celebrated picture-gallery in Munich, Bavaria. It is a magnificent building of yellow sandstone, 530 feet long, containing a very fine collection of pictures. Above the cornice on the southern side of the building stand 25 colossal statues of painters by Schwanthaler. The name Pinacotheca is also sometimes applied to other galleries of paintings, in particular to the collection in the Vatican, Rome. See *supra*.

☞ "The Pinakothek, with its elevated windows in the roof, has from the spot on which I am standing the appearance of a large hot-house or conservatory, and such it is. In the Pinakothek are all the varieties of glowing plants, and the saloons are equally as gorgeous as the flowers."
Hans Christian Andersen.

Pincian Hill. [Ital. *Monte Pincio*, Lat. *Collis Hortulorum*, the hill of pleasure-grounds.] A celebrated eminence at Rome, and the favorite promenade of the modern inhabitants of the city. It is not one of the original seven hills. The Pincian was once covered with the villas and gardens of Roman citizens.

☞ "The Monte Pincio itself is a space of only a few acres in extent, planted with trees and shrubbery. . . . The charm of this promenade consists in the splendid prospects which it commands on every side. On the north and east it overlooks the varied and undulating grounds of the Villa Borghese, with their fountains, their picturesque edifices, and the walks that wind and turn under broad canopies of oaks and pines. Beyond these a superb panorama of the Campagna and the Sabine and Alban hills is embraced at a glance. On the west . . . the view comprises the greater part of the modern city, including the Janiculum, the Vatican, St. Peter's, and the regular outline of Monte Mario, crowned with its dark line of cypresses. . . . Nowhere in the world is seen a greater variety of equipages than on the Pincio on a fine winter's afternoon."
Hillard.

☞ "The Pincian Hill is the favorite promenade of the Roman aristocracy. At the present day, however, like most other Roman possessions, it belongs less to the native inhabitants than to the barbarians from Gaul, Great Britain, and beyond the sea, who have established a peaceful usurpation over all that is enjoyable or memorable in the Eternal City." *Hawthorne.*

Pincio. See PINCIAN HILL.

Pineta, La. [The pine-grove.] A very celebrated pine-forest near the city of Ravenna in Italy. It was a favorite resort of Dante, of Byron, and of many other poets. Covino says, "Here grows a spacious pine forest, which stretches along the sea between Ravenna and Cervia."

A softly-breathing air, that no mutation
Had in itself, upon the forehead smote me
No heavier blow than of a gentle wind,
Whereat the branches lightly tremulous,
Did all of them bow downward toward
that side
Where its first-shadow casts the Holy
Mountain;
Yet not from their upright direction
swayed,
So that the little birds upon their tops
Should leave the practice of each art of
theirs;
But with full ravishment the hours of
prime,
Singing, received they in the midst of
leaves
That ever bore a burden to their rhymes,
Such as from branch to branch goes gathering on
Through the pine forest on the shore of
Chiassi,
When Eolus unlooses the Sirocco.
Dante, Purgatorio, XXVIII., Longfellow's Translation.

Sweet hour of twilight, — in the solitude
Of the pine-forest, and the silent shore
Which bounds Ravenna's immemorial
wood,
Rooted where once the Adrian wave flow'd
o'er,
To where the last Cesarean fortress stood,
Evergreen forest! which Boccaccio's lore
And Dryden's lay made haunted ground
to me,
How have I loved the twilight hour and
thee! *Byron.*

It [the basilica of St. Apollinaris-in-classe] is still seen standing in the midst of a solitary marshy plain near Ravenna, surrounded with rice-grounds, and on the verge of that vast melancholy *pine-forest* made famous in the works of Boccaccio, Dante, and Byron. *Mrs. Jameson.*

Pinkham Notch. A mountain pass in the White Mountain region in New Hampshire, in the township of Jackson. It was named after Capt. Daniel, who, about 1790, built a road through the notch.

Pinta, The. One of the three little vessels with which Columbus set sail for America from Palos, Spain, on the 3d of August, 1492. The *Pinta* was commanded by Alonzo Pinzon, a famous Spanish navigator.

As early voyagers over untried realms of waste, we have already observed the signs of land. The green twig and fresh red berry have floated by our bark; the odors of the shore fan our faces; nay, we may seem to descry the distant gleam of light, and hear from the more earnest observers, as Columbus heard, after midnight, from the mast-head of the *Pinta*, the joyful cry of *Land! Land!* and lo! a new world broke upon his early morning gaze. *C Sumner.*

Pio-Clementino, Museo. See MUSEO PIO-CLEMENTINO.

Piombi. See LEADS, THE.

Pioneer, The. An Arctic exploring ship which sailed from England under Capt. Belcher in 1852.

Pisa, Baptistery of. See BAPTISTERY OF PISA.

Pisa Cathedral. [Ital. *Duomo di Pisa.*] A beautiful and noted church, making one of the famous group of marble buildings in Pisa, the Cathedral, the Baptistery, the Leaning Tower, and the Campo Santo. It was erected in the eleventh century.

Pisa, Leaning Tower of. See LEANING TOWER.

Pisani Palace. [Ital. *Palazzo Pisani.*] A splendid fifteenth-century palace in Venice, Italy.

Pisaro Family. A celebrated picture by Titian (1477-1576), representing the members of that family engaged in adoring the Madonna and Child. In the church of S. Maria Gloriosa de' Frari, Venice, Italy.

Pitt Diamond. This stone, which is regarded as one of the most perfect diamonds in the world, was brought from India by Mr. Pitt (grandfather of William Pitt), and by him sold to the Regent of Orleans, in 1717, for £135,000. It was placed among the crown jewels of France, was set in the handle of Bonaparte's sword of state, and was shown in the Paris Exhibition of 1855. The weight of the Pitt diamond is 137 carats. It is also known as the Regent Diamond.

The grand *Pitt diamond*, — the Queen's own star of the garter, — a sample of otto of roses at a guinea a drop, would not be handled more curiously, or more respectfully, than this porcelain card of the Baroness. *Thackeray.*

Lifting the green veil, to see what invaluable it hid, they descried there, amid down and rich white wrappages, no *Pitt Diamond* or Hapsburg Regalia, but, in the softest sleep, a little red-colored Infant! *Carlyle.*

Pitt, Fort. See FORT DU QUESNE.

Pitti Palace. [Ital. *Palazzo Pitti.*] A royal palace in Florence, Italy. It was begun by Luca Pitti, the opponent of the Medici family, about the year 1435, and contains a very rich and noted collection of paintings. It is of immense size, the front being 460 feet in length, three stories (of 40 feet each) high in the centre, and with the centres of its windows 24 feet apart.

☞ "There is no palace in Europe to compare it to for grandeur, though many may surpass it in elegance. The design is said to have been by Brunelleschi, but it is doubtful how far this is the case, or, at all events, how much may be due to Michelozzi, who certainly assisted in its erection, or to Ammanati, who continued the building, left incomplete at Brunelleschi's death, in 1444." *Fergusson.*

☞ "I doubt if there is a more imposing palace in Europe; I have not seen one which leaves so grand and simple an impression." *Taine, Trans.*

And when the face was finished, throat and hands,
Her cameriera carried him, in hate
Of the English-fashioned shroud, the last brocade
She dressed in at the *Pitti*.
Mrs. Browning.

Some gas-lights tremble along squares and streets;
The *Pitti's palace*-front is drawn in fire.
Mrs. Browning.

Such conditions are not exactly fitted for ordinary treatment of design; yet the shop-front architect delights in ignoring them altogether, and in loading his upper stories with pediments, columns, niches, and cornices, just as if they stood on a basement as solid as that of the *Pitti Palace*. *C. L. Eastlake.*

Pius III. A remarkable portrait by Titian (1477-1576), of which there are many replicas and copies. In the Hermitage, St. Petersburg, Russia.

Place Dauphine. A place in Paris which was designed by Henry IV. in 1608, and so named in commemoration of the birth of his son, the Dauphin Louis XIII.

Place de Grève. See PLACE DE L' HÔTEL DE VILLE.

Place de la Bastille. This place in Paris was the scene of some of the fiercest struggles in June, 1848. The largest barricade was thrown up here, at the end of the Rue St. Antoine; and here Gen. Negrier and the Archbishop of Paris were struck down. Here stood the famous prison known as the Bastille. Here ends the line of the original boulevards, and here begins the Faubourg St. Antoine. See BASTILLE.

Poised in thy beauty o'er the vaults of doom,
Time was, ere thy bright presence bathed the "*Place*"
In borrowed sunshine, when the Bastille towers
Frowned on the passer-by.
George Gordon McCrae.

Place de la Concorde. A square in Paris, of peculiar interest, as connected with scenes of the Revolution. It has been called also Place Louis XV., and Place de la Revolution. In the centre stands the Obelisk de Luxor, which once stood in front of the temple of Thebes, as long ago as the reign of Sesostris, 1550 (?) years before Christ. It stands on the spot where the guillotine was erected in the "reign of terror," after the death of Louis XVI. Here the signal was given for the attack on the Bastille in 1789. In 1793, Louis XVI. and Marie Antoinette were beheaded here; and in 1848 the proclamation of the Republic was celebrated here with much rejoicing. It is one of the grandest and most imposing squares in Paris or in any city. See OBELISK OF LUXOR.

☞ "What is there in Europe—nay, in the world—equal to this? In the centre the mighty obelisk of red granite pierces the sky; on either hand showers of silver spray are thrown up from splendid bronze fountains; statues and pillars of gilded bronze sweep in a grand circle round the square; and on each side magnificent vistas lead the eye off, and combine the distant with the near, to complete this unparalleled view." *Bayard Taylor.*

☞ "The Place de la Concorde is a most splendid square, large enough for a nation to erect trophies in of all its triumphs; and on one side of it is the Tuileries, on the opposite side the Champs Elysées, and, on a third, the Seine, adown which we saw large cakes of ice floating, beneath the arches of a bridge." *Hawthorne.*

Place de la Pucelle. [Place of the Maid.] A place in Rouen, France, named in memory of Jeanne d'Arc, the Maid of Orleans, and serving to mark the spot where she was burned in 1431.

Here blooms the legend, fed by Time and Chance,
Fresh as the morning, though with centuries old,
The whitest lily on the shield of France,
With heart of virgin gold.
Maria Lowell.

Place de l' Hôtel de Ville. The large square in front of the Hôtel de Ville, Paris. Here was formerly the Place de Grève, the scene of many executions, and of some of the chief events in the revolutions of 1830, 1848, and 1872.

☞ "The Place de Grève is, in the history of Paris, one of the most revolting localities the stranger could be induced to visit. For many centuries it was the spot on which criminals were executed; and, besides having been thus appropriated to scenes of horror, its pavement has been stained with the blood of the victims of almost every revolution that has occurred. On the 17th of March, 1848, it was the scene of a frightful mutiny in favor of the Provisional Government; and on the 16th of the following month an attempt to overturn that Government was foiled here by the steady attitude of the National Guard." *Sir Francis B. Head.*

Place des Consuls. See PLACE MÉHÉMET ALI.

Place des Victoires. A circular space in Paris built in 1686 by Mansard, and surrounded by houses. A statue of Louis XIV., in the centre, raised by the Duc de la Feuillade, was destroyed during the Revolution. Its place is now taken by another of the same monarch.

Place du Carrousel. A large public square in Paris, near the Tuileries, which derives its name from a tournament held here by

Louis XIV. in 1662. A portion of the place is called the Court of the Tuileries, and at the entrance of this court stands a triumphal arch erected by Napoleon in 1806. The long gallery of French pictures, which connects the Louvre with the Tuileries, is on the south side of this square. The Revolutionary guillotine was first set up here. Until the beginning of the present century the space occupied by this square was covered with houses, churches, etc.; and the work of clearing the land between the Tuileries and the Louvre was begun by Napoleon I., and continued by Louis Philippe. Napoleon III., before the close of the year 1858, removed the remaining houses, finished the palatial structures, and carried out the whole plan for the magnificent Place du Carrousel, at an expense of £1,600,000. See ARC DU CARROUSEL.

Place du Palais Royal. On the south front of the Palais Royal, Paris. Here was a small square which was the scene of a severe conflict between some of the Municipal Guard and the insurgents in 1848.

Place du Trône. A large space in Paris at the end of the Rue St. Antoine. Here was the guillotine (afterwards removed to the Place de la Concorde) from June 9 to July 27, 1794; and here 1,270 persons were executed by that instrument.

Place Méhémet Ali. A large square in Alexandria, Egypt, formerly called Place des Consuls, but usually known among English-speaking people as the *Great Square*. It is the European centre of the city. Here are the chief shops, business offices, and hotels, while the interior of the square forms an agreeable promenade.

Place of Wailing of the Jews. A famous spot in Jerusalem, being a narrow enclosed space near the Mosque of Omar. It is a section of the ancient wall of the Haram, which includes the site of the old temple on Mount Moriah, and is believed to be the only part remaining of Solomon's temple wall. To this place the Jews have for centuries come once a week, every Friday, to mourn over the desolation of Israel. Men, women, and children may be seen there in every variety of attitude indicative of grief and despondency, bewailing their dishonored sanctuary.

☞ "I have said how proud and prosperous looked the Mosque of Omar, with its marble buildings, its green lawns, the merry children, and gay inmates making holiday; all these ready and eager to stone to death on the instant any Jew or Christian who should dare to bring his homage to the sacred spot. This is what we saw within the walls. We next went round the outside, till we came, by a narrow, crooked passage, to a desolate spot, occupied by desolate people. Under a high, massive, very ancient wall, was a dusty, narrow, enclosed space, where we saw the most mournful groups I ever encountered. This high ancient wall, where weeds are springing from the crevices of the stones, is believed to be a part, and the only part remaining, of Solomon's temple wall; and here the Jews come, every Friday, to their Place of Wailing as it is called, to mourn over the fall of their Beautiful House, and pray for its restoration. What a contrast did these humbled people present to the proud Mohammedans within! The women were sitting in the dust, — some wailing aloud, some repeating prayers with moving lips, and others reading them from books on their knees. A few children were at play on the ground; and some aged men sat silent, their heads drooped on their breasts. Several younger men were leaning against the wall, pressing their foreheads against the stones, and resting their books on their clasped hands in the crevices. With some, this wailing is no form; for I saw tears on their cheeks." *Miss Martineau.*

Place Royale. A square in Paris, built in the beginning of the seventeenth century, on part of the site of the Palais des Tournelles.

Place St. Sulpice. A place in Paris which has lately been ornamented with trees, and in which a flower-market is held. In its centre stands a beautiful fountain erected by Napoleon the First. This fountain is in the form of a pavilion, and is adorned with figures of Fénelon, Bossuet, Fléchier, and Massillon.

Place Vendôme. This square in Paris was designed by Lóuis XIV., who began it to contain public buildings, such as the Mint, Royal Library, etc. This design was, however, abandoned except so far as the formation of a square was concerned. In 1806 a grand triumphal column was erected by Napoleon in honor of the victories achieved by the French armies. This column is constructed from the metal of cannon taken from the Austrians and Prussians, and is 140 feet in height. It is surmounted by a statue of Napoleon, and is ornamented by bas-reliefs of some of the principal scenes in the campaign of 1805; also with helmets, cannon, and military implements of various kinds. See COLONNE VENDÔME.

The sun unveiled himself in beauty bright,
The eyes of all beamed gladness and delight,
When, with unruffled visage, thou didst come,
Hero of France! unto the *Place Vendôme*
To mark thy column towering from the ground,
And the four eagles ranged the base around.
Victor Hugo, Trans.

Placentia. A place on the Hudson, near Poughkeepsie, formerly the home of James K. Paulding (1779–1860).

Placidia. See MAUSOLEUM OF GALLA PLACIDIA.

Plaine-des-Recollets. A fine public square in Ghent, Belgium.

Plains of Abraham. See ABRAHAM.

Plains of Chalmette. A level tract about five miles from New Orleans, La., bordering on the Mississippi River, and surrounded by cypress-swamps. It is the site of the engagement known as the "Battle of New Orleans," Jan. 8, 1815, between the American forces under Gen. Jackson and the British under Pakenham, in which the latter were defeated. A marble monument has been erected on the spot.

Plantes, Jardin des. See JARDIN DES PLANTES.

Playford Hall. An ancient country mansion in England, for many years the residence of Thomas Clarkson (1760–1846), the philanthropist. It is said to be the oldest fortified house of the kind in England, and the only one that has water in the moat by which it is surrounded.

☞ "The place [Playford Hall] is a specimen of a sort of thing which does not exist in America. It is one of those significant landmarks which unite the present with the past, and for which we must return to the country of our origin." *Mrs. H. B. Stowe.*

Plaza de las Cortes. A well-known public square in Madrid, Spain, in front of the Spanish House of Commons. In this enclosure is a statue of Miguel de Cervantes.

Plaza de Oriente. A well-known public square in Madrid, Spain. It is of an oval form, and is surrounded with 44 colossal statues.

Plaza Mayor. [The Great Square.] The chief square in Madrid, Spain, on which, in former times, executions, *autos-da-fé*, and royal bull-fights were celebrated. The elevation of this square above the level of the sea is some 2,450 feet.

Pleiad. See LOST PLEIAD.

Pleissenburg Castle. An ancient citadel of historic interest in Leipsic, Germany.

Plessis les Tours. A famous castle in the commune of La Riche, near Tours, France, once the royal residence of Louis XI. Portions only of the original building are now standing. Sir Walter Scott, in his novel of "Quentin Durward," has given a graphic description of this castle.

Pliny's Doves. A mosaic, perhaps the most celebrated in the world, now in the Museum of the Capitol, Rome, representing doves drinking from a basin surrounded by a border. It derives its name from the supposition that it is a work described by Pliny, in the 35th book of his Natural History, who says that at Pergamos there is a wonderful mosaic, by Sosus, of a dove drinking, and casting the shadow of her head upon the water, while others are pluming themselves upon the lip of the vessel.

Ploughing in Nivernais. [*Labourage Nivernais.*] A noted picture by Rosa Bonheur (b. 1822), and esteemed her masterpiece. In the Gallery of the Luxembourg, Paris.

☞ "I hear as I write the cry of the ox-drivers — incessant, musical, monotonous. I hear it not in imagination, but coming to my open window from the fields; . . . white oxen of the noble Charolais breed, sleek, powerful beasts, whose moving muscles show under their skins like the muscles of trained athletes. When the gleams of sunshine fall on these changing groups, I see in nature that picture of Rosa Bonheur's, 'Ploughing in the Nivernois.'" *Hamerton.*

Plover, The. An Arctic exploring ship which sailed from England in the expedition of Capt. Maguire in 1852.

Plummer Hall. A fine building in Salem, Mass., containing several libraries, and an elegant hall adorned with portraits of distinguished men of the colonial period.

Plymouth Church. A large plain church edifice in Brooklyn, N.Y., noted as that in which Henry Ward Beecher preaches.

Plymouth Rock. The famous rock or ledge on which the Pilgrims are believed to have landed when they first stepped from their boats in the harbor of what is now Plymouth, Mass. The main rock is on Water Street, and is surmounted by a stone canopy. A portion of the rock was removed in 1775 to the vicinity of Pilgrim Hall, but has been recently restored to its original place, and is now under the canopy.

This rock has become an object of veneration in the United States. *De Tocqueville.*

But if he [Davis] bar New England out in the cold, what then? She is still there. And, give it only the fulcrum of *Plymouth Rock*, an idea will upheave the continent. *W. Phillips.*

From the deck of the Mayflower, from the landing at *Plymouth Rock*, to the Senate of the United States, is a mighty contrast, covering whole spaces of history — hardly less than from the wolf that suckled Romulus and Remus to that Roman Senate, which, on curule chairs, swayed Italy and the world. *Charles Sumner.*

An' then they bust out in a kind of a raptur
About their own vartoo, an' folks's stone-blindness
To the men that 'ould actilly do 'em a kindness, —
The American eagle, — the Pilgrims thet landed, —
Till on ole *Plymouth Rock* they git finally stranded. *Lowell, Biglow Papers.*

For well she keeps her ancient stock,
The stubborn strength of *Pilgrim Rock*;
And still maintains, with milder laws,
And clearer light, the Good Old Cause! *Whittier.*

Pnyx, The. A place of public assembly for the citizens of ancient Athens. It was cut out of a hill about a quarter of a mile from the Acropolis, and was of a semicircular form like a theatre.

Where stands the vane of Theseus, there she dwells,
Within the shadow of Minerva's shrine.
The cavern dungeon where old Socrates
The hemlock drank; the azure-vaulted *Pnyx*,
Where great Demosthenes the state controlled
With matchless eloquence, are near the spot
Wherein she dwells. *S. G. W. Benjamin.*

Pocahontas, Baptism of. See BAPTISM OF POCAHONTAS.

Poetry. See PARNASSUS.

Poets' Corner. An angle in the south transept of Westminster Abbey, London, popularly so called from the fact that it contains the tombs of Chaucer, Spenser, and other eminent English poets, and memorial tablets, busts, statues, or monuments, to many who are buried in other places. Addison says that here there are "many poets who have no monuments, and many monuments which have no poets." The name is first mentioned by Goldsmith.

☞ "I passed some time in Poets' Corner, which occupies an end of one of the transepts or cross aisles of the abbey. The monuments are generally simple, for the lives of literary men afford no striking themes for the sculptor. Shakespeare and Addison have statues erected to their memories; but the greater part have busts, medallions, and sometimes mere inscriptions. Notwithstanding the simplicity of these memorials, I have always observed that the visitors to the abbey remained longest about them." *Irving.*

While we surveyed the *Poets' Corner*, I said to him [Goldsmith], "Forsitan et nostrum nomen miscebitur istis." When we got to Temple Bar, he stopped me, pointed to the heads upon it, and slyly whispered, "Forsitan et nostrum nomen miscebitur istis." *Dr. Johnson.*

And over him the kindred dust was strewed
Of *Poets' Corner*. O misnomer strange!
The poet's confine is the amplitude
Of the whole earth's illimitable range
O'er which his spirit wings its flight,
Shedding an intellectual light,
A sun that never sets, a moon that knows no change. *Horace Smith.*

O World, what have your poets while they live
But sorrow and the finger of the scorner?
And, dead, the highest honor you can give
Is burial in a corner.

Here in Westminster's sanctuary, where
Some two-three kings usurp one-half the Abbey,
Whole generations of the poets share
This nook so dim and shabby.

So when we come to see Westminster's lions,
The needy vergers of the Abbey wait us;
And while we pay to see the royal scions,
We see the poets gratis.
Robert Leighton.

Poggia Reale. A favorite promenade of the lower classes of Naples, Italy, in the neighborhood of that city. A palace with extensive gardens formerly stood on the spot.

Pola, Amphitheatre of. A celebrated Roman ruin in the town of Pola, Austria.

Polaris, The. An Arctic exploring vessel which sailed for the Northern seas under Commander Hall, in 1870. By travelling on the ice on a sledge, Capt. Hall penetrated as far as to lat. 82° 16′ N.

Pole, Cardinal. A portrait by Sebastian del Piombo (1485–1547), pronounced "a magnificent work." It is now in the Hermitage at St. Petersburg, Russia.

Pollice Verso. A picture by Jean Léon Gérôme (b. 1824), the French painter.

Pollux. See CASTOR AND POLLUX.

Polyphemus. A picture by Nicolas Poussin (1594–1665), the celebrated French painter.

Poussin's magnificent "*Polyphemus*" (I only know a print of that marvellous composition) has perhaps suggested the first-named picture [one by Gudin]. *Thackeray.*

Polytechnique, École. See ÉCOLE POLYTECHNIQUE.

Pompeian, Maison. See MAISON POMPEIAN.

Pompey's Pillar. This pillar, which presents a fine appearance to one approaching Alexandria, in Egypt, from the sea, stands on a lonely eminence about a third of a mile south of the present walls of the city. It is 98 feet 9 inches in height. There is an inscription upon it purporting that it was erected by Publius in honor of Diocletian. Abdallatif, the ancient scholar and traveller, asserts that this column was called by the Arabs "the pillar of the colonnades," and that he himself had seen more than 400 similar ones on the seashore. He says also that these pillars had evidently supported a roof; and he believes them to be the remains of the famous Serapéum built by Alexander, and in the stoa or portico of which Aristotle taught.

☞ "Pompey's Pillar is by no means so big as the Charing Cross trophy. This venerable column has not escaped ill treatment either. Numberless ships' companies, travelling cockneys, etc., have affixed their rude marks upon it. Some daring ruffian even painted the name of 'Warren's blacking' upon it, effacing other inscriptions — one, Wilkinson says, 'of the second Psammetichus.'" *Thackeray, Cornhill to Cairo.*

When Victory's Gallic column shall but rise,
Like *Pompey's Pillar*, in a desert's skies,
The rocky isle that holds or held his dust
Shall crown the Atlantic like the hero's bust. *Byron.*

Is *Pompey's Pillar* really a misnomer?
Had Thebes a hundred gates, as sung by Homer? *Horace Smith.*

Pillar of Pompey! gazing o'er the sea,
In solemn pride, and mournful majesty!
When on thy graceful shaft, and towering head,
In quivering crimson, day's last beams are shed,
Thou look'st a thing some spell with life supplies,
Or a rich flame ascending to the skies. *Nicholas Michell.*

Pompey's Statue. [Otherwise called the *Spada Pompey.*] A colossal figure of Parian marble, discovered in 1553, and now in the Spada Palace at Rome. It is generally considered to be the identical statue which once stood in the Curia of Pompey, and the one at the base of which "great Cæsar fell," although this has been a subject of dispute among antiquaries. This statue narrowly escaped destruction during the siege of Rome by the French in 1849, shots from their batteries having penetrated the building where it stands, but it escaped unharmed.

☞ "I saw in the Palazzo Spada the statue of Pompey,—the statue at whose base Cæsar fell. A stern, tremendous figure! I imagined one of greater finish, of the last refinement, full of delicate touches, losing its distinctness in the giddy eyes of one whose blood was ebbing before it, and settling into some such rigid majesty as this, as Death came creeping over the upturned face." *Dickens.*

☞ "Every one knows that it was found below the foundation walls of two houses, in a lane near the site of the Curia of Pompey—that the proprietors, unable to settle to which of them it belonged, the head being under one house and the feet under the other, imitated the judgment of Solomon, and resolved to cut it in two, and that a cunning cardinal, hearing of this, persuaded the Pope to buy it, and to make him a present of it." *Eaton.*

☞ "In a more civilized age this statue was exposed to an actual operation; for the French, who acted the Brutus of Voltaire in the Coliseum, resolved that their Cæsar should fall at the base of that Pompey which was supposed to have been sprinkled with the blood of the original dictator. The nine-foot hero was therefore removed to the arena of the amphitheatre, and, to facilitate its transport, suffered the temporary amputation of its right arm. The republican tragedians had to plead that the arm was a restoration; but their accusers do not believe that the integrity of the statue would have protected it." *Byron.*

This was the unkindest cut of all;
For when the noble Cæsar saw him stab,
Ingratitude, more strong than traitors' arms,
Quite vanquished him; then burst his mighty heart;
And in his mantle muffling up his face,
Even at the base of Pompey's statua,
Which all the while ran blood, great Cæsar fell. *Shakespeare.*

And thou, dread statue! yet existent in
The austerest form of naked majesty,
Thou who beheldest, 'mid the assassin's din,
At thy bathed base the bloody Cæsar lie,
Folding his robe in dying dignity,
An offering to thine altar from the queen
Of gods and men, great Nemesis! *Byron.*

Pons Elius (Ælius). See BRIDGE OF ST. ANGELO.

Pont du Gard. A magnificent aqueduct, a grand relic of Roman times, at Nîmes, in Southern France.

☞ "The famous Pont du Gard served the double purpose of a bridge and an aqueduct. It crossed the river Gardon between two mountains some leagues from Nîmes. Three ranges of arcades, superposed, decreasing in size from the lowest range, and constructed of hewn stone lain without mortar or cement, constituted this marvellous work. Rain has not been able to penetrate the seams of this uncemented structure, nor has time been able to dislocate its joints. The Pont du Gard is in the style of the best Roman epoch. It is attributed to Agrippa, who came to Nîmes in A.D. 19, and who had the superintendence of the waters at Rome. No Roman monument is more admired." *Lefèvre, Tr. Donald.*

☞ "Such confidence had they [the Romans] in the stability of their empire, that they provided for the day when repairs might be necessary for the Pont du Gard!" *Mérimée, Trans.*

☞ "The sound of my footsteps in these immense vaults made me fancy that I heard the loud voice of those who

had built them. I felt lost like an insect in this immensity."
Rousseau, Trans.

Rousseau came out of one of his sad self-torturing fits, as he cast his eye on the arches of the old Roman aqueduct, the *Pont du Gard.* *Holmes.*

Here it [the Bridge of Alcantara] exceeds every thing I have seen, even the *Pont du Gard,* which is more remarkable than the aqueducts about Rome.
George Ticknor.

As the arches of the *Pont du Gard,* suspended in their power amidst that solitude, produce an overmastering feeling of awe; so the huge fabric of the Lucretian system, hung across the void of Nihilism, inspires a sense of terror, not so much on its own account, as for the Roman sternness of mind that made it. *J. A. Symonds.*

Pont Neuf. [The New Bridge.] This bridge is one of the most important in Paris, as it connects the bank of the Seine with the island of the city, and is frequented by crowds of people. It was finished by Henry IV., of whom a statue was erected in the open space between the two bridges in 1818. An older statue of that ruler on the same spot was melted to make cannon in 1792; and to form the present statue the statues of Napoleon from the Place Vendôme and the column of Boulogne sur Mor, and of Desaix from the Place des Victoires, were likewise melted down. This, the longest bridge of Paris, was the second built over the Seine.

1643, Dec. 24. Over the Seine is a stately bridge called *Pont Neuf,* begun by Henry III. in 1578, finished by Henry IV., his successor. It is all of hewn free-stone, found under the streets, but more plentifully at Mont-Martyre, and consists of 12 arches, in the midst of which ends the poynt of an island on which are built handsome artificers houses. There is one large passage for coaches and two for foot passengers three or four feet higher and of convenient breadth for eight or ten to go abreast. *John Evelyn, Diary.*

His [Lulli's] drowsy pieces are played still to the most sprightly audience that can be conceived; and even though Rameau, who is at once a musician and a philosopher, has shown, both by precept and example, what improvements French music may still admit of, yet his countrymen seem little convinced by his reasonings; and the *Pont-neuf* taste, as it is called, still prevails in their best performances. *Goldsmith.*

When I was in full training as a *flaneur,* I could stand on the *Pont Neuf* with the other experts in the great science of passive cerebration, and look at the river for half an hour with so little mental articulation, that when I moved on it seemed as if my thinking-marrow had been asleep and was just waking up refreshed after its nap. *Holmes.*

Pontack's. A tavern in Abchurch Lane, London, erected after the Great Fire of 1666. It was resorted to by Swift.

Ponte alle Grazie. A well-known bridge in Florence, Italy, erected in the middle of the thirteenth century, and taking its name from a neighboring shrine of the Madonna.

Ponte dei Sospiri. See BRIDGE OF SIGHS.

Ponte di Rialto. See RIALTO.

Ponte Molle. A bridge across the Tiber in Rome, built by Pope Pius VII. in 1815. It is the site of the old Roman bridge called the Pons Milvius, after M. Emilius Scaurus by whom it was built. The golden candlestick from the Temple of Jerusalem is believed to have been thrown into the river from this bridge.

I have stood upon the *Ponte Molle* to enjoy the sublime spectacle of the close of day. The summits of the Sabine Hills appeared of lapis lazuli and gold, while their bases and sides were bathed in vapors of violet or purple. This rich decoration does not vanish so quickly as in our climate. *Chateaubriand, Trans.*

I should like to live long enough to see the course of the Tiber turned, and the bottom of the river thoroughly dredged. I wonder if they would find the seven-branched golden candlestick, brought from Jerusalem by Titus, and said to have been dropped from the *Milvian bridge.* *Holmes.*

We crossed the *Ponte Molle,* looking back often to the dome of St. Peter's, and the castle of St. Angelo, as we caught glimpses of them between the villas and over the hills. *George Ticknor.*

Ponte Rotto. [The Broken Bridge.] A bridge over the Tiber at Rome, built upon the site of the ancient Pons Æmilius. The modern bridge has been several times rebuilt. Two of its arches were carried away in 1598, their place being since supplied by a suspension span. The derivation of the modern name from the condition of the stone structure is obvious.

☞ "In constructing a suspension bridge the piles of the *Ponte Rotto* were used as a foundation, which last structure was erected in the Middle Ages upon the foundations of the Pons Palatinus, finished under the censorship of Scipio Africanus. Scipio Africanus and a suspension bridge, such are the contrasts which can be found nowhere but in Rome."

Ampère, Trans.

Ponte San Angelo. See BRIDGE OF ST. ANGELO.

Ponte SS. Trinita. A well-known bridge in Florence, Italy, constructed in the fourteenth century, but more than once restored.

Ponte Vecchio. [The Old Bridge,] A celebrated bridge across the Arno in Florence, Italy, built in the fourteenth century, and, like the Rialto in Venice, a street of shops, appropriated to jewellers, goldsmiths, and other workers in metal.

☞ "The space of one house, in the centre, being left open, the view beyond is shown as in a frame; and that precious glimpse of sky, and water, and rich buildings, shining so quietly among the huddled roofs and gables on the bridge, is exquisite. Above it, the Gallery of the Grand Duke crosses the river. It was built to connect the two great palaces by a secret passage; and it takes its jealous course among the streets and houses, with true despotism: going where it lists, and spurning every obstacle away, before it."

Dickens.

☞ "I returned homeward over the Ponte Vecchio, which is a continuous street of ancient houses, except over the central arch, so that a stranger might easily cross the river without knowing it." *Hawthorne.*

Taddeo Gaddi built me. I am old —
Five centuries old. I plant my foot of stone
Upon the Arno, as St. Michael's own
Was planted on the dragon.
. . . .
I can remember when the Medici
Were driven from Florence; longer still ago
The final wars of Ghibelline and Guelf.
Florence adorns me with her jewelry;
And when I think that Michael Angelo
Hath leaned on me, I glory in myself.

Longfellow.

Pontine Marshes. This is a name given to a marshy plain in the Papal States, about 24 miles long by 10 broad, infected with miasmata, which for ages have given rise to malarial fevers. Many attempts have been made to drain these marshes. The tract is supposed to have been at one time a gulf of the sea; and within the historical period it was a fertile neighborhood, containing towns and a considerable population.

Pool, The. A name given to a part of the river Thames, just below London Bridge, where the stream is divided into two channels by the rows of vessels anchored in it.

Pool of Bethesda. A fountain in Jerusalem alluded to in the Bible (John v. 2-7). Its situation is not established beyond question, but it is by Dr. Robinson and others identified with the intermittent spring called the Fountain of the Virgin. See FOUNTAIN OF THE VIRGIN.

☞ "I could not but wish that it might have been Bethesda; but it cannot be reasonably supposed so."

Miss Martineau.

Pool of Siloam. This celebrated pool is near the Valley of Jehoshaphat at Jerusalem. It is a rectangular reservoir of stone, which is now crumbling, and overrun by a weedy growth, which adds beauty and grace to the scene. It is fed from a fountain high up in the rock. Its waters, once sacred to the Temple, are now used to irrigate the neighboring valleys. It is only three times referred to in the Scriptures.

The waters of *Siloah* that flow softly.

Isa. viii. 6.

The wall of the *pool* of *Siloah* by the king's garden. *Neh.* iii. 15.

Go wash in the *pool* of *Siloam*. . . . He went his way, therefore, and washed and came seeing. *John* ix. 17.

—— or if Sion hill
Delight thee more, and *Siloa's* brook that flowed
Fast by the oracle of God, I thence
Invoke thy aid to my advent'rous song.

Milton.

By cool *Siloam's* shady rill
How sweet the lily grows!

Heber.

Pools of Solomon. Three reservoirs in Palestine, receiving their supply from a subterranean fountain which furnished water for the Holy City, the "Pools of Solomon" serving to render the supply of water constant.

Pope's Head. A noted tavern in London, in existence as early as 1464, and still standing in 1756.

Popolo. See PIAZZA DEL POPOLO and PORTA DEL POPOLO.

Porcelain Tower. A celebrated tower in the city of Nanking, China. It was built the ninth century before Christ by King A-yon, was rebuilt in the fourth century of the Christian era, and, having been again destroyed, was rebuilt for the last time in 1413 by Hoang-li-Tai. The edifice, which was the most splendid of its kind in China, was octagonal in shape and 261 feet high. It was made of white brick, and the cost of the edifice is said to have been between $35-000,000 and $40,000,000. This superb tower was destroyed during the Tae Ping occupation of the city in 1853.

☞ "When the introduction of Buddhism into the country necessitated the use of high towers, the Chinese achieved marvels in this kind of structure. The Great Porcelain Tower at Nankin attains a height of 350 feet. Originally eight chains of iron, falling from the summit at each of the eight angles, sustained 72 brass bells. Eighty other bells hung from the roofs of the nine stories, which were ornamented also with 128 lamps. From the summit rose a great mast, surrounded with a spiral cage in open-work, and crowned with a globe of an extraordinary size. This Porcelain Tower is so named because of the brilliant porcelain ornaments with which its walls and roofs are decked." *Lefèvre, Tr. Donald.*

The *Tower of Porcelain*, strange and old,
Uplifting to the astonished skies
Its ninefold painted balconies,
With balustrades of twining leaves,
And roofs of tile, beneath whose eaves
Hang porcelain bells that all the time
Ring with a soft, melodious chime;
While the whole fabric is ablaze
With varied tints, all fused in one
Great mass of color, like a maze
Of flowers illumined by the sun.
Longfellow.

Porch, The. See STOA.

Porchester Castle. An ancient fortress in the harbor of Portsmouth, England. Its origin is referred by some to the time of the Roman occupation.

Port Coon Cave. A natural curiosity in the county of Antrim, Ireland. It is an extraordinary excavation in the basaltic rocks into which boats may row a long distance.

Port Royal des Champs. A famous abbey, now in ruins, about eight miles from Versailles in France, the headquarters of the Jansenists. It was destroyed in 1709 through the influence of the Jesuits. In the seventeenth century a society of learned men gathered here for purposes of study, and published many works. From their place of residence they are known in history as the Port Royalists.

☞ "France has many a lovelier prospect, though this is not without its beauty, and many a field of more heart-stirring interest, though this, too, has been ennobled by heroic daring; but through the length and breadth of that land of chivalry and song, the traveller will in vain seek a spot so sacred to genius, to piety, and to virtue. The round tower of the dove-cote and the bases of the piers of the abbey chapel are all that remain of the once crowded monastery of Port Royal. In those woods Racine first learned the language of poetry. Under the roof of that humble farm-house, Pascal, Arnauld, Nicole, De Sacy, and Tillemont meditated those works which as long as civilization and Christianity survive will retain their hold on the gratitude and reverence of mankind. . . . To this seclusion retired the heroine of the Fronde, Ann Génévieve, Duchess of Longueville, to seek the peace the world could not give. Madame de Sévigné discovered here a place 'tout propre à inspirer le désir de faire son salut.' From Versailles there came hither to worship God many a courtier and many a beauty, heart-broken or jaded with the very vanity of vanities — the idolatry of their fellow-mortals. Survey French society in the seventeenth century from what aspect you may, at Port Royal will be found the most illustrious examples of whatever imparted to that motley assemblage any real dignity or permanent regard." *Stephen.*

Porta Aurea. See ARCH OF TRAJAN.

Porta del Popolo. [Gate of the People.] A gate of Rome, upon the north, and not far from the site of the ancient Porta Flaminia, which was the entrance of the old Flaminian Way. The Porta del Popolo was built in 1561 from designs by Michael Angelo.

☞ "The first entrance of Rome is prodigiously striking. It is by a noble gate designed by Michael Angelo and adorned with statues; this brings you into a large square, in the midst of which is a large obelisk of granite, and in the front you have at one view two churches of a handsome architecture, and so much alike that they are called the twins, with three streets, the middlemost of which is one of the largest in Rome." *Addison.*

Hence turning on the right out of the *Porto del Popolo* we came to Justinian's gardens neere the Muro torto, so prominently built as threatening every moment to fall, yet standing so for these thousand yeares. *John Evelyn*, 1644.

Porta di San Giovanni. [Gate of St. John.] A modern gate of Rome, built by Gregory XIII. in the sixteenth century. It is near the ancient Porta Asinaria, which is now walled up, but which is the best preserved of those of the Aurelian wall, and is the one through which Belisarius first entered the city, and through which the treachery of the Isaurians allowed Totila to pass.

Porta di San Paolo. [Gate of St. Paul.] A celebrated ancient gate in Rome, and one of the most picturesque entrances to the city. It was rebuilt by Belisarius, and a portion of it is thought to be older than his time.

Porta di San Sebastiano. [Gate of St. Sebastian.] One of the ancient gateways of Rome.

Porta Flaminia. [The Flaminian Gate.] One of the ancient gates of Rome, the place of which is now supplied by the Porta del Popolo. See PORTA DEL POPOLO.

Porta Maggiore. [The Greater Gate.] The finest of the city gates of Rome, and a noble monument of ancient architecture. It was originally an arch of the aqueduct of Claudius.

Porta Nigra. [The Black Gate.] A noted ruin and relic of Roman times at Trèves, in Rhenish Prussia. It was a provincial gate of justice.

☞ "It is the only example of its class which we possess in any thing like its original state. Notwithstanding its defects of detail, there is a variety in the outline of this building and a boldness of profile that render it an extremely pleasing example of the style adopted, and, though exhibiting many of the faults incidental to the design of the Colosseum, it possesses all that repetition of parts and Gothic feeling of design which gives value to such dimensions." *Fergusson.*

Porta Ostiensis. [The Ostian Gate.] One of the old Roman gates, leading to the seaport Ostia. Its place is now occupied by the Porta San Paolo. See PORTA DI SAN PAOLO.

Porta Santa. [The Holy Gate.] A door adjoining the main entrance to St. Peter's in Rome, which is walled up and marked by a cross in the middle. It is pulled down by the pope in person on the Christmas-eve of the Jubilee which has taken place at the expiration of every period of 25 years (except 1850) since the time of Sixtus IV. The pope himself begins the destruction of the door by striking it with a silver hammer. The dates of the two preceding jubilees are afterwards placed over the entrance. There are three other basilicas in Rome, besides St. Peter's, viz.: St. John Lateran, Sta. Maria Maggiore, and St. Paolo *fuori le Mura*, which enjoy the dignity of a *Porta Santa*.

☞ "These holy years and doors were originally invented by Boniface VIII., at the termination of the thirteenth century, who proclaimed a jubilee throughout the Christian world, with plenary indulgence and remission of sins to all who in the course of that year should visit the shrines of the apostles and martyrs of Christianity at Rome; and commanded this festival to be held for evermore at the expiration of every century. . . . But it was found so lucrative to the Holy See from the heaps of gold the piety of wealthy pilgrims poured on the altars, that instead of one the number was gradually multiplied to four jubilees or holy years in every age. Thus after the holy doors have been walled up, and the brazen cross upon them devoutly pressed by the lips and rubbed by the foreheads and chins of the pious for five and twenty years, they are thrown open, and the Pope, followed by every good Christian, walks into the four churches through them, but always walks out by some door not holy." *Eaton.*

☞ "After preliminary prayers from Scripture, singularly apt, the pope goes down from his throne, and, armed with a silver hammer, strikes the wall in the doorway, which, having been cut round from its jambs and lintel, falls at once inwards, and is cleared away in a moment by the San Pietrini. The pope then, bareheaded and torch in hand, first enters the door, and is followed by his cardinals and other attendants to the high altar, where the first vespers of Christmas Day are chanted as usual. The other doors of the church are then flung open, and the great queen of churches is filled." *Cardinal Wiseman.*

Porta Westphalica. [The Westphalian Gate.] A pass in the mountain range called the Wiehengebirge near Minden, Germany.

Portage Bridge. A famous wooden bridge at Portage, N.Y., 800 feet long, and 234 feet high. It is said to have been the largest wooden structure of the kind in the world. It is now replaced by an iron structure.

Portamento della Croce. [Bearing of the Cross.] A fine picture by Gaudenzio Ferrari (1484–1550).

Porte St. Denis. A triumphal arch, 76 feet in height, in Paris, built in 1672 in honor of the victories of Louis XIV. The walls of Paris at that time ran where the Boulevards now are, and this arch was one of the gates of the city. The tops of this arch and of the Porte St. Martin were occupied and held by the insurgents in 1830.

☞ "It commemorates some of the wonderful feats of arms of Ludovicus Magnus, and abounds in ponderous allegories — nymphs and river-gods, and pyramids crowned with fleurs-de-lis; Louis passing over the Rhine in triumph, and the Dutch lion giving up the ghost, in the year of our Lord 1672." *Thackeray.*

He [Voltaire] is properly their god, — such god as they are fit for. Accordingly all persons, from the Queen Antoinette to the Douanier at the *Porte St. Denis*, do they not worship him? *Carlyle.*

Porte St. Martin. A triumphal arch in Paris, 57 feet high and 57 feet wide, erected in 1675 in honor of the victories of Louis XIV. See PORTE ST. DENIS.

Portland Vase. This beautiful work of art was found in a sarcophagus in a sepulchre near Rome about the year 1560. It was formerly the principal ornament of the Barberini palace in Rome, but afterwards became the property of the Duchess of Portland, and after her death was deposited in the British Museum. It is composed of glass and enamel, out of which figures are cut in the manner of a cameo. There are different opinions as to the designs of these figures, but all agree as to the value and beauty of the work. Copies of it were executed by Wedgwood, one of which may be seen in the British Museum. The original vase was broken in 1845, but the pieces were so skilfully put together that scarcely a blemish can be detected. It is kept in the medal-room of the museum.

Portman Square. A well-known public square in London.

Portsmouth, The. A vessel of the United States navy, with which, aided by the *Levant*, Admiral Foote attacked and took the four Barrier-forts in Canton, China, in 1856.

Portugal Street. A street in London which has acquired considerable notoriety from the court for the relief of insolvent debtors being held there.

Posilipo, Grotta di. See GROTTA DI POSILIPO.

Potiphar's Wife accusing Joseph. A picture by Rembrandt van Ryn (1607-1669), the Dutch painter. It is now in the Hermitage at St. Petersburg, Russia.

Potomac, The. A noted frigate of the United States navy, in service in the war of 1812. She was built at Washington.

Potter's Field. An ancient burial place for strangers at Jerusalem. It is on a hill overlooking the Valley of Hinnom.

Poulterer's Shop. A picture by Gerard Dow (1613-1680), the Dutch *genre*-painter. In the National Gallery, London.

Poultry. A well-known street in London anciently occupied by poulterers, whence the name.

Poverty. A picture by Hans Holbein the Younger (1498?-1543), well known by engravings. The original perished at Whitehall in 1698.

Powderham Castle. A noble mansion, the seat of the Earl of Devon, near Kenton, England.

Pozzi. See WELLS, THE.

Praça do Commercio. A large and handsome public square in Lisbon, Portugal.

Prado, El. [The Meadow.] The grand boulevard of Madrid, Spain, converted by Charles III. from a meadow, as the name indicates, into a delightful promenade.

☞ "The interior of the city of Madrid, taken as a whole, is far from handsome. It should not, however, be forgotten that no city in Europe can boast within its walls so fine a walk as the Prado." *George Ticknor.*

☞ "To me the Prado is an inexhaustible source of amusement. In the first place, it is in itself the finest public walk I have ever seen within the walls of any city. . . . Anciently it was an uneven meadow of little beauty, but famous for being the scene of the plots, murders, duels, and intrigues of the city and court. It was not, however, until the middle of the last century that Charles III. levelled it, and made it the beautiful walk it now is. . . . During the forenoon, and nearly all the afternoon, no part of the city in summer is so silent and deserted as this. At five o'clock the whole Prado is watered, to prevent the dust which would otherwise be intolerable. Just before sundown the carriages and crowd begin to appear, and about half an hour the exhibition is in its greatest splendor. On your left hand are two rows of carriages slowly moving up and down on each side, while the king and the *infantas* dash up and down in the middle with all the privileges of royalty, and compel everybody on foot to take off his hat as he passes, and everybody in a carriage to stop and stand up. Every time I see this singularly picturesque crowd mingled with the great number of the officers of the guard that are always there in splendid uniforms, and contrasted with the still greater number of priests and monks in their dark, severe costumes, I feel persuaded anew that it is the most striking moving panorama the world can afford." *George Ticknor.*

Prairie Avenue. A well-known and prominent street in Chicago, Ill.

Prarie de Lacken. A landscape picture by Peter Paul Rubens (1577-1640), now in Buckingham Palace, London.

Prater, The. A celebrated promenade in Vienna, Austria, consisting of avenues nearly four miles in length, and greatly frequented.

☞ "In the afternoon we drove out to the Prater — the famous Prater. It is a great public garden and drive, intersected with many pleasant walks and roads, ornamented with fine old trees, and parts of it enlivened with large numbers of deer, while other parts are rendered still more lively with coffee-houses, puppet-shows, and shows of animals. But we enjoyed very much the drive into the more picturesque parts, where the deer were browsing undisturbed, and oaks a thousand years old cast their shade upon us, as they had perchance in their youth upon the court of Charlemagne." *George Ticknor.*

Prato della Valle. A well-known public square in Padua, Italy, containing a large number of colossal statues.

Pratt Street. A street in Baltimore, Md. It was while passing along this street on the 19th of April, 1861, that the 6th Massachusetts regiment was attacked, having three of their number killed, and eighteen wounded.

Praxiteles, Faun of. See FAUN.

Praying Boy. See BOY PRAYING.

Pré aux Clercs. A district near St. Germain des Prés, Paris, now occupied by houses, but once, owing to the disputed ownership of the land, a place for lawlessness and debauchery, rioting and duels.

Pré Catelan. A prettily-laid-out garden in the Bois de Boulogne, Paris. The Pré Catelan is patronized by the upper classes, and concerts are given here several times a week.

Prebischthor. A remarkable natural arch, 90 feet high, in the region known as the Saxon Switzerland.

Preble, Fort. See FORT PREBLE.

Presentation of the Virgin. [Ital. *La Presentazione.*] A favorite subject of representation by the great painters of the Middle Ages, based upon a legendary incident, in which the Virgin, as a child, is consecrated to the service of the Temple. Among the more noted compositions which treat of this subject the following may be mentioned: —

Presentation of the Virgin. A picture by Ghirlandaio (1449-1498), "a composition full of life and character, . . . with luxury of accessories and accompaniments." In the church of S. Maria Novella, Florence, Italy.

Presentation in the Temple. A picture by Rembrandt van Ryn (1606-1669), the Dutch painter. In the Gallery of the Hague, Holland.

Presentation of the Virgin. A picture by Guido Reni (1574?-1642). In the Louvre, Paris.

Presentation of the Virgin. A picture by Titian (1477-1576). In the Accademia delle Belle Arti, Venice, Italy.

Presentation in the Temple. A picture by Jacopo Robusti, called Tintoretto (1512-1594). In the church of S. Maria del Orto, Venice, Italy.

Presentation in the Temple. A picture by Fra Bartolommeo (1469-1517), the Italian painter. Now at Venice, Italy.

Presentation in the Temple. A picture by Stephan Lochner, called Meister Stephan (d. 1451), a German painter of rare merit. It is now in the Museum at Darmstadt, Germany.

Presentation of the Virgin. A large altar-picture by Titian (1477-1576). It is now in the Accademia delle Belle Arti, in Venice, Italy.

☞ "This famous picture is so well known through the numerous engravings that I have not thought it necessary to reproduce it here. In the general arrangement Titian seems to have been indebted to Carpaccio, but all that is simple and poetical in the latter becomes in Titian's version sumptuous and dramatic. The number of portrait-heads adds to the value and interest of the picture."

Mrs. Jameson.

Presentation of the Virgin. A picture by Taddeo Gaddi (1300-1352?). In the church of Santa Croce, Florence, Italy.

Presepio, Il. [The Manger.] A chapel in the church of Ara-Cœli at Rome, which contains the famous image of the Bambino. See BAMBINO.

President, The. 1. A war-vessel of the old United States navy. She was built in 1794 at New York, and carried 44 guns.

So off he goes and tells his crew;
  The sails were quickly bent, sir;
A better ship you never knew,
  She's called the *Presi-dent*, sir.

Old Song.

2. An American steamer which left New York for Liverpool in April, 1841. She was never heard from afterwards.

There is another passenger very much wrapped up, who has been frowned down by the rest, and morally trampled upon and crushed, for presuming to inquire with a timid interest how long it is since the poor *President* went down. *Dickens.*

Primrose Hill. An elevation near

Regent's Park, London, which has been converted into a public garden, and commands an extensive view. It is so called from the primroses which once grew upon it in great abundance.

> As I was going up *Primrose Hill*, —
> Primrose Hill was dirty, —
> There I met a pretty miss,
> And she dropped me a courtesy.
>
> Little miss, pretty miss,
> Blessings light upon you!
> If I had half-a-crown a day,
> I'd spend it all upon you.
> *Mother Goose.*

> I shall not omit to speak of one genius, in drab breeches and gaiters, and an Arcadian hat, who had a violent propensity to the pastoral, but whose rural wanderings had been confined to the classic haunts of *Primrose Hill* and the solitudes of the Regent's Park. *Irving.*

Prince Adolphus. See SAMSON THREATENING HIS FATHER.

Prince Albert. **1.** An Arctic exploring ship which sailed from England under Commander Kennedy, in 1851, Lady Franklin having equipped the expedition.

2. An armor-plated ship of the British navy, launched May 23, 1864.

Prince Consort. An armor-plated ship of the British navy, launched June 26, 1862.

Prince Eugène, Boulevart de. See VOLTAIRE, BOULEVART DE.

Prince of Orange landing at Torbay. A picture by Joseph Mallord William Turner (1775-1851). In the National Gallery, London.

Prince of Wales's Theatre. A well-known place of entertainment in London, formerly known as the Queen's Theatre.

Princes Street. A noted street in the New Town of Edinburgh, Scotland, regarded as almost unrivalled for the magnificent view it commands of the Old Town (the street being only built upon on the north side), and constituting one of the finest promenades to be found in any city.

Princess's Theatre. A theatre in Oxford Street, London, celebrated for the reproduction, under the management of Mr. Charles Kean, of Shakespeare's historic plays. It was opened to the public Sept. 30, 1841.

Princeton, The. A United States frigate. By the bursting of a gun during an experimental firing, while a distinguished party of visitors were on board, the Secretary of State, A. P. Upshur, and others, were killed, in February, 1844.

Printing House Square. **1.** A retired court in London. It derives its name from the office of the King's Printer, which stood here till nearly the close of the last century, and was marked by the royal arms over the doorway.

> I went one day with a good friend to the "Times" office, which was entered through a pretty garden-yard, in *Printing-House Square.* *Emerson.*

2. A noted square in the city of New York, the centre of the great news-purveying industry of the United States, where are assembled the offices of the chief metropolitan journals, the *Tribune*, the *Herald*, the *Times*, the *World*, the *Sun*, and others, some of which occupy costly and imposing buildings.

Prison of Socrates. This name is applied to one of three chambers hewn in the rock at the base of the hill Museum, at Athens, Greece. The dome of the inner chamber is funnel-shaped, with an aperture to let in the light from the top. These excavations are sometimes called ancient baths.

Prisoner of Chillon. A picture by Ferdinand Victor Eugène Delacroix (1799-1863), the celebrated French historical painter.

Procuratie Nuove. The new or modern palace of the Procurators. In Venice, Italy, fronting on the Piazza of St. Mark.

Procuratie Vecchie. The ancient palace of the Procurators. In Venice, Italy, fronting upon the Square of St. Mark.

Prodigal Son. A noted picture by

Bartolomé Esteban Murillo (1618–1682). Now in the Gallery of Stafford House, London.

Prodigal Son. A picture by David Teniers the Younger (1610-1694?), the Belgian *genre*-painter. It is now in the Louvre, in Paris.

Profile, The. A huge and very interesting rock-conformation upon the side of Profile Mountain in the Franconia range (White Mountains), New Hampshire. From a certain point of view at a distance, it bears a wonderful resemblance to the outline of a human face. This remarkably complete and distinct profile is nearly 1,500 feet above the little lake below it, and is from 60 to 80 feet in length. It is also popularly known as the OLD MAN OF THE MOUNTAIN. Hawthorne refers to it in "The Great Stone Face."

Beyond them, like a sun-rimmed cloud,
  The great Notch mountains shone,
Watched over by the solemn-browed
  And awful face of stone! *Whittier*

'Tis the musical Pemigewasset,
  That sings to the hemlock-trees
Of the pines on the Profile Mountain,
  Of the stony Face that sees,
Far down in the vast rock-hollows
  The waterfall of the Flume.
Lucy Larcom.

Propaganda. [Ital. *Collegio di Propaganda Fede.*] A religious establishment at Rome, founded by Gregory XV. in 1622, to educate young foreigners from heretical countries, in order that they might afterward return as missionaries and spread the Catholic faith among the people of their different nations. The annual examination of the pupils takes place in January. At the time of the French Revolution, the name Propaganda was given to the secret societies which aimed to disseminate democratic ideas, and it is often used at the present day to denote any institution or organization which seeks to promote special schemes either in politics or religion.

☞ "The origin of the Propaganda is properly to be sought in an edict of Gregory XIII., by which the direction of Eastern missions was confided to a certain number of cardinals, who were commanded to promote the printing of catechisms in the less-known tongues. . . . It was at the suggestion of the great preacher Girolamo da Narni that the idea was first conceived of extending the above-named institution. At his suggestion a congregation was established in all due form, and by this body regular meetings were to be held for the guidance and conduct of missions in every part of the world."
Ranke.

☞ "We may with equal justice call Propaganda an universal academy, or a Noah's Ark, just as we feel disposed. Young men from all parts of the world are educated here for missionaries. Here are children from California to China, from Ireland to the Cape of Good Hope: every one of them repeats a poem by rote in his native tongue. But a man must be a Mezzofanti to profit by this Babel-like anthology. . . . The less the audience [at the Feast of Languages in the Propaganda] understand of these poems, the more they applaud: it was so at least on this occasion, when I heard them cheer loudest an Ethiopian and two Chinese, their languages sounding most like gibberish and awaking the loudest laughter." *Hans Christian Andersen.*

Propylæa. This structure, at Athens, Greece, the *Vestibule* of the citadel, built of Pentelic marble, was begun in the year 437 B.C., and was completed by the architect Mnesicles five years later, or about the time of the beginning of the Peloponnesian war. It covered the whole of the western end of the Acropolis. The Greeks admired the Propylæa more than any other of their buildings. Some walls and a few columns are still standing, and the entrance has been recently cleared.

☞ "The grand flight of the Propylæum is on the right. A high rampart serves as the basement for the little temple of the Wingless Victory, demolished in 1687 by the Turks, and afterward built up again, stone by stone, by two German architects. Athens dedicated it to her divine protectress Athena. The friezes represented the combats in which this goddess assured victory to her people, and upon the balustrade, the Victories, her winged messengers, seemed to await her orders." *Lefevre, Trans.*

☞ "The *Propylæa* still form a portal which divides two worlds. You leave modern and mediæval associations behind you, and are alone with the Past." *Bayard Taylor.*

Proserpine. A well-known ideal bust by Hiram Powers (b. 1805), the American sculptor.

☞ "The popularity of this work has caused its incessant reproduction; few modern works of the chisel are more exquisitely and gracefully ornamental to boudoir, salon, or library." *Tuckerman.*

Proserpine, Rape of. See RAPE OF PROSERPINE.

Prospect Park. A fine pleasure-ground in Brooklyn, N.Y., covering nearly 600 acres, including hills, meadows, and groves, and a beautiful lake. The park was begun in 1866, and is said to have cost, together with two boulevards connected with it, nearly $12,000,000.

Protestant Cemetery. [At Rome.] The Protestant Burial-ground in Rome, near the Pyramid of Caius Cestius, containing the graves of many English and American travellers and other foreign residents at Rome. The Old Protestant Cemetery, now closed, contains the grave of Keats, and in the New Burial-ground is a monument to Shelley.

☞ "It would almost make one in love with death to be buried in so sweet a place." *Percy Bysshe Shelley.*

Protomoteca. The name given to a suite of seven rooms in the Capitol of Rome, presented to the Arcadian Academy by Leo XII. They contain many busts of illustrious men, including some which were formerly in the Pantheon.

Province House. A noted mansion of colonial times, which formerly stood on Washington Street, Boston, Mass. It had a fine lawn in front. The building was of brick, three stories in height, with stone steps. It was erected in 1679. In 1715 it was purchased by the Province as a residence for the governors, who from a portico in front were in the habit of addressing the citizens. In the early part of the present century it became private property, and a block of stores was erected in front of it, the old building degenerating into a hall for negro concerts. It was destroyed by fire in 1864, but the walls remain, and have been used as the exterior of a new building. Nathaniel Hawthorne has given a description of the Province House in his "Twice-Told Tales."

O my God! — for that free spirit, which of old in Boston town
Smote the *Province House* with terror, struck the crest of Andros down!
Whittier.

Prytaneum. [Gr. πρυτανεῖον, the President's Hall, or Town Hall.] A public building in ancient Greek cities. In Athens, the hall in which the magistrates had their meals, and where they entertained at the public cost foreign ambassadors. Citizens also of high public merit, and the children of those who fell in battle, were often rewarded by a seat at this public table. Socrates, on his trial, when asked to name his punishment, adjudged himself entitled to be supported in the Prytaneum.

What, then, is suitable to a poor man, a benefactor, and who has need of leisure in order to give you good advice? There is nothing so suitable, O Athenians, as that such a man should be maintained in the *Prytaneum*. . . . If, therefore, I must award sentence according to my just deserts, I award this, maintenance in the Prytaneum.
Plato, Apology of Socrates.

Psyche. A beautiful relic of ancient sculpture, now in the museum at Naples, Italy, well known by the numerous reproductions of it in marble and plaster. It apparently represents her listening to a Cupid who may be supposed to stand on her right. This figure was found in the amphitheatre at Capua.

☞ "The charming Naples *Psyche*. This refined youthful torso, with its delicate *distingué* head, is likewise not of the great epoch of sculpture." *Taine, Trans.*

Psyche and the Butterfly. See CUPID CATCHING A BUTTERFLY.

Ptarmigan Hill. A picture by Sir Edwin Landseer (1803-1873), the most celebrated modern painter of animals.

Pucelle, Place de la. See PLACE DE LA PUCELLE.

Puck. 1. An admired picture by Sir Joshua Reynolds (1723-1792).
2. A work of sculpture by Harriet G. Hosmer (b. 1830).

Pudding Lane. A narrow street or lane in London. It was here that the Great Fire of 1666 began.

Puente de Alcantara. [The Bridge of Alcantara.] An interesting and impressive Roman ruin in the town of Alcantara, Spain. The bridge, built of immense stones, which here spans the Tagus, was built for the Emperor Trajan, A.D. 105. It consists of six arches, the central span being 110 feet. The bridge is about 670 feet in length, and 210 in height, and is constructed of granite without cement.

☞ "One of the most remarkable of these [bridges] is that which Trajan erected at Alcantara in Spain. The roadway is perfectly level, as is generally the case in Roman bridges, though the mode by which this is attained, of springing the arches from different levels, is perhaps not the most pleasing. To us, at least, it is unfamiliar, and has never, I think, been adopted in modern times." *Fergusson.*

Puente del Diablo. [The Devil's Bridge.] A famous old Roman aqueduct — called by the Spaniards el Puente, the bridge — at Segovia in Spain.

☞ "The first thing we went to see was the cathedral; . . . the next, the Roman Aqueduct, called by the people 'Puente del Diabolo,' for they have no idea such a stupendous work could be achieved by a personage of less authority and power. . . . It begins outside of the city, and traverses the valley on 159 arches in the upper row, but not quite so many below. It is built of square-hewn stones, without cement or clamps, and is nevertheless so perfectly preserved, that it still serves the purpose for which it was built as well as when it was new. . . . It is certainly one of the most solid and magnificent monuments that have come down to us from antiquity." *George Ticknor.*

Puerta de Alcala. [Gate of Alcala.] A grand triumphal gate affording an entrance to the city of Madrid, Spain, on the east. It consists of five arches, and was erected by Charles III. to commemorate his entrance to Madrid.

☞ "It should not be forgotten that no city in Europe can boast within its walls so fine a walk as the Prado, that Rome alone, so far as I know, has an entrance equal to that by the *Gate of Alcala.*" *George Ticknor.*

Puerta del Sol. [Gate of the Sun.] A celebrated public square in Madrid, Spain. It is now in the middle of the capital, although it was once the east gate on which the rising sun shone. It is the centre of the busy life of the city, and at all times a crowded rendezvous of idlers.

Pullins, The. A natural curiosity in the county of Donegal, Ireland. It is an extraordinary ravine, presenting in succession a series of cascades, caves, wild cliffs, with a foaming river and a natural bridge.

☞ "A description can but faintly convey the extraordinary character of these lovely scenes." *Mr. and Mrs. Hall.*

Pulpit [of Nicholas of Pisa]. In the cathedral of Siena, Italy. A celebrated and very elaborate work of sculpture. Another by the same artist, very similar, in the Duomo at Pisa.

☞ "I have no words to express the originality and richness of invention displayed in this pulpit. It is as peculiar as it is beautiful. . . . On the panels a labyrinth of crowded figures — a long octagonal procession, the Nativity, the Passion, the Last Judgment — envelops the marble with a marble covering." *Taine, Trans.*

Purgatory, St. Patrick's. See ST. PATRICK'S CAVE AND PURGATORY.

Puritans going to Church. A picture by George H. Boughton, a painter of landscapes and *genre*.

Puttina, La. [The Girl.] An admired portrait by Titian (1477-1576). In the Palazzo Strozzi, Florence, Italy.

Pylades and Orestes. A picture by Benjamin West (1738-1820). In the National Gallery, London.

Pyramids, The. A general name for the sepulchral monuments of ancient Egypt, in all about 60, but specially applied to the Pyramids of Gheezeh, about 12 miles from Cairo, consisting of two large and several smaller pyramids.

☞ "Let us now turn to the Pyramids — the oldest, largest, and most mysterious of all the monuments of man's art now existing. All those in Egypt are situated on the left bank of the Nile, just beyond the cultivated ground, and on the edge of the desert, and all the principal examples within what may fairly be called the Necropolis of Memphis. Sixty or seventy of these have been discovered and explored, all of which appear to be royal sepulchres. This alone, if true, would suffice to justify us in assigning a duration of 1,000 years at least to the dynasties of the pyramid builders. . . . The three great pyramids of Gizeh are the best known and the most remarkable of all those in Egypt. Of these the first, erected by Cheops, or as he is now more correctly named, Suphis, is the largest; but the next by Chepheren, his successor, is scarcely inferior in dimensions; the third, that of Mycerinus, is very much smaller. . . . All the pyramids (with one exception) face exactly north, and have their entrance on that side. . . . The small residuum we get from all these pyramid discussions is, that they were built by the kings of the early dynasties of the old kingdom of Egypt as their tombs. The leading idea that governed their forms was that of durability. By concealment of the entrance, the difficulties of the passages, and the complicated but most ingenious arrangement of portcullises, these ancient kings hoped to be allowed to rest in undisturbed security for at least 3,000 years. Perhaps they were successful, though their tombs have been since so shamefully profaned." *Fergusson.*

☞ "Nothing can express the variety of sensations which they provoke. The height of their summit, the steepness of their slope, the vastness of their surface, their tremendous weight, the memory of the times they have outlived, and above all the reflection that these mountains of masonry have been reared by petty and insignificant man who creeps at their feet — all impress the beholder, and fill at once the heart and the mind with astonishment, terror, humiliation, admiration, and respect." *Volney.*

The *Pyramids* themselves, doting with age, have forgotten the names of their founders. *Thomas Fuller.*

And Morning opes with haste her lids,
To gaze upon the *Pyramids*. *Emerson.*

Pyramid of Abooroash. A ruined pyramid about five miles distant from the Pyramids of Gheezeh in Egypt.

Pyramids of Abooseer. A group of four pyramids, a few miles distant from the Pyramids of Gheezeh, in Egypt.

Pyramid of Caius Cestius. A sepulchral pyramid — the only one in Rome — situated near the Porta di San Paolo, and immediately adjoining the Protestant Burial-ground. It was erected to Caius Cestius, a tribune of the people. The pyramid is over 100 feet in height, and contains in the centre a small sepulchral chamber.

☞ "This pyramid, of more than 100 feet in height, is entirely built of marble, but time has changed its color and defaced its polish. The gray lichen has crept over it, and wild evergreens hang from its crevices. But what it has lost in splendor, it has gained in picturesque beauty; and there are few remains of antiquity within the bounds of the Eternal City, that the eye rests upon with such unwearying admiration, as this gray pyramid." *Eaton.*

☞ "It is the most imperishable of the antiquities, a beautiful pyramid, 113 feet high, built into the ancient wall of Rome, as perfect after 1,800 years as if it were built but yesterday." *N. P. Willis.*

☞ "From one part of the city, looking out beyond the walls, a squat and stunted pyramid (the burial-place of Caius Cestius) makes an opaque triangle in the moonlight. But, to an English traveller, it serves to mark the grave of Shelley too, whose ashes lie beneath a little garden near it. Nearer still, almost within its shadow, lie the bones of Keats, 'whose name is writ in water,' that shines brightly in the landscape of a calm Italian night." *Dickens.*

☞ "When I am inclined to be serious I love to wander up and down before the tomb of Caius Cestius. The Protestant burial-ground is there. . . . It is a quiet and sheltered nook, . . . and the pyramid that overshadows it gives it a classic and singularly solemn air." *Rogers.*

Eastward hence,
Nigh where the *Cestian pyramid* divides
The mouldering wall, behold yon fabric huge.
John Dyer.

Within the shadow of the *Pyramid*
Of Caius Cestius was the Daisy found,
White as the soul of Keats in Paradise.
T. B. Aldrich.

Pyramid of Cheops. See GREAT PYRAMID.

Pyramid of Cholula. A celebrated ruined pyramid constructed of clay and brick, at Cholula, an Indian town, near Pueblo, in Mexico. It was built by the ancient inhabitants of Mexico. It is over 1,400 feet square at the base, and 177 feet in height, and is ascended by a flight of steps, 120 in number. On the summit is a chapel erected by the Spaniards.

The fact teaches him how Belus was worshipped, and how the Pyramids were built, better than the discovery by Champollion of the names of all the workmen and the cost of every tile. He finds Assyria and the *Mounds of Cholula* at his door, and himself has laid the courses.
Emerson.

Q.

Quadrant, The. See Regent St.

You will observe a town dandy getting fidgetty after his second turn in the *Quadrant*, while you will meet the same Frenchman there from noon till dusk, bounding his walk by those columns, as if they were the bars of a cage.
N. P. Willis.

Quarr Abbey. A famous monastic establishment upon the Isle of Wight, erected in the twelfth century, of which the ruins only now remain.

Quarters of the World. See Four Quarters of the World.

Quartier Latin. [Latin Quarter.] A large district in Paris, on the south of the Seine. Here the principal colleges and schools have been situated for many centuries, and here the numerous students have lived; whence this quarter derives its name.

☞ "Though the colleges are now converted into private houses or into public schools, the Pays Latin is still inhabited by many thousand students in letters, science, law, and medicine, leading a life of gayety and freedom from restraint which is hardly to be understood by an Englishman. They and their associates, male and female, form the staple of a large portion of the well-known novels of Paul de Kock." *Murray's Handbook.*

☞ "The life of the young artist here is the easiest, merriest, dirtiest existence possible. He comes to Paris, probably at sixteen, from his province; his parents settle forty pounds a year on him, and pay his master; he establishes himself in the Pays Latin; . . . he arrives at his atelier at a tolerably early hour, and labors among a score of companions as merry and as poor as himself." *Thackeray.*

Quatre Fils Aymon. A ruined castle near Spa in Belgium, associated with historic and romantic traditions.

Quebec Citadel. A vast fortress, from its lofty commanding situation one of the strongest in the world, is the principal defence of the city of Quebec, Can. It covers 40 acres.

Queen Anne's Farthing. The belief generally obtains in England that a Queen Anne's farthing is a very rare possession: indeed, it is supposed that there are but three, of which two are in the public keeping, and that one which is missing would bring a fabulous price; but the fact is, that it is no more rare than any other coinage of the mint of equal antiquity, and that the poor country people who occasionally take long journeys to London to dispose of so great a curiosity which has fallen into their hands, find that the numismatist to whom they apply is already the possessor of several.

Queen Elizabeth. See Death of Queen Elizabeth.

Queen Elizabeth's Pocket Pistol. The popular name of an ancient piece of brass ordnance, 24 feet in length, cast in 1514, and presented by the States General of Holland to Queen Elizabeth. It is preserved in Dover Castle.

Queen of Sheba. See Embarkation of the Queen of Sheba.

Queen of the West. A powerful United States "ram," in the War of the Rebellion. She was sent down the Mississippi, and, running the batteries at Vicksburg, destroyed several transport vessels on the Lower Mississippi and on the Red River, but was finally lost on the latter river through the treachery of a pilot.

Queen's Arms. A tavern in St. Paul's Churchyard, London.

Queen's Bench. See King's Bench and Queen's Bench.

Queen's College. A foundation of the University of Cambridge, England. Established in 1448.

Queen's Head. A noted hostelry in the olden time in Islington, London.

The *Queen's Head* and Crown in Islington town
Bore, for its brewing, the highest renown.

Queen's Prison. See KING'S BENCH AND QUEEN'S BENCH.

Queen's State Coach. See CORONATION COACH.

Queen's Theatre. See PRINCE OF WALES'S THEATRE.

Queensberry House. The seat of the Duke of Buccleuch, near Richmond, England.

Quinze Vingts. A hospital for the blind, in the Faubourg St. Antoine, Paris.

Quirinal Hill. [Lat. *Mons Quirinus.*] One of the original seven hills of Rome, now covered with palaces and churches, among which the most noticeable is the Palace of the Pope on the Monte Cavallo, the summit of the hill. The modern name, Monte Cavallo, is derived from the marble groups of Castor and Pollux with their horses, discovered in the Baths of Constantine, which now stand before the obelisk in the Piazza di Monte Cavallo.

Hence we went to *Monte Cavallo*, heretofore called Mons Quirinalis, where we saw those two rare horses, the worke of the rivals Phidias and Praxitiles, as they were sent as a present to Nero out of Armenia. They were placed on pedestals of white marble by Sixtus V., by whom I suppose their injuries are repair'd. They are govern'd by 4 naked slaves like those at the foot of the Capitol.
John Evelyn, 1644.

Quirinal Palace. The papal palace on Monte Cavallo, Quirinal Hill, Rome. The present structure was begun by Gregory XIII. in 1574, and continued and enlarged by succeeding popes. The meeting of the conclave for the election of the popes takes place in the Quirinal Palace, and from the balcony opening upon the Piazza di Monte Cavallo the name of the new pope is proclaimed to the people.

☞ "That palace-building, ruin-destroying Pope, Paul III., began to erect the enormous palace on the Quirinal Hill, and the prolongation of his labors by a long series of successive pontiffs has made it one of the largest and ugliest buildings extant."
C. A. Eaton.

What is most charming here is what you encounter on the way unexpectedly; now the *Quirinal Palace* on the summit of a hill entirely detached in the gray atmosphere, and, in front, its horses and colossi of marble. *Taine, Trans.*

Nor heed those blood stains on the wall,
Not Tiber's flood can wash away,
Where, in thy stately *Quirinal*,
Thy mangled victims lay! *Whittier.*

I have climbed Trajan's column, and saw thence
The *Quirinal* here, and there the Vatican.
Théodore Aubanel, Trans.

Quoit-Thrower, The. See DISCOBOLUS.

R.

Rabenstein. [Ravenstone.] An ancient feudal castle, of late partially restored, near Streitberg, in Franconia, Germany.

Raboteur, Le. [The Planer.] A picture by Annibale Caracci (1560–1609), representing Joseph "planing a board, while Jesus, a lovely boy about six or seven years old, stands by watching the progress of the work. Mary is seated on one side plying her needle." This picture is in the collection of the Earl of Suffolk at Charlton, England.

☞ "The great fault of this picture is the subordinate and commonplace character given to the Virgin Mary; otherwise it is a very suggestive and dramatic subject, and one which might be usefully engraved in a cheap form for distribution." *Mrs. Jameson.*

Raby Castle. One of the finest and best-preserved of the ancient northern castles of England, the seat of the Duke of Cleveland. King Canute presented it with other offerings at the shrine of St. Cuthbert, but it passed out of the hands of the monks in 1131. Portions of the older building are so skilfully incorporated with the new that it seems a perfect specimen of a castle of the fourteenth century. The castle is of great size and strength, and the walls surrounding it occupy about two acres of ground. The pleasure-grounds and park are of a magnificence commensurate with that of the castle itself, and command lovely prospects.

Rachel. See Jacob and Rachel.

Rachel's Tomb. A small structure near Bethlehem is known as the "sepulchre of Rachel." Jews, Moslems, and Christians unite in affirming the authenticity of this sepulchre, although the building is modern.

They journeyed from Bethel, and there was but a little way to come to Ephrath. . . . And Rachel died, and was buried on the way to Ephrath, which is Bethlehem. *Gen.* xxxv. 16-19.

Radcliffe Library. An imposing library building connected with the University of Oxford, founded by Dr. John Radcliffe (d. 1714).

Radical Road. The name given to a promenade under the cliff called Salisbury Crags in Edinburgh, Scotland. The name is derived from the circumstance that the road was built in 1819 by disaffected people who were out of employment.

Rainbow, The. According to Aubrey, the Rainbow, in Fleet Street, the second coffee-house established in London, was opened about 1656. It is now a tavern, and the old coffee-room has been destroyed.

The coffee-house was the Londoner's house; and those who wished to find a gentleman commonly asked, not whether he lived in Fleet Street or Chancery Lane, but whether he frequented "the Grecian" or "the *Rainbow*." *Macaulay.*

Rainbow Falls. A beautiful cascade in the Adirondack region of New York, near the foot of the Ausable Ponds.

Rainbow Landscape. The name given to a celebrated picture by Peter Paul Rubens (1577–1640). Now in the Bethnal Green Museum, London.

Rainy Season in the Tropics. A noted picture by Frederic Edwin Church (b. 1826), the American landscape-painter.

Raising of Lazarus. A picture by Sebastian del Piombo (1485–1547), and considered one of the most important works of the sixteenth century, executed for Giulio de' Medici, afterward Pope Leo X.

It is now in the National Gallery, London.

☞ "This is in many respects one of the noblest pictures existing, — a dramatic combination and pictorial completeness which few would now hesitate to prefer to the Transfiguration by Raphael."
Eastlake, Handbook of Painting.

Raising of Lazarus. An admired painting by Benjamin West (1738-1820), serving as an altar-piece in Winchester Cathedral, England.

Raising of Lazarus. A picture by Benjamin Robert Haydon (1786-1846). In the National Gallery, London.

Raising the Body of St. Hubert of Liège. An altar-piece, ascribed to Gerard van Meire, the Flemish painter, but which has also been ascribed to Dierick Bouts and to other painters. It is in the National Gallery of London.

Rake's Progress. A famous dramatic and satirical picture by William Hogarth (1697-1764).

☞ "It would be suppressing the merits of his heart to consider him only a promoter of laughter. . . . Mirth colored his pictures, but benevolence designed them. He smiled, like Socrates, that men might not be offended at his lectures, and might learn to laugh at their own follies." *Lord Orford.*

Rákos, Field of. [Rákos Mezo.] See FIELD OF RÁKOS.

Raleigh's House. See MYRTLE GROVE.

Ramaseum [or Memnonium]. An ancient Egyptian palace and temple at Thebes, the residence of Rhamses the Great. It is now a wreck, but the ruins indicate that it was of immense size. Within the palace are the remains of the statue of Rhamses, the largest found in Egypt. The walls are covered with wonderful sculptures, illustrating the adventures and victories of the great king, and his offerings to the gods. [Written also *Rhamession.*]

☞ "The Rhamession was built wholly by the great Rhamses, in the fifteenth century B.C.; . . . and it may be considered as a typical example of what an Egyptian temple of this age was intended to have been. Its façade is formed by two great pylons, or pyramidal masses of masonry, which, like the two western towers of a Gothic cathedral, are the most imposing part of the structure externally. . . . They [the palace-temples] do not seem to have been appropriated to the worship of any particular god, but rather for the great ceremonials of royalty, of kingly sacrifice to the gods for the people, and of worship of the king himself by the people." *Fergusson.*

And thou hast walked about — how strange a story!
In Thebes's streets, three thousand years ago;
When the *Memnonium* was in all its glory,
And time had not begun to overthrow
Those temples, palaces, and piles stupendous,
Of which the very ruins are tremendous.
Horace Smith.

Rambla. A beautiful promenade in Barcelona, Spain. The name is derived from the Arabic, and signifies a river-bed, which in Spain, being often dry in summer, is used as a road. It is the centre of fashion and amusement.

Ramble, The. A lovely region in Central Park, in the city of New York, with labyrinthine foot-paths winding through acres of woody hills, bordered by a lake.

Rambouillet. See HÔTEL DE RAMBOUILLET.

Rameses III., Tomb of. See HARPERS' TOMB.

Ranelagh Gardens. A place of amusement in London, no longer in existence, but very popular from its opening in 1742 till the beginning of the present century. Ranelagh, spoken of by Smollett as being like the "enchanted palace of genii," was a sort of rival to Vauxhall.

☞ "The prince, princess, duke, much nobility, and much mob besides, were there." *Walpole (in 1742).*

☞ "Ranelagh has totally beat Vauxhall. Nobody goes anywhere else — everybody goes there."
Walpole (in 1744).

☞ "Ranelagh was a very pleasing

place of amusement. There persons of inferior rank mingled with the highest nobility of Britain."
Samuel Rogers.

Accordingly, Mr. Stryver inaugurated the Long Vacation with a formal proposal to take Miss Manette to Vauxhall Gardens; that failing, to *Ranelagh;* that unaccountably failing too, it behooved him to present himself in Soho, and there declare his noble mind. *Dickens.*

Vauxhall and *Ranelagh!* I then had heard
Of your green groves, and wilderness of lamps
Dimming the stars, and fireworks magical,
And gorgeous ladies, under splendid domes,
Floating in dance, or warbling high in air
The song of spirits. *Wordsworth.*

Rape of Europa. A picture by Paul Veronese (1530?-1588). In the Doge's Palace, Venice.

Rape of Ganymede. 1. The masterpiece of the Athenian sculptor Leochares (fl. 372-338 B.C.) Copies in marble of the bronze original abound. One, and perhaps the best existing, is in the Museo Pio-Clementino, of the Vatican, Rome. There is another copy in the Library of St. Mark's, Venice.

2. A well-known picture by Rembrandt van Ryn (1606-1669), the Dutch painter. Now in the Dresden Gallery.

Rape of Proserpine. A picture by Francesco Primaticcio (1490-1570), the pupil of Raphael. Now in the Stafford House Gallery.

Rape of Proserpine. A picture, "with a rich, fantastically lighted landscape," by Niccolo dell' Abbate, called also Niccolo da Modena (1512-1571). In the gallery of Stafford House.

Rape of Proserpine. A picture by Peter Paul Rubens (1577-1640). Now at Blenheim, England.

Rape of the Sabines. A celebrated group in marble by Giovanni da Bologna (1524-1608), and regarded as his masterpiece. In the Loggia de' Lanzi, Florence, Italy.

☞ "John of Bologna, after he had finished a group of a young man, holding up a young woman in his arms, with an old man at his feet, called his friends together to tell him what name he should give it, and it was agreed to call it the *Rape of the Sabines.*"
Sir Joshua Reynolds.

Raphael and his Fencing Master. A picture in the Louvre, Paris, by some attributed to Pontormo.

Raphael and Michael Angelo. A noted picture by Horace Vernet (1789-1863), the French painter.

☞ "As clever a picture as can be, — clever is just the word, — the groups and drawing excellent, the coloring pleasantly bright and gaudy; and the French students study it incessantly: there are a dozen who copy it for one who copies Delacroix." *Thackeray.*

Raphael Sanzio. A celebrated portrait of himself by the painter. In the collection of autograph portraits in the Uffizi Gallery, Florence, Italy. There is another in the Louvre, Paris.

Raphael, Stanze of. See STANZE OF RAPHAEL.

Raphael's Cartoons. See CARTOONS OF RAPHAEL.

Raphael's Loggia. See LOGGIA OF RAPHAEL.

Raphael's House. [Ital. *Casa da Raffaello.*] A well-known house in Florence, Italy, in which Raphael was born and lived.

Ras-et-Teen, Palace of. This palace, built by Mohammed Ali, is situated at the western end of the peninsula of the same name, near Alexandria, Egypt.

Ratcliffe Highway. A famous London thoroughfare, now called St. George's Street, noted from its association in former times with murders and robberies.

☞ "Many can remember the terror which was on every face, the careful barring of doors, the providing of blunderbusses and watchmen's rattles."
Macaulay.

☞ "Look at a marine-store dealer's, in that reservoir of dirt, drunkenness, and drabs: thieves, oysters, baked potatoes, and pickled salmon, — *Ratcliff Highway.*" *Dickens.*

Rattler, The. The first naval vessel propelled by a screw. She was built by the English Admiralty, and launched at Sheerness in 1843.

Ravenscraig Castle. A ruined fortress near Kirkcaldy, in Scotland.

Moor, moor the barge, ye gallant crew,
And, gentle lady, deign to stay!
Rest thee in *Castle Ravensheugh*,
Nor tempt the stormy Firth to-day.
Old Ballad of Rosabelle.

Yon's *Ravenscraig*, wi' riven ha',
A thousand winters shook its wa'—
Tired Time let scythe an' san'-glass fa',
To breathe awhile at Ugie.
William Thom.

Reading Magdalen. See MAGDALEN.

Reale, Villa. See VILLA REALE.

Rebecca. A picture by Horace Vernet (1789–1863), the French painter.

☞ "His [Vernet's] 'Rebecca' is most pleasing; and not the less so for a little pretty affectation of attitude and needless singularity of costume." *Thackeray.*

Red Bull. An old London theatre referred to by Knight as being in 1583 one of the chief London theatres.

☞ "I have seen the Red Bull playhouse, which was a large one, so full, that as many went back for want of room as had entered; and, as meanly as you now think of these drolls, they were then acted by the best comedians." *Kirkman*, 1672.

Red Convent. An ancient monastery of Coptic Christians in Upper Egypt.

Red Deer of Chillingham. A picture by Sir Edwin Landseer (1803–1873), the most celebrated modern painter of animals.

Red Horse. See VALE OF THE RED HORSE.

Redentore, Il. [The Redeemer.] A grand and noted church of the sixteenth century in Venice, Italy.

Redwood Library. A Doric building in Newport, R.I., erected in 1750, containing a small but choice collection of books, with some works of art. Some of the volumes in this library were presented by the King of England, and others by Bishop Berkeley.

Reform Club. 1. A fine building in Pall Mall, London, is owned and occupied by the Reform Club, which was founded by Liberal members of the British Parliament, about the time the Reform Bill was passed, 1830-32. The club is composed of 1,000 members, not including those belonging to Parliament.

☞ "Let all strangers who come to London for business, or pleasure, or curiosity, or for whatever cause, not fail to visit the Reform Club. In an age of utilitarianism, and of the search for the comfortable, like ours, there is more to be learned here than in the ruins of the Coliseum, of the Parthenon, or of Memphis." *Viscountess de Malleville.*

No Carlton Clubs, *Reform Clubs*, nor any sort of clubs or creatures or of accredited opinions or practices, can make a Lie Truth, can make Bribery a Propriety. *Carlyle.*

2. A marble club-house in Philadelphia, Penn.

Reformation, The. A well-known picture by Wilhelm Kaulbach (1805–1874), the eminent German painter. [Called also the *Epoch of the Reformation.*]

Reformation, Oak of. See OAK OF REFORMATION.

Regalia. A general term, usually applied to a valuable collection of jewels and plate kept in the Tower, London. That portion of the Tower where the regalia is now kept is called the Wakefield Tower. A desperate but unsuccessful attempt was made in the reign of Charles II., by the ruffian Blood, to carry off the crown jewels. Blood, though captured, contrived by his great audacity to secure his own release, and even frightened the king into granting him a pension of £500 a year.

Regent Diamond. See PITT DIAMOND.

Regent Street. A street in London, nearly a mile in length, designed by John Nash in 1813, and named from his patron the Prince Regent. The street trends northwest by a *Quadrant*, giving a very ornamental appearance by its elegant shop-fronts.

☞ "Regent Street has appeared to me the greatest and most oppressive solitude in the world. . . . Here, it is wealth beyond competition, exclusiveness and indifference perfectly unapproachable." *N. P. Willis.*

The gay old boys are paunchy old men in the disguise of young ones, who frequent tne Quadrant and *Regent Street* in the daytime. *Dickens.*

King Arthur's self
Was commonplace to Lady Guenever;
And Camelot to minstrels seemed as flat,
As *Regent Street* to poets.
Mrs. Browning.

Regents, The. A picture by Ferdinand Bol (1611-1680), the Dutch painter, and considered his best work. It is in the "Leprosenhuys" at Amsterdam, Holland.

Regent's Park. An extensive common or pleasure-ground in London, comprising 472 acres. It contains within its boundaries several handsome private residences.

☞ "*Regent's Park* is larger than the Jardin des Plantes and the Luxembourg put together." *Taine, Trans.*

He only left Bombay yesterday morning, was seen in the Red Sea on Tuesday, is engaged to dinner this afternoon in the *Regent's Park*, and (as it is about two minutes since I saw him in the court-yard) I make no doubt he is by this time at Alexandria or Malta. *Thackeray.*

Regicides' Cave. A cavern in a rock near New Haven, Conn., where the "regicides" Edward Whalley and William Goffe, two of the judges who had condemned Charles I. to death, and afterwards on the restoration of the Stuarts had escaped from England, were secreted and lived for some time.

Reichenberg Castle. An interesting ruined castle overlooking the Rhine, near Goarshausen. It was built in 1284.

Reichsveste. An ancient imperial castle at Nuremberg, Germany.

Relay House. The name formerly given to what is now called Washington Junction, a station on the Baltimore and Ohio Railroad, nine miles from Baltimore, Md. It was noted in the Civil War as the spot seized by Gen. Butler, and from which he pushed on with the Massachusetts and New York troops to the occupation of Baltimore on the night of May 13, 1861.

Religion and Philosophy. A noted picture by Taddeo Gaddi (1300-1352?). In the church of Sta. Maria Novella, Florence, Italy.

Reliquary of St. Ursula. A celebrated shrine in the chapel of St. John's Hospital at Bruges, about four feet in length, the whole exterior of which is covered with miniature designs in oil by Hans Memling (d. 1495), the Flemish painter, representing scenes in the life of St. Ursula. These little pictures are described as among the best productions of the Flemish school.

Reliques, Grandes. See GRANDES RELIQUES.

Rendezvous de Chasse. A picture by Adrian van de Velde (1639-1672), the Dutch painter. In the possession of Mr. Baring, London.

Repentance Tower. A monument near Ecclefechan, Scotland, which has a singular history. According to the account in the "Minstrelsy of the Scottish Border," it was built by a certain Lord Herries as an act of penance for having on a voyage from England thrown overboard a number of prisoners. It bears the inscription "Repentance" over the door, with a serpent on one side and a dove on the other.

Repentant Eve. A work of sculpture by Edward S. Bartholomew (b. 1822). In possession of Joseph Harrison, Philadelphia.

Reply to Hayne. See WEBSTER'S REPLY to HAYNE.

Repose in Egypt. A very common and most pleasing subject of representation by the mediæval painters, exhibiting the Holy Family as resting on their journey, or at the close of their journey, and seated in a landscape. Of numerous compositions upon this subject, greatly varying in details, the following may be named as among the more important and better known.

Repose in Egypt. A picture by Anthony van Dyck (1599-1641). In the Palazzo Pitti, Florence, Italy.

Repose in Egypt. A beautiful picture by Sir Anthony van Dyck (1599-1641), often copied and engraved. Now in the Grosvenor Gallery.

Repose in Egypt. A well-known picture by Correggio. See MADONNA DELLA SCODELLA.

Repose in Egypt. A picture by Domenico Zampieri, called Domenichino (1581-1641). In the Louvre, Paris.

Repose in Egypt. A picture by Raphael Sanzio (1483-1520), representing the Virgin "kneeling and holding the Child in her arms; St. John also kneels, and presents fruits; Joseph leading an ass by the bridle is in the act of raising St. John." This picture is now in the Imperial Gallery in Vienna, Austria.

Repose in Egypt. A picture by Antonio Allegri, surnamed Correggio (1494-1534). In the gallery at Parma, Italy. Called also La Zingarella (the Gypsy), *q.v.*

Repose in Egypt. A picture by Lucas Cranach (1472-1553), a German painter. It is now in the Sciarra Colonna palace at Rome.

☞ "In a singular and charming *Riposo* by Lucas Cranach, the Virgin and Child are seated under a tree; to the left of the group is a fountain, where a number of little angels appear to be washing linen; to the right Joseph approaches, leading the ass, and in the act of reverently removing his cap."
Mrs. Jameson.

Representation of Human Life. A noted picture by Jan Steen (1636-1689), the Dutch *genre*-painter. In the Museum of the Hague.

Rescue, The. A group of statuary by Horatio Greenough (1805-1852), "intended to illustrate the struggle between the Anglo-Saxon races and the aborigines." At the Capitol, Washington.

Rescue, The. An American exploring ship in the expedition of De Haven and Kane to the Arctic regions in 1850-51.

Research, The. An armor-plated ship of the British navy, launched Aug. 15, 1863.

Resignation of Washington at Annapolis. A large picture by John Trumbull (1756-1843), executed under commission from Congress, for the Rotunda of the Capitol at Washington. It is well known by engravings.

Resistance, The. An armor-plated ship of the British navy. She was launched April 11, 1861.

Resolute, The. An Arctic exploring ship which sailed from England, April 15, 1852, in Sir Edward Belcher's expedition. On the 25th of August in the same year she was abandoned in the ice. On the 10th of September, 1855, she was found drifting on the high seas by Capt. Buddington of the American whaling ship *George Henry*. All claim to the Resolute having been relinquished by the British government, the vessel was purchased by Congress for the sum of $40,000, and sent to Queen Victoria, as a present, and was formally presented to her by Capt. Hartstein of the United States navy, Dec. 16, 1856.

Resurrection, The. A noted fresco by Giotto di Bondone (1276-1336). In the Arena Chapel, Padua, Italy.

Resurrection, The. A fresco painting by Luca Signorelli (da Cortona) (1439-1521). In the Cathedral of Orvieto, Italy.

Resurrection, The. A picture by Francesco Albani (1578-1660). In the S. Maria de Galeria, Bologna, Italy.

Retable de Poissy. An altar-piece, now in the Louvre, Paris, which represents in the centre scenes in the Passion of the Saviour, and on the sides events which took place in the lives of St. John the Evangelist and St. John the Baptist. Jean de France, Duc de Berry, brother of Charles VI., and his wife, gave it to the church of Poissy.

Return from the Flight into Egypt. A picture by Peter Paul Rubens (1577-1640). Now at Blenheim, England.

Revelation, Book of. See BOOK OF REVELATION.

Rex Tibicen. A picture by Jean Léon Gérôme (b. 1824), the French painter.

Rheinfels. [The Rock of the Rhine.] This fortress is considered one of the most beautiful ruins on the banks of the Rhine. It was founded in 1245, and belonged alternately to the Hessians and the French, until in 1794 it fell into the hands of the French revolutionary army, and three years later it was blown up. It now belongs to the Emperor of Germany. It is the most extensive ruin on the Rhine, and was originally built partly as a stronghold where toll could be collected upon merchandise passing on the Rhine. An increase in the duties levied led to an unsuccessful siege of the castle for 15 months by the neighboring burghers. From this and other circumstances originated the union of 60 German and Rhenish cities, which resulted in the breaking-up of this and many other robber strongholds upon the Rhine.

Rheinstein. [The Stone of the Rhine.] A conspicuous castle on the Rhine. The original castle was of great antiquity. It was rebuilt by Frederic of Prussia in 1825-29, and a chapel has since been added.

Rhodian Colossus. See COLOSSUS OF RHODES.

Rhymer's Glen. A locality near Abbotsford in Scotland, so named because of legendary traditions connected with Thomas of Ercildoune (Thomas the Rhymer).

Rialto, The. [Ital. *Ponte di Rialto.*] A famous bridge over the Grand Canal in Venice, deriving its name from the quarter of the city in which it is situated. This section — so called from *Rivo-alto* — is one of the islands upon which Venice is built, and gave its name first to the Exchange which was built upon it, and later to the bridge by which it was reached. The Rialto was long the centre of trade and commercial life in the city. The bridge, which has shops upon it, was begun in 1588.

☞ "The Venice of modern fiction and drama is a thing of yesterday, a mere efflorescence of decay, a stage-drama, which the first ray of daylight must dissipate into dust. No great merchant of Venice ever saw that Rialto under which the traveller now pauses with breathless interest."

Ruskin.

Shy. Signior Antonio, many a time and oft,
In the *Rialto*, you have rated me
About my moneys, and my usances:
Still have I borne it with a patient shrug;
For suffrance is the badge of all our tribe.

Shakespeare.

[This allusion is probably to the Exchange, though it might be taken to refer to the island, but hardly to the bridge.]

Ours is a trophy which will not decay
With the *Rialto*; Shylock and the Moor,
And Pierre, cannot be swept or worn away.

Byron.

Soprano, basso, even the contra-alto
Wished him five fathom under the *Rialto*.

Byron.

Shylock still darkens the *Rialto* with his frown; the lordly form of Othello yet stalks across the piazza of St. Mark's, and every veil that flutters in the breeze shrouds the roguish black eyes of Jessica.

Hillard.

The soul's *Rialto* hath its merchandise:
I barter curl for curl upon that mart.

Mrs. Browning.

Pisa's patron saint hath hallowed to himself the joyful day,
Never on the thronged *Rialto* showed the Carnival more gay.

T. W. Parsons.

Riccardi Palace. [Ital. *Palazzo Riccardi.*] A celebrated palace in Florence, erected in the fifteenth century. The chapel contains some fine frescos.

☞ "The Riccardi Palace is at the corner of the Via Larga. It was built by the first Cosmo di Medici, the old banker, more than four centuries ago. . . . It looks fit to be still the home of a princely race, being nowise dilapidated nor decayed externally, nor likely to be so. . . . This mansion gives the visitor a stately notion of the life of a commercial man in the days when merchants were princes. . . . It must have been, in some sense, a great man who thought of founding a homestead like this, and was capable of filling it with his personality, as the hand fills a glove." *Hawthorne.*

Richelieu, Rue. A well-known street in Paris. In this street is the house where Molière died.

Those two splendidly dressed ladies are milliners from the *Rue Richelieu*, who have just brought over, and disposed of, their cargo of summer fashions. *Thackeray.*

Riches. A picture by Hans Holbein the Younger (1498?-1543), well known by engravings. The original perished at Whitehall in 1698. There is a drawing of this picture in the British Museum. See TRIUMPH OF RICHES.

Richmond, The. A noted vessel of the United States navy, one of the vessels of Commodore Farragut's flotilla, which ran the gauntlet of the forts of Mississippi on the 24th April, 1862, and led to the taking of New Orleans.

Richmond, Fort. See FORT RICHMOND.

Richmond Palace. An ancient and celebrated royal residence at Richmond, on the Thames, ten miles from London. The palace, of which only the ruins are now standing, was also called *Shene* (shining), from its beautiful situation.

Richmond Park. An ancient and famous park or pleasure-ground of the royal manor of Richmond, about nine miles from London, overlooking the Thames, and comprising fine forest scenery. It is eight miles in circumference, and is the most beautiful of the royal parks in the vicinity of the metropolis. It is a favorite resort of Londoners.

Rideau Hall. The official residence of the Governor-General of Canada, in New Edinburgh, Ontario.

Riegersburg. A remarkable mediæval stronghold, now fallen into ruin, on an eminence near Feldbach, in Southern Austria.

Rienzi's House. A noted building in Rome, built of brick, and thought to have been the house in which "The Last of the Tribunes" may have lived. It has been called also, without apparent reason, the House of Pilate.

☞ "By what inexplicable absurdity it has obtained the name of the House of Pilate, it is impossible to conceive, unless, from the cruel and iniquitous judgments that disgraced the conclusion of Rienzi's reign, he may himself have acquired that nickname among the people of Rome." *C. A. Eaton.*

Riesenburg. A remarkable natural curiosity, — a sort of cave with the top taken off, — near Streitberg, in the region known as the Franconian Switzerland.

Rigi, Spectre of the. See SPECTRE OF THE RIGI.

Rimini. See FRANCESCA DA RIMINI.

Ring of Brogarth. A remarkable monument of antiquity at Stenniss, in the Orkneys, consisting of a great circle of erect and prostrate stones, of unknown origin and use. Allusion is made to one of them in Scott's novel of "The Pirate."

Rinuccini Palace. [Palazzo Rinuccini.] A palace in Florence, Italy, built in the sixteenth century by Luigi Cardi Cigoli. It contains some fine pictures.

Ripetta, Via. See VIA RIPETTA.

Riposo, Il. [The Repose (in Egypt).] See REPOSE IN EGYPT.

☞ "The subject generally styled a *Riposo* is one of the most graceful and most attractive in the whole range of Christian art." *Mrs. Jameson.*

But for the occasion and the appellation, it would be quite impossible to distinguish the Loves that sport round Venus and Adonis, from the Cherubim, so called, that hover above a Nativity or a *Riposo;* and the little angels, in his [Albano's] Crucifixion, cry so like naughty little boys, that one longs to put them in a corner. *Mrs. Jameson.*

Ripresa dei Barberi. The end of the Corso, Rome, and the place where, in the races of the carnival, the horses are stopped by a piece of cloth suspended across the street. It derives its name from the Barbary horses which were the original racers.

Rising. See CASTLE RISING.

Rittenhouse Square. A public park in Philadelphia, Penn., surrounded by handsome mansions.

Riva dei Schiavoni. A street or promenade in Venice, Italy, facing the harbor.

'Twas so
When I came here. The galley floats within
A bow-shot of the "*Riva di Schiavoni.*"
Byron.

Riviera. [Bank or shore.] A name of general application, but frequently given in particular to the Mediterranean coast in the neighborhood of Genoa, Italy.

Riviera di Chiaia. See CHIAJA.

Rivoli, Rue de. One of the finest streets in Paris. Napoleon I. began the Rue de Rivoli.

This ostentatious architecture, which arrived in Judea by cargoes, these hundreds of columns all of the same diameter, the ornament of some insipid *Rue de Rivoli*, such is what he called "the kingdoms of the world and all their glory." *Renan.*

In our black, orderless, zigzag streets, we can show nothing to compare with the magnificent array of the *Rue de Rivoli.* *Thackeray.*

Roaring Meg. A celebrated piece of ordnance preserved in Londonderry, Ireland. It was presented to the city by the Fishmongers' Company of London.

☞ "In the yard of the court-house is the far-famed 'Roaring Meg,' so called from the loudness of her voice, which is said hourly to have cheered the hearts of the besieged, and appalled those of the besiegers." *Mr. and Mrs. Hall.*

Rob Roy's Cave. A cavern in a rock near Inversnaid, Scotland, sometimes called also Bruce's cave, because Bruce lay hid there for a night.

Robin Hood Society. A debating club which met, in the time of George II., in Essex Street, Strand, London. Here was heard some of Burke's earliest eloquence. Goldsmith was an occasional visitor.

Bobuste, La. An ancient piece of ordnance captured at San Juan d'Ulloa, now preserved as a trophy in the United States Navy-yard, Brooklyn, N.Y.

Rocco, San. See SAN ROCCO.

Roch, St. See ST. ROCH.

Roche. See CASTLE ROCHE.

Roche Guyon, La. A large and imposing château on the banks of the Seine, in France, near Bonnières. It dates from the twelfth century, and is the property of the Rochefoucauld family.

Rocher Percé, Le. [The pierced rock.] A natural curiosity near Gaspé, in the Province of Quebec, Canada. It is a remarkable promontory, rising 280 feet above the water, with an opening or archway through which fishing-smacks can pass.

Rochester Castle. The venerable fortress in the Medway, at Rochester, England, one of the most interesting remains of feudal architecture in the kingdom.

Rocio, The. A fine public square in Lisbon, Portugal.

Rock of Abooseer. An almost perpendicular crag, 200 feet high, on the shore of the Nile, commanding a fine view of the second cataract, and of the desert and Arabian hills.

☞ "I doubt whether a more striking scene than this, to English eyes, can be anywhere found. It is thoroughly African, thoroughly tropical, very beautiful, — most majestic, and most desolate." *Miss Martineau.*

☞ "This is the *ultima Thule* of Egyptian travellers."
Murray's Handbook.

Rock of Cashel. A famous hill in Tipperary County, Ireland, surmounted by the most interesting and impressive ruins in the island.

☞ "The rock, rising above the adjacent country, is seen from a very long distance and from every direction by which it is approached; its summit crowned by the venerable remains that have excited the wonder and admiration of ages, and will continue to do for ages yet to come."
Mr. and Mrs. Hall.

☞ "That noble ruin, an emblem as well as a memorial of Ireland, — at once a temple and a fortress, the seat of religion and nationality; where councils were held; where princes assembled; the scene of courts and of synods; and on which it is impossible to look without feeling the heart at once elevated and touched by the noblest as well as the most solemn recollections."
R. L. Shiel.

Royal and saintly *Cashel!* I would gaze
Upon the wreck of thy departed powers,
Not in the dewy light of matin hours,
Nor the meridian pomp of summer's blaze,
But at the close of dim autumnal days.
—— At such a time, methinks
There breathes from thy lone courts and voiceless aisles
A melancholy moral; such as sinks
On the lone traveller's heart, amid the piles
Of vast Persepolis on her mountain stand,
Or Thebes half-buried in the desert sand.
Sir Aubrey de Vere.

Rock of Dunamase. One of the most striking and interesting objects in Ireland, situated in Queen's County. It is a solitary rock in the midst of a fertile plain, covered from base to top with the ruins of an ancient and powerful fortress.

☞ "Although from its great natural strength the castle would seem impregnable, it was several times taken and retaken by the 'ferocious Irish,' and the English invaders."
Mr. and Mrs. Hall.

Rock (and Fortress) of Gibraltar. A fortification of immense strength, at the southern extremity of Spain, in Andalusia. It belongs to England, and is regarded as an impregnable stronghold. Vast sums of money have been spent in adding to the natural defences of the situation. Numerous caverns and galleries several miles in length have been cut in the solid rock. The chief defences are upon the western side.

☞ "The vast Rock rises on one side with its interminable works of defence; and Gibraltar Bay is shining on the other, out on which from the terraces immense cannon are perpetually looking, surrounded by plantations of cannon-balls and beds of bomb-shells, sufficient, one would think, to blow away the whole Peninsula. . . . So we took leave of this famous Rock, — this great blunderbuss, — which we seized out of the hands of the natural owners 140 years ago, and which we have kept ever since tremendously loaded and cleaned and ready for use."
Thackeray.

Rock of Horeb. A large granite block in the neighborhood of Mount Sinai, in Arabia Petræa, pointed out as the rock which Moses smote with his rod, and from which water poured forth. There are several seams in the rock, which by the faithful are believed to be the impressions of the rod.

Rocket, The. A locomotive engine produced by the two Stephensons, and the first which proved a practical success. In October, 1829, the Rocket gained the prize offered by the directors of the Liverpool and Manchester Railroad, and settled the question as to the superiority of the locomotive steam-engine as a motive-power.

Rocks of Fontainebleau. A picture by Rosa Bonheur (b. 1822), the celebrated French painter of animals.

Rocky Mountains. A picture by Albert Bierstadt (b. 1829), and considered one of his best works. In possession of Mr. James McHenry.

☞ "No more genuine and grand American work has been produced than Bierstadt's *Rocky Mountains.*"
Tuckerman.

☞ "Bierstadt's great picture of the Rocky Mountains represents a vast plain, over which groups of Indians in their primitive condition, and their wigwams, are scattered; huge cottonwood trees, oaks and pines, occupy a portion of the foreground; beyond flows a river, on the opposite shore of which rise beetling cliffs, and lofty snow-crowned mountains, — the highest peak Mount Lander. The picture made a great impression."

Sarah Tytler.

Rodenstein. A ruined fortress of the Middle Ages, near Erbach in Germany, famous as being the seat of the legend of the Wild Huntsman.

Roderberg. An eminence overlooking the Rhine near Mehlem. It is an extinct volcano, with a crater 100 feet in depth.

Roger de Coverley. See SIR ROGER DE COVERLEY GOING TO CHURCH.

Rokeby. A place on the Hudson, near Rhinebeck, belonging to the Astor family.

Roland. A famous tocsin-bell in the ancient Belfry-tower of Ghent, Belgium. Its tolling called the citizens together to arms or for debate. It bears the following inscription in Dutch: "Mynen naem is Roelant, als ick clippe dan ist brandt; als ick luyde, dan ist Storm im Vlaenderlandt."

Toll! *Roland*, toll!
Bell never yet was hung,
Between whose lips there swung
So grand a tongue! *T. Tilton.*

Roland's Breach. See BRÈCHE DE ROLAND.

Rolandseck Castle. A well-known ruined castle on the Rhine, near Oberwinter. It is associated with a legendary story which Schiller has made the subject of his ballad of "The Knight of Toggenburg."

Rolls Chapel. A chapel in London, first erected in the time of Henry III., and rebuilt in 1617 by Inigo Jones. Bishops Atterbury, Butler, and Burnet were preachers here. The chapel contains a noble and beautiful tomb by Torregiano.

Roman Forum. See FORUM ROMANUM.

Roman Wall. See HADRIAN'S WALL.

Romans of the Decadence. A well-known picture by Thomas Couture (b. 1815). In the Luxembourg, Paris.

Rome. See SIEGE OF ROME UNDER PORSENNA.

Romeo and Juliet. A picture by Wilhelm Kaulbach (1805-1874), the eminent German painter.

Römer. An ancient and celebrated building in Frankfort-on-the-Main, Germany. It is the guild-hall, or town-house, of the city, and contains the room in which the electors met to choose a new emperor, and that in which he gave his first banquet. The building is thought to have derived its name from the Italians, commonly called Römer (Romans), who at the great fairs of the town lodged their goods in it.

Römerberg, The. A celebrated public square in Frankfort-on-the Main, where formerly the emperors were crowned. In this square is situated the ancient structure called the Römer or town-house.

Rondinini Faun. A relic of Greek sculpture formerly in the Rondinini Palace at Rome. Now in the British Museum, London. See BARBERINI FAUN, FAUN, etc.

Rondinini Medusa. A celebrated work of ancient sculpture, so named after its former possessors, and now in the Glyptothek at Munich, Bavaria.

Rosamund's Tower (*or* **Bower**). In the park of Blenheim, England, near the place where the ancient palace of Woodstock was built. It was a concealed labyrinth built by Henry II. as a residence for Rosamund, a daughter of Walter de Clifford, that she might escape the observation of his wife Queen Eleanor. It consisted of subterranean vaults of brick and stone. According to Holinshed, "the Queene found hir [Rosamond] out by a silken thridde which the King had drawne after him out of hir chamber with his foote, and dealt with her in such sharpe and cruell wise that she lived not long after."

☞ "Rosamond's Labyrinth, whose ruins, together with her Well, being paved with square stones in the bottom, and also her Bower, from which the Labyrinth did run, are yet remaining, being vaults arched and walled with stone and brick, almost inextricably wound within one another, by which, if at any time her lodging were laid about by the Queen, she might easily avoid peril imminent, and, if need be, by secret issues, take the air abroad, many furlongs about Woodstock, in Oxfordshire." *Michael Drayton.*

Yea Rosamonde, fair Rosamonde,
Her name was called so,
To whom our queene, dame Ellinor,
Was known a deadlye foe.

The king therefore, for her defence
Against the furious queene,
At Woodstocke builded such a bower,
The like was never seene.

Most curiously that bower was built
Of stone and timber strong,
An hundered and fifty doors
Did to this bower belong:

And they so cunninglye contriv'd
With turnings round about,
That none but with a clue of thread,
Could enter in or out. *Percy's Reliques.*

Roscommon Castle. An ancient fortress in Ireland, and one of the finest in the kingdom.

Rose, The. A celebrated cask, filled with fine hock, some of it a century and a half old, in the cellars underneath the Rathhaus in Bremen, Germany. A companion cask is called the Twelve Apostles.

This is the *Rose* of roses:
The older she grows, the sweeter she blossoms,
And her heavenly perfume has made me happy,
It has inspired me, — has made me tipsy;
And were I not held by the shoulder fast
By the Town-Cellar Master of Bremen,
I had gone rolling over!
Henrich Heine, Trans.

Rose, The. A famous tavern in Covent Garden, London, frequented, in the seventeenth and eighteenth centuries, by persons from various classes of society. It was near the Drury Lane Theatre, and was resorted to by dramatists, poets, courtiers, and persons of doubtful character.

Some sing Molly Mogg of the *Rose*,
And call her the Oakingham pelle;
Whilst others does farces compose,
On peautiful Molle Lepelle.
Welsh ballad.

Rose, The. An old tavern which was situated in Marylebone, London, and was formerly much frequented. There was a Rose tavern in Tower Street before the Great Fire.

Rose, The. A place of amusement referred to by Knight as being, in 1853, one of the chief London theatres.

Scenery, dresses, and decorations such as would now be thought mean and absurd, but such as would have been thought incredibly magnificent by those who, early in the seventeenth century, sat on the filthy benches of the Hope, or under the thatched roof of the *Rose*, dazzled the eyes of the multitude. *Macaulay.*

Rose, Golden. See GOLDEN ROSE.

Rosemary Lane. A street in London.

You must understand that I have been these sixteen years Merry Andrew to a puppet show: last Bartholomew Fair my master and I quarrelled, beat each other and parted; he to sell his puppets to the pincushion-makers in *Rosemary Lane*, and I to starve in St. James's Park. *Goldsmith.*

Rosenborg. [Castle of the Roses.] A royal palace in Copenhagen, Denmark. Here are kept the regalia of the Danish kings.

Roseneath. A beautiful peninsula stretching out into the Clyde, Scotland. The Duke of Argyle has an elegant Italian mansion upon it, also called Roseneath.

Roses. See FEAST OF ROSES and MIRACLE OF ROSES OF ST. FRANCIS.

Roses of Pæstum. The roses of Pæstum (an ancient city in Southern Italy, now in ruins) were much celebrated by the Latin poets Virgil, Propertius, Ausonius, and others, for their beauty and fragrance. These roses have disappeared, though it is said a few may be found flowering in May near the ruins of the temples. The violets of Pæstum, lauded by Martial, were nearly as celebrated as its roses.

☞ "I suppose no one who has read his Virgil at school crosses the plain between Salerno and Pæstum without those words of the Georgics ringing in his ears: *biferique rosaria Pæsti.* . . . The poets of Rome seem to have felt the magic of this phrase; for Ovid has imitated the line in his Metamorphoses; Martial sings of *Pæstane rosæ.* . . . Even Ausonius, at the very end of Latin literature, draws from the rosaries of Pæstum a pretty picture of beauty doomed to a premature decline.

'Vidi Pæstano guadere rosaria cultu
Exoriente nova roscida Lucifero.'

('I have watched the rose-beds that luxuriate on Pæstum's well-tilled soil, all dewy in the young light of the rising dawn-star.')

"What a place this was, indeed, for a rose-garden, spreading far and wide along the fertile plain, with its deep loam reclaimed from swamps, and irrigated by the passing of perpetual streams! But where are the roses now? As well ask, *où sont les neiges d'antan?*" *John A. Symonds.*

Rosetta Gate. The eastern entrance to a large *circuit*, near the modern town of Alexandria, Egypt, the walls of which enclose an area about 10,000 feet in length, and from 1,600 to 3,200 feet in breadth. This space, till recently uninhabited, is now being settled, and may be regarded as again a part of Alexandria.

Rosetta Stone. A piece of black basalt, the most valuable existing relic of Egyptian history, inscribed in hieroglyphics and in Greek. It was found by Boussard, a French officer, near Rosetta, in Egypt, in 1799. It is now in the British Museum, London. The stone is a trilingual slab or tablet, bearing an inscription in honor of one of the Ptolemies, written in Greek, hieroglyphic, and demotic characters. A comparison of the Greek letters with the other characters upon the stone enabled Dr. Young and Champollion to read the whole inscription, thus giving the clew to the deciphering of the ancient sacred writings of the Egyptians. The Rosetta Stone is fragmentary.

Rosewell. A fine old mansion, now deserted, near the York River, above Yorktown, Va., once the country-seat of Gov. Page, said to be the largest private house in the Old Dominion. Its materials were imported from England, and the cost of its erection ruined the owner.

Roslin Castle. An ancient ruined castle near Edinburgh, Scotland. It has under it a set of curious excavations, similar to those at Hawthornden. It was the seat of the St. Clair family, Lords of Roslin.

O'er *Roslin*, all that dreary night
A wondrous blaze was seen to gleam:
'Twas broader than the watchfire's light,
And redder than the bright moonbeam.

It glared on *Roslin's* castled rock,
It ruddied all the copsewood glen;
'Twas seen from Deyden's groves of oak,
And seen from caverned Hawthornden.
Scott.

Roslin Chapel. A beautiful ruin near Edinburgh, Scotland. The chapel was built by William St. Clair in 1446, and was the burial-place of the Barons of Roslin, who were all laid here in their armor, as described by Sir Walter Scott in his poem. It is noted for the profuseness of its decorations.

☞ "This little gem of florid architecture is scarcely a ruin, so perfect are its arches and pillars, its fretted cornices and its painted windows." *N. P. Willis.*

☞ "It is the rival of Melrose, but more elaborate: in fact, it is a perfect cataract of architectural vivacity and ingenuity, as defiant of any rules of criticism and art as the leaf-embowered arcades and arches of our American forest cathedrals." *Mrs. H. B. Stowe.*

August and hoary, o'er the sloping dale
The Gothic abbey rears its sculptured towers;
Dull through the roofs resounds the whistling gale;
Dark solitude among the pillars lowers.
Mickle.

Rospigliosi Aurora. See AURORA.

Rospigliosi Palace. [Ital. *Palazzo Rospigliosi.*] A palace in Rome, built in 1603, chiefly remarkable as possessing the celebrated fresco of Aurora by Guido.

Ross Castle. An interesting ruin in the county of Kerry, Ireland, situated on a peninsula in the Lower Lake of Killarney. It is a tall, square embattled building, with machicolated defences, and is a very conspicuous object in the landscape. It is celebrated for its exquisite views.

Rossmarkt, The. A public square in Frankfort-on-the-Main, Germany. It contains a monument to Guttenberg, the inventor of printing.

Rosso Palace. See BRIGNOLE SALE PALACE.

Rostellan. The seat of the Marquis of Thomond, near Cloyne, Ireland.

Rota, The. A political club in London, founded in 1659, and so called from a project for annually changing by *rotation* a certain number of members of Parliament. The Rota (or Coffee Club) was a sort of debating club for the spread of republican ideas. Aubrey, who became a member in 1659, says that here Milton and Marvell, Cyriac Skinner, Harrington (the author of "Oceana"), Nevill, and their friends, discussed abstract political questions, and that they had "a balloting box, and balloted how things should be carried, by way of Tentamens. The room was every evening as full as it could be crammed." The Rota broke up after the Restoration.

> But Sidrophel, as full of tricks
> As *Rota*-men of politics. *Butler.*

Rotello del Fico. A famous picture by Leonardo da Vinci (1452-1519), representing a horrid monster, said to have been composed by him after having collected serpents, lizards, and other obnoxious animals, with a view to producing the most horrid image possible.

Rotherhithe. A district in London, the headquarters of sailors.

Rotten Row. A road in Hyde Park, London, used only by equestrians, and greatly frequented by them during the London season. Its name is said by some to be derived from *rotteran*, to muster; but others pronounce it a corruption of *Route de Roi*, King's Drive.

> But yesterday a naked sod,
> The dandies sneered from *Rotten Row*,
> And sauntered o'er it to and fro,
> And see 'tis done! *Thackeray.*

Rotten Row, this half-mile to which the fashion of London confines itself as if the remainder of the bright green Park were forbidden ground, is now fuller than ever. *N. P. Willis.*

> I hope I'm fond of much that's good,
> As well as much that's gay:
> I'd like the country if I could,
> I like the Park in May;
> And when I ride in *Rotten Row*,
> I wonder why they called it so.
> *Frederick Locker.*

Rotto, Ponte. See PONTE ROTTO.

Rotonda, La. See PANTHEON.

Rotunda, The. A circular hall in the centre of the Capitol at Washington. It is 96 feet in diameter, and 180 feet high, and is over-arched by the great dome. The rotunda contains eight large historical paintings.

Rotunda, The. A public enclosure and favorite resort in Dublin, Ireland.

Rotzberg Castle. An old fortress in Switzerland, on the shore of the Alpnach lake. It is the subject of legendary song.

Rouen Cathedral. See NOTRE DAME [de Rouen].

Round Hill School. A famous but short-lived classical school on a beautiful hill near Northampton, Mass., established in 1823 by George Bancroft and J. G. Cogswell.

☞ "They aimed to found a private school with the character of a great public school, without any public foundation, and to supply its wants from its annual receipts. It was a romantic enterprise, and carried on in a quixotic or poetical spirit; and it is even remarkable that the school survived its first lustre. There never was before, and probably never will be again, such a school in America, or perhaps in the world. It was composed, as to pupils, almost exclusively of the sons of rich men; and they came from the cities of the North and the South, many being children of men well known in public life, or of historical families. . . . Probably no American college had at the time so large, varied, well-paid, and gifted a faculty as the *Round Hill School*. It outnumbered Harvard and Yale in the corps of its teachers, and put a complete circle about them in the comprehensiveness of its scheme of education. The first gymnasium in the country was set up in its playground, under Dr. Follen, who afterwards planted a similar one in the Delta at Cambridge. The school had a regular professor of manners, a *Custos Morum*, who spent his time with the boys in their play-hours, with special purpose to correct ill-speech or violence or ungentlemanliness." *H. W. Bellows.*

About the first of August we went to *Round Hill* and Hanover, but that is all. *George Ticknor.*

Round Robin. This name is given to a written petition or protest, signed by a number of persons, in a circular form, so that it may not appear who signed it first. Sometimes the names are written around a ring or circle enclosing the memorial or remonstrance, and sometimes they are appended to it, arranged within a circle of their own, from the centre of which they radiate as the spokes of a wheel do from the nave. It has been said that the officers of the French government first used the Round Robin as a means of making known their grievances; but this is doubtless a mistake, as the same device seems to have been in use among the ancient Romans, and also among the Greeks, with whom it perhaps originated. The most celebrated Round Robin ever written was addressed to Dr. Johnson by several friends of Oliver Goldsmith, for whose monument in Westminster Abbey Johnson had written a Latin inscription. The following is a copy of this famous paper:—

We, the circumsubscribers, having read with great pleasure an intended epitaph for the monument of Dr. Goldsmith, which, considered abstractedly, appears to be, for elegant composition and masterly style, in every respect worthy of the pen of its learned author, are yet of opinion that the character of the deceased as a writer, particularly as a poet, is, perhaps, not delineated with all the exactness which Dr. Johnson is capable of giving it. We, therefore, with deference to his superior judgment, humbly request that he would at least take the trouble of revising it, and of making such additions and alterations as he shall think proper on a further perusal. But, if we might venture to express our wishes, they would lead us to request that he would write the epitaph in English rather than in Latin; as we think the memory of so eminent an English writer ought to be perpetuated in the language to which his works are likely to be so lasting an ornament, which we also known to have been the opinion of the late doctor himself.

JOS. WARTON.	J. REYNOLDS.
EDM. BURKE.	W. FORBES.
THOS. FRANKLIN.	T. BARNARD.
ANT. CHANVIER.	R. B. SHERIDAN.
GEO. COLMAN.	P. METCALFE.
WM. VACHELL.	E. GIBBON.

[These names were signed around a circle enclosing the petition.]

☞ The term Round Robin is of uncertain derivation. Some say it comes from the French words *rond*, round, and *ruban*, a ribbon; but this is mere assertion, and lacks even plausibility to support it. In some parts of England a pancake is called a Round Robin; and it may, fairly enough, be conjectured that the circular form of petition, which is also so called, was named from its resemblance to a pancake. But the question then arises, Why was the pancake so called? This is not easily answered. It may even have happened that the pancake was named from its resemblance to the petition. *Robin* is an old and familiar form of *Robert* (Robin Redbreast, by the by, means Robert Redbreast); and it would not be strange if some forgotten person of that name, who proposed to his associates this ingenious method of declaring their wishes or sentiments, was the occasion of the designation. Or he may have been the happy inventor of the pancake, and have left no memorial of himself except that useful article of food and its provincial name. There is, however, another conjecture, which, as it has greater probability, deserves to be mentioned. The small pieces of spun-yarn or marline which are used to confine the upper edge of a sail to the yard or gaff, are called *rope-bands*, —corrupted by sailors to *robands*, or *robbins*. Now, a robbin of this sort encircling a yard bears an easily recognizable, though rather fanciful, resemblance to a ring enclosing a petition or other writing. As Round Robins are frequently made use of by British sailors, it is quite possible that this is the true origin of the name.

No *round robin* signed by the whole main-deck of the Academy or the Porch. *De Quincey.*

Round Table [of King Arthur]. An ancient painted oaken table of a circular form, in the County Hall of Winchester, England. The tradition is, that this table is the same around which King Arthur and his knights used to assemble. This table was exhibited in 1522 to the Emperor Charles V. of Germany. It is described as "a circle divided into 25 green and white compartments radiating from the centre, which is a large double rose. . . . Resting upon the rose, is a canopied niche, in which is painted a royal figure, bearing the orb and sword, and wearing the royal crown."

"For his own part," he said, "and in the land where he was bred, men would as soon take for their mark King Arthur's *Round Table*, which held sixty knights around it." *Scott.*

Where Venta's Norman castle still uprears
Its raftered hall,—
High hung remains, the pride of warlike years,
Old Arthur's board;—on the capacious round
Some British pen has sketched the names renowned,
In marks obscure, of his immortal peers.
Though joined by magic skill with many a rhyme
The Druid frame, unhonored, falls a prey
To the slow vengeance of the wizard Time,
And fade the British characters away;
Yet Spenser's page, that chants in verse sublime
Those chiefs, shall live, unconscious of decay. *Thomas Warton.*

Full fifteen years and more were sped,
Each brought new wreaths to Arthur's head,
And wide were through the world renown'd
The glories of his *Table Round*. *Scott.*

Round Table. See KING ARTHUR'S ROUND TABLE.

Round Top. See LITTLE ROUND TOP.

Round Tower. See OLD STONE MILL.

Rousseau's House. On the Grand Rue, Geneva, Switzerland. In this house Jean Jacques was born, and spent his early life.

Rowallan Castle. A feudal mansion of great antiquity near Kilmarnock, Scotland.

Roxburgh Castle. An ancient fortress, made a royal palace by David I. in 1124, near Teviot Bridge, over the Tweed, in Scotland. It is now in ruins. In a churchyard adjoining is the grave of Edie Ochiltree, a character in Scott's novel of "The Antiquary." His real name was Andrew Gemmel. In the same neighborhood is a monument to the memory of the poet Thomson, the author of "The Seasons," who was born here.

Roxburgh! how fallen, since first in Gothic pride,
Thy frowning battlements the war defied. *Leyden.*

Roxburghe Club. This club in London derives its foundation from the sale, in 1812, of the library of John, third Duke of Roxburghe (died 1804), after whom it is named. It was avowedly instituted for the reprinting of rare and old specimens of ancient literature; each member to "reprint a scarce piece of ancient lore, to be given to the members, one copy being on vellum for the chairman, and only as many copies as members." The Roxburghe Club gave elaborate dinners. It is still in existence.

Royal Academy. A Society of Artists in London, organized in 1768, of which Sir Joshua Reynolds was the first president. The Academy occupied rooms for a time in Somerset House, but in 1838 removed to the National Gallery.

Royal Academy of Music. An academy in London, for teaching all branches of music, founded in 1822 by the late Earl of Westmoreland.

Royal Adelaide. A British steamer wrecked off Margate, March 30, 1850, with a loss of 200 lives.

Royal Alfred. An armor-plated ship of the British navy, launched Oct. 15, 1864.

Royal Charter. A British steamer, bound from Australia to Liverpool, wrecked on the English coast, Oct. 25, 1859, with a loss of 459 lives and nearly $4,000,000 worth of gold. A good part of the latter was recovered.

Royal Exchange. A building erected for the use of merchants and bankers in London, opened by Queen Victoria in 1844. The hour of 'Change — the busy period — is from 3½ to 4½ P.M. Tuesday and Friday are the principal days on 'Change. Lloyd's is situated in the Royal Exchange. Sir Thomas Gresham (sixteenth century) built the first Royal Exchange, which was destroyed in the Great Fire of 1666. It was rebuilt, and again burnt in 1838.

Proclaim through every high street of the city,
This place be no longer called a Burse;
But since the building's stately, fair, and strange,
Be it forever called — the *Royal Exchange*.
Heywood.

Observe the humors of th' *Exchange*,
That universal mart. *Tom Brown.*

Royal George. One of the finest ships in the British navy, commanded by Admiral Kempenfeldt. Requiring repairs near the keel, she was careened at Portsmouth; but, being turned over too much, she filled and went down with all on board. Nearly 900 lives were lost.

☞ "The Royal George, of 108 guns, whilst undergoing a partial careening in Portsmouth Harbor, was overset about 10, A.M. Aug. 29, 1782. The total loss was believed to be near 1,000 souls." *Palgrave.*

Toll for the brave! the brave that are no more!
All sunk beneath the wave, fast by their native shore!
Eight hundred of the brave, whose courage well was tried,
Had made the vessel heel, and laid her on her side.
A land-breeze shook the shrouds, and she was overset;
Down went the *Royal George*, with all her crew complete!

Weigh the vessel up, once dreaded by our foes,
And mingle with our cup the tear that England owes!
Her timbers yet are sound, and she may float again,
Full charged with England's thunder, and plough the distant main.
But Kempenfeldt is gone, his victories are o'er;
And he and his eight hundred shall plough the waves no more. *Cowper.*

Royal Institution of Great Britain. A society formed in London in 1799 for the pursuit of natural science. It has been called "the workshop of the Royal Society." In the laboratory of the Institution Sir Humphry Davy and Professor Faraday made some of their most brilliant discoveries.

Royal Naval Club. This club in London, formed in 1765, numbered among its members Boscawen, Rodney, Sir Philip Durham, and was a favorite resort of William IV. when Duke of Clarence. The precursor of this club was the Naval Club, founded about 1674. The Royal Naval Club was confined to members of the naval service. The club dined at the Thatched House, on the anniversaries of the battle of the Nile.

Royal Oak. A famous pollard oak on the borders of Worcestershire, England, in which, according to tradition, King Charles II. secreted himself from his pursuers, who passed around and under the tree without discovering him. On account of the king's escape, it became a custom to wear oak on the anniversary of the king's birthday. At the Restoration the oak was destroyed, through the eagerness to obtain relics of the king's hiding-place; but another tree, which grew from one of its acorns, is still standing It is said that the king planted two acorns from the old tree in Hyde Park, and that the tree which sprang from one of them is now flourishing.

There is no need that the personages on the scene be a King and Clown; that the scene be the Forest of the *Royal Oak*, "on the borders of Staffordshire:" need only that the scene lie on this old firm Earth of ours, where we also have so surprisingly arrived; that the personages be *men*, and *seen* with the eyes of a man. *Carlyle.*

And I will work in prose and rhyme,
And praise thee more in both
Than bard has honored beech or lime,
Or that Thessalian growth

In which the swarthy ringdove sat,
And mystic sentence spoke;
And more than England honors that,
Thy famous brother-oak,

Wherein the younger Charles abode
Till all the paths were dim,
And far below the Roundhead rode,
And hummed a surly hymn.
Tennyson.

Royal Oak. An armor-plated ship of the British navy, launched Sept. 10, 1862.

Royal Society. A society established in London for the study of natural science, about the year 1645, and said to be the oldest society of its kind in Europe, with the exception of the Lincean Academy in Rome, of which Galileo was a member. Sir Isaac Newton was one of the presidents of the society. The greater part of its collections have been transferred to the British Museum.

Royal Society Club. This club in London is said to have been founded about 1743 as the Club of Royal Philosophers, which name it bore until 1786. It was established "for the convenience of certain members [of the Royal Society] who lived in various parts, that they might assemble and dine together on the days when the Society held its evening meetings." Many distinguished persons have been guests of the club. Ward, in 1709, humorously refers to the "Virtuoso's Club" as first established by some of the principal members of the Royal Society, and says its chief design "was to propagate new whims, advance mechanical exercises, and to promote useless as well as useful experiments." The Royal Society Club has changed its place for dining several times: in 1857 they removed to the Thatched House, where they remained until that tavern was taken down.

Royal Sovereign. An armor-plated ship of the British navy, launched March 8, 1864.

Rubens, The Two Sons of. A picture of his two sons by Peter Paul Rubens (1577-1640), and considered one of his masterpieces. It is in the collection of Prince Lichtenstein at Vienna.

Rubicon, The. The ancient name of a little stream which divided Italy from Cisalpine Gaul. It is at the present time identified with the Uso. Julius Cæsar's passage of this stream in the year 49 is famous as being the initiative act of civil war; and from this circumstance to "pass the Rubicon" became a proverb, signifying the entrance upon any undertaking from which there can be no retreat.

Now near the banks of *Rubicon* he stood;
When lo! as he surveyed the narrow flood,
Amidst the dusky horrors of the night,
A wondrous vision stood confest to sight.
Her awful head Rome's reverend image reared,
Trembling and sad the matron form appeared;
A tow'ry crown her hoary temples bound,
And her torn tresses rudely hung around.
Lucan, Trans.

☞ "Cæsar paused upon the brink of the Rubicon. What was the Rubicon? The boundary of Cæsar's province. From what did it separate his province? From his country. Was that country a desert? No: it was cultivated and fertile; rich and populous! . . . What was Cæsar, that stood upon the brink of that stream? A traitor, bringing war and pestilence into the heart of that country! No wonder that he paused! No wonder if, in his imagination, wrought upon by his conscience, he had beheld blood instead of water, and heard groans instead of murmurs. No wonder if some Gorgon horror had turned him into stone upon the spot. But, no! he cried, 'The die is cast!' He plunged! he crossed! and Rome was free no more." *J. S. Knowles.*

Alas! why pass'd he, too, the *Rubicon*,—
The *Rubicon* of man's awaken'd rights,
To herd with vulgar kings and parasites?
Byron.

Rue [Street]. For names beginning with Rue, see the next prominent word.

Rufus's Oak. See Rufus's Stone.

Rufus's Stone (*and* **Oak**). A triangular stone erected in the New Forest, near Southampton, England, on the spot where formerly stood the famous oak, on which, according to the inscription, "an arrow shot by Sir Walter Tyrrel at a stag, glanced and struck King William II., named Rufus, in the breast, of which he instantly died, on the 2d of August, A.D. 1100." The spot is visited by great numbers of people every year.

O'er the New Forest's heath-hills bare,
Down steep ravine, by shaggy wood,
A pilgrim wandered, questing where
The relic-tree of Rufus stood.
. . . .
Some monument he found, which spoke
What erst had happened on the spot;
But for that old avenging oak,
Decayed long since, he found it not.
John Kenyon.

Rugby. A famous school in the town of the same name in the county of Warwick, England. It is noted as the scene of Dr. Arnold's life and labors. The school was founded in the reign of Elizabeth, and has fine cloistered buildings.

Ruhmeshalle, Die Baierische. See HALL OF FAME.

Rump Steak, *or* **Liberty Club.** This political club, in opposition to Sir Robert Walpole, was in existence in 1733-4. See BEEF-STEAK SOCIETY [CLUB].

Russell Square. A well-known public square in London, upon the site of the old palace of the Dukes of Bedford.

Rutgers College. A collegiate establishment in New Brunswick, N.J. It was founded in 1770.

Ruth and Naomi. A picture by Ary Scheffer (1795-1858).

Ruthwell Cross. A remarkable Runic monument in the parish of Ruthwell, near Dumfries, Scotland. It is a stone cross, bearing an inscription in Runic and in Latin characters. This stone is said to have been broken in two in the last century by direction of the General Assembly, as being an object of superstitious veneration, and to have been afterwards put together.

Rutland House. A noble mansion which formerly stood in Charterhouse Square, London.

Rydal Mount. The picturesque and celebrated residence of the poet Wordsworth, standing on the projection of a hill near the little village of Rydal, near Ambleside, in the "Lake District" of England. Wordsworth's dwelling commanded a fine view, embracing the lake of Rydal and a part of Windermere. The poet is sometimes called the "Bard of Rydal Mount."

☞ "A lovely cottage-like building, almost hidden by a profusion of roses and ivy." *Mrs. Hemans.*

This day without its record may not pass,
In which I first have seen the lowly roof
That shelters Wordsworth's age.
Fitting place I found
Blest with rare beauty, set in deepest calm;
Looking upon still waters, whose expanse
Might tranquillize all thought, and bordered round
By mountains. *Henry Alford.*

Of him whose whitened locks on *Rydal Mount*
Are lifted yet by morning breezes blowing
From the green hills, immortal in his lays.
Whittier.

Rye House. A frequent resort of anglers from London, and the scene, according to some authorities, of the celebrated alleged conspiracy of 1683, known as the Rye House Plot. It is situated between London and Newmarket. By other authorities the scene of the plot is referred to an ancient mansion, called the Rye House, in the parish of Stanstead, Hertfordshire.

Ryknield St. See FOSSE, THE.

S.

Sabines, Rape of the. See RAPE OF THE SABINES.

Sacer, Mons. See MONS SACER.

Sachem's Plain. A locality near Norwich, Conn., noted as the scene of a battle between the Narragansetts and Mohegans in 1642. A granite monument to the memory of Miantonomoh, the Narragansett chief who fell in the action, was erected on this battlefield in 1841.

Sackville Street. A noble street in Dublin, Ireland, the principal thoroughfare of the city, midway in which is Nelson's Pillar.

☞ "The street is exceedingly broad and handsome. Even in this, the great street of the town, there is scarcely any one; and it is as vacant and listless as Pall Mall in October." *Thackeray.*

Sacra Conversazione. [Holy Conversation.] The name given by the Italians to pictures of the Holy Family in which the sacred persons are represented as a *devotional* group, in distinction from a merely domestic or historical group. For examples see under HOLY FAMILY.

Sacra Famiglia. See HOLY FAMILY.

Sacra, Via. See VIA SACRA.

Sacrament. See DISPUTE OF THE SACRAMENT.

Sacraments. See SEVEN SACRAMENTS.

Sacred and Profane Love. A well-known picture by Titian (1477–1576). In the Palazzo Borghese, Rome.

☞ "Out of Venice, there is nothing of Titian's to compare to his *Sacred and Profane Love*. Description can give no idea of the consummate beauty of this composition." *Eaton.*

☞ "The Sacred and Profane Love by Titian is still another masterpiece of the same spirit. A beautiful woman dressed appears by the side of another naked. By their side is a sculptured fountain, and behind them a broad landscape of a blue tone with warm patches of earth intersected by the darks of sombre forests, and in the distance the sea; two cavaliers are visible in the background, also a spire and a town. . . . The eye passes from the simple tones of that ample and healthy flesh to the rich subdued tints of the landscape, as the ear passes from a melody to its accompaniment." *Taine, Trans.*

Sacred College. A name given to the body of cardinals or princes of the Roman Catholic Church. It is the Sacred College assembling in conclave, which elects a new pope whenever a vacancy occurs in the holy see.

Sacred Mount. See MONS SACER and MONTE SACRO.

Sacred Way. See VIA SACRA.

Sacrément, St. See ST. SACRÉMENT.

Sacrifice of Isaac. 1. A fresco by Raphael Sanzio (1483–1520), in the Stanza of the Heliodorus, in the Vatican, Rome.

2. A picture by David Teniers the Younger (1610–1694 ?), the Belgian *genre*-painter.

Sacro (*or* **Santo**) **Eremo.** A collection of 24 hermitages, established by Saint Romualdo near the convent of Camaldoli in Italy. The rules and observances of the hermitage are strict and severe.

☞ "Here [at Camaldoli] we passed the night, and next morning rode up by the steep traverses to the Santo Eremo, where Saint Romualdo lived and established

de' tacenti cenobiti il coro,
L'arcane penitenze, ed i digiuni
Al Camaldoli suo.

The Eremo is a city of hermits,

walled round, and divided into streets of low detached cells. Each cell consists of two or three naked rooms, built exactly on the plan of the Saint's own tenement, which remains just as Romualdo left it 800 years ago, now too sacred and too damp for a mortal tenant. The unfeeling Saint has here established a rule which anticipates the pains of Purgatory. No stranger can behold without emotion a number of noble, interesting young men bound to stand erect chanting at choir for eight hours a day; their faces pale, their heads shaven, their beards shaggy, their backs raw, their legs swollen, and their feet bare. . . . The sickly novice is cut off in one or two winters, the rest are subject to dropsy, and few arrive at old age." *Forsyth.*

At Casentino's foot
A river crosses named Archiano, born
Above the Hermitage in Apennine.
Dante, Purgatorio, Longfellow's Trans.

Sacro, Monte. See MONTE SACRO and MONS SACER.

Sadler's Wells. A place of amusement for the populace, on the banks of the New River near Islington, England. It contains a medicinal spring, of much repute in old times. The public-house on the place is represented in the background of Hogarth's print of "Evening." The site is now occupied by a theatre. See SADLER'S WELLS THEATRE.

Sadler's Wells Theatre. One of the oldest theatres in London, named from a mineral spring in the neighborhood. The present house was erected in 1764, and rebuilt in 1876-77. See SADLER'S WELLS.

Her [Mademoiselle Clairon's) hands are not alternately stretched out, and then drawn in again, as with the singing women at *Sadler's- Wells:* they are employed with graceful variety, and every moment please with new and unexpected eloquence. *Goldsmith.*

Is it the skilfullest Anatomist that cuts the best figure at *Sadler's Wells?* or does the Boxer hit better for knowing that he has a flexor longus and a flexor brevis? *Carlyle.*

Sages, The Chaldean. See CHALDEAN SAGES.

Saidnâya. A convent of great antiquity in Northern Palestine, in the neighborhood of Damascus, containing a shrine of the Virgin which is a favorite resort of pilgrims belonging to the Greek Church.

St. Agnes. A well-known picture by Andrea del Sarto (1488-1530). In the cathedral at Pisa, Italy. See also EVE OF ST. AGNES and MARTYRDOM OF ST. AGNES.

St. Aignan, Hôtel. See HÔTEL ST. AIGNAN.

St. Alban's Abbey. An ancient monastic establishment in the vicinity of St. Albans, in Hertfordshire, England. It was once the wealthiest and most brilliant of all the religious houses of Great Britain. It is now restored, and is one of the finest cathedral-churches in England.

☞ "The surviving ruins convey a more imposing sense of the ancient magnificence than Melrose, or Fountains, or Glastonbury." *Froude.*

St. Angelo. The celebrated fortress of Papal Rome, anciently the mausoleum of Hadrian, erected by him as his family tomb, the last imperial niche in the mausoleum of Augustus having been occupied by the ashes of Nerva. It derives its present name from the Church tradition, that while Gregory the Great was leading a procession to St. Peter's with the object of offering up a solemn service to avert the plague which followed the inundation of 589, there appeared to him a vision of the Archangel Michael standing on the summit of the mausoleum in the act of sheathing his bloody sword, to indicate that the pestilence was stayed. The pope, in memory of this vision, built a chapel on the summit; but this was afterwards replaced by a statue of the archangel. The history of this fortress during the Middle Ages is almost the history of the city itself during that period. It has suffered much from siege and mutilations, and is now but the skeleton of the ancient mausoleum of the emperors. The tomb of Hadrian is thought to have been first turned into a fortress about A.D. 423,—in the time of Honorius. Merivale speaks of the effort of imagination required to transform the present scarred and shapeless bulk into the "graceful pile which rose column upon column, surmounted by a gilded dome of span almost unrivalled;" and Procopius says of the original mausoleum, in the sixth century, that it was built of Parian marble, the square blocks fitting closely without cement; that it had four equal sides, each a stone's throw in length, and rising above the walls of the city, while on the summit were statues of men and horses, of admirable workmanship. The castle of St. Angelo has often served as a prison, and part of it is now so used. Benvenuto Cellini was confined here, and the pretended cell of Beatrice Cenci is shown by the custode. For an account of the celebrated display of fireworks formerly exhibited from the castle at Easter, see GIRANDOLA. See BRIDGE OF ST. ANGELO.

☞ "No building in the world has probably lived through a more eventful existence, and none, if there were tongues in stones, could tell a tale of more varied interest."

George S. Hillard.

☞ "This proud fabric is an instance how completely vanity defeats its own ends. It was destined by Hadrian to hold his remains forever. Had he chosen a more humble monument, his imperial dust might probably still have remained undisturbed. As it is, his ashes are long since scattered, his very name has passed away, and the place which was destined to be sacred to the greatest of the dead now serves for the punishment of the vilest of the living." *C. A. Eaton.*

Turn to the mole which Hadrian rear'd
on high,
Imperial mimic of old Egypt's piles,
Colossal copyist of deformity,
Whose travell'd phantasy from the far
Nile's
Enormous model, doom'd the artist's toils
To build for giants, and for his vain earth,
His shrunken ashes, raise this dome! How
smiles
The gazer's eye with philosophic mirth,
To view the huge design which sprung
from such a birth! *Byron.*

Think also whether thou hast known no Public Quacks, on far higher scale than this, whom a *Castle of St. Angelo* could never get hold of; and how, as Emperors, Chancellors (having found much fitter machinery), they could run their Quack-career; and make whole kingdoms, whole continents, into one huge Egyptian Lodge, and squeeze supplies, of money or blood, from it at discretion? *Carlyle.*

The cannon of *St. Angelo*,
And chanting priest and clanging bell,
And beat of drum and bugle blow,
Shall greet thy coming well!

Whittier.

St. Angelo, Bridge of. See BRIDGE OF ST. ANGELO.

St. Anna. A picture by Bartholomew Zeitblom (b. 1410–1450), a German painter. It is now in the museum at Berlin, Prussia.

St. Anna (and the Virgin). A well-known picture by Leonardo da Vinci (1452–1520), in the Louvre, at Paris. It is thought by some to have been only executed from a cartoon by Leonardo.

St. Anne's. Of several churches of this name in London, one of the oldest and most noted is that in Soho, finished in 1686.

Kettles and pans,
Say the bells at *St. Ann's*.
Mother Goose.

St. Anthony. See TEMPTATION OF ST. ANTHONY.

St. Antoine, Rue. A street in Paris which has been closely connected with every revolution. This wide and irregular street leads from the Hôtel de Ville, forms a continuation of the Rue de Rivoli to the Place de la Bastille, where the Bastille formerly stood, beyond which it continues as the Rue du Faubourg St. Antoine.

St. Antoine. See FAUBOURG ST. ANTOINE.

St. Antony. An ancient Coptic monastery in the Eastern Desert of Egypt, and the principal one in the country.

St. Augustine and his Mother. A picture by Ary Scheffer (1795–1858).

St. Barbara. A grand altar-piece by Jacopo Palma, called Palma Vecchio (1480?–1548?), in the church of Santa Maria Formosa at Venice, Italy.

☞ "She is no saint, but a blooming young girl, the most attractive and lovable that one can imagine."
Taine, Trans.

St. Bartholomew's Hospital. The first institution of the kind in London. It is in Smithfield, and was originally part of the Priory of St. Bartholomew, founded in 1102 by Rahere. The hospital escaped the Great Fire in 1666, and since that time has been much enlarged. St. Bartholomew's enjoys an excellent reputation as a medical school.

St. Basil. A famous church in Moscow, Russia, built during the reign of Ivan the Terrible. It consists of an agglomeration of towers each enclosing a chapel, so that as many as a dozen or fifteen saints have their shrines under one roof.

☞ "What is it? A church, a pavilion, or an immense toy? All the colors of the rainbow, all the forms and combinations which straight and curved lines can produce, are here compounded. It seems to be the product of some architectural kaleidoscope, in which the most incongruous things assume a certain order and system, for surely such another bewildering pile does not exist. It is not beautiful; for beauty requires at least a suggestion of symmetry, and here the idea of proportion or adaptation is wholly lost. Neither is it offensive; because the maze of colors, in which red, green, and gold predominate, attracts and cajoles the eye. . . . I cannot better describe this singular structure than by calling it the Apotheosis of Chimneys."
Bayard Taylor.

St. Bavon. A cathedral in Ghent, Belgium, one of the finest Gothic churches, containing celebrated works of art; in particular, the "Adoration of the Lamb," by Hubert and John Van Eyck.

Toll! Roland, toll!
In old *St. Bavon's* tower,
At midnight hour,
The great bell Roland spoke!

. . . . .

Toll! Roland, toll!
Not now in old *St. Bavon's* tower—
Not now at midnight hour—
Not now from River Scheldt to Zuyder Zee,
But here,—this side the sea!
T. Tilton.

St. Bernard. See HOSPICE OF ST. BERNARD and VISION OF ST. BERNARD.

St. Botolph's. A well-known church in Aldersgate, London.

At *Saint Botulphe*, and Saint Anne of Buckstone;

. . . . .

Praying to them to pray for me
Unto the blessed Trinitie.
Heywood.

St. Bride's. A church at the foot of Fleet Street, London. It was rebuilt by Wren, after the Great Fire of 1666. Dwellers in London are fond of the bells of St. Bride's. The old church contained the graves of Wynkin de Worde, Sackville the poet, Lovelace, Sir Richard Baker. John Milton lodged in the churchyard of St. Bride, and here wrote several of his treatises, and in defence of the house in which he lived composed his sonnet beginning,—

"Captain, or colonel, or knight in arms."

Richardson the novelist was buried in the present church.

St. Calixtus, Catacomb of. See CATACOMB OF ST. CALIXTUS.

St. Catherine. A Greek convent situated on the slope of one of the peaks of Mount Sinai in Arabia. It is said to have been founded by the Emperor Justinian, and contains interesting MS. and other relics.

☞ "Though the interior presents a scene of the most hopeless confusion when looked down upon from the guest-chambers, there is not wanting a certain quaint picturesqueness and charm, which is heightened in spring by the bright green of the trellised vines. Two tiers of loopholes are still visible in the west wall; and some few of the vaults and arches within remain intact, but they are for the most part broken down, and filled with all manner of filth. Over, above, and within them are the buildings of after ages, mosques, chapels, bakeries, distilleries, and stables, some themselves gone to ruin, and serving as foundations for still later erections of mud and sun-dried bricks, which are daily adding their mite to the general confusion. The quadrangle is now completely filled with buildings; and through them, turning and twisting in every direction,

now ascending, now descending, exposed to the full force of the sun, or passing through dark tunnels, is a perfect labyrinth of narrow passages."
C. W. Wilson.

☞ "M. Seetzen has fallen into a mistake in calling the convent by the name of St. Catherine. It is dedicated to the Transfiguration, or, as the Greeks call it, the Metamorphosis, and not to St. Catherine, whose relics are only preserved here." *Burckhardt.*

☞ "Before we went, we called this the Convent of St. Catherine, as everybody does. We had read of it under that name, and seen that name under every print of the place that had come before our eyes. Our surprise was therefore great when a monk, who had taken the vows twenty years before, declared that he did not know it by that name. Being asked whether the convent had nothing to do with St. Catherine, he replied, only by the bones of a hermitess named Catherine, having been found on the mountain above the convent which bears her name. Perplexed by this, I was yet more surprised when I observed a little Catherine-wheel rudely carved over one of the posterns; and a picture of the saint, leaning on her wheel, in the library, with her name at length. In the chapel also her relics lie in state, —those bones which were found on the mountain-top, and were brought hither by the monks a few years after the establishment of the convent. The monk, however, stuck to his declaration that the convent had no connection with St. Catherine."
Miss Martineau.

St. Catherine. 1. A picture by Raphael Sanzio (1483–1520). In the National Gallery, London. See also MARTYRDOM OF ST. CATHERINE and MARRIAGE OF ST. CATHERINE.

2. A picture by Heinrich Karl Anton Mücke (b. 1806), which has become popular through engravings. It represents the saint borne by four angels over sea and land to Mount Sinai.

☞ "The floating onward movement of the group is very beautifully expressed." *Mrs. Jameson.*

St. Catherine's House. A house still standing in Sienna, Italy, and distinguished as the residence of St. Catherine of Sienna (1347–1380), remarkable for her fervent charity and devotion. Over the doorway is inscribed in gold, "Sposæ Christi Katharinæ domus" (the house of Catherine the bride of Christ).

☞ "Her fame was universal throughout Italy before her death; and the house from which she went forth to preach, and heal the sick, and comfort plague-stricken wretches whom kith and kin had left alone to die, was known and well-beloved by all her citizens. From the moment of her death, it became, and has continued to be, the object of superstitious veneration to thousands." *Symonds.*

And the house midway hanging see
That saw Saint Catherine bodily.
Felt on its floors her sweet feet move,
And the live light of fiery love
Burn from her beautiful, strange face.
Swinburne.

St. Cecilia. A picture by Domenico Zampieri, called Domenichino (1581-1641). In the Louvre, Paris. Another upon the same subject by this painter, formerly in the Palazzo Borghese, Rome, is now in Lansdowne House, London.

St. Cecilia. A picture by Carlo Dolce (1616-1686). In the Dresden Gallery. There are several repetitions of this picture in other places.

St. Cecilia. A celebrated altar-picture by Raphael Sanzio (1483–1520), representing St. Cecilia, as patroness of music, standing in the centre, with two saints on each side, instruments of secular music, the pipe, the flute, etc., lying broken and scattered at her feet, she herself raising her eyes to the angels in the clouds above, and apparently listening to the heavenly song. This picture was originally painted for the church of San Giovanni-in-Monte, near Bologna, Italy, and is now in the gallery of that city Raphael's original drawing for this picture, engraved by Marc Antonio, is highly admired.

☞ "The most celebrated of the modern representations of St. Cecilia, as patroness of music, is the picture by Raphael, painted by him for the altar-piece of her chapel in the church of San Giovanni-in-Monte, near Bologna. She stands in the centre, habited in a rich robe of golden tint, and her hair confined by a band of jewels. In her hand she bears a small organ, — but seems about to drop it as she looks up, listening with ecstatic expression to a group of angels, who are singing above. Scattered and broken at her feet, lie the instruments of secular music, the pipe, flute, tabor, etc. To the right of St. Cecilia stands St. Paul, leaning on his sword; behind him is St. John the Evangelist, with the eagle at his feet; to the left, in front, the Magdalene, as already described; and behind her St. Augustine. . . . Sir Joshua Reynolds has given us a parody of this famous picture, in his portrait of Mrs. Billington; but, instead of the organ, he has placed a music-book in her hands, a change which showed both his taste and his judgment, and lent to the borrowed figure an original significance. It gave occasion also to the happy compliment paid to the singer by Haydn. 'What have you done?' said he to Sir Joshua: 'you have made her listening to the angels: you should have represented the angels listening to *her!*'"

Mrs. Jameson.

There are five saints there, side by side, who in no wise concern us, but whose existence is so perfect that we wish the picture could continue forever

Goethe, Trans.

St. Cecilia. A picture by Van Eyck (1366–1426). In the museum at Berlin, Prussia.

St. Christopher. A large altar-piece by Hans Memling (d. 1495), the Flemish painter, executed for Willem Moreel, and bearing date 1484. It is in the collection of the Academy at Bruges, Belgium.

St. Christopher. A picture by Hans Memling (d. 1495), the Flemish painter. Erroneously called Albert Dürer. It is now at the Duke of Devonshire's seat, Holker Hall, Lancashire.

St. Christopher. A gigantesque fresco painting by Mateo Perez de Alesio (d. 1600). "The figure of the saint is 33 feet high, and his leg is three feet across the calf." In the cathedral of Seville, Spain.

St. Chrysostom. An altar-picture by Sebastian del Piómbo (1485–1547). In the church of S. Giovanni Crisostomo, at Venice, Italy.

St. Clement-Danes. A church in London, built under the supervision of Sir Christopher Wren (1632–1723). Strype derives the name of St. Clement Danes from the account that when the Danish people were expelled by Alfred in 886, those who had married English women were allowed to remain here. Stow, however, tells how the body of Harold, the illegitimate son of King Canute, was exhumed from Westminster by the legitimate Hardicanute, and cast into the Thames, and how it was afterwards recovered by a fisherman, and buried upon this spot.

☞ "We pass from the open Place where St. Clement-Danes stands, — one of the most Dutch-like spots in London, to which idea the quaint and rather elegant tower lends itself. To hear its chimes, not at midnight, but on some December evening, when the steeple is projected on a cold blue background, while you can see the shadows of the ringers in the bell-tower, is a picturesque feeling. They fling out their janglings more wildly than any peal in London: they are nearer the ground, and the hurly-burly is melodious enough. Those tones the Doctor often heard in Gough Square and Bolt Court; and inside he had his favorite seat, to this day reverently marked by a plate and inscription. Yet St. Clement's is in a precarious condition, and when the Law Courts are completed its fate will be decided." *Fitzgerald.*

☞ "The church of *St. Clement*, in the Strand, is dedicated to this saint [St. Clement]. The device of the parish is an anchor, which the beadles and other officials wear on their buttons, etc., and which also surmounts the weathercock on the steeple. To choose the anchor — the symbol of stability — for a weathercock, appears strangely absurd till we know the reason. There are in England 47 churches dedicated to St. Clement." *Mrs. Jameson.*

That Church of *St. Clement Danes*, where Johnson still *worshipped* in the era of Voltaire, is to me a venerable place.

Carlyle.

How Samuel Johnson, in the era of Voltaire, can purify and fortify his soul, and hold real communion with the Highest, "in the Church of *St. Clement Danes:*" this too stands all unfolded in his Biography, and is among the most touching and memorable things there. *Carlyle.*

Where the fair columns of *St. Clement* stand,
Whose straitened bounds encroach upon the Strand. *Gay.*

Oranges and lemons,
Say the bells of *St. Clement's.*
Mother Goose.

St. Clement's Well. This holy well in the Strand, London, was much resorted to by the youth of the city in the reign of Henry II. A pump now stands on the spot.

St. Cloud. A magnificent royal residence in France, on the southern slope of a hill overlooking the Seine. The château contains several suites of rooms, which are highly ornamented with Gobelin tapestry, paintings, statues, and mosaics. Its history is closely connected with that of the French monarchs. It derives its name from Cleodald, a grandson of Clovis, who escaped assassination by concealing himself in a hermitage in the woods on the summit of the hill. The palace commands a most lovely prospect, and the adjoining park is celebrated for its beauty. St. Cloud was the favorite residence of Napoleon I. In October, 1870, the French destroyed it by shells from Mont Valérien, that it might not serve to shelter the Prussians.

They resembled those loathsome slanders which Goldsmith, and other abject libellers of the same class, were in the habit of publishing about Bonaparte, how he hired a grenadier to shoot Dessaix at Marengo, how he filled *St. Cloud* with all the pollutions of Capreæ. *Macaulay.*

Soft spread the southern summer night
Her veil of darksome blue;
Ten thousand stars combined to light
The terrace of *St. Cloud.*
The evening breezes gently sighed,
Like breath of lover true,
Bewailing the deserted pride
And wreck of sweet *St. Cloud.* *Scott.*

St. Cuthbert's Beads. These beads are portions of the fossilized remains of animals, called crenoids. They consist of a series of flat plates with a hole in the centre of each piece, through which they may be strung like a rosary. They are found on the shore of the island of Lindisfarne; and the legend is, that in violent storms, on dark nights, St. Cuthbert used to sit on a rock in the spray and mist, and with another rock forge these beads; and after the storm the shore was found to be strewn with them.

On a rock, by Lindisfarne,
St. Cuthbert sits, and toils to frame
The sea-born beads that bear his name:
Such tales had Whitby's fishers told,
And said they might his shape behold,
And hear his anvil sound;
A deadened clang, — a huge dim form,
Seen but, and heard, when gatherin storm
And night were closing round.
Scott's Marmion.

St. Cuthbert's Shrine. See SHRINE OF ST. CUTHBERT.

St. Denis, Abbey Church of. A religious edifice in St. Denis, France, rich in historical associations, and celebrated as the burial-place of the monarchs of France from the earliest times. It has suffered much from the revolutions and wars which have swept over France, but the restorations which it has recently undergone entitle it to rank among the most splendid Gothic edifices in the world. The present church dates from the twelfth century. According to tradition here was the burial-place of St. Denis, and here in very early times a Benedictine abbey was founded.

St. Denis du Marais. See ST. SACRÉMENT.

St. Denis, Porte. See PORTE ST. DENIS.

St. Denis, Rue. One of the ancient streets of Paris. According to tradition, St. Denis frequently passed over the old *chaussée*, and the street is supposed to have been so named in his memory.

☞ "Thence we turned into the Rue St. Denis, which is one of the oldest streets in Paris, and is said to have been first marked out by the track of the saint's footsteps, where, after his martyrdom, he walked along it, with his head under his arm, in quest of a burial-place. This legend may account for any crookedness of the street; for it could not reasonably be asked of a headless man that he should walk straight." *Hawthorne.*

☞ "The street which we enter, that of the Faubourg St. Denis, presents a strange contrast to the dark uniformity of a London street, where every thing, in the dingy and smoky atmosphere, looks as though it were painted in India-ink. Here, on the contrary, is a thousand times more life and color. Before you, shining in the sun, is a long glistening line of *gutter*, — not a very pleasing object in a city, but in a picture invaluable. On each side are houses of all dimensions and hues; some but of one story, some as high as the Tower of Babel. From these the haberdashers (and this is their favorite street) flaunt long strips of gaudy calicoes, which give a strange air of rude gayety to the street. Gay wine-shops, painted red, and smartly decorated with vines and gilded railings, are filled with workmen taking their morning's draught. That gloomy-looking prison on your right is a prison for women." *Thackeray.*

St. Dolough. A famous wonder-working well and pilgrim-resort in the county of Waterford, Ireland.

St. Dunstan's. Two churches in London of this name, one known as St. Dunstan's-in-the-East, the other as St. Dunstan's-in-the-West. Both the existing churches are of modern construction. The clock of the old church of St. Dunstan's-in-the-West was one of the sights of London. Above the dial were two wooden figures of savages as large as life, and each striking with a club the quarter-hours upon a bell, at the same time moving his head.

When labor and when dulness, club in hand,
Like the two figures at *St. Dunstan's* stand. *Cowper.*

St. Elisius. A picture by the Flemish painter, Petrus Cristus, painted (1449) for the Goldsmiths' Guildhall, Antwerp, Belgium. Now in the Oppenheim Collection at Cologne, Germany.

St. Elizabeth of Hungary. A piece of sculpture by Benjamin Akers, called also Paul Akers, the American sculptor (1825–1862), which has been admired and often repeated.

St. Elmo. A well-known hill in Naples, Italy, on the summit of which is the celebrated Castel Sant' Elmo.

St. Elmo. [Ital. *Castel Sant' Elmo.*] The great fortress of Naples, Italy, built, in its present form, in the sixteenth century, by Pedro de Toledo. It was in former times a fortification of great strength, but is incapable of resisting the weapons of attack used in modern warfare.

The morrow after our arrival, in the afternoone, we hired a coach to carry us about the town. First we went to the *Castle of St. Elmo*, built on a very high rock, whence we had an intire prospect of the whole Citty, which lyes in the shape of a theatre upon the sea brinke, with all the circumjacent islands. This Fort is the bridle of the whole Citty, and was well stor'd and garrisoned with native Spanyards. *John Evelyn*, 1644.

Naples, thou white sun-lit city! The swarms of beings with song and shout flow like streaming lava through thy streets; we hear the sounds; town after town winds like a serpent about the bay, Naples is this serpent's head, and *St. Elmo* the crown it bears. *Hans Christian Andersen.*

St. Erasmus. See MARTYRDOM OF ST. ERASMUS.

St. Etienne. A monastic church in Caen, France, founded by William the Conqueror, and dedicated by him in 1077. It contains the grave of the king, which has been several times despoiled. [Called also *Abbaye aux Hommes.*]

St. Etienne du Mont. [St. Stephen of the Mount.] A noted church in Paris, France, situated in the square of the name, near the Pantheon. The present building was begun in 1517, and completed in 1626. The style is a union of Gothic and Renaissance. This church is celebrated for its choir, pulpit, and the grave of St. Genoveva.

I wandered through the haunts of men,
From Boulevard to Quai,
Till frowning o'er *St. Etienne*,
The Pantheon's shadow lay. *Holmes.*

I used very often, when coming home from my morning's work at one of the public institutions of Paris, to step in at the dear old church of *St. Etienne du Mont.* *Holmes.*

St. Eustache. A noted church in Paris, France, in the Rue Trainée. It is second only in size to Notre Dame, and belongs to one of the richest parishes in the city. The building was begun in 1532, and finished in 1641. The style is Gothic in the general arrangement, but Renaissance in the details. A façade was added on the western side in 1752.

St. Francis. A large altar-picture painted about 1514 for the Franciscan convent at Carpi by Antonio Allegri, surnamed Correggio (1494–1534), representing the Madonna enthroned with St. Francis and St. Anthony of Padua on the left, and on the right St. John the Baptist and St. Catherine. In the Dresden Gallery.

St. Francis. See COMMUNION OF ST. FRANCIS, DEATH OF ST. FRANCIS, ECSTASY OF ST. FRANCIS, MIRACLE OF ROSES OF ST. FRANCIS.

St. Francis receiving the Stigmata. A small picture by Jan van Eyck (1370-1441). Now in the possession of Lord Heytesbury.

St. Francis wedded to Poverty. A fresco painting by Giotto di Bondone (1276-1336), the early Italian painter. In the lower church of S. Francesco, Assisi, Italy.

St. Felicitas. See MARTYRDOM OF SANTA FELICITÀ.

St. Geneviève. See PANTHEON (2).

St. George. 1. A picture by Raphael Sanzio (1483-1520), representing the saint attacking the dragon with his sword, having already pierced him with a lance. This picture has suffered somewhat from injuries. It is now in the Louvre, Paris.

☞ "As for St. George and the Dragon — from the St. George of the Louvre, — Raphael's, — who sits his horse with the elegant tranquillity of one assured of celestial aid, down to him who 'swings on a sign-post at mine hostess's door' — he is our familiar acquaintance." *Mrs. Jameson.*

2. There is another St. George by Raphael, in which the dragon is killed by the spear alone. It was executed for the Duke of Urbino, and intended by him as a present for Henry VII. of England. It is considered one of the most finished works of Raphael. Now in the Hermitage at St. Petersburg.

St. George. A picture by Antonio Allegri, surnamed Correggio (1494–1534), representing the Madonna enthroned, with St. George and other saints at the sides. This picture is noteworthy, like the St. Jerome (*q. v.*), on account of the bright daylight diffused through it. In the Dresden Gallery.

St. George's. A London church, situated in Hanover Square, famous for the number of aristocratic weddings which have taken place in it. It is stated that upwards of a thousand marriages have been solemnized here within a single year.

St. George's Fields. A district between Lambeth and Southwark in London, formerly occupied for political meetings and low amusements.

St. George's Hall. A noted building in Liverpool, England, of the Corinthian order, and including a large concert-room.

St. George's Hospital. At Hyde Park Corner, London. It was originated in 1733, and was rebuilt in 1831. This hospital, built on the site of Lanesborough House, is supported by voluntary contributions as a hospital for sick and lame persons.

St. Germain des Prés. One of the oldest churches in Paris. King Childebert, A.D. 550, founded the abbey to which this church was joined. St. Germanus is said to have advised Childebert to found this abbey in the meadows (*prés*) along the left bank of the Seine, whence the name. Only the church and part of the abbot's house remain of this celebrated establishment, the church being the only building of size in the Romanesque style now standing in Paris. Only a few fragments remain of the original edifice of Childebert, in fact, nothing earlier than the first of the twelfth century. Externally the church is plain and simple, but it has been decorated in a style not in sympathy with the original architecture.

☞ "Most of the Merovingian monarchs of France in the sixth and seventh centuries were buried in the church of St. Germain; but their tombs were rifled at the Revolution, and a few only of their monuments are now preserved in the church of St. Denis."
Murray's Handbook.

St. Germain l'Auxerrois. This church, situated in the place of the same name, opposite the eastern façade of the Louvre, in Paris, was commenced in the fourteenth century. It is remarkable for the beauty of its architecture, its richly painted windows, and the magnificence of its decorations. It was the bell of this church that tolled the signal for the commencement of the massacre of St. Bartholomew, Aug. 24, 1572. Members of the royal family were generally baptized in this church. It has undergone numerous additions and restorations.

St. Gervais. A fine Gothic church in Paris, finished in 1820. A classical façade was added to the original structure in 1616. In the windows of this church is what is still the finest glass in Paris, by Cousin and Pinaigrier. Scarron, the husband of Madame de Maintenon, Crébillon, and other celebrities of the seventeenth century, were buried here.

St. Giles's. A celebrated locality in London, once the resort of the most degraded and abandoned portion of the populace. It has undergone great changes within a few years; churches, schools, and reformatory institutions of every class having been erected.

☞ "*St. Giles* has been especially venerated in England and Scotland. In 1117, Matilda, wife of Henry I., founded an hospital for lepers outside the city of London, which she dedicated to St. Giles, and which has since given its name to an extensive parish."
Mrs. Jameson.

☞ "It is noteworthy that places dedicated to this saint, 'abbot and martyr,' were almost always outside some great town. This was because St. Giles (St. Egidius) was the patron saint of lepers, and where a place was called by his name a lazar-house always existed."
Hare.

☞ "The Puritans made stout efforts to reform its morals; and, as the parish books attest, 'oppressed tipplers' were fined for drinking on the Lord's day, and vintners for permitting them; fines were levied for swearing oaths, travelling and brewing on a fast-day, etc. Again, St. Giles's was a refuge for the persecuted tipplers and ragamuffins of London and Westminster in those days; and its blackguardism was increased by harsh treatment. It next became the abode of knots of disaffected foreigners, chiefly Frenchmen, of whom a club was held in Seven Dials. Smollett speaks, in 1740, of 'two tatterdemalions from the purlieus of St. Giles's, and between them both there was but one shirt and a pair of breeches.' Hogarth painted his moralities from St. Giles's. . . . Here were often scenes of bloody fray, riot, and chance-medley; for in this wretched district were grouped herds of men but little removed from savagery."
Timbs.

A friend of mine who was sitting unmoved at one of the sentimental pieces was asked how he could be so indifferent. "Why, truly," says he, "as the hero is but a tradesman, it is indifferent to me whether he be turned out of his counting-house on Fish-street hill, since he will still have enough left to open shop in *St. Giles's*." *Goldsmith.*

Be all the bruisers cull'd from all *St. Giles'*,
That art and nature may compare their styles;
While brawny brutes in stupid wonder stare,
And marvel at his lordship's "stone shop" there. *Byron.*

St. Giles's. 1. One of the oldest and most venerable churches in London (Cripplegate). Here Milton was buried, and Oliver Cromwell was married. The church was built in 1545. Its bells are celebrated.

Brickbats and tiles,
Say the bells of *St. Giles'*.
Mother Goose.

2. A noted church in the High Street of the Old Town of Edinburgh, Scotland, memorable from its associations with some of the most important events in the religious history of Scotland.

☞ "The parish church of Edinburgh existed under the invocation of St. Giles, as early as 1359."
Mrs. Jameson.

☞ "There are 146 churches in England dedicated to St. Giles. They are frequently near the outskirts of a city or town; St. Giles, Cripplegate, St. Giles-in-the-Fields, St. Giles, Camberwell, were all on the outside of London as it existed when these churches were erected, and there are other examples at Oxford, Cambridge, etc."
Mrs. Jameson.

St. Giles's Hospital. A hospital for lepers, St. Giles's, London, built about 1118, and dissolved at the Reformation. The church of St. Giles-in-the-Fields commemorates the hospital and vicinity.

St. Giles in the Fields. A church in London, built in 1730–34. Andrew Marvel was buried here; here is a tomb to George Chapman; and in the churchyard are buried Lord Herbert of Cherbury, Shirley the dramatist, George Villiers, Duke of Buckingham, and others.

St. Gothard. See DOGS OF ST. GOTHARD and HOSPICE OF ST. GOTHARD.

St. Helen's. An old and noted church in Bishopsgate, London, restored in 1866.

You owe me ten shillings,
Say the bells at *St. Helen's*.
Mother Goose.

St. Hippolitus. See MARTYRDOM OF ST. HIPPOLITUS.

St. Honoré, Rue. One of the principal streets of Paris. This long and irregular street reaches from the Marché des Innocens to the Rue Royal, beyond which it further continues as the Rue du Faubourg St. Honoré.

☞ "We issued forth at about eleven, and went down the Rue St. Honoré, which is narrow, and has houses of five or six stories on either side, between which run the streets like a gully in a rock. . . . As we went down the Rue St. Honoré, it grew more and more thronged, and with a meaner class of people. The houses still were high, and without the shabbiness of exterior that distinguishes the old part of London, being of light-colored stone; but I never saw any thing that so much came up to my idea of a swarming city as this narrow, crowded, and rambling street."
Hawthorne.

☞ "This Rue St. Honoré is one of the old streets in Paris, and is that in which Henry IV. was assassinated."
Hawthorne.

If the banker in Lombard Street emerges from the twilight of his counting-house to make a morning call, he steps into a Piccadilly omnibus, in a claret-colored frock of the last fashion at Crockford's, a fresh hat, and (if he is young) a pair of cherished boots from the *Rue St. Honoré.*
N. P. Willis.

St. Hubert of Liège. See RAISING THE BODY OF ST. HUBERT OF LIÈGE.

St. Ildefonso. See GRANJA, LA.

St. Isaac's. See IZAK CHURCH.

St. Jacques. A noted church in Antwerp, Belgium. The altar-piece is a Holy Family by Rubens.

St. Jacques la Boucherie. A Gothic bell-tower in Paris, 187 feet in height, begun in 1508 and completed in 1522. The church to which it belonged was pulled down in 1797. The region around the tower has been cleared: the tower itself has been restored, and now forms one of the most picturesque and beautiful monuments of Paris.

St. James [of Compostella]. See SHRINE OF ST. JAMES.

St. James Baptizing. A picture by Andrea Mantegna (1431–1506). In the Eremitani Chapel, Padua, Italy.

St. James's. This was once a part of the parish of St. Martins-in-the Fields, London. The phrase, "The Court of St. James's," is said to date from the burning of Whitehall in the reign of William III., when St. James's became the royal residence. "In the reign of Queen Anne it had acquired the distinction of the Court quarter."

The inhabitants of *St. James's*, notwithstanding they live under the same laws and speak the same language, are a distinct people from those of Cheapside, who are likewise removed from those of the Temple on one side, and those of Smithfield on the other, by several climates and degrees in their way of thinking and conversing together. *Addison, Spectator*

☞ St. James's Street and St. James's Place are familiar localities near the Palace of St. James, and have been the residence of many eminent men in past times.

Half St. Giles in frieze
Was bidden to meet *St. James* in cloth of gold,
And, after contract at the altar, pass
To eat a marriage-feast on Hampstead Heath. *Mrs. Browning.*

St. James's Coffee-house. A Whig coffee-house in St. James's Street, London, famous from the reign of Queen Anne till the early part of the present century. It was closed, according to Mr. Cunningham, about 1806. It was frequented by Swift, Goldsmith, Garrick, and many others.

☞ "That I might begin as near the fountain-head as possible, I first of all called in at St. James's, where I found the whole outward room in a buzz of politics; the speculations were but very indifferent towards the door, but grew finer as you advanced to the upper end of the room, and were so much improved by a knot of theorists, who sat in the inner room, within the steams of the coffee-pot, that I there heard the whole Spanish monarchy disposed of, and all the line of Bourbons provided for in less than a quarter of an hour." *Addison, Spectator.*

If it be fine weather, we take a turn into the Park till two, when we go to dinner; and if it be dirty, you are entertained at piquet or basset at White's, or you may talk politics at the Smyrna or *St. James's*. *Journey through England*, 1714.

He [Thomas Wharton] was quite as dexterous a canvasser among the embroidered coats at the *St. James's Coffee-house*, as among the leathern aprons at Wycombe and Aylesbury. *Macaulay.*

St. James's Court. See St. James's.

St. James's Hall. A modern building in London, fronting upon Piccadilly and Regent Street, containing a large hall and two smaller halls, used for concerts and lectures.

St. James's Palace. A royal palace in London, formerly the residence of the sovereigns, very interesting from its historical associations. It was built upon the site of a hospital dedicated to St. James. After the burning of Whitehall in 1697, the palace was used for state ceremonies, whence dates *the Court of St. James*. Since the accession of Queen Victoria, the palace has only been used for levees, drawing-rooms, and state-balls.

Thus this palace [of the Cæsars] was, as it were, the *St. James's* of Rome. *Hare.*

St. James's Park. An ancient common or pleasure-ground in London, contiguous to St. James's Palace. It comprises 91 acres. Since the time of Charles II. the park has been open to the public.

☞ "St. James's is far the prettiest of the London parks, and the most frequented by the lower orders. On Sundays they come by thousands to sit upon the seats, . . . and they bring bread to feed the water-fowl, which are the direct descendants of those introduced and fed by Charles II. . . . Till the present century, the Mall continued to be the most fashionable promenade of London; but the trees were then ancient and picturesquely grouped, and the company did not appear as they do now by Rotten Row, for the ladies were in full dress, and the gentlemen carried their hats under their arms." *Hare.*

☞ "*St. James's Park* is a genuine piece of country, and of English country." *Taine, Trans.*

I remember to have read in some philosopher — I believe in Tom Brown's works — that let a man's character, sentiments, or complexion be what they will, he can find company in London to match them. If he be splenetic, he may every day meet companions on the seats in *St. James's Park*, with whose groans he may mix his own, and pathetically talk of the weather. *Goldsmith.*

I fancy it was a merrier England, that of our ancestors, than that which we inhabit. . . . They played all sorts of games, which, with the exception of cricket and tennis, have quite gone out of our manners now. In the old prints of *St. James's Park* you still see the marks along the walk to note the balls when the Court played at mall. *Thackeray.*

A nymph of quality admires our knight;
He marries, bows at court, and grows polite;
Leaves the dull cits, and joins (to please the fair)
The well-bred cuckolds in *St. James's* air.
Pope.

St. James's Street. A well-known street in London, noted for its club-houses. In this street lived Waller the poet, Pope, Lord Byron; and here Gibbon died.

The Campus Martius of *St. James's-street*,
Where the beaux cavalry pace to and fro.
Before they take the field in Rotten Row.
R. B. Sheridan.

If our Government is to be a No-Government, what is the matter who administers it? Fling an orange-skin into *St. James's Street*; let the man it hits be your man. *Carlyle.*

Come, and once more together let us greet
The long-lost pleasures of *St. James's-street.* *Tickell.*

St. James's Street, of classic fame!
The finest people throng it!
St. James's Street? I know the name!
I think I've passed along it!
Why, that's where Sacharissa sighed
When Waller read his ditty;
Where Byron lived, and Gibbon died,
And Alvanley was witty.
Frederick Locker

St. James's. A small theatre in King Street, St. James's, London, well patronized in the height of the London season.

St. Januarius, Blood of. See BLOOD OF ST. JANUARIUS.

St. Jerome. A noted picture by Titian (1477–1576). In the Brera, at Milan, Italy. Vandyke is said to have derived some of his highest inspirations from the study of this picture.

St. Jerome. A picture by George Pencz (1500?–1554?), a German painter. In the chapel of St. Maurice at Nuremberg, Germany.

St. Jerome. A well-known picture by Antonio Allegri, surnamed Correggio (1494–1534), representing the Virgin and Child together with St. Jerome and Mary Magdalen. Sometimes called "The Day" (Il Giorno), in contrast with La Notte, or the "Adoration of the Shepherds," at Dresden. This picture is in the gallery of Parma, Italy.

☞ "The pure light of day is diffused over the picture; the figures seem surrounded, as it were, by a radiant atmosphere. The Magdalen is equally the perfection of female beauty and of Correggio's art; other portions, however, are not quite free from affectation."
Eastlake, Handbook of Painting.

☞ "In the celebrated *St. Jerome* of Correggio, she [the Magdalen] is on the left of the Madonna, bending down with an expression of the deepest adoration to kiss the feet of the infant Christ, while an angel behind holds up the vase of ointment."
Mrs. Jameson.

St. Jerome. See COMMUNION OF ST. JEROME.

St. Jerome in his Study. A celebrated and well-known print by Albert Dürer (1471–1528), the German painter and engraver. It is familiar through photographic and heliotype reproductions.

☞ "A perfect contrast to the Melancholy [see Melencolia] is to be found in its contemporary print of *St. Jerome in his Study*. There, too, we see the figure of a man sunk in deep thought, and a chamber filled with various apparatus. The whole is arranged with the most ingenious fancy, but pervaded by a serenity and grace which keep aloof all the dreams and visionary forms created by the imagination, and bring before us the simple reality of homely life in its most pleasing form. Gerard Dow, the most feeling of the Dutch *genre*-painters, has produced nothing so pleasing and touching as this print, which even in the most trifling accessories bears the impress of a lofty and gentle nature."
Kugler, Handbook of Painting.

☞ "Very celebrated is an engraving of this subject [St. Jerome] by Albert Dürer. The scene is the interior of a cell at Bethlehem: two windows on the left pour across the picture a stream of sunshine. St. Jerome is seen in the background, seated at a desk, most intently writing his translation of the Scriptures. In front the lion is crouching, and a fox is seen asleep. The execution of this print is a miracle of art, and it is very rare."
Mrs. Jameson.

St. Joachim. See ST. JOSEPH AND ST. JOACHIM.

St. John, Grotto of. See GROTTO OF ST. JOHN.

St. John Lateran. [Ital. *S. Giovanni in Laterano.*] A celebrated basilica in Rome, dedicated to St. John the Baptist, and long regarded as the first of Christian churches. It derives its name of *Lateran* from a rich patrician family. The present building is the fourth which has been erected, and has itself undergone many alterations. The first basilica was built in 324 by Constantine; the present one by Urban V. (1362–70). The west front bears the inscription, "Sacrosancta Lateranensis ecclesia, omnium urbis et orbis Ecclesiarum Mater et Caput." The Chapter of the Lateran takes precedence even over that of St. Peter's, and the coronation of each newly-elected pope takes place here. This basilica owes its chief celebrity to the five General Councils held in it, known as the Lateran Councils, the last of which occurred May 3, 1512. St. John Lateran is one of the four basilicas which enjoy the distinction of having a "Porta Santa."

☞ "The basilica of St. John Lateran is held in peculiar reverence from its venerable antiquity and from its having long been regarded as the mother church of Christendom. . . . As there has never been a total demolition and destruction, the chain of association remains unbroken; and the reverend form of the first Christian Emperor, whose statue stands in the vestibule, is still the presiding genius of the place. The interior is rich and imposing, though not in the purest taste."
Hillard.

The next day there was much ceremony at *St. John de Lateran*, so as the whole week was spent in running from church to church, all the town in busie devotion, greate silence, and unimaginable superstition. *John Evelyn*, 1644.

St. John Nepomuck. A famous bronze statue upon the Carlsbrücke, a bridge over the Moldau in Prague, Austria. St. John Nepomuck is the patron saint of bridges.

☞ "He was a priest many centuries ago, whom one of the kings threw from the bridge into the Moldau, because he refused to reveal to him what the queen confessed. The legend says the body swam for some time on the river with five stars around its head."
Bayard Taylor.

The story of the saint having been thrown from the bridge is now proved to be an invention.

St. John Nepomuck, Shrine of. See SHRINE OF ST. JOHN NEPOMUCK.

St. John the Baptist. A small but delicately executed picture by Hans Memling (d. 1495), the Flemish painter. Formerly in possession of Cardinal Bembo, but now in the Pinakothek at Munich, Bavaria.

St. John the Baptist. A picture by Titian (1477–1576). In the Academy at Venice, Italy.

St. John the Baptist. A picture by Salvator Rosa (1615-1673). In Florence, Italy.

St. John the Baptist. See BEHEADING OF ST. JOHN.

St. John the Divine, Monastery of. This celebrated monastery, on the island of Patmos, off the west coast of Asia Minor, was built in the twelfth century by the Byzantine emperors. The building has the appearance of a Middle Age fortress. Not far distant is the famous cavern or grotto where the Apocalypse is said to have been written by St. John.

St. John the Evangelist. A picture attributed to Raphael Sanzio (1483-1520), representing him mounted on the back of an eagle and soaring heavenward, holding in one hand a tablet, in the other a pen. In the Museum at Marseilles, France.

St. John the Evangelist. A picture by Antonio Allegri, surnamed Correggio (1494-1534). One of the series of the Evangelists in the Cathedral at Parma, Italy.

St. John the Evangelist. A half-length portrait by Domenico Zampieri, surnamed Domenichino (1581-1641), well-known by Müller's engraving of it. In the collection of Prince Narischkin, at St. Petersburg. There is a repetition of the same at Castle Howard, England.

St. John the Evangelist. A picture by Carlo Dolce (1616–1686), and one of his best works. In the Museum at Berlin, Prussia.

St. John in the Wilderness. A noted picture by Raphael Sanzio (1483–1520). In the Uffizi Gallery in Florence, Italy.

☞ "His glorious form in the fair proportions of ripening boyhood, the grace of his attitude, with the arm lifted eloquently on high, the divine inspiration which illumines his young features, chain the step irresistibly before it. It is one of those triumphs of the pencil which few but Raphael have accomplished, — the painting of *spirit* in its loftiest and purest form."
Bayard Taylor.

St. John's. A church in Clerkenwell, London. It was in the crypt of this church that the investigation was made in regard to the so-called Cock-Lane Ghost. See Cock Lane.

Pokers and tongs,
Say the bells at *St. John's.*
Mother Goose.

St. John's. An interesting church edifice in Richmond, Va., built before the Revolution, and connected with many historical events. In 1775 the Virginia Convention held its sessions here, during which Patrick Henry made his famous address. The Convention for ratifying the Federal Constitution also assembled in this church.

St. John's Gate. A relic of the old and splendid monastery of the Knights of St. John of Jerusalem, in London. In 1845 it underwent repairs and restorations. The first number of the "Gentleman's Magazine" was printed in an office established here, the magazine still bearing the Gate as a vignette.

How he [Johnson] sits there, in his rough-hewn, amorphous bulk, in that upper room at *St. John's Gate*, and trundles off sheet after sheet of those Senate-of Lilliput Debates, to the clamorous Printer's Devils waiting for them, with insatiable throat, down stairs; himself perhaps *impransus* all the while. . . . If to Johnson himself, then much more to us, may that *St. John's Gate* be a place we can "never pass without veneration."
Carlyle.

At the time of Johnson's appearance, there were still two ways on which an author might attempt proceeding: there were the Mæcenases proper in the West End of London; and the Mæcenases virtual of *St. John's Gate* and Paternoster Row.
Carlyle.

St. John's Wood. A district in London, situated to the west of Regent's Park.

St. Joseph and St. Joachim. A picture by Albert Dürer (1471–1528), the German painter and engraver. In the Gallery of Munich, Bavaria.

St. Julian. A picture by Cristoforo Allori (1577–1619). In the Pitti, Florence, Italy.

St. Just. See Yuste.

St. Justina and the Duke of Ferrara. A noted picture by Alessandro Bonvicino, called Il Moretto di Brescia (1514–1564). In the Belvedere, Vienna, Austria.

☞ "Every one who has been at Vienna will probably remember the *St. Justina* of the Belvedere, so long attributed to Pordenone, but now known to be the production of a much greater man, Bonvicino of Brescia (Il Moretto)."
Mrs. Jameson.

St. Katherine Docks. Well-known docks in London, opened for use in 1828. It is said that over 1,200 houses were pulled down, and more than 11,000 inhabitants were removed, to clear the ground for this great undertaking. The cost was £1,700,000. These docks were united in 1863 with the London Docks (*q. v.*), under one management.

This London City, with all its houses, palaces, steam-engines, cathedrals, and huge immeasurable traffic and tumult, what is it but a Thought, but millions of Thoughts made into One, — a huge immeasurable Spirit of a *Thought*, embodied in brick, in iron, smoke, dust, Palaces, Parliaments, Hackney Coaches, *Katherine Docks*, and the rest of it!
Carlyle.

St. Kevin's Kitchen. A noted ruin in the county of Wicklow,

Ireland, being an ancient church invested with much legendary lore.

St. Keyne's Well. A celebrated well in Cornwall, England, which is described in the following rhymes: —

In name, in shape, in quality,
  This well is very quaint;
The name to lot of Keyne befell,
  No over-holy saint.
The shape — four trees of divers kind,
  Withy, oak, elm, and ash,
Make with their roots an arched roof,
  Whose floor the spring doth wash.
The quality — that man and wife,
  Whose chance or choice attains,
First of this sacred stream to drink,
  Thereby the mastery gains. *Carew.*

You drank of the well, I warrant, betimes?
  He to the Cornishman said;
But the Cornishman smiled as the stranger spake,
  And sheepishly shook his head.
I hastened as soon as the wedding was done,
  And left my wife in the porch;
But i' faith she had been wiser than me,
  For she took a bottle to church!
Southey.

St. Kieran's Chair. A very ancient and venerated stone chair in Kilkenny, Ireland, reputed to be the seat of the saint who preceded St. Patrick in his mission by thirty years, and who was the first to preach Christianity in Ireland.

St. Lazare. A house of detention and correction for disorderly women in the Faubourg St. Denis, Paris. Here was formerly a celebrated convent.

Well, let us take a look at this guinguette [at the bal Perron at the Barrière du Trône]; a hundred low grisettes, and fifty women of the town whose acquaintance with *St. Lazare* and the Prefecture of Police you recognize at once.
Taine, Trans.

St. Leonard's Crags. The popular name of a cottage in Edinburgh, Scotland, once the home of Effie Deans, the heroine of Scott's tale of "The Heart of Mid-Lothian."

St. Louis. A noted frigate of the United States navy, in service in the war of 1812. She was built at Washington.

St. Luke. [Ital. *Accademia di San Luca.*] An academy of fine arts in Rome, founded in the last part of the sixteenth century, and composed of painters, sculptors, and architects. It occupies part of the site of the Forum of Julius Cæsar, and contains, besides numerous designs and models, a collection of pictures by various artists. Among these works is St. Luke painting the portrait of the Virgin and Child, ascribed to Raphael, of which Mrs. Jameson says that it is the most famous of all pictures upon this favorite subject. The skull of Raphael was for a long time thought to be among the treasures of the Academy, until the discovery of the genuine one in the Pantheon.

St. Luke. A statue by Giovanni da Bologna, called Il Fiammingo (1524–1608). In the church of Or S. Michele, Florence, Italy.

St. Luke. 1. A famous picture by Raphael Sanzio (1483-1520), representing St. Luke as kneeling on a footstool before an easel, and painting the Virgin and Child, who appear to him in the clouds of heaven. Behind St. Luke, Raphael stands looking on. In the Academy of St. Luke at Rome.

2. There is another picture, usually ascribed to Raphael, upon the same subject, in the Grosvenor Gallery, London.

St. Luke. A picture by Roger van der Weyden (d. 1464), the Flemish painter. It was originally placed on the altar of the Guild of St. Luke at Brussels, Belgium, but is now in the Gallery of Munich, Bavaria.

St. Madem's Well. A holy well in Cornwall, England. It was in Catholic times a favorite resort for invalids, who attempted to propitiate the saint by offerings of pins and pebbles. Since the seventeenth century it has been little visited.

St. Margaret. A famous picture of this saint by Raphael Sanzio (1483–1520), painted for Francis I. in compliment to his sister Margaret of Navarre. Now in the Louvre at Paris.

St. Margaret (and the Dragon).

An altar-picture attributed to Raphael Sanzio (1483–1520), but probably by his pupil Giulio Romano, (1492–1546), representing the saint "issuing from a cave, with the monster crouching around her, while she raises the crucifix against him." This picture is in the Gallery of Vienna, Austria.

St. Margaret's. An old and celebrated church in the parish of Westminster, London. It was repaired at the expense of Parliament in 1735.

> Bull's eyes and targets,
> Say the bells of *St. Marg'ret's*.
> *Mother Goose.*

St. Marguérite. A church in the Rue St. Bernard, Faubourg St. Antoine, Paris. It is built in the Italian style.

St. Mark. A celebrated colossal figure of the apostle by Fra Bartolommeo (1469–1517), the Italian painter. In the Pitti Palace, Florence, Italy.

☞ "Among the devotional pictures of St. Mark, one of the most famous is that of Fra Bartolommeo, in the Palazzo Pitti. He is represented as a man in the prime of life, with bushy hair, and a short reddish beard, throned in a niche, and holding in one hand the Gospel, in the other a pen." *Mrs. Jameson.*

St. Mark. See Miracle of St. Mark.

St. Mark preaching in Alexandria. A picture by Gentile Bellini (1421–1501). In the Brera, Milan, Italy.

St. Mark's. The cathedral church of Venice, Italy, and one of the most celebrated and interesting buildings in the world. The original church edifice was destroyed by fire in 976. The present building was dedicated to St. Mark, the patron saint of Venice, in 1085.

☞ "The church is lost in a dim twilight, to which the eye must be accustomed for some moments before the form of the building can be traced; and then there opens before us a vast cave, hewn out into the form of a cross, and divided into shadowy aisles by many pillars. Round the domes of its roof the light enters only through narrow apertures like large stars; and here and there a ray or two from some far-away casement wanders into the darkness, and casts a narrow phosphoric stream upon the waves of marble that heave and fall in a thousand colors along the the floor." *Ruskin.*

☞ "It is impossible to find fault with plain surfaces when they are covered with such exquisite gold mosaics as those of St. Mark's, or with the want of accentuation in the lines of the roof, when every part of it is more richly adorned in this manner than any other church of the Western world. Then, too, the rood-screen, the pulpit, the *pala d'oro*, the whole furniture of the choir, are so rich, so venerable, and on the whole so beautiful, and seen in so exquisitely subdued a light, that it is impossible to deny that it is perhaps the most impressive interior in Western Europe." *Fergusson.*

☞ "This singular edifice can neither be described nor forgotten. It is a strange jumble of architectural styles; partly Christian and partly Saracenic, in form a Greek cross, crowned with the domes and minarets of a mosque. . . . And yet in spite of architectural defects, this church is one of the most interesting buildings in the world. It is a vast museum, filled with curious objects collected with religious zeal, and preserved with religious care. It is the open lap of Venice into which the spoils of the East have been poured." *Hillard.*

☞ "The church, which the mighty bell-tower and the lofty height of the palace-lines make to look low, is in no wise humbled by the contrast, but is like a queen enthroned amid upright reverence. The religious sentiment is deeply appealed to, I think, in the interior of St. Mark's; but if its interior is heaven's, its exterior, like a good man's daily life, is earth's; and it is this winning loveliness of earth that first attracts you to it, and when you emerge from its portals, you enter upon spaces of such sunny length and breadth, set round with such exquisite architecture, that it makes you glad to be living in this world." *W. D. Howells.*

☞ "St. Mark's of Venice is a St. Sophia in miniature, a reduction on the scale of an inch to the foot of the immense structure of Justinian. Its architects had the advantage of seeing St. Sophia in all its integrity and splendor before it had been profaned by Mahomet II. in the year 1453." *Théophile Gautier.*

Before *St. Mark* still glow his steeds of brass,
Their gilded collars glittering in the sun;
But is not Doria's menace come to pass?
Are they not bridled? *Byron.*

Fair as the palace builded for Aladdin,
Yonder *St. Mark* uplifts its sculptured splendor,—
Intricate fretwork, Byzantine mosaic,
Color on color, column on column,
Barbaric, wonderful, a thing to kneel to!
T. B. Aldrich.

St. Mark's. See FORT ST. MARK'S.

St. Mark's Campanile. The great belfry tower of the Cathedral of Venice. It was begun in 888, but not completed till the beginning of the sixteenth century. It is a very conspicuous object in any view of the city; and from its summit, which is ascended by an easy incline, without steps, a magnificent prospect is obtained.

Between those pillars [at the entrance of the Piazza of St. Mark], there opens a great light; and in the midst of it, as we advance slowly, the vast *tower of S. Mark* seems to lift itself visibly forth from the level field of chequered stones. *Ruskin.*

At the corner of the new Procuratie, a little distant from the church, stands the steeple of St. Mark. This is a quadrangular tower, about 300 feet in height. I am told that it is not uncommon in Italy for the church and steeple to be in this state of disunion. This shocked a clergyman of my acquaintance very much. . . . The gentleman was clearly of the opinion that church and steeple ought to be as inseparable as man and wife, that every church ought to consider its steeple as mortar of its mortar, and stone of its stone. An old captain of a ship, who was present, declared himself of the same way of thinking, and swore that a church, divorced from its steeple, appeared to him as ridiculous as a ship without a mast.
Dr. John Moore.

St. Mark's Column. A famous granite pillar in Venice, Italy, on the summit of which rests the Lion of St. Mark. It was brought from the Holy Land in the twelfth century.

St. Mark's Square *or* Place. [Ital. *Piazza S. Marco.*] The famous piazza, or square, in Venice, near or around which are grouped all the more celebrated edifices,—the Doge's Palace, the Church of St. Mark with its Campanile or bell-tower, the Horologe of Petrus Lombardus, and the other structures which have given to the city its great renown.

☞ "St. Mark's Place is the heart of Venice. The life which has fled from the extremities still beats strongly here. Apart from all associations, it is one of the most imposing architectural objects in Europe." *Hillard.*

☞ "Of all the open spaces in the city, that before the Church of St. Mark alone bears the name of Piazza, and the rest are merely called *Campi*, or fields. But if the company of the noblest architecture can give honor, the Piazza San Marco merits its distinction, not in Venice only, but in the whole world; for I fancy that no other place in the world is set in such goodly bounds." *W. D. Howells.*

St. Mark yet sees his lion where he stood
Stand, but in mockery of his wither'd power,
Over the proud Place where an emperor sued,
And monarchs gazed and envied in the hour
When Venice was a queen with an unequall'd dower. *Byron.*

Were Genoa's galleys riding in the port,
Were civil fury raging in *St. Mark's*,
You are not to be wrought on, but would fall,
As you have risen, with an unalter'd brow.
Byron.

Not a stone
In the broad pavement, but to him who has
An eye, an ear, for the inanimate world,
Tells of past ages. *Samuel Rogers.*

Hushed is the music, hushed the hum of voices;
Gone is the crowd of dusky promenaders,
Slender-waisted, almond-eyed Venetians,
Princes and paupers. Not a single footfall
Sounds in the arches of the Procuratie.
One after one, like sparks in cindered paper,
Faded the lights out in the goldsmiths' windows.
Drenched with the moonlight lies the still *Piazza.* *T. B. Aldrich.*

St. Martin. 1. A picture by Anthony van Dyck (1599-1641), in the church of Savelthem near Brussels, Belgium, representing the saint as dividing his mantle with a beggar.

2. Also a picture upon the same subject, by the same painter, now at Windsor Castle.

St. Martin, Boulevard. A fine avenue in Paris, France.

St. Martin de Tours. A famous abbey church in Tours, France, of which at present only two towers remain, the rest of the building having been destroyed in the

Revolution of 1790. The existing portions are of the twelfth century. This celebrated shrine was a place of great resort for ages. It possessed immense treasures in gold and silver, which were plundered by the Huguenots in 1562.

St. Martin, Porte. See PORTE ST. MARTIN.

St. Martin, Rue. A long narrow street in Paris, running from the river to the boulevards, and continuing under the name of Rue du Faubourg St. Martin, to the Barrière de la Villette on the north of the city. The Boulevart de Sébastopol has deprived it of much of its importance as a thoroughfare.

St. Martin's in the Fields. A church on the east side of Trafalgar Square, London, built in 1721–26, and having for its best feature a Greek portico. There was a church upon this spot as early as 1222.

St. Martin's Ludgate. An old and noted church in Ludgate Street, London, rebuilt after the Great Fire by Sir Christopher Wren. An epitaph in the old church, bearing date 1590, has become very celebrated.

Earth goes to Earth treads on Earth as to Earth shall to	Earth	As mold to mold Glittering in gold Return here should Goe ere he would
Earth upon Earth goes to Earth though on Earth shall from	Earth	Consider may Passed away Is stout and gay Passe poor away.

Half-pence and farthings,
Say the bells of *St. Martin's*.
Mother Goose.

St. Martin's le Grand. A well-known street in London. The general post-office is situated on this street.

St. Mary-le-Bow. See BOW CHURCH.

St. Mary-le-Strand. An interesting old church in the Strand, London.

St. Mary's College. A celebrated institution in Winchester, England, founded by William of Wykeham. The building, which is architecturally fine, was begun in 1387 and finished in 1393.

St. Maurice. A noted abbey, said to be the most ancient monastic establishment among the Alps, in the town of the same name in Switzerland.

St. Maurice. See CONVERSION OF ST. MAURICE BY ERASMUS.

St. Médard. A church in Paris, the nave and choir of which date from the end of the sixteenth century, though the latter was altered in the latter part of the eighteenth century.

St. Merri. A large church in Paris, begun in 1520 and completed in 1612. It has suffered some injudicious alterations. It is in the Flamboyant style.

St. Michael. A picture by Giovanni da Fiesole, called Fra Angelico (1387-1455). In the Uffizi Palace, Florence, Italy.

St. Michael. A celebrated picture by Raphael Sanzio (1483-1520), representing the archangel treading on the neck of the dragon, and attacking him with a sword. It is in the Louvre at Paris.

☞ "St. Michael — not standing, but hovering on his poised wings, and grasping his lance in both hands — sets one foot lightly on the shoulder of the demon, who, prostrate, writhes up, as it were, and tries to lift his head and turn it on his conqueror with one last gaze of malignant rage and despair. The archangel looks down upon him with a brow calm and serious: in his beautiful face is neither vengeance nor disdain, in his attitude no effort. . . . The form of the demon is human, but vulgar in its proportions; but, from the attitude into which he is thrown, the monstrous form is so fore-shortened that it does not disgust, and the majestic figure of the archangel fills up nearly the whole space, — fills the eye — fills the soul — with its victorious beauty." *Mrs. Jameson.*

St. Michael. A picture by Guido Reni (1574?–1642). In the church of the Cappucini, Rome.

☞ "It seems agreed that as a work

of art there is only the *St. Michael* of Guido which can be compared with that of Raphael." *Mrs. Jameson.*

☞ "Like the Belvedere god, the archangel breathes that dignified vengeance which animates without distorting, while the very devil derives importance from his august adversary, and escapes the laugh which his figure usually provokes." *Forsyth.*

St. Michael's. 1. A famous church on the hill of the Kremlin in Moscow, Russia. It contains the sarcophagi of the early Tzars from Ivan I. to Alexis, father of Peter the Great, and a splendid silver coffin, enclosing the body of a boy, believed to be that of the last prince of the house of Ruric. This body is worshipped as a holy relic.

2. The finest old church now remaining in Scotland, in point of size and architecture. It was a royal chapel at Linlithgow, founded by David I.

St. Michael's Chair. The vulgar designation of a stone lantern on a tower at St. Michael's Mount, Cornwall, England, just large enough to admit of one person being seated in it. The attempt to sit in it is attended with danger on account of its exposed position, and the popular superstition is that, of a married couple, whichever party first succeeds in occupying it, thereby acquires marital sovereignty.

Rebecca his wife had often wished
To sit in *St. Michael's Chair;*
For she should be the mistress then,
If she had once sat there.
Southey.

St. Michael's Mount. A celebrated rocky eminence near Penzance in Cornwall, England. It is surmounted by a chapel, founded in the fifth century, and is associated with much romantic legend. It is asserted that the archangel Michael appeared to some hermits upon one of its crags, to which tradition has given the name of St. Michael's Chair. At high tide the rock is surrounded by the sea.

Or whether thou to our moist vows deny'd,
Sleep'st by the fable of Bellerus old,
Where the great vision of the guarded *Mount*
Looks towards Namancos and Bayona's hold,
Look homeward, angel, now, and melt with ruth,
And, O ye dolphins, waft the hapless youth.
Milton.

If we had the Spaniards established at Land's End, with impregnable Spanish fortifications on *St. Michael's Mount*, we should perhaps come to the same conclusion. *Thackeray.*

St. Nicolas des Champs. A florid Gothic church of the fifteenth and sixteenth centuries, in the Rue St. Martin, Paris. Here were buried Gassendi and Mdlle. de Scudéry.

St. Olave's. An old and interesting church in Hart Street, London.

St. Ouen. [Fr. *Église de St. Ouen.*] A fine Gothic church in Rouen, France, and one of the few ancient ecclesiastical monuments of the Continent which are completed. It is named after the Archbishop of Rouen, who died in 678.

St. Pancras. One of the parishes of London, and the most populous.

St. Pancras-in-the-Fields. An old and noted church in London, said to have been the last church in England whose bell tolled for mass, and in which the Roman Catholic rites were celebrated before the Reformation. This church was restored and enlarged in 1858.

In passing and returning by *St. Pancras* church, he [Dr. Johnson] fell into prayer, and mentioned, upon Dr. Brocklesby inquiring why the Catholics chose that spot for their burial-place, that some Catholics in Queen Elizabeth's time had been burnt there. *Windham's Diary.*

St. Patrick's. A cathedral in Dublin, Ireland. It is in the minds of many associated with Jonathan Swift, the English satirist, who was appointed to the deanery in 1713, and retained it till his death, being known as the Dean of St. Patrick's.

St. Patrick's. The Roman Catholic cathedral in the city of New York. It is an imposing edifice of white marble, of the decorated Gothic order, with two marble spires each over 325 feet in height. It was begun in 1858, and is situated upon the highest point of Fifth Avenue.

St. Patrick's Cave [and **Purgatory**]. A locality in Ireland, upon a small island in Lough Derg, famous throughout Europe in the Middle Ages by reason of the legendary associations connected with the saint, who is here supposed to have opened a descent into purgatory for living sinners who wished to undergo expiation for their misdeeds.

☞ "St. Patrick's Purgatory has been famous from a very early period. The lake upon which it is situated is about six miles in length by four in breadth. The 'holy islands' it contains are little more than bare rocks. The one to which the pilgrims resort, 'Station Island,' is about half a mile from the shore, and rises very little above the surface of the lake; a ferry-boat carries them across, and of course a considerable income is derived from this source. The station commences on the 1st of June, and continues till the 15th of August; and we learn that the whole number of pilgrims visiting the Lough would amount during the season to above 19,000, the great majority being women; and many of them will have travelled a distance of 200 miles to arrive at the scene of their devotions, this too at a season of the year when labor is particularly needful and profitable. There are few intelligent persons of any creed who will not rejoice that 'St. Patrick's Purgatory' has fallen from its high estate, and that the gross superstitions connected with it are becoming every year more and more a mere record of by-gone degradations." *Mr. and Mrs. Hall.*

☞ "Who has not heard of *St. Patrick's Purgatory*, of its mysterious wonders, and of the crowds of devotees who have for ages been attracted by its reputed sanctity? There it stands, with its chapels and its toll-houses; and thither repair yearly crowds of pious pilgrims, who would wash away at once, by a visit to these holy shores, the accumulated sins of their lives." *Wright.*

Patrick. This cave, Egerio, which you see, concealeth
Many mysteries of life and death,
Not for him whose hardened bosom feeleth
Nought of true repentance or true faith.
But he who freely enters, who revealeth
All his sins with penitential breath,
Shall endure his purgatory then,
And return forgiven back again.
Calderon, Trans.

St. Paul. See BEHEADING OF ST. PAUL, CONVERSION OF ST. PAUL, and PAUL AND BARNABAS.

St. Paul and St. Anthony. A striking picture by Guido Reni (1574?-1642). In the Museum at Berlin.

St. Paul preaching at Athens. See PAUL PREACHING AT ATHENS.

St. Paul visiting St. Peter in Prison. A picture by Filippino Lippi (1460-1505). In the church of S. M. del Carmine, Florence, Italy.

St. Paul's. 1. The metropolitan church of London, and the third cathedral dedicated to that saint, built upon very nearly the same site as its predecessors. The first church was founded, according to Bede, about A.D. 610, by Ethelbert, King of Kent, but destroyed by fire in 1087. The second church, "Old St. Paul's," was destroyed in the Great Fire, 1666. The corner-stone of the present building was laid June 21, 1675. It was finished in 35 years under one architect, Sir Christopher Wren (1632-1723). It is in the form of a Latin cross. Wren was buried in the crypt of St. Paul's, where is a tablet to his memory, bearing the inscription, "Si monumentum requiris, circumspice."

☞ "Other edifices may crowd close to its foundation, and people may tramp as they like about it; but still the great cathedral is as quiet and serene as if it stood in the middle of Salisbury Plain. There cannot be any thing else in its way so good in the world as just this effect of St. Paul's in the very heart and densest tumult of London." *Hawthorne.*

☞ "The whole cost, £747,954 2*s.* 9*d.*, was paid by a tax on every chaldron of coal brought into the port of

London, on which account it is said that the cathedral has a special claim of its own to its smoky exterior."
Hare.

☞ "The roof from which the dome springs is itself as high as the spires of most other churches; blackened for two hundred years with the coal smoke of London, it stands like a relic of the giant architecture of the early world." *Bayard Taylor.*

He sette not his benefice to huyre,
And lefte his scheep encombred in the myre,
And ran to Londone, unto *seynte Poules*,
To seeken him a chaunterie for soules.
Chaucer, Prologue.

We're all in the dumps,
For diamonds are trumps,
The kittens are gone to *St. Paul's!*
The babies are bit,
The moon's in a fit,
And the houses are built without walls.
Mother Goose.

As I was walking o'er little Moorfields,
I saw *St. Paul's* a-running on wheels,
With a fee, fo, fum.
Then for further frolics I'll go to France,
While Jack shall sing and his wife shall dance,
With a fee, fo, fum.
Mother Goose.

Right down by smoky *Paul's* they bore,
Till, where the street grows straiter,
One fixed forever at the door,
And one became head-waiter.
Tennyson.

St. Paul's high dome amidst the vassal bands
Of neighboring spires, a regal chieftain stands. *Joanna Baillie.*

2. An interesting and important church, though architecturally plain, situated in Covent Garden, London, built by Inigo Jones, and the first Protestant church of consequence erected in England. The interior was mostly destroyed by fire in 1795.

St. Paul's. See SAN PAOLO.

St. Paul's Churchyard. An irregular circle of houses enclosing St. Paul's Church and burial-ground, in London.

No place so sacred from such fops is barr'd,
Nor is Paul's church more safe than *Paul's churchyard.* *Pope.*

St. Paul's Cross. A canopied cross, rising from stone steps, in the graveyard of St. Paul's, London. Before the time of the Commonwealth, sermons were delivered here on Sunday afternoons. It was destroyed by order of Parliament in 1643.

☞ "Paul's Cross was the pulpit not only of the cathedral: it might almost be said, as preaching became more popular, and began more and more to rule the public mind, to have become that of the Church of England. . . . Paul's Cross was not only the great scene for the display of eloquence by distinguished preachers: it was that of many public acts, some relating to ecclesiastical affairs, some of mingled cast, some simply political. Here Papal Bulls were promulgated; here excommunications were thundered out; here sinners of high position did penance; here heretics knelt, and read their recantations, or, if obstinate, were marched off to Smithfield."
Dean Milman.

St. Paul's, Great Bell of. See GREAT BELL OF ST. PAUL'S.

St. Paul's School. An establishment near St. Paul's Cathedral, London, founded in 1514 by Dean Colet. It was designed for 153 poor children, the number corresponding to that of the fishes taken by St. Peter. John Milton went to school here between the ages of 11 and 16.

☞ "In 1877 the Mercers' Company purchased 16 acres of ground in Hammersmith, whither it is intended to remove the school." *Hare.*

St. Paul, Hôtel. See HÔTEL ST. PAUL.

St. Peter. A well-known bronze statue of St. Peter in the basilica of St. Peter's, Rome, having one foot extended, the toe of which is reverently kissed by devout Catholics. By some antiquaries it is thought to have been cast by St. Leo from the bronze statue of Jupiter Capitolinus; others maintain that it is the identical statue of Jupiter, transformed into that of the Apostle. It is probable, however, that it is not a work of classical times, but belongs to the early ages of Christianity.

☞ "Long since would that toe have been kissed away, had it not been guarded by a sort of brass slipper; for no good Roman Catholic, from the pope to the beggar, ever enters the church without fervently pressing his lips to

it, and then applying his forehead and chin to its consecrated tip."
C. A. Eaton.

St. Peter. See CRUCIFIXION OF ST. PETER and DELIVERANCE OF ST. PETER.

St. Peter and St. John curing the Lame Man at the Beautiful Gate of the Temple. See PETER AND JOHN AT THE BEAUTIFUL GATE.

St. Peter and St. Paul. An imposing Roman Catholic church edifice, built of red sandstone, in Philadelphia, Penn. It has a dome over 200 feet in height.

St. Peter delivered from Prison. A picture by Filippino Lippi (1460-1505). In the church of Sta. Maria del Carmine, Florence, Italy.

St. Peter liberated by an Angel. A picture by Washington Allston (1779-1843). Now in the church of Ashby-de-la-Zouch, England.

St. Peter Martyr. A noted picture by Titian (1477-1576), in which his greatest qualities as a figure and landscape painter were displayed. It was formerly in the church of SS. Giovanni e Paolo, in Venice, but was destroyed by fire in 1866.

St. Peter's. **1.** [Ital. *S. Pietro in Vaticano.*] The chief metropolitan church of Rome, and the most magnificent of Christian temples. As early as A.D. 90, an oratory was built on the site of the present building to mark the spot where, according to tradition, the Apostle Peter was interred, and where many of the early Christian martyrs had sufferred. In 306 Constantine the Great built a basilica on the same spot. The present edifice was dedicated by Urban VIII. in 1626. St. Peter's is one of the seven basilicas in Rome, of which four are within the walls, and three without. They derive their name from the *Basilicæ* or Courts of Justice of the later period of the empire, upon the plan of which, and often upon the sites of which, the first Christian churches were built. The space covered by the buildings of St. Peter's is said to be 240,000 square feet, or about 5½ English acres. Its façade is 357 feet in length, and 144 feet in height. A line upon the pavement marks the size of the other great Christian churches, according to which the length of St. Peter's is 613½ feet; St. Paul's, London, 520½ feet; Milan Cathedral, 443 feet. It is only by degrees that one receives the impression of its vast size. The dome, which is double, was begun by Michael Angelo, and was completed when he died in 1563.

☞ "A work so vast and various must be approached in the spirit of knowledge and docility. Most buildings have an unity of plan; and their different parts, and the successive changes in structure and detail, are like variations upon one musical theme. Not so with St. Peter's. It awakens no ideas of unity or simplicity. It is a great representative structure, which gathers within itself the convergent rays of innumerable lights. It is a temple, a museum, a gallery of art, and a mausoleum. If a fanciful comparison may be pardoned, other churches are gardens, but St. Peter's is a landscape. Its growth and history embrace nearly three hundred and fifty years. . . . Its foundation was nearly coeval with the invention of printing; before the sacristy was completed, the splendid researches of Watt had been crowned with success; and in the interval had occurred the discovery of America, and the Reformation. Religion, politics, literature, art, and manners had gone through whole cycles of mutation, and the web of society had been unravelled and re-woven. All these considerations should be borne in mind by him who would form a true judgment of this unique building. It should be examined in that historical spirit in which we study the Roman law or the English constitution."
Hillard.

☞ "The building of St. Peter's surpasses all powers of description. It appears to me like some great work of nature, a forest, a mass of rocks, or something similar, for I never can realize the idea that it is the work of man."
Mendelssohn, Trans.

☞ "No architecture ever surpassed in effect the interior of this pile when illuminated at Easter by a single cross of lamps. The immediate focus of glory — all the gradations of light and darkness — the sombre of the deep perspectives — the multitude kneeling round the Pope — the groups in the distant aisles — what a world of pictures for men of art to copy or combine! What fancy was ever so dull or so disciplined or so worn as to resist the enthusiasm of such a scene?"

Forsyth.

☞ "St. Peter's surpasses all other churches not more in magnitude than in magnificence. . . . The treasures and the taste of the world seem to have been exhausted in its embellishment."

C. A. Eaton.

☞ "I have been twice to St. Peter's, and was impressed more than at any former visit by a sense of breadth and loftiness, and, as it were, a visionary splendor and magnificence."

Hawthorne.

But thou, of temples old, or altars new,
Standest alone, with nothing like to thee,
Worthiest of God, the holy and the true.
Since Zion's desolation, when that He
Forsook his former city, what could be
Of earthly structures, in his honor piled,
Of a sublimer aspect? Majesty,
Power, glory, strength, and beauty, all are aisled
In this eternal ark of worship undefiled.

Enter: its grandeur overwhelms thee not;
And why? It is not lessened; but thy mind,
Expanded by the genius of the spot,
Has grown colossal. *Byron.*

And while still stands
The austere Pantheon, into heaven shall soar
A dome [*St. Peter's*], its image, while the base expands
Into a fane surpassing all before,
Such as all flesh shall flock to kneel in.

Byron.

The hand that rounded *Peter's dome*,
And groined the aisles of Christian Rome,
Wrought in a sad sincerity.
Himself from God he could not free:
He builded better than he knew;
The conscious stone to beauty grew.

Emerson.

A spiritual empire there embodied stood;
The Roman Church there met me face to face;
Ages, sealed up, of evil and of good,
Slept in that circling colonnade's embrace.

Aubrey de Vere.

And mark! our church hath its own atmosphere,
That varies not with seasons of the year,
But ever keeps its even, temperate air,
And soft, large light without offensive glare. *W. W. Story.*

2. A number of churches of this name in London. That in Cornhill, rebuilt by Sir Christopher Wren (1632–1723) after the Great Fire, is one of the oldest and best known.

Pancakes and fritters,
Say the bells of *St. Peter's*.

Mother Goose.

St. Peter's Chains. See San Pietro in Vincoli.

St. Peter's Chair. See Chair of St. Peter.

St. Peter's College. A foundation of the University of Cambridge, England. Established in 1257. [Called also *Peterhouse*.]

St. Peter's College. See Westminster School.

St. Peter's, Obelisk of. See Obelisk of St. Peter's.

St. Petronia. A picture by Francesco Barbieri, called Guercino (1590–1666). In the Museum of the Capitol, Rome. See also Martyrdom of S. Petronilla.

☞ "The body is being taken out of the ground while the soul is received into Paradise. This is a composite work; the artist, according to the practice of schools not primitive, having assembled together three or four kinds of effect. . . . The entire subject — death, cold and lugubrious, contrasted with a happy triumphant resurrection — serves to arrest the attention of the multitude, and excite its emotion. Painting thus regarded leaves its natural limits, and approaches literature."

Taine, Trans.

St. Petronilla. See Santa Petronilla.

St. Philippe. The parish church of the Faubourg St. Honoré, Paris, built in 1784.

St. Roch. A large and fashionable church in Paris, in the Rue St. Honoré. Here were buried Corneille, Descartes, and the Abbé de l'Epée. The chapels contain numerous paintings and sculptures of the last century, and the church shows the change from the style of architecture of the time of Louis XIV. to that of Louis XV.

Then and there Napoleon ascended his throne; and the next day, from the steps of *St. Roche*, thundered forth the cannon which taught the mob of Paris, for the first time, that it had a master. That was the commencement of the Empire. So the Anti-slavery movement commenced unheeded in that "obscure hole" which Mayor Otis could not find, occupied by a printer and a black boy. *W. Phillips.*

St. Roch distributing Alms. A picture by Annibale Caracci (1560-1609), and regarded as one of his chief works. In the Gallery at Dresden, Germany.

St. Sacrément. A modern Italian church in Paris, also known as St. Dénis du Marais.

St. Saviour (Southwark). A church in London, near London Bridge, a remnant of the priory of St. Mary Overy, but known as St. Saviour's before 1510. The choir and Lady Chapel remain excellent specimens of early English church architecture. In the former are the graves of Philip Massinger, John Fletcher, and Edward Dyer the poet; and here is the tomb of John Gower (Moral Gower).

St. Sebaldus. See SHRINE OF ST. SEBALDUS.

St. Sebastian. 1. A celebrated picture in the church of S. Maria degli Angeli, at Rome.

2. A picture by Domenico Zampieri, surnamed Domenichino (1581-1641). In the Städel Institut, Frankfort-on-the-Main, Germany.

☞ "Visitors to picture and sculpture galleries are haunted by the forms of two handsome young men, — Sebastian and Antinous. Both were saints: the one of decadent Paganism, the other of mythologizing Christianity. According to the popular beliefs to which they owed their canonization, both suffered death in the bloom of earliest manhood for the faith that burned in them. There is, however, this difference between the two: that, whereas Sebastian is a shadowy creature of the pious fancy, Antinous preserves a marked and unmistakable personality. . . . The pictures of Sebastian vary according to the ideal of adolescent beauty conceived by each successive artist. In the frescos of Perugino and Luini he shines with the pale pure light of saintliness. On the canvas of Sodoma he reproduces the voluptuous charm of youthful Bacchus, with so much of anguish in his martyred features as may serve to heighten his dæmonic fascination. . . . Under Guido's hand he is a model of mere carnal comeliness. And so forth through the whole range of the Italian painters." *J. A. Symonds.*

St. Sebastian. A series of pictures representing the history of the saint, by Paul Veronese (1530?-1588). In the sacristy of the church of S. Sebastiano, Venice, Italy.

☞ "Paul Veronese's '*St. Sebastian*' . . . appeared to me when last I saw it one of the finest dramatic pictures I had ever beheld. It struck me as a magnificent scene played before me with such a glow of light and life and movement and color, . . . that I felt as if in a theatre, . . . and inclined to clap my hands and cry 'Bravo!'" *Mrs. Jameson.*

St. Sebastian. A picture by Guido Reni (1574?-1642). In the Capitol, Rome.

St. Sebastian. A celebrated votive picture by Antonio Allegri, surnamed Correggio (1494-1534), representing the Virgin and Child "enthroned on clouds and surrounded by a circle of infant angels; below are St. Sebastian, St. Geminianus, and St. Roch." This picture is in the Gallery at Dresden, Germany.

☞ "The figure of St. Sebastian is one of the most beautiful by Correggio, and the picture is thought to represent the most perfect period of the master." *Eastlake, Handbook of Painting.*

St. Sebastian. A noted and admired picture by Giovanni Antonio Cavaliere Razzi, called Il Sodoma (1479?-1550?). In the Uffizi Gallery, Florence, Italy.

St. Sebastian. See also CATACOMB OF ST. SEBASTIAN and MARTYRDOM OF ST. SEBASTIAN.

St. Sepulchre's. A well-known church in London, near Newgate, containing one of the oldest and largest organs in the city. By a legacy left to this church in 1605, a person was employed to toll a hand-bell before the cells of those prisoners at Newgate who were condemned to death, on the night before their execution, reciting these lines: —

All you that in the condemned hole do lie,
Prepare you, for to-morrow you shall die;
. . . .
And when St. Sepulchre's bell to-morrow tolls,
The Lord have mercy on your souls!

Unreasonable people are as hard to reconcile as the vanes of *St. Sepulchre's* tower, which never looked all four upon one point in the heavens. *Howell.*

St. Sernin. An ancient church of the Romanesque order in Toulouse, France. It was dedicated in 1090 by Pope Urban II.

St. Séverin. A fine Gothic church in Paris, in the form of a central nave and two aisles, and rows of chapels on either side. This church, on the site of an older structure of the eleventh century, was begun as early as 1489.

St. Simeon the Prophet. [*S. Simeone Profeta.*] A noted statue by Marco Romano. In the church of S. Simeone Grande, Venice, Italy.

St. Simon's Pillar. The famous column upon the summit of which St. Simon Stylites (b. 388), the Eastern hermit, lived for 37 years. After his death, his admirers built a church upon the spot, enclosing the pillar on which he had so long lived. The pedestal upon which this column stood is still remaining among the ruins of Kul'at Sim'ân, between Antioch and Aleppo, in Syria.

St. Sophia. A mosque in Constantinople, Turkey, and the principal place of Mohammedan worship in the world. It is a very fine example of Byzantine architecture. The mosque was originally a Christian church built by the Emperor Justinian in 531, and was converted into a Moslem temple by Mohammed II. in 1453. The building is in the form of a Greek cross, and is surmounted by a lofty dome with several lesser domes and minarets. The building is of brick, but is lined in the interior with costly marbles. Many of the temples of Greece and Egypt were pillaged to enrich this mosque.

☞ "When Justinian exclaimed, 'I have surpassed thee, O Solomon,' he took an exaggerated view of the work of his predecessor, and did not realize the extent to which his building excelled the Jewish temple. The latter was only equal to a small church, with a wooden roof, supported by wooden posts, and covering some 7,200 square feet. Sta. Sophia covers ten times that area, is built of durable materials throughout, and far more artistically ornamented than the temple of the Jews ever could have been. But Justinian did more than accomplish this easy victory. Neither the Pantheon nor any of the vaulted halls at Rome equal the nave of Sta. Sophia in extent, or in cleverness of construction, or in beauty of design. Nor was there any thing erected during the ten centuries which elapsed from the transference of the capital to Byzantium till the building of the great mediæval cathedrals, which can be compared with it. Indeed, it remains even now an open question whether a Christian church exists anywhere, of any age, whose interior is so beautiful as that of this marvellous creation of old Byzantine art." *Fergusson.*

☞ "It is certain that no domical building of modern times can at all approach *Sta. Sophia's*, either for appropriateness or beauty. If we regard it with a view to the purposes of Protestant worship, it affords an infinitely better model for imitation than any thing our own mediæval architects ever produced." *Fergusson.*

☞ "Its immense dome is said to be more wonderful than St. Peter's; but its dirt is much more wonderful than its dome, though they never mention it." *Mark Twain.*

I have beheld *Sophia's* bright roofs swell
Their glittering mass i' the sun, and have surveyed
Its sanctuary the while the usurping Moslem prayed. *Byron.*

Poor child! I would have mended it with gold,
Until it gleamed like *St. Sophia's dome*
When all the faithful troop to morning prayer. *Mrs. Browning.*

O, Stamboul! once the empress of their reign?
Though turbans now pollute *Sophia's* shrine,
And Greece her very altars eyes in vain. *Byron.*

St. Stephen. The name by which the great bell in Westminster

Palace, London, is known. The weight of this bell is $11\frac{1}{2}$ tons.

St. Stephen. See MARTYRDOM OF ST. STEPHEN.

St. Stephen's. 1. The cathedral of Vienna, Austria. One of the most imposing specimens of Gothic architecture in the world. It was begun in 1359 and finished in 1480.

☞ "St. Stephen's Cathedral in the centre of the old city is one of the finest specimens of Gothic architecture in Germany. Its unrivalled tower, which rises to the height of 428 feet, is visible from every part of Vienna. It is entirely of stone, most elaborately ornamented, and is supposed to be the strongest in Europe. The inside is solemn and grand, but the effect is injured by the number of small chapels and shrines." *Bayard Taylor.*

☞ "No one with a trace of poetry in his composition can stand under the great cavernous western porch [of St. Stephen's], and not feel that he has before him one of the most beautiful and impressive buildings in Europe. A good deal of this may be owing to the color. The time-stain in the nave is untouched, the painted glass perfect, and the whole has a venerable look, now too rare. The choir is being smartened up, and its poetry is gone. Meanwhile no building can stand in more absolute contrast with the cathedral at Cologne, than this one at Vienna. The former fails, because it is so coldly perfect: this impresses, though offending against all rules, because it was designed by a poet." *Fergusson.*

2. An admired church, in the rear of the Mansion House, London, the work of Sir Christopher Wren (1632-1723).

☞ "If the material had been as lasting, and the size as great, as St. Paul's, this church would have been a greater monument to Wren than the cathedral." *Fergusson.*

St. Stephen's Chapel. In the Old Palace at Westminster, London. See ST. STEPHEN'S HALL.

☞ "St. Stephen's Chapel was a beautiful specimen of rich Decorated Gothic, its inner walls being covered with ancient frescos relating to the Old and New Testament history: it was used as the House of Commons from 1547 till 1834; and its walls resounded to the eloquence of Chatham, Pitt, Fox, Burke, Grattan, and Canning." *Hare.*

St. Stephen's Court. The English Exchequer.

That cupboard, where the mice disport,
I liken to *St. Stephen's Court.*
Matt. Prior (Erle Robert's Mice).

St. Stephen's Hall. A room in the New Palace at Westminster, London, leading from Westminster Hall. It derives its name from occupying the same space as St. Stephen's Chapel of the old palace, and is lined by twelve statues of eminent parliamentary statesmen and orators. See ST. STEPHEN'S CHAPEL.

What is the good of men collected, with effort, to debate on the benches of *St. Stephen's*, now when there is a *Times* Newspaper? Not the discussion of questions; only the ultimate voting of them (a very brief process, I should think!) requires to go on, or can veritably go on, in *St. Stephen's* now. *Carlyle.*

St. Sulpice. This church, on the Place St. Sulpice in Paris, was commenced by Anne of Austria in 1646, but was not completed until 1745. It is in the form of a Latin cross. The exterior is very fine, and within, the high altar surrounded by statues of the Twelve Apostles is very imposing.

St. Sulpice. See PLACE ST. SULPICE.

St. Theodore's Column. A well-known pillar of granite in Venice, Italy, on the summit of which is a statue of St. Theodore resting upon a crocodile. It was brought from the Holy Land in the early part of the twelfth century. St. Theodore was the first patron of Venice; but he was deposed, and St. Mark adopted, when the bones of the latter were brought from Alexandria.

St. Theresa delivering St. Bernardino de Mendoza from Purgatory. A picture by Peter Paul Rubens (1577-1640). It is in the Museum of Antwerp, Belgium.

St. Theresa. A statue by Giovanni Lorenzo Bernini (1598-1680). In the church of Santa Maria della Vittoria, in Rome.

☞ "She is adorable. In a swoon of ecstatic happiness lies the saint, with pendant hands, naked feet, and half-closed eyes, fallen in transports of blissful love. Her features are emaciated, but how noble! Words cannot render the sentiment of this affecting rapturous attitude." *Taine, Trans.*

St. Thomas. See INCREDULITY OF ST. THOMAS.

St. Thomas d'Aquin. A fashionable church in the most aristocratic quarter of the Faubourg St. Germain, Paris. It formerly belonged to a Dominican convent. Here, among other modern pictures, is one by Ary Scheffer, of St. Thomas calming the waves in a tempest.

St. Thomas's Hospital. A hospital in London, originally founded in 1213 as an almshouse. Queen Victoria laid the first stone of the present building in 1868.

St. Ursula. A well-known church in Cologne, Germany, containing the famous relics of the saint and of the 11,000 virgins.

☞ "The whole church is full of virgins. The altar-piece is a vast picture of the slaughter, not badly painted. Through various glass openings you perceive that the walls are full of the bones and skulls. Did the worship of Egypt ever sink lower in horrible and loathsome idolatry?" *Charles Beecher.*

St. Ursula. A picture by the distinguished Flemish painter Jan van Eyck (1370–1441), representing St. Ursula seated before a rich Gothic tower — her attribute. The picture bears the date 1437, and is in the Museum at Antwerp, Belgium.

St. Ursula. See RELIQUARY OF ST. URSULA.

St. Veronica. A picture by Roger van der Weyden (d. 1464), the Flemish painter, and one of his later works. It represents the saint with the Sudarium on which the countenance of Christ is impressed. The picture is now in the Städel Institut at Frankfort-on-the-Main, Germany.

St. Winifred's Well. This was once the most celebrated holy well in Great Britain. It was situated in Holywell in the county of Flint, England. In the Middle Ages it was regarded with great veneration. It is said to derive its name from the following legend: "Winifred, a noble British maiden of the seventh century, was beloved by a certain Prince Cradocus. She repulsed his suit, and he in revenge cut off her head. The prince was immediately struck dead, and the earth opening swallowed him up. Winifred's head rolled down the hill, and from the spot where it rested a spring gushed forth. St. Bueno picked up the head, and re-united it to the body, so that Winifred lived for many years a life of great sanctity; and the spring to which her name was given became famous for its curative powers." The Countess of Richmond, mother of Henry VII., built a court-house over this celebrated well. In the seventeenth century it was visited by thousands, but has since fallen into comparative neglect.

St. Zaccaria. An admired church in Venice, Italy, built in the middle of the fifteenth century. Its façade is regarded by Fergusson as one of the finest in Italy.

St. Zenobius, Burial of. A picture by Ridolfo Ghirlandajo (1482–1560), the Italian painter, and considered one of his *chefs-d'œuvre.* In the Louvre, Paris.

St. Zenobius raising a dead child. A picture by Ridolfo Ghirlandajo (1482–1560), the Italian painter, and considered his masterpiece. It is in the Louvre in Paris.

Sainte Chapelle. [Holy Chapel.] A small but beautiful religious edifice in the courtyard of the Palais de Justice in Paris, formerly the royal chapel. It was begun in 1244, and finished in 1248. It is in two stories, to correspond with the floors of the ancient palace. The upper chapel was for the royal family, and the lower for the servants. This chapel is attractive from its historical associations as well as from the delicacy and beauty of its architecture, which is Gothic, and one of the most exquisite specimens existing of that style. It was built by St. Louis for the reception of reliques of the Saviour, — the crown of thorns, a piece of the true cross, and the spear-head which pierced our Saviour's side. The stained-glass windows of the chapel are very splendid: four of them are illustrative of the principal events in the life of St. Louis and his two crusades. St. Chapelle is said to now present "the completest, perhaps the finest, example of the religious architecture of the middle of the thirteenth century."

☞ "It only wants increased dimensions to merit the title of a sublime specimen of Gothic art."
Fergusson.

Mabille at the present day is so well known, both in France and in other countries, it is so frequented by people of fashion, by princes even, who in their passage through the city visit it with as much interest as Notre Dame and the *Sainte Chapelle*, and give it renown, that to call the Château des Fleurs its brother is to confer upon it the highest eulogy.
Larousse, Trans.

Sainte Clotilde. The chief modern Gothic church in Paris. It was begun in 1846, and is said to have cost £320,000. The style is that of the fourteenth century. It has two conspicuous spires, and is richly ornamented.

Sainte Gudule. A cathedral church in Brussels, Belgium. It was built in 1273, and is famous for its painted windows, statues, and pulpit.

Sainte Trinité. An ancient monastic establishment in Caen, France, founded and consecrated by Matilda, wife of William the Conqueror, 1066. [Also called *Abbaye aux Dames.*]

Sakkárah, Tablet of. See TABLET OF SAKKÁRAH.

Sala a Croce Greca. [Hall of the Greek Cross.] A noble apartment in the Vatican, Rome.

☞ "Whoever would seek for the luxury of architecture in its highest perfection will find it in the Hall of the Greek Cross. The finest materials are used to embellish the noblest proportions. . . . Every thing is rich, airy, and exhilarating."
Hillard.

Sala del Cambio. [Exchange Hall.] A building in Perugia, Italy, once an exchange, but now no longer used for that purpose. It is noted for its fine frescos by Perugino (1446–1524).

This is still more apparent in the *Cambio*, a kind of exchange or guildhall of the merchants. Perugino was intrusted with its decoration in the year 1500
Taine, Trans.

Sala degli Animali. [Hall of Animals.] An apartment in the Vatican, at Rome, containing representations of animals in marble and alabaster.

☞ "The Hall of Animals is a fresh revelation of the resources of Greek sculpture. Here is a motionless menagerie in marble, — horses, dogs, centaurs, crocodiles, wild boars, lions, bulls, and serpents. In some cases the colors of life are attempted, . . . the general effect of each type is given with nice discrimination."
Hillard.

Sala della Biga. [Hall of the Biga.] A well-known apartment in the Vatican, Rome.

☞ "The Hall of the Biga is a circular chamber in which is preserved a representation in white marble of an ancient Biga, or chariot, with two wheels. Very little of the original work remains; but it has been restored with great taste and skill, and forms a curious and interesting object."
Hillard.

Sala di Constantino. [Hall of Constantine.] A hall in the Vatican Palace, Rome, adorned with frescos by the pupils of Raphael, after designs by that master.

Sala Ducale. [Ducal Hall.] A room in the Vatican Palace, in Rome, in which the popes formerly gave audience to foreign princes.

Sala Regia. [Royal Hall.] A room in the Palace of the Vatican, Rome, used as a hall of audience for ambassadors.

Salisbury Cathedral. A famous church, the most elegant of its kind in England, at Salisbury, the capital of Wiltshire. It was erected in the thirteenth century. The spire, which is greatly admired for its beauty, is more than 400 feet in height.

Salisbury Court Theatre. See DUKE'S THEATRE.

Salisbury Crags. The foremost, but not the highest, of a precipitous range of hills on the eastern side of Edinburgh, and south of Holyrood Palace. They are said to derive their name from the Earl of Salisbury, who was with Edward III. in his expedition to the north. The rocks, with the buildings upon them, give to the city its imposing appearance. See ARTHUR'S SEAT and CALTON HILL.

☞ "These Salisbury Crags which overlook Edinburgh have a very peculiar outline: they resemble an immense elephant crouching down."
Mrs. H. B. Stowe.

Salisbury Plain. A bare, barren tract, affording pasturage for sheep, about eight miles north of Salisbury, Wiltshire, England. It contains the druidical remains of Stonehenge, and is associated also with the hero of Hannah More's popular story of the "Shepherd of Salisbury Plain."

☞ "After dinner, we walked to *Salisbury Plain*. On the broad downs, under the gray sky, not a house was visible, nothing but Stonehenge, which looked like a group of brown dwarfs in the wide expanse. Far and wide a few shepherds with their flocks sprinkled the plain." *R. W. Emerson.*

Other edifices may crowd close to its foundation, and people may tramp as they like about it; but still the great cathedral [St. Paul's] is as quiet and serene as if it stood in the middle of *Salisbury Plain.*
Hawthorne.

Sallust's House and Gardens. [Lat. *Horti Pretiosissimi.*] Celebrated palace and pleasure-grounds in ancient Rome, once belonging to the historian Sallust (86–34 B.C.), and after his death purchased for the emperors. They were the favorite retreat of Vespasian, Nerva, and Aurelian. Many fine buildings once stood here, which were destroyed when Rome was taken by Alaric, A.D. 410, and only a few ruins now remain.

Salon, El. See SALOON, THE.

Salon Carré. In the Louvre, Paris. Here are the finest paintings of the Italian, Flemish, Spanish, and French schools.

Saloon, The. [Span. *El Salon.*] A well-known promenade in the Prado, at Madrid, Spain. It is 1,450 feet in length, and 250 feet broad.

☞ "As you enter it [the Prado], you find yourself in a superb wide opening called the *Saloon;* on your right hand a double walk, and on your left first the place where carriages parade, and afterwards another double walk, the whole ornamented with fountains and trees and statues."
George Ticknor.

Salt Pond. A natural curiosity in Giles County, Va. It is described as a lake of "fresh water sunk in the mountain [Salt Pond Mountain] at an elevation of 4,500 feet above the level of the sea, and is fed by no visible stream. . . . The lake is said to have been gradually enlarging instead of diminishing since 1804, when it was first discovered. It is without fish; and, though some were placed in it, they have disappeared. Among its mysterious attractions is the singular fact that its depth is unfathomable, — a line 300 feet in depth touched no bottom. . . . The origin of this singular lake is undiscovered."

Saltero's, Don. See DON SALTERO'S.

Salpêtrière. A house of refuge and hospital for poor, insane, aged, and incurable women, Boulevard de l' Hôpital, Paris. It was founded under Louis XIV.

☞ "This magnificent hospital, commonly called 'La Salpêtrière,'— from its standing on ground formerly occupied as a saltpetre manufactory, — and which in the year 1662 contained nearly 10,000 poor, is 120 yards more than a quarter of a mile in length, by 36 yards more than the fifth of a mile in breadth." *Sir Francis B. Head.*

My neighbor said to a vulgar creature who was dancing: "Has the *Salpêtrière* come down to the bal du Trône to-day?" — "No, but Mazas has emptied itself to-day into the bal du Trône." A distinction is made between them.

Taine, Trans.

Saltram Gallery. An interesting collection of paintings formed chiefly by Sir Joshua Reynolds, in the possession of the Earl of Morley at his country seat, Saltram, in Devonshire, England.

Saltram House. The seat of the Earl of Morley, near Lyneham, England.

Salutation, The. A picture by Mariotto Albertinelli (1475?-1520?), and considered his *chef d'œuvre*. In the Uffizi Gallery, Florence, Italy.

Salutation. A tavern of this name, well known in the eighteenth century, was situated in Tavistock Street, Covent Garden, London. The name Salutation was not confined to this tavern. See SALUTATION AND CAT.

There hath been great sale and utterance of Wine,
Besides Beere, and Ale, and Ipocras fine,
In every country, region, and nation,
But chiefly in Billingsgate, at the *Salutation*.

Newes from Bartholomew Fayre.

Salutation and Cat. A tavern in Newgate Street, London, resorted to in the last century. Lamb and Coleridge met here. See SALUTATION.

For me, I'm much concerned I cannot meet
"At *Salutation Tavern*, Newgate-street,"
Your notice, like your verse, so sweet and short!
If longer, I'd sincerely thank you for it.

Samuel Richardson.

Salvation. See FOUNT OF SALVATION.

Salvator Mundi. [The Saviour of the World.] A picture bearing this name, by Fra Bartolommeo (1469-1517), the Italian painter. In the Pitti Palace at Florence, Italy.

Salvator Mundi. A head of Christ, represented as the Saviour of the world, by Jan van Eyck (1370-1441), the Flemish painter. It bears date 1438, and is in the Museum at Berlin, Prussia.

Samaritan. See GOOD SAMARITAN.

Samaritan Synagogue. This little chapel, in which the few remaining Samaritans meet to worship, is on Mount Gerizim, not far from Jerusalem. The priests exhibit, but do not allow the visitor to touch, a very valuable copy of the Pentateuch which they believe to be 3,500 years old.

Samian Sibyl. A picture by Francesco Barbieri, called Guercino (1590-1666). In the Tribune of the Uffizi, Florence, Italy.

☞ "It is a glorious work. With her hands clasped over her volume, she is looking up with a face full of deep and expressive sadness. A picturesque turban is twined around her head, and bands of pearls gleam amidst her rich dark brown tresses. Her face bears the softness of dawning womanhood." *Bayard Taylor.*

Samson and Delilah. 1. A picture by Anthony van Dyck (1599-1641), and considered by some one of his finest works. It is in the Gallery of Vienna, Austria.

2. A picture by Lucas Cranach (1472-1553), a German painter. It is now in the Royal Gallery at Augsburg, Bavaria.

Samson blinded by the Philistines. A picture by Rembrandt van Ryn (1606-1669), the Dutch painter. In the collection of Count Schönborn at Vienna, Austria.

Samson threatening his Father-in-law. A picture by Rembrandt van Ryn (1607-1669), the Dutch painter. In the Museum at Berlin, Prussia. [Sometimes called *Prince Adolphus of Gueldres threatening his imprisoned father*.]

San Agostino. [St. Augustine.] A well-known church at Rome in the piazza of the same name.

☞ "It [San Agostino] is a transitional specimen between the pillared styles, which were then struggling for the mastery. It may either be regarded as the last of the old race, or the first of the new style which was so soon destined to revolutionize the architectural world."

Fergusson.

San Carlo. [St. Charles.] A famous opera-house in Naples, and one of the largest in Europe. It was first opened in 1737. Having been burned down in the year 1816, it was rebuilt in the original form. Some of the chief masterpieces of music were first brought out on this stage.

☞ "There are six rows of boxes in this theatre: the house is magnificent, the light is not strong, not dazzling. The science of humoring the eye, and indeed all the senses, is well understood here. They do not heap the audience together, as at the 'Grand Opéra,' or at the 'Italiens' in Paris."

Taine, Trans.

San Francesco. **1.** A beautiful and remarkable building of Assisi, Italy, so called from St. Francis of Assisi (1182–1226), the founder of one of the four orders of mendicant monks, called Franciscans. This interesting convent is now suppressed.

Worn with travel, tired and lame,
To Assisi's walls I came:
Sad, and full of homesick fancies,
I addressed me to St. Francis.

T. W. Parsons.

2. The hermitage of San Francesco, situated in a picturesque gorge near the convent of San Francesco at Assisi, Italy, and remarkable as the solitary retreat of St. Francis.

San Giorgio. An important and noted church of the sixteenth century in Venice, Italy.

San Giorgio-in-Velabro. A church in Rome, founded in the fourth century after Christ, and which has been several times rebuilt. For the origin of the name see VELABRUM.

☞ "St. George and the dragon, and his martyrdom, are the usual subjects in the many churches dedicated to this saint. His church at Rome, at the foot of the Palatine, called from its situation San Giorgio-in-Velabro, was built by Leo II. in 682. In a casket under the altar is preserved, as a precious relic, a fragment of his banner; and on the vault of the apsis is an ancient painting, the copy of a more ancient mosaic, which once existed there. In the centre stands the Redeemer between the Virgin and St. Peter; on one side, St. George on horseback with his palm as martyr, and his standard as the 'Red-cross Knight;' on the other side, St. Sebastian standing, bearded, and with one long arrow."

Mrs. Jameson.

San Giovanni, Baptistery of. See BAPTISTERY OF SAN GIOVANNI.

San Giovanni e San Paolo. A noted church in Venice, erected in the thirteenth century.

☞ "Their famous church at Venice, the SS. Giovanni e Paolo, can never be forgotten by those who have lingered around its wondrous and precious monuments." *Mrs. Jameson.*

San Giovanni, Porta. See PORTA SAN GIOVANNI.

San Gregorio. A church in Rome, founded in the seventh century, and so named from Gregory the Great, who was for many years a monk in the adjoining monastery. The church contains in one of its chapels the two celebrated rival frescos by Guido and Domenichino, of which Annibal Caracci said that the work of Guido was that of the master, but the picture of Domenichino the work of the scholar who knew more than the master.

San Ildefonso. See GRANJA, LA.

San Jacinto. A frigate of the United States navy, noted as being the vessel into which Mason and Slidell, the Confederate emissaries, were forcibly taken by her commander, Capt. Wilkes, from the British mail steamer *Trent*, on the 8th of November, 1861.

San Juan d'Ulloa. A famous fortress now more than 250 years old, commanding the harbor of Vera Cruz, Mexico.

San Lorenzo. A famous church in Florence, Italy, consecrated by St. Ambrose in 373, rebuilt by Brunelleschi and Antonio Manetti. This church contains the famous monuments of the Medicis, executed by Michael Angelo.

☞ "No church can be freer from bad taste than this one; and there is no false construction, nor any thing to offend the most fastidious."
Fergusson.

San Lorenzo. See MARTYRDOM OF SAN LORENZO.

San Lorenzo fuori le Murà. [St. Laurence without the Walls.] One of the seven basilicas of Rome, situated a short distance from the city, on the way to Tivoli. The basilica is now almost swallowed up in the burial-ground of San Lorenzo, the great modern public cemetery of Rome.

San Lorenzo in Lucinà. A well-known church, situated on the Corso, Rome.

San Luca, Accademia di. See ST. LUKE.

San Marco. A well-known monastic establishment in Florence, Italy, now used as a museum, and containing some fine frescos.

San Marco, Piazza. See ST. MARK'S SQUARE.

San Michele. A famous monastery crowning an eminence in the neighborhood of Turin, Italy. See also OR SAN MICHELE.

San Miniato al Monte. A celebrated and beautiful church near Florence, Italy, so named after the Florentine St. Miniato (or S. Minias), who, according to the legend, served in the Roman army under Decius, and suffered martyrdom in the year 254. The place now serves as a burial-ground — a Florentine *Campo Santo.*

☞ "A mass of buildings conspicuous from their position and castellated appearance. The church, parts of which belong to the eleventh century, is an imposing structure, and is, to a considerable extent, built of the fragments of ancient Roman edifices, which, when we compare their original destination with their present position, remind us of a palimpsest manuscript, from which a hymn to Apollo has been expunged, and a holy legend written in its place."
Hillard.

Who, that remembers Florence, does not remember well the *San Miniato-in-Monte* towering on its lofty eminence above the city, and visible along the Lung' Arno from the Ponte alle Grazie to the Ponte alla Carraja? *Mrs. Jameson.*

Fired with the patriots' zeal,
Where *San Miniato's* glow
Smiled down upon the foe,
Till Treason won the gates that mocked the invader's steel. *C. P. Cranch.*

San Pancrazio. [St. Pancras.] An ancient church in Rome, Italy. It adjoins the grounds of the Villa Pamphili. The church was founded in the sixth century, and restored in the seventeenth, and has been the scene of many interesting events. In the siege of Rome in 1849 by the French, the building was taken by storm.

As they passed
The gate of *San Pancrazio*, human blood
Flowed ankle-high about them, and dead men
Choked the long street with gashed and gory piles. *Whittier.*

San Paolo fuori le Murà. [St. Paul's without the Walls.] One of the great churches of Rome. The original temple, which was one of the most interesting monuments of the early Church, having been founded by the Emperor Theodosius in 386 to commemorate the martyrdom of St. Paul, and in which Christian worship had been performed uninterruptedly for 1,500 years, was destroyed by fire, July 16, 1824. A splendid edifice, though far inferior to its predecessor, has since been built upon the same site, which is pointed out as the burial-place of St. Paul. It was opened by Pius IX., in 1854.

☞ "The very abandonment of this huge pile standing in solitary grandeur on the banks of the Tiber was one source of its value. . . . It remained genuine, though bare, as S. Apollinare in Classe, at Ravenna, the city eminently of unspoiled basilicas."
Cardinal Wiseman.

☞ "The church of San Paolo fuori le Murà was almost an exact counterpart of St. Peter's, both in design and dimensions. The only important variations were, that the transept was made of the same width as the central nave, and that the pillars separating the nave from the side aisles were joined by arches instead of by a horizontal architrave. Both these were undoubted improvements; the first giving space and dignity, the latter not only adding height, but giving it, together with lightness, that apparent strength requisite to support the high wall placed over the pillars." *Fergusson.*

San Paolo, Porta di. See PORTA DI SAN PAOLO.

San Pietro in Montorio. A well-known and interesting church in Rome founded by Constantine the Great, and rebuilt by the Spanish sovereigns Ferdinand and Isabella. The name Montorio (Monte d' Oro) is thought to be derived from the yellowish sand of the hill on which it stands.

San Pietro in Vincoli. [St. Peter in Chains.] A celebrated church in Rome, on the Esquiline Hill, near the Baths of Titus; originally founded, according to the legend, by Theodora, sister of Hermes, prefect of Rome, A.D. 109; but probably built by the Empress Eudoxia, wife of Valentinian III., who placed in it one of the famous chains with which St. Peter is said to have been bound, and which now gives to this church its great attraction to Catholic pilgrims. The chains are in fragments, many links having been broken off and sent as presents to differerent monarchs. The longest is some five feet. They are not publicly exhibited except on the occasion of the festival of St. Peter, on the 1st of August and the following eight days. The church contains Michael Angelo's celebrated statue of Moses.

☞ "San Pietro in Vincoli is one of the noblest churches in Rome, comprising a nave separated from two aisles by fluted marble columns of the Doric order." *Hillard.*

San Placido. See MARTYRDOM OF SAN PLACIDO AND SANTA FLAVIA.

San Rocco, Scuola di. A building in Venice, erected in the sixteenth century, containing some of the best works of Tintoretto and other Venetian painters.

☞ "Among other buildings of this date [the sixteenth century], the palatial fraternity-houses — the so-called schools — take foremost rank; as for example the superb Scuola di San Rocco, extravagantly adorned with colored marble wainscoating and a wealth of plastic ornament." *Lübke.*

San Sebastiano. [St. Sebastian.] A Roman basilica, or metropolitan church, situated about two miles beyond the gate of the same name, on the Via Appia. See DOMINE QUO VADIS and CATACOMBS.

San Sebastiano, Porta di. See PORTA DI SAN SEBASTIANO.

Sân, Stone of. See STONE OF SÂN.

San Vitale. A celebrated Byzantine church in Ravenna, Italy, containing some fine mosaics. It was erected in the sixth century, but has undergone great restorations.

Sancho Panza and the Duchess. A picture by Charles Robert Leslie (1794–1859). In the National Gallery, London.

Sancta Sanctorum. [Holy of Holies.] A celebrated Gothic chapel in the basilica of St. John Lateran, in Rome, containing a famous portrait of the Saviour, of Greek workmanship, attributed by the faithful to St. Luke, and said to be an exact likeness of Christ at the age of 12. This chapel is regarded as so extremely sacred that no one but the pope can officiate in it; and it is only open even to the clergy on the day before Palm Sunday. See HOLY OF HOLIES.

Sanctuary, The. A picture by Sir Edwin Landseer (1803–1873), the most celebrated modern painter of animals. This picture was painted in 1842, and is now the property of Queen Victoria. Its motto was taken from the poem of *Loch Maree:* —

"Poor hunted hart! the painful struggle o'er,
How blest the shelter of that island shore!
There while he sobs, his panting heart to rest,
Nor hound nor hunter shall his lair molest."

Sandringham Hall. The seat of the Prince of Wales, not far from Lynn, England.

Sans Souci. A famous palace in the vicinity of Potsdam, near Berlin, Prussia. It was built by Frederick the Great (1712–1786), and was his favorite residence. Voltaire lived here for a time. The name Philosopher of Sans Souci was given to Frederick the Great. He was a disciple of Voltaire, and the author of several political and philosophical treatises.

On the whole, we must pity Frederic, environed with that cluster of Philosophers: doubtless he meant rather well; yet the French at Rosbach, with guns in their hands, were but a small matter, compared with these French in *Sans Souci*. *Carlyle.*

Nay, what is better, I have not the trouble of entertaining them. My estate is a perfect *Sans Souci*, where every one does as he pleases, and no one troubles the owner. *Irving.*

Potsdam, thou cradle of a line of kings,
Quiet in thy greatness, a historic crown
Rests well upon thee and on *Sanssouci*,
The home of him whom sternly gained renown
Calls "Great" forever.
Arthur von Rapp.

Santa Annunziata. A noted church in Florence, Italy. It was built in the thirteenth century, but has undergone restorations. It contains, among other chapels, one of the Annunciation built by Pietro de Medici.

☞ "It [the chapel] is a very beautiful piece of architecture — a sort of canopy of marble, supported on pillars; and its magnificence within, in marble and silver, and all manner of holy decoration, is quite indescribable." *Hawthorne.*

☞ "In the inner part of this chapel is preserved a miraculous picture of the '*Santissima Annunziata*' painted by angels, and held in such holy repute that $40,000 have lately been expended in providing a new crown for the sacred personage represented." *Hawthorne.*

After dinner we went to the church of *Annunciata*, where the Duke and his Court were at their devotions; for here is a shrine that dos greate miracles [proved] by innumerable votive tablets, &c., covering almost the walles of the whole church. This is the image of Gabriel who saluted the Bl. Virgin, and which the artist performed so well he was in despair of finishing the Virgin's face, whereupon it was miraculously don for him whilst he slept; but others say it was painted by St. Luke himself. Whoever it was, infinite is the devotion of both sexes to it. *John Evelyn*, 1644.

Sant' Apollinare in Classe. A famous Byzantine church on the site of the old Roman town of Classis, in the neighborhood of Ravenna, Italy, dating from the sixth century.

☞ "A vast lonely structure, bearing its huge long back against the low horizon, like some monster antediluvian saurian, the fit denizen of this marsh world. It is the venerable Basilica of S. Apollinare in Classe." *Trollope.*

☞ "On the spot where he [St. Apollinaris of Ravenna] suffered, about 534 years afterwards, was built and dedicated to his honor the magnificent basilica of St. Apollinaris-in-Classe. It is still seen standing in the midst of a solitary marshy plain near Ravenna, surrounded with rice-grounds, and on the verge of that vast melancholy pine-forest made famous in the works of Boccaccio, Dante, and Byron." *Mrs. Jameson.*

Santa Casa. [The Holy House.] A celebrated religious sanctuary in the church of the same name in the city of Loreto, Italy. For five centuries it has been a centre of pilgrimage, its fame and sanctity drawing crowds of votaries from all parts of the Christian world. It is a small brick house, enclosed in a marble casing, and contains the statue of the Virgin [Our Lady of Loretto], said to have been sculptured by St. Luke from the cedar-wood of Lebanon. According to the Romish legend, the Casa Santa was the birthplace of the Virgin, the scene of the Annunciation and Incarnation, and the place where the Holy Family found shelter after the flight out of Egypt. It is said to have been miraculously transported from Nazareth by angels, and finally deposited, in 1295, on the spot it now occupies.

☞ "Every one knows the story of the House of Loreto. The devotion of one-half the world, and the ridicule of the other half, has made us familiar with the strange story, written in all the languages of Europe round the walls of that remarkable sanctuary. But the 'wondrous flitting' of the Holy House is not the feature in its history which is most present to the pilgrims who frequent it. It is regarded by them simply as an actual fragment of the Holy Land, sacred as the very spot on which the mystery of the Incarnation was announced and begun. In proportion to the sincerity and extent of this belief is the veneration which attaches to what is undoubtedly the most frequented sanctuary in Christendom." *Dean Stanley.*

☞ "Nazareth was taken by Sultan Khalil in 1291, when he stormed the last refuge of the Crusaders in the neighboring city of Acre. From that time, not Nazareth only, but the whole of Palestine, was closed to the devotions of Europe. The Crusaders were expelled from Asia, and in Europe the spirit of the crusades was extinct. But the natural longing to see the scenes of the events of the Sacred History — the superstitious craving to win for prayer the favor of consecrated localities — did not expire with the crusades. Can we wonder, that, under such circumstances, there should have arisen the feeling, the desire, the belief, that, if Mahomet could not go to the mountain, the mountain must come to Mahomet? The house of Loretto is the petrifaction, so to speak, of the 'last sigh of the crusades.'" *Dean Stanley.*

It is worthy of notice also, in the history of this extraordinary chair [Shakespeare's], that it partakes something of the volatile nature of the *Santa Casa* of Loretto, or the flying chair of the Arabian enchanter; for, though sold some few years since to a northern princess, yet, strange to tell, it has found its way back again to the old chimney-corner. *Irving.*

Thou see'st my father's house, so German, there,
As if in airy flight such angel-pair,
As bore *Loretto's house of charity*,
Right from the Rhine had brought thee o'er the sea.
Graf von Auersperg, Trans.

Forms, features, worshipped while we breathe or move,
Be, by some spirit of your dreaming hour,
Borne, like *Loretto's chapel*, through the air
To the green land I sing, then wake: you'll find them there.
Fitz-Greene Halleck.

I scanned
That house walled round with sculptured forms divine,
Labor illustrious of a Tuscan hand.
. . . . .
Of song-raised temples we have heard ere now:
Lo, here a visible hymn in marble graven!
Aubrey de Vere.

Santa Conversazione. [The Holy Conversation.] A name given to a style of representations of the Madonna, or the Holy Family, in which numerous figures are grouped around the Virgin and Child, usually amid retired and beautiful country landscapes. Palma Vecchio (1475-1528) seems to have invented the larger form of this composition, of which frequent examples are found among his works.

Santa Croce. [Holy Cross.] A famous church of the Black Friars in Florence, Italy. As a favorite place of interment of the Florentines, it has often been styled the "Westminster Abbey" of the city.

☞ "In Santa Croce, as at Westminster Abbey, the present destination of the building [as a place of interment] was no part of the original design. . . . Thus it came to pass, as if by accident, that in the vault of the Buonarotti was laid Michael Angelo; in the vault of the Viviani, the preceptor of one of their house, Galileo. From these two burials the church gradually became the recognized shrine of Italian genius." *Dean Stanley.*

☞ "This morning . . . to the church of Santa Croce, the great monumental deposit of Florentine worthies. . . . I threw my eyes about the church, and came to the conclusion, that, in spite of its antiquity, its size, its architecture, its painted windows, its tombs of great men and all the reverence and interest that broods over them, it is not an impressive edifice. Any little Norman church in England would impress me as much or more." *Hawthorne.*

☞ "This church of Santa Croce contains perhaps the most brilliant assemblage of the dead in Europe." *Mme. de Staël.*

In *Santa Croce's* holy precincts lie
Ashes which make it holier, dust which is
Even in itself an immortality,
Though there were nothing save the past, and this
The particle of those sublimities
Which have relapsed to chaos: — here repose

Angelo's, Alfieri's bones, and his,
The starry Galileo, with his woes;
Here Machiavelli's earth, return'd to whence it rose. *Byron.*

Henceforward, Dante! now my soul is sure
That thine is better comforted of scorn,
And looks down from the stars in fuller cure,
Than when, in *Santa Croce* church, forlorn
Of any corpse, the architect and hewer
Did pile the empty marbles as thy tomb!
Mrs. Browning.

There's a verse he set
In *Santa Croce* to her memory.
Mrs. Browning.

Santa Croce and the dome of St. Peter's are lame copies after a divine model.
Emerson.

Santa Croce in Gerusalemme. [Holy Cross in Jerusalem.] One of the great Roman basilicas. It derives its name from the *Title of the True Cross* (Titulus Crucis), — a plank of wood bearing the inscription in Greek, Hebrew, and Latin, Jesus Nazarene King, — deposited here by the Empress Helena, and from the earth from Jerusalem which was brought and mixed with the foundations of the church.

☞ "The Church of Santa Croce in Gerusalemme stands on the lonely expanse of the Esquiline Hill, close by the walls of Rome, . . . built by St. Helena, mother of Constantine the Great. Unspeakable are the obligations the Roman Catholic world lies under to this exemplary saint and empress, not only for bringing into the world the first Christian emperor, but for going all the way to Jerusalem on purpose to make the discovery of the True Cross (which nobody on the spot had been able to find for 300 years), and bringing it to this church, where every true believer may see it." *C. A. Eaton.*

Santa Culla. [The Holy Cradle.] A relic preserved in a costly reliquary in the Basilica of Santa Maria Maggiore in Rome, and believed by the devout to be the identical cradle in which the Saviour was carried into Egypt. It is publicly exhibited on Christmas Day.

Sant' Elmo. See St. Elmo.

Santa Felicità. See Martyrdom of Santa Felicità.

Santa Flavia. See Martyrdom of San Placido and Santa Flavia.

Santa Liparata. See Santa Maria del Fiore.

Santa Maria. One of the three vessels with which Columbus set sail for America. The *Santa Maria* was commanded by Columbus in person. These little ships set sail from Palos, Spain, on the 3d of August, 1492.

☞ "The departure from Palos, where, a few days before, he had begged a morsel of bread and a cup of water for his wayworn child, — his final farewell to the Old World at the Canaries, — his entrance upon the trade-winds, which then, for the first time, filled a European sail, — the portentous variation of the needle, never before observed, — the fearful course westward and westward, day after day, and night after night, over the unknown ocean,— the mutinous and ill-appeased crew; — at length, when hope had turned to despair in every heart but one, the tokens of land, — the cloud-banks on the western horizon, — the logs of drift-wood, — the fresh shrub, floating with its leaves and berries, — the flocks of land-birds, — the shoals of fish that inhabit shallow water,— the indescribable smell of the shore, — the mysterious presentiment that seems ever to go before a great event, — and finally, on that ever-memorable night of the 12th of October, 1492, the moving light seen by the sleepless eye of the great discoverer himself, from the deck of the Santa Maria, and in the morning the real, undoubted land, swelling up from the bosom of the deep, with its plains, and hills, and forests, and rocks, and streams, and strange new races of men; — these are incidents in which the authentic history of the discovery of our Continent excels the specious wonders of romance, as much as gold excels tinsel, or the sun in the heavens outshines the flickering taper."
E. Everett.

Santa Maria ad Martyres. See Pantheon.

Santa Maria degli Angeli. [Holy Mary of the Angels.] A Roman church built by Michael Angelo out of a portion of the ruins of the Baths of Diocletian.

☞ "One of the largest and handsomest churches in Rome. It is Diocletian's bathing-room. Immense columns, each a single block of granite,

still stand proudly and unchanged from his time. In this church there is something very pleasant and refreshing, as if one were in the open air under the shade of the pine-trees, and at the same time all is so solitary, solemn, really Catholic! The walls display some of the finest paintings. Here is Domenichino's 'St. Sebastian,' and Carlo Maratti's 'Baptism of Christ.'"
Hans Christian Andersen.

Santa Maria dei Gesuiti. [St. Mary of the Jesuits.] A church in Venice, Italy. It contains an "Assumption" by Tintoretto, and a "Martyrdom of St. Lawrence" by Titian. [Called also *S. Maria Assunta.*]

☞ "In order to see this taste in full display, it is necessary to visit the Gèsu, . . . the central monument of the society [the Jesuits], built by Vignolles and Jacques della Porta in the last quarter of the sixteenth century. The grand pagan renaissance perpetuates itself here, but with modifications. . . . With the solidity of its foundation and the soundness of its forms, with the pompous majesty of its pilasters crowned with gilded capitals, its painted domes eddying with grand figures, its paintings framed in with borderings of sculptured gold, . . . this church resembles a magnificent banqueting hall, some regal *hôtel de ville* decked out with all its silver and glass . . . to receive a monarch and do him the honors of a city." *Taine, Trans.*

Santa Maria del Fiore. [Holy Mary of the Flower.] The cathedral or Duomo of Florence, Italy, begun in 1294, and finished by Brunelleschi in 1446. It is so called in allusion to the lily in the city arms of Florence, which perpetuates the tradition of its having been founded in a flowery field. The cupola is one of the largest domes in the world, and can be compared only to that of St. Peter's. Many eminent architects were engaged in the construction of this church, among whom in particular Giotto may be mentioned, by whom the famous campanile, or bell-tower, was designed. When Michael Angelo was asked to make the dome of St. Peter's excel that of the Cathedral of Florence, he said that he would make "its sister, greater, but not more beautiful."

☞ "As patroness of Florence in her own right, the Virgin bears the title of *Santa Maria del Fiore*, and in this character she holds a flower, generally a rose, or is in the act of presenting it to the Child." *Mrs. Jameson.*

☞ "Florence extended her walls for the third time. Arnolfo de Lapo, the famous architect, began to build the churches which yet stand there as the greatest and finest, and among them, most distinguished of all, Santa Maria del Fiore. He built it in a new style, — the Gothic, or as the Italians called it, the German, the free upward-rising proportions of which took the place of the more heavy and wide-spreading dimensions in which they had been built hitherto."
Grimm, Trans.

☞ "Around the Duomo, there is strife and bustle at all times: crowds come and go; men buy and sell; boys laugh and quarrel; but, in the midst of this, there is the Duomo unharmed and unpolluted, at the same time a prayer and poem." *Pascarel, Trans.*

☞ "The charm of the past in Florence is like the beauty of the majestic Duomo." *Pascarel, Trans.*

☞ "Among the greatest and most complete examples of Italian Gothic is the church of Sta. Maria dei Fiori, the cathedral of Florence, one of the largest and finest churches produced in the Middle Ages, — as far as mere grandeur of conception goes, perhaps the very best, though considerably marred in execution from defects of style which are too apparent in every part."
Fergusson.

Santa Maria del Popolo. A church in Rome, near the Porta del Popolo, said to have been founded in 1099.

☞ "A church of the fifteenth century, modernized by Bernini, but still impressive. Wide arcades in rows separate the great nave from the lesser ones, and the effect of these bold curves is grave and grand."
H. Taine, Trans.

Santa Maria dell' Ara Cœli. See ARA CŒLI.

Santa Maria della Salute. [Our Lady of Salvation.] A noble and conspicuous church in Venice, Italy, built in the early part of the seventeenth century, and fronting on the Grand Canal. It is a votive church, having been built as an offering to the Virgin for having stayed a pestilence which was devastating the city, from which circumstance the church takes its name.

When at last that boat darted forth upon the breadth of silver sea, across which the front of the Ducal Palace, flushed with its sanguine veins, looks to the snowy dome of *Our Lady of Salvation*, it was no marvel that the mind should be so deeply entranced by the visionary charm of a scene so beautiful and so strange, as to forget the darker truths of its history and its being. *Ruskin.*

Santa Maria di Rotonda. See PANTHEON.

Santa Maria Gloriosa dei Frari See FRARI, etc.

Santa Maria in Trastevere. A church in Rome, said to have been the first in the city consecrated to the Virgin. It was founded by St. Calixtus in 224, and was in early times known as Fons Olei, from a spring of oil which is said to have appeared there at the time of the Saviour's birth. The church was afterwards rebuilt, and has since been largely altered.

Santa Maria Maggiore. [St. Mary the Greater.] One of the principal Roman churches, and the third in rank. It was founded A.D. 352, by Pope Liberius, — hence often styled the *Liberian Basilica*, — and was originally called S. Maria ad Nives, from a legend that it was founded in fulfilment of a vision representing a fall of snow which covered the precise space to be occupied. This legend is the subject of two fine pictures by Murillo in the Gallery at Madrid. The basilica afterwards took its present name from being the principal of all the churches of Rome dedicated to the Virgin. This basilica is one of those which possesses a Porta Santa.

☞ "The basilica of Santa Maria Maggiore has little to be commended externally; but the interior, through all the changes which it has undergone, still retains the features of the basilica essentially unimpaired, and a single glance at its noble and harmonious proportions vindicates the taste and judgment of those who adapted that form to the purposes of Christian worship." *Hillard.*

☞ "This basilica, standing upon a large eminence, surmounted with its domes, rises nobly upwards, at once simple and complete; and when you enter it, it affords still greater pleasure. It belongs to the fifth century: on being rebuilt at a later period, the general plan, its antique idea, was preserved. An ample portico with a horizontal roof is sustained by two rows of white Ionic columns. You are rejoiced to see so fine an effect produced by such simple means." *Taine, Trans.*

Santa Maria Novella. [The New Church of the Holy Virgin.] A fine Gothic church in Florence, Italy, containing some fine paintings. The square in front of this church is the scene of many of the public festivities of the city. Michael Angelo thought this church very beautiful, and called it "the bride" (la Sposa).

☞ "The interior of Santa Maria Novella is spacious and in the Gothic style, though differing from English churches of that order of architecture. Its old walls are yet stalwart enough to outlast another set of frescos, and to see the beginning and the end of a new school of painting as long-lived as Cimabue's. I should be sorry to have the church go to decay, because it was here that Boccaccio's dames and cavaliers encountered one another." *Hawthorne.*

And, past the quays, Maria Novella's Place,
In which the mystic obelisks stand up
Triangular, pyramidal, each based
On a single trine of brazen tortoises,
To guard that fair church, Buonarotti's Bride,
That stares out from her large blind dial-eyes,
Her quadrant and armillary dials, black
With rhythms of many suns and moons, in vain
Inquiry for so rich a soul as his.
Mrs. Browning.

Or enter, in your Florence wanderings,
Santa Maria Novella church.
Mrs. Browning.

Santa Maria sopra Minerva. [The Holy Virgin upon Minerva.] The principal Gothic church in Rome, so called because it was built upon the ruins of a temple of Minerva. It contains many interesting relics of art and history.

Santa Petronilla. A famous picture by Giovanni Francesco Barbieri, called Guercino (1590–1666), representing the saint as "being raised from her tomb to be shown to Flaccus, her betrothed." In the Capitol at Rome.

Santa, Porta. See PORTA SANTA.

Santa Reparata. See SANTA MARIA DEL FIORE.

Santa Saba. This ancient convent is on a mountainous height overlooking the Dead Sea. It is about three hours ride from Jerusalem. The situation is wild and dreary in the extreme. It was founded by St. Saba in the fifth century, and tradition says that 14,000 anchorites followed him hither. Cyril, John Damascenus, and Euphemius lived here. It is said that this convent contains many inestimable manuscripts, but only Turks are allowed to see them. The building occupies a situation of wild grandeur, the irregular groups of towers, walls, and chapels being lodged upon narrow terraces in the rock, and clinging to the faces of precipices. Women are not allowed to enter the convent under any circumstances, the monks being, as Miss Martineau says, too holy to be hospitable.

Santa Scala. [The Holy Staircase.] A famous staircase consisting of 28 marble steps, on the north side of the Basilica of St. John Lateran at Rome. According to the church tradition, they belonged to the house of Pilate, and are the very steps descended by the Saviour when he left the judgment-seat. Penitents can ascend only upon their knees, and the multitude of the faithful who visit them is so great that it has been found necessary to protect the steps by planks of wood. For 1500 years this staircase has been regarded with special veneration by the Roman Church. In a chapel of a church on the summit of the Kreuzberg, near Bonn, on the Rhine, is a marble staircase built by the Elector Clement Augustus, in 1725, in *imitation* of the Scala Santa, which, like the latter, is believed by the faithful to be the identical staircase which led to Pilate's Judgment Hall, and which no one is allowed to ascend except on his knees.

☞ "These holy steps that pious knees have worn till they are almost worn away, have now been cased in wood. . . . Go when you will, except on a grand *festa* — you cannot fail to see various sinners creeping up it on their knees, repeating on every step a Paternoster and an Ave Maria. . . . I am told the ascenders of this Holy Staircase gain three thousand years' indulgence every time of mounting; but what temptation is that in a church where indulgences for thirty-nine thousand years may be bought on the festa of the patron saint?" *C. A. Eaton.*

☞ "It is covered with wood, and the devout ascend it on their knees. I have just seen these people staggering and climbing up: it takes half an hour thus to hoist themselves to the top, clinging to its steps and walls with their hands the better to become impregnated with the sanctity of the place. It is worth while to see their earnestness, their large fixed eyes. . . . One would imagine himself in a Buddhist country: there is gilding for the better and relics for the poorer classes — such is the comprehension of worship in Italy for the last two hundred years." *Taine, Trans.*

☞ "I never, in my life, saw any thing at once so ridiculous, and so unpleasant, as this sight, — ridiculous in the absurd incidents inseparable from it; and unpleasant in its senseless and unmeaning degradation. There are two steps to begin with, and then a rather broad landing. The more rigid climbers went along this landing on their knees, as well as up the stairs; and the figures they cut, in their shuffling progress over the level surface, no description can paint. Then, to see them watch their opportunity from the porch, and cut in where there was a place next the wall! And to see one man with an umbrella (brought on purpose, for it was a fine day) hoisting himself, unlawfully, from stair to stair! And to observe a demure lady of fifty-five or so, looking back, every now and then, to assure herself that her legs were properly disposed! There were such odd differences in the speed of different people too. Some got on as if they were doing a match against time; others stopped to say a prayer on every step. This man touched every stair with his forehead, and kissed it; that man scratched his head all the way. . . . But most of the Peni-

tents came down very sprightly and fresh, as having done a real good substantial deed, which it would take a good deal of sin to counterbalance."
Dickens.

The pious monk [Luther] climbing the *Santa Scala* painfully on his knees among the retinue of pilgrims. *Chr. Examiner.*

Brother Martin Luther went to accomplish the ascent of the *Santa Scala*, which once, they say, formed part of Pilate's house. *Schönberg-Cotta Chronicles.*

Santissimo Bambino. See BAMBINO.

Santo Chiodo. [The Holy Nail.] See IRON CROWN.

Santo Eremo. See SACRO EREMO.

Santo Spirito. A well-known and interesting church of the fourteenth century, in Florence, Italy.

Santo Volto. [Holy Face.] A crucifix preserved in the cathedral of Lucca, Italy, and held in the utmost veneration by the people. The tradition is, that it is the work of Nicodemus, who sculptured it from memory. There are references to be found also to another Santo Volto in the church of Santa Croce at Florence.

The other sank, and rose again face downward;
But the demons, under cover of the bridge,
Cried: "Here the *Santo Volto* has no place!

Here swims one otherwise than in the Serchio;
Therefore, if for our gaffs thou wishest not,
Do not uplift thyself above the pitch."
Dante, Inferno, Trans. of Longfellow.

Sappho's Leap. The name given to a white cliff or promontory anciently called Leucadia, now Cape Ducato, at the southern extremity of Santa Maura, one of the Ionian Islands. It was so called because Sappho, the poetess, is reported to have thrown herself from this height into the sea. A criminal, with birds attached to him to break his fall, was thrown from this cliff at the annual festival of Apollo; and, if he reached the water unhurt, he was picked up by boats placed there for the purpose. This is the rock from which, according to the story, lovers threw themselves in order to be free from the pangs of love.

☞ "I shall in this paper discharge myself of the promise I have made to the public by obliging them with a translation of the little Greek manuscript, which is said to have been preserved in the Temple of Apollo upon the promontory of Leucate. It is a short history of the 'Lover's Leap.' [Here follows a humorous account of various persons who threw themselves from the precipice.] . . . Sappho the Lesbian arrived at the Temple of Apollo, habited like a bride. After having sung a hymn to Apollo, she hung up her garland on one side of his altar and her harp on the other. She then tucked up her vestments like a Spartan virgin, and amidst thousands of spectators who were anxious for her safety, marched directly forward to the utmost summit of the promontory, where, after having repeated a stanza of her own verses, which we could not hear, she threw herself off the rock with such an intrepidity as was never before observed in any one who had attempted that dangerous leap. . . . Alcæus, the famous lyric poet, who had been some time passionately in love with Sappho, arrived at the promontory of Leucate that very evening in order to take the leap upon her account; but hearing that Sappho had been there before him, and that her body could be nowhere found — he very generously lamented her fall, and is said to have written his hundred and twenty-fifth ode upon that occasion."
Addison, Spectator.

"Sappho's Leap of course was the great point of interest. It is a precipice about two hundred feet in height, near the southern extremity of the island, and, I should judge, well adapted for the old lady's purpose."
Bayard Taylor.

There stands a rock, from whose impending steep
Apollo's fane surveys the rolling deep;
There injured lovers, leaping from above,
Their flames extinguish and forget to love.
Deucalion once with hopeless fury burned,
In vain he loved — relentless Pyrrha scorned:
But when from hence he plunged into the main,
Deucalion scorned, and Pyrrha loved in vain
Haste, Sappho, haste, from high Leucadia throw
Thy wretched weight, nor dread the deeps below!
Ovid, Tr. Pope.

'Twas on a Grecian autumn's gentle eve
Childe Harold hailed Leucadia's cape afar
. . . .

But when he saw the evening star above
Leucadia's far-projecting cape of woe,
And hailed the last resort of fruitless love,
He felt, or deemed he felt, no common
glow. *Byron.*

Saratoga. A mansion near Berryville, Va., once the residence of Gen. Daniel Morgan (1736–1802), who is said to have built the house with the help of Hessians taken prisoners at Saratoga.

Saratoga, The. A noted vessel, the flag-ship of the American fleet under Commodore Macdonough, in the naval battle on Lake Champlain in September, 1814. The Saratoga took the *Confiance*, the flag-ship of the British fleet.

Sardanapalus. A picture by Ferdinand Victor Eugène Delacroix (1799–1863), the celebrated French historical painter.

Sarto, Andrea del. See ANDREA DEL SARTO.

Sasso di Dante. See DANTE'S STONE.

Saturday Club. An old club in London. Swift writes to Stella in 1711 that there were Lord Keeper, Lord Rivers, Mr. Secretary, Mr. Harley, and himself; and again, in 1713, "I was of the original Club, when only poor Lord Rivers, Lord Keeper, and Lord Bolingbroke came; but now Ormond, Anglesey, Lord Stewart, Dartmouth, and other rabble intrude, and I scold at it; but now they pretend as good a title as I; and, indeed, many Saturdays I am not there. The company being too many, I don't love it."

Saturn, Temple of. See TEMPLE OF SATURN.

Saturnian Hill. See CAPITOLINE HILL.

Saul and the Witch of Endor. A picture by Washington Allston (1779–1843). Formely in possession of Col. T. H. Perkins, Boston.

Savin Rock. A bluff on Long Island Sound, near New Haven, Conn., and a favorite place of resort for the inhabitants.

Saviour, St. See ST. SAVIOUR.

Savoir Vivre Club. See BOODLE'S CLUB.

Savonarola. A portrait by Fra Bartolommeo (*Della Porta*) (1469–1517). In the Museum of St. Mark, Florence, Italy.

Savoy, The. A noted palace which once stood in London, all remains of which were removed upon the building of Waterloo Bridge. The Savoy was built on ground granted to Peter, Earl of Savoy, and magnificently rebuilt by Henry, first Duke of Lancaster, it having been purchased by Queen Eleanor. There lived the captive King John of France, who died there in 1364. The poet Chaucer was married in the Savoy to Philippa de Ruet. The palace was destroyed by the rebels under Wat Tyler in 1381, but was rebuilt as a hospital by Henry VII. Part of the Savoy was used as a prison.

☞ "Still aiming at the lawyers, the people attacked the Temple and burned it, with the records which it contained. They proceeded next to destroy the Savoy Palace belonging to the Duke of Lancaster, the most beautiful house in England, and afterwards the Hospital of the Knights of Rhodes, the bloody axe beating time to their march, and every supposed enemy of popular rights that was unable to escape being dragged to the block." *Froude.*

The comons brent the *Sauoye* a place fayre
For evill wyll the hand unto Duke John:
Wherefore he fled northwarde in great dispayre
Into Scotlande. *Hardyng's Chronicle.*

Cade. So, sirs. — Now go some and pull down the *Savoy*. *King Henry VI., Part II.*

Not content with the easy victories which he [Dr. William Sherlock] gained over such feeble antagonists as those who were quartered at Clerkenwell and the *Savoy*, he had the courage to measure his strength with no less a champion than Bossuet, and came out of the conflict without discredit. *Macaulay.*

Scala, La. A celebrated theatre in Milan, Italy, of great size, surpassed only by that of San Carlo at Naples.

He carried me immediately to his box in the great theatre *Della Scala;* for here everybody goes every evening to the play, and what society there is . . . is at this great exchange and lounge.
George Ticknor (*in* 1817).

I fancy that to find good Italian opera you must seek it somewhere out of Italy, — though possibly it might be chanced upon at *La Scala* in Milan, or San Carlo in Naples.
W. D. Howells.

Scala dei Giganti. See GIANT'S STAIRCASE.

Scala d'Oro. See GOLDEN STAIRCASE.

Scala Regia. [Royal Staircase.] A staircase in the palace of the Vatican in Rome, a magnificent work of Bernini, leading to the Sala Regia.

Scaligers, Tombs of the. See TOMBS OF THE SCALIGERS.

Sceleratus, Vicus. See VICUS SCELERATUS.

Schaffhausen. See FALL OF SCHAFFHAUSEN.

Schiava di Tiziano. [Titian's Slave.] A picture in the Barberini Palace, Rome. It is now attributed to Jacopo Palma, called Palma Vecchio (1480?-1548).

Schiavi, Torre di. See TORRE DI SCHIAVI.

Schleissheim. A deserted palace in the vicinity of Munich, which once contained a celebrated gallery of pictures. It still contains the Crucifixion, by Tintoretto, one of the largest pictures in the world.

Schönberg. A ruined castle on the Rhine, near Oberwesel, associated with romantic legends.

Schönberg Cotta House. The famous house in Eisenach, Germany, in which Martin Luther once lived. "The house has an antique, tumble-down appearance, owing to its top-heavy style, but was evidently rather a fine house in its day, though the interior arrangements must always have been inferior. The rooms are very small, with tiny windows. The bedroom is like a prison-cell, and the sitting-room is only a trifle larger." Mrs. E. R. Charles wrote "Chronicles of the Schönberg-Cotta Family."

Schönbrunn. The summer palace of the Emperor of Austria, about two miles from Vienna. It derives its name from a beautiful fountain (Schöne Brunnen) at the end of one of the alleys in the garden. The palace was built by the Empress Maria Theresa, and was occupied by Napoleon in 1809, when Vienna was in the hands of the French.

Shall Belgium feel, and gallant France,
By Vendome's pile and *Schoenbrun's* wall,
And Poland, gasping on her lance,
The impulse of our cheering call?
Whittier.

Schöne Brunnen. [Beautiful Fountains.] A fine work of monumental art in the market-place at Nuremberg, Germany.

☞ "One of the most unexceptionable pieces of German design in existence. It much resembles the contemporary crosses erected by our Edward I. to the memory of his beloved queen Eleanor; but it is larger and taller, the sculpture better, and better disposed, and the whole design perhaps unrivalled among monuments of its class."
Fergusson.

Schönforst. A ruined castle near Aix-la-Chapelle in Rhenish Prussia.

School of Athens. The popular title of a celebrated fresco by Raphael Sanzio (1483-1520) in the *Camera della Segnatura* of the Vatican Palace in Rome. Its proper subject is PHILOSOPHY, and it is one of four paintings which the chamber contains, the other three illustrating respectively THEOLOGY, POETRY, and JURISPRUDENCE, and which were intended to exhibit the lofty subjects of thought with which the human mind is occupied.

☞ "The general arrangement of this subject [the School of Athens] is masterly. The style is grand and free; a picturesque unity of effect seems to have been the artist's aim throughout, and this aim he has attained most per-

fectly. . . . The group of youths in particular assembled around Archimedes, is among the most interesting and natural of Raphael's creations."
Eastlake.

☞ "In the composition and execution of the 'School of Athens,' Raphael had recovered, so to speak, the long-lost thread of the manner and taste of antiquity, and had at length connected with the eternal models of the true and beautiful the chain of modern inventions."
Quatremère de Quincy.

Schoolmaster. See TITIAN'S SCHOOLMASTER.

Schuyler, Fort. See FORT SCHUYLER.

Schwedenstein. [Stone of the Swede.] A monument erected on the battle-field of Lützen, Germany, to mark the spot where Gustavus Adolphus fell Nov. 6, 1632.

Sciarra Palace. [Ital. *Palazzo Sciarra.*] A palace on the Corso, Rome, built in 1603 by Labacco, and containing a small gallery of pictures in which are some fine works of art.

Sciences, Académie des. One of the five academies embraced in the Institut, the most important learned society of France. It is devoted to purely scientific, moral, and political objects. It was founded in 1795, suppressed by Napoleon in 1803, and re-established by the government of Louis Philippe in 1832. See INSTITUT.

Scimia, Torre della. See TORRE DELLA SCIMIA.

Scipios, Tombs of the. See TOMBS OF THE SCIPIOS.

Scollop Shell Cave. A natural curiosity in the island of Staffa, in Scotland. It derives its name from the peculiar shape of the basaltic columns, which are bent in such a way as to give them the appearance of a ship's timbers, or of a scollop shell.

Scone Palace. The parish of Scone with its castle was formerly one of the most important places in Scotland. The Scottish kings were crowned in the abbey which stood here, and of which only a part of an aisle and a cross remain. On the ancient site near Perth stands a modern mansion, called Scone Palace, the seat of Lord Mansfield. See STONE OF SCONE.

This castle hath a pleasant seat: the air
Nimbly and sweetly recommends itself
Unto our gentle senses. *Shakespeare.*

Scone, Stone of. See STONE OF SCONE.

Scorpion, The. An armor-plated ship of the British navy, launched July 4, 1863.

Scotland Yard. A place in London said to derive its name from the fact of its being the site of a palace in which the kings of Scotland were received when they came to England, and now widely known as the headquarters of the metropolitan police. Scotland Yard is near the Banqueting House, Whitehall. It remained in the possession of the kings of Scotland from 959 (the time of King Edgar) till the rebellion of William of Scotland (reign of Henry II.). Milton, Inigo Jones, Sir John Denham, Sir Christopher Wren, lived in Scotland Yard. No one could be arrested for debt within the limits of Scotland Yard.

Much of this had occurred before the intelligence of *Scotland Yard* had been set to work by Judge Bramber.
Anthony Trollope.

Scott Monument. A memorial structure 200 feet in height, in Edinburgh, Scotland, erected in 1844 in honor of Sir Walter Scott (1771-1832), and designed to imitate Melrose Abbey. It consists of a pile of arches diminishing in size towards the top, with 56 niches for statues of some of the chief characters in the stories of the great novelist. Beneath the main arches is a statue of Scott himself and his dog, by Steele.

☞ "Most conspicuous and beautiful of all objects, rises 200 feet an elaborate brown-stone Gothic spire in the shape of a mediæval cross, and noblest example of that style ever reared, — indeed, one of the noblest open-air monuments on earth, the just and honorable memorial of Scotland to Sir Walter Scott." *J. F. Hunnewell.*

Scottish Raid. A picture by Rosa Bonheur (b. 1822), the celebrated French painter of animals.

Scriblerus Club. This famous association in London, formed in 1714 by Dean Swift in place of the Brothers Club, was of a literary rather than political character. Arbuthnot, Pope, Gay, Oxford, and St. John were members. The chief object of the club was to satirize the abuse of human learning; but violent disagreements between Oxford and Bolingbroke, which Swift tried in vain to settle, led to the final dissolution of the society. Scott says that the violence of political faction "dispersed this little band of literary brethren, and prevented the accomplishment of a task for which talents so various, so extended, and so brilliant, can never again be united." The "Memoirs of P. P., Clerk of the Parish," and the famous "Gulliver's Travels," preserve the memory of the Scriblerus Club. Dyce says, "In the *Miscellanies* of Pope and Swift, was printed, for the first time, *Martinus Scriblerus* ΠΕΡΙ ΒΑΘΟΥΣ, *or the Art of Sinking in Poetry*, of which the greater part, if not the whole, was composed by Pope. It was intended to form a portion of that larger work, which the members of the Scriblerus Club, particularly Pope, Swift, Arbuthnot, and Lord Oxford, had projected many years before."

☞ "Polite letters never lost more than by the defeat of this scheme, in which each of this illustrious triumvirate [Pope, Swift, and Arbuthnot] would have found exercise for his own peculiar talent, besides constant employment for that they all held in common. For Arbuthnot was skilled in every thing which related to science; Pope was a master in the fine arts; and Swift excelled in a knowledge of the world. Wit they had all in equal measure; and this so large, that no age perhaps ever produced three men to whom nature had more bountifully bestowed it, or art had brought it to higher perfection." *Warburton.*

☞ "The name originated as follows: Oxford used playfully to call Swift *Martin*, and from this sprung Martinus Scriblerus. *Swift*, as is well known, is the name of one species of swallow (the largest and most powerful flyer of the tribe), and Martin is the name of another species, the wall-swallow, which constructs its nest in buildings." *Timbs.*

Scuola di San Rocco. See San Rocco.

Scylla. Now called Sciglio. A celebrated promontory of Italy on the Strait of Messina. It is opposite to Charybdis, where are numerous rocks and shoals with strong currents, making the passage between the headlands and the whirlpool somewhat difficult, and giving rise to the proverbial expression, to "avoid Scylla and fall on Charybdis." According to ancient fable, a terrible monster named Scylla inhabited a cave in the promontory called after him, and devoured the rash voyagers who approached too near.

☞ "Scylla and Charybdis are far-famed names. . . . Where is Scylla? 'Yes, she still lives.' They pointed to a little jutting rock, with a dark ruinous tower, on the wild coast of Calabria. There was a heavy surf here, though the sea was tolerably calm. Blackish gray rocks jutted forth, against which the waves dashed with angry roar. It was Scylla's howling dog we saw. I think they may be able to hear it in a storm from the sandy isthmus of Messina." *Hans Christian Andersen.*

Thus when I shun *Scylla*, your father,
I fall into Charybdis, your mother.
Shakespeare.

Seal, The Great. See Great Seal.

Sealed Knot. An old Royalist club of London. Just before the Restoration it had arranged for a general uprising in favor of the king; but the leaders, having been informed against, were arrested and imprisoned.

Seasons. See Four Seasons.

Sebald. See ST. SEBALD'S TOMB.

Sebaldus. See SHRINE OF ST. SEBALDUS.

Sebastian, St. See ST. SEBASTIAN and CATACOMBS OF ST. SEBASTIAN.

Sebastiano, San. See SAN SEBASTIANO and PORTA DI SAN SEBASTIANO.

Sébastopol, Boulevart de. A wide, magnificent street in Paris, one of the new boulevards, lined with trees, and reaching from the Strasbourg Railway terminus to the Seine, the part between the railway-station and the B. St. Denis being known as the Boulevart de Strasbourg. See BOULEVARDS.

☞ "Any one who has traced on an old map of Paris the labyrinth of dark and narrow streets through which the Rue de Rivoli has boldly cut, or who can remember the former aspect of those quarters now intersected by the Boulevart Sébastopol and other thoroughfares, will bear witness to the almost magical effect of a transformation which the social economist or the sanitary commissioner indeed may view with satisfaction, but which the artist and antiquarian cannot but deplore."
C. L. Eastlake.

Secchia Rapita. [The Stolen Bucket.] A famous relic, and the subject of Tassoni's celebrated poem of the same name, now preserved in the Ghirlandina, or bell-tower, of Modena, Italy.

If thou shouldst ever come by choice or chance
To Modena, where still religiously
Among her ancient trophies is preserved
Bologna's bucket (in its chain it hangs
Within that reverend tower, the Guirlandine).
Rogers.

Sefton Park. A fine pleasure-ground in Liverpool, England, covering 200 acres and elaborately laid out.

Segnatura, Stanza della. See STANZE OF RAPHAEL.

Segovia, Bridge of. See PUENTE DEL DIABLO.

Seine, Rue de. A well-known street in Paris, France.

1644, March 1. I went to see the Count de Liancourt's palace in the *Rue de Seine*, which is well built. *John Evelyn, Diary*,

They have no Rue de la Harpe or Rue St. Denis here [Ostia]: I was reminded of nothing at Paris but the *Rue de Seine*, or the Quai des Augustins.
Montaigne, Trans.

Passing from thence up the picturesque *Rue de Seine*, let us walk to the Luxembourg, where bonnes, students, grisettes, and old gentlemen with pigtails, love to wander in the melancholy, quaint old gardens. *Thackeray.*

Ah, Clemence! when I saw thee last
Trip down the *Rue de Seine*,
And turning, when thy form had passed,
I said, "We meet again." *Holmes.*

Selsker Abbey. A beautiful monastic ruin of the twelfth century in Wexford county, Ireland. The name is a corruption of St. Sepulchre.

Selva de' Filosofi. [Wood of the Philosophers.] A picture by Salvator Rosa (1615-1673). In the Pitti Palace, Florence, Italy.

Seminary Ridge. An eminence in the western part of the town of Gettysburg, Penn., famous in connection with the great battle of July 3, 1863. The hill was occupied by the troops of Gen. Lee, and from this point three columns advanced into the valley and charged the Federal lines.

Senator, Palace of the. See PIAZZA DEL CAMPIDOGLIO.

Sennacherib's Palace. The great metropolitan palace of Nineveh, built by Sennacherib, the Assyrian king. It stands upon a mound about a mile and a half in circumference.

☞ "Judging even from what has as yet been uncovered, it is, of all the buildings of antiquity, alone surpassed in magnitude by the great palace-temple at Karnak; and when we consider the vastness of the mound on which it was raised, and the richness of the ornaments with which it was adorned, a doubt arises whether it was not as great or at least as expensive a work as the great palace-temples of Thebes. The latter, however, were built with far higher motives, and designed to last through ages, while the palace at Nineveh was built only to gratify the bar-

baric pride of a wealthy and sensual monarch, and perished with the ephemeral dynasty to which he belonged."
Fergusson.

Septimius Severus, Arch of. See ARCH OF SEPTIMIUS SEVERUS.

Sepulchre's, St. See ST. SEPULCHRE'S.

Seraglio, The. The former palace of the Sultan of Turkey in Constantinople. It is beautifully situated on a point of land extending into the sea, and contains, within the area of nine miles which are embraced by its walls, several mosques, gardens, and buildings, capable of accommodating 15,000 or 20,000 persons.

☞ "The palace of the Seraglio, the cloister with marble pillars, the hall of the ambassadors, the impenetrable gate guarded by eunuchs and ichoglaus, have a romantic look in print; but not so in reality. Most of the marble is wood, almost all the gilding is faded, the guards are shabby, the foolish perspectives painted on the walls are half cracked off. The place looks like Vauxhall in the daytime." *Thackeray.*

☞ "The old Seraglio is a dark-red, noble-looking pile, but somewhat heavy in comparison with the rest of the environs. The new Seraglio looks handsome and invites the eye. Round about stand splendid kiosks, where rich marble columns support the glittering spiral roofs."
Hans Christian Andersen.

Serapéum (*or* **Serapion**), **The.** This ancient edifice of Alexandria, Egypt, was founded by Ptolemy Soter, in honor of Serapis, a foreign deity, to whom he erected a statue. It was the last stronghold of the Pagans in Alexandria, and was besieged by the Christians and zealously defended by the Pagans, A.D. 389, when Theodosius put an end to the conflict by an imperial order that the idols of Alexandria should be destroyed. According to some ancient writers Pompey's Pillar is a relique of this magnificent building. Three hundred thousand volumes, of the 700,000 of which the Alexandrian Library consisted, were in the Serapeum.

☞ "Gibbon says that the temple of Serapis, which "rivalled the pride and magnificence of the Capitol, was erected on the spacious summit of an artificial mount, raised 100 steps above the level of the adjacent parts of the city; and the interior cavity was strongly supported by arches, and distributed into vaults and subterraneous apartments. The consecrated buildings were surrounded by a quadrangular portico: the stately halls, the exquisite statues, displayed the triumph of the arts; and the treasures of ancient learning were preserved in the famous Alexandrian Library, which had arisen with new splendor from its ashes." He adds with reference to the conflict of the Christians and Pagans and the final destruction of the Serapeum: "The votaries of Serapis, whose strength and numbers were much inferior to those of their antagonists, rose in arms, at the instigation of the philosopher Olympius, who exhorted them to die in defence of the altars of the gods. These Pagan fanatics fortified themselves in the temple, or rather fortress of Serapis, repelled the besiegers by daring sallies and a resolute defence. . . . The efforts of the prudent magistrate were usefully exerted for the establishment of a truce, till the answer of Theodosius should determine the fate of Serapis. The two parties assembled without arms in the principal square; and the imperial rescript was publicly read. But when a sentence of destruction against the idols of Alexandria was pronounced, the Christians set up a shout of joy and exultation, whilst the unfortunate Pagans, whose fury had given way to consternation, retired with hasty and silent steps, and eluded by their flight or obscurity the resentment of their enemies. Theophilus proceeded to demolish the temple of Serapis, without any other difficulties than those which he found in the weight and solidity of the materials; but these obstacles proved so insuperable, that he was obliged to leave the foundations, and to content himself with reducing the edifice itself to a heap of rubbish. . . . The colossal statue of Serapis was involved in the ruin of this temple and religion. . . . The huge idol was overthrown and broken to pieces; and the parts of Serapis were ignominiously dragged through the streets of Alexandria."

☞ "The Serapeum was the Palladium of the Egyptian religion and of the Greek philosophy. At the time of its destruction it represented the alliance which these two had completed against their enemy, the Christian religion." *M. Ampère, Trans.*

Rome herself had received with rapture the strange rites of Nilotic and of Syrian superstition. . . . In his villa at Tivoli, he [Hadrian) built a *Serapeum.*
J. A. Symonds.

Serapeum. See APIS MAUSOLEUM.

Serapion. See SERAPEUM.

Serapis, The. A British frigate captured off Scarborough, England, in 1779, by John Paul Jones, commander of the *Bon Homme Richard.*

Serbonian Bog. A swamp of great extent in ancient times near Damietta in Egypt.

A gulf profound, as that *Serbonian bog*
Betwixt Damiata and Mount Casius old,
Where armies whole have sunk.
Milton.

Much of this barrenness is, I am persuaded, to be charged to the philosophy of Kant, which for nearly 20 years ruled unquestioned, and absorbed and perverted all the talents of the land. It was a vast "*Serbonian bog*, where armies whole have sunk," and from which even the proud and original genius of Schiller hardly escaped. *George Ticknor.*

Sermon on the Mount. A fresco painting by Cosimo Rosselli (1439–1506). In the Sistine Chapel, Rome.

Serpentine, The. A pool of water covering 50 acres in Hyde Park, London, formed by order of Caroline, queen of George II., and so called in distinction from the previous straight canals. Here 200,000 persons are said to bathe annually. In the winter it is used as a skating-field.

Serra Palace. [Ital. *Palazzo Serra.*] A noted palace in Genoa, Italy.

Serrant. A château in France, near Angers, the country-seat of Count Walsh.

Servant Maid. See IDLE SERVANT MAID.

Servius Tullius. See AGGER OF SERVIUS TULLIUS.

Sethi I., Tomb of. See BELZONI'S TOMB.

Seven Churches [of Asia]. A collective name given to the Christian churches established at Ephesus, Smyrna, Pergamos, Thyatira, Sardis, Philadelphia, and Laodicea, all in Asia Minor. They are spoken of in the Book of Revelation i. 4.

Seven Dials. A celebrated locality in St. Giles's, London, formerly notorious for its degraded condition, but now much improved. It was so named from a pillar, removed in 1773, bearing a seven-faced dial, and standing at the point of divergence of seven streets. See ST. GILES'S.

Where famed St. Giles's ancient limits spread,
An in-rail'd column rears its lofty head;
Here to seven streets seven dials count their day,
And from each other catch the circling ray. *Gay.*

I went to see the building near St. Giles's, where seven streets made a star, from a Doric pillar placed in the centre of a circular area, said to be built . . . in imitation of those at Venice. *Evelyn.*

There are many by-streets [in New York] almost as neutral in clean colors, and positive in dirty ones, as by-streets in London; and there is one quarter, commonly called the Five Points, which, in respect of filth and wretchedness, may be safely backed against *Seven Dials*, or any other part of famed St. Giles's. *Dickens.*

Seven Hills [of Rome]. The heights or eminences upon which the ancient city of Rome was built, though not all of them obvious at a glance, can be recognized without much difficulty, and are usually enumerated as follows: the Capitoline, the Palatine, the Aventine, the Cœlian, the Esquiline, the Quirinal, and the Viminal. See these hills under their respective names.

But I will sing above all monuments,
Seven Roman hills — the world's seven wonderments.
. . . .
Jove fearing, least if she should greater growe,
The Giants old should once againe uprise,
Her whelm'd with hills, these Seven Hils which be nowe
Tombes of her greatnes which did threate the skies:
Upon her head he heapt Mount Saturnal,
Upon her bellie th' antique Palatine,
Upon her stomacke laid Mount Quirinal,
On her left hand the noysome Esquiline,
And Coelian on the right: but both her feete
Mount Viminal and Aventine doo meete.
Spenser, The Ruins of Rome.

Seven Joys of Mary. [Ger. *Die sieben Freuden Maria.*] A noted picture by Hans Memling (d. 1499?). In the Gallery at Munich, Bavaria.

Seven Pines. A locality a few miles from Richmond, Va., on the Williamsburg road, so called from seven large pines. At this spot, on the 31st of May, 1862, a severe but indecisive battle was fought between the Union and the Confederate armies, under the command of Gen. McClellan and Gen. Johnston respectively.

Seven Sacraments. A picture by Roger van der Weyden (d. 1464), the Flemish painter. It was executed for Jean Chevrot, Bishop of Tournai, and is now in the Museum of Antwerp, Belgium.

Seven Sacraments. A series of pictures by Nicholas Poussin (1594–1665), the French painter, and among his most important works. Now in England.

Seven Towers. A state prison in Constantinople, Turkey, near the former palace of the Sultan, the Seraglio.

> But then they never came to the *Seven Towers.* *Byron.*

Seven Wonders of the World. The seven wonders of the ancient world have been differently enumerated, but the following list is that generally received: the Pyramids of Egypt, the Pharos of Alexandria, the walls and hanging gardens of Babylon, the temple of Diana at Ephesus, the statue of Jupiter by Phidias at Olympia, the Mausoleum built by Artemisia at Halicarnassus, and the Colossus of Rhodes.

Seven Works of Mercy. A picture by David Teniers the Younger (1610-1694?), the Belgian *genre*-painter. Now in the Louvre, at Paris.

Seven Years of Famine. A fresco painting illustrating the history of Joseph, by Friedrich Overbeck (1789–1869). In the villa of the consul-general Bartholdy, in Rome.

Sevendroog Castle. A tower erected by Sir W. James on Shooter's Hill near London, to commemorate his capture of a fort of the same name in India.

1789, Club of. See FEUILLANT CLUB.

Séverin, St. See ST. SÉVERIN.

Severus (Septimius), Arch of. See ARCH OF SEPTIMIUS SEVERUS.

Severus' Wall. See HADRIAN'S WALL.

Shadow of Death. A noted picture by William Holman Hunt (b. 1827), representing Christ in the carpenter's shop. It was sold for £10,000.

Shadwell Street. A street in London, and one of the poorest and most wretched districts.

> ☞ "Shadwell . . . is close at hand; by the vastness of its distress and by its extent, it is in keeping with the hugeness and wealth of London. I have seen the bad quarters of Marseilles, of Antwerp, of Paris: they do not come near to it." *Taine, Trans.*

Shaftesbury House. A noble mansion, formerly the residence of the Earl of Shaftesbury, still standing in Aldersgate Street, London.

Shakespeare and his Contemporaries. A picture by Thomas Faed (b. 1826), well known by numerous repetitions. The original is in the Corcoran Gallery, Washington.

Shakespeare Tavern. A well-known theatrical tavern which was situated in Covent Garden, London. It is said to have been the first tavern in Covent Garden, and the first in the metropolis that had rooms. There was another of the same name opposite Drury-lane Theatre.

Shakespeare's Cliff. A bold cliff of chalk at Dover, England, so called from the description in

"King Lear," which it is thought to have suggested.

There is a cliff whose high and bending head
Looks fearfully in the confinèd deep.
Shakespeare.

Shakespeare's House. 1. The famous house in which the poet was born, situated in Henley Street, Stratford-on-Avon, England. It has recently been purchased by subscription, with a view to the careful preservation of it and of its contents for the inspection of future generations.

☞ "It is a small, mean-looking edifice of wood and plaster, a true nestling-place of genius, which seems to delight in hatching its offspring in by-corners. The walls of its squalid chambers are covered with names and inscriptions in every language, by pilgrims of all nations, ranks, and conditions, from the prince to the peasant; and present a simple but striking instance of the spontaneous and universal homage of mankind to the great poet of nature." *Irving.*

☞ "The part of the house which is shown consists of a lower room which is floored with flat stones very much broken. It has a wide, old-fashioned chimney on one side, and opens into a smaller room back of it. From thence you go up a rude flight of stairs to a low-studded room, with rough-plastered walls, where the poet was born. . . . Though scrupulously neat and clean, the air of it is ancient and rude. The roughly-plastered walls are so covered with names that it seemed impossible to add another. The name of almost every modern genius, names of kings, princes, dukes, are shown here; and it is really curious to see by what devices some very insignificant personages have endeavored to make their own names conspicuous in the crowd." *Mrs. H. B. Stowe.*

☞ "Neglect, subdivision, and base uses had reduced this house at the beginning of the present century to a very forlorn and unsightly condition. But as late as 1769 it preserved enough of its original form to show that William Shakespeare was born and passed his childhood and his adolescent years in a home which was not only pretty and picturesque, but very comfortable and unusually commodious for a man in his father's station in the middle of the sixteenth century. . . . In 1847 the Shakespeare house passed into the hands of an association, under whose care it has been renovated; but unfortunately, like some of the Shakespeare poetry, not restored to a close resemblance to its first condition; though that was perhaps impossible." *Richard Grant White.*

Coleridge was singularly destitute of sympathy with local associations, which he regarded as interfering with the pure and simple impression of great deeds or thoughts, denied a special interest to the pass of Thermopylæ; and, instead of subscribing to purchase "*Shakespeare's House*," would scarcely have admitted the peculiar sanctity of the spot which enshrines his ashes. *T. N. Talfourd.*

2. An old house still standing in Aldersgate, London, to which Shakespeare's name has been affixed without any apparent warrant. It was formerly, under the name of the Half Moon Tavern, a great resort of literary men.

Shakespeare's Monument. On the north wall of the church in Stratford-on-Avon, just above the grave of the poet, a monument was erected to his memory, the precise date of which is unknown. From references to it in the first folio edition of Shakespeare's plays, it is certain that the monument was erected prior to 1623. It exhibits a bust of the poet in the act of writing. Beneath is a tablet with the following inscription:—

IVDICIO PYLIVM, GENIO SOCRATEM, ARTE MARONEM
TERRA TEGIT, POPVLVS MÆRET, OLYMPVS HABET.

Stay Passenger, why goest thov by so fast?
Read if thov canst, whom enviovs Death hath plast,
With in this monvment, Shakspeare with whome
Qvick natvre dide, whose name doth deck ys Tombe
Far more then cost: Sich all yt He hath writ it,
Leaves living art, but page, to serve his witt.

Obiit ano Dó. 1616
Ætatis, 53, Die 23 A D.

☞ "The last line of this inscription, and a tradition unheard of until Oldys wrote his notes in Langbaine, have raised the question whether Shakespeare died on the same day of the month on which he is supposed to have been born. . . . Dugdale tells us that his monument was the work of Gerard Johnson, an eminent sculptor of the period; others have attributed it to Thomas Stanton, and experts have supposed that the face was modelled from a cast taken after death. Be that as it may, the bust must be accepted as the most authentic likeness that we have of Shakespeare. It was originally colored after life. The eyes were light hazel, the hair and beard auburn, the complexion fair; the doublet was scarlet; the tabard, or loose gown without sleeves thrown over the doublet, black; the neck and wristbands white; the upper side of the cushion green, the under, crimson; its cord and tassels, gilt. The colors were renewed in 1749; but in 1793 Malone, tastelessly and ignorantly classic, had the whole figure painted white by a house painter." *Richard Grant White.*

Shakespeare's Tomb. In the church at Stratford-on-Avon. The grave, which is just in front of the chancel rail, is covered by a flat stone, bearing the inscription: —

Good frend for Jesvs sake forbeare,
to digg the dvst encloased heare:
Bleste be ye man yt spares thes stones,
and cvrst be he yt moves my bones.

Shane's Castle. A ruined castle in the county of Antrim, Ireland, the seat of the O'Neils, which "for centuries has been the chosen realm of the Banshee."

The Banshee mournful wails
In the midst of the silent, lonely night:
Plaintive she sings the song of death.

Shanklin Chine. A curious and celebrated ravine on the Isle of Wight, not far from Ventnor, much visited by tourists.

Shannon, The. A British war-ship which engaged in a duel with the American ship *Chesapeake*, off the coast of Marblehead, Mass., in June, 1813, and captured her. See CHESAPEAKE.

Shanter. A farm near Maybole, Scotland, where formerly lived Douglas Grahame, the original of Burns's Tam O'Shanter.

Sheepshanks Collection. A collection of 234 oil-paintings, etc., gathered by the late John Sheepshanks, and by him presented to the British nation. The collection is valued at £60,000, and is now in the South Kensington Museum, London.

Shelton Abbey. The seat of the Earl of Wicklow, in the county of Wicklow, Ireland.

Shelton Oak. A famous oak in the parish of Shelton, near Shrewsbury, England, measuring 44 feet and 3 inches in circumference.

Shenandoah, The. A Confederate privateer in the War of the Rebellion. During her cruise she destroyed a great part of the United States whaling fleet in the Pacific. She surrendered to the British government at Liverpool, Nov. 9, 1865.

☞ "The Shenandoah was another active English-Confederate sea-rover that sailed from England. She went around Cape Horn, crossed the Pacific Ocean, and sailed up the eastern coast of Asia to Behring Strait, to spread havoc among the New England whaling ships engaged in fishing in those waters. These vessels held a sort of convention in that high latitude (June 28, 1865), when the *Shenandoah*, disguised as a merchantman, and flying the American flag, ran in among the ships unsuspected. Then she revealed her true character, captured ten of them, placed eight of them in a group before midnight, and set them on fire, lighting up the ice-floes of the Polar Sea by the incendiary flames. This was the last act of hostility in the American Civil War in 1861-1865." *Lossing.*

Shene Palace. See RICHMOND PALACE.

Shepherd and Shepherdess. A famous picture by Edward Bendemann (b. 1811).

Shepherd Boy in a Shower. A picture by Thomas Gainsborough (1727–1788).

Shepherd Martius. A celebrated bronze statue in the Hall of the Conservators, Rome, representing a youth extracting a thorn from his foot.

Shepherds, Adoration of the. See ADORATION OF THE SHEPHERDS.

Shepherd's Bible. A picture by Sir Edwin Landseer (1803–1873), the celebrated English painter of animals.

Shepherd's Chief Mourner. See OLD SHEPHERD'S CHIEF MOURNER.

Sherwood Forest. An ancient forest adjoining the town of Mansfield, near Nottingham, in England. It is famous as having been the scene of Robin Hood's chief exploits. At the present time the region is for the most part bare of trees.

☞ "A few solitary and battered oaks standing here and there, the last melancholy remnant of these vast and ancient woods, the beautiful springs, swift and crystalline brooks, and broad sheets of water lying abroad amid the dark heath, and haunted by numbers of the wild ducks and the heron, still remain. But at the Clipstone extremity of the forest, a remnant of its ancient woodlands remains, unrifled, except of its deer, a specimen of what the whole once was, . . . extending about five miles in length and one or two in width, — a forest of oaks, clothed with the most impressive aspect of age that can perhaps be presented to the eye in these kingdoms."
William Howitt.

☞ "The relics of the old forest are few and scattered; but as to the bold outlaw who once held a kind of freebooting sway over it, there is scarce a hill or dale, a cliff or cavern, a well or fountain, in this part of the country, that is not connected with his memory." *Irving.*

A monarch bade thee from that wild arise,
Where *Sherwood's* outlaws once were wont to prowl;
And Superstition's crimes, of various dyes,
Sought shelter in the priest's protecting cowl. *Byron.*

Or Marmion's acts of darkness, fitter food
For *Sherwood's* outlaw tales of Robin Hood? *Byron.*

Ship Tavern. A former noted place of entertainment near Temple Bar, London.

Shipbuilder and his Wife. A picture by Rembrandt van Ryn (1606–1669), the Dutch painter. In Buckingham Palace, London.

Shipwreck of Æneas. A picture by Peter Paul Rubens (1577–1640). Now in the collection of H. T. Hope, Esq., London.

Shipwreck of the Medusa. A noted picture by Jean Louis Théodore André Géricault (1790–1824), and regarded as his masterpiece. In the Louvre, Paris.

☞ "Géricault died, they say, for want of fame. He was a man who possessed a considerable fortune of his own, but pined because no one in his day would purchase his pictures, and so acknowledge his talent. At present a scrawl from his pencil brings an enormous price. All his works have a grand *cachet:* he never did any thing mean. When he painted the 'Raft of the Medusa,' it is said he lived for a long time among the corpses which he painted, and that his studio was a second morgue. If you have not seen the picture you are familiar probably with Reynolds's admirable engraving of it. A huge black sea; a raft beating upon it; a horrid company of men dead, half-dead, writhing, and frantic with hideous hunger or hideous hope; and far away, black against a stormy sunset, a sail. The story is powerfully told, and has a legitimate tragic interest."
Thackeray.

☞ "His [Géricault's] picture has come to be regarded as 'one of the principal attractions' of the French portion of the gallery. The results of the terrible shipwreck, with its living and dead victims, are only too signally effective, and seem made to shake, if not to overthrow, traditional art. They are like the rough expression of the living present, beside the most scholarly fruit of the dead past. Géricault was not thirty when he painted the Raft of the Medusa." *Sarah Tytler.*

Shobeck. An ancient stronghold in Arabia Petræa, near the city of Petra. It is in a very fair state of preservation, and affords a refuge for several hundred Arabs. It was an important castle in the time of the Crusades.

Shockhoe Hill. An eminence in Richmond, Va., surmounted by the State Capitol and other buildings. Also a cemetery.

Shoreditch. A district of immoral reputation in London. The name is traditionally derived from Jane Shore, as shown by the ancient ballad entitled "Jane Shore's Lament;" but Pennant says that it was originally Soersditch, from its lord, Sir John Soerditch, a learned lawyer trusted by Edward III. Here were situated two theatres of Shakespeare's time, — "the Theatre," and "the Curtain."

Cromwell, Blake, Marlborough, Chatham, Nelson, and Wellington are not to be trifled with, and the brutal strength which lies at the bottom of society, the animal ferocity of the quays and cockpits, the bullies of the costermongers of *Shoreditch*, Seven Dials, and Spitalfields, they know how to wake up. *Emerson.*

When I grow rich,
Say the bells at *Shoreditch.*
Mother Goose.

Shrine of Our Lady of Walsingham. The chapel and image of the Virgin in the priory of Walsingham, England, of great renown throughout Europe in the Middle Ages, and a favorite resort of pilgrims. It was even more frequented than the shrine of St. Thomas à Becket at Canterbury. See WALSINGHAM PRIORY.

Shrine of St. Cuthbert. This shrine at the Cathedral of Durham, in England, was visited by multitudes for more than 500 years, in consequence of the belief that the incorruptible body of the patron saint was miraculously preserved during all this time. The shrine was splendidly adorned with gold, silver, and precious stones. The body being disinterred in 1827, it was discovered that a fraud had been practised, as it was plain that the wrappings had been wound around a skeleton.

He kneel'd before *Saint Cuthbert's shrine,*
With patience unwonted at rites divine;
He abjured the gods of heathen race,
And he bent his head at the font of grace.
Scott.

Shrine of St. James [at Compostella]. This shrine at Santiago de Compostella, Spain, was a favorite resort of pilgrims in the Middle Ages, on account of the legend that the body of St. James was discovered there in the ninth century, and placed in a chapel under the altar of the cathedral. St. James is held in the highest veneration by the Spaniards, since they believe that in the battle of Clavijo, in the year 841, he appeared in the field armed with a sword, and mounted on a white horse, whose housings were adorned with scallop shells, and that he slew 60,000 of the Moorish infidels, thus gaining the day for Christianity. It is said that over 2,000 persons left England for Santiago in one year in the fifteenth century.

A stupendous metamorphosis was performed in the ninth century, when from a peaceful fisherman of the Lake of Gennesareth, the apostle James was transformed into a valorous knight, who charged at the head of Spanish chivalry in battles against the Moors. The gravest historians have celebrated his exploits, the miraculous shrine of *Compostella* displayed his power; and the sword of a military order, assisted by the terrors of the inquisition, was sufficient to remove every objection of profane criticism. *Gibbon.*

Shrine of St. John Nepomuck. A gorgeous silver shrine enclosing the body of the saint, in the cathedral of Prague, Austria.

☞ "On each side hang four massive lamps of silver constantly burning. The pyramid of statues, of the same precious metal, has at each corner a richly carved urn, three feet high, with a crimson lamp burning at the top. Above, four silver angels, the size of life, are suspended in the air, holding up a splendid drapery of crimson and gold." *Bayard Taylor.*

Shrine of St. Sebaldus. A famous work of monumental sculpture in the church of St. Sebald at Nuremberg, Germany, executed by Peter Vischer (1460?–1540), the old German sculptor. Regarded as his *chef d'œuvre*, and as one of the finest works of the plastic art of that period.

☞ "Never has a work of German sculpture combined the beauty of the South with the deep feeling of the North more richly, more thoughtfully, and more harmoniously." *Lübke, Trans.*

Shrine of St. Thomas à Becket. Formerly a famous shrine in the chapel of the Holy Trinity in the cathedral of Canterbury, England. The pavement of the chapel is deeply worn by the knees of the countless pilgrims who have resorted to this shrine.

☞ "It was a national as well as a religious feeling that drew great multitudes to the shrine of Becket, the first Englishman, who, since the Conquest, had been terrible to foreign tyrants." *Macaulay.*

When that Aprille, with his schowres swoote,
The drought of Marche hath perced to the roote.
. . . .
Thanne longen folk to go on pilgrimages,
And palmers for to seeken straunge strondes;
And specially, from every schires ende
Of Engelond, to Canterbury they wende,
The holy blisful martir for to seeke,
That hem hath holpen whan that they were seeke. *Chaucer.*

Shrine of the Black Virgin of Altötting. A famous resort of pilgrims, at Altötting, in Bavaria, one of the most ancient and celebrated shrines in Europe. The image of the Madonna, which is thought to have come from the East, has stood almost uninterruptedly for 1,200 years in its present situation.

Shrine of the Black Virgin. A famous resort of pilgrimage in the monastery of Czenstochau, Poland. The convent contains a dark-colored picture of the Virgin, probably of Byzantine origin, alleged to have been painted by St. Luke, and which is held in great veneration.

Shrine of the Three Kings of Cologne. A famous reliquary in the cathedral of Cologne, Germany, which formerly contained treasures of extraordinary magnificence. During the French revolution some of these were disposed of, and their place supplied by cheap imitations. The bones of the three kings, or Magi, are publicly exhibited on Sundays and holidays.

Si Quis Door. The name popularly given to a door in the north aisle of St. Paul's Church, London, from the circumstance that posters beginning "Si quis invenerit" (i.e., "If any one has found") were affixed to it.

Saw'st thou ever *Si quis* patched on Paul's church door? *Bishop Hall.*

Sibyl, The. [Lat. *sibylla*, a prophetess.] The ancient sibyls, or women endowed with the gift of prophecy, of whom there are commonly reckoned ten, residing in different parts of Persia, Greece, and Italy, were made a very common subject of representation by the painters of the Middle Ages. For SIBYLLA ERYTHRÆA, SIBYLLA CUMÆA, SIBYLLA DELPHICA, etc., see ERYTHRÆAN SIBYL, CUMÆAN SIBYL, DELPHIC SIBYL, etc.

☞ "The Sibyls were much the fashion in the classic times of the sixteenth century: Michael Angelo and Raphael have left us consummate examples. . . . In general, if there be only two, they are the Tiburtina, who showed the vision to Augustus, and the Cumæan Sibyl, who foretold the birth of our Saviour." *Mrs. Jameson.*

Sibyl, Temple of the. See TEMPLE OF THE SIBYL.

Sibyls. See FOUR SIBYLS.

Sibyl's Cave. [Ital. *Grotta della Sibilla.*] A celebrated tunnel leading from the Lake Avernus, near the Bay of Baiæ, Italy. It is cut through a hill of volcanic tufa, and is interesting from its connection with the poetical legends of Virgil's Æneid. [Also called *Grotta Giulia.*] There is also another cave of the Sibyl at Cumæ.

Siddons, Mrs., as the Tragic Muse. A noted allegorical picture by Sir Joshua Reynolds (1723-1792), the most celebrated English portrait-painter.

Sidney Sussex College. A foundation of the University of Cambridge, England. Established in 1598.

Sidney's Oak. See PENSHURST.

Siege of Namur. A picture by Joon van Huchtenberg (1646-1733), and his masterpiece. In the Gallery of Vienna, Austria.

Siege of Rome under Porsenna. A picture by Martin Fesele, a German painter. In the Gallery of Munich, Bavaria.

Siena Cathedral. A famous church in the city of Siena, Italy, and one of the most glorious structures in the world.

☞ "This church is the most purely Gothic of all Italian cathedrals designed by national architects. Together with that of Orvieto, it stands alone to show what the unassisted genius of the Italians could produce when influenced by mediæval ideas. It is built wholly of marble, and overlaid inside and out with florid ornaments of exquisite beauty." *Symonds.*

☞ "The architecture has a variety which does not produce the effect of eccentricity, an exuberant imagination flowering out in stone. . . . How much pride, love, and reverence in the lapse of ages must have clung to the sharp points of all this sculpture. The cathedral is a religion in itself — something worth dying for to those who have an hereditary interest in it." *Hawthorne.*

☞ "The impression is incomparable. That of St. Peter's does not approach it: a surprising richness and sincerity of invention, the most admirable of Gothic flowers." *Taine, Trans.*

Sighs, Bridge of. See BRIDGE OF SIGHS.

Signoria, Palazzo della. See PALAZZO VECCHIO.

Signoria, Piazza della. See PIAZZA DELLA SIGNORIA.

Sîk, The. The principal street of Petra in Arabia. It is two miles long, and is the chief entrance to the city. On each side are precipices from 100 to 700 feet in height. Its width is from 10 to 30 feet. It is dimly lighted, as the sky is in places almost entirely hidden by the rocks, which nearly meet. The pavement and rocks are now covered by various vegetable growth, vines, flowers, ferns, and bushes.

☞ "How strange must have been the strong echoes of city noises in this gorge! — the cry of the camel-drivers, the rattle of chariots, the common talk and laugh of citizens, and the play of children! And what different people must have been met there from the few we saw to-day! Instead of Eastern merchants and Roman soldiers, and a Greek traveller or two, I saw to-day a group of goats and their herdsmen, entering into the deepest shadow from a reach of sunshine; and a child standing with two kids on a point of rock above my head; and a wild troop of shaggy Arabs, clattering their arms as I passed; and here and there a solitary figure, with his matchlock, brown tunic, and white teeth, perched on a pinnacle, or striding over a distant slope." *Harriet Martineau.*

☞ "Nothing could surpass the awful grandeur of this ravine; and one cannot repress a shudder on looking up from its gloomy depths, through the gradually narrowing fissure, to the irregular streak of blue sky far overhead. Constantly winding, too, one seems at every new turn to be shut in on all sides, and hopelessly imprisoned in the very bowels of the earth. Yet here, in this cleft, from whence the light of day is well-nigh excluded, into the depths of which no solitary ray of sunlight can penetrate, traces of art and industry are everywhere visible. Remains of ancient pavement cover the bottom, once the highway to a proud city; along the sides are niches hewn in the smooth cliff to receive statues; and tablets, too, are there, *once* inscribed with some records; on the left is an aqueduct tunnelled in the rock, and high up on the right is a conduit of earthen pipes let into the precipice. These, the works of man, are now all ruinous and time-worn; statue and inscription, form, name, and story, are alike gone." *Murray's Handbook.*

Silence de la Vierge. See SILENTIUM and VIERGE AU VOILE.

Silentium. [Silence.] The name given to representations of the Virgin and Child, in which the latter is represented as sleeping. For an example, among others, see VIERGE À LA DIADÈME.

Silenus. A mythological picture by Giuseppe Ribera, called Lo Spagnoletto (1588-1656). In the Public Gallery at Naples, Italy.

Silenzio, Il. [Silence.] See SILENTIUM.

Siloam, Pool of. See POOL OF SILOAM.

Simeon and Lazarus. A picture by Albert Dürer (1471-1528), the German painter and engraver. In the Gallery of Munich, Bavaria.

Simeon, St. See ST. SIMEON.

Sion College. A hall, library, and almshouse in London, founded in the time of Charles I. for the use of the clergy. Fuller here wrote his "Church History."

Sion House. The seat of the Duke of Northumberland, near Twickenham, England. It is a very large and imposing structure, said to contain 365 windows to equal the number of days in the year. The grounds are laid out with great taste. The interior is very splendid, with many fine treasures of art.

Sir Roger de Coverley going to Church. A picture by Charles Robert Leslie (1794–1859), and one of his principal works. There is a repetition in the collection of the Marquis of Lansdowne, England.

Sistine Chapel, *or* **Sixtine Chapel.** [Ital. *Capella Sistina.*] A celebrated room in the Vatican Palace, Rome, built from designs of Bacio Pintelli in 1473, for Pope Sixtus IV., whence its name. The lower part of the walls was formerly intended to be hung on festival days with the tapestries executed from the cartoons of Raphael. The ceiling is covered with frescos by Michael Angelo, and the upper part of the walls by the works of eminent masters of the fifteenth century. The end of the chapel is occupied by Michael Angelo's vast fresco entitled "The Last Judgment." The chapel was designed for the religious services performed during Passion Week, for which purpose it is still used. The *Miserere* is chanted in this chapel with great solemnity in the presence of the pope, on the afternoon of Wednesday preceding Easter Sunday.

☞ "At the present day the ceiling of the Sistine Chapel is partly injured as regards the brightness of its coloring, by the rising smoke and dust, and has partly faded from length of time. Cracks have appeared in the dome, and water has trickled down through them. Three centuries and a half the paintings have stood there, and it is not possible by any means to oppose the slow decay to which they must be subject. Still a happy fate has been theirs in that they are thoroughly inaccessible to human hands; they would have to be shot at, or the roof broken through from above, to be injured intentionally." *Grimm, Trans.*

☞ "The ceiling of the Sistine Chapel contains the most perfect works done by Michael Angelo in his long and active life." *Kugler.*

☞ "The religious character of this chapel, in the view of Protestants at least, is quite lost in the admiration for that immortal artist who has left here such wonderful monuments of his genius. It seems really dedicated to Michael Angelo, and he is the presiding divinity of the place." *Hillard.*

Whether he [Michael Angelo] drew, or sung,
Or wrought in stone, or hung
The Pantheon in the air;
Whether he gave to Rome
Her *Sistine walls* or dome,
Or laid the ponderous beams, or lightly wound the stair. *C. P. Cranch.*

Sistine Madonna. See MADONNA DI SAN SISTO.

Sitt Miriam. [*El Moallâka.*] An interesting church situated at a considerable height from the ground in one of the towers of the Roman Gateway of Babylon, in Egypt. The title *El Moallâka* (the suspended) is given to it on account of its elevation. This church contains many remarkable and interesting objects,—sculptures, paintings, carvings, mosaics, etc.

Six Hundred, The. A name often popularly applied to the British light cavalry brigade (670 in number), which at the battle of Balaclava, in the Crimea, Oct. 25, 1854, charged the Russian infantry and cavalry in position, owing to a misunderstanding of orders. It was a feat almost unparalleled in military history. The charge occupied less than half an hour, during which two-thirds of the assailing party were killed or wounded.

Half a league, half a league,
Half a league onward,
All in the valley of Death
Rode the six hundred.
"Forward, the Light Brigade!
Charge for the guns!" he said:
Into the valley of Death
Rode the six hundred.
Tennyson.

Sixtine Chapel. See SISTINE CHAPEL.

Skerryvore Lighthouse. An important lighthouse on the west coast of Scotland, begun in 1838, and finished in 1843. This structure, containg four and one-half times as much masonry as the Eddystone lighthouse and twice as much as the Bell Rock tower, was built under the charge of Mr. Alan Stevenson, and is an example of great engineering skill.

Slaughter's. 1. A celebrated coffee-house in St. Martin's Lane, London, so called after its first landlord, Thomas Slaughter, 1692. During the last century it was noted as a rendezvous of painters and sculptors. It was frequented by Hogarth, Benjamin West, Roubiliac, Wilkie, and others. After the opening of another "Slaughter's" in the same street, the original coffee-house was known as "Old Slaughter's" till its destruction in the first half of the present century.

2. A coffee-house opposite Northumberland House in the Strand.

I remember to have read in some philosopher, — I believe in Tom Brown's works, — that, let a man's character, sentiments, or complexion be what they will, he can find company in London to match them. . . . If he be passionate, he may vent his rage among the old orators at *Slaughter's* coffee-house, and damn the nation because it keeps him from starving. *Goldsmith.*

Slave. A statue by Michael Angelo (1474-1564). In the Louvre, Paris. [Called also *The Captive.*] See GREEK SLAVE.

Slave Ship. A well-known picture by Joseph Mallord William Turner (1775-1851). It is now in the possession of Miss Alice Hooper, Boston.

☞ "I believe, if I were reduced to rest Turner's immortality upon any single work, I should choose the *Slave Ship*. Its daring conception, ideal in the highest sense of the word, is based on the purest truth, and wrought out with the concentrated knowledge of a life." *Ruskin.*

☞ "Thackeray, when speaking of 'The Slave Ship' by the same amazing artist, says with delightful *naïveté*, 'I don't know whether it is sublime or ridiculous.'" *Dr. Brown's Spare Hours.*

☞ "The following opinion, expressed by an intelligent and accomplished American artist, Mr. George Inness, is interesting for its frankness: 'Turner's 'Slave Ship' is the most infernal piece of clap-trap ever painted. There is nothing in it. It has as much to do with human affections and thought as a ghost. It is not even a fine bouquet of color. The color is harsh, disagreeable, and discordant.' This is severe, and I think its severity is partly due to re-action against Mr. Ruskin's eloquent praises." *P. G. Hamerton.*

Slavino di San Marco. A singular mass of rocks and *débris* in the valley of the Adige, near Trent, Italy, supposed to have been occasioned by an avalanche.

☞ "The traveller cannot fail to notice a vast tract called the *Slavini di Marco*, covered with fragments of rock torn from the sides of the neighboring mountains by an earthquake, or perhaps by their own unsupported weight, and hurled down into the plains below. They spread over the whole valley, and in some places contract the road to a very narrow space." *Eustace.*

Such as that ruin is which in the flank
Smote, on this side of Trent, the Adige,
Either by earthquake or by failing stay.
Dante, Inferno, Longfellow's Trans.

Sleeping Ariadne. See ARIADNE.

Sleeping Faun. 1. An admired statue found in 1756 at Herculaneum, and now in the Museum at Naples. See FAUN, BARBERINI FAUN, DANCING FAUN.

2. A work of sculpture by Harriet G. Hosmer (b. 1830).

Sleepy Hollow. A quiet valley near Tarrytown, on the Hudson, New York, immortalized by Washington Irving in his "Legend of Sleepy Hollow" (in "The Sketch Book"). There is a hamlet of the same name.

☞ "If ever I should wish for a retreat, whither I might steal from the world and its distractions, and dream quietly away the remnant of a troubled life, I know of none more promising than this little valley. From the listless repose of the place, and the peculiar character of its inhabitants, who are descendants from the original Dutch settlers, this sequestered glen has long been known by the name of Sleepy Hollow, and its rustic lads are called the Sleepy Hollow Boys throughout all the neighboring country. A drowsy, dreamy influence seems to hang over the land, and to pervade the very atmosphere. Some say that the place was bewitched by a High German doctor during the early days of the settlement; others, that an old Indian chief, the prophet or wizard of his tribe, held his powwows there before the country was discovered by Master Hendrick Hudson. Certain it is, the place still continues under the sway of some witching power, that holds a spell over the minds of the good people, causing them to walk in a continual revery. They are given to all kinds of marvellous beliefs, are subject to trances and visions, and frequently see strange sights, and hear music and voices in the air. The whole neighborhood abounds with local tales, haunted spots, and twilight superstitions." *Irving.*

Sloane Museum. A collection of curiosities belonging to Sir Hans Sloane, and offered by him to the English Parliament for £20,000. The offer was accepted, and the collection was used as the nucleus of the present British Museum.

Smailholm Tower. A lofty tower now in ruins, and commanding an extensive view of a part of Scotland with which many very interesting associations are connected. It is not far from Melrose and Dryburgh Abbeys, and is the scene of Scott's ballad of "The Eve of St. John."

Then rose those crags, that mountain tower,
Which charmed my fancy's wakening hour.
. . . .
And still I thought that shattered tower
The mightiest work of human power.
Marmion.

Smith College. A well-endowed institution in Northampton, Mass., designed for the higher education of women.

Smithfield. The ancient market of London. The name signifies smooth plain, from the Saxon *smeth*, smooth. It was the largest live-market in the world, and its characteristic features are well described by Dickens in "Oliver Twist." In 1852 it was condemned by law to be removed to Islington. Smithfield is famous for its tournaments, executions, and burnings. Here too, from Sept. 3 to 6, was held the celebrated Bartholomew Fair, noted not only for its sales of cloth, but as a scene of license and revelry. See BARTHOLOMEW FAIR.

☞ "It was market morning. The ground was covered nearly ankle-deep with filth and mire; and a thick steam perpetually rising from the reeking bodies of the cattle, and mingling with the fog, which seemed to rest upon the chimney-tops, hung heavily above. All the pens in the centre of the large area, and as many temporary ones as could be crowded into the vacant space, were filled with sheep; and tied up to posts by the gutter-side were long lines of beasts and oxen three or four deep. Countrymen, butchers, drovers, hawkers, boys, thieves, idlers, and vagabonds of every low grade, were mingled together in a dense mass: the whistling of drovers, the barking of dogs, the bellowing and plunging of beasts, the bleating of sheep, and grunting and squeaking of pigs; the cries of hawkers, the shouts, oaths, and quarrelling on all sides, the ringing of bells, and the roar of voices that issued from every public-house; the crowding, pushing, driving, beating, whooping, and yelling: the hideous and discordant din that resounded from every corner of the market; and the unwashed, unshaven, squalid, and dirty figures constantly running to and fro, and bursting in and out of the throng, rendered it a stunning and bewildering scene which quite confused the senses." *Dickens.*

So I came into *Smithfield;* and the shameful place, being all asmear with filth, and fat, and blood, and foam, seemed to stick to me.
Pip (Dickens, Great Expectations).

Falstaff. Where's Bardolph?
Page. He's gone into *Smithfield* to buy your worship a horse. *Shakespeare.*

For, in the earlier part of the seventeenth century, a speculator who had dared to affirm that the human soul is by its nature mortal, and does, in the great majority of cases, actually die with the body, would have been burned alive in *Smithfield.* *Macaulay.*

The midnight of Bartholomew,— the stake
Of *Smithfield.* *Whittier.*

Smith's Cave. See WAYLAND SMITH'S CAVE.

Smithsonian Institution. A noble building of red sandstone and of Gothic architecture, in Washington. The main hall, which is 200 feet in length by 50 feet in width, and 25 feet high, contains the National Museum of curiosities, with natural history and ethnological collections. The institution was founded by James Smithson, a native of England, born in the last century, who, although he had never visited this country, and was totally unacquainted with any one in America, for reasons unknown left the whole of his property, amounting to over half a million of dollars, "to the United States of America, to found at Washington, under the name of the Smithsonian Institution, an establishment for the increase and diffusion of knowledge among men."

Smolnoi Church. A noted white-marble church in St. Petersburg, Russia. It is surmounted with five blue domes.

And *Smolnoi's* wealth of spangled blue
Beams all the dusky distance through!
E. D. Proctor.

Smoo, Cave of. A cavern in the North of Scotland, in the neighborhood of Durness. It is described by Sir Walter Scott.

Smyrna, The. A former coffee-house in Pall-Mall, London, famous in the reign of Queen Anne. The "Tatler" suggested "to all ingenious gentlemen in and about the cities of London and Westminster who have a mind to be instructed in the noble sciences of music, poetry, and politics, that they repair to the Smyrna Coffee-house, in Pall-Mall, betwixt the hours of eight and ten at night, where they may be instructed gratis."

If it be fine weather, we take a turn into the Park till two, when we go to dinner; and if it be dirty, you are entertained at piquet or basset at White's, or you may talk politics at the *Smyrna* or St. James.
Journey through England, 1714.

You then, O ye beggars of my acquaintance, whether in rags or lace; whether in Kent-street or in the Mall; whether at *Smyrna* or St. Giles's; might I advise you as a friend, never seem in want of the favor you solicit. *Goldsmith.*

Snow Hill. A well-known locality in London. Snow Hill was formerly remarkable for its steepness of ascent, a difficulty now obviated by the Holborn Viaduct.

Who has not heard the Scourer's midnight fame?
Who has not trembled at the Mohocks' name?
I pass their desperate deeds and mischief, done
Where from *Snow Hill* black steepy torrents run,
How matrons, hooped within the hogshead's womb,
Were tumbled furious thence. *Gay.*

Soane Museum. An interesting and valuable art-collection in London, founded by Sir John Soane.

Yes, to see England well needs a hundred years; for, what they told me was the merit of *Sir John Soane's Museum*, in London,—that it was well packed and well saved,—is the merit of England.
Emerson.

Society of the Pin. An association consisting chiefly of foreigners, formed in London in the fourteenth century. It is supposed to have derived its name from the city of Le Puy, in Auvergne, where was a famous statue of the Virgin, much visited by pilgrims. The object of the association seems to have been to promote good-will and good-fellowship. They held a great festival on the first Sunday after Trinity.

Socrates, Prison of. See PRISON OF SOCRATES.

Soho. A district in London, in which many French have settled at various times. See SOHO SQUARE.

It is natural to me to go where I please, to do what I please. . . . I digress into *Soho*, to explore a bookstall. Methinks I have been thirty years a collector. There is nothing strange nor new in it.
Charles Lamb.

Fancy the three [Fielding and his companions] in a great wainscoted room, in Covent Garden or *Soho*, lighted by two or three candles in silver sconces, and a bottle of Florence wine on the table.
Thackeray.

Soho Square. A square in London, built in the reign of Charles II. It was formerly sometimes called King's Square from its surveyor and architect, Gregory

King. It was a very fashionable quarter of London until within the last century. Here Sir Roger de Coverley is made to reside; and here Evelyn went in 1690 to pass the winter "in Soho, in the great square."

☞ "Soho Square . . . was to our ancestors a subject of pride with which their posterity will hardly sympathize." *Macaulay.*

But it [the answer to Bentley's "Dissertation on the Epistles of Phalaris"] had its day of noisy popularity. It was to be found not only in the studies of men of letters, but on the tables of the most brilliant drawing-rooms of *Soho Square* and Covent Garden. *Macaulay.*

Soho Theatre. A theatre in London, opened in 1840, now called the New Royalty.

Sol, Puerta del. See PUERTA DEL SOL.

Soldiers' Home. An asylum for disabled soldiers of the regular army, situated in the environs of Washington. It was established in 1851. The buildings are of marble, enclosed in a large and beautiful park. The cost of the establishment was defrayed by a forced levy on the inhabitants of the city of Mexico, during the occupation of the place by Gen. Scott. Some of the Presidents have made the Soldiers' Home their summer residence.

Soldiers Bathing in the Arno. A celebrated cartoon by Michael Angelo (1475–1564). It represents a body of soldiers suddenly called to arms while bathing. The work never went beyond this cartoon, which was begun in 1504 and exhibited in 1506.

Solferino, Tour de. See TOUR DE SOLFERINO.

Solomon. See JUDGMENT OF SOLOMON and POOLS OF SOLOMON.

Solomon's Temple. The famous temple at Jerusalem built by King Solomon (B.C. 1015), after the model of the Tabernacle, the plan of which the Jews considered to have been divinely revealed to them through Moses, in the desert of Sinai, and from which they never departed in any of their subsequent erections. Of this celebrated temple not one stone now remains upon another. It is now agreed by all topographers that the site of the Temple at Jerusalem is within the limits of the area which is now called the Haram, but its precise extent is a matter of uncertainty. It was of rectangular shape, measuring, according to Josephus, a stadium, or 600 Greek feet, on each side.

☞ "There is perhaps no building of the ancient world which has excited so much attention since the time of its destruction as the Temple which Solomon built at Jerusalem, and its successor as rebuilt by Herod. Its spoils were considered worthy of forming the principal illustration of one of the most beautiful of Roman triumphal arches, and Justinian's highest architectural ambition was that he might surpass it. Throughout the Middle Ages it influenced to a considerable degree the forms of Christian churches, and its peculiarities were the watchwords and rallying points of all associations of builders. Since the revival of learning in the sixteenth century its arrangements have employed the pens of numberless learned antiquarians, and architects of every country have wasted their science in trying to reproduce its forms. But it is not only to Christians that the Temple of Solomon is so interesting: the whole Mohammedan world look to it as the foundation of all architectural knowledge; and the Jews still recall its glories and sigh over their loss with a constant tenacity, unmatched by that of any other people to any other building of the ancient world. The Temple was a very insignificant building in size; the truth being, that, like the temples of the Semitic nations, it was more in the character of a shrine or treasury intended to contain certain precious works in metal. The principal ornaments of its façade were two brazen pillars, Jachin and Boaz, which seem to have been wonders of metal-work, and regarding which more has been written, and, it may be added, more nonsense, than regarding almost any other known architectural objects." *Fergusson.*

Somerset, The. A British line-of-battle ship stationed in Boston harbor in 1775.

Where swinging wide at her moorings lay
The *Somerset*, British man-of-war;
A phantom ship, with each mast and spar
Across the moon like a prison bar,
And a huge black hulk that was magnified
By its own reflection in the tide.
Longfellow.

Somerset, The. A club occupying a fine mansion on Beacon Street, Boston, Mass.

Somerset House. A public building in London occupying the site of the old palace of the same name. It is used for government offices, and contained the rooms of the Royal Society, the Society of Antiquaries, and other literary and scientific institutions. The old Somerset House, interesting from its historic connection with royal personages, was built in 1549.

☞ "If you would see something quite dreadful, go to the enormous palace in the Strand, called Somerset House. Massive, heavy architecture, of which the recesses seem dipped in ink, the porticos smeared with soot. . . . What can men do in such a catacomb?" *Taine, Trans.*

Dan Stuart once told us that he did not remember that he ever deliberately walked into the exhibition at *Somerset House* in his life. *Charles Lamb.*

For the science, he [Carlyle] had, if possible, even less tolerance, and compared the savans of *Somerset House* to the boy who asked Confucius "how many stars in the sky?" Confucius replied, "he minded things near him." Then said the boy, "how many hairs are there in your eyebrows?" Confucius said, "he didn't know and didn't care." *Emerson.*

Sommeil de Jésus. See SILENTIUM and VIERGE À LA DIADÈME.

Sonneck. A ruined mediæval stronghold of the thirteenth century, on the Rhine, near Lorch.

Sophia, The. An Arctic exploring-ship which sailed from England under the command of Capt. Stewart, April 13, 1850.

Sophia, St. See ST. SOPHIA.

Sorbonne, The. A university in Paris, named for its founder, Robert de Sorbonne, confessor to St. Louis. It was established in the thirteenth century. The old building having fallen into decay, it was restored by Cardinal Richelieu, in 1629. The chapel of the institution contains the tomb of the cardinal, a superior work of art. The disputations and decisions of the Sorbonne in theological matters acquired great fame and power. It is now the seat of three of the five Faculties of the Academy of Paris, — theology, sciences, and letters. The building contains large lecture. rooms, collections, etc.

Thence to the *Sorbonne*, an ancient fabric built by one Robert de Sorbonne, whose name it retains, but the restauration which the late Cardinal de Richlieu has made to it renders it one of the most excellent moderne buildings.
John Evelyn, Diary 1644, 4 *Jan.*

So, too, in matters spiritual, what avails it that a man be Doctor of the *Sorbonne*, Doctor of Laws, of Both Laws, and can cover half a square foot in pica-type with the list of his fellowships, arranged as equilateral triangle, at the vertex an "&c." over and above, and with the parchment of his diplomas could thatch the whole street he lives in: what avails it? *Carlyle.*

I compared them [the professors' houses at Oxford] to those of our scholars, resembling cages, to the third floor in a great city, to the dismal lodgings of the *Sorbonne*. *Taine, Trans.*

Voltaire, in the days of Lewis the Fourteenth, would probably have been, like most of the literary men of the time, a zealous Jansenist, eminent among the defenders of efficacious grace, a bitter assailant of the lax morality of the Jesuits and the unreasonable decisions of the *Sorbonne*. *James Parton.*

Sortie from Gibraltar. A painting by John Trumbull (1756–1853), and considered his masterpiece. Now in the Museum of Fine Arts, Boston, Mass.

Sospiri, Ponte dei. See BRIDGE OF SIGHS.

South Kensington Museum. A national collection of art and manufactures in London. It contains many valuable paintings and other works of art, including the Vernon and Sheepshanks Collection, belonging to the National Gallery.

☞ "However much opinions may differ as to the system of instruction in design adopted in that Department, there can be no doubt that the truly magnificent collection of objects assembled there, and the facility afforded students who may desire to inspect and

study them, reflect the highest credit upon the authorities intrusted with its care. By such means, the art-workman, his employer, and the public, whose encouragement and patronage are necessary to both, may learn that which alone can rescue English manufacture from its recent degradation, viz., the formation of a sound taste."
C. L. Eastlake.

South Sea House. The office of the famous South Sea Company, which was organized in 1711. The original building stood in Old Broad Street, London; and the new building, which is now let for chambers, stands in Threadneedle Street.

☞ "Reader, in thy passage from the Bank — where thou hast been receiving thy half-yearly dividends (supposing thou art a lean annuitant like myself) — to the Flower Pot, to secure a place for Dalston, or Shacklewell, or some other thy suburban retreat northerly, — didst thou never observe a melancholy-looking, handsome, brick and stone edifice, to the left — where Threadneedle Street abuts upon Bishopsgate? I dare say thou hast often admired its magnificent portals ever gaping wide, and disclosing to view a grave court, with cloisters, and pillars, with few or no traces of goers-in or comers-out, — a desolation something like Balclutha's. This was once a house of trade, — a centre of busy interests. The throng of merchants was here — the quick pulse of gain — and here some forms of business are still kept up, though the soul be long since fled. Here are still to be seen stately porticos, imposing staircases, offices roomy as the state apartments in palaces, — deserted, or thinly peopled with a few straggling clerks; the still more sacred interiors of court and committee-rooms, with venerable faces of beadles, door-keepers — directors seated in form on solemn days (to proclaim a dead dividend), at long worm-eaten tables, that have been mahogany, with tarnished gilt-leather coverings, supporting massy silver inkstands long since dry; huge charts, which subsequent discoveries have antiquated; dusty maps of Mexico, dim as dreams — and soundings of the Bay of Panama! The long passages hung with buckets, appended, in idle row, to walls whose substance might defy any, short of the last, conflagration: — with vast ranges of cellarage under all, where dollars and pieces-of-eight once lay, an 'unsunned heap,' for Mammon to have solaced his solitary heart withal, — long since dissipated, or scattered into air at the blast of the breaking of that famous BUBBLE." *Charles Lamb.*

Southampton House. A former mansion of London. The last vestiges of it were destroyed in 1876. The site is marked by Southampton Buildings. The Earl of Southampton, father of Lady Rachel Russell, died here.

Southwark. The district, "called by the Saxons Southverke, or the South Work," on the south side of the Thames, London. It is interesting for its old inns, as the "White Hart" and "Tabard." Here was the Marshalsea Prison.

Southwark Bridge. One of the great bridges across the Thames, at London, connecting the City with the borough of Southwark, first opened to the public, April 1819. It was built by John Rennie.

Sovereign of the Seas. The first three-decker in the English navy, launched in 1637.

Spa Fields. A locality in London, England, formerly a place of popular gatherings. It was not occupied by houses until the present century.

Spada Palace. [Ital. *Palazzo Spada.*] A Roman palace, near the Palazzo Farnese, built in 1564, and chiefly remarkable for the celebrated statue which goes under the name of the Spada Pompey. See POMPEY'S STATUE.

I saw in the *Palazzo Spada* the statue of Pompey; the statue at whose base Cæsar fell. *Dickens.*

Returning home I saw the palace of Cardinal *Spada*, where is a most magnificent hall painted by Daniele da Volterra and Giulio Piocentino, who made the fret in the little court, but the rare perspectives are of Bolognesi. *John Evelyn*, 1644.

Spada Pompey. See POMPEY'S STATUE.

Spagna, Piazza di. See PIAZZA DI SPAGNA.

Spalatro. A picture by Washington Allston (1779-1843). In the possession of John Taylor Johnston, New York. This picture is said to have been pronounced by the painter his best work.

Spanish Armada. See ARMADA, THE SPANISH.

Spanish Dwarf. A great pearl in the Green Gallery (Das grüne Gewölbe) in Dresden. It is nearly as large as a pullet's egg.

Spanish Square. See PIAZZA DI SPAGNA.

Spanish Steps. A magnificent flight of steps leading from the Piazza di Spagna, or Spanish Square, in Rome, to the church of Trinità de' Monti on the Pincian Hill.

☞ "Behind the fountain [in the Piazza di Spagna] rises a flight of stone stairs. They are as broad as a street, and as high as the neighboring houses. It is the so-called Spanish Stairs, which lead to the French cloister for nuns, to the French Academy, as well as to the finest and most frequented promenades. These stairs once bore a disreputable name on account of the midnight assaults that took place there. During the day, this place swarms with beggars with withered limbs; some hop like frogs, using their hands to spring on; others lie down at full length and show their decrepit limbs."

Hans Christian Andersen.

Spasimo, Lo. [The spasm, or convulsion.] A not unfrequent subject of representation by the mediæval painters, in which is exhibited the affliction of Mary as she witnessed the sorrowful procession to Calvary, and her divine Son sinking under the weight of the cross. The most celebrated of these compositions is the well known picture entitled Lo Spasimo di Sicilia. [See *infra.*]

Spasimo di Sicilia. A celebrated altar-picture by Raphael Sanzio (1483-1520), representing the affliction [*spasimo*, spasm, or convulsion] of Mary at the moment when Christ is sinking under the weight of the cross. This picture derives its name from the circumstance that it was originally painted for the altar of the convent-church of Santa Maria dello Spasimo, at Palermo, Sicily. The composition of this picture is believed to have been imitated from Albert Dürer. It is now in the gallery of Madrid, Spain.

☞ "The veneration at all times entertained for this picture was probably enhanced by a remarkable fact in its history. Raphael painted it towards the close of the year 1517; and when finished, it was embarked at the port of Ostia, to be consigned to Palermo. A storm came on, the vessel foundered at sea, and all was lost except the case containing this picture, which was floated by the currents into the Bay of Genoa, and on being landed the wondrous masterpiece of art was taken out unhurt. The Genoese at first refused to give it up, insisting that it had been preserved and floated to their shores by the miraculous interposition of the Blessed Virgin herself; and it required a positive mandate from the Pope before they would restore it to the Olivetan fathers."

Passavant's Rafael, referred to by Mrs. Jameson.

Spectre of the Brocken. A singular optical phenomenon which is occasionally seen at sunrise or sunset from the summit of the Brocken (or Blocksberg, *Mons Bructerus*), the highest of the Harz Mountains, in Prussian Saxony. It consists of a gigantic projection of the observer, or observers, upon misty clouds which rise out of the valley on the side of the mountain opposite to the sun. The apparition, which is commonly seen eight or nine times during the year, was formerly looked upon with superstitious awe.

☞ "Among the various legends current in that wild country, there is a favorite one, which supposes the Hartz to be haunted with a kind of tutelar demon, in the shape of a wild man, of huge stature, his head wreathed with oak-leaves, and his middle cinctured with the same, bearing in his hand a pine torn up by the roots. It is certain that many profess to have seen such a form, traversing with huge strides, in a line parallel to their own course, the opposite ridge of a mountain, when divided from it by a narrow glen; and, indeed, the fact of the apparition is so generally admitted, that modern scepticism has only found refuge by ascribing it to optical deception."

Sir Walter Scott

☞ "The cause is very simple. It is always seen at sunrise, when the eastern side of the Brocken is free from clouds, and at the same time the mist rises from the valley on the opposite side. The shadow of every thing on the Brocken is then thrown in grand proportions upon the mist, and is seen surrounded with a luminous halo. It is somewhat singular that such a spectacle can be seen upon the Brocken alone, but this is probably accounted for by the formation of the mountain, which collects the mist at just such a distance from the summit as to render the shadow visible." *Bayard Taylor.*

☞ "If the fog is very dry, you see not only yourself but your neighbor; if very damp, only yourself, surrounded by a rainbow-colored glory, which becomes more lustrous and beautiful the damper and thicker the fog is, and the nearer it approaches." *Howitt.*

Spectre of the Rigi. An atmospheric phenomenon observed on the summit of the Rigi in Switzerland, and similar to the spectre of the Brocken in the Harz Mountains. It is simply a magnified shadow of objects projected upon a wall of mist.

Speedwell, The. One of the two vessels in which the Pilgrims embarked at Southampton for America in 1620. Soon after leaving port, the Speedwell was declared unseaworthy, and the two vessels put back into the port of Plymouth. Here the company was divided; and those regarded as most desirable for colonists went on board the *Mayflower*, which proceeded on the voyage alone.

Before the *Speedwell's* anchor swung,
Ere yet the Mayflower's sail was spread,
While round his feet the Pilgrims clung,
The pastor spake, and thus he said :—
Holmes.

Speyer Cathedral. A noble church structure in Speyer, or Spires, Germany. It contains the tombs of many German emperors.

☞ "Although the cathedral of Spires cannot boast of the elegance and finish of that of Worms, it is perhaps, taken as a whole, the finest specimen in Europe of a bold and simple building conceived, if the expression may be used, in a truly Doric spirit. . . . There is a simple grandeur about this building which gives a value to the dimensions unknown in later times, and it may be questioned if there is any other mediæval church which impresses the spectator more by its appearance of size than this." *Fergusson.*

Sphinx, The. This ancient and unique monument near Cairo, in Egypt, was supposed to have been cut out from the solid rock in the reign of Thothmes III. or IV.; but the researches of M. Mariette have shown that the Sphinx is anterior to Cheops — of even greater antiquity than the Pyramids. According to Pliny it was 143 feet in length, and the circumference of its head round the forehead was 102 feet, and the paws extended 50 feet. Tablets and an altar were found between the paws; and other evidences show that processions passed up to this altar and offered sacrifices, from which it is evident that the Sphinx (which was an imaginary animal often found as the emblem of royalty in the Pharaonic remains) was deified by the Egyptians, and worshipped as the Sun. Only the head, shoulders, and back can now be seen, the rest being buried in the sand. It has been called, with its half-human, half-animal form, "the best welcome, and the best farewell, to the history and religion of Egypt." We can only wonder what it must have been "when," says Dean Stanley, "on its head there was the royal helmet of Egypt; on its chin the royal beard; when the stone pavement by which men approached the Pyramids ran up between its paws; when immediately under its heart an altar stood, from which the smoke went up into the gigantic nostrils of that nose, now vanished from the face, never to be conceived again!" ⁂ The Sphinx (Σφίγξ) of Greek and Roman mythology was a famous monster described as having the head of a woman, the body of a lion or of a dog, the paws of a lion, and sometimes as having also the wings of a bird. The Sphinx proposed this riddle to travellers: "What animal walks on four legs in the morning, on two at noon, and on three at night?" As those who could not solve this question were torn in pieces, the Sphinx became a very uncomfortable monster; and King Creon offered his crown and his daughter Jocasta to any one who should solve the riddle. Œdipus accomplished the feat by explaining that it was man, who creeps on all fours when an infant, walks on two feet when a man, and uses a stick (for a third foot) when old. The Sphinx then destroyed herself.

☞ "One of our party said, on our arrival [at the Pyramids], 'When we were passing the Sphinx'—'Oh, the Sphinx!' cried I, 'you don't mean that you have seen the Sphinx!' To be sure they had; and they insisted on it that I had too,—that I must have seen it,—could not have missed it. I was utterly bewildered. It was strange enough to have forgotten it; but not to have seen it was inexplicable. However, on visiting it later in the day I found I had seen it. Being intent on the Pyramid before me, I had taken the Sphinx for a capriciously-formed rock, like so many that we had passed—forgetting that I should not meet with limestone at Geezeh. I rather doubt whether any traveller would take the Sphinx for any thing but a rock unless he was looking for it, or had his eye caught by some casual light. . . . Now I was half afraid of it. The full, serene gaze of its round face, rendered ugly by the loss of the nose, which was a very handsome feature of the old Egyptian face,—this full gaze, and the stony calm of its attitude, almost turn one to stone. So life-like,—so huge, so monstrous,—it is really a fearful spectacle. I saw a man sitting in a fold of the neck,—as a fly might settle on a horse's mane. In that crease he reposed, while far over his head extended the vast pent-house of the jaw; and above that the dressed hair on either side the face,—each bunch a mass of stone which might crush a dwelling-house. . . . Fancy the long, well-opened eyes, in such proportion as this,—eyes which have gazed unwinking into vacancy, while mighty Pharaohs, and Hebrew law-givers, and Persian princes, and Greek philosophers, and Antony with Cleopatra by his side, and Christian anchorites, and Arab warriors, and European men of science, have been brought hither in succession by the unpausing ages to look up into those eyes,—so full of meaning, though so fixed!"

Miss Martineau.

☞ "The face is (supposing the nose restored) much like the Berber countenance. The long mild eye, the thick but not protuberant lips, and the projecting jaw; with the intelligent, gentle expression of the whole face, are very like what one sees in Nubia at every village." *Miss Martineau.*

☞ "Comely the creature is, but the comeliness is not of this world: the once worshipped beast is a deformity and a monster to this generation, and yet you can see that those lips so thick and heavy were fashioned according to some ancient mould of beauty." *A. W. Kinglake.*

Everywhere greatness and littleness seemed so inexplicably blended: Nature, like the *Sphinx*, her emblem, with her fair woman's face and neck, showed also the claws of a Lioness. *Carlyle.*

This human mind wrote history, and this must read it. The *Sphinx* must solve her own riddle. *Emerson.*

The *Sphinx* is drowsy,
Her wings are furled;
Her ear is heavy,
She broods on the world.
"Who'll tell me my secret,
The ages have kept?—
I awaited the seer,
While they slumbered and slept."
Emerson.

And she—
Colossal Woman, couchant in the sands,
Who has a lion's body, paws for hands,
(If she was winged, like the Theban one,
The wide-spread wings are gone:)
Nations have fallen round her, but she stands;
Dynasties came and went, but she went not;
She saw the Pharaohs and the Shepherd Kings,
Chariots and horsemen in their dread array,—
Cambyses, Alexander, Antony,
The hosts of standards, and the eagle wings,
Whom, to her ruinous sorrow, Egypt drew:
She saw, and she forgot.
R. H. Stoddard.

Behold!
The *Sphinx* is Africa. The bond
Of silence is upon her.
Joaquin Miller.

Spielberg. A famous castle, formerly the citadel of Brünn, the capital of Moravia, but now a prison. It is noted as the prison of Silvio Pellico (1789–1854), who was arrested in October, 1820, as a member of the Carbonari, and in 1822 was sentenced to 15 years of imprisonment (*carcere duro*), and was confined here until August, 1830. His well-known narrative "Mie Prigioni" (My Prisons) tells the story of his imprisonments.

And, such proved possible, thy throne to me
Shall seem as holy a place as Pellico's
Venetian dungeon; or as *Spielberg's* grate,
Where the fair Lombard woman hung the rose
Of her sweet soul, by its own dewy weight,
(Because her sun shone *inside* to the close!)
And pining so, died early, yet too late
For what she suffered!
Mrs. Browning.

Safe now is *Spielberg's* dungeon cell,
Safe drear Siberia's frozen hell:
With Slavery's flag o'er both unrolled,
What of the New World fears the Old?
Whittier.

No prisoner in *Spielberg* was ever more cautiously deprived of writing materials.
Lowell.

Spitalfields. A district in London, formerly belonging to the Priory of St. Mary Spital, now thickly settled by weavers.

☞ "Spittlefields and the parts adjoining became a great harbor for poor Protestant strangers, Walloons and French, who, as in former days, so of late, have been found to become exiles from their own country for their religion, and for the avoiding cruel persecution. Here they found quiet and security, and settled themselves in their several trades and occupations, weavers especially." *Stow.*

Cromwell, Blake, Marlborough, Chatham, Nelson, and Wellington are not to be trifled with; and the brutal strength which lies at the bottom of society, the animal ferocity of the quays and cockpits, the bullies of the costermongers of Shoreditch, Seven Dials, and *Spitalfields*, they know how to wake up. *Emerson.*

'Twas August; and the fierce sun overhead
Smote on the squalid streets of Bethnal Green,
And the pale weaver, through his windows seen
In *Spitalfields*, looked thrice dispirited.
Matthew Arnold.

Sposalizio, Lo. [The Marriage.] A familiar subject of representation by the great painters of the Middle Ages, in connection with both the Virgin and Joseph, and with St. Catherine and the Saviour. See MARRIAGE OF THE VIRGIN and MARRIAGE OF ST. CATHERINE, also MARRIAGE AT CANA.

Spring Garden. A region in St. James's Park, London, formerly noted for its sights and amusements. The name was also applied to other public gardens. *Vauxhall* was once called by this name.

In the company of that charming guide [the "Spectator" and "Tatler"] . . . we can take boat at Temple Stairs, and accompany Sir Roger de Coverley and Mr. Spectator to *Spring Garden.*
Thackeray.

Spring Grove. A well-known and beautiful cemetery three miles from Cincinnati, O., approached by a fine avenue. The cemetery comprises about 450 acres. It was established in 1845.

Springfield Arsenal. A large building in Springfield, Mass., belonging to the United States, in which some 175,000 stand of arms are stored.

This is the *Arsenal.* From floor to ceiling,
Like a huge organ rise the burnished arms;
But from their silent pipes no anthem pealing
Startles the villages with strange alarms.
Longfellow.

Squire's. A coffee-house in London, near Gray's Inn, which was so named from one Squire, by whom it was kept, and who died in 1717. Sir Roger de Coverley and the "Spectator" visited Squire's.

Staalhof. See TRUSTEES OF THE STAALHOF.

Staffa Madonna. A Holy Family by Raphael (1483-1520), and one of his earliest paintings. In the Palazzo Connestabile in Perugia, Italy.

Stafford Gallery. See BRIDGEWATER HOUSE.

Stafford House. The city residence of the Duke of Sutherland, in St. James's Park, London, called the finest private mansion in the city. It contains a fine collection of pictures known as the Sutherland Gallery.

Why is it that the virtue of Exeter Hall and *Stafford House* can tolerate this fact [the contempt of the native population by the British in India], without a blush, yet condemn with pharisaic zeal the social inequality of the negro and the white races in America? *Bayard Taylor.*

Stag Hunt. A picture by Peter Paul Rubens (1577-1640). In the Museum at Berlin, Prussia. See also HUNTED STAG.

Stahleck. An ancient feudal fortress now in ruins near Bacharach on the Rhine. It was formerly the residence of the Electors Palatine.

Staircase, Holy. See SANTA SCALA.

Stampede, The. A well-known picture by Rosa Bonheur (b. 1822), the French painter of animals. It has been reproduced.

Standard, Battle of the. See BATTLE OF THE STANDARD.

Standing Stones of Stennis. An ancient and curious monument in the Orkneys, consisting of two circles of erect stones, with a few lying prostrate.

☞ "They are thought to be of pre-Scandinavian or of Celtic origin. They were erected over 900 years ago, and, as Pagan relics, are second, in Great Britain, only to the celebrated Stonehenge, near Salisbury." *J. F. Hunnewell.*

Stannaries. The name given to the districts of Cornwall and Devon, in which the tin-mines are situated (Lat. *stannum*, tin). The miners enjoy certain privileges of suing and being sued only in their own courts.

Stanza d'Eliodoro [of Heliodorus]. See STANZE OF RAPHAEL.

Stanza del Incendio. One of the four rooms in the Vatican at Rome, known as the Stanze of Raphael, because decorated with paintings by that artist.

Stanza delle Maschere. A small apartment in the Vatican, Rome, so called from the masks (*Maschere*) which form the subject of the mosaic on the floor.

☞ "In an adjoining room, the richness, beauty, and delicacy of which almost transport us into the fabled regions of enchantment, supported by columns and pilasters of transparent alabaster, adorned with ancient bassi-relievi of exquisite sculpture, and floored with the bright pictured mosaics of imperial palaces — in this beautiful chamber are arranged in marble niches the famous Ganymede, perhaps the finest extant, the crouching Venus, the Faun of Hadrian's villa, a beautiful Bacchante, etc. . . . This beautiful apartment is called the *Stanza delle Maschere*." *Eaton.*

Stanza della Segnatura. See STANZE OF RAPHAEL.

Stanze of Raphael. [*Stanza*, room.] The name given to four rooms in the palace of the Vatican at Rome, decorated with frescos by Raphael. They are called, respectively, the *Stanza della Segnatura*, from a judicial assembly once held here; the *Stanza* of the *Incendio del Borgo*, from a picture of the fire in the Leonine City in 847; the *Stanza d'Eliodoro*, from a picture of Heliodorus driven from the Temple; and the *Sala di Constantino*, or Hall of Constantine.

☞ "You return and make your first circuit of the four celebrated *Stanze* of Raphael. These were the apartments of Julius II.: here the Pope transacted business, and in one of them signed his briefs. The painter here is secondary: the apartment was not made for his work, but it for the apartment." *Taine, Trans.*

Staple Inn. One of the Inns of Chancery, London. It became such in the reign of Henry V.

☞ "Behind the most ancient part of Holborn . . . is a little nook composed of two irregular quadrangles called *Staple Inn.* It is one of those nooks, the turning into which out of the clashing street imparts to the relieved pedestrian the sensation of having put cotton in his ears, and velvet soles on his boots." *Dickens.*

☞ "I went astray in Holborn through an arched entrance over which was '*Staple Inn*,' and here likewise seemed to be offices; but in a court opening inwards from this, there was a surrounding seclusion of quiet dwelling-houses with beautiful green shrubbery and grass plots. . . . There was not a quieter spot in England than this, and it was very strange to have drifted into it so suddenly out of the bustle and rumble of Holborn." *Hawthorne.*

Star and Garter. An old tavern in Pall Mall, London. It is no longer standing. The Literary

Club held meetings here. In a room of this tavern was fought, in 1765, the duel between Lord Byron (not the poet) and Mr. Chaworth, which resulted in the death of the latter. The first cricket-club was formed here in 1774.

> Confess how many times you have read Béranger, and how many Milton? If you go to the *Star and Garter*, don't you grow sick of that vast, luscious landscape, and long for the sight of a couple of cows, or a donkey, and a few yards of common? *Thackeray.*

Star Chamber. The council-chamber of the Old Palace at Westminster, London, "in which the king sat in extraordinary cases," built by Henry VIII. The last buildings used for this purpose were taken down in the early part of the present century. This chamber was so called from the stars upon the ceiling. Here was the court where could be inflicted every punishment but death.

> These poor men [the Puritans], driven out of their own country, not able well to live in Holland, determine on settling in the New World. Black untamed forests are there, and wild savage creatures; but not so cruel as *Star-chamber* hangmen. *Carlyle.*

> *Shallow.* Sir Hugh, persuade me not; I will make a *Star-chamber* matter of it: If he were twenty sir John Falstaffs, he shall not abuse Robert Shallow, esquire. *Shakespeare.*

> Here in England, in those days, earthly masters were still apt to put their heels on the necks of men. The *Star Chamber* was gone, but Jeffreys had not yet reigned. *Anthony Trollope.*

Star Chamber. A famous apartment in the Mammoth Cave, Kentucky. It is a magnificent hall, with arched sides and a flat roof. The latter is of a dark hue, and is relieved by brilliant substances resembling stars, which, when illuminated by Bengal lights, produce a wonderful effect.

Star of Empire. A picture by Emmanuel Leutze (1816-1868). In the Rotunda of the Capitol at Washington.

Star of the South. A celebrated diamond found by a negro in Brazil in 1853. It originally weighed 254½ carats, but by cutting this weight has been reduced to 125 carats.

Star of the West. A vessel formerly belonging to the government of the United States. At the close of 1860, while engaged in taking supplies to the garrison in Fort Sumter in the harbor of Charleston, S.C., she was fired upon by the insurgents who were preparing to attack the fort.

Starkenburg. A ruined castle between Darmstadt and Heidelberg, Germany.

State Coach. See CORONATION COACH.

State House Row. A line of ancient buildings in Philadelphia, Penn., the central one of which is Independence Hall. They are now used for municipal purposes. See INDEPENDENCE HALL.

State Street. **1.** The chief business street in Boston, Mass., in or near which is the centre of the banking and moneyed interests of the city and of New England.

> Thus a king or a general does not need a fine coat, and a commanding person may save himself all solicitude on that point. There are always slovens in *State Street* or Wall Street, who are not less considered. If a man have manners and talent he may dress roughly and carelessly. *Emerson.*

2. A main thoroughfare in Chicago, Ill., called the "Broadway" of the city.

Stationers' Hall. A building in London belonging to the Company of Stationers, one of the ancient city guilds. It existed as a fraternity long before the introduction of printing. The privilege was granted them by James I., in 1603, of the sole printing of "Prymers, Psalters and Psalms, as well as Almanacks, and prognostications and the Latin books used in the grammar schools." The proprietor of every published work is required to register his claim in the books of the Stationers' Company, before any legal proceeding can take place. From early times the Stationers' Company has been celebrated for it sumptuous state, and its attendance upon the Lord Mayor's shows. In the Hall, on Almanack Day, in November, are published the Almanacks printed for the Company, which still contain astrological predictions.

What does it signify whether a poor dear dead dunce is to be stuck up in Surgeons' or in *Stationers' Hall?* Is it so bad to unearth his bones as his blunders? *Byron.*

Statue. For statues, etc., see the proper name following; e.g., STATUE OF MARCUS AURELIUS, see MARCUS AURELIUS.

Staubbach. [Stream of Dust.] A famous waterfall at Lauterbrunnen, Switzerland, one of the loftiest in Europe.

☞ "It [the *Staubbach*] is neither mist nor water, but a something between both; its immense height gives it a wave or curve, — a spreading here or condension there, — wonderful and indescribable. The torrent is in shape like the tail of a white horse streaming in the wind, — such as it might be conceived would be that of the 'pale horse' on which Death is mounted in the Apocalypse." *Lord Byron.*

Staunton Harold. The seat of Earl Ferrers, in the county of Leicester, England.

Stein. An ancient Austrian castle and stronghold, now in ruins, near Baden, Switzerland.

Stennis, Standing Stones of. See STANDING STONES OF STENNIS.

Stephen. See ST. STEPHEN, MARTYRDOM OF ST. STEPHEN, and STONING OF ST. STEPHEN.

Stephen's, St. See ST. STEPHEN'S.

Sternberg. One of two ruined castles on the Rhine, near Boppart, both crowning the top of a high rock. The other castle is called the Liebenstein, and the two together are known as the Brothers.

Stirling Castle. This castle in Stirling, Scotland, on the summit of a hill overlooking the river Forth, commands a charming view. The fortress has been identified with the fortunes of Scotland, having repeatedly fallen into the hands of the English and been rescued by Scottish heroism. It has also been a royal residence. Its date and origin are unknown.

☞ "This fortress is one of the four to be kept always in repair, and garrisoned according to the terms of the 'union' of England and Scotland. . . . So that, although antiquated, and indeed almost useless as a stronghold now, Stirling Castle will continue to present a military aspect." *J. F. Hunnewell.*

☞ "One could not but think of the old days Scott has described.

'The castle gates were open flung,
The quivering drawbridge rocked and rung,
And echoed loud the flinty street,
Beneath the coursers' clattering feet,
As slowly down the steep descent
Fair Scotland's king and nobles went,
While all along the crowded way,
Was jubilee and loud huzza.'

"The place has been long deserted as a palace; but it is one of the four fortresses which, by the articles of union between Scotland and England, are always to be kept in repair." *Mrs. H. B. Stowe.*

I have been sinuous as the Links of Forth seen from *Stirling Castle*, or as that other river which threads the Berkshire valley, and runs, a perennial stream, through my memory. *Holmes.*

From *Stirling Castle* we had seen
The mazy Forth unravelled;
Had trod the banks of Clyde and Tay,
And with the Tweed had travelled.
Wordsworth.

Stoa. A celebrated porch, or roofed colonnade, in ancient Athens, in which the philosopher Zeno and his successors taught. From this place the disciples of Zeno derived their name of Stoics. [Also called the *Porch*.]

But, above all, the mysticism of Fichte might astonish us. The cold, colossal, adamantine spirit, standing erect and clear, like a Cato Major among degenerate men: fit to have been the teacher of the *Stoa*, and to have discoursed of Beauty and Virtue in the groves of Academe! *Carlyle.*

Stoke Park. The seat of Lord Taunton, about 17 miles from London.

☞ "The house is large, but not very good-looking outside. Inside, however, it is fine and filled with fine works of art, ancient and recent, among them the last four bas-reliefs by Thorwaldsen. . . . Of course I was taken to see the Old Manor-house, the scene of Gray's 'Long Story,' that begins, 'In Briton's Isle and Arthur's days.' It is well cared for, and is an excellent specimen of the Elizabethan style. The church, too, and above all the churchyard, which gave the world the undying Elegy. They are most poetical places; the architecture, the position, and the plantations being just what you would like to have them, and treated with the respect they deserve."

George Ticknor.

Stolzenfels. This is a royal castle on the banks of the Rhine, three miles above Coblenz, the highest point of which is 410 feet above the river. It was in the Middle Ages a residence of the archbishops; but in 1688 it fell into the hands of the French, and was nearly destroyed. During this century it has been entirely restored. The view from the castle is exquisitely lovely, and scarcely surpassed by any on the Rhine.

Stone of Destiny. See STONE OF SCONE.

Stone of Sân. A famous trilingual stone, discovered at Sân (Tanis), and now preserved in the Museum of Egyptian Antiquities at Cairo, Egypt. It is known to English students of Egyptian antiquities as the Decree of Canopus. The French call it *La Pierre de Sân.* It bears the inscription in three characters, Greek, hieroglyphic, and demotic, of a decree issued by the Egyptian priests at Canopus in the ninth year of Ptolemy Euergetes (254 B.C.). There is a plaster cast of this monument in the British Museum, London.

Stone of Scone. On this stone, of legendary fame, which is now enclosed within the older of the two Coronation Chairs in Westminster Abbey, the Scottish kings had for ages been crowned. The "Fatal" or "Prophetic" Stone of Scone, so called from the Scottish belief that the power of the nation would decline if the stone were lost, was brought from the Abbey of Scone by Edward I., and by him placed in Westminster Abbey and enclosed in a wooden chair. At an earlier date it had been transferred from Ireland to the Abbey of Scone. It was also called Jacob's Pillow, from the legend that it was the pillow upon which the patriarch slept when he beheld the vision of the ladder reaching to heaven. See CORONATION CHAIR.

☞ "The legends of the old historians inform us that this is the very stone on which the patriarch Jacob laid his head in the plain of Luz; that it was brought from Egypt into Spain by Gathelus, the supposed founder of the Scottish nation; that it was thence transported into Ireland." *Taylor.*

Ni fallit fatum, Scoti quocunque locatum
Invenient lapidem, regnare tenentur
ibidem.

In the Minster of Scone, within Scotlȧd
grȯnd,
Sittyng upon the regal stone full sound,
As all the Kynges there used had afore,
On Sainct Andrewes day, with al joye
therefore.

Stonehenge. A famous monument of antiquity, being probably the remains of a Druid temple, though antiquaries are not fully agreed as to its origin or object. It is situated in a plain near Amesbury, and about eight miles from Salisbury, England. It consists of a number of immense stones arranged in two circles, with flat pieces partly connecting them at the top.

☞ "It is evident that Stonehenge was at one time a spot of great sanctity. A glance at the ordnance map will show that the tumuli cluster in great numbers round and within sight of it; within a radius of three miles, there are about three hundred burial-mounds, while the rest of the country is comparatively free from them. If, then, we could determine the date of these tumuli, we should be justified, I think, in referring the Great Temple itself to the same period. . . . Stonehenge, then, may, I think, be regarded as a monument of the Bronze age, though apparently it was not all erected at one time, the inner circle of small unwrought blue stones being probably older than the rest." *Sir John Lubbock.*

☞ "On the broad downs, under the gray sky, not a house was visible, nothing but Stonehenge, which looked like a group of brown dwarfs in the wide expanse, — Stonehenge and the barrows — which rose like green bosses about the plain, and a few hayricks. On the top of a mountain the old temple would not be more impressive. Far and wide a few shepherds with their flocks sprinkled the plain, and a bagman drove along the road. It looked as if the wide margin given in this crowded isle to this primeval temple were accorded by the veneration of the British race to the old egg out of which all their ecclesiastical structures and history had proceeded. Stonehenge is a circular colonnade, with a diameter of a hundred feet, and enclosing a second and third colonnade within. We walked around the stones and clambered over them, to wont ourselves with their strange aspect and groupings, and found a nook sheltered from the wind among them where C. [Carlyle] lighted his cigar. It was pleasant to see that just this simplest of all simple structures — two upright stones and a lintel laid across — had long outstood all later churches, and were like what is most permanent on the face of the planet: these, and the barrows — mere mounds (of which there are a hundred and sixty within a circle of three miles about Stonehenge) like the same mound upon the plain of Troy, which still makes good to the passing mariner on Hellespont, the vaunt of Homer and the fame of Achilles. . . . We counted and measured by paces the biggest stones, and soon knew as much as any man can suddenly know of the inscrutable temple. There are ninety-four stones, and there were probably once one hundred and sixty. The temple is circular and uncovered, and the situation fixed astronomically — the grand entrances here, and at Abury, being placed exactly north-east, as all the gates of the old cavern temples are. . . . The chief mystery is that any mystery should have been allowed to settle on so remarkable a monument in a country on which all the Muses have kept their eyes now for eighteen hundred years. We are not yet to learn much more than is known of this structure." *R. W. Emerson.*

Stone is laid on the top of stone, just as it comes to hand: a trowel or two of biographic mortar, if perfectly convenient, being perhaps spread in here and there, by way of cement; and so the strangest pile suddenly arises; amorphous, pointing every way but to the zenith, — here a block of granite, there a mass of pipe-clay; till the whole finishes, when the materials are finished, — and you leave it standing to posterity, like some miniature *Stonehenge*, a perfect architectural enigma. *Carlyle.*

I have, in the abstract, no disrespect for Jews. They are a piece of stubborn antiquity, compared with which *Stonehenge* is in its nonage. They date beyond the pyramids. *Charles Lamb.*

Rocks scattered about. — *Stonehenge-like monoliths. Holmes.*

Stones of Clava. An interesting sepulchral monument of antiquity, and one of the most extensive remains of the kind in Britain, near Culloden, Scotland. It consists of a circle of stones surrounding a line of cairns.

Stones of Stennis. See STANDING STONES OF STENNIS.

Stoning of Stephen. A cartoon by Raphael Sanzio (1483-1520), from which one of the tapestries in the Vatican at Rome was executed.

Stonyhurst. An ancient and celebrated baronial residence in Lancashire, England. It is now the chief Jesuit College in the kingdom.

Storm in the Rocky Mountains. A well-known picture by Albert Bierstadt (b. 1829).

☞ "No picture that we have ever seen has more entirely conveyed a sense of natural sublimity, and there is so much to study that the spectator is detained before it for a long time." *Saturday Review.*

Storm King. An eminence on the Hudson River near West Point. It was formerly called the Boterberg, by the Dutch skippers, but received its present name from N. P. Willis. It commands a beautiful view.

Stowe. The magnificent seat of the Duke of Buckingham, in the parish of the same name near Buckingham, England. It is one of the finest residences in the kingdom.

It puzzles much the sages' brains,
Where Eden stood of yore:
Some place it in Arabia's plains,
Some say it is no more.

But Cobham can these tales confute,
As all the curious know;
For he has proved beyond dispute
That Paradise is *Stowe*.
Nathaniel Cotton.

Strada Balbi. [*Strada*, street.] One of the two finest streets in Genoa, Italy. It is adorned with palaces of superb architecture.

When shall I forget the Streets of Palaces: the Strada Nuova and the *Strada Balbi!* *Dickens.*

Strada di Costanza. A name sometimes given to the territory between Perugia and Foligno in Italy, after St. Constantius, bishop of Perugia in the third or fourth century.

Strada di Roma. See TOLEDO.

Strada Nuova. [New Street.] A famous street in Genoa, Italy, sometimes called the street of palaces on account of the noble old palaces that front upon it.

When shall I forget the Streets of Palaces: the *Strada Nuova* and the Strada Balbi! or how the former looked one summer day, when I first saw it underneath the brightest and most intensely blue of summer skies: with its narrow perspective of immense mansions, reduced to a tapering and most precious strip of brightness, looking down upon the heavy shade below! *Dickens.*

Straight Street. An ancient street in Damascus, Syria, beginning at one of the gates of the city and extending about a mile, formerly in a straight direction, but at present with many windings. It was originally without question a broad promenade, but is now in places hardly more than a narrow lane. Of its identity with the street mentioned in the New Testament there can be no doubt; and many localities connected with the history of Paul are pointed out, such as the house in which he lodged, and the spot where he escaped from the city in a basket.

They led him [Paul] by the hand, and brought him to Damascus. . . . And the Lord said unto him [Ananias], Arise and go into the street which is called *Straight*, and inquire in the house of Judas for one called Saul, of Tarsus; for, behold, he prayeth. *Acts* ix. 8, 11.

Strand, The. 1. A great thoroughfare in the city of London, extending from Temple Bar to Charing Cross, and skirting the margin of the river Thames, of which it was formerly the strand, or shore. The Strand was for three centuries a street of palaces, but these palaces are now gone.

☞ "You would think London Strand the main artery of the world. I suppose there is no thoroughfare on the face of the earth where the stream of human life runs with a tide so overwhelming. In any other street in the world you catch the eye of the passer-by. In the Strand no man sees another except as a solid body whose contact is to be avoided. You are safe nowhere on the pavement without the vigilance of your senses." *N. P. Willis.*

The *Strand*, that goodly thorow-fare betweene
The Court and City; and where I have seene
Well-nigh a million passing in one day.
George Wither.

For who would leave, unbribed, Hibernia's land,
Or change the rocks of Scotland for the *Strand?* *Samuel Johnson.*

I often shed tears in the motley *Strand* from fulness of joy at so much life.
Lamb to Wordsworth.

After an hour's walk in the *Strand* . . . one has the spleen, one meditates suicide.
Taine, Trans.

Cheapside, the *Strand*, Fleet Street, and Ludgate Hill,
Each name a very story in itself.
Robert Leighton.

2. A favorite promenade in Calcutta, India.

Strasbourg, Boulevart de. See SÉBASTOPOL, BOULEVART DE.

Strasburg Cathedral. This cathedral, which is one of the grandest Gothic structures in the world, was founded in 510, and destroyed by lightning in 1007. Its restoration was commenced in the eleventh century. The sculptures above the portal are said to belong to the thirteenth and fourteenth centuries. The upper part of the spire was erected by Johann Hultz, of Cologne, at the commencement of the fifteenth century. Its height is 468 feet, which is greater than that of any building in Europe. The design of this cathedral is ascribed to Erwin of Steinbach, whose plans are still preserved. This church suffered some damage during the bombardment of Strasburg in the Franco-Prussian war, but the injuries have been repaired.

☞ "Next in rank to Cologne among German cathedrals is that at Strasburg. It is, however, so much smaller as hardly to admit of a fair comparison. The whole of the eastern part of this church belongs to an older basilica built in the eleventh and twelfth centuries, and is by no means remarkable for its beauty or its size, besides being so overpowered by the nave which has been added to it, as to render its appearance somewhat insignificant. The nave and the western front are the glory and the boast of Alsace, and possess in a remarkable degree all the beauties and the defects of the German style. It is not known when the nave was commenced, but it seems to have been finished about the year 1275, a date which, if authentic, is quite sufficient to settle the controversy as to whether any part of Cologne is of an earlier age, every thing we see in Strasburg being of an older style than any thing in that church. . . . Altogether the façade of the cathedral at Strasburg is imposing from its mass, and fascinating from its richness; but there is no building in France or England where such great advantages have been thrown away in so reckless a manner and by such an unintelligent hand."
Fergusson.

☞ "We climbed the spire, we gained the roof. . . . Here I saw the names of Goethe and Herder. . . . But the inside! — a forest-like firmament, glorious in holiness; windows many-hued as the Hebrew psalms; a gloom solemn and pathetic as man's mysterious existence, a richness gorgeous and manifold as his wonderful nature. In this Gothic architecture we see earnest Northern races whose nature was a composite of influences from pine forest, mountain and storm, expressing in vast proportions and gigantic masonry, those ideas of infinite duration and existence which Christianity opened before them. A barbaric wildness mingles itself with fanciful, ornate abundance; it is the blossoming of northern forests."
Beecher.

☞ "I once ascended the spire of Strasburg Cathedral, which is the highest, I think, in Europe. It is a shaft of stone filagree-work, frightfully open, so that the guide puts his arms behind you to keep you from falling. To climb it is a noonday nightmare, and to think of having climbed it crisps all the fifty-six joints of one's twenty digits. While I was on it, 'pinnacled dim in the intense inane,' a strong wind was blowing, and I felt sure that the spire was rocking. It swayed back and forward like a stalk of rye or a cat-o'-nine-tails (bulrush) with a bobolink on it."
Holmes.

Santa Croce and the Dome of St. Peter's are lame copies after a divine model. *Strasburg Cathedral* is a material counterpart of the soul of Erwin of Steinbach.
Emerson.

A great master of his craft,
Erwin von Steinbach; but not he alone,
For many generations labored with him.
Children that came to see these Saints in stone,
As day by day out of the blocks they rose,
Grew old and died, and still the work went on,
And on, and on, and is not yet completed.
Longfellow.

Up the stone lace-work chiselled by the wise
Erwin of Steinbach, dizzily up to where
In the noon-brightness the great minster's tower,
Jewelled with sunbeams on its mural crown,
Rose like a visible prayer.
Whittier.

Strasburg Clock. A famous clock, — a wonder of art, — in the cathedral of Strasburg, Germany. The original, which was made centuries ago, having fallen into decay, a German artist of the present century has reproduced the complete mechanism of the old clock. At the stroke of noon, the Twelve Apostles issue from the side door of a chapel, and move in procession before the Saviour, who bows his head in blessing as they pass, the cock crows and flaps his wings, Satan watches Judas, while the bells chime and the organ is played. Upon the dial of this clock are marked the minutes, hours, days, weeks, months, the phases of the moon, and the constellations.

Three of us stood in the Strasburg streets,
In the wide and open square,
Where, quaint and old, and touched with the gold
Of a summer morn, at stroke of noon
The tongue of the great cathedral tolled,
And into the church with the crowd we strolled
To see their wonder, the famous Clock.
Anonymous.

Strathfieldsaye. The seat of the Duke of Wellington near Silchester, England.

Straw Hat. See CHAPEAU DE PAILLE.

Straw Street. [Fr. *Rue du Fouarre.*] A famous old street in Paris, originally called Rue de l'Ecole, the University having been founded there. Fouarre is the old French for *foin*, and it was formerly a hay and straw market. Rabelais speaks of it as the place where Pantagruel first disputed with the learned doctors, and Petrarch frequently refers to it in his Latin writings, and always with a sneer.

It is the light eternal of Sigier,
Who, reading lectures in the *Street of Straw*,
Did syllogize invidious verities.
Dante, Paradiso.

☞ "A common idealist would have been rather alarmed at the thought of introducing the name of a street in Paris — Straw Street (Rue du Fouarre) — into the midst of a description of the highest heavens. . . . What did it matter to Dante, up in heaven there, whether the mob below thought him vulgar or not? Sigier *had* read in Straw Street. That was the fact, and he had to say so, and there is an end." *Ruskin.*

Strawberry Girl. A picture by Sir Joshua Reynolds (1723–1792). It is familiar through reproductions.

☞ "A sweet and innocent little maiden creeping timidly along, and looking about with great black eyes. Sir Joshua always held that this was one of the half-dozen original things which he had done."

Strawberry Hill. The name of the celebrated residence of Horace Walpole, situated near Twickenham, Surrey, England. It contained many fine specimens of *vertu* collected by him, which were sold at auction in 1842. A private printing-press was also established here, from which several rare and valuable works issued under his immediate direction. It is now the residence of Countess Waldegrave.

They [the English] delight in a freak as the proof of their sovereign freedom. . . . *Strawberry Hill* of Horace Walpole, Fonthill Abbey of Mr. Beckford, were freaks; and Newstead Abbey became one in the hands of Lord Byron. *Emerson.*

Street Scene in Cairo. A picture by Jean Léon Gerôme (b. 1824).

☞ "It is a precious example of delicate and elaborate workmanship; its careful drawing will be enjoyed by all lovers of form, who will also like its profoundly-studied modelling, and the faithfulness which is everywhere observed in the rendering of textures of light and shade." *Athenæum.*

Strozzi Chapel. A chapel in the church of Santa Maria Novella, in Florence, Italy.

I met with this legend again in the famous *Strozzi Chapel* in the S. Maria Novella at Florence. The great frescos of the Last Judgment, so often pointed out as worthy of especial attention, generally engross the mind of the spectator to the exclusion of minor objects; few, therefore, have examined the curious and beautiful old altar-piece, also by Orcagna (A.D. 1349). *Mrs. Jameson.*

Strozzi Maddalena. A well-known portrait by Raphael Sanzio (1483–1520). In the Uffizi Gallery, Florence, Italy.

Strozzi Palace. [Ital. *Palazzo Strozzi.*] A splendid palace in Florence, Italy, erected towards the close of the fifteenth century after designs by Cronaca (1454–1509).

☞ "Taking into account the age when it was built, and the necessity of security combined with purposes of state to which it was to be applied, it will be difficult to find a more faultless design in any city of modern Europe." *Fergusson.*

Stuarts, Tombs of the. See TOMBS OF THE STUARTS.

Studley Royal. The seat of Earl de Grey, near Ripon, England.

Styx, The. A torrent in the Aroanian mountains, in the north-east part of Arcadia, Greece, and emptying into the Crathis. The waterfall of the Styx, well described by Homer and Hesiod, is by far the highest in Greece. From the wildness and gloom of the spot the Styx was early regarded with superstitious reverence and terror. The Greek and Roman poets transferred the Styx to the nether world, of which it is the principal river. According to Herodotus, the Styx has its source near to the Arcadian town of Nonacris.

Styx, The. A well-known subterranean river in the Mammoth Cave, Kentucky; named after the river of hell in ancient Greek and Roman mythology.

Subeibeh. See Bânîâs.

Sublime Porte. [The High Gate.] The gate of the imperial palace at Constantinople, at which justice was administered. Hence applied as a designation of the Turkish government, or the court of the sultan.

Suburra, The. A quarter in ancient Rome, upon the Esquiline Hill, largely occupied by the poorer classes.

Hence we walked to the *Suburra*, where yet remain some ruines and inscriptions.
John Evelyn, 1644.

Sudarium. [Ital. *Il Sudario*; Fr. *Le Saint Suaire.*] The napkin, or, as some say, the veil, which, according to the ancient legend, was used to wipe away the drops of sweat from the brow of the Saviour while bearing his cross on his way to Calvary, and upon which his features were miraculously impressed. See Veronica.

During the interval between the closing of the ancient and the opening of the modern age, the faith of Christians had attached itself to symbols and material objects little better than fetishes. . . To such concrete actualities the worshippers referred their sense of the invisible divinity. The earth of Jerusalem, the Holy Sepulchre, the House of Loreto, the *Sudarium of* St. Veronica, aroused their deepest sentiments of aweful adoration.
J. A. Symonds.

Suffolk House. See Northumberland House.

Sukhrah. See Mosque of Omar.

Suleimaine Mosque. A superb Mohammedan temple in Constantinople, Turkey. It was erected by Solyman the Magnificent, between 1550 and 1555.

☞ "Externally the mosque suffers, like all the buildings of the capital, from the badness of the materials with which it was constructed. Its walls are covered with stucco, its dome with lead; and all the sloping abutments of the dome have to be protected by a metal covering. This, no doubt, detracts from the effect; but still the whole is so massive — every window, every dome, every projection, is so truthful, and tells so exactly the purpose for which it was placed where we find it, that the general result is most satisfactory."
Fergusson.

Suli Castle. A castle standing on an isolated rock 1,000 feet below the summit of the Suliot ridge, in Greece.

Sulpice, St. See St. Sulpice and Place St. Sulpice.

Sumter, The. A noted Confederate privateer, in the War of the Rebellion, under a commission from Jefferson Davis, in the spring of 1861. Her career was brief but very destructive. She ran the blockade at the mouth of the Mississippi, cruised among the West Indies, captured many merchant vessels, and was the terror of the American mercantile marine, being everywhere welcomed in British ports, but was finally driven into the port of Gibraltar, where, in 1862, she was sold.

Sumter, Fort. See Fort Sumter.

Sundwich Höhle. [Sundwich Cave.] A cavern in Westphalia, near Hemar, interesting in a geological regard on account of the fossil remains discovered in it.

Sunium. See Temple of Sunium.

Sunrise in a Mist. A well-known picture by Joseph Mallord William Turner (1775-1851), the English landscape-painter, and regarded one of his best works. Now in the National Gallery, London.

Sunny Side. An ancient mansion on the Hudson River, near Irvington, N.Y., the former home of Washington Irving. The front of the building is covered with ivy from a slip brought from Abbotsford by Irving, who received it from Sir Walter Scott. This old mansion, which was erected in the seventeenth century, was formerly known as

Wolfert's Roost. Irving says that Wolfert inscribed over the door his favorite Dutch motto, "Lust in Rust" (pleasure in quiet), and that the mansion was "thence called Wolfert's Rust (Wolfert's Rest), but by the uneducated, who did not understand Dutch, Wolfert's Roost."

Reader! the Roost still exists. Time, which changes all things, is slow in its operations on a Dutchman's dwelling. The stout Jacob Van Tassel, it is true, sleeps with his fathers; and his great goose-gun with him; yet his stronghold still bears the impress of its Dutch origin. *Irving.*

Suonatore, Il. See VIOLIN PLAYER.

Superga, La. A well-known and celebrated church, situated on an eminence near Turin, Italy. It has been the place of interment for the royal family of Sardinia.

Supper at Emmaus. A famous picture by Titian (1477-1576), originally painted for the Sala de' Pregadi, in the Ducal Palace, Venice. Now in the Gallery of the Louvre, Paris.

☞ "The disciple on the right of the Saviour, raising his hand with no more vehemence of surprise than might become the greatest monarch of his time, is supposed to be the portrait of the Emperor Charles V.; the disciple on the left . . . with round shaven face and a pilgrim's hat, that of Cardinal Ximenes; while the page, with plumed cap, is meant for the Infant, afterwards Philip II." *Lady Eastlake.*

Supper at Emmaus. A well-known and interesting picture by Paul Veronese (1530?-1588), in which "the painter has introduced a large family, supposed to be his own, with an exquisite group of two girls in the centre, caressing a large dog." This picture is in the Louvre, Paris.

Supper, The Last. See LAST SUPPER.

Surgeons, College of. See COLLEGE OF SURGEONS.

Surrender of Breda. A painting by Diego Rodriguez de Silva y Velasquez (1599-1660), and regarded one of the first historical pictures in the world. In the Gallery at Madrid, Spain.

Surrender of Burgoyne. A large picture by John Trumbull (1756-1843), executed under commission from Congress for the Rotunda of the Capitol at Washington. It is well known by engravings.

Surrender of Cornwallis. A large picture by John Trumbull (1756-1843), executed under commission from Congress for the Rotunda of the Capitol at Washington. It is well known by engravings.

Surrey Chapel. A noted place of worship in London, opened as a free and independent church by the Rev. Rowland Hill in 1783.

Since you departed, we have been passing with a kind of comprehensive skip and jump over remaining engagements. And first, the evening after you left, came off the presentation of the inkstand by the ladies of *Surrey Chapel*. *Mrs. H. B. Stowe.*

Surrey Theatre. A theatre in Blackfriars Road, London, built in 1806 on the site of a former edifice burnt, and again built in 1866.

Susannah, History of. A picture by Albert Altdorfer (d. 1538), a German painter. It bears date 1526, and is now in the gallery of Munich, Bavaria.

Suspense. A picture by Sir Edwin Landseer (1803-1873), the celebrated English painter of animals. It is in the National Gallery, London.

Sutherland Gallery. See STAFFORD HOUSE.

Sutro Tunnel. A famous tunnel driven through Mount Davidson in Nevada, for the purpose of intercepting the Great Comstock Lode, at a depth of 2,000 feet. The tunnel is almost four miles long, and is said to have cost $5,000,000. It was named after its projector, Mr. Sutro. See COMSTOCK LODE.

Swamp Angel. A huge piece of ordnance used in the attack by the Union forces upon Fort Wagner, one of the defences of Charleston, S.C., in the War of the Rebellion. It was so named from the fact that it was mounted upon a rampart which had been erected upon piles driven into the deep mud of the swampy land surrounding the fortification.

Swan Theatre. One of the chief London theatres in the age of Shakespeare.

Swedes' Church. See OLD SWEDES' CHURCH.

Sweetheart Abbey. See NEW ABBEY.

Sweno's Stone. A curious monument of antiquity near Forres, in Scotland, supposed to have been erected by Malcolm II. or Macbeth, in memory of the expulsion of the Danes. It is a pillar of sandstone, 23 feet high, covered with figures.

☞ "These figures are arranged closely in five divisions, forming, as it were, so many passages of the story."
Muir.

Symonds Inn. Formerly one of the inns of Chancery in London.

☞ "A little, pale, wall-eyed, woe-begone inn like a large dust-bin of two compartments and a sifter." *Dickens.*

Synodalni Dom. See HOLY SYNOD, HOUSE OF THE.

T.

Tabard, The. An ancient inn formerly situated in Southwark, London, the traditional "hostelry where Chaucer and the other pilgrims met, and, with their host, accorded about the manner of their journey to Canterbury." The buildings of Chaucer's time have disappeared, but were standing in 1602; the oldest now remaining is of the age of Elizabeth, and the most interesting portion is a stone-colored wooden gallery, in front of which is a picture of the Canterbury pilgrimage, said to have been painted by Blake. Instead of the ancient sign of the Tabard, the ignorant landlord (says Aubrey) put up about the year 1676, the sign of Talbot, which it now bears.

Befell that in that season, on a day
At Southwark at the *Tabard* as I lay,
Readie to wander on my pilgrimage
To Canterbury with devout courage,
At night was come into that hostelrie
Well nine and twenty in a companie
Of sundrie folke, by adventure yfall
In fellowship, and pilgrims were they all,
That toward Canterbury woulden ride.
Chaucer.

The name of Chaucer is not more identified with the *Tabard Inn* at Southwark, nor Scott's with the Trosachs and Loch Katrine, . . . than that of Byron with the Ducal Palace. *Hillard.*

Tabernacle, The. A frequent designation for the chapels or places of worship of some of the religious sects. The original building which has given its name to succeeding structures of the kind was built in Moorfields, London, in 1752, and was so called in allusion to the tabernacle of the Israelites in the Wilderness. Whitefield and Wesley both preached in this building. The building known as the Metropolitan Tabernacle, in London, was built for Mr. Spurgeon in 1861, and is capable of seating 6,500 persons.

Tabernacle, The. An immense wooden building in Salt Lake City, Utah Territory, the chief religious edifice or temple of Mormon worship. Though built of wood it has 46 sandstone pillars upon which rests its huge dome-shaped roof. The building is oval in form, and will accommodate nearly or quite 10,000 persons. It is said to be the largest building in America with a "self-supporting roof."

Table Rock. A mass of rock at Niagara Falls, from which the finest front view of the entire falls is obtained. Formerly this rock overhung the water to a large extent, but in 1850 a huge piece of the ledge, some 200 feet in length and 100 feet in thickness broke off and fell into the chasm, carrying with it an omnibus which happened to be standing upon it. At present but little of the rock projects over the water.

☞ "You may stand by the water just where it falls off, and if your head does not swim you may proceed to the brink of *Table Rock*, and look down into the gulf beneath. This is all froth and foam and spray; as you stand here it looks as if all the water of the globe was collected around this circle, and pouring down here into the centre of the earth. . . . There the grand spectacle has stood for centuries, from the beginning of the creation, as far as we know, without change. From the beginning it has shaken as it now does the earth and the air, and its unvarying thunder existed before there were human ears to hear it." *Daniel Webster.*

☞ "It was not until I came on Table Rock and looked — Great Heaven — on what a fall of bright green water, that it came upon me in its might and majesty. Then when I felt how near to my Creator I was standing, the first effect and the enduring one — instant and lasting — of the tremendous spectacle was Peace. Niagara was at once stamped upon my heart, an Image of Beauty to remain there changeless and indelible until its pulses cease to beat forever." *Dickens.*

Close to the cataract, exactly at the spot from whence in former days the *Table Rock* used to project from the land over the boiling caldron below, there is now a shaft down which you will descend to the level of the river. *Anthony Trollope.*

Tablet of Abydos. 1. An historical monument giving a genealogy of the early Egyptian kings. It was discovered at Abydos, in Upper Egypt, in 1818. Now in the British Museum, London.

2. A monument of historical importance discovered in 1865 in the Temple of Sethi I., at Abydus, Egypt, is conjectured by M. Mairette to be the original of the one now in the British Museum. It contains a list of 76 kings from Menes to Sethi I.

Tablet of Sakkárah. A famous monument found at Sakkárah, now preserved in the Museum of Egyptian Antiquities at Cairo, Egypt. This tablet, which has been of much use in the solution of the problem of the dynasties of Egypt, has inscribed upon it the names of 58 kings which correspond with those in the list of Manetho.

Tabularium. An ancient ruin in Rome, of which only a few remains are now standing, once the public Record Office, where the *tabulæ*, or engraved decrees, of the Roman Senate were preserved.

☞ "After his lecture was over this morning, Mr. Bunsen took us into the *Tabularium*, and explained it to us in a very interesting manner. It has been fully explored, only within a few years, and is now one of the grandest monuments of ancient Rome." *George Ticknor.*

Taj Mahal. A renowned monument — justly considered one of the wonders of the world — at Agra in Hindostan. Its cost is estimated at $16,000,000.

☞ "The distant view of this matchless edifice satisfied me that its fame is well deserved. So pure, so gloriously perfect, did it appear, that I almost feared to approach it lest the charm should be broken. It is a work inspired by love and consecrated to Beauty. Shah Jehan — the 'Selim' of Moore's poem — erected it as a mausoleum over his queen Noor Jehan. . . . Few persons of the thousands who sigh over the pages of Lalla Rookh are aware that the 'Light of the Harem' was a real personage, and that her tomb is one of the wonders of the world. . . . A building which has no counterpart in Europe, or even in the East. . . . The remains of Moorish art in Spain approach nearest to its spirit, but are only the scattered limbs, the torso, of which the Taj is the perfect type. If there were nothing else in India, this alone would repay the journey. . . . It is an octagonal building of the purest white marble, little inferior to that of Carrara. Every part — even the basement, the dome, and the upper galleries of the minarets — is inlaid with ornamental designs in marble of different colors, principally a pale brown and a bluish-violet variety. The building is perfect in every part. . . . The dome of the Taj contains an echo more sweet, pure, and prolonged than that in the Baptistery of Pisa, which is the finest in Europe. The Taj is, as I have said, a poem. Did you ever build a castle in the air? Here is one brought down to earth and fixed for the wonder of ages; yet so light it seems, so airy, and when seen from a distance, so like a fabric of mist and sunbeams, with its great dome soaring up, a silvery bubble about to burst in the sun, that even after you have touched it, and climbed to its summit, you almost doubt its reality." *Bayard Taylor.*

Tak Kesra. A well-known and important ruin on the site of the ancient Ctesiphon in Mesopotamia.

☞ "It was apparently originally erected as a hunting-box on the edge of the desert for the use of the Persian king, and preserves all the features we are familiar with in Sassanian palaces. It is wholly of brick, and contains in the centre a tri-apsal hall, once surmounted by a dome." *Fergusson.*

Tancarville. A mediæval stronghold on the banks of the Seine below Rouen. It was pillaged at the time of the Revolution, but has now reverted to the descendants of its original owners, the Montmorencys.

Tantallon Castle. An ancient and ruined baronial fortress, of unknown age, occupying a high rock which projects into the German Ocean, near Berwick in Scotland.

But scant three miles the band had rode,
When o'er a height they passed;
And, sudden, close before them showed
His towers, *Tantallon* vast.

The train from out the castle drew;
But Marmion stopped to bid adieu:—
"Though something I might plain," he said,
"Of cold respect to stranger guest,
Sent hither by your king's behest,
While in *Tantallon's* towers I staid,—
Part we in friendship from your land."
Sir Walter Scott.

Tapestries [of the Vatican]. A series of ornamental hangings, after designs by Raphael Sanzio (1483–1520), wrought at Arras in Flanders, first hung in the Sistine Chapel on St. Stephen's day, 26th of December, 1519. They were afterwards carried off to France, but subsequently restored, and are now, it is supposed, hanging in a dilapidated condition, in the upper rooms of the Vatican. One of them, at least, has long been lost. Besides the series of tapestries in the Sistine, another series, twelve in number, of which the cartoons are lost, are still preserved in the Vatican. They are known as "Arazzi della Scuola Nuova," the others being called "Arazzi della Scuola Vecchia."

☞ "The tapestries are the only work of Raphael which does not seem insignificant after seeing Michael Angelo's ceiling in the Sistine Chapel."
Goethe, Trans.

Tapestry Weavers, The. [Hilanderas.] A noted picture by Diego Rodriguez de Silva y Velasquez (1599–1660), of which Mengs said that it seemed to be painted rather by the mind than the hand. In the Gallery at Madrid, Spain.

Tappan Zee. An expansion of the Hudson River beginning at Dobbs's Ferry. It is about ten miles long and from two to five miles in breadth.

He was never seen afterwards, but may be heard plying his oars, as above mentioned, being the Flying Dutchman of the *Tappan Sea*, doomed to ply between Kakiat and Spiting Devil until the day of judgment. *Washington Irving.*

Tara Hill. An eminence in the parish of Tara, in Leinster, Ireland, formerly the seat of the Irish kings, and from which the famous coronation stone was brought to Scotland. See STONE OF SCONE.

☞ According to Cambrensis, there is "in Mieth, an hill, called the Hill of Taragh, wherein is a plaine twelve score long, which was named the Kempe his hall; where the countrie had their meetings and folkmotes, as a place that was accounted the high palace of the monarch. The Irish historians hammer manie tales in this forge, of Fin Mac Coile and his champions. But doubtlesse seemeth to beare the shew of an ancient and famous monument."

The harp that once through *Tara's* halls.
Moore.

Tarpeian Rock. [Lat. *Tarpeius mons*, Ital. *Monte Tarpeia.*] A rocky eminence or cliff on the southern summit of the Capitoline Hill in Rome, from which criminals sentenced to death were frequently thrown. It was so named to commemorate the treachery of Tarpeia, who, during the war with the Sabines, in the early period of Roman history, longing for the golden bracelets of the enemy and allured by the promise of receiving that which they wore upon their arms, opened the fortress to the Sabines, and was rewarded by being crushed by their shields which they threw upon her in passing.

☞ "The Tarpeian rock is on the southern side of the Capitoline Hill. The soil has gathered round the base in considerable quantities, so that the formidable impressions conveyed by Roman writers are not confirmed by the sight. But a very respectable precipice may still be seen, and a traitor who should now leap from the top would probably be as harmless ever after as Clodius or Catiline." *Hillard.*

The tribune with unwilling steps withdrew,
While impious hands the rude assault renew;
The brazen gates with thundering strokes resound,
And the *Tarpeian* mountain rings around.
Lucan, Trans.

Then on to the *Tarpeian rock* he leads
The way, and to the Capitol, now decked
With gold, then rough with bushes wild.
Virgil, Trans. of Cranch.

And when upon their hinges were turned
round
The swivels of that consecrated gate,
Which are of metal, massive and sonorous,
Roared not so loud, nor so discordant
seemed
Tarpeia, when was ta'en from it the good
Metellus, wherefore meagre it remained.
Dante, Purgatorio, Longfellow's Trans.

On the *Tarpeian rock*, the citadel
Of great and glorious Rome, queen of the
earth,
So far renown'd, and with the spoils enriched
Of nations. *Milton.*

Thou hast the whole Universe against thee. No more success: mere sham-success, for a day and days; rising ever higher, — towards its *Tarpeian Rock*. *Carlyle.*

On the 23d May, 1618, the delegates of the Protestants of Bohemia cast from the windows of the royal castle of Prague two Catholic members of the Council of Regency. They pretended it was an old custom of the country, and that like the Romans they precipitated traitors from the top of this *Tarpeian Rock*. *Henri Martin.*

— where the steep
Tarpeian? fittest goal of Treason's race,
The promontory whence the Traitor's
Leap
Cured all ambition. *Byron.*

Tassoni's Bucket. See SECCHIA RAPITA.

I liked the town [Modena] as I drove in; and, after sleeping an hour or two, I went out in search of "*Tassoni's Bucket.*" *N. P. Willis.*

Tasso's Prison. A cell in the Hospital of S. Anna in Ferrara, Italy, pointed out as the prison in which the poet Tasso was confined by the Duke of Ferrara.

And Tasso is their glory and their shame.
Hark to his strain! and then survey his
cell!
And see how dearly earned Torquato's
fame,
And where Alfonso bade his poet dwell.
Byron.

Tattersall's. A celebrated sporting rendezvous and auction-mart for horses in London, established by Richard Tattersall in 1766. The betting throughout the country is governed by the betting at Tattersall's.

On the Proposal for a *Cast-metal King*: gradually a light kindled in our Professor's eyes and face, a beaming, mantling, loveliest light; through those murky features, a radiant, ever-young Apollo looked; and he burst forth like the neighing of all *Tattersall's*, — tears streaming down his cheeks, pipe held aloft, foot clutched into the air, — loud, long-continuing, uncontrollable. *Carlyle.*

And they look at one another with the seriousness of men prepared to die in their opinion, — the authentic seriousness of men betting at *Tattersall's*, or about to receive judgment in Chancery. *Carlyle.*

Taymouth Castle. The seat of the Marquis of Breadalbane near Kenmore, Scotland.

Tazza Farnese. [The Farnese Cup.] A celebrated onyx cup, a relic of ancient art, highly ornamented with figures in relief. Now in the Museum at Naples, Italy.

Te, Palazzo del. A noble palace in Mantua, Italy.

☞ "Giulio Romano's masterpiece." *J. A. Symonds.*

Tebaldeo. A portrait by Sebastian del Piombo (1485-1547). In the Scarpa collection at La Motta, Italy.

Tecumseh, The. A noted iron-clad vessel of the United States navy in the Civil War in 1861-65. She was one of Admiral Farragut's fleet in the attack upon the defences of Mobile, Ala., Aug. 5, 1864. She was suddenly destroyed by the explosion of a torpedo.

☞ "The *Tecumseh* was about 300 yards ahead of the *Brooklyn* when she was suddenly uplifted, and almost as suddenly disappeared beneath the waters, carrying down with her Capt. Craven and nearly all his officers and crew. Only 17 of 130 were saved. The *Tecumseh* had struck a percussion-torpedo, which exploded directly under her turret, making a fearful chasm, into which the water rushed in such volume that she sunk in a few seconds." *Lossing.*

Telegraph Hill. An eminence at the northern extremity of San Francisco, Cal., commanding a fine view.

Tell's Chapel. 1. A building situated on a ledge of rock on the slope of the Axenfluh, washed by the waters of the Lake of Uri, Switzerland. It is a small chapel built in memory of William Tell (b. thirteenth century), and on the very spot where he sprang out of Gessler's boat, as he was being carried away a prisoner. The chapel was rebuilt in 1879, in strict adherence to the original design.

2. A chapel in a village near Altorf, Switzerland, built in 1522 on the spot where the house stood which was occupied by William Tell.

Téméraire. See FIGHTING TÉMÉRAIRE.

Tempe. A narrow rocky gorge in Greece, about five miles in length, between Mount Olympus on the north and Mount Ossa on the south, through which flows the river Peneus. On the right side of the vale is the inscription cut in the rock: "Lucius Cassius Longinus, the Proconsul, made the road through Tempe." According to the legends of the Greek mythology, this fissure was cut through by Neptune with a stroke of his trident, thus opening a passage for the waters imprisoned in Thessaly, the defile receiving from this circumstance the name of *Tempe* (from Gr. τέμνω), or *The Cuts*.

From *Tempe's* vale next ancient Peneus came,
That fertile vale immortalized in fame!
Catullus, Trans.

Lapped in Thessalia's forest-mantled hills
Lies the fair vale of *Tempe*. *Ovid, Trans.*

Passing from Italy to Greece, the tales
Which poets of an elder time have feigned
To glorify their *Tempe*, bred in me
Desire of visiting that Paradise.
To Thessaly I came, and, living private,
I, day by day, frequented silent groves
And solitary walks.
Ford. (Lover's Melancholy.)

The smooth Peneus from his glassy flood
Reflects purpureal *Tempe's* pleasant scene.
Fair *Tempe!* haunt beloved of sylvan powers,
Of nymphs and fauns; where in the golden age
They played in secret on the shady brink
With ancient Pan. *Akenside.*

Yet in famed Attica such lovely dales
Are rarely seen; nor can fair *Tempe* boast
A charm they know not. *Byron.*

Temperaments. See FOUR TEMPERAMENTS.

Temple, The. A liberty or district of London, lying between Fleet Street and the Thames, so called from the Knights Templars. See INNER TEMPLE and INNS OF COURT.

☞ "There are still worse places than the Temple on a sultry day, for basking in the sun or resting idly in the shade." *Dickens.*

This privileged spot [Whitefriars or "Alsatia"] stood in the same relation to the *Temple* as Alsace did to France and the central powers of Europe. In the *Temple*, students were studying to observe the law; and in Alsatia, adjoining, debtors to avoid and violate it. *Cunningham.*

Temple, The. Nothing is now left of this old fortress and prison in Paris, though much of it was standing a century ago. There were two Commanderies of the Knights Templars at Paris in the thirteenth century, of which this strong and important feudal fortress was one. It was granted to the Knights of St. John (subsequently the Knights of Malta) after the suppression of the order of Templars in 1312. Louis XVI., with Marie Antoinette his queen, his son the Dauphin, his daughter and his sister, were confined in the prison in the tower of the Temple in 1792. The tower was subsequently used as a prison, but was pulled down in the early part of the present century. Sir Sidney Smith, Toussaint l'Ouverture, and Pichegru were imprisoned in the tower.

Temple. See PRESENTATION IN THE TEMPLE.

Temple Bar. A noted historic boundary in London, between the east end of the Strand and the west end of Fleet Street, dividing the City of London from the liberty of Westminster. The original division was by posts and rails, a chain and a *bar* placed across the street and named from its immediate vicinity to the Temple. The *Bar*, or house of stone, which until lately stood on this site, was erected by Sir Christopher Wren. It had a large flattened arch in the centre for the carriage-way, and a smaller arch on each side for foot passengers. Above the centre, on iron spikes, were formerly placed the heads and limbs of persons executed for treason. The last of these spikes was not removed till the present century. Mr. Rogers, the poet, who died in

1855, remembered "one of the heads of the rebels upon a pole at Temple Bar." The gates were originally shut at night and guarded by watchmen, and have occasionally been in recent times closed in cases of apprehended tumult. It was formerly the case upon the visit of the sovereign to the city, to keep the gates closed until admission was formally demanded, when the gates were opened, and the lord-mayor surrendered the city sword to the sovereign, who re-delivered it to his lordship. This noted structure is now taken down and removed.

☞ "With the removal of Temple Bar an immensity of the associations of the past will be swept away. Almost all the well-known authors of the last two centuries have somehow had occasion to mention it. Fleet Street, just within its bounds, is still the centre for the offices of nearly all the leading newspapers and magazines." *Hare.*

"It is my practice, when I am in want of amusement, to place myself for an hour at Temple Bar, and examine one by one the looks of the passengers; and I have commonly found that between the hours of eleven and four every sixth man is an author." *Dr. Johnson.*

While we surveyed the Poets' Corner, I said to him [Goldsmith], "Forsitan et nostrum nomen miscebitur istis." When we got to *Temple Bar* he stopped me, pointed to the heads upon it, and slyly whispered, "Forsitan et nostrum nomen miscebitur istis." *Dr. Johnson.*

How they exult in the idea that the King himself dare not enter the city, without first knocking at the gate of *Temple Bar*, and asking permission of the Lord Mayor; for if he did, heaven and earth! there is no knowing what might be the consequence. *Irving.*

The raw afternoon is rawest, and the dense fog is densest, and the muddy streets are muddiest, near that leaden-headed old obstruction, appropriate ornament for the threshold of a leaden-headed old corporation: *Temple Bar.* *Dickens.*

Each man an Ascapart, of strength to toss
For quoits both *Temple-bar* and Charing-cross. *Pope.*

The earth is rich in man and maid;
With fair horizons bound;
This whole wide earth of light and shade
Comes out, a perfect round.
High over roaring *Temple Bar*,
And, set in Heaven's third story,
I look at all things as they are,
But through a kind of glory.
Tennyson.

Once more I greet thee, *Temple Bar*,
That hast so often from afar
Risen amid my dreams;
When avalanches round me roared,
Or where the Tagus, sunlit, poured
Its stately golden streams.
Walter Thornbury.

Temple Church. A church situated in the rear of Fleet Street, London, one of the four circular churches built in England after the Templars' return from the Crusades, containing many effigies of feudal warriors. John Selden was buried in this church. In the Temple "Round," as the church was called, lawyers conferred with their clients.

Retain all sorts of witnesses,
That ply i' the Temple under trees;
Or walk the Round with Knights o' the Posts,
About the cross-legg'd knights, their hosts.
Butler.

Temple Emanuel. The principal Jewish synagogue in the city of New York, an imposing building, in the Saracenic style, with a magnificent interior. It is considered the finest specimen of architecture of its kind in America.

Temple Gardens. An open space belonging to the Inns of Court, London, fronting the Thames. Here Shakespeare represents the choice of the York and Lancastrian roses as emblems by the partisans of the two houses.

Suffolk. Within the Temple Hall we were too loud:
The garden here is more convenient. . . .
Plantagenet. Let him that is a true-born gentleman,
And stands upon the honour of his birth,
If he suppose that I have pleaded truth,
From off this briar pluck a white rose with me.
Somerset. Let him that is no coward, nor no flatterer,
But dare maintain the party of the truth,
Pluck a red rose from off this thorn with me. . . .
Plantagenet. Hath not thy rose a canker, Somerset?
Somerset. Hath not thy rose a thorn, Plantagenet? . . .
Warwick. This brawl to-day,
Grown to this faction in the *Temple Gardens*,
Shall send, between the red rose and the white,
A thousand souls to death and deadly night.
Shakespeare. First Part of Henry VI.

Stand in *Temple Gardens*, and behold
London herself on her proud stream afloat. *Shakespeare.*

Temple of Aboo-Simbel. This and a smaller temple near it are among the most interesting objects in Egypt. They were hewn out of the solid rock. The great temple is remarkable for its magnificent colossi, the most beautiful in Egypt. They are 66 feet in height, and represent Rameses the Great. The façade of the temple is about 100 feet high. Within are eight Osirides precisely alike, all carrying the crozier and flagellum. There are eight rooms opening into the large hall, the walls of which are covered with sculptures representing the offerings to the gods. In the adytum are figures of four gods. The warlike deeds of Rameses are represented on the walls as offerings to the gods. See Lady of Aboshek.

☞ "Nothing more interesting than these temples is to be found beyond the limits of Thebes. . . . The faces of Rameses outside (precisely alike) are placid and cheerful, — full of moral grace; but the eight Osirides within (precisely alike, too) are more. They are full of soul." *Miss Martineau.*

This is the shrine of Silence, sunk and hewn
Deep in the solid rock: its pillars rise
From floor to roof, like giants, with fixed eyes,
And palms crossed on their breasts; e'en at mid-noon
A dim light falls around, as though the moon
Were peering at the temple from the skies. *J. B. Norton.*

The mighty shapes that guard the solemn pile,
Unburied, after ages, from the tomb
Heaped on them by the blast of the simoom,
Sit at the portal, gazing, night and day,
O'er the lone desert, stretching far away,
And on the eternal flood of Father Nile.
J. B. Norton.

Temple of Antoninus and Faustina. A temple erected by the Senate to the memory of Antoninus Pius and his wife Faustina, in the Forum at Rome. It is now in ruins.

Temple of Apollo [at Delphi]. The site of this structure is now regarded as definitely determined, from the discovery of what are thought to be, in all probability, the foundations of the temple. The temple of Apollo was reckoned one of the largest and most beautiful in Greece; having been burnt in 548 B.C, it was rebuilt by the Alcmæonidæ. The "Ion" of Euripides contains an interesting record of the ornaments with which it was decorated. Here was the oracular chasm with the issuing vapor, which moved the destiny of empires; here, too, was the elliptical stone looked upon as the centre of the earth.

Temple of Apollo. A striking and picturesque ruin at Tivoli, in the neighborhood of Rome.

Temple of Apollo Epicurius. One of the finest and best-preserved temples in Greece, built, in a place which was called Bassæ, in the time of the Peloponnesian War, by Ictinus, who was also one of the architects of the Parthenon. It was dedicated to Apollo *Epicurius* (the Helper) in gratitude for the relief afforded by Apollo during a plague. Pausanias speaks of the harmony of construction, and beauty of the stone, of this temple as surpassing all works of the same kind in the Peloponnesus.

☞ "Such is the seclusion in which the Temple of Bassæ stands, that for many ages its very existence was either unknown or forgotten. Like the temples at Pæstum in this respect, it was not till after the middle of the eighteenth century that this, the most beautiful and most perfect of all the remains of Greek architecture in the Peloponnesus, was discovered in nearly the same state as when visited more than a thousand years before by Pausanias." *C. Wordsworth.*

Temple of Belus. See Birs Nimrood.

Temple of Bubastis. This magnificent temple at the town of the same name in Egypt is not now standing. It was built of the finest red granite. The name Bubastis is derived from the goddess Pasht, to whom this temple was dedicated. Herodotus describes the temple as forming a peninsula, surrounded by water (two canals from the Nile) on all sides except the one by which you enter, and as being situated in a low space in the centre of the town, from which you could look down upon it; the town having been raised, while the temple retained its original level.

☞ "Other temples may be grander, and may have cost more in the building, but there is none so pleasant to the eye as this of Bubastis." *Herodotus.*

Temple of Castor and Pollux. An ancient temple in Rome, of which three columns only are now standing. This ruin has also been designated by various other names.

Temple of Denderah. This temple of the Nile, though not of the remotest antiquity, is interesting and imposing. It was built by the Cæsars, and bears the names of Tiberius (in whose reign the inscription was made), Caligula, Claudius, and Nero. It also bears upon its walls portraits of Cleopatra and her son Neo-Cæsar. It is in better preservation than most of the Egyptian ruins.

☞ "The building of the temple of Denderah was begun in the reign of the eleventh Ptolemy, and completed in that of the Emperor Tiberius; but the sculptures and decorations were not finished till the time of Nero." *Murray's Handbook.*

☞ "Of the temple of Dendara I will say nothing. The oldest names it bears are those of Cleopàtra and her son Cæsarion; and it has not therefore the interest of antiquity; while its beauty is of the same kind as that of the Isna temple. At Dendara, as at Isna, the Pasha has caused the building to be cleaned out; for which the world is obliged to him: and it would have been more so, if he had not run a mud-brick wall directly up against the middle of the front; so that no complete view of the portico can be had from any point." *Miss Martineau.*

What yonder rises? 'Tis *Tentyra's fane*,
That stands like some dark giant, on the plain;
Rival of Karnak, Edfou, stern and lone,
It looks to Heaven, its founder, date, unknown. *Nicholas Michell.*

Or, lodged by an Arab guide, ventured to render a
General view of the ruins at *Denderah*. *Lowell.*

Temple of Diana. An interesting Roman temple at Nîmes, France.

☞ "Throughout this building the details of the architecture are unsurpassed for variety and elegance by any thing found in the metropolis, and are here applied with a freedom and elegance bespeaking the presence of a Grecian mind, even in this remote corner of the empire." *Fergusson.*

Temple of Ephesus. A famous temple of Artemis, or Diana, in ancient Ephesus, Asia Minor. The original temple, erected in the sixth century B.C., was intentionally burned by Herostratus, with a view to gaining notoriety, on the same day on which Alexander the Great was born, B.C. 356. The new temple, which occupied more than two centuries in building, was one of the largest and most gorgeous of all those erected by the Greeks, and was regarded one of the wonders of the world. Scanty remains of it still exist.

☞ "According to Pindarus, the first temple of Ephesus was built by the Amazons at the time when they made war upon Theseus. Strabo attributes it to the architect Ctesiphon. After Erostratus burnt it in 356 B.C., says Strabo, the gifts brought from all parts, the donations of pious women, the presents of the colonies, and the valuable articles deposited by the kings in the ancient sanctuary, enabled the people to rebuild the temple on a still more magnificent scale. All Asia joined in the undertaking, and the structure took no less than 220 years to raise. It was placed on a marshy soil to insure it against earthquakes, and in order to obtain sufficiently strong foundations for such a considerable mass, a bed of ground carbon was laid down, and a bed of wool above that. The entire temple was 425 feet long and 220 feet wide. . . . In the thirteenth century A.D., the Persians first, and afterwards the Scythians, pillaged and burnt the temple of Ephesus. What of destruction was left unaccomplished by these was completed by the Goths and Mahomet the Great." *Lefèvre, Tr. Donald.*

☞ "Strange to say, till very recently even its situation was unknown; and even now that it has been revealed by the energy and intelligence of Mr. Wood, scarcely enough remains to enable him to restore the plan with any

thing like certainty. This is the more remarkable, as it was found buried under seventeen or twenty feet of mud, which must have been the accumulation of centuries, and might, one would have thought, have preserved considerable portions of it from the spoiler."
Fergusson.

Temple of Fortuna Virilis. A very ancient building in Rome, supposed to date back to the times of the Republic, which has undergone many restorations, and is now a Christian church.

Temple of Glory. A celebrated picture by Anton Rafael Mengs (1728-1779). In Madrid, Spain.

Temple of Greenan. A singular pile of ruined buildings of very great antiquity, near Derry, Ireland. By some it is thought to have been a temple for sun-worship, by others a royal residence.

☞ "To the casual observer, the first appearance of the edifice is that of a truncated cairn of extraordinary dimensions; but on inspection it will be found to be a building constructed with every attention to masonic regularity. In the centre are the remains of the altar, or place of sacrifice. The stones of which the building is formed are of the common gray schistus, but evidently selected with care, and, considering their exposure to the Atlantic storms for so many centuries, the decomposition is wonderfully small."
Dublin Penny Journal.

Temple of Herod. See HEROD'S TEMPLE.

Temple of Isis [at Philæ]. This is the principal temple at Philæ, and of great interest. It was built by the Ptolemies, though many of the sculptures are of the time of the Roman Emperors. It contains among its many objects of interest ten colossal columns, completely covered with sculptures in a variety of brilliant and beautiful colors, all of which are not merely ornamental, but also emblematic.

☞ "No Gothic architect in his wildest moments ever played so freely with his lines and dimensions, and none, it must be added, ever produced any thing so beautifully picturesque as this. It contains all the play of light and shade, all the variety of Gothic art, with the massiveness and grandeur of the Egyptian style; and as it is still tolerably entire, and retains much of its color, there is no building out of Thebes that gives so favorable an impression of Egyptian art as this. It is true, it is far less sublime than many, but hardly one can be quoted as more beautiful."
Fergusson.

Temple of Isna. A vast and celebrated temple at Isna, on the left bank of the Nile, in Upper Egypt, not far from Thebes.

☞ "I think I had better say little of Isna, whose temple is so universally praised that every one knows all about it. Those have heard of it who are ignorant of almost every thing else about Egypt. If it were ancient, I could not refrain from giving my impressions of it; but the only relic of the old edifice supposed to exist is a small red door-jamb bearing date in the time of Thothmes I., mentioned by Champollion. The portico bears the names of the Cæsars; and, however greatly the world is obliged to them for erecting a very majestic and elegant temple, we are not aided by it in our researches into the affairs of the old Egyptians. . . . If I were to enlarge on any thing in regard to this temple, it would be the amount of inscriptions. But it is indescribable, — unrememberable, — incredible anywhere but on the spot. I have already said all that language can say on this point; and I will leave it."
Miss Martineau.

Temple of Janus. A temple in ancient Rome dedicated to Janus, one of the early Roman deities, which was opened at the commencement of every war, and continued open while the war lasted. The tradition is that it was only closed three times in a period of 700 years, one of those times being at the birth of Christ in the reign of Augustus Cæsar.

Temple of Jupiter Latialis. A temple of Jupiter, the remains of which are still in existence, on the summit of Mount Albano, or Monte Cavo, near Rome, Italy.

Temple of Jupiter Stator. Three well-known beautiful columns near the base of the Palatine Hill, Rome, are usually supposed to be the remains of this temple; but they have been the subject of much antiquarian dispute.

Temple of Kalabsheh. This temple was the largest in Nubia, and is a magnificent ruin. It was built by the Cæsars, of stones which had belonged to an older edifice. Its interest lies mainly in its vastness, and the remarkable preservation of its coloring.

Temple of Karnak. One of the most imposing and best-preserved temples in Egypt. It stands on the east bank of the Nile, amid the ruins of Thebes. It occupies an area of nine acres, which is covered with gigantic columns, courts, and avenues of sphinxes.

☞ "The palace temple at Karnak—perhaps the noblest effort of architectural magnificence ever produced by the hand of man. Its principal dimensions are 1,200 feet in length by about 360 in width; and it covers, therefore, about 430,000 square feet, or nearly twice the area of St. Peter's at Rome, and more than four times that of any mediæval cathedral existing. This, however, is not a fair way of estimating its dimensions; for our churches are buildings entirely under one roof, but at Karnak a considerable portion of the area was uncovered by any buildings, so that no such comparison is just. The great hypostyle hall, however, is internally 340 feet by 170, and with its two pilons, it covers more than 88,000 square feet, a greater area than the cathedral of Cologne, the largest of all our Northern cathedrals; and when we consider that this is only a part of the great whole, we may fairly assert that the entire structure is among the largest, as it undoubtedly is one of the most beautiful, buildings in the world."
Fergusson.

☞ "The earliest name found on any of the buildings of the Great Temple is that of Osirtasen I., and the latest that of Alexander II."
Murray's Handbook.

Who would not feel and satisfy this want,
Watching, as I, in *Karnak's* roofless halls,
Subnuvolar lights of evening sharply slant
Through pillared masses and on wasted walls? *Lord Houghton.*

Here let me sit in *Karnak's* gorgeous hall,
Firm as when reared each massy pictured wall. *Nicholas Michell.*

Temple of Luxor. A palace-temple in Egypt, on the east bank of the Nile, built by Amunoph III. and Rameses II., forming a part of the ruins of Thebes. Though inferior in size to Karnak, it is reckoned superior in point of architecture. Two monolithic obelisks of granite formerly stood in front of Luxor, one of which is now in the Place de la Concorde, in Paris.

Those unexampled temples sempitern—
Luxor and Karnak, twain, yet linked in one
By avenue of sphinxes, multiplied,
To endless view. *J. Ellis.*

Temple of Mars Ultor. [Mars the Revenger.] An ancient Roman temple, of which only a few beautiful pillars now remain.

Temple of Minerva [at Ægina.] One of the oldest temples in Greece, formerly thought to have been a temple of Zeus Panhellenius, probably built in the sixth century B.C. It is now in ruins. Some of the sculptures of the pediment are now preserved at Munich, Bavaria. Of these there are casts in the British Museum.

Temple of Minerva Medica. An interesting ruin in Rome. It is now thought to be misnamed.

☞ "It [this temple] commonly goes by the name of the Temple of Minerva Medica, though this is certainly a misnomer. Recently it has become the fashion to assume that this was the hall of some bath; no building of that class, however, was known to exist in that neighborhood. . . . It certainly belongs to the last days of the Roman empire, if, indeed, it be not a Christian building, which I am very much inclined to believe it is. . . . Taking it altogether, the building is certainly, both as concerns construction and proportion, by far the most scientific of all those in ancient Rome, and in these respects as far superior to the Pantheon, as it is inferior to that temple in size. Indeed, there are few inventions of the Middle Ages that are not attempted here; so much so, indeed, that I cannot help believing it is much more modern than is generally supposed." *Fergusson.*

Temple of Neptune. A famous ruined temple at Pæstum in Southern Italy, regarded as the finest specimen of Greek architecture outside of Athens.

☞ "Of the three temples of Pæstum, the best preserved ranks among the most beautiful works of antiquity, and is situated between the two others. Neptune was the god to whom it was dedicated. Its fluted columns, of which there are six on the façade and fourteen on the sides, rest upon three broad steps of most harmonious proportions. Between the columns the space is little more than the diameter of the pillars. This makes the play of light and shade among them very striking." *Lefèvre, Tr. Donald.*

☞ "Study of these buildings, so sublime in their massiveness, so noble in the parsimony of their decoration, so dignified in their employment of the simplest means for the attainment of an indestructible effect of harmony, heightens our admiration for the Attic genius which found in this grand manner of the elder Doric architects resources as yet undeveloped." *J. A. Symonds.*

Yet there, a lovely dream,
There Grecian temples gleam,
Whose form and mellowed tone
Rival the Parthenon.

Temple of Phthah. A famous temple at Garf Hoseyn, a large village in Nubia, on the banks of the Nile.

☞ "It may be remembered that this was the deity [Phthah] to whom, according to tradition, the first temple was raised in Egypt; when Menes, having redeemed the site of Memphis from the waters, began the city there, and built the great temple of Phthah, renowned for so many years afterwards. Memphis and this Garf Hoseyn formerly bore the same name, derived from their deity, viz., Phthahei or Thyphthah. His temple has been found by some travellers as imposing as any on the Nile. It has been compared even with Aboo-Simbil. . . . We saw nothing ruder than this temple, which yet is grand in its way." *Miss Martineau.*

Temple of Saturn. An old Roman temple, of which a few fragments, in the shape of eight Ionic columns, still remain in the Forum at Rome.

Temple of Sunium. A ruined temple, dedicated to the tutelary goddess of Attica, at Sunium, now Cape Colonna, the most southern point of Attica, is magnificently situated at the extremity of the promontory, 269 feet above the Ægean Sea, and commands an extensive view. It was built of white marble. Sixteen columns are now standing.

☞ "The marble columns of the ruins of Sunium's temple on Cape Colonna stood forth with a shining whiteness in the warm sunshine. Sea-birds fluttered around on the gray desert coast." *H. C. Andersen.*

☞ "In all Attica, if we except Athens itself and Marathon, there is no scene more interesting than Cape Colonna. To the antiquary and artist, sixteen columns are an inexhaustible source of observation and design; to the philosopher, the supposed scene of some of Plato's conversations will not be unwelcome; and the traveller will be struck with the beauty of the prospect over '*Isles that crown the Ægean deep:*' but, for an Englishman, Colonna has yet an additional interest, as the actual spot of Falconer's Shipwreck. Pallas and Plato are forgotten, in the recollection of Falconer and Campbell:

'Here in the dead of night by Lonna's steep,
The seaman's cry was heard along the deep.'

This temple of Minerva may be seen at sea from a great distance." *Byron.*

Save where Tritonia's airy shrine adorns
Colonna's cliff, and gleams along the wave.
Byron.

Temple of the Latter Day Saints. See Mormon Temple.

Temple of the Sibyl. A famous temple, of the Corinthian Order, at Tivoli, near Rome, "which has probably sat for its likeness more often than any building on earth." It is now a ruin crowning a cliff, with ten of its original eighteen columns still standing.

☞ "The building, when perfect, placed anywhere would have been an elegant structure, and its remains have formed a most satisfactory ruin; but no fabric of man ever owed more to its situation. . . . The relation between the temple and the rock is like that between the capital and the shaft: each seems to require the other as its complement. Nature and art never worked together more harmoniously, and to call the combination merely picturesque is to do it injustice. It is a picture which requires nothing to be added to or taken from it to make it perfect." *Hillard.*

Temple of the Sun. A ruined temple at Ba'albek, in Syria, and the most perfect of the existing remains in that country. It was considerably larger than the Parthenon at Athens. The most interesting portion of the building at present remaining is the Great Gateway, 42 feet in height by 20 feet in width. What was left of this temple was much injured by the earthquake of 1759, which threw down many of the columns. [Also called the *Temple of Jupiter* and *Temple of Apollo*.]

Temple of the Sun. A ruined temple in Palmyra, Northern Palestine, and one of the finest ruins in Syria. About 100 columns are still standing.

Temple of the Wingless Victory. A small but very beautiful temple at Athens, Greece, "only 27 feet long, 18 feet broad, and, from the lowest step to the top of the pediment, not more than 23 feet high." This temple of Νίκη ἄπτερος had entirely disappeared a century ago, but in 1835 its fragments were discovered and skilfully restored to their original places. It is not mentioned among the works of Pericles, and is thought to have been built by Cimon.

☞ "The little temple [of *Nike Apteros*, or Wingless Victory] is a jewel of a structure, not half so large as that of Vesta at Rome, and consists only of a cella with four Ionic columns at each end. Nevertheless it lightens wonderfully the heavy masses of masonry against which it stands." *Bayard Taylor.*

Temple of Vespasian. An old Roman temple, of which a few fragments, in the shape of three beautiful columns, are still standing in the Forum. This ruin was formerly called the Temple of Jupiter Tonans.

Temple of Vesta. A celebrated Roman temple, of a circular form, standing on the banks of the Tiber, near where the Cloaca Maxima empties into the river. By some antiquaries this temple is thought to be misnamed. It is surrounded by a row of marble columns nineteen in number. In place of the entablature, which has fallen, a roof of red tiles is laid directly upon the capitals of the columns.

☞ "It is a pretty toy of a building; too small — to borrow an expression of Horace Walpole's — to live in, and too large to hang at one's watch-chain. Its form and features are multiplied in an immense progeny of bronze models and inkstands to which it has given birth." *Hillard.*

☞ "The picture of this perfect temple and the beautiful purpose of its consecration have always been prominent in my imaginary Rome. It is worthy of its association — an exquisite round temple, with its simple circle of columns from the base to the roof, a faultless thing in proportion, and as light and floating to the eye as if the wind might lift it. It needed not the heavenly moonlight that broke across its columns to make it a very shrine of fancy." *N. P. Willis.*

Temptation of Christ. A picture by Ary Scheffer (1795-1858).

Temptation of St. Anthony. 1. A picture by Joachim Patenier (d. 1548?), the Flemish painter, and one of his masterpieces. It is now at Madrid, and there is also a copy of it in the Museum of Berlin, Prussia.

2. A picture by David Teniers the Younger (1610-1694). In the Museum at Berlin, Prussia.

Ten Thousand Saints. See MARTYRDOM OF THE TEN THOUSAND SAINTS.

Tenebrario. A famous and beautiful candlestick of bronze, modelled after Solomon's Temple, in the cathedral of Seville, Spain. It was executed by Bartolomé Morel, who lived in the reign of Philip II.

Tennessee, The. A noted Confederate iron-clad ram, taken in the harbor of Mobile, Ala., Aug. 5, 1864, by Admiral Farragut's fleet.

☞ "Admiral Farragut believed the fierce combat was ended; for, as darkness closed in, the forts were silent. He was mistaken. Just before nine o'clock the *Tennessee* came down under a full head of steam, and made directly for the *Hartford*. All the national vessels were immediately signalled to close in upon and destroy the monster. It was not an easy task, for it appeared absolutely invulnerable for several hours. The *Monongahela* first struck it a blow square in the side, and fired an eleven-inch shot upon it with very little effect. The *Lancaster*, running at full speed, struck the 'ram,' and crushed in her own stem. Now the *Hartford* tried her powers upon the sea-giant. She gave the *Tennessee* a glancing blow and a broadside of ten-inch shells at a few feet distance. . . . Thus beset and badly crippled, the *Tennessee* struck her colors, and became Farragut's prisoner after fighting all night and until ten o'clock in the morning. Her commander was badly wounded, and six of her crew were killed." *Lossing.*

Tenterden Steeple. A church in Tenterden, Kent, England, which has acquired notoriety from a supposed connection between it and the formation of the dangerous shoal known as the Goodwin Sands; the tradition being that the money which should have been used to maintain the sea-wall was diverted to the building of the church.

☞ "Mr. Moore was once sent in commission into Kent, to help to try out (if it might be) what was the cause of Goodwin Sands, and the shelf that stopped up Sandwich haven. Thither cometh Mr. Moore, and calleth the country afore him; such as were thought to be men of experience, and men that could, of likelihood, best certify him of that matter, concerning the stopping of Sandwich haven. Among others, came in before him an old man, with a white head; and one that was thought to be little less than an hundred years old. When Mr. Moore saw this aged man, he thought it expedient to hear him say his mind in this matter; for, being so old a man, it was likely that he knew most of any man in that presence and company. So Mr. Moore called this old man unto him, and said, 'Father,' said he, 'tell me, if you can, what is the cause of this arising of the sands and shelves here about this haven; the which stop it up that no ships can arrive here; ye are the eldest man that I can espy in all this company; so that if any man can tell any cause of it, ye of likelihood can say most in it; or, at leastwise, more than any other man assembled.'—'Yea, forsooth, good master,' quoth this old man, 'for I am well nigh an hundred years old; and no man here in this company any thing near unto mine age.'—'Well, then,' quoth Mr. Moore, 'how say you in this matter? what think ye to be the cause of these shelves and flats that stop up Sandwich haven?'—'Forsooth, say ye,' quoth he, 'I am an old man; I think that Tenterden Steeple is the cause of Goodwin Sands; for I am an old man,' quoth he; 'and I may remember the building of Tenterden Steeple, and I may remember when there was no steeple at all there; and before that Tenterden Steeple was in building, there was no manner of speaking of any flats or sands that stopped the haven; and, therefore, I think that Tenterden Steeple is the cause of the destroying and decay of Sandwich haven.' And even so to my purpose is preaching of God's word the cause of rebellion, as Tenterden Steeple was the cause that Sandwich haven is decayed."
Bishop Latimer, Sermons.

Thus, however, it was that *Tenterden Steeple* brought an influx of the Atlantic on us, and so Godwin Sands. *Carlyle.*

Terrace, The. An imposing pile of architecture in Central Park, New York, comprising corridors and stairways, and broad avenues adorned with statuary.

Terrapin Tower. An observatory which formerly stood on a little isle at Niagara, and afforded a fine view of the falls. It was destroyed in 1873.

☞ "I do not quite approve of that tower, seeing that it has about it a gingerbread air. Nevertheless the tower is worth mounting. Here the mystery is lost, but the whole fall is seen."
Anthony Trollope.

Terror, The. An Arctic exploring vessel which sailed from England in company with the Erebus, under Sir John Franklin, in May, 1845, and never returned. See EREBUS.

Testaccio, Monte. See MONTE TESTACCIO.

Thames Embankments. A series of great improvements effected in London since 1850, consisting of stone embankments on both the north and the south side of the Thames, by which many acres that were formerly mud-banks have been reclaimed, roads a hundred feet wide constructed, with landing-stages from the river-steamers, the interior being laid out in ornamental gardens forming a pleasant promenade. The Victoria embankment, on the north side of the river, was opened in 1870. The Albert, on the opposite side, was opened in 1869.

Thames Street. A well-known street in London, extending from Blackfriars to the Tower.

Thames Tunnel. A brick arched double roadway under the river Thames at London, executed by Brunel at a cost of £614,000. It was opened to the public March 25, 1843. Since 1865 it has been used for a railway-tunnel by the East London Railway Company.

Thatched House. This celebrated tavern in St. James's Street, London, is no longer standing. For about two centuries it was noted for its club meetings and its dinners. As late as 1860 more than 25 societies and clubs were entertained at the Thatched House. Part of its site is now occupied by the house of the Civil Service Club.

> Was it never thy hard fortune, good reader, to attend any meeting convened for public purposes; any Bible Society, Reform, Conservative, *Thatched-Tavern*, Hogg-Dinner, or other such meeting?
> *Carlyle.*

Thavies Inn. Formerly an inn of court in London, and one of the oldest. It was destroyed by fire towards the close of the last century.

> According to Mr. Guppy in Dickens's novel of "Bleak House," it was "round the corner" from Lincoln's Inn. "We just twist up Chancery Lane, an' cut along Holborn, and there we are in four minutes' time as near as a toucher."

Théâtre Français. A theatre in Paris, Rue Richelieu, on the south-west side of the Palais Royal. Here are acted the regular French dramas, the modern as well as the more classic productions of Molière, Racine, Corneille, and others. Richelieu built the Théâtre du Palais Royal, upon the site of which the present house was erected in 1787. Molière was manager from 1658 till his death in 1673.

Théâtre Lyrique. A recent theatre in Paris, on the Place du Châtelet, devoted to the lyric drama and operas.

> Twice a week he goes to the theatre; he prefers the Palais-Royal: perhaps twice more he takes upon his arm one of the figurantes of the *Théâtre Lyrique.*
> *Taine, Trans.*

Theatre of Marcellus. An interesting ruin in Rome, of which only a few arches now remain. The building is supposed to have been capable of holding 20,000 spectators. It was a fortress in the Middle Ages, and subsequently passed into the possession of the Orsini family.

Theobalds. A palace in the parish of Chishurst, near London, formerly the residence of Sir William Cecil (Lord Burleigh). It passed into possession of the Stuart kings, who often resided here. The building is described as one of great magnificence, but has now entirely disappeared.

Theodore's, St., Column. See St. Theodore's Column.

Theodoric's Palace. 1. A celebrated ruin in Ravenna, Italy, the old residence of the Gothic king. This palace was despoiled of many of its treasures by Charlemagne.

2. Well-known and picturesque ruins at Terracina, on the route between Rome and Naples, Italy.

Theodoric's Tomb. An interesting and celebrated sepulchral monument, of a circular form, built by the Gothic king Theodoric, and standing in the midst of a plain near Ravenna, Italy.

Theology. See Dispute of the Sacrament.

Theresa, St. See St. Theresa.

Thermæ. See Baths.

Thermes, Palais des. See Palais des Thermes.

Theseum. A monumental temple in Athens, Greece, finished about 465 B.C., and built to receive the bones of Theseus. The Theseum is thought to have furnished the model for the Parthenon.

☞ "It is a memorial at the same time of the hero's friend Heracles, and of the alliance between the cities which the two represent, Athens and Argos. . . . Very appropriately this temple is now occupied as a museum of relics of ancient Greek art." *T. Chase.*

☞ "The oldest temple of this class [the Doric temples built in the forty or fifty years which succeeded the defeat of the Persians at Salamis] is that best known as the Theseium or Temple of Theseus, at Athens, though it is nearly certain that it ought more properly to be considered the temple of the god Mars. It constitutes a link between the archaic and the perfect age of Grecian art; more perfect than the temple at Ægina or any that preceded it, but falling short of the perfection of the Parthenon, its near neighbor both in locality and in date." *Fergusson.*

☞ "This edifice, the best preserved of all ancient temples, stands on a mound at the foot of the Areopagus, on its western side, overlooking a part of the modern city. Its outer colonnade of Doric pillars, tinted with a rich golden stain, is entire; the cella is for the most part so, and little but the roof is wanting. It is small, but very beautiful, and with such a background! — the olive-groves of the Academy, Colonos, and Parnes." *Bayard Taylor.*

Theseus. An ancient Greek statue. Now in the British Museum, London.

☞ "The Apollo Belvedere as compared with the Theseus in the British Museum — perhaps the best work now left to us of the best period of Grecian art — is like Dryden's Alexander's Feast as compared with Milton's Ode on the Nativity. The latter is the production of the greater genius, but nine readers out of ten will prefer the former." *Hillard.*

Thetis bearing the Armor of Achilles. A noted picture by François Gérard (1770-1837), the eminent French painter.

Thiergarten. An extensive public park adjacent to the Brandenburg Gate in Berlin, Prussia.

Thomas à Becket. See CONSECRATION OF THOMAS À BECKET and SHRINE OF THOMAS À BECKET.

Thomas d'Aquin, St. See ST. THOMAS D'AQUIN.

Thomas. See INCREDULITY OF ST. THOMAS.

Thomas's Hospital, St. See ST. THOMAS'S HOSPITAL.

Thornbury Castle. An ancient castellated mansion of historical interest, begun by the Duke of Buckingham in the reign of Henry VIII. It is in the town of the same name in Gloucestershire, England.

Threadneedle Street. [Or Threeneedle Street.] A street in London said to derive its name from *three needles*, the sign on the shield of the Needle-makers' Company's arms. The Bank of England is situated in this street, and is sometimes referred to as the "Old Lady of Threadneedle Street."

Contrive to talk well, you will get to heaven, the modern heaven of the English. Do not talk well, only work well, and heroically hold your peace, you have no chance whatever to get thither: with your utmost industry you may get to *Threadneedle Street*, and accumulate more gold than a dray-horse can draw. *Carlyle.*

Nay, if M'Croudy offered his own life for *sale* in *Threadneedle Street*, would anybody buy it? Not I, for one. *Carlyle.*

Even so, ye indigent millionnaires, and miserable bankrupt populations rolling in gold, — whose note-of-hand will go to any length in *Threadneedle Street*, and to whom in heaven's bank the stern answer is, "No effects!" Bankrupt, I say; and Californias and Eldorados will not save us. *Crabbe.*

Threave Castle. The ancient seat of the Douglas family, situated on an island of the Dee, in Scotland, and inaccessible by land except in a very dry season. It is now a ruin.

Three Ages. A noted picture by Titian (1477-1576). "A youth and a maiden — she playing the lute — sit in the foreground; children, undisturbed by a cupid, sleep in the middle distance; and, further from the eye, an old man contemplates two skulls on the ground." In the Bridgewater Gallery.

☞ "One of the most beautiful idyllic groups of modern creation." *Kugler, Handbook of Painting.*

Three Brothers of Antwerp. The name given to three celebrated rubies. They are alluded to in Sir Walter Scott's "Anne of Geierstein."

Three Cranes in the Vintry. A famous old tavern in London. It figures in Scott's novel of "Kenilworth," and was one of the taverns of Ben Jonson's time.

> There hath been great sale and utterance of Wine,
> Besides Beere, and Ale, and Ipocras fine,
> In every country, region, and nation,
> But chiefly in Billingsgate, at the Salutation;
> And the Bor's Head . . *Three Cranes in the Vintry.*
>
> *Newes from Bartholomew Fayre.*

Three Fates. A remarkable picture usually ascribed to Michael Angelo, but the correctness of this ascription is doubted. In the Palazzo Pitti, Florence, Italy.

☞ "In the Pitti Palace, a picture of the Three Fates is ascribed to Michael Angelo. It was executed, however, by Rosso Fiorentino." *Kugler.*

☞ "Michael Angelo's Fates are three very grim and pitiless old women, who respectively spin, hold, and cut the thread of human destiny, all in a mood of sombre gloom, but with no more sympathy than if they had nothing to do with us. I remember seeing an etching of this when I was a child, and being struck even then with the terrible, stern, passionless severity, neither loving nor hating us, that characterizes these ugly old women. . . . They are a great work, containing and representing the very idea that makes a belief in fate such a cold torture to the human soul." *Hawthorne.*

Three Graces. A mythological picture by Raphael Sanzio (1483–1520), and one of his earlier compositions. It is in the Dudley Gallery, London.

Three Graces. A group in one of the frescos in the Farnesina, Rome, executed wholly or in part by Raphael Sanzio (1483–1520).

Three Graces. A well-known picture by Giacomo Palma, called Il Vecchio (1480?–1548?). This picture is said to represent the painter's daughters. It is in the Gallery at Dresden, Germany.

Three Kings of Cologne, Shrine of. See SHRINE.

Three Marys. A well-known picture by Annibale Caracci (1560–1609), "of singular grandeur and pathos." It is now at Castle Howard, England.

Three Moors. See DREI MOHREN.

Three Sisters. Romantic islets at Niagara Falls, from which is obtained the best view of the rapids at their widest and most disturbed part. "The Three Sisters are mere fragments of wilderness, clumps of vine-tangled woods, planted upon masses of rock; but they are parts of the fascination of Niagara which no one resists."

Three Trees. A celebrated picture by Paul Rembrandt van Ryn (1606–1669). It is known through reproductions.

> And ye *Three Trees* of Rembrandt, black in shadow against the blaze of sunlight; and thou Rosy Cottager of Sir Joshua,—thy roses hinted by the peppery burin of Bartolozzi; ye, too, of lower grades in nature, yet not unlovely nor unrenowned, Young Bull of Paulus Potter, and Sleeping Cat of Cornelius Visscher: welcome once more to my eyes! *Holmes.*

Thule. See ULTIMA THULE.

Thunder, Castle. See CASTLE THUNDER.

Thunderbolt. A beautiful pleasure-ground on the Warsaw River, near Savannah, Ga.

Thuron. A picturesque ivy-clad ruined castle on the Moselle, in Rhenish Prussia. The fortress was built in 1209.

Ticonderoga, Fort. See FORT TICONDEROGA.

Tiffagnes. A ruined castle in France, between Nantes and Poitiers. It is said to have been one of the haunts of the famous Gilles de Retz, the "Blue Beard of the Loire."

Tigellum Sororis. [The Sister's Beam.] A name given to a structure, in the form of a yoke, in ancient Rome, erected to commemorate the legend of the last of the Horatii, who, being sentenced to death for the murder of his sister, had his punishment commuted, at the intercession of his father, to passing under a yoke. It is said that this structure was still standing in Rome as late as the fifth century of our era.

Tih, Tomb of. See TOMB OF TIH.

Tinker, The. A well-known picture by Franz van Mieris (1635–1681), the Dutch *genre*-painter, and considered one of his masterpieces. It is in the Gallery of Dresden, Saxony.

Tintagel. A famous ruined castle, near the town of Camelford in England, reputed to have been the birthplace of King Arthur, and the residence of Queen Isolde. [Also written *Tintadgel.*]

> Four of the train combined to rear
> The terrors of *Tintadgel's* spear.
> *Scott.*

Tintern Abbey. 1. A famous and picturesque ruin, four miles from Chepstow, England. The monastery was founded in 1131. The existing remains are the property of the Duke of Beaufort. They are associated with one of Wordsworth's most admired poems.

> The men who called their passion piety,
> And wrecked this noble argosy of faith,—
> They little thought how beauteous could be death,
> How fair the face of time's aye-deepening sea! *Lord Houghton.*

2. A ruined abbey in Wexford county, Ireland.

Tiryns, Ruins of. Tiryns, one of the oldest cities of Greece, was situated a short distance southeast of Argos, and 12 stadia from Nauphlia. According to the fable, Tiryns was built for Prœtus by the Cyclopes, about 1379 B.C. The walls are well preserved.

Titania, The. An English iron yacht belonging to Mr. R. Stephenson, which was beaten in the ocean race of Aug. 28, 1851, by the United States yacht the *America.*

Titian. A portrait of himself by the painter. In the collection of autograph portraits in the Uffizi, Florence, Italy.

Titian and his Mistress. A picture, bearing this name, by Titian (1477 - 1576), representing "a beautiful woman, with a male figure holding a mirror behind her." This picture, of which there are many repetitions, is in the Louvre, Paris.

Titian's Beauty. See BELLA DI TIZIANO.

Titian's Daughter. See DAUGHTER OF TITIAN.

Titian's House. At Tai Cadore, Italy.

Titian's Slave. See SCHIAVA DI TIZIANO.

Titian's Schoolmaster. A picture called by this title, but misnamed, in the Duke of Sutherland's gallery, in Stafford House, England. It was painted by Giovanni Battista Moroni (1510–1578).

Titus, Arch of. See ARCH OF TITUS.

Titus, Baths of. See BATHS OF TITUS.

Tivoli Gardens. 1. A beautiful place of public resort in the city of Mexico, situated on San Cosme Avenue. The trees and fountains and singing birds and tropical luxuriance of these gardens make them a spot of rare attractiveness.

2. A place of amusement in Paris.

> On my return home, I found all Paris in motion in the upper part of the city, chiefly with a *fête* at the *Gardens of Tivoli.* *George Ticknor.*

Tobit. 1. A picture by Rembrandt van Ryn (1606–1669), the Dutch painter, representing the family of Tobit adoring the departing angel. It bears date 1637, and is now in the Louvre, Paris.

2. A picture by Gerard Dow (1613–1674?), the Dutch *genre*-painter, representing the blind Tobit going to meet his son. In Wardour Castle, England.

Todtenleuchter. [Lantern of the Dead.] An ancient and curious monumental structure near Vienna, Austria. It is 30 feet in height, and the date inscribed upon it is 1381. "There is a small door at a height of about five feet from the ground, and near the summit a chamber with six glazed windows in which the light was exhibited."

Toilet of Venus. A picture by Francesco Albani (1578–1660), and one of his best works. In the Louvre, Paris.

Tolbooth. A building which formerly stood on the Castle Hill in Edinburgh, Scotland, and which served the various purposes of a House of Parliament, a Court of Justice, and a jail for common criminals, and for insolvent debtors. After degenerating into a mere prison, it was taken down in 1817. This prison is poetically known as the "Heart of Mid-Lothian." The word Tolbooth is a general name for a jail.

☞ "A massive, turreted, five-storied stone structure of various ages. . . . At a later period the structure served for a prison, once under the name of the old Tolbooth, but since, and probably for coming time, distinguished as the 'Heart of Mid-Lothian.' . . . The entrance door and the huge padlock and key were removed to Abbotsford, where they now appear among the many curiosities collected by Scott." *J. F. Hunnewell.*

His [Scott's] house itself is a kind of collection of fragments of history; architectural ornaments, — copies from Melrose in one part, the old identical gate of the *Tolbooth*, or rather the stone part of it, through which the Porteous mob forced its way, in another.
George Ticknor.

But whar's the gude *Tolbooth* gane now?
Whar's the auld Claught, wi' red and blue? *Scott.*

The *Tolbooth* felt, — for marble sometimes can,
On such occasions, feel as much as man, —
The Tolbooth felt defrauded of his charms,
If Jeffrey died, except within her arms.
Byron.

Arthur's steep summit nodded to its base,
The surly *Tolbooth* scarcely kept her place. *Byron.*

Toledo, The. A celebrated street in Naples, Italy, and the chief business avenue of the city, about a mile and a half in length. It was built in 1540 by Don Pedro de Toledo, and separates the ancient from the modern city. It swarms with people, and has been pronounced the noisiest street in Europe. It is now called the Strada di Roma.

You remember J——, and what a dandy he was, the faultlessness of his boots and cravats, the brilliancy of his waistcoats and kid-gloves: we have seen his splendor in Regent Street, in the Tuileries, or on the *Toledo*. *Thackeray.*

Tom, Great. See GREAT TOM.

Tomb of Aaron. See AARON'S TOMB.

Tomb of Abelard and Eloise. This tomb is in Père-la-Chaise, the celebrated cemetery in Paris. Abelard died in 1142, and Heloise in 1163.

Come to yon stately dome,
With arch and turret, every shapely stone
Breathing the legends of the Paraclete,
Where slumber Abelard and Heloise,
'Neath such a world of wreaths, that scarce ye see
Their marble forms recumbent, side by side. *Mrs. L. H. Sigourney.*

Fair saint of passion, placidly reclining,
Thy glowing breast contained in marble death,
While Love's soft planet on thy brow is shining,
A sister heart to thine would lend its breath.

'Tis with a thrill of joy I see beside thee
The form that might not pass the convent grate,
And gather that the happiness denied thee
On earth makes blessed thine immortal state. *Julia Ward Howe.*

An avenue of tombs! I stand before
The tomb of *Abelard and Eloise*.
A long, a dark bent line of cypress-trees
Leads past and on to other shrines; but o'er
This tomb the boughs hang darkest and most dense,
Like leaning mourners clad in black.
Joaquin Miller.

Tomb of Alexander. See ALEXANDER'S TOMB.

Tomb of Atreus. A subterranean dome, constructed under the slope of the hill at Mykenæ, Greece. Here was stored the wealth of the early kings, cars and armor, with treasures of decoration in embroidery, purple, and gold.

Tomb of Cecilia Metella. A circular tower, 70 feet in diameter, resting upon a quadrangular base, situated upon the Appian Way, two or three miles from Rome. It was built to the memory of Cecilia Metella, the daughter of Quintus Metellus (called Creticus) and wife of Crassus, and is one of the best-preserved of the ancient monuments near Rome.

☞ "This tomb of a woman has become the dungeon keep of a castle, and all the care that Cecilia Metella's husband could bestow to secure endless peace for her beloved relics, only sufficed to make that handful of precious ashes the nucleus of battles, long ages after her death." *Hawthorne.*

There is a stern round tower of other days,
Firm as a fortress, with its fence of stone,
Such as an army's baffled strength delays,
Standing with half its battlements alone,
And with two thousand years of ivy grown,
The garland of eternity, where wave
The green leaves over all by time o'erthrown;—
What was this tower of strength? Within its cave
What treasure lay so locked? so hid?—
A woman's grave. *Byron.*

Tomb of Dante. See DANTE'S TOMB.

Tomb of Rameses III. See HARPERS' TOMB.

Tomb of St. Sebald. See ST. SEBALD'S TOMB.

Tomb of Sethi I. See BELZONI'S TOMB.

Tomb of the Volumnii. A noted ancient sepulchre, containing cinerary urns, in the immediate neighborhood of Perugia, Italy.

Tomb of Theodoric. See THEODORIC'S TOMB.

Tomb of Tih. An interesting and (so far as it remains) excellently preserved specimen of an Old Empire tomb in Egypt. The sculptures and representations on the walls are in wonderfully good condition, having kept their delicacy of outline and their color. They are considered in some respects superior to those at Beni Hassan.

Tomb of Virgil. See VIRGIL'S TOMB.

Tomb of Washington. See WASHINGTON'S TOMB.

Tombs, The. A massive stone building of Egyptian architecture in New York, serving as a city prison.

Tombs of Beni Hassan. See BENI HASSAN.

Tombs of the Judges. A group of sepulchral monuments near Jerusalem.

☞ "These are ornamented by a tympanum of a Greek or Roman temple filled with scroll-work of a rich but debased pattern." *Fergusson.*

Tombs of the Kings. A group of sepulchral monuments near Jerusalem.

☞ "They still retain traces of the original design, sufficient to fix their date within or subsequently to the Herodian period, without much possibility of doubt." *Fergusson.*

Tombs of the Prophets. The name given to a series of tombs excavated in the side of Olivet near Jerusalem. The origin and history of these caves are involved in obscurity. They probably derive their name from the "tombs of the prophets" alluded to by Christ in Matt. xxiii. 29.

Tombs of the Scaligers. A group of admired sepulchral monuments in Verona, Italy, erected to the memory of the Scaligeri, the family who ruled over the city in the thirteenth and fourteenth centuries.

☞ "The tombs of the Scaligers stand in the centre of the town, with a highly ornamental railing about them, and are a perfect mockery of death with their splendor. If the poets and scholars whom these petty princes drew to their court had been buried in these airy tombs beside them, one would look at them with some interest. *Now* one asks, 'Who were the Scaligers, that their bodies should be lifted high in air in the midst of a city, and kept for ages, in marble and precious stones?'" *N. P. Willis.*

Tombs of the Stuarts. In St. Peter's. Church, Rome, with a monument by Canova (1757–1822) to the memory of *James the Third, Charles the Third, and Henry the Ninth, Kings of England.*

☞ "To those who speak the English tongue, the most interesting of the monuments in St. Peter's is that erected by Canova to the last three of the Stuart family. . . . It is a marble structure, in form resembling a truncated obelisk. . . . Its interest is independent of its merit as a work of art." *Hillard.*

Tombs of the Scipios. [Ital. *Sepolcri degli Scipioni.*] These ancient tombs which are situated on the Appian Way, not far from the Porta S. Sebastiano, Rome, were discovered towards the close of the last century, and are among the most interesting historical monuments that have been brought to light. The inscriptions which were found in them have been removed to the Vatican.

The *Scipios' tombs* contain no ashes now:
The very sepulchres lie tenantless
Of their heroic dwellers. *Byron.*

Tompkins Square. A public park in New York, noted as a place of parade for the soldiery, and of gatherings of workingmen.

Tom's. A noted coffee-house in London, so called after the original proprietor, one Thomas West. It was situated in Russell Street, Covent Garden, and was taken down in 1865. In the same street were the two other celebrated coffee-houses, Will's, and Button's. In the reign of Queen Anne, Tom's was frequented by many persons of rank; and the balcony is said to have been seen "crowded with noblemen in their stars and garters, drinking their tea and coffee exposed to the people." It is described as being at that time a favorite resort for the best company, after the play, where they could enjoy "playing at piquet and the best conversation till midnight. Here you will see blue and green ribbons, with stars, sitting familiarly and talking with the same freedom as if they had left their quality and degrees of distance at home." A club, comprising nearly 700 persons, seems to have been established here in 1764, and was patronized by the nobility, gentry, and men of genius of the period. The list of members includes many noted names. Johnson and his biographer Boswell first met here. There was another Tom's in Cornhill, resorted to by Garrick.

Tonquédec. A large and well-preserved feudal castle in Brittany, France, near Lannion. It was built in the thirteenth century, and was used as a royal fortress.

☞ "To the antiquary, precious as a specimen of the military architecture of the thirteenth century. For the sketcher they combine the requisites to form a lovely landscape." *Trollope.*

Tooley Street. A street in Southwark, London. The "Three Tailors of Tooley Street" are characters said by Canning to have addressed a petition about popular grievances to the House of Commons, and to have headed the petition, "We, the people of England."

The honorable gentleman whom you interrupt here, he, in his official capacity, is not an individual now, but the embodiment of a Nation; he is the "People of England" engaged in the work of Secretaryship, this one; and cannot forever afford to let the three Tailors of *Tooley Street* break in upon him at all hours! *Carlyle.*

Tooloon. See MOSQUE OF AHMED EBN TOOLOON.

Tor de' Specchi. An aristocratic conventual establishment at Rome, Italy.

The young Countess Bolognetti, one of the famous Cenci family, took the veil at the Tor de' Specchi, the fashionable rich convent of the nobility here. *Ticknor.*

Tor di Babele. A well-known mediæval tower of the Colonna family in Rome.

Torlonia Palace. [Ital. *Palazzo Torlonia.*] A palace in Rome, built about 1650 by Fontana for the Bolognetti family, and bought early in this century by the Roman banker Torlonia, from whom it takes its present name.

Toro Farnese. See FARNESE BULL.

Torre degli Asinelli. A well-known leaning tower in Bologna, Italy, erected in the twelfth century, and so called from its builder, Gherardo degli Asinelli. See GARISENDA.

☞ "The leaning towers of brick, one of which furnished to Dante a most characteristic and picturesque illustration, impressed me. We read so much of the leaning tower of Pisa, that we feel something like a sense of injury at finding it does not incline more. These towers in Bologna are very ugly; and one half suspects them to have bent over on purpose to attract that attention which in their normal state they could not secure." *Hillard.*

In the devotional pictures he [St. Petronius] holds in his hand the city of Bologna, distinguished by the tall central tower, the *Torre Asinelli*, and the leaning tower near it. *Mrs. Jameson.*

Torre dei Conti. An immense brick tower in Rome, erected by Innocent III. (1198–1216), one of the Conti family, from whom it gets its name. It was resorted to as a place of safety in the Middle Ages.

Torre del Gallo. See GALILEO'S TOWER.

Torre del Grillo. A well-known mediæval tower in Rome.

Torre del Orologio. See HOROLOGE OF PETRUS LOMBARDUS.

Torre della Fame. [The Tower of Famine.] A famous tower which once stood in Pisa, Italy, but of which now no vestiges remain. It was the scene of the sufferings of Count Ugolino della Gherardescha, immortalized by Dante. Ugolino, as head of the Guelphs, had doubtless sought to enslave his country, and had committed various tyrannical acts. He was overcome in 1288 by the Archbishop Ruggiero Rubaldino, chief of the Ghibellines, and was afterwards imprisoned, with his two sons and two grandsons in this tower, where they starved to death.

☞ "The Pisans, who had imprisoned Count Ugolino and his two sons and two grandsons, children of Count Guelfo, as we have before mentioned, in a tower on the Piazza degli Anziani, ordered the door of the tower to be locked, and the keys to be thrown into the Arno, and forbade any food should be given to the prisoners, who in a few days died of hunger. And the five dead bodies, being taken together out of the tower, were ignominiously buried; and from that day forth the tower was called the Tower of Famine, and shall be forevermore." *Villani.*

Of the erl Hugilin of Pise the langour
Ther may no tonge telle for pite.
But litel out of Pise stant a tour,
In whiche tour in prisoun put was he;
And with him been his litel children thre,
Theldest skarsly fyf yer was of age;
Allas! fortune! it was gret cruelte
Suche briddes to put in such a cage.
Dampnyd he was to deye in that prisoun,
For Roger, which that bisschop was of Pise,
Had on him maad a fals suggestioun;
Thurgh which the peple gan on him arise,
And putte him in prisoun in such wise
As ye have herd.
. . . .
Who so wil it hiere in lenger wise,
Rede the gret poet of Itaile
That highte Daunt, for he can it devise,
Fro poynt to poynt nought oon word wil he fayle.
Chaucer, The Monkes Tale.

Thou hast to know I was Count Ugolino,
And this one was Ruggieri the Archbishop;
Now I will tell thee why I am such a neighbor.
That, by effect of his malicious thoughts,
Trusting in him I was made prisoner,
And after put to death, I need not say;
But ne'ertheless what thou canst not have heard,
That is to say, how cruel was my death,
Hear shalt thou, and shalt know if he has wronged me.
A narrow perforation in the mew,
Which bears because of me the title of Famine,
And in which others still must be locked up,
Had shown me through its opening many moons
Already, when I dreamed the evil dream
Which of the future rent for me the veil.
Dante, Inferno, Longfellow's Trans.

A human Mother and Father had said to themselves, What shall we do to escape starvation? We are deep sunk here, in our dark cellar; and help is far. Yes, in the *Ugolino Hunger-tower* stern things happen; best-loved little Gaddo fallen dead on his Father's knees! *Carlyle.*

There stands the *Tower of Famine.* It is built
Upon some prison-homes, whose dwellers rave
For bread, and gold, and blood. *Shelley.*

But those, the human savages, explore
All paths of torture, and insatiate yet,
With *Ugolino* hunger prowl for more.
Byron.

Torre della Scimia. [Tower of the Ape.] A mediæval tower in Rome, the subject of a curious legend. It relates how a baby, snatched by an ape and borne to the top of the battlements, was restored in safety to its parents in answer to a vow which they made that they would cause a lamp to burn nightly forever before an image of the Virgin upon the summit. The building is also known as Hilda's Tower from the part which it plays in Hawthorne's romance of the "Marble Faun."

☞ "Connected with this old tower and its lofty shrine, there is a legend; and for centuries a lamp has been burning before the Virgin's image, at noon, at midnight, at all hours of the twenty-four, and must be kept burning forever, as long as the tower shall stand, or else the tower itself, the palace, and whatever estate belongs to it, shall pass from its hereditary possessor, in accordance with an ancient vow, and become the property of the church."
Hawthorne, The Marble Faun.

They brought at once to mind the flocks that Hilda watches from her tower window, in Hawthorne's Roman romance.
Richard Grant White.

Torre delle Milizie. A well-known tower in the city of Rome, Italy.

☞ "On the slope of the Quirinal Hill . . . stands a square brick tower, seven stories high. It is a conspicuous object in any general view of Rome; for there are few others so tall, and there is not a single spire or steeple in the city. It is the Torre delle Milizie. It was begun by Pope Gregory the Ninth, and finished near the end of the thirteenth century by his vigorous and warlike successor, Boniface the Eighth. Many such towers were built for the purposes of private warfare, in those times when the streets of Rome were the fighting-places of its noble families; but this is perhaps the only one that now remans undiminished in height and unaltered in appearance. It was a new building when Dante visited Rome; and it is one of the very few edifices that still preserve the aspect they then presented."
C. E. Norton.

Torre di Schiavi. An elevation about three miles from the Porta Maggiore, Rome, upon which are some ruins of a villa of the Emperor Gordian.

Torre Guelfa. A noted tower in Pisa, Italy, at the extremity of the Lung' Arno.

Torre, Palazzo delle. An ancient Roman building in Turin, Italy.

☞ "In this building, to which no more precise date can be assigned than that of the age between Justinian and Charlemagne, is probably seen the last expiring effort of Romanesque architecture in a Gothic country, though the paucity of contemporary examples renders it extremely difficult to trace the exact history of the style at this age."
Fergusson.

Torrigiani Palace. [*Palazzo Torrigiani.*] A well-known palace in Florence, Italy, containing some art treasures.

Torso Belvidere. A celebrated fragment of Greek sculpture found in the Baths of Caracalla, Rome, and now in the *Museo Pio-Clementino* of the Vatican. It is generally supposed to be a figure of Hercules, wrought, according to the inscription on its base, by Apollonius, son of Nestor of Athens. Michael Angelo declared he owed his power of representing the human form to this statue; and when old and blind, he was sometimes led up to it that he might place his hands upon it.

☞ "Here are the masterpieces; and first the *Torso*, so lauded by Michael Angelo: indeed, in its life, in its grandeur of style, in the vigorous setting of the thighs, in its spirited action, and in the mingling of human passion with ideal nobleness, it is in conformity with his manner."
Taine, Trans.

And dost thou still, thou mass of breathing stone
(Thy giant limbs to night and chaos hurled),
Still sit as on the fragment of a world,
Surviving all, majestic and alone?
Rogers.

It is like the new virtue shown in some unprized old property, as when a boy finds that his pocket-knife will attract steel filings and take up a needle; or when the old horse-block in the yard is found to be a *Torso Hercules* of the Phidian age.
Emerson.

Torso Farnese. See Bacchus.

Torso of Hercules. See Torso Belvidere.

Torto, Muro. See Muro Torto.

Tothill Fields. A region in London between Pimlico and the Thames, formerly a place of recreation. The name is thought to be derived from the French *tout le champ*.

Tottenham Court Road. An important avenue in London. It was the old road from St. Giles's to the Manor of Totham or Totten Hall.

And Hogsdone, Islington, and *Tothnam Court*,
For cakes and creame, had then no small resort.
Wither.

As for the smaller fry, who swarm in shoals
From silly Hafiz up to simple Bowles,
Why should we call them from their dark abode,
In broad St. Giles's or in *Tottenham-road?*
Byron.

At seven we started for New York on board a great North-River steamboat, which was so crowded with passengers that the upper deck was like the box-lobby of a theatre between the pieces, and the lower one like *Tottenham Court Road* on a Saturday night. *Dickens.*

Tour de Cordouan. A celebrated and important light-house begun at the mouth of the Garonne in 1584, but not completed for a number of years afterwards. But little is known of the two or more predecessors of the present structure. The first light-house is traditionally said to have been built by Louis the Débonnair, but some think that it was erected here not till the thirteenth century at the request of the merchants of Cordova, and the foreign traders with whom they dealt. The second tower was built here by order of the Black Prince in the fourteenth century.

The cock upon the village church
Looks northward from his airy perch,
As if beyond the ken of man
To see the ships come sailing on,
And pass the Isle of Oléron,
And pass the *Tower of Cordouan.*
Longfellow.

Tour de Montgomery. A circular tower of the Palais de Justice, Paris.

Tour de Nesle. The site of this former tower, or castle, in Paris is now occupied by the Palais de l'Institut. It formed the end of the city wall on the south side of the river. It was often inhabited by royal personages, and a number of crimes are said to have been committed here.

Tour de Solferino. A modern tower, on the hill of Montmartre, Paris, which commands a view over the city.

Tour d'Ordre. A celebrated light-house, or pharos, at Boulogne, of which little or nothing now remains. Suetonius tells us that it was originally erected as a triumphal tower, or monument of his achievements, by the Emperor Caligula. It is thought to have been used as a light-house as early as 191 A.D., and served for that purpose as late as the seventeenth century, when it finally fell, together with part of the cliff on which it was built. It is said to have been octagonal in shape, and 192 feet in circumference, growing smaller and smaller towards the top. The height is variously given from 124 feet to 200 feet. It was built of stone and brick. *Tour d'Ordre* has been popularly, but doubtless wrongly, regarded as a corruption of *Turris ardens.*

Tour de Peyberland. A fine mediæval belfry tower in Bordeaux, France, 300 feet in height, including the spire. It was built in 1430.

Tour Magne. [Great Tower.] A celebrated monument, and relic of Roman times, at Nîmes, France.

☞ "It consists of an octagonal tower 50 feet in diameter, and now about 120 feet high. . . . Within the basement is a great chamber, covered by a dome of rubble masonry, to which no access could have been obtained from without, but the interior may have been reached through the eye of the dome. From the terrace an important flight of steps led upward to — what? It is almost impossible to refrain from answering, to a cella, like those which crowned the tomb-temples of Assyria. That the main object of the building was sepulchral seems hardly doubtful, but we have no other instance in Europe of a tomb with such a staircase leading to a chamber above it." *Fergusson.*

Tournament, A. A picture by Peter Paul Rubens (1577–1640). In the Louvre Gallery in Paris.

Tournelles, Palais des. See PALAIS DES TOURNELLES.

Touro Park. A park in Newport, R.I., given by Judah Touro, a Jew, and containing within its enclosure the celebrated Old Stone Mill, or Round Tower. See OLD STONE MILL.

Tower. For names beginning with

Tower, see the next prominent word. See also *infra*.

Tower, The. The ancient and famous citadel of London. It stands on the north bank of the Thames, about a mile below London Bridge, and in the oldest part of the metropolis. Its foundation has been ascribed to Julius Cæsar; but the tradition is unsupported by evidence, though it is probable that the Romans had a fortification here. The oldest portion of the present fortress is the keep, or White Tower, so named from its having been originally whitewashed. It was built about 1078 for William the Conqueror. The Tower is memorable for the distinguished persons who have been confined within its walls as prisoners of state. It has been from early times the depository of the national arms; and since the restoration of Charles II. the regalia, or crown jewels, have been kept here on exhibition.

☞ "This Tower is a citadel to defend or command the City; a royal palace; a prison of state for the most dangerous offenders; the armory for warlike provisions; the treasury of the ornaments and jewels of the Crown; and general conserver of most of the records of the King's courts of justice at Westminster." *Stow.*

☞ "Here [in the White Tower] we were shown the Council Chamber of the ancient kings of England, hardly altered at all; the very room in which Richard III. bared his arm, and accused Hastings of witchcraft in shrivelling it. We went to the very window where he stood, when he witnessed the instant execution of his victim, and saw the very spot, at the corner of the old chapel, where the block was laid for it." *Ticknor.*

Prince. Where shall we sojourn till our coronation?
Gloster. Where it seems best unto your royal self.
If I may counsel you, some day or two
Your highness will repose you at the *Tower*.
Prince. I do not like the *Tower*, of any place.—
Did Julius Cæsar build that place, my lord?
Buck. He did, my gracious lord, begin that place,
Which since succeeding ages have re-edified.
Prince. Is it upon record, or else reported
Successively from age to age, he built it?
Buck. Upon record, my gracious lord.
Shakespeare.

Methought that I had broken from the *Tower*,
And was embarked to cross to Burgundy.
Shakespeare.

How pleasing Atterbury's softer hour,
How shone his soul unconquered in the *Tower*. *Pope.*

Ye towers of Julius, London's lasting shame,
With many a foul and midnight murder fed. *Gray.*

From all the batteries of the *Tower*
Pealed loud the voice of fear;
And all the thousand masts of Thames
Sent back a louder cheer. *Macaulay.*

Merry Margaret, as Midsomer flowre,
Gentyll as faucon and hawke of the *Towre*.
Skelton.

Where London's towres theire turrets show
So stately by the Thames's side,
Faire Arabella, childe of woe!
For many a day had sat and sighed.
Old Ballad.

And have they fixed the where and when?
And shall Trelawny die?
Here's twenty thousand Cornish men
Will know the reason why!

Out spake their captain brave and bold,
A merry wight was he:
"If *London Tower* were Michael's hold,
We'll set Trelawny free!"
Robert S. Hawker.

Tower Hill. The high ground adjoining the Tower of London, on the north-west. Here formerly stood a large scaffold and gallows for the execution of traitors and other criminals.

12 May, 1641. I beheld on *Tower Hill* the fatal stroke which severed the wisest head in England from the shoulders of the Earl of Strafford, whose crime coming under the cognizance of no human law, a new one was made, not to be a precedent, but his destruction, to such exorbitance were things arrived. *John Evelyn, Diary.*

Mr. and Mrs. Quilp resided on *Tower Hill;* and in her bower on *Tower Hill*, Mrs. Quilp was left to pine the absence of her lord. *Dickens, Old Curiosity Shop.*

It would be a noble feat to bring their necks to the block. Above all, it would be delightful to see Nottingham's long solemn face on *Tower Hill.* *Macaulay.*

Tower of Babel. A structure believed to have been built in the most primitive times in the plain of Shinar, according to the account given in Gen. xi. 1-10, and to have been abandoned through the confusion of tongues then occasioned by the Divine displeasure. This tower has been thought to be identified with the ruin known as Birs Nimrood. See BIRS NIMROOD.

His Sicilian-Italian, and Laquais-de-Place French, garnished with shreds from all European dialects, was wholly intelligible to no mortal; a *Tower-of-Babel* jargon, which made many think him [Count Cagliostro] a kind of Jew. *Carlyle.*

The press, that giant machine, pours forth incessantly new materials for its work — the entire human race is upon the scaffolding, every spirit is mason, every day a new course is raised, . . . there is also a confusion of languages, incessant acting, — a refuge secured to intelligence against a new deluge; it is the second *Tower of Babel* of the human race. *Victor Hugo.*

Tower of Babel. A well-known painting by Wilhelm von Kaulbach (1805–1874). In the Museum at Berlin, Prussia.

Tower of David. This name is generally applied to a massive tower of the citadel of Jerusalem. A "Castle of David" is referred to here in the thirteenth century, and the historians of the crusades mention a "Tower of David" built of immense hewn stones. The structure now known as the Tower of David is thought to be identical with the ancient "Tower of Hippicus," frequently referred to by Josephus.

☞ "The so-called Tower of David appears to be the oldest portion of the citadel: it has a sloping escarp of masonry. . . . Above which the tower rises in a solid mass to the height of 29 feet. . . . The whole, when perfect, must have presented a smooth surface difficult to escalade, and, from the solidity of the mass, unassailable by the battering-ram." *Capt. Wilson.*

Tower of Drusus. See DRUSUS, TOWER OF.

Tower of Famine. See TORRE DELLA FAME.

Tower of Hollows. A Border tower, 70 feet in height, in Scotland, near Canobie.

Tower of the Ape. See TORRE DELLA SCIMIA.

Tower of the Conti. See TORRE DEI CONTI.

Tower of the Winds. An octagonal tower of marble — the Horologe of Andronicus Cyrrhestes — built at Athens, Greece, about 100 years before our era. Its sides face the eight principal points of the compass, and are marked by figures of the winds from each of those points. It was surmounted by a Triton for a weathercock, and contained a clepsydra in the interior. It served as a town-clock, and was a double measure of time with its sun-dials on the outside, and its clepsydra within. The Horologium is called by Delambre "the most curious existing monument of the practical gnomonics of antiquity."

☞ "At the end of the broad street, there is an extensive place, uneven from its torn-down clay huts and ruined walls. The Tower of the Winds rises, half dug out of the earth and grass, where the dervishes lived in the time of the Turks. Two tall cypresses point mournfully towards heaven." *H. C. Andersen.*

Townley Collection [or Townley Marbles]. A large collection of remains of Greek and Roman art, gathered by Mr. Charles Townley, at Rome, between 1765 and 1772, and afterwards purchased by the British Museum, where they are now deposited.

Townley Venus. A beautiful Greek statue, now in the British Museum. One of the so-called Townley Marbles, *q.v.*

Trafalgar Square. A place in London so named from the last victory of Nelson, to whom a column is erected in the square. See NELSON COLUMN.

☞ "'The finest site in Europe,' as Trafalgar Square has been called by some obstinate British optimist, is disfigured by trophies, fountains, columns, and statues, so puerile, disorderly, and hideous, that a lover of the arts must hang the head of shame as he passes, to see our dear old queen city arraying herself so absurdly." *Thackeray.*

Traitors' Gate. A gate in the Tower of London, through which state prisoners were introduced.

Old London Bridge was soon passed, and old Billingsgate Market, with its oyster-boats and Dutchmen, and the White Tower, and *Traitor's Gate,* and we were in among the tiers of shipping. *Dickens.*

On through that gate through which before
Went Sidney, Russell, Raleigh, Cranmer, More. *Rogers.*

Trajan, Arch of. See Arch of Trajan.

Trajan's Column. [Ital. *La Colonna Trajana.*] An interesting relic of ancient Rome, and the most beautiful historical column in the world. It was dedicated to the Emperor Trajan, as the inscription says, by the Senate and Roman people, A.D. 114. On the summit formerly stood a lofty statue of Trajan holding in his hand a gilded globe. This globe is now in the Museum of the Capitol. Towards the end of the sixteenth century Pope Sixtus V. erected a statue of St. Peter upon the column in place of that of Trajan, which had fallen to the ground. The ashes of the emperor rest under this column.

Whose arch or pillar meets me in the face,
Titus, or *Trajan's?* No — 'tis that of Time:
Triumph, arch, pillar, all he doth displace
Scoffing; and apostolic statues climb
To crush the imperial urn, whose ashes slept sublime,
Buried in air, the deep blue sky of Rome,
And looking to the stars. *Byron.*

Historic figures round the shaft embost
Ascend, with lineaments in air not lost:
Still as he turns, the charmed spectator sees
Group winding after group, with dream-like ease.

. . . . .

Memorial pillar! 'mid the wrecks of time,
Preserve thy charge with confidence sublime, —
The exultations, pomps, and cares of Rome,
Whence half the breathing world received its doom. *Wordsworth.*

Trajan's Forum. See Forum of Trajan.

Tramontana. [Across the mountains.] A name given in Italy to a prevailing north wind, which sweeps over the Alps.

A chilling *tramontana* . . . was blowing; and the barren, rocky, desolate shore suggested Norway rather than Greece. *Bayard Taylor.*

Transfiguration, The. 1. A painting by Raphael Sanzio (1483–1520), in the gallery of the Vatican in Rome, executed for the cathedral of Narbonne in France. It is considered the first picture in the world. Raphael was engaged in painting this picture when he was seized with his last illness, and after his death it was suspended over his body as he lay in state. The lower part, which he left unfinished, was completed by his pupil Giulio Romano. It was carried to Paris in 1797, but afterwards restored to the Vatican. The picture is divided into two parts; the upper part representing the three disciples lying prostrate upon Mount Tabor, while above them is the figure of Christ in glory with Moses and Elijah on each side. The lower part represents a crowd of people bearing along a boy possessed with an evil spirit. The two parts of the picture are united by the uplifted look and appealing gesture of some of the figures in the crowd below, who seem to point for help to the Saviour on the Mount. This picture is well known through the engraving by Raphael Morghen (1758-1833).

☞ "All great actions have been simple, and all great pictures are. The *Transfiguration*, by Raphael, is an eminent example of this peculiar merit. A calm, benignant beauty shines over all this picture, and goes directly to the heart. It seems almost to call you by name. The sweet and sublime face of Jesus is beyond praise, yet how it disappoints all florid expectations! This familiar, simple, home-speaking countenance is as if one should meet a friend." *Emerson.*

Glances we do seem to find of that ethereal glory, which looks on us in its full brightness from the *Transfiguration* of Rafaelle, from the Tempest of Shakespeare. *Carlyle.*

The real value of the Iliad, or the *Transfiguration*, is as signs of power; billows or ripples they are of the stream of tendency; tokens of the everlasting effort to produce, which even in its worst estate the soul betrays. *Emerson.*

2. A picture by Hans Holbein the Elder (d. 1524). In the Gallery of Augsburg, Germany.

Trappe, La. A famous monastery

near Mortagne in Normandy, France. It owes its celebrity to the rigid asceticism practised by its inmates in obedience to the rules of the order. The abbey was suppressed in 1790 by the National Assembly, but the monks were afterwards allowed to return.

Endowments, faculties, enough we have: it is her [Nature's] wise will too that no faculty imparted to us shall rust from disuse; the miraculous faculty of Speech, once given, becomes not more a gift than a necessity; the Tongue, with or without much meaning, will keep in motion, and only in some *La Trappe*, by unspeakable self-restraint, forbear wagging. *Carlyle.*

Trastevere. [Lat. *Regio Transtiberina*, the region on the other side of the Tiber.] The largest of the *Rioni*, or quarters, into which modern Rome is divided. It extends along the foot of Mount Janiculum, and is inhabited by a peculiar and in many respects a distinct race, said to be the direct descendants of the ancient Romans.

☞ "In Trastevere there are no remains of antiquity, but abundance of monuments of superstitions, —churches full of the shrines of saints, and convents full of imprisoned sinners, — plenty of houses, but few inhabitants. These inhabitants, however, boast of being descended from the ancient Romans, and look on the upstart race on the other side of the river with sovereign contempt." *Eaton.*

Traunstein Profile. A remarkable freak of nature on the hill called the Traunstein, near Lambach in Austria.

☞ "The rough back of the mountain forms the exact profile of the human countenance, as if regularly hewn out of the rock. What is still more singular, it is said to be a correct portrait of the unfortunate Louis XVI. The landlord said it was immediately recognized by all Frenchmen." *Bayard Taylor.*

Travellers' Club. A celebrated club in London, founded in 1815. According to one of the rules no person can be considered eligible to the Travellers' Club "who shall not have travelled out of the British Islands to a distance of at least 500 miles from London in a direct line." The present club-house, adjoining the Athenæum in Pall Mall, was built in 1832 from designs by Barry.

☞ "Close at hand is another place, — the *Travellers' Club*, — how well they know how to organize comfort!" *Taine, Trans.*

Not a cab stands yet at the *Travellers*, whose members, noble or fashionable, are probably at this hour in their dressing-gowns of brocade, or shawl of the Orient, smoking a hookah over Balzac's last romance. *N. P. Willis.*

Not to know Brown was, at the West End, simply to be unknown. Brookes was proud of him, and without him the *Travellers* would not have been such a *Travellers* as it is. *Anthony Trollope.*

To call a hill aristocratic seems affected or absurd; but the difference between these hills and the others is the difference between Newgate Prison and the "*Travellers' Club*," for instance: both are buildings; but the one stern, dark, and coarse; the other rich, elegant, and festive. *Thackeray.*

Tre Fontane. [The Three Fountains.] A locality anciently called Aqua Salvias, about two miles from Rome, outside the Ostian Gate, where, according to the Church tradition, St. Paul was beheaded by the sword.

☞ "In all the melancholy vicinity of Rome, there is not a more melancholy spot than the Tre Fontane. A splendid monastery, rich with the offerings of all Christendom, once existed there. The ravages of the malaria have rendered it a desert; yet there is a sort of dead beauty about the place, something hallowed, as well as sad, which seizes on the fancy." *Mrs. Jameson.*

Treaty Elm. The famous tree in the environs of Philadelphia, Penn., under which William Penn negotiated the treaty with the Indian chiefs, of which it has been said that it is "the only one ever made without an oath, and the only one never broken." The tree is no longer standing, but a monument marks its place.

Treaty Stone. An object of curiosity in Limerick (the "city of the violated treaty"), Ireland. It is the stone upon which the celebrated treaty-document of the 3d of October, 1691, was signed, whereby Limerick and other fortresses in the hands of the Irish were surrendered, with the proviso that the garrisons should be allowed to march out with the honors of war, and conveyed to France, or elsewhere, at the cost of the British Government, and granting certain privileges and immunities to Roman Catholics.

☞ "That both the letter and the spirit of this solemn compact were broken, no unprejudiced mind can entertain a doubt; and it is the merest sophistry to contend that the king had no power to ratify the bargain he had made by his agents, and subsequently confirmed under the great seal of England." *Mr. and Mrs. S. C. Hall.*

Tremont Street. A well-known street in Boston, Mass. It is called after the original name of Boston, *Tremont*, which was given to the city on account of the three hills on which it is built.

Tremont Temple. A well-known building on Tremont Street, Boston, Mass., used as a place of worship on Sundays, and at other times for lectures, public meetings, and various gatherings.

Trenc-le-mer. The flag-ship of Richard I., Cœur-de-Lion (1157–1199).

Ah, never braver bark and crew,
 Nor bolder flag, a foe to dare,
Had left a wake on ocean blue
 Since Lion-Heart sailed *Trenc-le-mer!*
H. H. Brownell.

Trent, The. A vessel, under command of Franklin, sent, in company with the Dorothea, under Buchan, on an expedition to the Arctic regions in 1818.

Trent, The. A British mail-steamer, noted as being the vessel from which the Confederate emissaries, Mason and Slidell, were forcibly taken, Nov. 8, 1861, by Capt. Wilkes of the U.S. frigate *San Jacinto*.

Treves. See ELECTORS OF TREVES, CASTLE OF THE.

Trevi, Fountain of. See FONTANA DI TREVI.

Trianon. See GRAND TRIANON and PETIT TRIANON.

Trianon de Porcelaine. See GRAND TRIANON.

Tribune, The. A name given to an apartment in the Uffizi Palace in Florence, Italy, appropriated to works of art, and containing some of the most celebrated specimens of sculpture and painting, such as the Venus de' Medici, the Dancing Faun, the Fornarina, and others. See UFFIZI.

They then led us into a large square room, in the middle of which stood a Cabinet of an octangular form, so adorned and furnish'd with chrystals, sculptures, and so forth, as exceeds any description. This cabinet is called the *Tribuna*, and in it is a pearle as big as a hazel nut. *John Evelyn*, 1644.

☞ "With feelings of high-wrought expectation, we entered the presence-chamber; a crimson, octagonal hall of the gallery called the Tribune, where, bright in eternal youth and matchless beauty, 'stands the statue that enchants the world.'" *Eaton.*

☞ "The *Tribune*, that noble room unsurpassed by any in the world for the number and value of the gems it contains." *Bayard Taylor.*

Tribute Money. A picture by Masaccio (Tommaso Guidi) (1402?–1443?). In the church of S. M. del Carmine, Florence, Italy.

Tribute Money. See CHRIST WITH THE TRIBUTE MONEY.

Trient, Gorges du. See GORGES DU TRIENT.

Trifels. A castle and ruined mediæval fortress in the neighborhood of Heidelberg, Germany, famous as the place where Richard *Cœur de Lion* was imprisoned by the Duke of Austria, and beneath the walls of which the minstrel Blondel, by his song and the response it awakened, discovered his royal master.

Trimurti. See ELEPHANTA, CAVE-TEMPLES OF.

Trinita de' Monti. A church in Rome, well known from its conspicuous position above the Piazza di Spagna. It contains the celebrated painting of the Descent from the Cross by Volterra.

1644, 22, Feb. I went to *Trinità del Monte*, a monastery of French, a noble Church, built by Lewis XI. and Charles VIII.; the Chapells well painted, especially that by Zuccari, Volterra, and the cloyster with the miracles of their St. Francis di Paulo and the heads of the French kings . . . This convent, so eminently situated on Mons Pincius, has the intire prospect of Campus Martius, and has a faire garden. *John Evelyn.*

☞ "This church, formerly belonging to the Franciscan monks, suffered severely from the destructive propensities of the French soldiers who were quartered in the adjoining convent during the French occupation of Rome in the first revolution. Many of the pictures were destroyed or irreparably injured, and the building itself was abandoned and closed from 1798 to 1816, when it was restored by Louis XVIII., after the designs of a French architect. The old pictures which had disappeared were replaced by new ones, painted by students of the French Academy in Rome; a compensation which will remind the classical reader of the old joke of Lucius Mummius." *Hillard.*

☞ "From the height of Trinità de' Monti, the bell-towers and the distant edifices appear like the effaced sketches of a painter, or like the inequalities of a seacoast dimly discerned from the deck of an anchored vessel. Rome is asleep in the midst of these ruins." *Chateaubriand, Trans.*

☞ "Ascending the Spanish Stairs, we behold the church Trinità dei Monti: a crowd of strangers flock here every Sunday morning to hear the singing and music of the holy sisters. It seems to be the weeping of angels dissolved in harmony." *Hans Christian Andersen.*

A convent like the *Trinità del Monte* with the air of a closed fortress, a fountain like that of Trevi, a palace massive and monumental like those of the Corso and of the great square of Venice, denote beings and tastes not of the ordinary stamp. *Taine, Trans.*

Trinità, Ponte SS. See PONTE SS. TRINITÀ.

Trinité, La. This church in Paris is a fine example of the modern Renaissance style. It is in the Rue St. Lazare.

Trinity, The. A large altar-piece representing the Trinity between the Virgin and the Baptist, by Jean Bellegambe, the Flemish painter. It was originally placed (1511–1519) on the high altar of the abbey church of Auchin, but is now in the sacristy of Notre Dame at Douai, France.

Trinity, The. A wood-cut by Albert Dürer (1471–1528), the German painter and engraver. "A well-known and grand composition."

Trinity, The. A picture by Roger van der Weyden (d. 1464), the Flemish painter, and one of his later works. It is now in the Städel Institute at Frankfort-on-the-Main, Germany.

Trinity, Adoration of the. See ADORATION OF THE TRINITY.

Trinity Church. A noted ecclesiastical edifice in New York, of Gothic architecture, with a steeple 284 feet in height. It is reputed to be the wealthiest church in America (the society is said to be worth over $10,000,000); its revenues accruing from a large tract of land on Manhattan island, given to it by Queen Anne in 1705. Trinity Church is situated on Broadway, a short distance above the Battery. Its lofty spire, 284 feet high, is a popular place of ascent for the sake of the magnificent view over the city and surroundings. The first church on the present site was built in 1696. In the graveyard are buried a number of noted men, among others Alexander Hamilton.

Trinity Church. A fine modern church in Boston, Mass.

Trinity College. A foundation of the University of Cambridge, England. Established in 1546. Also well-known institutions at Dublin, Ireland, founded in 1591, and at Hartford, Conn., founded in 1823.

Trinity House. A public building on the north side of Tower Hill, in London, erected in 1793 for the ancient guild or fraternity of mariners, established for the encouragement of the science of navigation, etc. The office of Master of the Corporation has been at various times held by princes and statesmen. The Corporation has in charge the light-houses, licensing of pilots, etc. Its arms are a cross between four ships under sail. It was founded by charter of Henry VIII., the document opening with the statement that "Out of the sincere and complete love and devotion which we have for the very glorious and indivisible Trinity, and also for Saint Clement the Confessor, His Majesty grants and gives license for the establishment of a corporation, or perpetual brotherhood, to certain of his subjects and their associates." The general oversight of the merchant marine (and of the royal fleet, under certain conditions) was given to them by charters which they received from Elizabeth, James I., Charles II., and James II.

Triomphe, Arc de. See ARC DE L'ÉTOILE.

Triumph of Death. A celebrated fresco in the Campo Santo, Pisa, Italy, usually ascribed to Andrea di Cione, called Orcagna (d. 1389); though recently some have claimed the authorship of it for the Sienese brothers Giovanni and Pietro Lorenzetti.

Triumph of Galatea. See GALATEA.

Triumph of Religion in the Arts. See INFLUENCE OF CHRISTIANITY IN THE ARTS.

Triumph of Riches. A large picture in distemper by Hans Holbein the Younger (1498–1543), the German painter, executed at the request of the company of German merchants in London. There was also a companion picture, the "Triumph of Poverty," both of which were greatly admired, and by some placed on a level with the works of Raphael. Their subsequent history cannot be traced later than the year 1616, and it is thought that they may have perished in the fire at Whitehall in 1697.

Triumph of the Church. See FOUNT OF SALVATION.

Triumph of Trajan. A celebrated picture by Anton Rafael Mengs (1728–1779). In Madrid, Spain.

Triumphal March of Alexander. A work of sculpture executed by Albert Bertel Thorwaldsen (1770–1844) for the Emperor Napoleon.

Triumphs of Julius Cæsar. A series of nine colored designs by Andrea Mantegna (1431–1506), the Italian painter, representing the different parts of a Roman triumphal procession. They were executed as decorations for the theatre at Mantua, Italy. They are now at Hampton Court, England.

Trocadéro. This elevation, opposite the Champ de Mars, Paris, is a popular resort of the *bourgeoisie* on Sundays. From its top a fine view of the city is obtained. It was so called from a French victory in Spain.

Trois Frères Provençaux. [The Three Brothers of Provence.] A celebrated restaurant in Paris, France.

— O boys — that were — actual papas and possible grandpapas — some of you with crowns like billiard-balls — some in locks of sable silvered, and some of silver sabled — do you remember, as you doze over this, those after-dinners at the *Trois Frères*, when the Scotch-plaided snuff-box went round, and the dry Lundy-Foot tickled its way along into our happy sensoria?

Holmes.

Here we are, however, at the *Trois Frères*; and there goes my unconscious model deliberately up stairs. We'll follow him, and double his orders; and, if we dine not well, there is no eating in France.

N. P. Willis.

One does not dine at the *Trois Frères* without contracting a tenderness for the very name of Burgundy. *N. P. Willis.*

Trône, Barrière du. See BARRIÈRE DU TRÔNE.

Trône, Place du. See PLACE DU TRÔNE.

Trophonius' Cave. See CAVE OF TROPHONIUS.

Trou de Han. [The Hole of Han.] A singular cavern in the region of the Ardennes, in Belgium.

Troy House. A seat of the Duke of Beaufort, near Monmouth, England.

True Cross. See CROSS, THE TRUE.

Trumbull, Fort. See FORT TRUMBULL.

Trustees of the Staalhof. A well-known picture by Rembrandt van Ryn (1606–1669). In the Gallery at Amsterdam, Holland.

Tuckerman's Ravine. A tremendous gulf in the White Mountains, New Hampshire. It is in the southerly side of Mount Washington, and receives its name from Edward Tuckerman, an enthusiastic explorer of the White Hills. It contains nearly every year a beautiful "Snow Arch," or cave of snow, which does not disappear until the last of August.

Tufts College. This institution at Medford, Mass., under the care of the Universalist Church, was founded in 1852.

Tuileries, The. A royal palace of France, now destroyed. It was commenced in 1564, as a residence for Catherine de' Medicis, and was completed by Henry IV. After the restoration it was habitually the residence of the royal family. It was situated on the banks of the river Seine; and on the spot where it stood were formerly tile-fields, whence the name is derived, the word Tuilerie signifying a tile-kiln. These fields were converted into gardens in 1665, containing about 67 acres, beautifully laid out, ornamented with flowers, trees, and statuary, open to the public, and much resorted to by the people. This palace was sacked by the Revolutionary mob of 1792, and was again attacked and taken in the insurrection of 1830, and in that of 1848. It was partially burned by the leaders of the Commune, prior to the entrance into the city of the German army in May, 1871, and has never been rebuilt.

Truly, this same world may be seen in Mossgiel and Tarbolton, if we look well, as clearly as it ever came to light in Crockford's, or the *Tuileries* itself. *Carlyle.*

In the Château of the *Tuileries*, for instance, I perceive the same jumble of contrarieties that marks the French character; the same whimsical mixture of the great and the little, the splendid and the paltry, the sublime and the grotesque. *Irving.*

A spittin' tobacker ez proud ez you please
On Victory's bes' carpets, or loafin' at ease
In the *Tool'ries* front-parlor, discussin' affairs
With our heels on the backs o' Napoleon's new chairs.
Lowell, Biglow Papers.

An' turnin' quite faint in the midst of his fooleries,
Sneaks down stairs to bolt the front-door o' the *Tooleries.*
Lowell, Biglow Papers.

The Henriade, as we see it completed, is a polished, square-built *Tuileries;* Hamlet is a mysterious, star-paved Valhalla, and dwelling of the gods. *Carlyle.*

—Ah, the old *Tuileries*
Is pulling its high cap down on its eyes,
Confounded, conscience-stricken, and amazed
By the apparition of a new fair face
In those devouring mirrors.
Mrs. Browning.

No house, though it were the *Tuileries* or the Escurial, is good for any thing without a master. *Emerson.*

To me, the Prado is an inexhaustible source of amusement. In the first place, it is in itself the finest public walk I have ever seen within the walls of any city, not excepting either the *Tuileries* or the Chiaja. *George Ticknor.*

I finished this day with a walk in the great garden of the *Thuilleries*, which is rarely contrived for privacy, shade, or company, by groves, plantations of tall trees, especially that in the middle being of elmes, another of mulberys. . . . From a terrace in this place we saw so many Coaches as one would hardly think could be maintained in the whole Citty, going, late as it was in the year, towards the Course, which is a place adjoyning, of near an English mile long, planted with 4 rows of trees.
John Evelyn, Diary, 1644, *Feb.* 4.

Tullamore Park. The seat of the Earl of Roden, near Newcastle, in the county of Down, Ireland.

Tullian Prison. See MAMERTINE PRISONS.

Tullius. See AGGER OF SERVIUS TULLIUS.

Tulp, Nicholas, and his pupils. See ANATOMICAL LECTURE.

Tun of Heidelberg. This huge reservoir is in a cellar of the Castle of Heidelberg, which, "next to the Alhambra of Granada," says Longfellow, "is the most magnificent ruin of the Middle Ages." The original tun was begun in the year 1589, and finished in 1591; it held 528 hogsheads of wine. The present tun was made in 1751. It is of copper, bound with iron hoops, and is 36 feet long by 24 in height. Its capacity is 49,000 gallons, or 283,000 bottles. For nearly 20 years it was kept full of the best Rhenish wine, and its annual replenishment at the time of vintage was celebrated by dances on the platform that covered the top. Notwithstanding its large proportions, it is much smaller than some of the beer-vats of the British brewers, one of which, in the establishment of the Messrs. Barclay and Perkins of London, holds 108,000 gallons, or more than twice as much as the Tun of Heidelberg.

☞ "It is as high as a common two-story house; on the top is a platform upon which people used to dance after it was filled, to which one ascends by two flights of steps. I forget exactly how many casks it holds, but I believe 800. It has been empty for 50 years."
Bayard Taylor.

The kitchen was crowded with good cheer; the cellars had yielded up whole oceans of *Rhein-wein* and *Ferne-wein;* and even the great *Heidelberg tun* had been laid under contribution. *Irving.*

Tunnel, The. See THAMES TUNNEL.

Tuolumne Grove. A noted group of mammoth trees in the Yosemite Valley, California, 24 in number, the largest being 36 feet in diameter. See CALAVERAS and also MARIPOSA.

Turk's Head. Several coffee-houses in London have borne this name. One situated in Change Alley was opened about 1662. Another house of the same name in the Strand was frequented by Dr. Johnson and Boswell. In Soho was a Turk's Head, at which the Literary Club was founded. The Rota Club met at another house of this name in Westminster.

☞ "We concluded the day at the *Turk's Head* Coffee-house [Strand] very socially." *Boswell.*

☞ "At this time of year the Society of the *Turk's Head* [Soho] can no longer be addressed as a corporate body, and most of the individual members are probably dispersed: Adam Smith, in Scotland; Burke in the shades of Beaconsfield; Fox, the Lord or the devil knows where."
Gibbon, August, 1777.

☞ "Ah! I would have liked a night at the Turk's Head, even though bad news had arrived from the colonies, and Doctor Johnson was growling against the rebels, to have sat with him and Goldy; and to have heard Burke — the finest talker in the world, and to have had Garrick flashing in with a story from his theatre!"
Thackeray.

Turk's Head Club. A club founded by Edmund Burke, in connection with Johnson and Reynolds in 1763, at the "Turk's Head" in Gerard Street, London. The chief men of the day belonged to it. Also called the Literary Club.

☞ "'I believe Mr. Fox will allow me to say,' remarked the Bishop of St. Asaph, 'that the honor of being elected into the Turk's Head Club is not inferior to that of being the representative of Westminster or Surrey.'"
Forster.

Turner's Gap. A pass in the South Mountain about five miles from Harper's Ferry, Va. It was the scene of a great battle between the National and Confederate troops on the 14th of September, 1862.

Tuscaloosa, The. A Confederate privateer in the War of the Rebellion. She was originally a United States trading vessel, named the *Conrad,* which had been captured by Capt. Raphael Semmes in the *Alabama.*

Tushielaw Castle. An old mediæval mansion, on the bank of the river Ettrick, in Scotland, once the finest castle in that region.

Tussaud, Mme., Wax Works of. See MADAME TUSSAUD'S EXHIBITION.

Twa Brigs [of Ayr]. Two bridges across the river Ayr in Scotland, connecting the town of Ayr with its suburbs, and immortalized by Burns in his famous metrical dialogue, the "Twa Brigs of Ayr."

Twelve Apostles. Figures executed in chiaroscuro, after de signs by Raphael, in an apartment of the Vatican, Rome. Some of them were destroyed by alterations in the apartment, and others have been repainted.

Twelve Apostles. See Rose, The.

Two Ambassadors, The. A picture by Hans Holbein the Younger (1498–1543), the German painter, and considered one of his most important works. It is in the collection of Lord Radnor at Longford Castle, England.

Two Boxers. A well-known statue by Antonio Canova (1757–1822). In the Vatican, Rome.

☞ "The Two Boxers are carefully executed in anatomical details, but they are wanting in refinement. . . . A Greek sculptor in executing a statue of an athlete would have made him first a man, and secondly an athlete. But in Canova's Boxers we see only an accurate transcript of brute animal force." *Hillard.*

290. See Alabama, The.

Two Misers. A celebrated picture by Quentin Massys (1466-1530), the Flemish painter. It is now in Windsor Castle, England.

Two Philosophers. A picture so called, by Rembrandt van Ryn (1606-1669), the Dutch painter. Now in the Louvre, Paris.

Tyburn. An ancient place of execution for felons in London, used for this purpose as early as the reign of Henry IV. It derived its name from a brook called Tyburn, which flowed into the Thames. The bodies of Cromwell, Ireton, and Bradshaw, were exposed at Tyburn, Jan. 30, 1661. The last execution here took place Nov. 7, 1783. Tyburn road is the modern Oxford Street. The criminals were carried, "thief and parson in a Tyburn cart," from Newgate. The famous triangle on three legs, where the executions took place, was known as the "Tyburn Tree," and sometimes as the "Three-Legged Mare." See Tyburnia.

☞ "The manor of Tyburn was formerly held by Richard Jaquett, where felons were for a long time executed; from whence we have Jack Ketch."
A writer in "Notes and Queries," quoting from Lloyd's MS. Collections in the British Museum.

If, in calculating the numbers of the people, we take in the multitudes that emigrate to the plantations, from whence they never return, those that die at sea and make their exit at *Tyburn*, together with the consumption of the present war by sea and land, in the Atlantic, Mediterranean, . . . we may fairly state the loss of men during the war at 100,000.
Goldsmith (1762).

Cloaks and fur-pelisses avail little against the January-cold; "time and hours" are, once more, the only hope: but lo, at the tenth mile, this *Tyburn*-coach breaks down! *Carlyle.*

The history of those gods and saints which the world has written, and then worshipped, are documents of character. The ages have exulted in the manners of a youth who owed nothing to fortune, and who was hanged at the *Tyburn* of his nation. *Emerson.*

Tyburn-Tree. The name given to the famous gibbet erected in Tyburn, from which so many memorable executions have taken place. See Tyburn and Tyburnia.

Tyburnia. The Latinized name given to a district of London, once occupied by the Tyburn, or place of execution for criminals. It is now one of the most reputable quarters of the city. It has been built up between 1839 and 1850. See Tyburn.

☞ "How the times have changed! On the spot where Tom Idle made his exit from this wicked world, and where you see the hangman smoking his pipe as he reclines on the gibbet, and views the hills of Harrow or Hampstead beyond, — a splendid marble arch, a vast and modern city, — the abodes of wealth and comfort, the elegant, the prosperous, the polite *Tyburnia* rises, the most respectable district in the habitable globe!" *Thackeray.*

That is a source of prospective pleasure in which the inhabitants of Belgravia and *Tyburnia* cannot indulge. *Eastlake.*

Tyropœon. A valley in Jerusalem, mentioned by Josephus, but not alluded to in the Bible. It is generally understood as being the region which extended around two sides of Mount Zion, separating it from Akra on the north, and Moriah and Ophel on the east.

Tzar Kolokol. See EMPEROR OF BELLS.

Tzarsko Selo. A celebrated summer palace and park of the Emperor of Russia, at a town of the same name near St. Petersburg. The grounds are said to be 18 miles in circumference, and are at all times open to the public, and a favorite pleasure-resort for the inhabitants of the capital. The palace was founded by Peter the Great in 1710, was destroyed by fire in 1822, but has been rebuilt with great splendor.

U.

Uffizi. [*The Offices.*] A public edifice in Florence, Italy, erected by Cosmo de' Medici (1389–1464), and containing one of the richest and most celebrated collections of art in the world. It is connected by a covered passage with the Pitti Palace on the other side of the Arno. See TRIBUNE.

☞ "Perhaps it is the picturesque variety of the Uffizi — the combination of painting, sculpture, gems, and bronzes — that makes the charm. The Tribune, too, is the richest room in all the world, a heart that draws all hearts to it." *Hawthorne.*

☞ "I paid another visit to the Uffizi Gallery this morning, and found that the Venus is one of the things the charm of which does not diminish on better acquaintance." *Hawthorne.*

The Transfiguration, the Last Judgment, the Communion of St. Jerome, and what are as transcendent as these, are on the walls of the Vatican, the *Uffizi*, or the Louvre, where every footman may see them. *Emerson.*

Ugbrooke House. A noble mansion, the seat of Lord Clifford, near Chudleigh, England.

Ugolino's Tower. See TORRE DELLA FAME.

Ulm Minster. At Ulm in Würtemberg. One of the finest Gothic cathedrals in Germany, begun in 1377. Its tower is over 300 feet in height.

Ultima Thule. [The most remote *Thule.*] A name applied by the Latin poets, on account of its distance from Rome, to the island of Thule, the situation and existence of which are involved in the greatest obscurity. The first mention of such a northern island is by a traveller from Massilia (Marseilles) in the fourth century B.C., who claimed to have arrived at a spot, some six days' journey from Britain, where nature had put a bar to all further progress, since there was no longer either water or land or air, but a mixture of all the elements, through which no passage could be made. According to Strabo and Pliny, this island reached to the Polar Circle, within a day's journey of an ever-frozen sea. Many articles have been written upon the subject of this semi-fabulous island. The south-west coast of Norway has been fixed upon by some as its probable location. Maltebrun thinks that Jutland was meant. Others, and the majority, give the preference to the Shetland Isles. The phrase *ultima Thule* is now commonly and poetically applied to the extreme limit of any journey, undertaking, or pursuit. A little volume by Longfellow has recently appeared under the title of "Ultima Thule."

This [the Rock of Abooseer] is the *Ultima Thule* of Egyptian travellers. *Murray's Handbook.*

Ulysses and Nausicaa. A picture by Peter Paul Rubens (1577–1640). In the Pitti Palace, Florence, Italy.

Ulysses deriding Polyphemus. A picture by Joseph Mallord William Turner (1775–1851), the English landscape-painter, and regarded one of his best works. In the National Gallery, London.

☞ "Ulysses is on the poop [of a gilded galley] with hands uplifted, shouting derisively to the blinded giant, while his companions, thickly clustered on mast and yard, unfurl in haste the vast sails, and one by one the red oars are thrust forth from the vessel's burnished sides, ready to sweep away from the inhospitable shore, and out of the reach of the missiles the monster may hurl after them." *Redgrave.*

Ulysses, Return of. A picture by Francesco Primaticcio (1490–1570), the pupil of Raphael. Now at Castle Howard, England.

Undercliff. A romantic spot and natural curiosity on the Isle of Wight, near Ventnor.

☞ "A strip of land some six miles long by a half mile wide, which appears to have slipped down toward the sea, exhibiting a jumble of rocks, overturned and broken mounds of earth, deep hollows, and numerous springs, forming falls of water, collecting into pools, and hurrying toward the sea." *M. Simond.*

The moonbeam sleeps on *Undercliff*,
The sea is lulled and calm,
The honey-bee has left the rose,
The lily lies in balm.
Allan Cunningham.

Undine. An admired picture by Thomas Buchanan Read (1822–1872).

Union Club. A club in London composed chiefly of politicians, merchants, professional men, and, according to James Smith, of "gentlemen at large." The club-house, Trafalgar Square, was built in 1824. The Union Club has always been noted for its *cuisine*. Also an association in Boston, Mass., having a house on Park Street.

Union College (University). An old and well-endowed institution at Schenectady, N.Y. It was founded in 1795 by a union of several religious denominations, from which circumstance it derives its name.

Union League House. A noble building, with a fine interior, on Broad Street, Philadelphia, Penn., occupied by the Union League, an organization formed in 1862 for patriotic purposes. It has a large number of members.

Union Square. A well-known public park in the city of New York, surrounded with fine hotels and shops, with statues of Washington and of Lincoln.

United Service Club. This club in London was formed in 1816, and is one of the oldest of the modern clubs. It was a favorite resort of the Duke of Wellington. The present building, in Pall Mall, was built in 1826. The United Service Club is for officers of rank not lower than major in the army and commander in the navy; and the club-house is considered one of the best-managed and most commodious in London. See JUNIOR UNITED SERVICE CLUB.

Let no man despair of Governments who looks on these two sentries at the Horse-Guards and our *United-Service Clubs!* *Carlyle.*

United Service Museum. The museum of the United Service Institution, London, founded in 1830, containing models of ships and weapons, and specimens of naval and military uniforms.

United States. A frigate of the United States navy, launched at Philadelphia in 1797. Before the war of 1812 she went by the nickname of the Old Wagon, on account of her poor sailing qualities; but these were subsequently so much improved that she was able to chase, overtake, and capture the British frigate *Macedonian*, which she brought into port as a prize in 1812.

United States Bank. An imposing marble structure on Chestnut Street in Philadelphia, built in 1824 at a cost of half a million of dollars. It is now used as a custom-house.

☞ "Looking out of my chamber window, before going to bed, I saw, on the opposite side of the way, a handsome building, of white marble, which had a mournful, ghost-like aspect, dreary to behold. I attributed this to the sombre influence of the night, and on rising in the morning looked out again, expecting to see its steps and portico thronged with groups of people passing in and out. The door was still tight shut, however; the same cold, cheerless air prevailed; and the building looked as if the marble statue of Don Guzman could alone have any business to transact within its gloomy walls. I hastened to inquire its name and purpose, and then my surprise vanished. It was the tomb of many fortunes; the Great Catacomb of investment; the memorable United States Bank. The stoppage of this bank, with all its ruinous consequences, had cast (as I was told on every side) a gloom on Philadelphia, under the depressing effect of which it yet labored." *Dickens* (*American Notes*).

United States Military Academy. A national institution for the education of young men in academic and military studies, at West Point on the Hudson, N. Y. It opened in 1812. The buildings are fine structures of stone. A library, observatory, and museum are connected with the academy. Each congressional district is entitled to send annually one young man to this school. [Familiarly known as West Point.]

United States Naval Academy. A national school for the training of midshipmen, founded in 1845, situated in Annapolis, Md. During the war of the Rebellion, the school was transferred to Newport, R.I.

University Club. A London club, Suffolk Street, Pall Mall East, founded in 1824, chiefly composed of members of Parliament who have been educated at some university, several judges, and a number of clergymen.

University College. A proprietary institution in London, for the "general advancement of literature and science," built in 1827–28. It contains the Flaxman Museum, in which are models of the chief works of John Flaxman.

University of London. See LONDON UNIVERSITY.

University of the City of New York. A fine building of marble in New York, the seat of the university, founded in 1831. It has numerous professors and students.

University of Vermont. An institution of learning in Burlington, Vt., founded in 1791.

Unspunnen Castle. A ruined feudal mansion in Switzerland, near Interlaken, where Byron's *Manfred* is reputed to have lived.

Unter den Linden. [Under the Lindens.] A noted street in Berlin, Prussia, extending from the royal palace to the Brandenburg gate. It is adorned with four rows of lime-trees, an equestrian statue of Frederick the Great, and many fine buildings.

Urbino Palace. A grand and stately palace in Urbino, Italy, once the residence of the Dukes of Urbino, now unused and fallen into neglect, but still containing many interesting remains of art.

Urdos. An extraordinary fortification in southern France, not far from Pau. It is excavated in a rock, rising in successive stages to a height of 500 feet. It was 10 years in constructing, and is capable of holding 3,000 men.

Uriel in the Sun. A picture by Washington Allston (1779–1843), the American painter. Now in possession of the Duke of Sutherland.

☞ "I have never seen Uriel represented by name, or alone, in any sacred edifice. In the picture of Uriel painted by Allston, he is the 'Regent of the Sun,' described by Milton; not a sacred or scriptural personage."

Mrs. Jameson.

Urquhart Castle. A ruined castle in Scotland, near Inverness. It is the property of the clan Grant.

Urr, Moot of. See MOOT OF URR.

Ursula, St. See ST. URSULA and EMBARKATION OF ST. URSULA.

V.

Val d'Arno. [Vale of the Arno.] In Tuscany, Italy. It is renowned for its beauty and its poetic associations.

> A dream alone to me is *Arno's* vale,
> And the Alhambra's halls are but a traveller's tale.
> *Whittier.*

Val de Grace. **1.** An extensive military hospital in Paris. Here was formerly a convent of Benedictine nuns.

2. A church in Paris, built in the Italian style. It was begun in 1645 for Anne of Austria. The dome forms a conspicuous object in views over Paris.

Val d'Emo. See CERTOSA OF THE VAL D'EMO.

Val Tremola. [Ger. *Trümmeln Thal*, Trembling Valley.] A gully on the St. Gothard Pass in Switzerland, so called from the fears formerly excited by the terrors of the passage.

Vale of the Red Horse. A locality in Warwick county, England, near Edgehill, the scene of the battle between Charles I. and the Parliamentary forces. It is so called from the colossal figure of a horse cut on the side of the hill.

Valentino, Il. A fine old palace in Turin, Italy.

Valérien, Mont. See MONT VALÉRIEN.

Valhalla. A celebrated Grecian temple or Hall of Fame, overlooking the Danube, near Regensburg, Bavaria, and deriving its name from the mythological palace of immortality, inhabited by the souls of heroes slain in battle. It was built by the king of Bavaria as a monument to the great men of Germany, and contains many statues of her heroes, statesmen, and poets, from the earliest times to the present. It is a magnificent structure of marble, and was completed in 1842 at a cost of over $3,000,000.

> Chivalry this, if not as they do chivalry in Drury Lane or West-End drawing-rooms, yet as they do it in *Valhalla* and the General Assembly of the Gods.
> *Carlyle.*

> Crowned doubly by man's blessing and God's grace,
> Thy future is secure:
> Who frees a people makes his statue's place
> In Time's *Valhalla* sure.
> *Whittier.*

Valiant, The. An armor-plated ship of the British navy, launched Oct. 14, 1863.

Vallée du Sang. [Valley of Blood.] A valley reputed to have, in ancient times, separated France from Bretagne.

> When the Vale of Blood she neared,
> All that ghastly band with speed
> Following in pursuit appeared
> Close behind her coal-black steed.
> *Anon, Tr. L. S. Costello.*

Valley-farm, The. A picture by John Constable (1776-1837). In the National Gallery, London.

Valley of Jehoshaphat. This valley of Jerusalem which is beneath the hill Mount Moriah, on which the ancient Jewish temple stood (now occupied by the Mosque of Omar), is about half a mile long, extending from the village of Siloam to the Garden of Gethsemane. Its sides are full of tombs, and the brook Kedron runs through it. The Jews believe that the Last Judgment will take place in this valley, according to the prediction found in Joel iii. 12, "Let the heathen be wakened, and come up to the valley of Jehoshaphat: for there will I sit, to judge all the heathen round about."

Vallombrosa. [The Shady Valley.] A famous convent and sanctuary near Florence, Italy. Its original name was Acqua Bella. The conventual buildings were erected in 1637, and with the surrounding forest are now chiefly interesting from the allusions to them in literature.

Thick as autumnal leaves that strew the brooks
In *Vallombrosa*, where the Etrurian shades,
High over-arch'd embower. *Milton.*

Swelling the outcry dull, that long resounds
Portentous through her old woods' trackless bounds,
Vallombre, mid her falling fanes, deplores,
Forever broke, the Sabbath of her bowers.
Wordsworth.

He [Milton] nevermore was thirsty when God's will
Had shattered to his sense the last chain-link
By which he had drawn from Nature's visible
The fresh well-water. Satisfied by this,
He sang of Adam's paradise, and smiled,
Remembering *Vallombrosa*. Therefore is
The place divine to English man and child,
And pilgrims leave their soul here in a kiss. *E. B. Browning.*

Not a grand nature. Not my chestnut-woods
Of *Vallombrosa*, cleaving by the spurs
To the precipices. *Mrs. Browning.*

Valle Crucis Abbey. A beautiful and picturesque ruined monastery, founded in 1200, near Llangollen, in Wales.

Vanity and Modesty. See Modesty and Vanity.

Varuna, The. An iron-clad vessel of the United States navy, sunk April 24, 1862, after destroying five of the enemy's fleet in the battle on the Mississippi, below New Orleans.

Who has not heard of the dauntless *Varuna?*
Who has not heard of the deeds she has done?
Who shall not hear, while the brown Mississippi
Rushes along from the snow to the sun?
Crippled and leaking she entered the battle,
Sinking and burning she fought through the fray;
Crushed were her sides, and the waves ran across her,
Ere, like a death-wounded lion at bay,
Sternly she closed in the last fatal grapple,
Then in her triumph moved grandly away. *G. H. Boker.*

Vase, Hall of the. See Hall of the Vase.

Vassar College. A noted women's college situated in Poughkeepsie, N. Y. It was founded and endowed by Matthew Vassar, from whom it takes its name. It was organized in 1865.

Vatican, The. The ancient palace of the popes, and the most magnificent in the world, built upon one of the hills of Rome, on the right bank of the Tiber. It is rather a collection of separate buildings, constructed at various times, than one regular structure. Its extent is enormous. It has 8 grand staircases, 200 smaller staircases, 20 courts, and, it is said, 11,000 apartments of different sizes. Its riches in marbles, bronzes, and frescos, in ancient statues and gems, and in paintings, are unequalled in the world. It also possesses a library with a large and choice collection of manuscripts.

☞ "The palace of the Vatican bears the same relation to other palaces that St. Peter's does to other churches. It is, indeed, not a palace, but a congress of palaces. One of the stories with which every traveller at Rome is amused is, that the Vatican with its gardens and St. Peter's occupy as much space as the city of Turin; and, as it has never been contradicted, it is probably true. The Vatican comprises a papal palace, a library, and a museum. As a museum of art, it is the first in the world. In sculpture it not only surpasses any other collection, but all other collections put together. The whole of Europe could furnish nothing to rival the Vatican. It also comprises the highest triumphs of painting, in the frescos of Raphael and Michael Angelo. He who has seen the Vatican has seen the utmost point reached by the human mind and hand in these two arts. The world is no more likely to witness any thing beyond what is here visible than to have a nobler epic than the Iliad, or a greater dramatist than Shakespeare."
Hillard.

The *Vatican* is great; yet poor to Chimborazo or the Peake of Teneriffe: its dome is but a foolish Big-endian or Little-endian chip of an egg-shell, compared with that star-fretted Dome where Arcturus and Orion glance for ever. *Carlyle.*

That Leicester shoe-shop, had men known it, was a holier place than any *Vatican* or Loretto-shrine. *Carlyle.*

On that sad mountain slope whose ghostly dead,
Unmindful of the gray exorcist's ban,
Walk, unappeased, the chambered *Vatican*,
And draw the curtains of Napoleon's bed!
Whittier.

Vatican Library. This library, in the Vatican Palace, Rome, has been called the largest in the world, not because it has the most books, but because it occupies the largest space. It is really a small collection, though exceedingly rich in ancient and rare manuscripts, the number of which is said to be over 30,000. Among the precious treasures here preserved are a famous copy of Virgil of the age of Constantine, and early manuscripts of the Scriptures. The books in this library are invisible, being shut up in wooden presses.

Vatican, Obelisk of the. See OBELISK OF ST. PETER'S.

Vaucluse, Fountain of. See FOUNTAIN OF VAUCLUSE.

Vauxhall. The region on the bank of the Thames above Lambeth, London. See VAUXHALL GARDENS.

How, in a word, . . . shall it, at length, be made manifest, and kept continually manifest to the hearts of men, that the Good is not properly the highest, but the Beautiful; that the true Beautiful (differing from the false, as Heaven does from *Vauxhall*) comprehends in it the Good? *Carlyle.*

Vauxhall Bridge. An iron bridge across the Thames at London.

Vauxhall Gardens. A place of public amusement in London for nearly two centuries. It was so named from its site in the manor of "La Sale Faukes." The gardens were first laid out about 1661. They were finally closed July 25, 1859, and the property sold. Buildings have since been erected, and roads laid out upon their site. We are told in Rogers's "Table Talk" that the proprietors of Vauxhall and Ranelagh used to send fashionably dressed persons to walk among the ladies and gentlemen in the Mall, and to exclaim every now and then, "What charming weather for Ranelagh!" or "for Vauxhall!" See RANELAGH GARDENS.

The lights everywhere glimmering through scarcely moving trees; the full-bodied concert bursting on the stillness of night; the natural concert of the birds in the more retired part of the grove, vying with that which was formed by art; the company gayly dressed, looking satisfied; and the tables spread with various delicacies, — all conspired to fill my imagination with the visionary happiness of the Arabian lawgiver, and lifted me into an ecstasy of admiration."
Goldsmith, Citizen of the World.

Vauxhall and Ranelagh! I then had heard
Of your green groves, and wilderness of lamps
Dimming the stars, and fireworks magical,
And gorgeous ladies, under splendid domes,
Floating in dance, or warbling high in air
The songs of spirits! *Wordsworth.*

The narrow lanes [in Genoa] have great villas opening into them, whose walls (outside walls, I mean) are profusely painted with all sorts of subjects, grim and holy. But time and the sea-air have nearly obliterated them; and they look like the entrance to *Vauxhall Gardens* on a sunny day. *Dickens.*

It was a curious phenomenon, in the withered, unbelieving, second-hand Eighteenth Century, that of a Hero starting up, among the artificial pasteboard figures and productions, in the guise of a Robert Burns. Like a little well in the rocky desert places, — like a sudden splendor of Heaven in the artificial *Vauxhall!* *Carlyle.*

Vecchio, Palazzo. See PALAZZO VECCHIO.

Vecchio, Ponte. See PONTE VECCHIO.

Véfour's. A noted restaurant in Paris.

We are not prepared to say what sums were expended upon the painting of Véry's, *Véfour's*, or of other places of public resort in the capital. *Thackeray.*

Veiled Image [at Sais]. A concealed or draped image said to have stood in the temple of Minerva at Sais, the ancient metropolis of Lower Egypt, and held in great veneration. It has been made the subject of many poetical allusions. Schiller has a poem entitled *Das verschleierte Bild zu Sais.*

He spoke and raised the veil! And ask ye what
Unto the gaze was there within revealed?
I know not. Pale and senseless, at the foot
Of the dread statue of Egyptian Isis,
The priests beheld him at the dawn of day;
But what he saw, or what did there befall,
His lips disclosed not. Ever from his heart
Was fled the sweet serenity of life,
And the deep anguish dug the early grave:
"Woe, woe to him," — such were his warning words,
Answering some curious and impetuous brain, —
"Woe — for she never shall delight him more!
Woe, — woe to him who treads through guilt to Truth." *Schiller, Trans.*

An awful statue, by a veil half hid,
At Sais stands. *R. C. Trench.*

Velabrum. In ancient Rome, a marsh, or fen, occupying the interval between the Capitoline and Palatine hills, caused by the overflow of the Tiber. Varro derives the name from *vehere*, to carry, from the ferry which was used to carry travellers across. See SAN GIORGIO-IN-VELABRO.

Vendôme. See COLONNE VENDÔME and PLACE VENDÔME.

Venetia. A well-known portrait of Venetia, wife of Sir Kenelm Digby, by Anthony van Dyck (1599–1641). In the Louvre, Paris.

Vengeance, La. A noted French frigate, attacked and put to flight by the United States man-of-war the *Constellation*, Commodore Truxtun, Feb. 1, 1800.

☞ "The combatants fought desperately at pistol-shot distance, until one o'clock in the morning. Suddenly the French frigate disappeared in the gloom. Truxtun, after small repairs, bore away to Jamaica, and it was some time before he knew that he had fought the vessel he was searching for, La Vengeance, 54 guns, with 400 men. The frigate, dreadfully crippled, had run away in the darkness, and escaped to Curaçoa. This victory made the navy immensely popular. Congress gave Truxtun the thanks of the nation, and voted him a gold medal." *Lossing.*

Venice. A picture by Joseph Mallord William Turner (1775–1851), the celebrated English painter.

Venice, Approach to. See APPROACH TO VENICE.

Venice paying Homage to Catherine Cornaro. See CATHERINE CORNARO.

Venice, Queen of the Sea. A picture by Jacopo Robusti, called Tintoretto (1512–1594). In the Doge's Palace, Venice, Italy.

Venus. A renowned statue by the Greek sculptor Alcamenes (fl. 444–400 B.C.), in which Phidias is supposed to have assisted.

Venus. A statue by Giovanni da Bologna, called Il Fiammingo (1524–1608). At the Villa of Petrarca, Florence, Italy.

Venus. A well-known statue by Antonio Canova (1757–1822). In the Pitti Palace, Florence, Italy.

☞ "Although undoubtedly a figure of great beauty, it by no means struck me as possessing that exquisite and classic perfection which has been ascribed to it." *Bayard Taylor.*

Venus. A well-known statue by Antonio Canova (1757–1822). In the gallery of Stafford House, London.

Venus à la Coquille. [Venus of the Shell.] A mythological picture by Titian (1477–1576). "A single figure rising from the sea, and drying her hair, a shell floating near her." In the Orleans Gallery.

Venus Anadyomene. [Gr. Ἀφροδίτη ἀναδυομένη, Venus rising from the sea.] A celebrated statue of Venus in the Vatican Palace, Rome. The name Anadyomene is applied to several other statues of Venus, one or two of which are in the Museum at Naples, Italy.

There was in ancient times a celebrated picture bearing this name, by the Greek painter Apelles. It is said to have been executed for the temple of Asclepius at Cos, and to have been taken to Rome by the Emperor Augustus, and placed in the temple of Cæsar.

Venus and Adonis. A statue by Antonio Canova (1757–1822), and regarded as one of the most beautiful of his works. Now in Naples, Italy.

Venus and Cupid. A mythological fresco in the Vatican, Rome, designed by Raphael (1483–1520), but executed by his pupils.

Venus and Cupid. A picture by George Pencz (1500–1550), a German painter. In the Gallery at Munich, Bavaria.

Venus and Mercury teaching Cupid his Letters. A picture by Antonio Allegri, surnamed Correggio (1494–1534). In the National Gallery, London.

Venus at Cytherea. See LANDING OF VENUS AT CYTHEREA.

Venus, Birth of. See BIRTH OF VENUS.

Venus Callipyge. An admired statue found at Rome among the ruins of Nero's Golden House, and which has been attributed to Praxiteles. It is now in the Museum at Naples.

☞ "The Venus Callipygis, apparently a boudoir ornament, reminding one of the pretty license of our eighteenth century." *Taine, Trans.*

Venus, The Cnidian. See CNIDIAN VENUS.

Venus coming from the Bath. A well-known statue by Antonio Canova (1757–1822), of which there are several repetitions. One is in the Palazzo Pitti, Florence, another in the possession of Lord Lansdowne.

Venus coming from the Bath. An admired statue by Giovanni da Bologna (1524–1608), "remarkable for delicacy and grace" [Flaxman].

Venus de' Medici. A famous statue, and one of the most perfect remains of ancient art. Now in the Tribune of the Uffizi Palace in Florence, and is supposed to be the work of the Greek sculptor Cleomenes (fl. 363? B.C.). It is a figure of the goddess, of small but beautiful proportions, regarded as an example of perfect art in its class. It was discovered in the villa of Hadrian, near Tivoli, about the year 1680.

☞ "Her modest attitude is partly what unmakes her as the heathen goddess, and softens her into woman. On account of the skill with which the statue has been restored, she is just as whole as when she left the hands of the sculptor. One cannot think of her as a senseless image, but as a being that lives to gladden the world, incapable of decay or death; as young and fair as she was three thousand years ago, and still to be young and fair as long as a beautiful thought shall require physical embodiment." *Hawthorne.*

☞ "The Venus stands somewhat aside from the centre of the room, and is surrounded by an iron railing, a pace or two from her pedestal in front and less behind. I think she might safely be left to the reverence her womanhood would win, without any other protection. She is very beautiful, very satisfactory, and has a fresh and new charm about her unreached by any cast or copy." *Hawthorne.*

There, too, the Goddess loves in stone, and fills
The air around with beauty; we inhale
The ambrosial aspect, which, beheld, instils
Part of its immortality; the veil
Of heaven is half undrawn; within the pale
We stand, and in that form and face behold
What mind can make, when Nature's self would fail;
And to the fond idolaters of old
Envy the innate flash which such a soul could mould:
We gaze and turn away, and know not where,
Dazzled and drunk with beauty, till the heart
Reels with its fulness; there—forever there,—
Chain'd to the chariot of triumphal Art,
We stand as captives, and would not depart. *Byron.*

Why is yonder simpering *Venus de' Medicis* to be our standard of beauty, or the Greek tragedies to bound our notion of the sublime? *Thackeray.*

Venus del Pardo. A picture by Titian (1477–1576). In the Louvre, Paris.

Venus del Vasto. A picture by Titian (1477–1576). In the Gallery at Vienna, Austria.

Venus di Milo. See VENUS OF MILO.

Venus lamenting over Adonis. A mythological picture by Giuseppe Ribera, called Lo Spagnoletto (1588–1656). In the Palazzo Corsini, Rome.

Venus of Quinipily. A singular granite statue in the garden of a ruined château near Baud in the Department of Morbihan, France. Its origin is wrapped in obscurity. It is thought by some to be a statue of Isis. The name Venus is given to it from an inscription on the pedestal in 1689. It was worshipped as late as the seventeenth century, and is an object of superstitious veneration by the peasantry.

Venus of the Capitol. A celebrated statue of the goddess, of Pentelic marble, found in the *Suburra* of Rome, and now preserved in the Museum of the Capitol.

Venus, Toilet of. See TOILET OF VENUS.

Venus, Townley. See TOWNLEY VENUS.

Venus of Milo [*or* of Melos]. A celebrated statue, found in 1820 in the island of Milo. It is in the Louvre, Paris.

☞ "This is a statue which is so called from having been dug up piecemeal in the Island of Milos. There was quite a struggle for her between a French naval officer, the English, and the Turks. The French officer carried her off like another Helen, and she was given to Paris, old Louis Philippe being bridegroom by proxy."
Beecher.

☞ "If we heard it said of a modern artist that he had even equalled the works of the Greek masters, the *Venus of Milo* would rise before us in her divine smiling beauty, in derision of all other statues we might try and place beside her." *Grimm, Trans.*

Yon bare-footed girl filling her pitcher at the fountain would have been a *Venus of Milo* in a higher social sphere.
Bayard Taylor.

Venus triumphant! so serene and tender,
In thy calm after-bloom of life and love,
More fair than when of old thy sea-born splendor
Surprised the senses of Olympian Jove.
S. H. Whitman.

O Goddess of that Grecian isle
Whose shore the blue Ægean laves,
Whose cliffs repeat with answering smile
Their features in its sun-kissed waves,—

An exile from thy native place,
We view thee in a northern clime,
Yet mark on thy majestic face
A glory still undimmed by time.
J. L. Stoddard.

Venus Rising from the Sea. See VENUS ANADYOMENE.

Venus Victrix. [Venus Victorious.] An admired statue by Antonio Canova (1757–1822). In the Villa Borghese, Rome. It represents the Princess Pauline Borghese, sister of Napoleon I.

Vergine, Colonna della. See COLONNA DELLA VERGINE.

Verhelst Family. A picture by Gonzales Coques (1618–1684), and his masterpiece. In the Queen's collection, Buckingham Palace, London.

Verlorenes Loch. [The Lost Gulf.] A celebrated gallery or tunnel in the so-called Via Mala, among the Swiss Alps. See VIA MALA.

Vermont, The. An old line-of-battle ship, now used as a receiving ship, moored off shore at the United States Navy Yard in Brooklyn, N.Y.

Vermont, University of. See UNIVERSITY OF VERMONT.

Vernia, La. A celebrated Franciscan convent, near Bibieno, Italy, established by St. Francis of Assisi in the early part of the thirteenth century, and held in veneration on account of his residence in it.

☞ "This singular convent, which stands on the cliffs of a lofty Apennine, was built by St. Francis himself, and is celebrated for the miracle which the motto records. Here reigns all the terrible of nature,—a rocky mountain, a ruin of the elements, broken, sawn, and piled in sublime confusion,—precipices crowned with old, gloomy, visionary woods,—black chasms in the rock, where curiosity shudders to look down,—haunted caverns, sanctified by miraculous crosses,—long excavated stairs that restore you to daylight."
Forsyth.

On the rude rock 'twixt Tiber and the Arno
From Christ did he receive the final seal,
Which during two whole years his members bore.
Dante, Paradiso, Longfellow's Trans.

Vernon Gallery. A collection of paintings of the English school, consisting of 162 pictures presented to the nation by Mr. Robert Vernon (d. 1849), and now deposited in the South Kensington Museum, London.

Vernon, Mount. See MOUNT VERNON.

Verona Amphitheatre. See ARENA.

Veronica, The. [The True Image.] A famous Catholic relic preserved in St. Peter's Church, Rome, said to be the impress of the countenance of the Saviour upon the handkerchief of Santa Veronica, with which he wiped his brow on the way to Calvary. [Sometimes called also *Volto Santo*, or *Santo Volto* (Holy Face).]

☞ "Properly speaking, the Veronica (*vera icon*) is the true likeness of Our Lord; and the same name has been given to the holy woman who obtained it, because the name of this holy woman was uncertain. According to some, she was a pious Jewess, called Seraphia; according to others, she was Berenice, niece of Herod. It is impossible to decide between the different traditions, some of which make her a virgin, and others the wife of Zaccheus. . . . When she saw Our Lord pass, bearing his cross, covered with blood, spittle, sweat, and dust, she ran to meet him, and, presenting her kerchief, tried to wipe his adorable face. Our Lord, leaving for an instant the burden of the cross to Simon the Cyrenian, took the kerchief, applied it to his face, and gave it back to the pious woman, marked with the exact imprint of his august countenance." — *Collin de Plancy*. Longfellow, from whose notes on Dante this extract is taken, says: "Of the Veronica there are four copies in existence, each claiming to be the original; one at Rome, another at Paris, a third at Laon, and a fourth at Xaen in Andalusia."

☞ "There is nothing regarded with so much reverence as this: the people prostrate themselves on the earth before it, most of them with tears rolling down their cheeks, and all uttering cries of commiseration."

Montaigne, Trans.

☞ "In St. Peter's at Rome, one of the chapels under the dome is dedicated to St. Veronica. An ancient image of our Saviour, painted on linen, and styled the Vera Icon (whence it is supposed that the name of *Veronica* is derived), is regarded by the people as the veritable napkin of St. Veronica, and is exhibited among the relics of the Church."

Mrs. Jameson.

☞ "To-day we gazed on the Veronica, — the holy impression left by our Saviour's face on the cloth Sta. Veronica presented to him to wipe his brow, bowed under the weight of the cross. We had looked forward to this sight for days, for seven thousand years of indulgence from penance are attached to it. But when the moment came we could see nothing but a black board hung with a cloth, before which another white cloth was held. In a few minutes this was withdrawn, and the great moment was over, the glimpse of the sacred thing on which hung the fate of seven thousand years."

E. R. Charles, Schönberg-Cotta Chronicles.

☞ "The strangest thing about the incident that has made her name so famous is, that, when she wiped the perspiration away, the print of the Saviour's face remained upon the handkerchief, a perfect portrait, and so remains unto this day. We knew this, because we saw this handkerchief in a cathedral in Paris, in another in Spain, and in two others in Italy. In the Milan cathedral it costs five francs to see it, and at St. Peter's at Rome it is almost impossible to see it at any price. No tradition is so amply verified as this of St. Veronica and her handkerchief."

Mark Twain.

As he who peradventure from Croatia
Cometh to gaze at our *Veronica*,
Who through its ancient fame is never sated,
But says in thought, the while it is displayed,
"My Lord, Christ Jesus, God of very God
Now was your semblance made like unto this?"

Dante, Paradiso, Trans. of Longfellow.

1644, 11 April. *St. Veronica's handkerchief* [with the impression of our Saviour's face] was exposed, and the next day the speare with a world of ceremonie.

John Evelyn.

Veronica, St. See ST. VERONICA.

Verplanck House. An old colonial mansion near Fishkill, N.Y., for a time the headquarters of Baron Steuben, in the Revolutionary War. Here in 1783 the Society of the Cincinnati was instituted.

Versailles. A magnificent palace in the city of the same name, 10 miles from Paris. It was built by Louis XIV. in 1661. It became a royal residence in 1681. It was attacked by the mob at the outbreak of the Revolution in 1789. The palace is now used as an historical museum, and its immense galleries are adorned with paintings and statues arranged in chronological order. A grand park is connected with the palace.

☞ "Before us lies the palace dedicated to all the glories of France. Honored pile! Time was when tall musketeers and gilded body-guards allowed none to pass the gate. Fifty years ago, ten thousand drunken women from Paris broke through the charm; and now a tattered commissioner will conduct you through it for a penny, and lead you up to the sacred entrance of the palace. Let them disguise the place, however, as they will, and plaster the walls with bad pictures as they please, it will be hard to think of any family but one, as one traverses this vast, gloomy edifice. It has not been humbled to the ground, as a certain palace of Babel was of yore; but it is a monument of fallen pride, not less awful, and would afford matter for a whole library of sermons. The cheap defence of nations expended a thousand millions in the erection of this magnificent dwelling-place. Armies were employed, in the intervals of their warlike labors, to level hills or pile them up; to turn rivers, and to build aqueducts, and transplant woods, and construct smooth terraces and long canals. A vast garden grew up in a wilderness, and a stupendous palace in the garden, and a stately city round the palace; the city was peopled with parasites who daily came to do worship before the creator of these wonders, — the Great King. 'Dieu seul est grand,' said courtly Massillon; but next to him, as the prelate thought, was certainly Louis, his vice-gerent here upon earth, — God's lieutenant, governor of the world, before whom courtiers used to fall upon their knees, and shade their eyes, as if the light of his countenance, like the sun, which shone supreme in heaven, the type of him, was too dazzling to bear." *Thackeray.*

☞ "Versailles is the most complete type of the classic style. That palace was the seat and tomb of the old dynasty of French monarchs, and has held a great place in the history of France. Louis XIII. built at Versailles a sort of feudal château, flanked by four large pavilions at the angles, encircled by ditches with drawbridges. Louis XIV. continued his father's labors, but in his additions the feudal character is no longer seen. The modest hunting rendezvous of Louis XIII. presents towards the town a façade in stone and brick, the arrangement of which forms an agreeable perspective. The buildings were commenced a little after the death of Mazarin, in 1661, under the direction of Levan, and were continued by Mansart from 1670 to 1684. They were severely criticised by court retainers. Saint-Simon declared that the place chosen was 'unpleasant, sad, without view, without wood, without water, without land, because the ground was sandy and marshy.' To this complaint the finished structures are a victorious answer, opening as they do upon beautiful gardens, with a thousand fine views and vistas, and numberless sheets of water. It is only fair to say that the architects themselves experienced a hundred difficulties in carrying out this undertaking. The chief difficulty was to obtain funds. 90,000,000 of francs (which at the present day would be worth 400,000,000) were sunk at Versailles under Louis XIV., and Mirabeau valued the total expense at 1,200,000,000. There is no doubt that these enormous expenses affected the economy of the public finances, and largely contributed to the embarrassments which resulted in the fall of the monarchy. The façade overlooking the garden was a repetition of the arrangements common to all the great buildings of the reigns of Louis XIV. and Louis XV. Seen at sunset from near the Swiss lake, the profile of the façade produces a grand impression of nobleness and simplicity. The interior arrangement is imperfect; the vestibules are ill-placed; and the stairs do not correspond with the richness and grandeur of the apartments. But these defects are more than compensated for by the splendid pictures of Lebrun, Audran, Coypel, Jouvenet, Lafosse, and Lemoyne. Ancient statues, the rarest marbles, fine specimens of the goldsmith's art, jewels, and curiosities of every description, were formerly lavished on these empty saloons. We may still judge of the former splendor of Versailles by the famous Mirror Gallery. It is 228 feet long by 33. Its 17 great crosses correspond with the mirrors, which reflect the gardens and the lakes." *Lefèvre, Trans. Donald.*

He [Admiral Torrington] had long been in the habit of exacting the most abject homage from those who were under his command. His flagship was a little *Versailles.* *Macaulay.*

Versailles! Up the chestnut alleys,
All in flower, so white and pure,
Strut the red and yellow lacqueys
Of this Madame Pompadour.
Walter Thornbury.

I do not think that on this earth,
Mid its most notable plantations,
Has been a spot more praised, more famed,
More choice, more citied, oftener named,
Than thy most tedious park, *Versailles!*
Alfred de Musset, Trans.

John saw *Versailles* from Marlé's height,
And cried, astonished at the sight,
"Whose fine estate is that there here?"
"State! Je vous n'entends pas, Monsieur."
C. Dibdin.

Véry's. A noted restaurant in Paris.

I had eaten for a week at *Véry's* before I discovered that since Pelham's day that gentleman's reputation has gone down. He is a subject for history at present. *N. P. Willis.*

We are not prepared to say what sums were expended upon the painting of *Véry's* . . . or of other places of public resort in the capital. *Thackeray.*

Vespasian, Temple of. See TEMPLE OF VESPASIAN.

Vesta, Temple of. See TEMPLE OF VESTA.

Via Appia. [Appian Way.] One of the great avenues leading from ancient Rome, and the principal line of communication with Southern Italy, Greece, and the East. It was begun by Appius Claudius Cæcus, the Censor, B.C. 312, from whom it derived its name. Under Pope Pius IX. this ancient road was laid open in the most interesting part of its extent. The Appian Way is about 11 Roman miles in length, and is remarkable for the number and magnificence of the tombs which lined it, and for the solid and durable construction of its pavement, which is now exposed for parts of its extent.

☞ "The Via Appia is a magnificent promenade amongst ruinous tombs, the massive remains of which extend for many miles over the Roman Campagna. The powerful families of ancient Rome loved to build monuments to their dead by the side of the public road, probably to exhibit at once their affection for their relations and their own power and affluence." *Frederika Bremer.*

☞ "The best known of the Roman roads, the Appian Way, . . . forms the most travelled route between Rome and Naples. . . . Such roads could not have been constructed unless the very workmen who wrought upon them had been impressed with the idea of the eternal duration of Rome." *Hillard.*

☞ "Even the Pyramids form hardly a stranger spectacle, or a more alien from human sympathies, than the tombs of the Appian Way, with their gigantic height, breadth, and solidity, defying time and the elements, and far too mighty to be demolished by ordinary earthquakes." *Hawthorne.*

Then you must build up or uncover the massive tombs, now broken or choked with sand, so as to restore the aspect of vast streets of tombs like those on the *Appian Way*, out of which the Great Pyramid would rise like a cathedral above smaller churches. *A. P. Stanley.*

"Is there time," I asked,
"In these last days of railroads, to stop short
Like Cæsar's chariot (weighing half a ton)
On the *Appian road* for morals?"
Mrs. Browning.

Awe-struck I gazed upon that rock-paved way,
The *Appian Road;* marmorean witness still
Of Rome's resistless stride and fateful will,
Which mocked at limits, opening out for aye
Divergent paths to one imperial sway.
Aubrey de Vere.

Via Babuino. One of three streets diverging from the Piazza del Popolo in Rome. It extends to the Piazza di Spagna.

Via Balbi. The principal street in Genoa, Italy, containing many fine palaces.

Via de' Bardi. An ancient and historic street in Florence, Italy, which has of late in great part disappeared as a consequence of city improvements.

The color of these objects was chiefly pale or sombre; the vellum bindings, with their deep-ridged backs, gave little relief to the marble livid with long burial, the dark bronzes wanted sunlight upon them to bring out their tinges of green, and the sun was not yet high enough to send gleams of brightness through the narrow windows that looked on the *Via de' Bardi.* *George Eliot.*

Via Dolorosa. A narrow street about a mile in length, which pursues a winding or zigzag course through the city of Jerusalem from the Mount of Olives to Golgotha, and which has borne its present name for the last few centuries. On this street the credulous may find the scenes of all the historical and legendary events connected with the Crucifixion. Here are situated the birthplace of the Virgin Mary, the house of St. Veronica, upon whose handkerchief or veil, used to wipe away his blood and sweat, the face of Jesus was miraculously impressed, and the church said to have been erected upon the spot where Mary swooned and fell at the time when her Son sank under the weight of the cross.

☞ "One cannot help wondering how the good old monks could manifest such childish simplicity in their inventions. A schoolboy in England would naturally ask how the present lane, with its sharp turns and numerous windings, happens so exactly to correspond with the ancient one; or how arches, and walls, and staircases, and particular stones, and whole houses could remain intact, and be identified, after the total destruction of the city by the Romans, and the lapse of so many centuries. And yet so it is. Not a word is heard of the Via Dolorosa, and its *eight stations*, from monk or priest, traveller or pilgrim, previous to the fourteenth century. . . . There is something deeply interesting in it also to the artist and the historian; for here are the originals, if we may so call them, of some of the most celebrated works of European art, and here is the fountain-head of some of the most famous of European superstitions."
Murray's Handbook.

☞ "The Procession to Calvary (*Il Portamento del Croce*) followed a path leading from the gate of Jerusalem to Mount Calvary, which has been kept in remembrance and sanctified as the *Via Dolorosa.*" *Mrs. Jameson.*

☞ "Yonder steep, tortuous lane before us, flanked by ruined walls on either side, has borne, time out of mind, the title of *Via Dolorosa;* and tradition has fixed the spots where the Saviour rested, bearing his cross to Calvary." *Thackeray.*

Via Felice. A well-known street in Rome, Italy, near the Piazza Barberini.

Thence to *Via Felix*, a straite and noble streete but very precipitous, till we came to the Fountains of Lepidus, built at the abuttments of four stately wayes.
John Evelyn, 1644.

'Twas in the *Via Felice*
My friend his dwelling made,
The Roman Via Felice,
Half sunshine, half in shade.
Julia Ward Howe.

Via Flaminia. [Flaminian Way.] Formerly the chief northern road of Italy, so called from Caius Flaminius, by whom it was begun during his censorship in the third century B.C. It entered the city near the present Porta del Popolo.

Via Mala. A celebrated Alpine gorge in the canton of the Grisons, Switzerland, in which the opposite walls of limestone rock rise in towering precipices on both sides, sometimes to the height of 1,500 feet. The road crosses the river Rhine three times, and the scenery is grand in the extreme.

Via Mala Bergamesca. A remarkable gorge among the Italian Alps near Lovere.

Via Nuova. [The New Street.] A well-known street in Genoa, Italy.

Via Ripetta. One of three streets which diverge from the Piazza del Popolo in Rome. It leads somewhat in the direction of the Castle of St. Angelo and St. Peter's.

Via Sacra. [Sacred Way.] A street in ancient Rome, and one over which triumphal processions passed, extending from the Arch of Fabius to that of Titus. It was a favorite promenade of the poet Horace.

Ibam forte *Viâ Sacrâ*, sicut meus est mos,
Nescio quid meditans nugarum, et totus in illis. *Sat. lib.* i. ix.

Along the *Sacred Way*
Hither the triumph came, and, winding round
With acclamation, and the martial clang
Of instruments, and cars laden with spoil,
Stopped at the sacred stair that then appeared. *Samuel Rogers.*

Who would have thought that the saucy question, "Does your mother know you're out?" was the very same that Horace addressed to the bore who attacked him in the *Via Sacra?*

Interpellandi locus hic erat: Est tibi mater?
Cognati, queis te salvo est opus?
Holmes.

Victoires, Place des. See PLACE DES VICTOIRES.

Victoria Bell. A large bell at Leeds, England, hung in the town-hall. It weighs 4 tons 1 cwt., and its diameter at the mouth is 6 ft. 2 in.

Victoria Bridge. A celebrated bridge across the St. Lawrence at Montreal, Canada. It was erected in 1854–59, and is 9,184 feet in length, with 24 spans of 242 ft. each, and a centre span of 330 ft., at a height of 60 ft. above the river. The cost of the bridge was nearly $7,000,000.

Victoria Docks. The docks bearing this name, which occupy 200 acres on the left bank of the Thames, London, were opened in 1856.

Victoria Embankment. See THAMES EMBANKMENTS.

Victoria Hall. A building in Edinburgh, Scotland, used for the meetings of the General Assembly of the Church of Scotland.

Victoria Park. An extensive pleasure-ground in London, originated by act of Parliament in the fourth and fifth years of the reign of Queen Victoria.

Victoria Theatre. A theatre in Waterloo Bridge Road, Lambeth, London, originally called The Coburg.

Victoria Square. A public ground in Montreal, Can.

Victoria Tower. See WESTMINSTER PALACE.

Victory. A statue by Giovanni da Bologna, called Il Fiammingo (1530?–1608). In the Palazzo Vecchio, Florence, Italy.

Victory, The. A famous vessel of the British navy. She was the flagship of Admiral Nelson (1758–1805) at Trafalgar, and on her deck he received a fatal wound. The ship is anchored at Portsmouth, England, and is kept on exhibition.

Victory, The. An Arctic exploring-ship which sailed from England in 1829 under the command of Sir John Ross (1777–1856). The Victory was abandoned in the ice in 1832.

Victory of Alexander the Great over Darius. A celebrated picture by Albert Altdorfer (d. 1538), a German painter, and considered his masterpiece. It was painted in 1529 for Duke William of Bavaria, and is now in the Gallery of Munich, Bavaria.

☞ "It is in truth a little world on a few square feet of canvas; the hosts of combatants who advance on all sides against each other are innumerable, and the view into the background appears interminable. In the distance is the ocean, with high rocks and a rugged island between them; ships of war appear in the offing, and a whole fleet of vessels. On the left the moon is setting — on the right the sun is rising; both shining through the opening clouds — a clear and striking image of the events represented. . . . The character and execution of the figures is most masterly and profound."

Frederic Schlegel, Trans.

Victory of Constantine. A fresco by Raphael Sanzio (1483–1520). In the Vatican, Rome.

Vicus Judæorum. See GHETTO.

Vicus Sceleratus. [The Accursed Street.] A street in ancient Rome, reputed to be the one in which the daughter of Servius Tullius drove over the corpse of her father, after he had been murdered by the emissaries of Tarquin, her husband.

Vierge à la Diadème. [The Virgin with the Diadem.] "The Madonna, kneeling, is lifting the veil from the sleeping Child, in order to show it to the little St. John, who kneels in joyful adoration. In the background a rich landscape." This picture, which has been considerably injured, is now in the Louvre, Paris. [Called also *Vierge au Linge*.]

☞ "The subject of the Sleeping Christ is beautifully varied by the introduction of St. John, as where Mary lifts the veil, and shows her Child to the little St. John kneeling with folded hands. Raphael's well-known 'Vierge à la Diadème' is an instance replete with grace and expression."

Mrs. Jameson.

Vierge à la Victoire. See MADONNA DELLA VITTORIA.

Vierge à l'Oreiller verd. [Virgin of the Green Pillow.] A beautiful picture of the Madonna and Child by Andrea Solario, the early Italian painter. The picture derives its name from the color of the pillow on which the Child is lying. In the Louvre, Paris.

Vierge au bas-relief. A picture of the Madonna and Child by Leonardo da Vinci (1452–1520), the Italian painter. It is so called from the small sculptured stone in the corner, and is supposed to have been executed about 1490. "This is probably one of the earliest specimens of that arrangement of the Holy Family which Raphael afterwards consecrated." It is now in the possession of Lord Monson at Gatton Park. A very similar picture to this by Leonardo is in the Hermitage at St. Petersburg.

Vierge au Donataire. See MADONNA DI FOLIGNO.

Vierge au Lapin. [Virgin with the Rabbit.] A beautiful picture of the Madonna and Child by Titian (1477–1576). In the Gallery of the Louvre, Paris.

☞ "This Arcadian sentiment is carried as far as could well be allowed in a picture by Titian known as the *Vierge au Lapin*. The Virgin holds a white rabbit, towards which the infant Christ, in the arms of St. Catherine, eagerly stretches his hand."
Mrs. Jameson.

Vierge au Linge. See VIERGE À LA DIADÈME.

Vierge au Palmier. See HOLY FAMILY OF THE PALM-TREE.

Vierge au Panier. [The Virgin with the Work-basket.] A well-known picture of the Madonna, by Antonio Allegri, surnamed Correggio (1494–1534), in which the Virgin is represented dressing her Child, with a work-basket standing beside her. This picture is now in the National Gallery, London.

☞ "Mary holds the Child upon her knee, looking down upon him fondly. . . . A finished example of that soft yet joyful maternal feeling for which Correggio was remarkable."
Mrs. Jameson.

☞ "This picture shows that Correggio was the greatest master of aërial perspective of his time." *Mengs.*

Vierge au Voile. See VIERGE À LA DIADÈME.

Vierge aux Candélabres. See MADONNA DELLA CANDELABRA.

Vierge aux Cerises. [Virgin with Cherries.] A well-known picture of the Madonna and Child by Annibale Caracci (1560–1609), in which Joseph is seen presenting cherries. Now in the Louvre, Paris.

☞ "It is related, that before the birth of our Saviour, the Virgin Mary wished to taste of some cherries which hung upon a tree high above her head: she requested Joseph to procure them for her, and, he reaching to pluck them, the branch bowed down to his hand."
Mrs. Jameson.

Vierge aux Rochers. [Madonna of the Rocks.] A picture of the Madonna and Child, by Leonardo da Vinci (1452-1520), the Italian painter. It derives its name from the dismal dark cavern with stalactite forms in which the figures are placed. It is thought that others beside Leonardo had a hand in this composition. There are similar pictures in the Louvre, the Naples Museum, and elsewhere, which are undoubtedly the work of pupils, and probably taken from Leonardo's cartoon of the subject. This picture was formerly at Milan, but is now in possession of the Earl of Suffolk at Charlton Park.

Vierge au Silence. [The Silent Virgin.] The name given to pictures of the Madonna and Child, in which the latter is represented as sleeping. For an example, among others, see VIERGE À LA DIADÈME. See also SILENTIUM.

Vierge aux Anges [with Angels]. A picture by Peter Paul Rubens (1577–1640), representing the Virgin and Child surrounded by a host of children. In the Gallery of the Louvre, Paris.

☞ "Rubens has more than once committed the same fault against ecclesiastical canons and decorum (i.e., introducing into a glory round the Virgin, female angels), for instance in his *Madonna aux Anges* in the Louvre."
Mrs. Jameson.

Vigilant, The. A French frigate captured by the British frigate *Massachusetts* at the taking of Louisbourg in 1745.

Villa Adriana. See HADRIAN'S VILLA.

Villa Albani. A Roman villa built in 1760 by Cardinal Albani, and now owned by Prince Torlonia. It contains a collection of sculptures and paintings, once of great merit, but now of reduced value in consequence of the loss of 294 of its best specimens which were taken to Paris by Napoleon, and there sold. Among the treasures of art in the villa, are the bronze Apollo Sauroctonos, *q. v.*, and a beautiful rilievo of Antinous, *q.v.*

Villa Aldobrandini. A celebrated villa in Frascati, near Rome. It was erected towards the close of the sixteenth century by Cardinal Aldobrandini, nephew of Pope Clement VIII. It is famous for its water-works, the water being made to flow in every fantastic form.

1644, 5 May. We tooke coach and went 15 miles out of the Cittie to Frascati, formerly Tusculanum, a villa of Cardinal *Aldobrandini*, built for a country house, but surpassing, in my opinion, the most delicious places I ever beheld for its situation, elegance, plentifull water, groves, ascents and prospects. Just behind the palace (which is of excellent architecture) in the centre of the enclosure rises an high hill or mountaine all overclad with tall wood, and so formed by nature as if it had been cut out by art, from the sum'it whereof falls a cascade, seeming rather a great river than a streame precipitating into a large theater of water. Under this is made an artificial grott, wherein are curious rocks, hydraulic engines and all sorts of singing-birds moving and chirping by force of the water, with severall other pageants and surprising inventions.
John Evelyn.

☞ "This is the Italian rural palace constructed for a noble of classic tastes, one who relished nature according to the landscapes of Poussin and Claude Lorraine. In the interior the walls are decorated with 'Apollo and the Nine Muses,' 'The Cyclops and Vulcan at his Forge,' . . . 'David and Goliath,' and a 'Judith,' simple and beautiful, by Domenichino."
Taine, Trans.

Villa Borghese. A villa or country house just outside the Porta del Popolo, Rome, belonging to the Borghese family. It contains a collection of sculptures. The grounds connected with this villa are very beautiful.

☞ "The scenery is such as arrays itself to the imagination when we read the beautiful old myths, and fancy a brighter sky, a softer turf, a more picturesque arrangement of venerable trees, than we find in the rude and untrained landscapes of the Western world. . . . A seclusion, but seldom a solitude; for priest, noble, and populace, stranger and native, all who breathe the Roman air, find free admission, and come hither to taste the languid enjoyment of the day-dream which they call life."
Hawthorne.

☞ "The *Villa Borghese* is a vast park four miles in circumference, with buildings of all kinds scattered over it. . . . Here is a little temple, there a peristyle, further on a ruined colonnade, a portico, balustrades, large round vases, and a sort of amphitheatre. The undulating surface rises and falls in beautiful meadows, red with the delicate trembling anemone. Fountains murmur at every turn of the avenues, and in small valleys grand old oaks send up their valiant, heroic, antique forms."
Taine, Trans.

I walked to the *Villa Borghesi*, a house and ample garden on Mons Pincius, yet somewhat without the Citty walls, circumscribed by another wall full of small turrets and banqueting-houses, which makes it appeare at a distance like a little towne. Within it is an elysium of delight, having in the centre a noble Palace, but the entrance of the garden presents us with a very glorious fabrick or rather dove-case adorned with excellent marble statues. This garden abounded with all sort of delicious fruit and exotiq simples, fountains, groves, and rivulets.
John Evelyn.

☞ "I was never weary of seeing from the Villa Borghese the sun go down behind the cypresses of Monte Mario, and the pines of the Villa Pamphili planted by Le Notre."
Chateaubriand, Trans.

Villa Farnesina. See FARNESINA.

Villa Gherardesca. A villa at San Domenica di Fiesole, in the environs of Florence, known as the residence of Walter Savage Landor, and since called by his name.

☞ "I found him [Landor] noble and courteous, living in a cloud of pictures at his Villa Gherardesca, a fine house commanding a beautiful landscape." *Emerson.*

Villa Landore. See VILLA GHERARDESCA.

Villa Ludovisi. A beautiful villa in Rome, built early in the eighteenth century by Cardinal Ludovisi, nephew of Gregory XV., now owned by the Duke and Duchess Sora. It contains a fine collection of sculptures, among which the most celebrated is the Ludovisi Juno, a colossal head, greatly admired by Goethe.

☞ "The Villa Ludovisi, though its grounds are a mile in circumference, is within the walls of Rome. The principal building, inhabited by the prince, is not shown. A smaller structure, or casino, is appropriated to sculpture; and it contains one of the finest private collections in Rome." *Hillard.*

☞ "1644, Nov. 10. We went to see Prince *Ludovisio's villa*, where was formerly the Viridarium of the poet Sallust. The house is very magnificent, and the extent of the ground is exceeding large, considering it is a Citty; in every quarter of the garden are antiqu statues, and walkes planted with cypresse." *John Evelyn.*

☞ "The villa is charming. This kind of landscape is unique: you find the vegetation of all climates mingled and grouped together. And a still more peculiar sight is the old walls of Rome, a veritable natural ruin, that serves as an enclosure. Hot-houses are supported against red arcades; lemon-trees in pale rows hug the disjointed bricks, and in the vicinity fresh green grass is growing abundantly." *Taine, Trans.*

Villa Madama. A deserted villa near Rome, containing some interesting frescos.

One event in nature, on the contrary, like a sunset from the *Villa Madama*, one work of art like the much-revered Juno, make a deep and inspiring impression. *Goethe, Trans.*

Villa Medici. A villa upon a beautiful situation in Rome, built in 1540, afterwards passing into the possession of the Medici family, and now the seat of the French Academy. It contains a valuable collection of casts.

☞ "The grounds of the Villa Medici are laid out in the old fashion of straight paths, with borders of box. There are green alleys with long vistas overshadowed by ilex-trees, . . . and in their season a profusion of roses from which the genial sun of Italy distils a fragrance, to be scattered abroad by the no less genial breeze." *Hawthorne.*

Villa Massimo. A villa in Rome near the Church of S. Maria Maggiore, and formerly one of the most beautiful in the city. [Called also *Villa Negroni* and *Villa Massimo Negroni.*]

Villa Mozzi. A noted villa in the vicinity of Florence, Italy, once the residence of Lorenzo de' Medici.

Villa Nazionale. See VILLA REALE.

Villa Negroni. See VILLA MASSIMO.

Villa Pamfili-Doria. A beautiful villa in Rome, called by the Italians Belrespiro. It contains some statues and pictures.

Villa Reale. [Now called *Villa Nazionale.*] The Public Garden of Naples, in the street called the Chiaja, and the favorite promenade of the inhabitants. It is nearly a mile in length, and 200 feet in breadth, bordering upon the sea, from which it is separated by a wall and parapet. It is planted with orange-trees, myrtles, acacias, and evergreen oaks, and is laid out partly in the Italian and partly in the English style of gardening.

☞ "The brightest and gayest aspect in Europe. . . . Here is every thing that can restore the weary, or amuse the idle, — a prospect of indescribable beauty; the breezes and voices of the sea; the rich foliage of the south, gay faces of men and women, and children sporting round the fountains." *Hillard.*

Ville, Hôtel de. See HÔTEL DE VILLE.

Viminal Hill. [Lat. *Mons Viminalis.*] One of the seven hills of ancient Rome, scarcely distinguishable at the present time. It is supposed to derive its name from the osiers (*vimina*) which grew upon it.

☞ "The Viminal Hill is to me *terra incognita.* It is, or was, situated between the Esquiline and the Quirinal; and, I suppose, 'if it be not gone, it must be there still.' But I have already confessed my incapacity to discover it; and though I have frequently since most diligently renewed my scrutiny, I have been able to descry nothing that, by any latitude of interpretation, can be construed into the least resemblance to a hill. The truth is, that it has sustained, between its two puissant neighbors (the Esquiline and the Quirinal) that extinction which a small state sometimes suffers between two large ones." *C. A. Eaton.*

Vincennes, Barrière de. See BARRIÈRE DU TRÔNE.

Vinci. See LEONARDO DA VINCI.

Vintage of Noah. A fresco painting by Bennozo Gozzoli (1408–1478). In the Campo Santo, Pisa, Italy.

Violets of Pæstum. See ROSES OF PÆSTUM.

Violin Player. [*Il Suonatore.*] A well-known picture by Raphael Sanzio (1483-1520), representing a young man holding in his hand the bow of a violin and a wreath of laurel. It is supposed to be the portrait of one Antonio Marone, a Brescian improvvisatore, and is regarded as one of Raphael's best portraits. This picture is now in the Sciarra Palace in Rome.

☞ "Two precious pictures here [in the Sciarra Palace] are under glass, the first and most beautiful being the *Violin-player* by Raphael. This represents a young man in a black cap and green mantle, with a fur collar, and thick brown hair descending over it. The young man slowly turns his head, fixing his eye on the spectator. The nobleness and calmness of the head are incomparable, also its gentleness and intelligence: you cannot imagine a more beautiful, a more delicate spirit." *Taine, Trans.*

One of these peasants, with long black hair and pale dignified face, resembles the *Suonatore* of Raphael. *H. Taine, Trans.*

Viper, The. A noted frigate of the United States navy, in service in the war of 1812. She was built at Washington.

Virgen de la Serviletta. [Virgin of the Napkin.] A picture by Bartolomé Estevan Murillo (1618–1682), so called in allusion to the dinner-napkin on which it was painted.

Virgil's Tomb. That which is known as the tomb of Virgil (70–19 B.C.) is on the promontory of Pausilippo, overlooking the Bay of Naples. It bears the inscription: "Mantua me genuit: Calabri rapuere: tenet nunc Parthenope: cecini pascua, rura, duces." See GROTTA DI POSILIPPO.

☞ "*Virgil's Tomb* is so called, I believe, on the single authority of Donatus. . . . And who is this Donatus? — an obscure grammarian, or rather his counterfeit. The structure itself resembles a ruined pigeon-house, where the numerous *columbaria* would indicate a family-sepulchre: but who should repose in the tomb of Virgil, but Virgil alone? Visitors of every nation, kings and princes, have scratched their names on the stucco of this apocryphal ruin, but the poet's awful name seems to have deterred them from versifying here." *Forsyth.*

☞ "The epitaph, which, though not genuine, is yet ancient, was inscribed by order of the Duke of Pescolangiano, then proprietor of the place, on a marble slab placed in the side of the rock opposite the entrance of the tomb, where it still remains." *Eustace.*

"Why dost thou still mistrust?" my Comforter
Began to say to me turned wholly round;
"Dost thou not think me with thee, and that I guide thee?
'Tis evening there already where is buried
The body within which I cast a shadow;
'Tis from Brundusium ta'en, and Naples has it."
Dante, Purgatorio, Longfellow's Trans.

Virgin. See MADONNA. Also see CORONATION OF THE VIRGIN; DEATH OF THE VIRGIN; MAR-

RIAGE OF THE VIRGIN; PRESENTATION OF THE VIRGIN, etc. See GROTTO DE LA VIERGE.

Virgin and Angel Annunciate. A picture by Gheerardt David (1484–1523), the Flemish painter. Now in the collection of the Prince of Hohenzollern at Sigmaringen.

Virgin and Child. A small altarpiece by Hans Memling (d. 1495), the Flemish painter, and considered one of his finest works. By Horace Walpole this picture was ascribed to Jan van Eyck. It is now in the possession of the Duke of Devonshire at Chiswick, England.

Virgin and Child. A picture by Albert Dürer (1471–1528), the German painter and engraver, and regarded as one of his finest works. "In the centre of the landscape is the Virgin, seated, with the Child, and crowned by two angels; on her right is a Pope with priests kneeling, on the left the Emperor Maximilian with knights . . . all being crowned with garlands of roses by the Virgin, the Child, St. Dominick, — who stands behind the Virgin, — and by angels." This picture is now in the monastery of Strahow at Prague. There is also a copy in the Museum at Lyons, France.

Virgin and Child. A votive picture by Hans Memling (d. 1495), the Flemish painter. Now in possession of Count Duchâtel, of Paris.

Virgin and Child with Mary Magdalen. A picture by Luc Jacobsz, commonly called Lucas van Leyden (1494–1533), a Flemish painter. It is a beautiful and finely-executed work. Now in the Gallery of Munich, Bavaria.

Virgin and Child with Saints. A picture by Gheerardt David (1484–1523), a Flemish painter. It is now in the Museum of Rouen, France.

Virgin and Saints. A picture by the Flemish painter, Petrus Cristus. Now in the Städel Museum at Frankfort-on-the-Main, Germany.

Virgin and Child with the little St. John. A picture by Anthony van Dyck (1599–1641). In the Munich Gallery.

Virgin, Assumption of the. See ASSUMPTION, THE.

Virgin between S. Anthony and S. Sebastian. A large altarpiece by Alessandro Bonvicino, called Il Moretto di Brescia (1514–1564). In the Städel Institute, Frankfort-on-the-Main, Germany.

Virgin in a Bower of Roses. A picture by Martin Schongauer, commonly called Martin Schön (b. 1420?), a German painter, and considered to be his most important work. It is in St. Martin's church at Colmar, Germany.

Virgin in the Meadow. A well-known picture by Raphael Sanzio (1483–1520), in which the Madonna is "represented in a beautiful landscape with both hands supporting the infant Christ, who stands before her; her head inclined toward the little St. John, who, kneeling at the side, offers a reed cross to his companion." This picture is now in the Belvedere Gallery at Vienna, Austria.

Virgin, Iron. See IRON VIRGIN.

Virgin, Joys and Sorrows of the. A beautiful picture by Hans Memling (d. 1495), the Flemish painter, described as representing "the principal events of the life of Christ and the Virgin (the seven joys of the Virgin); not in separate compartments, but as one great whole, united in a landscape with an endless number of subordinate events, — a whole world of life and joy and sorrow, all executed with wonderful grace and beauty." It was painted for Pierre Baltynck, a currier of Bruges, and was formerly in the Boisserée Collection, but is now at Munich, Bavaria.

Virgin, Life of the. A series of wood-cuts by Albert Dürer (1471–1528), the German painter and engraver, and considered to be among the best of his works which have descended to us.

Virgin nursing the Child. A picture by Roger van der Weyden (d. 1464), the Flemish painter, and one of his later works. It is now in the Städel Institute, Frankfort-on-the-Main, Germany.

Virgin of the Burgomaster Meyer. See MADONNA OF THE BURGOMASTER MEYER.

Virgin Staying the Plague at Brescia. A picture by Alessandro Bonvicino, called Il Moretto (1514–1564). In the Gallery of Dresden, Germany.

Virgin with the Goldfinch. See MADONNA DEL CARDELLINO.

Virgin with the Seven Sorrows. A picture by Joachim Patenier (d. 1545?), a Flemish painter. It is now in the Museum at Brussels, Belgium.

Virginia, The. An old line-of-battle ship in one of the ship-houses of the United States Navy Yard at Charlestown, Mass. She has been on the stocks for half a century.

Virginia Water. A beautiful artificial lake seven miles from Windsor, near London.

Virginius, The. A vessel sailing under the American flag from New York for the West Indies, on the 4th of October, 1869. On the 31st of October she was captured by a Spanish ship and taken to Havana. Being accused of hostile designs against Spain, the American commander, Capt. Fry, with 36 of his crew, and 18 others, were shot without trial. After much diplomacy, the Virginius was formally surrendered to the United States navy on the 16th of December, 1873, but, on the way to New York, sank off Cape Fear.

Virgin's Chapel and Tomb. A venerable and picturesque building in Jerusalem, believed by the faithful to be the place where the Virgin Mary was laid. Near the chapel is the spot where her *Assumption* is supposed to have occurred, together with a rock that bears the marks of the girdle she let fall to convince the incredulous Thomas.

Virgin's Tree. A name applied to an old sycamore-tree, near the village of Matareeah, Egypt, under which the Holy Family are said to have rested after the flight into Egypt.

Vision of a Knight. A small allegorical picture by Raphael Sanzio (1483–1520), representing a young knight sleeping upon his shield, with a female figure on each side. "One in a plain purple robe is offering him a book and a sword; the other, richly dressed, is presenting flowers as symbols of the pleasures of life. . . . The original pen-and-ink drawing by the master, with punctured outlines from which the picture was traced, hangs by its side." There is an engraving of it by L. Gruner. This picture was formerly in the Borghese Gallery in Rome, but is now in the National Gallery, London.

Vision of Ezekiel. A picture by Raphael Sanzio (1483–1520). It is in the Pitti Palace, Florence, Italy. A copy of this picture, which was for a time regarded as the original, and which was formerly in the Orleans Gallery, is now at Stratton, in England.

☞ "All direct imitation of nature was by the best painters carefully avoided. In this respect how fine is Raphael's 'Vision of Ezekiel'! How sublime and true in feeling and conception! where the Messiah comes floating along, upborne by the Four Creatures, . . . animals in form, but in all else unearthly, and the winged ox not less divine than the winged angel."

Mrs. Jameson.

Vision of Jacob. A celebrated picture by Rembrandt van Ryn (1606–1669). In the Dulwich Gallery.

☞ "In a print by Rembrandt, he has emulated, in picturesque and poetical treatment, his famous *Vision of Jacob* in the Dulwich Gallery."
Mrs. Jameson.

Vision of St. Bernard. A picture by Filippino Lippi (1460?-1505), and his chief work. In the Badia at Florence, Italy.

Vision of St. Bernard. A noted and admired picture by Parmigiano (1503-1540). In the National Gallery, London.

Vision of the Holy Cross. A fresco in the Sala di Costantino, in the Vatican, Rome, executed by Giulio Romano (1492?-1546), after a design by Raphael.

Visitation, The. A favorite subject of representation by the painters of the Middle Ages, exhibiting the visit of the Virgin Mary to Elisabeth, according to the account in Luke i. 39, *et seq.* Of the numerous compositions which treat of this subject, may be mentioned as among the more noted the following.

Visitation, The. A picture designed by Raphael Sanzio (1483-1520), the execution probably by Francesco Penni (1488-1528). Now in the Gallery of Madrid, Spain. It represents the visit of Mary to Elisabeth.

☞ "In the composition by Raphael [The Visitation] there are the two figures only [Mary and Elisabeth]; and I should object to this otherwise perfect picture, the bashful conscious look of the Virgin Mary."
Mrs. Jameson.

Visitation, The. A picture by Mariotto Albertinelli (1475?-1520?), the Italian painter, and regarded as his masterpiece. It is now in the Gallery of the Uffizi, Florence, Italy.

☞ "The simple, majestic composition of Albertinelli. . . . The work in its large and solemn beauty and religious significance, is worthy of being placed over an altar, on which we might offer up the work of Rembrandt [see *infra*], as men offer incense, gems, and gold."
Mrs. Jameson.

Visitation, The. A richly colored group by Sebastian del Piombo (1485-1547). This picture is now in the Louvre, Paris.

Visitation, The. A picture by Rembrandt van Ryn (1606-1669), the Dutch painter. Now in the Grosvenor Gallery.

☞ "— the small but exquisitely finished composition by Rembrandt. . . . Nothing can be more poetical than the treatment, more intensely true and noble than the expression of the diminutive figures, more masterly and finished than the execution, more magical and lustrous than the effect of the whole."
Mrs. Jameson.

Visitation, The. A picture in the Museum of Berlin, ascribed to Gerard van Meire, the Flemish painter. There is another well-preserved and interesting picture of the same name, ascribed to the same artist, in the collection of Baron Speek von Sternburg, at Lütschena, near Leipzig, Germany.

Vitale, San. See San Vitale.

Vittoria, The. One of the ships with which Fernando Magellan (1470?-1521) made his famous voyage of discovery in 1520. The Vittoria, after the death of Magellan, under the command of Sebastian del Cano returned to Spain, and was the first vessel that circumnavigated the globe.

Vittorio Emanuele. See Galleria Vittorio Emanuele.

Volks Denkmal. [The People's Monument.] A Gothic cross of iron, 160 feet in height, erected upon an eminence near Berlin, Prussia, to commemorate the deliverance of Prussia from the French, and the recovery of national independence. The monument bears an inscription, together with statues of Prussian warriors, executed by Rauch and Tieck.

Voltaire, Boulevart de. A magnificent street in Paris, one of the new boulevards, and formerly known as the Boulevart de Prince Eugène. See Boulevards.

Voltaire, Quai de. This quay, on the river Seine in Paris, derives its name from the fact that the philosopher Voltaire died in the house at the corner of the quay and the Rue de Beaume.

Volto Santo. See SANTO VOLTO.

Volumnii. See TOMB OF THE VOLUMNII.

Voyage of Life. An allegorical picture by Thomas Cole (1801–1848). In the collection of John Taylor Johnston, New York.

Vulcan's Forge. See FORGE OF VULCAN.

Vulture, The. A British sloop-of-war, in which Major André went up the Hudson, when arranging terms of surrender with Benedict Arnold.

Vyverberg. A fine square and pleasure-ground in the Hague, Holland.

W.

Wabash, The. The flag-ship of Admiral Dupont, in the attack upon the Sea Islands of South Carolina in 1861.

Wabash Avenue. A noted street in Chicago, Ill. It is lined with stately edifices, and adorned with trees.

Wachusetts, The. A noted vessel of the United States navy in the War of the Rebellion. She captured the celebrated Confederate privateer, the *Florida*, in the Brazilian port of Bahia, or San Salvador. This capture was in violation of neutrality, and produced considerable excitement. The prize was soon after brought into Hampton Roads.

Wadsworth Athenæum. A building in Hartford, Conn., containtaining a library and gallery of sculpture and paintings.

Wafers, The Miraculous. See MIRACULOUS WAFERS.

Wagner, Fort. See FORT WAGNER.

Wailing-place of the Jews. See PLACE OF WAILING.

Wakefield Tower. See REGALIA, THE.

Waldburg. An ancient castle near Ravensburg, Germany, famous for its magnificent views.

Walden Pond. A beautiful sheet of water near Concord, Mass., now a favorite pleasure-resort, and celebrated for its associations with H. D. Thoreau (1817-1862), the scholar and naturalist, who, in 1845, built on the shore of this pond a small house in which he lived two years as a hermit in studious retirement, afterwards publishing an account of this portion of his life, under the title of "Walden."

Wall, London. See LONDON WALL.

Wall of Antoninus. A wall, or rampart, erected during the Roman occupation of Britain, with the design of preventing the incursion of the northern tribes into the lowlands. It extended from the Forth to the Clyde, a distance of 27 miles, and was guarded by 10 forts. There is a stone in Glasgow College which preserves the name of the builder, Lollius Urbicus. [Often known as *Graham's Dyke*.]

☞ "The wall of Antoninus, or Graham's or Grime's Dyke, crossed from the Forth to the Clyde, on the line on which previously Agricola had erected a series of forts. It consisted of a new line of forts connected together by an immense continuous rampart of earth and turf, raised by the Proprætor Lollius Urbicus in the reign of Antoninus, and named after that emperor. Inscribed stones have been from time to time found along its course, expressive of the work done by different troops and cohorts of the Roman army." *L. Jewitt.*

If we carefully trace the distance from the *Wall of Antoninus* to Rome, and from thence to Jerusalem, it will be found that the great chain of communication from the north-west to the south-east point of the empire was drawn out to the length of four thousand and eighty Roman miles.
Gibbon.

Wall of China. See GREAT WALL OF CHINA.

Wall Street. This street in New York City, running east from Broadway, opposite Trinity Church, is the centre for bankers and brokers in New York, and is in fact the centre of the financial interests of the whole country. The Stock Exchange in Wall Street presents an exciting scene during business hours.

Free institutions, general education, and the ascendancy of dollars, are the words written on every paving-stone along Fifth Avenue, down Broadway, and up *Wall Street.* *Anthony Trollope.*

Thus a king or a general does not need a fine coat, and a commanding person may save himself all solicitude on that point. There are always slovens in State Street or *Wall Street*, who are not less considered. If a man have manners and talent, he may dress roughly and carelessly. *Emerson.*

Just where the Treasury's marble front
Looks over *Wall Street's* mingled nations;
Where Jews and Gentiles most are wont
To throng for trade and last quotations;
Where, hour by hour, the rates of gold
Outrival, in the ears of people,
The quarter-chimes, serenely tolled
From Trinity's undaunted steeple.
E. C. Stedman.

Wallace Tower. A monument 133 feet high in the town of Ayr, Scotland, erected in 1832 upon the site of an ancient tower in which, according to tradition, Sir William Wallace (1270-1305), the celebrated Scotch hero and patriot, was imprisoned, and from which, by the aid of his friends, he contrived to escape.

Wallack's. A theatre in the city of New York, devoted chiefly to the legitimate comedy.

Wallenstein. A picture erroneously supposed to be the portrait of Wallenstein, by Anthony van Dyck (1599-1641). It is in the gallery of Prince Lichtenstein at Vienna, Austria.

Wallenstein Palace. A famous palace in Prague, Bohemia, built by the great general Albert, duke of Friedland (1583-1634). The building, which was one of surprising magnificence, has undergone extensive restorations. It is said that 100 houses were pulled down to make room for its erection, and that even the stables were profusely ornamented with marble.

Walmer Castle. A sea-side fortress near Deal, England, erected by Henry VIII. It was the official residence of the Duke of Wellington until his death in 1852. The castle is supposed to stand on the very spot where Julius Cæsar landed at the time of his invasion of Britain.

Walsingham Priory. Walsingham is a little spot in Norfolk, England, much resorted to formerly by pilgrims. It was the rival of Our Lady of Loretto and St. James of Compostella. The chapel was founded in 1061, and was a perfect copy of the Santa Casa, or home of the Virgin Mary, at Nazareth. The splendid priory built soon after was granted to the Order of St. Augustine, and in 1420 a fine church was built at the side of the shrine. Erasmus says of the church: "The church is splendid and beautiful," and of the shrine: "If you look in, you will say it is the seat of the Gods, so bright and shining as it is all over with jewels, gold, and silver." It was despoiled of its treasures by Henry VIII., and there remain now only a few ruins of the priory church.

Wanderer, The. A ship engaged in the African slave-trade which came to this country in 1859, and on her voyage experienced an unexampled mortality as the consequence of her frightfully crowded condition.

Wapping. A long street in London, extending from Lower East Smithfield on the north bank of the Thames to New Crane. It is noted for its nautical signs, its ship and boat builders, rope-makers, ship-chandlers, and sail-makers. Its name Wapping was probably derived from the ship's rope called a *wapp*. Pirates and sea-rovers were hung at *Execution Dock* in Wapping.

☞ "Wapping is a neighborhood of which many persons know the name, but nothing more. . . . Wapping, too, may be remembered as having afforded a principal link in the chain of evidence against the notorious impostor who claimed the Tichborne estate. Immediately on his arrival at London, he went to Wapping (which Roger Tichborne would never have done), and there he was recognized as a former resident of the place. Wapping is a narrow strip of old London, which lies below the Tower and between London docks and the river. It is, as might be expected, wholly occupied by mariners, or those who supply their wants. It is very damp and very dingy, and everybody in it seems to smell of oakum."
Richard Grant White.

Your Molly has never been false, she declares,
Since last time we parted at *Wapping Old Stairs*,
When I swore that I still would continue the same,
And gave you the 'bacco box marked with my name. *Wapping Old Stairs.*

[The "Stairs" were steps by which people formerly descended to the river.]

But if this be a defect, what must be the entire perversion of scenical decorum, when, for instance, we see an actress that might act the *Wapping* landlady without a bolster, pining in the character of Jane Shore, and, while unwieldy with fat, endeavoring to convince the audience that she is dying with hunger? *Goldsmith.*

No longer a poor Jack Tar, frolicking in the low taverns of *Wapping*, he might roll through London in his coach, and perchance arrive, like Whittington, at the dignity of Lord Mayor. *Irving.*

The same insular limitation pinches his [the Englishman's] foreign politics. He sticks to his traditions and usages, and, so help him God! he will force his island by-laws down the throat of great countries, like India, China, Australia, and not only so, but impose *Wapping* on the Congress of Vienna, and trample down all nationalities with his taxed boots. *Emerson.*

You might be as well impressed with *Wapping* as with your first step on Egyptian soil. *Thackeray.*

You forget that the town [Gibraltar] is at all like *Wapping*, and deliver yourself up entirely to romance. *Thackeray.*

The new spirit at once showed itself in Dickens, whose broad, bright, kindly, aggressive democracy, making the hero of his story a friendless workhouse boy instead of a knight at arms, and its scene a city lane or *Wapping* instead of a stately castle or a historic land, was the representative of the changed feeling and the new day. *Harper's Magazine.*

Wardour Castle. A ruined feudal fortress near Salisbury, in Wiltshire, England.

If rich designs of sumptuous art may please,
Or nature's loftier views august and old,
Stranger! behold this spreading scene.
W. L. Bowles.

Ware, Great Bed of. See GREAT BED OF WARE.

Warren. See DEATH OF WARREN.

Warren, Fort. See FORT WARREN.

Warrior, The. An armor-plated ship of the British navy, launched Dec. 29, 1860.

And then through the familiar examples till we come to such ships as the 'Wellington' and 'Marlborough' of yesterday, and the '*Warrior*' or 'Minotaur' of to-day. *Fergusson.*

Wartburg. A famous castle near Eisenach, Germany, in which Luther was imprisoned as a friendly act of protection against his enemies.

Safe in this *Wartburg* tower I stand,
Where God hath led me by the hand,
And look down with a heart at ease,
Over the pleasant neighborhoods,
Over the vast Thuringian woods.
Longfellow.

☞ "The castle on the Wartburg is historically the most important edifice of its class in Germany, and its size and state of preservation render it remarkable in an artistic point of view. It was in one of its halls that the celebrated contest was held between the six most eminent poets of Germany in the year 1206, which, though it nearly ended fatally to one of them at least, shows how much importance was attached to the profession of literature at even that early period. Here the sainted Elizabeth of Hungary lived with her cruel brother-in-law, here she practised those virtues and endured those misfortunes that render her name so dear and so familiar to all the races of Germany; and it was in this castle that Luther found shelter, and where he resided under the name of Ritter George. . . . It resembles the older palaces at Venice more than any other buildings of the class It has been recently restored, apparently with considerable judgment; and it well deserves the pains bestowed upon it as one of the best illustrations of its style still existing in Europe." *Fergusson.*

Methinks I see him sitting, the heroic student, in his chamber in the *Warteburg*, with his midnight lamp before him, seen by the late traveller in the distant plain of Bischofsroda, as a star on the mountain! *Coleridge.*

Warwick Castle. The magnificent mansion of the Earl of Warwick, and one of the finest of the residences of the English nobility. Its architecture is greatly admired. Its two towers are called the most beautiful in the world. Its situation, on a rock washed by the Avon, is very picturesque, overlooking the river and surrounded by beautiful grounds. The ancient castle of which we first hear in the reign of Henry II. was destroyed in the reign of Henry III. The present castle was begun in the time of Edward

III. Additions and improvements have since been made at intervals. The most ancient part of the building, Cæsar's tower, is 147 feet high. Guy's tower, erected in 1394, is 128 feet high. A fire occurred at Warwick Castle in 1871, which did much damage.

☞ "The principal features are the battlements, towers, and turrets of the old feudal castle, encompassed by grounds on which has been expended all that princely art of landscape-gardening for which England is famous,—leafy thickets, magnificent trees, openings and vistas of verdure, and wide sweeps of grass, short, thick, and vividly green as the velvet moss we sometimes see growing on rocks in New England. The pains that are taken in sowing, tending, cutting, clipping, rolling, and otherwise nursing and coaxing the grass, being seconded by the misty breath and often-falling tears of the climate, produce results which must be seen to be appreciated." *Mrs. H. B. Stowe.*

Then *Warwick Castle* wide its gate displayed,
And peace and pleasure this their dwelling made. *George Crabbe.*

I look with respect at houses six, seven, eight hundred, or, like *Warwick Castle*, nine hundred years old. *Emerson.*

Warwick Vase. A celebrated and very beautiful antique vase, found at Tivoli, Italy, and capable of holding 168 gallons. It is preserved in the greenhouse connected with Warwick Castle, in England.

☞ "On a pedestal, surrounded by all manner of flowering shrubs, stands this celebrated antique. . . . They say that it holds 136 gallons; constructed, I suppose, in the roistering old drinking times of the Roman emperors, when men seem to have discovered that the grand object for which they were sent into existence was to perform the functions of wine-skins. It is beautifully sculptured with grape-leaves, and the skin and claws of the panther—these latter certainly not an inappropriate emblem of the god of wine, beautiful but dangerous." *Mrs. H. B. Stowe.*

Washington. A well-known statue of the first President of the United States, executed by Jean Antoine Houdon (1741–1828), a French sculptor. It is now at the Capitol, Richmond, Va.

Methinks I see his venerable form now before me, as presented in the glorious statue by Houdon, now in the capital of Virginia. He is dignified and grave; but his concern and anxiety seem to soften the lineaments of his countenance. *Daniel Webster.*

Washington. A portrait by Rembrandt Peale (1778–1860), considered the best ever taken of Washington, and of which there are many copies.

Washington. A statue by Horatio Greenough (1805–1852). At the Capitol, Washington.

☞ "I regard Greenough's *Washington* as one of the greatest works of sculpture of modern times." *Edward Everett.*

Washington. A statue by Thomas Crawford (1814–1857), cast in bronze at Munich.

Washington. A fine equestrian statue on Commonwealth Avenue, Boston, by Thomas Ball (b. 1819).

Washington. See APOTHEOSIS OF WASHINGTON and RESIGNATION OF WASHINGTON.

Washington Avenue. A wide and fine avenue in St. Louis, Mo. It leads directly to the great bridge over the Mississippi.

Washington crossing the Delaware. A picture by Thomas Sully (1783–1872), which is very familiar in America. Now in the Boston Museum.

Washington crossing the Delaware. A well-known picture by Emmanuel Leutze (1816–1868).

Washington Elm. A well-known tree in Cambridge, Mass., supposed to be nearly or quite 300 years old. Under this tree, July 3, 1775, Washington assumed command of the American forces.

☞ "You know the 'Washington elm,' or, if you do not, you had better rekindle your patriotism by reading the inscription, which tells you that under its shadow the great leader first drew his sword at the head of an American army." *Holmes.*

Beneath our consecrated elm
A century ago he stood,
Famed vaguely for that old fight in the wood,
Whose red surge sought, but could not overwhelm
The life foredoomed to wield our rough-hewn helm. *Lowell.*

Washington, Fort. See FORT WASHINGTON.

Washington Market. A noted market in New York, and the chief one in the city.

Washington Monument. A noted monumental structure in Washington, begun in 1848, and intended to be in the form of an obelisk 600 feet in height, and to contain the tomb of Washington. It is now in an unfinished state, being at present 174 feet high. In a building adjoining the monument is a collection of memorial stones sent by different countries and states for the decoration of the interior. It is uncertain whether this monument will ever be carried forward to completion, or whether the material used in its construction will be adapted to some other commemorative use.

Washington Monument. An imposing memorial structure in Baltimore, Md. It consists of a marble shaft upwards of 176 feet in height, rising from a base 20 feet high, and crowned by a colossal statue of Washington. There is a stairway in the interior of the shaft leading to the summit, from which is a fine and extensive view of the city and its surroundings. The monument was erected between the years 1815 and 1829.

Washington Street. The chief thoroughfare of Boston, Mass.

> If I like Broadway better than *Washington Street*, what then? I own them both, as much as anybody owns either.
> *Holmes.*

Washington's Headquarters. An old colonial mansion in Cambridge, Mass., occupied by Washington as headquarters during the siege of Boston. It is now the residence of Henry W. Longfellow, the poet.

Washington's Headquarters. An old stone mansion in Newburgh, N.Y., containing a museum of historical relics. It was occupied by Washington as his headquarters while the American army was on the Hudson. The building is now owned by the State of New York.

Washington's Tomb. On the estate of Mount Vernon, Va. The remains rest within a marble sarcophagus near the mansion-house. They were removed in 1837 from the old tomb, which is rapidly going to decay, to their present situation.

Wasp, The. An American sloop-of-war under the command of Capt. Jacob Jones, in the war of 1812. She captured the British sloop *Frolic*, for which achievement the Legislature of Delaware, the Corporation of New York City, and Congress, voted thanks and gold medals. The victory caused great exultation throughout the country.

> The foe bravely fought, but his arms were all broken,
> And he fled from his death-wound, aghast and affrighted;
> But the *Wasp* darted forward her death-going sting,
> And full on his bosom, like lightning, alighted.
> She pierced through his entrails, she maddened his brain,
> And he writhed and he groaned as if torn with the colic;
> And long shall rue the terrible day
> He met the American *Wasp* on a Frolic.
> *Old Song.*

Water Carrier of Seville. A noted picture by Diego Rodriguez de Silva y Velasquez (1599-1660), the Spanish painter. Now in Apsley House, London.

Water-Mill, The. A picture by Rembrandt van Ryn (1606-1669), the Dutch painter. In the collection of Lord Lansdowne, England.

Waterloo, Battle of. See BATTLE OF WATERLOO.

Waterloo Bridge. A magnificent stone bridge spanning the Thames at London, first opened June 18, 1817, called by Dupin a "colossal monument, worthy of Sesostris and the Cæsars," and by Canova the "noblest bridge in the world."

☞ "Canova, when he was asked during his visit to England what struck him most forcibly, is said to have replied that the trumpery Chinese Bridge, then in St. James's Park, should be the production of the Government, whilst that of Waterloo was the work of a Private Company." *Quarterly Review.*

Waterloo Place. A public square in London, and a centre of social and political life. It occupies the site of Carlton House.

Watervliet Arsenal. A great United States establishment for the manufacture of war supplies. It is situated in West Troy, N.Y.

Watier's Club. This club in London, noted as a gambling-house, was established in 1807, and dissolved in 1819. The favorite game was Macao.

☞ "The Club did not endure for twelve years altogether; the pace was too quick to last: it died a natural death in 1819, from the paralyzed state of its members; the house was then taken by a set of blacklegs, who instituted a common bank for gambling."
Thomas Raikes.

Watkins Glen. A remarkable rocky ravine in the town of Watkins, Schuyler County, in New York, one of the greatest natural curiosities in the United States.

☞ "It [Watkins Glen] suggests Vaucluse in the pellucid clearness and sparkle of the water. It faintly suggests the sombre magnificent Pass of the Finstermunz in the Tyrol, but is infinitely brighter and more varied. It suggests Trenton Falls, but is wilder and deeper." *Grace Greenwood.*

☞ "In all my travels I have never met with scenery more beautiful and romantic than that embraced in this wonderful Glen; and the most remarkable thing of all is, that so much magnificence and grandeur should be found in a region where there are no ranges of mountains." *Bayard Taylor.*

Watling Street. A street in London considered to have been the principal thoroughfare of Roman London, and one of the great Roman ways in Britain. What remains of it is narrow and inconvenient for passage. It extended across South Britain, beginning at Dover and running through Canterbury to London and from London across the island to Chester. In the time of the Britons it was a mere forest-road; but the Romans converted it into a great military highway, and it is still an important road in some parts of its extent. The name Watling Street was also very generally applied in England, during the Middle Ages, to the "Milky Way" (Via Lactea). Chaucer says: —

"Se yondir, lo, the galaxie,
The wiche men clepe the milky way,
For it is white; and some, parfay,
Y-callin it han *Watlinge-street.*"

The name is of uncertain origin, and is variously said to be derived from *Vitellius*, from *Vitellianus*, from the *Wætlings*, from the Saxon *Atheling* (noble), from *wattles* (hurdles or *fascines*), and from a number of other sources.

☞ "Who the Wætlings were, and how they came to give their name both to an earthly and a heavenly street, we do not know." *Grimm.*

Who would of *Watling-street* the dangers share,
When the broad pavement of Cheapside is near? *Gay.*

Wax Works of Madame Tussaud. See MADAME TUSSAUD'S EXHIBITION.

Wayland Smith's Cave [or Forge]. A cavern of great antiquity, on the western boundaries of Berkshire, England, near the town of Wantage. "In an early deed of the estate to which it belongs, of a date previous to the Norman Conquest, it is called Weland's Smithy; and the legend connected with it is, that a traveller wishing his horse shod had only to take him to the cave, and, leaving a piece of money on the copestone, retire to a distance. On returning he would find the horse shod, and that the money had been taken away." Three flat stones supporting a fourth are still pointed out as his smithy. In the Anglo-Saxon mythology Weland was the representative of Vulcan. Walter Scott has introduced this legend of Wayland Smith into one of his most interesting novels, "Kenilworth," making him a living person of the time of Elizabeth.

Wayland Wood. A tract of woodland near Watton, England, where, according to tradition, the murder of the two children by order of their uncle occurred on which is founded the famous ballad of the "Children in the Wood."

Wayside Inn. An old tavern still standing in the town of Sudbury, Mass., a "busy place" in the old colonial days of New England, and made famous by the poems of Longfellow entitled "The Wayside Inn."

As ancient is this hostelry
As any in the land may be,
Built in the old Colonial day,
When men lived in a grander way,
With ampler hospitality.

Weber Cañon. A stupendous ravine, forming a natural gateway through the Wahsatch range of mountains in Utah Territory. It is one of the most remarkable sights in the West. The trains of the Union Pacific Railroad pass through this gorge.

Webster. See DEATH OF WEBSTER.

Webster, Daniel. A statue of the great American statesman by Hiram Powers (b. 1805).

☞ "It is the second cast of the statue, the first having been shipped some months ago on board of a vessel which was lost; and, as Powers observed, the statue now lies at the bottom of the Atlantic Ocean, somewhere in the vicinity of the telegraphic cable. . . . Happy is Webster to have been so truly and adequately sculptured; happy the sculptor in such a subject, which no idealization of a demigod could have supplied him with. Perhaps the statue at the bottom of the sea will be cast up in some future age, when the present race of man is forgotten, and, if so, that far posterity will look up to us as a grander race than we find ourselves to be." *Hawthorne.*

Webster's Reply to Hayne. A well-known picture by G. P. A. Healy (b. 1808). In Faneuil Hall, Boston. This picture contains 130 portraits.

Wedding. See PEASANT WEDDING.

Wednesday Club. An old London club.

☞ "In Friday-street, Cheapside, was held the Wednesday Club, at which, in 1695, certain conferences took place under the direction of William Paterson, which ultimately led to the establishment of the Bank of England. Such is the general belief; but Mr. Saxe Bannister, in his *Life of Paterson*, p. 93, observes: 'It has been a matter of much doubt whether the Bank of England was originally proposed from a Club or Society in the City of London.'" *Timbs.*

Weehawken, The. A war-vessel of Admiral Dupont's flotilla in the attack upon the defences of Charleston, S. C., in the war of the Rebellion (1861–1865).

Weibertreue. [Woman's Fidelity.] The popular name of a ruined castle at Weinsberg, near Heilbronn, Germany, celebrated for a romantic legend connected with it, which relates how, when the garrison were threatened with death on the taking of the castle, the women, who had been allowed to depart with their valuables, carried off their husbands on their backs, each in a sack. The German poet Bürger has made this incident the subject of a well-known ballad, which has been translated by C. T. Brooks. See also the "Spectator," No. 449.

Welbeck Abbey. The seat of the Duke of Portland, near Worksop, England.

Wellesley College. A well-endowed institution of learning for young women, in Wellesley, Mass. It has an elegant building finely situated.

Wellington. A fine equestrian statue of the duke by Sir Francis Chantrey (1782–1841). In front of the Royal Exchange, London.

Wellington's Funeral Car. This car, constructed from the guns taken in the battles in which he was engaged, is preserved as a monumental trophy in St. Paul's Church, London.

Wells, The. [Ital. *I Pozzi.*] A series of prison-cells, one beneath the other, in the ancient state prison of Venice, Italy, adjoining the Ducal Palace, with which it is connected by the "Bridge of Sighs."

☞ "I descended from the cheerful day into two ranges, one below the other, of dismal, awful, horrible, stone cells. They were quite dark. Each had a loop-hole in its massive wall, where, in the old time, a torch was placed, to light the prisoners within for half an hour. The captives, by the glimmering of these brief rays, had cut and scratched inscriptions in the blackened vaults. I saw them. For their labor with the rusty nail's point had outlived their agony and them through many generations." *Dickens.*

☞ "What fables concerning these cells have not been uttered and believed! . . . I do not say that they are calculated to enamour the unimpounded spectator with prison life, but they are certainly far from being as bad as I hoped. They are not joyously light nor particularly airy; but their occupants could have suffered no extreme physical discomfort, and the thick wooden casing of the interior walls evidences at least the intention of the state to inflict no wanton hardship of cold or damp." *W. D. Howells.*

The *Pozzi* and the Piombi were in vain;
They might wring blood from me, but treachery never. *Byron.*

Wells of Moses. See FOUNTAINS OF MOSES.

Wentworth House. A noted mansion, and one of the largest private residences in Europe, formerly the abode of the famous Earl of Strafford, near Wakefield, England.

Wentworth Mansion. An old colonial house near Portsmouth, N. H., once occupied by Gov. Wentworth, and containing the old provincial council-chamber and many historical relics.

Werrington House. A seat of the Duke of Northumberland, on the river Tamar, near Launceston, England.

Wesleyan University. An institution of learning under the care of the Methodist Church, at Middletown, Conn.

West, Benjamin. See BENJAMIN WEST.

West India Docks. Extensive docks, covering 295 acres, on the left bank of the Thames, London, opened in 1802. William Pitt laid the first stone in 1800. See EAST INDIA DOCKS.

West Point. See UNITED STATES MILITARY ACADEMY.

West Rock. A rocky hill near New Haven, Conn., much resorted to, and affording a fine view.

Western Emigration. An historical picture by Emanuel Leutze (1816-1868). In the Capitol at Washington.

Westminster Abbey. The renowned Abbey-church of London. Its earliest foundation is enveloped in obscurity. Edward the Confessor built an abbey on this site, which was dedicated on the festival of the Holy Innocents, Dec. 28, 1065. In 1862 it was discovered that the lower half of the south cloister wall consists of masonry of the age of Edward the Confessor. The Abbey, as it now exists, was for the most part rebuilt by Henry III. (1245-1272), out of regard to the memory of the Confessor. Its general plan is cruciform. Besides the nave, choir, and transepts, it contains 12 chapels, of which 10 are nearly filled with monumental tombs. No less than 17 English kings, from the Confessor to George II., and 10 queens, lie within the Abbey, amid statesmen, poets, divines, scholars, and artists. Dean Stanley says: "The Abbey of Westminster owes its traditions and its present name, revered in the bosoms of the people of England, to the fact that the early English kings were interred within its walls, and that through its associations the Norman rulers learnt to forget their foreign paternity, and to unite in fellowship and affection with their Saxon fellow-citizens. There is no other church in the world, except, perhaps, the Kremlin at Moscow, with which Royalty is so intimately associated."

☞ "The eye gazes with wonder at clustered columns of gigantic dimensions, with arches springing from them to such an amazing height. It seems as if the awful nature of the place presses down upon the soul, and hushes the beholder into noiseless reverence. We feel that we are surrounded by the congregated bones of the great men of past times, who have filled history with their deeds, and earth with their renown." *Irving.*

☞ "When I am in a serious humor, I very often walk by myself in Westminster Abbey; where the gloominess of the place, and the use to which it is applied, with the solemnity of the building, and the condition of the people who lie in it, are apt to fill the mind with a kind of melancholy, or rather thoughtfulness, that is not disagreeable." *Addison.*

☞ "The moment I entered Westminster Abbey I felt a kind of awe pervade my mind which I cannot describe: the very silence seemed sacred." *Burke.*

☞ "The superb nave, the admirable Gothic architecture, of Westminster Abbey, are alone adapted to the climate: this labyrinth of forms, these sweeping and huge mouldings, this profusion of delicate sculptures, are required to fill the dim air and people the void of such sombre interiors." *Taine, Trans.*

Here, where the end of earthly things
Lays heroes, patriots, bards, and kings,
. . . .
Here, where the fretted aisles prolong
The distant notes of holy song,
. . . .
If ever from an English heart,
Oh, here let prejudice depart! *Scott.*

Be mine, in hours of fear
Or grovelling thought, to seek a refuge here,
And through the aisles of *Westminster* to roam,
Where bubbles burst, and folly's dancing foam
Melts, if it crosses the threshold. *Wordsworth.*

Westminster Bridge. An elegant bridge across the Thames at London, built 1856-62, in place of a stone bridge (the second upon the spot) built in 1739-50. Wordsworth has a sonnet on the view from Westminster Bridge, beginning: —

"Earth hath not any thing to show more fair."

As I was going o'er *Westminster Bridge,*
I met with a Westminster scholar;
He pulled off his cap, *an' drew* off his glove,
And wished me a very good morrow.
What is his name? *Mother Goose.*

Westminster Hall. An ancient hall originally added to the Palace at Westminster, London, by William Rufus, who held his first court here, 1099. It has long been used for the sittings of the Royal Courts and of the Parliaments, for Coronation-feasts, and other similar purposes; and the name Westminster Hall is not unfrequently used for the law itself. It is called the *Great Hall* to distinguish it from the *Lesser* Hall, the House of Commons after the fire of 1834. It is one of the noblest and most venerable architectural relics in Europe, and the largest room unsupported by pillars in the world. Westminster Hall was the place of trial of the Earl of Strafford, of Charles I., and of Warren Hastings.

☞ "One of these halls, Westminster Hall, which serves for great state trials, is immense and of the greatest beauty. . . . The effect of the whole is rich and grave." *Taine, Trans.*

Those who have attended to the practice of our literary tribunal are well aware that, by means of certain legal fictions similar to those of *Westminster Hall*, we are frequently enabled to take cognizance of cases lying beyond the sphere of our original jurisdiction. *Macaulay.*

Thus he [Cromwell] subdued a spirit that had been often troublesome to the most sovereign power, and made *Westminster Hall* as obedient and subservient to his commands as any of the rest of his quarters. *Edward Hyde.*

The clothed, embodied Justice that sits in *Westminster Hall*, with penalties, parchments, tipstaves, is very visible. But the *un*embodied Justice, whereof that other is either an emblem, or else is a fearful indescribability, is not so visible. *Carlyle.*

Especially what member of the legal profession, unless his heart be as dry as parchment and worn as the steps of a court-house, can fail to do honor to the genius of a place [the Roman Forum] where jurisprudence was reared into a perfect system, while Druids were yet cutting mistletoe on the site of *Westminster Hall?* *Hillard*

The fight in the street, which is backed for gold. —
The plea of the lawyers in *Westminster Hall.* *Mrs. Browning.*

Westminster Palace. The English Houses of Parliament in London, occupying the site of the Royal Palace of the monarchs of England from Edward the Confessor to Queen Elizabeth. The first stone of the New Palace was laid April 27, 1840. It is the largest public edifice in England, probably the largest Gothic edifice in the world, and is considered in respect to the arrangement of its apartments for the transaction of business, lighting, ventilation, etc., to be the most perfect building in Europe. It covers about eight acres, and has four principal fronts, the eastern or river front being 940 feet in length. The architect was Sir Charles Barry. The Royal or Victoria Tower at the south-west angle, containing the royal entrance, rises to the height of about 340 feet, and is one of the most stupendous works of the kind in the world.

☞ "Though the Palace of Westminster may not have realized the highest qualities of the architecture which it is popularly supposed to represent, it has at least proved an excellent school for the encouragement of ancient art. It has educated many a sculptor, stone-mason, metal-worker, decorator, and cabinetmaker, who would otherwise have grown up ignorant of every phase of ornament save that which had reached him by a perverted tradition. Barry, to whose talent are due the merits of the general design, wisely intrusted to Pugin the design of those details which were to enrich his structure." *Eastlake.*

☞ "We proceed to the Houses of Parliament; as a whole, the architecture constantly repeats a rather poor idea, and does not show great invention. . . . It is Gothic, accommodated to the climate. The palace magnificently mirrors itself in the shining river. In default of genius, the architects have had good sense."

Taine, Trans.

Westminster School, *or* **St. Peter's College.** A public school, in London, for "Grammar, Rethoricke, Poetrie, and for the Latin and Greek languages," founded by Henry VIII., and re-established in 1560 by Queen Elizabeth. Among the names of eminent men who were scholars here are Ben Jonson, George Chapman, Jaspar Mayne, Giles Fletcher, William Cartwright, Cowley, Nathaniel Lee, Dryden, Prior, Rowe, Churchill, Dyer, Cowper, Southey, Sir Harry Vane the younger, Hakluyt, Sir Christopher Wren, Locke, South, Warren Hastings, Atterbury, Gibbon, the elder Colman, Cumberland, Lord John Russell.

Westphalica, Porta. See PORTA WESTPHALICA.

Weyer's Cave. A natural curiosity in Augusta County, Va., regarded as one of the greatest wonders of its class in the United States. The cave is more than 1,600 feet in length, and contains many calcareous formations of great variety and beauty. It was discovered in 1804.

What Cheer Rock. A rock in a cove near Providence, R.I. The tradition is that Roger Williams, the founder of the Rhode Island colony, on his banishment from Massachusetts landed on this rock, where he was hailed by the Indians with the words, "What cheer, Netop? (friend.)"

Wheatland. The estate and residence for many years of James Buchanan, the 15th President of the United States. It is situated about a mile from the city of Lancaster, Penn.

Wheel of Fortune. A water-color painting by Hans Holbein the Younger (1498-1543), the German painter. It is now at Chatsworth, England.

Whirlpool Rapids. At Niagara Falls, N.Y. Here the waters from the Great Lakes rush with terrible fury through a narrow gorge. The velocity and volume of these rapids is so great that the stream is thirty or forty feet higher in the centre than at the sides. See MAID OF THE MIST.

Whispering Gallery. A gallery in St. Paul's Cathedral, London, so called because the slightest whisper is transmitted with great rapidity and distinctness from one side of the gallery to the other. Another instance of a "Whispering Gallery" in a church is found in the Whitefield Church of Newburyport, Mass.

> Nor had Fancy fed
> With less delight upon that other class
> Of marvels, broad-day wonders permanent:
> The river proudly bridged; the dizzy top
> And *Whispering Gallery* of St. Paul's.
> *Wordsworth.*

White Conduit House. A public-house on the extreme verge of London. It derived its name from the conduit near by, which was built for the use of the Charter-house. It had, both in and around it, ample accommodations for tea-drinking, and was a very popular place of resort in the early part of this century. It was celebrated for its White Conduit rolls.

> All public dinners in London, from the Lord Mayor's annual banquet at Guildhall, to the Chimney-sweepers' anniversary at *White Conduit House;* from the Goldsmiths' to the Butchers', from the Sheriffs' to the Licensed Victuallers'—are amusing scenes. *Dickens.*

White Convent. A monastery of Coptic Christians in Upper Egypt, standing upon the edge of the desert, supposed to be of the time of the Empress Helena, but probably of a later date.

White Hart. 1. An ancient tavern situated in Southwark, London, near London Bridge. It was the headquarters of Jack Cade and his rebel forces in 1450. It was partly demolished and partly burnt. Dickens in the "Pickwick Papers" has described the modern building of this name.

> Hath my sword therefore broke through London gates, that you should leave me at the *White Hart*, in Southwark?
> *Shakespeare.*

☞ "A great, rambling, queer old place, with galleries and passages and staircases, wide enough and antiquated enough to furnish materials for a hundred ghost-stories." *Dickens.*

2. An old London tavern, Bishopsgate Without. It was standing in the first part of the present century.

White Horse of Berkshire. Between Abingdon and Uffington, in the county of Berks, England, is a vale called the "Vale of the White Horse." It takes its name from a colossal figure of a galloping horse rudely fashioned on the side of a steep chalk hill (893 feet high) by removing the overlying turf. The figure is about 374 feet in length, and can be seen 10 or 12 miles in a fair day, when the sun is shining upon it. At what period or by whom it was cut, is not known. It has been variously ascribed to the Saxons, to the Danes, and to the Druids. Local tradition attributes it to King Alfred, and regards it as a monument of the victory won by him over the Danes in the great battle of Ashdown, in 871. He is said to have carved a horse, rather than any other object, because that was the device borne on the Saxon standard. The earliest historical notice of the White Horse is contained in a cartulary, or register of the Abbey of Abingdon, written in the year 1171, and preserved in the British Museum. As, in the course of time, the trench which forms the figure of the horse would naturally get filled up and grown over, the people living in the neighborhood have a custom of meeting for the purpose of "scouring" or cleaning it; and they make this the occasion of a "pastime," or festival, at which manly games and sports, with prizes, are exhibited. Thomas Hughes has written a work called "The Scouring of the White Horse," which gives, in story form, an interesting account of a great pastime held on the 18th of September, 1857, and embodies all the scattered legends and traditions of the vicinity, and all the authentic historical notices relating to the old monument.

White House. The executive or presidential mansion at Washington. It is a large freestone building, painted white, from which latter circumstance it derives its name. It is said to have been modelled after the palace of the Duke of Leinster. The executive mansion was first occupied by President Adams in 1800, was destroyed by the British in 1814, and rebuilt a few years later.

The President's house — or the *White House*, as it is now called all the world over — is a handsome mansion fitted for the chief officer of a great republic.
Anthony Trollope.

Ef you git *me* inside the *White House*,
Your head with ile I'll kin' o' 'nint
By gittin' *you* inside the Light-house
Down to the eend o' Jaalam Pint.
Lowell, Biglow Papers.

At a moment when the *White House* itself is in danger of conflagration, instead of all hands uniting to extinguish the flames, we are contending about who shall be its next occupant. When a dreadful crevasse has occurred, which threatens inundation and destruction to all around it, we are contesting and disputing about the profits of an estate which is threatened with total submersion. *H. Clay.*

Before the *White House* portals
The careless eyes behold
Three iron bombs uplifted,
Adusk in summer gold.
J. J. Piatt.

White House. See CASA BLANCA.

White Tower. See TOWER, THE.

Whitechapel. A wide and spacious street in London.

In spirituals and temporals, in field and workshop, from Manchester to Dorsetshire, from Lambeth Palace to the Lanes of *Whitechapel*, wherever men meet and toil and traffic together, — Anarchy, Anarchy. *Carlyle.*

Two sticks and an apple,
Say the bells at *Whitechapel.*
Mother Goose.

Whitefield Church. A name by which the Old South (Presbyterian) church in Newburyport, Mass., is sometimes known. The remains of George Whitefield (1714–1770), the founder of Calvinistic Methodism, rest in a vault under the pulpit of this church. In this church is a noted whispering-gallery, said to be equalled only by that at St. Paul's, London.

Long shall the traveller strain his eye
From the railroad-car, as it plunges by,
And the vanishing town behind him search
For the slender spire of the *Whitefield Church.* *Whittier.*

"Yonder spire
Over gray roofs, a shaft of fire;
What is it, pray?" — "The *Whitefield Church!*
Walled about by its basement stones,
There rest the marvellous prophet's bones." *Whittier.*

Whitefriars. A district in London, which long possessed the privileges of sanctuary, and hence became the asylum of debtors, cheats, and gamblers, who were here protected from arrest. From this circumstance it derived the cant name of *Alsatia*, perhaps from the Landgraviate of Alsace, which stood in much the same relation to France as Whitefriars did to the *Temple*. In the Temple students were studying to observe the law, and in *Alsatia*, adjoining, debtors to avoid and violate it. Alsatia, or Whitefriars, has been immortalized by Sir Walter Scott in "The Fortunes of Nigel;" and here is laid the scene of Shadwell's comedy of "The Squire of Alsatia."

☞ "Though the immunities legally belonging to the place extended only to cases of debt, cheats, false witnesses, forgers, and highwaymen found refuge there. For amidst a rabble so desperate no peace-officer's life was in safety. At the cry of 'Rescue!' bullies with swords and cudgels, and termagant hags with spits and broomsticks, poured forth by hundreds; and the intruder was fortunate if he escaped back into Fleet Street, hustled, stripped, and pumped upon." *Macaulay.*

☞ "It is not unlikely that the Landgraviate of Alsace [Ger. *Elsass*, Lat. *Alsatia*] — now the frontier province of France [at present (1881) a part of the German empire], long a cause of contention, often the seat of war, and familiarly known to many British soldiers — suggested the application of the name *Alsatia* to the precinct of Whitefriars." *Cunningham.*

We shall not charge upon a whole party the profligacy and baseness of the horseboys, gamblers, and bravos, whom the hope of license and plunder attracted from all the dens of *Whitefriars* to the standard of Charles, and who disgraced their associates by excesses which under the stricter discipline of the Parliamentary armies were never tolerated.
Macaulay.

Whitehall. A district of Westminster, London, and the site of the Royal Palace of Whitehall from 1530 to 1697. It was formerly called York Place from having been the town residence of the Archbishops of York. Cardinal Wolsey lived here for a long time upon his fall from office in 1529. York Place was taken from him by Henry VIII., and the name of the palace changed to Whitehall, perhaps from some new buildings constructed of white stone. The present banqueting-house, which is about all that is left of the palace, was built by Inigo Jones between 1619 and 1622, and is considered one of the finest buildings in London. James I. had previously rebuilt the old banqueting-house, but his structure was burnt in 1619.

☞ "Little did James think that he was raising a pile from which his son [Charles I.] was to step from the throne to a scaffold." *Pennant.*

☞ "Poetry, painting, music, and architecture were all called in to make them rational amusements: and I have no doubt that the celebrated festivals of Louis the Fourteenth were copied from the shows exhibited at Whitehall, in its time the most polite court in Europe. Ben Jonson was the laureate, Inigo Jones the inventor of the decorations; Laniere and Ferabosco composed the symphonies; the king, the queen, and the young nobility danced in the interludes." *Walpole.*

☞ "Whitehall, when he [Charles the Second] dwelt there, was the focus of political intrigue and of fashionable gayety. Half the jobbing and half the flirting of the metropolis went on under his roof." *Macaulay.*

You must no more call it York-place,
that is past;
For since the Cardinal fell, that title's
lost:
'Tis now the king's, and call'd *Whitehall.*
Shakespeare.

The king, with wonder and surprise,
Will swear the seas grow bold;
Because the tides still higher rise
Than e'er they did of old,
But let them know it is our tears
Bring floods of grief to *Whitehall* stairs.
Lord Dorset.

I see, I see, where two fair cities bend
Their ample bow, a new *Whitehall* ascend!
Pope.

The furious German comes, with his clarions and his drums,
His bravoes of Alsatia, and pages of *Whitehall.* *Macaulay.*

All the town was in an uproar of admiration of his poem, the "Campaign," which Dick Steele was spouting at every coffee-house in *Whitehall* and Covent Garden. *Thackeray.*

White's Chocolate House. See WHITE'S.

White's. A famous club in St. James's Street, London, first established in 1698 as "White's Chocolate House." White's has from the first been noted as a gaming-house.

☞ "I have heard that the late Earl of Oxford, in the time of his ministry, never passed by White's Chocolate-house (the common rendezvous of infamous sharpers and noble cullies) without bestowing a curse upon that famous Academy, as the bane of half the English nobility." *Swift.*

☞ "The Club, which is at this time limited to 500 members, was formerly composed of the high Tory party, but, though Conservative principles may probably prevail, it has now ceased to be a political club, and may rather be termed 'aristocratic.' Several of the present members have belonged to the Club upwards of half a century, and the ancestors of most of the noblemen and men of fashion of the present day who belong to the Club were formerly members of it. The Club has given magnificent entertainments in our time. On June 20, 1814, they gave a ball at Burlington House to the Emperor of Russia, the King of Prussia, and the allied sovereigns then in England: the cost was £9,849, 2*s.* 6*d.* Three weeks after this, the Club gave to the Duke of Wellington a dinner, which cost £2,480, 10*s.* 9*d.*" *Timbs.*

Gambling he [Harley] held in aversion; and it was said that he never passed *White's*, then the favorite haunt of noble sharpers and dupes, without an exclamation of anger. *Macaulay.*

Aimwell. Pray, sir, han't I seen your face at Will's coffee-house?
Gibbet. Yes, sir, and at *White's* too.
Farquhar, Beaux' Stratagem.

While softer chairs the tawdry load convey
To court, to *White's*, assemblies, or the play,
Rosy-complexioned Health thy steps attends,
And exercise thy lasting youth defends.
Gay.

His grace will game: to *White's* a bull be led,
With spurning heels and with a butting head:
To *White's* be carried, as to ancient games,
Fair coursers, vases, and alluring dames.
Pope.

Or chair'd at *White's*, amidst the doctors sit,
Teach oaths to gamesters, and to nobles wit. *Pope.*

Whittington Club. A London club—now in existence—established in 1846 at the Crown and Anchor Tavern. Douglas Jerrold, the originator of the club, was its first president.

Wie die Alten sungen, so pfeifen auch die Jungen. A noted picture, illustrating this proverb, by Jan Steen (1636-1689). Now at the Hague, Holland.

Wigmore Castle. An ancient and famous fortress, now in ruins, adjoining the town of the same name in Herefordshire, England.

Wild-boar Hunt. A picture by Jan Fyt (1625-1671), the Flemish painter, and one of his principal works. In Ravensworth Castle, England.

Wild Deer of Chillingham. A picture by Sir Edwin Landseer (1803–1873), the most celebrated modern painter of animals.

Wilderness, The. A wild and gloomy tract near the Rapidan River, about 15 miles from Fredericksburg, Va., the scene of a great battle between Gen. Grant and Gen. Lee, May 5 and 6, 1864.

Wilhelm Strasse. [William Street.] A noted street in Berlin, Prussia.

Wilhelma Palace. A celebrated show-palace at Cannstadt, on the Neckar, in Germany, built in 1851.

Wilhelms Platz. [William's Square.] A well-known public square in Berlin, Prussia.

Wilhelmshöhe. A famous palace and summer residence in the neighborhood of Cassel, Germany. It has been called the German Versailles. The Emperor Napoleon III. lived here for a time as a prisoner-of-war after his defeat in the battle of Sedan, Sept. 1, 1870. See GIANT'S CASTLE.

It is incalculable how much that royal big-wig cost Germany. Every prince imitated the French king, and had his Versailles, his *Wilhelmshöhe*, his court and its splendors, his fountains and water-works and Tritons. *Thackeray.*

Willey House. A famous dwelling-house at the base of Willey Mountain in the Notch of the White Mountains, New Hampshire. In former years terrible slides of soil and rock at times came thundering down the sides of the mountain. On the night of Aug. 28, 1826, during a violent storm, one of these avalanches occurred; and the whole Willey family, who then lived in the house, were killed. The story is, that Mr. Willey, fearing a slide from the mountain, had built farther down the valley what he considered a safe shelter to which they could flee on hearing the approach of an avalanche. The whole family and two hired men, warned by the crash of the expected slide, rushed out of doors towards the supposed shelter, but were overtaken and overwhelmed by the torrent of rocks, while the house which they had just abandoned remained uninjured, as would its inmates, had they staid within it. See NOTCH, THE.

William and Mary College. A collegiate establishment in Williamsburg, Va. It was founded in 1692, and is the oldest institution of the kind in the country, next to Harvard College.

William, Fort. See FORT WILLIAM and FORT WILLIAM HENRY.

Williams College. An institution of learning at Williamstown, Mass. It was founded in 1793. The cluster of buildings comprised in the college is beautifully situated.

Willis's Rooms. See ALMACK'S.

Williston Seminary. A well-endowed educational establishment in Easthampton, Mass.

Will's. This noted coffee-house and famous resort was in Russell Street, London. In the time of Dryden, who here presided over those celebrated as the wits and poets of the period, it was called the Wits' Coffee-house, and was much frequented. After Dryden's death the wits resorted to Button's. See BUTTON'S.

☞ "It was Dryden who made Will's Coffee-house the great resort of the wits of his time."
Pope, Spence's Anecdotes.

☞ "That celebrated house, situated between Covent Garden and Bow Street, was sacred to polite letters. There the talk was about poetical justice and the unities of place and time. . . . Under no roof was a greater variety of figures to be seen, — earls in stars and garters, clergymen in cassocks and bands, pert templars, sheepish lads from the universities, translators and index-makers in ragged coats of frieze. The great press was to get near the chair where John Dryden sate." *Macaulay.*

And, upon my going into *Will's*, I found their discourse was gone off, from the death of the French King, to that of Monsieur Boileau, Racine, Corneille, and several other poets, whom they regretted on this occasion as persons who would have obliged the world with very noble elegies on the death of so great a prince, and so eminent a patron of learning.
Addison, Spectator.

The loose atheistical wits at *Will's* might write such stuff to divert the painted Jezebels of the court: but did it become a minister of the gospel to copy the evil fashions of the world? *Macaulay.*

His fame travelled to London: he [Charles Montague] was thought a clever lad by the wits who met at *Will's;* and the lively parody which he wrote, in concert with his friend and fellow-student Prior, on Dryden's Hind and Panther, was received with great applause. *Macaulay.*

Be sure at *Will's* the following day
Lie snug, and hear what critics say.
Swift.

☞ There was another *Will's* at the corner of Serle and Portugal Streets, London.

Wilton House. A famous mansion, the seat of the Earls of Pembroke, and in which Sir Philip Sidney wrote his "Arcadia." It adjoins the town of Wilton, in England.

☞ "At Wilton House, the 'Arcadia' was written, amidst conversations with Fulke Greville, Lord Brooke, a man of no vulgar mind, as his own poems declare him." *Emerson.*

From Pembroke's princely dome, where mimic art
Decks with a magic hand the dazzling bowers,
Its living hues where the warm pencil pours,
And breathing forms from the rude marble start,
How to life's humbler scene can I depart?
My breast all glowing from those gorgeous towers,
In my low cell, how cheat the sullen hours? *Thomas Warton.*

Winchester Cathedral. A noted church in Winchester, England, of great size and magnificence. The nave, 250 feet in length, is regarded as one of the finest in England. William Rufus was buried in this church, and also Izaak Walton. It contains also a celebrated painting by West of the "Raising of Lazarus."

Winds, Cave of the. See CAVE OF THE WINDS.

Windsor Castle. A royal residence, and the principal seat of the British sovereigns, in the town of Windsor, near London. It surpasses in antiquity and in beauty of situation all the other palaces of Europe. The date of the old castle is uncertain. It undoubtedly belongs to a period much earlier than the Conquest. The history of the present castle, which was founded by William the Conqueror, begins with Edward III., by whom it was almost rebuilt. The castle stands upon a promontory overlooking the valley of the Thames. Edward IV. re-erected St. George's Chapel nearly as it now stands, one of the finest ecclesiastical buildings in the country. Henry VII. also erected a fine though small chapel, which is still standing. Queen Elizabeth caused the terrace to be made which is one of the grand characteristics of the place, and regarded as the noblest walk of its kind in Europe. Charles II. added what is known as the Star-building, which contains the rooms shown to the public. The state apartments contain valuable pictures, ancient decorative furniture, Gobelin tapestries, plate, and other articles of value.

☞ "It is a place full of storied and poetical associations. . . . I have visited Vaucluse with as much enthusiasm as a pilgrim would visit the shrine at Loretto; but I have never felt more poetical devotion than when contemplating the old Tower and the little garden at Windsor, and musing over the romantic loves of the Lady Jane and the Royal Poet of Scotland." *Irving*.

As I have fancied I could read the French character in the national palace of the Tuileries, so I have pictured to myself some of the traits of John Bull in his royal abode of *Windsor Castle*. *Irving*.

Although the palace has not attained any thing like its full growth, yet what exists is quite big enough for the monarch of such a little country; and Versailles or *Windsor* has not apartments more nobly proportioned. *Thackeray*.

Search *Windsor Castle*, elves, within, without,
Strew good luck, ouphes, on every sacred room,
That it may stand till the perpetual doom
In state as wholesome as in state 'tis fit,
Worthy the owner and the owner it.
Shakespeare.

Home of my heart! to me more fair
Than gay Versailles or *Windsor's* halls,
The painted, shingly town-house where
The freeman's vote for Freedom falls!
Whittier.

Windsor Forest. A tract of woodland said to be 56 miles in circumference, adjoining the town of Windsor, England, and having many historical and legendary associations. See HERNE'S OAK.

Thy forest, Windsor! and thy green retreats,
At once the Monarch's and the Muses' seats,
Invite my lays. *Pope*.

Long shalt thou flourish, Windsor! bodying forth
Chivalric times, and long shall live around
Thy Castle the old oaks of British birth,
Whose gnarled roots, tenacious and profound,
As with a lion's talons grasp the ground.
Campbell.

Outstretched beneath the leafy shade
Of *Windsor Forest's* deepest glade,
A dying woman lay:
Three little children round her stood,
And there went up from the greenwood
A woful wail that day.
Caroline Bowles Southey.

Windsor Knights. The name given to a body of superannuated military officers who are provided with accommodations in Windsor Castle, and who receive a daily allowance. The establishment was founded by Edward the Third.

Wingfield Manor-house. A fine mansion in Derbyshire, England. It was built by Ralph, Lord Cromwell, Treasurer of England in the time of Henry VI. Mary, Queen of Scots, was imprisoned here, under the care of the Earl of Shrewsbury.

Winifred's Well. See ST. WINIFRED'S WELL.

Winter Palace. A gigantic pile of buildings in St. Petersburg, Russia, used by the emperor as his residence when at home in his capital. It is one of the largest and most splendid royal edifices in the world, the interior especially being very gorgeous. The present building was erected upon the site of another bearing the same name, which was destroyed by fire in 1837. It is said that 6,000 persons occupy this palace during the period of the emperor's residence in it. It contains a regalia-room and a picture-gallery. Of the *old* Winter Palace, Kohl says: "The suites of apartments were perfect labyrinths, and even the chief of the imperial household, who had filled that post for 12 years, was not perfectly acquainted with all the nooks and corners of the building." The new palace, though not so intricate, is of equal size.

☞ "To me the most delightful part of the Winter Palace was the garden. It forms one of the suite of thirty halls, some of them three hundred feet long, on the second story. In this garden . . . rise clumps of Italian cypress and laurel from beds of emerald turf and blooming hyacinths. Lamps of fretted glass hang among the foliage, and diffuse a mellow golden moonlight over the enchanted ground." *Bayard Taylor*.

Winthrop, Fort. See FORT WINTHROP.

Wisdom Victorious over the Vices. An allegorical picture by Andrea Mantegna (1430-1506), the Italian painter. Now in the Louvre, Paris.

Witch Hill. A hill in Salem, Mass., bearing this name because of the executions of the so-called witches which took place upon it during the witchcraft delusion in 1692. [More commonly called *Gallows Hill*.]

☞ "Whether Witch Hill be the first or last place visited, it is there

Salem witchcraft culminates. There is seen, approaching by the railway, a bleak and rocky eminence bestrewn with a little soil. On the summit is a tolerably level area of several acres. Not a tree was growing on it when I was there. The bleak winds sweep over it without hinderance. . . . John Adams mentions a visit to this hill in 1766, then called Witchcraft Hill. In 1793, Dr. Morse notes that the graves might still be traced." *Drake.*

Over this seems to lie a certain tenderness for humanity in general, bred out of life-long trial, I should say, but sharply streaked with fiery lines of wrath, at various individual acts of wrong, especially if they come in an ecclesiastical shape, and recall to him the days when his mother's great-grandmother was strangled on *Witch Hill*, with a text from the Old Tesment for her halter. *Holmes.*

Witch House. An ancient house in Salem, Mass., one of the oldest, if not the very oldest building, now standing in this part of the country. It is said to have been built in 1631. Here were tried persons suspected of witchcraft during the terrible delusion which spread over New England. A modern addition has been made to the building.

☞ "In appearance the original house might have been transplanted out of old London. Its peaked gables, with pine-apples carved in wood surmounting, its latticed windows and colossal chimney, put it unmistakably in the age of ruffs, Spanish cloaks, and long rapiers. It has long been divested of its antique English character, now appearing no more than a reminiscence of its former self." *Drake.*

Witch of Endor. A picture by Washington Allston (1779–1843).

Wittinagemot Club. The name Wittinagemot was applied to a corner box of the coffee-room of the Chapter Coffee-house in Paternoster Row, London, noted, in the eighteenth century, as a favorite resort of publishers, booksellers, men of letters, and others. The Chapter Coffee-house, also famed for its newspapers, pamphlets, and for its punch, was altered into a tavern in 1854.

Wittlesbach Ancestors. Twelve statues, so called, in the Hall of the Throne, in the New Palace of Munich, Bavaria.

Wivern, The. An armor-plated ship of the British navy. It was launched Aug. 27, 1863.

Woburn Abbey. The seat of the Duke of Bedford, near the town of Woburn, Bedford, England. The modern mansion, which is of the last century, includes a part of the ancient abbey from which it derives its name.

☞ "He [an American] would sooner have built Jones's tenth block, with a prospect of completing a twentieth, than settle himself down at rest for life as the owner of a Chatsworth or a *Woburn*." *Trollope.*

Wokey Hole. A remarkable and romantic cavern, near Glastonbury, England.

Wolf Hunt. A picture by Peter Paul Rubens (1577–1640), and considered one of his most magnificent works. It was once in the collection of Lord Ashburton, England.

Wolf of the Capitol. A famous bronze figure of unknown antiquity in the Capitol at Rome. Some regard this as the bronze wolf described by Dionysius as standing at the temple of Romulus under the Palatine; while others consider that it is one referred to by Cicero in one of his harangues against Catiline, which was struck by lightning in the time of that orator, and which is also commemorated by Virgil in his well-known lines. The wolf is undoubtedly ancient, but the twins are modern.

And thou, the thunder-stricken nurse of Rome!
She-wolf! whose brazen-imaged dugs impart
The milk of conquest yet within the dome
Where, as a monument of antique art,
Thou standest: Mother of the mighty heart,
Which the great founder suck'd from thy wild teat,
Scorch'd by the Roman Jove's ethereal dart,
And thy limbs black with lightning — dost thou yet
Guard thine immortal cubs, nor thy fond charge forget? *Byron.*

Wolfe. See DEATH OF WOLFE.

Wolfert's Roost. See SUNNYSIDE

Woman sick with the Dropsy. A picture by Gerard Dow (1613–1674?), the Dutch *genre*-painter, and considered to be his masterpiece. It is in the National Gallery, London. There is another in the Louvre, Paris.

Woman taken in Adultery. A celebrated picture by Rembrandt van Ryn (1607–1669), the Dutch painter. It is now in the National Gallery, London.

☞ "In this work a touching truthfulness and depth of feeling, with every other grand quality peculiar to Rembrandt, are seen in their highest perfection." *Handbook of Painting.*

Women of Algiers. A noted picture by Ferdinand Victor Eugène Delacroix (1799–1863), the celebrated French historical painter. This picture, which appeared in 1834, procured for the artist a high reputation as a colorist.

Wonders of the World. See SEVEN WONDERS OF THE WORLD.

Woodland. A cemetery in Philadelphia, Penn., with many fine and costly monuments.

Woodlawn. A cemetery a few miles from New York, containing fine monuments.

Woodward Avenue. One of the principal streets in Detroit, Mich.

Woodward's Gardens. A pleasure-resort in San Francisco, Cal.

Woolwich Arsenal. The largest depot of military stores in the world, at Woolwich, near London. It covers an area of more than 100 acres, and contains over 20,000 pieces of ordnance, besides a great variety of warlike material.

Wood Street. A street in London, which has now disappeared.

At the corner of *Wood Street* when daylight appears,
Hangs a thrush that sings loud, — it has sung for three years;
Poor Susan has passed by the spot, and has heard
In the silence of morning the song of the bird. *Wordsworth.*

Woolsack, The. A large sack of wool covered with red cloth, the seat of the Lord Chancellor of England in the House of Lords.

Consider . . . if it is not yet, in these last days, by very much the same means . . . that the like result is brought about: and from the *Woolsack* down to the Treadmill, from Almack's to Chalk Farm and the West-end of Newgate, the incongruous whirlpool of life is forced and induced to whirl with some attempt at regularity? *Carlyle.*

That he who sat in Chancery, and rayed out speculation from the *Woolsack*, was now a man that squinted, now a man that did not squint? *Carlyle.*

Wooster, Fort. See FORT WOOSTER.

Worcester College. A college in Oxford, England, founded in 1714, one of the 19 colleges which are included in the university.

At *Worcester College* an ample sheet of water, on which swans float, moistens with its slow undulations the greensward constellated with flowers. *Taine, Trans.*

Worcester House. A noble mansion which formerly stood in the Strand, London, the residence of the Bishops of Carlisle.

Worksop Manor. The seat of the Duke of Norfolk, near the town of Worksop, England.

World, The. An old London club.

☞ "There was a club held at the King's Head, in Pall Mall, that arrogantly called itself 'The World.'" *Spence's Anecdotes.*

☞ On one occasion, after dinner, when each member proposed an epigram to be written upon the glasses, Dr. Young, who was present as a guest, refused to make one because he had no diamond with which to write it, whereupon Lord Stanhope handed him his, and he immediately wrote the following: —

Accept a miracle, instead of wit:
See two dull lines with Stanhope's pencil writ.

Worms Cathedral. A noble cathedral in Worms, Germany, regarded as one of the finest Romanesque churches in the world. It has ten towers.

Worsley Hall. The seat of the Earl of Ellesmere, near Manchester, England.

Wotton House. A mansion in Surrey, England, once the residence of John Evelyn. It was built in the age of Elizabeth. John Evelyn describes the house as "large and ancient, suitable to those hospitable times, and so sweetly environed with delicious streams and venerable woods. It has rising grounds, meadows, woods, and water in abundance."

Wounded Gladiator. A famous relic of ancient sculpture. Now in the Museum at Naples. See BORGHESE GLADIATOR and DYING GLADIATOR.

Wrestlers, The. [Ital. *I Lottatori.*] An ancient statue, now in the Tribune of the Uffizi Palace, Florence, Italy.

☞ "In the famous group of the Wrestlers, the flexibility of the intwined limbs, the force of the muscles, and the life and action of the figures are wonderful; . . . their fixed, immovable countenances have no marks even of that corporeal exertion, much less of that eager animation and passion, which men struggling with each other in the heat of contest would naturally feel." *Eaton.*

Wyandotte Cave. A noted cavern in Crawford County, Indiana, thought to be not much inferior in interest to the famous Mammoth Cave in Kentucky. It has been explored over 20 miles.

Wych Street. A London street, famous for the exploits of Jack Sheppard.

Wyndham Club. A club in London, so called from William Wyndham, a former occupant of the house, founded by Lord Nugent, "to secure a convenient and agreeable place of meeting for a society of gentlemen, all connected with each other by a common bond of literary or personal acquaintance."

X.

Xanthian Marbles. See LYCIAN GALLERY.

Xerxes, Hall of. A magnificent ruin in ancient Persepolis, regarded the finest building of which any remains exist in that part of the world.

☞ "Presuming this structure to have been sculptured and painted as richly as others of its age and class, which it no doubt was, it must have been not only one of the largest, but one of the most splendid, buildings of antiquity. In plan it was a rectangle of about 300 feet by 350, and consequently covered 105,000 square feet; it was thus larger than the hypostyle hall at Karnac, or any of the largest temples of Greece or Rome. It is larger, too, than any mediæval cathedral except that of Milan; and although it has neither the stone roof of a cathedral, nor the massiveness of an Egyptian building, still its size and proportions, combined with the lightness of its architecture, and the beauty of its decorations, must have made it one of the most beautiful buildings ever erected. Both in design and proportion, it far surpassed those of Assyria, and though possessing much of detail or of ornament that was almost identical, its arrangements and proportions were so superior in every respect that no similar building in Nineveh can be compared with this — the great architectural creation of the Persian Empire."
Fergusson.

Y.

Yale College. An institution of learning in New Haven, Conn., chartered in 1701, and holding rank among the first colleges in the country. It includes the various departments of law, divinity, medicine, and art, which constitute a university.

Yardley Oak. A venerable oak in the parish of Yardley, England.

> This sole survivor of a race
> Of giant oaks, where once the wood
> Rang with the battle or the chase,
> In stern and lonely grandeur stood.
>
> From age to age it slowly spread
> Its gradual boughs to sun and wind;
> From age to age its noble head
> As slowly withered and declined.
> *James Montgomery.*

Yellow Tower. The ruin of an ancient abbey-church in Trim, Meath County, Ireland.

Yellowstone. See GRAND CAÑON OF THE YELLOWSTONE.

Yes, or No? A picture by John Everett Millais (b. 1829).

Yester House. The seat of the Marquis of Tweeddale, near Longniddry in Scotland.

York Column. A pillar of Scotch granite in Carlton House Gardens, London, 124 feet high, surmounted by a statue of the Duke of York, second son of George III.

York House. A former palace of London, so called from the Archbishops of York. Here Lord Bacon was born in 1560. York House was finally sold and removed. Its "Watergate" on the Thames still remains.

☞ "There was a costly magnificence in the *fêtes* at York House, the residence of Buckingham, of which few but curious researchers are aware: they eclipsed the splendors of the French Court." *Isaac Disraeli.*

York Minster. A noble church at York, the finest structure of its kind in England. It was mostly built in the thirteenth and fourteenth centuries. Its extreme length is 486 feet, length of transept 223 feet. It has a magnificent west front, flanked by two towers, 196 feet in height.

☞ "Owing to the great width attempted for the nave, York has not the usual perfection of length affected by other English cathedrals, and loses in effect accordingly. Its great peculiarity is the simplicity and squareness of its plan." *Fergusson.*

In the history of art, it is a long way from a cromlech to *York minster;* yet all the intermediate steps may still be traced in this all-preserving island. *Emerson.*

If there were a building on it [the moon] as big as *York minster*, as big as the Boston Coliseum, the great telescopes like Lord Rosse's would make it out. *Holmes.*

> Open your gates, ye everlasting piles!
> Types of the spiritual church which God hath reared,
> Thou, stately *York!* and ye, whose splendors cheer
> Isis and Cam, to patient science dear!
> *Wordsworth.*

York Place. The name by which the palace of Whitehall, in London, was formerly known, from the circumstance that the Archbishops of York resided there when in town. The last Archbishop of York who lived there was Cardinal Wolsey; and on his fall, in 1529, the name was changed to White Hall.

> You must no more call it *York-Place*, that is past;
> For since the Cardinal fell, that title's lost:
> 'Tis now the king's, and called Whitehall. *Shakespeare.*

Yosemite Valley. **1.** A picture by Albert Bierstadt (b. 1829). Now in possession of Mr. James Lenox.

2. A picture by Thomas Hill (b. 1829).

Young Bull. See BULL, THE YOUNG.

Young Courtesan. A picture by Xavier Sigalon (1788-1837), well known by engravings. In the Louvre, Paris.

Yuste. A monastic edifice near Plasencia in the province of Estremadura, Spain, celebrated as the place of retirement of the Emperor Charles V. on his abdication of the throne in 1556. It was the property of the Jeronymite monks, and derives its name from the little stream, the Yuste, which flows beneath it. It was founded in 1404. The convent and the surrounding estate now belongs to the Duke of Montpensier. It is now in ruins.

So Charles the emperor, whose mighty reign
The globe itself scarce held within its bound,
At *Yuste*, a fair abbey of our Spain,
A lowly home and quiet haven found.
Luis Capata, Trans.

In *Saint Just* the silent bowers
Hear a drowsy funeral lay:
Bells are humming from the towers
For the monk who died to-day.
Graf von Auersperg, Trans.

Z.

Zaccaria, St. See ST. ZACCARIA.

Zamek. A royal castle at Cracow, the ancient capital of Poland, built in the fourteenth century, but mainly rebuilt in 1610.

Zealous, The. An armor-plated ship of the British navy, launched March 7, 1864.

Zechariah's Tomb. A rock-cut tomb near Jerusalem, adorned with Ionic pillars and square piers, and surmounted with a pyramidal roof.

☞ "Perhaps this building should properly be called a cenotaph, as it is perfectly solid, and no cave or sepulchral vault has been found beneath it; though, judging from analogies, one might yet be found, if properly looked for." *Fergusson.*

Zemzem. A holy spring in Mecca, Arabia. It is said to have gushed out on this spot to the succor of Ishmael and his mother when perishing of thirst. It is carefully enclosed and joined with the tower of the Kaabah by a railing.

☞ "The Well Zemzem has its name from the bubbling sound of the waters, *zem-zem:* they think it is the well which Hagar found with her little Ishmael in the wilderness: the aërolite and it have been sacred now, and had a Caabah over them, for thousands of years." *Carlyle.*

Zeno Chapel. A chapel in St. Mark's Church, Venice, Italy, built by Cardinal Zeno in the early part of the sixteenth century.

Zenobia. A statue by Harriet Hosmer (b. 1831).

☞ "This morning I went to Miss Hosmer's studio to see her statue of Zenobia. . . . [It] stood in the centre of the room, as yet unfinished in the clay, but a very noble and remarkable statue indeed, full of dignity and beauty." *Hawthorne.*

Zenobius, St. See ST. ZENOBIUS.

Zingarella, La. [The Gypsy.] A beautiful picture of the Madonna and Child by Antonio Allegri, surnamed Correggio (1494-1534), representing the Virgin with an Oriental turban (hence the name). This picture is now in the Museum at Naples. There is another upon the same subject bearing this name at Parma, Italy. See REPOSE IN EGYPT.

The painter's wife, whom he married in 1520, is supposed to have been his model for La Zingarella. This picture is also called Madonna del Coniglio from the rabbit (*coniglio*) which appears in the foreground.

Zion. See MOUNT ZION.

Zocodover. The principal square and fashionable promenade of Toledo, Spain.

Zodiac of Denderah. A celebrated astronomical drawing upon the ceiling of the portico of the Temple of Denderah in Egypt. It was formerly supposed to be of the age of the early Pharaohs, but is now referred to the time of the Ptolemies.

Zoölogical Gardens. An enclosure contiguous to Regent's Park, London, belonging to the Zoölogical Society, and containing a large and rare collection of animals. The Gardens were first opened to the public in 1828, and the menagerie is now the finest public bivarium in Europe.

In the *Zoölogical Gardens*, I saw a baboon who always got into a furious rage when his keeper took out a letter or book. *C. Darwin.*

Zuccone, Lo. [The Bald Head.] A bronze statue of David by Donatello (1383-1466). In the Uffizi, Florence, Italy.

Zwinger, The. A public building in Dresden, Saxony. It contains a valuable collection of works of art and scientific treasures. The word is a general name for a prison or any confined place.